RUNNING
LINUX

Other Linux resources from O'Reilly

Related titles

Linux Cookbook™
Linux Desktop Hacks™
Linux Desktop Pocket Guide
Linux in a Nutshell
Linux in a Windows World
Linux Multimedia Hacks™
Linux Network
    Administrator's Guide

Linux Pocket Guide
Linux Server Hacks™
Linux Server Security
LPI Linux Certification
    in a Nutshell
OpenOffice.org Writer
SELinux
Version Control with
    Subversion

**Linux Books
Resource Center**

linux.oreilly.com is a complete catalog of O'Reilly's books on Linux and Unix and related technologies, including sample chapters and code examples.

ONLamp.com is the premier site for the open source web platform: Linux, Apache, MySQL, and either Perl, Python, or PHP.

Conferences

O'Reilly brings diverse innovators together to nurture the ideas that spark revolutionary industries. We specialize in documenting the latest tools and systems, translating the innovator's knowledge into useful skills for those in the trenches. Visit *conferences.oreilly.com* for our upcoming events.

Safari Bookshelf (*safari.oreilly.com*) is the premier online reference library for programmers and IT professionals. Conduct searches across more than 1,000 books. Subscribers can zero in on answers to time-critical questions in a matter of seconds. Read the books on your Bookshelf from cover to cover or simply flip to the page you need. Try it today for free.

RUNNING
LINUX

FIFTH EDITION

Matthias Kalle Dalheimer
and Matt Welsh

O'REILLY®

Beijing · Cambridge · Farnham · Köln · Paris · Sebastopol · Taipei · Tokyo

Running Linux, Fifth Edition

by Matthias Kalle Dalheimer and Matt Welsh

Copyright © 2006, 2002, 1999, 1996, 1995 O'Reilly Media, Inc. All rights reserved.
Printed in the United States of America.

Published by O'Reilly Media, Inc., 1005 Gravenstein Highway North, Sebastopol, CA 95472.

O'Reilly books may be purchased for educational, business, or sales promotional use. Online editions
are also available for most titles (*safari.oreilly.com*). For more information, contact our corporate/insti-
tutional sales department: (800) 998-9938 or *corporate@oreilly.com*.

Editor:	Andy Oram
Production Editor:	Adam Witwer
Production Services:	Argosy Publishing
Cover Designer:	Edie Freedman
Interior Designer:	David Futato

Printing History:

May 1995:	First Edition.
August 1996:	Second Edition.
August 1999:	Third Edition.
December 2002:	Fourth Edition.
December 2005:	Fifth Edition.

Nutshell Handbook, the Nutshell Handbook logo, and the O'Reilly logo are registered trademarks of
O'Reilly Media, Inc. The *Linux* series designations, *Running Linux*, images of the American West, and
related trade dress are trademarks of O'Reilly Media, Inc.

Many of the designations used by manufacturers and sellers to distinguish their products are claimed as
trademarks. Where those designations appear in this book, and O'Reilly Media, Inc. was aware of a
trademark claim, the designations have been printed in caps or initial caps.

While every precaution has been taken in the preparation of this book, the publisher and authors
assume no responsibility for errors or omissions, or for damages resulting from the use of the
information contained herein.

ISBN: 0-596-00760-4
[M]

Table of Contents

Part II.   System Administration

Preface

*Technical knowledge is not enough. One must
transcend techniques so that the art becomes an artless
art, growing out of the unconscious.*
—Daisetsu Suzuki (1870–1966)

This is a book about Linux, a free, open source operating system that's changing the world of computing. In this book, we show how you can completely change the way you work with computers by exploring a powerful and free operating system. Linux goes against the traditional computing mainstream, being developed by a loosely organized group of thousands of volunteers across the Internet. Linux started as a real underground movement—guerrilla hacking, if you will—and brings a lot of excitement, discovery, and self-empowerment back into today's corporate-dominated computing culture. We invite you to dive in, enjoy yourself, and join the throng of people who know what it means to tweak your dot clocks and *rdev* your kernel image.

The Zen quote at the beginning of this preface summarizes our philosophy in this book. We're targeting readers who are inquisitive and creative enough to delve full-tilt into the world of Linux, and who want to get at the heart of the system. Linux represents a rebellion against commercial and proprietary operating systems, and many of its users like living on the edge of the latest technological trends. Of course, the casual reader can set up and run a Linux system (or hundreds of them!) without much trouble, but the purpose of this book is to dig more deeply into the system—to bring you completely into the Linux mentality, to reach Linux "enlightenment." Rather than gloss over messy details, we explain the concepts by which the system actually works so that you can troubleshoot problems on your own. By sharing the accumulated expertise of several Linux experts, we hope to give you enough confidence to call yourself a true Linux Guru. (Your first koan: what is the sound of one user hacking?)

You have in your hands the fifth edition of *Running Linux*, and by most accounts this book is considered the classic text on installing, maintaining, and learning to use a

Linux system. The first edition was published way back in 1996, and had its roots in a free book called *Linux Installation and Getting Started*, which was written by Matt Welsh and is still floating around the Internet. Since Matt conceived and wrote *Running Linux*, the book has gone through a lot of expansion and improvement to keep up-to-date with the latest developments in the Linux world.

Kalle Dalheimer, a developer and consultant bringing a great deal of experience with both Linux development and desktop applications, has become the lead author on the past three editions. Other contributors over time have included Lar Kaufman (material on printing and other first-edition material), Tom Adelstein (updates to the introductory chapter and substantial material on VMWare, rdesktop, VNC, and FreeNX), Aaron Weber (GNOME, Evolution, Red Carpet, and ZENworks), Sam Hiser (OpenOffice), Jay Ts (Samba), John H. Terpstra (updates to Samba and NFS), Jeff Tranter (multimedia, sources of Linux information), Kyle Rankin (games), Breckin Loggins (GnuCash), Rod Smith (substantial printing material, including CUPS), Kyle Dent (Postfix), Terry Dawson (material on security), Brian Vincent (Wine and CodeWeaver), Chris Lawrence (Debian packaging), Vatafu Valerica (LAMP chapter), Marc Mutz (material on public-key encryption and encypted file-systems), Steffen Hansen (material on the GIMP, OpenGL, Postfix, and ProFTPd), Till Adam (material on groupware solutions for Linux), Jesper Pedersen (material on kimdaba and Procmail, updates to the Python section), Michel Boyer de la Giroday (PHP), Ivan Ristic (updates to Apache and LAMP chapters), and Jeffrey Dunitz (updates to the backup chapter).

As Linux attracts more and more development, becoming increasingly appealing in new areas of use, the challenge for a book like this is to continue its mission with an ever-increasing scope. This edition is much bigger than any of the previous ones, and covers topics such as desktop tools that made only cursory appearances earlier. No book can adequately capture *everything* there is to know about Linux, so we've tried to ask at each turn what information is most valuable for a person exploring the system and trying to get a firm basis for further self-education. Our approach has worked remarkably well over the many editions, and we think this book will be of use to you for a long time to come.

In the preface to the first edition, we said that "Linux has the potential to completely change the face of the PC operating system world." Looking back, it's clear that our prediction was right! Linux has erupted into the computing mainstream with an amazing force: it has been covered by every major media channel, has helped usher in the so-called Open Source Revolution, and is widely claimed as the most viable competitor to Microsoft's dominance in the operating systems market. Today, most estimates place the number of Linux users worldwide at well over 300 million. Linux has matured to the point where many people can dive in and start using Linux without knowing most of the hairy details behind device drivers, XFree86 configuration files, and bootloaders. Actually, a good Linux distribution these days is just as easy to install as its commercial competitors such as Microsoft Windows. Still, we think it's best to give you some of the behind-the-scenes views, so you have an understanding of the workings of the system, even if it's not strictly necessary for casual Linux use.

Organization of This Book

Each chapter of this book contains a big chunk of information. It takes you into a world of material that could easily take up several books. But we move quickly through the topics you need to know.

Part I of the book, "Enjoying and Being Productive on Linux," introduces Linux and brings you to the point where you can do all the standard activities people do on other systems: emailing, web surfing, playing games, watching videos, and so on.

Chapter 1, *Introduction to Linux*
> Tries to draw together many different threads. It explains why Linux came to be and what it offers that continues to attract new users and developers.

Chapter 2, *Preinstallation and Installation*
> Describes preliminary tasks that you may have to do before installation, such as partitioning your disk, and guidance for initial Linux installation and configuration.

Chapter 3, *Desktop Environments*
> Helps you get comfortable navigating the desktop and the most important tools, including the Evolution utility for mail, calendar, and managing contacts.

Chapter 4, *Basic Unix Commands and Concepts*
> Offers a system administrator's introduction to Unix. It is intended to give you enough tools to perform the basic tasks you'll need to do throughout the book. Basic commands are covered, along with some tips for administrators and some concepts you should know.

Chapter 5, *Web Browsers and Instant Messaging*
> Shows neat tricks and advanced uses for some of the popular and basic computer activities: web browsing and instant messaging.

Chapter 6, *Electronic Mail Clients*
> Introduces other mail clients, for people who want to try something besides Evolution, and shows ways to secure email.

Chapter 7, *Games*
> Explains the impressive array of games supported on Linux, both standalone and client/server.

Chapter 8, *Office Suites and Personal Productivity*
> Explains how you can be just as productive in your office work on Linux as on the proprietary alternatives. The main topics are the OpenOffice office suite, KOffice office suite, and the GnuCash financial application, along with an introduction to groupware.

Chapter 9, *Multimedia*

Discusses audio and video, covering concepts you'll find useful, configuration for systems where the tools don't work automatically, and a few common applications. The GIMP is also introduced for image manipulation.

Part II of the book, "System Administration," shows you how to set up your Linux system and its environment for such tasks as printing and sharing files with other systems; it also shows you how to take care of your system in other ways.

Chapter 10, *System Administration Basics*

Covers system administration topics such as filesystems and swap space that are normally handled automatically during installation, but sometimes need user intervention.

Chapter 11, *Managing Users, Groups, and Permissions*

Shows you the fundamental building blocks of security on Linux: managing users and access rights (permissions).

Chapter 12, *Installing, Updating, and Compiling Programs*

Covers system updates, which are important both to get new features and applications and to fix security flaws.

Chapter 13, *Networking*

Is a basic introduction to networking, which is usually set up during installation but is worth understanding at a deeper level. The chapter shows you how to configure your system so that it can work on a local area network or communicate with an Internet service provider using Point-to-Point Protocol (PPP). ISDN and ADSL are also covered.

Chapter 14, *Printing*

Shows you how to get Linux to recognize printers and to manage document printing.

Chapter 15, *File Sharing*

Covers file sharing, with a particular focus on Samba, which allows both file and printer sharing with Windows systems.

Chapter 16, *The X Window System*

Shows you how to configure the X Window System, which underlies the desktops introduced in Chapter 3. We show you how to overcome problems you might encounter when your distribution installs the software and how to configure it for the best performance on your video hardware.

Chapter 17, *System Start and Shutdown*

Covers system startup and shutdown. Topics include the GRUB bootloader, which lets you choose between operating systems at startup time, and how to get the right services going.

Chapter 18, *Configuring and Building the Kernel*

Explains how to update the kernel and its modules, which may be necessary to run new Linux features or get drivers installed for your hardware.

Part III of the book, "Programming," starts exploring interesting advanced topics that make Linux a powerful asset, such as programming.

Chapter 19, *Text Editing*

Offers in-depth tutorials on *vi* and Emacs, valuable text editors. Covers text processing, an alternative to using word processors to format text documents.

Chapter 20, *Text Processing*

Describes tools for producing formatted documents from markup languages, including XML and the older languages TEX, *troff*, and Texinfo.

Chapter 21, *Programming Tools*

Is a wide-ranging introduction to programming on Linux, introducing a number of languages, as well as tools that you may find it useful to understand even if you are not a programmer.

Part IV of the book, "Network Services," introduces several services and other advanced networking activities.

Chapter 22, *Running a Web Server*

Shows you how to set up and configure Apache, the most popular web server in the world.

Chapter 23, *Transporting and Handling Email Messages*

Covers the easy-to-use Postfix mail server and some other useful mail tools, such as SpamAssassin.

Chapter 24, *Running an FTP Server*

Shows a secure way to offer files for download.

Chapter 25, *Running Web Applications with MySQL and PHP*

Covers the M and P in the well-known acronym LAMP, introducing the basic configuration and use of MySQL and PHP for use with Apache.

Chapter 26, *Running a Secure System*

Covers the ProFTPD web server, which is convenient for serving documents to colleagues or the general public.

Chapter 27, *Backup and Recovery*

Basic techniques for the critical task of safeguarding your data.

Chapter 28, *Heterogeneous Networking and Running Windows Programs*

A wealth of ways to get the best out of two diffferent environments.

Appendix, *Sources of Linux Information*

Tells you about useful online documentation for Linux and other sources of help.

Conventions Used in This Book

The following is a list of the typographical conventions used in this book:

Italic

> Is used for file and directory names, command names, command-line options, email addresses and pathnames, usernames, hostnames, site names, and all new terms.

`Constant Width`

> Is used in examples to show the contents of files or the output from commands, to indicate environment variables and keywords that appear in code, and for Emacs commands.

`Constant Width Bold`

> Is used in examples to show commands or other text that should be typed literally by the user.

`Constant Width Italic`

> Is used to indicate variable options, keywords, or text that the user is to replace with an actual value.

> This icon designates a note, which is an important aside to the nearby text.

> This icon designates a warning relating to the nearby text.

Using Code Examples

This book is here to help you get your job done. In general, you may use the code in this book in your programs and documentation. You do not need to contact us for permission unless you're reproducing a significant portion of the code. For example, writing a program that uses several chunks of code from this book does not require permission. Selling or distributing a CD-ROM of examples from O'Reilly books does require permission. Answering a question by citing this book and quoting example code does not require permission. Incorporating a significant amount of example code from this book into your product's documentation does require permission.

We appreciate, but do not require, attribution. An attribution usually includes the title, author, publisher, and ISBN. For example: "*Running Linux*, Fifth Edition by Matthias Kalle Dalheimer and Matt Welsh. Copyright 2006 O'Reilly Media, Inc., 0-596-00760-4."

If you feel your use of code examples falls outside fair use or the permission given above, feel free to contact us at *permissions@oreilly.com*.

How to Contact Us

We have tested and verified the information in this book to the best of our ability, but you may find that features have changed (or even that we have made mistakes!). Please let us know about any errors you find, as well as your suggestions for future editions, by writing to:

O'Reilly Media, Inc.
1005 Gravenstein Highway North
Sebastopol, CA 95472
800-998-9938 (in the U.S. or Canada)
707-829-0515 (international or local)
707-829-0104 (fax)

You can send us messages electronically. To be put on the mailing list or to request a catalog, send email to:

info@oreilly.com

To ask technical questions or to comment on the book, send email to:

bookquestions@oreilly.com

We have a web site for the book, where we'll list examples, errata, and any plans for future editions. You can access this page at:

http://www.oreilly.com/catalog/runlinux5

For more information about this book and others, see the O'Reilly web site:

http://www.oreilly.com

Safari® Enabled

 When you see a Safari® Enabled icon on the cover of your favorite technology book, that means the book is available online through the O'Reilly Network Safari Bookshelf.

Safari offers a solution that's better than e-books. It's a virtual library that lets you easily search thousands of top tech books, cut and paste code samples, download chapters, and find quick answers when you need the most accurate, current information. Try it for free at *http://safari.oreilly.com*.

Acknowledgments

This book is the result of many people's efforts, and as expected, it would be impossible to list them all here. First of all, we would like to thank Andy Oram, who did an excellent job of editing, writing, and whip-cracking to get this book into shape.

Apart from being the overall editor, Andy contributed the Unix tutorial chapter and the Gaim section as well as material for the X and Perl sections. It was Andy who approached us about writing for O'Reilly in the first place, and he has demonstrated the patience of a saint when waiting for our updates to trickle in.

Because this book has grown so much in size and scope, its topics have become too diverse for one person, or even a small set of coauthors. Therefore, we have drawn in experts in a number of subject areas, listed near the beginning of the preface, to write substantial material.

We would also like to thank the following people for their work on the Linux operating system—without all of them, there wouldn't be anything to write a book about: Linus Torvalds, Richard Stallman, Donald Becker, Alan Cox, Remy Card, Eric Raymond, Ted T'so, H. J. Lu, Miguel de Icaza, Ross Biro, Drew Eckhardt, Ed Carp, Eric Youngdale, Fred van Kempen, Steven Tweedie, Patrick Volkerding, Dirk Hohndel, Matthias Ettrich, and all of the other hackers, from the kernel grunts to the lowly docos, too numerous to mention here.

Special thanks to the following people for their contributions to the Linux Documentation Project, technical review of this book, or general friendliness and support: Phil Hughes, Melinda McBride, Bill Hahn, Dan Irving, Michael Johnston, Joel Goldberger, Michael K. Johnson, Adam Richter, Roman Yanovsky, Jon Magid, Erik Troan, Lars Wirzenius, Olaf Kirch, Greg Hankins, Alan Sondheim, Jon David, Anna Clark, Adam Goodman, Lee Gomes, Rob Walker, Rob Malda, Jeff Bates, and Volker Lendecke.

For the third edition, we thank Phil Hughes, Robert J. Chassell, Tony Cappellini, Craig Small, Nat Makarevitch, Chris Davis, Chuck Toporek, Frederic HongFeng, and David Pranata for wide-ranging comments and corrections. Particularly impressive were the efforts put in by an entire team of Debian developers and users, organized for us by Ossama Othman and Julian T. J. Midgley. Julian set up a CVS repository for comments, and the book was examined collectively by him, Chris Lawrence, Robert J. Chassell, Kirk Hilliard, and Stephen Zander.

For the fourth edition, we thank David Collier-Brown, Oliver Flimm, Phil Hughes, Chris Lawrence, Rich Payne, Craig Small, Jeff Tranter, and Aaron Weber for their reviews.

For the fifth edition, we thank Ben Hyde, Cheridy Jollie, Chris Lawrence, Ellen Siever, and Jeff Tranter.

Kalle would like to thank Valerica Vatafu from Buzau, Romania, for lots of help with the chapter about LAMP. He would also like to thank his colleagues in his company Klarälvdalens Datakonsult AB—Michel Boyer de la Giroday, Tanja Dalheimer, Steffen Hansen, Jesper Pedersen, Lutz Rogowski, Karl-Heinz Zimmer, Tobias Larsson, Romain Pokrzywka, David Faure, Marc Mutz, Tobias Larsson, and Till Adam—for their constructive comments on drafts of the book as well as for being general "Linux thought amplifiers."

## PART I

Enjoying and Being Productive on Linux

This part of the book introduces Linux and brings you to the point where you can do all the standard activities people do on other systems: emailing, web surfing, playing games, watching videos, and so on.

Chapter 2 is worth reading even if you plan to install Linux from an easy-to-use distribution. Fundamental considerations, such as how much disk space to devote to different parts of your system, indicate that some planning lies behind every installation.

The vast majority of Linux installations go well and make the features discussed in this part of the book available to system users. If you have trouble, though, the more advanced material in other parts of the book can help you, along with online documentation and more specialized texts.

## CHAPTER 1

Introduction to Linux

Welcome to *Running Linux*, Version 5! When we wrote the first edition of this book, Linux had barely arrived on the scene. Our task seemed simple: help readers learn the basics of a new operating system that required a pretty fixed and predictable set of tasks. Few if any observers expected Linux would become a best-of-breed operating system, supported by the vast majority of hardware and software manufacturers on the planet. Who would have known that Linux would grow from a small user base of 30,000 people in 1995 to hundreds of millions only 10 years later? People use Linux everywhere on the planet and in some cases in outer space and under the ocean.

To the casual observer, Linux looks like a fairly simple personal computer desktop built on the same chassis as any IBM PC. People use Linux to browse the Internet, exchange email, listen to music, watch videos, and instant message their friends and coworkers. Students and office workers create documents with word processors, perform numerous tasks with spreadsheet programs, and make slide presentations.

The same Linux operating system also drives sonar arrays in nuclear submarines, indexes every document on the Internet, unifies large corporate data centers, runs nearly 70% of all web sites in the world, records your television programs, works in your cellular phone, and runs the switches that allow you to connect with your friends and family anywhere on the globe. Linux runs systems on the international space station as well as the shuttles that take astronauts there. It protects you from spam and computer viruses on numerous routers and back-end systems.

You can benefit directly from installing Linux on a system at home, at school, or in the office, and having all that power at your fingertips. Not only can you carry on everyday surfing and office work, but you can also learn how to write database queries, administer a web server, filter mail for spam and viruses, automate your environment through scripting languages, access web services, and participate in the myriad of other cutting-edge activities provided by modern computing.

How does Linux do all those things? Linux distributions harvest vast amounts of diverse technology, especially new and innovative developments in hardware. Developers have access to all the code that makes up the operating system. Although many people consider Linux the largest cooperative software development project in human history, Linux developers don't need to even know each other. If someone wants to write a software application, all he has to do is download the Linux code or visit its documentation site. If you started counting people who have contributed to the development of Linux and its associated projects, you would see hundreds of thousands of individuals.

Linux and open source software developers come from many walks of life. Major computer vendors such as IBM, HP, Novell, Red Hat, Sun, Dell, and others pay portions of their staffs to work on Linux. Universities around the globe sponsor projects and foundations that contribute to Linux. The U.S. Department of Defense, NASA, and the National Security Agency have paid for numerous pieces of the Linux operating system. Developing countries such as China, Brazil, Malaysia, South Africa, and Viet Nam, to mention a few, have added to the Linux base. Industrial giants such as Germany, Australia, Japan, the United Kingdom, and others have also made their presence felt. But in the very midst of those giants, many individuals such as you and me have also contributed to Linux.

During the 1990s, Linux generated more excitement in the computer field than any other development since the advent of microprocessor technology. Linux rejuvenated a dying technology sector following the fall of the dot-com boom in the spring of 2001. Today, Linux has surpassed the expectations of informed observers worldwide, including the authors of this book.

Early on, Linux inspired and captured the loyalty of its users. Technologists interested in the server side of the Internet needed to become familiar with the operating systems that ran web sites, domain name services, and email and service providers. Traditional software manufacturers priced their systems out of the range of those wanting to gain webmaster-type skills. Many people viewed Linux as a godsend because you could download it for free and gain the skills necessary to become a webmaster or system administrator while working on relatively low-cost hardware.

Originally, people saw Linux as simply an operating system kernel, offering the basic services of process scheduling, virtual memory, file management, and handling of hardware peripherals such as hard drives, DVDs, printers, terminals, and so forth. Other Internet operating systems belonged to the Unix family, which became available for commercial sale only after the breakup of AT&T and the Bell Operating Systems.

To skirt the legal issues surrounding AT&T's Unix, the Free Software Foundation (FSF) created a plethora of applications that performed many of the functions of basic Unix while using totally original FSF code instead of code produced by Bell

Labs. This collection of FSF software was called GNU. To become a complete operating system, however, FSF needed a kernel. Although their own efforts in that area stalled, an operating system fitting the bill arose unexpectedly from efforts by a student at the University of Helsinki in Finland: Linus Torvalds.

People now use the term "Linux" to refer to the complete system—the kernel along with the many applications that it runs: a complete development and work environment including compilers, editors, graphical interfaces, text processors, games, and more. FSF proponents ask that this broader collection of software be known as "GNU/Linux."

About This Book

This book provides an overview and guide to Linux as a desktop and a back-office system. We present information on topics to satisfy novices and wizards alike. This book should provide sufficient material for almost anyone to choose the type of installation they want and get the most out of it. Instead of covering many of the volatile technical details—those things that tend to change with Linux's rapid development—we give you the information that helps you over the bumps as you take your first steps with popular distributions, as well as background you will need if you plan to go onto more advanced Linux topics such as web services, federated identity management, high-performance computing, and so on.

We geared this book for those people who want to understand the power that Linux can provide. Rather than provide minimal information, we help you see how the different parts of the Linux system work, so you can customize, configure, and troubleshoot the system on your own. Linux is not difficult to install and use. Many people consider it easier and faster to set up than Microsoft Windows. However, as with any commercial operating system, some black magic exists, and you will find this book useful if you plan to go beyond desktop Linux and use web services or network management services.

In this book, we cover the following topics:

- The design and philosophy of the Linux operating system, and what it can do for you.
- Information on what you need to run Linux, including suggestions on hardware platforms and how to configure the operating system depending on its specified role (e.g., desktop, web server, database and/or application server).
- How to obtain and install Linux. We cover the Red Hat, SUSE, and Debian distributions in more detail than others, but the information is useful in understanding just about any distribution.
- An introduction, for new users, to the original Linux/Unix system philosophy, including the most important commands and concepts still in use.

- Personal productivity through slick and powerful office suites, image manipulation, and financial accounting.
- The care and feeding of the Linux system, including system administration and maintenance, upgrading the system, and how to fix things when they don't work.
- Expanding the basic Linux system and desktop environments with power tools for the technically inclined.
- The Linux programming environment. The tools of the trade for programming and developing software on the Linux system.
- Using Linux for telecommunications and networking, including the basics of TCP/IP configuration, PPP for Internet connectivity over a modem, ISDN configuration, ADSL, cable, email, news, and web access—we even show how to configure a Linux system as a web and database server.
- Linux for fun: audio, video, and games.

Many things exist that we'd love to show you how to do with Linux. Unfortunately, to cover them all, this book would be the size of the unabridged *Oxford English Dictionary* and would be impossible for anyone (let alone the authors) to maintain. Instead we've included the most salient and interesting aspects of the system and show you how to find out more.

Although much of the discussion in this book is not overly technical, you'll find it easier to navigate if you have some experience with the command line and the editing of simple text files. For those who don't have such experience, we have included a short tutorial in Chapter 4. Part 2 of the book is an exploration of system administration that can help even seasoned technicians run Linux in a server mode.

If you are new to Linux and want more system-oriented information, you'll want to pick up an additional guide to command-line basics. We don't dwell for long on the fundamentals, preferring instead to skip to the fun parts of the system. At any rate, although this book should be enough to get you functional and even seasoned in the use of Linux, you may have requirements that will take you into specialized areas. See Appendix A for a list of sources of information.

Who's Using Linux?

Application developers, system administrators, network providers, kernel hackers, students, and multimedia authors are just a few of the categories of people who find that Linux has a particular charm.

Programmers are increasingly using Linux because of its extensibility and low cost—they can pick up a complete programming environment for free and run it on inexpensive PC hardware—and because Linux offers a great development platform for portable programs. In addition to the original FSF tools, Linux can utilize a number of development environments that have surfaced over the last three years, such as Eclipse (*http://eclipse.org*). Eclipse is quite a phenomenon: a tribute to both the creativity of the open source community and the fertility of a collaboration between an open source community and a major vendor (Eclipse was originally developed and released by IBM). It is an open source community focused on providing an extensible development platform and application frameworks for building software.

Eclipse's tools and frameworks span the software development life cycle, including support for modeling; language development environments for Java™, C/C++, and other languages; testing and performance; business intelligence; rich client applications; and embedded development. A large, vibrant ecosystem of major technology vendors, innovative startups, universities, and research institutions and individuals extend, complement, and support the Eclipse platform.

Networking is one of Linux's strengths. Linux has been adopted by people who run large networks because of its simplicity of management, performance, and low cost. Many Internet sites make use of Linux to drive large web servers, e-commerce applications, search engines, and more. Linux is easy to merge into a corporate or academic network because it supports common networking standards. These include both old stand-bys, such as the Network File System (NFS) and Network Information Service (NIS), and more prominent systems used in modern businesses, such as Microsoft file sharing (CIFS and related protocols) and Lightweight Directory Access Protocol (LDAP). Linux makes it easy to share files, support remote logins, and run applications on other systems. A software suite called Samba allows a Linux machine to act as a Windows server in Active Directory environments. The combination of Linux and Samba for this purpose is faster (and less expensive) than running Windows Server 2003. In fact, given the ease with which Linux supports common networking activities—DHCP, the Domain Name System, Kerberos security, routing—it's hard to imagine a corporate networking task for which it's unsuited.

One of the most popular uses of Linux is in driving large enterprise applications, including web servers, databases, business-to-business systems, and e-commerce sites. Businesses have learned that Linux provides an inexpensive, efficient, and robust system capable of driving the most mission-critical applications.

As just one example among the many publicized each month, Cendant Travel Distribution Services put its Fares application on a Linux Enterprise Server with IBM xSeries and BladeCenter servers as the hardware platforms. The move reduced expenditures by 90% while achieving 99.999% availability and handling 300 to 400 transactions per second.

Linux's ease of customization—even down to the guts of the kernel—makes the system very attractive for companies that need to exercise control over the inner workings of the system. Linux supports a range of technologies that ensure timely disk access and resistance to failure, from RAID (a set of mechanisms that allow an array of disks to be treated as a single logical storage device) to the most sophisticated storage area networks. These greatly increase reliability and reduce the costs of meeting new regulatory demands that require the warehousing of data for as long as 30 years.

The combination of Linux, the Apache web server, the MySQL database engine, and the PHP scripting language is so common that it has its own acronym—LAMP. We cover LAMP in more detail in Chapter 25.

Kernel hackers were the first to come to Linux—in fact, the developers who helped Linus Torvalds create Linux are still a formidable community. The Linux kernel mailing lists see a great deal of activity, and it's the place to be if you want to stay on the bleeding edge of operating system design. If you're into tuning page replacement algorithms, twiddling network protocols, or optimizing buffer caches, Linux is a great choice. Linux is also good for learning about the internals of operating system design, and an increasing number of universities make use of Linux systems in advanced operating system courses.

Finally, Linux is becoming an exciting forum for multimedia because it's compatible with an enormous variety of hardware, including the majority of modern sound and video cards. Several programming environments, including the MESA 3D toolkit (a free OpenGL implementation), have been ported to Linux; OpenGL is introduced in "Introduction to OpenGL Programming" in Chapter 21. The GIMP (a free Adobe Photoshop work-alike) was originally developed under Linux, and is becoming the graphics manipulation and design tool of choice for many artists. Many movie production companies regularly use Linux as the workhorse for advanced special-effects rendering—the popular movies *Titanic* and *The Matrix* used "render farms" of Linux machines to do much of the heavy lifting.

Linux systems have traveled the high seas of the North Pacific, managing telecommunications and data analysis for oceanographic research vessels. Linux systems are used at research stations in Antarctica, and large "clusters" of Linux machines are used at many research facilities for complex scientific simulations ranging from star formation to earthquakes, and in Department of Energy laboratories helping to bring new sources of energy to everyone. On a more basic level, hospitals use Linux to maintain patient records and retrieve archives. The U.S. judiciary uses Linux to manage its entire infrastructure, from case management to accounting. Financial institutions use Linux for real-time trading of stocks, bonds, and other financial instruments. Linux has taken over the role that Unix used to play as the most reliable operating system.

System Features

Linux has surpassed the features found in implementations of Unix and Windows. With the changes offered by IBM's Power Architecture, for example, Linux provides functionality for commodity hardware normally only found on the most expensive mainframes. Additionally, the latest kernels include the structure of Security Enhanced Linux (SELinux) provided by the National Security Agency (*http://www. nsa.gov/selinux*). SELinux provides the most trusted computing environment available today.

Now add Linux's ability to provide virtualization at the kernel level. Through Xen (*http://sourceforge.net/projects/xen*), Linux can securely execute multiple virtual machines, each running its own operating system, on a single physical system. This allows enterprises to stop server sprawl and increase CPU utilization.

A Bag of Features

This section provides a nickel tour of Linux features.

Linux is a complete multitasking, multiuser operating system (as are all other versions of Unix). This means that many users can be logged onto the same machine at once, running multiple programs simultaneously. Linux also supports multiprocessor systems (such as dual-Pentium motherboards), with support for up to 32 processors in a system,* which is great for high-performance servers and scientific applications.

The Linux system is mostly compatible with a number of Unix standards (inasmuch as Unix has standards) on the source level, including IEEE POSIX.1, System V, and BSD features. Linux was developed with source portability in mind: therefore, you will probably find features in the Linux system that are shared across multiple Unix implementations. A great deal of free Unix software available on the Internet and elsewhere compiles on Linux out of the box.

If you have some Unix background, you may be interested in some other specific internal features of Linux, including POSIX job control (used by shells such as the C shell, *csh*, and *bash*), pseudoterminals (*pty* devices), and support for national or customized keyboards using dynamically loadable keyboard drivers. Linux also supports *virtual consoles*, which allow you to switch between multiple login sessions from the system console in text mode. Users of the *screen* program will find the Linux virtual console implementation familiar (although nearly all users make use of a GUI desktop instead).

Linux can quite happily coexist on a system that has other operating systems installed, such as Windows 95/98, Windows NT/2000/XP, Mac OS, and Unix-like operating systems such as the variants of BSD. The Linux bootloader (LILO) and the GRand Unified Bootloader (GRUB) allow you to select which operating system to

---

* On a 32-bit architecture; on a 64-bit architecture, up to 64 CPUs are supported, and patches are available that support up to 256 CPUs.

start at boot time, and Linux is compatible with other bootloaders as well (such as the one found in Windows XP).

Linux can run on a wide range of CPU architectures, including the Intel x86 (the whole Pentium line), Itanium, SPARC/UltraSPARC, AMD 64 ("Hammer"), ARM, PA-RISC, Alpha, PowerPC, MIPS, m68k, and IBM 390 and zSeries mainframes. Linux has also been ported to a number of embedded processors, and stripped-down versions have been built for various PDAs, including the PalmPilot and Compaq iPaq. In the other direction, Linux is being considered for top-of-the-line computers as well. Hewlett-Packard has a supercomputer with Linux as the operating system. A large number of scalable clusters—supercomputers built from arrays of PCs—run Linux as well.

Linux supports various filesystem types for storing data. Some filesystems, such as the Second Extended Filesystem (*ext2fs*), have been developed specifically for Linux. Other Unix filesystem types, such as the Minix-1 and Xenix filesystems, are also supported. The Windows NTFS, VFAT (Windows 95/98), and FAT (MS-DOS) filesystems have been implemented as well, allowing you to access Windows files directly. Support is included for Macintosh, OS/2, and Amiga filesystems as well. The ISO 9660 CD-ROM filesystem type, which reads all standard formats of CD-ROMs, is also supported. We talk more about filesystems in Chapter 2 and Chapter 10.

Networking support is one of the greatest strengths of Linux, in terms of both functionality and performance. Linux provides a complete implementation of TCP/IP networking. This includes device drivers for many popular Ethernet cards, PPP and SLIP (allowing you to access a TCP/IP network via a serial connection or modem), Parallel Line Internet Protocol (PLIP), and ADSL. Linux also supports the modern IPv6 protocol suite, and many other protocols, including DHCP, Appletalk, IRDA, DECnet, and even AX.25 for packet radio networks. The complete range of TCP/IP clients and services is supported, such as FTP, Telnet, NNTP, and Simple Mail Transfer Protocol (SMTP), the Sun RPC protocols allowing NFS and NIS, and the Microsoft protocols allowing participation in a Microsoft domain. The Linux kernel includes complete network firewall support, allowing any Linux machine to screen network packets and prevent unauthorized access to an intranet, for example.

It is widely held that networking performance under Linux is superior to other operating systems. We talk more about networking in Chapter 13 and Part IV.

Kernel

The *kernel* is the guts of the operating system itself; it's the code that controls the interface between user programs and hardware devices, the scheduling of processes to achieve multitasking, and many other aspects of the system. The kernel is not a separate process running on the system. Instead, you can think of the kernel as a set of routines, constantly in memory, to which every process has access. Kernel routines can be called in a number of ways. One direct method to utilize the kernel is for a process to execute a *system call*, which is a function that causes the kernel to execute some code on behalf of the process. For example, the *read* system call will read data from a file descriptor. To the programmer, this looks like any other C function, but in actuality the code for *read* is contained within the kernel.

The Linux kernel is known as a *monolithic* kernel, in that all core functions and device drivers are part of the kernel proper. Some operating systems employ a *micro-kernel* architecture whereby device drivers and other components (such as filesystems and memory management code) are *not* part of the kernel—rather, they are treated as independent services or regular user applications. There are advantages and disadvantages to both designs: the monolithic architecture is more common among Unix implementations and is the design employed by classic kernel designs, such as System V and BSD. Linux does support loadable device drivers (which can be loaded and unloaded from memory through user commands); this is covered in Chapter 18.

The Linux kernel on Intel platforms is developed to use the special protected-mode features of the Intel x86 processors (starting with the 80386 and moving on up to the current Pentium 4). In particular, Linux makes use of the protected-mode descriptor-based memory management paradigm and many of the other advanced features of these processors. Anyone familiar with x86 protected-mode programming knows that this chip was designed for a multitasking system such as Unix (the x86 was actually inspired by Multics). Linux exploits this functionality.

Like most modern operating systems, Linux is a multiprocessor operating system: it supports systems with more than one CPU on the motherboard. This feature allows different programs to run on different CPUs at the same time (or "in parallel"). Linux also supports *threads*, a common programming technique that allows a single program to create multiple "threads of control" that share data in memory. Linux supports several kernel-level and user-level thread packages, and Linux's kernel threads run on multiple CPUs, taking advantage of true hardware parallelism. The Linux kernel threads package is compliant with the POSIX 1003.1c standard.

The Linux kernel supports demand-paged loaded executables. That is, only those segments of a program that are actually used are read into memory from disk. Also, if multiple instances of a program are running at once, only one copy of the program code will be in memory. Executables use dynamically linked shared libraries, meaning that executables share common library code in a single library file found on disk. This allows executable files to occupy much less space on disk. This also means that a single copy of the library code is held in memory at one time, thus reducing overall memory usage. There are also statically linked libraries for those who wish to maintain "complete" executables without the need for shared libraries to be in place. Because Linux shared libraries are dynamically linked at runtime, programmers can replace modules of the libraries with their own routines.

In order to make the best use of the system's memory, Linux implements so-called *virtual memory* with disk paging. That is, a certain amount of *swap space** can be allocated on disk. When applications require more physical memory than is actually installed in the machine, it will swap inactive pages of memory out to disk. (A *page* is simply the unit of memory allocation used by the operating system; on most architectures, it's equivalent to 4 KB.) When those pages are accessed again, they will be read from disk back into main memory. This feature allows the system to run larger applications and support more users at once. Of course, swap is no substitute for physical RAM; it's much slower to read pages from disk than from memory.

The Linux kernel keeps portions of recently accessed files in memory, to avoid accessing the (relatively slow) disk any more than necessary. The kernel uses all the free memory in the system for caching disk accesses, so when the system is lightly loaded a large number of files can be accessed rapidly from memory. When user applications require a greater amount of physical memory, the size of the disk cache is reduced. In this way physical memory is never left unused.

To facilitate debugging, the Linux kernel generates a *core dump* of a program that performs an illegal operation, such as accessing an invalid memory location. The core dump, which appears as a file called *core* in the directory that the program was running, allows the programmer to determine the cause of the crash. We talk about the use of core dumps for debugging in the section "Examining a Core File" in Chapter 21.

Commands and Shells

The most important utility to many users is the *shell*. The shell is a program that reads and executes commands from the user. In addition, many shells provide features such as *job control* (allowing the user to manage several running processes at once—not as Orwellian as it sounds), input and output redirection, and a command language for writing *shell scripts*. A shell script is a file containing a program in the shell command language, analogous to a "batch file" under Windows.

Many types of shells are available for Linux. The most important difference between shells is the command language. For example, the C shell (*csh*) uses a command language somewhat like the C programming language. The classic Bourne shell uses a different command language. One's choice of a shell is often based on the command language it provides. The shell that you use defines, to some extent, your working environment under Linux.

---

* If you are a real OS geek, you will note that swap space is inappropriately named: entire processes are not swapped, but rather individual pages of memory are paged out. Although in some cases entire processes will be swapped out, this is not generally the case. The term "swap space" originates from the early days of Linux and should technically be called "paging space."

No matter what Unix shell you're accustomed to, some version of it has probably been ported to Linux. The most popular shell is the GNU Bourne Again Shell (*bash*), a Bourne shell variant. *bash* includes many advanced features, such as job control, command history, command and filename completion, an Emacs-like (or optionally, a *vi*-like) interface for editing the command line, and powerful extensions to the standard Bourne shell language. Another popular shell is *tcsh*, a version of the C shell with advanced functionality similar to that found in *bash*. Recently, *zsh*, with very advanced completion facilities, has found a lot of followers. Other shells include the Korn shell (*ksh*), BSD's *ash*, and *rc*, the Plan 9 shell.

What's so important about these basic utilities? Linux gives you the unique opportunity to tailor a custom system to your needs. For example, if you're the only person who uses your system, and you prefer to use the *vi* editor and the *bash* shell exclusively, there's no reason to install other editors or shells. The "do it yourself" attitude is prevalent among Linux hackers and users.

Text Processing and Word Processing

Almost every computer user has a need for some kind of document preparation system. (In fact, one of the authors has almost entirely forgotten how to write with pen and paper.) In the PC world, *word processing* is the norm: it involves editing and manipulating text (often in a "what you see is what you get" [WYSIWYG] environment) and producing printed copies of the text, complete with figures, tables, and other garnishes.

As you will see in this book, Linux supports attractive and full-featured WYSIWYG tools. In Chapter 8 we'll discuss OpenOffice (a free version of a propriety product, StarOffice, released by Sun Microsystems when it bought the suite's manufacturer), and KOffice, both of which are tightly integrated suites that support word processing, spreadsheets, and other common office tasks. These don't support all the features of Microsoft Office, but by the same token, they have some valuable features that Microsoft Office lacks. If you want to run Microsoft Office, you can do so through Wine, which we mention later.

There is a role for other ways to create documents, though. The system configuration files you need to edit on Linux from time to time, as well as programming for application development, require the use of simple *text processing*. The most popular tools for creating such documents are *vi* and Emacs, described in detail in Chapter 19.

Text processing can also be used with separate formatting tools to create very readable and attractive documents. With a text processing system, the author enters text using a "typesetting language" that describes how the text should be formatted. Once the source text (in the typesetting language) is complete, a user formats the text with a separate program, which converts the source to a format suitable for printing. This is somewhat analogous to programming in a language such as C, and "compiling" the document into a printable form.

The most famous text formatting language is HTML, the markup language used by virtually every page on the World Wide Web. Another popular text processing language is DocBook XML, a kind of industry-standard set of tags for marking up technical documentation, which is also used by the Linux Documentation Project (to be discussed later in this chapter).

We'll look at several text formatting systems in Chapter 20, *Text Processing*: TEX (developed by Donald Knuth of computer science fame) and its dialect LATEX, *groff*, the GNU version of the classic *troff* text formatter originally developed by Bell Labs); Texinfo (an extension to TEX used for software documentation by the Free Software Foundation); and Docbook.

Commercial Applications

In addition to the more than fifteen hundred Linux applications maintained by Linux distributors such as Debian, a groundswell of support exists from commercial application developers for Linux. These products include office productivity suites, word processors, scientific applications, network administration utilities, ERP packages such as Oracle Financials and SAP, and large-scale database engines. Linux has become a major force in the commercial software market, so you may be surprised to find how many popular commercial applications are available for Linux. We can't possibly discuss all of them here, so we'll only touch on the most popular applications and briefly mention some of the others.

Oracle, IBM, Informix, Sybase, and Interbase have released commercial database engines for Linux. Many of the Linux database products have demonstrated better performance than their counterparts running on Windows servers.

One very popular database for Linux is MySQL, a free and easy-to-use database engine. Because MySQL is easy to install, configure, and use, it has rapidly become the database engine of choice for many applications that can forego the complexity of the various proprietary engines. Furthermore, even though it's free software, MySQL is supported professionally by the company that developed it, MySQL AB. We describe the basic use of MySQL in Chapter 25.

MySQL does not include some of the more advanced features of the proprietary databases, however. Some database users prefer the open source database PostgresSQL, and Red Hat features it in some of its products. On the other hand, MySQL is catching up really quickly; the next version will contain support for distributed databases, for example.

A wide range of enterprise applications is available for Linux in addition to databases. Linux is one of the most popular platforms for Internet service hosting, so it is appropriate that high-end platforms for scalable web sites, including JBoss, BEA

WebLogic, and IBM WebSphere, have been released for Linux. Commercial, high-performance Java Virtual Machines and other software are available from Sun, IBM, and other vendors. IBM has released the popular Lotus Domino messaging and web application server, as well as the WebSphere MQ (formerly MQSeries) messaging platform.

Scientists, engineers, and mathematicians will find that a range of popular commercial products are available for Linux, such as Maple, Mathematica, MATLAB, and Simulink. Other commercial applications for Linux include high-end CAD systems, network management tools, firewalls, and software development environments.

Programming Languages and Utilities

Linux provides a complete Unix programming environment, including all the standard libraries, programming tools, compilers, and debuggers that you would expect to find on other Unix systems. The most commonly used compiler on Linux is the GNU's Compiler Collection, or *gcc*. *gcc* is capable of compiling C, C++, Objective C (another object-oriented dialect of C), Chill (a programming language mainly used for telecommunications), FORTRAN, and Java. Within the Unix software development world, applications and systems programming is usually done in C or C++, and *gcc* is one of the best C/C++ compilers around, supporting many advanced features and optimizations.

Java is an object-oriented programming language and runtime environment that supports a diverse range of applications such as web page applets, Internet-based distributed systems, database connectivity, and more. Java is fully supported under Linux. Several vendors and independent projects have released ports of the Java Development Kit for Linux, including Sun, IBM, and the Blackdown Project (which did one of the first ports of Java for Linux). Programs written for Java can be run on any system (regardless of CPU architecture or operating system) that supports the Java Virtual Machine. A number of Java "just in time" (or JIT) compilers are available, and the IBM and Sun Java Development Kits (JDKs) for Linux come bundled with high-performance JIT compilers that perform as well as those found on Windows or other Unix systems.

Some of the most popular and interesting tools associated with Java are open source. These include Eclipse, an integrated development environment (IDE) that is extendable to almost anything through plugins; JBoss, an implementation of Java 2 Enterprise Edition (J2EE) that has actually gone through the expense of becoming certified after a complaint by Sun Microsystems; and Gluecode, another application platform company bought by IBM in May 2005.

gcc is also capable of compiling Java programs directly to executables, and includes limited support for the standard JDK libraries.

Besides C, C++, and Java, many other compiled and interpreted programming languages have been ported to Linux, such as Smalltalk, FORTRAN, Pascal, LISP, Scheme, and Ada. In addition, various assemblers for writing machine code are available. An important open source project sponsored by Novell has developed an environment called Mono that provides support for Microsoft's .NET environment on Unix and Linux systems. Perhaps the most important class of programming languages for Linux is the many scripting languages, including Perl (the script language to end all script languages), Python (the first scripting language to be designed as object-oriented from the ground up), and Ruby (a fiercely object-oriented scripting language that has been heralded as very good for rapid application development).

Linux systems make use of the advanced *gdb* debugger, which allows you to step through a program to find bugs or examine the cause for a crash using a core dump. *gprof*, a profiling utility, will give you performance statistics for your program, letting you know where your program is spending most of its time. The Emacs and *vim* text editors provide interactive editing and compilation environments for various programming languages. Other tools that are available for Linux include the GNU *make* build utility, used to manage compilation of large applications, as well as source-code control systems such as CVS and *Subversion*.

Linux is an ideal system for developing Unix applications. It provides a modern programming environment with all the bells and whistles, and many professional Unix programmers claim that Linux is their favorite operating system for development and debugging. Computer science students can use Linux to learn Unix programming and to explore other aspects of the system, such as kernel architecture. With Linux, not only do you have access to the complete set of libraries and programming utilities, but you also have the complete kernel and library source code at your fingertips. Chapter 20 of this book is devoted to the programming languages and tools available for Linux.

The X Window System

The X Window System is the standard GUI for Unix systems. It was originally developed at MIT in the 1980s with the goal of allowing applications to run across a range of Unix workstations from different vendors. X is a powerful graphical environment supporting many applications. Many X-specific applications have been written, such as games, graphics utilities, programming and documentation tools, and so on.

Unlike Microsoft Windows, the X Window System has built-in support for networked applications: for example, you can run an X application on a server machine and have its windows display on your desktop, over the network. Also, X is extremely customizable: you can easily tailor just about any aspect of the system to your liking. You can adjust the fonts, colors, window decorations, and icons for your personal taste. You can go so far as to configure keyboard macros to run new applications at a keystroke. It's even possible for X to emulate the Windows and Macintosh desktop environments, if you want to keep a familiar interface.

The X Window System is freely distributable. However, many commercial vendors have distributed proprietary enhancements to the original X software. The version of X available for Linux is known as X.org, which is a port of X11R6 (X Window System Version 11, Release 6) made freely distributable for PC-based Unix systems, such as Linux.* X.org supports a wide range of video hardware, including standard VGA and many accelerated video adapters. X.org is a complete distribution of the X software, containing the X server itself, many applications and utilities, programming libraries, and documentation. It comes bundled with nearly every Linux distribution.

The look and feel of the X interface are controlled to a large extent by the *window manager*. This friendly program is in charge of the placement of windows, the user interface for resizing, iconifying, and moving windows, the appearance of window frames, and so on.

The X distribution and the major Linux distributions also contain programming libraries and include files for those wily programmers who wish to develop X applications. All the standard fonts, bitmaps, manual pages, and documentation are included.

Chapter 16 discusses how to install and use the X Window System on your Linux machine.

KDE and GNOME

Although the X Window System provides a flexible windowing system, many users want a complete desktop environment, with a customizable look and feel for all windows and widgets (such as buttons and scrollbars), a simplified user interface, and advanced features such as the ability to "drag and drop" data from one application to another. The KDE and GNOME projects are separate efforts that are striving to provide such an advanced desktop environment for Linux. By building up a powerful suite of development tools, libraries, and applications that are integrated into the desktop environment, KDE and GNOME aim to usher in the next era of Linux desktop computing. In the spirit of the open source community, these projects work together to provide complete interoperability so that applications originating in one environment will work on the other. Both systems provide a rich GUI, window manager, utilities, and applications that rival or exceed the features of systems such as the Windows XP desktop.

---

* X.org actually derives from another PC-based version of the X Window System, XFree86. Political quarrels that we do not want to go into here have led to a split into XFree86 and X.org; most Linux distributions these days ship the X.org version. This is not relevant for you, though, unless you plan to help with the continued development of the X Window System.

With KDE and GNOME, even casual users and beginners will feel right at home with Linux. Most distributions automatically configure one of these desktop environments during installation, making it unnecessary to ever touch the text-only console interface.

Both KDE and GNOME aim to make the Linux environment more user-friendly, and each has its fans and partisans. We discuss both in Chapter 3. As with X, both KDE and GNOME provide open source libraries that let you write programs conforming to their behavior and their look and feel.

Networking

Linux boasts one of the most powerful and robust networking systems in the world—more and more people are finding that Linux makes an excellent choice as a network server. Linux supports the TCP/IP networking protocol suite that drives the entire Internet, as well as many other protocols, including IPv6 (a new version of the IP protocol for the next-generation Internet), and UUCP (used for communication between Unix machines over serial lines). With Linux, you can communicate with any computer on the Internet, using Ethernet (including Fast and Gigabit Ethernet), Token Ring, dial-up connection, wireless network, packet radio, serial line, ADSL, ISDN, ATM, IRDA, AppleTalk, IPX (Novell NetWare), and many other network technologies. The full range of Internet-based applications is available, including World Wide Web browsers, web servers, FTP, email, chat, news, *ssh*, Telnet, and more.

Most Linux users use either a dial-up or a DSL connection through an ISP to connect to the Internet from home. Linux supports the popular PPP and SLIP protocols, used by most ISPs for dial-in access. If you have a broadband connection, such as a T1 line, cable modem, DSL, or other service, Linux supports those technologies as well. You can even configure a Linux machine to act as a router and firewall for an entire network of computers, all connecting to the Internet through a single dial-up or broadband connection.

Linux supports a wide range of web browsers, including Mozilla (the open source spin-off of the Netscape browser), Konquerer (another open source browser packaged with KDE), and the text-based Lynx browser. The Emacs text editor even includes a small text-based web browser.

Linux also hosts a range of web servers. Linux played an important role in the emergence of the popular and free Apache web server. In fact, it's estimated that Apache running on Linux systems drives more web sites than any other platform in the world. Apache is easy to set up and use; we show you how in Chapter 22.

A full range of mail and news readers is available for Linux, such as MH, Elm, Pine, and mutt, as well as the mail/news readers included with the Mozilla web browser. Many of these are compatible with standard mail and news protocols such as IMAP and POP. Whatever your preference, you can configure your Linux system to send and receive electronic mail and news from all over the world.

A variety of other network services are available for Linux. Samba is a package that allows Linux machines to act as a Windows file and print server. NFS allows your system to share files seamlessly with other machines on the network. With NFS, remote files look to you as if they were located on your own system's drives. FTP allows you to transfer files to and from other machines on the network. Other networking features include NNTP-based electronic news systems such as C News and INN; the Sendmail, Postfix, and Exim mail transfer agents; *ssh*, *telnet*, and *rsh*, which allow you to log in and execute commands on other machines on the network; and *finger*, which allows you to get information on other Internet users. There are tons of TCP/IP-based applications and protocols out there.

If you have experience with TCP/IP applications on other systems, Linux will be familiar to you. The system provides a standard socket programming interface, so virtually any program that uses TCP/IP can be ported to Linux. The Linux X server also supports TCP/IP, allowing you to display applications running on other systems on your Linux display. Administration of Linux networking will be familiar to those coming from other Unix systems, as the configuration and monitoring tools are similar to their BSD counterparts.

In Chapter 13, we discuss the configuration and setup of TCP/IP, including PPP, for Linux. We also discuss configuration of web browsers, web servers, and mail software.

Laptop Support

Linux includes a number of laptop-specific features, such as PCMCIA (or "PC Card") support and APM and the newer ACPI, as well as the wireless networking built into Centrino laptops. The PCMCIA Tools package for Linux includes drivers for many PCMCIA devices, including modems, Ethernet cards, and SCSI adapters. APM allows the kernel to keep track of the laptop's battery power and perform certain actions (such as an automated shutdown) when power is low; it also allows the CPU to go into "low-power" mode when not in use. This is easy to configure as a kernel option. Various tools interact with APM, such as *apm* (which displays information on battery status) and *apmd* (which logs battery status and can be used to trigger power events). These should be included with most Linux distributions. ACPI has a similar purpose, but is newer and more featureful. With ACPI, you can even use the so-called "suspend to disk" facility with it, where the current state of the computer is written to your hard disk, and the computer turned off. You can then turn it on later and resume your work exactly where you left off. GUI tools such as *kpowersave* let you control this from a friendly graphical environment.

Interfacing with Windows

Various utilities exist to interface with the world of Windows and MS-DOS. The most well-known application is a project known as Wine—a platform for Microsoft Windows applications on the X Window System under Linux. Wine allows Microsoft Windows applications to run directly under Linux and other Intel-based operating systems. Wine is in a process of continual development, and now runs a wide variety of Windows software, including many desktop applications and games. We discuss Wine in Chapter 28.

Linux provides a seamless interface for transferring files between Linux and Windows systems. You can mount a Windows partition or floppy under Linux, and directly access Windows files as you would any others. In addition, there is the *mtools* package, which allows direct access to MS-DOS-formatted floppies, as well as *htools*, which does the same for Macintosh floppy disks.

Another legacy application is the Linux MS-DOS Emulator, or DOSEMU, which allows you to run many MS-DOS applications directly from Linux. Although MS-DOS-based applications are rapidly becoming a thing of the past, there are still a number of interesting MS-DOS tools and games that you might want to run under Linux. It's even possible to run the old Microsoft Windows 3.1 under DOSEMU.

Although Linux does not have complete support for emulating Windows and MS-DOS environments, you can easily run these other operating systems on the same machine with Linux, and choose which operating system to run when you boot the machine. Many distributions know how to preserve another operating system that's already installed when you add Linux to the computer, and set up a working LILO or GRUB bootloader to let you to select between Linux, Windows, and other operating systems at boot time. In this book we'll show you how to set up the LILO bootloader, in case you need to do it yourself.

Another popular option is to run a system-level virtual machine, which literally allows you to run Linux and Windows *at the same time*. A *virtual machine* is a software application that emulates many of the hardware features of your system, tricking the operating system into believing that it is running on a physical computer. Using a virtual machine, you can boot Linux and then run Windows at the same time—with both Linux and Windows applications on your desktop at once. Alternatively, you can boot Windows and run Linux under the virtual machine. Although there is some performance loss when using virtual machines, many people are very happy employing them for casual use, such as running a Windows-based word processor within a Linux desktop. The most popular virtual machines are VMware (*http://www.vmware.com*), which is a commercial product, and Bochs (*http://bochs.sourceforge.net*), which is an open source project. We describe VMware in Chapter 28.

Finally, remote logins allow you to work on another system from your Linux system. Any two computers running the X Window System (mostly Linux, BSD, and Unix systems) can share work this way, with a user on one system running a program on another, displaying the graphical output locally, and entering commands from the local keyboard and mouse. RDP, an acronym that has been expanded to both Remote Desktop Protocol and Remote Display Protocol, allows a Linux system to run programs on remote Windows systems in the same way. A Virtual Network Connection (VNC) client and server perform the same task with even greater flexibility, letting different operating systems on different computers work together. In "Remote Desktop Access to Windows Programs" we show you how to set up these services, and in "FreeNX: Linux as a Remote Desktop Server" we discuss the FreeNX remote communication system, which allows the same transparent networking as X with a tremendous speed advantage. Both of these sections are in Chapter 28.

Other Applications

A host of miscellaneous applications are available for Linux, as one would expect from an operating system with such a diverse set of users. Linux's primary focus is currently for personal Unix computing, but this is rapidly changing. Business and scientific software are expanding, and commercial software vendors have contributed a growing pool of applications.

The scientific community has wholly embraced Linux as the platform of choice for inexpensive numerical computing. A large number of scientific applications have been developed for Linux, including the popular technical tools MATLAB and Mathematica. A wide range of free packages is also available, including FELT (a finite-element analysis tool), Spice (a circuit design and analysis tool), and Khoros (an image/digital signal processing and visualization system). Many popular numerical computing libraries have been ported to Linux, including the LAPACK linear algebra library. There is also a Linux-optimized version of the BLAS code upon which LAPACK depends.

Linux is one of the most popular platforms for parallel computing using *clusters*, which are collections of inexpensive machines usually connected with a fast (gigabit-per-second or faster) network. The NASA Beowulf project first popularized the idea of tying a large number of Linux-based PCs into a massive supercomputer for scientific and numerical computing. Today, Linux-based clusters are the rule, rather than the exception, for many scientific applications. In fact, Linux clusters are finding their way into increasingly diverse applications—for example, the Google search engine runs on a cluster of Linux machines (over 250,000 of them in December 2004, according to an MIT paper)!

As with any operating system, Linux has its share of games. A number of popular commercial games have been released for Linux, including Quake, Quake II, Quake

III Arena, Doom, SimCity 3000, Descent, and more. Most of the popular games support play over the Internet or a local network, and clones of other commercial games are popping up for Linux. There are also classic text-based dungeon games such as Nethack and Moria; MUDs (multiuser dungeons, which allow many users to interact in a text-based adventure) such as DikuMUD and TinyMUD; and a slew of free graphical games, such as *xtetris*, *netrek*, and *Xboard* (the X11 frontend to *gnuchess*).

For audiophiles, Linux has support for a wide range of sound hardware and related software, such as CDplayer (a program that can control a CD-ROM drive as a conventional CD player, surprisingly enough), MIDI sequencers and editors (allowing you to compose music for playback through a synthesizer or other MIDI-controlled instrument), and sound editors for digitized sounds. You can play your MP3 and OGG/Vorbis files on Linux, and with the tools in some distributions you can handle more proprietary formats as well.

Can't find the application you're looking for? A number of web sites provide comprehensive directories of Linux applications. The best known is Freshmeat (*http://www.freshmeat.net*); a couple others are listed in Appendix A. Take a look at these sites just to see the enormous amount of code that has been developed for Linux.

If you absolutely can't find what you need, you can always attempt to port the application from another platform to Linux. Or, if all else fails, you can write the application yourself. That's the spirit of free software—if you want something to be done right, do it yourself! While it's sometimes daunting to start a major software project on your own, many people find that if they can release an early version of the software to the public, many helpers pop up in the free software community to carry on the project.

About Linux's Copyright

Linux is covered by what is known as the GNU GPL. The GPL, which is sometimes referred to as a "copyleft" license, was developed for the GNU project by the Free Software Foundation. It makes a number of provisions for the distribution and modification of "free software." "Free," in this sense, refers to freedom, not just cost. The GPL has always been subject to misinterpretation, and we hope that this summary will help you to understand the extent and goals of the GPL and its effect on Linux. A complete copy of the GPL is available at *http://www.gnu.org/copyleft/gpl.html*.

Originally, Linus Torvalds released Linux under a license more restrictive than the GPL, which allowed the software to be freely distributed and modified, but prevented any money changing hands for its distribution and use. The GPL allows people to sell and make profit from free software, but doesn't allow them to restrict the right for others to distribute the software in any way.

A Summary of Free Software Licensing

First, we should explain that "free software" covered by the GPL is *not* in the public domain. Public domain software is software that is not copyrighted and is literally owned by the public. Software covered by the GPL, on the other hand, is copyrighted to the author or authors. This means that the software is protected by standard international copyright laws and that the author of the software is legally defined. Just because the software may be freely distributed doesn't mean it is in the public domain.

GPL-licensed software is also not "shareware." Generally, shareware software is owned and copyrighted by the author, but the author requires users to send in money for its use after distribution. On the other hand, software covered by the GPL may be distributed and used free of charge.

The GPL also allows people to take and modify free software, and distribute their own versions of the software. However, any derived works from GPL software must also be covered by the GPL. In other words, a company could not take Linux, modify it, and sell it under a restrictive license. If any software is derived from Linux, that software must be covered by the GPL as well.

People and organizations can distribute GPL software for a fee and can even make a profit from its sale and distribution. However, in selling GPL software, the distributor can't take those rights away from the purchaser; that is, if you purchase GPL software from some source, you may distribute the software for free or sell it yourself as well.

This might sound like a contradiction at first. Why sell software for profit when the GPL allows anyone to obtain it for free? When a company bundles a large amount of free software on a CD-ROM and distributes it, it needs to charge for the overhead of producing and distributing the CD-ROM, and it may even decide to make profits from the sale of the software. This is allowed by the GPL.

Organizations that sell free software must follow certain restrictions set forth in the GPL. First, they can't restrict the rights of users who purchase the software. This means that if you buy a CD-ROM of GPL software, you can copy and distribute that CD-ROM free of charge, or you can resell it yourself. Second, distributors must make it obvious to users that the software is indeed covered by the GPL. Third, distributors must provide, free of charge, the complete source code for the software being distributed, or they must point their customers on demand to where the software can be downloaded. This will allow anyone who purchases GPL software to make modifications to that software.

Allowing a company to distribute and sell free software is a very good thing. Not everyone has access to the Internet to download software, such as Linux, for free. The GPL allows companies to sell and distribute software to those people who do not have free (cost-wise) access to the software. For example, many organizations sell

Linux on floppy, tape, or CD-ROM via mail order, and make a profit from these sales. The developers of Linux may never see any of this profit; that is the understanding that is reached between the developer and the distributor when software is licensed by the GPL. In other words, Linus knew that companies might wish to sell Linux and that he might not see a penny of the profits from those sales. (If Linus isn't rich, at least he's famous!)

In the free-software world, the important issue is not money. The goal of free software is always to develop and distribute fantastic software and to allow anyone to obtain and use it. In the next section, we'll discuss how this applies to the development of Linux.

SCO and Other Challenges

In March 2003, a company called SCO—which had a tortuous history of mergers and divestitures that involved purchasing some rights to Unix—claimed that Linux contained some source code to which SCO had rights, and therefore that SCO had rights to Linux as well. The company started by suing IBM, a bold choice (to say the least) because few companies in the computer field could be more familiar with litigation or be better prepared for it. In any case, SCO made it clear that their complaints went far beyond IBM; indeed, that they were owed something by anyone using Linux. In December 2003, according to news reports, SCO even sent letters to a large number of Fortune 1000 companies advising them to send licensing fees to SCO.

Red Hat and other companies joined the fray. Novell, which by then had bought SUSE and become a solid member of the Linux community, added some zest to the already indigestible controversy by citing its own rights to Unix. Over time the whole affair became a tangle of lawsuits, countersuits, motions to dismiss, public relations grand-standing, and general mud-slinging.

As of this writing, the SCO case is unresolved, but the results seem salutary. Few observers believe Linux is in trouble; rather, it is SCO that is financially threatened. The network of companies, individuals, and key organizations that support Linux has handled the challenge well. Some major vendors strengthened their support for Linux by offering their customers indemnification. The next edition of this book, we hope, will contain little more than a footnote about the whole affair.

Finally, Linus Torvalds and the OSDL have recognized that the old method of accepting code with no strings attached should be tightened. Starting in May 2004, anyone submitting code to the kernel has been asked to include their contact information and to declare informally that they have a right to the code they are submitting. The new system is lightweight and simple, but allows challenges (of which none have been received yet) to be tracked back to the people responsible for the code in question.

Further copyright challenges to Linux are unlikely; patents, however, could be used against it. But every programmer and software company has to worry about software patents; Linux and free software are no more at risk than any other software. Although the workings of free software are entirely open to inspection, and therefore might be more tempting to target with a patent lawsuit, the only purpose of such a lawsuit would be to maliciously shut down a project, because free software cannot support license fees.

Open Source and the Philosophy of Linux

When new users encounter Linux, they often have a few misconceptions and false expectations of the system. Linux is a unique operating system, and it's important to understand its philosophy and design in order to use it effectively. At the center of the Linux philosophy is a concept that we now call open source software.

Open source is a term that applies to software for which the source code—the inner workings of the program—is freely available for anyone to download, modify, and redistribute. Software covered under the GNU GPL, described in the previous section, fits into the category of open source. Not surprisingly, though, so does software that uses copyright licenses that are similar, but not identical, to the GPL. For example, software that can be freely modified but that does not have the same strict requirements for redistribution as the GPL is also considered open source. Various licenses fit this category, including the BSD License and the Apache Software License.

The so-called open source and free software development models started with the Free Software Foundation and were popularized with Linux. They represent a totally different way of producing software that opens up every aspect of development, debugging, testing, and study to anyone with enough interest in doing so. Rather than relying upon a single corporation to develop and maintain a piece of software, open source allows the code to evolve, openly, in a community of developers and users who are motivated by a desire to *create good software*, rather than simply to make a profit.

O'Reilly has published two books, *Open Sources 1.0* and *Open Sources 2.0*, that serve as good introductions to the open source development model. They're collections of essays about the open source process by leading developers (including Linus Torvalds and Richard Stallman). Another popular text on this topic—so often cited that it is considered nearly canonical—is *The Cathedral and the Bazaar*, by Eric S. Raymond.

Open source has received a lot of media attention, and some are calling the phenomenon the next wave in software development, which will sweep the old way of doing things under the carpet. It still remains to be seen whether that will happen, but there have been some encouraging events that make this outcome seem likely. For example, Netscape Corporation has released the code for its web browser as an open source project called Mozilla, and companies such as Sun Microsystems, IBM, and Apple have released certain products as open source in the hopes that they will flourish in a community-driven software development effort.

Open source has received a lot of media attention, and Linux is at the center of all of it. In order to understand where the Linux development mentality is coming from, however, it might make sense to take a look at how commercial software has traditionally been built.

Commercial software houses tend to base development on a rigorous policy of quality assurance, source and revision control systems, documentation, and bug reporting and resolution. Developers are not allowed to add features or to change key sections of code on a whim: they must validate the change as a response to a bug report and consequently "check in" all changes to the source control system so that the changes can be backed out if necessary. Each developer is assigned one or more parts of the system code, and only that developer may alter those sections of the code while it is "checked out."

Internally, the quality assurance department runs rigorous test suites (so-called regression tests) on each new pass of the operating system and reports any bugs. It's the responsibility of the developers to fix these bugs as reported. A complicated system of statistical analysis is employed to ensure that a certain percentage of bugs are fixed before the next release, and that the system as a whole passes certain release criteria.

In all, the process used by commercial software developers to maintain and support their code is very complicated, and quite reasonably so. The company must have quantitative proof that the next revision of the software is ready to be shipped. It's a big job to develop a commercial software system, often large enough to employ hundreds (if not thousands) of programmers, testers, documenters, and administrative personnel. Of course, no two commercial software vendors are alike, but you get the general picture. Smaller software houses, such as startups, tend to employ a scaled-down version of this style of development.

On the opposite end of the spectrum sits Linux, which is, and more than likely always will be, a hacker's operating system.* Although many open source projects have adopted elements of commercial software development techniques, such as source control and bug tracking systems, the collaborative and distributed nature of Linux's development is a radical departure from the traditional approach.

---

* Our definition of "hacker" is a feverishly dedicated programmer—a person who enjoys exploiting computers and generally doing interesting things with them. This is in contrast to the common connotation of "hacker" as a computer wrongdoer or an outlaw.

Recently, there has been a lot of talk about so-called agile development practices like XP (extreme programming). Linux and open source adepts are often a bit surprised about this, since these "lightweight" software development methods have always been a central idea of open source development.

Linux is primarily developed as a group effort by volunteers on the Internet from all over the world. No single organization is responsible for developing the system. For the most part, the Linux community communicates via various mailing lists and web sites. A number of conventions have sprung up around the development effort: for example, programmers wanting to have their code included in the "official" kernel should mail it to Linus Torvalds. He will test the code and include it in the kernel (as long as it doesn't break things or go against the overall design of the system, he will more than likely include it). As Linux has grown, this job has become too large for Linus to do himself (plus, he has kids now), so other volunteers are responsible for testing and integrating code into certain aspects of the kernel, such as the network subsystem.

The system itself is designed with a very open-ended, feature-rich approach. A new version of the Linux kernel will typically be released about every few weeks (sometimes even more frequently than this). Of course, this is a very rough figure; it depends on several factors, including the number of bugs to be fixed, the amount of feedback from users testing prerelease versions of the code, and the amount of sleep that Linus has had that week.

Suffice it to say that not every single bug has been fixed and not every problem ironed out between releases. (Of course, this is always true of commercial software as well!) As long as the system appears to be free of critical or oft-manifesting bugs, it's considered "stable" and new revisions are released. The thrust behind Linux development is not an effort to release perfect, bug-free code; it's to develop a free implementation of Unix. Linux is for the developers, more than anyone else.

Anyone who has a new feature or software application to add to the system generally makes it available in an "alpha" stage—that is, a stage for testing by those brave users who want to bash out problems with the initial code. Because the Linux community is largely based on the Internet, alpha software is usually uploaded to one or more of the various Linux web sites (see the Appendix), and a message is posted to one of the Linux mailing lists about how to get and test the code. Users who download and test alpha software can then mail results, bug fixes, or questions to the author.

After the initial problems in the alpha code have been fixed, the code enters a "beta" stage, in which it's usually considered stable but not complete (that is, it works, but not all the features may be present). Otherwise, it may go directly to a "final" stage in which the software is considered complete and usable. For kernel code, once it's complete, the developer may ask Linus to include it in the standard kernel, or as an optional add-on feature to the kernel.

Keep in mind these are only conventions, not rules. Some people feel so confident with their software that they don't need to release an alpha or test version. It's always up to the developer to make these decisions.

What happened to regression testing and the rigorous quality process? It's been replaced by the philosophy of "release early and often." Real users are the best testers because they try out the software in a variety of environments and in a host of demanding real-life applications that can't be easily duplicated by any software quality assurance group. One of the best features of this development and release model is that bugs (and security flaws) are often found, reported, and fixed within *hours*, not days or weeks.

You might be amazed that such an unstructured system of volunteers programming and debugging a complete Unix system could get anything done at all. As it turns out, it's one of the most efficient and motivated development efforts ever employed. The entire Linux kernel was written *from scratch*, without employing any code from proprietary sources. A great deal of work was put forth by volunteers to port all the free software under the sun to the Linux system. Libraries were written and ported, filesystems developed, and hardware drivers written for many popular devices.

The Linux software is generally released as a *distribution*, which is a set of prepackaged software making up an entire system. It would be quite difficult for most users to build a complete system from the ground up, starting with the kernel, then adding utilities, and installing all necessary software by hand. Instead, there are a number of software distributions including everything you need to install and run a complete system. Again, there is no standard distribution; there are many, each with its own advantages and disadvantages. In this book, we describe how to install the Red Hat, SUSE, and Debian distributions, but this book can help you with any distribution you choose.

Despite the completeness of the Linux software, you still need a bit of Unix know-how to install and run a complete system. No distribution of Linux is completely bug-free, so you may be required to fix small problems by hand after installation. Although some readers might consider this a pain, a better way to think about it is as the "joy of Linux"—that of having fun tinkering with, learning about, and fixing up your own system. It's this very attitude that distinguishes Linux enthusiasts from mere users. Linux can be either a hobby, an adventure sport, or a lifestyle. (Just like snowboarding and mountain biking, Linux geeks have their own lingo and style of dress—if you don't believe us, hang out at any Linux trade show!) Many new Linux users report having a great time learning about this new system, and find that Linux rekindles the fascination they had when first starting to experiment with computers.

Hints for Unix Novices

Installing and using your own Linux system doesn't require a great deal of background in Unix. In fact, many Unix novices successfully install Linux on their systems. This is a worthwhile learning experience, but keep in mind that it can be very frustrating to some. If you're lucky, you will be able to install and start using your Linux system without any Unix background. However, once you are ready to delve into the more complex tasks of running Linux—installing new software, recompiling the kernel, and so forth—having background knowledge in Unix is going to be a necessity. (Note, however, that many distributions of Linux are as easy to install and configure as Windows and certainly easier than Windows 2000 or XP.)

Fortunately, by running your own Linux system, you will be able to learn the essentials of Unix necessary to perform these tasks. This book contains a good deal of information to help you get started. Chapter 4 is a tutorial covering Unix basics, and Part II contains information on Linux system administration. You may wish to read these chapters before you attempt to install Linux at all; the information contained therein will prove to be invaluable should you run into problems.

Just remember that nobody can expect to go from being a Unix novice to a Unix system administrator overnight. A powerful and flexible computer system is never maintenance-free, so you will undoubtedly encounter hang-ups along the way. Treat this as an opportunity to learn more about Linux and Unix, and try not to get discouraged when things don't always go as expected!

Hints for Unix Gurus

Even those people with years of Unix programming and system administration experience may need assistance before they are able to pick up and install Linux. There are still aspects of the system Unix wizards need to be familiar with before diving in. For one thing, Linux is not a commercial Unix system. It doesn't attempt to uphold the same standards as other Unix systems you may have come across. But in some sense, Linux is *redefining* the Unix world by giving all other systems a run for their money. To be more specific, while stability is an important factor in the development of Linux, it's not the *only* factor.

More important, perhaps, is functionality. In many cases, new code will make it into the standard kernel even though it's still buggy and not functionally complete. The assumption is that it's more important to release code that users can test and use than delay a release until it's "complete." Nearly all open source software projects have an alpha release before they are completely tested. In this way, the open source community at large has a chance to work with the code, test it, and develop it further, while those who find the alpha code "good enough" for their needs can use it. Commercial Unix vendors rarely, if ever, release software in this manner.

Even if you're a Unix ultra-wizard who can disassemble Solaris kernels in your sleep and recode an AIX superblock with one hand tied behind your back, Linux might take some getting used to. The system is very modern and dynamic, with a new kernel release approximately every few months and new utilities constantly being released. One day your system may be completely up to date with the current trend, and the next day the same system is considered to be in the Stone Age.

With all of this dynamic activity, how can you expect to keep up with the ever-changing Linux world? For the most part, it's best to upgrade incrementally; that is, upgrade only those parts of the system that *need* upgrading, and then only when you think an upgrade is necessary. For example, if you never use Emacs, there is little reason to continuously install every new release of Emacs on your system. Furthermore, even if you are an avid Emacs user, there is usually no reason to upgrade it unless you find that a missing feature is in the next release. There is little or no reason to always be on top of the newest version of software.

Keep in mind that Linux was developed by its users. This means, for the most part, that the hardware supported by Linux is that which users and developers actually have access to. As it turns out, most of the popular hardware and peripherals for 80x86 systems are supported (in fact, Linux probably supports more hardware than any commercial implementation of Unix). However, some of the more obscure and esoteric devices, as well as those with proprietary drivers for which the manufacturers do not easily make the specifications available, aren't supported yet. As time goes on, a wider range of hardware will be supported, so if your favorite devices aren't listed here, chances are that support for them is forthcoming.

Another drawback for hardware support under Linux is that many companies have decided to keep the hardware interface proprietary. The upshot of this is that volunteer Linux developers simply can't write drivers for those devices (if they could, those drivers would be owned by the company that owned the interface, which would violate the GPL). The companies that maintain proprietary interfaces write their own drivers for operating systems, such as Microsoft Windows; the end user (that's you) never needs to know about the interface. Unfortunately, this does not allow Linux developers to write drivers for those devices.

Little can be done about the situation. In some cases, programmers have attempted to write hackish drivers based on assumptions about the interface. In other cases, developers work with the company in question and attempt to obtain information about the device interface, with varying degrees of success.

Sources of Linux Information

As you have probably guessed, many sources of information about Linux are available, apart from this book.

Online Documents

If you have access to the Internet, you can get many Linux documents via web and anonymous FTP sites all over the world. If you do not have direct Internet access, these documents may still be available to you; many Linux distributions on CD-ROM contain all the documents mentioned here and are often available off the retail shelf.

A great number of web and FTP archive sites carry Linux software and related documents. Appendix A contains a listing of some of the Linux documents available via the Internet.

Examples of available online documents are the Linux FAQ, a collection of frequently asked questions about Linux; the Linux HOWTO documents, each describing a specific aspect of the system—including the Installation HOWTO, the Printing HOWTO, and the Ethernet HOWTO; and the Linux META-FAQ, a list of other sources of Linux information on the Internet.

Additional documentation, individually hosted "HOWTOs," blogs, knowledge bases, and forums exist that provide significant material to help individuals use Linux. Distributors maintain diverse mailing lists and forums dealing with a variety of subjects from using Linux on a laptop to configuring web servers. Such web sites and digests of mailing lists have largely taken over for Linux-related Usenet newsgroups; see "Usenet Newsgroups" later in this chapter.

The central Linux Documentation home page is available to web users at *http://www.tldp.org*. This page contains many HOWTOs and other documents, as well as pointers to other sites of interest to Linux users, including the Linux Documentation Project manuals (see the following section).

Books and Other Published Works

There are a number of published works specifically about Linux. In addition, a number of free books are distributed on the Internet by the Linux Documentation Project (LDP), a project carried out over the Internet to write and distribute a bona fide set of "manuals" for Linux. These manuals are analogs to the documentation sets available with commercial versions of Unix: they cover everything from installing Linux to using and running the system, programming, networking, kernel development, and more.

The LDP manuals are available via the Web, as well as via mail order from several sources. O'Reilly has published the *Linux Network Administrator's Guide* from the LDP.

Aside from the growing number of Linux books, books about Unix still exist (though many have ceased publication). In general, these books are equally applicable to Linux. So far as using and programming the system is concerned, simpler Linux tasks don't differ greatly from original implementations of Unix in many respects. Armed with this book and some other Linux or Unix books on specialized topics, you should be able to tackle a majority of Linux tasks.

There are monthly magazines about Linux, notably *Linux Journal* and *Linux Magazine*. These are an excellent way to keep in touch with the many goings-on in the Linux community. Languages other than English have their own Linux print publications as well. (European, South American, and Asian publications have become commonplace in the last few years.)

Usenet Newsgroups

Usenet is a worldwide electronic news and discussion forum with a heavy contingent of so-called newsgroups, or discussion areas devoted to a particular topic. Much of the development of Linux has been done over the waves of the Internet and Usenet, and not surprisingly, a number of Usenet newsgroups are available for discussions about Linux.

There are far too many newsgroups devoted to Linux to list here. The ones dealing directly with Linux are under the *comp.os.linux* hierarchy, and you'll find others on related topics such as *comp.windows.x*.

Internet Mailing Lists

If you have access to Internet electronic mail, you can participate in a number of mailing lists devoted to Linux. These run the gamut from kernel hacking to basic user questions. Many of the popular Linux mailing lists have associated web sites with searchable archives, allowing you to easily find answers to common questions. We list some of these resources in the Appendix.

Getting Help

First, we should mention that Linux has a rich community of volunteers and participants who need help and offer help for free. A good example of such a community is Ubuntu (*http://www.ubuntulinux.org*). Supported by a commercial company, Canonical Ltd., that offers low-cost professional support, Ubuntu has a large and enthusiastic community ready to provide old-style Linux support. Ubuntu, a derivative of Debian, employs a number of paid developers who also help maintain the Debian project.

Distributions such as Red Hat, Novell's SUSE, and Mandriva have become quite adept at providing commercial support for their own distributions of Linux and for other open source projects. Following a concept originated by Bernard Golden called the Open Source Maturity Model, Linux companies have done an excellent job in demonstrating their ability to compete using the open source paradigm. They have demonstated the ability to provide:

- Adequate support and maintenance
- Continued innovation
- Product road maps and commitments to adhere to them
- Functionality and ease of use for IT managers, particularly across enterprise-size environments
- Stable business models to fund new development and expand into new product areas
- Structured and scalable partner ecosystems devoted to enabling customer success

Additionally, these Linux companies have established community projects to keep them from becoming stale.

Mature Linux companies also provide extended business offerings, including training, professional sales and support ($24 \times 7 \times 365$), indemnification, and quality documentation.

In addition to the companies already mentioned, you will find a channel full of their business partners who have considerable expertise in providing commercial Linux support. Their web sites contain ways to find a business partner that can assist Linux users in a variety of ways.

As you become more accustomed to running Linux, you will probably discover many facets that may pleasantly surprise you. Many people not only use Linux but consider the community their home base. Good luck in the coming days.

CHAPTER 2
Preinstallation and Installation

This chapter represents your first step in installing Linux. We describe how to obtain the Linux software, in the form of one of the various prepackaged distributions, and how to prepare your system. We include ways to partition disks so that Linux can coexist with Windows or another operating system.

As we have mentioned, there is no single "official" distribution of the Linux software; there are, in fact, many distributions, each serving a particular purpose and set of goals. These distributions are available via anonymous FTP from the Internet and via mail on CD-ROM and DVD, as well as in retail stores.

Distributions of Linux

Because Linux is free software, no single organization or entity is responsible for releasing and distributing the software. Therefore, anyone is free to put together and distribute the Linux software, as long as the restrictions in the GPL (and other licenses that may be used) are observed. The upshot of this is that there are many distributions of Linux, available via anonymous FTP or mail order.

You are now faced with the task of deciding on a particular distribution of Linux that suits your needs. Not all distributions are alike. Many of them come with just about all the software you'd need to run a complete system—and then some. Other Linux distributions are "small" distributions intended for users without copious amounts of disk space.

You might also want to consider that distributions have different target groups. Some are meant more for businesses, others more for the home user. Some put more emphasis on server use, others on desktop use.

How can you decide among all these distributions? If you have access to Usenet news, or another computer conferencing system such as web-based discussion boards, you might want to ask there for opinions from people who have installed Linux. Even better, if you know someone who has installed Linux, ask him for help and advice. In actuality, most of the popular Linux distributions contain roughly the same set of software, so the distribution you select is more or less arbitrary.

A particularly interesting type of distribution is the so-called live CD, such as Knoppix (*http://www.knoppix.org*). These distributions boot from CD and do not require any installation at all; they keep all information in RAM, but can still access your hard drive and other hardware. Besides being a very convenient way of test-driving Linux without having to wipe out anything else, they are also a very good way of rescuing a system that has become unbootable. More about salvaging booting problems will follow later in this book.

Getting Linux via Mail Order or Other Hard Media

If you don't have high-speed Internet access, you can get many Linux distributions via mail order on CD-ROM or DVD. Many distributors accept credit cards as well as international orders, so no matter where you live, you should be able to obtain Linux in this way.

Linux is free software, but distributors are allowed by the GPL to charge a fee for it. Therefore, ordering Linux via mail order might cost you between U.S. $5 and U.S. $150, depending on the distribution. However, if you know people who have already purchased or downloaded a release of Linux, you are free to borrow or copy their software for your own use. Linux distributors are not allowed to restrict the license or redistribution of the software in any way. If you are thinking about installing an entire lab of machines with Linux, for example, you need to purchase only a single copy of one of the distributions, which can be used to install all the machines. There is one exception to this rule, though: in order to add value to their distribution, some vendors include commercial packages that you might not be allowed to install on several machines. If this is the case, it should be explicitly stated on the package.

Another advantage with buying a distribution is that you often get installation support; that is, you can contact the distributor by phone or email and get help if you run into trouble during the installation.

Many Linux user groups offer their own distributions; see if there's a user group near you. For special platforms like Alpha, a user group may be an excellent place to get Linux.

Getting Linux from the Internet

If you have access to the Internet, the easiest way to obtain Linux is via anonymous FTP. One major FTP site is *ftp://ftp.ibiblio.org*, and the various Linux distributions can be found there in the directory */pub/Linux/distributions*. In many countries, there are local mirrors of this server from which you should be able to get the same software faster.

When downloading the Linux software, be sure to use binary mode for all file transfers (with most FTP clients, the command *binary* enables this mode).

You might run into a minor problem when trying to download files for one system (such as Linux) with another system (such as Windows), because the systems are not always prepared to handle each other's files sensibly. However, with the hints given in this chapter, you should be able to complete the installation process nevertheless.

Some distributions are released via anonymous FTP as a set of disk images. That is, the distribution consists of a set of files, and each file contains the binary image of a floppy. In order to copy the contents of the image file onto the floppy, you can use the *RAWRITE.EXE* program under Windows. This program copies, block for block, the contents of a file to a floppy, without regard for disk format. *RAWRITE.EXE* is available on the various Linux FTP sites, including *ftp://ftp.ibiblio.org* in the directory */pub/Linux/system/Install/rawwrite*.

Be forewarned that this is a labor-intensive way of installing Linux: the distribution can easily come to more than 50 floppies. Therefore, only few distributions still provide an installation option that uses floppy disks exclusively. However, combinations of a few floppy disks for the initial booting procedure plus one or more CD-ROMs for the actual software installation are not uncommon.

To proceed, download the set of floppy images and use *RAWRITE.EXE* with each image in turn to create a set of floppies. Boot from the so-called boot floppy, and you're ready to roll. The software is usually installed directly from the floppies, although some distributions allow you to install from a Windows partition on your hard drive, while others allow you to install over a TCP/IP network. The documentation for each distribution should describe these installation methods if they are available.

If you have access to a Unix workstation with a floppy drive, you can also use the *dd* command to copy the file image directly to the floppy. A command such as dd of=/dev/rfd0 if=foo bs=18k will "raw write" the contents of the file *foo* to the floppy device on a Sun workstation. Consult your local Unix gurus for more information on your system's floppy devices and the use of *dd*.

Each distribution of Linux available via anonymous FTP should include a *README* file describing how to download and prepare the floppies for installation. Be sure to read all available documentation for the release you are using.

Today, some of the bigger Linux distributions are also distributed as one or a few ISO images that you can burn on a CD-ROM or DVD. Downloading these is feasible only for people with big hard disks and a broadband connection to the Internet, due to the enormous amounts of data involved (but remember that you only need the disk space for one ISO image at a time; you can delete the image after having burnt it, and before downloading the next one).

Preparing to Install Linux

After you have obtained a distribution of Linux, you're ready to prepare your system for installation. This takes a certain degree of planning, especially if you're already running other operating systems. In the following sections, we describe how to plan for the Linux installation.

Installation Overview

Although each release of Linux is different, in general the method used to install the software is as follows:

1. *Repartition your hard drive(s)*. If you have other operating systems already installed, you will need to repartition the drives in order to allocate space for Linux. This is discussed in "Repartitioning Concepts" later in this chapter. In some distributions (such as SUSE), this step is integrated into the installation procedure. Check the documentation of your distribution to see whether this is the case. Still, it won't hurt you to follow the steps given here and repartition your hard drive in advance.

2. *Boot the Linux installation medium*. Each distribution of Linux has some kind of installation medium—usually a boot floppy or a bootable CD-ROM—that is used to install the software. Booting this medium will either present you with some kind of installation program, which will step you through the Linux installation, or allow you to install the software by hand.

3. *Create Linux partitions*. After repartitioning to allocate space for Linux, you create Linux partitions on that empty space. This is accomplished with the Linux *fdisk* program, covered in "Editing /etc/fstab," or with some other distribution-specific program, such as the Disk Druid, which comes with Red Hat Linux.

4. *Create filesystems and swap space*. At this point, you will create one or more filesystems, used to store files, on the newly created partitions. In addition, if you plan to use swap space (which you should, unless you have really huge amounts of physical memory, or RAM), you will create the swap space on one of your Linux partitions. This is covered in the sections "Creating Swap Space" and "Editing /etc/fstab."

5. *Install the software on the new filesystems*. Finally, you will install the Linux software on your newly created filesystems. After this, if all goes well, it's smooth sailing. This is covered in "Installing the Software." Later, in "Running into Trouble," we describe what to do if anything goes wrong.

People who want to switch back and forth between different operating systems sometimes wonder which to install first: Linux or the other system? We can testify that some people have had trouble installing Windows 95/98/ME after Linux. Windows 95/98/ME tends to wipe out existing boot information when it's installed, so you're safer installing it first and then installing Linux afterward using the information in this chapter. Windows NT/2000/XP seems to be more tolerant of existing boot information, but installing Windows first and then Linux still seems to be the safer alternative.

Many distributions of Linux provide an installation program that will step you through the installation process and automate one or more of the previous steps for you. Keep in mind throughout this chapter and the next that any number of the previous steps may be automated for you, depending on the distribution.

 While preparing to install Linux, the best advice we can give is to take notes during the entire procedure. Write down everything you do, everything you type, and everything you see that might be out of the ordinary. The idea here is simple: if (or when!) you run into trouble, you want to be able to retrace your steps and find out what went wrong. Installing Linux isn't difficult, but there are many details to remember. You want to have a record of all these details so that you can experiment with other methods if something goes wrong. Also, keeping a notebook of your Linux installation experience is useful when you want to ask other people for help—for example, when posting a message to one of the Linux-related Usenet groups or web discussion forums. Your notebook is also something you'll want to show to your grandchildren someday.[*]

Repartitioning Concepts

In general, hard drives are divided into *partitions*, with one or more partitions devoted to an operating system. For example, on one hard drive you may have several separate partitions—one devoted to, say, Windows, another to FreeBSD, and another two to Linux.

If you already have other software installed on your system, you may need to resize those partitions in order to free up space for Linux. You will then create one or more Linux partitions on the resulting free space for storing the Linux software and swap space. We call this process *repartitioning*.

Many Windows systems utilize a single partition inhabiting the entire drive. To Windows, this partition is known as C:. If you have more than one partition, Windows names them D:, E:, and so on. In a way, each partition acts like a separate hard drive.

On the first sector of the disk is a *master boot record* along with a *partition table*. The boot record (as the name implies) is used to boot the system. The partition table contains information about the locations and sizes of your partitions.

---

[*] Matt shamefully admits that he kept a notebook of all his tribulations with Linux for the first few months of working with the system. It is now gathering dust on his bookshelf.

There are three kinds of partitions: *primary*, *extended*, and *logical*. Of these, primary partitions are used most often. However, because of a limit on the size of the partition table, you can have only four primary partitions on any given drive. This is due to the poor design of MS-DOS and Windows; even other operating systems that originated in the same era do not have such limits.

The way around this four-partition limit is to use an extended partition. An extended partition doesn't hold any data by itself; instead, it acts as a "container" for logical partitions. Therefore, you could create one extended partition, covering the entire drive, and within it create many logical partitions. However, you are limited to only one extended partition per drive.

Linux Partition Requirements

Before we explain how to repartition your drives, you need an idea of how much space you will be allocating for Linux. We discuss how to create these partitions later in this chapter, in "Editing /etc/fstab."

On Unix systems, files are stored on a *filesystem*, which is essentially a section of the hard drive (or other medium, such as CD-ROM, DVD, or floppy) formatted to hold files. Each filesystem is associated with a specific part of the directory tree; for example, on many systems, there is a filesystem for all the files in the directory */usr*, another for */tmp*, and so on. The *root filesystem* is the primary filesystem, which corresponds to the topmost directory, /.

Under Linux, each filesystem lives on a separate partition on the hard drive. For instance, if you have a filesystem for / and another for */usr*, you will need two partitions to hold the two filesystems.[*]

Before you install Linux, you will need to prepare filesystems for storing the Linux software. You must have at least one filesystem (the root filesystem), and therefore one partition, allocated to Linux. Many Linux users opt to store all their files on the root filesystem, which, in most cases, is easier to manage than several filesystems and partitions.

However, you may create multiple filesystems for Linux if you wish—for example, you may want to use separate filesystems for */usr* and */home*. Those readers with Unix system administration experience will know how to use multiple filesystems creatively. In "Creating Filesystems" in Chapter 10 we discuss the use of multiple partitions and filesystems.

Why use more than one filesystem? The most commonly stated reason is safety; if, for some reason, one of your filesystems is damaged, the others will (usually) be

---

[*] Notice that this applies to filesystems only, not to directories. Of course, you can have any number of directory trees off the root directory in the same filesystem.

unharmed. On the other hand, if you store all your files on the root filesystem, and for some reason the filesystem is damaged, you may lose all your files in one fell swoop. This is, however, rather uncommon; if you back up the system regularly, you should be quite safe.

On the other hand, using several filesystems has the advantage that you can easily upgrade your system without endangering your own precious data. You might have a partition for the users' home directories, and when upgrading the system, you leave this partition alone, wipe out the others, and reinstall Linux from scratch. Of course, nowadays distributions all have quite elaborate update procedures, but from time to time, you might want a fresh start.

Another reason to use multiple filesystems is to divvy up storage among multiple hard drives. If you have, say, 300 MB free on one hard drive, and 2 GB free on another, you might want to create a 300-MB root filesystem on the first drive and a 2-GB /usr filesystem on the other. It is possible to have a single filesystem span multiple drives by using a tool called *Logical Volume Manager* (LVM), but setting this up requires considerable knowledge, unless your distribution's installation program automates it for you.

In summary, Linux requires at least one partition, for the root filesystem. If you wish to create multiple filesystems, you need a separate partition for each additional filesystem. Some distributions of Linux automatically create partitions and filesystems for you, so you may not need to worry about these issues at all.

Another issue to consider when planning your partitions is swap space. *Swap space* is a portion of the disk used by an operating system to temporarily store parts of programs that were loaded by the user but aren't currently in use. You are not required to use swap space with Linux, but if you have less than 256 MB of physical RAM, it is strongly suggested that you do.

You have two options. The first is to use a *swap file* that exists on one of your Linux filesystems. You will create the swap file for use as virtual RAM after you install the software. The second option is to create a *swap partition*, an individual partition to be used only as swap space. Most people use a swap partition instead of a swap file.

A single swap file or partition may be up to 2 GB.* If you wish to use more than 2 GB of swap (hardly ever necessary), you can create multiple swap partitions or files—up to 32 in all.

Setting up a swap partition is covered in "Creating Swap Space," later in this chapter, and setting up a swap file is discussed in "Managing Swap Space" in Chapter 10. For instance, if you want to run *fdisk* on the first SCSI disk in your system, use the command:

```
# fdisk /dev/sda
```

---

* This value applies to machines with Intel processors. On other architectures it can be both higher and lower.

/dev/hda (the first IDE drive) is the default if you don't specify one.

If you are creating Linux partitions on more than one drive, run *fdisk* once for each drive:

```
# fdisk /dev/hda

Command (m for help):
```

Here *fdisk* is waiting for a command; you can type m to get a list of options:

```
Command (m for help): m
Command action
   a   toggle a bootable flag
   b   edit bsd disklabel
   c   toggle the dos compatibility flag
   d   delete a partition
   l   list known partition types
   m   print this menu
   n   add a new partition
   o   create a new empty DOS partition table
   p   print the partition table
   q   quit without saving changes
   s   create a new empty Sun disklabel
   t   change a partition's system id
   u   change display/entry units
   v   verify the partition table
   w   write table to disk and exit
   x   extra functionality (experts only)

Command (m for help):
```

The n command is used to create a new partition. Most other options you won't need to worry about. To quit *fdisk* without saving any changes, use the q command. To quit *fdisk* and write the changes to the partition table to disk, use the w command. This is worth repeating: so long as you quit with q without writing, you can mess around as much as you want with *fdisk* without risking harm to your data. Only when you type w can you cause potential disaster to your data if you do something wrong.

The first thing you should do is display your current partition table and write the information down for later reference. Use the p command to see the information. It is a good idea to copy the information to your notebook after each change you have made to the partition table. If, for some reason, your partition table is damaged, you will not access any data on your hard disk any longer, even though the data itself is still there. But by using your notes, you might be able to restore the partition table and get your data back in many cases by running *fdisk* again and deleting and re-creating the partitions with the parameters you previously wrote down. Don't forget to save the restored partition table when you are done.

Here is an example of a printed partition table (of a very small hard disk), where blocks, sectors, and cylinders are units into which a hard disk is organized:

```
Command (m for help): p

Disk /dev/hda: 16 heads, 38 sectors, 683 cylinders
Units = cylinders of 608 * 512 bytes
   Device Boot  Begin   Start    End  Blocks  Id  System
/dev/hda1    *      1       1    203   61693   6  DOS 16-bit >=32M

Command (m for help):
```

In this example, we have a single Windows partition on */dev/hda1*, which is 61693 blocks (about 60 MB).* This partition starts at cylinder number 1 and ends on cylinder 203. We have a total of 683 cylinders in this disk; so there are 480 cylinders left on which to create Linux partitions.

To create a new partition, use the n command. In this example, we'll create two primary partitions (*/dev/hda2* and */dev/hda3*) for Linux:

```
Command (m for help): n
Command action
  e   extended
  p   primary partition (1-4)
  p
```

Here, *fdisk* is asking which type of the partition to create: extended or primary. In our example, we're creating only primary partitions, so we choose p:

```
Partition number (1-4):
```

fdisk will then ask for the number of the partition to create; because partition 1 is already used, our first Linux partition will be number 2:

```
Partition number (1-4): 2
First cylinder (204-683):
```

Now, we'll enter the starting cylinder number of the partition. Because cylinders 204 through 683 are unused, we use the first available one (numbered 204). There's no reason to leave empty space between partitions:

```
First cylinder (204-683): 204
Last cylinder or +size or +sizeM or +sizeK (204-683):
```

fdisk is asking for the size of the partition we want to create. We can either specify an ending cylinder number, or a size in bytes, kilobytes, or megabytes. Because we want our partition to be 80 MB in size, we specify +80M. When specifying a partition size in this way, *fdisk* will round the actual partition size to the nearest number of cylinders:

```
Last cylinder or +size or +sizeM or +sizeK (204-683): +80M
```

---

* A block, under Linux, is 1024 bytes.

If you see a warning message such as this, it can be ignored. *fdisk* prints the warning because it's an older program and dates back before the time that Linux partitions were allowed to be larger than 64 MB.

Now we're ready to create our second Linux partition. For sake of demonstration, we'll create it with a size of 10 MB:

```
Command (m for help): n
Command action
   e   extended
   p   primary partition (1-4)
p
Partition number (1-4): 3
First cylinder (474-683): 474
Last cylinder or +size or +sizeM or +sizeK (474-683): +10M
```

At last, we'll display the partition table. Again, write down all this information—especially the block sizes of your new partitions. You'll need to know the sizes of the partitions when creating filesystems. Also, verify that none of your partitions overlaps:

```
Command (m for help): p

Disk /dev/hda: 16 heads, 38 sectors, 683 cylinders
Units = cylinders of 608 * 512 bytes
    Device Boot  Begin   Start    End  Blocks   Id  System
/dev/hda1   *        1       1    203   61693    6  DOS 16-bit >=32M
/dev/hda2          204     204    473   82080   83  Linux native
/dev/hda3          474     474    507   10336   83  Linux native
```

As you can see, */dev/hda2* is now a partition of size 82,080 blocks (which corresponds to about 80 MB), and */dev/hda3* is 10,336 blocks (about 10 MB).

Note that most distributions require you to use the t command in *fdisk* to change the type of the swap partition to "Linux swap," which is numbered 82. You can use the l command to print a list of known partition type codes, and then use the t command to set the type of the swap partition to that which corresponds to "Linux swap."

This way the installation software will be able to automatically find your swap partitions based on type. If the installation software doesn't seem to recognize your swap partition, you might want to rerun *fdisk* and use the t command on the partition in question.

In the previous example, the remaining cylinders on the disk (numbered 508 to 683) are unused. You may wish to leave unused space on the disk, in case you want to create additional partitions later.

Finally, we use the w command to write the changes to disk and exit *fdisk*:

```
Command (m for help): w
#
```

Keep in mind that none of the changes you make while running *fdisk* takes effect until you give the w command, so you can toy with different configurations and save them when you're done. Also, if you want to quit *fdisk* at any time without saving the changes, use the q command. Remember that you shouldn't modify partitions for operating systems other than Linux with the Linux *fdisk* program.

You may not be able to boot Linux from a partition using cylinders numbered over 1023. Therefore, you should try to create your Linux root partition within the sub-1024 cylinder range, which is almost always possible (e.g., by creating a small root partition in the sub-1024 cylinder range). If, for some reason, you cannot or do not want to do this, you can simply boot Linux from floppy, use the rescue option of the installation CD or DVD, or boot a Linux live CD like Knoppix.

Some Linux distributions require you to reboot the system after running *fdisk* to allow the changes to the partition table to take effect before installing the software. Newer versions of *fdisk* automatically update the partition information in the kernel, so rebooting isn't necessary. To be on the safe side, after running *fdisk* you should reboot from the installation medium before proceeding.

Creating Swap Space

If you are planning to use a swap partition for virtual RAM, you're ready to prepare it.* In "Managing Swap Space" in Chapter 10, we discuss the preparation of a swap file, in case you don't want to use an individual partition.

Many distributions require you to create and activate swap space before installing the software. If you have a small amount of physical RAM, the installation procedure may not be successful unless you have some amount of swap space enabled.

The command used to prepare a swap partition is *mkswap*, and it takes the following form:

```
mkswap -c partition
```

where *partition* is the name of the swap partition. For example, if your swap partition is */dev/hda3*, use the command

```
# mkswap -c /dev/hda3
```

With older versions of *mkswap*, you had to specify the size of the partition, which was dangerous, as one typo could destroy your disk logically.

The -c option tells *mkswap* to check for bad blocks on the partition when creating the swap space. Bad blocks are spots on the magnetic medium that do not hold the data correctly. This occurs only rarely with today's hard disks, but if it does occur, and you do not know about it, it can cause you endless trouble. Always use the -c option to have *mkswap* check for bad blocks. It will exclude them from being used automatically.

---

* Again, some distributions of Linux prepare the swap space for you automatically, or via an installation menu option.

If you are using multiple swap partitions, you need to execute the appropriate *mkswap* command for each partition.

After formatting the swap space, you need to enable it for use by the system. Usually, the system automatically enables swap space at boot time. However, because you have not yet installed the Linux software, you need to enable it by hand.

The command to enable swap space is *swapon*, and it takes the following form:

```
swapon partition
```

After the *mkswap* command shown, we use the following command to enable the swap space on */dev/hda3*:

```
# swapon /dev/hda3
```

Creating the Filesystems

Before you can use your Linux partitions to store files, you must create filesystems on them. Creating a filesystem is analogous to formatting a partition under Windows or other operating systems. We discussed filesystems briefly in "Linux Partition Requirements," earlier in this chapter.

Several types of filesystems are available for Linux. Each filesystem type has its own format and set of characteristics (such as filename length, maximum file size, and so on). Linux also supports several third-party filesystem types, such as the Windows filesystem.

The most commonly used filesystem types are the *Second Extended Filesystem*, or *ext2fs* and the *Third Extended Filesystem*, or *ext3fs*. The *ext2fs* and *ext3fs* filesystems are two of the most efficient and flexible filesystems; they allows filenames of up to 256 characters and filesystem sizes of up to 32 terabytes. In "Filesystem Types" in Chapter 10, we discuss the various filesystem types available for Linux. Initially, however, we suggest you use the *ext3fs* filesystem.

To create an *ext3fs* filesystem, use the command

```
mke2fs -j -c partition
```

where *partition* is the name of the partition. (Notice that the same command, mke2fs is used for creating both *ext2* and *ext3* filesystems; it's the -*j* that makes it a journalled, *ext3*, filesystem.) For example, to create a filesystem on */dev/hda2*, use the command

```
# mke2fs -j -c /dev/hda2
```

If you're using multiple filesystems for Linux, you need to use the appropriate mke2fs command for each filesystem.

If you have encountered any problems at this point, see "Running into Trouble," later in this chapter.

Installing the Software

Finally, you are ready to install the software on your system. Every distribution has a different mechanism for doing this. Many distributions have a self-contained program that steps you through the installation. On other distributions, you have to *mount* your filesystems in a certain subdirectory (such as */mnt*) and copy the software to them by hand. On CD-ROM distributions, you may be given the option to install a portion of the software on your hard drive and leave most of the software on the CD-ROM. This is often called a "live filesystem." Such a live filesystem is convenient for trying out Linux before you make a commitment to install everything on your disk.

Some distributions offer several different ways to install the software. For example, you may be able to install the software directly from a Windows partition on your hard drive instead of from floppies. Or you may be able to install over a TCP/IP network via FTP or NFS. See your distribution's documentation for details.

For example, the Slackware distribution requires you to do the following:

1. Create partitions with *fdisk*.
2. Optionally create swap space with *mkswap* and *swapon* (if you have 16 MB or less of RAM).
3. Run the *setup* program to install the software. *setup* leads you through a self-explanatory menu system.

The exact method used to install the Linux software differs greatly with each distribution.

You might be overwhelmed by the choice of software to install. Modern Linux distributions can easily contain a thousand or more packages spread over several CD-ROMs. There are basically three methods for selecting the software package:

Selection by task
> This is the easiest means of selection for beginners. You don't have to think about whether you need a certain package. You just pick whether your Linux computer should act as a workstation, a development machine, or a network router, and the installation program will pick the appropriate packages for you. In all cases, you can then either refine the selection by hand or come back to the installation program later.

Selection of individual packages by series
> With this selection mechanism, all the packages are grouped into series such as "Networking," "Development," or "Graphics." You can go through all the series and pick the individual packages there. This requires more decisions than if you choose selection by task, because you have to decide whether you need each package; however, you can skip an entire series when you are sure that you are not interested in the functions it offers.

Selection of individual packages sorted alphabetically
> This method is useful only when you already know which packages you want to install; otherwise, you won't see the forest for the trees.

Choosing one selection method does not exclude the use of the others. Most distributions offer two or more of the aforementioned selection mechanisms.

It might still be difficult to decide which package to pick. Good distributions show a short description of each package on screen to make it easier for you to select the correct ones, but if you are still unsure, our advice is this: when in doubt, leave it out! You can always go back and add packages later.

Modern distributions have a very nifty feature, called *dependency tracking*. Some packages work only when some other packages are installed (e.g., a graphics viewer might need special graphics libraries to import files). With dependency tracking, the installation program can inform you about those dependencies and will let you automatically select the package you want along with all the ones it depends on. Unless you are very sure about what you are doing, you should always accept this offer, or the package might not work afterward.

Installation programs can help you make your selection and avoid mistakes in other ways. For example, the installation program might refuse to start the installation when you deselect a package that is absolutely crucial for even the most minimal system to boot (like the basic directory structure). Or, it might check for mutual exclusions, such as cases in which you can only have one package or the other, but not both.

Some distributions come with a large book that, among other things, lists all the packages together with short descriptions. It might be a good idea to at least skim those descriptions to see what's in store for you, or you might be surprised when you select the packages and are offered the 25th text editor.

Creating the Boot Floppy or Installing GRUB

Every distribution provides some means of booting your new Linux system after you have installed the software. In many cases, the installation procedure suggests you create a boot floppy, which contains a Linux kernel configured to use your newly created root filesystem. In order to boot Linux, you could boot from this floppy; control is transferred to your hard drive after you boot. On other distributions, this boot floppy is the installation floppy itself. If your system does not contain a floppy drive any more (like many newer systems), be assured that there are always other ways of booting Linux, such as booting directly from CD.

Many distributions give you the option of installing GRUB on your hard drive. GRUB is a program that resides on your drive's master boot record. It boots a number of operating systems, including Windows and Linux, and allows you to select which one to boot at startup time.

In order for GRUB to be installed successfully, it needs to know a good deal of information about your drive configuration: for example, which partitions contain which operating systems, how to boot each operating system, and so on. Many distributions, when installing GRUB, attempt to "guess" at the appropriate parameters for your configuration. Occasionally, the automated GRUB installation provided by some distributions can fail and leave your master boot record in shambles (however, it's very doubtful that any damage to the actual data on your hard drive will take place).

In many cases, it is best to use a boot floppy until you have a chance to configure GRUB yourself, by hand. If you're exceptionally trusting, though, you can go ahead with the automated GRUB installation if it is provided with your distribution.

In "Using GRUB" in Chapter 17, we'll cover in detail how to configure and install GRUB for your particular setup.

 There are other boot loaders besides GRUB, including the older Linux Leader (LILO). The general concepts are the same, though; only the installation and configuration differ.

If everything goes well, congratulations! You have just installed Linux on your system. Go have a cup of tea or something; you deserve it.

In case you ran into trouble, "Running into Trouble," later in this chapter, describes the most common sticking points for Linux installations, and how to get around them.

Additional Installation Procedures

Some distributions of Linux provide a number of additional installation procedures, allowing you to configure various software packages, such as TCP/IP networking, the X Window System, and so on. If you are provided with these configuration options during installation, you may wish to read ahead in this book for more information on how to configure this software. Otherwise, you should put off these installation procedures until you have a complete understanding of how to configure the software.

It's up to you; if all else fails, just go with the flow and see what happens. It's doubtful that anything you do incorrectly now cannot be undone in the future (knock on wood).

Post-Installation Procedures

After you have completed installing the Linux software, you should be able to reboot the system, log in as *root*, and begin exploring the system. (Each distribution has a different method for doing this; follow the instructions given by the distribution.)

Before you strike out on your own, however, there are some tasks you should do now that may save you a lot of grief later. Some of these tasks are trivial if you have the right hardware and Linux distribution; others may involve a little research on your part, and you may decide to postpone them.

Creating a User Account

In order to start using your system, you need to create a user account for yourself. Eventually, if you plan to have other users on your system, you'll create user accounts for them as well. But before you begin to explore you need at least one account.

Why is this? Every Linux system has several preinstalled accounts, such as *root*. The root account, however, is intended exclusively for administrative purposes. As *root* you have all kinds of privileges and can access all files on your system.

However, using *root* can be dangerous, especially if you're new to Linux. Because there are no restrictions on what *root* can do, it's all too easy to mistype a command, inadvertently delete files, damage your filesystem, and so on. You should log in as *root* only when you need to perform system administration tasks, such as fixing configuration files, installing new software, and so on. See "Maintaining the System" in Chapter 10 for details.*

For normal usage, you should create a standard user account. Unix systems have built-in security that prevents users from deleting other users' files and corrupting important resources, such as system configuration files. As a regular user, you'll be protecting yourself from your own mistakes. This is especially true for users who don't have Unix system administration experience.

Many Linux distributions provide tools for creating new accounts. These programs are usually called *useradd* or *adduser*. As *root*, invoking one of these commands should present you with a usage summary for the command, and creating a new account should be fairly self-explanatory.

Most modern distributions provide a generic system administration tool for various tasks, one of which is creating a new user account.

---

* A side note: on a Windows 95/98/ME system, the user is always the equivalent of a *root* user, whether that power is needed or not.

Again, other distributions, such as SUSE Linux, Red Hat Linux, or Mandriva, integrate system installation and system administration in one tool (e.g., *yast* or *yast2* on SUSE Linux).

If all else fails, you can create an account by hand. Usually, all that is required to create an account is the following:

1. Edit the file */etc/passwd* to add the new user. (Doing this with *vipw*—instead of editing the file directly—will protect you against concurrent changes of the password file, but *vipw* is not available on all distributions.)

2. Optionally edit the file */etc/shadow* to specify "shadow password" attributes for the new user.

3. Create the user's home directory.

4. Copy skeleton configuration files (such as *.bashrc*) to the new user's home directory. These can sometimes be found in the directory */etc/skel*.

We don't want to go into great detail here: the particulars of creating a new user account can be found in virtually every book on Unix system administration. We also talk about creating users in "Managing User Accounts" in Chapter 11. You should be able to find a tool that takes care of these details for you.

Keep in mind that to set or change the password on the new account, you use the passwd command. For example, to change the password for the user *duck*, issue the following command:

```
# passwd duck
```

This will prompt you to set or change the password for *duck*. If you execute the passwd command as *root*, it will not prompt you for the original password. In this way, if you have forgotten your old password but can still log in as *root*, you can reset it.

Getting Online Help

Linux provides online help in the form of manual pages. Throughout this book, we'll be directing you to look at the manual pages for particular commands to get more information. Manual pages describe programs and applications on the system in detail, and it's important for you to learn how to access this online documentation in case you get into a bind.

To get online help for a particular command, use the man command. For example, to get information on the passwd command, type the following command:

```
$ man passwd
```

This should present you with the manual page for passwd.

Usually, manual pages are provided as an optional package with most distributions, so they won't be available unless you have opted to install them. However, we very strongly advise you to install the manual pages. You will feel lost many times without them.

In addition, certain manual pages may be missing or incomplete on your system. It depends on how complete your distribution is and how up-to-date the manual pages are.

Linux manual pages also document system calls, library functions, configuration file formats, and kernel internals. In "Manual Pages" in Chapter 4, we describe their use in more detail.

Besides traditional manual pages, there are also so-called Info pages. These can be read with the text editor Emacs, the command `info`, or one of many graphical info readers available.

Many distributions also provide documentation in HTML format that you can read with any web browser, such as Konqueror, as well as with Emacs.

Finally, there are documentation files that are simply plain text. You can read these with any text editor or simply with the command `more`.

If you cannot find documentation for a certain command, you can also try running it with either the `-h` or `-help` option. Most commands then provide a brief summary of their usage.

Editing /etc/fstab

In order to ensure that all your Linux filesystems will be available when you reboot the system, you may need to edit the file */etc/fstab*, which describes your filesystems. Many distributions automatically generate the */etc/fstab* file for you during installation, so all may be well. However, if you have additional filesystems that were not used during the installation process, you may need to add them to */etc/fstab* in order to make them available. Swap partitions should be included in */etc/fstab* as well.

In order to access a filesystem, it must be *mounted* on your system. Mounting a filesystem associates that filesystem with a particular directory. For example, the root filesystem is mounted on /, the */usr* filesystem on */usr*, and so on. (If you did not create a separate filesystem for */usr*, all files under */usr* will be stored on the root filesystem.)

We don't want to smother you with technical details here, but it is important to understand how to make your filesystems available before exploring the system. For more details on mounting filesystems, see "Mounting Filesystems" in Chapter 10, or any book on Unix system administration.

The root filesystem is automatically mounted on / when you boot Linux. However, your other filesystems must be mounted individually. Usually, this is accomplished with the command:

```
# mount -av
```

in one of the system startup files in */etc/rc.d* or wherever your distribution stores its configuration files. This tells the `mount` command to mount any filesystems listed in the file */etc/fstab*. Therefore, in order to have your filesystems mounted automatically at boot time, you need to include them in */etc/fstab*. (Of course, you could always mount the filesystems by hand, using the `mount` command after booting, but this is unnecessary work.)

Here is a sample */etc/fstab* file, shortened by omitting the last two parameters in each line, which are optional and not relevant to the discussion here. In this example, the root filesystem is on */dev/hda1*, the */home* filesystem is on */dev/hdb2*, and the swap partition is on */dev/hdb1*:

```
# /etc/fstab
# device       directory   type    options
#
/dev/hda1      /           ext3    defaults
/dev/hdb2      /home       ext3    defaults
/dev/hdb1      none        swap    sw
/proc          /proc       proc    defaults
```

The lines beginning with the "#" character are comments. Also, you'll notice an additional entry for */proc*. */proc* is a "virtual filesystem" used to gather process information by commands such as `ps`.

As you can see, */etc/fstab* consists of a series of lines. The first field of each line is the device name of the partition, such as */dev/hda1*. The second field is the *mount point*—the directory where the filesystem is mounted. The third field is the type; Linux *ext3fs* filesystems should use ext3 for this field. `swap` should be used for swap partitions. The fourth field is for mounting options. You should use `defaults` in this field for filesystems and `sw` for swap partitions.

Using this example as a model, you should be able to add entries for any filesystems not already listed in the */etc/fstab* file.

How do we add entries to the file? The easiest way is to edit the file, as *root*, using an editor such as *vi* or Emacs. We won't get into the use of text editors here. *vi* and Emacs are both covered in Chapter 19.

After editing the file, you'll need to issue the command:

```
# /bin/mount -a
```

or reboot for the changes to take effect.

If you're stuck at this point, don't be alarmed. We suggest that Unix novices do some reading on basic Unix usage and system administration. We offer a lot of introductory material in upcoming chapters, and most of the remainder of this book is going to assume familiarity with these basics, so don't say we didn't warn you.

Shutting Down the System

You should never reboot or shut down your Linux system by pressing the reset switch or simply turning off the power. As with most Unix systems, Linux caches disk writes in memory. Therefore, if you suddenly reboot the system without shutting down cleanly, you can corrupt the data on your drives. Note, however, that the "Vulcan nerve pinch" (pressing Ctrl-Alt-Delete in unison) is generally safe: the kernel traps the key sequence and passes it to the init process, which, in turn, initiates a clean shutdown of the system (or whatever it is configured to do in this case; see "init, inittab, and rc Files" in Chapter 17). Your system configuration might reserve the Ctrl-Alt-Delete for the system administrator so that normal users cannot shut down the network server that the whole department depends upon. To set permissions for this keystroke combination, create a file called */etc/shutdown.allow* that lists the names of all the users who are allowed to shut down the machine.

The easiest way to shut down the system is with the *shutdown* command. As an example, to shut down and reboot the system immediately, use the following command as *root*:

```
# shutdown -r now
```

This will cleanly reboot your system. The manual page for *shutdown* describes the other available command-line arguments. Instead of now, you can also specify when the system should be shut down. Most distributions also provide *halt*, which calls *shutdown now*. Some distributions also provide *poweroff*, which actually shuts down the computer and turns it off. Whether it works depends on the hardware and the BIOS (which must support APM or ACPI), not on Linux.

Running into Trouble

Almost everyone runs into some kind of snag or hang-up when attempting to install Linux the first time. Most of the time, the problem is caused by a simple misunderstanding. Sometimes, however, it can be something more serious, such as an oversight by one of the developers or a bug.

This section describes some of the most common installation problems and how to solve them. It also describes unexpected error messages that can pop up during installations that appear to be successful.

In general, the proper boot sequence is as follows:

1. After booting from the LILO prompt, the system must load the kernel image from floppy. This may take several seconds; you know things are going well if the floppy drive light is still on.

2. While the kernel boots, SCSI devices must be probed for. If you have no SCSI devices installed, the system will hang for up to 15 seconds while the SCSI probe continues; this usually occurs after the line:

```
lp_init: lp1 exists (0), using polling driver
```

appears on your screen.

3. After the kernel is finished booting, control is transferred to the system bootup files on the floppy. Finally, you will be presented with a login prompt (either a graphical or a textual one) or be dropped into an installation program. If you are presented with a login prompt such as:

```
Linux login:
```

you should then log in (usually as *root* or install—this varies with each distribution). After you enter the username, the system may pause for 20 seconds or more while the installation program or shell is being loaded from floppy. Again, the floppy drive light should be on. Don't assume the system is hung.

Problems with Booting the Installation Medium

When attempting to boot the installation medium for the first time, you may encounter a number of problems. Note that the following problems are *not* related to booting your newly installed Linux system. See "Problems After Installing Linux," later in this chapter, for information on these kinds of pitfalls.

A floppy or medium error occurs when attempting to boot
The most popular cause for this kind of problem is a corrupt boot floppy. Either the floppy is physically damaged, in which case you should re-create the disk with a brand-new floppy, or the data on the floppy is bad, in which case you should verify that you downloaded and transferred the data to the floppy correctly. In many cases, simply re-creating the boot floppy will solve your problems. Retrace your steps and try again.

If you received your boot floppy from a mail-order vendor or some other distributor, instead of downloading and creating it yourself, contact the distributor and ask for a new boot floppy—but only after verifying that this is indeed the problem. This can, of course, be difficult, but if you get funny noises from your floppy drive or messages like *cannot read sector*, chances are that your medium is damaged.

The system hangs during boot or after booting
After the installation medium boots, you see a number of messages from the kernel itself, indicating which devices were detected and configured. After this, you are usually presented with a login prompt, allowing you to proceed with installation (some distributions instead drop you right into an installation program of some kind). The system may appear to hang during several of these steps. Be patient; loading software from floppy is very slow. In many cases, the system has

not hung at all, but is merely taking a long time. Verify that there is no drive or system activity for at least several minutes before assuming that the system is hung.

Each activity listed at the beginning of this section may cause a delay that makes you think the system has stopped. However, it is possible that the system actually may hang while booting, which can be due to several causes. First of all, you may not have enough available RAM to boot the installation medium. (See the following item for information on disabling the ramdisk to free up memory.)

Hardware incompatibility causes many system hangs. Even if your hardware is supported, you may run into problems with incompatible hardware configurations that are causing the system to hang. See "Hardware Problems," later in this chapter, for a discussion of hardware incompatibilities. "Hardware Requirements" in Chapter 16 lists the currently supported video chipsets, which are a major issue in running graphics on Linux.

The system reports out-of-memory errors while attempting to boot or install the software

This problem relates to the amount of RAM you have available. Keep in mind that Linux itself requires at least 8 MB of RAM to run at all; almost all current distributions of Linux require 32 MB or more. On systems with 16 MB of RAM or less, you may run into trouble booting the installation medium or installing the software itself. This is because many distributions use a *ramdisk*, which is a filesystem loaded directly into RAM, for operations while using the installation medium. The entire image of the installation boot floppy, for example, may be loaded into a ramdisk, which may require more than 1 MB of RAM.

The solution to this problem is to disable the ramdisk option when booting the install medium. Each distribution has a different procedure for doing this. Please see your distribution documentation for more information.

You may not see an out-of-memory error when attempting to boot or install the software; instead, the system may unexpectedly hang or fail to boot. If your system hangs, and none of the explanations in the previous section seems to be the cause, try disabling the ramdisk.

The system reports an error, such as "Permission denied" or "File not found," while booting

This is an indication that your installation boot medium is corrupt. If you attempt to boot from the installation medium (and you're sure you're doing everything correctly), you should not see any such errors. Contact the distributor of your Linux software and find out about the problem, and perhaps obtain another copy of the boot medium if necessary. If you downloaded the boot disk yourself, try re-creating the boot disk, and see if this solves your problem.

The system reports the error "VFS: Unable to mount root" when booting

This error message means that the root filesystem (found on the boot medium itself) could not be found. This means that either your boot medium is corrupt or you are not booting the system correctly.

For example, many CD-ROM/DVD distributions require you to have the CD-ROM/DVD in the drive when booting. Also be sure that the CD-ROM/DVD drive is on, and check for any activity. It's also possible the system is not locating your CD-ROM/DVD drive at boot time; see "Hardware Problems" for more information.

If you're sure you are booting the system correctly, your boot medium may indeed be corrupt. This is an uncommon problem, so try other solutions before attempting to use another boot floppy or tape. One handy feature here is Red Hat's new `mediacheck` option on the CD-ROM/DVD. This will check if the CD is OK.

Hardware Problems

The most common problem encountered when attempting to install or use Linux is an incompatibility with hardware. Even if all your hardware is supported by Linux, a misconfiguration or hardware conflict can sometimes cause strange results: your devices may not be detected at boot time, or the system may hang.

It is important to isolate these hardware problems if you suspect they may be the source of your trouble. In the following sections, we describe some common hardware problems and how to resolve them.

Isolating hardware problems

If you experience a problem you believe is hardware related, the first thing to do is attempt to isolate the problem. This means eliminating all possible variables and (usually) taking the system apart, piece by piece, until the offending piece of hardware is isolated.

This is not as frightening as it may sound. Basically, you should remove all nonessential hardware from your system (after turning the power off), and then determine which device is actually causing the trouble—possibly by reinserting each device, one at a time. This means you should remove all hardware other than the floppy and video controllers, and, of course, the keyboard. Even innocent-looking devices, such as mouse controllers, can wreak unknown havoc on your peace of mind unless you consider them nonessential. So, to be sure, really remove everything that you don't absolutely need for booting when experimenting, and add the devices one by one later when reassembling the system.

For example, let's say the system hangs during the Ethernet board detection sequence at boot time. You might hypothesize that there is a conflict or problem with the Ethernet board in your machine. The quick and easy way to find out is to pull the Ethernet board and try booting again. If everything goes well when you reboot, you know that either the Ethernet board is not supported by Linux, or there is an address or IRQ conflict with the board. In addition, some badly designed network boards (mostly ISA-based NE2000 clones, which are luckily dying out by now) can hang the entire system when they are auto-probed. If this appears to be the case for you, your best bet is to remove the network board from the system during the installation and put it back in later, or pass the appropriate kernel parameters during boot-up so that auto-probing of the network board can be avoided. The most permanent fix is to dump that card and get a new one from another vendor that designs its hardware more carefully.

What does "address or IRQ conflict" mean, you may ask? All devices in your machine use an *interrupt request line*, or IRQ, to tell the system they need something done on their behalf. You can think of the IRQ as a cord the device tugs when it needs the system to take care of some pending request. If more than one device is tugging on the same cord, the kernel won't be able to determine which device it needs to service. Instant mayhem.

Therefore, be sure all your installed non-PCI/AGP devices are using unique IRQ lines. In general, the IRQ for a device can be set by jumpers on the card; see the documentation for the particular device for details. Some devices do not require an IRQ at all, but it is suggested you configure them to use one if possible (the Seagate ST01 and ST02 SCSI controllers are good examples). The PCI bus is more cleverly designed, and PCI devices can and do quite happily share interrupt lines.

In some cases, the kernel provided on your installation medium is configured to use a certain IRQ for certain devices. For example, on some distributions of Linux, the kernel is preconfigured to use IRQ 5 for the TMC-950 SCSI controller, the Mitsumi CD-ROM controller, and the bus mouse driver. If you want to use two or more of these devices, you'll need first to install Linux with only one of these devices enabled, then recompile the kernel in order to change the default IRQ for one of them. (See "Building a New Kernel" in Chapter 18 for information on recompiling the kernel.)

Another area where hardware conflicts can arise is with DMA channels, I/O addresses, and shared memory addresses. All these terms describe mechanisms through which the system interfaces with hardware devices. Some Ethernet boards, for example, use a shared memory address as well as an IRQ to interface with the system. If any of these are in conflict with other devices, the system may behave unexpectedly. You should be able to change the DMA channel, I/O, or shared memory addresses for your various devices with jumper settings. (Unfortunately, some devices don't allow you to change these settings.)

The documentation for your various hardware devices should specify the IRQ, DMA channel, I/O address, or shared memory address the devices use, and how to configure them. Of course, a problem here is that some of these settings are not known before the system is assembled and may thus be undocumented. Again, the simple way to get around these problems is to temporarily disable the conflicting devices until you have time to determine the cause of the problem.

Table 2-1 lists IRQ and DMA channels used by various "standard" devices found on most systems. Almost all systems have some of these devices, so you should avoid setting the IRQ or DMA of other devices to these values.

Table 2-1. Common device settings

Device	I/O address	IRQ	DMA
ttyS0 (COM1)	3f8	4	n/a
ttyS1 (COM2)	2f8	3	n/a
ttyS2 (COM3)	3e8	4	n/a
ttyS3 (COM4)	2e8	3	n/a
lp0 (LPT1)	378 - 37f	7	n/a
lp1 (LPT2)	278 - 27f	5	n/a
fd0, fd1 (floppies 1 and 2)	3f0 - 3f7	6	2
fd2, fd3 (floppies 3 and 4)	370 - 377	10	3

Problems recognizing hard drive or controller

When Linux boots, you see a series of messages on your screen, such as the following:

```
Console: switching to colour frame buffer device 147x55
Real Time Clock Driver v1.12
Serial: 8250/16550 driver $Revision: 1.7 $ 48 ports, IRQ sharing enabled
ttyS0 at I/O 0x3f8 (irq = 4) is a 16550A
ttyS1 at I/O 0x2f8 (irq = 3) is a 16550A
Using anticipatory io scheduler
Floppy drive(s): fd0 is 1.44M
FDC 0 is a post-1991 82077
...
```

Here, the kernel is detecting the various hardware devices present on your system. At some point, you should see a line like the following:

```
hda: hda1 hda2 hda3 hda4 < hda5 hda6 hda7 >
```

If, for some reason, your drives or partitions are not recognized, you will not be able to access them in any way.

Several conditions can cause this to happen:

Hard drive or controller not supported

If you are using a hard drive or controller (IDE, SCSI, or otherwise) not supported by Linux, the kernel will not recognize your partitions at boot time.

Drive or controller improperly configured

Even if your controller is supported by Linux, it may not be configured correctly. (This is a problem particularly for SCSI controllers; most non-SCSI controllers should work fine without additional configuration.)

Refer to the documentation for your hard drive and controller for information on solving these kinds of problems. In particular, many hard drives will need to have a jumper set if they are to be used as a slave drive (e.g., as the second hard drive). The acid test for this kind of condition is to boot up Windows or some other operating system known to work with your drive and controller. If you can access the drive and controller from another operating system, the problem is not with your hardware configuration.

See the previous section, "Isolating hardware problems," for information on resolving possible device conflicts and the following section, "Problems with SCSI controllers and devices," for information on configuring SCSI devices.

Controller properly configured, but not detected

Some BIOS-less SCSI controllers require the user to specify information about the controller at boot time. The following section, "Problems with SCSI controllers and devices," describes how to force hardware detection for these controllers.

Hard drive geometry not recognized

Some older systems, such as the IBM PS/ValuePoint, do not store hard drive geometry information in the CMOS memory where Linux expects to find it. Also, certain SCSI controllers need to be told where to find drive geometry in order for Linux to recognize the layout of your drive.

Most distributions provide a boot option to specify the drive geometry. In general, when booting the installation medium, you can specify the drive geometry at the LILO boot prompt with a command such as:

```
boot: linux hd=cylinders,heads,sectors
```

where *cylinders*, *heads*, and *sectors* correspond to the number of cylinders, heads, and sectors per track for your hard drive.

After installing the Linux software, you can install LILO, allowing you to boot from the hard drive. At that time, you can specify the drive geometry to the LILO installation procedure, making it unnecessary to enter the drive geometry each time you boot. See "Using GRUB" in Chapter 17 for more about LILO.

Problems with SCSI controllers and devices

Presented here are some of the most common problems with SCSI controllers and devices, such as CD-ROMs, hard drives, and tape drives. If you are having problems getting Linux to recognize your drive or controller, read on. Let us again emphasize that most distributions use a modularized kernel and that you might have to load a module supporting your hardware during an early phase of the installation process. This might also be done automatically for you.

The Linux SCSI HOWTO contains much useful information on SCSI devices in addition to that listed here. SCSIs can be particularly tricky to configure at times.

It might be a false economy, for example, to use cheap cables, especially if you use wide SCSI. Cheap cables are a major source of problems and can cause all kinds of failures, as well as major headaches. If you use SCSI, use proper cabling.

Here are common problems and possible solutions:

A SCSI device is detected at all possible IDs
> This problem occurs when the system straps the device to the same address as the controller. You need to change the jumper settings so that the drive uses a different address from the controller itself.

Linux reports sense errors, even if the devices are known to be error-free
> This can be caused by bad cables or by bad termination. If your SCSI bus is not terminated at both ends, you may have errors accessing SCSI devices. When in doubt, always check your cables. In addition to disconnected cables, bad-quality cables are a common source of troubles.

SCSI devices report timeout errors
> This is usually caused by a conflict with IRQ, DMA, or device addresses. Also, check that interrupts are enabled correctly on your controller.

SCSI controllers using BIOS are not detected
> Detection of controllers using BIOS will fail if the BIOS is disabled, or if your controller's "signature" is not recognized by the kernel. See the Linux SCSI HOWTO for more information about this.

Controllers using memory-mapped I/O do not work
> This happens when the memory-mapped I/O ports are incorrectly cached. Either mark the board's address space as uncacheable in the XCMOS settings, or disable the cache altogether.

When partitioning, you get a warning "cylinders > 1024," or you are unable to boot from a partition using cylinders numbered above 1023
> BIOS limits the number of cylinders to 1024, and any partition using cylinders numbered above this won't be accessible from the BIOS. As far as Linux is concerned, this affects only booting; once the system has booted, you should be able to access the partition. Your options are to either boot Linux from a boot floppy or to boot from a partition using cylinders numbered below 1024. See "Creating the Boot Floppy or Installing GRUB," earlier in this chapter.

CD-ROM drive or other removable media devices are not recognized at boot time
> Try booting with a CD-ROM (or disk) in the drive. This is necessary for some devices.

If your SCSI controller is not recognized, you may need to force hardware detection at boot time. This is particularly important for SCSI controllers without BIOS. Most distributions allow you to specify the controller IRQ and shared memory address when booting the installation medium. For example, if you are using a TMC-8xx controller, you may be able to enter:

```
boot: linux tmx8xx=interrupt,memory-address
```

at the LILO boot prompt, where *interrupt* is the controller IRQ, and *memory-address* is the shared memory address. Whether you can do this depends on the distribution of Linux you are using; consult your documentation for details.

Problems Installing the Software

Installing the Linux software should be trouble-free if you're lucky. The only problems you might experience would be related to corrupt installation media or lack of space on your Linux filesystems. Here is a list of common problems:

System reports "Read error, file not found" or other errors while attempting to install the software

This is indicative of a problem with your installation medium. If you are installing from floppy, keep in mind that floppies are quite susceptible to media errors of this type. Be sure to use brand-new, newly formatted floppies. If you have a Windows partition on your drive, many Linux distributions allow you to install the software from the hard drive. This may be faster and more reliable than using floppies.

If you are using a CD-ROM, be sure to check the disk for scratches, dust, or other problems that might cause media errors.

The cause of the problem may also be that the medium is in the incorrect format. For example, many Linux distributions require floppies to be formatted in high-density Windows format. (The boot floppy is the exception; it is not in Windows format in most cases.) If all else fails, either obtain a new set of floppies, or re-create the floppies (using new ones) if you downloaded the software yourself.

System reports errors such as "tar: read error" or "gzip: not in gzip format"

This problem is usually caused by corrupt files on the installation medium itself. In other words, your floppy may be error-free, but the data on the floppy is in some way corrupted. For example, if you downloaded the Linux software using text mode, rather than binary mode, your files will be corrupt and unreadable by the installation software. When using FTP, just issue the *binary* command to set that mode before you request a file transfer.

System reports errors such as "device full" while installing

This is a clear-cut sign that you have run out of space when installing the software. If the disk fills up, not all distributions can clearly recover, so aborting the installation won't give you a working system.

The solution is usually to re-create your filesystems with the *mke2fs* command, which will delete the partially installed software. You can then attempt to reinstall the software, this time selecting a smaller amount of software to install. If you can't do without that software, you may need to start completely from scratch and rethink your partition and filesystem sizes.

System reports errors such as "read_intr: 0x10" while accessing the hard drive

This is usually an indication of bad blocks on your drive. However, if you receive these errors while using *mkswap* or *mke2fs*, the system may be having trouble accessing your drive. This can either be a hardware problem (see "Hardware Problems" earlier in this chapter), or it might be a case of poorly specified geometry. If you used the option:

```
hd=cylinders,heads,sectors
```

at boot time to force detection of your drive geometry and incorrectly specified the geometry, you could receive this error. This can also happen if your drive geometry is incorrectly specified in the system CMOS.

System reports errors such as "file not found" or "permission denied"

This problem can occur if the necessary files are not present on the installation medium or if there is a permissions problem with the installation software. For example, some distributions of Linux have been known to have bugs in the installation software itself; these are usually fixed rapidly and are quite infrequent. If you suspect that the distribution software contains bugs, and you're sure that you have done nothing wrong, contact the maintainer of the distribution to report the bug.

If you have other strange errors when installing Linux (especially if you downloaded the software yourself), be sure you actually obtained all the necessary files when downloading.

For example, some people use the FTP command:

```
mget *.*
```

when downloading the Linux software via FTP. This will download only those files that contain a "." in their filenames; files without the "." will not be downloaded. The correct command to use in this case is:

```
mget *
```

The best advice is to retrace your steps when something goes wrong. You may think that you have done everything correctly, when in fact you forgot a small but important step somewhere along the way. In many cases, just attempting to redownload or reinstall the Linux software can solve the problem. Don't beat your head against the wall any longer than you have to!

Also, if Linux unexpectedly hangs during installation, there may be a hardware problem of some kind. See "Hardware Problems" for hints.

Problems After Installing Linux

You've spent an entire afternoon installing Linux. In order to make space for it, you wiped your Windows and OS/2 partitions and tearfully deleted your copies of Sim-City 2000 and Railroad Tycoon 2. You reboot the system and nothing happens. Or, even worse, *something* happens, but it's not what should happen. What do you do?

In "Problems with Booting the Installation Medium," earlier in this chapter, we covered the most common problems that can occur when booting the Linux installation medium; many of those problems may apply here. In addition, you may be a victim of one of the following maladies.

Problems booting Linux from floppy

If you are using a floppy to boot Linux, you may need to specify the location of your Linux root partition at boot time. This is especially true if you are using the original installation floppy itself and not a custom boot floppy created during installation.

While booting the floppy, hold down the Shift or Ctrl key. This should present you with a boot menu; press Tab to see a list of available options. For example, many distributions allow you to boot from a floppy by entering:

```
boot: linux root=partition
```

at the boot menu, where *partition* is the name of the Linux root partition, such as */dev/hda2*. SUSE Linux offers a menu entry early in the installation program that boots your newly created Linux system from the installation boot floppy. Consult the documentation for your distribution for details.

Problems booting Linux from the hard drive

If you opted to install LILO instead of creating a boot floppy, you should be able to boot Linux from the hard drive. However, the automated LILO installation procedure used by many distributions is not always perfect. It may make incorrect assumptions about your partition layout, in which case you need to reinstall LILO to get everything right. Installing LILO is covered in "Using GRUB" in Chapter 17.

Here are some common problems:

System reports "Drive not bootable—Please insert system disk"
> You will get this error message if the hard drive's master boot record is corrupt in some way. In most cases, it's harmless, and everything else on your drive is still intact. There are several ways around this:

- While partitioning your drive using *fdisk*, you may have deleted the partition that was marked as "active." Windows and other operating systems attempt to boot the "active" partition at boot time (Linux, in general, pays no attention to whether the partition is "active," but the Master Boot Records installed by some distributions like Debian do). You may be able to boot MS-DOS from floppy and run *fdisk* to set the active flag on your MS-DOS partition, and all will be well.

  Another command to try (with MS-DOS 5.0 and higher, including Windows 95/98/ME) is:

  ```
  FDISK /MBR
  ```

  This command will attempt to rebuild the hard drive master boot record for booting Windows, overwriting LILO. If you no longer have Windows on your hard drive, you'll need to boot Linux from floppy and attempt to install LILO later. This command does not exist on Windows NT/2000/XP; here the procedure is more involved.

- If you created a Windows partition using Linux's version of *fdisk*, or vice versa, you may get this error. You should create Windows partitions only by using Windows' version of *fdisk*. (The same applies to operating systems other than Windows.) The best solution here is either to start from scratch and repartition the drive correctly, or to merely delete and re-create the offending partitions using the correct version of *fdisk*.

- The LILO installation procedure may have failed. In this case, you should boot either from your Linux boot floppy (if you have one) or from the original installation medium. Either of these should provide options for specifying the Linux root partition to use when booting. At boot time, hold down the Shift or Ctrl key and press Tab from the boot menu for a list of options.

When you boot the system from the hard drive, Windows (or another operating system) starts instead of Linux

First of all, be sure you actually installed LILO or GRUB when installing the Linux software. If not, the system will still boot Windows (or whatever other operating system you may have) when you attempt to boot from the hard drive. In order to boot Linux from the hard drive, you need to install LILO or GRUB (see the section "Using GRUB" in Chapter 17).

On the other hand, if you *did* install LILO, and another operating system boots instead of Linux, you have LILO configured to boot that other operating system by default. While the system is booting, hold down the Shift or Ctrl key and press Tab at the boot prompt. This should present you with a list of possible operating systems to boot; select the appropriate option (usually just linux) to boot Linux.

If you wish to select Linux as the default operating system to boot, you will need to reinstall LILO.

It also may be possible that you attempted to install LILO, but the installation procedure failed in some way. See the previous item on installation.

Problems logging in

After booting Linux, you should be presented with a login prompt:

```
Linux login:
```

At this point, either the distribution's documentation or the system itself will tell you what to do. For many distributions, you simply log in as *root*, with no password. Other possible usernames to try are *guest* or *test*.

Most Linux distributions ask you for an initial root password. Hopefully, you have remembered what you typed in during installation; you will need it again now. If your distribution does not ask you for a root password during installation, you can try using an empty password.

If you simply can't log in, consult your distribution's documentation; the username and password to use may be buried in there somewhere. The username and password may have been given to you during the installation procedure, or they may be printed on the login banner. Another option is to log into Linux in single-user mode by typing linux simple at the boot prompt.

One possible cause of this password impasse may be a problem with installing the Linux login and initialization files. If this is the case, you may need to reinstall (at least parts of) the Linux software, or boot your installation medium and attempt to fix the problem by hand.

Problems using the system

If login is successful, you should either be presented with a shell prompt (such as # or $) or be directly taken to a graphical desktop environment such as KDE or Gnome, and can happily roam around your system. The next step in this case is to try the procedures in Chapter 4. However, some initial problems with using the system sometimes creep up.

The most common initial configuration problem is incorrect file or directory permissions. This can cause the error message:

```
Shell-init: permission denied
```

to be printed after logging in. (In fact, anytime you see the message permission denied, you can be fairly certain it is a problem with file permissions.)

In many cases, it's a simple matter of using the *chmod* command to fix the permissions of the appropriate files or directories. For example, some distributions of Linux once used the incorrect file mode 0644 for the root directory (/). The fix was to issue the command:

```
# chmod 755 /
```

as *root*. (File permissions are covered in the section "File Ownership and Permissions" in Chapter 11.) However, in order to issue this command, you need to have booted from the installation medium and mounted your Linux root filesystem by hand—a hairy task for most newcomers.

As you use the system, you may run into places where file and directory permissions are incorrect or software does not work as configured. Welcome to the world of Linux! Although most distributions are quite trouble-free, you can't expect them to be perfect. We don't want to cover all those problems here. Instead, throughout the book we help you to solve many of these configuration problems by teaching you how to find them and fix them yourself. In Chapter 1, we discussed this philosophy in some detail. In Part II, we give hints for fixing many of these common configuration problems.

## CHAPTER 3

Desktop Environments

If you installed one of the popular Linux distributions, it came up with a rather attractive graphical interface. This chapter tells you how to use this interface to get work done more quickly and pleasantly. Most Linux systems with graphical interfaces offer a comprehensive graphical environment called a *desktop*.

This chapter covers both of the popular Linux desktops, the K Desktop Environment (KDE) and GNOME. Readers who have trouble getting their graphical interfaces to work at all, or who want to delve deeper into the guts of Linux graphics, can find help in Chapter 16.

Why Use a Graphical Desktop?

If you plan to run your Linux machine as a server, there is no need to install any of the packages described in this chapter (unless you want to use graphical administration tools). X and the desktop systems require significant memory, CPU time, and disk space, and if your system never has a monitor attached to it, installing them is a waste of time and resources. Similarly, if you will just be doing programming and have no interest in viewing results graphically or using graphical integrated development environments (IDEs), you could well get by without these conveniences.

But for all other systems, KDE and GNOME make Linux appropriate for mass use. They do the kinds of things the average user expects his computer to do for him, such as the following:

- Display many different kinds of content automatically when their icons are clicked, without the user having to specify the program used for display

- Cut and paste both text and pictures from one window to another, even when these windows run different applications that store data in different formats

- Save and restore sessions, so the user can log back in and pick up as much as possible just where she left off

- Aid the user with hints as to where he is, such as thumbnail images and tool tips

- Offer a wealth of beautiful backgrounds, screen savers, and themes
- Allow a dizzying extent of customization—but in a subtle way that allows most users to feel happy with defaults

To offer all these features, both KDE and GNOME require hefty computing power and memory. Modern hardware can handle them comfortably (and they're both getting trimmer over time), but some users prefer to use more lightweight graphical systems that lack some of the power. If you want something partway between a plain command-line console and the resource-intensive environments of KDE or GNOME, try the xfce window manager. It comes with many distributions and can be downloaded from *http://www.xfce.org*, along with its documentation. With a much smaller footprint than KDE or GNOME, it offers a surprisingly rich range of features.

Because KDE and GNOME were designed to be intuitive and borrowed many ideas from other popular graphical environments, their basic use is intuitive for most computer users. In this chapter we'll explore some of the neat things that they and their key applications offer, but which you might not have found out through everyday experimentation.

The K Desktop Environment

KDE is an open source software project that aims at providing a consistent, user-friendly, contemporary desktop for Unix, and hence, Linux systems. Since its inception in October 1996, it has made great progress. This is partly due to the choice of a very high-quality GUI toolkit, Qt, as well as the consequent choice of using C++ and its object-oriented features for the implementation.

KDE employs a component technology called KParts that makes it possible to embed one application into another transparently, such that, for example, the web browser Konqueror can display PDF documents in its own browser window by means of the PDF display program KPDF, without Konqueror having to have a PDF display component of its own. The same goes for the KOffice suite (see *http://koffice.kde.org*), discussed in Chapter 8, where, for example, the word processor KWord can embed tables from the spreadsheet application KSpread seamlessly.

KDE is in ever-continuing development, but every few months the KDE team puts out a so-called official release that is considered very stable and suitable for end users. The KDE team makes these available in source form, and most distributions provide easy-to-install binary packages within days of a source release. If you don't mind fiddling around with KDE and can stand an occasional bug, you can also live on the bleeding edge and download daily snapshots of KDE, but this is not for the fainthearted. At the time of this writing, the current stable release was 3.4.2. To stay current with KDE development, visit *http://www.kde.org*, the official web site of the KDE project, often.

General Features

One of the goals of the KDE team is to make everything in KDE configurable by GUI dialogs. Underneath the configuration system lies a set of text files in a fairly simple *parameter=value* format; you can edit these if you prefer, but you never need to. Even the most experienced users usually admit that in order to do simple things, such as change the background color of the desktop, it's faster to click a few buttons than to read the manual page, find the syntax for specifying the background color, open the configuration file, edit it, and restart the window manager.

Besides easy configuration, KDE sports a few other features that were previously unheard of on Linux. For example, it integrates Internet access fully into the desktop. It comes with a file manager that doubles as a web browser (or the other way around), and browsing files on some FTP sites is just the same as browsing your local hard disk. You can drag and drop icons that represent Internet locations to your desktop and thus easily find them again later. KDE integrates search engines and other Internet resources into your desktop and even lets you define your own favorite search engines and Internet links with ease. In addition, almost all KDE application are able to open and save files in remote locations, not just via FTP or HTTP, but also to and from a digital camera, or using *SSH* encryption, or in other ways.

Drag-and-drop, commonplace on Windows or the Macintosh, is also widely used in KDE. For example, to open a file in the text editor, you just grab its icon in the file manager window and drop it onto the editor window. This works no matter where the file is located; if it is on a remote server, KDE automatically downloads the file for you before opening it in the text editor or whichever application you choose to open it with. The same goes for multimedia files. Just by clicking an icon for an MP3 file on a remote server, you can download it in the background and play it locally.

Although manual pages are designed well to give programmers instant access to terse information about system libraries, they are not really very well suited for end-user documentation. KDE therefore uses standard HTML files (which are generated from XML files in the background) and comes with a fast help viewer, the KDE Help Center. The viewer also knows how to display manual page and Info files so that you can access all the documentation on your system from one application. In addition, most KDE applications support context-sensitive help.

For the past few releases, the X Window System has supported a feature called *session management*. When you leave your X environment, log off, or reboot, an application that understands session management will reappear at the same positions and in the same configuration. Unfortunately, this very user-friendly feature was rarely supported by X applications. KDE uses it extensively. KDE provides a session manager that handles session management, and all KDE applications are written to behave properly with that feature. KDE will also support other modern X11 features such as anti-aliasing if your X server supports them (most X servers do, by means of the so-called *RENDER extension*).

KDE contains a window manager, kwin, and an excellent one at that, but that is only one part of KDE. Some of the others are the file manager, the web browser, the panel, a pager, the control center for configuring your desktop, and many, many more. If you want to, you can even run KDE with another window manager, but you might lose some of the integration features. Also, KDE comes with tons of applications, from a full office productivity suite to PostScript and PDF viewers to multimedia software to games.

You might be thinking, "Well, this all sounds very nice, but I have a couple of normal X applications that I want to run." In this case, you will be delighted to hear that you can continue to do that. Yes, you can run all X applications on a KDE desktop, and KDE even provides some means of integrating them as far as possible into the overall desktop. For example, if you desire, KDE can try to reconfigure your other X applications to use the same colors as the overall desktop so that you get a nice consistent environment. Of course, non-KDE applications will not support some of KDE's advanced features such as drag-and-drop or session management, but you can continue to use the programs you have grown accustomed to until someone releases KDE applications that address the same needs (or perhaps KDE versions of your favorite programs themselves).

Installing KDE

Most Linux distributions come with KDE nowadays, but if yours doesn't, or you want to use a newer version of KDE, you can download it from the Internet. *http://www.kde. org* is your one-stop shop for everything KDE related, including documentation, screenshots, and download locations. *ftp://ftp.kde.org* is the KDE project's FTP site, but it is often overloaded, so you might be better off trying a mirror instead. *http://www. kde.org/mirrors/* gives you a list of mirrors.

KDE consists of a number of packages. These include the following:

aRts
> *aRts* is short for "a real-time sequencer" and forms the base of most of the multimedia capabilities of KDE.

kdelibs
> The KDE libraries. They contain the basic application frame, a number of GUI widgets, the configuration system, the HTML display system, and many other things. Without this package, nothing in KDE will run.

kdebase
> In this package, you will find the basic KDE applications that make a desktop a KDE desktop, including the file manager/web browser, the window manager, and the panel. You definitely need this package if you want to use KDE.

kdegames

A number of games, including card games, action games, and strategy games. Everybody will probably want to install these, but only to get acquainted with the system, of course.

kdegraphics

A number of graphics-related programs such as a *dvi* viewer, a PostScript viewer, and an icon editor.

kdeutils

Some productivity tools, such as text editors, a calculator, printer managers, and so on.

kdemultimedia

As the name implies, this package contains multimedia programs, including a CD player, a MIDI player, an MP3 player, and—of all things—a Karaoke player.

kdenetwork

Here, you will find programs for use with the Internet, including a news reader, and some network management tools. The KDE mail program is not contained in this package, but rather in the package kdepim (see below).

kdeadmin

This package contains some programs for the system administrator, including a user manager, a run-level editor, and a backup program.

kdepim

Considered by many the centerpiece of KDE these days, kdepim contains software for personal information management, most notably the Kontact integration package that unites under a common surface the time planner and task tracker KOrganizer, the KDE email package KMail, an address book, PDA synchronization software, and many other useful tools.

kdeedu

As the name implies, this package contains a set of educational programs, ranging from vocabulary trainers to programs teaching you the movements of the planets and stars.

kaccessibility

This package contains tools that make it possible, or easier, for people with disabilities to use computers, such as screen magnifiers. The goal of the KDE project is to fully comply with the Americans with Disabilities Act.

kartwork

This package contains graphics artwork for KDE, including different sets of icons, wallpapers, and so forth.

kde-i18n

There are a large number of packages starting with *kde-i18n-*. Each of these contains translations for one particular language. (American) English is the default, even in the KDE world, so if that's the language you want to use, you do not need any of the *kde-i18n-* packages. But if you are British and frown at the spelling, there even is a UK English package.

kdetoys

This package contains a number of smaller programs that do not really have a very useful purpose, but are often funny or interesting to use or to look at. Try, for example, AMOR, the Amusing Misuse of Resources.

kdewebdev

If you are developing web pages, you may want to install this package. It contains tools such as the Quanta HTML editor.

koffice

KOffice is no less than a complete feature-rich office productivity suite. It may have a few rough edges here and there, but many people use it already for their daily work.

The release cycle of KOffice is today decoupled from KDE's release cycle. At the time of this writing, the current version was 1.3.5. You can read all about KOffice at *http://koffice.kde.org*.

Developer tools

There are a number of packages for developers of KDE applications. *kdesdk* contains tools, scripts, and information for developers of KDE programs (if you plan to develop your own KDE programs, you may also want to see *http://developer. kde.org*), *kdebindings* contains bindings for developing KDE programs in programming languages other than the default C++, and finally, *KDevelop* is a complete integrated development environment, not only for developing KDE applications, but for developing all kinds of applications.

In addition to the packages mentioned here, which are officially provided by the KDE team, literally hundreds of other KDE programs have been developed. See *http: //www.kde.org/applications.html* for a list of applications that are currently available.

Once you have selected which packages to install, your procedure for the actual installation depends on which Linux distribution you use and whether you install a binary package or compile KDE yourself from the source code. If your distribution contains KDE, you will also be able to install KDE during your system installation.

Once the software is loaded onto your hard disk, there are only a few steps left to take. First, you have to make sure that the directory containing the KDE applications is in your PATH environment variable. The default location of the executable KDE programs is */opt/kde3/bin*, but if you have chosen to install KDE to another location, you will have to insert your path here.* You can add this directory to your PATH variable by issuing:

```
export PATH=/opt/kde3/bin:$PATH
```

---

* Some distributions might put the KDE programs elsewhere, such as in */usr/bin*.

To make this permanent, add this line to either the *.bashrc* configuration file in your home directory, or the system-wide configuration file, */etc/profile*.

Next, do the same with the directory containing the KDE libraries (by default */opt/kde3/lib*) and the environment variable `LD_LIBRARY_PATH`:

```
export LD_LIBRARY_PATH=/opt/kde3/lib:$LD_LIBRARY_PATH
```

Now you are almost done, but you still need to tell X that you want to run the KDE desktop when X starts. This is done in the file *.xinitrc* in your home directory. Make a backup copy first. Then remove everything in this file and insert the following single line:

```
exec startkde
```

startkde is a shell script provided with KDE that simply starts up the KDE window manager *kwin* and a number of system services. Distributions will usually install a somewhat more complex *.xinitrc* file that may even start non-KDE applications and services.

If, for some reason, you plan to install KDE packages in more than one directory tree, you will also need to set the environment variable `KDEDIRS` to contain the path to all the trees. Normally, this is not necessary.

Using KDE

Using KDE is quite easy. Most things are very intuitive, so you can often simply guess what to do. We will, however, give you some hints for what you can do with KDE here, to encourage you to explore your KDE desktop further.

The KDE panel and the K menu

When you start KDE for the first time, it looks like Figure 3-1. Along the lower border of the screen, you see the so-called *panel*. The panel serves several purposes, including fast access to installed applications and the currently opened windows. KDE also opens a configuration program that lets you configure the initial settings when started for the first time.

KDE provides a number of workspaces that are accessible via the buttons in the middle of the panel, labeled One to Eight by default. Try clicking those buttons. You can see that windows that you have opened are visible only while you are in workspace One, whereas the panel and the taskbar are always visible. Now go to workspace Two and start a terminal window by clicking the terminal icon on the panel. When the panel appears, change workspaces again. You will see that the terminal window is visible only while you are in workspace Two, but its label is visible on the taskbar that appears in all workspaces. When you are in any other workspace, click the terminal label in the taskbar. This will immediately bring you back to the workspace where your terminal is shown.

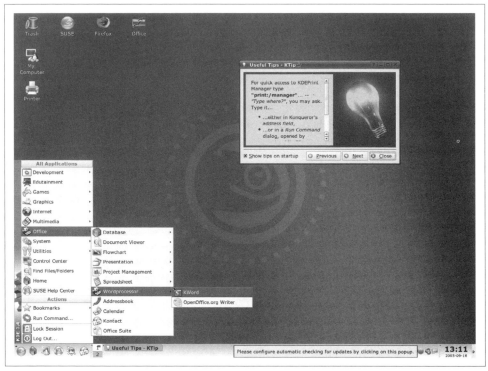

Figure 3-1. The KDE desktop at startup

To try another nifty feature, push the small button that looks like a pushpin in the titlebar of the terminal window. Now change workspaces again. You will see that the terminal window is now visible on every workspace—it has been "pinned down" to the background of the desktop, so to speak.

If you grow tired of seeing the terminal window in every workspace, simply click the pin again. If you want to get rid of the window as a whole, click the button with the little x on it in the upper-right corner.

KDE can be configured in many different ways, and the window decorations are just one thing. It might therefore be that you do not have the little pushpin button, because your configuration does not include it. In that case, you can left-click on the application in the left corner of the title frame and select To Desktop → All Desktops instead.

There are lots of things that you can do with windows in KDE, but we'll switch now to a short exploration of the so-called *K menu*. You open the K menu by clicking the icon with the gear-and-K symbol to the far left of the panel. Besides some options for configuring the K menu and the panel itself, you will find all installed KDE applications here, grouped into submenus. To start one of those applications, select the menu entry.

We have promised that you can run old X applications on your KDE desktop. You can do that either by opening a terminal window and typing the application name on the command line or by pressing Alt-F2 and entering the application name in the small command line that appears in the middle of the screen. But, with a little more work, you can also integrate non-KDE applications into the K menu and the panel, which then displays icons that you can click to run the associated programs.

Depending on how you have installed KDE, it may well be that there is already a submenu of non-KDE programs in your K menu that contains a number of non-KDE applications. If you don't have this, run the application KAppfinder, which you can either find in the System submenu or start from the command line with kappfinder. This searches your system for a number of applications that it has in its database and integrates each one into the KDE desktop by generating a so-called *.desktop* file for it. If the program that you want to integrate into KDE is not included in the Appfinder's database, you will have to write such a *.desktop* file yourself. But as always in KDE, there are dialogs for doing this where you just have to fill in the required information. See the KDE documentation at *http://www.kde.org/documentation/index.html*.

By default, the panel already contains a number of icons to start the most often used programs, but you can easily add your own. To do this, right-click somewhere on the panel where it does not contain any items and select Add to Panel → Application from the menu that pops up. A copy of the whole K menu pops up. Find the application whose icon you want to add to the panel and select it, just as if you wanted to start it. KDE will then add the icon for this application to the panel. You can even add submenus to the panel by selecting the first menu entry (Add This Menu) in a submenu in the Add → Button tree. The icon will then have a small black arrow in it, which indicates that clicking the icon opens a menu instead of starting an application.

There are other things besides application starter buttons that you can add to the panel as well: for example, panel *applets*, small programs that are designed to run inside the panel and cannot run as standalones. Just explore the Add to Panel submenus, and you will find many interesting things.

There is only limited space on the panel, so you might need to remove some icons of programs that you do not often use. Just click with the right mouse button on the icon and select the Remove menu item (they will be called different things depending on what you are trying to remove). This does not remove the program, just its icon. In general, you can get at a lot of functionality in KDE by clicking the right mouse button!

The KDE Control Center

Next, we will show you how to configure your KDE desktop to your tastes. As promised, we will not edit any configuration files to do this.

Configuration is done in the KDE Control Center, which you can start from the K menu. (On some distributions, the Control Center is at the top level of the K menu; in others, such as Debian, it is in a submenu such as Settings.) Configuration options are grouped into different types of operations. When you start up the Control Center, you will see the top-level groups. By clicking the plus signs, you can open a group to see the entries in this group.

Configuring the background. As an example, we will now change the background color to something else. To do this, open the Appearance & Themes group and choose Background. The configuration window for configuring the background will appear (see Figure 3-2).

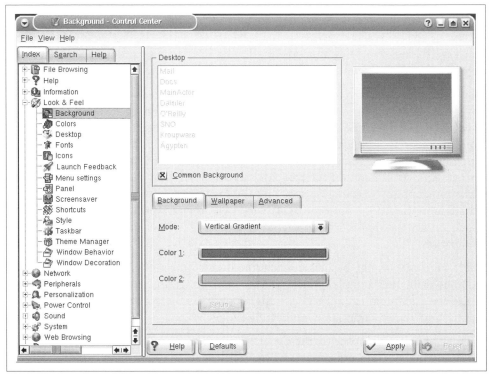

Figure 3-2. Configuring the background of the KDE desktop

You can select a single-colored background, a two-colored background with a number of gradients where one color is slowly morphed into another, a wallpaper (predefined or an image of your own choice), or a blending effect that combines various choices. To select colors, click on either of the two color buttons; a color selection dialog pops up where you can select a color to your taste. When you close the color selection dialog, the new color is displayed in the monitor in the upper-right corner of the configuration window. When you configure KDE, you often see such monitors that allow you to preview your choice. However, you also have the option to see what your choice looks like when in full use. Simply click the Apply button at the lower border of the configuration window, and your change is automatically applied. There is no need to restart the desktop. If you do not see any changes in the monitor, check whether the Picture option is checked. If that is the case, the selected picture will overlay your background color selection in some modes (such as Scaled, which resizes the selected picture to fill the whole background). But try selecting a picture and then experiment with the blending effects to get a combination of background colors (possibly with gradients) and your picture.

If all you want is a monocolored background, select "No picture" in the Background group, and Colors: Single Color in the Options group. You will see that the second color button is grayed out then. Select the color you want with the first color button.

If you want a background picture, but cannot find a suitable one among either your own or the ones provided with your distribution, click the Get New Wallpapers button and you will get a huge list of wallpapers that have been contributed by KDE users; there surely is something for every taste!

You can do more things with the background, but we'll leave it at that for now and look at something else: configuring the styles and colors of the windows.

Configuring window styles and colors. With normal window managers, you can configure the color of the window decorations, but not the window contents. KDE is different. Because KDE is an integrated desktop, color and other settings apply to both the window decorations painted by the window manager and the window contents painted by the applications. We'll now set off to configure a little bit of the appearance.

In the Control Center, open the Appearance & Themes group, and choose Colors. You'll see a preview window and a selection list where you can pick a color scheme. KDE works not by configuring individual colors but by defining so-called color schemes. This is because it does not make sense to change only one color; all colors must fit together to achieve a pleasing and eye-friendly look.

Although KDE lets you create your own color schemes, doing so is a task that requires some knowledge about color psychology and human vision. We therefore suggest that you pick one of the predefined color schemes. Check in the preview monitor whether you like what you see. Now comes the fun part: click the Apply button and watch how all running applications flicker a bit and suddenly change colors—without you having to restart them. Although Windows users tend to take this for granted, it was never seen on Unix before KDE.

The same feature applies to other settings. For example, open the Appearance & Themes group and choose Style. Here, you can select among a large number of so-called styles. The styles determine how the user interface elements are drawn—for example, as in Windows (style MS Windows 9x), as in Motif (style Motif), as on an SGI workstation (style SGI), or even something original such as the "Light" styles or the all-time KDE favorites "Plastik" and "Keramik."* You can change this setting by clicking Apply and watch your running applications change their style. The same goes, by the way, for the fonts that you can select on the Font page.

Internationalization. There are many more things to configure in KDE, but we cannot go through all the options here. Otherwise there would not be much space left for other topics in this book. But there's one more thing that we'd like to show you. You will especially like this if English is not your native language or if you frequently converse in another language.

Go to the Country → Region & Language page in the Regional & Accessibility group (see Figure 3-3). Here, you can select the country settings and the language in which your KDE desktop and the KDE applications should be running. Currently, KDE lets you choose from more than 80 country settings and languages. Note that you need to have a language module installed in order to be able to select a particular language. You can either download those from the KDE FTP server (as explained earlier) or install them from your distribution medium.

You might be wondering why you can select more than one language. The reason is that the KDE programs are translated by volunteers, and not all the applications are translated at the same time. Thus, a particular application might not be available in the language that you have chosen as your first language (the topmost one in the Language list). In this case, the next language is chosen automatically for that application, and if no translation is available for this application in that language either, the next language is chosen, and so on. If all else fails, KDE uses U.S. English, which always is present.

While speaking about different languages, it might also be worthwhile to briefly go into keyboard layouts. Most European languages, even those based on the Latin alphabet, have special characters that are either not available on other keyboards or are just awkward to type. KDE comes with a nifty little program that lets you quickly change keyboard layouts. Of course, it cannot change the labeling on your keys, but quickly changing layouts may already be helpful if you are regularly moving in different worlds such as some of the authors of this book do. To turn on this feature, go to the Keyboard Layout page in the Regional & Accessibility group and check the Enable keyboard layouts box. Then select the Active layouts that you plan to use among the Available layouts. Once you click on Apply, a little flag button will appear on the right-hand side of the panel (in the so-called *system tray*); clicking on this flag lets you change keyboard layouts on the fly.

There is much more to say about using the KDE desktop, but we'll let you explore it yourself. Besides the obvious and intuitive features, there are also some that are not

---

* If by now you are wondering about the strange spelling of many terms in KDE, think about the first letter of the desktop's name.

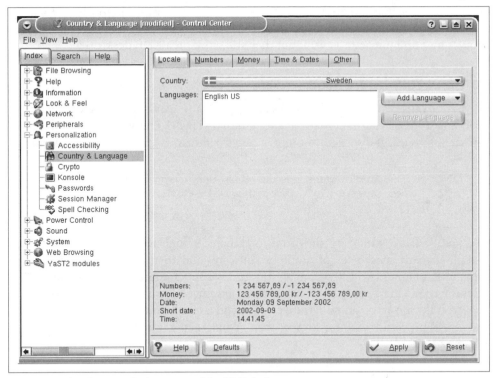

Figure 3-3. Configuring the language of the KDE desktop

so obvious but are very useful nevertheless, so be sure to check the documentation at *http://www.kde.org/documentation/index.html.*

KDE Applications

Thousands of programs are available for KDE. They range from basic utilities (such as *konsole*, the terminal emulator, and *OClock*, a rudimentary clock) to editors, programming aids, games, and multimedia applications. The most we can provide here is a tiny slice of the software available for KDE. In this section, we'll present those applications that all KDE users should know how to use. These aren't necessarily the most exciting programs out there, but they should certainly be part of your toolbox.

There are many, many more KDE applications than the few we can list here. You will make the acquaintance of some of them, such as KWord, the word processor, and Kontact, the personal information manager and mail user agent (and much else), elsewhere in this book. But others haven't found space in this book, so you should search through your favorite Linux archive for more exciting KDE programs; there are thousands of them to discover.

Also remember that if there really is no KDE program for a task you have to solve, you can always resort to one of the classic X applications, if available. These do not look as nice and integrate as well, but they still work on a KDE desktop.

konsole: Your Home Base

Let's start our exploration of X applications with the workhorse that you might be spending a lot of your time with in the terminal. This is simply a window that contains a Unix shell. It displays a prompt, accepts commands, and scrolls like a terminal.

 Traditionally, *xterm* was the classic Unix terminal emulator. It has been superseded by *konsole* in the KDE desktop environment.

Perhaps you are struck by the irony of buying a high-resolution color monitor, installing many megabytes of graphics software, and then being confronted by an emulation of an old VT100 terminal. But Linux is much more than a point-and-click operating system. There are plenty of nice graphical applications, but a lot of the time you'll want to do administrative tasks, and a command-line interface still offers the most powerful tool for doing that. You'll get a glimpse of these tasks in Chapter 4.

So let's take look at a *konsole* window. Figure 3-4 shows one containing a few commands.

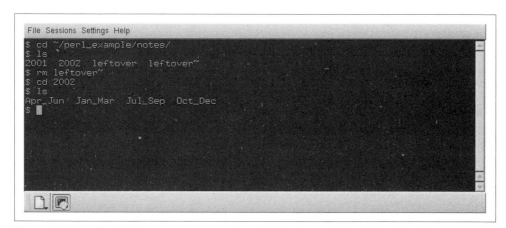

Figure 3-4. konsole window

Starting up konsole

You can start *konsole* in one of several ways, as with all KDE programs:

- Start it from the panel, if you have a *konsole* icon there. This will be the default setup with most distributions.
- Select it from the K menu, where *konsole* can be found in Utilities → System → Konsole.
- Type Alt-F2, and then type konsole in the small command window that opens.
- If you already have a *konsole* open, type konsole there and press Enter in order to get a whole new window running the program, or pull down the Session → New Shell screen.

When you open a *konsole* window, a "Tip of the Day" window will open that gives you useful hints about using *konsole*. You can turn this off, but we suggest keeping it on for a while, as you will learn many useful things this way. You can also read through all the tips by clicking the Next button in that window repeatedly. Many KDE applications have such a Tip of the Day.

konsole allows you to run several sessions in one *konsole* window. You can simply open a new session by selecting a session type from the Session menu or by clicking the New tab button. The tab bar or the View menu lets you then switch between sessions. If you don't see any tab bar, select Settings → Tab Bar (and then either Top or Bottom) from the menu to make it visible.

Cutting and pasting selections

Actually, *konsole* offers a good deal more than a VT100 terminal. One of its features is a powerful cut-and-paste capability.

Take another look at Figure 3-4. Let's say we didn't really want the *notes* directory; we wanted to look at *~/perl_example/for_web_site* instead.

First, we'll choose the part of the cd command that interests us. Put the mouse just to the left of the c in cd. Press the left mouse button, and drag the mouse until it highlights the slash following example. The result is shown in Figure 3-5.

When the highlighted area covers just the right number of characters, click the middle button.* *konsole* pastes in what you've selected on the next command line. See the result in Figure 3-6. Now you can type in the remainder of the directory name *for_website* and press the Enter key to execute the command.

You can select anything you want in the window—output as well as input. To select whole words instead of characters, double-click the left mouse button. To select whole lines, triple-click it. You can select multiple lines too. Selecting multiple lines is not useful when you're entering commands but is convenient if you're using the *vi* editor and want to cut and paste a lot of text between windows.

---

* If the middle mouse button does not work for you, or you have a two-button mouse, please see "Configuring X.org" in Chapter 16 for how to set up your mouse.

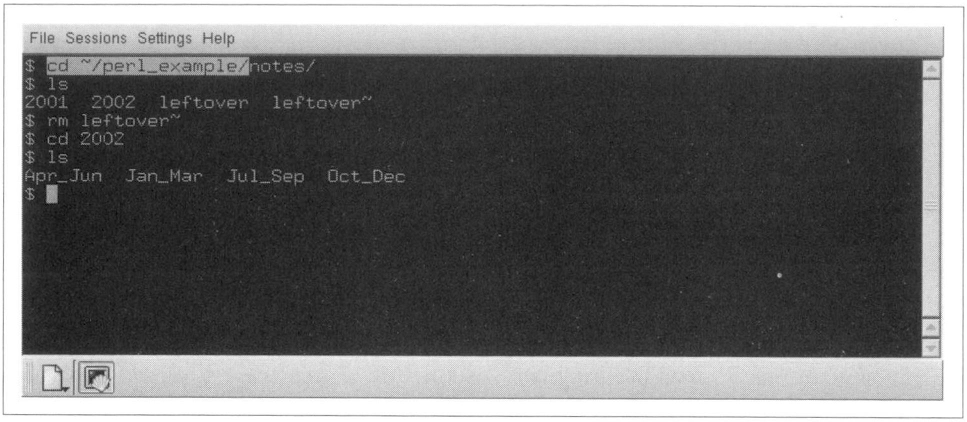

Figure 3-5. Selected text in konsole

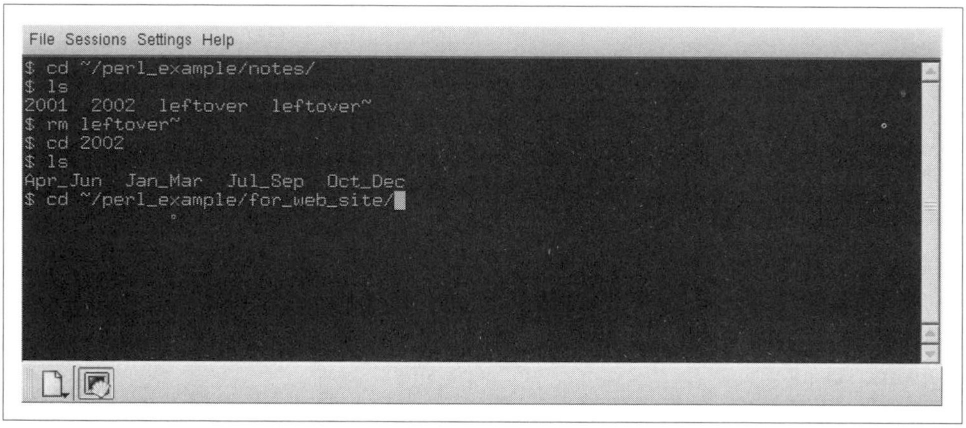

Figure 3-6. konsole window after text is pasted

Note that if you are more used to the drag-and-drop style of copying text, *konsole* supports that as well.

Copying and pasting of text is even integrated between *konsole* and the graphical KDE applications. For example, if you are viewing a directory with the Konqueror file manager/web browser, you can just drag those icons to a *konsole* window. *konsole* will either offer to paste the filenames as they are or prepend them with a cd, cp, mv, or ln command.

More konsole tricks

There are lots of things you can configure in *konsole*. You can select fonts, color schemes, whether the scrollbar should be shown to the left, to the right, or not at all, and so on. The most often used settings are available in the Settings menu, and if you can't find what you are looking for, go to Settings → Configure Konsole. There you can select the line spacing, whether the cursor should blink, and so on.

A particularly useful feature in *konsole* is the ability to watch for output or silence in one of the sessions.

What is this feature good for? Imagine that you are working on a large program that takes a long time to compile. Nonprogrammers can imagine that you download a large file in a terminal window with *wget* or that you are computing a complex POV-RAY image. While the compilation is running, you want to do something else (why do you have a multitasking operating system, after all?) and start composing an email message to a friend in your KDE mail client. Normally, you would have to check the console window every so often to see whether compilation is finished and then continue to work on your program. With the watcher, you can get a visual or audible notification when compilation completes. In order to set this up, simply switch to the session you want to watch and select View → Monitor for Silence. You will get a notification as soon as your compiler doesn't output any more messages for a while and can divert your attention from your mail client back to your *konsole* window. Of course, you can also watch for output instead of silence, which might be useful in long-running network operations that don't show any progress indicators.

Clocks

How can your screen be complete if it is unadorned by a little clock that tells you how much time you are wasting on customizing the screen's appearance? You can have a clock just the way you want it, square or round, analog or digital, big or small. You can even make it chime.

KDE contains a number of clocks, but usually you will want to run the small panel applet, as screen real estate is always at a premium, regardless of your screen resolution. The clock should appear by default at the bottom-right corner of your screen, in the confines of the panel (this is called a *panel applet*, or a small application that runs within the panel). If your distribution hasn't set up things this way, you can also right-click anywhere on the panel background and select Add to Panel → Applet → Clock from the menu, which will make the clock appear on the panel. If you'd rather have it somewhere else on the panel, you can right-click the small striped handle to the left of the clock, select Move from the context menu that appears, and move the clock with the mouse to the desired position. Other panel objects will automatically make room for the clock.

The panel clock applet has a number of different modes that you can select by right-clicking the clock itself and selecting Type as well as the desired mode from the context menu. There is a plain, a digital, an analog, and, most noteworthy, a fuzzy clock. The fuzzy clock is for everybody who doesn't like being pushed around by his clock. For example, if you run the fuzzy clock, it will show *Middle of the week*. If that is a bit too fuzzy for you, you can select Configure Clock → Appearance from the clock's context menu and select the degree of fuzziness here. For example, I am typing this at 9:53 A.M. on a Thursday, and the four degrees of fuzziness are *Five to ten*, *Ten o' clock*, *Almost noon*, and the aforementioned *Middle of the week*.

The clock applet also lets you configure the date and time format and the time zone to be used, as well as set the system clock (you need root permissions to do that; if you are logged in as a normal user, a dialog will pop up and ask you for the root password). You can even copy the current date and time in a number of formats into the system clipboard.

KGhostview: Displaying PostScript and PDF

Adobe PostScript, as a standard in its own right, has become one of the most popular formats for exchanging documents in the computer world. Many academics distribute papers in PostScript format. The Linux Documentation Project offers its manuals in PostScript form, among others. This format is useful for people who lack the time to format input, or who have sufficient network bandwidth for transferring the enormous files. When you create documents of your own using *groff* or TEX you'll want to view them on a screen before you use up precious paper resources by printing them.

KGhostview, a KDE application, offers a pleasant environment for viewing Post-Script on the X Window System that, besides PostScript files, can also view files in Adobe's Portable Document Format (PDF). However, there is another application that is specific for viewing PDF files in KDE as well, *kpdf*. KGhostview is really mostly a more convenient frontend to an older application, Ghostview, so you can also get the functionality described here with Ghostview. The user experience is much better with KGhostview, however, so that's what we describe here.

Using KGhostview is very simple: invoke it with the name of the file to be displayed —for instance:

```
eggplant$ kghostview article.ps
```

or simply click the icon of any PostScript or PDF file anywhere in KDE.

Since we are interested only with viewing existing files here, we do not need to concern ourselves much with the benefits of PostScript and PDF. Both can be considered standards to the extent that many programs write them (and a few can read them), but both have been defined by one company, Adobe Systems. PDF is a bit more portable and self-contained, as it can even contain the fonts necessary to display the document. Also, PDF is better known on Microsoft Windows and the Macintosh, so you are more likely to come across PDF files than PostScript files on the Internet. And finally, whereas PostScript is really meant for printing, PDF has some features for interactive viewing, such as page icons, hyperlinks, and the like.

KGhostview is not a perfect PDF viewer, even though it is sufficient for most documents. If you have problems with a particular document, you may want to try either Adobe's own Acrobat Reader (which is not free software, but can be downloaded at no cost from *http://www.adobe.com*), or the KDE program *kpdf*, which comes in the same package as KGhostview.

The Ghostview window is huge; it can easily take up most of your screen. The first page of the document is displayed with scrollbars, if necessary. There is a menu bar and a toolbar, as in most KDE programs, as well as a page scroller and a page list on the left side of the window.

Like most X applications, KGhostview offers both menu options and keys (accelerators) for common functions. Thus, to view the next page, you can pull down the View menu and choose the Next Page option. Or you can just press the PgDn key (or the Space key, if you don't have a PgDn key, such as on a laptop).[*]

To go back to the previous page, choose Previous Page from the View menu. To go to any page you want, press the left mouse button on its number in the Page Number column. To exit, choose Quit from the File menu, or just press Ctrl-Q.

Documents from different countries often use different page sizes. The Ghostview default is the standard U.S. letter size (but it can be overridden by comments in the PostScript file, and this is often done by PostScript tools set up on Linux distributions that are configured for European customs). You can select a different size from the Paper Size submenu in the View menu.

Ghostview lets you enlarge or reduce the size of the page, a useful feature for checking the details of your formatting work. (But be warned that fonts on the screen are different from the fonts on a printer, and therefore the exact layout of characters in Ghostview will not be the same as that in the hard copy.) To zoom in on a small part of the page, press Ctrl-+; to zoom out, use Ctrl-−. You can also use the toolbar buttons or the Zoom In → Zoom Out menu entries in the View menu.

You can also adjust the window size to exactly fit the document's page width by selecting Fit To Page Width from the View menu.

To print a page, choose Print from the File menu or press Ctrl-P anywhere in the window. The standard KDE printer dialog will appear that lets you—among other things—choose the printer to use.

You can also print only the current page or a range of pages; just specify your selection in the printer dialog. This can also be combined with the PageMarks feature. The PageMarks menu lets you mark and unmark individual or groups of pages.

---

[*] There is a subtle difference between the Space key and the PgDn key: the PgDn key will always take you to the next page, while the Space key will first take you to the bottom of the current page if the window is too small to display the whole page on the screen at once. A second press of the Space key will then take you to the next page.

Marked pages are displayed with a little red flag in the page list. If you mark some pages and select the printing functionality, the dialog will pop up with the marked pages already filled in as the selection of pages to print. Of course, you can override this setting before finally sending the document to the printer.

Reading Documentation with Konqueror

Konqueror is not only a high-class web browser and file manager but also serves as a documentation reader, besides the Help Center built into KDE and described previously. KDE's documentation is displayed using HTML format, but Konqueror is capable of displaying other documentation formats, such as Info and manpages, that you will learn about later in this book. For example, in order to show the manpage for the ls command, just open a mini command-line window by pressing Alt-F2 and typing the following in that window:

```
man:ls
```

KDE will recognize that you want to read the manpage of the ls command, open a Konqueror window, and display the manpage. The result is also much more nicely formatted than how the original *man* command (or its X11 replacement, xman) would do it.

This works similarly for Info pages. For example, the documentation of the GNU C compiler, *gcc*, comes in info format. Just type:

```
info:gcc
```

either in a mini command line or in the Konqueror URL entry line, and the requested Info page will pop up (assuming it is installed, of course). If you have cursed at the really user-unfriendly command-line *info* program and weren't too happy with programs such as *xinfo* either, this feature may be a boon for you.

But Konqueror doesn't stop here when it comes to getting information. Want to use a search engine on the Internet? To find pages about Tux (the Linux mascot) on, let's say, the AltaVista search engine, simply type the following in a mini command line or the Konqueror URL entry line:

```
av:tux
```

and a Konqueror window with (at the time of this writing) 3,360,000 search results pops up. This works with many other search engines as well. See Table 3-1 for some of the most popular search engines together with their prefixes.

Table 3-1. Popular search engines and their prefixes

Search Engine	Prefix
AltaVista	av:
SourceForge	sf:
Excite	ex:

Table 3-1. Popular search engines and their prefixes (continued)

Search Engine	Prefix
Google	`gg:`
Merriam-Webster Dictionary	`dict:`

If your favorite search engine is not configured (which is quite unlikely, actually), you can configure it yourself by opening a Konqueror window and selecting Settings, Configure Konqueror, and then Web Shortcuts. The list contains all the preconfigured search engines and even lets you add your own.

Burning CDs with K3b

KDE comes with a very user-friendly and popular application for burning CDs and DVDs, K3b. If you insert an empty CD-R or DVD-R, KDE will offer to start K3b automatically; otherwise, you can start it from the command line with k3b; your distribution may even have it preconfigured in the K menu.

K3b usually detects your CD and DVD drives automatically, but if it should not do so in your case, select Settings → Configure K3b → Devices. Here you can see a list of recognized CD and DVD drives, sorted into readers and writers. If you are missing devices here, try clicking the Refresh button first; if that does not work, click on Add Device and enter your device manually. K3b expects the device file here; many distributions use symbolic links with telling names such as */dev/cdrom* or */dev/cdrecorder*. If you have specified the correct device file, K3b is usually able to detect all parameters, such as read and write speeds, automatically.

The K3b screen is separated into two halves. In the upper half, you see a view of your filesystem; in the lower half, you see project icons for common tasks such as creating a new data DVD or copying a CD. Other, less common, tasks such as burning a previously created ISO image on CD can be found in the Tools and File → New Project menu.

As an example, let's look into how you create a data CD with a backup of your digital pictures from your last holiday. Click on the New Data CD Project icon. You get an empty list of files and can now drag files from the filesystem view above (or from any Konqueror window) into this list. Just grab the directory that contains your holiday pictures and drag it into the list—that's all you need to do. You will see a green bar at the bottom of the K3b window that tells you how much space the currently selected files will occupy on the CD so that you know whether you can add another batch.

Once you are done selecting the files, click on the Burn button that is a bit hidden in the lower-right corner. A dialog with a lot of settings pops up; you should quickly check these settings, but you can leave most of them as they are. We usually suggest to select the "Verify written data" box on the Writing page so that you can be sure that the CD was written correctly (this will double the time for creating the CD, though). You may also want to change the Volume name (the name of the CD) and add yourself as the Publisher on the Volume Desc page. If you plan to read the CD on both Windows and Linux, it is a good idea to check that both the "Generate Rock Ridge extensions" and "Generate Joliet extensions" are selected on the Filesystem page. Once you are satisfied with all your settings, hit the Burn button in the upper right, lean back, and watch the progress bar move on until your CD is finished.

The GNOME Desktop Environment

The GNOME desktop environment, like KDE, is a complete desktop suite, from the desktop background up to a set of applications. As with KDE, GNOME can run any X application, and both KDE and GNOME rely on standards set by the Freedesktop. org group. In fact, the distinction between the two desktops is, in many ways, of interest more to developers choosing toolkits than to users, who in most cases mix and match applications without having to worry about the underpinnings.

The primary goals of the GNOME project are simplicity and ease of use. Applications must comply with extensive human interface guidelines to become part of the official GNOME desktop. Because GNOME makes an excellent platform for development in C, C++, Python, Java, and C#, unofficial and third-party applications are numerous. In some cases (notably the XML system), GNOME libraries appear in command-line and server-based applications.

Of course, for our purposes, the interesting parts are the core desktop and its associated applications. In the following sections, we go over the GNOME look and feel, talk a little bit about the customization options it offers to you, and then give a quick tour of major applications, such as Evolution and Nautilus.

Most Linux distributions include GNOME, but if you haven't installed it yourself, or if you want a newer version, you can visit *http://gnome.org* or your distribution's web page for downloads.

Core Desktop Interface

The GNOME desktop is designed to be familiar to anyone who has used a computer before. Although you can change the settings in almost any way, a typical installation will have a desktop with icons on it and a panel along the top and bottom. The panels are among the most important GNOME tools because they are so versatile and they allow a wide range of interactions with your system. Panels can exist along one edge of your screen, like the Windows control panel; along a portion of it, like the Macintosh Dock, and more. They can contain buttons to launch applications and small applications called *applets* such as clocks, system monitors, and even tiny games.

Basic GNOME tasks

Here is a quick explanation of how to perform the most common tasks. Once you get the hang of these, you can probably guess how to do anything else.

Open or activate an item in the panel
> Click once with the left button.

Start a program
> Buttons known as *launchers* cause a program to open when left-clicked; GNOME desktops typically have such buttons both in panels and on the desktop. Furthermore, when you click on a file, an appropriate program opens that file, as described shortly.

Move items around on the desktop
> Click and drag with the left mouse button.

Move items in the panel
> Clicking and dragging with the left mouse button works for launchers, but for some applets, the left mouse button is used to control the applet. In that case, middle-click and drag. This is also the case for moving windows by their borders—left-click will expand the window, but middle-click lets you move it.

Organize items on the desktop
> Right-click the desktop background and select Clean Up by Name. Items will be arranged in alphabetical order, with two exceptions: the first item, in the upper left, is always your home directory, and the last item in the list is always the Trash folder.

Open or activate an item on the desktop
> Double-click it. If you double-click a folder icon, it opens the folder in the Nautilus file management tool. If you double-click a spreadsheet document, the Gnumeric spreadsheet starts up and opens the document. If you have a window open and Shift-click or middle-click a folder in it, the current folder will close as a new one opens in its place.

Get a list of options or set preferences for any object
> Click with the right mouse button to get a menu of available options for any object. For example, you can change the desktop background by right-clicking the background and choosing Change Desktop Background. More general preferences are available in the GNOME Control Center, which you can access by choosing System → Personal Settings or Applications → Desktop Preferences, or by typing gnome-control-center at the command line. The exact menu arrangements may vary slightly depending on your distribution and version.

Paste text into any text area
> As with other operating systems, Ctrl-C copies, Ctrl-X cuts, and Ctrl-V pastes in every application except Emacs and XChat. You can also use the more traditional Unix mode pasting by selecting any text and then middle-clicking.

The panel

The preset configuration for many systems has a thin panel along the top and bottom of the screen. The top panel has a set of menus along the upper left, and a few buttons and a clock at the right. The bottom panel contains the window list applet, which should feel familiar to Microsoft Windows users; it displays a list of all open windows so you can switch applications easily.

To create a new panel, click any blank space in an existing panel, and choose Panel → Create New Panel, then select the type of panel you would like. To change a panel's properties, such as its size and color, right-click it and choose Properties (the menu panel at the top of the screen has no available properties; it is preconfigured for one position and size). Experiment with different kinds of panels and with different sizes to see which ones you like best. If you use a smaller screen, such as a laptop screen, you will want to choose a smaller panel size than if you have plenty of screen real estate to use.

To add application launcher buttons to your panels, you can drag them from menus, or right-click the panel and choose Panel → Add to Panel Launcher. Then, enter the name of the application you want to run, and choose an icon. You may also choose a description of the launcher that will display as a tool tip when you hover the mouse over the icon in your panel. If you want to launch the application from a terminal, check the "Run in Terminal" box.

For more information on the panel, right-click any empty spot in the panel and select Panel → Panel Manual.

Panel applets are small applications that run inside the panel. You can add them to the panel from the Add to Panel menu or just run them by clicking Applications → Applets. Panel applets come in a bewildering variety of flavors, from games to utilities. Some of the most common are the following:

Notification Area
> The notification area is similar to the Windows system tray and holds a variety of system status displays. Applications such as the Gaim instant messenger tool (described in "Instant Messaging" in Chapter 5) and the Rhythmbox music player use it as a control area that allows users to access them without keeping any windows open. System alerts and print queues will also display in this area. Both KDE and GNOME make use of the same notification area system, so applets that use the notification area will work in both desktops.

Netapplet
> Netapplet runs in the notification area and allows you to browse and choose available wired and wireless network connections. This is particularly useful for laptop users who need to use Wi-Fi (802.11x) connections. To run Netapplet, you must also be running netdaemon.

System Monitor

A graph that displays the load on your system resources for the past few seconds. To get a more detailed system report, including a list of all running processes and applications, right-click on the applet and select *Open System Monitor*.

Workspace Switcher

In most installations, this applet will already be running when you log in, and is typically set to four workspaces. Each workspace is the equivalent of a new screenful of desktop space, and you can have as many as you like. The workspace switcher displays all the virtual workspaces you have created, and displays each window on the desktop as a tiny box. You can use the left mouse button to drag a window from one workspace to another. Right-click and select the Properties menu item to change the number or arrangement of workspaces.

Window List

Like the workspace applet, the Window List is included in most default configurations. It displays the windows that you have open so that you can switch easily among them, even when they are minimized. If you have multiple windows for a single application, they will be grouped under a single entry. To turn this feature off, or to set other options for the applet, right-click the Window List and select Properties.

Battery Charge Monitor

The Battery Charge Monitor displays the remaining battery life for laptop systems. You can also use the Battery Charge Monitor to put your system into "sleep" or "suspend" mode by right-clicking on the applet and selecting *Suspend Computer*. Resuming operation from suspend mode is faster than rebooting, but the mechanism for operation will vary depending on your hardware and distribution. Older systems with the Advanced Power Management system use the command *apm -s*. Newer systems with ACPI support need to be sure that they have ACPI events configured properly in */etc/acpi/events/default*, although your distribution will probably have a convenient GUI for this task. For both ACPI and APM, SUSE Linux uses *powersaved*, and the sleep command is *powersave --suspend*.

Nautilus: your desktop and file manager

Nautilus is the name of the GNOME desktop and file manager. It controls the display of your background image and the files on your desktop, allows you to interact with files without using a terminal, and keeps track of your trash for you. In other words, it's the GNOME equivalent of Windows Explorer, the Macintosh Finder, and KDE's Konqueror. Like those other applications, Nautilus lets you drag items from one place to another. You can also copy files using Ctrl-C, cut with Ctrl-X, and paste with Ctrl-V.

In most cases, Nautilus will be running when you log in. If you *don't* want to run Nautilus at all, you can remove it from your session with the Session Properties tool in the Control Center. If you change your mind and want to start it, the command is *nautilus*.

The quickest way to get started with Nautilus is to double-click the home icon in the upper-left corner of your desktop, labeled as your home. This will open your home directory. Nautilus varies from other file management systems in that a window not only displays a folder, but *is* the folder: if you open a folder, then double-click it to open it again, it will merely raise the first window. For that reason, the location bar you may expect at the top of a window is not present. Instead, press Ctrl-L to enter a file location.

 Experts and those familiar with other file management systems will appreciate that Nautilus, although simple at first look, has a variety of conveniences and shortcuts that make advanced use much quicker. The first is Ctrl-L, which works not only in Nautilus but in all GNOME-related file selection dialogs to allow you to type a filename instead of clicking to choose a file. In web browsers, you can also use Ctrl-L to enter a web page instead of selecting the location bar with the mouse.

Opening windows: To avoid opening several windows at once, Shift-click or middle-click to close the current window when opening a new one.

Shortcuts for places: The combination Alt-Up opens the parent of the current folder, and Alt-Home opens your home directory.

If you prefer a more complex file display, right-click on any directory and choose *Browse Folder*. Browse mode includes the location bar absent from the normal Nautilus display mode, and also includes the left-side pane. At the top of the left pane is a selector for different information displays:

Information
Displays basic information about the current folder.

Emblems
Displays a list of available emblems, small badges you can add to any file's icon. Drag them from the side pane onto any file to mark it. For example, if you have several similar images in a folder, you might want to drag the "Cool" or "Favorite" emblem to remind you which one you like best. You can also set emblems by selecting Edit → Background and Emblems.

History
Shows a list of previous locations you have displayed in Nautilus. Double-click any folder to return to it.

Notes

> Allows a note to be kept on a particular folder. Each folder has a different page of notes.

Tree

> Perhaps the most useful of the side-pane tools, this allows you to navigate a complex folder hierarchy with convenient spin-down triangles. Each folder in the tree is displayed with a triangle next to it; click the folder to open it, or click the triangle to display any subfolders without actually visiting the folder itself.

Some neat Nautilus features include the following:

- Instead of a generic image icon for graphics files, Nautilus uses scaled-down thumbnails of the image itself. This makes it easy to organize directories full of images, such as those pulled from a digital camera.

- If you hover your mouse over a music file, the file will begin to play.

- For text files, the plain document icon is decorated by the actual text contents of the file. That way, you can remember how the file starts without having to open it, even if you didn't give it the most descriptive name.

- You can stretch icons by right-clicking them and choosing Stretch Icon. If you stretch a text icon enough, you can see the entire contents of the file, and use it as a desktop notepad.

- Select Edit → Backgrounds and Emblems to choose different emblems to decorate icons. You can also drag colors and patterns from this area to set your desktop and panel background. To set an image as the desktop background, right-click on the desktop and choose Change Desktop Background.

All in all, Nautilus is a versatile tool that you can learn to use just by poking around a little. For additional help, just choose Help and then Nautilus User Manual from any Nautilus window.

Expert Settings: GConf

GConf is a centralized, XML-based configuration system for desktop applications. It allows applications to share keyboard shortcuts, themes, and other preferences, and uses a daemon to notify applications when preferences change, so you don't have to restart the application to see a change take effect.

GConf can also be used to lock down a desktop system with a finer degree of granularity than traditional Unix file locking. An administrator might wish to lock GConf settings to permit some, but not all, behavior for a given application, and allow some, but not all, changes in preferences. Administrators of kiosks, public computer labs, and other security- and support-conscious deployments find system lockdown to be indispensable. Therefore, most applications provide a *lockdown* section in their GConf files. If you have users you want to keep out of trouble, explore these options in greater detail. One good resource is the GNOME System Administrator's Guide, available at *http://www.gnome.org*.

In this book, we assume that you're not interested in locking preferences down, but in opening things up and tweaking them to your taste. That's where *gconf-editor* comes in handy. You can, of course, edit the XML files in *~/.gconf* yourself, but the gconf-editor application makes things a little more convenient.

To get started, run the command *gconf-editor*. On the left side of the window is the GConf hierarchy, arranged like a file tree starting at /. The tree corresponds to actual settings files stored in the *~/.gconf* directory, so changing something in the /applications tree alters files stored in *~/.gconf/applications*. On the right side of the window is the list of available settings, called keys, and a place for documentation about the selected key.

We're mostly interested in items under the */apps* tree. The */desktop* and */GNOME* trees hold information not tied to a specific application, such as session data and desktop-wide lockdown settings. Systemwide configuration is stored in */system*, and information about the way GConf stores settings is kept in */schemas*. Avoid changing anything in the */schemas* tree.

For now, let's try adjusting an application setting, to give you a feel for what can be done. Normally, the files on your desktop come from the *~/Desktop* folder. However, you can force Nautilus to display your home directory on the desktop instead. Select */apps/nautilus/preferences/desktop_is_home_dir* and check the box. Now, Nautilus will display the contents of your home directory on your desktop.

Other applications have similar "hidden" preferences you can change. Try the following:

- Metacity window manager: Check the box in */apps/metacity/reduced_resources* to make Metacity use as few system resources as possible. This will make it look less attractive, but may improve system performance.

- Epiphany web browser: Normally, a middle click in the Epiphany web browser turns on the vertical scroll feature familiar to users of Internet Explorer. However, users of traditional UNIX browsers may prefer to check the box for */apps/epiphany/general/middle_click_open_url* and turn on the "paste URL" feature. Select a URL in any application, then middle-click in a non-text-entry area of a web page, and Epiphany will load the text you have selected.

GNOME Applications

Now that you have a feel for the desktop and how to get around it, let's take a look at some of the applications that are built to go with it. Note that these applications aren't restricted to the GNOME desktop, and they aren't the only applications you can run on the GNOME desktop—they're just built from the same materials and work particularly well together.

Evolution: Mail, Calendar, and Contacts

Evolution is what's known as a groupware suite; it combines email with a calendar and an address book so that communication and scheduling tasks all fall into one convenient package. We don't have room to go into depth regarding all three, but a complete manual is included in the Help menu and is available online at *http://gnome. org/projects/evolution*.

You can start Evolution by selecting Evolution from your Applications menu, or by typing evolution at the command line. A screen like the one in Figure 3-7 should come up.

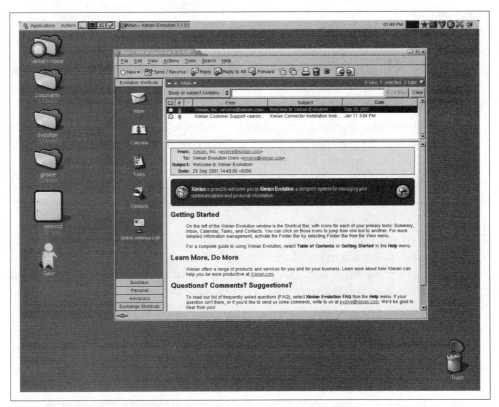

Figure 3-7. Evolution on the GNOME desktop

The first time you run Evolution, you'll be asked to create an email account by entering information about yourself and your email access. You can copy this information from your existing mail program, or ask your system administrator or ISP.

Evolution works with standard mail server protocols and can be used in almost any network environment. It lets you leave your mail on the server (if it's running the IMAP protocol), download mail to your local system (if it runs either the IMAP or the POP protocol), or use mail spools on your local system (if you're running your own mail server). In addition, Evolution supports Microsoft Exchange 2000 and later and Novell GroupWise 6.5 and later for mail, calendar, and address functions.

Once you've created an account, you will be presented with the main Evolution window. On the left side of the Evolution window is a shortcut bar, with a list of available tools at the bottom and a list of available sources of data at the top. Click the buttons at the bottom to switch among email, calendar, task list, contacts, and Microsoft Exchange tools.

The following sections describe Evolution's major features.

Evolution mail

To start using Evolution mail, click the Inbox button in the shortcut bar. The mail view is divided into two portions: in the top half, a list of messages, and in the bottom half, the display of your selected message. You can change the proportions by dragging the gray bar between them, or hide the message preview area entirely by selecting View → Preview Pane or pressing Ctrl - '.

In general, the mail features are fairly simple: click the Send and Receive button to check for new mail and send mail you've queued for later delivery, and click the New Message button to compose a new message.

What distinguishes Evolution from other mail programs are the speed of its searches, the power and simplicity of its filters, and its unique vFolders, a sort of combination of searches and filters.

The search bar is located at the top of the message list. To search your mail, go to any mail folder, select a portion of the message to search (just the message body, the sender, the entire message, and so forth), enter a word into the text box, and press Enter. Evolution pre-indexes your mail, so the results are returned to you faster than with other tools.

Filters add an action to the end of a search: every time you get mail, Evolution performs a search that you specify on the new messages, and then takes actions based on those results. The most common uses of filters are to automatically file messages based on the senders, and to delete messages that are flagged as spam.

To create a filter, go to any mail view and open your list of filters by selecting *Tools* → Filters. Then

1. Click the *Add* button to add a filter.
2. In the top half of the dialog, select a set of criteria you'll use to pick messages for the filter. For example, if you select Sender Contains in the first drop-down item,

and enter gnome.org in the text box that appears next to it, your filter will act on mail that comes to you from all *gnome.org* email addresses.

3. In the bottom half of the window, select one or more actions for your messages. For example, if you select Move to Folder, you'll be offered a button labeled Click to Select Folder. Click that, select a destination folder, and your filter will file all mail from *gnome.org* addresses in your GNOME email folder.

4. Click OK in the filter creation box, and OK in the filter list. You're done.

If you find that you need more flexibility than filters offer you, you can use vFolders. A vFolder, or virtual folder, is essentially a complex saved search that looks like a folder. That also means that although an email message can exist only in a single standard folder, you can find it in several vFolders.

When you create a vFolder, you select criteria just as you would for a filter, but instead of choosing what to do with them, you specify where you want to look for these messages. Once you've created a vFolder, it appears in a list of vFolders at the bottom of your folder tree. Then, every time you open it, it searches your mail folders for messages that match the criteria you chose when you created it. So if you create your filters to file mail depending on its sender, you can create a vFolder that holds mail with a given subject, no matter who sent it.

Mail on GroupWise and Exchange servers works in a similar way, with only a few exceptions. On GroupWise servers, event notifications are delivered directly to the Calendar folder rather than to your inbox or to the calendar itself. Once you have accepted a meeting, it appears in your calendar. For Exchange servers, your folder tree contains shared or public folders available to you. To subscribe to shared and public folders, click the *Exchange* button in the shortcut bar and select Actions → Subscribe to Other User's Folder.

Evolution calendar

The Evolution calendar allows you great flexibility in creating and viewing your schedule. To get started, click the Calendar button in the shortcut bar. You'll be presented with an empty work-week spread out before you, devoid of appointments. On the left side of the window is a list of available calendars, and on the right side is your calendar view. You can check the boxes next to the calendar names in the shortcut bar to show or hide the events for each calendar. Each set of events is color-coded to prevent confusion, and the overlay helps you reduce clutter when you want to see only one type of event, while allowing you to compare schedules if you need to coordinate or avoid conflicts.

Calendars are listed in several categories: On this Computer, On the Web, Contacts, and, depending on your groupware server, Exchange or GroupWise. When you start, you will have at least two calendars. The first, your default personal calendar, is empty. The second, Birthdays and Anniversaries, shows any dates you have entered into address cards in the contacts tool.

To add a new calendar, select New → Calendar and choose the type of calendar you'll be creating: On this Computer or On the Web. The first type of calendar requires only that you pick a name and a color and click OK. For subscription-only web calendars, you'll need to enter that information, plus the URL of the calendar file and the frequency with which Evolution will check for changes as well.

The GroupWise and Contacts calendars are created automatically, and you can have only one of each. To create a new Exchange calendar, use the Exchange tool to subscribe to a calendar folder on the Exchange server.

To show a different range of time in the calendar display, select a range of days in the small calendar in the upper-right side of the window or click one of the prebuilt ranges of days in the toolbar: today, one day, five days, a week, or a month.

Once you have a feel for how to page through your datebook, you'll want to start scheduling events. To schedule an event, click the New Appointment button. Pick which calendar you want it to go in, enter a summary of the event, choose a time, and (optionally) enter a longer description. Note that you can't add events to every calendar: web calendars and your contact calendar, for example, are read-only.

At the lower right, you can select from a list of categories for this event. Events with categories, recurrences, or reminders are displayed with small icons in the calendar view: an alarm clock for reminders, arrows moving in a circle for recurrences, a birthday cake for birthdays, and so forth.

You can also schedule reminders and recurrences. For example, if you have an important meeting next week, you can schedule a reminder to pop up 15 minutes beforehand so that you have time to prepare. Just click the Reminder tab and choose a time and type of reminder, then click Add to add it to the list. Recurrences are similar: click the Recurrence tab, and choose how often you'd like to repeat the event. Is it just this Thursday and next Tuesday? Is it every Wednesday from now until Christmas? Is it a holiday that happens every year? Choose the recurrence rules, click Save and Close, and you've added the event to your calendar.

All that's left is to coordinate this event with other people. Select Actions, and then Forward as iCalendar to create an email message that has the event attached to it. When the recipients receive the message, they can click a single button to add the event to their calendars and send a note to you letting you know whether they'll attend.

Evolution contacts

The Evolution contact manager, or address book, is perhaps the least glamorous tool in the suite. However, it is interwoven with the email tools quite thoroughly. You can create contact cards by clicking the New Contact button in the contacts view, but you can also create a card by right-clicking any email address in an email someone has sent you.

 If you enter birthday and anniversary information for your contacts, the dates will show up in a special calendar dedicated to your contacts.

If you're looking at your address book for someone's email address, you can right-click his card and have the option to send him a message, or to send his card to someone else, with just two clicks.

To have a look at the contact manager, click the Contacts button in the shortcut bar, or select any contact folder from the folder bar. You'll see a simple list of cards. If you prefer to have your contacts arranged as a phone list, select View, Current View, and then Phone List. You can also choose to display the list by organization rather than just by name.

GNOME and Office Software

GNOME integrates with the OpenOffice suite to allow users a consistent experience for word processing, spreadsheets, and presentations. OpenOffice has excellent file compatibility with Microsoft Office and offers the vast majority of features necessary for day to day use.

Other options are also available, however. The Gnumeric spreadsheet application handles certain files more capably than OpenOffice does, and has more complex financial calculations, although its graphics capabilities are not as strong. AbiWord is an excellent word processor for most tasks, and simpler than OpenOffice. Both take up far less disk space and run faster, and are suitable for low-resource situations.

For more information about office suites, see Chapter 8.

Movies and Music: Totem and Rhythmbox

The discussion of video and music playback inevitably involves the discussion of licensing. Because the group that defines the MP3 format has patented the encoding and decoding algorithms and requires that every distributor keep track of, and pay for, each copy of MP3 playing or recording software, there are no free, legal MP3 playback or recording devices. Similar license restrictions from the DVD Copy Control Association (*dvdcca.org*) have prevented the development of a free application that will display the DVD movies you can buy in a store.

Unlicensed MP3 and DVD applications are easy enough to build, as anyone with a search engine can find out quickly enough, but they also aren't necessary. You can still record and play music CDs with the free Ogg Vorbis format, and you can still record and play movies stored in MPEG and MOV formats—including unencrypted DVDs such as those made by home DVD recorders.

To play those songs, start up Rhythmbox, a music player modeled after features from Apple's iTunes. Rhythmbox will require a few moments to index your music collection before you use it. If it doesn't index your music library immediately, or if it doesn't find all your songs, select Music → Import Folder.

Once your files are indexed by the Rhythmbox library, you'll see a strikingly familiar interface: a list of music sources on the left, including Library, Radio, and any playlists you have created. To the right of the music sources is a list of artists and albums you can use to browse your collection, and below that is a list of individual songs that match the artist and album you've selected. You can also search for items in the artist, album, and song title categories in the Search bar at the top.

Select a song and press Play. As you listen, right-click on a song and select Properties. The first tab, Basic, shows you a little information about the track, but the second tab, Details, shows you how often you've played the song, where it's stored, and the exact length; it also lets you rate the song on a scale of 0 to 5. If you don't rate the song yourself, Rhythmbox will guess at ratings based on how often you play a song.

The other major feature in Rhythmbox is its playlists. To create a playlist, select Music → Playlist → New Playlist. Enter a name for your playlist, and it will appear in your list of available sources. Then, drag songs from the library to the list, and you've got a playlist.

To import a song into Rhythmbox, you must have an application known as Sound Juicer installed, which is often included with Rythmbox, but not always. Select File → Import CD to start ripping. Sound Juicer will check the CD title and track listings online with the MusicBrainz service, and ask you to confirm them before it proceeds. It will record in the Ogg Vorbis format unless you specify otherwise by selecting Edit → Preferences.

For movie playback, Totem makes things as easy as hitting Ctrl-O to open a file (or Ctrl-L to open a video stream on the Web). Totem provides a very clean interface to the extremely complex world of video encoding algorithms, but it is not always possible to hide from the sometimes bewildering array of file types. Totem supports several video formats by default, including the formats used by most video cameras.

 You don't need to mount a DVD or video disc: just press Play. You do, however, need to be sure that the /dev/dvd or /media/dvd device exists on your system.

Tinkerers will note that Totem uses the Xine backend, which is as configurable as Totem is simple. For example, not all QuickTime video subformats (there are several) are supported, but users of most recent x86-based hardware can copy the QuickTime DLLs from a Windows installation into */usr/lib/win32* and access their system's hardware support. In addition, if you have RealPlayer for Linux installed, Totem is able to display the RealVideo format using RealPlayer's own binary codecs. For more information about media playback on Linux, including performance tuning hints, updates to the Xine libraries, and links to other media playback systems, visit *http://www.xinehq.de*.

Additional Applications and Resources

There are dozens, if not hundreds, of other GNOME applications, from software development tools to games to flowcharting and diagramming tools. The best ways to explore them are to visit the *http://gnome.org* web site and browse the software map or to try installing a few from your update system, whether it's Red Carpet, *up2date*, *apt-get*, or YaST.

If you get stuck, there are several places to turn for help. In addition to the Nautilus help system and the *gnome.org* web site, try looking for help in chat systems. Developers can be found on `irc.gnome.org` in #gnome, so if you have software development questions, go there. A web search on the text of an error message can often turn up the solution to a problem. Searching Google for an error message you've seen can turn up postings to public forums from people who have seen (and hopefully solved) the same error.

CHAPTER 4
Basic Unix Commands and Concepts

If you've come to Linux from Windows or another non-Unix operating system, you have a steep learning curve ahead of you. We might as well be candid on this point. Unix is a world all its own, even though it has become *a lot* more user-friendly over the last few years.

In this chapter, we introduce the rudiments of Unix for those readers who have never had exposure to this operating system. If you are coming from Microsoft Windows or other environments, the information in this chapter will be absolutely vital to you. Unlike other operating systems, Unix is not at all intuitive. Many of the commands have seemingly odd names or syntax, the reasons for which usually date back many years to the early days of this system. And, although many of the commands may appear to be similar to their counterparts in the Windows command-line interpreter, there are important differences.

Instead of getting into the dark mesh of text processing, shell syntax, and other issues, in this chapter we strive to cover the basic commands needed to get you up to speed with the system if you're coming from a non-Unix environment. This chapter is far from complete; a real beginner's Unix tutorial would take an entire book. It's our hope that this chapter will give you enough to keep you going in your adventures with Linux, and that you'll invest in some more advanced books once you have a need to do so. We'll give you enough background to make your terminal usable, keep track of jobs, and enter essential commands.

Part 2 of this book contains material on system administration and maintenance. This is by far the most important part of the book for anyone running his own Linux system. If you are completely new to Unix, the material found in Part II should be easy to follow once you've completed the tutorial here.

One big job we merely touch on in this chapter is how to edit files. It's one of the first things you need to learn on any operating system. The two most popular editors for Linux, *vi* and Emacs, are discussed in Chapter 19.

Logging In

Let's assume that your installation went completely smoothly, and you are facing the following prompt on your screen:

```
Linux login:
```

Some Linux users are not so lucky; they have to perform some heavy tinkering when the system is still in a raw state or in single-user mode. But for now, we'll talk about logging into a functioning Linux system.

Logging in, of course, distinguishes one user from another. It lets several people work on the same system at once and makes sure that you are the only person to have access to your files.

You may have installed Linux at home and are thinking right now, "Big deal. No one else shares this system with me, and I'd just as soon not have to log in." But logging in under your personal account also provides a certain degree of protection: your account won't have the ability to destroy or remove important system files. The system administration account (covered in the next chapter) is used for such touchy matters.

If you connect your computer to the Internet, even via a modem, make sure you set nontrivial passwords on all your accounts. Use punctuation and strings that don't represent real words or names. Although Unix systems are not as susceptible to random brute-force attacks from the outside world as Windows systems are (according to some sources, it takes about 20 minutes from connecting a Windows box to the Internet until that computer is attacked, whereas it takes about 40 minutes to download the security fixes from Microsoft), you certainly do not want anybody to snoop around in your files.

Note that some distributions install a so-called graphical login manager right away, so you might not be greeted by the somewhat arcane login: prompt in white letters on black background, but with a fancy graphical login screen, possibly even presenting you with the user accounts available on your system (maybe even with a little picture for each user) as well as different modes to log into. The basic login procedure is the same as described here, however: you still type your username and password.

You were probably asked to set up a login account for yourself when you installed Linux. If you have such an account, type the name you chose at the Linux login: prompt. If you don't have an account yet, type root because that account is certain to exist. Some distributions may also set up an account called *install* or some other name for fooling around when you first install the system.

After you choose your account, you see:

```
Password:
```

and you need to enter the correct password. The terminal turns off the normal echoing of characters you enter for this operation so that people looking at the screen cannot read your password. If the prompt does not appear, you should add a password to protect yourself from other people's tampering; we'll go into this later.

By the way, both the name and the password are case-sensitive. Make sure the Caps Lock key is not set because typing `ROOT` instead of `root` will not work.

When you have successfully logged in, you will see a prompt. If you're *root*, this may be a simple:

```
#
```

For other users, the prompt is usually a dollar sign ($). The prompt may also contain the name you assigned to your system or the directory you're in currently. Whatever appears here, you are now ready to enter commands. We say that you are at the "shell level" here and that the prompt you see is the "shell prompt." This is because you are running a program called the *shell* that handles your commands. Right now we can ignore the shell, but later in this chapter we'll find that it does a number of useful things for us.

As we show commands in this chapter, we'll show the prompt simply as $. So if you see:

```
$ pwd
```

it means that the shell prints $ and that `pwd` is what you're supposed to enter.

Setting a Password

If you don't already have a password, we recommend you set one. Just enter the command *passwd*. The command will prompt you for a password and then ask you to enter it a second time to make sure you enter it without typos.

There are standard guidelines for choosing passwords so that they're hard for other people to guess. Some systems even check your password and reject any that don't meet the minimal criteria. For instance, it is often said that you should have at least six characters in the password. Furthermore, you should mix uppercase and lowercase characters or include characters other than letters and digits.

If you think it is a good idea to pick an ordinary, but rarely used word as your password, think again. There are password attack programs available that come with an English dictionary and just try all words in that dictionary in order to find the correct one so that the account can be compromised. Also, never use the account name for the password. This is sometimes called a "joe," and is likely to be the first thing a password attacker is going to try.

A good trick for choosing a good password is to take a full phrase that you can remember (maybe a line from your favorite song), and then just take the first letters.

Then blend in a digit and maybe a special character. For example, if your line is *I'd really like to go fishing now*, your password could be *Irl2gfn!*. But do not use exactly this one; the fact that it has been published in this book makes it a bad password. There are even programs available (not unlikely integrated into the graphical user management tools of your distribution) that generate a random password from random characters, but of course these passwords are difficult to remember—if you have to write the password down in order to remember it, it is a bad password as well.

To change your password, just enter the `passwd` command again. It prompts you for your old password (to make sure you're you) and then lets you change it.

Virtual Consoles

As a multiprocessing system, Linux gives you a number of interesting ways to do several things at once. You can start a long software installation and then switch to reading mail or compiling a program simultaneously.

Most Linux users, when they want this asynchronous access, will employ the X Window System (see Chapter 16). But before you get X running, you can do something similar through virtual consoles. This feature appears on a few other versions of Unix, but is not universally available.

To try out virtual consoles, hold down the left Alt key and press one of the function keys, F1 through F8. As you press each function key, you see a totally new screen complete with a login prompt. You can log in to different virtual consoles just as if you were two different people, and you can switch between them to carry out different activities. You can even run a complete X session in each console. The X Window System will use virtual console 7 by default. So if you start X and then switch to one of the text-based virtual consoles, you can go back again to X by typing Alt-F7. If you discover that the Alt-+ function key combination brings up an X menu or some other function instead of switching virtual consoles, use Ctrl + Alt + function key. You can even have two X servers running the X Window System; the second one would then be on virtual console 8.

Popular Commands

The number of commands on a typical Unix system is enough to fill a few hundred reference pages. And you can add new commands too. The commands we'll tell you about here are just enough to navigate and to see what you have on the system.

Directories

As with Windows and virtually every modern computer system, Unix files are organized into a hierarchical directory structure. Unix imposes no rules about where files have to be, but conventions have grown up over the years. Thus, on Linux you'll find a directory called */home* where each user's files are placed. Each user has a subdirectory under */home*. So if your login name is *mdw*, your personal files are located in */home/mdw*. This is called your home directory. You can, of course, create more subdirectories under it.

If you come from a Windows system, the slash (/) as a path separator may look odd to you because you are used to the backslash (\). There is nothing tricky about the slash. Slashes were actually used as path separators long before people even started to think about MS-DOS or Windows. The backslash has a different meaning on Unix (turning off the special meaning of the next character, if any).

As you can see, the components of a directory are separated by slashes. The term *pathname* is often used to refer to this slash-separated list.

What directory is */home* in? The directory named */,* of course. This is called the root directory. We have already mentioned it when setting up filesystems.

When you log in, the system puts you in your home directory. To verify this, use the "print working directory," or pwd, command:

```
$ pwd
/home/mdw
```

The system confirms that you're in */home/mdw*.

You certainly won't have much fun if you have to stay in one directory all the time. Now try using another command, cd, to move to another directory:

```
$ cd /usr/bin
$ pwd
/usr/bin
$ cd
```

Where are we now? A cd with no arguments returns us to our home directory. By the way, the home directory is often represented by a tilde (~). So the string *~/programs* means that *programs* is located right under your home directory.

While we're thinking about it, let's make a directory called *~/programs*. From your home directory, you can enter either:

```
$ mkdir programs
```

or the full pathname:

```
$ mkdir /home/mdw/programs
```

Now change to that directory:

```
$ cd programs
$ pwd
/home/mdw/programs
```

The special character sequence .. refers to the directory just above the current one. So you can move back up to your home directory by typing the following:

```
$ cd ..
```

You can also always go back to your home directory by just typing:

```
$ cd
```

no matter where in the directory hierarchy you are.

The opposite of mkdir is rmdir, which removes directories:

```
$ rmdir programs
```

Similarly, the rm command deletes files. We won't show it here because we haven't yet shown how to create a file. You generally use the *vi* or Emacs editor for that (see Chapter 19), but some of the commands later in this chapter will create files too. With the *-r* (recursive) option, *rm* deletes a whole directory and all its contents. (Use with care!)

At this point, we should note that the graphical desktop environments for Linux, such as KDE and GNOME, come with their own file managers that can perform most of the operations described in this chapter, such as listing and deleting files, creating directories, and so forth. Some of them, like Konqueror (shipped with KDE) and the web browser in that environment, are quite feature-rich. However, when you want to perform a command on many files, which perhaps follow a certain specification, the command line is hard to beat in efficiency, even it takes a while to learn. For example, if you wanted to delete all files in the current directory and all directories beneath that which start with an *r* and end in *.txt*, the so-called Z shell (*zsh*) would allow you to do that with one line:

```
$ rm **/r*.txt
```

More about these techniques later.

Listing Files

Enter *ls* to see what is in a directory. Issued without an argument, the *ls* command shows the contents of the current directory. You can include an argument to see a different directory:

```
$ ls /home
```

Some systems have a fancy ls that displays special files—such as directories and executable files—in bold, or even in different colors. If you want to change the default colors, edit the file */etc/DIR_COLORS*, or create a copy of it in your home directory named *.dir_colors* and edit that.

Like most Unix commands, ls can be controlled with options that start with a hyphen (-). Make sure you type a space before the hyphen. One useful option for *ls* is *-a* for "all," which will reveal to you riches that you never imagined in your home directory:

```
$ cd
$ ls -a
.                       .bashrc                 .fvwmrc
..                      .emacs                  .xinitrc
.bash_history           .exrc
```

The single dot refers to the current directory, and the double dot refers to the directory right above it. But what are those other files beginning with a dot? They are called *hidden files*. Putting a dot in front of their names keeps them from being shown during a normal *ls* command. Many programs employ hidden files for user options—things about their default behavior that you want to change. For instance, you can put commands in the file *.Xdefaults* to alter how programs using the X Window System operate. Most of the time you can forget these files exist, but when you're configuring your system you'll find them very important. We list some of them later.

Another useful *ls* option is *-l* for "long." It shows extra information about the files. Figure 4-1 shows typical output and what each field means. Adding the *-h* ("human" option) shows the file sizes rounded to something more easily readable.

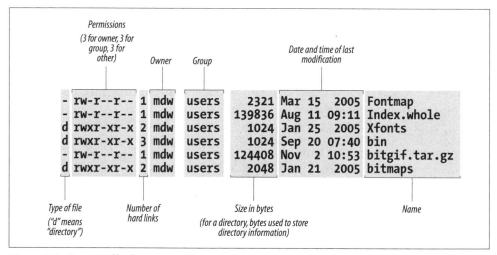

Figure 4-1. Output of ls -l

We discuss the permissions, owner, and group fields in a later chapter, Chapter 11. The ls command also shows the size of each file and when it was last modified.

Viewing Files, More or Less

One way to look at a file is to invoke an editor, such as:

```
$ xemacs .bashrc
```

But if you just want to scan a file quickly, rather than edit it, other commands are quicker. The simplest is the strangely named cat command (named after the verb *concatenate* because you can also use it to concatenate several files into one):

```
$ cat .bashrc
```

But a long file will scroll by too fast for you to see it, so most people use the more command instead:

```
$ more .bashrc
```

This prints a screenful at a time and waits for you to press the spacebar before printing more. more has a lot of powerful options. For instance, you can search for a string in the file: press the slash key (/), type the string, and press Return.

A popular variation on the more command is called *less*. It has even more powerful features; for instance, you can mark a particular place in a file and return there later.

Symbolic Links

Sometimes you want to keep a file in one place and pretend it is in another. This is done most often by a system administrator, not a user. For instance, you might keep several versions of a program around, called *prog.0.9*, *prog.1.1*, and so on, but use the name *prog* to refer to the version you're currently using. Or you may have a file installed in one partition because you have disk space for it there, but the program that uses the file needs it to be in a different partition because the pathname is hard-coded into the program.

Unix provides *links* to handle these situations. In this section, we'll examine the *symbolic link*, which is the most flexible and popular type. A symbolic link is a kind of dummy file that just points to another file. If you edit or read or execute the symbolic link, the system is smart enough to give you the real file instead. Symbolic links work a lot like shortcuts under MS-Windows, but are much more powerful.

Let's take the *prog* example. You want to create a link named *prog* that points to the actual file, which is named *prog.1.1*. Enter the following command:

```
$ ln -s prog.1.1 prog
```

Now you've created a new file named *prog* that is kind of a dummy file; if you run it, you're really running *prog.1.1*. Let's look at what ls -l has to say about the file:

```
$ ls -l prog
lrwxrwxrwx   2 mdw      users        8 Nov 17 14:35 prog -> prog.1.1
```

The l at the beginning of the output line shows that the file is a link, and the little -> indicates the real file to which the link points.

Symbolic links are really simple, once you get used to the idea of one file pointing to another. You'll encounter links all the time when installing software packages.

Shells

As we said before, logging into the system in console mode puts you into a shell. If your system is configured with a graphical login, logging in brings you to the graphical interface where you can open an *xterm* (or similar) window in order to get a shell. The shell interprets and executes all your commands. Let's look a bit at different shells before we keep going, because they're going to affect some of the material coming up.

If it seems confusing that Unix offers many different shells, just accept it as an effect of evolution. Believe us, you wouldn't want to be stuck using the very first shell developed for Unix, the Bourne shell. Although it was a very powerful user interface for its day (the mid-1970s), it lacked a lot of useful features for interactive use—including the ones shown in this section. So other shells have been developed over time, and you can now choose the one that best suits your way of working.

Some of the shells available on Linux are as follows:

bash
> Bourne Again shell. The most commonly used (and most powerful) shell on Linux. POSIX-compliant, compatible with the Bourne shell, created and distributed by the GNU project (Free Software Foundation). Offers command-line editing, history substitution, and Bourne shell compatibility.

csh
> C shell. Developed at Berkeley. Mostly compatible with the Bourne shell for interactive use, but has a very different interface for programming. Does not offer command-line editing, although it does have a sophisticated alternative called history substitution. On Linux, *csh* is just another name for the newer *tcsh*.

ksh
> Korn shell. Perhaps the most popular on Unix systems generally, and the first to introduce modern shell techniques (including some borrowed from the C shell) into the Bourne shell. Compatible with the Bourne shell. Offers command-line editing.

sh
> Bourne shell. The original shell. Does not offer command-line editing.

tcsh
> Enhanced C shell. Offers command-line editing.

zsh

Z shell. The newest of the shells. Compatible with the Bourne shell. Offers command-line editing. Has very powerful completion features. If you do not know any shell yet, and your Linux distribution carries *zsh*, go with that choice from the start.

Try the following command to find out what your shell is. It prints out the full pathname where the shell is located. Don't forget to type the dollar sign:

```
$ echo $SHELL
```

You are probably running *bash*, the Bourne Again shell, because that is the most popular one on Linux. If you're running something else, this might be a good time to change to *bash* or *zsh*. They are both powerful, POSIX compliant, well supported, and very popular on Linux. Use the chsh command to change your shell:

```
$ chsh
Enter password: Type your password here – this is for security's sake
Changing the login shell for mdw
Enter the new value, or press return for the default

      Login Shell [/bin/sh]:/bin/bash
```

(Use /usr/bin/zsh or /bin/zsh, depending on your distribution, for *zsh*.)

Before a user can choose a particular shell as a login shell, that shell must be installed and the system administrator must make it available by entering it in */etc/shells*.

There are a couple of ways to conceptualize the differences between shells. One is to distinguish Bourne-compatible shells from *csh*-compatible shells. This will be of interest to you when you start to program with the shell, also known as writing shell scripts. The Bourne shell and C shell have different programming constructs. Most people now agree that Bourne-compatible shells are better, and there are many Unix utilities that recognize only the Bourne shell.

Another way to categorize shells is to identify those that offer command-line editing (all the newer ones) versus those that do not. *sh* and *csh* lack this useful feature.

When you combine the two criteria—being compatible with the Bourne shell and offering command-line editing—your best choice comes down to *bash*, *ksh*, or *zsh*. Try out several shells before you make your choice; it helps to know more than one, in case someday you find yourself on a system that limits your choice of shells.

Useful Keys and How to Get Them to Work

When you type a command, pressing the Backspace key should remove the last character. Ctrl-U should delete the line from the cursor to the beginning of the line; thus, this key combination will delete the whole line if the cursor is at the end of the line. When you have finished entering a command, and it is executing, Ctrl-C should abort it, and Ctrl-Z should suspend it. (When you want to resume the suspended program, enter *fg* for "foreground.")

Ctrl-S stops the terminal output until you turn it off again with Ctrl-Q. This is probably less useful today, as most terminal emulations provide scrolling facilities anyway, but it's important to know if you have hit Ctrl-S by accident and the terminal all of a sudden "becomes unresponsive." Just hit Ctrl-Q to make it respond again; it was just waiting for you.

If any of these keys fail to work, your terminal is not configured correctly for some reason. You can fix it through the stty command. Use the syntax:

    stty *function key*

where *function* is what you want to do, and *key* is the key that you press. Specify a control key by putting a circumflex (^) in front of the key.

Here is a set of sample commands to set up the functions described earlier:

```
$ stty erase ^H
$ stty kill ^U
$ stty intr ^C
$ stty susp ^Z
```

The first control key shown, ^H, represents the ASCII code generated by the Backspace key.

By the way, you can generate a listing of your current terminal settings by entering *stty -a*. But that doesn't mean you can understand the output: *stty* is a complicated command with many uses, some of which require a lot of knowledge about terminals.

Here is another use of stty that can prove useful quite often: if your shell gets confused (as can often happen if you output binary data to it), and does not react as you are used to, try entering:

```
$ stty sane
```

That will usually succeed in bringing the shell to reason and making it operate as expected again.

Typing Shortcuts

If you've been following along with this tutorial at your terminal, you may be tired of typing the same things over and over. It can be particularly annoying when you make a mistake and have to start again. Here is where the shell really makes life easier. It doesn't make Unix as simple as a point-and-click interface, but it can help you work really fast in a command environment.

This section discusses command-line editing. The tips here work if your shell is *bash*, *ksh*, *tcsh*, or *zsh*. Command-line editing treats the last 50 or so lines you typed as a buffer in an editor (this is also called the *command history*). You can move around within these lines and change them the way you'd edit a document. Every time you press the Return key, the shell executes the current line.

Word Completion

First, let's try something simple that can save you a lot of time. Type the following, without pressing the Return key:

```
$ cd /usr/inc
```

Now press the Tab key. The shell will add `lude` to complete the name of the directory */usr/include*. Now you can press the Return key, and the command will execute.

The criterion for specifying a filename is "minimal completion." Type just enough characters to distinguish a name from all the others in that directory. The shell can find the name and complete it—up to and including a slash, if the name is a directory.

You can use completion on commands too. For instance, if you type:

```
$ ema
```

and press the Tab key, the shell will add the `cs` to make `emacs` (unless some other command in your path begins with `ema`).

What if multiple files match what you've typed? If they all start with the same characters, the shell completes the word up to the point where names differ. Beyond that, most shells do nothing. *bash* has a neat enhancement: if you press the Tab key twice, it displays all the possible completions. For instance, if you enter:

```
$ cd /usr/l
```

and press the Tab key twice, *bash* prints something like the following:

```
lib        local
```

zsh even goes a step further: if you press the Tab key yet another time, the first of the possible choices will be selected; if you press it yet again, the second is selected, and so on. This way, you can keep your finger on the Tab key and don't have to supply additional characters in order to disambiguate your entry.

Moving Around Among Commands

Press the up arrow, and the command you typed previously appears. The up arrow takes you back through the command history, and the down arrow takes you forward. If you want to change a character on the current line, use the left or right arrow keys.

As an example, suppose you tried to execute:

```
$ mroe .bashrc
bash: mroe: command not found
```

Of course, you typed mroe instead of more. To correct the command, call it back by pressing the up arrow. Then press the left arrow until the cursor lies over the o in mroe. You could use the Backspace key to remove the o and r and retype them correctly. But here's an even neater shortcut: just press Ctrl-T. It will reverse o and r, and you can then press the Return key to execute the command.

Some shells even go a step further: if you type in a nonexistent command such as mroe, but there is a similar existing one, such as more, the shell will offer to correct your typing mistake and select this other option. Of course, before accepting this generous offer, you should first check what you are getting so that it is not a dangerous command that, for example, deletes your files.

Many other key combinations exist for command-line editing. But the basics shown here will help you quite a bit. If you learn the Emacs editor, you will find that most keys work the same way in the shell. And if you're a *vi* fan, you can set up your shell so that it uses *vi* key bindings instead of Emacs bindings. To do this in *bash*, *ksh*, or *zsh*, enter the command:

```
$ export VISUAL=vi
```

In *tcsh*, enter:

```
$ setenv VISUAL vi
```

Filename Expansion

Another way to save time in your commands is to use special characters to abbreviate filenames. You can specify many files at once by using these characters. This feature of the shell is sometimes called "globbing."

The Windows command-line interpreter offers a few crude features of this type. You can use a question mark to mean "any character" and an asterisk to mean "any string of characters." Unix provides these wildcards too, but in a more robust and rigorous way.

Let's say you have a directory containing the following C source files:

```
$ ls
inv1jig.c   inv2jig.c   inv3jig.c   invinitjig.c   invpar.c
```

To list the three files containing digits in their names, you could enter:

```
$ ls inv?jig.c
inv1jig.c   inv2jig.c   inv3jig.c
```

The shell looks for a single character to replace the question mark. Thus, it displays *inv1jig.c*, *inv2jig.c*, and *inv3jig.c*, but not *invinitjig.c* because that name contains too many characters.

If you're not interested in the second file, you can specify the ones you want using brackets:

```
$ ls inv[13]jig.c
inv1jig.c   inv3jig.c
```

If any single character within the brackets matches a file, that file is displayed. You can also put a range of characters in the brackets:

```
$ ls inv[1-3]jig.c
inv1jig.c   inv2jig.c   inv3jig.c
```

Now we're back to displaying all three files. The hyphen means "match any character from 1 through 3, inclusive." You could ask for any numeric character by specifying 0-9, and any alphabetic character by specifying [a-zA-Z]. In the latter case, two ranges are required because the shell is case-sensitive. The order used, by the way, is that of the ASCII character set.

Suppose you want to see the *init* file, too. Now you can use an asterisk because you want to match any number of characters between the inv and the jig:

```
$ ls inv*jig.c
inv1jig.c   inv2jig.c   inv3jig.c   invinitjig.c
```

The asterisk actually means "zero or more characters," so if a file named *invjig.c* existed, it would be shown too.

Unlike the Windows command-line interpreter, the Unix shells let you combine special characters and normal characters any way you want. Let's say you want to look for any source (*.c*) or object (*.o*) file that contains a digit. The resulting pattern combines all the expansions we've studied in this section:

```
$ ls *[0-9]*.[co]
```

Filename expansion is very useful in shell scripts (programs), where you don't always know exactly how many files exist. For instance, you might want to process multiple log files named *log001*, *log002*, and so on. No matter how many there are, the expression *log** will match them all.

Again, *zsh* goes a bit further than the other shells. With *zsh*, you can look for certain files in the current directory *and* all subdirectories thereof, using ** as the directory specification. If we repeat the previous example of searching for certain C source files, but this time want to find them in the whole tree, the command would look like this:

```
$ ls **/inv?jig.c
inv1jig.c   inv2jig.c   inv3jig.c   old/inv1jig.c
old/veryold/inv1jig.c
```

Filename expansions are not the same as regular expressions, which are used by many utilities to specify groups of strings. Regular expressions are beyond the scope of this book, but are described by many books that explain Unix utilities. A taste of regular expressions appears in Chapter 19.

Saving Your Output

System administrators (and other human beings too) see a lot of critical messages fly by on the computer screen. It's often important to save these messages so that you can scrutinize them later, or (all too often) send them to a friend who can figure out what went wrong. So, in this section, we'll explain a little bit about redirection, a powerful feature provided by Unix shells. If you come from Windows, you have probably seen a similar, but more limited, type of redirection in the command-line interpreter there.

If you put a greater-than sign (>) and a filename after any command, the output of the command will be sent to that file. For instance, to capture the output of ls, you can enter:

```
$ ls /usr/bin > ~/Binaries
```

A listing of */usr/bin* will be stored in your home directory in a file named *Binaries*. If *Binaries* had already existed, the > would wipe out what was there and replace it with the output of the ls command. Overwriting a current file is a common user error. If your shell is *csh* or *tcsh*, you can prevent overwriting with the command:

```
$ set noclobber
```

In *bash*, you can achieve the same effect by entering:

```
$ noclobber=1
```
                   It doesn't have to be 1; any value will have the same effect.

Another (and perhaps more useful) way to prevent overwriting is to append new output. For instance, having saved a listing of */usr/bin*, suppose we now want to add the contents of */bin* to that file. We can append it to the end of the *Binaries* file by specifying two greater-than signs:

```
$ ls /bin >> ~/Binaries
```

You will find the technique of output redirection very useful when you are running a utility many times and saving the output for troubleshooting.

Most Unix programs have two output streams. One is called the standard output, and the other is the standard error. If you're a C programmer you'll recognize these: the standard error is the file pointer named *stderr* to which you print messages.

The > character does not redirect the standard error. It's useful when you want to save legitimate output without mucking up a file with error messages. But what if the error messages are what you want to save? This is quite common during troubleshooting. The solution is to use a greater-than sign followed by an ampersand. (This construct works in almost every modern Unix shell.) It redirects both the standard output and the standard error. For instance:

```
$ gcc invinitjig.c >& error-msg
```

This command saves all the messages from the *gcc* compiler in a file named *error-msg*. On the Bourne shell and *bash* you can also say it slightly differently:

```
$ gcc invinitjig.c &> error-msg
```

Now let's get really fancy. Suppose you want to save the error messages but not the regular output—the standard error but not the standard output. In the Bourne-compatible shells you can do this by entering the following:

```
$ gcc invinitjig.c 2> error-msg
```

The shell arbitrarily assigns the number 1 to the standard output and the number 2 to the standard error. So the preceding command saves only the standard error.

Finally, suppose you want to throw away the standard output—keep it from appearing on your screen. The solution is to redirect it to a special file called */dev/null*. (Have you heard people say things like "Send your criticisms to */dev/null*"? Well, this is where the phrase came from.) The */dev* directory is where Unix systems store special files that refer to terminals, tape drives, and other devices. But */dev/null* is unique; it's a place you can send things so that they disappear into a black hole. For example, the following command saves the standard error and throws away the standard output:

```
$ gcc invinitjig.c 2>error-msg >/dev/null
```

So now you should be able to isolate exactly the output you want.

In case you've wondered whether the less-than sign (<) means anything to the shell: yes, it does. It causes commands to take their input from a file. But most commands allow you to specify input files on their command lines anyway, so this "input redirection" is rarely necessary.

Sometimes you want one utility to operate on the output of another utility. For instance, you can use the sort command to put the output of other commands into a more useful order. A crude way to do this would be to save output from one command in a file and then run sort on it. For instance:

```
$ du > du_output
$ sort -nr du_output
```

Unix provides a much more succinct and efficient way to do this using a *pipe*. Just place a vertical bar between the first and second commands:

```
$ du | sort -nr
```

The shell sends all the output from the du program to the sort program.

In the previous example, du stands for "disk usage" and shows how many blocks each file occupies under the current directory. Normally, its output is in a somewhat random order:

```
$ du
10          ./zoneinfo/Australia
13          ./zoneinfo/US
```

```
9          ./zoneinfo/Canada
4          ./zoneinfo/Mexico
5          ./zoneinfo/Brazil
3          ./zoneinfo/Chile
20         ./zoneinfo/SystemV
118        ./zoneinfo
298        ./ghostscript/doc
183        ./ghostscript/examples
3289       ./ghostscript/fonts
    .
    .
    .
```

So we have decided to run it through sort with the -n and -r options. The -n option means "sort in numerical order" instead of the default ASCII sort, and the -r option means "reverse the usual order" so that the highest number appears first. The result is output that quickly shows you which directories and files hog the most space:

```
$ du | sort -rn
34368       .
16005       ./emacs
16003       ./emacs/20.4
13326       ./emacs/20.4/lisp
4039        ./ghostscript
3289        ./ghostscript/fonts
    .
    .
    .
```

Because there are so many files, we had better use a second pipe to send output through the more command (one of the more common uses of pipes):

```
$ du | sort -rn | more
34368       .
16005       ./emacs
16003       ./emacs/20.4
13326       ./emacs/20.4/lisp
4039        ./ghostscript
3289        ./ghostscript/fonts
    .
    .
    .
```

An alternative to more could be using the head command here, which only shows the first few lines (10 by default). Of course, if there is a head command, there also needs to be a tail command, which just shows the last few lines.

You may have noticed that when using du alone, the output starts appearing fairly quickly and is then added to as the command finishes more computations, whereas when the output is piped to sort, it will take quite a while (if your hard disk is large and well filled) until the output appears. That is because the sort command needs all the data first in order to be able to sort, and not because the piping would delay things.

What Is a Command?

We've said that Unix offers a huge number of commands and that you can add new ones. This makes it radically different from most operating systems, which contain a strictly limited table of commands. So what are Unix commands, and how are they stored? On Unix, a command is simply a file. For instance, the ls command is a binary file located in the directory *bin*. So, instead of ls, you could enter the full pathname, also known as the *absolute pathname*:

```
$ /bin/ls
```

This makes Unix very flexible and powerful. To provide a new utility, a system administrator can simply install it in a standard directory where commands are located. There can also be different versions of a command—for instance, you can offer a new version of a utility for testing in one place while leaving the old version in another place, and users can choose the one they want.

Here's a common problem: sometimes you enter a command that you expect to be on the system, but you receive a message such as "Not found." The problem may be that the command is located in a directory that your shell is not searching. The list of directories where your shell looks for commands is called your *path*. Enter the following to see what your path is (remember the dollar sign; otherwise, you won't see the contents of the environment variable, but only its name, which you know anyway!):

```
$ echo $PATH
/usr/local/bin:/usr/bin:/usr/X11R6/bin:/bin:/usr/lib/java/bin:\
/usr/games:/usr/bin/TeX:.
```

This takes a little careful eyeballing. First, the word PATH is specially recognized by the shell and is called an *environment variable*. It's a short moniker for useful information—in this case, a list of directories where the shell should search for commands. There are lots of environment variables; we saw another one called SHELL in the section "Shells." When you specify an environment variable, include a dollar sign before the name.

The output of our echo command is a series of pathnames separated by colons. The first pathname, for this particular user, is */usr/local/bin*. The second is */usr/bin*, and so on. So if two versions of a command exist, one in */usr/local/bin* and the other in */usr/bin*, the one in */usr/local/bin* will execute. The last pathname in this example is simply a dot; it refers to the current directory. Unlike the Windows command-line interpreter, Unix does not look automatically in your current directory. You have to tell it to explicitly, as shown here. Some people think it's a bad idea to look in the current directory, for security reasons. (An intruder who gets into your account might copy a malicious program to one of your working directories.) However, this mostly applies to root, so normal users generally do not need to worry about this.

If a command is not found, you have to figure out where it is on the system and add that directory to your path. The manual page should tell you where it is. Let's say you find it in */usr/sbin*, where a number of system administration commands are installed. You realize you need access to these system administration commands, so you enter the following (note that the first PATH doesn't have a dollar sign, but the second one does):

```
$ export PATH=$PATH:/usr/sbin
```

This command adds */usr/sbin*, but makes it the last directory that is searched. The command is saying, "Make my path equal to the old path plus */usr/sbin*."

The previous command works for some shells but not others. It's fine for most Linux users who are working in a Bourne-compatible shell like *bash*. But if you use *csh* or *tcsh*, you need to issue the following command instead:

```
set path = ( $PATH /usr/sbin )
```

Finally, there are a few commands that are not files; cd is one. Most of these commands affect the shell itself and therefore have to be understood and executed by the shell. Because they are part of the shell, they are called built-in commands.

Putting a Command in the Background

No matter whether you are using the X Window System (described later) or virtual consoles, you may at times still want to run several commands simultaneously from the same shell, if only in order to avoid having to switch between windows or consoles all the time. You can take advantage of Unix's multitasking features and achieve this by simply putting an ampersand at the end of commands, as shown in this example:

```
$ gcc invinitjig.c &
[1] 21457
```

The ampersand puts the command into the background, meaning that the shell prompt comes back and you can continue to execute other commands while the gcc command is compiling your program. The [1] is a job number that is assigned to your command. The 21457 is a process ID, which we'll discuss later. Job numbers are assigned to background commands in order and therefore are easier to remember and type than process IDs.

Of course, multitasking does not come for free. The more commands you put into the background, the slower your system runs as it tries to interleave their execution.

You wouldn't want to put a command in the background if it required user input. If you do so, you see an error message, such as:

```
Stopped (tty input)
```

You can solve this problem by bringing the job back into the foreground through the *fg* command. If you have many commands in the background, you can choose one of them by its job number or its process ID. For our long-lived gcc command, the following commands are equivalent:

```
$ fg %1
$ fg 21457
```

Don't forget the percent sign on the job number; that's what distinguishes job numbers from process IDs.

To get rid of a command in the background, issue a *kill* command:

```
$ kill %1
```

If you have started a program in the foreground, but want to put in the background later, most shells allow you to type Ctrl-Z. That key combination temporarily suspends the current foreground program. You can then type either *fg* as described before, to put it back in the foreground, or *bg*, to put it in the background.

Remote Logins and Command Execution

You are probably connected to a network, either within your own home or office, or through dial-up to the Internet. Sometimes you want to log in to another system, or copy a file to or from another system.

If you need help setting up networking, check Chapter 13 and the following chapters. In this section we assume you are on the network already. If you can view a web page in a browser, you're connected and can carry out the commands in this section. We'll use a package called SSH that's installed on most, if not all, Linux distributions.

SSH stands for Secure Shell, and denotes the project developers' focus on protecting your communications from snooping and hijacking. SSH has become an extremely respected and popular protocol for communicating between systems, and is supported on many different types of systems, such as the Putty graphical interface for Windows (*http://www.chiark.greenend.org.uk/~sgtatham/putty*).

Linux uses OpenSSH, a free software implementation (*http://www.openssh.com*). It rarely has bugs (although one will turn up once in a while, so for security reasons you should keep up with your distribution's updates), and it supports the latest standard, SSH protocol version 2. If you decide to do some heavy internetworking with SSH, you can get quite deep into it through *SSH, The Secure Shell: The Definitive Guide* (O'Reilly).

This section lays out the four or five commands you'll use most often. Suppose you have an account named *mdw* on a remote system called *eggplant*. You can log in as follows:

```
$ ssh -l mdw eggplant
```

The -1 specifies the account on the remote system. Another syntax with identical effects is:

```
$ ssh mdw@eggplant
```

If your account name is the same on the local and remote systems, you can omit the name and just enter:

```
$ ssh eggplant
```

Each time you start an ssh session, it prompts for the password of the account on the remote system.

During the session, if you have to do something on your local machine, you don't have to log out or switch windows. Suspend the remote login session by entering a tilde character (~) followed by Ctrl-Z. (Sometimes the tilde is not caught by SSH; if it isn't, try again. You're successful if the tilde is not displayed.) To pick up the session you suspended, use *fg* as for local programs you suspend.

You might want to run a single command instead of starting up a shell on the remote system; if so, just enter the command after the hostname:

```
$ ssh -1 mdw eggplant rm logfiles/temp_junk
```

Or, if you can omit your name:

```
$ ssh eggplant rm logfiles/temp_junk
```

Filenames such as *logfiles/temp_junk* are interpreted as if you were located in your home directory (the directory you'd be in if you logged in). Use absolute pathnames (such as */home/mdw/logfiles/temp_junk*) if you want to make sure you're naming the right file in the right location.

The manpage for *ssh* can fill in interesting details, such as how to run X Window System graphical programs over SSH, and how to eliminate the annoyance of having to enter your password at each invocation of the command. (To be really robust, though, you may have to play around with configuration files beyond what the manpage tells you.)

You can copy files using another command from the SSH suite, scp. The following copies a file from your local system to *eggplant*:

```
$ scp logfiles/temp_junk mdw@eggplant:
```

Once again, the username and @ can be omitted if it's the same on both systems. (But the *-l* syntax doesn't work on *scp*; it uses a different *-l* option for a different purpose.)

Be sure to include the final colon; without it, you simply copy the file to a new file named *eggplant* on your local system. On *eggplant*, the default directory is your home directory (as with *ssh*). You can specify that the file be copied to any directory you have access to, with a path relative to the home directory or with an absolute pathname.

To do the reverse operation—copy a file from the remote system to your own—enter:

```
$ scp mdw@eggplant:logfiles/temp_junk .
```

We used a single dot here to denote the local directory where you're executing the command. Any relative or absolute pathname could be specified instead.

To copy a directory, add the -r option:

```
$ scp -r mdw@eggplant:logfiles .
```

Manual Pages

The most empowering information you can get is how to conduct your own research. Following this precept, we'll now tell you about the online help system that comes built into Unix systems. It is called *manual pages*, or *manpages* for short.

Actually, manual pages are not quite the boon they ought to be. This is because they are short and take a lot of Unix background for granted. Each one focuses on a particular command and rarely helps you decide why you should use that command. Still, they are critical. Commands can vary slightly on different Unix systems, and the manual pages are the most reliable way to find out what your system does. (The Linux Documentation Project deserves a lot of credit for the incredible number of hours they have put into creating manual pages.) To find out about a command, enter a command, such as the following:

```
$ man ls
```

Manual pages are divided into different sections depending on their purpose. User commands are in section 1, Unix system calls in section 2, and so on. The sections that will interest you most are 1, 5 (file formats), and 8 (system administration commands). When you view manpages online, the section numbers are conceptual; you can optionally specify them when searching for a command:

```
$ man 1 ls
```

But if you consult a hardcopy manual, you'll find it divided into actual sections according to the numbering scheme. Sometimes an entry in two different sections can have the same name. (For instance, *chmod* is both a command and a system call.) So you will sometimes see the name of a manual page followed by the section number in parentheses, as in *ls*(1).

There is one situation in which you will need the section number on the command line: when there are several manual pages for the same keyword (e.g., one for a command with that name and one for a system function with the same name). Suppose you want to look up a library call, but the man command shows you the command because its default search order looks for the command first. In order to see the manual page for the library call, you need to give its section number.

Look near the top of a manual page. The first heading is NAME. Under it is a brief one-line description of the item. These descriptions can be valuable if you're not quite sure what you're looking for. Think of a word related to what you want, and specify it in an apropos command:

```
$ apropos edit
```

The previous command shows all the manual pages that have something to do with editing. It's a very simple algorithm: apropos simply prints out all the NAME lines that contain the string you request.

Many other utilities, particularly those offered by the desktops discussed in Chapter 3, present manual pages attractively.

Like commands, manual pages are sometimes installed in strange places. For instance, you may install some site-specific programs in the directory */usr/local*, and put their manual pages in */usr/local/man*. The man command will not automatically look in */usr/local/man*, so when you ask for a manual page you may get the message "No manual entry." Fix this by specifying all the top *man* directories in a variable called MANPATH. For example (you have to put in the actual directories where the manual pages are on your system):

```
$ export MANPATH=/usr/man:/usr/local/man
```

The syntax is like PATH, described earlier in this chapter. Each pair of directories is separated by a colon. If your shell is *csh* or *tcsh*, you need to say:

```
$ setenv MANPATH /usr/man:/usr/local/man
```

Another environment variable that you may want to set is MANSECT. It determines the order in which the sections of the manual pages are searched for an entry. For example:

```
$ export MANSECT="2:3:1:5:4:6:7:8:n:9"
```

searches in section 2 first.

Have you read some manual pages and still found yourself confused? They're not meant to be introductions to new topics. Get yourself a good beginner's book about Unix, and come back to manual pages gradually as you become more comfortable on the system; then they'll be irreplaceable.

Manual pages are not the only source of information on Unix systems. Programs from the GNU project often have Info pages that you read with the program *info*. For example, to read the Info pages for the command find, you would enter:

```
info find
```

The *info* program is arcane and has lots of navigation features; to learn it, your best bet is to type Ctrl-H in the *info* program and read through the Help screen. Fortunately, there are also programs that let you read Info pages more easily, notably *tkinfo* and *kdehelp*. These commands use the X Window System to present a graphical interface. You can also read Info pages from Emacs (see "Tutorial and Online Help" in Chapter 19) or can use the command pinfo, available on some Linux distributions, which works more like the Lynx web browser.

In recent times, more and more documentation has been provided in the form of HTML pages. You can read those with any web browser (see Chapter 5). For example, in the Konqueror web browser, you select Open Location from the Location menu and press the button with the folder symbol, which opens an ordinary file selection dialog where you can select your documentation file. Some documentation may also come in PDF files; these can be read with either the proprietary Acrobat Reader, which comes with many Linux distributions and can otherwise be downloaded from *http://www.adobe.com*, or with *xpdf* and the KDE program *KGhostview*.

Startup Files

Configuration is a strong element of Unix. This probably stems from two traits commonly found in hackers: they want total control over their environment, and they strive to minimize the number of keystrokes and other hand movements they have to perform. So all the major utilities on Unix—editors, mailers, debuggers, X Window System clients—provide files that let you override their default behaviors in a bewildering number of ways. Many of these files have names ending in *rc,* which means *resource configuration.*

Startup files are usually in your home directory. Their names begin with a period, which keeps the ls command from displaying them under normal circumstances. None of the files is required; all the affected programs are smart enough to use defaults when the file does not exist. But everyone finds it useful to have the startup files. Here are some common ones:

.bashrc

> For the *bash* shell. The file is a shell script, which means it can contain commands and other programming constructs. Here's a very short startup file that might have been placed in your home directory by the tool that created your account:

```
PS1='\u$'         # The prompt contains the user's login name.
HISTSIZE=50        # Save 50 commands for when the user presses the up arrow.
# All the directories to search for commands.
PATH=/usr/local/bin:/usr/bin:/bin:/usr/bin/X11
# To prevent the user from accidentally ending a login session,
# disable Ctrl-D as a way to exit.
IGNOREEOF=1
stty erase "^H"        # Make sure the backspace key erases.
```

.bash_profile

> For the *bash* shell. Another shell script. The difference between this script and *.bashrc* is that *.bash_profile* runs only when you log in. It was originally designed

so that you could separate interactive shells from those run by background processors such as *cron* (discussed in Chapter 10). But it is not very useful on modern computers with the X Window System because when you open a new terminal window, only *.bashrc* runs. If you start up a window with the command xterm -ls, it will run *.bash_profile* too.

.zshrc

Like *.bashrc*, but for *zsh*.

.zprofile

Like *.bash_profile*, but for *zsh*.

.cshrc

For the C shell or *tcsh*. The file is a shell script using C shell constructs.

.login

For the C shell or *tcsh*. The file is a shell script using C shell constructs. Like *.bash_profile* in the *bash* shell, this runs only when you log in. Here are some commands you might find in *.cshrc* or *.login*:

```
set prompt='$ '         # Simple $ for prompt.
set history=50          # Save 50 commands for when the user presses the up arrow.
# All the directories to search for commands.
set path=(/usr/local/bin /usr/bin /bin /usr/bin/X11)
# To prevent the user from accidentally ending a login session,
# disable Ctrl-D as a way to exit.
set ignoreeof
stty erase "^H"         # Make sure the backspace key erases.
```

.emacs

For the Emacs editor. Consists of LISP functions. See "Tailoring Emacs" in Chapter 19.

.exrc

For the *vi* editor (a visual editor that incorporates the older *ex* editor). Each line is an editor command. See "Extending vi" in Chapter 19.

.newsrc

For news readers. Contains a list of all newsgroups offered at the site.

.xinitrc

For the X Window System. Consists of shell commands that run whenever you log in to an X session. See "Running X" in Chapter 16 for details on using this file.

.kde/share/config

This is actually a whole directory with configuration files for the K Desktop Environment (KDE). You will find a lot of files here, all starting with the name of the program they configure and ending in *rc*. Note that you should normally not need to edit these files manually; the respective programs all come with their own configuration dialogs. Depending on the KDE version, this path might start with *.kde2* or *.kde3*.

.gnome

Like the previous entry, a whole directory of configuration files, this time for the GNOME graphical desktop.

Important Directories

You already know about */home*, where user files are stored. As a system administrator and programmer, several other directories will be important to you. Here are a few, along with their contents:

/bin

The most essential Unix commands, such as *ls*.

/usr/bin

Other commands. The distinction between */bin* and */usr/bin* is arbitrary; it was a convenient way to split up commands on early Unix systems that had small disks.

/sbin

Very common commands used by the superuser for system administration.

/usr/sbin

Commands used less often by the superuser for system administration.

/boot

Location where the kernel and other files used during booting are sometimes stored.

/etc

Files used by subsystems such as networking, NFS, and mail. Typically, these contain tables of network services, disks to mount, and so on. Many of the files here are used for booting the system or individual services of it and will be discussed elsewhere in this book.

/var

Administrative files, such as log files, used by various utilities.

/var/spool

Temporary storage for files being printed, sent by UUCP, and so on.

/usr/lib

Standard libraries, such as *libc.a*. When you link a program, the linker always searches here for the libraries specified in *-l* options.

/usr/lib/X11

The X Window System distribution. Contains the libraries used by X clients, as well as fonts, sample resources files, and other important parts of the X package. This directory is usually a symbolic link to */usr/X11R6/lib/X11*.

/usr/include

Standard location of include files used in C programs, such as *<stdio.h>*.

/usr/src

Location of sources to programs built on the system.

/usr/local

Programs and datafiles that have been added locally by the system administrator.

/etc/skel

Sample startup files you can place in home directories for new users.

/dev

This directory contains the so-called device files, the interface between the filesystem and the hardware (e.g., */dev/modem* represents your modem in the system).

/proc

Just as */dev* is the interface between the filesystem and the hardware devices, */proc* is the interface between the filesystem and the running processes, the CPU, and memory. The files here (which are not real files, but rather virtual files generated on the fly when you view them) can give you information about the environment of a certain process, the state and configuration of the CPU, how your I/O ports are configured, and so forth.

/opt

The */opt* directory is often used for larger software packages. For example, it is quite likely that you will find the KDE Desktop Environment in */opt/kde3* (or */opt/kde4*, once version 4 is out), the office productivity suite OpenOffice in */opt/OpenOffice.org*, and the Firefox web browser in */opt/firefox*.

Basic Text Editing

Now that you have come across configuration files, we want to give you at least a small head start on how to edit them. We save the real discussion of various text editors for Chapter 19.

We use the Emacs editor as an example here because it is both widely available and fairly user-friendly. Other editors, such as vi, are even more widely available, but not very user-friendly for a beginner. Again, others are more user-friendly, but may not be available on your Linux installation. We talk more about vi and the other editors later.

Emacs comes in two different incarnations: GNU Emacs and XEmacs. GNU Emacs is started by issuing:

```
$ emacs filename
```

and XEmacs is started with:

```
$ xemacs filename
```

If you are not running from a graphical environment, add the -nw option (for "no windows"):

```
$ xemacs -nw filename
```

It is very likely that either GNU Emacs or XEmacs is available on your installation, and for the simple things we are going to do now, the differences do not matter. If you have both at your disposal, we would personally recommend XEmacs.

At this point, there are only very few things you need to know: how to enter and edit text, how to save your edits, and how to terminate the editor. Of course, Emacs can do many more advanced things, but we'll save those for later.

When you have started Emacs, you will see the file you specified on the command line loaded into its buffer. You can freely type away, edit, enter new text, delete existing text using the Backspace key, and move around with the cursor keys. When you want to save your file, you use the key combination C-x C-s. This is Emacs jargon for "hold down the Control key, press the X key, release both, hold down the Control key, press the S key, release both." This may sound arcane to you, but when you have done this a couple of times, you will have the combination "in your fingers" and will not even think about it. Some Emacs installations even come with graphical menus like you may be used to from other operating systems, but these are not universally available, so we stick to what is guaranteed to be there for now.

When you are done with your edits and have saved your file, you will probably want to leave Emacs. This is done with the key combination C-x C-c. You can probably guess it by now: this means "hold down the Control key, press the X key, release both, hold down the Control key, press the C key, release both." This will get you back to the command line.

Advanced Shells and Shell Scripting

In this section, we will look at some of the more advanced things you can do with your trusty shell, the Linux command-line interpreters.

Setting Terminal Attributes

setterm is a command that sets various characteristics of your terminal (say, each virtual console), such as the keyboard repeat rate, tab stops, and text colors.

Most people use this command to change the colors for each virtual console. In this way, you can tell which virtual console you're currently looking at based on the text color. (Notice that this only applies to the virtual consoles in text mode. X11 windows with shells in them are configured differently.)

For example, to change the color of the current terminal to white text on a blue background, use the command:

```
$ setterm -foreground white -background blue
```

Some programs and actions cause the terminal attributes to be reset to their default values. In order to store the current set of attributes as the default, use:

```
$ setterm -store
```

setterm provides many options (most of which you will probably never use). See the *setterm*(1) manual page or use *setterm -help* for more information.

If your terminal settings get really messed up (as happens, for example, if you try to look at the contents of a binary file with *cat*), you can try typing *setterm -reset* blindly, which should reset your terminal to reasonable settings.

Shell Programming

In "Shells," earlier in this chapter, we discussed the various shells available for Linux, but shells can also be powerful and consummately flexible programming tools. The differences come through most clearly when it comes to writing shell scripts. The Bourne shell and C shell command languages are slightly different, but the distinction is not obvious with most normal interactive use. The Z shell command language is a superset of the Bourne shell. Many of the distinctions arise only when you attempt to use bizarre, little-known features of either shell, such as word substitution or some of the more oblique parameter expansion functions.

The most notable difference between Bourne and C shells is the form of the various flow-control structures, including if ...then and while loops. In the Bourne shell, an if ...then takes the following form:

```
if list
then
   commands
elif list
then
   commands
else
   commands
fi
```

where *list* is just a sequence of commands to be used as the conditional expression for the if and elif (short for "else if") commands. The conditional is considered to be true if the exit status of the *list* is zero (unlike Boolean expressions in C, in shell terminology an exit status of zero indicates successful completion). The *commands* enclosed in the conditionals are simply commands to execute if the appropriate *list* is true. The then after each *list* must be on a new line to distinguish it from the *list* itself; alternately, you can terminate the *list* with a ;. The same holds true for the *commands*.

An example is:

```
if [ "$PS1" ]; then
   PS1="\h:\w% "
fi
```

This sequence checks to see whether the shell is a login shell (that is, whether the prompt variable PS1 is set), and if so, it resets the prompt to \h:\w%, which is a prompt expansion standing for the hostname followed by the current working directory. For example:

```
loomer:/home/loomer/mdw%
```

The [...] conditional appearing after the if is a *bash* built-in command, shorthand for *test*. The *test* command and its abbreviated equivalent provide a convenient mechanism for testing values of shell variables, string equivalence, and so forth. Instead of using [...], you could call any set of commands after the if, as long as the last command's exit value indicates the value of the conditional.

Under *tcsh*, an if ...then compound statement looks like the following:

```
if (expression) then
   commands
else if (expression) then
   commands
else
   commands
endif
```

The difference here is that the *expression* after the if is an arithmetic or logical expression evaluated internally by *tcsh*, whereas with *bash* the conditional expression is a command, and the expression returns true or false based on the command's exit status. Within *bash*, using *test* or [...] is similar to an arithmetic expression as used in *tcsh*.

With *tcsh*, however, if you wish to run external commands within the *expression*, you must enclose the command in braces: {*command*}.

The equivalent of the previous *bash* sequence in *tcsh* is:

```
if ($?prompt) then
   set prompt="%m:%/%% "
endif
```

where *tcsh*'s own prompt special characters have been used. As you can see, *tcsh* boasts a command syntax similar to the C language, and expressions are arithmetically and logically oriented. In *bash*, however, almost everything is an actual command, and expressions are evaluated in terms of exit-status values. There are analogous features in either shell, but the approach is slightly different.

A similar change exists with the while loop. In *bash*, this takes the following form:

```
while list
do
    commands
done
```

You can negate the effect by replacing the word while with until. Again, *list* is just a command sequence to be executed, and the exit status determines the result (zero for success and nonzero for failure). Under *tcsh* the loop looks like this:

```
while (expression)
    commands
end
```

where *expression* is a logical expression to be evaluated within *tcsh*.

This example should be enough to get a head start on understanding the overall differences of shell scripts under *bash* and *tcsh*. We encourage you to read the bash(1) and tcsh(1) manual pages (although they serve more as a reference than a tutorial) and Info pages, if you have them available. Various books and tutorials on using these two shells are available as well; in fact, any book on shell programming will do, and you can interpolate the advanced features of *bash* and *tcsh* into the standard Bourne and C shells using the manual pages. *Learning the bash Shell* by Cameron Newham and Bill Rosenblatt and *Using csh and tcsh* by Paul DuBois (both from O'Reilly) are also good investments.

Being More Efficient with the Z Shell

The Z shell (*zsh*) is particularly appreciated for its many features that make you more efficient on the command line. To start with, *zsh* does not have one command prompt, but rather two: one for the lefthand side, and one for the righthand side. The lefthand one is set as usual by assigning to the environment variable PROMPT; for the righthand side, the environment variable RPROMPT is used. For example:

```
export PROMPT="%n@%m"
export RPROMPT="%~%"
```

gives you your username and hostname to the left of the entry line, and the current directory to the right. The smart thing about the right prompt is that it disappears when you "need the space"; that is, it gets out of the way when your typing comes close.

An interesting thing about *zsh* is the many, many options that you can set with the setopt command. The manual page *zshoptions* will list all of them, but we'd like to mention at least one very useful one here, the ALL_EXPORT option. By specifying:

```
setopt ALL_EXPORT
```

any environment variable that you set will automatically be exported. This is very useful if you, like us, keep setting environment variables for processes other than the shell and then forget to export them, and wonder why they are not picked up by the processes started from the shell. You can turn this off with setopt noALL_EXPORT.

You have already seen how to use the cd command. Of course, *zsh* knows about cd as well, but it does some other interesting stuff. For example, if you specify – (a dash) as the argument, you will be returned to the working directory that was your working directory before the last cd command (for the following example, we have moved the display of the current directory back to the lefthand side):

```
~%> cd kdesvn/kdelibs/kdecore
~/kdesvn/kdelibs/kdecore> pwd
/home/kalle/kdesvn/kdelibs/kdecore
~/kdesvn/kdelibs/kdecore> cd /usr/local
/usr/local> cd -
~/kdesvn/kdelibs/kdecore
~/kdesvn/kdelibs/kdecore>
```

Also, if you type in a command that *zsh* does not recognize (i.e., it is neither an executable in your PATH nor a built-in command), but there is a directory with the name of that command, *zsh* will interpret that as a request to change the working directory to that directory:

```
~> Documents
~/Documents>
```

Another neat feature is the autocorrection of commands. If you, like us, keep typing mroe instead of more, turn on the autocorrection by issuing:

```
setopt CORRECT
```

Now *zsh* will come up with suggestions if it cannot understand your command:

```
~/Documents> mroe /etc/motd
zsh: correct 'mroe' to 'more' [nyae]? y
Welcome to tigger...
```

Even when it comes to completion, *zsh* has a number of features that sets it apart from other shells. There are few things that it does not attempt completion on. You know already that you can press the Tab key half way during typing a command or filename, and most shells will attempt to complete what you have started. But *zsh* also has the following features:

```
rpm --erase <TAB> # shows installed packages

rpm -q<TAB> # shows suboptions of the 'q' option

fg % <TAB> # shows the names of background processes that could be
            promoted to foreground processes

cvs checkout <TAB> # shows possible modules to check out
```

```
make -f Makefile <TAB> # shows the targets in Makefile

cd <TAB> # shows directories only
```

There are many, many more completions built into *zsh*, and you can even program your own. The manual page *zshcompctl* tells you all about this.

## CHAPTER 5

Web Browsers and Instant Messaging

For the everyday communications that millions of people love to use—web browsing and instant messaging, including Internet Relay Chat—Linux provides free software tools that match or exceed most proprietary offerings.

The World Wide Web

Everybody who has even the slightest connection with computers and has not heard about, or used, the World Wide Web, most have spent some serious time under a rock. Like word processors or spreadsheets some centuries ago, the Web is what gets many people to use computers at all in the first place. We cover here some of the tools you can use to access the Web on Linux.

Linux was from the beginning intimately connected to the Internet in general and the Web in particular. For example, the Linux Documentation Project (LDP) provides various Linux-related documents via the Web. The LDP home page, located at *http://www.tldp.org*, contains links to a number of other Linux-related pages around the world. The LDP home page is shown in Figure 5-1.

Linux web browsers usually can display information from several types of servers, not just HTTP servers sending clients HTML pages. For example, when accessing a document via HTTP, you are likely to see a page such as that displayed in Figure 5-1—with embedded pictures, links to other pages, and so on. When accessing a document via FTP, you might see a directory listing of the FTP server, as seen in Figure 5-2. Clicking a link in the FTP document either retrieves the selected file or displays the contents of another directory.

The way to refer to a document or other resource on the Web, of course, is through its *Uniform Resource Locator*, or URL. A URL is simply a pathname uniquely identifying a web document, including the machine it resides on, the filename of the document, and the protocol used to access it (FTP, HTTP, etc.). For example, the Font

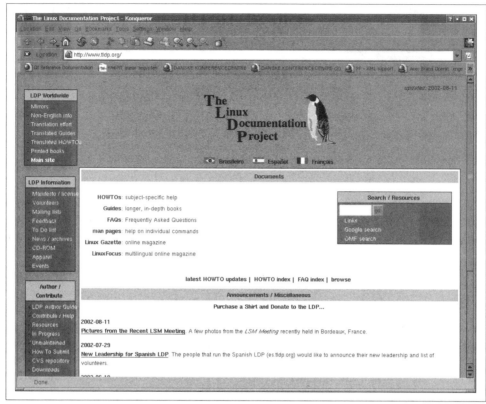

Figure 5-1. LDP home page on the World Wide Web

HOWTO, an online document that describes the optimal use of fonts on Linux, has the following URL:

> *http://www.tldp.org/HOWTO/html_single/Font-HOWTO/index.html*

Let's break this down. The first part of the URL, *http:*, identifies the protocol used for the document, which in this case is HTTP. The second part of the URL, *//www.tldp.org*, identifies the machine where the document is provided. The final portion of the URL, *HOWTO/html_single/Font-HOWTO/index.html*, is the logical pathname to the document on *www.tldp.org*. This is similar to a Unix pathname, in that it identifies the file *index.html* in the directory *HOWTO/html_single/Font-HOWTO*. Therefore, to access the Font HOWTO, you'd fire up a browser, telling it to access *http://www.tldp.org/HOWTO/html_single/Font-HOWTO/index.html*. What could be easier?

Actually, the conventions of web servers do make it easier. If you specify a directory as the last element of the path, the server understands that you want the file

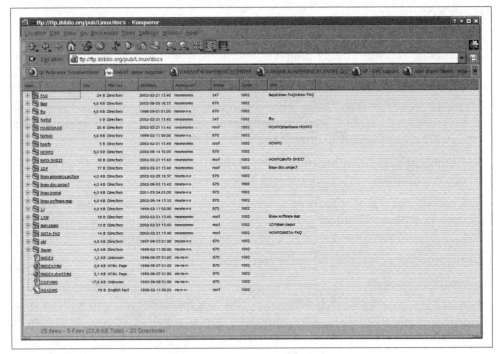

Figure 5-2. FTP directory as displayed in the Konqueror web browser

index.html in that directory. So you can reach the Font HOWTO with a URL as short as:

> *http://www.tldp.org/HOWTO/html_single/Font-HOWTO/*

To access a file via anonymous FTP, we can use a URL, such as:

> *ftp://ftp.ibiblio.org/pub/linux/docs/FAQ*

This URL retrieves the Linux FAQ. Using this URL with your browser is identical to using *ftp* to fetch the file by hand.

The best way to understand the Web is to explore it. In the following section we'll explain how to get started with some of the available browsers. Later in the chapter, we'll cover how to configure your own machine as a web server for providing documents to the rest of the Web.

Of course, in order to access the Web, you'll need a machine with direct Internet access (via either Ethernet or PPP). In the following sections, we assume that you have already configured TCP/IP on your system and that you can successfully use clients, such as *ssh* and *ftp*.

Using Konqueror

Konqueror is one of the most popular browsers for Linux. It features JavaScript and Java support, can run Firefox plug-ins (which allow you to add functions such as viewing Flash presentations), and is well integrated into the KDE desktop described in "The K Desktop Environment" in Chapter 3. Actually, when you install KDE, Konqueror will be installed as an integral part of the system. In the section on KDE, we have already described how to use Konqueror to read local information files. Now we are going to use it to browse the Web.

Most things in Konqueror are quite obvious, but if you want to read more about it, you can use Konqueror to check out *http://www.konqueror.org*.

Here, we assume that you're using a networked Linux machine running X and that you have Konqueror installed. As stated before, your machine must be configured to use TCP/IP, and you should be able to use clients, such as *ssh* and *ftp*.

Starting Konqueror is simple. Run the command:

```
eggplant$ konqueror url
```

where *url* is the complete web address, or URL, for the document you wish to view. If you don't specify a URL, Konqueror will display a splash screen, as shown in Figure 5-3.

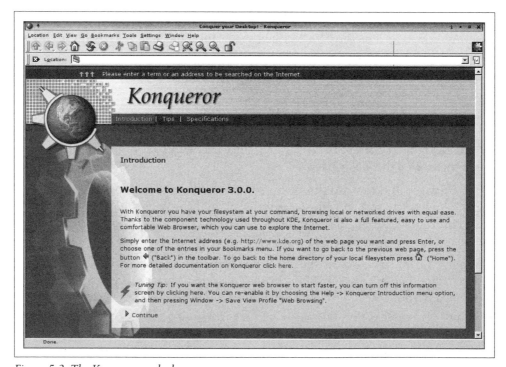

Figure 5-3. The Konqueror splash screen

If you run Konqueror from within KDE, you can simply type Alt-F2 to open the so-called *minicli* window, and type the URL. This will start up Konqueror and point it directly to the URL you have specified.

We assume that you have already used a web browser to browse the Web on some computer system, so we won't go into the very basics here; we'll just point out a few Linux-specific things.

Keep in mind that retrieving documents on the Web can be slow at times. This depends on the speed of the network connection from your site to the server, as well as the traffic on the network at the time. In some cases, web sites may be so loaded that they simply refuse connections; if this is the case, Konqueror displays an appropriate error message. At the bottom edge of the Konqueror window, a status report is displayed, and while a transfer is taking place, the KDE gear logo in the upper-right corner of the window animates. Clicking the logo, by the way, will open a new Konqueror window.

As you traverse links within Konqueror, each document is saved in the *window history*, which can be recalled using the Go menu. Pressing the Back button (the one that shows an arrow pointing to the left) in the top toolbar of the Konqueror window moves you back through the window history to previously visited documents. Similarly, the Forward button moves you forward through the history.

In addition, the sidebar in Konqueror can show you previously visited web sites; that is a very useful feature if you want to go to a web site that you have visited some time ago—too long ago for it to still appear in the Go menu—but you do not remember the name any more. The History pane of the sidebar has your visited URLs sorted by sites. If you do not have a sidebar in your Konqueror window, it may be hidden; press F9 in that case, or select Window → Show Navigation Panel from the menu bar. The sidebar has several panels, of which one at a time is shown; the one you want in this case is the one depicted by a little clock. Click on the clock icon to see the previously visited sites.

You can also bookmark frequently visited web sites (or URLs) to Konqueror's "bookmarks." Whenever you are viewing a document that you might want to return to later, choose Add Bookmark from the Bookmarks menu, or simply press Ctrl-B. You can display your bookmarks by choosing the Bookmarks menu. Selecting any item in this menu retrieves the corresponding document from the Web. Finally, you can also display your bookmarks permanently in another pane of the sidebar by clicking on the yellow star. And of course, Konqueror comes with ample features for managing your bookmarks. Just select Bookmarks → Edit Bookmarks, and sort away!

You can also use the sidebar for navigating your home directory, your hardware, your session history, and many other things. Just try it, and you will discover many useful features.

Besides the sidebar, another feature that can increase your browsing experience considerably is the so-called *tabbed browsing*. First made popular by the open source browser Mozilla (see later in this chapter), Konqueror has really taken tabbed browsing to its heart and provides a number of useful features. For example, when you are reading a web page that contains an interesting link that you might want to follow later, while continuing on the current page now, you can right-click that link and select Open in New Tab from the context menu. This will create a new tab with the caption of that page as its header, but leave the current page open. You can finish reading the current page and then go on to one of those that you had opened while reading. Since all pages are on tabs in the single browser window, this does not clutter your desktop, and it is very easy to find the page you want. In order to close a tab, just click on the little icon with the tabs and the red cross.

As mentioned previously, you can access new URLs by running konqueror with the URL as the argument. However, you can also simply type the URL in the location bar near the top of the Konqueror window. The location bar has autocompletion: if you start typing an address that you have visited before, Konqueror will automatically display it for your selection. Once you are done entering the URL (with or without help from autocompletion), you simply press the Enter key, and the corresponding document is retrieved.

Konqueror is a powerful application with many options. You can customize Konqueror's behavior in many ways by selecting Settings → Configure Konqueror. The sections Web Behavior and Web Shortcuts provide particularly interesting settings. In the section Cookies, you can configure whether you want to accept cookies domain by domain and even check the cookies already stored on your computer. Compare this to browsers that hide the cookies deep in some hidden directory and make it hard for you to view them (or even impossible without the use of extra programs!).

Finally, one particular feature deserves mention. Web browsers register themselves with the server using the so-called User Agent string, which is a piece of text that can contain anything, but usually contains the name and version of the web browser, and the name and version of the host operating system. Some notably stupid webmasters serve different web pages (or none at all!) when the web browser is not Internet Explorer because they think that Internet Explorer is the only web browser capable of displaying their web site.[*] But by going to the Browser Identification section, you can fool the web server into believing that you are using a different browser, one that the web server is not too snobbish to serve documents to. Simply click New, select the domain name that you want to access, and either type an Identification string of your own, or select one of the predefined ones.

---

[*] A web site that can be browsed with only one browser or that calls itself "optimized for browser X" should make you virtually run away, wringing your hands in wrath over such incompetence on the part of the webmaster.

Other Web Browsers

Konqueror is not the only browser that reads web documents. Another browser available for Linux is Firefox, a descendant of Mozilla, which in turn started its life as the open source version of Netscape Navigator, the browser that made the Web popular to many in the first place. If your distribution does not contain Firefox already, you can get it from *http://www.mozilla.org/products/firefox/*. Firefox's features are in many aspects similar to Konqueror's, and most things that you do with one you should be able to do with the other. Konqueror wins over Firefox in terms of desktop integration if you use the KDE desktop, of course, and also has more convenience features, whereas Firefox is particularly strong at integrating nonstandard technologies such as Flash. Firefox also comes with a very convenient pop-up blocker that will display a little box at the top of your browser window when it has blocked one of those annoying pop-ups. You can select to always block it (and not be told about it anymore), always allow pop-ups from that site (they could be important information about your home banking account), or allow the pop-up once.

Firefox has one particular powerful feature that is often overlooked: its extensions. By selecting Tools → Extensions from the menu bar, a dialog with installed extensions pops up; it is quite likely that you initially don't have any (unless your distributor or system administrator has preinstalled some for you). Click on the *Get More Extensions* link, and a long list with extensions that have been contributed to Firefox will show up. By default, you will see the list of the most popular and the list of the newest extensions, but take some time to discover all categories that seem interesting to you, there are a lot of goodies in here.

We would like to point out two extensions that we have found particularly interesting. Adblock adds a small overlay that looks like a tab to parts of the rendered web page that it suspects to be banner advertising. Just click on that little tab, click OK in the dialog that pops up (or edit the URL to be blocked, maybe to be even more general), and enjoy web pages without banner ads. It can actually become an addiction to refine the blocking patterns so much that you do not see any banner advertising anymore while surfing the Web. But just zapping a single one is a source of joy.

The other extension that we found particularly interesting is ForecastFox. It lets you select a number of locations on the earth and then displays small icons in the status bar (or other locations at your discretion) that show the current weather at those locations. Hover the mouse over one of those icons, and you will get a tooltip with more detailed information.

As with Konqueror, you should plan to spend some time with Firefox in order to explore all its possibilities. In many aspects, such as security, privacy, and browsing convenience, it beats the most often used browser on the Web these days hands down.

Yet another versatile browser is w3m. It is a text-based browser, so you miss the pictures on a web site. But this makes it fast, and you may find it convenient. You can also use it without the X Window System. Furthermore, when you want to save a page as plain text, w3m often provides a better format than other browsers, because text-based rendering is its main purpose in life. Then there is the ad-financed browser Opera, which has become quite popular lately, and finally, for those who never want to leave Emacs, there is Emacs/W3, a fully featured web browser you can use within Emacs or XEmacs.

Instant Messaging

Although various forms of chat have been widespread among computer users for decades, a very rich and easy-to-use kind of chat called instant messaging (IM) has become popular with the growth of Internet use. AOL Instant Messenger (AIM), Yahoo! Messenger, and MSN Messenger are just a few versions of this medium. Although each service provides its own client (and prefers that you use their client, so they can send advertisements your way), you can get access to all the most popular IM systems through open source programs such as Gaim, Kopete, and a variety of Jabber clients. These are very full-featured clients that have a number of powerful features that in terms of functionality put them ahead of the clients that the commercial services foist on you (although the open source clients are missing some of the eye candy in the commercial clients).

Unfortunately, instant messaging has as many different protocols as there are commercial services. None of the protocols communicates with the others. This is because each instant messaging provider wants to force people to use its client and receive its ads. And since the services are offered for free, one could make a good case for their right to recoup their costs this way. At least one popular service (Yahoo!) offers a Linux client, and it's quite decent.

But this is an age where digital recorders can zip right through the ads on TV. In the same way, open source clients can serve up instant messaging plain and simple, without pushing weather updates or pictures of last month's pop star in your face. Most important, open source clients let you use a single program to control all your accounts; you don't need to run multiple programs in the background and enter configuration information in each one. Eventually, commercial providers may give in and standardize on the Extensible Messaging and Presence Protocol (XMPP), which is the stiff-sounding name Jabber had to adopt to be accepted as a bona fide standard (more specifically, a set of RFCs put out by an IETF committee). For now, use a multi-protocol client.

All these clients are intuitive to use, but there are some neat tricks you should be aware of. This section shows how to use Gaim, the most popular messaging program among Linux users. Kopete, a KDE client, is probably the next most popular.

Most Linux distributions put Gaim right on your desktop, usually somewhere under a menu item for Internet services. If you see a menu item labeled something such as "instant messaging," it probably runs Gaim (or Kopete). Naturally, if Gaim is installed, you can run *gaim* from the command line. And if it isn't installed, it's easy to get from *http://gaim.sourceforge.net* and install yourself.

Here we'll cover Version 1.2.1 for Linux. A new version was expected at the time of this writing that would have different pull-down menus and other interface changes, but would offer the same functions overall.

Initial Configuration

This book doesn't deal with how to set up an instant messaging account; for that you have to go to the web site provided by the service you want to use and follow its simple procedure. After you get an account (which involves finding a screen name no one has taken yet—not always so easy), you have to configure Gaim to know about it. Gaim should show you an Accounts screen the first time it runs (see Figure 5-4). If Gaim shows you its Buddy List screen instead, press Ctrl-A to show the Accounts screen, or pull down the Tools menu and select Accounts.

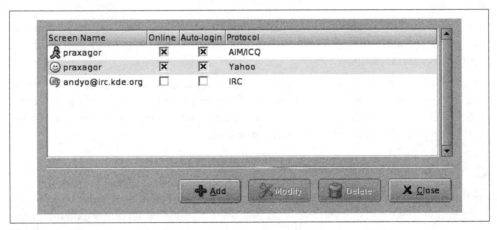

Figure 5-4. Gaim's Accounts screen

Press the Add button, and fill out the information on the Add Account screen that pops up:

Protocol
> Make sure to choose the service you're using. The default is AIM/ICQ, which is the most popular service, but if you're using a different service you can just choose it from the drop-down menu. One of the options is IRC, so Gaim can be used to participate in the IRC sites that are so popular among Linux users and developers.

Screen name

This is the account name you use to log in, such as simplesimonpi or alljazzedtogo.

Password

You chose this when you signed up for the account.

Alias

This is the name you see for yourself when you're typing in a chat; it has no effect on what other people see when they chat with you.

There are also a variety of options in this dialog box. For instance, if you need to connect through a proxy, you can specify the protocol after pressing the "Show more options" button. You can also get access to this option (and scads of others) from the Buddy List screen, by pulling down the Tools menu and choosing Preferences, or simply by pressing Ctrl-P. Note that the Preferences menu sets a default for all accounts, and that you can override the default for individual accounts.

If you have a desktop or laptop that's usually Internet connected, it's extremely convenient to have Gaim remember your password and log you in automatically. But if you don't use instant messaging often, or are afraid of nosy people getting their hands on your system while you're logged in, you may decide to leave these options unchecked.

We haven't yet done anything special to give you a real personality on the Internet (we do that later under "Advanced Configuration"), but you have accomplished enough to communicate.

When you're done, save your account. Back in the Accounts screen, click the Online box. If you have Internet connectivity, it will log you in and you're ready to go. If the login fails, click Modify and check all the items you entered. Did you choose the right protocol? Try re-entering your password.

Chatting

At this point, using Gaim is straightforward. Most people allow IM only with people they know, and only after explicitly adding them to a list of accounts called a *buddy list*. If you have already added buddies in another client, most services store the information, and they'll show up in Gaim's buddy list.

To add new buddies, pull down the Buddies menu. First add a few groups such as Work, Family, and Political Debaters. (You'll appreciate having groups after a few weeks, when you realize how many people you want to chat with. Some authors of this book chat with family members who are in the next room. Hey, isn't it better than shouting?)

Then add buddies to these groups. How do you find the buddies? Like signing up for an IM account, that's an "out of band" procedure—a computer science term meaning "It's up to you to do it and we don't care how." Most people exchange account names through email or written slips of paper. But one convenient search method for AIM/ICQ is through Tools → Account Actions → Search for Buddy by Email.

To start a conversation, double-click on somebody from the buddy list who's logged in. To start a multiperson chat with two or more buddies who use the same service, pull down the Buddies menu and choose "Join a chat." Here you can pick the service you're using and any name you like; then invite other buddies in one at a time by pressing the Invite button, choosing a buddy from the pull-down menu, and entering a bit of text to let her know what you're inviting her to. You can carry on separate chats with buddies on different services (for instance, AOL and MSN) but you can't combine buddies from two different services in a single chat because each service uses its own protocol.

One of the most valuable features of instant messaging—making it a real business tool, not just a pastime—is the ability to save the text from chats so you can refer later to your "speech acts" (the promises you made). During the chat, choose Conversations → Save As and you can save the text in HTML format. What you save is what has already appeared in the window; if more text you want is added later, you have to resave it. It may be convenient for you to make all chats or instant messages logged by default; you can do this through the Logging item on the Preferences menu, but you will probably end up saving a lot of trash you don't care about.

The HTML in the logs is ugly, but it's sufficiently human-readable for you to extract the text you want later. If timestamps are just a lot of junk to you, turn off time-stamping under the Options drop-down menu.

The little boxes with A in them show different types of formatting (italic, bold, and even color) that you can apply: use a mouse to highlight the text you want to change, and click the button. Instead of a button, you can change highlighted text to bold with Ctrl-B or to italic with Ctrl-I, put a strike-through line through it with Ctrl-S, or underline it with Ctrl-U. If something is highlighted and you want to remove the formatting, click the button or Ctrl key again to undo the action.

Long before IM, users of text-only programs such as email, Net news, and Internet Relay Chat (IRC) exercised a great deal of ingenuity making up the famous little strings such as :-) and :-< that are known as smileys or emoticons. Running in a graphical environment, IM adds another dimension by providing sets of graphical smileys. And if you're bold or uncivilized enough to use a smiley, you might as well replace the defaults in Gaim with a bold or uncivilized set downloaded from the Gaim web site. (Choose the Themes link on the right side of the main page.) Download a tarball that looks intriguing—unfortunately, you get to see only one representative smiley until you install the theme—and unpack the tarball into its constituent *.png* files in the *smileys* subdirectory of your Gaim configuration directory, usually *~/.gaim/smileys*.

You can type or paste a URL into a chat, and it will automatically turn into a link. But if you want more sophisticated formatting, where an arbitrary piece of text such as My Home Page turns into a link, press the little button with a metal chain link. You can then enter both a URL and the text that appears in your message to link to the URL. Sending a file from your system to your buddy is as easy as choosing Conversation → Send File. However, the transfer does not take place until the buddy accepts your request.

Advanced Configuration

You wouldn't leave home without your shadow, and you should similarly feel that your IM experience would be incomplete without a number of personalized items to present to the world:

- Buddy information (known in some other clients as a *profile*)—free-form text that describes you
- A small icon
- A punchy set of Away messages to tell your buddies your status, a hot topic in communications research called *presence*

We'll also discuss some other customizations you'll find useful in this section, including how to find out what your buddies are doing.

Buddy information can be entered and changed from Tools → Account Actions → Set User Info. Note that this information (and all the items set in this section) is tied to the Gaim client you're working in. If you use Gaim on a different system or run a different IM client, you have to re-enter all the information to make it appear to buddies. Consider typing a small summary of your work and including a URL that points to a web page with more information.

Like other IM clients, Gaim lets you attach a picture to your account, so it will show up when people include you in their buddy lists and chat with you. When you configure your account using the Add Account or Modify Account dialog, click the Open button next to the "Buddy icon" label and drill through your file hierarchy till you find an image you like. You can also pull up, in the file manager on your desktop, a folder containing the picture you want to use as your icon, and drag the icon from the desktop folder to the Modify Accounts window. Gaim supports lots of popular formats, including JPEG, GIF, and PNG. Depending on the support available in the GTK+ libraries, Gaim converts the file's format to a format your service accepts if necessary.

AIM imposes quite restrictive size limits on the image you use, and Gaim does not tell you that you have exceeded the limits. For many services, furthermore, you must be careful to provide a perfect square, because the image may otherwise be stretched and come out quite unflattering. The GIMP (described in Chapter 9) is useful for adjusting pictures to fit requirements, once you have determined what they are.

Now create a series of apt Away messages that you can put up when you leave your terminal. From the Tools → Preferences dialog, choose "Away messages" and press the Add button to bring up a dialog that lets you add and save a new message. (Or use Tools → Away → New Away Message.) For each message, assign a title that will appear in your menus, and in the larger box underneath the title type the actual text that buddies will see.

When you leave your desk, you can choose an appropriate Away message from Tools → Away → Custom, and it's very helpful to your associates to do so. But setting a message can often be too much trouble to remember, so Gaim sets one automatically when your terminal is idle for a while. We recommend you replace the boring default (if you don't think it's boring, look at what it says) with a message of your own choice. Do this from the Preferences dialog, reached by pressing Ctrl-P. The Away/Idle item in this dialog lets you set the default Away message, as well as how long the terminal has to be idle before it appears.

If your Away message is set through the idle timer just described, Gaim automatically replaces it with an Available message when you move the mouse or start typing again. If you have set an Away message explicitly, you need to explicitly indicate when you've returned by choosing Tools → Away → Back. The Available message shown when you're at your terminal can be set through Tools → Account Actions → Set Available message.

Gaim automatically checks your spelling and underlines misspelled words as you type. Because a rebellious air of reckless informality has always hung over instant messaging, it strikes us as the tool where accurate spelling is least important. The feature works quite well and adapts to the user's locale (that is, the language and nationality you chose when installing your distribution), but it can be turned off in the Message Text box under Preferences if you like.

A more useful feature for busy and bumbling typists is text replacement. This is provided as one of the many plug-ins you can enable in the Preferences dialog. Click on Plugins and enable "Text replacement." Then type in abbreviations you'd like to use for common phrases. For instance, one author of this book has defined the string newrl to expand to *Running Linux, 5th Edition* to make it easy to refer to that book. You must enter the string as a separate word for Gaim to recognize and expand it.

We described earlier how to let buddies know your changes in presence. Gaim can also display their presence, but by default it does not pop up a message (as some IM clients do) to let you know every time a buddy has arrived or left. You can add this feature through the guifications plug-in. Download it from *http://guifications.sourceforge.net*, install it, and enable it in the Preferences dialog box under Plugins.

Even without the guifications feature, you have fine-grained control over presence notifications: you can tell Gaim to notify you when a particular buddy has logged in, logged out, gone idle, returned, and so forth. Thus, you may choose on a particular day to be told when somebody logs in or returns, because you're in a hurry to reach him to discuss a particular task. The mechanism for doing all this is called a *buddy pounce*.

To use this feature, choose Tools → Buddy Pounce → New Buddy Pounce. In the dialog that appears, you can indicate exactly whom you want to track, what changes in presence you want to be notified about, and how you want to be notified. The buddy is not informed of any of this snooping unless you choose "Send a message." You could use that feature to have a box such as "Please call home right away" appear on the buddy's screen at the moment his or her presence changes.

## CHAPTER 6

Electronic Mail Clients

Modern email readers have graphical interfaces and tend to offer similar features in a similar manner. In addition to delivering your electronic mail, most allow you to maintain contact lists and many include calendars. Email readers usually also let you read newsgroups, which are one of the oldest features in computer networking and still offer valuable communities and quick sources of information (if you can find groups untainted by scads of unsolicited commercial postings).

One of the most popular email readers and contact managers, Evolution, was described in Chapter 3. In this chapter, we show you some interesting ways to use other graphical email readers productively, and give you the background you need to carry out some more advanced tasks, such as delivering mail from a server to a local system using *fetchmail*, and protecting your mail with encryption.

Linux supports older, text-based tools for doing these things too. Elm and Pine are fast text-based readers that have managed to keep up pretty well with changes in modern email conventions, such as displaying files of different types and following URLs. A few people like the tried-and-true `mail` program, but it's generally used more in scripts to send mail automatically. These older tools are not discussed in this book.

At this point, it may be worthwhile to point out the difference between a Mail User Agent (MUA) and a Mail Transport Agent (MTA). The program that you interact with when reading or writing email messages is the Mail User Agent, like the ones described in this chapter. Mail Transport Agents are the software that then relays the messages across the Internet to the receiving party, which gets the message delivered into the inbox of his or her Mail User Agent. An example of a Mail Transport Agent is Postfix, which we describe in "The Postfix MTA" in Chapter 23.

Using KMail

KMail is a very user-friendly, feature-rich mailer that comes with KDE and integrates mail smoothly with other utilities. For example, if an email message you receive contains a link to a web page, you can click this link in the message, and the KDE web browser Konqueror will pop up and display the web page. Or, if the email contains an MP3 file as an attachment, you can click it to play the file with one of KDE's MP3 players. Figure 6-1 shows a screenshot of KMail at work.

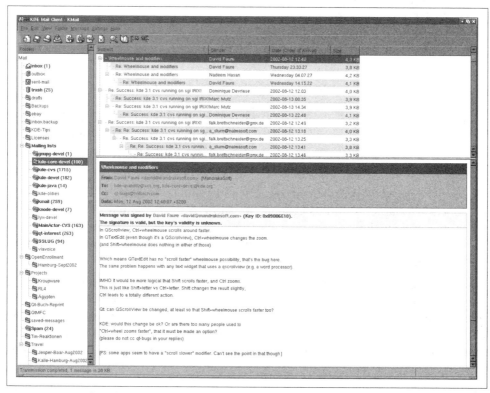

Figure 6-1. KMail mailer

KMail has a lot of features and settings, but we'll just cover some that get you started quickly and leave it to you to explore KMail further. As you can see in Figure 6-1, the KMail window is divided by default into three parts. On the left, you see a tree of your folders (at first startup, you will have only the default folders, of course). The upper part of the right side shows a listing of messages in the currently selected folder, and the lower part of the right side shows the currently selected message. You can change how the space is distributed between these parts by dragging the separator lines between them. The latest KMail versions even have a fourth part that lets you drill further into the structure of an individual message by displaying the MIME parts the message is composed of. However, this display is turned off by default, as most people do not need it.

Before you can use KMail, you have to set up some information in it. Select Configure KMail from the Settings menu and then open the configuration group Identities by clicking its icon. You can create a number of different identities here; for example, you may want to use different return addresses when emailing as an employee of your company or as a private person. Click Add to create a new entity; a subsequent dialog lets you choose between starting from scratch, using the settings from the KDE Control Center (useful only if you have configured your email settings there), and copying the values from an existing identity (which of course is possible only if you already have one and only makes sense if you intend to edit the copy afterwards). If you are setting up KMail, you will want to select creating an entirely new identity here. Give the identity a name, such as "Work" or "Home," and click OK. For starters, it is sufficient to fill in the Name and Email Address fields on the General tab (see Figure 6-2) of the identity editor.

Next, go to the Accounts configuration group. Here, you need to create at least one account for outgoing mail and one for incoming mail.

Let's start with the outgoing mail, which you will find on the Sending tab of the Configure dialog box (see Figure 6-3.) Click the Add button. You will be asked whether you want to use SMTP or talk to a *Sendmail* installation directly. In almost all cases, if you have an MTA installed locally, you will want to select SMTP. Then, on the General tab of the SMTP transport configuration, give the transport a name (which you can choose arbitrarily because it exists only for you to recognize the settings later and will not be used in any network communication). In any case, you need to enter the hostname of the port. The port is almost always 25; the hostname should be given to you by your provider. If you have a local MTA installed and want to use it, simply enter localhost. If your mail server requires authentication (check with your provider if you are unsure), check the appropriate checkbox and fill in the login name and password. This is less common than you would think, however; most ISPs protect themselves against being used as spam relays either by only accepting outgoing mail from IP addresses that they have provided themselves, or by asking you to fetch your email (which always requires a login) first, and then sending outgoing email within a certain amount of time.

This should be enough to let you send outgoing email, but we recommend that you take a few additional steps to make this as secure as possible. KMail makes this easy for you by autodetecting the security settings of the SMTP server you are using. Go to the Security tab and click the button labeled "Check what the server supports." KMail will check the connection to the server and use the settings with the highest supported security and encryption. Alas, many providers run their mail servers without any encryption at all.

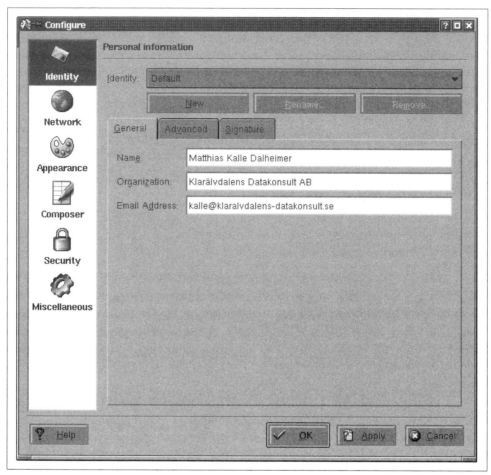

Figure 6-2. KMail identity configuration

Now let's continue by configuring the receiving end. Close all subdialogs until you are back at the Network configuration group, and select the Receiving tab. Here you can set up a number of accounts to be queried. This can be useful if you have more than one provider that stores email for you. Click the Add button and select the type of mail server. If you run your own MTA locally, you need to select Local Mailbox. Usually, you can then accept the defaults on the next page (but change the name to something more appropriate than "Default").

If you retrieve your messages directly from your provider's server, you need to select either POP3 or IMAP, depending on what your provider supports. In the dialog that appears again enter a name of your own choice, then specify your login name, your password, the name of the host that stores your email, and the port (usually 110 for POP3 and 143 for IMAP). All this information should be given to you by your

Figure 6-3. KMail identity for outgoing mail

provider or system administrator. You can leave all other options as they are for now, and experiment later with them.

As an aside, recent KMail versions have a feature for retrieving your messages that make it stand apart from many other email clients. Traditionally, the IMAP protocol required an online connection to the IMAP server that is storing your messages because no messages are stored locally. KMail, however, also sports a mode called *disconnected IMAP* that caches your messages locally so that you can both use the benefits of IMAP, such as having the same view on your mailbox from different computers (e.g., your workstation and your laptop), and still work offline when the need arises. Intelligent synchronization mechanisms make sure that all computers always have the same view of your mailbox (of course, only after you have performed synchronizations).

Close all dialogs with the OK button. You should now be ready to retrieve your email. To do so, select File → Check Mail from the menu. This will retrieve all messages from all incoming mailboxes that you have specified. If it does not work or you get any error messages, check all the values you entered on the various configuration pages again and compare them to the information given to you by your provider or system administrator. The most typical error is a typo in the hostname, username, or password.

If you are using disconnected IMAP, the Check Mail menu item does a lot more than checking the server mailbox for new messages: it ensures that the server and your local mailbox are in the same state, which may include deleting messages from the server, changing flags, and so forth.

To send a message, press Ctrl-N or select Message → New Message. A composer window opens where you can type in the recipient's address, the subject, and the actual message body. An intelligent autocompletion will come up with suggestions as you type; these suggestions are pulled both from your address book (if you keep one) and from mails you have sent and received recently.

If you have configured more than one identity, you can also select the one to be used for this message. When you are done composing your message, press Ctrl-N. Depending on how you have configured your outgoing mail transport, the message will either be put into the output folder and wait there for further handling (this is the default) or be transmitted directly. If you want to override your setting for a particular email, just select Message → Queue or Message → Send Now from the menu bar of the composer window.

Messages put into the output folder are by default not sent automatically. (You can, however, configure KMail to always send messages in the outbox when it checks for incoming messages.) To send all messages in your outbox, select File → Send Queued from the menu bar of the main KMail menu. We have made it a habit never to send any message automatically and always review our outbox before sending the messages therein, which saves a lot of embarrassment that could result from sending email to the wrong people. Reviewing complaint mails that you have written in anger after your anger has cooled down may also keep you a few more friends and business contacts.

If you have problems sending your messages, check the settings you have made for typos. As mentioned earlier, to prevent the relaying of unsolicited commercial email (so-called spam) via their servers, some providers require that you check your mailbox on the server (providing your username and password as you go) in order to identify yourself before you can send any email via that server. After you have checked your incoming email, you have a certain period of time (often 15 minutes) to send your outgoing email.

You should now know enough about how to use KMail in order to continue exploring the mailer on your own. One of the first things you may want to do (especially if you have a large number of messages to handle everyday) is to create folders by selecting Folder → New Folder and then set up filters by selecting Settings → Configure Filters. This lets you redirect messages with certain characteristics (e.g., certain senders or subjects) to predefined folders. For example, you may want to gate all messages from a mailing list to a folder dedicated to that purpose. If all you want to do is file messages sent to a certain mailing list, recipient, or with a certain subject, you can also right-click on that message header and select Create Filter from the context menu that pops up; a submenu lets you select what to filter on. After selecting this, the filter configuration dialog will pop up with the criteria already filled in correctly; all you have to do is to specify what should happen to that message, such as moving it to a folder or deleting it right away.

If you find you are not only using KMail regularly but also the address book and calendaring components that come with the KDE desktop, KAddressbook and KOrganizer, and if you would like those applications to be integrated into a common main window, you should take a look at Kontact. It is a wrapper application that "swallows" the individual application components using the KParts technology and presents them with a common interface, as shown in Figure 6-4.

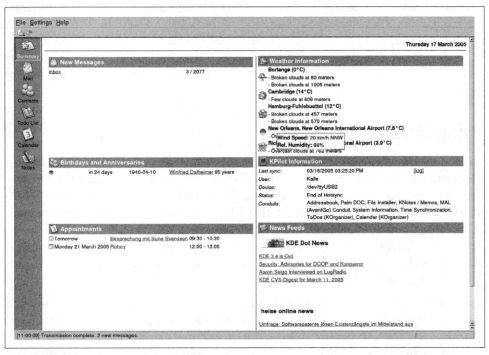

Figure 6-4. The Kontact overview window

All the individual components that are available appear on the button bar on the left side of the window, where you can click on them to bring the respective component to the front. In most of the Kontact applications, these buttons also act as targets for drag-and-drop operations, which means you can, for example, drag an email message on to the Todo view button to create a new task based on that email. Experiment with dragging things onto the different buttons and see what happens.

It should be noted that the components available inside Kontact are exactly the same applications that are available standalone, such as KMail or KAddressbook. This means that you can start one of them individually, whenever you do not want to start Kontact for some reason, and keep working with the same data and settings. All of the functionality available in Kontact is also available with the standalone applications. Since Kontact uses KParts, it can be extended with other components, not just the ones that are shipped with it; several third-party components already exist, such as a news feed reader component. To find out which components are currently installed and available, use Select Components from the Settings menu.

One of the most prominent integrative features of Kontact is the summary view. Click the Summary button on the sidebar to activate it. The page that appears is filled with information from each of the application components. The mail part shows a configurable summary of folders with unread mail. Clicking one of the listed folders will take you directly into that folder in the mail part. Similarly, the calendaring component shows any upcoming events, birthdays of people in your address book, and currently open tasks. To configure the summary view in detail, select Configure Summary View from the Settings menu. The individual areas of the summary view can be rearranged by dragging them by the header area in recent versions of Kontact.

Using Mozilla Mail & News

Mozilla Mail & News is the mail client that comes with the Mozilla web browser if you install more than the minimal installation (which only contains the browser and the composer itself). Chances are that your distribution already carries Mozilla, but if it doesn't, or you'd rather have a newer version, you can download it from *http://www.mozilla.org*. A freestanding version of Mozilla Mail & News is Thunderbird, which you can find at *http://www.mozilla.org/products/thunderbird/*. Thunderbird is particularly good at filtering junk mail and preventing email viruses from entering your system.

The concepts for setting up and using Mozilla Mail are quite similar to those for KMail, so we will cover only the differences here. To open the mail client, start Mozilla and select Windows → Mail and Newsgroups from the menu. If you are starting the mailer for the first time, a wizard will pop up that lets you configure your email. Check "Email account" on the first page, and your identity information on the second page (Mozilla's account handling is slightly less flexible than KMail's because it ties identities to accounts, whereas you can change identities at will with KMail).

On the third page, select whether you get your incoming mail via POP or IMAP (it's not possible to retrieve your email locally with Mozilla Mail & News, a big drawback), and specify the incoming and outgoing server name (specify *localhost* both times if you are running your own MTA). Complete the remaining information on the next pages, and you are ready to run Mozilla Mail & News. The screen layout is by default the same as that of KMail.

As when using KMail, one of the first things you probably want to set up when using Mozilla Mail & News is additional folders and filters that sort your incoming messages into these folders. You can create new folders by right-clicking the folder list and selecting New Folder in the context menu that appears. You can configure the filter rules by selecting Tools → Message Filters.

This concludes our discussion of email clients on Linux. As you can see, many options, from simple to sophisticated, are available to help you administer and digest the daily flood of email messages.

Getting the Mail to Your Computer with fetchmail

If your provider stores your mail for you until you fetch it, and you do not want to use your mailer to download the mail, you need a program that retrieves the mail from your provider's computer. There are a lot of programs for doing this; we will discuss *fetchmail* here briefly because it is both robust and flexible and can handle both POP3 and IMAP.

You can get *fetchmail* from your friendly Linux archive; chances are that your distribution carries it, too. If you download a source distribution of *fetchmail*, unpack, build, and install it according to the installation instructions. At the time of this writing, the current version was 6.2.5. The official home page for *fetchmail* is *http://www.catb.org/~esr/fetchmail/*.

You can control *fetchmail*'s behavior via both command-line options and a configuration file. It is a good idea to first try to fetch your mail by passing the necessary information on the command line, and when this works, to write the configuration file.

As an example, let's assume that my provider is running the POP3 protocol, that my username there is *joeuser*, and that my password is secret. The hostname of the machine where the POP3 server is running is *mail.isp.com*. I can then retrieve my mail with the following command:

```
fetchmail --protocol POP3 --username joeuser mail.isp.com
```

fetchmail then asks me for my password and, after I specify it correctly, retrieves the mail waiting for me and passes it on to my MTA for further delivery. This assumes that an SMTP server is running on port 25 of my machine, but this should be the case if I have set up my MTA correctly.

While you are experimenting with *fetchmail*, it might be a good idea to also specify the option *--keep*. This prevents *fetchmail* from deleting the messages from your POP3 account. Normally, all messages are deleted from your provider's hard disk once they are safely stored on your own machine. This is a good thing because most providers limit the amount of mail you can store on their machines before retrieving them, and if you don't delete the messages after fetching them, you might reach this limit quite quickly. On the other hand, while testing, it is a good idea to be on the safe side and use *--keep* so as not to lose any mail.

With the aforementioned options to *fetchmail*, you should be able to get your mail in most cases. For example, if your provider uses the newer IMAP protocol, simply specify IMAP in the command line instead of POP3. If your provider has some unusual setup, you might need one of the other options that the *fetchmail*(1) manual page tells you about.

Once you are satisfied with the download process, you can write a *fetchmail* configuration file in order not to have to enter all the options each time you use the command. This configuration file is called *.fetchmailrc* and should reside in your home directory. Once you are done editing it, make sure it has the permission value 0600 so that nobody except yourself can read it because this file might contain your password:

```
chmod 0600 ~/.fetchmailrc
```

The full syntax of the configuration file is detailed in the *fetchmail* manpage, but in general you need only very simple lines that start with poll. To specify the same data as on the command line in the previous example, but this time include the password, put the following line into your configuration file:

```
poll mail.isp.com with proto pop3 username joeuser password secret
```

Now you can run *fetchmail* without any parameters. Because *fetchmail* already knows about your password from the configuration file, it will not prompt you for it this time. If you want to play it safe while testing, add the word keep to the poll line.

Using *fetchmail* with a configuration file has one additional advantage: you can fetch mail from as many mailboxes as you want. Just add more poll lines to your *.fetchmailrc* file, and *fetchmail* happily retrieves your mail from one server after the other.

When and how you run *fetchmail* depends on your connection to the Internet. If you have a permanent connection or a cheap, flat rate, you might want to have *fetchmail* invoked by *cron* at a suitable interval (such as once an hour). However, if your Internet connection is nonpermanent (dial-up) and costly, you might want to choose to run *fetchmail* by hand whenever you actually want to fetch and read your mail so as to minimize your Internet connection time. Finally, if you are using PPP for dialing in to your Internet service provider, you might want to invoke *fetchmail* from the ip-up script, which is invoked as soon as an Internet connection is made. With this setup, when you browse a web page and your computer dials up your provider, your mail is fetched automatically.

So what happens to your email messages once *fetchmail* has pulled them from your account? We have said previously that it passes them on to your MTA. Your MTA then usually puts the messages into a so-called local spool file, often */var/spool/mail/<username>*. You can then set up your MUA to pull in the messages from this spool file. Each MUA should have such a setting; in KMail, for example, you create a "local receiving account."

OpenPGP Encryption with GnuPG

Using the GNU Privacy Guard, or GnuPG for short, you can encrypt individual files and emails, and digitally sign them. The main command-line tool of GnuPG is *gpg*, thus called because it started out as a replacement for PGP, which was the first encryption tool available to everyone that had strong cryptography built into it. PGP, which stands for Pretty Good Privacy, was written by Phil Zimmermann in the early 1990s. OpenPGP is the standard that describes the file format of PGP version 5.0 and later. GnuPG and PGP both implement this standard, and hence are able to read each other's files.

Symmetric Encryption

The simplest way to encrypt a file with GnuPG is to encrypt it with a passphrase.[*] This method is called *symmetric encryption*. The actual cryptography underlying this is beyond the scope of this book. Suffice it to say that the passphrase is used as the encryption key to the file. Everyone knowing the passphrase will be able to decrypt and read the file.[†]

To encrypt the file *music.ogg*, you simply type **gpg --symmetric music.ogg**. GnuPG will prompt you for a passphrase, and then again to confirm the passphrase in order to avoid typos. The encrypted file is written to *music.ogg.gpg*. If you prefer another output file name, use *--output outfile*, like this:

```
gpg --output music.gpg -c music.ogg
```

Here, we used the *-c* and *-o* shortcuts for *--symmetric* and *--output*, respectively.

---

[*] A *passphrase* is just a long password, usually a sentence.

[†] Of course, you can encrypt any kind of file, not just text files, so when we talk about "reading a file," you could just as well substitute "listen to audio files" or "watch movie files."

To decrypt the file, simply call gpg *file*. For instance, to continue the previous example:

```
gpg music.ogg.gpg
```

As with encryption, you can request the output to be written to a file other than the default one by using -o *outfile*.

Public-Key Cryptography

Although symmetric encryption works well for short-term and casual use, you will run into problems managing the plethora of passphrases accumulated when you encrypt lots of files. The obvious solution of using the same passphrase over and over again poses much the same problems as using the same lock for all your doors. Among others, losing one key locks you out of everything, and if one key is stolen, everything is open to the thief. This can be described as the problem of "Everyone who knows the passphrase can read the contents."

Another problem is that of "Everybody who needs to read the contents also needs to know the passphrase." If you encrypt files not for archiving but for sharing with friends, collegues, or business partners, you run into this problem. You cannot reuse passphrases because it's insecure, as already mentioned, and because each new file might target another set of recipients. For instance, if you reuse a passphrase that was used to encrypt a message to Alice and Bob to now encrypt another message, this time to Alice and Charlie, then Alice, Bob, and Charlie can all read both messages, even though only Alice was intended to be able to read both messages.

You cannot create a new passphrase for each new message, because your recipients will not know the passphrase. And if you have a secret channel to tell them the new passphrase, why would you need to use encryption in the first place?

The only solution using simple encryption, then, is to negotiate a passphrase with each recipient separately, and encrypt the message to each of the recipients separately. But this, too, becomes prohibitively complex, because there must be a passphrase (or another shared secret) for each *pair* of people wishing to exchange messages; the problem is said to be of $O(n^2)$ complexity.

These problems haunted cryptography until the mid-1970s, when Whitfield Diffie and Martin Hellman invented a new method of key exchange that no longer required a shared secret. They used asymmetrical encryption, where the encryption key is public, but the decryption key is secret. In this scheme, everyone can encrypt a message to, say, Alice, but only Alice can decrypt it with her secret key.

This makes it easy to address the situation described earlier: encrypt the message to each recipient using that recipient's public keys. Only the intended recipients can read the message. In addition, there is only one key for each person, instead of one per pair of persons; the problem is said to be reduced to $O(n)$ complexity. Glossing over the new problem of ensuring that a public key marked as belonging to Alice actually does belong to her, encrypting a message to another person is as easy as downloading her public key from a keyserver, and then encrypting the message to that key. (We discuss the problem we glossed over here in "The Web of Trust" later in this chapter.)

Creating a New Key Pair

To be able to send and receive messages using public-key encryption, you have to own a secret and a public key—that is, a key pair. They can be created using the command gpg --gen-key. In this mode, GnuPG will prompt you with a series of questions, at the end of which it has generated a new key pair. The following shows a screen capture of the procedure for GnuPG 1.4.0. GnuPG asks for a passphrase that is used to protect (lock away) your secret key. It is *not* used to encrypt any messages later on.

```
$ gpg --gen-key
gpg (GnuPG) 1.4.0; Copyright (C) 2004 Free Software Foundation, Inc.
This program comes with ABSOLUTELY NO WARRANTY.
This is free software, and you are welcome to redistribute it
under certain conditions. See the file COPYING for details.

Please select what kind of key you want:
  (1) DSA and Elgamal (default)
  (2) DSA (sign only)
  (5) RSA (sign only)
Your selection? 1
DSA keypair will have 1024 bits.
ELG-E keys may be between 1024 and 4096 bits long.
What keysize do you want? (2048) 2048
Requested keysize is 2048 bits
Please specify how long the key should be valid.
     0 = key does not expire
  <n>  = key expires in n days
  <n>w = key expires in n weeks
  <n>m = key expires in n months
  <n>y = key expires in n years
Key is valid for? (0) 5y
Key expires at Tue Mar 2 10:33:35 2010 CET
Is this correct? (y/N) y

You need a user ID to identify your key; the software constructs the user ID
from the Real Name, Comment and Email Address in this form:
   "Heinrich Heine (Der Dichter) <heinrichh@duesseldorf.de>;"

Real name: John Doe
Email address: john@doe.example.net
Comment: work
You selected this USER-ID:
   "John Doe (work) <john@doe.example.net>;"

Change (N)ame, (C)omment, (E)mail or (O)kay/(Q)uit? o
You need a Passphrase to protect your secret key.
```

```
Enter passphrase:
Re-enter passphrase:
We need to generate a lot of random bytes. It is a good idea to perform
some other action (type on the keyboard, move the mouse, utilize the
disks) during the prime generation; this gives the random number
generator a better chance to gain enough entropy.
+++++.+++++++++++++++++++++++++++++++++++++++++.++++++++++.++++++++++.+++++++++++++
++++++++...+++++.+++++++++++++++++++++..+++++...++++++++++++++++++++++++>+++++.++
+++..+++++
++++++++++++++++++++++++++++++++++++++++++++++++++++++++++++++.++++++++++.++++
+.+++++..++++++++++++++.+++++.+++++.+++++++++++++++++++..+++++++++++++++..
.+++++>++++++++++.....>+++++.................................>+++++..........
.........<+++++...........+++++^^^^
gpg: key 461BA2AB marked as ultimately trusted
public and secret key created and signed.

gpg: please do a --check-trustdb
pub   1024D/461BA2AB 2005-03-03 [expires: 2010-03-02]
    Key fingerprint = E880 E195 62A8 9EFD ED83 3CD7 0B38 4F5D 461B A2AB
uid         John Doe (work) <john@doe.example.net>;
sub   2048g/6D18BF84 2005-03-03 [expires: 2010-03-02]
```

After creating the key pair, GnuPG stores it in the local key ring, usually in *~/.gnupg*. You can check that the key has been properly added using the commands gpg --list-keys, which lists all keys in your public keyring, and gpg --list-secret-keys, which lists all keys in your secret keyring.

To make this key available for others to encrypt messages to you using it, you have to upload it to a keyserver using

```
gpg --keyserver wwwkeys.pgp.net --send key-id
```

where *key-id* is the ID of the key (461BA2AB in the case of the key created above). The keyserver can be hardcoded into *~/.gnupg/gpg.conf* so you do not need to give it on the command line every time you upload or download keys. You do not need to upload a key to more than one server, because the *pgp.net* servers synchronize new and changed keys among each other.

It is important at this point to take precautions for the case of a lost passphrase: If the key gets compromised, or you simply forget the passphrase, you want other people to know that this key should no longer be used. This is the purpose of a *revocation certificate*. A revoked key can no longer be used as an encryption target. To create a revocation certificate, however, you need to know the passphrase to unlock your secret key. So in order to have a revocation certificate ready for publishing in the case of emergency, you have to create one while you still remember the passphrase, and then store it somewhere safe.

To create such a revocation certificate, you can use the command *gpg --armour --output rev-cert.gpg --gen-revoke key-id*. This will create a revocation certificate and save it in *rev-cert.gpg*. The *--armour* option tells GnuPG to create a printable version instead of a binary file. This way, you can print the certificate and store it on paper as backup in case of hard disk failures.

To apply the revocation certificate, simply import it by using gpg < rev-cert.gpg, and then upload the changed key using gpg --send *key-id*, as shown earlier.

 Keys uploaded to a keyserver cannot be removed. Furthermore, they can only be added to; no data will ever be removed from them. This includes additional user IDs and third-party signatures (discussed shortly), as well as revocations.

Encrypting with Public Keys

As mentioned earlier, when doing public-key encryption, you need to have the recipient's public keys. For GnuPG, this means they need to be downloaded from a keyserver, and that there should be a trust path (see "The Web of Trust," later in this chapter) from your key to the recipient's key.

For now, we can make do with a speciality of GnuPG: encrypting to untrusted keys.

First you need to find the key on the keysever. You can use the GnuPG search interface for this: gpg --search *name-or-email*. GnuPG will list all matching keys (which can be hundreds) in a list, from which you can choose one to import.

If you already know the key ID of the recipient's key, then you can download it directly using gpg --recv *key-id*.

Next, you can encrypt a file using one or more keys. Be aware that GnuPG does not necessarily encrypt using your key, too (this is an option in the config file), so you might not be able to decrypt the message any more. The command to use is:

```
gpg --encrypt --recipient recip_1 --recipient recip_2 ... file
```

A shortcut notation for this is:

```
gpg -e -r recip_1 -r recip_2 ... file
```

Both versions create the encrypted message in a file called *file.gpg*, unless the *--output* (*-o*) option is used to redirect the output to a non-standard file. No matter to how many recipients you encrypt, there will always be only one output file—it will just be generated such that all the recipients are able to decrypt it.

To decrypt a file, simply run GnuPG on it: *gpg file.gpg*. GnuPG asks for your passphrase and then saves the decrypted file into *file* (i.e., the name of the input file stripped of the *.gpg* extension).

If you want to encrypt a lot of files in one go, consider using *--multifile*, like this:

```
gpg --multifile -e -r recip_1 ... file1 file2 ...
```

Digital Signatures

Public-key cryptography is valuable not only for encryption, but for authentication. Digital signatures are a way to ascertain that a given file has not been modified since it was signed. Very simply put, the system encrypts a checksum of the data with your secret key. This works because, on the other end, the public key can decrypt data encrypted with the secret key.

So to verify the signature, the recipient calculates the same checksum of the data, and then compares the value with the value stored in the signature. If they match, two things have been proved: first, that the data has not been changed since it was signed, and second, that the message was signed using your secret key. If the data was changed, the checksum would not come out the same. Likewise, if the original checksum was encrypted with some other key than yours, the decryption result when using your public key would be gibberish, and the checksums would also fail to compare.

OpenPGP allows two different types of signatures: clearsigned and detached. In clearsigning, the original message is modified to include the data and the signature of the data in one file. Detached signatures, on the other hand, do not modify the original file, but write the signature to a second file, usually with *.gpg* or *.asc* appended. You should use only detached signatures, becuase they work for all types of files, while clearsigning works only with (plain) text files.

To sign a file, you need only your secret key. Use the following command to create a detached signature of a file named *music.ogg*:

```
gpg --sign music.ogg
```

The signature file will be named *music.ogg.gpg*. As usual, you can redirect the data to another file by using the *--output (-o)* option. The shortcut for *--sign* is *-s*.

It will not come as a surprise to you to learn that verifying a signature works by just running GnuPG on the signature file: gpg `music.ogg.gpg`.

Signing and encrypting can be combined into a single operation. Indeed, this is the usual mode of operation:

```
gpg -es -r recip_1 -r recip_2 ... file
```

Note that in this case of combined operation, the signature is encrypted together with the signed data, so that there is no third file containing the signature. It is all nicely packaged into the *.gpg* file.

Note that as of this writing, signing does not yet work with *--multifile*. You have to revert to using a shell for loop:

```
for i in *.ogg; do gpg --sign $i ; done
```

The Web of Trust

We have noted earlier that for public-key cryptography to work, one needs to be certain that the public key obtained from the keyserver is actually authentic and has not been changed or created by an impersonator.

To this end, OpenPGP uses the concept of a Web of Trust, in which keys known to belong to the person described by a user ID can in turn certify that another key is authentic. This is done using signatures on the key material, that is, the public key and the associated user ID.

As an example, consider the scenario where Alice wants to send an encrypted message to Bob, the ex of her friend Carol. She does not know Bob personally, and so she cannot be certain that the public key she finds when searching for Bob on the keyservers indeed belongs to Bob.

However, she knows Carol personally, and they have in the past cross-certified their keys. This means that Carol's key now contains a signature by Alice stating more or less, "I, Alice, confirm that this key does belong to the owner listed in the user ID— that is, Carol."

Carol, in turn, knows Bob, of course.* From their time together, they still have their keys cross-signed, although it has been a long while since they were used to send secret love letters.

If Alice *trusts* Carol to not be careless about certifying other people's keys, she can use Carol's key to create a *trust path* from herself to Bob: her own signature on Carol's key makes that key *valid*. She trusts the owner of the key to certify other keys, and has indicated this to GnuPG by specifying a corresponding *ownertrust* value for Carol's key. Because Bob's key carries Carol's signature of certification, Bob's key is also valid from Alice's point of view.

This example illustrates two fundamental points:

- The validity of a given key is not an absolute. It is always relative to another key and to that key's owner's trust in other people, as expressed by the assigned ownertrust values. If Alice did not trust Carol to certify other keys, she could not ascertain Bob's key's validity.
- The Web of Trust model works incredibly well in your own socioecological vicinity. However, it is hard or downright impossible to make it work across more than one or two hops (i.e., intermediate keys).

In recent years, however, the global Web of Trust has exploded, so the latter point becomes less and less of a problem. Thanks to the analysis tools implemented and run fortnightly by Drew M. Streib and Jason Harris, we now know that the global Web of Trust contains one large *strongly connected* set, a set of keys with the property that each key from the set has a trust path to any other key from the set. This big set currently encompasses 28,418 keys, and its diameter is on the order of 15 hops. Another 60,000 keys can be reached from any key in this set with up to 30 hops. Usually, around 10,000 keys are reachable with no more than three hops. The mean

---

* Although she sometimes wished she didn't.

square distance to the best-connected key from any key in the cluster is currently about 3.6 hops. In contrast to the big set, the next biggest sets have only 147, 117, and 79 keys in turn.

In order to enter the strongly connected set, all you need is to cross-sign your keys with at least one of its members. If you live in North America or Europe, this is usually not much of a problem. Visiting a conference or fair with Debian or KDE developers lets you take part in one of the numerous key signing parties that are often held during these events. In other parts of the world, however, it can be very hard.

The commands to sign other keys and change the ownertrust are all available using gpg --edit *key-id*. This enters a GnuPG shell where commands such as sign and trust are available to perform key maintainance.

Using gPG-agent

After using GnuPG for a while, you will notice that you need to type in your passphrase quite often. But do not let this fool you into choosing a short passphrase! Instead, consider using the *gpg-agent* tool.

Much like *ssh-agent*, *gpg-agent* can be configured to maintain a cache of recently entered passphrases and reuse them instead of prompting the user. *gpg-agent* is part of the GnuPG 2, the next-generation GnuPG. You can download GnuPG 2 from *ftp://ftp.gnupg.org/gcrypt/alpha/gnupg*; its packages are called *gnupg-1.9.n*. Even though *gpg-agent* is packaged alongside GnuPG 2, it works just fine with GnuPG Version 1.2.6 or higher. Note that *gpg-agent* uses the pinentry package to prompt the user for a passphrase. Versions of pinentry are currently available for Qt (KDE), GTK (GNOME), and ncurses (text terminal).

To make GnuPG use the agent, you first have to start it: eval `gpg-agent --daemon`. The eval feeds back the output of the command in the backticks into the current shell; that is important because the gpg-agent command outputs environment variable assignments that are necessary for GnuPG to use the agent; in this case, the environment variable GPG_AGENT_INFO will be set. If you start GnuPG from this shell (or any other shell spawned from it), and pass it the *--use-agent* option (either on the command line or in *~/.gnupg/gpg.conf*), then GnuPG will contact *gpg-agent* to obtain the passphrase instead of prompting the user directly.

To make *gpg-agent* cache the passphrase instead of asking each time anew, create *~/.gnupg/gpg-agent.conf* with the following contents:

```
default-cache-ttl
         3600
```

This instructs gpg-agent to cache the passphrase for 3,600 seconds—that is, one hour.

Gaming

Gaming under Linux has long had a bad reputation. Even very experienced Linux users often keep a Windows partition around to dual boot into only for games. In many ways this problem is due to a chicken-or-egg approach from game developers: games aren't ported to Linux because not enough people game on the platform, and not enough people game on the platform because there aren't enough games ported to it.

The fact is, though, that gaming under Linux continues to improve every year. Not only are the major video card manufacturers making sure their cards have full 3D acceleration support under X, but a number of software companies, such as Id Software and Epic Games, have consistently released Linux ports of their titles either on the same CD as the Windows software or as separate downloads released a bit after the initial launch date. Of course, some of this good will toward the community keeps in mind the strength of Linux as a server platform. The idea is that if the companies promote Linux clients, the community will be more likely to run the Linux servers for the game.

When you examine the different commercial games that have been ported to Linux, you will notice that many if not most of them are in the FPS (first-person shooter) genre. Doom, the full Quake series, the Unreal Tournament series, Return to Castle Wolfenstein, Tribes 2, and many other FPSs have Linux ports. This doesn't mean that other genres are unrepresented—for instance, games such as Railroad Tycoon and Neverwinter Nights have been ported to Linux—just that the FPS games seem to get ported more readily.

Even if your favorite game hasn't been ported to Linux, there's still a chance that the Windows binary can install and run in a Wine or Cedega environment. These environments translate the Windows system calls to Linux system calls, and many games play very well. Cedega is a commercial product released by Transgaming that is based on Wine and focused on getting all of the latest games running under Linux.

There is an extensive list of games that Cedega supports, rated by how well they perform under Linux, that you can browse on their site. The list includes games such as Warcraft III, Max Payne II, and Battlefield 1942. If you decide to use Cedega, you can sign up on a subscription basis at *www.transgaming.com* for $5 a month. The site contains a number of FAQs for the different games it supports to help you through the installation process.

A number of true game emulators also exist for Linux. If you have ROM images for arcade or console cartridges, you can use arcade emulators such as Xmame or console emulators such as Nestra and Snes9x to play those games directly on your Linux system. Some people have developed their own personal arcade cabinet, complete with a large collection of games and arcade-style joysticks, on a Linux platform.

Gaming under Linux isn't limited to commercial titles; Linux also has a large number of free software titles. These games range from simple card games to board games such as chess and backgammon and from arcade games such as xgalaga to adventure games such as rogue and nethack. There has also been development of free 3D games, such as Tux Racer. Most distributions include a number of these games on the CD, so you aren't limited simply to Solitaire, Freecell, and Minesweeper. The KDE Desktop Environment comes with more than 30 basic games, including Solitaire, Backgammon, a Minesweeper clone, a Tetris-like game, and video poker.

So if you like games, you will find plenty to keep you amused under Linux, and maybe even some reasons to get rid of that dual-boot gaming platform you keep around. In this chapter are introductions to a few Linux-native games including instructions to install, play, and if applicable, run a game server.

Quake III

The Quake series has long been a favorite among FPS fans for its addictive yet simple gameplay and its graphics, which have always pushed the envelope for the time. Although Quake and Quake 2 were initially single-player games, both became very popular for multiplayer deathmatch games over a network. With Quake III, Id Software took the Quake universe and created a game strictly aimed at multiplayer gaming. In Quake III there is a single-player mode, but it revolves around playing a series of deathmatch games against one or more computer opponents in an arena style. As you progress in the game the opponents get more difficult to defeat; in the final round, you are one-on-one with an incredibly accurate opponent. In many ways the single-player mode is practice for multiplayer games on the network.

The entire Quake series has Linux binaries available for download from *ftp. idsoftware.com*. When Quake III was first released, Linux binaries weren't available; however, a special tin box edition of the game containing Linux binaries was released in stores some time after the initial Windows version. Even if you didn't get the special tin box edition, you can still use your Windows CD and download the Linux installer.

Installation

To install Quake III under Linux, download the latest version of the installer from the *ftp.idsoftware.com/idstuff/quake3/linux* directory. Once you have downloaded the file, use chmod +x filename to make it executable and then run the installer from a console as root. Accept the licensing agreement to then see the main installer window (Figure 7-1). The installer will default to putting the game files into */usr/local/games/quake3*. The installer from the Linux retail CD will copy the *.pk3* data files from the CD-ROM, but the installer that you download will not. Therefore, if you used the downloaded installer, mount the Linux or Windows Quake III CD and copy *pak0.pk3* from the *Quake3/baseq3* directory on the CD to */usr/local/games/quake3/baseq3*. If you also have the Team Arena CD-ROM, you can mount that CD and copy *pak0.pk3* from the *Setup/missionpack* directory to */usr/local/games/quake3/missionpack/*.

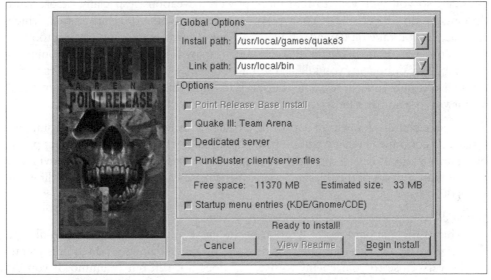

Figure 7-1. Quake III Installer

Once Quake III is installed, click the corresponding icon in your KDE or GNOME menu, or type quake3 in a console. Quake III relies on OpenGL as its graphics library, so make sure that you have 3D hardware acceleration with OpenGL support. Unlike with the Windows version, the Linux version of Quake III does not require you to have the CD-ROM in the drive to start the game. Once the game begins for the first time, a *.q3a* directory is created in your home directory to store settings and saved games. You can edit the configuration files directly if you wish, or you can change game options through the Setup menu on the main screen.

Single Player

In single-player mode you can either start with the first arena match and move map by map through the game, or you can immediately get to the action and click the skirmish button inside the single-player screen. A skirmish is a quick match that doesn't count toward the standard single-player game. You can choose any map and also how many and which bots to play against on the map, along with their difficulty. Skirmish mode is very useful to hone your skills on a particular map, especially before you move to a multiplayer game.

The rules for a standard deathmatch are pretty simple—kill everyone else. When a match starts, your player is spawned in one of the many spawn points on the map. Once the match starts the object is to have the most frags, or kills, before the time limit lapses. Scattered across the map are weapons; items such as health, ammo, and armor, and your opponents. You start off with a simple machine gun and your gauntlet, so you will want to find more powerful weapons, especially before your opponents do (Figure 7-2). Your player starts out with 100 hit points, which decrease as you take on damage. If you reach zero or fall into one of the bottomless pits on the map, your character dies and you "respawn" at a random spawn point on the map. Any opponents you kill also respawn in this way. There are no limits to the number of times you can respawn, but keep in mind that you lose any weapons and armor you previously had, so try to keep respawning to a minimum.

The Quake series is known for supplying a basic set of weapons to choose from, and Quake III continues in that tradition by including many favorite weapons from previous games without having too much overlap in weapon functions. It is worthwhile to get familiar with all of the different weapons because each can be useful in different types of combat.

Gauntlet
> This is the standard melee weapon of the game and a weapon that you always have with you. This electrified fist does not do much damage and requires you to be very close to your enemy to use, but does not run out of ammo. If you do manage to kill an enemy with the gauntlet the announcer will yell "humiliation" to alert all of the players to your opponent's shame at being killed by such a weak weapon.

Machine gun
> This is the default weapon that a player starts with. It does a minimum amount of damage but has a lot of ammo and can be an effective weapon if used accurately.

Shotgun
> Like most shotguns in FPSs, this shotgun causes a lot of damage when used at close range, and the damage tapers off the farther away you are from your enemy.

Figure 7-2. Quake III game

Grenade launcher

Very effective as a defensive weapon, the grenade launcher fires grenades that either explode upon direct contact with an enemy or after a short delay. The grenade launcher is a useful weapon when running away from a pursuing enemy backwards.

Rocket launcher

A powerful weapon, the rocket launcher not only is useful for mid- to long-range combat, but the rockets can damage opponents (and you) just by being near them when they explode. Thus, you can fire at walls and the floor near an opponent and still damage him.

Lightning gun

The lightning gun fires a stream of lightning at your opponent. This is a better weapon at shorter ranges, and is useful to encourage an aggressive opponent to keep his distance.

Railgun

The popular sniper weapon, the railgun fires a depleted uranium slug quickly at your opponent. The railgun has a weakness in that it needs to charge for a second between firing, so keep that in mind if you are using it in the middle of fast-paced combat.

Plasma gun

> This weapon fires balls of plasma at an enemy in rapid succession. This weapon also has some "splash damage" like the rocket launcher so you can inflict damage on an opponent even if you just miss him.

BFG

> The BFG in Quake III is somewhat different from the weapon in Quake II. This BFG is more like a souped-up plasma gun. It fires green balls of plasma that cause large amounts of damage, and is the most powerful weapon in the game.

Along with weapons, there are a few other items you will find in the maps, some of which give you extra abilities. There are the normal health and ammo packs that regenerate across the map, and on some maps there is a Quad Damage item. If a player picks up this item, the announcer says "Quad Damage" and the player shines a bright blue that makes him easy to see from a distance. If you pick up Quad Damage, all of your weapons inflict four times their damage for a limited time, useful for racking up quick kills. Be careful, though: if you are killed with time remaining, the Quad Damage will be left behind, so other players have an incentive to kill you.

Multiplayer

Quake III was primarily designed to be played in multiplayer mode. The multiplayer mode is not much different from single-player mode except that you are fighting other people instead of computer-controlled bots. When you click the Multiplayer option from the main menu, you are taken to the Quake III server browser. Here you can see a list of available game servers you can connect to, along with the map and game type currently in progress and the number of players on the server. You can also specify a particular server to connect to by IP address.

If you want to create your own server, click Create and select a map and number of bots for your own server and click Fight to launch the server. If you change the Dedicated option before you launch the server, the server will launch in the background. Otherwise, the server will start and you will immediately be connected to it. If you want to create your own customized dedicated server, particularly one that runs without the client from the command line, check out some of the great Quake III server HOWTOs on the Internet. A good place to start is *http://www.planetquake. com/quake3/q3aguide/server-setup_a.shtml*.

There are a number of multiplayer game types, and many of them require special mods or maps to be installed on your system. The basic game types are baseq3, which is the standard multiplayer deathmatch, and CTF, which is a standard two-team capture-the-flag match. Once you find a game you wish to join, click on the server and then click the Fight button at the bottom of the screen to connect.

Mods

Like the previous versions of Quake, Quake III has a large number of community-created mods for it. Some of these mods are simplistic and add a new weapon or new basic game type, whereas other mods are very extensive and change maps, weapons, and even the major rules of the game. To find mods, skins, and maps to add to your Quake III install, visit *www.planetquake.com*.

Among the many mods and files hosted on that site is a popular mod called Rocket Arena 3 (RA3) at *http://www.planetquake.com/servers/arena/*. Rocket Arena 3 is the continuation of the Rocket Arena mods that were available for Quake and Quake II; it takes deathmatch play and changes a few of the rules to result in a unique style of game play. First, by default in Rocket Arena 3, you start with all of the weapons fully loaded. This means no longer running around a map trying to find the more powerful weapons—you can get right to fragging. Second, your player is not hurt by his own splash damage. This means you can do manuevers like rocket jumps (firing a rocket below you as you jump, launching you high into the air) without any damage. These two changes in the rules, combined with a completely new set of maps result in a very different deathmatch game. On RA3 servers, you can select to play directly against another player one-one-one or in a team deathmatch. Unlike in standard deathmatch, you only have one life, so when you die you must wait until the current match ends before you can get back in the game.

Installing RA3 takes only a few steps. First go to the RA3 site and find the Linux/Mac installer on the downloads page, a 135Mb *.zip* file. Then unzip the file into */usr/local/games/quake3/* where it should create an *arena* directory. To play RA3 start Quake III from the command line with quake3 +set fs_game arena or select "arena" from the Mods menu in Quake III. If you want to host your own RA3 server, a sample server script has already been created for you called *ra3server* in the *arena* directory. Launch it to start a dedicated RA3 server. Read the *readsrv.txt* file in the *arena* directory for more information on how to customize the RA3 server.

Return to Castle Wolfenstein

For many gamers, Wolfenstein 3D was their first exposure to a 3D first-person shooter. In the game you are a captured American soldier inside a Nazi prison. Your goal is to escape the prison and shoot any guards who get in your way. Id Software has released an updated version of the classic called Return to Castle Wolfenstein (RTCW) that shares the same basic objectives but expands the game play and provides updated graphics and sounds.

Unfortunately the native Linux client is not included with the Return to Castle Wolfenstein CD, so you will need to download the latest version of the installer from *ftp://ftp.idsoftware.com/idstuff/wolf/linux*. Updates are also provided in the directory, so be sure to download the full installer (it will be a larger file and not have the word update in the filename).

Installation

To install RTCW, become root, add executable permissions to the installer with chmod +x filename, and run the installer script. The installer provides a basic GUI that lets you configure a few installation settings, including where to install the binaries (Figure 7-3). By default the installer will put files in */usr/local/games/wolfenstein*.

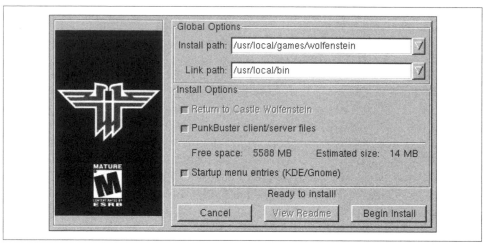

Figure 7-3. RTCW installer

Unlike some Linux game installers, the Wolfenstein installer will not install the compressed game files that are on your CD. The *README* file that comes with the installer instructs you to copy seven files from your Windows install of the game to the */usr/local/games/wolfenstein/main* directory. These files are *mp_pak0.pk3*, *mp_pak1.pk3*, *mp_pak2.pk3*, *pak0.pk3*, *sp_pak1.pk3*, and *sp_pak2.pk3*. If you have not installed the game under Windows, your other option is to run the CD installer under Wine and then copy the files. If you have trouble with the installer, you can check out the official FAQ for the Linux client, found at *zerowing.idsoftware.com/linux*.

Single Player

Once you launch RTCW, you will probably want to click on Options and familiarize yourself with and change the default key bindings and other settings to suit you. In the Options section you can also launch various mods you have downloaded and installed for the game. Click Play to start a game. The default mode for RTCW is a single-player game that puts you into a similar situation as the first Wolfenstein 3D —you are freed from your Nazi prison cell when you attack and kill a guard (Figure 7-4). Your goal is to advance through enemy lines and escape prison.

Figure 7-4. RTCW start

As you move through the game, at different times you will want to employ stealth by walking slowly (hit the Caps Lock key) and peeking around corners (Q and E lean to the left and to the right, respectively), or react quickly without regard to noise and sprint through an area (hold down the Shift key when you move) and kick in doors (the X key) and jump over obstacles (spacebar). When you find items such as weapons or supplies, you can pick them up just by walking over them. Some objects in the game, such as alarms, can be activated and deactivated with the Enter key. Of course, you can also deactivate an alarm by shooting at it.

There are a number of weapons in the game to help you fight the enemy. You start with a basic knife and quickly pick up the guard's pistol. As you progress in the game you get more powerful weapons, such as submachine guns, rifles, grenades, and rockets. Some of the weapons share ammunition, so be aware of your ammo counts. Also, some of the autofire guns overheat if fired too much in a short time, so be sure to fire them only in short bursts. Certain levels contain mounted machine guns. To use these weapons, step up to them until the hand icon appears on the screen and then press F or Enter to mount or dismount from the machine gun. When mounted, you view through the machine gun's crosshairs and can aim and fire at your enemies.

Multiplayer

RTCW also has a multiplayer mode that is rather different from the single-player game. In multiplayer mode there are two teams—the Axis and the Allies. In the default multiplayer mode both teams have one or more objectives they must accomplish within a time limit. The first team that completes the objective wins the round. In stopwatch mode the game changes a bit. After each round of play, the teams switch sides and must beat the other team's time for completing the objective. Checkpoint mode is somewhat like capture the flag. There are a number of checkpoint flags scattered across the map. The first team that controls all of the different checkpoints simultaneously wins. If time runs out, the team that controls the most checkpoints wins the round.

Multiplayer mode also differs from single player in that there are four different character classes to choose from, each with different abilities and roles in the game. A successful team will have members from each of the roles working together.

Soldier

> This is a standard fighting role. The soldier can use all of the two-handed weapons, such as the sniper rifle. This is a good default role to pick if you are starting out and aren't sure what to do.

Engineer

> The engineer's primary focus is demolitions, and the engineer is the only player who can use dynamite to destroy objectives. In addition, the engineer can repair stationary guns and disarm dynamite that enemies lay.

Medic

> A medic is an important team member. Medics can help heal and even revive dead team members on the battlefield. Medics also are equipped with health packs that they can drop for other teammates to pick up. If you have a medic on the team, then all players will spawn with an additional 10 hits points. Also, the health of a medic slowly regenerates over time.

Lieutenant

> A lieutenant's primary duties are back a bit from the main battle and involve tactical decisions. A lieutenant can drop a smoke grenade on an area to signal an airstrike. Also, lieutenants can use binoculars to call in artillery attacks on a location. Lieutenants can drop ammo packs for other teammates, much in the way medics drop health packs.

Unlike in some other tactical multiplayer FPSs, in RTCW players have multiple lives and respawn, but with a twist. When a player dies, he is placed in "limbo" and must wait until the next reinforcement period occurs to respawn. During this period he can change character classes and weapons, and even switch teams. You can also choose to wait for a medic to revive you instead of waiting in limbo. In that case, you can get back into the game immediately once a medic revives you.

You can play multiplayer games either locally on a LAN or on servers on the Internet. The multiplayer interface provides a server browser that will scan for currently open servers to connect to, otherwise you can directly enter the IP address of a server. You can also host your own server. Included in the Linux binary is a file called *QUICKSTART* that goes through the basics of running a dedicated server.

The dedicated server is called `wolfded` and game options are changed through arguments on the command line or by specifying a config file to execute. To get a basic server up, run:

```
$ wolfded +set com_hunkmegs 64 +set sv_maxrate 9000 +set com_zonemegs 32 +set \
    dedicated 2 +set sv_hostname "my server" +set g_motd "my motd" +map mp_villiage
```

Included with the install is a basic map rotation script in *main/rotate.cfg*. You can specify this on the command line to start a basic server that will cycle through the different maps:

```
$ wolfded +set com_hunkmegs 64 +set sv_maxrate 9000 +set com_zonemegs 32 +set \
    dedicated 2 +set sv_hostname "my server" +set g_motd "my motd" +exec rotate.cfg \
    +vstr m_rotate1
```

Unlike with standard single-player or multiplayer mode, you do not have to have a valid CD key to host a dedicated server.

To update to the latest version of RTCW, download the latest version of the installer (or to save bandwidth, the *-update* file of the same version) from *ftp.idsoftware.com* and execute it as root. You will see an interface just like that of the original installer, and updated files will overwrite the old versions once you click Install.

Unreal Tournament 2004

Some FPS games attempt to shun the stereotype that FPS games lack depth and generally rely more on quick reflexes than thinking or strategy by adding a basic storyline along with a single-person mode. The storyline usually puts the character in some sort of hostile environment as a pretense to fire at anything that moves. The fact is, however, that while some players might play through the single-person mode now and then, the majority spend their time in a head-to-head deathmatch with other players.

The Unreal Tournament (UT) series has no such pretense, and instead focuses completely on arena-style play. Because of this focus, UT has become the favorite for many players over the Net, as it includes many different arena maps and styles of network play, from basic deathmatch and capture the flag to bombing runs and other games that start to blur the line between an FPS and the sports genre.

Installation

Like its predecessors Unreal Tournament and Unreal Tournament 2003, Unreal Tournament 2004 (or UT2K4) has native Linux support both for the client and the server. *Unlike* many other Linux-native FPSs from other companies, however, UT2K4 ships with the Linux binaries and installer in the same box as the Windows binaries. This means you don't have to search for a fast mirror and download a large .sh file, much less wait for weeks or months for a Linux port—you can get to gaming immediately.

UT2K4 chooses its installation directory based on what user runs the installer. If a regular user starts the installer, UT2K4 creates a *ut2004* directory under the user's home directory. Although the game will run fine for a single user either way, if you do have root privileges on a machine, it is better to install it for every user in case you decide to switch users. If you run linux-installer.sh as root, it will install to */usr/local/games/ut2004/* by default and be made available to all users on the system.

To install UT2K4, mount CD1, also labeled the Install Disc, on your Linux system and execute the file called linux-installer.sh. Most file managers will execute the file if you click on it; otherwise, you can open a terminal and type:

```
# /mnt/cdrom/linux-installer.sh &
```

After you accept the licensing agreement, you will see the primary screen for the Linux installer, as shown in Figure 7-5.

In this primary screen you can change many of the installation settings, including where to install, what language to use, and whether to add menu entries for KDE and GNOME. The install uses about 5 GB of space, so make sure you have enough free space cleared up; otherwise, the Begin Install button will be disabled. Once you click Begin Install, the installer will prompt you for your CD key and then start copying files from the CD-ROM to the hard drive. If you purchased the default CD edition of UT2K4, you will be prompted to switch CDs throughout the process. If you purchased the DVD special edition, you can install the full game without swapping discs.

Once the install finishes, you can click the Start button in the final window to start the game, you can select it from your KDE or GNOME menu, or you can simply type ut2004 in a terminal. Unlike in Windows, you do not need to have the play disc mounted in the CD-ROM drive to play.

Play

One of the first things you will want to do when you start UT2K4 for the first time is go over all of the configuration settings and key bindings and make sure they are to your liking. All of these settings can be configured in the Settings menu on the main screen. All of the game options, from screen resolution to special visual effects and

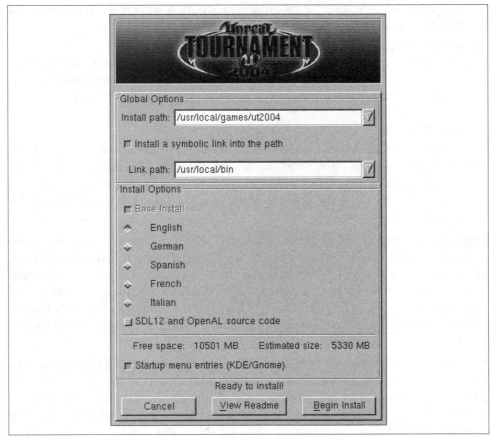

Figure 7-5. Primary UT2K4 install screen

your player's skin and name, can be configured here. Your options and saved games are then stored in the *~/.ut2004* directory. You can even tweak the text configuration files (they end in *.ini*) under *~/.ut2004/System/* by hand if you so choose.

UT2K4 has a variety of play options. The first is to play in single-player mode, which places you as the captain of a team of arena fighters you choose. Your team then moves up the ranks playing different types of team games:

Capture the Flag
> Like traditional capture the flag in other FPSs, your team attempts to penetrate the opposing team's base, grab its flag, and return it to your flag while preventing them from doing the same to you. You score points for each flag you capture.

Bombing Run
> This game is a bit like basketball. A ball is placed in the middle of the map, and each team has a goal on its side. Points are scored when a player picks up the

ball and fires it through the opposing team's goal. If you kill the player with the ball, the ball is dropped and you can pick it up.

Double Domination

A variant on capture the flag, in this game the map has two "domination points" that are initially set to neutral. The object is to run over both domination points, which sets them to your side, and keep both domination points set for 10 seconds to score.

Assault

This game operates with a series of rounds. Each round-one team takes the role of attacker and the other takes the role of defender. The attacker team has a series of goals to accomplish within a time limit, such as reaching a certain location on the map, and the defender team tries to stop them. Once the round is over, the roles reverse.

Single-player mode is useful to get acquainted with the different maps and game types, as the game slowly increases in difficulty. Your progress is saved at each point in the game, so you can pick up where you left off last time. If you want to get right to the action instead, try Instant Action. This lets you choose the type of game and map to play on, along with the number of bots and their difficulty. Instant Action is useful to hone skills on a certain map or to practice without applying wins or losses to your single-player record.

Be sure to become acquainted with each of the different weapons and their alternate firing modes. Also, some weapons offer combos, such as the shock rifle. Fire the alternate fire on the shock rifle to send a plasma charge, and then fire on that charge with the primary fire to create a large explosion that causes a great deal of damage (Figure 7-6). The most successful players are those who have mastered multiple weapons and can quickly switch between them as necessary.

If you are ready to play against others on the Internet or at a LAN party, click Join Game. You can then choose whether to search for LAN or Internet games, and UT2K4 will search and list all the available games. Joining in is as simple as selecting a game and clicking Join, but keep in mind that the lower your ping to a server, the more responsive game play will be.

Game Server

You can also host your own UT2K4 server as the Host Game option. This lets you configure your own game scenario much like with Instant Action, so you can choose maps, number of players, number of bots, and other settings, and then start your own custom server that others can join whether on the local LAN or on the Internet. Once you have configured your server, you can either click Listen or Dedicated to start the server. Listen starts the server and immediately connects you to it. Dedi-

Figure 7-6. UT2K4 shock combo

cated starts the server in the background and exits, which is ideal if you want to host a server but not play yourself. You can also start a dedicated server directly from the command line. Change to the *ut2004/System* directory, and then run ucc with the server argument, and then the name of the map to use:

```
# cd /usr/local/games/ut2004/System
# ./ucc server DOM-SunTemple
```

Another advantage to starting the server this way is that you can run servers on machines with no 3D acceleration or graphics support at all. All of the options you can change inside the GUI can be changed on the command line as well, and there are a number of tutorials on the Internet that cover the different command-line options. If you have configured previous Unreal Tournament servers, you will find that many of the options are the same in UT2K4.

Updates

If you intend on playing UT2K4 on the Internet, you will want to keep up with your patches. Sometimes patches fix more than bugs—they prevent cheats, so in that case you will need the latest patch to connect to a server. Patches are announced on the official Unreal Tournament site at *www.unrealtournament.com*, but check sites such as *www.icculus.org* and *www.linuxgames.com* for links to the Linux patches. Click Join Game and you will see your current version in the upper right-hand corner.

These patches come in .tar.bz2 format, and to apply them you will want to first extract the patch directory and then overwite your current files with the patched version:

```
# tar -xjf ut2004-lnxpatchversion.tar.bz2
# cd UT2004-Patch
# /bin/cp -a * /usr/local/games/ut2004/
```

Emulators

Modern games with detailed graphics, sophisticated soundtracks, and fast-paced network play are certainly fun, but sometimes you want to hearken back to a simpler time—a time with 8- or 16-bit graphics when arguably gameplay was more important than fancy graphics. Linux has a number of emulators so you can take a trip back to the days of plunking quarters into Pacman—only, as with Linux, the arcade is free. These emulators work from ROM images that have been extracted from the arcade or console game, and emulate the environment necessary for the ROM to function, so you can use your keyboard or even a joystick and play the games directly from your computer.

MAME

Probably the most famous and popular console emulator is MAME (Multiple Arcade Machine Emulator). The focus of the MAME project (*www.mame.net*) is to create an emulator for the various different arcade platforms that have been in use over the years. In this respect the MAME project is much more complicated than many of the other console emulation projects because it supports many different platforms. Currently MAME supports thousands of arcade titles and the list continues to grow. You can view the list of currently supported titles on *www.mame.net/gamelist.html*.

MAME was originally a project for the Windows platform only; however, a Linux port, called Xmame, has been created. Xmame is based directly on the MAME source code, with changes being made only when necessary to run under Linux. Because of this you can treat Xmame under Linux like MAME under Windows, and ROMS that work on one will work on the other.

Xmame is a popular program and should already be packaged for your particular distribution, but if it isn't you can download the latest source from the project's site at *x.mame.net*. There are a number of different display options for Xmame, and some distributions package the different display options separately:

X11

The standard Xmame display option is output to a window under X.

SVGAlib

Xmame can also use SVGAlib to display to the console, allowing you to use Xmame without running X.

GL

Xmame can output to an X11 display using OpenGL libraries to take advantage of hardware acceleration on your video card.

SDL

Xmame can also use SDL libraries for output under an X11 environment. Similar to the OpenGL libraries, SDL lets Xmame take advantage of hardware acceleration where available.

Glide

As with OpenGL, Xmame can use the Glide libraries for hardware acceleration both under X and with SVGAlib for 3DFX cards.

To start, you will want to use the X11 display method because it is the default and is most likely to work with your system. The first time, just run xmame from the command line without any arguments. Xmame will search */etc/xmame/xmamerc* for system-wide defaults and will create a local configuration directory under *~/.xmame*. Copy the */etc/xmame/xmamerc* file to *~/.xmame* so you can tweak settings specific to your user. This file contains all the different settings for Xmame, but the first setting you will probably want to change is rompath. This setting controls in what directory Xmame looks for ROMs, so if your user has a local folder for MAME ROMs, put it here and save the file. Now you will be able to play any game you have a ROM for simply by passing the name of the ROM as an argument to Xmame. ROMs generally come in .zip files that contain a number of different files the emulator needs all in one package. To play your *pacman.zip* ROM, you would simply run:

```
$ xmame pacman
```

on the command line (Figure 7-7).

Now that the game is running, what do you do? Xmame uses the same keybindings as the DOS version of MAME. Table 7-1 lists some of the primary key bindings you will find yourself using.

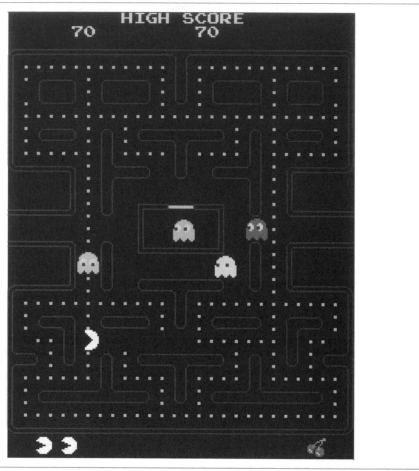

Figure 7-7. Xmame with Pacman

Table 7-1. Xmame key bindings

Key	Action
P	Pause the game
F3	Reset the game
F8	Reduce frame skip
F9	Increase frame skip (useful to speed up games on slower machines)
ESC	Exit emulator
left-Shift + Pgup	Increase scale (makes game larger for higher-resolution displays)
left-Shift + Pgdn	Decrease scale
left-Shift + Insert	Normal window
left-Shift + Home	DGA fullscreen mode

In addition, individual games have their own key bindings. These vary from game to game, but there are some standard key bindings most games use for common buttons (Table 7-2).

Table 7-2. Common button bindings

Key	Action
Arrow keys	Move left, right, up, and down
1	Select one player
2	Select two players
5	Insert a coin
Ctrl	Button 1
Alt	Button 2

Because some arcade games just have a joystick, and others have six or more buttons, the button mappings to a keyboard will sometimes vary. For basic games, Ctrl and Alt work as the first and second buttons but more complicated games will require some experimentation to discover the key bindings. By default, Xmame will play a game in its original resolution, so on a high-resolution computer screen you might want to increase the scale of the game once or twice with left-Shift and PageUp.

Xmame can use your mouse for applicable games as well. A good example of using a mouse in an arcade game is Centipede, which by default uses a large trackball mouse. You can either use your mouse or the arrow keys for movement.

Xmame also supports use of a joystick, although this isn't turned on by default. Either change the joytype option in your *xmamerc* file or pass -joytype *number* on the command line. The number corresponds to the type of joystick you use (Table 7-3).

Table 7-3. Joystick mapping

Number	Joystick type
0	No joystick
1	i386 joystick driver
2	Fm Town Pad support
3	X11 input extensions joystick
4	New i386 Linux joystick driver
5	NetBSD USB joystick driver
6	PS2-Linux native pad
7	SDL joystick driver

Nestra

Arcade games are incredibly fun, but there are some games that seem to only exist on certain game consoles, such as the original Nintendo Entertainment System (NES). As with the MAME project, there is software you can use to emulate the NES hardware and play ROMs directly on your computer. Under Linux, the software is Nestra.

Nestra will already be packaged for you depending on your distribution, but if it isn't, you can download and build the source directly from *nestra.linuxgames.com*. Once installed, using Nestra is as simple as running nestra with the path to the ROM you want to play as an argument. So, to play the original Metroid, you would type:

```
$ nestra Metroid.nes
```

See Figure 7-8.

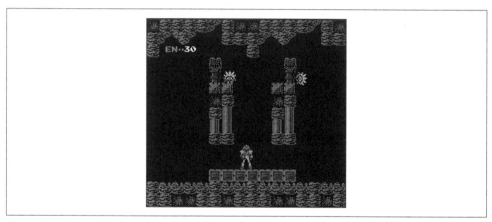

Figure 7-8. Metroid under Nestra

Nestra key bindings are the same across games and correspond to the standard NES controller (Table 7-4).

Table 7-4. Nestra key mappings

Key	Function
Arrow keys	Arrow pad
Spacebar	Button A
z, x	Button B
Enter	Start
Tab	Select
Pause, Break	Reset
Esc	Exit Nestra

Table 7-4. Nestra key mappings (continued)

Key	Function
1–9	Adjust the emulation speed. 1 is the normal speed, 2 is double speed, etc.
-	Run at half speed
0	Pause the emulator

Some games, such as Zelda, save games on the game cartridge itself. Since you are dealing with ROMs here, Nestra will place saved games in a file in the directory containing the ROM you are running, or will put the saved games in *~/.nestra* if the directory exists.

SNES9x

The NES definitely had a lot of fun games, and when the next generation of Nintendo's consoles was released—the Super Nintendo Entertainment System, or SNES —many of the classics, such as Super Mario Bros, Zelda, and Metroid, found their way onto the new platform. You can play all of your favorite SNES ROMs under Linux using the *Snes9x* program.

Snes9x is an SNES emulator that runs on Windows, Linux, Mac OSX, and other platforms. The Linux port is packaged by most distributions, or you can download and build the source from the official Snes9x page at *www.snes9x.com*.

Once installed, running Snes9x is similar to Nestra—simply type snes9x followed by the path to the SNES ROM as an argument. To run Zelda 3, for example, you would type

```
$ snes9x zelda3.smc
```

Unlike Nestra, Snes9x has a large number of options you can pass on the command line. For instance, the *-y* option enables "TV mode," which scales the image by two and inserts an extra blended pixel between each scan line. The end result of TV mode is a larger, easier-to-read screen that looks more like a regular television screen.

Snes9x uses a standard set of key bindings to correspond to the buttons on an SNES controller. The standard key bindings are shown in Table 7-5.

Table 7-5. Snes9x key mappings

Key	Function
Escape	Quit the emulator
Pause, Scroll Lock	Pause the emulator
Up arrow, u	Up direction
Down arrow, j, n	Down direction
Left arrow, h	Left direction
Right arrow, k	Right direction

Table 7-5. Snes9x key mappings (continued)

Key	Function
a, v, q	TL button
z, b, w	TR button
s, m, e	X button
x, ',', r	Y button
d, '.', t	A button
c, y	B button
Enter	Start button
Spacebar	Select button
Shift F1–F9	Save the game in one of nine different slots
F1–F9	Restore the saved game in the specified slot

Snes9x has support for joysticks, and by default will scan for */dev/js0*, or you can specify the joystick device to use with the *-joydev1* argument. You can also control the mapping for the eight different SNES buttons with the *-joymap1* and *-joymap2* options (for joystick 1 and joystick 2, respectively) followed by the eight different buttons in order. For instance, the default is 0 1 2 3 4 5 6 7, which corresponds to A B X Y TL TR Start Select.

There are so many different options to Snes9x, in fact, that a couple of graphical frontends have been created to make the process of configuring Snes9x easier. Snes9express is an easy-to-use frontend that makes it easy to organize your SNES ROMs and experiment with different settings. You can download the latest version from *www.linuxgames.com/snes9express* or use the package that comes with your distribution. Snes9express supports skinning and even includes a skin that makes it look like the original SNES console (Figure 7-9).

Click Console → Preferences and give *snes9express* the path to your SNES ROM directory, and then you can click the ROM Selector button for a window to pop up with a full list of available games to run. Select the game you want to play and then click Power to start. The Snes9express window will disappear while the game is running, and reappear once you exit the game.

To change Snes9x settings from within Snes9express, click on the different settings tabs in the the main window. Sound, video, controller, and other settings can be configured in these tabs and the GUI makes it easy to toggle an option, or to change your joystick settings quickly.

Frozen Bubble

Some of the most fun games, the games that have the highest replay value, are often the simplest ones. Frozen Bubble is a puzzle game similar to Puzzle Bobble or Bust-a-

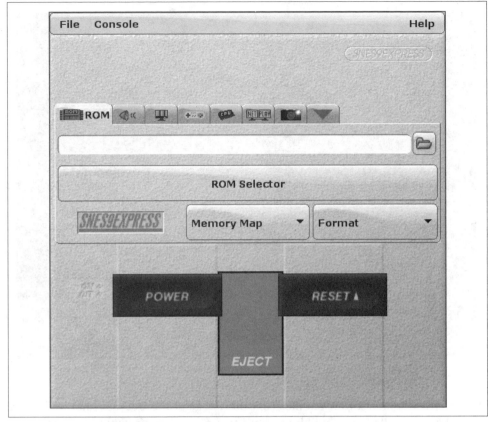

Figure 7-9. Snes9express

Move. The object of Frozen Bubble is to remove all of the different colored bubbles that are arranged on the top of the screen (Figure 7-10). Your player is given a single colored bubble, and you aim from the bottom of the screen and attempt to hit a bubble at the top of the screen that has a matching color. If you hit a bubble with a matching color, it and all of the bubbles connected below it will disappear. If you don't hit a match, your bubble becomes another bubble to eliminate. You beat a level by eliminating all of the bubbles from the level. If you don't remove bubbles fast enough, the board shifts down closer to the bottom. Once a bubble hits the bottom of the board, you lose.

Frozen Bubble is a common game and should be packaged by your distribution. Otherwise, you can download and compile the source from the official site at *www.frozen-bubble.org*. Start Frozen Bubble from a menu or type `frozen-bubble` on the command line. You can choose one- or two-player games, and can even create your own levels from the included level editor.

The single-player game pits you against the clock. The controls are basic and easy to pick up. Left and right arrows adjust your aim to the left and right, respectively, and

Figure 7-10. Frozen Bubble

the up arrow launches your bubble. Take advantage of the fact that bubbles bounce from the side walls to get bubbles to hard-to-reach places. If your aim is good you can sometimes complete a level with a single well-placed bubble.

The double-player games pits you head-to-head against another player (Figure 7-11). Both players use the keyboard, so player 1 aims left with X, right with V, and launches with the C key. The second player uses the standard arrow keys. In two-player mode both players are playing side by side at the same time with their own puzzle. The first player to complete the level wins that round.

The included level editor allows you to customize your own levels so you can arrange the number, color, and location of bubbles however you choose. Right-click on a bubble to remove it, and click on the colored bubbles on the side of the screen to choose the color to use. You can change any of the 100 included levels with the level editor.

Tux Racer

What would a chapter on Linux games be without a game featuring the Linux mascot Tux? Tux Racer is a 3D racing game, but instead of a car or other vehicle, you

RedBrazil.com

www.redbrazil.com

FREE SHIPPING*

LOW NEW BOOK PRICES
Fast Google Checkout, PayPal or Secure Pay
A Real Alternative to Amazon

- Over One Million Fiction and Nonfiction Book and Audio Book Titles Available
- Specializing in New Computer and Business Books
- Red-hot Discounts on Select Best-selling Computer Books from O'Reilly Press
- *Free shipping <u>in the USA</u> when you order three or more books

If you have been pleased with the products you have received from Auriga Distribution Services, you may want to visit our sister company www.redbrazil.com for all your new book needs. We feature some of the lowest prices on the web for new books, audio books and O'Reilly Media titles. We feature the same excellent service you have come to expect from Auriga.

We pack your new books with the care they deserve. Each book is packed in its own sturdy box OR double packed in two bubble wrap envelopes and shipped promptly and efficiently from our state-of-the-art facilities.

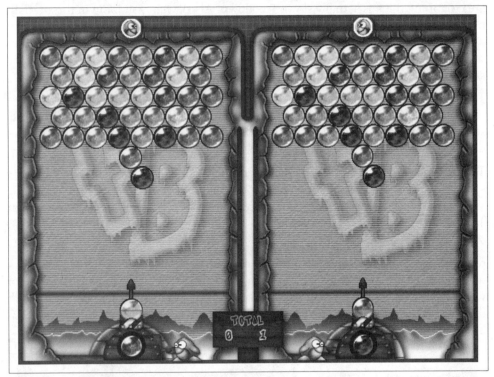

Figure 7-11. Frozen Bubble two-player mode

race Tux the penguin down an ice hill on his stomach. Success depends on how quickly you complete the race and the number of herrings you eat along the way.

Tux Racer began as a completely open source project up through Version 0.61. With the increased success and improvements to the game, Tux Racer 1.0 was released as a boxed commercial product from Sunspire Studios. Although you could purchase Tux Racer 1.0 from the official site at *www.tuxracer.com*, the open source 0.61 release was still available for download at *tuxracer.sourceforge.net*. This release is what is commonly included with most distributions.

Start Tux Racer either through your menu or by typing tuxracer on the command line. The opening menu gives you the option to enter an event or practice. The events are a series of races, and each race requires that you complete the previous races to advance. As you select from the available races, you can see the maximum time and number of herrings needed to advance. If either of those requirements aren't met, you will have to try the race again.

The controls in Tux Racer are fairly simple to learn, but the finer points of controlling Tux can take time to master. The left and right arrow keys steer Tux through the race. The up arrow causes Tux to flap his fins, which does different things depending on where you are in a race. If you are moving slowly (particularly when you start a race), flap the fins to increase Tux's speed. Once your speed reaches the yellow area, flapping the fins actually slows Tux down. Also, when you jump in the air, flapping his fins allows Tux to stay in the air longer, and lets you adjust his direction while flying. The down arrow serves as a brake and slows Tux down. You can combine the down arrow with the left and right arrows to perform a hard turn in the game.

Tux can also jump in the game with the E key. Holding down this key charges Tux's "Energometer"; the fuller the Energometer, the higher Tux will jump. If Tux gets stuck in some area of the map, you can use the Backspace key to reset Tux's position, or, if you want to completely give up, you can press the Q key to quit.

Tux Racer saves its files in the *~/.tuxracer* directory. You can edit Tux Racer options such as whether to run in full-screen mode, by editing the *~/.tuxracer/options* file. You can also use the options file to change the keyboard and joystick bindings that Tux Racer uses.

The practice levels provide quick access to the different levels in Tux Racer without requiring you to beat any levels or even meet any requirements. This lets you pick out your favorite level and play a quick game without worrying about the time or whether you picked up enough herring. A favorite is the "Who said penguins can't fly" level, which is designed like a bobsled run to get Tux moving as quickly as possible (Figure 7-12).

Figure 7-12. Who said penguins can't fly?

There are some strategies that you can use to get better times in the races. For one, not all surfaces are the same to Tux's stomach. The fastest surface is the slick ice, the second fastest is the snow, and the slowest is the rough ground. The latter will actually slow you down when you slide over it, so try to avoid it. Also, be sure to flap Tux's fins only when you are below the yellow line in speed; otherwise, you will be slowed down. You can also pick up a great deal of speed by flying through the air. You can use angled sections of the race track as ramps to propel Tux through the air. Upon his descent Tux picks up a great deal of speed and also avoids obstacles on the track that might slow him down. Of course, keep in mind that flying too much might mean missing valuable herring you need to pick up along the course.

## CHAPTER 8

Office Suites and Personal Productivity

Linux has come a long way since the early days. When people started to use Linux not just for tinkering with the system, but rather in order to get actual work done, various kinds of servers such as email or web servers were the normally used applications. Typical desktop and personal productivity applications such as word processors, spreadsheets, or collaboration tools were mostly unknown on Linux.

This situation has changed fundamentally. A variety of office suites and other personal productivity applications are available, and this chapter describes some of the options. The focus is on OpenOffice, probably the most feature-complete office suite available for Linux today, but we also talk about other options, as well as collaboration tools.

Using OpenOffice

By now, OpenOffice has become the leading full-function free and open source office suite program for GNU/Linux and is included by default on most distributions, including SUSE, Red Hat, Debian, and others.

This should not take credit away from the other free and open source office suite development projects—KOffice and AbiWord come quickest to mind—but OpenOffice gains the stage here due to the relative maturity of its code base and the elegance of its native open XML file format (which even KOffice has) as well as the suite's ability to run on Windows and its compatibility with the popular proprietary file formats.

"OpenOffice" Versus "OpenOffice.org"

Certain conventions of language used in this chapter would be confusing if they are not highlighted. The term "OpenOffice," or its abbreviated form "OOo," typically refers to the software, the code, the product, the office suite itself. In referring to the development project, the terms "OpenOffice.org" or "OOo project" or "OpenOffice.org development project" apply exclusively. To make things even more confusing, there is also StarOffice, which is based on the same code base, but sold by Sun Microsystems as a commercial product.

The Modules of OpenOffice

One among several hallmarks of OOo is the tight integration of its word processor, spreadsheet, and all other modules, which leads to a strong consistency in features, menu placement, and ease of use. The OpenOffice modules are listed in Table 8-1.

Table 8-1. The modules of OpenOffice

Module name	Function	Label under File → New
OOoWriter	Word processor	Text Document
OOoCalc	Spreadsheet program	Spreadsheet
OOoImpress	Presentation editor	Presentation
OOoDraw	Graphics editor	Drawing
OOoHTML	Web (HTML) editor	HTML Document
OOoMath	Math formulas editor	Formula

We cover OOoWriter, OOoCalc, and OOoImpress in this chapter, omitting the remaining modules because they are less frequently used and their features and functions are well supported in the leading reference texts and online documentation for the users who still depend upon them.

OpenDocument and OpenOffice 2

This section of the book was written for OpenOffice 1.1 and therefore will be most helpful to users of Versions 1.1.1 through 1.1.5. By the time of publication, however, the OpenOffice.org development project will have released OpenOffice Version 2 worldwide.

Generally, OpenOffice 2 looks and feels more like the modern versions of Microsoft Office. This should help smooth transitions to the open source office suite, on both Linux and other platforms.

The most significant development in Version 2 is the new native file format, called "OASIS OpenDocument." This has already been widely embraced by technologists and government IT organizations (a web search for "Massachusetts" and "OpenDocument" offers a revealing start).

OpenDocument is an open XML file format, represented in OpenOffice 2 by the new filename extensions *.odt* for a text file, *.ods* for a spreadsheet, and *.odp* for a presentation file, among others. (Version 1 uses the filename extensions *.sxw*, *.sxc*, and *.sxi*, respectively.) OpenDocument is an upgrade of the same OASIS-based open XML file format used in Version 1; however, OpenDocument has some additional capabilities that make it incompatible with the earlier iteration of the format.

Accordingly, OpenOffice software prior to 1.1.5 cannot open or create files in the OpenDocument file format, and therefore cannot handle files created by users of OpenOffice 2. However, OpenOffice.org put the OpenDocument filters into Version 1.1.5 so that users of the 1.1 version can easily upgrade to a version that works the way they are familiar with and still open the new OpenDocument files. Users of Version 1.1 or earlier will need to upgrade to OpenOffice 2 in order to gain all the latest functionality and be able to create OpenDocument files themselves.

OpenOffice Writer

OpenOffice Writer (also known as OOoWriter) is the word processor module included as one of six key components of OpenOffice. By now, OOoWriter is designed to be familiar to users of Microsoft Word.

Launching OOoWriter

Configuration of the Launch or Start menu may vary across the Linux distributions. On the Java Desktop System, for example, starting OOoWriter from the Launch menu brings up the Templates and Documents—New Document window, where you can select the New Document icon in the left-hand index, then Text Document from the list in the central pane.

You can launch OOoWriter directly if you have created a dedicated Launcher icon on the desktop, taskbar panel, or both. Create a Launcher icon for any module of OpenOffice that you use frequently.

Keep in mind, you may launch any alternative module from within any open module of OpenOffice: on the main menu, select File → New → [module].

Opening files

To open an OOoWriter or MS Word file, either open the directory where the file is located and double-click on the file's icon or select File → Open on the main menu. Then, in the Open window, browse to the appropriate folder, highlight the filename and select the Open button.

Note that MS Office files—those in the *.doc* format—open in OpenOffice in the same way a native OpenOffice document opens. You can edit the MS Office document and save it either in its own format or in OpenOffice's native format. See Table 8-2 for a complete list of file formats available for saving.

Saving files

After editing a document, select File → Save. A new file will be saved to the user's /home/[user]/Documents directory by default. You can also save a file to its current directory or the default directory with one click of the Save Document icon on the function bar.

For information about the function bar, see "Identifying the toolbars" later in this chapter and Figure 8-2.

If you need to select a different target directory or change the filename or file type, select File → Save As. The Save As window then appears, and you can make the appropriate selections and click the Save button. This window is explored further in the following section.

Saving as different file types. If you open an existing document, it is saved by default in its original format. To save as a different file format, select File → Save As to open the Save As window. Here you can make the appropriate selections in the File Type drop-down menu, then click the Save button. The file types available in the File Type drop-down are listed in Table 8-2.

Table 8-2. Save files in many formats or file types

File format	File extension (suffix)
OpenOffice 6.0/7 Text Document	.sxw
OpenOffice 6.0/7 Text Document Template	.stw
MS Word 97/2000/XP	.doc
MS Word 95	.doc
MS Word 6.0	.doc
Adobe PDF	.pdf
Rich Text Format	.rtf
OOoWriter 5.0	.sdw
OOoWriter 5.0 Template	.vor
OOoWriter 4.0	.sdw
OOoWriter 4.0 Template	.vor
OOoWriter 3.0	.sdw
OOoWriter 3.0 Template	.vor
Text	.txt
Text Encoded	.txt
HTML Document (OpenOffice Writer)	.html;. htm
AportisDoc (Palm)	.pdb
DocBook (simplified)	.xml
Pocket Word	.psw

Note that you can save a native OOo text document file (with the *.sxw* extension) as several different versions of the legacy MS Office file types as well as in other standard formats, including the web page format of HTML.

You will be warned about a possible loss of formatting when saving to a format other than the native file format. That is, of course, because OOoWriter may support features that other word processors (and therefore their file formats) do not support. So if you want to be absolutely sure that you do not lose any formatting, macros, or other aspects of your documents at all, always save in the native file format, or at least keep a copy in the native file format.

Saving or exporting to common file formats. OpenOffice facilitates saving files in several different file types, including some very useful document standards such as PDF. By choosing the format in which you save a document, you can ensure that your work is viewable and editable in different software environments, such as Windows, Mac, Solaris, and others.

Saving in the MS Word file formats. Chose File → Save As from the main menu. In the Save As window, open the File Type drop-down menu and select the desired MS Office file format version. Choices include the following:

- Microsoft Word 97/2000/XP (.doc)
- Microsoft Word 95 (.doc)
- Microsoft Word 6.0 (.doc)

Exporting and sending files

There are occasions when it's convenient to quickly send a document in its current form to a colleague. OOo offers a few menu items to help you attach the current document to an email message in a choice of formats.

Export as Adobe PDF. In your current document, click the small, red Export to PDF icon on the menu, and the Export window will open with File Type preselected to Adobe PDF. Notice in Figure 8-1 that the Export window is similar to the Save As window.

Enter the filename, choose a folder in which to save the new PDF file, and press the Save button.

You can achieve the same result by selecting File → Export as PDF and filling out the Export window as instructed previously.

PDF is a great format for GNU/Linux users to get into the habit of using often. In a world of mixed computer systems, PDF is one of the most universally accepted file formats, and the security of locking down the content of your files as they get passed

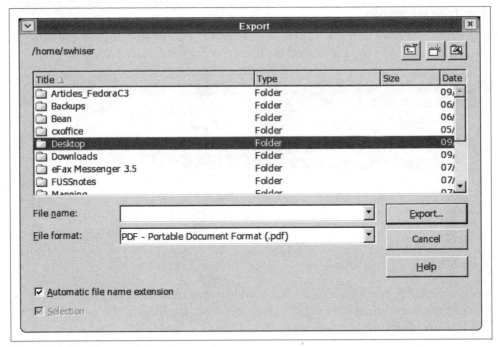

Figure 8-1. The Export window

around your organization and supply chain can reduce the chances of unhappy, confusing or surprising content alterations.

Sending a document as an email file attachment. OOoWriter offers a host of facilities for exporting or sending the current document to others through one or two mouse-clicks. To send the current document as an attachment to an email, select File → Send → Document as Email. This will call up your email program along with a new Compose window with the current OOoWriter document already attached. Fill in the address and subject lines as fitting, perhaps add a few words in the message window, and press the Send button.

This feature automatically sends the attached file in the native or default OpenOffice open XML (*.sxw*) file format.

Sending a document as a PDF attachment to an email. To send the current document as an Adobe PDF attachment to an email, select File → Send → Document as PDF Attachment. The PDF Options window appears and lets you select a page range or the whole document, and the amount of file compression. The default compression setting, Print optimized, is fine for most purposes.

Identifying the toolbars

The default toolbars of OOoWriter—to which we refer often—are the main menu, the function bar, the object bar, and the main toolbar (see Figure 8-2).

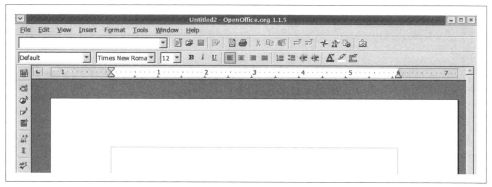

Figure 8-2. The toolbars of OOoWriter

These are merely the default toolbars available out of the box. Other toolbars can be invoked with customization. We cover toolbar customization in the section entitled "OOoWriter Customization," later in this chapter.

Basic formatting

This section covers basic formatting techniques for short and simple documents.

One-click character formatting. The text formatting buttons located on the object bar for bold, italic, and underline hardly need to be covered, because even beginning users know their purpose instinctively.

In addition to these one-click font-change object bar buttons, many people enjoy using the shortcut keystroke combinations Ctrl-B, Ctrl-I, or Ctrl-U to effect the same changes on any selected text. These changes affect any word in which the cursor sits, so text selection (using the Shift key and moving the cursor, or selecting text with the mouse) is not necessary unless you are changing multiple words of text.

Character, paragraph, and page formatting. For more customized or fine-grained formatting of textual characters, whole paragraphs, or entire pages, select Format on the main menu. The sequences Format → Character, Format → Paragraph, and Format → Page open the Character dialog, the Paragraph dialog, and the Page Style: Default dialog, respectively.

Inserting headers and footers. To insert a header, go to the main menu, select Insert → Header, and check Default in the drop-down menu. This opens a header frame in the current document where you can type or enter the appropriate content that will appear at the top of every page of the document.

Inserting a footer is similar to inserting a header, but select Insert → Footers, and check Default.

To change headers or footers in the middle of a document, see "Changing styles in mid-document," later in this chapter.

Page numbering. For most documents it's appropriate to place page numbers in a header or footer. To generate page numbers automatically, insert a header or footer (depending on where you intend the page number to go, at either the top or bottom of each page) and place the cursor inside the live header or footer frame by clicking once there. Then go to the main menu and select Insert → Fields. This invokes a drop-down menu with the following choices: Date, Time, Page Number, Page Count, Subject, Title, Author, and Other.

Selecting the Page Number choice inserts the page number automatically at the location of the cursor. If you wish the page number to be located flush right, simply click the Align Right justification icon on the object bar after inserting the page number.

To change or restart page numbering at a certain point in a document, see the section "Changing styles in mid-document."

Generating a table of contents. For a longer written work that is structured with chapters or headings, it is convenient to exploit OOoWriter's ability to autogenerate a table of contents. This feature is often used because manually generating tables and indexes is extremely time-consuming and repetitive—especially for larger documents.

To generate a table of contents that picks up the headings you've inserted into your document, choose Insert → Indexes and Tables and then, from the drop-down menu, Indexes and Tables once again. You can then insert a generic table of contents simply by pressing the OK button of the Insert Index/Tables window, as shown in Figure 8-3.

You can generate a number of different kinds of indexes and tables; the choices include Table of Contents, Alphabetical Index, Illustration Index, Index of Tables, User-Defined, Table of Objects, and Bibliography. Format these indexes and tables from the Insert Index/Table dialog, where you can designate the type of index or table, its layout, the number of heading levels, and other design characteristics.

Printing a document

Print the current document in one stroke by simply clicking the printer icon on the function bar.

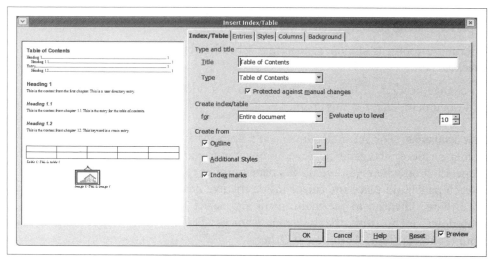

Figure 8-3. The Insert Index/Table window

More precise control is gained via the Print window: select File → Print from the main menu, or simply press Ctrl-P. Here, you can choose a nondefault printer (if one is set up), a limited page range, or a different number of copies (the default is 1) for the current print job. You can also elect to print to a file.

Advanced formatting

Although the following sections introduce the strong formatting features of templates and styles below, other advanced formatting features are outside the scope of this chapter. It may help just the same to mention some of the useful features we're unable to cover.

Long-form documents benefit from frames, borders, and sections. These facilities help you format sidebars, set apart quotations, or highlight elements you wish to distinguish from the running text. They provide opportunities for adding colored or shaded backgrounds, changing fonts, and using multiple columns. Text contained in frames can even be set to flow through multiple frames inserted throughout a document. This is especially useful in formatting newsletters, for example, and making them more visually engaging.

Templates

A variety of stock templates and a facility for creating, editing, importing, and managing templates are included with OOoWriter. You can access templates by clicking File → New → Templates and Documents to open the Templates and Documents window. Then highlight the Templates icon on the left-hand index, as shown in Figure 8-4.

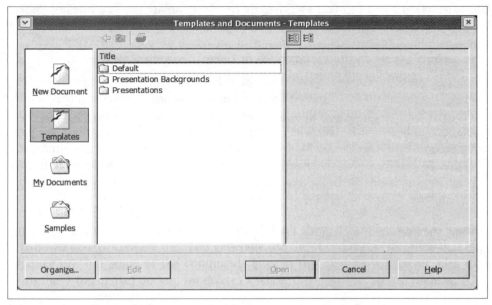

Figure 8-4. Templates and Documents—Templates

Here you can open one of the various stock templates and work away: edit and save it just as you would a normal document. Documents created this way, however, will not be linked to the template file from which they were derived. See "Template linkages," later in this chapter, for further detail.

Saving your own document as a template. Any of the documents you've created in your filesystem can perform as a template. Quite often users repurpose old files such as office memoranda, fax cover sheets, or business letters and use them to create new documents by simply replacing a few key words. This practice is fine and works well for many people; however, users could be more productive if they took full advantage of OOoWriter's template management facilities and particularly its linkage abilities.

Creating a new template. To create a new template, open a new text document (or use an existing document from your file store) and make the necessary formatting adjustments that you'd like to have in your template. Now, select File → Templates → Save from the main menu. This calls up the Templates window, which permits you to name the new template and select a template folder or category in which to store it. You can create any number of your own personal templates and store them this way.

Files saved as templates this way will automatically have the *.stw* file extension appended.

Editing templates. You can edit or generally treat a template file just like any other; however, we recommend editing a template with special care, because it can be easy to open a template file and then save it by mistake as a normal OOoWriter *.sxw* file, which would interfere with the template's linkages and storage location.

One direct way to edit a template is to select File → New → Templates and Documents. This opens up the Templates and Documents window directly in the Default folder. Click through the Templates folders to find the template you wish to edit. Click once to highlight it. This will light up the Edit button at the bottom of the window, second from the left. Clicking the Edit button will open your template, ready for edits. When you save via this route, the proper directory path and file format appear automatically in the Save dialog, so there's less opportunity to mishandle your template.

Managing templates. You can also save any of your own documents as a template or, later, move them into one of the Templates folders/categories using the Template Manager (Figure 8-5). Access the Template Manager from the main menu by selecting File → Templates → Organize.

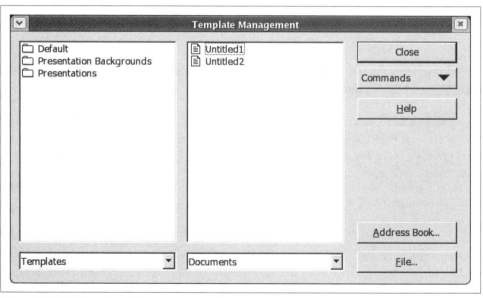

Figure 8-5. The Template Management window

You can browse documents in the right-hand pane of the Template Manager and drop them into folders in the templates pane on the left-hand side.

Template Manager also offers facilities for importing, updating, and adjusting the printer settings associated with templates.

Importing templates. The template files you encounter in the Template Management window's Default folder are actually stored in the */home/swhiser/OpenOffice. org/user/template* directory on the system. The templates you encounter in all the other Template Management folders are actually stored in the */home/swhiser/ OpenOffice.org/share/template/english* directory. (This allows individual users in a multiuser installation of OpenOffice to change their own default master templates without affecting other users on the network.)

To import template files from MS Word or from any trusted outside sources (including useful ones you find on the Web), you can manually copy the templates into the directories just discussed, and they will show up in the folders you expect in the Template Management window. Templates copied in this way will also be available when you use the AutoPilot to create documents from templates.

You can also use the Import Templates feature in the Templates Management window to get external templates into the correct place and into the proper file format (*.stw*). This ensures that templates and the files derived from them maintain their linkages (see the following section).

A third way to import a template is to select File → Save As, choose "OpenOffice.org Text Document Template (.stw)" as the File Type, and set the path to the appropriate one of the two directories mentioned previously.

Template linkages. Template files are linked to the documents that are derived from those templates. It helps to imagine the template file, or the source file, as the "parent," and the derived document as the "child." Parent-to-child linkage is one of the principal benefits of using templates. When you have a large number of child documents in your Documents folder, for example, you have the ability to update the formatting of all those files in one stroke by altering the formatting of the parent template file. Each time you open a child document, you are prompted to accept or reject the formatting alterations that were previously made to the source template, as illustrated in Figure 8-6.

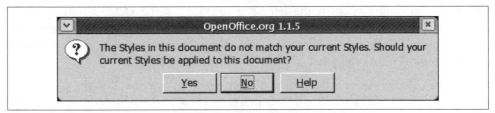

Figure 8-6. Accept the formatting changes to a subdocument

Linkage is broken, however, if you later save the source template file via File → Save As or via the Save icon on the object bar. Thus you should always save a template file via File → Templates → Save if you wish it to remain linked to its children or to keep using it as a template.

Change the default template for all new text documents. As mentioned earlier, the standard blank document that opens up when you select File → New → Text Document from the main menu is based on a default template file that is saved in the Templates and Documents—New Document window (Figure 8-7).

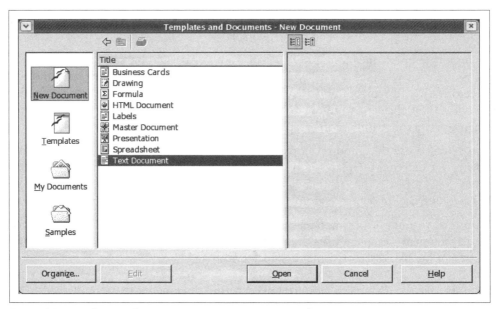

Figure 8-7. Templates and Documents—New Document window

To change the default template for all new text documents, first create a new template with the desired formatting (and add custom styles if desired) as described earlier in "Creating a new template." Save it by selecting File → Templates → Save, enter the filename (let's call it *newdefault*), and click once on Default in the Categories pane at the left to save it in that folder.

Then, go into the Template Management window by selecting File → Templates → Organize and double-click in the left pane to open up the Default folder, where you'll find your new template file, *newdefault*. Click once upon it to highlight *newdefault*, and click on the Command button at the far right to view the drop-down choices. Select "Set As Default Template" at the bottom of the list.

To restore the original text document default template, simply click the Command button once again and select Reset Default Template → Text Document.

AutoPilot: quick document creation. AutoPilot is like templates on steroids. It offers a way of creating customized documents that are much like templates, but it is a wizard that takes you through a few steps to customize the new document rapidly before launching it. AutoPilot is therefore a useful tool for first-time users who wish to get up and running in OOoWriter quickly.

Access AutoPilot via File → AutoPilot, where you'll see a drop-down menu, as shown in Figure 8-8.

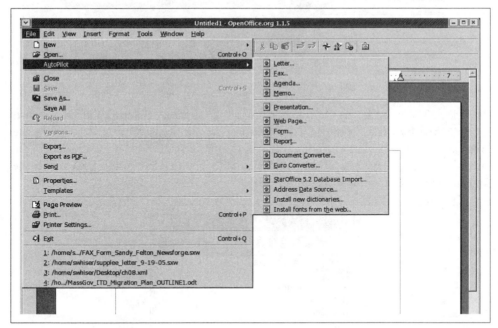

Figure 8-8. The AutoPilot

AutoPilot is a wizard that takes you through various steps to create an individual document from a generous list of different document types, including letters, faxes, agendas, memos, presentations, web pages, forms, and reports.

AutoPilot also contains several different utilities to manage document or content conversion: Document Converter, Euro Converter, StarOffice5.2 Database Import, and Address Data Source.

Styles

If you work with many people and want them all to make documents that look the same, you definitely need styles. Put another way, any formatting you can apply to text can be turned almost as quickly into a style, which you can then apply over and over through a couple of clicks.

Figure 8-9 shows the button on the function bar (third from right, highlighted) with which you can quickly open the Stylist in order to begin manipulating styles. Alternatively, open the Stylist by pressing the function key, F11.

Once open, the Stylist lets you toggle among the five different style types or style categories: paragraph styles, character styles, frame styles, page styles, and numbering styles. To switch from one style category to another, simply click the corresponding icon at the top left of the Stylist's toolbar.

Figure 8-9. The Stylist On/Off button

The Stylist. The interface to OOoWriter's Styles is a floating palette called the Stylist. It is invoked by pressing the function key F11 or the Stylist On/Off button on the function bar. The Stylist On/Off button looks like a page with a tiny hand on the lower-left corner. The default state of Stylist is to open in Paragraph Styles with the Automatic mode, as shown in Figure 8-10.

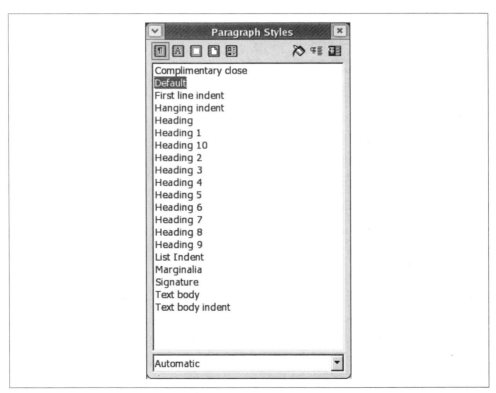

Figure 8-10. The Stylist opens to Paragraph Styles

Clicking through the icons on the Stylist's toolbar, you begin to get a feel for the different styles that come with OOoWriter out of the box.

Applying a character style. To apply character styles in the Stylist, click on the Character Styles icon (second from left, showing an A) at the top of the Stylist. This reveals all the default character styles available (the window is in All mode by default).

To apply an italics style, for example, highlight the "Emphasis" character style (fifth from the top of the list by default) with a single click and then click once on the paint can icon, which is third from right at the top of the Stylist (Figure 8-11).

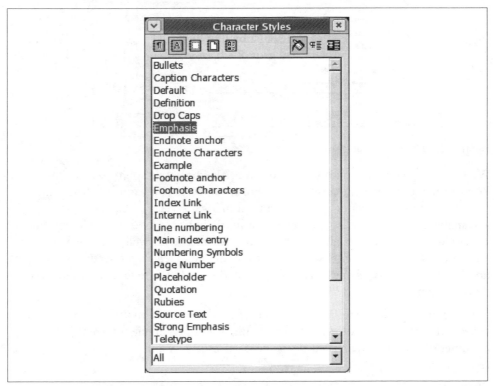

Figure 8-11. The Stylist, ready to paint italics

When you invoke the paint can, your cursor turns into a little paint can tool that makes it easy to apply your chosen style with precision. Click on a word you wish to italicize, or draw the paint can cursor across some text. The paint can now gives you a Midas touch that italicizes everything on which you click. You can turn off the style by pressing F11, clicking on the X icon at the top right of the Stylist box, or choosing a different style.

Modifying styles. To modify a style, press CtrlF11 to bring up the Style Catalog. The resulting window is shown in Figure 8-12. You can also invoke the Style Catalog from the main menu by selecting Format → Styles → Catalog.

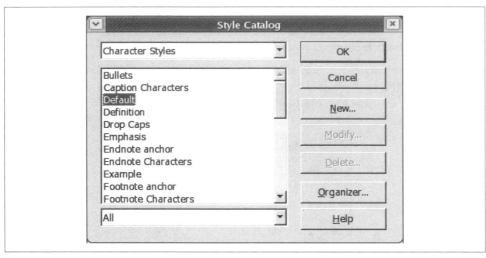

Figure 8-12. The Style Catalog

We've already shown you how to change a particular paragraph or set of characters. You can make similar changes to styles. For instance, if you want list items indented differently from the default indentation used in a list style, you can edit the list style and make it indent each list the way you want. When you modify a style, it immediately takes effect on all existing items in the document, as well as items you create afterward. This section shows you how to modify a style; a later section shows you how to create an entirely new style so you can do things the inventors of OOoWriter didn't anticipate.

Quick-flowing styles modification is one of the key productivity benefits for using styles rather than manual or direct formatting. It permits efficient formatting of large documents for work that is likely to be used by many different people or reused repeatedly.

The Style Catalog displays different styles depending on the style existing at the cursor's current location. This can be very convenient; if you wish to modify a certain style throughout an entire document, just place the cursor on one example of that style and proceed to modify it.

With the Style Catalog open, highlight the style you wish to alter and click the Modify button at the right of the Style Catalog window. This opens the Style Settings window for the highlighted style (in Figure 8-12 this is Default). The Style Settings window is shown in Figure 8-13: here you can change any characteristic that is available for modification.

An alternate way to modify a style is to right-click on the style in the Stylist and choose from New, Modify, or Delete. When you click Modify, the Style Settings window opens and you can make the desired changes.

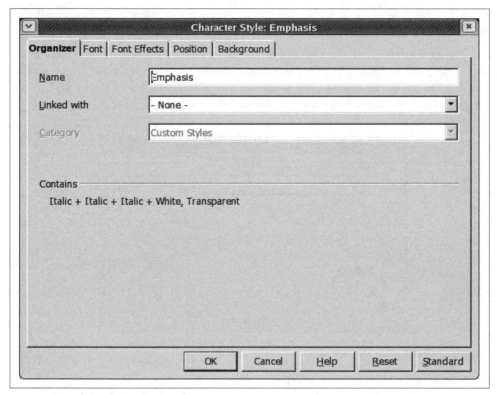

Figure 8-13. The Style Settings window

Updating styles. Short of creating a whole new style from scratch, you can quickly change an existing style by applying the format of a selected character, paragraph, or page.

To update a particular style, press the function key F11 to open the Stylist. Next, click the icon of the style type you want to update: paragraph, character, or page. Then, click once in the document in the place where you want to copy or update the style. For example, you may be "borrowing" paragraph formatting that you had previously applied manually. Next, in the Stylist, click on the style name you wish to update. Finally, click the Update Style icon at the far right of the Stylist toolbar.

Adding new styles (or creating styles). Although OOoWriter comes with many predefined styles, advanced situations will inevitably need *new* styles to be added. These styles are also known as custom styles, and they travel with the document with which they were created when it is saved.

To add a new style to the Stylist, first open the Stylist by pressing F11. Next, pick a style type and highlight an existing style in the Stylist that's similar to the new one you wish to create (if such a style exists). Right-click that style and select New. This opens the Style Settings window (shown in Figure 8-13). Here you can set all the characteristics you want for the new style, including its category.

There are two alternative ways to add a new style. One is by clicking the "New Style from Selection" button, which is the second button from the right at the top of the Stylist. This opens the Create Style window, where you can choose a new style from the given list and enter a name for the new style, as shown in Figure 8-14.

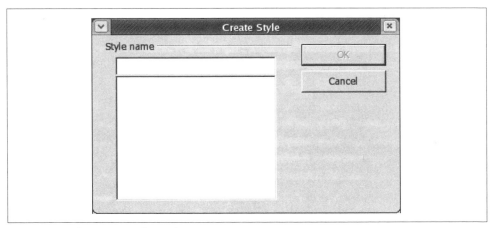

Figure 8-14. The Create Style window

Perhaps the best way to create a style that doesn't closely resemble any existing style is to press Ctrl-F11 to open the Style Catalog. Then click the New button on the right side. This opens the Style Settings window, where you can make all the desired selections to create your new style.

Changing styles in mid-document. To change page styles, headers, and footers, or to restart page numbering in mid-document, generally insert a manual break where the cursor sits by selecting Insert → Break from the main menu. The Insert Break dialog offers you the opportunity to select a new page style or to change the page number. Headers and footers can be changed at this point by creating new page styles with different header and footer content and invoking these new page styles when inserting the break.

Load (transfer) styles. You can transfer styles into the current document from another document or template by selecting Format → Styles → Load from the main menu. This calls up the Load Styles window, shown in Figure 8-15. Here you can specify a file containing the styles you want, and load any or all of these styles by checking the desired boxes along the bottom of the window.

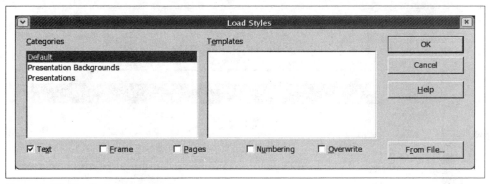

Figure 8-15. The Styles Load window

Collaboration with documents

When several people create and edit a document together by passing the draft around, it becomes useful to turn on changes tracking. This allows each person's changes and deletions to appear in a different color while the document circulates for drafting.

Changes tracking. To turn on Changes Tracking, select Edit → Changes from the main menu and single-click both Record and Show. Once turned on, these settings travel with the document when it is saved, and will stay on until someone un-checks them and saves the document again.

Comparing documents. To compare two different documents, open the first document and select Edit → Compare Document. This opens the Insert dialog, where you can select or type in the name of the second document. Click the Insert button at the bottom right of the window. The insert procedure merges the two documents and shows the results using the changes tracking feature, as if you had started with the second document and edited it to create the first. Typical results are shown in Figure 8-16.

Version control. OOoWriter's version control features allow you to keep track of numerous versions of a document from within a single file. This both saves disk storage space and provides ready and quick access to older versions of a document. Thus, if you make edits that you later regret, you can back them out. If somebody asks when a change was made, you can review earlier versions of the document.

Version control is accessed via the main menu under File → Versions. This launches the Versions window (see Figure 8-17).

To save a new version of a document on which you're working, choose File → Versions from the main menu and click the Save New Version button at the top left in the Versions window. The Insert Version Comment window (Figure 8-18) pops up,

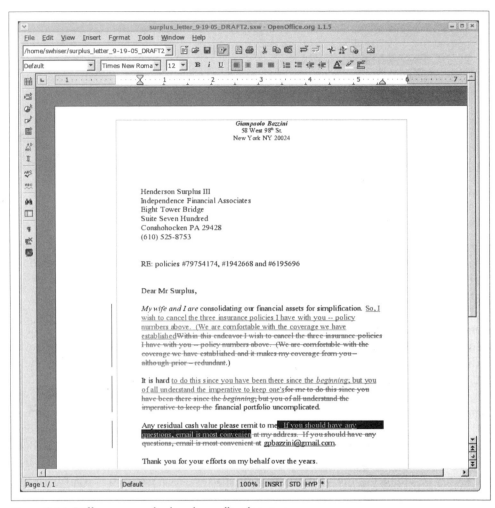

Figure 8-16. Differences are displayed as redlined content

permitting you to enter a few phrases to remind yourself and your collaborators later what changes you made and why. Documenting what you've done here lets you also distinguish versions later without having to open each one.

If you use File → Save As to save a version on which you are working, none of the version information is preserved; you have instead created a spanking new document. You could, of course, start again with this new document as a base, and use version control once again for future changes.

To open a specific version of a document listed in the Versions window, choose File → Versions, highlight the desired version, and click the Open button. This opens the indicated version of the document as a read-only file. You can, if you wish, save this

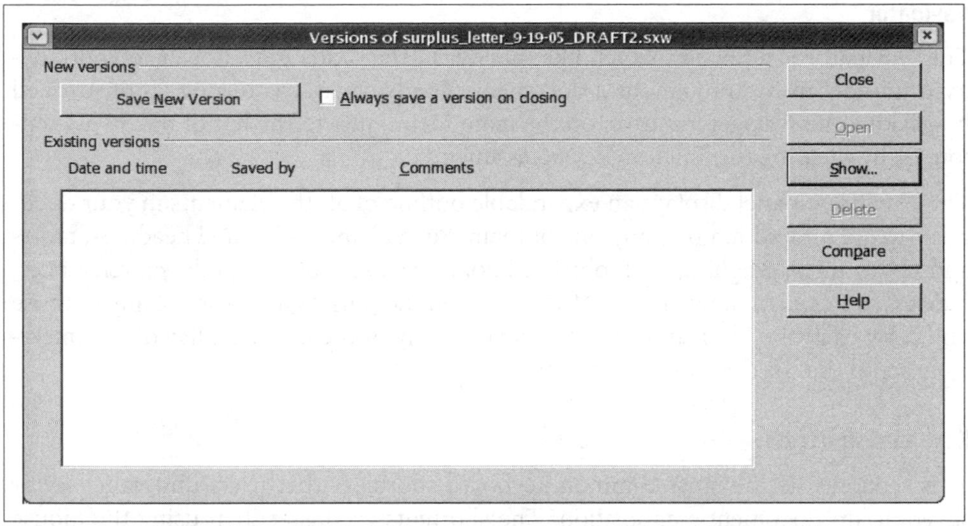

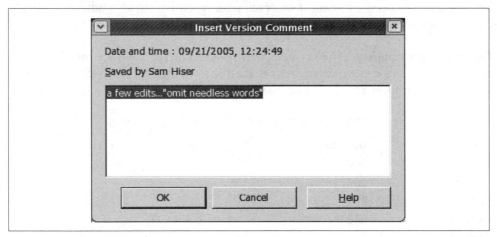

Figure 8-17. The Versions window

Figure 8-18. The Insert Version Comment window

version as a separate document, with no reference to other versions, past or future, by using the File → Save As menu option.

To track and show changes from one version to another, click the Compare button in the Versions window. This highlights all version differences (just as when using the Edit → Compare Document feature) in a document and gives you the chance to accept and reject each change.

Navigator

The Navigator is a floating panel, like the Stylist, that adds horsepower to your ability to rapidly move throughout a document. The Navigator is turned on or invoked by clicking the Navigator button on the main menu, just to the left of the Stylist button, or by pressing the function key F5 at any time.

The Navigator panel displays an expandable outline of all the elements in your document to aid a rapid jump to any one of them. Such elements include headings, tables and text frames, graphics, OLE objects, bookmarks, sections, hyperlinks, references, indexes, notes, and draw objects. If you click on the plus sign in front of any of those object types in the Navigator, you can click on any of the elements listed to immediately scroll the document to that location.

Keyboard shortcuts

This section lists the most common keyboard shortcuts that users find valuable for speeding up document composition. The shortcuts are faster than using the mouse and drop-down menus because the keystrokes allow you to keep both hands on the keyboard. Some people in danger of developing repetitive stress syndrome through excessive use of the mouse can find these shortcuts of particular value.

Custom keyboard mappings. The key mappings reflected in Table 8-3 are merely default settings. Users and system administrators are free to change them to reflect their personal or organizational taste or habit by selecting Tools → Configure → Keyboard.

Table 8-3. Common keystrokes to avoid the mouse

Function	Keystrokes
Copy text	Ctrl-C
Cut text	Ctrl-X
Paste text	Ctrl-V
Bold text	Ctrl-B
Italic text	Ctrl-I
Underline text	Ctrl-U

Adjustments to the Function Key defaults can be helpful, too, in the desktop migration process. OpenOffice offers four modes—F[1–12], Shift-F[1–12], Ctrl-F[1–12], and Shift-Ctrl-F[1–12]—which creates many openings for custom function key mappings that can aid speed and productivity.

Searching a document with Find & Replace

To find and replace characters in a document, press Ctrl-F to open the Find & Replace dialog. Alternatively, you can access the Find & Replace dialog from the main menu by selecting Edit → Find & Replace.

Enter the term you're searching for in the "Search for" field (top left), and, if you want to change it, the term you'd like to replace it with in the "Replace with" field. Proceed by pressing the Find button at the top right of the window, and the search will locate the term you're searching for in the nearest location in the document after the placement of the cursor. Continue by pressing the Replace button whenever appropriate. If you come to a term that you don't wish to replace, just press the Find button again to advance to the next example of the search term.

Inserting hyperlinks

Inserting hyperlinks—textual references to URLs on the Web—into documents has become essential. To insert a link, choose Insert → Hyperlink from the main menu. This invokes the Hyperlink window, where you can enter the name of the link (compete with http://) in the Target field and the text for the link in the document in the Text field, second from the bottom of the window. Other options are also offered, as shown in Figure 8-19.

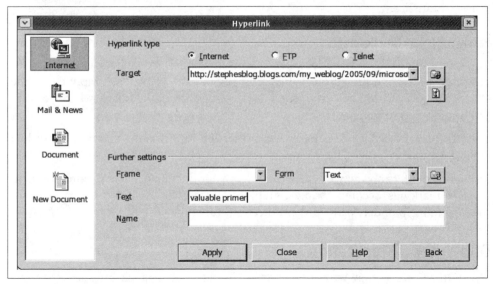

Figure 8-19. Inserting a hyperlink

Click the Apply button at the left of the series of buttons across the bottom of the window, and your text will appear highlighted and clickable in your document. Close the dialog by clicking the Close button. Test the link to see that it was spelled, punctuated, and typed correctly. If it is correct, clicking on the link in your document will wake up your browser with the target web page in it, and produce a little surge of joy in your heart.

Naming your hyperlinks is a good idea because that will enable you to move quickly among them with the Navigator, where the link names will be listed in outline form and clickable. To enter a name in the Hyperlink window, type a short but descriptive sequence in the Name field at the bottom of the dialog before you click the Apply button.

One may also make a hyperlink from existing text by highlighting the text sequence with the cursor, selecting Insert → Hyperlink, and filling out the dialog. Fill in at least the Target field and click the Apply button. Close the dialog by clicking the Close button.

Word count

Journalists, authors, and editors depend on this feature for their daily bread, so they can be forgiven anxiety at missing the word count feature. In fact, word count is present in OpenOffice, but it's in a surprising location. The feature is located in MS Word under Tools → Word Count, but in OOoWriter it's found under File → Properties → Statistics.

Password-protecting documents

You can secure OOoWriter documents from unwanted access by saving files with password protection turned on. When saving with File → Save As, simply check the "Save with password" box and enter and confirm your password when you are prompted to do so during the save.

To turn off whole document password protection at any time, simply choose File → Save As, uncheck the "Save with password" box, and complete the save.

OOoWriter offers a variety of ways to protect your documents against alterations to revision markings, sections, frames, graphics, objects, indexes, and tables. Consult the system Help under "passwords: protecting content."

OOoWriter Customization

OpenOffice offers many ways to customize its settings. A quick browse of the five tabs under OOoWriter's Tools → Configure (Menu, Keyboard, Status bar, Toolbars, Events) offers a good sense of the scope of OOoWriter's customization possibilities for the advanced user or system administrator.

OOoWriter toolbar customization

The workflow habits and nature of the business of each organization dictate the shape of its desktop toolset. So wide latitude in toolbar customization can help system administrators or power users bring the most frequently used toolbars or object elements to the top to increase productivity for themselves or all users in the workgroup.

In addition to the default toolbars available out of the box (main menu, function bar, object bar and main toolbar) the following additional toolbars are available through customization: table object bar, numbering object bar, frame object bar, draw object bar, control bar, text object bar/graphics, Bezier object bar, graphics object bar, objects, text object bar/Web, frame object bar/Web, graphics object bar/Web, object/Web, and user-defined no.1.

You can hide any of the toolbars (except main menu) by unchecking their names in the top half of the context menu that opens when you right-click in the empty space within any of the toolbars (Figure 8-20).

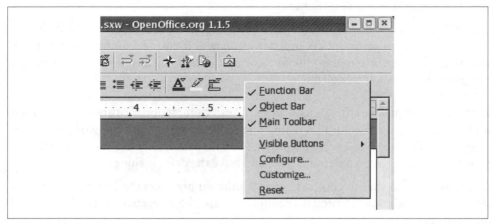

Figure 8-20. The context menu for configuring toolbars

You can further rearrange elements and redesign toolbars to your personal or work-group preference by choosing any of the other four choices in the bottom half of the contextual menu: Visible Buttons, Configure, Customize, and Reset. Changes made using these commands apply to the specific toolbar on which you right-clicked to call the context menu.

Adding an OOoWriter icon on the desktop or taskbar panel

Launching OOoWriter with a quick double-click of an icon is usually faster and pref-erable to wading through a series of cascading menus. You can add separate Launch-ers to open each of the OpenOffice modules directly. Here's the easiest way to set up a launcher specifically for OOoWriter on both your desktop workspace or the edge panel across the top or bottom of your desktop. The example is given from the GNOME environment; KDE will be different.

Right-click on an open space on the edge panel and select Add to Panel → Launcher from menu → Office → OpenOffice Text Document (the path may vary across differ-ent Linux distributions). This will place a OOoWriter icon onto that location on your Taskbar Panel. To add either an OOoCalc or OOoImpress icon, simply choose OpenOffice Spreadsheet or OpenOffice Presentation in the last step.

To add the same Launcher icon to the desktop space, simply drag and drop the OOoWriter icon you've just created on your taskbar panel onto your desktop workspace. This places a duplicate Launcher icon on the desktop, if that location is useful to you, and you can remove the taskbar panel icon if you wish by right-clicking it and selecting Remove From Panel on the context menu. To remove a desktop icon, right-click it and select Move to Trash in the context menu.

Adjusting unpopular default settings

OpenOffice is set by default to automatically complete words, replace certain characters, and capitalize initial letters in a new sentence. If you feel autocorrection to be intrusive while you are typing, the autocorrect settings are easy to adjust to be less intrusive or to turn off completely.

Word Completion (turning off). OOoWriter's Word Completion feature comes turned on by default. Some users find it distracting or annoying to have the word processor program appending the ends of words before they finish typing them. Others are content to ignore the completion action and leave the default alone.

If you like OOoWriter to complete your words, simply press the Enter key when its recommendations are felicitous; otherwise, press the spacebar to reject the program's offering.

To turn Word Completion off, select Tools → AutoCorrect/AutoFormat → Word Completion and uncheck the box before the phrase "Enable word completion" near the top of the window. Then click the OK button.

Auto-Replace (turning off). If you find Auto-Replace to be invasive—such as when you attempt to type (c) and it keeps replacing your keystrokes with the copyright symbol—you have two options: edit the replacement list, or turn off Auto-Replace altogether.

Editing the replacement list is straightforward. Select Tools → AutoCorrect/AutoFormat and go to the Replace tab. There, highlight the offending element and either press the Delete key or enter a different target result in the With: field.

To turn off the Auto-Replace function, select Tools → AutoCorrect/AutoFormat and click on the Options tab. The topmost option is "Use replacement table," with two checkboxes in front. By unchecking both boxes in the [M] and the [T] columns, you can turn off the specific substitutions listed in the replacement table. You can turn off all the other specific automatic replacement actions, too, by unchecking the respective boxes under [M] or [T] as you go down this list in the Options tab.

Customizing Auto-Replace. Note that in the Tools → AutoCorrect/AutoFormat dialog, the leftmost Replace tab contains the list of default replacements. This list is based on the OpenOffice developers' extensive knowledge of common keystroke errors and frequently used symbols (such as the copyright symbol). Leaving Auto-Replace turned on can aid your compositional productivity, especially if you customize the replacement list to make your own most frequent word, character, or symbol replacements. Add your own simply by typing elements into the Replace and With fields and then press the New button. Delete an entry by highlighting it in the list pane and pressing the Delete button.

Auto-Capitalization (turning off). OOoWriter is set to automatically capitalize the next character you type after a period. It also decapitalizes a second uppercase character typed in a sequence. This is beneficial most of the time when we fail to strike the Shift key, which is surprisingly often; however, when we type abbreviations or when we type acronyms that demand two initial capitals, these AutoCorrect actions are unwanted.

If the Auto-Capitalization feature offends your sensibilities or disturbs your workflow, you can turn it off by selecting Tools → AutoCorrect/AutoFormat and clicking on the Options tab. Uncheck the two boxes under the [M] and [T] columns in front of the second option, "Correct Two Initial Capitals," and the third option, "Capitalize the first letter of every sentence."

Auto-Capitalization (making exceptions). Auto-Capitalization can be very helpful when you integrate it into your typing repertoire. Consider keeping the feature turned on, and just add exceptions to make the Auto-Capitalization work for you instead of against you. You can adjust Auto-Capitalization exceptions by selecting Tools → AutoCorrect/AutoFormat and proceeding to the Exceptions tab.

At the Exceptions tab, you can add abbreviations you repeatedly use to the "Abbreviations (no subsequent capitals)" list in the upper window. These entries permit Auto-Capitalization to automatically capitalize the first letter of a new sentence, while it will not make such an invasive adjustment after any of the abbreviations listed.

Also at the Exceptions tab, you can add to the list of words or acronyms that demand two initial capitals. The default entries already there provide a source of examples. Among our own favorite exceptions of this type are OOo, OOoWriter, and the many variations on that sequence.

OpenOffice Calc

OpenOffice Calc (also known as OOoCalc) is the spreadsheet program included in the OpenOffice office suite. Users familiar with recent versions of Microsoft Excel will feel at home in OOoCalc.

Managing files

Opening, saving, sending, and exporting OOoCalc files is the same as with OOo-Writer files. See the previously described details for OOoWriter.

Entering labels (text)

Entering a label—that is, a word rather than a number—into a cell is the same in OOoCalc as in MS Excel: begin the character sequence with a ' (single quote) character, finish typing the rest of the characters, and press Enter.

Autofill

Fill a row or column of numbers quickly with a simple drag-and-drop motion. After entering the number 1, for example, in the cell A1, simply highlight the cell by clicking on it once; then, grab the small black square at the bottom right corner of the cell with a left-click and drag the square down or across to fill in numbers. Consecutive numbers fill in the cells upon release of the mouse button.

Entering simple formulas

This is basic stuff to experienced spreadsheet users. Formulas always begin with an equals sign (=). For example, to calculate the result of 1 + 1, you would type = 1 + 1 and press Enter.

To calculate a result based on other cells, type = in the cell where you want the result to appear, then click on the first cell in the formula. This will highlight the cell in a red outline. Type an operator such as + and click on the second cell. This will highlight that cell in a red outline. You can keep entering as many operators followed by cells or other values as you like. Finally, press Enter; the result will appear in the target cell.

Note that the formula field, just above the cell area of the spreadsheet, contains the formula just created. The alternative way of creating the same formula would be to simply type it directly into the formula field. First, click once on the desired cell. Then click once on the empty formula bar and type your formula directly in it and then press the Enter key.

Summing a column of numbers

To quickly sum an existing column of numbers, highlight the empty target result cell with a single click. Then, click the sigma icon on the formula bar. This automatically highlights in blue the most likely nearby column of numbers to be summed. If the highlighted group is appropriate, press the Enter key, and the result will appear in the target cell. If the appropriate group of numbers is not highlighted, you can grab the small blue square at the bottom right of the highlighted column and adjust the grouping to the precise numbers you wish to sum. Then, press the Enter key.

Moving cell contents

It's easier to move a range of cells in OOoCalc than it is to move a single cell entry. This task is the one that gives the most people trouble when they are adjusting to the new environment of OOoCalc, but it is quite simple once you've done it once or twice.

To move a range of cells, simply highlight the range by clicking in one cell at an extreme corner of the range and, while holding the left mouse key down, drag the mouse pointer across the rest of the cells in the range. When the whole range is blackened, release the left mouse key. Now, go back with the mouse pointer and make a single mouse click anywhere in the blackened range (while holding down the button) to grab the range and move it to its new location. Drop the range of cells in its new location by simply releasing the mouse button.

Moving a single cell entry requires the same procedure, but highlighting a single cell usually proves troublesome for new users. That's because the highlight motion with the left mouse button requires the user to left-click on the cell, move the mouse pointer outside the cell and back, release the mouse button, and then go back to grab and move the highlighted cell.

MS Office offers a single motion to move a single cell, while OOoCalc requires a double motion involving first a highlight and then a move. The OOoCalc process is annoying because it's more complicated, but in the end it's effective and not that difficult to master and remember (because the old method is soon forgotten).

Adjusting column widths and row heights

To change the width of a column, bring the mouse pointer up into the grid's column headings, labeled A, B, C, and so on. Note how the mouse pointer changes to a double horizontal arrow when it rolls over any column divider. While the arrow is visible, simply move it to the right or left to increase or decrease the width of the column immediately to the left of the divider. To put a column back to its default width, right-click on the column heading to call up the Column Width dialog. Check the empty box labeled "Default value" and press the OK button. The column will now snap back to its default width (0.89 inches).

To adjust the height of a row, apply the procedure just shown for adjusting column width, but with the mouse cursor on the top or bottom of a row heading at the left edge of the page. To restore a row's default height, apply the procedure just shown for restoring the default column width, but at the left edge of the page on the desired row heading.

Merging cells

To merge multiple cells, first highlight the group of cells you wish to merge, then select Format → Merge Cells → Define from the main menu. This will create one cell that contains the contents of the cells in the range you highlighted. OOoCalc's recognition of data can be quite sophisticated. For instance, if one column contains Jun and another contains 3, the date 06/03 followed by the current year appears in the merged cell.

Freezing and splitting windows

It's hard to navigate through larger spreadsheets because the column and row headings disappear from view. The Window → Freeze and Window → Split commands permit you to lock column and row headings into place while scrolling to view other sections of the spreadsheet.

To lock down your column and row headings, click on the cell where you want the freeze to take effect and select Window → Freeze from the main menu. This will put a check mark on the Freeze item on the drop-down menu and lock the columns to the left of the highlighted cell, as well as the rows above the cell. The spreadsheet initially shows just lines to outline the frozen cells, as can be seen in Figure 8-21.

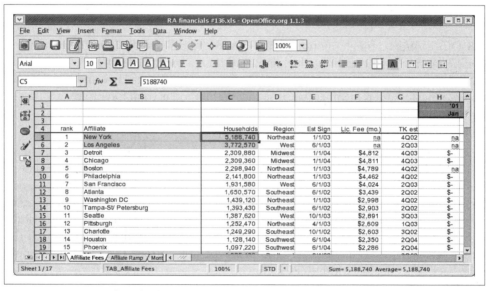

Figure 8-21. Freezing the column and row headings

Now you can move down and to the right. Note in Figure 8-22 how column headings stay fixed and visible as we move down the spreadsheet. A similar effect takes place with the column B row headings at the left if we scroll through the spreadsheet to the right.

Another interesting way to leave parts of your spreadsheet visible is to choose Windows → Split instead of Window → Freeze. Now you can click on any pane and scroll it. The pane you clicked on will move, along with one of the panes next to it

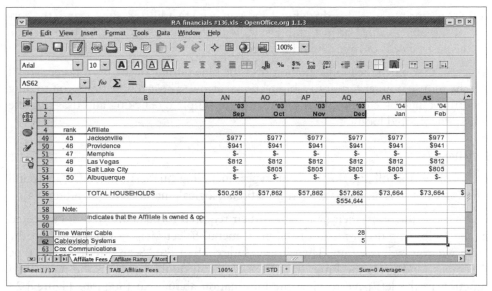

Figure 8-22. Column and row headings are frozen

depending on whether you scroll up and down or right and left. The other two panes will stay still.

To remove the Freeze or Split settings, simply click the checked selection on the drop-down menu, and the freeze or split lines will go away. Freeze and Split settings "travel" with a document when it is saved with either of the settings checked.

Page Break View

Page Break View offers a detailed view of the current spreadsheet's page breaks for printing. To turn on Page Break View, select View from the main menu and click on Page Break View in the drop-down menu. This sets a check mark at the selection. To turn off Page Break View, uncheck this selection on the drop-down menu.

You can quickly set or adjust page breaks by dragging the outside blue lines to cover the desired range, and just as easily move the page-dividing lines to include the desired columns and rows on the proper printed page. Page Break View also offers a way to view and navigate larger spreadsheets from a more distant perspective.

Setting the print range

When you create a new spreadsheet from scratch, it has no print range set. Such a spreadsheet appears gray when in Page Break View. To set a print range for your spreadsheet, make sure Page Break View is turned on, then highlight the full area you wish to print by clicking on the cell in one corner and dragging the mouse pointer across the entire range. Alternatively, select Format → Print Ranges → Define. Any spreadsheet content that's outside the range you set this way will not be printed.

If there is a print range already defined and you need to adjust it, simply grab the corner of the blue outline (or just grab a side) with the mouse and stretch it to include all the desired cells of your new print range.

To grab, first move the mouse pointer over the blue outline of the print range; you'll see the mouse pointer turn into a bidirectional arrow. The arrow permits you to drag the print range blue outline to a different place simply by clicking and dragging the line to the desired location.

Functions

OOoCalc has a full array of function types, including financial, database, temporal (date and time), array, statistical, informational, logical, mathematical, and textual.

OOoCalc's functions, their syntax, and their required formats are well documented in the Help drop-down menu of the main menu. Select Help → Contents, and the Help window will open up. Then, in the Index tab at the "Search term" field, type functions, and press the Enter key. Here, you can double-click on the name of a function in the left pane to view the information about that function. Figure 8-23 illustrates the Help Index and information on the financial function called PV, which calculates the present value of a stream of regular payments or cash flows. PV is a spreadsheet function that's understandably popular with MBAs and bankers.

When entering a function into a cell, remember always to precede the entry with an equals sign (=). The example offered in Figure 8-24 indicates what the PV function formula looks like in the formula field when it is correctly typed into a cell and the necessary information for the function is properly cell-referenced: =PV(B1;B2;B3).

The function in Figure 8-24 is a common mortgage problem. If you are guaranteed terms by your bank on a 30-year loan at 5% interest per annum, and you know that you have exactly $1,500 per month to spend on your new house, the question to answer is, "What is the purchase price that corresponds with my maximum monthly payment of $1,500?"

The PV function is perfect for solving such a problem. MBAs will fondly recall that mortgage payments made by you to the bank are outgoing and, therefore, negative. Make your payment input negative, or the resulting present value will be negative. The number of periods is 30 years times 12 months (360 periods), and the periodic interest rate is 5% per year divided by 12 months (0.42% per month), as indicated in Figure 8-24.

You could just as readily use the PMT (Payment) function to determine what the monthly payment is on your 10-million-Euro dream home.

It is possible also to enter numbers as well as cell references into the body of a function. In the Formula Field, this would look like the following:

```
=PV(.0042;360;-1500)
```

Figure 8-23. The PV (present value) function—Using Help

However, using cell references leaves room for easily trying alternative inputs or for generating a sensitivity analysis using a range of choices for one variable.

Worksheets, or sheets

One OOoCalc spreadsheet file (sometimes called a *Workbook*) contains three sheets by default, but can hold up to 256 sheets in total.

Figure 8-25 shows the three sheets of a standard, default spreadsheet file. In the figure, note from the white coloration of the sheet tab that sheet 1 is live or current. The gray coloration of sheets 2 and 3 indicate they are present but not visible.

To move among sheets, simply click on a sheet tab and it will become the live sheet.

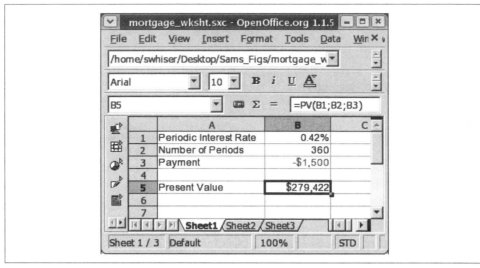

Figure 8-24. A common mortage problem, solved

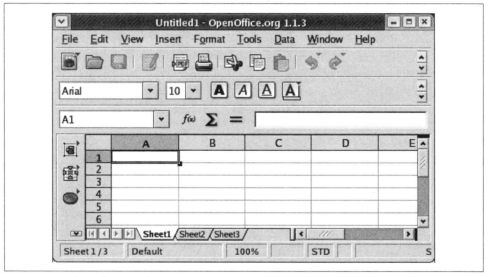

Figure 8-25. Three sheets to the wind

To add a new sheet, right-click on the sheet area or any one of the sheet tabs to call up the context menu. Then, select Insert Sheet from the menu and the Insert Sheet dialog box appears. Here, designate the names, positions, and number of the new sheets. Note that you can add multiple sheets. You can also bring in sheets from another file; after you browse and select a file, the names of its sheets are displayed for you to choose from.

To delete a sheet from a workbook, first select the sheet you wish to delete by clicking on its tab. Then right-click the sheet bar or live sheet tab and select Delete Sheet. Answer "Yes" in the confirmation dialog to delete the sheet.

To rename a live sheet, right-click the target sheet's tab and select Rename Sheet from the menu that appears. This activates the Rename Sheet dialog, where you can enter the new name for the sheet in the Name field.

To select more than one sheet at a time, hold down the Ctrl key while clicking on each sheet tab you wish to select.

Selecting concurrent sheets is useful when entering content, such as column headings or labels, that you wish to have on many sheets. It saves the repetition of setting up multiple sheets with the same information.

If you have a workbook with many sheets and wish to select a long range of contiguous sheets, click on the tab of the leftmost sheet in your target range. Then, while holding down the Shift key, click on the rightmost sheet tab of your target range. This selects all sheets included in that range.

To deselect that same group, hold down the Shift key while clicking on the tab of the first sheet (the leftmost sheet, in this case) you selected in that range.

To deselect a selected sheet (other than the live sheet, which always remains selected), hold down the Ctrl key while clicking on its sheet tab.

If you have a spreadsheet with many sheets, not all the tabs are visible at the bottom. To make a tab visible so you can select its sheet, you'll need to use the sheet navigation arrow buttons at the left of the sheet tabs.

Sorting data

To sort a list or chart of numerical or textual information, first highlight the full range to be sorted (including labels, but excluding unwanted data such as totals) and then select Data → Sort from the main menu. This launches the Sort dialog box, where you can designate the sorting order, among other parameters.

In the case illustrated in Figure 8-26, we want to reorder the data to put the largest responses at top. Therefore, in the Sort dialog we select to sort by the "Responses per Platform" column (where the numbers are) and set the radio button at the right to Descending. Then we press the OK button. Notice how rearranging the order of the source chart automatically registers the new order in the bar graph that was previously generated (see Figure 8-27).

Data sources

Instead of having its own database format, OOoCalc is designed to interact with many different varieties of external databases. Data Sources is the name for OOo-Calc's strong feature set for interacting with databases and for linking spreadsheets,

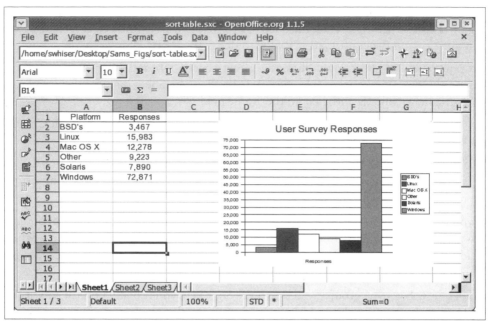

Figure 8-26. Sorting a simple table

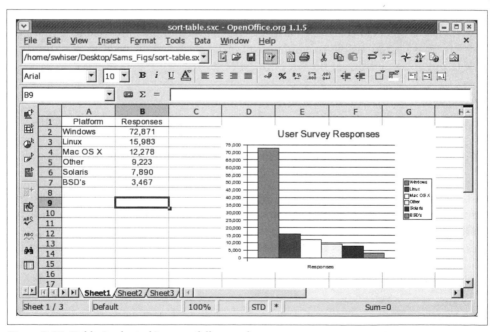

Figure 8-27. Table (and graph) successfully sorted

forms, and reports to information contained in databases. OOoCalc offers a variety of ways to link to a MySQL or Adabas D database, for example, or many other data sources, including MS Outlook, Outlook Express, Mozilla, and others.

In OOoCalc, call up the Data Source View by choosing Tools → Data Sources from the main menu, or simply pressing the function key F4. Press F4 again to close the Data Source window.

Having made such a promising introduction, it's a shame to say that Data Sources is outside the scope of this section. It's a shame because interacting with databases is becoming more relevant to the web-enabled desktop user. Furthermore, OpenOffice's database interactivity is a hot focus of development activity and promises to get stronger as well as easier for the average user to handle with each progressive release of the OpenOffice software.

Macros

Creating or handling macros in OOoCalc is not within the scope of this book. However, we can offer some general information that may be useful to macro users. Macros could come into play for all the different modules of OpenOffice (and MS Office), but here we deal strictly with their relevance to OOoCalc (and MS Excel).

OOoCalc uses its own macro scripting language called OpenOffice Basic (or Star-Basic). This is a different macro language from the one used by Microsoft in MS Office, which is called Visual Basic (or VBA).

VBA macros are not able to run in OOoCalc, creating a significant barrier for migration from MS Excel to OOoCalc for users with many large or significant VBA macros within their spreadsheets. VBA macros that come with MS Excel files currently must be rewritten in StarBasic for these files to be fully useful in OOoCalc.

Sun Microsystems has promised to release a Visual Basic-to-StarBasic macro conversion tool to facilitate the automatic conversion of VBA macros to StarBasic macros.

Meanwhile, OOoCalc is set by default to save VBA macros to be available and written back whenever a OOoCalc spreadsheet file is saved again in the MS Excel file format. This offers three options: (1) you can reimport a spreadsheet to Excel in order to run the stored VBA macros, (2) you can store the VBA macros in order to manually rewrite them in StarBasic, and (3) you can preserve them unused in OOoCalc, to be converted later to StarBasic when Sun's macro conversion tool becomes available.

Because VBA macros do not run in OOoCalc, the viruses associated with them pose no threat as long as you use OOoCalc. If you want to leave off the macros (for security reasons or because you just don't want them) when importing Excel files, turn off the default in Tools → Options → Load/Save → VBA Properties.

If you are interested in macros, feel free to consult the OpenOffice Basic Programmer's Guide at *http://docs.sun.com/db/doc/817-1826?q=star+basic*.

OpenOffice Impress

OpenOffice Impress (also known as OOoImpress) is the presentation module included in the OpenOffice suite. Users who are familiar with most recent versions of Microsoft PowerPoint will feel at home in OOoImpress.

Creating a presentation from scratch with AutoPilot

When opening the OOoImpress module from an icon on the desktop or Taskbar Panel, or when opening it from another OOo module via File → New → Presentation, you are confronted by the AutoPilot wizard, which can lead you through the creation of a presentation from scratch. In the wizard you can also choose to open an existing presentation or a presentation template.

Less experienced users can feel free to let the wizard take them through the process of creating a presentation, but experienced users can simply select the Create button at the lower right in the wizard and get right to working in a blank presentation document.

Opening an existing presentation

To open a presentation you have created earlier or received from someone else, simply click once on a presentation file's icon in its folder. Your Linux system is likely set up to open MS PowerPoint files (which have a *.ppt* file suffix) automatically in OOoImpress. By default, each file is saved in the same format it had when you opened it (PowerPoint, OOoImpress, etc.).

Alternatively, you can select File → Open from the main menu and browse your file system to find the existing file with which you'd like to work.

Saving a presentation

To save your current presentation in its existing location and format, click the Save icon (the little floppy disk image) on the function bar, and the file will be saved into its present location in your file system. The same result occurs if you select File → Save from the main menu.

If you are saving the presentation for the first time, the Save dialog window opens to allow you to select a folder and fill in the filename field. Do so, then click the Save button. By default, the Save dialog window opens to the *Documents* directory (folder) in your file system. That is, user *swhiser* by default saves documents to */home/swhiser/Documents*. This default also is consistent with other OpenOffice modules.

If you need to change the filename, folder, or format of the presentation file you are saving, save by selecting File → Save As and fill out the Save As dialog accordingly.

Export formats

One of the principal strengths of OOoImpress is the sheer number of file formats to which you may export your presentation. Table 8-4 lists the various export file formats available.

Table 8-4. OOoImpress file formats for export

Format	Name	File extension
BMP	Windows Bitmap	.bmp
EMF	Enhanced Metafile	.emf
EPS	Encapsulated Postscript	.eps
GIF	Graphics Interchange Format	.gif
HTML	Hypertext Markup Language	.html, .htm
JPEG	Joint Photographic Experts Group	.jpg, .jpeg, .jfif, .jif, .jpe
MET	OS/2 Metafile	.met
PBM	Portable Bitmap	.pbm
PCT	Mac Pict	.pct
PDF	Printable Document Format	.pdf
PGM	Portable Greymap	.pgm
PNG	Portable Network Graphic	.png
PPM	Portable Pixel Map	.ppm
PWP	Placeware	.pwp
RAS	Sun Raster Image	.ras
SVG	Scalable Vector Graphics	.svg
SVM	StarView Metafile	.svm
SWF	Macromedia Flash	.swf
SXI	OOoImpress native file format	.sxi
TIFF	Tagged Image File Format	.tif, .tiff
WMF	Windows Metafile	.wmf
XPM	X PixMap	.xpm

Export to HTML. Among the most useful facilities here is the ability to export a presentation to the HTML or web page format. This feature allows us to painlessly convert any presentation we've given to a format suitable to the Web so the audience—as well as those who were unable to attend—can visit the material from any Internet-enabled location on the planet at their own convenience.

Start by selecting File → Export from the main menu. This launches the Save As window. Here, change the File format drop-down box to HTML Document and designate the filename and directory of the resulting HTML files. Then click the Export button to kick off the HTML Export dialog series.

First, select a design. Leaving the default as is and clicking the Next button is fine for many situations. Now you can choose from a variety of publication types that affect how the presentation appears and can be manipulated once it's up on the Web. Among these types are standard HTML format, standard HTML with frames, automatic, and WebCast (requires a server).

The default works nicely. Click Next. Here you can alter the format of graphics in the output and the resolution of output, and turn sound effects on or off. Leaving the settings at their defaults works fine. Click Next. This screen permits you to enter information that appears on the title page of the new web presentation. Enter the desired information and click Next. Here you can set the look of the navigational elements you like, such as forward and backward arrows. Leaving the "Text only" box checked (the default setting) produces text links, but you also have a choice of four styles of colorful buttons.

Click Next. In this final screen of the export process, you can alter the default color scheme of the text. Leaving settings alone works fine for first-timers. Finally, click the Create button, and your presentation is ready to post to the Web.

Export to Macromedia Flash. Not to be overshadowed among the many output formats is Macromedia Flash. This is yet another universally acceptable file format (along with PDF and HTML, in particular), which guarantees that anyone with a web browser (that is, everyone with a desktop computer) can view your presentation. Many of the same benefits of converting a presentation to HTML web pages (described earlier) hold for the Flash format as well.

To export your presentation to Flash, proceed to the main menu and select File → Export. This opens the Export dialog box, where you should go to the File Format drop-down field and select "Macromedia Flash (SWF)(.swf)." In the Export dialog box, if you do not alter the folder or save path, the new Flash version of your presentation will automatically be placed in the same folder as the original .sxi presentation file. Now, click the Export button, and the Flash version of your presentation will be created.

OOoImpress workspace views

You can change the view setting from the main menu by selecting View → Workspace and checking the desired view setting in the drop-down menu. The five workspace views include Drawing View, Outline View, Slides View, Notes View and Handout View. Drawing View is the most commonly used view in which to work when building or editing a presentation.

The workspace views are easiest to change with a single click of the small icons arrayed vertically along the right edge of the OOoImpress window, toward the top, as shown in Figure 8-28.

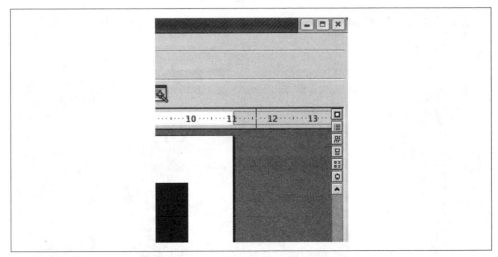

Figure 8-28. Workspace View icons

OOoImpress modes

Modes are states in which only certain editing functions can be performed or orientations/views can be elicited.

The three modes are accessed and altered from the main menu under View → Slide, View → Master, or View → Layers, where the active mode is evidenced by the check mark.

It's a recurring point of confusion for OpenOffice users that modes are accessed and changed under Views from the main menu. It makes it worse that OOoImpress changes the View settings based on mode settings. And, unforgivably, the mode icons at the bottom-left corner of the workspace (see Figure 8-29) have been mislabeled: the mouse roll-over labels for the three Mode icons read Slide View, Master View, and Layer View. These labels should read Slide Mode, Master Mode, and Layer Mode, respectively.

Due to the complexity of changing views and modes from the main menu, we recommend using the Mode icons (at the bottom-left edge of the workspace) and View icons (along the upper-right edge of the workspace) to change and visually confirm the current view or mode. Passing the mouse pointer over each icon and pausing will reveal its roll-over label if you need to know which icon is which. Figure 8-28 introduces the View icons, and Figure 8-29 shows where both sets of View and Mode icons are located on the workspace.

Editing a presentation

Altering an existing presentation is quite straightforward.

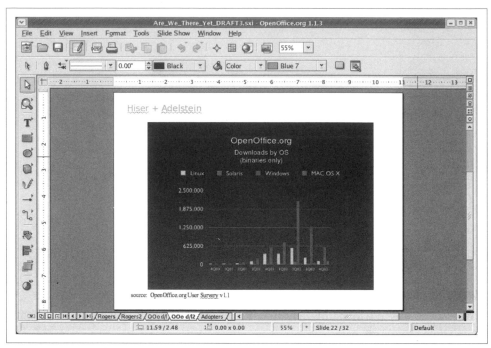

Figure 8-29. Control your modes and views

Entering text. To enter or edit an existing sequence of text, click once on the text. You will see a shaded block appear around the text with green squares at intervals around the box. Move the cursor to the appropriate place and enter changes. Clicking elsewhere in the slide will make the shaded block go away.

Using bullets. To introduce a bullet to a line of text, click once on the targeted text, then click the Bullets icon centrally located on the object bar. If you're not sure what to press, let the mouse hover over the icons and choose the one where the Bullets On/Off balloon appears.

To use advanced bullet formats, click the alternative Bullets icon at the extreme right of the object bar. This brings up a dialog box with a selection of bullet and numbering styles, and other formatting options.

Importing graphics, tables, and charts. To import a graphic, table, or chart from another program, web page, or module of OpenOffice, simple copy the element from its native source and paste it into your slide.

This, for example, might involve highlighting the item in its original application with a single click and pressing Ctrl-C to copy it (actually placing the element onto the desktop's clipboard), then clicking in your slide once and pressing Ctrl-V to paste in the element.

Adding slides. To add or insert a slide into your presentation, simply select Insert → Slide from the main menu, choose the desired AutoLayout format in the Insert Slide dialog that appears, and press the OK button.

Deleting slides. You can quickly delete a slide by right-clicking on its tab and selecting Delete from the contextual menu. Alternatively, from the main menu, select Edit → Delete Slide.

Moving slides around. The easiest way to move slides around within a presentation is to simply click, drag, and drop the tab of any slide into a new sequence among the tabs.

The presentation palette

Pressing the icon at the far right of the object bar opens the floating presentation palette, where you can execute functions quickly when building or editing your presentation. Functions include Insert Slide, Modify Slide Layout, Slide Design, Duplicate Slide, and Expand Slide. To turn off the presentation palette, click the icon again.

Putting on a slide show

Having created a presentation, putting on a slide show is a trivial undertaking. Press F9 to start the slide show and the Esc key to end.

Slides how transitions. To set the transition for a single slide, select Slide Show → Slide Transition from the main menu. Figure 8-30 shows the transition options available.

You can choose a slow, medium, or fast transition speed in the drop-down menu at the bottom of the Slide Transition window.

If you favor using a single kind of slide transition throughout your whole presentation, it's most efficient to set this up for all slides at the same time using AutoPilot when you first start building a presentation.

Custom slide shows. You can set up many different versions of the same presentation using only chosen slides and different settings. This is convenient for adapting different parts of one large presentation to specific audiences. You can also use it to pre-configure versions of a presentation that present increased detail, to which you can switch spontaneously during a presentation to cover some more intricate points that you would otherwise spare a general audience.

To define a new custom slide show, from the main menu of your live source presentation select Slide Show → Custom Slide Show, which opens the Custom Slide Shows dialog (Figure 8-31), where you should press the New button.

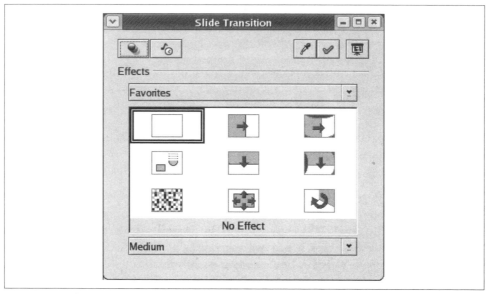

Figure 8-30. The Slide Transition window

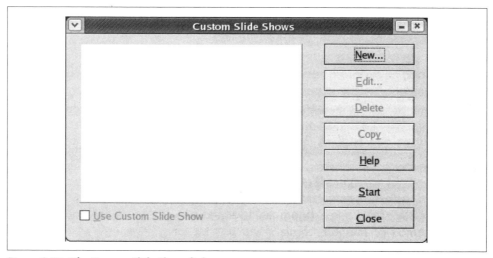

Figure 8-31. The Custom Slide Show dialog

This opens the Define Custom Slide Show dialog (Figure 8-32) where you can name the new version of your slide show and select which slides are to be included. To select a given slide for inclusion, highlight that slide in the "Existing slides" pane at the lefthand side of the dialog. Then, click the uppermost of the two arrow buttons and your chosen slide will be entered into the "Selected slides" pane at the righthand side of the dialog.

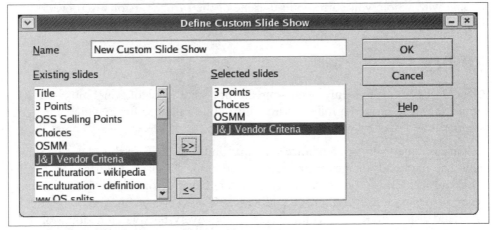

Figure 8-32. The Define Custom Slide Show dialog

Customizing OpenOffice

A couple of quick settings can save you a lot of time, depending on your needs.

Adding a Launcher icon

You can add an icon to launch either OpenOffice with no module or OpenOffice with any specific module ready to go.

We cover the procedure for adding an OOoWriter Launcher icon to the desktop or edge panel in the OOo Writer section "Adding an OOoWriter icon on the desktop or taskbar panel," earlier in this chapter. The procedure for adding OOoCalc or OOoImpress icons is analogous.

Defaulting to the MS Office file formats

To set OOoWriter to automatically save files in the MS Word .doc file format, select Tools → Options, then choose Load/Save in the left index of the Options dialog. In the index under Load/Save, click on General. This opens the Options-Load/Save-General dialog. Here, in the "Standard file format" section, your "Document type" drop-down is already set on "Text document." Leave that as is. In the "Always save as" drop-down at right, change the selection to one of the three available MS Word versions:

- Microsoft Word 6.0
- Microsoft Word 95
- Microsoft Word 97/2000/XP

Click the OK button. Use your best discretion when choosing a version. Microsoft Word 97/2000/XP has the most users at large; however, if your environment or the people with whom you correspond use one of the earlier versions (6.0 or 95), then that reality would inform your choice.

KOffice

OpenOffice is not the only open source office suite available on Linux; the KDE project has also created a fully featured office suite called KOffice, which adheres to standards and fits very well into the KDE desktop.*

KOffice is a highly integrated office suite that builds directly on the KDE technology. This has many advantages in terms of integration, features, performance, familiar look and feel, and so on. KOffice can therefore benefit from all of KDE's advanced technologies such as DCOP, KIO, and KParts. The KParts technology, in particular, is extended for the KOffice components to allow very flexible embedding of documents inside other documents. KOffice components can integrate very well into each other. So basically a spreadsheet can contain anything from charts to presentations, reports and even text documents. Likewise, almost any component can contain almost any other. Components are fully embedded, allowing the user to perform any operations that the standalone application would allow.

Because much technology is already present inside KDE itself, KOffice is a very lightweight office suite, which results in fast application startup and low memory consumption. This makes KOffice a very suitable office suite for older hardware as well, which can save lots of money in some cases.

Still, KOffice is quite rich and extensive in features. It is not limited to word processing, spreadsheets, or presentations, but also has components for image manipulation, flowcharts, business report generation, database management, and project management. Because of KDE's flexible component integration, smaller utilities, such as the diagram and chart engine, as well as the formula editor, are available as standalone tools. The straightforward and KDE-like approach in look and feel, as well as its familiar usability, make KOffice quite useful for daily office work.

The KOffice office suite is too large to list every detail. General features include document location abstraction, DCOP scripting, parts, and plug-ins. Take a look at the KOffice web site (*http://www.koffice.org*) to check on the latest state of the application.

KOffice adheres to the OASIS OpenDocument file format, so documents can be exchanged with other standards-conforming utilities, such as OpenOffice.

It is important for an office suite to use standards where possible, especially for the file format. In this way, a business can be sure that it can still open documents many

---

* This section was contributed by Raphael Langerhorst of the KOffice documentation team.

years into the future, regardless of what happens to current tools. The OASIS Open-Document file format specification is an open standard for office applications. Both KOffice and OpenOffice use the format, which means that files can be exchanged seamlessly between the suites.

KOffice has more components to offer than what is covered by the OASIS specification. Still, all components covered by the specifications actually use the OASIS OpenDocument file format.

Here are the components of KOffice:

Text processing and desktop publishing: KWord
> KWord is designed mainly for text processing, but includes many desktop publishing aspects. This creates a mixture of features that makes interesting layouts easily possible.

Spreadsheets: KSpread
> KSpread is a pretty standard spreadsheet application. It offers many functions as well as formatting, multiple sheets, charts, diagrams and more. Of course it can easily integrate any other KOffice component to extend its abilities.

Presentations: KPresenter
> KPresenter is a presentation component. It can be used to create on-screen presentations or to design and print transparencies.

Flowcharts and more: Kivio
> Kivio can be used for any kind of flowchart or diagram. Additional stencil sets can be used for custom needs. Even UML diagrams are possible.

Vector graphics: Karbon14
> Karbon14 is a vector drawing application.

Pixmap graphics: Krita
> Krita is a tool for creating high-quality pixmap graphics. It offers many plug-ins for image manipulation and supports various formats.

Business reports: Kugar
> Kugar can be used to create business-quality reports. A designer helps to easily design such reports.

Database management and forms: Kexi
> Kexi is a full-blown database management application. You can design forms for working with data. Many backends, such as PostgreSQL or MySQL, are possible. It is even capable of importing MS Access mdb database files.

Each KOffice component comes with its own manual. These manuals offer all the latest information about the various components KOffice has to offer and should be read to learn more about KOffice. The web site is also a good place to find out more.

The primary site on the Internet is *http://www.koffice.org*. You will also find information there about the user and developer mailing lists, as well as additional developer resources.

The Kexi project has an additional web site, which can be found at *http://www.kexi-project.org*.

The following two sections, instead of giving you a rundown of the standard features, explore two interesting features in more depth, in the hope that this will be mouthwatering enough to interest you in exploring KOffice further.

Hands On: Getting to Know KOffice

Now we will work through some examples with KOffice to get to know the office suite. You are very welcome to actually create the documents yourself and play around with the different components as we go along. The purpose of these examples is to get a feeling for KOffice, without trying to be a complete walkthrough, which would fill a complete book on its own. Remember that the handbooks included in the KOffice installation hold much more information that allows you to learn a lot about all the available components.

Using tabulators in KWord

You can use tabulators (tabs) to align text horizontally. This is very useful for simple tables or listings, where text needs to be vertically aligned. Tabulators can also be very useful to simply place text at an exact horizontal location.

KWord has various options for tabulators. You can set different alignments, such as left, right, centered, or alignment on a certain character (such as a comma). In particular, the last type is useful for listing numbers and prices.

Tabulators are part of the paragraph format. So you can configure everything related to tabulators in the Paragraph Settings dialog (Figure 8-33). This dialog can be reached through the Format → Paragraph menu entry.

Now we will create a couple of tab stops. We start with a very intuitive way of editing tabs and later look at some configuration details.

Start up KWord, choose the text-oriented U.S. letter template, and click OK (see Figure 8-34).

Then take a look at the top ruler of your document (Figure 8-35). The white space in the top ruler is exactly the width of the editable area of the document. This space can also be used to enter tab stops. In the top left corner is a small icon that represents the currently selected tab stop type. As already mentioned, tabs can be left aligned, right aligned, centered, or aligned on a certain character. You can change the type by simply clicking on that icon. See how it changes between different types of tab stops.

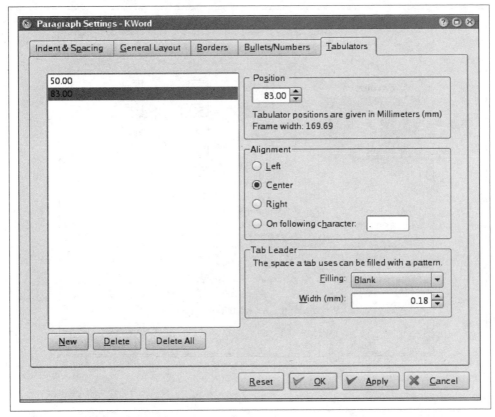

Figure 8-33. Configuring tabulators in KWord

Next you should insert some tab stops by choosing the correct types and placing them at the correct horizontal positions in the top ruler (Figure 8-36).

To do so, first choose the correct type in the upper-left corner and then left-click on the position in the top ruler. Do so for all four tab stops until your upper ruler looks like the one shown in the figure.

To see how the tab stops can be used, simply write some text at each tab stop:

1. Press the Tab key once. You are now at the first tab stop.

2. Write a few characters, such as How. You can see that the text is aligned on the right side with the tab, indicating that the first tab stop is right aligned.

3. Press the Tab key again. You are now at the second tab stop.

4. Write another word, such as are. The text is aligned on the left side with the tab, indicating that the second tab stop is left aligned.

5. Press the Tab key again. You are now at the third tab stop.

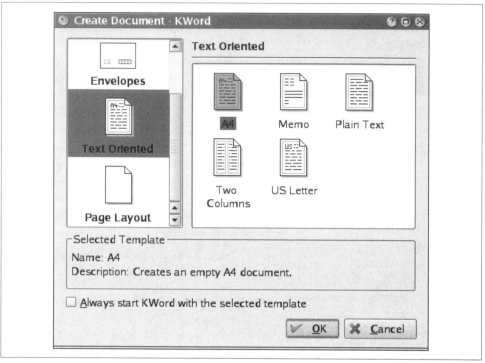

Figure 8-34. Selecting a text template

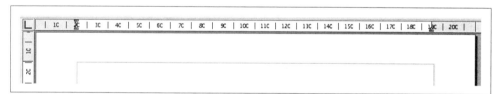

Figure 8-35. The KWord top ruler

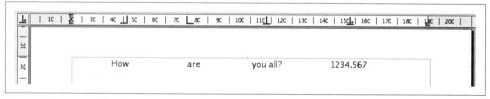

Figure 8-36. Inserted tab stops

6. Write more text, such as you all?. The text is centered on the tab stop, indicating that the third tab stop is center aligned.

7. Press the Tab key again, to come to the fourth and last tab stop.

8. Write a number such as 1234.567. Notice how the number is aligned at the decimal point. This type of tab stop is useful for numbers.

The text now looks like Figure 8-37.

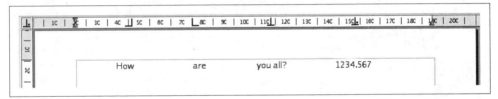

Figure 8-37. Inserted text at tab stops

To allow many more configuration options, use the paragraph format. A quick way to access these configuration options is to double-click on one of the tab stops in the top ruler. You can do this right away with the document you just created in the previous exercise. You will see the configuration dialog, just as at the beginning of this section. You can also get to the configuration options by choosing Paragraph from the Format menu, and then going to the Tabulators page. Play around with the options, which are pretty self-explanatory. You can also add or delete tab stops in this dialog.

If you need permanent tab stops for a specific style, use the Style Manager to edit the tabulators. You can find it in the Format menu as well.

Embedding charts into spreadsheets

KSpread is the spreadsheet component of KOffice. As such, it offers lots of calculation features as well as the ability to create charts to visualize data.

KSpread uses the KChart component for data visualization. KChart can also be used as a standalone charting application.

Now we will take a look at how simple charts can be created inside KSpread.

Assume that you are a company that deals with several products, and you want to see how much profit you can make with each product and compare the results. For this a nice chart is very useful.

Start KSpread with a blank worksheet. The application should look like Figure 8-38.

Entering data into the table is straightforward: simply go to the desired cell with the arrow keys or click on it with the mouse. Now enter data into the table, as shown in Figure 8-39. It does not matter much where you start. In this example, we have chosen cell B4 for the Expense text. After you have entered the data, select the area to create a chart from, as shown in Figure 8-40.

Now click on the Insert Chart toolbar icon, which you can see in Figure 8-40. The mouse cursor changes to a cross, indicating that you now have to select the area

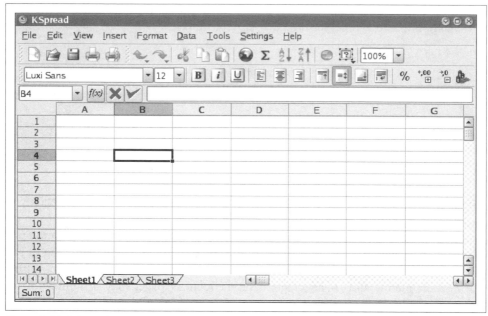

Figure 8-38. KSpread at startup

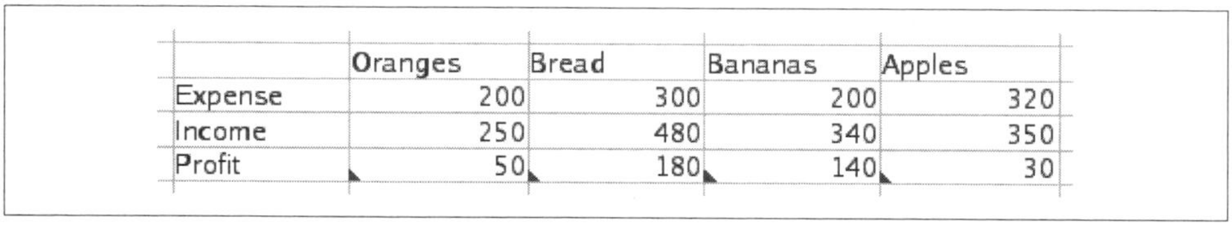

	Oranges	Bread	Bananas	Apples
Expense	200	300	200	320
Income	250	480	340	350
Profit	50	180	140	30

Figure 8-39. Entering data into a spreadsheet

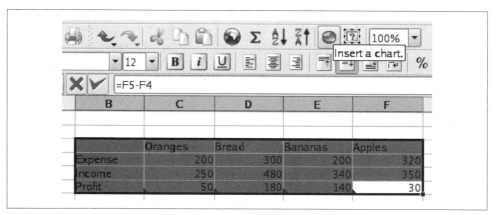

Figure 8-40. Selecting an area to be charted

where you want to place your chart. Simply draw a rectangle below the table with the left mouse button. After you release the mouse button, a wizard asks you for the chart type you want to insert. Use the default (Bar) and click Finish (Figure 8-41).

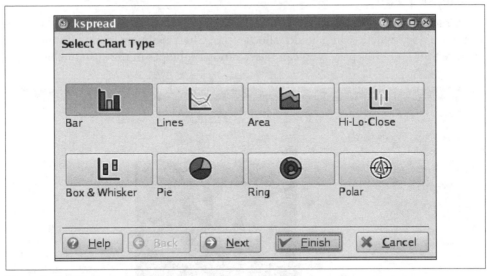

Figure 8-41. The chart wizard

The result will look like Figure 8-42. In this chart you see the expense (red on the screen, although it does not appear in color in the printed book), the income (green), and the profit (blue) for each product. If you would like the percentage shown for each of the products, simply double-click on the chart.

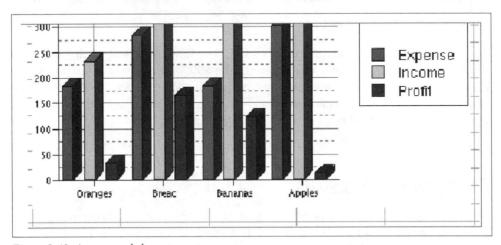

Figure 8-42. A generated chart

Note how the toolbars and the menu change. This is a good example of the tight integration in KOffice, which allows it to use components inside components very flexibly. The menu and the toolbar shown here are the ones that are relevant for the KChart component.

Now right-click on the chart and choose Configure Chart. This brings up a configuration dialog, where you should choose the Chart Subtype configuration page (Figure 8-43). On this page, you can select various subtypes of the current chart type.

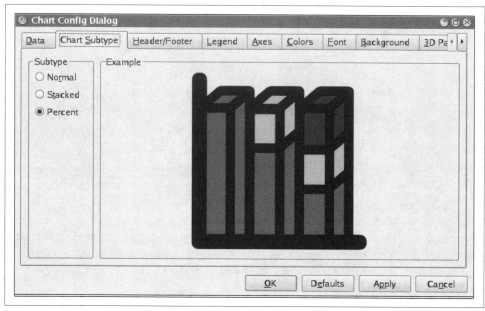

Figure 8-43. Selecting a chart subtype

For this example, select Percent and click OK. The final result will be the nice chart in Figure 8-44. Every product is scaled to fit the 100% mark, and we see how much expenses we have and how much income we get for each product. Finally, the profit shows the difference between income and expense. We can conclude that bananas make the most profit, whereas apples have very little.

Go ahead and try various configurations and see how the data is represented!

Other Word Processors

Although the word processors discussed so far are the most popular among Linux users, this book would not be fair to the rich environment in which Linux and free software thrive if it failed to mention some of the other alternatives.

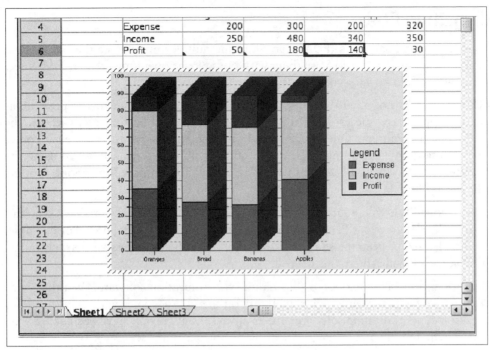

Figure 8-44. The final chart

Anyware Office, by VistaSource, Inc.

Anyware Office is an office suite that is commercially made but inexpensive for Linux. It includes not only a word processor but also a spreadsheet, a drawing program, a mail program, and other smaller tools. In some respects, Anyware Office behaves differently from word processors such as Microsoft Word or WordPerfect, but once you get used to it, it can be quite useful and handy. Especially noteworthy is its support for importing and exporting FrameMaker documents. The development seems to have stopped somewhat, though, and it is uncertain what will become of this product.

AbiWord

You can find information about this word processor at *http://www.abiword.org*.

LyX

The LyX package (also available as KLyX with a more modern user interface) provides a decent WYSIWYG X user interface that works with window managers from standard Linux distributions and uses the LᴬTEX and TEX packages to format the text for printing. If you can live with the formatting limits of the package (most of us can), you may find that LyX/KLyX is an excellent solution. LyX/KLyX does not know how to display some of the powerful formatting features that TEX provides, so if you are a power TEX user, this isn't for you. LyX/KLyX isn't part of most Linux distributions; to try it, you will have to get it from a Linux archive.

Synching PDAs

Personal digital assistants (PDAs) have become quite commonplace these days, and as Linux adepts, we want to use them with our favorite operating system. In this section, we explain how to synchronize PDAs with Linux desktops.

This section is not about running Linux *on* PDAs, even though this is possible as well. People have successfully run Linux and Linux application software on the HP/Compaq iPaq line. One PDA product line, the Sharp Zaurus series, even comes with Linux preinstalled, though it does not show up very obviously when using the device. *http://www.handhelds.org* has a lot of valuable information about running Linux on PDAs.

Using your PDA with your desktop means, for most intents and purposes, synchronizing the data on your PDA with the data on your desktop computer. For example, you will want to keep the same address book on both computers, and synchronization software will achieve this for you.

Do not expect PDA vendors to ship Linux synchronization software; even the Sharp Zaurus—which, as mentioned, runs Linux on the PDA—comes with only Windows desktop synchronization software. But as always, Linux people have been able to roll their own; a number of packages are available for this purpose.

Synchronizing your PDA with your desktop involves a number of steps:

- Creating the actual hardware connection and making the hardware (the PDA and its cradle or other means of connection) known to Linux.
- Installing software that handles special synchronization hardware such as HotSync buttons
- Installing software that handles the actual synchronization of data objects
- Using desktop software that ensures synchronization at the application level (e.g., between the PDA calendar and your desktop calendar software)

Checking the Connection

Let's have a look at the hardware first. PDAs are usually connected to the desktop by means of a so-called *cradle*, a small unit that is wired to the computer and accepts the PDA in order to connect it electrically. Sometimes, a direct sync cable is used, attached to both the desktop computer and the PDA. The connection on the desktop computer side is either a USB interface or—much less often these days—a serial interface.

The first step in getting the connection to work is to see whether your PDA is recognized by the kernel. So connect the cradle (or the direct cable) to your computer and your PDA. Take a look at the kernel log messages, which you can do by becoming *root* and typing *tail -f /var/log/messages*. (More information on kernel log messages is presented in "Managing System Logs" in Chapter 10.)

Now, while viewing the kernel log messages, force a synchronization attempt from the PDA, such as by pressing the HotSync button at the cradle or issuing a command in the user interface of the PDA that performs a synchronization. If the PDA is connected via USB, you should see something like the following (some lines were truncated to fit the book's page):

```
Jun 21 10:32:52 tigger kernel: ohci_hcd 0000:02:06.1: wakeup
Jun 21 10:32:52 tigger kernel: klogd 1.4.1, ---------- state change ----------
Jun 21 10:32:52 tigger kernel: usb 3-2: new full speed USB device using address
Jun 21 10:32:52 tigger kernel: usb 3-2: Product: Palm Handheld
Jun 21 10:32:52 tigger kernel: usb 3-2: Manufacturer: Palm, Inc.
Jun 21 10:32:52 tigger kernel: usb 3-2: SerialNumber: 30300630419440343035069090
Jun 21 10:32:52 tigger kernel: visor 3-2:1.0: Handspring Visor / Palm OS convert
Jun 21 10:32:52 tigger kernel: usb 3-2: Handspring Visor / Palm OS converter now
Jun 21 10:32:52 tigger kernel: usb 3-2: Handspring Visor / Palm OS converter now
```

In this case, a USB-connected Palm Tungsten T3 was found. If nothing shows up, several things could have gone wrong: the hardware connection could be broken, the synchronization request could not have been recognized, or the kernel could be missing the necessary driver modules. Chapter 18 has more information about locating and installing kernel driver modules, in case that's the problem.

KPilot Synchronization

Next, you need the software that synchronizes actual data over the wire. For the very common Palm family of PDA (which also includes the Sony Clié, the Handspring Visor, and many other look-alikes), this is the *pilot-link* package. The package is already included with many popular distributions; if you need to download it, you can find it at *http://www.pilot-link.org*. Usually, you are not going to use the programs contained in this package directly, but through other application software that builds on them. What this package contains, besides the building blocks for creating said application software, is *conduits*, small applications that support one particular type of data to be synchronized. There are conduits for the calendar, the address book, and so on.

Up to this point, the software and procedures we've described were dependent on the type of PDA you want to synchronize, and independent of your desktop software. The actual software that you are going to interact with, however, is different for different desktops. We look here at KPilot, a comprehensive package for the KDE desktop that synchronizes Palm-like PDAs with both KDE desktop applications such as KOrganizer and KAddressBook and GNOME desktop applications such as Evolution.

KPilot, at *http://www.kpilot.org*, consists of two programs, *kpilotDaemon* and *kpilot*. In theory, you need only *kpilotDaemon*, as this is the software that waits for the HotSync button to be pressed and then performs the synchronization. In practice, you will want to use the *kpilot* application at least initially, as it allows you to configure the daemon and check that everything works as expected.

Upon starting up KPilot (Figure 8-45), select Settings → Configure KPilot from the menu bar. The program offers to start the Configuration Wizard; click that button. On the first page, you need to provide two pieces of information: the username stored in the PDA (so that the data is synced with the right desktop data), and the desktop computer port to which the PDA is connected. KPilot offers to autodetect this, which you should always try. If it cannot autodetect your connection (and you have ensured that the actual hardware connection is working, as described in the previous section), try specifying either */dev/ttyUSB1* or */dev/ttyUSB2* (or even higher numbers) if you have a USB-connected PDA, and */dev/ttyS0* or */dev/ttyS1* if you have a serially connected PDA. On the next page, you will be asked which desktop application set you want to synchronize with; pick the right one for you here.

Once you are set up, you can give KPilot a try. It will have started *kpilotDaemon* automatically if it was not running yet.

During the following steps, keep an eye on the HotSync Log window in KPilot; there could be important information here that can help you troubleshoot problems. If you see the message "Pilot device /dev/ttyUSB2 does not exist. Probably it is a USB device and will appear during a HotSync" or something similar, that's nothing to worry about.

Now press the HotSync button on the cradle or force a synchronization in whichever way your PDA does this. If you see "Device link ready," plus many more progress messages about the various conduits, things should be going fine. Notice that if you have a lot of applications installed on your PDA, the synchronization progress can take quite a while.

What can you expect to work on Linux? Synchronizing the standard applications, such as calendar, address book, and notes, should work just fine. For many other commercially available PDA applications, there is no Linux software provided, but since KPilot is able to synchronize Palm databases without actually understanding their contents, you can at least back up and restore this data. You can also install the application packages themselves by means of KPilot's File Installer. Even the popular news channel synchronization software AvantGo works nicely on Linux.

Things that typically do not work (or are very difficult to get to work) are access to additional storage media such as CompactFlash cards, and applications that perform additional functionality for synchronization (such as downloading new databases from a web site as part of the synchronization process). A typical example of the latter category is airline timetable applications. So if you have a Windows computer available (or have configured your computer to be dual-boot for both Windows and Linux), it can be a good idea to still install the Windows desktop

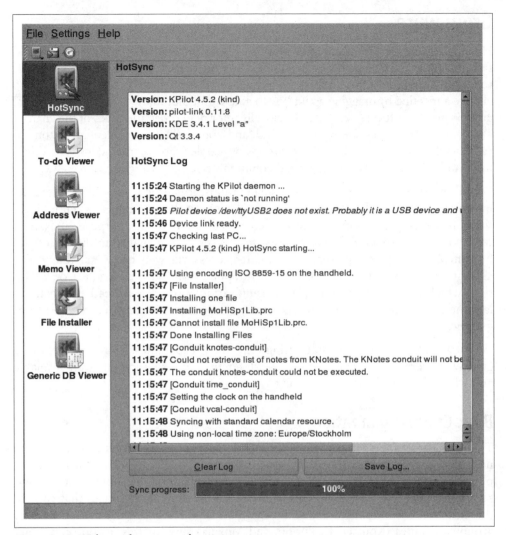

Figure 8-45. KPilot performs a synchronization

synchronization software. For day-to-day activities, Linux and your PDA (at least Palm-like PDAs) are an excellent combination.

Work is currently being done on creating a unified synchronization application called KitchenSync. Once this is ready, the intention is to replace not only KPilot and other PDA synchronization packages but also the many smaller packages for synchronizing your Linux desktop computer with various types of cellular phones. KitchenSync is a work in progress, and you can find more information about it at *http://www.handhelds.org/~zecke/kitchensync.html*. Another program that aims in a similar direction is OpenSync.

Groupware

Helping a group of people coordinate their work or private lives—their calendars and task lists, their notes and address books, and so forth—presents one of the rare opportunities for computers to actually solve a real, everyday problem. Imagine being able to change a meeting by dragging a text box to a new time slot in the calendar application, and having the software system automatically inform all other attendees of the change, ask them whether they still want to attend, and update their own calendars automatically. Such software, which supports groups of people who are interacting, coordinating with each other, and cooperating, is commonly referred to as *groupware*.

For all but the simplest needs of very small groups, it is usually sensible to store the information that is to be shared or exchanged between the members at a central location on the network. Often a computer is dedicated to this purpose; it is then referred to as a *groupware server*. Access to this server is managed in different ways by different groupware projects. Most offer access via web browsers. Many also allow users to work with full-fledged client applications such as Kontact or Evolution, which then connect to the server using various protocols to read and manipulate the data stored there. In this context such applications are often referred to as *groupware suites*.

We first look at what is possible using only client capabilites, without access to a groupware server, and then examine the different server solutions that are available and what addtional benefits they bring.

Basic Group Organization

Thanks to a set of established Internet standards, groupware users can collaborate not only using a single groupware server—within a single organization, for example—but also to a certain extent with partners using different groupware clients and servers on Linux or Windows. This is done by sending email messages that contain the groupware information as attachments back and forth. All the available Linux groupware suites (Kontact, Evolution, and Mozilla) support this, as do proprietary clients on Windows and Mac OS such as MS Outlook or Lotus Notes.

As an example, let's look at what ensues when you invite your friendly neighbor, who happens to still be running Windows and using MS Outlook, to your barbecue garden party on Wednesday. To do that you open your calendar to the current week and create a new event on Wednesday afternoon. (See Figure 8-46. We use Kontact in this example.) Add your neighbor as an attendee of the event and, since without him the party would be no fun, set his participation to be required. Once you've entered all the relevant information and closed the dialog, an email is constructed and sent to the email address of your neighbor. This message consists of a text part with the description of the event and an additional messsage part containing the details of the event in a certain format, which is specified in RFC 2446 and referred to as *iTip*.

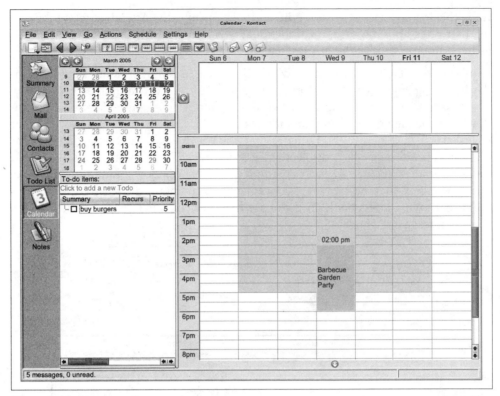

Figure 8-46. Creating a new event in Kontact

At the receiving end, your neighbor's Outlook mailer detects the incoming message as an invitation to an event and reads the relevant information from the attachments. One attachment asks your neighbor whether he'll be able to attend and whether the invitation should be accepted, declined, or accepted tentatively. Since he's not quite sure that Wednesday might be the night of a sports event he plans to watch, let's say he chooses to accept the event tentatively. The event is then added to his own calendar inside Outlook and a reply message is constructed and sent, again containing a special iTip attachment.

Once that message makes it back to you, Kontact will inform you that the person you invited has tentatively accepted the invitation, and will enter that information into your calendar. As soon as your neighbor decides to either decline or accept the invitation, an update message will be sent and the status updated accordingly in your calendar upon receipt of that message. Should you decide to delete the event from your calendar, such an update message would in turn be sent to all attendees automatically.

The described mechanisms work not only for events, but also for assigning and sending tasks to other people and being informed when those tasks have been completed. To do that, you can add participants to tasks in Kontact's Todo List view by right-clicking on a task, selecting Edit, and then opening the Attendees tab of the dialog that pops up. Of course, this functionality is also available in other clients, such as Evolution or Mozilla; the dialogs just look a bit different.

Similar to the iTip format (or iCal, which iTip is based on), there is an Internet standard for exchanging contact information called *vCard*. To communicate your new street address and phone number to your grandmother, who uses Mozilla on Windows for managing her many contacts, you could send her a message with your vCard attached (Figure 8-47). Using Kontact, this is as easy as right-clicking on your entry in the address book and selecting Send Contact. The resulting message should be easily understandable by most email programs on Windows, Linux, or the Mac. Most programs offer the user some convenient way to import the received vCard into his or her own address book. You can see how Kontact's mail component presents such a message in Figure 8-48.

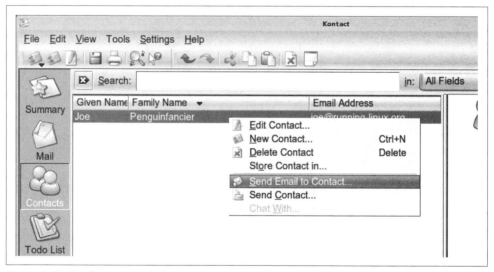

Figure 8-47. Sending your vCard

Figure 8-48. Receiving a vCard

As we have seen, it is quite possible to carry out basic group organization using only email mechanisms. This has two advantages: no groupware server is needed, and the operations work across different platforms and clients. On the other hand, things such as sharing a common calendar between several people or allowing read-only access to centrally managed information are not easily done with this scheme. This is where a groupware server starts to make sense.

Groupware Server Solutions

Linux is supported as a platform by a wide range of groupware server solutions, including both open source projects and proprietary products. They all offer a core set of functionality for email, calendaring, and address and task management, but also contain various extensions for things such as resource management, time tracking, and even project planning. In general, these systems can be extended with custom components to offer functionality that is not provided by the standard package. Such components are sometimes available from the creators themselves, but are also often developed by third-party developers or as part of individual consulting projects.

The following sections describe the most well-known solutions available as free software at the time of this writing, with their respective focus areas and peculiarities.

Kolab

The Kolab project grew out of a contract given by the German Federal Agency of IT Security to a group of companies to build a groupware solution accessible by both Outlook on Microsoft Windows and a KDE client on Linux. The developers created a sequence of concept documents and reference server implementations (called Kolab 1 and Kolab 2). They also built the ability to access these servers and operate on their data into the KDE Kontact suite client. Additionally, a closed-source plug-in for MS Outlook and a web-based client were developed.

The server implementation (Kolab 2) includes popular free software server components such as the Cyrus IMAP server for mail storage, the Postfix mail transfer agent, OpenLDAP as a directory service, and the Apache web server. It is a complete, standalone system that installs itself from scratch onto a basic Linux machine without any outside dependencies. The Kolab server is unique in that it does not store the groupware data in a relational database, like many of the others do, but instead uses mail folders inside the IMAP server for storage. Finally, it provides a unified management interface, written in PHP, to the components.

The Kolab server allows users to share calendars and contact folders with each other using fine-grained permissions for groups or individual people. It also offers management of distribution lists and resources such as rooms or cars, and the ability to check the free or busy state of people and resources. There is also a form of delegated authority, in which people can work on behalf of others, such as a secretary acting on behalf of his boss.

You can find more about Kolab at *http://www.kolab.org*.

OpenGroupware.org

The groupware server project (nicknamed OGo) came into being when Skyrix Software AG put its established commercial product under free software licenses and continued as the most significant contributor in the community to improve the product. This move worked out nicely for the company, as both its business and the groupware server project have been thriving ever since.

The OGo server provides a web-based interface to email, calendaring, contacts, and document and tasks management. In addition to the browser-based interface, all data can be accessed via several different standard protocols, so that access from Kontact or Evolution is also possible. Plug-ins that enable Windows users to connect to the server with Outlook exist as well, albeit as a commercial add-on product. Users can share calendars and address books as well as task lists, and can create arbitrary associations between individual entries.

To be fully functional, an OGo installation needs several additional components, such as an IMAP server, a PostgreSQL database, a working mail transfer agent, and a directory service such as OpenLDAP.

You can find more about OGo at *http://www.opengroupware.org*.

phpGroupWare and eGroupware

Coming from a common PHP codebase, phpGroupWare and eGroupware offer groupware functionality primarily through browser-based access. Users can manipulate and view their own and other people's calendars and contact information and manage files, notes, and news items. Several additional optional applications are available.

Both servers need to be installed on top of an existing web server and database and can make use of a mail server for sending and accessing mail via IMAP, if one is available.

More information about phpGroupware and eGroupware is available at the following URL: *http://www .phpgroupware.org* and *http://www.egroupware.org*.

OPEN-XCHANGE

The OPEN-XCHANGE server started out as a proprietary product, but has since been put under open source licenses. Like many other solutions, it builds on and works with other server components, such as the Apache web server and OpenLDAP. On top of those, it offers several standard modules, such as a calendar and contacts and tasks management, as well as document and project management, and discussion forum, knowledge base, and web mail components.

Technologically, OPEN-XCHANGE is different from many of the other solutions in that it is built using Java technologies. This makes it attractive if integration with existing Java-based applications is desired.

Read more about OPEN-XCHANGE at *http://www.open-xchange.org*.

Closed-source products

In addition to the free and open source solutions described in the previous sections, several commercial and nonfree alternatives are available as well. All of them are powerful and full-featured, and support Linux as a native platform either exclusively or along with other platforms. The most important ones include Novell Groupwise, Novell SUSE Linux Openexchange (based on OPEN-XCHANGE), Lotus Notes & Domino, Oracle Groupware, and Samsung Contact and Scalix (both based on HP Openmail). The web sites of the respective vendors and products have more information on each of them.

LDAP: Accessing Global Address Books

One of the benefits of having information centrally stored and maintained is that changes and updates need only be done in one place and are then available to everyone immediately. This is especially important for contact information, which is prone to change and become out of date. The ability to quickly search through large amounts of contacts flexibly is another requirement that becomes more important the larger the organization gets, with all its internal and external communication partners. To meet this need, so-called *directory services* have been developed, along with a standard protocol to access and query them. The protocol is Lightweight Directory Access Protocol (LDAP), shared by a number of implementations, including the open source implementation OpenLDAP and (with typical Microsoft extensions) Microsoft Active Directory. OpenLDAP can be integrated with many of the groupware systems described in the previous sections.

The address book components of all major groupware suites allow the administrator to tie them to one or several LDAP servers, which are then queried for contact information and will be used for email autocompletion when composing emails. In Kontact, the LDAP configuration dialog for adding a new LDAP query host looks like Figure 8-49.

Specify the hostname of the server to be used for queries, the port it listens on (the default should be fine), and a so-called *base DN*, which is the place in the LDAP hierarchy where searches should start. The choice of base DN can help tailor the LDAP queries to the needs of your users. If, for example, your company has a global address book with subtrees for each of its five continental branches, you might prefer to search only your local branch instead of the full directory. Your site's administrator should be able to tell you the values to be entered here. If the server only allows queries by authenticated users, enter your credentials as well.

Figure 8-49. Adding a new LDAP host in Kontact

With LDAP access set up, you can try opening up a mail composer in Kontact, for example, and typing someone's name in the recipient field. After a second or so a list of possible matches that were found in the central LDAP addressbook should be shown. You can then simply select the one you were thinking of from the list. Additionally all groupware suites offer the ability to search for and display someone's contact information, if you just want to look it up. In Kontact, the query dialog can be shown by clicking the LDAP Lookup button on the toolbar or from the Tools menu.

Managing Your Finances

By now you may have noticed there is an open source application for just about anything you could want to do with a computer. Managing finances is one of the most common things people do with their computers, so it should not come as a surprise that an open source application exists to do just that—it's called *GnuCash*.

GnuCash is the open source world's answer to popular personal financial applications such as Microsoft Money and Intuit's Quicken. Although it doesn't have all the bells and whistles of those applications, GnuCash has everything you need for keeping track of your money. With GnuCash you can keep tabs on your income, expenses, checking and savings accounts, debts, investments, and assets such as cars and houses. You will be able to see into the past to figure out where all your money has been going, keep an eye on your balances in the present to make sure you don't suffer any nasty surprises, and forecast your financial well-being into the distant and not-so-distant future.

If you use an off-the-shelf application such as Money or Quicken, you're in for a few surprises when you try GnuCash. Compared with those applications, the interface is extremely simple and straightforward. There are no fancy embedded web pages or advisors. You won't find endless options dialogs and wizards, and you can't pay your bills electronically from inside GnuCash. Instead, when you start GnuCash you are presented with a simple list of accounts. Double-clicking on an account opens an account register (which looks exactly like the one in your checkbook). You enter transactions in the account register, and the balance of each account is shown in the accounts list. You can view several reports to get an at-a-glance view of your financial life. That's almost all there is to GnuCash.

This simplicity is an asset, not a liability. When it comes to finances, simpler is better. The other major difference between GnuCash and those other applications has to do with the way you keep track of your money. We cover that in detail in "The Account," later in this chapter.

Getting Started

Start GnuCash from the desktop menu, if GnuCash is present there, or from the command line by typing *gnucash*. The GnuCash splash screen appears, showing you which modules are loading. The splash screen is then replaced by the Tip of the Day screen and the Welcome to GnuCash! dialog box.

The Tip of the Day screen presents a different piece of information each time you start GnuCash. You can also peruse the tips one at a time by clicking either the Prev or Next buttons. I would keep this screen around for a while because the information can be useful, but if you prefer not to see it you can always disable the feature by unchecking the "Display this dialog next time" checkbox. You can close the window by clicking the Close button, but not until you answer the question in the Welcome dialog.

The Welcome dialog (Figure 8-50) is only displayed the first time you use GnuCash. It gives you the option to create a new set of accounts, import data from Quicken (via QIF files), or open the new user tutorial. In this exercise, you are going to create a new set of accounts, which should be the default option, so click the OK button.

Figure 8-50. The GnuCash Welcome dialog

This launches the New Account Hierarchy Setup druid. A *druid* in Linux is analo-gous to a wizard in Windows; both are dialogs that take you click by click through a series of questions and setup screens to perform a complicated task. The first screen you see in the New Account Hierarchy Setup druid is an explanation of the druid. Click Next to go on to the important parts.

Choosing a currency

In Figure 8-51 you see the dialog for currency selection for new accounts. The default currency is USD (U.S. Dollar). If you use a different currency, select it by clicking the down arrow and choosing from the available options in the drop-down list. Click Next to continue.

Figure 8-51. The Choose Currency page

Choosing accounts

Figure 8-52 shows you the list of preset account structures. Each of these options creates one or more accounts for you. You can select multiple options (for example, if you wanted both A Simple Checkbook and Car Loan), but for now just select A Simple Checkbook. Once you select that option, you see a description and a list of the accounts that will be created. Don't worry about the number of available accounts; it may look confusing, but it will become clear by the end of this chapter. Click Next to continue.

Entering opening balances

The dialog in Figure 8-53 gives you the opportunity to give each account an opening balance, that is, the amount of money in that account when you first begin tracking it in GnuCash. If you want to put an opening balance in your checking account, just click that account to select it and enter the opening balance in the text box to the right. Click Next to continue.

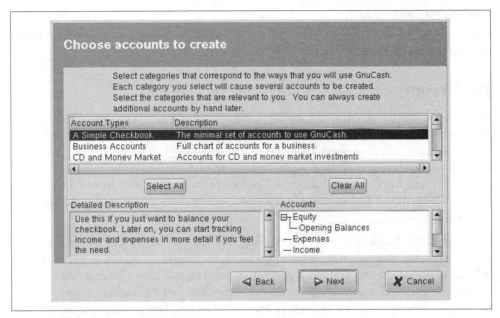

Figure 8-52. Account creation page

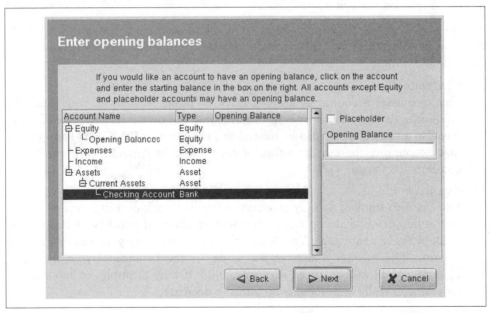

Figure 8-53. Opening balances page

Finishing your account setup

That's all there is to setting up an account hierarchy in GnuCash. Just click Finish, and the druid will close.

The Account

Fundamental to GnuCash is the account. An account is just what you think it is: a place where money comes in and money goes out. When most people think of accounts, they think of their bank accounts and credit card accounts. GnuCash treats these as accounts, but it treats everything else as an account too. You get a paycheck from work; where does the money come from? It comes from your Income account. You spend $30 at the grocery store; where does the money go? It goes to your Food account.

GnuCash uses the double-entry accounting method to keep track of your money. This is the same method that professional accountants and CPAs use to keep track of billions of dollars in corporate and government assets, and now you're going to use it too (don't you feel important?). In double-entry accounting, money always comes from one account and goes to another account. Always. The value of any account at a given time is either how much money is actually in that account or how much money has passed through it.

Not all accounts are treated equally in GnuCash. There are five types of accounts that will be covered in this introduction: assets, liabilities, income, expenses, and equity.

Asset accounts
> Think of asset accounts as keeping track of things you own. Your checking account is an asset. If money is in this account, you own it. If you have a house, it is also an asset. It can also be treated as an account in GnuCash. The value of that account is the current value of the home. In general, you want asset accounts to increase.

Liability accounts
> You can also think of liability accounts as keeping track of things you own. The only difference is that you don't want to own them! If you have a house, you probably have a mortgage. You "own" this promise to pay your lender a certain amount. The amount you have left to pay is the balance of your mortgage account. Credit card balances, car loans, and IOUs are examples of liabilities. In general, you really want liability accounts to decrease.

Income accounts
> Unlike asset and liability accounts, income accounts don't represent money you own (at least not directly). Think of the income account as a window into some-one else's (usually your employer's) check register. When your boss writes a check to you, it gets recorded on the withdrawals side of his register. If you can

imagine those records also showing up in your income account (giving you a glimpse into the portion of his checkbook that concerns you), then you have some idea of how income accounts work. Money doesn't usually stay in these accounts; it immediately goes into one of your asset accounts (usually your checkbook). The value of this account at any time is the total amount you have been paid. It probably goes without saying that you always want these accounts to increase.

Expense accounts

Expense accounts also don't represent money you own. You can think of them as a glimpse into the deposit side of the checkbooks of whomever you are paying at the time. The value of each expense account is the total amount you have paid to that person, business, or activity so far. Although you can't decrease the value of expense accounts (except via refunds and rebates), you do want to manage them well.

Equity accounts

Equity accounts are the odd man out of this group. Although there is a formal definition of equity in the accounting world, it is beyond the scope of this introduction. The easiest way to think of the equity account is as the place where opening balances come from. Remember we said that, in GnuCash, money must always come from some account and go to some other account. What about opening balances—where do they come from? They don't come from income, since it's not like you got a paycheck for that opening balance. Instead, they come from the equity account.

The GnuCash Accounts Window

The main window of GnuCash, shown in Figure 8-54, is the accounts window. This window shows all of your accounts in the currently open file. The accounts are listed in tree form because accounts can contain subaccounts (more on this later). For now, all you need to know is that a plus sign to the left of an account name indicates that is a parent account of one or more subaccounts, and that clicking on the plus sign expands the listing so you can see all accounts under the parent.

The accounts listing shows the account name, a description, and the current account total by default. If an account is a parent to one or more subaccounts, the account total is the combined total of all its subaccounts as well as the parent account itself. Clicking once on an account selects it. Right-clicking on an account shows a context menu with the options to create a new account, delete an account, edit an account's properties, and perform numerous other tasks. Double-clicking an account brings up the associated account ledger, or register. You will learn more about ledgers later.

Figure 8-54. The GnuCash accounts window

Creating new accounts

There are several ways to create a new account. The easiest way is to right-click on an empty area in the accounts window. Another way is to select New Account under the File menu. Create a new account now by selecting the Income account and right-clicking. In the context menu that appears, select New Account to begin.

Figure 8-55 shows the New Account screen. The first thing you need to do is give the account a name. Because you're going to record all the money you get from your job in this account, type Paycheck in the Account Name field. The Account Code and Description fields are for your personal use if you need to record an account code (such as an account number from your bank) or a more descriptive description. You can set the commodity of this account just as you did for the main accounts file. By default it uses the commodity (USD, Euro, GBP, etc.) and commodity type (currency) of the main file, but you can change this to use other commodities (for example, if you're a spy and have a numbered bank account in Zurich) or other commodity types. This is useful for tracking stocks, bonds, and other financial instruments. The available commodity types are determined by the account type you select.

Next up is the Account Type. In this box you find the five account types introduced earlier as well as other types used for special purposes. The point of our Paycheck account is to keep track of income, so scroll down until you find the Income entry, and select that. After Account Type is the Parent Account box. Accounts can be nested, which means that one account can exist as part of another account. You already have an account called Income, so click on the plus sign next to New Top Level Account. This expands the tree to show your existing accounts. Scroll down until you see the Income account and select it. This puts your Paycheck account under the Income account.

If you don't see the Account Type and Parent Account fields, it is probably because you need to resize the window to be taller. If the window is already as tall as your

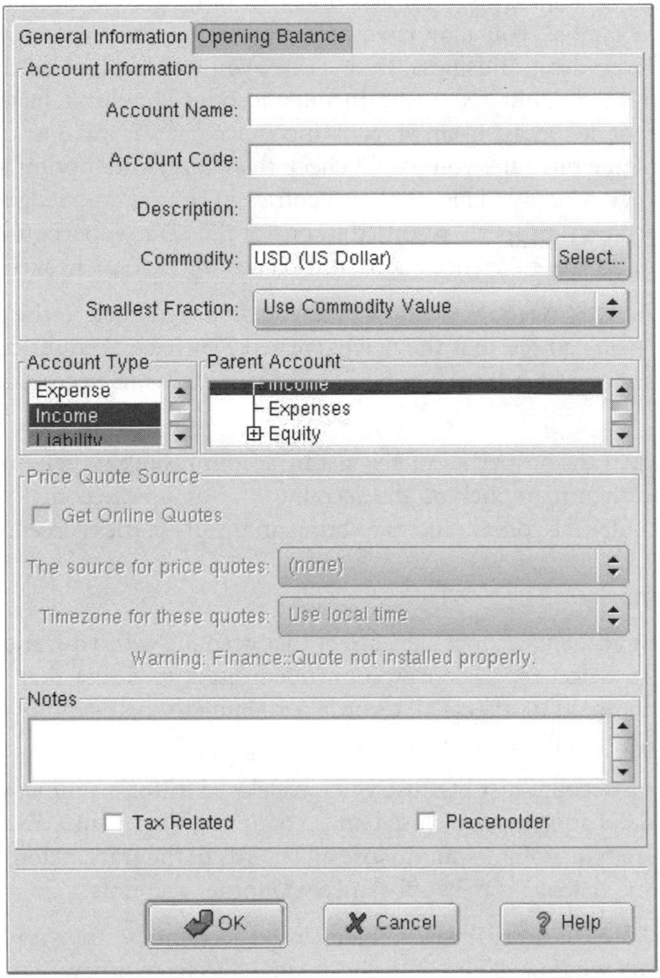

Figure 8-55. The New Account screen

screen allows, you probably need to adjust your screen resolution, which both KDE and GNOME allow through dialog boxes.

If this account was for stocks and other special commodities, you could set up a way to get price quotes (say, to check the value of a stock) online. But explaining this is beyond the purpose of this chapter. The Notes field just lets you add notes to yourself, which you can see later if you go back to this screen.

Finally, there are two checkboxes near the bottom: Tax Related and Placeholder. The Tax Related checkbox links this account with tax information so that certain tax values are automatically calculated. Using this property is beyond the scope of this chapter.

The Placeholder account is used for accounts that only serve as organizers for other accounts. For example, you may have three sources of income: job, parents, and your weekend web design business. In this case, you would place all three accounts under the Income account. Now the Income account shouldn't have any activity directly inside of it, because all of your income comes from one of these three sources. To enforce this rule, you would check the Placeholder option in the Income account's settings window. This disallows entries in the Income ledger, so you can be sure that income is properly recorded in one of the three subaccounts. You don't want this option for your Paycheck account, so keep the box unchecked.

Click OK on the New Account window, and you are taken back to the main account window page. You can see that the newly created Paycheck account has been highlighted. Also notice that it has been placed under the Income account, just like you wanted.

If you want to edit the properties of an existing account, simply click on that account to select it, and then right-click on the account to bring up the context menu. Select Edit Account under the context menu to bring up the properties screen.

Deleting accounts

If you create an account erroneously, select that account with your mouse and then right-click on it. Select the Delete Account menu item to delete that account from your file. Beware that this affects all records pertaining to this account and may leave your accounts in an unbalanced state.

Do not delete an account just because you have closed it (for example, you paid off a credit card and cut it up or you closed an account at an old bank). Even though the account is closed, you do not want to lose all records of the transactions contained in that account, and deleting it may unbalance your other accounts.

Unfortunately, there is no real way to hide closed accounts so they no longer appear in your accounts window. There is a cheat, though: create a new top-level account called Closed as a placeholder account, and move all closed accounts under that account (by setting the new Closed account as the parent account). Since you can click the minus sign to collapse the closed accounts, all you see is the parent account and not all of your old accounts under it. This trick isn't perfect or particularly elegant, but it works.

Transactions

If the heart of GnuCash is the account, transactions are the blood. Without transactions, you simply have a bunch of accounts listed in a window. This isn't terribly useful; you probably want to do something with all these accounts. Recording transactions is exactly what makes GnuCash useful.

A *transaction* in GnuCash is a record of a specific event. This event is usually money being transferred from one place to another, but it could also be the equivalent value in stocks, bonds, or real estate. For a concrete example of a transaction, look no further than your own checkbook. If you keep a register, the individual entries in that register are records of transactions. When you use GnuCash, you simply record those transactions in the computer instead of in your checkbook (of course, a prudent person would do both).

Entering transactions

To enter transactions, you must open an account's register window, shown in Figure 8-56. You can access the register window for any account by double-clicking on the account in the accounts window. Let's start by recording a simple income transaction. You just mowed the lawn for Aunt Alice, and she paid you $25.00 for your troubles. Here's how to record the transaction in GnuCash.

Expand your Assets account, followed by the Current Assets account, and then double-click on Checking Account to bring up the register.

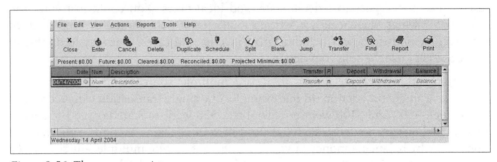

Figure 8-56. The account register

Today's date is already in the Date field. Hit the Tab key to move to the next field (Tab moves you forward through fields, and Shift-Tab moves you backward). The Num field lets you enter your check number or any other tracking number you need for this transaction. In this case, pretend that Aunt Alice gave you check number 100, so put 100 in the field.

Tab to the Description field and enter something, well, descriptive. Mowed Aunt Alice's Lawn is appropriate.

Tab to the Transfer field. This is one of the most important fields. Remember that in GnuCash, money always come from some account and goes to another. In this case you want money to come from your Income account and go into Checking Account. The good thing about this (and every other) field is that it autocompletes for you. Just enter In and it should display an account list and select the Income account automatically.

Since you are receiving money from Aunt Alice, tab to the Deposit field and enter 25.00.

When you press Enter, the transaction is recorded. When you close the register window and look at your accounts, you can see that both the Income account and the Checking Account have increased to $25.00. Notice also that the parent accounts of Checking Account also show $25.00. Parent accounts show the sum of all accounts below them. At a glance, you can see that you have made $25.00 in income so far and you have $25.00 in your checking account.

To delete a transaction, go to the register containing the transaction, right-click on the transaction, and select Delete. Doing this removes the transaction from all affected accounts. In the case of the check from Aunt Alice, the transaction is removed from the Income and Checking accounts.

Recording split transactions

Let's say you have a paycheck in hand, ready to enter into GnuCash. If you're like most people, the amount you get paid is different from the amount you earned. The rest of the money goes to federal, state, and local taxes. You could just enter the amount for which the check was written, but what if you wanted to keep track of total income and expenses, including gross income and taxes? The way to do this in GnuCash is to use the split transaction.

Split transactions provide a way to record multiple sources and destinations of money as a single transaction. In this example, one single transaction can record that you earned $500 and $100 went to federal tax, $50 went to state tax, and $50 went to local tax, leaving you with a $300 deposit to your checking account. Split transactions work by balancing money in versus money out among multiple sources and/or destinations. GnuCash allows you to have an unbalanced split, but it will complain loudly.

To enter a split transaction, follow these steps:

1. Open an account register. Split transactions are usually recorded at the logical source or destination. For a paycheck, it is common to record the transaction inside your checking account.

2. Enter the date and description as you would for any transaction.

3. Click the Split button on the Account Register's toolbar.

4. Press Tab to advance to the first subtransaction.

5. Enter each part of the transaction as you would a normal transaction. Here's the tricky part: Deposit and Withdrawal apply to the account you're transferring money to or from at the time. For our example transaction, you are withdrawing $500 from your Income:Paycheck account in the form of wages, and splitting that into several deposits in your Expenses and Assests:Current Assests: Checking Account. At first it may seem counterintuitive that taxes are a deposit

in an account, but if you reread the earlier definition for an Expense account it should make sense. Use Figure 8-57 as a guide for filling out this transaction. When you finish with a subtransaction, press Tab to go to the next subtransaction. I find it convenient to perform transactions like this by making my first split the withdrawal from the Income account. This makes the balancing that GnuCash automatically performs on the splits that follow work better.

6. Press the Enter key to finish the split transaction. If the transaction is not balanced (money in does not equal money out), GnuCash warns you and offers several solutions. GnuCash realizes that you're not as good at math as the computer, so it displays the amount remaining on the last subtransaction line. Once everything balances correctly, the split transactions collapse into a single line.

7. To see an already recorded split, select that transaction with the mouse and click the Split button on the toolbar.

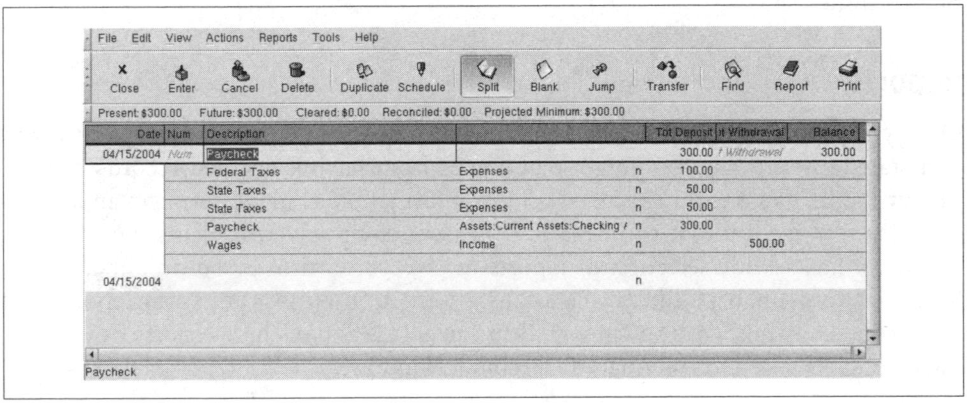

Figure 8-57. Example of a split transaction

The example in Figure 8-57 shows a good reason to create subaccounts under Expenses. If you create subaccounts called Federal, State, and Local, you can always see at a glance the amount you have paid so far in each respective category. This technique works just as well for categorizing other expenses and incomes.

Scheduling transactions

You probably pay certain bills every month at about the same time, and entering those transactions each time can become a chore. GnuCash's transaction scheduling feature allows you to create transactions that automatically recur at a certain interval. To schedule a transaction, follow these steps:

1. From the accounts window, select Actions → Scheduled Transactions → Scheduled Transaction Editor.

2. Click New.

3. Enter the name of the scheduled transaction (e.g., Electric Bill), the start date, frequency, and end date (if applicable).

4. There is a template transaction at the bottom of the window. This is where you tell GnuCash how much money to transfer at the specified intervals. Click in the Description field and create a transaction just like you would any other in your checking account. Remember, when you are paying a bill you are probably depositing money into an expense account and withdrawing money from your checking account. The template transaction needs to reflect both sides of the transaction. At the specified time interval, this transaction will occur in the accounts involved.

A quick way to make any transaction a scheduled transaction is by right-clicking on the transaction and selecting Schedule. If you are having trouble figuring out how to manually enter a template transaction, you can cheat by creating one this way, clicking the Advanced button, and seeing how GnuCash automatically creates the template transaction.

Reports

Once you have spent a few months entering your financial details into GnuCash, you will start to appreciate the power that comes from having detailed records of your money habits. It's one thing to have all this information available, and yet another to organize it in a form that can help you spot trends or solve problems. Fortunately, GnuCash has a wide selection of reports to give you a firm grasp on almost every aspect of your financial life. Table 8-5 lists some of the most common reports and what you can expect each to tell you. You can access any of these reports by navigating through the Reports menu in the accounts window.

Table 8-5. GnuCash reports

Report	What it tells you
Account Summary	Gives you an at-a-glance view of the balances for each account.
Asset Barchart/Piechart	Lets you see how your net worth is divided. For most people, their net worth is primarily in their house, bank accounts, and retirement funds.
Liability Barchart/Piechart	Breaks down your liabilities by percentage. For most people, houses and cars are the greatest liabilities, followed by credit cards, and consumer and student loans.
Net Worth Barchart	Assets – Liabilities = Net Worth. This is a graphical representation of that formula. In general you want the blue and green bars to get higher, and the red bar to get lower.
Expense Barcart/Piechart	Shows you where your money is going. If you spend 80% of your money each month on clothes, this will let you know (assuming you have structured your expense accounts correctly).
Income Barchart/Piechart	Shows you where your money comes from. You may think that most of your money comes from your job, but this report may surprise you with how much of your money comes from other sources, such as Mom and Dad and contract work (once again, assuming you have set up your accounts correctly).

Most of these reports require you to have an intricate account tree set up to be truly informative. For example, if you have one big Expenses account to which you send all of your money, then the Expense Report will show that 100% of your money goes to Expenses—not very helpful. To get the most out of the report, you must structure your account tree so that each category of expenses has an account under the main Expenses account, and ditto for Income, Liability, and Assets. The more structured your accounts, the more you will get out of GnuCash.

By default, GnuCash reports from the start of the current year to the current date. You can change this (e.g., to show expense allocations for April) by clicking on the Options button in the toolbar.

When you activate a report, it creates a tab to the far left of the window; above that tab you should also see Accounts. Use this to switch back and forth between the accounts window and your reports. Click the Close button on a toolbar to close a report.

Clicking Exit will exit GnuCash; it will not close the report window!

Real-Life Examples

Learning the basics of GnuCash is one thing—actually using it in day-to-day scenarios is quite another. You have already seen how to enter a paycheck so that total income and tax expenses are recorded. Here are several other real-life examples to get you started on the most common tasks.

Going to the grocery store

We mentioned the importance of setting up a sufficiently detailed account structure before, but what we didn't tell you is how easy it is to do. You don't have to set all those accounts up in advance. Knowing that you can create them as you go along gives you the motivation to do it right.

Here's what to do:

1. Open the Checking Account register.
2. Create a new transaction with today's date and Grocery Store as the description.
3. In the transfer field, enter Ex, and expenses will be selected automatically. Use the right arrow key to complete the auto entry. Now type :Food. The colon tells GnuCash to make Food a subaccount of Expenses.
4. Press Enter to accept your new category, and Tab to leave the transfer field. A dialog box will appear, asking you if you would like to create the Expenses:Food account. Click Yes.
5. The New Account window appears. The defaults should be fine, so click OK.
6. Skip the Deposit field, enter 50.00 in the Withdrawal field, and press Enter.

Congratulations! You have not only created a transaction recording your food purchase, but have also created the expense account for it. Future food transactions can now go into this account, and a quick glance at the accounts window will show you exactly how much you have spent on food.

GnuCash's autocomplete feature is very helpful. Once you have created subaccounts, typing a colon after an autocompleted account will jump directly to the end of that account and begin with a listing of its subaccounts.

Getting a tax refund

Most people think of tax refunds as income, but they aren't: they are rebates. If you keep track of your taxes from each paycheck, recording a tax refund is as simple as creating a rebate from your expense account to your checking account. Here's how it works:

1. Open the Checking Account register.
2. Create a new transaction with today's date and Tax Refund as the description.
3. Since we recorded federal taxes from our paycheck as going to the Expenses account, enter Expenses in the transfer field.
4. Enter 50.00 in the Deposit field.
5. Press Enter to complete the transaction.

You now have 50 more dollars in your checking account, but if you look at the accounts window, you will notice that your income has not increased. Instead, total assets have increased, and expenses have decreased. This is an accurate depiction of what happens when you get a tax refund. No longer can you fool yourself into thinking that a tax refund is extra money you make every year. You already earned it— you're just getting it back!

Buying a car

An automobile is a big expense. And if you're buying a vehicle on credit, it becomes an even more costly one. Luckily, GnuCash can keep track of every cent of the purchase, as well as what portion of your monthly payment goes toward principle and what portion is lost as interest. The process of setting up a car purchase is also a good example of how to handle a house purchase or other type of loan.

Here's the scenario: You've just bought a brand new car for $20,000. You put down $5000 and will be paying a $400 monthly payment for 60 months. You may have received an amortization table from your lender showing you how much money goes to principle and interest each month. If you didn't get an amortization table, you might want to ask your lender for one, or create one yourself using tools available at a web site such as *http://www.bankrate.com*. You will probably be surprised at how much money you spend on interest. To record a car payment transaction:

1. Begin by creating a new account. Call it Car Loan, set its Parent Account to New Top Level Account, and its account type to Liability.

2. Create a second new account called Car, set its Parent Account to Assets:Current Assets, and its account type to Asset.

3. Open the account register for the Car account.

4. Start a new transaction. Enter Buy Car as the description and then click the Split button on the toolbar.

5. The first subtransaction records the car's value. Enter Car Value as the description. The account will be Assets:Current Assets:Car, and the Increase value will be 20,000.

6. That 20 grand has to come from somewhere. The first place is your down payment. Enter Down Payment as the description and Assets:Current Assets:Checking Account as the account, and decrease the account by $5,000. (Yes, I know that in this example this makes your bank account negative. Don't try this at home!)

7. Unfortunately, tax, title, and license cost you another $1,500. Enter the description as TT&L and the account as Expenses, and increase the account by $1,500.

8. You now have a $16,500 balance for the transaction; this is your loan amount. Enter Loan Principle for the description and Car Loan for the account, and decrease the account by $16,500.

9. Complete the transaction. The accounts window should show the results of your hard work.

You've had the car for about a month and now it's time to pay the payment. A quick look at the lender's amortization table shows that $300 of your payment goes to interest and $100 goes to principle. Here's how to record that:

1. Open the Checking Account register.

2. Start a new transaction. Use today's date and enter Car Payment in the description field. Click the Split button to begin a split transaction.

3. Your payment is $400, so enter Payment as the description and Assets:Current Assets:Checking Account as the account, and withdraw $400.

4. $300 goes to interest, so enter Interest as the description and Expenses:Interest as the account (click Yes and OK after tabbing off the field to create the subaccount), and deposit $300 into the account.

5. The rest goes to principle. The $100 balance should already appear in the Deposit field, so just enter Principle in the description and Car Loan for the account. Press Enter to complete the transaction.

Looking at the accounts window, you see that the Car Loan account has decreased by $100 and the Expenses account has increased by $300, exactly as it should be. No longer will you have to consider all of your car payment as an expense, some of it goes to decreasing liability (and therefore increasing net worth), and now you can see it happening every month!

The preceding transaction is an excellent example of one that should be scheduled to recur every month, saving you the hassle of typing it in every time. With each payment, be sure to change the interest and principle amounts as the amortization table indicates.

## CHAPTER 9

Multimedia

This chapter is about multimedia on Linux. *Multimedia* is a rather vague and much abused term. For the purposes of this chapter, our loose definition is anything related to sound, graphics, or video.

Multimedia has historically been one of the more challenging areas of Linux, both for developers and users, and one that did not receive as much attention from Linux distributions as it should have, perhaps because Linux was initially embraced by so many as a server operating system. It was only recently that Linux has been seriously considered as a desktop solution for mainstream users. To be successful at attracting users from other popular operating systems, multimedia support is a requirement.

The good news is that, unlike a few years ago, most modern Linux distributions automatically detect and configure multimedia hardware for the user and provide a basic set of applications. And despite its historic use as a server, for a number of reasons Linux is well suited to audio and other multimedia applications.

We start off this chapter with a quick overview of multimedia concepts such as digital audio and video, and a description of the different types of multimedia hardware devices. Those familiar with the technology may wish to skip over this section. If you don't really care about how it all works or get lost in the first sentence of this section, don't worry, you can get applications up and running without understanding the difference between an MP3 and a WAV file. The section "Movies and Music: Totem and Rhythmbox" in Chapter 3 describes the basic playback tools offered on most Linux desktops.

We then discuss some of the issues related to multimedia support at the kernel level, which is a prerequisite for using the hardware. We then move on to applications, first those offered by some of the popular desktop environments, and then a sampling of more specialized applications broken down into different categories. If you want to develop your own applications, we briefly cover some of the popular toolkits and development environments. Finally, we wrap things up with a list of references in print and on the Web where you can find information that is more detailed and current.

Keep in mind that multimedia is an area where Linux development moves rapidly and new technologies quickly move from primitive prototypes to mainstream usage. In 1996, in a book on multimedia on Linux, we wrote about a technology called MPEG-1 layer 3, or MP3. At the time it was relatively unknown, used only by some obscure web sites to distribute music, and my then-current 40 MHz Intel 386 computer was barely able to decode it in real time. Not so many years later, it has become ubiquitous and the de facto standard file format for digital music on the Internet. At the same time, other technologies that appeared promising have fallen by the wayside, often not for technical reasons. To stay current, check the resources listed at the end of the chapter.

There are minor differences among Linux distributions. Although most of the information in this chapter is generic and applicable to most Linux distributions, for details you should consult the documentation that came with your system, contact your distribution vendor, or consult with fellow users.

Multimedia Concepts

This section very quickly covers some concepts relevant to digital audio, video, and sound cards. Understanding these basics will help you follow the rest of the material in this chapter.

Digital Sampling

Sound is produced when waves of varying pressure travel though a medium, usually air. It is inherently an *analog* phenomenon, meaning that the changes in air pressure can vary continuously over a range of values.

Modern computers are *digital*, meaning they operate on discrete values, essentially the binary ones and zeroes that are manipulated by the central processing unit (CPU). In order for a computer to manipulate sound, then, it needs to convert the analog sound information into digital format.

A hardware device called an *analog-to-digital converter* converts analog signals, such as the continuously varying electrical signals from a microphone, to digital format that can be manipulated by a computer. Similarly, a *digital-to-analog converter* converts digital values into analog form so they can be sent to an analog output device such as a speaker. Sound cards typically contain several analog-to-digital and digital-to-analog converters.

The process of converting analog signals to digital form consists of taking measurements, or *samples*, of the values at regular periods of time, and storing these samples as numbers. The process of analog-to-digital conversion is not perfect, however, and introduces some loss or distortion. Two important factors that affect how accurately the analog signal is represented in digital form are the *sample size* and *sampling rate*.

The *sample size* is the range of values of numbers that is used to represent the digital samples, usually expressed in bits. For example, an 8-bit sample converts the analog sound values into one of 2^8, or 256, discrete values. A 16-bit sample size represents the sound using 2^{16}, or 65,536, different values. A larger sample size allows the sound to be represented more accurately, reducing the sampling error that occurs when the analog signal is represented as discrete values. The trade-off with using a larger sample size is that the samples require more storage (and the hardware is typically more complex and therefore expensive).

The *sample rate* is the speed at which the analog signals are periodically measured over time. It is properly expressed as samples per second, although sometimes informally but less accurately expressed in Hertz (Hz). A lower sample rate will lose more information about the original analog signal, a higher sample rate will more accurately represent it. The *sampling theorem* states that to accurately represent an analog signal it must be sampled at at least twice the rate of the highest frequency present in the original signal.

The range of human hearing is from approximately 20 to 20,000 Hz under ideal situations. To accurately represent sound for human listening, then, a sample rate of twice 20,000 Hz should be adequate. CD player technology uses 44,100 samples per second, which is in agreement with this simple calculation. Human speech has little information above 4000 Hz. Digital telephone systems typically use a sample rate of 8000 samples per second, which is perfectly adequate for conveying speech. The trade-off involved with using different sample rates is the additional storage requirement and more complex hardware needed as the sample rate increases.

Other issues that arise when storing sound in digital format are the number of channels and the encoding format. To support stereo sound, two channels are required. Some audio systems use four or more channels.

Often sounds need to be combined or changed in volume. This is the process of *mixing*, and can be done in analog form (e.g., a volume control) or in digital form by the computer. Conceptually, two digital samples can be mixed together simply by adding them, and volume can be changed by multiplying by a constant value.

Up to now we've discussed storing audio as digital samples. Other techniques are also commonly used. *FM synthesis* is an older technique that produces sound using hardware that manipulates different waveforms such as sine and triangle waves. The hardware to do this is quite simple and was popular with the first generation of computer sound cards for generating music. Many sound cards still support FM synthesis for backward compatibility. Some newer cards use a technique called *wavetable synthesis* that improves on FM synthesis by generating the sounds using digital samples stored in the sound card itself.

MIDI stands for Musical Instrument Digital Interface. It is a standard protocol for allowing electronic musical instruments to communicate. Typical MIDI devices are music keyboards, synthesizers, and drum machines. MIDI works with events representing such things as a key on a music keyboard being pressed, rather than storing actual sound samples. MIDI events can be stored in a MIDI file, providing a way to represent a song in a very compact format. MIDI is most popular with professional musicians, although many consumer sound cards support the MIDI bus interface.

File Formats

We've talked about sound samples, which typically come from a sound card and are stored in a computer's memory. To store them permanently, they need to be represented as files. There are various methods for doing this.

The most straightforward method is to store the samples directly as bytes in a file, often referred to as *raw sound files*. The samples themselves can be encoded in different formats. We've already mentioned sample size, with 8-bit and 16-bit samples being the most common. For a given sample size, they might be encoded using signed or unsigned representation. When the storage takes more than 1 byte, the ordering convention must be specified. These issues are important when transferring digital audio between programs or computers, to ensure they agree on a common format.

A problem with raw sound files is that the file itself does not indicate the sample size, sampling rate, or data representation. To interpret the file correctly, this information needs to be known. Self-describing formats such as WAV add additional information to the file in the form of a header to indicate this information so that applications can determine how to interpret the data from the file itself. These formats standardize how to represent sound information in a way that can be transferred between different computers and operating systems.

Storing the sound samples in the file has the advantage of making the sound data easy to work with, but has the disadvantage that it can quickly become quite large. We earlier mentioned CD audio which uses a 16-bit sample size and a 44,100 sample per second rate, with two channels (stereo). One hour of this Compact Disc Digital Audio (CDDA) data represents more than 600 megabytes of data. To make the storage of sound more manageable, various schemes for compressing audio have been devised. One approach is to simply compress the data using the same compression algorithms used for computer data. However, by taking into account the characteristics of human hearing, it possible to compress audio more efficiently by removing components of the sound that are not audible. This is called *lossy compression*, because information is lost during the compression process, but when properly implemented there can be a major reduction of data size with little noticeable loss in audio quality. This is the approach that is used with MPEG-1 level 3 audio (MP3), which can achieve compression levels of 10:1 over the original digital audio. Another lossy compression algorithm that achieves similar results is Ogg Vorbis, which is popular with many Linux users because it avoids patent issues with MP3 encoding. Other compression algorithms are optimized for human speech, such as the GSM encoding used by some digital telephone systems. The algorithms used for encoding and decoding audio are sometimes referred to as *codecs*. Some codecs are based on open standards, such as Ogg and MP3, which can be implemented according to a published specification. Other codes are proprietary, with the format a trade secret held by the developer and people who license the technology. Examples of proprietary codecs are Real Networks' RealAudio, Microsoft's WMA, and Apple's Quick-Time.

We've focused mainly on audio up to now. Briefly turning to video, the storing of image data has much in common with sound files. In the case of images, the samples are pixels (picture elements), which represent color using samples of a specific bit depth. Large bit depths can more accurately represent the shades of color at the expense of more storage requirement. Common image bit depths are 8, 16, 24, and 32 bits. A bitmap file simply stores the image pixels in some predefined format. As with audio, there are raw image formats and self-describing formats that contain additional information that allows the file format to be determined.

Compression of image files uses various techniques. Standard compression schemes such as *zip* and *gzip* can be used. Run-length encoding, which describes sequences of pixels having the same color, is a good choice for images that contain areas having the same color, such as line drawings. As with audio, there are lossy compression schemes, such as JPEG compression, which is optimized for photographic-type images and designed to provide high compression with little noticeable effect on the image.

To extend still images to video, one can imagine simply stringing together many images arranged in time sequence. Clearly, this quickly generates extremely large files. Compression schemes such as that used for DVD movies use sophisticated algorithms that store some complete images, as well as a mathematical representation of the differences between adjacent frames that allows the images to be re-created. These are lossy encoding algorithms. In addition to the video, a movie also contains one or more sound tracks and other information, such as captioning.

We mentioned Compact Disc Digital Audio, which stores about 600 MB of sound samples on a disc. The ubiquitous CD-ROM uses the same physical format to store computer data, using a filesystem known as the ISO 9660 format. This is a simple directory structure, similar to MS-DOS. The Rock Ridge extensions to ISO 9660 were developed to allow storing of longer filenames and more attributes, making the format suitable for Unix-compatible systems. Microsoft's Joliet filesystem performs a similar function and is used on various flavors of Windows. A CD-ROM can be formatted with both the Rock Ridge and Joliet extensions, making it readable on both Unix-compatible and Windows-compatible systems.

CD-ROMs are produced in a manufacturing facility using expensive equipment. CD-R (compact disc recordable) allows recording of data on a disc using an inexpensive drive, which can be read on a standard CD-ROM drive. CD-RW (compact disc rewritable) extends this with a disc that can be blanked (erased) many times and rewritten with new data.

DVD-ROM drives allow storing of about 4.7 GB of data on the same physical format used for DVD movies. With suitable decoding hardware or software, a PC with a DVD-ROM drive can also view DVD movies. Recently, dual-layer DVD-ROM drives have become available, which double the storage capacity.

Like CD-R, DVD has been extended for recording, but with two different formats, known as DVD-R and DVD+R. At the time of writing, both formats were popular, and some combo drives supported both formats. Similarly, a rewritable DVD has been developed—or rather, two different formats, known as DVD-RW and DVD+RW. Finally, a format known as DVD-RAM offers a random-access read/write media similar to hard disk storage.

DVD-ROM drives can be formatted with a (large) ISO 9660 filesystem, optionally with Rock Ridge or Joliet extensions. They often, however, use the UDF (Universal Disc Format) file system, which is used by DVD movies and is better suited to large storage media.

For applications where multimedia is to be sent live via the Internet, often broadcast to multiple users, sending entire files is not suitable. *Streaming media* refers to systems where audio, or other media, is sent and played back in real time.

Multimedia Hardware

Now that we've discussed digital audio concepts, let's look at the hardware used. Sound cards follow a similar history as other peripheral cards for PCs. The first-generation cards used the ISA bus, and most aimed to be compatible with the Sound Blaster series from Creative Labs. The introduction of the ISA Plug and Play (PNP) standard allowed many sound cards to adopt this format and simplify configuration by eliminating the need for hardware jumpers. Modern sound cards now typically use the PCI bus, either as separate peripheral cards or as on-board sound hardware that resides on the motherboard but is accessed through the PCI bus. USB sound devices are also now available, some providing traditional sound card functions as well as peripherals such as loudspeakers that can be controlled through the USB bus.

Some sound cards now support higher-end features such as *surround sound* using as many as six sound channels, and digital inputs and outputs that can connect to home theater systems. This is beyond the scope of what can be covered in this chapter.

In the realm of video, there is obviously the ubiquitous video card, many of which offer 3D acceleration, large amounts of on-board memory, and sometimes more than one video output (multi-head).

TV tuner cards can decode television signals and output them to a video monitor, often via a video card so the image can be mixed with the computer video. Video capture cards can record video in real time for storage on hard disk and later playback.

Although the mouse and keyboard are the most common input devices, Linux also supports a number of touch screens, digitizing tablets, and joysticks.

Many scanners are supported on Linux. Older models generally use a SCSI or parallel port interface. Some of these use proprietary protocols and are not supported on Linux. Newer scanners tend to use USB, although some high-end professional models instead use FireWire (Apple's term for a standard also known as IEEE 1394) for higher throughput.

Digital cameras have had some support under Linux, improving over time as more drivers are developed and cameras move to more standardized protocols. Older models used serial and occasionally SCSI interfaces. Newer units employ USB if they provide a direct cable interface at all. They also generally use one of several standard flash memory modules, which can be removed and read on a computer with a suitable adapter that connects to a USB or PCMCIA port. With the adoption of a standard USB mass storage protocol, all compliant devices should be supported under Linux. The Linux kernel represents USB mass storage devices as if they were SCSI devices.

Kernel and Driver Issues

Configuring and building the kernel is covered elsewhere in this book. We cover here a few points relevant to multimedia. As mentioned earlier, most multimedia cards use the PCI bus and should be automatically detected and configured by the Linux kernel.

Sound Drivers

The history of sound drivers under Linux deserves some mention here, because it helps explain the current diversity in offerings. Early in the development of Linux (i.e., before the 1.0 kernel release), Hannu Savolainen implemented kernel-level sound drivers for a number of popular sound cards. Other developers also contributed to this code, adding new features and support for more cards. These drivers, part of the standard kernel release, are sometimes called OSS/Free, the free version of the Open Sound System.

Hannu later joined 4Front Technologies, a company that sells commercial sound drivers for Linux as well as a number of other Unix-compatible operating systems. These enhanced drivers are sold commercially as OSS/4Front.

In 1998 the Advanced Linux Sound Architecture, or ALSA project, was formed with the goal of writing new Linux sound drivers from scratch, and to address the issue that there was no active maintainer of the OSS sound drivers. With the benefit of hindsight and the requirements for newer sound card technology, the need was felt for a new design.

Some sound card manufacturers have also written Linux sound drivers for their cards, most notably the Creative Labs Sound Blaster Live! series.

The result is that there are as many as four different sets of kernel sound drivers from which to choose. This causes a dilemma when choosing a sound driver. Table 9-1 summarizes some of the advantages and disadvantages of the different drivers, in order to help you make a decision. Another consideration is that your particular Linux distribution will likely come with one driver, and it will be more effort on your part to use a different one.

Table 9-1. Sound driver comparison

Driver	Advantages	Disadvantages
OSS/Free	Free	Not all sound cards supported
	Source code available	Most sound cards not autodetected
	Part of standard kernel	Deprecated in 2.6 kernel
	Supports most sound cards	Does not support some newer cards
OSS/4Front	Supports many sound cards	Payment required
	Autodetection of most cards	Closed source
	Commercial support available	
	Compatible with OSS	
ALSA	Free	Not all sound cards supported
	Source code available	Not fully compatible with OSS
	Supports many sound cards	
	Actively developed/supported	
	Most sound cards are autodetected	
Commercial	May support cards with no other drivers	May be closed source
	May support special hardware features	May not be officially supported

In addition to the drivers mentioned in Table 9-1, kernel patches are sometimes available that address problems with specific sound cards.

The vast majority of sound cards are supported under Linux by one driver or another. The devices that are least likely to be supported are very new cards, which may not yet have had drivers developed for them, and some high-end professional sound cards, which are rarely used by consumers. You can find a reasonably up-to-date list of supported cards in the current Linux Sound HOWTO document, but often the best solution is to do some research on the Internet and experiment with drivers that seem likely to match your hardware.

Many sound applications use the kernel sound drivers directly, but this causes a problem: the kernel sound devices can be accessed by only one application at a time. In a graphical desktop environment, a user may want to simultaneously play an MP3 file, associate window manager actions with sounds, be alerted when there is new email, and so on. This requires sharing the sound devices between different applications. To address this, modern Linux desktop environments include a sound server that takes exclusive control of the sound devices and accepts requests from desktop applications to play sounds, mixing them together. They may also allow sound to be redirected to another computer, just as the X Window System allows the display to be on a different computer from the one on which the program is running. The KDE desktop environment uses the *artsd* sound server, and GNOME provides *esd*. Because sound servers are a somewhat recent innovation, not all sound applications are written to support them yet. You can often work around this problem by suspending the sound server or using a wrapper program such as *artswrapper*, which redirects accesses to sound devices to go to the sound server.

Installation and configuration

In this section we discuss how to install and configure a sound card under Linux.

The amount of work you have to do depends on your Linux distribution. As Linux matures, some distributions are now providing automatic detection and configuration of sound cards. The days of manually setting card jumpers and resolving resource conflicts are becoming a thing of the past as sound cards become standardized on the PCI bus. If you are fortunate enough that your sound card is detected and working on your Linux distribution, the material in this section won't be particularly relevant because it has all been done for you automatically.

Some Linux distributions also provide a sound configuration utility such as *sndconfig* that will attempt to detect and configure your sound card, usually with some user intervention. You should consult the documentation for your system and run the supplied sound configuration tool, if any, and see if it works.

If you have an older ISA or ISA PnP card, or if your card is not properly detected, you will need to follow the manual procedure we outline here. These instructions also assume you are using the OSS/Free sound drivers. If you are using ALSA, the process is similar, but if you are using commercial drivers (OSS/4Front or a vendor-supplied driver), you should consult the document that comes with the drivers, because the process may be considerably different.

The information here also assumes you are using Linux on an x86 architecture system. There is support for sound on other CPU architectures, but not all drivers are supported and there will likely be some differences in device names and other things.

Collecting hardware information

Presumably you already have a sound card installed on your system. If not, you should go ahead and install one. If you have verified that the card works with another operating system on your computer, that will assure you that any problem you encounter on Linux is caused by software at some level.

You should identify what type of card you have, including manufacturer and model. Determine if it is an ISA, ISA PnP, or PCI card. If the card has jumpers, you should note the settings. If you know what resources (IRQ, I/O address, DMA channels) the card is currently using, note that information as well.

If you don't have all this information, don't worry. You should be able to get by without it; you just may need to do a little detective work later. On laptops or systems with on-board sound hardware, for example, you won't have the luxury of being able to look at a physical sound card.

Configuring ISA Plug and Play (optional)

Modern PCI bus sound cards do not need any configuration. The older ISA bus sound cards were configured by setting jumpers. ISA PnP cards are configured under Linux using the ISA Plug and Play utilities. If you aren't sure if you have an ISA PnP sound card, try running the command *pnpdump* and examining the output for anything that looks like a sound card. Output should include lines like the following for a typical sound card:

```
# Card 1: (serial identifier ba 10 03 be 24 25 00 8c 0e)
# Vendor Id CTL0025, Serial Number 379791851, checksum 0xBA.
# Version 1.0, Vendor version 1.0
# ANSI string -->Creative SB16 PnP<--
```

The general process for configuring ISA PnP devices is as follows:

1. Save any existing */etc/isapnp.conf* file.
2. Generate a configuration file using the command *pnpdump >/etc/isapnp.conf*.
3. Edit the file, uncommenting the lines for the desired device settings.
4. Run the *isapnp* command to configure Plug and Play cards (usually on system startup).

Most modern Linux distributions take care of initializing ISA PnP cards. You may already have a suitable */etc/isapnp.conf* file, or it may require some editing.

For more details on configuring ISA PnP cards, see the manpages for *isapnp*, *pnp-dump*, and *isapnp.conf* and read the Plug-and-Play HOWTO from the Linux Documentation Project.

Configuring the kernel (optional)

In the most common situation, where you are running a kernel that was provided during installation of your Linux system, all sound drivers should be included as loadable modules and it should not be neccessary to build a new kernel.

You may want to compile a new kernel if the kernel sound driver modules you need are not provided by the kernel you are currently running. If you prefer to compile the drivers directly into the kernel rather than use loadable kernel modules, a new kernel will be required as well.

See Chapter 18 for detailed information on rebuilding your kernel.

Configuring kernel modules

In most cases the kernel sound drivers are loadable modules, which the kernel can dynamically load and unload. You need to ensure that the correct drivers are loaded. You do this using a configuration file, such as */etc/conf.modules*. A typical entry for a sound card might look like this:

```
alias sound sb
alias midi opl3
options opl3 io=0x388
options sb io=0x220 irq=5 dma=1 dma16=5 mpu_io=0x330
```

You need to enter the sound driver to use and the appropriate values for I/O address, IRQ, and DMA channels that you recorded earlier. The latter settings are needed only for ISA and ISA PnP cards because PCI cards can detect them automatically. In the preceding example, which is for a 16-bit Sound Blaster card, we had to specify the driver as sb in the first line, and specify the options for the driver in the last line.

Some systems use */etc/modules.conf* and/or multiple files under the */etc/modutils* directory, so you should consult the documentation for your Linux distribution for the details on configuring modules. On Debian systems, you can use the *modconf* utility for this task.

In practice, usually the only tricky part is determining which driver to use. The output of *pnpdump* for ISA PnP cards and *lspci* for PCI cards can help you identify the type of card you have. You can then compare this to documentation available either in the Sound HOWTO or in the kernel source, usually found on Linux systems in the */usr/src/linux/Documentation/sound* directory.

For example, a certain laptop system reports this sound hardware in the output of *lspci*:

```
00:05.0 Multimedia audio controller: Cirrus Logic CS 4614/22/24 [CrystalClear
         SoundFusion Audio Accelerator] (rev 01)
```

For this system the appropriate sound driver is cs46xx. Some experimentation may be required, and it is safe to try loading various kernel modules and see if they detect the sound card.

Testing the installation

The first step to verify the installation is to confirm that the kernel module is loaded. You can use the command *lsmod*; it should show that the appropriate module, among others, is loaded:

```
$ /sbin/lsmod
Module          Size   Used by
parport_pc      21256  1 (autoclean)
lp              6080   0 (autoclean)
parport         24512  1 (autoclean) [parport_pc lp]
3c574_cs        8324   1
serial          43520  0 (autoclean)
cs46xx          54472  4
soundcore       3492   3 [cs46xx]
ac97_codec      9568   0 [cs46xx]
rtc             5528   0 (autoclean)
```

Here the drivers of interest are cs46xx, soundcore, and ac97_codec. When the driver detected the card, the kernel should have also logged a message that you can retrieve with the *dmesg* command. The output is likely to be long, so you can pipe it to a pager command, such as *less*:

```
PCI: Found IRQ 11 for device 00:05.0
PCI: Sharing IRQ 11 with 00:02.0
PCI: Sharing IRQ 11 with 01:00.0
Crystal 4280/46xx + AC97 Audio, version 1.28.32, 19:55:54 Dec 29 2001
cs46xx: Card found at 0xf4100000 and 0xf4000000, IRQ 11
cs46xx: Thinkpad 600X/A20/T20 (1014:0153) at 0xf4100000/0xf4000000, IRQ 11
ac97_codec: AC97 Audio codec, id: 0x4352:0x5914 (Cirrus Logic CS4297A rev B)
```

For ISA cards, the device file */dev/sndstat* shows information about the card. This won't work for PCI cards, however. Typical output should look something like this:

```
$ cat /dev/sndstat
OSS/Free:3.8s2++-971130
Load type: Driver loaded as a module
Kernel: Linux curly 2.2.16 #4 Sat Aug 26 19:04:06 PDT 2000 i686
Config options: 0

Installed drivers:

Card config:
```

```
Audio devices:
0: Sound Blaster 16 (4.13) (DUPLEX)

Synth devices:
0: Yamaha OPL3

MIDI devices:
0: Sound Blaster 16

Timers:
0: System clock

Mixers:
0: Sound Blaster
```

If these look right, you can now test your sound card. A simple check to do first is to run a mixer program and verify that the mixer device is detected and that you can change the levels without seeing any errors. Set all the levels to something reasonable. You'll have to see what mixer programs are available on your system. Some common ones are *aumix*, xmix, and KMix.

Now try using a sound file player to play a sound file (e.g., a WAV file) and verify that you can hear it play. If you are running a desktop environment, such as KDE or GNOME, you should have a suitable media player; otherwise, look for a command-line tool such as *play*.

If playback works, you can then check recording. Connect a microphone to the sound card's mic input and run a recording program, such as *rec* or *vrec*. See whether you can record input to a WAV file and play it back. Check the mixer settings to ensure that you have selected the right input device and set the appropriate gain levels.

You can also test whether MIDI files play correctly. Some MIDI player programs require sound cards with an FM synthesizer, others do not. Some common MIDI players are Playmidi, KMid, and KMidi. Testing of devices on the MIDI bus is beyond the scope of this book.

A good site for general information on MIDI and MIDI devices is *http://midistudio.com*. The official MIDI specifications are available from the MIDI Manufacturers Association. Their web site can be found at *http://www.midi.org*.

Video Drivers

When configuring the Linux kernel, you can enable a number of video-related options and drivers. Under the Multimedia Drivers section, you can configure Video-ForLinux, which has support for video capture and overlay devices and radio tuner cards. Under the Graphics Support category, you can enable frame buffer support for various video cards so that applications can access the video hardware via the kernel's standardized frame buffer interface. For more information on building the kernel, see Chapter 18.

Your X server also needs support for your video hardware. The X windowing system software provided by your distribution vendor should have included all of the open source drivers. There may also be closed-source drivers available for your video card from the manufacturer. If these are not included in your distribution, you will have to obtain and install them separately. For more information on the X Window System, see Chapter 16.

Alternate Input Devices

When configuring the kernel, under the Input Device Support section you can enable support for various specialized mouse drivers, joysticks, and touchscreens.

For scanners and digital cameras, the kernel just needs to support the interface type that the devices use (serial, SCSI, USB, etc.). Communicating with the actual device will be done by applications or libraries such as SANE or libgphoto2.

Embedded and Other Multimedia Devices

Portable multimedia devices for playing music are very popular. The smaller devices use flash memory, whereas the larger ones use hard drives for increased storage capacity. Typically they can play music in MP3, WAV, or Windows WMA formats. Dedicated DVD players for watching movies are also available.

Files are transferred to these devices from a PC. Most current products do not officially support Linux as a host PC. Devices that use the standard USB mass storage protocol should work fine with Linux. Many devices tend to use proprietary protocols. A few of these now have Linux utilities that have been created, sometimes by reverse engineering. It may also be possible to run the Windows applications provided by the vendor under Wine. It is hoped that in the future more hardware vendors will officially support Linux.

Desktop Environments

This section discusses multimedia support offered by two major desktop environments, KDE and GNOME, discussed in Chapter 3. Note that these desktops are not mutually exclusive—you can run GNOME applications under KDE and vice versa. There are of course other desktop environments and window managers that offer unique features, KDE and GNOME are just the largest and most commonly offered by the major Linux distributions.

KDE

KDE is the K Desktop Environment, covered in Chapter 3. In the area of multimedia, KDE offers the following:

- A sound mixer (KMix)
- A sound recorder (Krec)
- Various media players supporting sound and video (Noatun, Juk, Kaboodle, Kaffeine, and others)
- A CD player (KsCD)
- A MIDI player (KMid)
- An audio CD ripping and encoding utility (KAudioCreator)
- A sound effects construction tool (*artsbuilder*)

Because the applications are all part of the same desktop environment, there is tight integration between applications. For example, the KDE web browser, Konqueror, can play audio and video files, and KDE applications can play sounds to notify the user of important events.

The multimedia support in KDE is based on aRts, the analog real-time synthesizer. Part of aRts is the sound server, *artsd*, which manages all sound output so that multiple applications can play sounds simultaneously. The sound server communicates with the underlying operating system's sound drivers, either OSS or ALSA on Linux.

There are also many KDE multimedia applications that are not officially part of the KDE release either because they are not yet of release quality or they are maintained as separate projects. The former can often be found in the *kdenonbeta* area of the KDE project. The latter can usually be found by using an index site such as *http://freshmeat.net* or *http://www.kde-apps.org*.

GNOME

GNOME is another free desktop project, covered in Chapter 3. Like KDE, GNOME offers a sound mixer, sound recorder, CD player, and various media player applications. Multimedia support is integrated into Nautilus, the GNOME file manager. GNOME uses the *esd* sound server to share sound resources among applications.

A problem when running a mixed environment of KDE and GNOME applications is that the sound servers can conflict when using sound resources. At the time of writing, both the KDE and GNOME projects were not totally satisfied with their sound server implementation and were having discussions to develop a replacement that could be shared between KDE and GNOME. This would finally make it possible to run KDE and GNOME multimedia applications at the same time without resource conflicts.

Windows Compatibility

The Wine project is a technology that allows running many Windows applications directly on Linux. It is covered in detail in Chapter 28. Some commercial multimedia applications run under Wine.

The commercial version of Wine from CodeWeavers called CrossOver supports a number of multimedia applications, including Adobe Photoshop, Apple iTunes, the Windows Media Player, and web browser plug-ins for QuickTime, Flash, and ShockWave.

TransGaming Technologies offers Cedega, which is optimized for running Windows games that require DirectX support. It is based on an alternate version of Wine known as ReWind, that has less restrictive licensing terms than Wine.

Some multimedia applications, such as MPlayer, can leverage Wine technology to directly load some Windows DLLs, providing support for proprietary codecs.

Multimedia Applications

Once you have your hardware configured under Linux, you'll want to run some multimedia applications. So many are available for Linux that they can't possibly be listed here, so we instead describe some of the general categories of programs that are available and list some popular representative applications. You can look for applications using the references listed at the end of the chapter. Toward the end of the chapter, you will also find more in-depth descriptions of some popular or particularly useful applications.

These are the major categories of multimedia applications that are covered:

- Mixer programs for setting record and playback gain levels
- Multimedia players for audio and video files and discs
- CD and DVD burning tools for authoring audio and video discs
- Speech tools, supporting speech recognition and synthesis
- Image, sound, and video editing tools for creating and manipulating multimedia files
- Recording tools for generating and manipulating sound files
- Music composition tools for creating traditional music scores or music in MIDI or MP3 format
- Internet telephone and conferencing tools for audio communication over computer networks
- Browser plug-ins for displaying multimedia data within a web browser

Sound Mixers

Sound mixers allow one to modify the hardware gain levels and input devices for your sound card. Most sound mixers are similar. If you are running KDE or GNOME you'll generally get the best results using the mixer provided with your desktop, which typically will appear as a speaker icon on your desktop's panel. Command line mixer programs such as *aumix* can be useful for use in scripts or startup files to set audio gains to desired levels during login, or when you are not running a graphical desktop, such as a remote login.

Figure 9-1 shows a screenshot of KMix, the mixer provided by KDE.

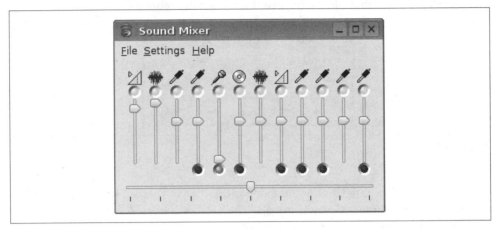

Figure 9-1. KMix

Multimedia Players

Media players are the area with the greatest selection of applications and widest range of features and user interfaces. No one application meets everyone's needs— some aim to be lightweight and fast, whereas others strive to offer the most features. Even within the KDE desktop, for example, a half dozen different players are offered.

If you are running a desktop environment, such as KDE or GNOME, you likely already have at least one media player program. If so, it is recommended that you use this player, at least initially, since it should work correctly with the sound server used by these desktop environments and provide the best integration with the desktop.

When choosing a media player application, here are some of the features you can look for:

- Support for different sound drivers (e.g., OSS and ALSA) or sound servers (KDE aRts and GNOME *esd*).

- An attractive user interface. Many players are "skinnable," meaning that you can download and install alternative user interfaces.

- Support for playlists, allowing you to define and save sequences of your favorite audio tracks.

- Various audio effects, such as a graphical equalizer, stereo expansion, reverb, voice removal, and visual effects for representing the audio in graphical form.

- Support for other file formats, such as audio CD, WAV, and video formats.

Here is a rundown of some of the popular media player applications:

Xmms

Xmms is one popular media player, with a default user interface similar to Winamp. You can download it from *http://www.xmms.org* if it is not included in your Linux distribution. A screenshot is shown in Figure 9-2.

Figure 9-2. Xmms

Xine

Xine is a full-featured audio and video media player that supports many file formats and streaming media protocols. The project is hosted at the following site: *http://xine.sourceforge.net*. A screenshot is shown in Figure 9-3.

Figure 9-3. Xine

MPlayer

MPlayer is another popular video player that supports a wide range of file formats, including the ability to load codecs from Windows DLLs. It supports output to many devices, using X11, as well as directly to video cards. The project's home page is *http://www.mplayer.hu*.

Due to legal issues, MPlayer is not shipped by most Linux distributions and so must be downloaded separately.

CD and DVD Burning Tools

If you are running KDE or GNOME, basic CD data and audio burning support is available within the file manager. If you want to go beyond this, or need more help to step you through the process, specialized applications are available.

Note that many of the graphical CD burning applications use command-line tools such as *cdrecord* and *cdrdao* to perform the actual CD audio track extraction, ISO image creation, and CD recording. For maximum flexibility, some advanced users prefer to use these tools directly.

X-CD-Roast

One of the first graphical CD burner applications was X-CD-Roast. Although newer applications may offer a more intuitive wizard interface, it is still a reliable and functional program. A screenshot is shown in Figure 9-4.

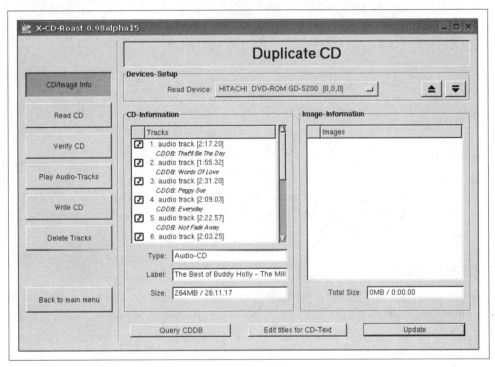

Figure 9-4. X-CD-Roast

K3b

K3b is a popular KDE CD burning tool. It presents a file manager interface similar to popular Windows CD burning utilities such as Easy CD Creator. A screenshot is shown in Figure 9-5. You can find an introduction to K3b in "Burning CDs with K3b," in Chapter 3.

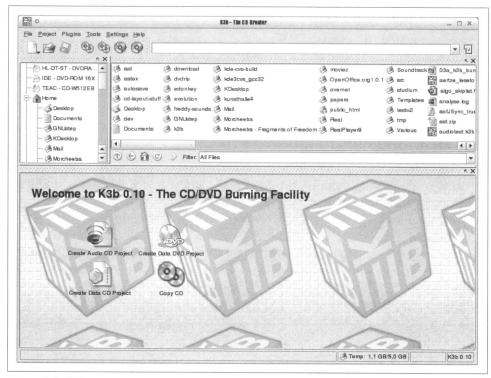

Figure 9-5. K3B

Gcombust

    Gcombust is a graphical burner application that uses the Gtk toolkit. The project's home page is *http://www.abo.fi/~jmunsin/gcombust*. A screenshot is shown in Figure 9-6.

Speech Tools

Speech synthesis and recognition have applications for accessibility and specialized applications, such as telephony, where only an audio path is available.

Speech synthesis devices fall into two major types. Dedicated hardware synthesizers are available that act as a peripheral to a computer and perform the text-to-speech function. These have the advantage of offloading the work of performing the speech conversion from the computer, and tend to offer good-quality output. Software synthesizers run on the PC itself. These are usually lower cost than hardware solutions but add CPU overhead and are sometimes of poor quality if free software is used.

Rsynth

    The Rsynth package provides a simple command-line utility called *say* that converts text to speech. It is included with or available for most Linux distributions.

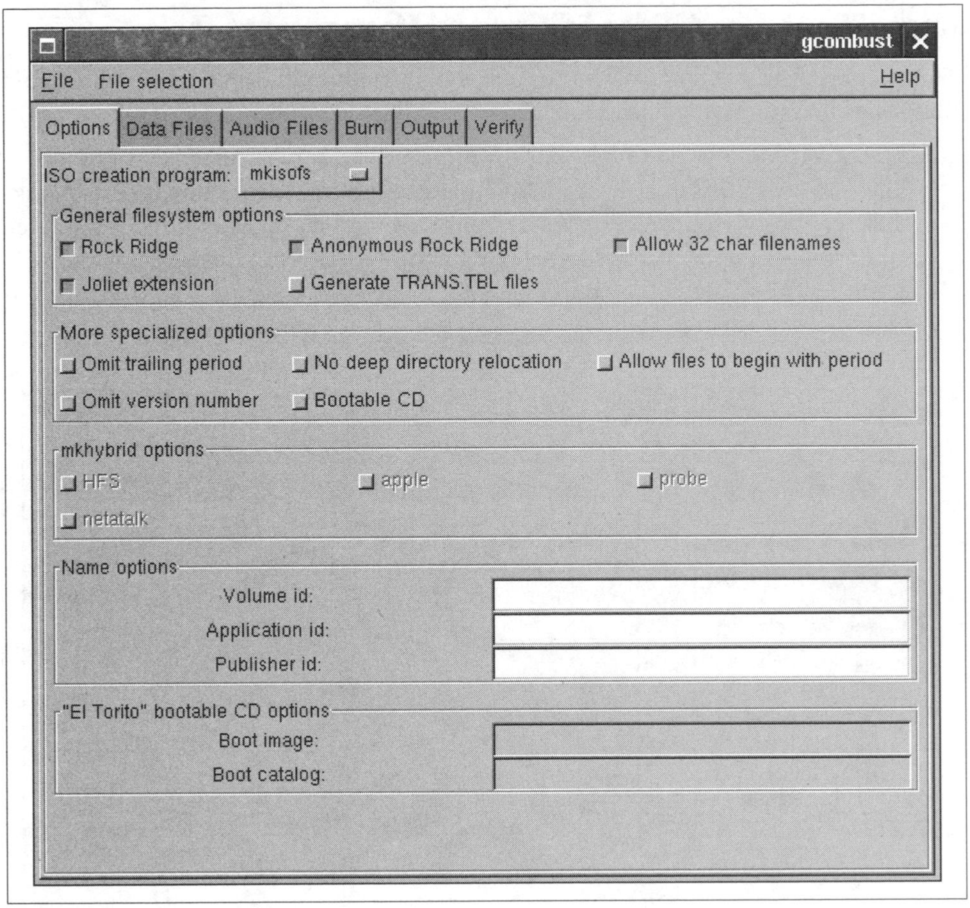

Figure 9-6. Gcombust

Emacspeak

Emacspeak is a text-based audio desktop for visually impaired users. It offers a screen reader that can be used with a hardware or software text-to-speech synthesizer. More information can be found on the project's web site, available here: *http://www.cs.cornell.edu/home/raman/emacspeak*.

Festival

Festival is a software framework for building speech synthesis systems. It supports multiple spoken languages and can be used to build systems programmed using the shell, C++, Java, and Scheme. The home page for the project is found at *http://www.cstr.ed.ac.uk/projects/festival*.

IBM ViaVoice

IBM offers a Linux version of the ViaVoice speech SDK that provides both text-to-speech conversion as well as speech recognition. This is a commercial (non-free) software product.

Image, Sound, and Video Editing and Management Tools

This section describes some of the popular tools for editing images, video, and sound files, as well as managing image collections:

The GIMP

> The GIMP is the GNU Image Manipulation Program. It is intended for tasks such as photo retouching, image composition, and image authoring. It has been in active development for several years and is a very stable and powerful program. A screenshot is shown in Figure 9-7. The official web site for the GIMP is *http://www.gimp.org*.

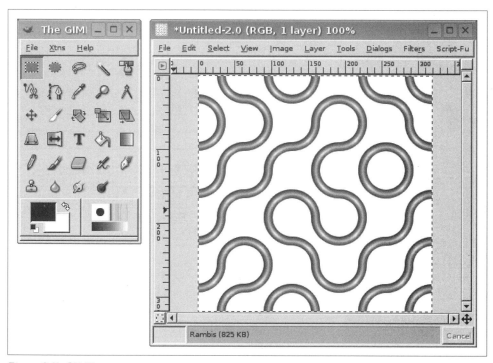

Figure 9-7. GIMP

CinePaint

> CinePaint, formerly called Film Gimp, is a painting and image retouching program designed for work with film and other high-resolution images. It is widely used in the motion picture industry for painting of background mattes and frame-by-frame retouching of movies. CinePaint is based on The GIMP but has added features for film editing, such as color depths up to 128 bits, easy navigation between frames, and support for motion picture file formats such as Kodak Cineon, ILM OpenEXR, Maya IFF, and 32-bit TIFF. A screenshot is shown in Figure 9-8. The CinePaint web site is *http://www.cinepaint.org*.

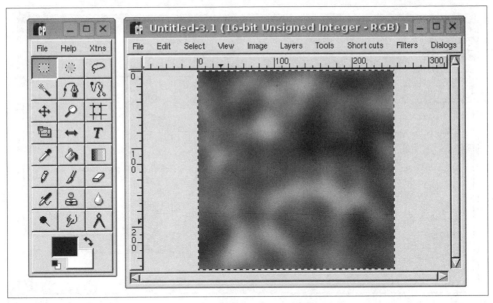

Figure 9-8. CinePaint

Gphoto2

Gphoto2 is a set of digital camera applications for Linux and other Unix-like systems. It includes the *libgphoto2* library, which supports nearly 400 models of digital cameras. The other major components are *gphoto2*, a command-line program for accessing digital cameras, and Gtkam, a graphical application. The project's home page is *http://www.gphoto.org*. A screenshot of Gtkam is shown in Figure 9-9.

Digikam

Digikam is the KDE digital camera application. It uses *libgphoto2* to interface to cameras. A screenshot is shown in Figure 9-10.

Kooka

Kooka is the KDE scanner program. It supports scanners using the SANE library. As well as basic image scanning, Kooka supports optical character recognition of text using several OCR modules. A screenshot is shown in Figure 9-11.

Imaging Tools

A variety of tools are available for acquiring, manipulating, and managing digital images on your computer. In this chapter, we look at some of them.

Image management with KimDaBa

Many applications for viewing images exist, and in our experience, they can be grouped into two main categories: those which are good at generating HTML pages

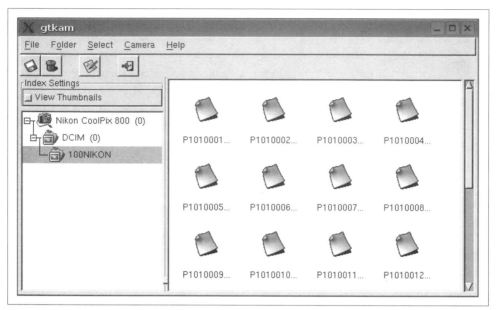

Figure 9-9. Gtkam

Figure 9-10. Digikam

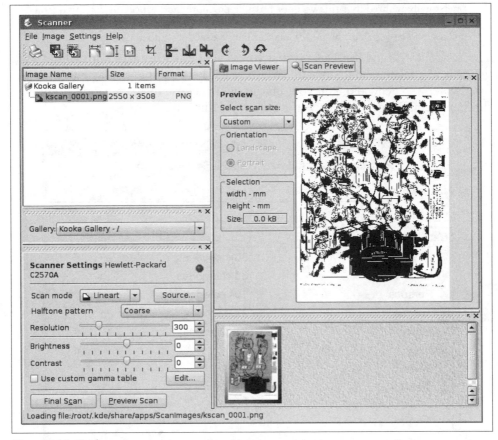

Figure 9-11. Kooka

from your image sets, and those which are cool for showing fancy slide shows. The number of applications in both categories is counted in hundreds if not thousands, mostly differing in things that would be considered *taste* or even *religion*. You can browse the Linux application sites for your favorite application. Here we focus on an application with a slightly different set of design goals.

KimDaBa (KDE Image DataBase) is best explained by the following quote from its home page:

> If you are like me you have hundreds or even thousands of images ever since you got your first camera, some taken with a normal camera, others with a digital camera. Through all the years you believed that until eternity you would be able to remember the story behind every single picture, you would be able to remember the names of all the persons on your images, and you would be able to remember the exact date of every single image.

I personally realized that this was not possible anymore, and especially for my digital images—but also for my paper images—I needed a tool to help me describe my images, and to search in the pile of images. This is exactly what KimDaba is all about.

The basic idea behind KimDaBa is that you categorize each image with who is in it, where it was taken, and a keyword (which might be anything you later want to use for a search). When looking at your images, you may use these categories to browse through them. Figure 9-12 shows the browser of KimDaBa.*

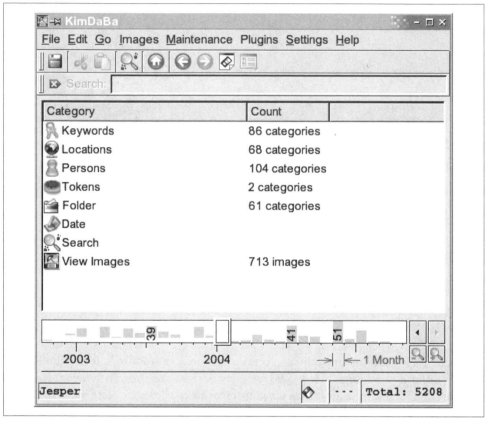

Figure 9-12. Browsing images with KimDaBa

Browsing goes like this: at the top of the list shown in Figure 9-12 you see items for Keywords, Locations, Persons, and so on. To find an image of, say, Jesper, you simply press Persons and, from the list that appears, choose Jesper. Now you are back to the original view with Keywords, Locations, Persons, and so forth. Now, however, you are *in the scope of* Jesper, meaning that KimDaBa only displays information

---

* You may add your own categories if the ones described do not fit your usage of KimDaBa.

about images in which Jesper appears. If the number of images is low enough for you to find the image you have in mind, then you may simply choose View Images. Alternatively, repeat the process. If you want to find images with Jesper *and* Anne Helene in them, then simply choose Persons again, and this time choose Anne Helene. If you instead want images of Jesper in Las Vegas, then choose Locations and, from that view, Las Vegas.

There is no such thing as a free lunch. For KimDaBa this means that you need to categorize all your images, which might be a rather big task—if you have thousands of images. KimDaBa is, however, up to this task—after all, one of its main design criteria is to scale up to tens or even hundreds of thousands of images.

There are two ways of categorizing images in KimDaBa, depending on your current focus, but first and foremost let's point out that the categorizing tasks can be done step by step as you have time for them.

The first way of categorizing images is by selecting one or more images in the thumbnail view (which you get to when you press *View Images*), and then press the right mouse button to get to the context menu. From the context menu, either choose Configure Images One at a *Time* (bound to Ctrl-1) or Configure All Images Simultaneously (bound to Ctrl-2).

Configure All Images Simultaneously allows you to set the location of all images from, say, Las Vegas with just a few mouse clicks, whereas Configure Images One at a Time allows you to go through all the images one by one, specifying, say, who is in them.

Figure 9-13 shows the dialog used for setting properties for the images. In this dialog you may either select items from the list boxes or start typing the name in question—KimDaBa will offer you alternatives as you type. (In the screenshot, I only typed J, and KimDaBa thus found the first occurrence that matched.)

The alternative way of specifying properties is to do it while you view your images (e.g., as a full-screen slide show). In this mode, you simply set a letter token on the image by pressing the letter in question. This usage is intended for fixing annotations later on—say you are looking at your images and realize that you forgot to mark that Jesper is in a given image. Once you have set a number of tokens, you can use these for browsing, just as you use persons, locations, and keywords. What you typically would do is simply to browse to the images with a given token, and then use the first method specified previously to set the person missing in the images.

Once you have annotated all your images, you can drive down memory lane in multiple ways. As an appetizer, here is a not-so-uncommon scenario derived from personal use of KimDaBa: you sit with your girlfriend on the living-room sofa, discussing how much fun you had in Mallorca during your vacation in 2000, and agree to grab your laptop to look at the images. You choose *Holiday Mallorca 2000*

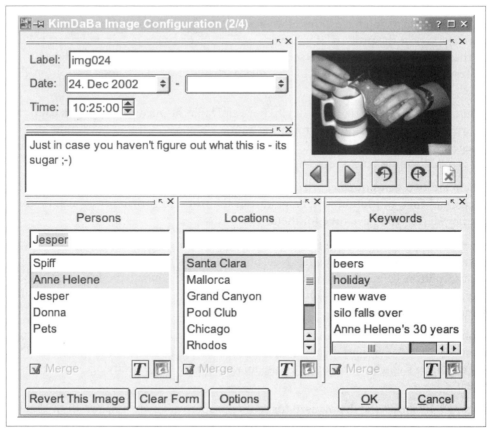

Figure 9-13. Configuring KimDaBa

from the keyword category, and start a slide show with all the images. As you go on, you see an image from when you arrived home. On that image is an old friend who you haven't talked to in a long time. In the full-screen viewer, you press the link with his name (all the information you typed in is available during viewing in an info box). Pressing his name makes KimDaBa show the browser, with him in scope. Using the date bar, you now limit the view to only show images of him from 1990 to 2000. This leads you to some images from a party that you attended many years ago, and again the focus changes, and you are looking at images from that party. Often, you end up getting to bed late those evenings when you fetch the laptop.

Image manipulation with the GIMP

Introduction. The GIMP is the GNU Image Manipulation Program. It is intended for tasks such as photo retouching, image composition, and image authoring. It has been in active development for several years and is a very stable and powerful program.

The GIMP's home is *http://www.gimp.org*, the online manual is available from *http://docs.gimp.org*, and additional plug-ins to expand GIMP's features can be found at *http://registry.gimp.org*.

It is possible to use GIMP as a simple pixel-based drawing program, but its strength is really image manipulation. In this book we present a small selection of useful tools and techniques. A complete coverage of the GIMP would require a whole book, so read this only as a teaser and for inspiration to explore GIMP.

At the time of writing the current version of GIMP was 2.2. Minor details in the feature set and user interface will be different in other versions, but the overall idea of the application is the same.

Selection tools. When GIMP is started, it shows the *toolbox window*, as seen in Figure 9-14. The upper part of the toolbox contains a number of buttons, each of which represents a tool. There is also a menubar with menus for creating new images, loading, saving, editing preferences, and so on. Below the buttons is a section showing the current foreground and background colors, selected pen, and so on. The lower part of the window shows the options for the current tool.

To create a new image, choose File → New. This gives us a blank image to use for experimenting with the tools.

The first five tools are selection tools: rectangle, ellipse, freehand, magic wand, by color, and shape-based selection. A *selection* is an area of the image that almost any tool and filter in GIMP will work on—so it is an important concept. The current selection is shown with "marching ants." You can show and hide the marching ants with Ctrl-Z.

The first three selection tools are, except for the shape of the selection made, quite similar. While dragging out a rectangular or elliptical selection, it is possible to keep a constant aspect ratio by holding down the Shift key. In the option window for each selection tool, it is possible to choose a selection mode to add to an existing selection, subtract from one, replace the current selection, and intersect with one.

All selection tools have a *feather* parameter that will control how soft the edges of the selection are. See Figure 9-15 for an example.

The magic wand allows you to click on a pixel in the image and thereby select a contiguous area around the pixel with similar color. Use the threshold slider to control how similar the colors must be. Selection by color works like the magic wand, but it selects *all* pixels with similar value—contiguous or not. Finally, selection by shapes allows you to place points in the image and try to connect the points with curves that follow edges in the image. When you have selected enough points to contain an area, click in the middle of that area to convert the traced curve to a selection.

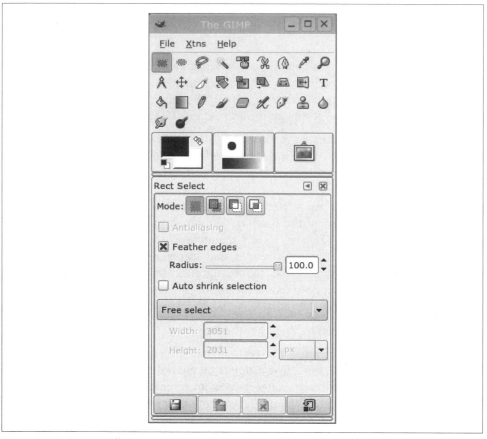

Figure 9-14. GIMP toolbox

Painting and erasing tools. To paint in an image, the Pencil, Paintbrush, Airbrush and Ink tools can be used. They differ in the way the shapes you draw look: Pencil paints with hard edges, and Paintbrush with soft edges, Airbrush paints semitransparently and Ink thickens the line when you paint slowly and thins the line when you paint quickly.

To fill in an area, make a selection and use the paintbucket or gradient fill tool to fill it with color. Selecting the pen style, color, and/or gradient can be done by clicking the controls in the middle of the toolbox window.

Some people have trouble drawing a straight line in GIMP, but since you have this clever book in your hands, you will know the secret: select one of the drawing tools, place the cursor where you want the line to start, press and hold Shift, and then move the mouse to where the line should end and click once with the left mouse button. Now either do the same again to draw another line segment or release the Shift key and enjoy your straight line.

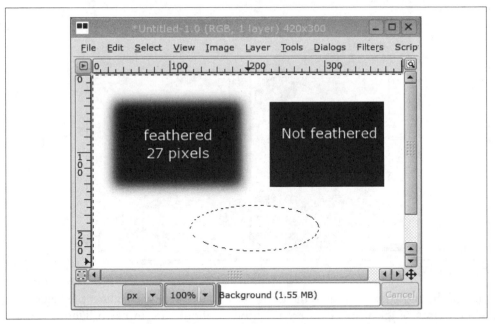

Figure 9-15. GIMP selections

If you make a mistake, use the most often used keyboard shortcut in GIMP: Ctrl-Z to undo. Multiple levels of undo are available. There is also an eraser tool that allows you to selectively erase pixels.

Everything you do with the painting tools will be confined to the currently selected area if there is a selection.

Photo retouching tools. The tools in this section are mostly for modifying digital photos in subtle (and not so subtle) ways. The Clone tool is very useful to remove blemishes from a photo. It works by first Ctrl-clicking in an image to set the source point, and then painting somewhere in an image. You will now paint with "copies" of the source area. Figure 9-16 shows the upper-right corner of a landscape photo that got a bit of the roof from a house into the frame. The left image is the original, and the right one has the undesired feature removed by using the clone tool with some other part of the clouds as the source area.

The last tool in the toolbox is the Dodge and Burn tool. It is used to lighten (dodge) and darken (burn) parts of an image by drawing on it. This tool can be used to fine-tune areas with shadows or highlights.

Color adjustment. During postprocessing of digital photos, it can be very useful to adjust the overall appearance of the light, color, and contrast of a photo. GIMP supports quite a number of tools for this. They are available in the Layer/Colors context menu.

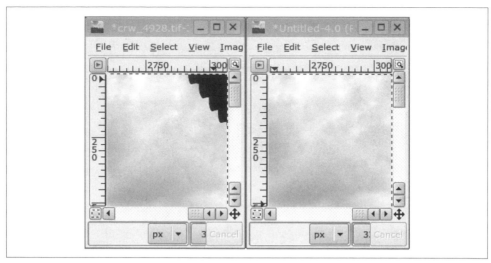

Figure 9-16. GIMP clone tool

One of the more useful tools is the Levels tool. It allows you to adjust the black and white points of an image. Figure 9-17 shows a photo shot in harsh lighting conditions. It has low contrast and looks hazy.

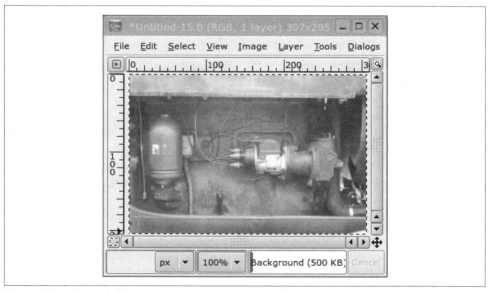

Figure 9-17. Original photo

Let's fix that problem using the Levels dialog! Open the dialog for the Levels tool by choosing Levels from the menu. The dialog can be seen in Figure 9-18.

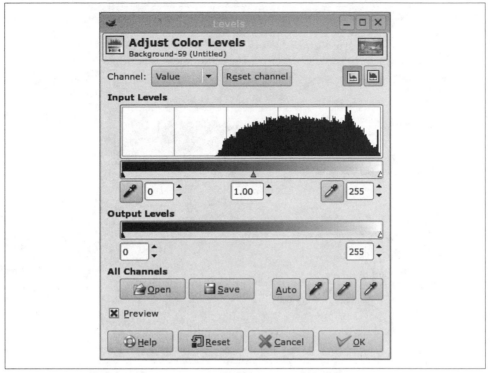

Figure 9-18. Levels dialog

The diagram seen under "Input Levels" is a histogram of the brightness values in the image. The left end of the histogram represents black, and the right end white. We see that that the lower 40% of the histogram is empty—this means that we are wasting useful dynamic range. Below the histogram are three triangular sliders. The black and the white ones are for setting the darkest and brightest point in the image, and the gray one is for adjusting how values are distributed within the two other ones. We can move the black point up as shown in Figure 9-19 to remove the haziness of the image. The result is shown in Figure 9-20.

Contrast enhancement can be done either with the Brightness-Contrast tool or with the Curves tool. The former is quite basic consisting of two sliders, one for brightness and one for contrast; the latter allows much more control. Figure 9-21 shows an original image and two modified versions with different curves applied. The middle image has the contrast-enhancing curve shown in Figure 9-22 applied, and the right image has the contrast-decreasing curve shown in Figure 9-23 applied. The curves describe a mapping from pixel values onto itself. A straight line at a 45-degree slope is the identity mapping; anything else will modify the image. Best results are obtained if you only deviate a little bit from the 45-degree straight line.

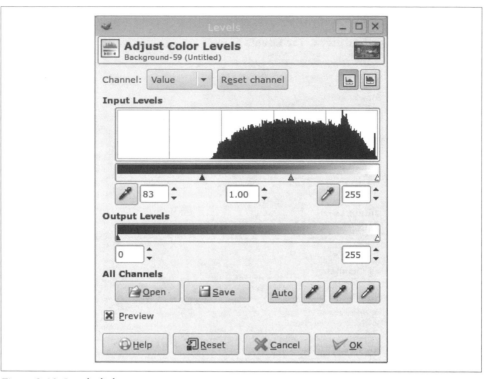

Figure 9-19. Levels dialog

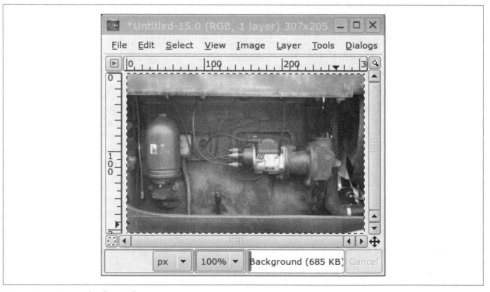

Figure 9-20. Level adjusted

Figure 9-21. Curve adjusted

Colors can be changed with several tools, such as the Color Balance and Hue-Saturation tools. The Levels and Curves tools can also be set to operate on individual color channels to achieve various effects. But there is also another tool available: the Channel Mixer. Unlike the other tools this is located in the Filters/Colors/Channel Mixer context menu. The Channel Mixer can be used to create a weighted mix of each color channel (red, green, and blue) for each of the output channels. It is particularly useful for converting color images to monochrome, often giving better results than simply desaturating the image. Figure 9-24 shows the Channel Mixer, and Figure 9-25 shows two monochrome versions of the same color image. The upper one is simply desaturated, and the lower one is based only on the blue channel and seems to emphasize the bird rather than the background. When judging how to convert a color image to monochrome, it can be helpful to examine each color component individually. See the paragraph about channels for more about this.

Layers and channels. The most convenient way to access layers and channels is through the combined layers, channels, paths, and undo history window. It can be accessed by right-clicking in the image's windows and selecting the Dialogs → Create New Dock → Layers, Channels & Paths menu item. Layers and channels allow you to view and manipulate different aspects of your images in a structured way.

Channels

An image is made up from one or more channel(s). True color images have three color channels, one for each of the red, green, and blue components. Index-colored and grayscale images have only one color channel. All types can have an optional alpha channel that describes the opacity of the image (white is completely opaque; black is completely transparent). By toggling the eye button for

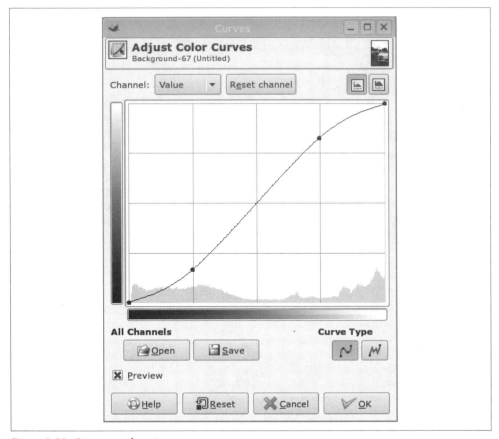

Figure 9-22. Contrast-enhancing curve

each channel, you can selectively view only a subset of the channels in an image. Channels can be selected or deselected for manipulation. For normal operation, all color channels are selected, but if you only want to paint into the red channel, for example, deselect the other channels. All drawing operations will then only affect the red channel. This can, for example, be used to remove the red flash reflection in your subjects' eyes. You can add additional channels to an image using the buttons at the bottom of the dialog. A very useful feature is that you can save a selection as a channel and convert a channel to a selection. This allows you to "remember" multiple selections for later use, and it makes it easier to fine-tune a selection because you can paint into a channel to add or remove areas to a selection. Figure 9-26 shows the Channel tab in the combined Layers, Channels dialog. The green and blue channels are visible, and the green channel is selected for editing.

Layers

Layers are a very powerful feature of the GIMP. Think of layers as a way of stacking multiple images on top of each other, affecting each other in various

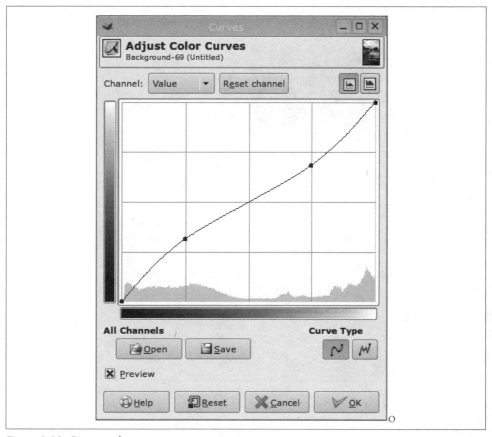

Figure 9-23. Contrast-decreasing curve

ways. If a layer has an alpha channel, the layers beneath it will show through in transparent areas of the layer. You can control the overall opacity of a layer by using the opacity slider shown in the dialog. Use the buttons at the bottom of the dialog to create, duplicate, and delete layers and to move layers up and down the stacking order. You can assign a name to a layer by right-clicking it and choosing Edit Layer Attributes. Figure 9-27 shows the Layers tab in the Layers, Channels dialog with an image loaded and two duplicate layers created.

Recall the image of the car from the curves example. The ground and car looked most interesting with the high-contrast curve, but the sky lost detail with this curve—it looked better with the low-contrast curve because it pulled out detail from the bright sky. Let us try to combine those two approaches. We'll leave the lowest layer alone—it will serve as a reference. Rename the middle layer "Ground" and the topmost one "Sky." Now make only the Ground layer visible, select it, and use the Curves tool to enhance contrast. Then make the topmost layer visible, select it, and apply a low-contrast curve to it. Now we need to

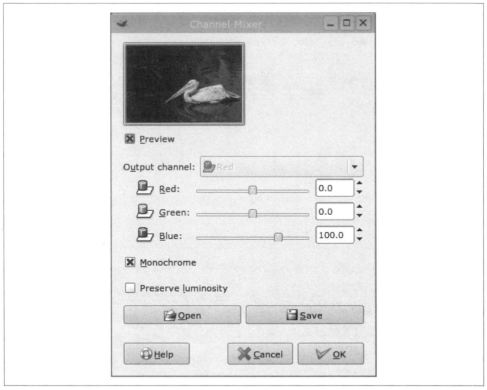

Figure 9-24. Channel Mixer

blend the two layers together. To do this, we add a *layer mask* to the topmost layer, but before we do that, we want to get a good starting point for the mask. Use the magic wand selection tool to select as much of the sky as possible without selecting any of the trees, cars, or the ground. Remember that Shift-clicking adds to a selection. When most of the sky is selected, right-click on the topmost layer and choose Add Layer Mask and then choose Selection in the dialog that pops up. Don't worry if the selection doesn't align perfectly at the pixel level with the horizon—we can fix that later. Press Ctrl-Shift-A to discard the current selection—we don't need it any more. Now the Layers dialog should look like Figure 9-28.

By clicking on either the layer thumbnail or the layer mask thumbnail, you can choose which one of them you want to edit. Choose the layer mask and zoom in on the boundary between the trees and the sky. Now the mask can be adjusted by simply painting on the image with a black or white pen. White makes the sky show through and black makes the trees show through. To see the mask itself instead of the image, right-click the mask in the Layers dialog and choose Show Mask. The result should look something like Figure 9-29.

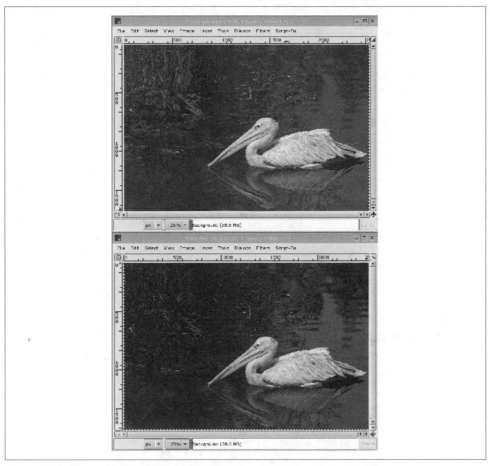

Figure 9-25. Channel Mixer example

So far we've only been using layers in Normal mode, but there are other modes as well. The other modes make a layer interact with the layers below it in interesting ways. It is possible to make the pixel values in a layer burn, dodge, multiply, and so forth, with the pixel values of the layer below it. This can be very powerful when used properly. Figure 9-30 shows the image from before with a new transparent layer added on top of it. This new layer contains the result of selecting a rectangle slightly smaller than the whole image, feathering the selection with a large radius (10% of the image height), inverting it, and filling out the selection with black paint. The mode of the layer is set to Overlay, which causes a slight darkening of the layers below it around the black areas near the borders. The effect looks as if the photo were taken with an old or cheap camera and adds to the mood of the scene. If we had used the Normal mode instead of Overlay, the effect would have been too much and looked unnatural. Try experimenting with the different modes yourself!

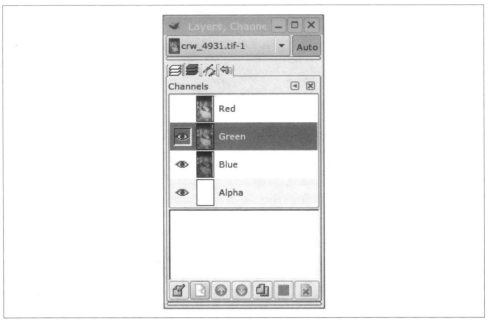

Figure 9-26. Channels dialog

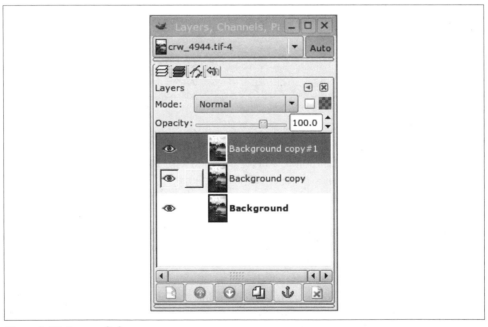

Figure 9-27. Layers dialog

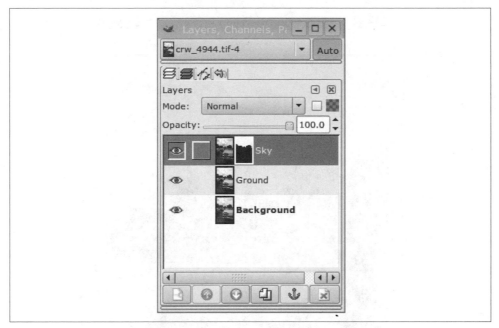

Figure 9-28. Layers and mask

Filters. The final major aspect of GIMP we cover here is its filters. Filters are effects that can be applied to an entire image or a selection. GIMP is shipped with a large number of different filters, and it is possible to plug in new filters to extend the capabilities of GIMP. Filters are located in the right mouse button Filters menu. The Channel Mixer is an example of such a filter. We discuss two useful filters, Gaussian Blur and Unsharp Mask, and apply them to the image from the previous example.

Gaussian Blur

This filter provides a nice smooth blurring effect. Try it with different blur radius settings. The IIR-type Gaussian blur seems to look better than RLE with most images.

For our example we are not going to blur the actual image. Instead, we are going to smooth out the transition between the high- and low-contrast layers. Do this by selecting the layer mask in the sky layer and applying Gaussian Blur. A radius of 8 seems to work well here. Zoom in on the border between the trees and the sky, and don't be afraid to experiment—you can always press Ctrl-Z to undo and try again. Figure 9-31 shows a closeup of before and after applying Gaussian Blur to the mask. The effect is subtle, but important for making the two layers blend seamlessly.

Unsharp Mask

Despite its name, Unsharp Mask is a filter for enhancing the perceived sharpness of images. It offers more control and often provides more pleasing results

Figure 9-29. Two layers

than the simple Sharpen filter. Unsharp Mask works like this: first it makes an internal copy of your image and applies a Gaussian blur to it. Then it calculates the difference between the original and the blurred image for each pixel, multiplies that difference by a factor, and finally adds it to the original image. The idea is that blurring affects sharp edges much more than even surfaces, so the difference is large close to the sharp edges in the image. Adding the difference back further emphasizes those sharp edges. The Radius setting for Unsharp Mask is the radius for the Gaussian blur step, the Amount is the factor that the differences are multipled by, and the Threshold setting is for ignoring differences smaller than the chosen value. Setting a higher threshold can help when working with images with digital noise in them so we don't sharpen the noise.

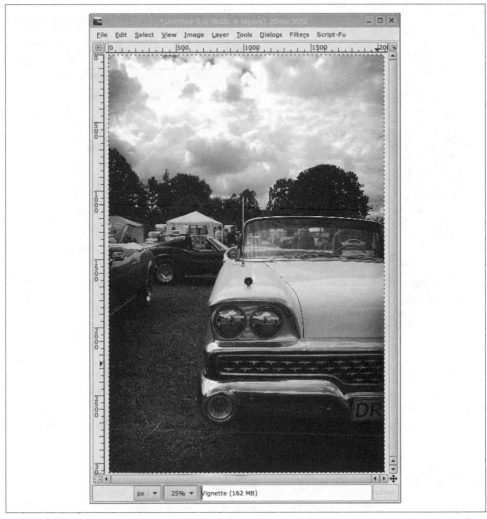

Figure 9-30. Two layers

Looking at our example with the sky and car again, we notice that the high-contrast part lost some details in the shadows when we pulled up the contrast. This can also be remedied with Unsharp Mask. To do this, we apply Unsharp Mask with a high radius and low amount. This technique is called "local contrast enhancement." Start out by making a copy of the whole image by pressing Ctrl-D and merging all layers in the copy. This is done by choosing Image → Flatten Image from the context menu. Then we want to scale the image for screen viewing. Open the scaling dialog by choosing Image → Scale Image from the context menu and choosing a suitable size and the bicubic (best) scaling algorithm. Now we are ready to apply Unsharp Mask for local contrast enhancement. A radius of 25, an amount of 0.15, and threshold of 0 seems to look good.

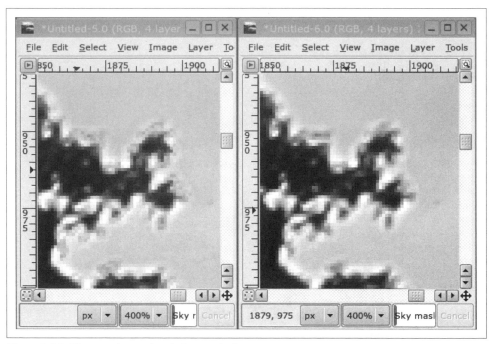

Figure 9-31. Blurring the mask—before and after

Finally, we want to sharpen up the edges a bit. To do this, we apply Unsharp Mask with a small radius (0.5) and higher amount (0.5) and with a threshold of 6. Figure 9-32 shows the unsharpened image on the left, the image with local contrast enhancement applied in the middle, and the image with the final sharpening pass applied on the right.

Recording Tools

If you want to create your own MP3 files, you will need an encoder program. There are also programs that allow you to extract tracks for audio CDs.

Although you can perform MP3 encoding with open source tools, certain patent claims have made the legality of doing so questionable. Ogg Vorbis is an alternative file format and encoder that claims to be free of patent issues. To use it, your player program needs to support Ogg Vorbis files because they are not directly compatible with MP3. However, many MP3 players, such as Xmms, support Ogg Vorbis already; in other cases, there are direct equivalents (such as ogg123 for mpg123). For video, Ogg has developed the Ogg Theoris codec, which is free and not encumbered by any patents.

This section lists some popular graphical tools for recording and manipulating multimedia.

Figure 9-32. Two passes of Unsharp Mask

Krec

KDE includes Krec as the standard sound recorder applications. You can record from any mixer source, such as a microphone or CD, and save to a sound file. Although it offers some audio effects, it is intended as a simple sound recorder application. A screenshot is shown in Figure 9-33.

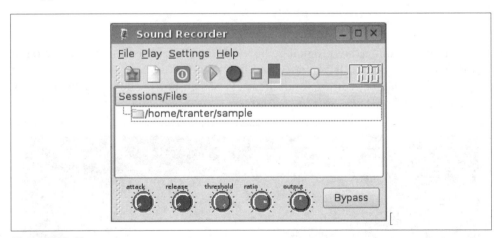

Figure 9-33. Krec

Audacity

Audacity is an audio editor that can record and play back sounds and read and write common sound file formats. You can edit sounds using cut, copy, and paste; mix tracks; and apply effects. It can graphically display waveforms in different formats.

A screenshot is shown in Figure 9-34. The project home page is *http://audacity.sourceforge.net*.

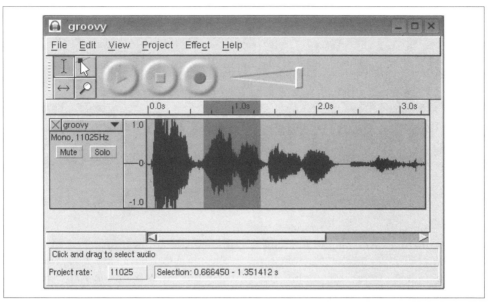

Figure 9-34. Audacity

Ardour

Ardour is a full-featured digital audio workstation designed to replace analog or digital tape systems. It provides multitrack and multichannel audio recording capability, mixing, editing, and effects. A screenshot is shown in Figure 9-35. The project home page is *http://ardour.org*.

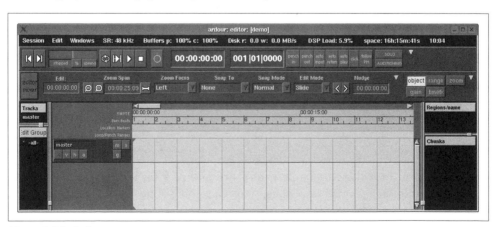

Figure 9-35. Ardour

Freevo

Freevo is an open source home theater platform based on Linux and open source audio and video tools. It can play audio and video files in most popular formats. Freevo can be used as a standalone personal video recorder controlled using a television and remote, or as a regular desktop computer using the monitor and keyboard.

A screenshot is shown in Figure 9-36. The project home page is *http:// freevo.sourceforge.net*.

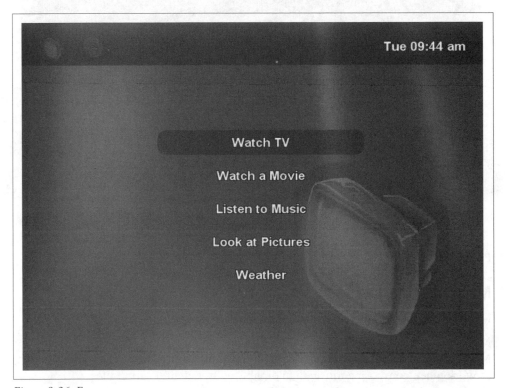

Figure 9-36. Freevo

MythTV

MythTV is a personal video recorder (PVR) application that supports a number of features, including

- Watching and recording television
- Viewing images
- Viewing and ripping videos from DVDs
- Playing music files
- Displaying weather and news and browsing the Internet
- Internet telephony and video conferencing

A screenshot is shown in Figure 9-37. The MythTV home page is *http://mythtv.org*.

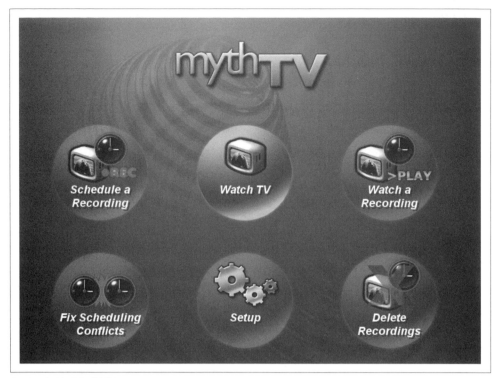

Figure 9-37. MythTV

Music Composition Tools

Many applications are available that help music composers.

MIDI sequencers allow a composer to edit and play music in MIDI format. Because MIDI is based on note events, tracks, and instruments, it is often a more natural way to work when composing music than directly editing digital sound files.

Scoring programs allow composers to work with traditional music notation and produce typeset sheet music. Some support other notation formats such as tablature for guitar and other instruments.

Some programs combine both MIDI sequencing and scoring, or can work with various standardized file formats for musical notation.

Brahms
> Brahms is a KDE-based MIDI sequencer application that allows a composer to edit tracks and play them back. You can work with MIDI events or a traditional music score using different editor windows. A screenshot is shown in Figure 9-38. The project home page is *http://brahms.sourceforge.net*.

Rosegarden

Rosegarden is an audio and MIDI sequencer, score editor, and general-purpose music composition and editing environment. It allows you to work with MIDI events or music notation. It is integrated with other KDE applications and has been localized into about 10 languages.

A screenshot is shown in Figure 9-39. The project home page is *http://www.rosegardenmusic.com*.

LilyPond

LilyPond is a music typesetter that produces traditional sheet music using a high-level description file as input. It supports many forms of music notation constructs, including chord names, drum notation, figured bass, grace notes, guitar tablature, modern notation (cluster notation and rhythmic grouping), tremolos, (nested) tuplets in arbitrary ratios, and more.

LilyPond's text-based music input language support can integrate into LATEX, HTML, and Texinfo, allowing documents containing sheet music and traditional text to be written from a single source. It produces PostScript and PDF output (via TEX), as well as MIDI.

The project home page is *http://lilypond.org*. There is a graphical front end to LilyPond called Denemo.

Internet Telephony and Conferencing Tools

Telephony over the Internet has recently become popular and mainstream. Using VOIP (Voice Over IP) technology, audio is streamed over a LAN or Internet connection. SIP (Session Initiation Protocol) is a standard for setting up multimedia sessions (not just audio). Either a sound card and microphone or dedicated hardware resembling a traditional telephone can be used. Internet telephony has a number of advantages, but the main one is cost—many users today have a full-time high-speed Internet connection that can be used to connect to anyone else in the world with compatible software. With a suitable gateway, you can make a call between a VOIP phone and the public telephone network.

There are many VOIP applications for Linux. KPhone is one popular KDE-based one. As well as audio, it supports instant messaging and has some support for video. The project's home page is *http://www.wirlab.net/kphone*.

There are also commercial applications that use proprietary protocols or extensions to protocols. One example is Skype, which offers a free client but requires subscription to a service to make calls to regular phones through a gateway. Skype can be found at *http://www.skype.com*.

H.323 is a standard for video conferencing over LANs. It is supported by Microsoft NetMeeting, which is included with Microsoft Windows. H.323-compliant

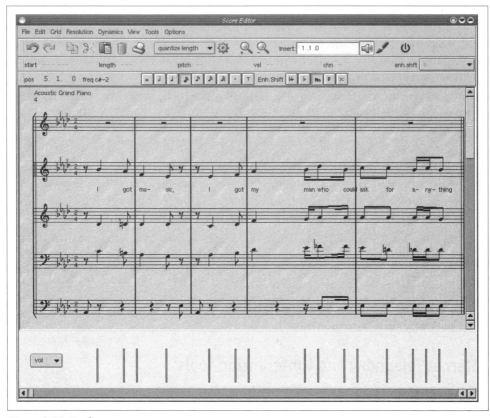

Figure 9-38. Brahms

applications are available on Linux, the most notable being GnomeMeeting. The project's home page is *http://www.gnomemeeting.org*.

Browser Plug-ins

Browser plug-ins allow data types other than HTML to be presented in your web browser. Some of these qualify as multimedia. They can be divided into three categories:

- Plug-ins that come with the browser or are available from the same source as the browser (e.g., Mozilla or Firefox).

- Native plug-ins from third parties, such as Adobe Acrobat, usually available at no cost although they may be closed source.

- Windows plug-ins that can run inside some Linux browsers using CodeWeaver's CrossOver (Wine) technology. This category includes plug-ins such as Apple QuickTime, Windows Media Player, and Adobe Shockwave. Many of these are not available as native Linux plug-ins.

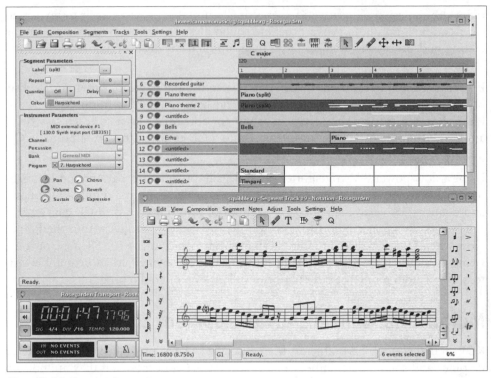

Figure 9-39. Rosegarden

The Netscape plug-in format is supported by Netscape, Mozilla, and some other browsers derived from Mozilla, such as FireFox. Netscape plug-ins are also supported by the KDE project's Konqueror browser.

Putting It All Together

This chapter has talked about a lot of different multimedia tools. Although most of these tools are straightforward to use and perform a well-defined function on their own, more powerful tasks can be performed by combining tools. Let's look at a real-life example.

I like to collect and restore old vacuum tube radios from the 1930s through 1950s. After I have restored a radio to working condition I like to display it. But when I turn it on, hearing the local sports or talk radio station doesn't seem appropriate. Wouldn't it be fun to hear some old radio shows from the era in which the radio was made coming out of the radio?

Lots of old-time radio broadcasts are available as free downloads on the Internet. I can download a number of these to my computer. It is also possible to buy CDs of old radio programs. I might even have an old vinyl record or cassette tape of old radio shows. Using Audacity and connecting a turntable or tape player to my sound card's audio input, I can convert them to sound files. The files can have some simple editing and processing done to clean them up, and they can be converted to MP3 format.

If I want to listen to them on my computer, I can use Juk to arrange them in playlists of my favorite programs arranged by type and have hours of continuous music or radio shows. I can save the MP3 files to my portable MP3 player to listen to when I am away from the computer, or burn them to a CD to listen to with a portable CD player.

Using a low-power AM transmitter, I can legally broadcast programming throughout my home. An inexpensive AM transmitter is available from a number of sources and connects either to the sound card output of my computer or a CD player, and can broadcast vintage radio programs on the AM band to radios within the house. Now when I turn on that old radio, I can hear Burns and Allen, *The Shadow*, or some swing music from the 1940s. I might even be able to convince the more gullible visitors to my radio room that old radios can still pick up old radio programs.

Multimedia Toolkits and Development Environments

KDE and GNOME have already been discussed. They provide basic support for graphics and sound that can be used for multimedia applications if they are not too demanding. If you want to do more, or if KDE or GNOME does not fit your needs, there are other toolkits available that are worth considering. This section briefly mentions some of the more popular multimedia toolkits and libraries available for Linux.

Simple DirectMedia Layer (SDL)
> Simple DirectMedia Layer (SDL) is a cross-platform multimedia library designed to provide low-level access to audio, keyboard, mouse, joystick, 3D hardware via OpenGL, and 2D video framebuffers. It is used by MPEG playback software, emulators, and many popular games, including the award-winning Linux port of Civilization: Call to Power.
>
> SDL is written in C, but works with C++ natively and has bindings to several other languages, including Ada, Eiffel, Java, Lua, ML, Perl, PHP, Pike, Python, and Ruby.
>
> The project home page is *http://www.libsdl.org*.

OpenGL
> OpenGL is a standardized API for 2D and 3D graphics programming developed by Silicon Graphics, Inc. (SGI). It supports rendering, texture mapping, special effects, and other powerful visualization functions. More information can be found at *http://www.opengl.org*.

There are several free implementations of OpenGL support under Linux. The most popular is Mesa. Because it is not licensed from SGI, it cannot officially be called OpenGL, but it is designed to be compatible. The Mesa project home page is *http://www.mesa3d.org*.

OpenAL

OpenAL is a cross-platform 3D audio API appropriate for use with gaming applications and many other types of audio applications. Conceptually, you can think of OpenAL as a 3D rendering library for audio just as OpenGL is a 3D rendering library for graphics.

The project's home page is *http://www.openal.org*.

JACK

JACK is a low-latency audio server, written for POSIX-conformant operating systems such as GNU/Linux and Apple's OS X. It can connect a number of different applications to an audio device, as well as allowing them to share audio between themselves. Its clients can run in their own processes (i.e., as normal applications), or they can run within the JACK server (i.e., as a plug-in).

The JACK home page is *http://jackit.sourceforge.net*.

GStreamer

GStreamer is a library that allows the construction of graphs of media-handling components, ranging from simple sound file playback to complex audio mixing and video nonlinear editing. Applications can take advantage of advances in codec and filter technology transparently. Developers can add new codecs and filters by writing a simple plug-in with a clean, generic interface.

The GStreamer web site is *http://gstreamer.freedesktop.org*.

Network Multimedia Middleware (NMM)

NMM is a multimedia middleware package that allows the creation of distributed multimedia applications. A number of plug-ins supporting various media types, operations, and I/O devices are included. NMM has been used to implement a multimedia application that provides an extensible home entertainment system for DVD/CD playback and frame grabbing, TV with time-shifting, video recording, and playlist creation and playback for all supported media types.

More information can be found at *http://www.networkmultimedia.org*.

Media Applications Server (MAS)

The Media Application Server (MAS) is a time-aware arbiter of video and audio hardware, meant to scale the gamut of systems, from embedded to massively parallel, from handheld devices to supercomputers, from a microphone source to a speech recognition engine sink. MAS is a multimedia routing server. It moves multimedia data across the Internet virtually in real time, ensuring quality presentation of video, audio, and other time-sensitive information.

For more information on MAS, see *http://www.mediaapplicationserver.net*.

Multimedia distributions

There are some Linux distributions being developed that are optimized to be used as multimedia platforms. One such project is AGNULA, which stands for A GNU/Linux Audio distribution. With funding from the European Commission, it is developing two reference Linux distributions of free software: DeMuDi (Debian-based Multimedia Distribution) and ReHMuDi (Red Hat-based Multimedia Distribution). The project's home page is *http://www.agnula.org*.

Solutions to Common Problems

Listed here are answers to some commonly asked questions and solutions to common problems related to multimedia hardware and software:

Why doesn't my distribution include an MP3 encoder or DVD player?

Due to legal issues related to patents, many Linux distributions do not ship an MP3 encoder or DVD player application. You may be able to download these separately after determining for yourself that they can be used legally in your jurisdication.

Are there free alternatives to MP3 and DVD that are not encumbered by patents?

The Ogg project by the Xiph.org Foundation has developed several encoding formats and free implementations that are free of patent issues including Ogg Vorbis for audio and Ogg Theoris for video. See *http://www.xiph.org* for more information.

Kernel modules not loaded

This could be caused by incorrect module configuration files. It will also occur if the kernel module loader (*kerneld* or *kmod*) is not running. Make sure the module is available for loading in the appropriate directory (typically something like */lib/modules/2.4.17/kernel/drivers/sound*).

Sound card not detected

You are probably using the wrong kernel driver or the wrong settings for I/O address, IRQ, or DMA channel.

IRQ/DMA timeout or device conflicts

You are using the wrong settings for I/O address, IRQ, and DMA, or you have a conflict with another card that is using the same settings.

No sound after rebooting

If sound was working and then stopped when the system was rebooted, you probably have a problem with the module configuration files. This can also occur if the system *init* scripts are not configured to initialize PnP cards or to load the modules. If the drivers are loaded, it could be that the mixer settings are set too low to hear any audio. Use a mixer program to adjust the sound levels while using a media player program to play a known good sound file.

If you are running KDE or GNOME, make sure that the appropriate sound server (*aRts* or *esd*) is running. On some systems, you may need to adjust the sound server settings using the control panel provided for this purpose. In the case of KDE you can also conveniently test the sound server from the control panel.

Sound works only for root

This probably indicates a permissions problem with the device files. Many systems allow only users who are members of the group "audio" to access the sound devices. Add the user(s) to this group or change the permissions on the audio devices using the chmod command. Some versions of the 2.6 Linux kernel do not respect the group file permissions for device files, and they need to be made readable to the user who is logged on.

No sound is heard but there are no error messages

If sound programs appear to be playing but nothing is heard, it is probably a problem with the mixer settings, or a problem with the connection of the speakers.

Unable to record audio

This could indicate a problem with the mixer settings. You need to set the levels and select the input device. You might also have a bad microphone or be using the wrong input jack on the sound card.

Device busy error

Either you have a device conflict, or another application is using the sound devices. This could be because you are running a sound server program, such as *esd* or *artsd*.

No sound when playing audio CD

To play audio CDs, you need a cable from the CD-ROM drive to your sound card. Make sure you have selected CD input using a mixer program. Try connecting headphones to the front-panel jack of the CD-ROM drive. If you can hear audio, the problem is not with the drive itself. If you can't hear audio from the headphones, the problem is with the drive or CD player program. (Note that some newer CD player programs support digital playback without a cable, but you may need to configure them to operate in this mode.)

Cannot play MIDI files

Some MIDI applications work only with a sound card that has an FM synthesizer, and not all cards have this hardware (or the kernel driver for the sound card may not support it). Try using another MIDI application that supports using the standard audio device.

References

Listed here are a few sources of information related to multimedia under Linux:

Sound and MIDI Software For Linux, a directory of multimedia applications and resources
    http://sound.condorow.net

SourceForge, the world's largest open source software development web site
    http://www.sourceforge.net

Freshmeat, a huge directory of open source and commercial software projects
    http://freshmeat.net

The Linux Sound HOWTO, available from the Linux Documentation Project
    http://www.tlpd.org

The Linux CD-ROM HOWTO, available from the Linux Documentation Project
    http://www.tlpd.org

The ALSA Project
    http://www.alsa-project.org

4Front Technologies
    http://www.opensound.com

The KDE project
    http://www.kde.org

The GNOME project
    http://www.gnome.org

The WINE project
    http://www.winehq.com

CodeWeavers, developers of CrossOver
    http://www.codeweavers.com

The ReWind project
    http://rewind.sourceforge.net

TransGaming Technologies, developers of Cedega
    http://www.transgaming.com

Linux Multimedia Guide (O'Reilly)
    http://www.oreilly.com/catalog/multilinux/

Linux Music and Sound (No Starch Press)
    http://www.nostarch.com/lms.htm

System Administration

In this part of the book we show you how to set up your Linux system and its environment to do pretty important things such as printing and sharing files with other systems; we also show you how to take care of your system in other ways. If you have more than one person using the system, the material in this section is particularly important. It's also important if your distribution failed to get networking up and running, or if you want to run any of the servers in Part IV of the book.

CHAPTER 10

System Administration Basics

If you're running your own Linux system, one of the first tasks at hand is to learn the ropes of system administration. You won't be able to get by for long without having to perform some kind of system maintenance, software upgrade, or mere tweaking to keep things in running order.

Running a Linux system is not unlike riding and taking care of a motorcycle.[*] Many motorcycle hobbyists prefer caring for their own equipment—routinely cleaning the points, replacing worn-out parts, and so forth. Linux gives you the opportunity to experience the same kind of "hands-on" maintenance with a complex operating system.

Although a passionate administrator can spend any amount of time tuning it for performance, you really have to perform administration only when a major change occurs: you install a new disk, a new user comes on the system, or a power failure causes the system to go down unexpectedly. We discuss all these situations over the next four chapters.

Linux is surprisingly accessible, in all respects—from the more mundane tasks of upgrading shared libraries to the more esoteric, such as mucking about with the kernel. Because all the source code is available and the body of Linux developers and users has traditionally been of the hackish breed, system maintenance is not only a part of daily life but also a great learning experience. Trust us: there's nothing like telling your friends how you upgraded from PHP 4.3 to PHP 5.0 in less than half an hour, and all the while you were recompiling the kernel to support the ISO 9660 filesystem. (They may have no idea what you're talking about, in which case you can give them a copy of this book.)

In the next few chapters, we explore your Linux system from the mechanic's point of view—showing you what's under the hood, as it were—and explain how to take care

---

[*] At least one author attests a strong correspondence between Linux system administration and Robert Pirsig's *Zen and the Art of Motorcycle Maintenance*. Does Linux have the Buddha nature?

of it all, including software upgrades, managing users, filesystems, and other resources, performing backups, and handling emergencies.

Once you put the right entries in startup files, your Linux system will, for the most part, run itself. As long as you're happy with the system configuration and the software that's running on it, very little work will be necessary on your part. However, we'd like to encourage Linux users to experiment with their system and customize it to taste. Very little about Linux is carved in stone, and if something doesn't work the way that you'd like it to, you should be able to change that. For instance, in earlier chapters we've shown you how to read blinking green text on a cyan background rather than the traditional white-on-black, if that's the way you prefer it, or to add applets to your desktop panel. But this book also shows you something even more important: after installing a Linux distribution, you usually have lots of services running that you may not need (such as a web server). Any of these services could be a potential security hole, so you might want to fiddle with the startup files to get only the services you absolutely need.

It should be noted that many Linux systems include fancy tools to simplify many system administration tasks. These include YaST2 on SUSE systems, the Mandriva Control Center on Mandriva systems, and a number of utilities on Red Hat systems. These tools can do everything from managing user accounts to creating filesystems to doing your laundry. These utilities can make your life either easier or more difficult, depending on how you look at them. In these chapters, we present the "guts" of system administration, demonstrating the tools that should be available on any Linux system and indeed nearly all Unix systems. These are the core of the system administrator's toolbox: the metaphorical hammer, screwdriver, and socket wrench that you can rely on to get the job done. If you'd rather use the 40-hp circular saw, feel free, but it's always nice to know how to use the hand tools in case the power goes out. Good follow-up books, should you wish to investigate more topics in Unix system administration, include the *Unix System Administration Handbook*, by Evi Nemeth et al. (Prentice Hall) and *Essential System Administration*, by Æleen Frisch (O'Reilly).

Maintaining the System

Being the system administrator for any Unix system requires a certain degree of responsibility and care. This is equally true for Linux, even if you're the only user on your system.

Many of the system administrator's tasks are done by logging into the *root* account. This account has special properties on Unix systems; specifically, the usual file permissions and other security mechanisms simply don't apply to *root*. That is, *root* can access and modify any file on the system, no matter to whom it belongs. Whereas normal users can't damage the system (say, by corrupting filesystems or touching other users' files), *root* has no such restrictions.

At this point, it should be mentioned that some distributions, such as Ubuntu, disable the *root* account and require users to use the *sudo* tool instead. With *sudo*, you cannot log in as *root*, but you can execute exactly one command with the rights of *root*, which amounts to the same thing, except that you have to prefix each command with *sudo*.

Why does the Unix system have security in the first place? The most obvious reason for this is to allow users to choose how they wish their own files to be accessed. By changing file permission bits (with the *chmod* command), users can specify that certain files should be readable, writable, or executable only by certain groups of other users, or by no other users at all. Permissions help ensure privacy and integrity of data; you wouldn't want other users to read your personal mailbox, for example, or to edit the source code for an important program behind your back.

The Unix security mechanisms also prevent users from damaging the system. The system restricts access to many of the raw device files (accessed via */dev*—more on this in "Device Files" later in this chapter) corresponding to hardware, such as your hard drives. If normal users could read and write directly to the disk-drive device, they could wreak all kinds of havoc—say, completely overwriting the contents of the drive. Instead, the system requires normal users to access the drives via the filesystem—where security is enforced via the file permission bits described previously.

It is important to note that not all kinds of "damage" that can be caused are necessarily malevolent. System security is more a means to protect users from their own natural mistakes and misunderstandings rather than to enforce a police state on the system. And, in fact, on many systems security is rather lax; Unix security is designed to foster the sharing of data between groups of users who may be, say, cooperating on a project. The system allows users to be assigned to groups, and file permissions may be set for an entire group. For instance, one development project might have free read and write permission to a series of files, while at the same time other users are prevented from modifying those files. With your own personal files, you get to decide how public or private the access permissions should be.

The Unix security mechanism also prevents normal users from performing certain actions, such as calling certain system calls within a program. For example, there is a system call that causes the system to halt, called by programs such as *shutdown* (more on this later in the chapter). If normal users could call this function within their programs, they could accidentally (or purposefully) halt the system at any time.

In many cases, you have to bypass Unix security mechanisms in order to perform system maintenance or upgrades. This is what the *root* account is for. Because no such restrictions apply to *root*, it is easy for a knowledgeable system administrator to get work done without worrying about the usual file permissions or other limitations. The usual way to log in as *root* is with the *su* command. *su* allows you to assume the identification of another user. For example:

```
su andy
```

will prompt you for the password for *andy*, and if it is correct it will set your user ID to that of *andy*. A superuser often wants to temporarily assume a regular user's identity to correct a problem with that user's files or some similar reason. Without a username argument, *su* will prompt you for the *root* password, validating your user ID as *root*. Once you are finished using the *root* account, you log out in the usual way and return to your own mortal identity.*

Why not simply log in as *root* from the usual login prompt? As we'll see, this is desirable in some instances, but most of the time it's best to use *su* after logging in as yourself. On a system with many users, use of *su* records a message, such as:

```
Nov  1 19:28:50 loomer su: mdw on /dev/ttyp1
```

in the system logs, such as */var/log/messages* (we talk more about these files later). This message indicates that the user *mdw* successfully issued an *su* command, in this case for *root*. If you were to log in directly as *root*, no such message would appear in the logs; you wouldn't be able to tell which user was mucking about with the *root* account. This is important if multiple administrators are on the machine: it is often desirable to find out who used *su* and when.

There is an additional little twist to the *su* command. Just running it as described previously will only change your user ID; it will not give you the settings made for this ID. You might have special configuration files for each user, but these are not executed when using *su* this way. To emulate a real login with all the configuration files being executed, you need to add a -, like this:

```
su - andy
```

or:

```
su -
```

for becoming *root* and executing *root*'s configuration files.

The *root* account can be considered a magic wand—both a useful and potentially dangerous tool. Fumbling the magic words you invoke while holding this wand can wreak unspeakable damage on your system. For example, the simple eight-character sequence `rm -rf /` will delete every file on your system, if executed as *root*, and if you're not paying attention. Does this problem seem far-fetched? Not at all. You might be trying to delete an old directory, such as */usr/src/oldp*, and accidentally slip in a space after the first slash, producing the following:

```
rm -rf / usr/src/oldp
```

---

* Notice that the Unix kernel does not care about the username actually being *root*: it considers everybody who has the user ID 0 to be the superuser. By default, the username *root* is the only username mapped to that user ID, but if you feel like it, you can always create a user named *thebigboss* and map that to user ID 0 as well. The next chapter will show you how to do that.

Also problematic are directory names with spaces in them. Let's say you have directories named *Dir\ 1* and *Dir\ 2*, where the backslash indicates that *Dir\ 1* is really one filename containing a space character. Now you want to delete both directories, but by mistake add an extra space again:

```
rm -rf Dir\  *
```

Now there are two spaces between the backslash and the asterisk. The first one is protected by the backslash, but not the second one, so it separates the arguments and makes the asterisk a new argument. Oops, your current directory and everything below it are gone.

Another common mistake is to confuse the arguments for commands such as dd, a command often used to copy large chunks of data from one place to another. For instance, in order to save the first 1024 bytes of data from the device */dev/hda* (which contains the boot record and partition table for that drive), one might use the command:

```
dd if=/dev/hda of=/tmp/stuff bs=1k count=1
```

However, if we reverse if and of in this command, something quite different happens: the contents of */tmp/stuff* are written to the top of */dev/hda*. More likely than not, you've just succeeded in hosing your partition table and possibly a filesystem superblock. Welcome to the wonderful world of system administration!

The point here is that you should sit on your hands before executing any command as *root*. Stare at the command for a minute before pressing Enter and make sure it makes sense. If you're not sure of the arguments and syntax of the command, quickly check the manual pages or try the command in a safe environment before firing it off. Otherwise you'll learn these lessons the hard way; mistakes made as *root* can be disastrous.

A nice tip is to use the *alias* command to make some of the commands less dangerous for *root*. For example, you could use:

```
alias rm="rm -i"
```

The *-i* option stands for *interactively* and means that the *rm* command will ask you before deleting each file. Of course, this does not protect you against the horrible mistake shown earlier; the *-f* option (which stands for *force*) simply overrides the *-i* because it comes later.

In many cases, the prompt for the *root* account differs from that for normal users. Classically, the *root* prompt contains a hash mark (#), whereas normal user prompts contain $ or %. (Of course, use of this convention is up to you; it is utilized on many Unix systems, however.) Although the prompt may remind you that you are wielding the *root* magic wand, it is not uncommon for users to forget this or accidentally enter a command in the wrong window or virtual console.

Like any powerful tool, the *root* account can be abused. It is important, as the system administrator, to protect the root password, and if you give it out at all, to give it only to those users who you trust (or who can be held responsible for their actions on the system). If you're the only user of your Linux system, this certainly doesn't apply—unless, of course, your system is connected to a network or allows dial-in login access.

The primary benefit of not sharing the *root* account with other users is not so much that the potential for abuse is diminished, although this is certainly the case. Even more important is that if you're the one person with the ability to use the *root* account, you have complete knowledge of how the system is configured. If anyone were able to, say, modify important system files (as we'll talk about in this chapter), the system configuration could be changed behind your back, and your assumptions about how things work would be incorrect. Having one system administrator act as the arbiter for the system configuration means that one person always knows what's going on.

Also, allowing other people to have the root password means that it's more likely someone will eventually make a mistake using the *root* account. Although each person with knowledge of the root password may be trusted, anybody can make mistakes. If you're the only system administrator, you have only yourself to blame for making the inevitable human mistakes as *root*.

That being said, let's dive into the actual tasks of system administration under Linux. Buckle your seatbelt.

Managing Filesystems

You probably created filesystems and swap space when you first installed Linux (most distributions help you do the basics). Here is a chance to fine-tune these resources. Most of the time, you do these things shortly after installing your operating system, before you start loading up your disks with fun stuff. But occasionally you will want to change a running system, for example, to add a new device or perhaps upgrade the swap space when you upgrade your RAM.

To Unix systems, a filesystem is some device (such as a hard drive, floppy, or CD-ROM) that is formatted to store files. Filesystems can be found on hard drives, floppies, CD-ROMs, and other storage media that permit random access. (A tape allows only sequential access, and therefore cannot contain a filesystem per se.)

The exact format and means by which files are stored is not important; the system provides a common interface for all *filesystem types* it recognizes. Under Linux, filesystem types include the Third Extended filesystem, or *ext3fs*, which you probably use to store Linux files; the Reiser filesystem, another popular filesystem for storing Linux files; the VFAT filesystem, which allows files on Windows 95/98/ME partitions and floppies to be accessed under Linux (as well as Windows NT/2000/XP partitions if they are FAT-formatted); and several others, including the ISO 9660 filesystem used by CD-ROM.

Each filesystem type has a very different underlying format for storing data. However, when you access any filesystem under Linux, the system presents the data as files arranged into a hierarchy of directories, along with owner and group IDs, permission bits, and the other characteristics with which you're familiar.

In fact, information on file ownership, permissions, and so forth is provided only by filesystem types that are meant to be used for storing Linux files. For filesystem types that don't store this information, the kernel drivers used to access these filesystems "fake" the information. For example, the MS-DOS filesystem has no concept of file ownership; therefore, all files are presented as if they were owned by *root*. This way, above a certain level, all filesystem types look alike, and each file has certain attributes associated with it. Whether this data is actually used in the underlying filesystem is another matter altogether.

As the system administrator, you need to know how to create filesystems should you want to store Linux files on a floppy or add additional filesystems to your hard drives. You also need to know how to use the various tools to check and maintain filesystems should data corruption occur. Also, you must know the commands and files used to access filesystems—for example, those on floppy or CD-ROM.

Filesystem Types

Table 10-1 lists the filesystem types supported by the Linux kernel as of Version 2.6.5. New filesystem types are always being added to the system, and experimental drivers for several filesystems not listed here are available. To find out what filesystem types your kernel supports, look at the file */proc/filesystems*. You can select which filesystem types to support when building your kernel; see "Kernel configuration: make config" in Chapter 18.

Table 10-1. Linux filesystem types

Filesystem	Type	Description
Second Extended filesystem	ext2	Used to be the most common Linux filesystem, but is slowly being made obsolete by the Reiser and Third Extended filesystems
Reiser filesystem	reiserfs	A journaling filesystem for Linux
Third Extended filesystem	ext3	Another journaling filesystem for Linux that is downward-compatible with *ext2*
JFS	jfs	IBM's implementation of a journaled filesystem for Linux; an alternative to *ext3* and *reiserfs*
Network File System (NFS)	NFS	Allows access to remote files on network
UMSDOS filesystem	umsdos	Installs Linux on an MS-DOS partition
DOS-FAT filesystem	msdos	Accesses MS-DOS files

Table 10-1. Linux filesystem types (continued)

Filesystem	Type	Description
VFAT filesystem	vfat	Accesses Windows 95/98/ME files
NT filesystem	ntfs	Accesses Windows NT/2000/XP files
/proc filesystem	proc	Provides process information for ps
ISO 9660 filesystem	iso9660	Used by most CD-ROMs
UDF filesystem	udf	The most modern CD-ROM filesystem
SMB filesystem	smbfs	Accesses files from a Windows server over the network
Coda filesystem	coda	An advanced network filesystem, similar to NFS
Cifs filesystem	cifs	The Common Internet File System, Microsoft's suggestion for an SMB successor; supported by Windows 2000, 2003, and XP, as well as the Samba server

Each filesystem type has its own attributes and limitations; for example, the MS-DOS filesystem restricts filenames to eight characters plus a three-character extension and should be used only to access existing MS-DOS floppies or partitions. For most of your work with Linux, you'll use the Second or Third Extended (*ext2* or *ext3*) filesystem, which were developed primarily for Linux and support 256-character filenames, a 32-terabyte maximum filesystem size, and a slew of other goodies, or you will use the Reiser (*reiserfs)*. Earlier Linux systems used the Extended filesystem (no longer supported) and the Minix filesystem. (The Minix filesystem was originally used for several reasons. First of all, Linux was originally cross-compiled under Minix. Also, Linus was quite familiar with the Minix filesystem, and it was straightforward to implement in the original kernels.) Some other obscure filesystems available in older Linux kernels are no longer supported.

The main difference between the Second Extended filesystem on the one hand and the Reiser and the Third Extended filesystem on the other hand is that the latter two are *journaled*. Journaling is an advanced technique that keeps track of the changes made to a filesystem, making it much easier (and faster!) to restore a corrupted filesystem (e.g., after a system crash or a power failure). Another journaled filesystem is IBM's Journaling File System, JFS.

You will rarely need the ROM filesystem, which is very small, does not support write operations, and is meant to be used in ramdisks at system configuration, startup time, or even in EPROMS. Also in this group is the Cram filesystem, which is used for ROMs as well and compresses its contents. This is primarily meant for embedded devices, where space is at a premium.

The UMSDOS filesystem is used to install Linux under a private directory of an existing MS-DOS partition. This is a good way for new users to try out Linux without repartitioning, at the expense of poorer performance. The DOS-FAT filesystem, on the other hand, is used to access MS-DOS files directly. Files on partitions created with Windows 95 or 98 can be accessed via the VFAT filesystem, whereas the NTFS filesystem lets you access Windows NT filesystems. The HPFS filesystem is used to access the OS/2 filesystem.

/proc is a virtual filesystem; that is, no actual disk space is associated with it. See "The /proc Filesystem," later in this chapter.*

The ISO 9660 filesystem (previously known as the High Sierra Filesystem and abbreviated *hsfs* on other Unix systems) is used by most CD-ROMs. Like MS-DOS, this filesystem type restricts filename length and stores only limited information about each file. However, most CD-ROMs provide the Rock Ridge Extensions to ISO 9660, which allow the kernel filesystem driver to assign long filenames, ownerships, and permissions to each file. The net result is that accessing an ISO 9660 CD-ROM under MS-DOS gives you 8.3-format filenames, but under Linux gives you the "true," complete filenames.

In addition, Linux now supports the Microsoft Joliet extensions to ISO 9660, which can handle long filenames made up of Unicode characters. This is not widely used now but may become valuable in the future because Unicode has been accepted internationally as the standard for encoding characters of scripts worldwide.

Linux also supports UDF, a filesystem that is meant for use with CD-RWs and DVDs.

Next, we have many filesystem types for other platforms. Linux supports the formats that are popular on those platforms in order to allow dual-booting and other interoperation. The systems in question include UFS, EFS, BFS, XFS, System V, and BeOS. If you have filesystems created in one of these formats under a foreign operating system, you'll be able to access the files from Linux.

Finally, there is a slew of filesystems for accessing data on partitions; these are created by operating systems other than the DOS and Unix families. Those filesystems support the Acorn Disk Filing System (ADFS), the Amiga OS filesystems (no floppy disk support except on Amigas), the Apple Mac HFS, and the QNX4 filesystem. Most of the specialized filesystems are useful only on certain hardware architectures; for instance, you won't have hard disks formatted with the Amiga FFS filesystem in an Intel machine. If you need one of those drivers, please read the information that comes with them; some are only in an experimental state.

Besides these filesystems that are used to access local hard disks, there are also network filesystems for accessing remote resources. We talk about those to some extent later.

---

* Note that the */proc* filesystem under Linux is not the same format as the */proc* filesystem under SVR4 (say, Solaris 2.x). Under SVR4, each running process has a single "file" entry in */proc*, which can be opened and treated with certain *ioctl()* calls to obtain process information. On the contrary, Linux provides most of its information in */proc* through *read()* and *write()* requests.

Finally, there are specialty filesystems, such as those that store the data in RAM instead of on the hard disk (and consequentially are much faster, but also lose all their data when the computer is powered off), and those that provide access to kernel objects and kernel data.

Mounting Filesystems

In order to access any filesystem under Linux, you must mount it on a certain directory. This makes the files on the filesystem appear as though they reside in the given directory, allowing you to access them.

Before we tell you how to mount filesystems, we should also mention that some distributions come with automounting setups that require you to simply load a diskette or CD into the respective drive and access it just as you would on other platforms. There are times, however, when everybody needs to know how to mount and unmount media directly. (We cover how to set up automounting yourself later.)

The *mount* command is used to do this and usually must be executed as *root*. (As we'll see later, ordinary users can use mount if the device is listed in the */etc/fstab* file and the entry has the user option.) The format of this command is:

```
mount -t type device mount-point
```

where *type* is the type name of the filesystem as given in Table 10-1, *device* is the physical device where the filesystem resides (the device file in */dev*), and *mount-point* is the directory on which to mount the filesystem. You have to create the directory before issuing mount.

For example, if you have a Third Extended filesystem on the partition */dev/hda2* and wish to mount it on the directory */mnt*, first create the directory if it does not already exist and then use the command:

```
mount -t ext3 /dev/hda2 /mnt
```

If all goes well, you should be able to access the filesystem under */mnt*. Likewise, to mount a floppy that was created on a Windows system and therefore is in DOS format, you use the command:

```
mount -t msdos /dev/fd0 /mnt
```

This makes the files available on an MS-DOS-format floppy under */mnt*. Note that using msdos means that you use the old DOS format that is limited to filenames of eight plus three characters. If you use vfat instead, you get the newer format that was introduced with Windows 95. Of course, the floppy or hard disk needs to be written with that format as well.

There are many options for the mount command, which can be specified with the -o switch. For example, the MS-DOS and ISO 9660 filesystems support "autoconversion" of text files from MS-DOS format (which contain CR-LF at the end of each line) to Unix format (which contain merely a newline at the end of each line). Using a command such as:

```
mount -o conv=auto -t msdos /dev/fd0 /mnt
```

turns on this conversion for files that don't have a filename extension that could be associated with a binary file (such as *.exe*, *.bin*, and so forth).

One common option to mount is *-o ro* (or, equivalently, *-r*), which mounts the filesystem as read-only. All write access to such a filesystem is met with a "permission denied" error. Mounting a filesystem as read-only is necessary for media such as CD-ROMs that are nonwritable. You can successfully mount a CD-ROM without the *-r* option, but you'll get the following annoying warning message:

```
mount: block device /dev/cdrom is write-protected, mounting read-only
```

Use a command such as:

```
mount -t iso9660 -r /dev/cdrom /mnt
```

instead. This is also necessary if you are trying to mount a floppy that has the write-protect tab in place.

The mount manual page lists all available mounting options. Not all are of immediate interest, but you might have a need for some of them, someday. A useful variant of using mount is *mount -a*, which mounts all filesystems listed in */etc/fstab* except those marked with the noauto option.

The inverse of mounting a filesystem is, naturally, unmounting it. Unmounting a filesystem has two effects: it synchronizes the system's buffers with the actual contents of the filesystem on disk, and it makes the filesystem no longer available from its mount point. You are then free to mount another filesystem on that mount point.

Unmounting is done with the *umount* command (note that the first "n" is missing from the word "unmount"). For example:

```
umount /dev/fd0
```

unmounts the filesystem on */dev/fd0*. Similarly, to unmount whatever filesystem is currently mounted on a particular directory, use a command such as:

```
umount /mnt
```

It is important to note that removable media, including floppies and CD-ROMs, should not be removed from the drive or swapped for another disk while mounted. This causes the system's information on the device to be out of sync with what's actually there and could lead to no end of trouble. Whenever you want to switch a floppy or CD-ROM, unmount it first using the *umount* command, insert the new disk, and then remount the device. Of course, with a CD-ROM or a write-protected floppy, there is no way the device itself can get out of sync, but you could run into other problems. For example, some CD-ROM drives won't let you eject the disk until it is unmounted.

Reads and writes to filesystems on floppies are buffered in memory, like they are for hard drives. This means that when you read or write data to a floppy, there may not be any immediate drive activity. The system handles I/O on the floppy asynchronously and reads or writes data only when absolutely necessary. So if you copy a small file to a floppy, but the drive light doesn't come on, don't panic; the data will be written eventually. You can use the sync command to force the system to write all filesystem buffers to disk, causing a physical write of any buffered data. Unmounting a filesystem makes this happen as well.

If you wish to allow mortal users to mount and unmount certain devices, you have two options. The first option is to include the user option for the device in */etc/fstab* (described later in this section). This allows any user to use the mount and umount command for a given device. Another option is to use one of the mount frontends available for Linux. These programs run *setuid* as *root* and allow ordinary users to mount certain devices. In general, you wouldn't want normal users mounting and unmounting a hard drive partition, but you could be more lenient about the use of CD-ROM and floppy drives on your system.

Quite a few things can go wrong when attempting to mount a filesystem. Unfortunately, the mount command will give you the same error message in response to a number of problems:

```
mount: wrong fs type, /dev/cdrom already mounted, /mnt busy, or other error
```

wrong fs type is simple enough: this means that you may have specified the wrong type to *mount*. If you don't specify a type, *mount* tries to guess the filesystem type from the superblock (this works only for *minix*, *ext2*, *ext3*, and *iso9660*). If *mount* still cannot determine the type of the filesystem, it tries all the types for which drivers are included in the kernel (as listed in */proc/filesystems*). If this still does not lead to success, mount fails.

device already mounted means just that: the device is already mounted on another directory. You can find out what devices are mounted, and where, using the *mount* command with no arguments:

```
rutabaga# mount
          /dev/hda2 on / type ext3 (rw)
          /dev/hda3 on /windows type vfat (rw)
          /dev/cdrom on /cdrom type iso9660 (ro)
          /proc on /proc type proc (rw,none)
```

Here, we see two hard drive partitions, one of type *ext3* and the other of type *vfat*, a CD-ROM mounted on */cdrom*, and the */proc* filesystem. The last field of each line (for example, (rw)) lists the options under which the filesystem is mounted. More on these soon. Note that the CD-ROM device is mounted in */cdrom*. If you use your CD-ROM often, it's convenient to create a special directory such as */cdrom* and mount the device there. */mnt* is generally used to temporarily mount filesystems such as floppies.

The error *mount-point* busy is rather odd. Essentially, it means some activity is taking place under *mount-point* that prevents you from mounting a filesystem there. Usually, this means that an open file is under this directory, or some process has its current working directory beneath *mount-point*. When using *mount*, be sure your root shell is not within *mount-point*; do a *cd /* to get to the top-level directory. Or, another filesystem could be mounted with the same *mount-point*. Use mount with no arguments to find out.

Of course, other error isn't very helpful. There are several other cases in which mount could fail. If the filesystem in question has data or media errors of some kind, mount may report it is unable to read the filesystem's *superblock*, which is (under Unix-like filesystems) the portion of the filesystem that stores information on the files and attributes for the filesystem as a whole. If you attempt to mount a CD-ROM or floppy drive and there's no CD-ROM or floppy in the drive, you will receive an error message such as

```
mount: /dev/cdrom is not a valid block device
```

Floppies are especially prone to physical defects (more so than you might initially think), and CD-ROMs suffer from dust, scratches, and fingerprints, as well as being inserted upside-down. (If you attempt to mount your Stan Rogers CD as ISO 9660 format, you will likely run into similar problems.)

Also, be sure the mount point you're trying to use (such as */mnt*) exists. If not, you can simply create it with the *mkdir* command.

If you have problems mounting or accessing a filesystem, data on the filesystem may be corrupt. Several tools help repair certain filesystem types under Linux; see "Checking and Repairing Filesystems," later in this chapter.

The system automatically mounts several filesystems when the system boots. This is handled by the file */etc/fstab*, which includes an entry for each filesystem that should be mounted at boot time. Each line in this file is of the following format:

```
device
mount-point
type
options
```

Here, *device*, *mount-point*, and *type* are equivalent to their meanings in the mount command, and *options* is a comma-separated list of options to use with the -o switch to mount.

A sample */etc/fstab* is shown here:

```
# device       directory      type      options
/dev/hda2      /              ext3      defaults
/dev/hda3      /windows       vfat      defaults
/dev/cdrom     /cdrom         iso9660   ro
```

```
/proc          /proc          proc      none

/dev/hda1      none           swap      sw
```

The last line of this file specifies a swap partition. This is described in "Managing Swap Space," later in this chapter.

The *mount*(8) manual page lists the possible values for *options*; if you wish to specify more than one option, you can list them with separating commas and no whitespace, as in the following examples:

```
/dev/cdrom     /cdrom         iso9660   ro,user
```

The user option allows users other than *root* to mount the filesystem. If this option is present, a user can execute a command such as:

```
mount /cdrom
```

to mount the device. Note that if you specify only a device or mount point (not both) to *mount*, it looks up the device or mount point in */etc/fstab* and mounts the device with the parameters given there. This allows you to mount devices listed in */etc/fstab* with ease.

The option `defaults` should be used for most filesystems; it enables a number of other options, such as `rw` (read-write access), `async` (buffer I/O to the filesystem in memory asynchronously), and so forth. Unless you have a specific need to modify one of these parameters, use `defaults` for most filesystems, and `ro` for read-only devices such as CD-ROMs. Another potentially useful option is `umask`, which lets you set the default mask for the permission bits, something that is especially useful with some foreign filesystems.

The command *mount -a* will mount all filesystems listed in */etc/fstab*. This command is executed at boot time by one of the scripts found in */etc/rc.d*, such as *rc.sysinit* (or wherever your distribution stores its configuration files). This way, all filesystems listed in */etc/fstab* will be available when the system starts up; your hard drive partitions, CD-ROM drive, and so on will all be mounted.

There is an exception to this: the *root filesystem*. The root filesystem, mounted on /, usually contains the file */etc/fstab* as well as the scripts in */etc/rc.d*. In order for these to be available, the kernel itself must mount the root filesystem directly at boot time. The device containing the root filesystem is coded into the kernel image and can be altered using the *rdev* command (see "Using a Boot Floppy" in Chapter 17). While the system boots, the kernel attempts to mount this device as the root filesystem, trying several filesystem types in succession. If at boot time the kernel prints an error message, such as

```
VFS: Unable to mount root fs
```

one of the following has happened:

- The root device coded into the kernel is incorrect.
- The kernel does not have support compiled in for the filesystem type of the root device. (See "Building the Kernel" in Chapter 18 for more details. This is usually relevant only if you build your own kernel.)
- The root device is corrupt in some way.

In any of these cases, the kernel can't proceed and panics. See "What to Do in an Emergency" in Chapter 27 for clues on what to do in this situation. If filesystem corruption is the problem, this can usually be repaired; see "Checking and Repairing Filesystems," later in this chapter.

A filesystem does not need to be listed in */etc/fstab* in order to be mounted, but it does need to be listed there in order to be mounted "automatically" by *mount -a*, or to use the user mount option.

Automounting Devices

If you need to access a lot of different filesystems, especially networked ones, you might be interested in a special feature in the Linux kernel: the *automounter*. This is a combination of kernel functionality, a daemon, and some configuration files that automatically detect when somebody wants to access a certain filesystem and mounts the filesystem transparently. When the filesystem is not used for some time, the automounter automatically unmounts it in order to save resources such as memory and network throughput.

If you want to use the automounter, you first need to turn this feature on when building your kernel. (See "Building the Kernel" in Chapter 18 for more details.) You will also need to enable the NFS option.

Next, you need to start the *automount* daemon. In order to check whether you have *automount* installed, look for the directory */usr/lib/autofs*. If it is not there, you will need to get the *autofs* package from your friendly Linux archive and compile and install it according to the instructions.

Note that there are two versions of automount support: Version 3 and Version 4. Version 3 is the one still contained in most distributions, so that's what we describe here.

You can automount filesystems wherever you like, but for simplicity's sake, we will assume here that you want to automount all filesystems below one directory that we will call */automount* here. If you want your automount points to be scattered over your filesystem, you will need to use multiple automount daemons.

If you have compiled the *autofs* package yourself, it might be a good idea to start by copying the sample configuration files that you can find in the *sample* directory and adapting them to your needs. To do this, copy the files *sample/auto.master* and *sample/auto.misc* into the */etc* directory, and the file *sample/rc.autofs* under the name autofs wherever your distribution stores its boot scripts. We'll assume here that you use *etc/init.d*. (Unfortunately, some distributions do not provide those sample files, even if they do carry the *autofs* package. In that case, it might still be a good idea to download the original package.)

The first configuration file to edit is *etc/auto.master*. This lists all the directories (the so-called *mount points*) below which the automounter should mount partitions. Because we have decided to use only one partition in this chapter's example, we will need to make only one entry here. The file could look like this:

```
/automount          /etc/auto.misc
```

This file consists of lines with two entries each, separated by whitespace. The first entry specifies the mount point, and the second entry names a so-called *map file* that specifies how and where to mount the devices or partitions to be automounted. You need one such map file for each mount point.

In our case, the file *etc/auto.misc* looks like the following:

```
cd              -fstype=iso9660,ro      :/dev/scd0
floppy          -fstype=auto            :/dev/fd0
```

Again, this file consists of one-line entries, each specifying one particular device or partition to be automounted. The lines have two mandatory and one optional field, separated by whitespaces. The first value is mandatory and specifies the directory onto which the device or partition of this entry is automounted. This value is appended to the mount point; thus, the CD-ROM will be automounted onto */automount/cd*.

The second value is optional and specifies flags to be used for the `mount` operation. These are equivalent to those for the `mount` command itself, with the exception that the type is specified with the option *-fstype=* instead of *-t*.

Finally, the third value specifies the partition or device to be mounted. In our case, we specify the first SCSI CD-ROM drive and the first floppy drive, respectively. The colon in front of the entry is mandatory; it separates the host part from the device/directory part, just as with *mount*. Because those two devices are on a local machine, there is nothing to the left of the colon. If we wanted to automount the directory *sources* from the NFS server `sourcemaster`, we would specify something like the following:

```
sources    -fstype=nfs,soft    sourcemaster:/sources
```

Please notice that the *etc/auto.misc* file must not be executable; when in doubt, issue the following command:

```
tigger# chmod a-x /etc/auto.misc
```

After editing the configuration files to reflect your system, you can start the *automount* daemon by issuing the following command (replace the path with the path that suits your system):

```
tigger# /etc/init.d/autofs start
```

Because this command is very taciturn, you should check whether the automounter has really started. One way to do this is to issue:

```
tigger# /etc/init.d/autofs status
```

but it is difficult to determine from the output whether the automounter is really running. Your best bet, therefore, is to check whether the automount process exists:

```
tigger# ps aux | grep automount
```

If this command shows the *automount* process, everything should be all right. If it doesn't, you need to check your configuration files again. It could also be the case that the necessary kernel support is not available: either the automount support is not in your kernel, or you have compiled it as a module but not installed this module. If the latter is the case, you can fix the problem by issuing

```
tigger# modprobe autofs
```

If that doesn't work, you need to use:

```
tigger# modprobe autofs4
```

instead.[*] When your automounter works to your satisfaction, you might want to put the modprobe call as well as the autofs call in one of your system's startup configuration files, such as */etc/rc.local*, */etc/init.d/boot.local*, or whatever your distribution uses.

If everything is set up correctly, all you need to do is access some directory below the mount point, and the automounter will mount the appropriate device or partition for you. For example, if you type

```
tigger$ ls /automount/cd
```

the automounter will automatically mount the CD-ROM so that ls can list its contents. The only difference between normal and automounting is that with automounting you will notice a slight delay before the output comes.

To conserve resources, the automounter unmounts a partition or device if it has not been accessed for a certain amount of time (the default is five minutes).

The automounter supports a number of advanced options; for example, you do not need to read the map table from a file but can also access system databases or even have the automounter run a program and use this program's output as the mapping data. See the manpages for *autofs*(5) and *automount*(8) for further details.

---

[*] We cover the modprobe command in "Loadable Device Drivers" in Chapter 18.

Creating Filesystems

You can create a filesystem using the *mkfs* command. Creating a filesystem is analogous to formatting a partition or floppy, allowing it to store files.

Each filesystem type has its own *mkfs* command associated with it—for example, MS-DOS filesystems may be created using *mkfs.msdos*, Third Extended filesystems using *mkfs.ext3*, and so on. The program *mkfs* itself is a frontend that creates a filesystem of any type by executing the appropriate version of *mkfs* for that type.

When you installed Linux, you may have created filesystems by hand using a command such as *mke2fs*, which, despite the name, can create both *ext2* and *ext3* filesystems. (If not, the installation software created the filesystems for you.) The programs are the same (and on many systems, one is a symbolic link to the other), but the *mkfs.fs-type* filename makes it easier for *mkfs* to execute the appropriate filesystem-type-specific program. If you don't have the *mkfs* frontend, you can use *mke2fs* or *mkfs.ext2* directly.

Assuming that you're using the *mkfs* frontend, you can create a filesystem using this command:

```
mkfs -t type device
```

where *type* is the type of filesystem to create, given in Table 10-1, and *device* is the device on which to create the filesystem (such as */dev/fd0* for a floppy).

For example, to create an *ext2* filesystem on a floppy (it does not make much sense to use journaling on a floppy disk, which is why we don't use *ext3* here), you use this command:

```
mkfs -t ext2 /dev/fd0
```

You could create an MS-DOS floppy using *-t msdos* instead.

We can now mount the floppy (as described in the previous section), copy files to it, and so forth. Remember to unmount the floppy before removing it from the drive.

Creating a filesystem deletes all data on the corresponding physical device (floppy, hard drive partition, whatever). *mkfs* usually does not prompt you before creating a filesystem, so be absolutely sure you know what you're doing.

Creating a filesystem on a hard drive partition is done as shown earlier, except that you use the partition name, such as `/dev/hda2`, as the *device*. Don't try to create a filesystem on a device such as `/dev/hda`. This refers to the entire drive, not just a single partition on the drive. You can create partitions using *fdisk*, as described in "Editing /etc/fstab" in Chapter 2.

You should be especially careful when creating filesystems on hard drive partitions. Be absolutely sure that the *device* and *size* arguments are correct. If you enter the wrong *device*, you could end up destroying the data on your current filesystems, and if you specify the wrong *size*, you could overwrite data on other partitions. Be sure that *size* corresponds to the partition size as reported by Linux `fdisk`.

When creating filesystems on floppies, it's usually best to do a low-level format first. This lays down the sector and track information on the floppy so that its size can be automatically detected using the devices */dev/fd0* or */dev/fd1*. One way to do a low-level format is with the MS-DOS `FORMAT` command; another way is with the Linux program *fdformat*. (Debian users should use `superformat` instead.) For example, to format the floppy in the first floppy drive, use the command

```
rutabaga# fdformat /dev/fd0
        Double-sided, 80 tracks, 18 sec/track. Total capacity 1440 kB.
        Formatting ... done
        Verifying ... done
```

Using the `-n` option with `fdformat` will skip the verification step.

Each filesystem-specific version of *mkfs* supports several options you might find useful. Most types support the `-c` option, which causes the physical media to be checked for bad blocks while creating the filesystem. If bad blocks are found, they are marked and avoided when writing data to the filesystem. In order to use these type-specific options, include them after the `-t` *type* option to *mkfs*, as follows:

```
mkfs -t type -c device blocks
```

To determine what options are available, see the manual page for the type-specific version of *mkfs*. (For example, for the Second Extended filesystem, see `mke2fs`.)

You may not have all available type-specific versions of *mkfs* installed. If this is the case, *mkfs* will fail when you try to create a filesystem of a type for which you have no *mkfs.<type>*. Many filesystem types supported by Linux have a corresponding *mkfs.<type>* available somewhere.

If you run into trouble using `mkfs`, it's possible that Linux is having problems accessing the physical device. In the case of a floppy, this might just mean a bad floppy. In the case of a hard drive, it could be more serious; for example, the disk device driver in the kernel might be having problems reading your drive. This could be a hardware problem or a simple matter of your drive geometry being specified incorrectly. See the manual pages for the various versions of *mkfs*, and read the sections in Chapter 2 on troubleshooting installation problems. They apply equally here.*

Checking and Repairing Filesystems

It is sometimes necessary to check your Linux filesystems for consistency and to repair them if there are any errors or if you lose data. Such errors commonly result

---

* Also, the procedure for making an ISO 9660 filesystem for a CD-ROM is more complicated than simply formatting a filesystem and copying files. See Chapter 9 and the CD-Writing HOWTO for more details.

from a system crash or loss of power, making the kernel unable to sync the filesystem buffer cache with the contents of the disk. In most cases, such errors are relatively minor. However, if the system were to crash while writing a large file, that file might be lost and the blocks associated with it marked as "in use," when in fact no file entry is corresponding to them. In other cases, errors can be caused by accidentally writing data directly to the hard drive device (such as */dev/hda*), or to one of the partitions.

The program *fsck* is used to check filesystems and correct any problems. Like *mkfs*, *fsck* is a frontend for a filesystem-type-specific *fsck.type*, such as *fsck.ext2* for Second Extended filesystems. (As with *mkfs.ext2*, *fsck.ext2* is a symbolic link to *e2fsck*, either of which you can execute directly if the *fsck* frontend is not installed.)

Use of *fsck* is quite simple; the format of the command is:

```
fsck -t type device
```

where *type* is the type of filesystem to repair, as given in Table 10-1, and *device* is the device (drive partition or floppy) on which the filesystem resides.

For example, to check an *ext3* filesystem on */dev/hda2*, you use:

```
rutabaga# fsck -t ext3 /dev/hda2
          fsck 1.34 (25-Jul-2003)
          /dev/hda2 is mounted.  Do you really want to continue (y/n)? y

          /dev/hda2 was not cleanly unmounted, check forced.
          Pass 1: Checking inodes, blocks, and sizes
          Pass 2: Checking directory structure
          Pass 3: Checking directory connectivity
          Pass 4: Checking reference counts.
          Pass 5: Checking group summary information.

          Free blocks count wrong for group 3 (3331, counted=3396).  FIXED
          Free blocks count wrong for group 4 (1983, counted=2597).  FIXED
          Free blocks count wrong (29643, counted=30341).  FIXED
          Inode bitmap differences: -8280.  FIXED
          Free inodes count wrong for group #4 (1405, counted=1406).  FIXED
          Free inodes count wrong (34522, counted=34523).  FIXED

          /dev/hda2: ***** FILE SYSTEM WAS MODIFIED *****
          /dev/hda2: ***** REBOOT LINUX *****
          /dev/hda2: 13285/47808 files, 160875/191216 blocks
```

First of all, note that the system asks for confirmation before checking a mounted filesystem. If any errors are found and corrected while using *fsck*, you'll have to reboot the system if the filesystem is mounted. This is because the changes made by *fsck* may not be propagated back to the system's internal knowledge of the filesystem layout. In general, it's not a good idea to check mounted filesystems.

As we can see, several problems were found and corrected, and because this filesystem was mounted, the system informed us that the machine should be rebooted.

How can you check filesystems without mounting them? With the exception of the root filesystem, you can simply *umount* any filesystems before running *fsck* on them. The root filesystem, however, can't be unmounted while running the system. One way to check your root filesystem while it's unmounted is to use a boot/root floppy combination, such as the installation floppies used by your Linux distribution. This way, the root filesystem is contained on a floppy, the root filesystem (on your hard drive) remains unmounted, and you can check the hard drive root filesystem from there. See "What to Do in an Emergency" in Chapter 27 for more details about this.

Another way to check the root filesystem is to mount it as read-only. This can be done using the option ro from the LILO boot prompt (see "Specifying boot-time options" in Chapter 17). However, other parts of your system configuration (for example, the programs executed by */etc/init* at boot time) may require write access to the root filesystem, so you can't boot the system normally or these programs will fail. To boot the system with the root filesystem mounted as read-only, you might want to boot the system into single-user mode as well (using the boot option single). This prevents additional system configuration at boot time; you can then check the root filesystem and reboot the system normally. To do this in GRUB, you would edit the command line in the GRUB screen interface by adding the ro option.

To cause the root filesystem to be mounted as read-only, you can either use the ro boot option, or use *rdev* to set the read-only flag in the kernel image itself.

Many Linux systems automatically check the filesystems at boot time. This is usually done by executing *fsck* from */etc/rc.d/boot.rootfsck* for the root filesystem and */etc/rc.d/boot.localfs* (filenames may vary from distribution to distribution). When this is done, the system usually mounts the root filesystem initially as read-only, runs *fsck* to check it, and then runs the command:

```
mount -w -o remount /
```

The *-o remount* option causes the given filesystem to be remounted with the new parameters; the *-w* option (equivalent to *-o rw*) causes the filesystem to be mounted as read-write. The net result is that the root filesystem is remounted with read-write access.

When *fsck* is executed at boot time, it checks all filesystems other than *root* before they are mounted. Once *fsck* completes, the other filesystems are mounted using *mount*. Check out the files in */etc/rc.d*, especially *rc.sysinit* (if present on your system), to see how this is done. If you want to disable this feature on your system, comment out the lines in the appropriate */etc/rc.d* file that executes *fsck*.

You can pass options to the type-specific *fsck*. Most types support the option *-a*, which automatically confirms any prompts that *fsck.type* may display; *-c*, which does bad-block checking, as with *mkfs*; and *-v*, which prints verbose information during the check operation. These options should be given after the *-t type* argument to *fsck*, as in

```
fsck -t type -v device
```

to run *fsck* with verbose output.

See the manual pages for *fsck* and *e2fsck* for more information.

Not all filesystem types supported by Linux have a *fsck* variant available. To check and repair MS-DOS filesystems, you should use a tool under MS-DOS, such as the Norton Utilities, to accomplish this task. You should be able to find versions of *fsck* for the Second and Third Extended filesystem, Reiser filesystem JFS, and Minix filesystem.*

In "What to Do in an Emergency" in Chapter 27, we provide additional information on checking filesystems and recovering from disaster. *fsck* will by no means catch and repair every error to your filesystems, but most common problems should be handled. If you delete an important file, there is currently no easy way to recover it—*fsck* can't do that for you. There is work under way to provide an "undelete" utility in the Second Extended filesystem. Be sure to keep backups, or use *rm -i*, which always prompts you before deleting a file.

Encrypted Filesystems

Linux has supported encrypted file systems since at least Version 2.2. However, due to export regulations regarding software containing cryptographic algorithms, this feature had to be distributed as a kernel patch, available from *http://www.kerneli.org/* (note the i for international, which indicates that the server was located outside the United States). This site is now no longer maintained.

In kernel Version 2.4, the *kerneli* patches were no longer actively maintained. The preferred method to encrypt filesystems was *loop-aes* (*http://loop-aes.sourceforge .net/*), which could be built as a kernel module, restricted itself to disk encryption with AES, and was more actively maintained.[†]

The 2.6 kernel series saw the end of the *kerneli* crypto framework, as a group of kernel developers created a new framework from scratch. This framework has been since integrated into the vanilla (Linus) kernel. This text restricts itself to the 2.6 kernel, although the user-space tools have not changed their interfaces much. For

---

* Actually, some distributions carry a command called *dosfsck/fsck.msdos*, but using this is not really recommended.

† AES stands for Advanced Encryption Standard. The algorithm underlying AES is called Rijndael. AES is the successor of DES, the 20-year-old Data Encryption Standard.

instance, all *losetup* commands work on the *kerneli* kernels, but the *mount* options may be different.

Configuring the kernel

Encrypted filesystem support works by using something called a transformed loopback block device (you may already know loopback devices from mounting CD-ROM ISO image files to access their contents).

To this end, you need to enable Device Drivers Loopback device support in the kernel's configuration, as well as Cryptoloop support in the same section.

Cryptoloop uses the cryptographic API of a v2.6 kernel, which you can enable in Cryptographic options. Usually, it is sufficient to build everything (ciphers, compression algorithms, and digests) as modules, which in newer kernels is also the default. You do not need the Testing module.

You build and install the kernel as you would any other. On reboot, if you compiled Cryptoloop as a module, use *modprobe cryptoloop* to load it into the kernel.

The final thing is to check for a *util-linux* package that can work with this kernel's cryptographic API. This package contains a number of system administration commands for working with the kernel cryptographic support. Unfortunately, as of this writing, the necessary patches had not been applied to the latest release of *util-linux*. Many distributions ship patched versions, though. Please check whether cryptoapi is supported in the documentation that comes with your *util-linux* package. If the losetup command (described in the next section) fails with an invalid argument error, the API probably is not in the distribution. In this case, compile it yourself after applying the patches as detailed in the Cryptoloop-HOWTO (*http://www.tldp.org/HOWTO/Cryptoloop-HOWTO/*).

Creating an encrypted filesystem

Encrypted filesystems can be created either on top of a whole partition, or with a regular file as the storage space. This is similar to setting up swap space. However, in order to mask which blocks have been written to, you should initialize the file or partition with random data instead of zeroes—that is, use:

```
dd if=/dev/urandom of=file-or-partition bs=1k count=size-in-kb
```

Omit the **count** argument when overwriting a partition, and ignore the resulting "device full" error.

Once the backing store is initialized, a loop device can be created on it using:

```
losetup -e cipher /dev/loop0 file-or-partition
```

Check */proc/crypto* for the list of available ciphers of the running kernel.

You will be prompted for a passphrase *once*. You are *not* requested to retype the passphrase. This passphrase needs to have enough randomness to frustrate dictionary attacks. We recommend generating a random key for a 128-bit cipher through the following command:

```
head -c16 /dev/random | mimencode
```

Replace *-c16* with *-c32* for a 256-bit cipher. Naturally, these passphrases are hard to remember. After all, they are pure randomness. Write them down on a piece of paper stored far away from the computer (e.g., in your purse).

When the command returns successfully, anything written to */dev/loop0* will now be transparently encrypted with the chosen cipher and written to the backing store.

Now create a filesystem on */dev/loop0* as you would for any other partition. As an example, use *mke2fs -j* to create an *ext3* filesystem. Once created, you can try mounting it using

```
mount -t ext3 /dev/loop0 mount-point
```

Write a text file into the encrypted filesystem and try to find the contents in the backing store, for example, using grep. Because they are encrypted, the search should fail.

After unmounting the filesystem with *umount /dev/loop0*, do not forget to tear down the loop device again, using *losetup -d /dev/loop0*.

Mounting the filesystem

Of course, setting up loopback devices and manually mounting them each time you need to access them is kind of tedious. Thankfully, you can make mount do all the work in setting up a loopback device.

Just add *-oencryption=cipher* to the mount command, like this:

```
mount -t ext3 -oencryption=cipher file-or-partition mount-point
```

encryption=cipher also works in the options column of */etc/fstab*, so you can allow users to mount and unmount their own encrypted filesystems.

Security Issues

When using encrypted filesystems, you should be aware of a few issues:

- Mounted filesystems can be read by anyone, given appropriate permissions; they are not visible just to the user who created them. Because of this, encrypted filesystems should not be kept mounted when they are not used.

- You cannot change the passphrase. It is hashed into the key used to encrypt everything. If you are brave, there is one workaround: set up two loop devices with losetup. Use the same encrypted filesystem as backing store for both, but supply the first one, say */dev/loop0*, with the old passphrase, while giving the second one, say *ldev/loop1*, the new passphrase. Double-check that you can mount both (one *after* the other, not both at the same time). Remember you are only asked for the new passphrase *once*. Unmount them again; this was only to be on the safe side.

Now, use *dd* to copy over data from the first loop device to the second one, like this:

```
dd if=/dev/loop0 of=/dev/loop1 bs=4k
```

The block size (*bs=* parameter) should match the kernel's page size, or the block size of the physical device, whichever is larger. This reads a block using the old passphrase and immediately writes it using the new passphrase. Better pray for no power outages while this is running, or buy a UPS.

Using the double loopback device trick, you can also change the cipher used to encrypt the data.

• The weak link in the system is really your passphrase. A cryptographic algorithm with a 256-bit key is no good if that key is hashed from a guessable passphrase. English text has about 1.3 bits of randomness (also called entropy) per character. So you'd need to type in a sentence about 200 characters long to get the full security of the cipher. On the other hand, using the mimencode-dev-random trick we suggested earlier, you need only type in about 40 characters, albeit pure random ones.

Managing Swap Space

Swap space is a generic term for disk storage used to increase the amount of apparent memory available on the system. Under Linux, swap space is used to implement *paging*, a process whereby memory pages are written out to disk when physical memory is low and read back into physical memory when needed (a page is 4096 bytes on Intel x86 systems; this value can differ on other architectures). The process by which paging works is rather involved, but it is optimized for certain cases. The virtual memory subsystem under Linux allows memory pages to be shared between running programs. For example, if you have multiple copies of Emacs running simultaneously, only one copy of the Emacs code is actually in memory. Also, text pages (those pages containing program code, not data) are usually read-only, and therefore not written to disk when swapped out. Those pages are instead freed directly from main memory and read from the original executable file when they are accessed again.

Of course, swap space cannot completely make up for a lack of physical RAM. Disk access is much slower than RAM access, by several orders of magnitude. Therefore, swap is useful primarily as a means to run a number of programs simultaneously that would not otherwise fit into physical RAM; if you are switching between these programs rapidly you'll notice a lag as pages are swapped to and from disk.

At any rate, Linux supports swap space in two forms: as a separate disk partition or a file somewhere on your existing Linux filesystems. You can have up to eight swap areas, with each swap area being a disk file or partition up to 2 GB in size (again, these values can differ on non-Intel systems). You math whizzes out there will realize that this allows up to 16 GB of swap space. (If anyone has actually attempted to use this much swap, the authors would love to hear about it, whether you're a math whiz or not.)

Note that using a swap partition can yield better performance because the disk blocks are guaranteed to be contiguous. In the case of a swap file, however, the disk blocks may be scattered around the filesystem, which can be a serious performance hit in some cases. Many people use a swap file when they must add additional swap space temporarily—for example, if the system is thrashing because of lack of physical RAM and swap. Swap files are a good way to add swap on demand.

Nearly all Linux systems utilize swap space of some kind—usually a single swap partition. In Chapter 2, we explained how to create a swap partition on your system during the Linux installation procedure. In this section we describe how to add and remove swap files and partitions. If you already have swap space and are happy with it, this section may not be of interest to you.

How much swap space do you have? The *free* command reports information on system-memory usage:

```
rutabaga% free
             total      used       free     shared    buffers     cached
Mem:       1034304   1011876      22428          0      18104     256748
-/+ buffers/cache:     737024     297280
Swap:      1172724     16276    1156448
```

All the numbers here are reported in 1024-byte blocks. Here, we see a system with 1,034,304 blocks (about 1 GB) of physical RAM, with 1,011,876 (slightly less) currently in use. Note that your system actually has more physical RAM than that given in the "total" column; this number does not include the memory used by the kernel for its own sundry needs.

The "shared" column lists the amount of physical memory shared between multiple processes. Here, we see that no pages are being shared. The "buffers" column shows the amount of memory being used by the kernel buffer cache. The buffer cache (described briefly in the previous section) is used to speed up disk operations by allowing disk reads and writes to be serviced directly from memory. The buffer cache size will increase or decrease as memory usage on the system changes; this memory is reclaimed if applications need it. Therefore, although we see that almost 1 GB of system memory is in use, not all (but most) of it is being used by application programs. The "cache" column indicates how many memory pages the kernel has cached for faster access later.

Because the memory used for the buffers and cache can easily be reclaimed for use by applications, the second line (`-/+ buffers/cache`) provides an indication of the memory actually used by applications (the "used" column) or available to applications (the "free" column). The sum of the memory used by the buffers and cache reported in the first line is subtracted from the total used memory and added to the total free memory to give the two figures on the second line.

In the third line, we see the total amount of swap, 1,172,724 blocks (about 1.1 GB). In this case, only very little of the swap is being used; there is plenty of physical RAM available (then again, this machine has generous amounts of physical RAM). If additional applications were started, larger parts of the buffer cache memory would be used to host them. Swap space is generally used as a last resort when the system can't reclaim physical memory in other ways.

Note that the amount of swap reported by *free* is somewhat less than the total size of your swap partitions and files. This is because several blocks of each swap area must be used to store a map of how each page in the swap area is being utilized. This overhead should be rather small—only a few kilobytes per swap area.

If you're considering creating a swap file, the *df* command gives you information on the amount of space remaining on your various filesystems. This command prints a list of filesystems, showing each one's size and what percentage is currently occupied.

Creating Swap Space

The first step in adding additional swap is to create a file or partition to host the swap area. If you wish to create an additional swap partition, you can create the partition using the `fdisk` utility, as described in "Editing /etc/fstab" in Chapter 2.

To create a swap file, you'll need to open a file and write bytes to it equaling the amount of swap you wish to add. One easy way to do this is with the `dd` command. For example, to create a 32-MB swap file, you can use the command:

```
dd if=/dev/zero of=/swap bs=1024 count=32768
```

This will write 32,768 blocks (32 MB) of data from */dev/zero* to the file */swap*. (*/dev/zero* is a special device in which read operations always return null bytes. It's something like the inverse of */dev/null*.) After creating a file of this size, it's a good idea to use the `sync` command to sync the filesystems in case of a system crash.

Once you have created the swap file or partition, you can use the `mkswap` command to "format" the swap area. As described in "Creating Swap Space" in Chapter 2, the format of the *mkswap* command is:

```
mkswap -c device size
```

where *device* is the name of the swap partition or file, and *size* is the size of the swap area in blocks (again, one block is equal to one kilobyte). You normally do not need to specify this when creating a swap area because mkswap can detect the partition size on its own. The *-c* switch is optional and causes the swap area to be checked for bad blocks as it is formatted.

For example, for the swap file created in the previous example, you would use the following command:

```
mkswap -c /swap 32768
```

If the swap area were a partition, you would substitute the name of the partition (such as */dev/hda3*) and the size of the partition, also in blocks.

If you are using a swap file (and not a swap partition), you need to change its permissions first, like this:

```
chmod 0600 /swap
```

After running mkswap on a swap file, use the sync command to ensure the format information has been physically written to the new swap file. Running *sync* is not necessary when formatting a swap partition.

Enabling the Swap Space

In order for the new swap space to be utilized, you must enable it with the *swapon* command. For example, after creating the previous swap file and running *mkswap* and *sync*, we could use the command:

```
swapon /swap
```

This adds the new swap area to the total amount of available swap; use the *free* command to verify that this is indeed the case. If you are using a new swap partition, you can enable it with a command such as:

```
swapon /dev/hda3
```

if */dev/hda3* is the name of the swap partition.

Like filesystems, swap areas are automatically enabled at boot time using the *swapon -a* command from one of the system startup files (usually in */etc/rc.d/rc.sysinit*). This command looks in the file */etc/fstab*, which, as you'll remember from "Mounting Filesystems" earlier in this chapter, includes information on filesystems and swap areas. All entries in */etc/fstab* with the *options* field set to sw are enabled by *swapon -a*.

Therefore, if */etc/fstab* contains the entries:

```
# device      directory    type    options
/dev/hda3     none         swap    sw
/swap         none         swap    sw
```

the two swap areas */dev/hda3* and */swap* will be enabled at boot time. For each new swap area, you should add an entry to */etc/fstab*.

Disabling Swap Space

As is usually the case, undoing a task is easier than doing it. To disable swap space, simply use the command:

```
swapoff device
```

where *device* is the name of the swap partition or file that you wish to disable. For example, to disable swapping on the device */dev/hda3*, use the command:

```
swapoff /dev/hda3
```

If you wish to disable a swap file, you can simply remove the file, using *rm*, *after* using *swapoff*. Don't remove a swap file before disabling it; this can cause disaster.

If you have disabled a swap partition using *swapoff*, you are free to reuse that partition as you see fit: remove it using *fdisk* or your preferred repartitioning tool.

Also, if there is a corresponding entry for the swap area in */etc/fstab*, remove it. Otherwise, you'll get errors when you next reboot the system and the swap area can't be found.

The /proc Filesystem

Unix systems have come a long way with respect to providing uniform interfaces to different parts of the system; as you learned in Chapter 4, hardware is represented in Linux in the form of a special type of file in the */dev* directory. We'll have a lot more to say about this directory in "Device Files," later in this chapter. There is, however, a special filesystem called the */proc* filesystem that goes even one step further: it unifies files and processes.

From the user's or the system administrator's point of view, the */proc* filesystem looks just like any other filesystem; you can navigate around it with the *cd* command, list directory contents with the *ls* command, and view file contents with the *cat* command. However, none of these files and directories occupies any space on your hard disk. The kernel traps accesses to the */proc* filesystem and generates directory and file contents on the fly. In other words, whenever you list a directory or view file contents in the */proc* filesystem, the kernel dynamically generates the contents you want to see.

To make this less abstract, let's see some examples. The following example displays the list of files in the top-level directory of the */proc* filesystem:

```
tigger # ls /proc
.      3759  5538  5679  5750  6137  9          filesystems  net
..     3798  5539  5681  5751  6186  966        fs           partitions
1      3858  5540  5683  5754  6497  acpi       ide          scsi
10     3868  5541  5686  5757  6498  asound     interrupts   self
11     3892  5542  5688  5759  6511  bluetooth  iomem        slabinfo
1138   3898  5556  5689  5761  6582  buddyinfo  ioports      splash
```

```
14    4     5572  5692  5800  6720  bus          irq        stat
15    4356  5574  5693  5803  6740  cmdline      kallsyms   swaps
1584  4357  5579  5698  5826  6741  config.gz    kcore      sys
1585  4368  5580  5701  5827  6817  cpufreq      kmsg       sysrq-trigger
1586  4715  5592  5705  5829  6818  cpuinfo      loadavg    sysvipc
16    4905  5593  5706  5941  6819  crypto       locks      tty
17    5     5619  5707  6     6886  devices      mdstat     uptime
18    5103  5658  5713  6063  689   diskstats    meminfo    version
19    5193  5661  5715  6086  6892  dma          misc       vmstat
2     5219  5663  5717  6107  6894  dri          mm
2466  5222  5666  5740  6115  6912  driver       modules
2958  5228  5673  5741  6118  7     execdomains  mounts
3     5537  5677  5748  6130  8     fb           mtrr
```

The numbers will be different on your system, but the general organization will be the same. All those numbers are directories that represent each of the processes running on your system. For example, let's look at the information about the process with the ID 3759:

```
tigger # ls /proc/3759
.      auxv      delay    fd           mem       oom_score  statm   wchan
..     cmdline   environ  mapped_base  mounts    root       status
attr   cwd       exe      maps         oom_adj   stat       task
```

(The output can be slightly different if you are using a different version of the Linux kernel.) You see a number of files that each contain information about this process. For example, the *cmdline* file shows the command line with which this process was started. *status* gives information about the internal state of the process, and *cwd* links to the current working directory of this process.

Probably you'll find the hardware information even more interesting than the process information. All the information that the kernel has gathered about your hardware is collected in the */proc* filesystem, even though it can be difficult to find the information you are looking for.

Let's start by checking your machine's memory. This is represented by the file */proc/meminfo*:

```
owl # cat /proc/meminfo
MemTotal:      1034304 kB
MemFree:        382396 kB
Buffers:         51352 kB
Cached:         312648 kB
SwapCached:          0 kB
Active:         448816 kB
Inactive:       141100 kB
HighTotal:      131008 kB
HighFree:          252 kB
LowTotal:       903296 kB
LowFree:        382144 kB
SwapTotal:     1172724 kB
SwapFree:      1172724 kB
Dirty:             164 kB
```

```
Writeback:            0 kB
Mapped:          294868 kB
Slab:             38788 kB
Committed_AS:    339916 kB
PageTables:        2124 kB
VmallocTotal:    114680 kB
VmallocUsed:      78848 kB
VmallocChunk:     35392 kB
HugePages_Total:      0
HugePages_Free:       0
Hugepagesize:      4096 kB
```

If you then try the command *free*, you can see that you get exactly the same information, only in a different format. *free* does nothing more than read */proc/meminfo* and rearrange the output a bit.

Most tools on your system that report information about your hardware do it this way. The */proc* filesystem is a portable and easy way to get at this information. The information is especially useful if you want to add new hardware to your system. For example, most hardware boards need a few I/O addresses to communicate with the CPU and the operating system. If you configured two boards to use the same I/O addresses, disaster is about to happen. You can avoid this by checking which I/O addresses the kernel has already detected as being in use:

```
tigger # more /proc/ioports
0000-001f : dma1
0020-0021 : pic1
0040-005f : timer
0060-006f : keyboard
0070-0077 : rtc
0080-008f : dma page reg
00a0-00a1 : pic2
00c0-00df : dma2
00f0-00ff : fpu
0170-0177 : ide1
01f0-01f7 : ide0
02f8-02ff : serial
0376-0376 : ide1
0378-037a : parport0
03c0-03df : vesafb
03f6-03f6 : ide0
03f8-03ff : serial
0cf8-0cff : PCI conf1
c000-cfff : PCI Bus #02
  c000-c0ff : 0000:02:04.0
    c000-c00f : advansys
  c400-c43f : 0000:02:09.0
    c400-c43f : e100
d000-d00f : 0000:00:07.1
  d000-d007 : ide0
  d008-d00f : ide1
d400-d4ff : 0000:00:07.5
  d400-d4ff : AMD AMD768 - AC'97
```

```
d800-d83f : 0000:00:07.5
  d800-d83f : AMD AMD768 - Controller
dc00-dcff : 0000:00:09.0
e000-e003 : 0000:00:00.0
```

Now you can look for I/O addresses that are free. Of course, the kernel can show I/O addresses only for boards that it has detected and recognized, but in a correctly configured system, this should be the case for all boards.

You can use the /proc filesystem for the other information you might need when configuring new hardware as well: /proc/interrupts lists the occupied interrupt lines (IRQs) and /proc/dma lists the DMA channels in use.

Device Files

Device files allow user programs to access hardware devices on the system through the kernel. They are not "files" per se, but look like files from the program's point of view: you can read from them, write to them, *mmap()* onto them, and so forth. When you access such a device "file," the kernel recognizes the I/O request and passes it a device driver, which performs some operation, such as reading data from a serial port or sending data to a sound card.

Device files (although they are inappropriately named, we will continue to use this term) provide a convenient way to access system resources without requiring the applications programmer to know how the underlying device works. Under Linux, as with most Unix systems, device drivers themselves are part of the kernel. In "Building the Kernel" in Chapter 18, we show you how to build your own kernel, including only those device drivers for the hardware on your system.

Device files are located in the directory /dev on nearly all Unix-like systems. Each device on the system should have a corresponding entry in /dev. For example, /dev/ttyS0 corresponds to the first serial port, known as COM1 under MS-DOS; /dev/hda2 corresponds to the second partition on the first IDE drive. In fact, there should be entries in /dev for devices you do not have. The device files are generally created during system installation and include every possible device driver. They don't necessarily correspond to the actual hardware on your system.

A number of pseudo-devices in /dev don't correspond to any actual peripheral. For example, /dev/null acts as a byte sink; any write request to /dev/null will succeed, but the data written will be ignored. Similarly, we've already demonstrated the use of /dev/zero to create a swap file; any read request on /dev/zero simply returns null bytes.

When using *ls -l* to list device files in /dev, you'll see something such as the following (if you are using a version of the *ls* command that supports colorized output, you should see the /dev/hda in a different color, since it's not an ordinary file):

```
brw-rw----  1 root disk 3, 0 2004-04-06 15:27 /dev/hda
```

This is *ldev/hda*, which corresponds to the first IDE drive. First of all, note that the first letter of the permissions field is b, which means this is a block device file. (Normal files have a - in this first column, directories a d, and so on; we'll talk more about this in the next chapter.) Device files are denoted either by b, for block devices, or c, for character devices. A block device is usually a peripheral such as a hard drive: data is read and written to the device as entire blocks (where the block size is determined by the device; it may not be 1024 bytes as we usually call "blocks" under Linux), and the device may be accessed randomly. In contrast, character devices are usually read or written sequentially, and I/O may be done as single bytes. An example of a character device is a serial port.

Also, note that the size field in the *ls -l* listing is replaced by two numbers, separated by a comma. The first value is the *major device number* and the second is the *minor device number*. When a device file is accessed by a program, the kernel receives the I/O request in terms of the major and minor numbers of the device. The major number generally specifies a particular driver within the kernel, and the minor number specifies a particular device handled by that driver. For example, all serial port devices have the same major number, but different minor numbers. The kernel uses the major number to redirect an I/O request to the appropriate driver, and the driver uses the minor number to figure out which specific device to access. In some cases, minor numbers can also be used for accessing specific functions of a device.

The naming convention used by files in */dev* is, to put it bluntly, a complete mess. Because the kernel itself doesn't care what filenames are used in */dev* (it cares only about the major and minor numbers), the distribution maintainers, applications programmers, and device driver writers are free to choose names for a device file. Often, the person writing a device driver will suggest a name for the device, and later the name will be changed to accommodate other, similar devices. This can cause confusion and inconsistency as the system develops; hopefully, you won't encounter this problem unless you're working with newer device drivers—those that are under testing. A project called *udev* should soon solve the problem of clashing device names.

At any rate, the device files included in your original distribution should be accurate for the kernel version and for device drivers included with that distribution. When you upgrade your kernel or add additional device drivers (see "Building a New Kernel" in Chapter 18), you may need to add a device file using the mknod command. The format of this command is:

```
mknod -m permissions name type major minor
```

where:

- *name* is the full pathname of the device to create, such as */dev/rft0*
- *type* is either c for a character device or b for a block device
- *major* is the major number of the device

- *minor* is the minor number of the device
- `-m` *permissions* is an optional argument that sets the permission bits of the new device file to *permissions*

For example, let's say you're adding a new device driver to the kernel, and the documentation says that you need to create the block device */dev/bogus*, major number 42, minor number 0. You would use the following command:

```
mknod /dev/bogus b 42 0
```

Making devices is even easier with the command */dev/MAKEDEV* that comes with many distributions—you specify only the kind of device you want, and *MAKEDEV* finds out the major and minor numbers for you.

Getting back to the `mknod` command, if you don't specify the *-m permissions* argument, the new device is given the permissions for a newly created file, modified by your current umask—usually 0644. To set the permissions for */dev/bogus* to 0660 instead, we use:

```
mknod -m 660 /dev/bogus b 42 0
```

You can also use `chmod` to set the permissions for a device file after creation.

Why are device permissions important? Like any file, the permissions for a device file control who may access the raw device, and how. As we saw in the previous example, the device file for */dev/hda* has permissions 0660, which means that only the owner and users in the file's group (here, the group *disk* is used) may read and write directly to this device. (Permissions are introduced in "File Ownership and Permissions" in Chapter 11.)

In general, you don't want to give any user direct read and write access to certain devices—especially those devices corresponding to disk drives and partitions. Otherwise, anyone could, say, run *mkfs* on a drive partition and completely destroy all data on the system.

In the case of drives and partitions, write access is required to corrupt data in this way, but read access is also a breach of security; given read access to a raw device file corresponding to a disk partition, a user could peek in on other users' files. Likewise, the device file */dev/mem* corresponds to the system's physical memory (it's generally used only for extreme debugging purposes). Given read access, clever users could spy on other users' passwords, including the one belonging to *root*, as they are entered at login time.

Be sure that the permissions for any device you add to the system correspond to how the device can and should be accessed by users. Devices such as serial ports, sound cards, and virtual consoles are generally safe for mortals to have access to, but most other devices on the system should be limited to use by *root* (and to programs running *setuid* as *root*).

A technique that some distributions follow is to assign a device file to the user *root*, but not to use *root* as the group, but rather something different. For example, on SUSE, the device file */dev/video0* that is the access point to the first video hardware (such as a TV card) is owned by user *root*, but group *video*. You can thus add all users who are supposed to have access to the video hardware to the group *video*. Everybody else (besides *root*, of course) will be forbidden access to the video hardware and cannot watch TV.[*]

Many files found in */dev* are actually symbolic links (created using ln -s, in the usual way) to another device file. These links make it easier to access certain devices by using a more common name. For example, if you have a serial mouse, that mouse might be accessed through one of the device files */dev/ttyS0*, */dev/ttyS1*, */dev/ttyS2*, or */dev/ttyS3*, depending on which serial port the mouse is attached to. Many people create a link named */dev/mouse* to the appropriate serial device, as in the following example:

```
ln -s /dev/ttyS2 /dev/mouse
```

In this way, users can access the mouse from */dev/mouse*, instead of having to remember which serial port it is on. This convention is also used for devices such as */dev/cdrom* and */dev/modem*. These files are usually symbolic links to a device file in */dev* corresponding to the actual CD-ROM or modem device.

To remove a device file, just use rm, as in:

```
rm /dev/bogus
```

Removing a device file does not remove the corresponding device driver from memory or from the kernel; it simply leaves you with no means to talk to a particular device driver. Similarly, adding a device file does not add a device driver to the system; in fact, you can add device files for drivers that don't even exist. Device files simply provide a hook into a particular device driver should such a driver exist in the kernel.

Scheduling Recurring Jobs Using cron

The original purpose of the computer was to automate routine tasks. If you must back up your disk at 1:00 A.M. every day, why should you have to enter the commands manually each time—particularly if it means getting out of bed? You should be able to tell the computer to do it and then forget about it. On Unix systems, cron exists to perform this automating function. Briefly, you use cron by running the crontab command and entering lines in a special format recognized by cron. Each line specifies a command to run and when to run it.

---

[*] A time will come when parents say to their children, "If you do not do your homework, I will remove you from the *video* group." Of course, clever kids will have cracked the *root* account already and won't care.

Behind your back, crontab saves your commands in a file bearing your username in the */var/spool/cron/crontabs* directory. (For instance, the *crontab* file for user *mdw* would be called */var/spool/cron/crontabs/mdw*.) A daemon called *crond* reads this file regularly and executes the commands at the proper times. One of the *rc* files on your system starts up crond when the system boots. There actually is no command named *cron*, only the *crontab* utility and the crond daemon.

On some systems, use of *cron* is limited to the *root* user. In any case, let's look at a useful command you might want to run as *root* and show how you'd specify it as a *crontab* entry. Suppose that every day you'd like to clean old files out of the */tmp* directory, which is supposed to serve as temporary storage for files created by lots of utilities.

Notice that *cron* never writes anything to the console. All output and error messages are sent as an email message to the user who owns the corresponding *crontab*. You can override this setting by specifying MAILTO=*address* in the *crontab* file before the jobs themselves.

Most systems remove the contents of */tmp* when the system reboots, but if you keep it up for a long time, you may find it useful to use *cron* to check for old files (say, files that haven't been accessed in the past three days). The command you want to enter is

```
ls -l filename
```

But how do you know which *filename* to specify? You have to place the command inside a *find* command, which lists all files beneath a directory and performs the operation you specify on each one.

Here, we'll specify */tmp* as the directory to search, and use the *-atime* option to find files whose last access time is more than three days in the past. The *-exec* option means "execute the following command on every file we find," the *-type d* option selects directories, and the \! inverts the selection, just choosing all items except directories (regular files, device files, and so on):

```
find /tmp \! -type d -atime +3 -exec ls -l {} \;
```

The command we are asking find to execute is *ls -l*, which simply shows details about the files. (Many people use a similar *crontab* entry to remove files, but this is hard to do without leaving a security hole.) The funny string {} is just a way of saying "Do it to each file you find, according to the previous selection material." The string \; tells find that the **-exec** option is finished.

Now we have a command that looks for old files on */tmp*. We still have to say how often it runs. The format used by *crontab* consists of six fields:

minute
hour
day

month
dayofweek
command

Fill the fields as follows:

1. Minute (specify from 0 to 59)
2. Hour (specify from 0 to 23)
3. Day of the month (specify from 1 to 31)
4. Month (specify from 1 to 12, or a name such as jan, feb, and so on)
5. Day of the week (specify from 0 to 6, where 0 is Sunday, or a name such as mon, tue, and so on)
6. Command (can be multiple words)

Figure 10-1 shows a cron entry with all the fields filled in. The command is a shell script, run with the Bourne shell *sh*. But the entry is not too realistic: the script runs only when all the conditions in the first five fields are true. That is, it has to run on a Sunday that falls on the 15th day of either January or July—not a common occurrence! So this is not a particularly useful example.

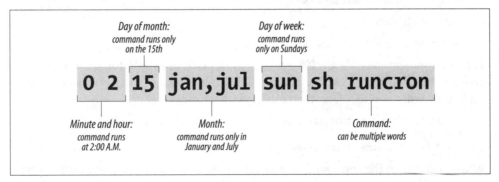

Figure 10-1. Sample cron entry

If you want a command to run every day at 1:00 A.M., specify the minute as 0 and the hour as 1. The other three fields should be asterisks, which mean "every day and month at the given time." The complete line in cron tab is:

```
0 1 * * * find /tmp -atime 3 -exec ls -l {} \;
```

Because you can do a lot of fancy things with the time fields, let's play with this command a bit more. Suppose you want to run the command just on the first day of each month. You would keep the first two fields, but add a 1 in the third field:

```
0 1 1 * * find /tmp -atime 3 -exec ls -l {} \;
```

To do it once a week on Monday, restore the third field to an asterisk but specify either 1 or mon as the fifth field:

```
0 1 * * mon find /tmp -atime 3 -exec ls -l {} \;
```

To get even more sophisticated, there are ways to specify multiple times in each field. Here, a comma means "run on the 1st and 15th day" of each month:

```
0 1 1,15 * * find /tmp -atime 3 -exec ls -l {} \;
```

A hyphen means "run every day from the 1st through the 15th, inclusive":

```
0 1 1-15 * * find /tmp -atime 3 -exec ls -l {} \;
```

A slash followed by a 5 means "run every fifth day," which comes out to the 1st, 6th, 11th, and so on:

```
0 1 */5 * * find /tmp -atime 3 -exec ls -l {} \;
```

Now we're ready to actually put the entry in our *crontab* file. Become *root* (because this is the kind of thing *root* should do) and enter the *crontab* command with the *-e* option for "edit":

```
rutabaga# crontab -e
```

By default, this command starts a *vi* edit session. If you'd like to use XEmacs instead, you can specify this before you start *crontab*. For a Bourne-compliant shell, enter the command:

```
rutabaga# export VISUAL=xemacs
```

For the C shell, enter:

```
rutabaga# setenv VISUAL xemacs
```

The environment variable EDITOR also works in place of VISUAL for some versions of crontab. Enter a line or two beginning with hash marks (#) to serve as comments explaining what you're doing, then put in your crontab entry:

```
# List files on /tmp that are 3 or more days old.  Runs at 1:00 AM
# each morning.
0 1 * * * find /tmp -atime 3 -exec ls -l {} \;
```

When you exit *vi*, the commands are saved. Look at your *crontab* entry by entering:

```
rutabaga# crontab -l
```

We have not yet talked about a critical aspect of our *crontab* entry: where does the output go? By default, *cron* saves the standard output and standard error and sends them to the user as a mail message. In this example, the mail goes to *root*, but that should automatically be directed to you as the system administrator. Make sure the following line appears in */usr/lib/aliases* (*/etc/aliases* on SUSE, Debian, and RedHat):

```
root: your-account-name
```

In a moment, we'll show what to do if you want output saved in a file instead of being mailed to you.

Here's another example of a common type of command used in *crontab* files. It performs a tape backup of a directory. We assume that someone has put a tape in the drive before the command runs. First, an *mt* command makes sure the tape in the

/dev/qft0 device is rewound to the beginning. Then a `tar` command transfers all the files from the directory */src* to the tape. A semicolon is used to separate the commands; that is standard shell syntax:

```
# back up the /src directory once every two months.
    0 2 1 */2 * mt -f /dev/qft0 rewind; tar cf /dev/qft0 /src
```

The first two fields ensure that the command runs at 2:00 A.M., and the third field specifies the first day of the month. The fourth field specifies every two months. We could achieve the same effect, in a possibly more readable manner, by entering:

```
0 2 1 jan,mar,may,jul,sep,nov * mt -f /dev/qft0 rewind; \
    tar cf /dev/qft0 /src
```

The section "Making Backups" in Chapter 27 explains how to perform backups on a regular basis.

The following example uses *mailq* every two days to test whether any mail is stuck in the mail queue, and sends the mail administrator the results by mail. If mail is stuck in the mail queue, the report includes details about addressing and delivery problems, but otherwise the message is empty:

```
0 6 */2 * * mailq -v | \
    mail -s "Tested Mail Queue for Stuck Email" postmaster
```

Probably you don't want to receive a mail message every day when everything is going normally. In the examples we've used so far, the commands do not produce any output unless they encounter errors. But you may want to get into the habit of redirecting the standard output to */dev/null*, or sending it to a logfile like this (note the use of two > signs so that we don't wipe out previous output):

```
0 1 * * * find /tmp -atime 3 -exec ls -l {} \; >> /home/mdw/log
```

In this entry, we redirect the standard output, but allow the standard error to be sent as a mail message. This can be a nice feature because we'll get a mail message if anything goes wrong. If you want to make sure you don't receive mail under any circumstances, redirect both the standard output and the standard error to a file:

```
0 1 * * * find /tmp -atime 3 -exec ls -l {} \; >> /home/mdw/log 2>&1
```

When you save output in a logfile, you get the problem of a file that grows continuously. You may want another *cron* entry that runs once a week or so, just to remove the file.

Only Bourne shell commands can be used in *crontab* entries. That means you can't use any of the convenient extensions recognized by bash and other modern shells, such as aliases or the use of ~ to mean "my home directory." You can use $HOME, however; cron recognizes the $USER, $HOME, and $SHELL environment variables. Each command runs with your home directory as its current directory.

Some people like to specify absolute pathnames for commands, such as */usr/bin/find* and */bin/rm*, in *crontab* entries. This ensures that the right command is always found, instead of relying on the path being set correctly.

If a command gets too long and complicated to put on a single line, write a shell script and invoke it from *cron*. Make sure the script is executable (use *chmod +x*) or execute it by using a shell, such as:

```
0 1 * * * sh runcron
```

As a system administrator, you often have to create crontab files for dummy users, such as *news* or *UUCP*. Running all utilities as *root* would be overkill and possibly dangerous, so these special users exist instead.

The choice of a user also affects file ownership: a crontab file for *news* should run files owned by *news*, and so on. In general, make sure utilities are owned by the user in whose name you create the crontab file.

As *root*, you can edit other users' crontab files by using the **-u** option. For example:

```
tigger # crontab -u news -e
```

This is useful because you can't log in as user *news*, but you still might want to edit this user's crontab entry.

Executing Jobs Once

With cron, you can schedule recurring jobs, as we have seen in the previous section. But what if you want to run a certain command just once or a limited number of times, but still at times when it is inconvenient to type in the command interactively? Of course, you could always add the command to the *crontab* and then remove it later, or pick a date selection that only applies very rarely. But there is also a tool that is made for this job, the at command.

at reads commands to be executed from a file or from standard input. You can specify the time in a number of ways, including natural-language specifications such as noon, midnight, or, interestingly, teatime (which, much to the dismay of British users, maps to 4 p.m.).

For at to work, the at daemon, atd, needs to run. How it is started depends on your distribution: rcatd start and /etc/init.d/atd start are good tries. In a pinch, you should also be able to just run */usr/sbin/atd* as *root*.

As an example, let's say that you want to download a large file from the Internet at midnight when your ISP is cheaper or when you expect the lines to be less congested so that the probability of success is higher. Let's further assume that you need to run a command connectinet for setting up your (dial-up) Internet connection, and disconnectinet for shutting it down. For the actual download in this example, we use the wget command:

```
tigger$ at midnight
warning: commands will be executed using /bin/sh
at> connectinet
at> wget ftp://overloadedserver.lotsastuff.com/pub/largefiles/reallylargefile.bz2
at> disconnectinet
at> <EOT>
job 1 at 2005-02-26 00:00
```

After typing at midnight, the at command first tells us that it is going to execute our commands with another shell (we are using the Z shell for interactive work here, whereas *at* will be using the Bourne shell) and then lets us enter our commands one after the other. When we are done, we type Ctrl-D, which at shows as <EOT>. at then shows the *job number* and the exact date and time for the execution. Now you can lean back in confidence that your command will be issued at the specified time—just don't turn off your computer!

If you are unsure which commands you have in the queue, you can check with the *atq* command:

```
tigger$ atq
1        2005-02-26 00:00 a kalle
```

This shows the job number in the first column, then the date of the planned execution, a letter specifying the queue used (here a, you can have more than queue—something that is rarely used and that we will not go into here), and finally the owner of the job.

If you decide that it wasn't such a good idea after all to submit that command, you can cancel a job if you know its job number—which you now know how to find out using the atq command, in case you have forgotten the output of the at command when you submitted the command in the first place.

Deleting a job from the queue is done using the *atrm* command. Just specify the job number:

```
tigger$ atrm 1
```

atrm is one of the more taciturn commands, but you can always use *atq* to see whether everything is as expected:

```
tigger$ atq
```

Not much talk, either, but your command is gone.

Managing System Logs

The *syslogd* utility logs various kinds of system activity, such as debugging output from sendmail and warnings printed by the kernel. *syslogd* runs as a daemon and is usually started in one of the *rc* files at boot time.

The file */etc/syslog.conf* is used to control where *syslogd* records information. Such a file might look like the following (even though they tend to be much more complicated on most systems):

```
*.info;*.notice    /var/log/messages
mail.debug         /var/log/maillog
*.warn             /var/log/syslog
kern.emerg         /dev/console
```

The first field of each line lists the kinds of messages that should be logged, and the second field lists the location where they should be logged. The first field is of the format:

```
facility.level [; facility.level ... ]
```

where *facility* is the system application or facility generating the message, and *level* is the severity of the message.

For example, *facility* can be mail (for the mail daemon), kern (for the kernel), user (for user programs), or auth (for authentication programs such as login or su). An asterisk in this field specifies all facilities.

level can be (in increasing severity): debug, info, notice, warning, err, crit, alert, or emerg.

In the previous */etc/syslog.conf*, we see that all messages of severity info and notice are logged to */var/log/messages*, all debug messages from the mail daemon are logged to */var/log/maillog*, and all warn messages are logged to */var/log/syslog*. Also, any emerg warnings from the kernel are sent to the console (which is the current virtual console, or a terminal emulator started with the -C option on a GUI).

The messages logged by *syslogd* usually include the date, an indication of what process or facility delivered the message, and the message itself—all on one line. For example, a kernel error message indicating a problem with data on an *ext2fs* filesystem might appear in the logfiles, as in:

```
Dec  1 21:03:35 loomer kernel: EXT2-fs error (device 3/2):
    ext2_check_blocks_bit map: Wrong free blocks count in super block,
    stored = 27202, counted = 27853
```

Similarly, if an su to the root account succeeds, you might see a log message such as:

```
Dec 11 15:31:51 loomer su: mdw on /dev/ttyp3
```

Logfiles can be important in tracking down system problems. If a logfile grows too large, you can empty it using *cat /dev/null > logfile*. This clears out the file, but leaves it there for the logging system to write to.

Your system probably comes equipped with a running *syslogd* and an */etc/syslog.conf* that does the right thing. However, it's important to know where your logfiles are and what programs they represent. If you need to log many messages (say, debugging messages from the kernel, which can be very verbose) you can edit *syslog.conf* and tell syslogd to reread its configuration file with the command:

```
kill -HUP `cat /var/run/syslog.pid`
```

Note the use of backquotes to obtain the process ID of *syslogd*, contained in */var/run/syslog.pid*.

Other system logs might be available as well. These include the following:

/var/log/wtmp

This file contains binary data indicating the login times and duration for each user on the system; it is used by the last command to generate a listing of user logins. The output of *last* might look like this:

```
mdw       tty3                    Sun Dec 11 15:25    still logged in
mdw       tty3                    Sun Dec 11 15:24 - 15:25  (00:00)
mdw       tty1                    Sun Dec 11 11:46    still logged in
reboot    ~                       Sun Dec 11 06:46
```

A record is also logged in */var/log/wtmp* when the system is rebooted.

/var/run/utmp

This is another binary file that contains information on users currently logged into the system. Commands such as *who*, *w*, and *finger* use this file to produce information on who is logged in. For example, the *w* command might print the following:

```
3:58pm  up  4:12,  5 users,  load average: 0.01, 0.02, 0.00
User      tty        login@  idle   JCPU  PCPU  what
mdw       ttyp3      11:46am    14                -
mdw       ttyp2      11:46am            1         w
mdw       ttyp4      11:46am                      kermit
mdw       ttyp0      11:46am    14                bash
```

We see the login times for each user (in this case, one user logged in many times), as well as the command currently being used. The *w*(1) manual page describes all the fields displayed.

/var/log/lastlog

This file is similar to *wtmp* but is used by different programs (such as *finger* to determine when a user was last logged in).

Note that the format of the *wtmp* and *utmp* files differs from system to system. Some programs may be compiled to expect one format, and others another format. For this reason, commands that use the files may produce confusing or inaccurate information—especially if the files become corrupted by a program that writes information to them in the wrong format.

Logfiles can get quite large, and if you do not have the necessary hard disk space, you have to do something about your partitions being filled too fast. Of course, you can delete the logfiles from time to time, but you may not want to do this, because the logfiles also contain information that can be valuable in crisis situations.

One option is to copy the logfiles from time to time to another file and compress this file. The logfile itself starts at 0 again. Here is a short shell script that does this for the logfile */var/log/messages*:

```
mv /var/log/messages /var/log/messages-backup
    cp /dev/null /var/log/messages

    CURDATE=`date +"%m%d%y"`

    mv /var/log/messages-backup /var/log/messages-$CURDATE
    gzip /var/log/messages-$CURDATE
```

First, we move the logfile to a different name and then truncate the original file to 0 bytes by copying to it from */dev/null*. We do this so that further logging can be done without problems while the next steps are done. Then, we compute a date string for the current date that is used as a suffix for the filename, rename the backup file, and finally compress it with *gzip*.

You might want to run this small script from *cron*, but as it is presented here, it should not be run more than once a day—otherwise the compressed backup copy will be overwritten because the filename reflects the date but not the time of day (of course, you could change the date format string to include the time). If you want to run this script more often, you must use additional numbers to distinguish between the various copies.

You could make many more improvements here. For example, you might want to check the size of the logfile first and copy and compress it only if this size exceeds a certain limit.

Even though this is already an improvement, your partition containing the logfiles will eventually get filled. You can solve this problem by keeping around only a certain number of compressed logfiles (say, 10). When you have created as many logfiles as you want to have, you delete the oldest, and overwrite it with the next one to be copied. This principle is also called *log rotation*. Some distributions have scripts such as *savelog* or *logrotate* that can do this automatically.

To finish this discussion, it should be noted that most recent distributions, such as SUSE, Debian, and Red Hat, already have built-in *cron* scripts that manage your logfiles and are much more sophisticated than the small one presented here.

Processes

At the heart of Unix lies the concept of a process. Understanding this concept will help you keep control of your login session as a user. If you are also a system administrator, the concept is even more important.

A *process* is an independently running program that has its own set of resources. For instance, we showed in an earlier section how you could direct the output of a program to a file while your shell continued to direct output to your screen. The reason that the shell and the other program can send output to different places is that they are separate processes.

On Unix, the finite resources of the system, such as the memory and the disks, are managed by one all-powerful program called the kernel. Everything else on the system is a process.

Thus, before you log in, your terminal is monitored by a *getty* process. After you log in, the *getty* process dies (a new one is started by the kernel when you log out) and your terminal is managed by your shell, which is a different process. The shell then creates a new process each time you enter a command. The creation of a new process is called *forking* because one process splits into two.

If you are using the X Window System, each process starts up one or more windows. Thus, the window in which you are typing commands is owned by an *xterm* process or a reloaded terminal program. That process forks a shell to run within the window. And that shell forks yet more processes as you enter commands.

To see the processes you are running, enter the command ps. Figure 10-2 shows some typical output and what each field means. You may be surprised how many processes you are running, especially if you are using X. One of the processes is the ps command itself, which of course dies as soon as the output is displayed.

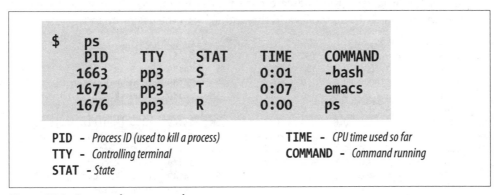

```
$   ps
    PID     TTY     STAT    TIME    COMMAND
    1663    pp3     S       0:01    -bash
    1672    pp3     T       0:07    emacs
    1676    pp3     R       0:00    ps
```

PID - *Process ID (used to kill a process)*   TIME - *CPU time used so far*
TTY - *Controlling terminal*   COMMAND - *Command running*
STAT - *State*

Figure 10-2. Output of ps command

The first field in the *ps* output is a unique identifier for the process. If you have a runaway process that you can't get rid of through Ctrl-C or other means, you can kill it by going to a different virtual console or X window and entering:

    $ kill *process-id*

The TTY field shows which terminal the process is running on, if any. (Everything run from a shell uses a terminal, of course, but background daemons don't have a terminal.)

The STAT field shows what state the process is in. The shell is currently suspended, so this field shows an S. An Emacs editing session is running, but it's suspended using Ctrl-Z. This is shown by the T in its STAT field. The last process shown is the ps that is generating all this input; its state, of course, is R because it is running.

The TIME field shows how much CPU time the processes have used. Because both bash and Emacs are interactive, they actually don't use much of the CPU.

You aren't restricted to seeing your own processes. Look for a minute at all the processes on the system. The **a** option stands for all processes, while the **x** option includes processes that have no controlling terminal (such as daemons started at runtime):

```
$ ps ax | more
```

Now you can see the daemons that we mentioned in the previous section.

Recent versions of the *ps* command have a nice additional option. If you are looking for a certain process whose name (or at least parts of it) you know, you can use the option -C, followed by the name to see only the processes whose names match the name you specify:

```
$ ps -C httpd
```

And here, with a breathtaking view of the entire Linux system at work, we end our discussion of processes (the lines are cut off at column 76; if you want to see the command lines in their full glory, add the option -w to the ps command):

```
kalle@owl:~ > ps aux
USER       PID %CPU %MEM   VSZ  RSS TTY      STAT START   TIME COMMAND
root         1  0.0  0.0   588  240 ?        S    14:49   0:05 init [3]
root         2  0.0  0.0     0    0 ?        S    14:49   0:00 [migration/0]
root         3  0.0  0.0     0    0 ?        SN   14:49   0:00 [ksoftirqd/0]
root         4  0.0  0.0     0    0 ?        S    14:49   0:00 [migration/1]
root         5  0.0  0.0     0    0 ?        SN   14:49   0:00 [ksoftirqd/1]
root         6  0.0  0.0     0    0 ?        S<   14:49   0:00 [events/0]
root         7  0.0  0.0     0    0 ?        S<   14:49   0:00 [events/1]
root         8  0.0  0.0     0    0 ?        S<   14:49   0:00 [kacpid]
root         9  0.0  0.0     0    0 ?        S<   14:49   0:00 [kblockd/0]
root        10  0.0  0.0     0    0 ?        S<   14:49   0:00 [kblockd/1]
root        11  0.0  0.0     0    0 ?        S    14:49   0:00 [kirqd]
root        14  0.0  0.0     0    0 ?        S<   14:49   0:00 [khelper]
root        15  0.0  0.0     0    0 ?        S    14:49   0:00 [pdflush]
root        16  0.0  0.0     0    0 ?        S    14:49   0:00 [pdflush]
root        17  0.0  0.0     0    0 ?        S    14:49   0:00 [kswapd0]
root        18  0.0  0.0     0    0 ?        S<   14:49   0:00 [aio/0]
root        19  0.0  0.0     0    0 ?        S<   14:49   0:00 [aio/1]
root       689  0.0  0.0     0    0 ?        S    14:49   0:00 [kseriod]
root       966  0.0  0.0     0    0 ?        S    14:49   0:00 [scsi_eh_0]
root      1138  0.0  0.0     0    0 ?        S    14:49   0:00 [kjournald]
root      1584  0.0  0.0     0    0 ?        S    14:49   0:00 [kjournald]
root      1585  0.0  0.0     0    0 ?        S    14:49   0:00 [kjournald]
root      1586  0.0  0.0     0    0 ?        S    14:49   0:00 [kjournald]
```

```
root      2466  0.0  0.0      0     0 ?       S    14:49   0:00 [khubd]
root      2958  0.0  0.0   1412   436 ?       S    14:49   0:00 [hwscand]
root      3759  0.0  0.0   1436   612 ?       Ss   14:49   0:00 /sbin/syslogd -a
root      3798  0.0  0.1   2352  1516 ?       Ss   14:49   0:00 /sbin/klogd -c 1
bin       3858  0.0  0.0   1420   492 ?       Ss   14:49   0:00 /sbin/portmap
root      3868  0.0  0.0   1588   652 ?       Ss   14:49   0:00 /sbin/resmgrd
root      3892  0.0  0.0   1396   544 ?       Ss   14:49   0:00 hcid: processing
root      3898  0.0  0.0   1420   528 ?       Ss   14:49   0:00 /usr/sbin/sdpd
root      4356  0.0  0.0      0     0 ?       S    14:49   0:00 [usb-storage]
root      4357  0.0  0.0      0     0 ?       S    14:49   0:00 [scsi_eh_1]
root      4368  0.0  0.1   4708  1804 ?       Ss   14:49   0:00 /usr/sbin/sshd -o
root      4715  0.0  0.1   2600  1240 ?       S    14:49   0:00 /usr/sbin/powersa
lp        4905  0.0  0.3   6416  3392 ?       Ss   14:49   0:00 /usr/sbin/cupsd
root      5103  0.0  0.1   4176  1432 ?       Ss   14:49   0:00 /usr/lib/postfix/
postfix   5193  0.0  0.1   4252  1512 ?       S    14:49   0:00 qmgr -l -t fifo -
root      5219  0.0  0.0   1584   704 ?       Ss   14:49   0:00 /usr/sbin/cron
root      5222  0.0  0.0  42624   784 ?       Ss   14:49   0:00 /usr/sbin/nscd
root      5537  0.0  0.1   2264  1216 ?       Ss   14:49   0:00 login -- kalle
root      5538  0.0  0.0   1608   608 tty2    Ss+  14:49   0:00 /sbin/mingetty tt
root      5539  0.0  0.0   1608   608 tty3    Ss+  14:49   0:00 /sbin/mingetty tt
root      5540  0.0  0.0   1608   608 tty4    Ss+  14:49   0:00 /sbin/mingetty tt
root      5541  0.0  0.0   1608   608 tty5    Ss+  14:49   0:00 /sbin/mingetty tt
root      5542  0.0  0.0   1608   608 tty6    Ss+  14:49   0:00 /sbin/mingetty tt
kalle     5556  0.0  0.1   4180  1996 tty1    Ss   14:50   0:00 -zsh
kalle     5572  0.0  0.0   3012   816 ?       Ss   14:50   0:00 gpg-agent --daemo
kalle     5574  0.0  0.1   4296  1332 ?       Ss   14:50   0:00 ssh-agent
kalle     5579  0.0  0.1   3708  1248 tty1    S+   14:50   0:00 /bin/sh /usr/X11R
kalle     5580  0.0  0.0   2504   564 tty1    S+   14:50   0:00 tee /home/kalle/.
kalle     5592  0.0  0.0   2384   652 tty1    S+   14:50   0:00 xinit /home/kalle
root      5593  3.4  4.5 106948 46744 ?       S    14:50   7:12 X :0 -auth /home/
kalle     5619  0.0  0.1   3704  1288 tty1    S    14:50   0:00 /bin/sh /usr/X11R
kalle     5658  0.0  1.0  24252 10412 ?       Ss   14:50   0:00 kdeinit Running..
kalle     5661  0.0  0.8  22876  8976 ?       S    14:50   0:00 kdeinit: dcopserv
kalle     5663  0.0  1.0  25340 10916 ?       S    14:50   0:00 kdeinit: klaunche
kalle     5666  0.0  1.7  31316 18540 ?       S    14:50   0:05 kdeinit: kded
kalle     5673  0.0  1.3  26480 14292 ?       S    14:50   0:00 kdeinit: kxkh
kalle     5677  0.0  0.5   9820  5736 ?       S    14:50   0:00 /opt/kde3/bin/art
kalle     5679  0.0  0.0   1372   336 tty1    S    14:50   0:00 kwrapper ksmserve
kalle     5681  0.0  1.1  24800 12116 ?       S    14:50   0:00 kdeinit: ksmserve
kalle     5683  0.0  1.4  27464 15512 ?       S    14:50   0:09 kdeinit: kwin -se
kalle     5686  0.0  1.8  30160 18920 ?       S    14:50   0:05 kdeinit: kdesktop
kalle     5688  0.1  1.8  31748 19460 ?       S    14:50   0:19 kdeinit: kicker
kalle     5689  0.0  1.0  25856 11360 ?       S    14:50   0:00 kdeinit: kio_file
kalle     5692  0.0  1.3  26324 14304 ?       S    14:50   0:02 kdeinit: klipper
kalle     5693  0.0  0.7  21144  7908 ?       S    14:50   0:00 kpowersave
kalle     5698  0.0  1.3  25840 13804 ?       S    14:50   0:00 kamix
kalle     5701  0.0  1.2  24764 12668 ?       S    14:50   0:00 kpowersave
kalle     5705  0.0  1.4  29260 15260 ?       S    14:50   0:01 suseplugger -capt
kalle     5706  0.0  1.2  24720 13376 ?       S    14:50   0:00 susewatcher -capt
kalle     5707  0.0  1.6  28476 16564 ?       S    14:50   0:00 kgpg
kalle     5713  0.0  1.2  25088 12468 ?       S    14:50   0:02 kdeinit: khotkeys
kalle     5715  0.0  1.9  30296 19920 ?       S    14:50   0:08 oooqs -caption Op
kalle     5717  0.0  1.5  28452 15716 ?       S    14:50   0:00 kdeinit: kio_uise
kalle     5740  0.0  1.0  26040 11260 ?       S    14:50   0:00 kdeinit: kio_file
```

```
kalle      5748   0.0   1.6  30084  16928  ?       S    14:50   0:05 kdeinit: konsole
kalle      5750   1.8   4.0  57404  42244  ?       S    14:50   3:48 kontact -session
kalle      5751   0.0   1.6  29968  16632  ?       S    14:50   0:00 kdeinit: konsole
kalle      5754   0.0   0.5  14968   5976  ?       S    14:50   0:00 /opt/kde3/bin/kde
kalle      5757   0.0   0.1   4188   1920  pts/2   Ss+  14:50   0:00 /bin/zsh
kalle      5759   0.0   0.1   4188   1944  pts/3   Ss   14:50   0:00 /bin/zsh
kalle      5761   0.0   0.2   4684   2572  pts/4   Ss+  14:50   0:00 /bin/zsh
kalle      5800   0.0   0.9  24484   9988  ?       S    14:50   0:00 kalarmd --login
kalle      5803   0.0   2.6  36264  27472  ?       S    14:50   0:05 xemacs
kalle      5826   0.0   0.1   3704   1172  pts/3   S+   14:51   0:00 sh ./sshtunnel
kalle      5827   0.0   0.2   4956   2348  pts/3   S+   14:51   0:02 ssh -X -L 23456:1
kalle      5829   0.1   1.9  31008  20204  ?       S    14:51   0:20 kdeinit: ksirc -i
kalle      6086   0.0   0.1   3444   1244  ?       S    15:07   0:00 /bin/sh /home/kal
kalle      6107   0.0   0.1   3704   1264  ?       S    15:07   0:00 /bin/sh /home/kal
kalle      6115   0.7   4.2  71184  43512  ?       S    15:07   1:29 /home/kalle/firef
kalle      6118   0.0   0.3   6460   3612  ?       S    15:07   0:00 /opt/gnome/lib/GC
kalle      6137   0.0   0.5   8232   5616  ?       S    15:08   0:03 perl /opt/kde3/bi
kalle      6186   0.0   2.9  42300  30384  ?       S    15:10   0:03 kdeinit: konquero
kalle      6497   0.1   1.6  30592  17424  ?       R    15:20   0:11 kdeinit: konsole
kalle      6498   0.0   0.2   4724   2624  pts/1   Ss+  15:20   0:00 /bin/zsh
kalle      6511   0.9   3.0  39932  31456  pts/1   S    15:20   1:37 xemacs
kalle      6720   0.0   0.2   4584   2500  pts/5   Ss   15:32   0:00 /bin/zsh
root       6740   0.0   0.1   3480   1264  pts/5   S    15:32   0:00 su
root       6741   0.0   0.1   3608   1732  pts/5   S    15:32   0:00 bash
kalle      6818   0.0   1.6  30152  17316  ?       S    15:39   0:00 kdeinit: konsole
kalle      6819   0.0   0.2   4492   2396  pts/6   Ss+  15:39   0:00 /bin/zsh
kalle      6948   0.0   1.6  29872  16564  ?       S    15:48   0:00 kdeinit: konsole
kalle      6949   0.0   0.1   4188   2040  pts/7   Ss   15:48   0:00 /bin/zsh
kalle      6982   0.0   0.1   4556   1908  pts/7   S+   15:50   0:00 ssh cvs.kdab.net
at         8106   0.0   0.0   1432    536  ?       Ss   17:24   0:00 /usr/sbin/atd
postfix    8672   0.0   0.1   4220   1448  ?       S    18:09   0:00 pickup -l -t fifo
postfix    8779   0.0   0.1   4208   1396  ?       S    18:15   0:00 proxymap -t unix
postfix    8796   0.0   0.1   4744   1784  ?       S    18:17   0:00 trivial-rewrite -
postfix    8797   0.0   0.1   4904   1848  ?       S    18:17   0:00 cleanup -z -t uni
postfix    8798   0.0   0.1   4376   1768  ?       S    18:17   0:00 local -t unix
root       8807   0.0   0.0   1584    700  ?       S    18:19   0:00 /USR/SBIN/CRON
kalle      8808   0.0   0.1   3112   1144  ?       Ss   18:19   0:00 fetchmail
root       8822   0.0   0.0   2164    688  pts/5   R+   18:20   0:00 ps aux
```

Programs That Serve You

We include this section because you should start to be interested in what's running on your system behind your back.

Many modern computer activities are too complex for the system simply to look at a file or some other static resource. Sometimes these activities need to interact with another running process.

For instance, take FTP, which you may have used to download some Linux-related documents or software. When you FTP to another system, another program has to be running on that system to accept your connection and interpret your commands. So there's a program running on that system called *ftpd*. The *d* in the name stands for *daemon*, which is a quaint Unix term for a server that runs in the background all the time. Most daemons handle network activities.

You've probably heard of the buzzword *client/server* enough to make you sick, but here it is in action—it has been in action for decades on Unix.

Daemons start up when the system is booted. To see how they get started, look in the */etc/inittab* and */etc/xinetd.conf* files, as well as distribution-specific configuration files. We won't go into their formats here. But each line in these files lists a program that runs when the system starts. You can find the distribution-specific files either by checking the documentation that came with your system or by looking for pathnames that occur frequently in */etc/inittab*. Those normally indicate the directory tree where your distribution stores its system startup files.

To give an example of how your system uses */etc/inittab*, look at one or more lines with the string getty or agetty. This is the program that listens at a terminal (tty) waiting for a user to log in. It's the program that displays the login : prompt we talked about at the beginning of this chapter.

The */etc/inetd.conf* file represents a more complicated way of running programs—another level of indirection. The idea behind */etc/inetd.conf* is that it would waste a lot of system resources if a dozen or more daemons were spinning idly, waiting for a request to come over the network. So, instead, the system starts up a single daemon named inetd. This daemon listens for connections from clients on other machines, and when an incoming connection is made, it starts up the appropriate daemon to handle it. For example, when an incoming FTP connection is made, inetd starts up the FTP daemon (*ftpd*) to manage the connection. In this way, the only network daemons running are those actually in use.

There's a daemon for every service offered by the system to other systems on a network: *fingerd* to handle remote *finger* requests, *rwhod* to handle *rwho* requests, and so on. A few daemons also handle non-networking services, such as *kerneld*, which handles the automatic loading of modules into the kernel. (In Versions 2.4 and up, this is called kmod instead and is no longer a process, but rather a kernel thread.)

## CHAPTER 11

Managing Users, Groups, and Permissions

Managing User Accounts

Even if you're the only actual human being who uses your Linux system, understanding how to manage user accounts is important—even more so if your system hosts multiple users.

User accounts serve a number of purposes on Unix systems. Most prominently, they give the system a way to distinguish between different people who use the system for reasons of identification and security. Each user has a personal account with a separate username and password. As discussed in "File Ownership and Permissions," later in this chapter, users may set permissions on their files, allowing or restricting access to them by other users. Each file on the system is "owned" by a particular user, who may set the permissions for that file. User accounts are used to authenticate access to the system; only those people with accounts may access the machine. Also, accounts are used to identify users, keep system logs, tag electronic mail messages with the name of the sender, and so forth.

Apart from personal accounts, there are users on the system who provide administrative functions. As we've seen, the system administrator uses the *root* account to perform maintenance—but usually not for personal system use. Such accounts are accessed using the *su* command, allowing another account to be accessed after logging in through a personal account.

Other accounts on the system may not involve human interaction at all. These accounts are generally used by system daemons, which must access files on the system through a specific user ID other than *root* or one of the personal user accounts. For example, if you configure your system to receive a newsfeed from another site, the news daemon must store news articles in a spool directory that anyone can access but only one user (the news daemon) can write to. No human being is associated with the *news* account; it is an "imaginary" user set aside for the news daemon only.

One of the permission bits that can be set on executables is the *setuid* bit, which causes the program to be executed with the permissions of the owner of that file. For example, if the news daemon were owned by the user *news*, and the *setuid* bit were set on the executable, it would run as if by the user *news*. *news* would have write access to the news spool directory, and all other users would have read access to the articles stored there. This is a security feature. News programs can give users just the right amount of access to the news spool directory, but no one can just play around there.

As the system administrator, it is your job to create and manage accounts for all users (real and virtual) on your machine. This is actually a painless, hands-off task in most cases, but it's important to understand how it works.

The passwd File

Every account on the system has an entry in the file */etc/passwd*. This file contains entries, one line per user, that specify several attributes for each account, such as the username, real name, and so forth.

Each entry in this file is of the following format:

```
username:password:uid:gid:gecos:homedir:shell
```

The following list explains each field:

username
> A unique character string, identifying the account. For personal accounts, this is the name the user logs in with. On most systems it is limited to eight alphanumeric characters—for example, *larry* or *kirsten*.

password
> An encrypted representation of the user's password. This field is set using the passwd program to set the account's password; it uses a one-way encryption scheme that is difficult (but not impossible) to break. You don't set this by hand; the passwd program does it for you. Note, however, that if the first character of the *password* field is * (an asterisk), the account is "disabled"; the system will not allow logins as this user. See "Creating Accounts," later in this chapter.

uid
> The user ID, a unique integer the system uses to identify the account. The system uses the *uid* field internally when dealing with process and file permissions; it's easier and more compact to deal with integers than byte strings. Therefore, both the user ID and the *username* identify a particular account: the user ID is more important to the system, whereas the *username* is more convenient for humans.

gid

> The group ID, an integer referring to the user's default group, found in the file */etc/group*. See "The Group File," later in this chapter.

gecos

> Miscellaneous information about the user, such as the user's real name, and optional "location information" such as the user's office address or phone number. Such programs as *mail* and *finger* use this information to identify users on the system; we'll talk more about it later. By the way, *gecos* is a historical name dating back to the 1970s; it stands for *General Electric Comprehensive Operating System*. GECOS has nothing to do with Unix, except that this field was originally added to */etc/passwd* to provide compatibility with some of its services.

homedir

> The user's home directory, for the user's personal use; more on this later. When the user first logs in, the shell finds its current working directory in the named home directory.

shell

> The name of the program to run when the user logs in; in most cases, this is the full pathname of a shell, such as */bin/bash* or */bin/tcsh*.

Many of these fields are optional; the only required fields are *username*, *uid*, *gid*, and *homedir*. Most user accounts have all fields filled in, but "imaginary" or administrative accounts may use only a few.

Here are two sample entries you might find in */etc/passwd*:

```
root:ZxPsI9ZjiVd9Y:0:0:The root of all evil:/root:/bin/bash
aclark:BjDf5hBysDsii:104:50:Anna Clark:/home/aclark:/bin/bash
```

The first entry is for the *root* account. First of all, notice that the user ID of *root* is 0. This is what makes *root root*: the system knows that uid 0 is "special" and that it does not have the usual security restrictions. The gid of *root* is also 0, which is mostly a convention. Many of the files on the system are owned by *root* and the *root* group, which have a uid and gid of 0, respectively. More on groups in a minute.

On many systems, *root* uses the home directory */root*, or just */*. This is not usually relevant because you most often use su to access *root* from your own account. Also, it is traditional to use a Bourne-shell variant (in this case */bin/bash*) for the *root* account, although you can use the C shell if you like. (Shells are discussed in Chapter 4.) Be careful, though: Bourne shells and C shells have differing syntax, and switching between them when using *root* can be confusing and lead to mistakes.

The second entry is for an actual human being, username *aclark*. In this case, the *uid* is 104. The *uid* field can technically be any unique integer; on many systems, it's customary to have user accounts numbered 100 and above and administrative accounts in the sub-100 range. The gid is 50, which just means that *aclark* is in whatever group is numbered 50 in the */etc/group* file. Hang on to your hats; groups are covered in "The Group File," later in this chapter.

Home directories are often found in */home*, and named for the username of their owner. This is, for the most part, a useful convention that avoids confusion when finding a particular user's home directory. You can technically place a home directory anywhere, but it must exist for you to be able to log into the system. You should, however, observe the directory layout used on your system.

Note that as the system administrator, it's not usually necessary to modify the */etc/passwd* file directly. Several programs are available that can help you create and maintain user accounts; see "Creating Accounts," later in this chapter. If you really want to edit the raw */etc/passwd* data, consider using a command such as vipw that protects the password file against corruption from simultaneous editing.

Shadow Passwords

To some extent, it is a security risk to let everybody with access to the system view the encrypted passwords in */etc/passwd*. Special crack programs are available that try a huge number of possible passwords and check whether the encrypted version of those passwords is equal to a specified one.

To overcome this potential security risk, *shadow passwords* have been invented. When shadow passwords are used, the password field in */etc/passwd* contains only an x or a *, which can never occur in the encrypted version of a password. Instead, a second file called */etc/shadow* is used. This file contains entries that look very similar to those in */etc/passwd*, but contain the real encrypted password in the password field. */etc/shadow* is readable only by *root*, so normal users do not have access to the encrypted passwords. The other fields in */etc/shadow*, except the username and the password, are present as well, but normally contain bogus values or are empty.

Note that in order to use shadow passwords, you need special versions of the programs that access or modify user information, such as passwd or login. Nowadays, most distributions come with shadow passwords already set up, so this should not be a problem for you. Debian users should use "shadowconfig on" instead to ensure that shadow passwords are enabled on their systems.

There are two tools for converting "normal" user entries to shadow entries and back. pwconv takes the */etc/passwd* file, looks for entries that are not yet present in */etc/shadow*, generates shadow entries for those, and merges them with the entries already present in */etc/shadow*.

pwunconv is rarely used because it gives you less security instead of more. It works like pwconv, but generates traditional */etc/passwd* entries that work without */etc/shadow* counterparts.

Modern Linux systems also provide something called *password aging*. This is sort of an expiry date for a password; if it approaches, a warning is issued, a configurable number of days before the password expires, and the user is asked to change his password. If he fails to do so, his account will be locked after a while. It is also possible to set a minimum number of days before a changed or created password can be changed again.

All these settings are configured with the passwd command. The *-n* option sets the minimum number of days between changes, *-x* the maximum number of days between changes, *-w* the number of days a warning is issued before a password expires, and *-i* the number of days of inactivity between the expiry of a password and the time the account is locked.

Most distributions provide graphical tools to change these settings, often hidden on an *Advanced Settings* page or similar.

PAM and Other Authentication Methods

You might think that having two means of user authentication, */etc/passwd* and */etc/shadow*, is already enough choice, but you are wrong. There are a number of other authentication methods with strange names, such as Kerberos authentication (so named after the dog from Greek mythology that guards the entrance to Hell). Although we think that shadow passwords provide enough security for almost all cases, it all depends on how much security you really need and how paranoid you want to be.

The problem with all those authentication methods is that you cannot simply switch from one to another because you always need a set of programs, such as login and passwd, that go with those tools. To overcome this problem, the *Pluggable Authentication Methods (PAM)* system has been invented. Once you have a PAM-enabled set of tools, you can change the authentication method of your system by reconfiguring PAM. The tools will automatically get the code necessary to perform the required authentication procedures from dynamically loaded shared libraries.

Setting up and using PAM is beyond the scope of this book, but you can get all the information you need from *http://www.kernel.org/pub/linux/libs/pam/*. Most modern distributions will set up PAM for you as well.

The Group File

User groups are a convenient way to logically organize sets of user accounts and allow users to share files within their group or groups. Each file on the system has both a user and a group owner associated with it. Using *ls -l*, you can see the owner and group for a particular file, as in the following example:

```
rutabaga$ ls -l boiler.tex
-rwxrw-r--   1 mdw        megabozo    10316 Oct  6 20:19 boiler.tex
rutabaga$
```

This file is owned by the user *mdw* and belongs to the *megabozo* group. We can see from the file permissions that *mdw* has read, write, and execute access to the file; that anyone in the *megabozo* group has read and write access; and that all other users have read access only.

This doesn't mean that *mdw* is in the *megabozo* group; it simply means the file may be accessed, as shown by the permission bits, by anyone in the *megabozo* group (which may or may not include *mdw*).

This way, files can be shared among groups of users, and permissions can be specified separately for the owner of the file, the group to which the file belongs, and everyone else. An introduction to permissions appears in "File Ownership and Permissions," later in this chapter.

Every user is assigned to at least one group, which you specify in the *gid* field of the */etc/passwd* file. However, a user can be a member of multiple groups. The file */etc/group* contains a one-line entry for each group on the system, very similar in nature to */etc/passwd*. The format of this file is

```
groupname:password:gid:members
```

Here, *groupname* is a character string identifying the group; it is the group name printed when using commands such as *ls -l*.

password is an optional encrypted password associated with the group, which allows users not in this group to access the group with the `newgrp` command. Read on for information on this.

gid is the group ID used by the system to refer to the group; it is the number used in the *gid* field of */etc/passwd* to specify a user's default group.

members is a comma-separated list of usernames (with no whitespace in between), identifying those users who are members of this group but who have a different *gid* in */etc/passwd*. That is, this list need not contain those users who have this group set as their "default" group in */etc/passwd*; it's only for users who are additional members of the group.

For example, */etc/group* might contain the following entries:

```
root:*:0:
bin:*:1:root,daemon
users:*:50:
bozo:*:51:linus,mdw
megabozo:*:52:kibo
```

The first entries, for the groups *root* and *bin*, are administrative groups, similar in nature to the "imaginary" accounts used on the system. Many files are owned by groups, such as *root* and *bin*. The other groups are for user accounts. Like user IDs, the group ID values for user groups are often placed in ranges above 50 or 100.

The *password* field of the *group* file is something of a curiosity. It isn't used much, but in conjunction with the *newgrp* program it allows users who aren't members of a particular group to assume that group ID if they have the password. For example, using the command

```
rutabaga$ newgrp bozo
Password: password for group bozo
rutabaga$
```

starts a new shell with the group ID of bozo. If the *password* field is blank, or the first character is an asterisk, you receive a permission denied error if you attempt to *newgrp* to that group.

However, the *password* field of the *group* file is seldom used and is really not necessary. (In fact, most systems don't provide tools to set the password for a group; you could use passwd to set the password for a dummy user with the same name as the group in */etc/passwd* and copy the encrypted *password* field to */etc/group*.) Instead, you can make a user a member of multiple groups simply by including the username in the *members* field for each additional group. In the previous example, the users *linus* and *mdw* are members of the *bozo* group, as well as whatever group they are assigned to in the */etc/passwd* file. If we wanted to add *linus* to the *megabozo* group as well, we'd change the last line of the previous example to:

```
megabozo:*:52:kibo,linus
```

The command groups tells you which groups you belong to:

```
rutabaga$ groups
users bozo
```

Giving a list of usernames to groups lists the groups to which each user in the list belongs.

When you log in, you are automatically assigned to the group ID given in */etc/passwd*, as well as any additional groups for which you're listed in */etc/group*. This means you have "group access" to any files on the system with a group ID contained in your list of groups. In this case, the group permission bits (set with *chmod g+...*) for those files apply to you (unless you're the owner, in which case the owner permission bits apply instead).

Now that you know the ins and outs of groups, how should you assign groups on your system? This is really a matter of style and depends on how your system will be used. For systems with just one or a handful of users, it's easiest to have a single group (called, say, *users*) to which all personal user accounts belong. Note that all the system groups—those groups contained within */etc/group* when the system is first installed—should probably be left alone. Various daemons and programs may depend upon them.

If you have a number of users on your machine, there are several ways to organize groups. For example, an educational institution might have separate groups for students, faculty, and staff. A software company might have different groups for each design team. On other systems, each user is placed into a separate group, named identically to the username. This keeps each pigeon in its own hole, so to speak. Files can also be assigned to special groups; many users create new groups and place files into them for sharing the files between users. However, this requires adding users to the additional groups, a task that usually requires the system administrator to intervene (by editing */etc/group* or using utilities, such as gpasswd on Debian systems). It's really up to you.

Another situation in which groups are often used is special hardware groups. Let's say that you have a scanner that is accessed via */dev/scanner*. If you do not want to give everybody access to the scanner, you could create a special group called *scanner*, assign */dev/scanner* to this group, make this special file readable for the group and nonreadable for everybody else, and add everybody who is allowed to use the scanner to the *scanner* group in the */etc/groups* file.

Creating Accounts

Creating a user account requires several steps: adding an entry to */etc/passwd*, creating the user's home directory, and setting up the user's default configuration files (such as *.bashrc*) in her home directory. Luckily, you don't have to perform these steps manually; nearly all Linux systems include a program called *adduser* to do this for you. Some Linux systems, such as Red Hat or SUSE, use a different set of tools for account creation and deletion. If the sequence of inputs in this section does not work for you, check the documentation for your distribution. (Red Hat allows accounts to be managed through the *control-panel* tool, and SUSE does it via *yast2*; Debian includes an *adduser* script (interactive in some versions and noninteractive on others) that automatically sets up users based on the configuration file */etc/adduser.conf*). In addition, there are graphical user management programs, such as *KUser* from KDE and the GNOME System Tools.

Running adduser as *root* should work as follows. Just enter the requested information at the prompts; many of the prompts have reasonable defaults you can select by pressing Enter:

```
Adding a new user. The username should not exceed 8 characters
in length, or you many run into problems later.

Enter login name for new account (^C to quit): norbert

Editing information for new user [norbert]
```

```
Full Name: Norbert Ebersol
GID [100]: 117

Checking for an available UID after 500
First unused uid is 501

UID [501]: (enter)
Home Directory [/home/norbert]: (enter)
Shell [/bin/bash]: (enter)
Password [norbert]: (norbert's password)

Information for new user [norbert]:
Home directory: [/home/norbert] Shell: [/bin/bash]
Password: [(norbert's password)] uid: [501] gid: [117]

Is this correct? [y/N]: y

Adding login [norbert] and making directory [/home/norbert]
Adding the files from the /etc/skel directory:
././.emacs -> /home/norbert/././.emacs
././.kermrc -> /home/norbert/././.kermrc
././.bashrc -> /home/norbert/././.bashrc
... more files ...
```

There should be no surprises here; just enter the information as requested or choose the defaults. Note that adduser uses 100 as the default group ID, and looks for the first unused user ID after 500 (500 is used as the minimum on SUSE and Red Hat; Debian uses 1000). It should be safe to go along with these defaults; in the previous example, we used a group ID of 117 because we designated that to be the group for the user, as well as the default user ID of 501.

After the account is created, the files from *etc/skel* are copied to the user's home directory. *etc/skel* contains the "skeleton" files for a new account; they are the default configuration files (such as *.emacs* and *.bashrc*) for the new user. Feel free to place other files here if your new user accounts should have them.

After this is done, the new account is ready to roll; *norbert* can log in, using the password set using *adduser*. To guarantee security, new users should always change their own passwords, using *passwd*, immediately after logging in for the first time.

root can set the password for any user on the system. For example, the command:

```
passwd norbert
```

prompts for a new password for *norbert*, without asking for the original password. Note, however, that you must know the *root* password in order to change it. If you forget the *root* password entirely, you can boot Linux from an emergency disk (as discussed previously), and clear the *password* field of the *etc/passwd* entry for *root*. See "What to Do in an Emergency" in Chapter 27.

Some Linux systems provide the command-line-driven *useradd* instead of *adduser*. (And, to make things even more confusing, on some other systems, the two commands

---

are synonyms.) This program requires you to provide all relevant information as command-line arguments. If you can't locate *adduser* and are stuck with *useradd*, see the manual pages, which should help you out.

Deleting and Disabling Accounts

Deleting a user account is much easier than creating one; this is the well-known concept of entropy at work. To delete an account, you must remove the user's entry in */etc/passwd*, remove any references to the user in */etc/group*, and delete the user's home directory, as well as any additional files created or owned by the user. For example, if the user has an incoming mailbox in */var/spool/mail*, it must be deleted as well.

The command *userdel* (the yin to *useradd*'s yang) deletes an account and the account's home directory. For example:

    userdel -r norbert

will remove the recently created account for *norbert*. The *-r* option forces the home directory to be removed as well. Other files associated with the user—for example, the incoming mailbox, *crontab* files, and so forth—must be removed by hand. Usually these are quite insignificant and can be left around. By the end of this chapter, you should know where these files are, if they exist. A simple way to find the files associated with a particular user is through the following command:

    find / -user username -ls

This will give an *ls -l* listing of each file owned by *username*. Of course, to use this, the account associated with *username* must still have an entry in */etc/passwd*. If you deleted the account, use the *-uid num* argument instead, where *num* is the numeric user ID of the dearly departed user.

Temporarily (or not so temporarily) disabling a user account, for whatever reason, is even simpler. You can either remove the user's entry in */etc/passwd* (leaving the home directory and other files intact) or add an asterisk to the first character of the *password* field of the */etc/passwd* entry, as follows:

    aclark:*BjDf5hBysDsii:104:50:Anna Clark:/home/aclark:/bin/bash

This will disallow logins to the account in question. Note that if you use shadow passwords, you need to do the same thing in */etc/shadow*. But why would you want to do that? Well, imagine that an employee is leaving the company, and you want to prevent him from logging in any more, but you still want to keep his files around in case there is anything his colleagues still need. In this case, it is convenient to be able to disable the account without actually deleting the home directory (and other related files such as the mail spool).

Modifying User Accounts

Modifying attributes of user accounts and groups is usually a simple matter of editing */etc/passwd* and */etc/group*. Many systems provide commands such as usermod and groupmod to do just this; it's often easier to edit the files by hand.

To change a user's password, use the passwd command, which will prompt for a password, encrypt it, and store the encrypted password in the */etc/passwd* file.

If you need to change the user ID of an existing account, you can do this by editing the uid field of */etc/passwd* directly. However, you should also chown the files owned by the user to that of the new user ID. For example:

```
chown -R aclark /home/aclark
```

will set the ownership for all files in the home directory used by *aclark* back to *aclark*, if you changed the uid for this account. If *ls -l* prints a numeric user ID, instead of a username, this means there is no username associated with the uid owning the files. Use chown to fix this.

File Ownership and Permissions

Ownership and permissions are central to security. It's important to get them right, even when you're the only user, because odd things can happen if you don't. For the files that users create and use daily, these things usually work without much thought (although it's still useful to know the concepts). For system administration, matters are not so easy. Assign the wrong ownership or permission, and you might get into a frustrating bind such as being unable to read your mail. In general, the message:

```
Permission denied
```

means that someone has assigned an ownership or permission that restricts access more than you want.

What Permissions Mean

Permissions refer to the ways in which someone can use a file. There are three such permissions under Unix:

- *Read* permission means you can look at the file's contents.
- *Write* permission means you can change or delete the file.
- *Execute* permission means you can run the file as a program.

When each file is created, the system assigns some default permissions that work most of the time. For instance, it gives you both read and write permission, but most of the world has only read permission. If you have a reason to be paranoid, you can set things up so that other people have no permissions at all.

Additionally, most utilities know how to assign permissions. For instance, when the compiler creates an executable program, it automatically assigns execute permission.

There are times when defaults don't work, though. For instance, if you create a shell script or Perl program, you'll have to assign execute permission yourself so that you can run it. We show how to do that later in this section, after we get through the basic concepts.

Permissions have different meanings for a directory:

- Read permission means you can list the contents of that directory.
- Write permission means you can add or remove files in that directory.
- Execute permission means you can list information about the files in that directory.

Don't worry about the difference between read and execute permission for directories; basically, they go together. Assign both or neither.

Note that if you allow people to add files to a directory, you are also letting them remove files. The two privileges go together when you assign write permission. However, there is a way you can let users share a directory and keep them from deleting each other's files. See "Upgrading Software Not Provided in Packages" in Chapter 12.

There are more files on Unix systems than the plain files and directories we've talked about so far. These are special files (devices), sockets, symbolic links, and so forth—each type observing its own rules regarding permissions. But you don't need to know the details on each type.

Owners and Groups

Now, who gets these permissions? To allow people to work together, Unix has three levels of permission: owner, group, and other. The "other" level covers everybody who has access to the system and who isn't the owner or a member of the group.

The idea behind having groups is to give a set of users, such as a team of programmers, access to a file. For instance, a programmer creating source code may reserve write permission to herself, but allow members of her group to have read access through a group permission. As for "other," it might have no permission at all so that people outside the team can't snoop around. (You think your source code is *that* good?)

Each file has an owner and a group. The owner is generally the user who created the file. Each user also belongs to a default group, and that group is assigned to every file the user creates. You can create many groups, though, and assign each user to multiple groups. By changing the group assigned to a file, you can give access to any collection of people you want. We discussed groups earlier in "The Group File."

Now we have all the elements of our security system: three permissions (read, write, execute) and three levels (user, group, other). Let's look at some typical files and see what permissions are assigned.

Figure 11-1 shows a typical executable program. We generated this output by executing *ls* with the *-l* option.

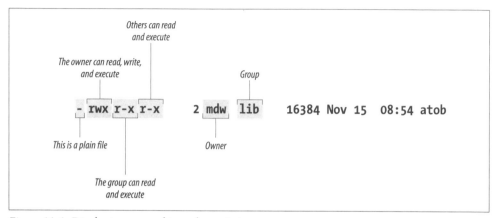

Figure 11-1. Displaying ownership and permissions

Two useful facts stand right out: the owner of the file is an author of this book and your faithful guide, *mdw*, and the group is *lib* (perhaps a group created for programmers working on libraries). But the key information about permissions is encrypted in the set of letters on the left side of the display.

The first character is a hyphen, indicating a plain file. The next three bits apply to the owner; as we would expect, *mdw* has all three permissions. The next three bits apply to members of the group: they can read the file (not too useful for a binary file) and execute it, but they can't write to it because the field that should contain a w contains a hyphen instead. And the last three bits apply to "other"; they have the same permissions in this case as the group.

Here is another example. If you asked for a long listing of a C source file, it would look something like this:

```
$ ls -l
-rw-rw-r--    1 kalle    kalle      12577 Apr 30 13:13 simc.c
```

The listing shows that the owner has read and write (rw) privileges, and so does the group. Everyone else on the system has only read privileges.

Now suppose we compile the file to create an executable program. The file *simc* is created by the *gcc* compiler:

```
  $ gcc -osimc simc.c
  $ ls -l
  total 36
```

```
-rwxrwxr-x    1 kalle    kalle      19365 Apr 30 13:14 simc
-rw-rw-r--    1 kalle    kalle      12577 Apr 30 13:13 simc.c
```

In addition to the read and write bits, *gcc* has set the executable (x) bit for owner, group, and other on the executable file. This is the appropriate thing to do so that the file can be run:

```
$ ./simc
(output here)
```

One more example—a typical directory:

```
drwxr-xr-x    2 mdw      lib          512 Jul 17 18:23 perl
```

The leftmost bit is now a d to show that this is a directory. The executable bits are back because you want people to see the contents of the directory.

Files can be in some obscure states that aren't covered here; see the *ls* manual page for gory details. But now it's time to see how you can change ownership and permissions.

Changing the Owner, Group, and Permissions

As we said, most of the time you can get by with the default security the system gives you. But there are always exceptions, particularly for system administrators. To take a simple example, suppose you are creating a directory under */home* for a new user. You have to create everything as *root*, but when you're done you have to change the ownership to the user; otherwise, that user won't be able to use the files! (Fortunately, if you use the adduser command discussed earlier in "Creating Accounts," it takes care of ownership for you.)

Similarly, certain utilities and programs such as the MySQL database and News have their own users. No one ever logs in as *mysql* or *News*, but those users and groups must exist so that the utilities can do their job in a secure manner. In general, the last step when installing software is usually to change the owner, group, and permissions as the documentation tells you to do.

The *chown* command changes the owner of a file, and the *chgrp* command changes the group. On Linux, only *root* can use *chown* for changing ownership of a file, but any user can change the group to another group to which he belongs.

So after installing some software named *sampsoft*, you might change both the owner and the group to *bin* by executing:

```
# chown bin sampsoft
# chgrp bin sampsoft
```

You could also do this in one step by using the dot notation:

```
# chown bin.bin sampsoft
```

The syntax for changing permissions is more complicated. The permissions can also be called the file's "mode," and the command that changes permissions is *chmod*. Let's start our exploration of this command through a simple example. Say you've written a neat program in Perl or Tcl named *header*, and you want to be able to execute it. You would type the following command:

```
$ chmod +x header
```

The plus sign means "add a permission," and the x indicates which permission to add.

If you want to remove execute permission, use a minus sign in place of a plus:

```
$ chmod -x header
```

This command assigns permissions to all levels: user, group, and other. Let's say that you are secretly into software hoarding and don't want anybody to use the command but yourself. No, that's too cruel—let's say instead that you think the script is buggy and want to protect other people from hurting themselves until you've exercised it. You can assign execute permission just to yourself through the command:

```
$ chmod u+x header
```

Whatever goes before the plus sign is the level of permission, and whatever goes after is the type of permission. User permission (for yourself) is *u*, group permission is g, and other is o. So to assign permission to both yourself and the file's group, enter:

```
$ chmod ug+x header
```

You can also assign multiple types of permissions:

```
$ chmod ug+rwx header
```

You can learn a few more shortcuts from the chmod manual page in order to impress someone looking over your shoulder, but they don't offer any functionality besides what we've shown you.

As arcane as the syntax of the mode argument may seem, there's another syntax that is even more complicated. We have to describe it, though, for several reasons. First of all, there are several situations that cannot be covered by the syntax, called *symbolic mode*, that we've just shown. Second, people often use the other syntax, called *absolute mode*, in their documentation. Third, there are times you may actually find the absolute mode more convenient.

To understand absolute mode, you have to think in terms of bits and octal notation. Don't worry, it's not too hard. A typical mode contains three characters, corresponding to the three levels of permission (user, group, and other). These levels are illustrated in Figure 11-2. Within each level, there are three bits corresponding to read, write, and execute permission.

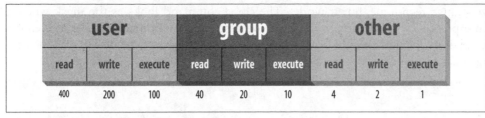

user			group			other		
read	write	execute	read	write	execute	read	write	execute
400	200	100	40	20	10	4	2	1

Figure 11-2. Bits in absolute mode

Let's say you want to give yourself read permission and no permission to anybody else. You want to specify just the bit represented by the number 400. So the chmod command would be:

```
$ chmod 400 header
```

To give read permission to everybody, choose the correct bit from each level: 400 for yourself, 40 for your group, and 4 for other. The full command is:

```
$ chmod 444 header
```

This is like using a mode *+r*, except that it simultaneously removes any write or execute permission. (To be precise, it's just like a mode of *=r*, which we didn't mention earlier. The equal sign means "assign these rights and no others.")

To give read and execute permission to everybody, you have to add up the read and execute bits: 400 plus 100 is 500, for instance. So the corresponding command is:

```
$ chmod 555 header
```

which is the same as *=rx*. To give someone full access, you would specify that digit as a 7: the sum of 4, 2, and 1.

One final trick: how to set the default mode that is assigned to each file you create (with a text editor, the > redirection operator, and so on). You do so by executing a umask command, or putting one in your shell's startup file. This file could be called *.bashrc*, *.cshrc*, or something else depending on the shell you use (we discussed startup files in Chapter 4).

The umask command takes an argument like the absolute mode in chmod, but the meaning of the bits is inverted. You have to determine the access you want to grant for user, group, and other, and subtract each digit from 7. That gives you a three-digit mask.

For instance, say you want yourself to have all permissions (7), your group to have read and execute permissions (5), and others to have no permissions (0). Subtract each bit from 7 and you get 0 for yourself, 2 for your group, and 7 for other. So the command to put in your startup file is

```
umask 027
```

A strange technique, but it works. The chmod command looks at the mask when it interprets your mode; for instance, if you assign execute mode to a file at creation time, it will assign execute permission for you and your group, but will exclude others because the mask doesn't permit them to have any access.

## CHAPTER 12

Installing, Updating, and Compiling Programs

In this chapter, we show you how to upgrade software on your system. Although most Linux distributions provide some automated means to install, remove, and upgrade specific software packages on your system, it is sometimes necessary to install software by hand.

Non-expert users will find it easiest to install and upgrade software by using a *package* system, which most distributions provide. If you don't use a package system, installations and upgrades are more complicated than with most commercial operating systems. Even though precompiled binaries are available, you may have to uncompress them and unpack them from an archive file. You may also have to create symbolic links or set environment variables so that the binaries know where to look for the resources they use. In other cases, you'll need to compile the software yourself from sources.

Upgrading Software

Linux is a fast-moving target. Because of the cooperative nature of the project, new software is always becoming available, and programs are constantly being updated with newer versions.

With this constant development, how can you possibly hope to stay on top of the most recent versions of your system software? The short answer is, you can't. In this section, we talk about why and when to upgrade and show you how to upgrade several important parts of the system.

When should you upgrade? In general, you should consider upgrading a portion of your system only when you have a demonstrated *need* to upgrade. For example, if you hear of a new release of some application that fixes important bugs (that is, those bugs that actually affect your personal use of the application), you might want to consider upgrading that application. If the new version of the program provides new features you might find useful, or has a performance boost over your present version, it's also a good idea to upgrade. When your machine is somehow connected to the Internet, another good reason for upgrading would be plugging a security hole that has been recently reported. However, upgrading just for the sake of having the newest version of a particular program is probably silly. In some, luckily rare, cases, newer versions are even regressions, that is, they introduce bugs or performance hits compared with the previous version.

Upgrading can sometimes be a painful thing to do. For example, you might want to upgrade a program that requires the newest versions of the compiler, libraries, and other software in order to run. Upgrading this program will also require you to upgrade several other parts of the system, which can be a time-consuming process. On the other hand, this can be seen as an argument for keeping your software up to date; if your compiler and libraries are current, upgrading the program in question won't be a problem.

How can you find out about new versions of Linux software? The best way is to watch the Usenet newsgroup *comp.os.linux.announce* (see the section "Usenet Newsgroups" in Chapter 1), where announcements of new software releases and other important information are posted. If you have Internet access, you can then download the software via FTP and install it on your system. Another good source to learn about new Linux software is the web site *http://www.freshmeat.net*. Many individual packages have mailing lists that update you about new versions of just that particular package.

If you don't have access to Usenet or the Internet, the best way to keep in touch with recent developments is to pay for a CD-ROM subscription. Here you receive an updated copy of the various Linux FTP sites, on CD-ROM, every couple of months. This service is available from a number of Linux vendors. It's a good thing to have, even if you have Internet access.

This brings us to another issue: what's the best upgrade method? Some people feel it's easier to completely upgrade the system by reinstalling everything from scratch whenever a new version of their favorite distribution is released. This way you don't have to worry about various versions of the software working together. For those without Internet access, this may indeed be the easiest method; if you receive a new CD-ROM only once every two months, a great deal of your software may be out of date.

It's our opinion, however, that reinstallation is not a good upgrade plan at all. Most of the current Linux distributions are not meant to be upgraded in this way, and a complete reinstallation may be complex or time-consuming. Also, if you plan to upgrade in this manner, you generally lose all your modifications and customizations to the system, and you'll have to make backups of your user's home directories and any other important files that would be deleted (or at least endangered) during a reinstallation. Finally, adapting a drastic approach to upgrading means that, in practice, you probably will wait longer than you should to upgrade software when critical security flaws are announced. In actuality, not much changes from release to release, so a complete reinstallation is usually unnecessary and can be avoided with a little upgrading know-how.

General Upgrade Procedure

As discussed in the previous section, it's usually easier and best to upgrade only those applications you need to upgrade. For example, if you never use Emacs on your system, why bother keeping up-to-date with the most recent version of Emacs? For that matter, you may not need to stay completely current with oft-used applications. If something works for you, there's little need to upgrade.

Modern Linux systems provide various ways of upgrading software, some manual (which ultimately are the most flexible, but also the most difficult), others quite automated. In this section, we look at three different techniques: using the RPM package system, using the Debian package system, and doing things manually.

We'd like to stress here that using packages and package systems *is* convenient, and even if you are a power user, you might want to use these techniques because they save you time for other, more fun stuff. Here is a short summary of the advantages:

- You have everything that belongs to a software package in one downloadable file.
- You can remove a software package entirely, without endangering other packages.
- Package systems keep a dependency database and can thus automatically track dependencies. For example, they can tell you if you need to install a newer version of a library in order to run a certain application you are about to install (and will refuse to remove a library package as long as packages are installed that use the libraries this package provides).

Of course, package systems also have a few disadvantages, some of which we discuss when we talk about RPM and the Debian package system. A generic problem is that once you start using a package system (which is a requirement if you use the distributions' automated installation interfaces) you ought to really install everything through packages. Otherwise, you can't keep track of the dependencies. For the same reason, mixing different package systems is a bad idea.

Every day some program you use is likely to be updated—all too often because of an important security flaw, unfortunately. Some grizzled system administrators insist on checking security reports regularly and upgrading every package manually, using the means shown in this section, so they can control every aspect of their systems and make sure no change breaks existing functionality. That's a noble cause to dedicate yourself to, and one that's feasible on systems with dedicated purposes (such as mail servers or routers) and a limited set of software.

For more general-purpose systems, though, keeping everything you use regularly up-to-date becomes a major part-time job. For this reason, all major distributions provide automated update services. We explore a few of them later in this chapter, but you'll want to understand general package management first. It shows what the update services are doing, and is important when you want to install new software or do something else that isn't offered by those services.

Using RPM

RPM, which originally expanded to Red Hat Package Manager but now just stands as a name on its own, is a tool that automates the installation of software binaries and remembers what files are needed so that you can be assured the software will run properly. Despite the name, RPM is not Red Hat-specific, but is used in many other distributions nowadays, including SUSE. Using RPM makes installing and uninstalling software a lot easier.

The basic idea of RPM is that you have a database of packages and the files that belong to a package. When you install a new package, the information about this package is recorded in the database. Then, when you want to uninstall the package for every file of the package, RPM checks whether other installed packages are using this file too. If this is the case, the file in question is not deleted.

In addition, RPM tracks dependencies. Each package can be dependent on one or more other packages. When you install a package, RPM checks whether the packages the new package is dependent on are already installed. If not, it informs you about the dependency and refuses to install the package.

The dependencies are also used for removing packages: when you want to uninstall a package that other packages are still dependent upon, RPM tells you about this, too, and refuses to execute the task.

The increased convenience of using RPM packages comes at a price, however: first, as a developer, it is significantly more difficult to make an RPM package than to simply pack everything in a *tar* archive. And second, it is not possible to retrieve just one file from an RPM package; you have to install everything or nothing.

If you already have an RPM system, installing RPM packages is very easy. Let's say that you have an RPM package called *SuperFrob-4.i386.rpm* (RPM packages always have the extension *.rpm*; the *i386* indicates that this is a binary package compiled for Intel x86 machines). You could then install it with:

```
tigger # rpm -i SuperFrob-4.i386.rpm
```

Instead of -i, you can also use the long-named version of this option; choose whatever you like better:

```
tigger # rpm --install SuperFrob-4.i386.rpm
```

If everything goes well, there will be no output. If you want RPM to be more verbose, you can try:

```
tigger # rpm -ivh SuperFrob-4.i386.rpm
```

This prints the name of the package plus a number of hash marks so that you can see how the installation progresses.

If the package you want to install needs another package that is not yet installed, you will get something like the following:

```
tigger # rpm -i SuperFrob-4.i386.rpm
failed dependencies:
        frobnik-2 is needed by SuperFrob-4
```

If you see this, you have to hunt for the package *frobnik-2* and install this first. Of course, this package can itself be dependent on other packages.

If you want to update a package that is already installed, use the *-U* or *--update* option (which is just the *-i* option combined with a few more implied options):

```
tigger # rpm -U SuperFrob-5.i386.rpm
```

Uninstalling a package is done with the *-e* or *--erase* option. In this case, you do not specify the package file (you might not have that around any longer), but rather, the package name and version number:

```
tigger # rpm -e SuperFrob-5
```

Besides the options described so far that alter the state of your system, the *-q* option provides various kinds of information about everything that is recorded in the RPM database as well as package files. Here are some useful things you can do with *-q*:

- Find out the version number of an installed package:

```
tigger# rpm -q SuperFrob
SuperFrob-5
```

- Get a list of all installed packages:

```
tigger# rpm -qa
SuperFrob-5
OmniFrob-3
...
glibc-2.3.4-23.4
```

- Find out to which package a file belongs:

```
tigger# rpm -qf /usr/bin/dothefrob
SuperFrob-5
tigger# rpm -qf /home/kalle/.xinitrc
file /home/kalle/.xinitrc is not owned by any package
```

- Display information about the specified package:

```
tigger# rpm -qi rpm
Name       : rpm                    Relocations: (not relocatable)
Version    : 4.1.1                       Vendor: SUSE LINUX Products GmbH,
Nuernberg, Germany
```

```
Release      : 208.2                    Build Date: Sat 11 Jun 2005 01:53:04
AM CEST
Install date: Tue 28 Jun 2005 10:02:18 AM CEST      Build Host: purcell.suse.de
Group        : System/Packages           Source RPM: rpm-4.1.1-208.2.src.rpm
Size         : 5970541                           License: GPL
Signature    : DSA/SHA1, Sat 11 Jun 2005 01:58:41 AM CEST, Key ID a84edae89c800aca
Packager     : http://www.suse.de/feedback
Summary      : The RPM Package Manager
Description :
RPM Package Manager is the main tool for managing the software packages
of the SuSE Linux distribution.
...
Distribution: SuSE Linux 9.3 (i586)
```

- Show the files that will be installed for the specified package file:

```
tigger# rpm -qpl SuperFrob-5.i386.rpm
/usr/bin/dothefrob
/usr/bin/frobhelper
/usr/doc/SuperFrob/Installation
/usr/doc/SuperFrob/README
/usr/man/man1/dothefrob.1
```

What we've just finished showing are the basic modes of operation, which are supplemented by a large number of additional options. You can check those in the manual page for the *rpm*(8) command.

If you are faced with an RPM package that you want to install, but have a system such as Slackware or Debian that is not based on RPM, things get a little bit more difficult.

You can either use the fairly self-explanatory command *alien* that can convert between various package formats and comes with most distributions, or you can build the RPM database from scratch.

The first thing you have to do in this latter case is to get the *rpm* program itself. You can download it from *http://www.rpm.org*. Follow the installation instructions to build and install it; if you have the C compiler *gcc* installed on your system, there should be no problems with this. It should be mentioned that some newer versions of *rpm* have experienced stability problems, so if you do not use the *rpm* version that your distribution provides, you should be a bit careful and look out for unexpected results. Version 4.1.1 seems to be reasonably stable, though.

The next task is to initialize the RPM database. Distributions that come with RPM do the initialization automatically, but on other systems you will have to issue the following command:

```
tigger # rpm --initdb
```

This command creates several files in the directory */var/lib/rpm*. The directory */var/lib* should already exist; if it doesn't, create it with the *mkdir* command first.

Now you can install RPM packages the normal way, but because you have not installed the basic parts of the system, such as the C library with RPM, you will get errors like the following:

```
tigger # rpm -i SuperFrob-4.i386.rpm
failed dependencies:
        libm.so.5 is needed by SuperFrob-4
        libdl.so.1 is needed by SuperFrob-4
        libc.so.5 is needed by SuperFrob-4
```

because those files are not recorded in the RPM database. Of course, you really do have those files on your system; otherwise most programs wouldn't run. For RPM to work, you must tell it not to care about any dependencies. You do this by specifying the command-line option *--nodeps*:

```
tigger # rpm -i --nodeps SuperFrob-4.i386.rpm
```

Now, RPM will install the package without complaining. Of course, it will run only if the libraries it needs are installed. The mere fact that you use *--nodeps* doesn't save you when the "dependent" library or software is not installed on your system.

With this information, you should be able to administer your RPM-based system. If you want to know more, read the manual page for the *rpm* command, or check out *http://www.rpm.org*.

Some commercial companies sell automated upgrade services based on RPM. As a subscriber to these services, you can have your system upgraded automatically; the service finds out which new packages are available and installs them for you. If you use the SUSE distribution, SUSE provides such a service (called "YOU") for free. Even the Debian distribution (whose package system is described in the next section) has an automated upgrade system (described there). However, some security experts consider these automated upgrades a security risk.

Using dpkg and apt

After *rpm*, the most popular package manager for Linux distributions is *dpkg*, which is used to manage *.deb* archives. As the name implies, the *.deb* format is tied to the Debian distribution, so it is also used by distributions based on Debian, such as Ubuntu and Kubuntu, Libranet, and Xandros. Like the RPM format, the *.deb* format keeps track of dependencies and files to help ensure your system is consistent.

The technical differences between the two formats are actually fairly small; although the RPM and *.deb* formats are incompatible (for example, you can't install a Debian package directly on Red Hat), you can use *alien* to translate *.deb* packages for other distributions (and vice versa). The main difference between the formats is that *.deb* packages are built using tools that help make sure they have a consistent layout and generally conform to policies (most notably, the Debian Policy Manual, provided in the *debian-policy* package) that help developers create high-quality packages.

While *dpkg* is the low-level interface to the Debian package manager, most functions are usually handled through either the *apt* suite of programs or frontends such as *dselect*, *aptitude*, *gnome-apt*, *synaptic*, or *KPackage*.

Installing *.deb* packages on a Debian system is quite easy. For example, if you have a package named *superfrob_4-1_i386.deb*, you can install it with:

```
tiger # dpkg -i superfrob_4-1_i386.deb
Selecting previously deselected package superfrob.
(Reading database ... 159540 files and directories currently installed.)
Unpacking superfrob (from superfrob_4-1_i386.deb) ...
Setting up superfrob (4-1) ...
```

If the *superfrob* package is missing a dependency, *dpkg* will issue a warning message:

```
tiger # dpkg -i superfrob_4-1_i386.deb
Selecting previously deselected package superfrob.
(Reading database ... 159540 files and directories currently installed.)
Unpacking superfrob (from superfrob_4-1_i386.deb) ...
dpkg: dependency problems prevent configuration of superfrob:
 superfrob depends on frobnik (>> 2); however:
  Package frobnik is not installed.
dpkg: error processing superfrob (--install):
 dependency problems - leaving unconfigured
Errors were encountered while processing:
 superfrob
```

The output indicates that you would need *frobnik* Version 2 or later for the package to install completely. (The files in the package are installed, but they may not work until *frobnik* is installed too.)

Unlike RPM, *dpkg* doesn't make a distinction between installing a new package and upgrading an existing one; the *-i* (or *--install*) option is used in both cases. For example, if we want to upgrade *superfrob* using a newly downloaded package *superfrob_5-1_i386.deb*, we'd simply type:

```
tiger # dpkg -i superfrob_5-1_i386.deb
(Reading database ... 159546 files and directories currently installed.)
Preparing to replace superfrob 4-1 (using superfrob_5-1_i386.deb) ...
Unpacking replacement superfrob ...
Setting up superfrob (5-1) ...
```

To uninstall a package, you can use either the *-r* (*--remove*) or *-P* (*--purge*) options. The *--remove* option will remove most of the package, but will retain any configuration files, while *--purge* will remove the system-wide configuration files as well. For example, to completely remove *superfrob*:

```
tiger # dpkg -P superfrob
(Reading database ... 159547 files and directories currently installed.)
Removing superfrob ...
```

dpkg can also be used to find out what packages are installed on a system, using the *-l* (*--list*) option:

```
tigger $ dpkg -l
Desired=Unknown/Install/Remove/Purge/Hold
| Status=Not/Installed/Config-files/Unpacked/Failed-config/Half-installed
|/ Err?=(none)/Hold/Reinst-required/X=both-problems (Status,Err: uppercase=bad)
||/ Name            Version        Description
+++-= == == == == == == =-= == == == == == == =-= == == == == == == == == == == == == == == == == == == ==
== == =
ii  a2ps            4.13b-15       GNU a2ps 'Anything to PostScript' converter
ii  aalib1          1.4p5-10       ascii art library
ii  abcde           2.0.3-1        A Better CD Encoder
...
ii  zlib1g-dev      1.1.3-19       compression library - development
```

The first three lines of the output are designed to tell you what the first three columns before each package's name mean. Most of the time, they should read *ii*, which means the package is correctly installed. If they don't, you should type *dpkg --audit* for an explanation of what is wrong with your system and how to fix it.

You can also use the *-l* option with a package name or glob-style pattern; for example, you could find out what version of *superfrob* is installed using the following:

```
tigger $ dpkg -l superfrob
Desired=Unknown/Install/Remove/Purge/Hold
| Status=Not/Installed/Config-files/Unpacked/Failed-config/Half-installed
|/ Err?=(none)/Hold/Reinst-required/X=both-problems (Status,Err: uppercase=bad)
||/ Name            Version        Description
+++-= == == == == == == =-= == == == == == == =-= == == == == == == == == == == == == == == == == == == ==
== == =
ii  superfrob       4-1            The superfrobulator
```

dpkg can also be used to find out the package to which a particular file belongs:

```
tigger $ dpkg --search /bin/false
shellutils: /bin/false
tigger $ dpkg --search /home/kalle/.xinitrc
dpkg: /home/kalle/.xinitrc not found.
```

You can also display information about an installed package or *.deb* archive:

```
tigger $ dpkg --status dpkg
Package: dpkg
Essential: yes
Status: install ok installed
Priority: required
Section: base
Installed-Size: 3156
Origin: debian
Maintainer: Dpkg Development <debian-dpkg@lists.debian.org>
Bugs: debbugs://bugs.debian.org
Version: 1.9.19
Replaces: dpkg-doc-ja
Pre-Depends: libc6 (>= 2.2.4-4), libncurses5 (>= 5.2.20020112a-1), libstdc++2.10-
glibc2.2 (>= 1:2.95.4-0.010810)
Conflicts: sysvinit (<< 2.80)
Conffiles:
```

```
/etc/alternatives/README 69c4ba7f08363e998e0f2e244a04f881
/etc/dpkg/dpkg.cfg 1db461ac9a1d4f4c8b47f5061078f5ee
/etc/dpkg/dselect.cfg 190f7cf843556324495ef12759b752e3
/etc/dpkg/origins/debian 24926c0576edec3e316fd9f6072b8118
Description: Package maintenance system for Debian
This package contains the programs which handle the installation and
removal of packages on your system.
 .
The primary interface for the dpkg suite is the 'dselect' program;
a more low-level and less user-friendly interface is available in
the form of the 'dpkg' command.
 .
In order to unpack and build Debian source packages you will need to
install the developers' package 'dpkg-dev' as well as this one.
```

tigger $ **dpkg --info** *reportbug_1.43_all.deb*
```
 new debian package, version 2.0.
 size 66008 bytes: control archive= 1893 bytes.
      40 bytes,     2 lines      conffiles
    1000 bytes,    24 lines      control
     986 bytes,    15 lines      md5sums
    1014 bytes,    41 lines    * postinst           #!/bin/sh
     147 bytes,     5 lines    * postrm             #!/bin/sh
     416 bytes,    19 lines    * prerm              #!/bin/sh
 Package: reportbug
 Version: 1.43
 Section: utils
 Priority: standard
 Architecture: all
 Depends: python
 Recommends: python-newt
 Suggests: postfix | mail-transport-agent, gnupg | pgp, python-ldap (>= 1.8-1)
 Conflicts: python (>> 2.3), python-newt (= 0.50.17-7.1)
 Installed-Size: 195
 Maintainer: Chris Lawrence <lawrencc@debian.org>
 Description: Reports bugs in the Debian distribution.
  reportbug is a tool designed to make the reporting of bugs in Debian
  and derived distributions relatively painless.  Its features include:
  .
   * Integration with the mutt, af, and mh/nmh mail readers.
   * Access to outstanding bug reports to make it easier to identify
     whether problems have already been reported.
   * Support for following-up on outstanding reports.
   * Optional PGP/GnuPG integration.
  .
  reportbug is designed to be used on systems with an installed mail
  transport agent, like exim or sendmail; however, you can edit the
  configuration file and send reports using any available mail server.
```

dpkg can also list the files and directories included in a *.deb* archive:

```
tigger $ dpkg --contents superfrob_4-1_i386.deb
-rwxr-xr-x root/root     44951 2002-02-10 12:16:48 ./usr/bin/dothefrob
-rwxr-xr-x root/root     10262 2002-02-10 12:16:48 ./usr/bin/frobhelper
...
```

dpkg, like *rpm*, has numerous other options; for more details, refer to the manual pages for *dpkg* and *dpkg-deb*.

In addition to *dpkg*, Debian and other Debian-based distributions provide the *apt* suite of programs.* *apt* stands for "advanced package tool," and is designed as an archive-independent system that can handle multiple package formats. Perhaps the most important feature of *apt* is its ability to resolve dependencies automatically; if, for example, *superfrob* requires Version 2 or later of *frobnik*, *apt* will try to find *frobnik* from the sources that are available to it (including CD-ROMs, local mirrors, and the Internet).

The most useful interface to *apt* is the *apt-get* command. *apt-get* manages the list of available packages (the "package cache") and can be used to resolve dependencies and install packages. A typical session would start with an update of the *apt* cache:

```
tiger # apt-get update
Get:1 http://http.us.debian.org stable/main Packages [808kB]
Get:2 http://http.us.debian.org stable/main Release [88B]
Hit http://non-us.debian.org stable/non-US/main Packages
Hit http://non-us.debian.org stable/non-US/main Release
Get:3 http://security.debian.org stable/updates/main Packages [62.1kB]
Get:4 http://security.debian.org stable/updates/main Release [93B]
Fetched 870kB in 23s (37kB/s)
Reading Package Lists... Done
Building Dependency Tree... Done
```

The output indicates that there have been updates to the stable distribution, so we may want to upgrade the packages already installed on the system. To do this automatically, we can use *apt-get*'s *upgrade* option:

```
tiger # apt-get upgrade
The following packages have been kept back:
  gnumeric
17 packages upgraded, 0 newly installed, 0 to remove and 1 not upgraded.
Need to get 16.3MB of archives.  After unpacking 5kB will be freed.
Do you want to continue? [Y/n] y
Get:1 http://http.us.debian.org stable/main base-passwd 3.4.6 [17.2kB]
Get:2 http://security.debian.org stable/updates/main ssh 1:3.1.6p4-1 [600kB]
...
(Reading database ... 159546 files and directories currently installed.)
Preparing to replace ssh 1:3.0.3p2-6 (using .../ssh_1%3a3.1.6p4-1_i386.deb) ...
Unpacking replacement ssh ...
...
```

One thing you will notice is that unlike most Linux commands, the actions taken by *apt* commands are specified *without* dashes. *apt-get* does allow some options, but they are used only to change the behavior of the main action specified.†

---

* Some RPM-based distributions now include *apt* as well because *apt* was designed to work with any packaging format.

† Some other Linux commands, such as *cvs*, also act this way.

Note that *gnumeric* was not automatically upgraded, probably because it would have required additional packages to be installed. To upgrade it and resolve dependencies, we can use *apt-get*'s *install* option, with the names of one or more packages: [*]

```
tigger # apt-get install gnumeric
The following extra packages will be installed:
  libgal36 libglade3
The following NEW packages will be installed:
  libgal36
2 packages upgraded, 1 newly installed, 0 to remove and 0 not upgraded.
Need to get 8.3MB of archives.  After unpacking 503kB will be used.
Do you want to continue? [Y/n] y
...
```

Another useful feature of *apt* is its ability to find information about packages in the repository. The *apt-cache* command is used to look up information about packages that are available for installation. One common use of *apt-cache* is to find packages based on keywords in the package's description, by using words, complete phrases (in quotes), or regular expressions. For example, if you want to find a package that allows you to play Ogg Vorbis-encoded music files, you can use the search option to find appropriate packages:

```
tigger $ apt-cache search "ogg vorbis"
audacity - A fast, cross-platform audio editor
bitcollider-plugins - bitcollider plugins
cplay - A front-end for various audio players
gqmpeg - a GTK+ front end to mpg321/mpg123 and ogg123
libapache-mod-mp3 - turns Apache into a streaming audio server
libvorbis0 - The Vorbis General Audio Compression Codec
mp3blaster - Full-screen console mp3 and ogg vorbis player
mp3burn - burn audio CDs directly from MP3s or Ogg Vorbis files
oggtst - Read comments in ogg vorbis files
python-pyvorbis - A Python interface to the Ogg Vorbis library
vorbis-tools - Several Ogg Vorbis Tools
xmms - Versatile X audio player that looks like Winamp
xmms-dev - XMMS development static library and header files
mq3 - a mp3/ogg audio player written in Qt.
```

Now, if we are interested in one of these packages, we can find out more about it using the show option of *apt-cache*:

```
tigger $ apt-cache show xmms
Package: xmms
Priority: optional
Section: sound
Installed-Size: 4035
Maintainer: Josip Rodin <jrodin@jagor.srce.hr>
...
```

---

[*] Note that *apt-get* does not install packages directly from *.deb* archives; *dpkg*'s *--install* option should be used instead for an archive that you have in a *.deb* archive on disk or have downloaded directly from the Internet. When using *dpkg*, you will need to resolve the dependencies yourself.

```
Description: Versatile X audio player that looks like Winamp
 XMMS (formerly known as X11Amp) is an X/GTK+ based audio player
 for various audio formats.
 .
It's able to read and play:
 * Audio MPEG layer 1, 2, and 3 (with mpg123 plug-in),
 * WAV, RAW, AU (with internal wav plug-in and MikMod plug-in),
 * MOD, XM, S3M, and other module formats (with MikMod plug-in),
 * CD Audio (with CDAudio plug-in), with CDDB support,
 * .cin files, id Software,
 * Ogg Vorbis files.
It has eSound, OSS, and disk writer support for outputting sound.
 .
It looks almost the same as famous Winamp, and includes those neat
features like general purpose, visualization and effect plug-ins,
several of which come bundled, then spectrum analyzer, oscilloscope,
skins support, and of course, a playlist window.
```

Although a full exploration of *apt*'s features is beyond the scope of this chapter, the *apt* manual page (and the manual pages it references) along with the APT HOWTO (available in the *apt-howto-en* package) should answer any questions you may have.

In addition to the command-line tools, a number of easy-to-use text-based and graphical frontends have been developed. One of the most mature frontends is *KPackage*, which is part of the KDE Desktop Environment, but can be used with other desktops, such as GNOME. *KPackage* can be run from the command line or found in the System menu of KDE. Figure 12-1 shows a sample screen from *KPackage*.

The main window of *KPackage* displays a list of all the packages available for your system on the left, with a box to the right; when you choose a package in the list, the box to the right includes information about the package you selected. You can install or uninstall packages by selecting them and choosing Install or Uninstall from the Packages menu, or by clicking the column labeled Mark to place a check mark next to them and then clicking the "Install marked" or "Uninstall marked" buttons. You can also install *.deb* packages directly by clicking the Open button on the toolbar to the left of the screen and selecting the file, or dragging *.deb* icons from KDE file manager windows into *KPackage*'s window. *KPackage* also has tools for finding packages with particular names. Like all KDE applications, *KPackage* has help available by pressing F1 or using the Help menu.

Automated and Bulk Upgrades

Nearly every distribution now includes a convenient update mechanism. SUSE ships one as part of YaST, and Red Hat uses an application called *up2date* that connects to the Red Hat Network. Debian, of course, has the *apt-get* utility described in the previous section. There are other tools out there, but you'll have to install them first. Usually there's no reason to go to all that trouble.

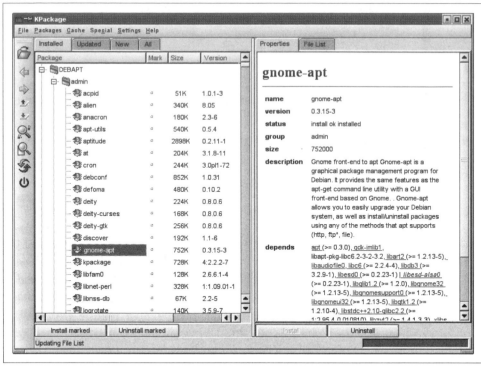

Figure 12-1. KPackage package manager

The update systems are designed to be ultra-simple and therefore are mostly intuitive to use. We will briefly introduce two here: YOU, which comes from the SUSE world, and ZENworks, which comes from the Red Hat world.

YaST Online Update: Automated Updates

YOU ("YaST Online Update") is SUSE's automated update tool. The service is free to use (i.e., it is not a subscription-based service). You run it whenever you feel like it (but doing it regularly might be a good idea if you plan to use such a tool at all). YOU is integrated into the YaST system administration tool; in the Software section, you'll find the Online Update icon. Click this, and the online update screen will appear. At first it is empty, because it needs to load the list of available servers. This can change dynamically over time. You can browse the drop-down list "Installation source" to choose a location that is close to you network-wise.

If you check the checkbox Manually Select Patches and click Next, you will, after a period of time during which the list of updated packages is loaded, be taken to another page (see Figure 12-2) where you can select the packages to update. Those updates that are relevant to you (in other words, that apply to packages you have installed) are already checked. It might still be a good idea to browse down the list, though, because YOU even gets you some packages that are, for legal reasons, not on the installation media. For example, the package `fetchmsttfonts` lets you download and install TrueType fonts provided by Microsoft (isn't that ironic?). Drivers for various WLAN cards are another example of packages that are only available via the online update. Because these do not update existing packages, they are never checked by default initially, so you may want to choose the manual update selection at least once and check them.

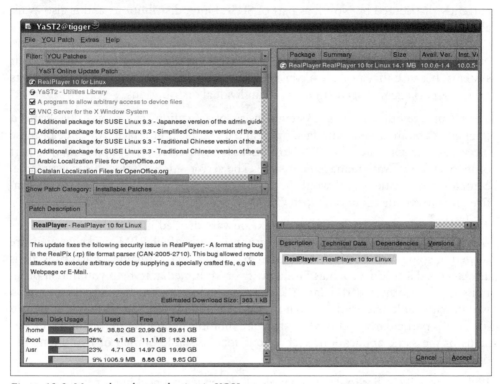

Figure 12-2. Manual package selection in YOU

If you do not check the Manually Select Patches box, the update selection step will be skipped, and the update will be performed immediately.

Another nice little gadget that comes with YOU is the SUSE Watcher. This is a panel applet for your KDE desktop that monitors the package update sites and alerts you when security patches are available by switching into a red ball (see Figure 12-3). Right-clicking that ball opens a context menu that lets you start the online update.

Figure 12-3. SUSE Watcher indicates available security patches

Red Carpet and ZENworks Linux Management: Alternative Package Management Tools

This section looks at another tool for automated update management, called Red Carpet (now part of the ZENworks Linux Management tools from Novell), and explains some of the advantages of different approaches to package management.

Originally developed as an updater for GNOME desktop software, Red Carpet is currently distributed by Novell as part of SUSE Linux distributions and is also available from other sources as a standalone system updater. It can install updates from a variety of servers, including apt repositories and ZENworks servers. Administrators of several flavors of Linux will appreciate having the Red Carpet tools on all their systems, because they provide a consistent interface and command set that abstracts away the package management quirks of individual distributions.

The client side of the package system consists of a daemon (*rcd*, soon to be changed to *zmd*), a command-line interface (*rug*), and a graphical interface. All three of these pieces are free software, although Novell sells a proprietary server application as part of its overall software management suite. The server side is designed for very large, complex organizations and won't be covered here, but we will cover a free alternative for software distribution, Open Carpet.

The ZENworks system distributes Linux software divided into channels, like television shows. Each channel contains a group of individual RPM packages that are related in some way: core operating system, for example, or games. Each package is also assigned a section, such as Productivity or Multimedia, to help you find applications that perform a particular task. You can subscribe to channels the way you would with cable television, so that they can show only software you are interested in. This is particularly useful when there are multiple channels offering different versions of the same application, such as one for the stable branch of Evolution, and one for unstable developer snapshots.

Red Carpet, like other tools, will handle all dependency checking for you: if you try to install a new version of Evolution, and it requires that you upgrade gtkhtml, the program will offer to upgrade that as well. Similarly, if you try to remove software that is required, Red Carpet will warn you that, to keep a clean package database, it will be removing everything upstream from that. For example, if you try to remove the gtk+ package, you'll also have to tear out most of your GNOME desktop tools, which almost universally require that library.

Installing Red Carpet

You can download Red Carpet RPM packages from *ftp://ftp.novell.com* or from your Linux distribution's web site. You may also wish to check *http://rpmfind.net* or *http://open-carpet.org* for additional sources. You will need the daemon package *rcd* or *zmd* and at least one of the *rug* (command-line) or Red Carpet (GUI) interface tools.

The packages have few dependencies, so you should be able to install them no trouble using the command *rpm -Uvh*.

Using the Red Carpet GUI

The Red Carpet graphical update tool can be invoked either from a menu or with the *red-carpet* command. When you first start it, it will tell you that there are no updates available, because you have not subscribed to any channels. To change your channel subscriptions, click the Channels button and select the items you want.

Once you have subscribed to channels, the start screen of Red Carpet will display new versions of packages you already have installed, if any are available. Each update is displayed with its name, the version you have and the version of the updated package, plus a recommendation as to how important that update is, ranging from "minor" for small enhancements to "urgent" and "necessary" for more important bugs such as security problems.

To install updates, select the packages you want to update and click the Mark for Installation button, or just click Update All. Then, click the Run Now button. Red Carpet will ask you to confirm the operation, and then perform it.

Near the top of the Red Carpet window is a set of tabs—Installed Software, Available Software, and Search—that let you see longer lists of software. The first one lists software you already have, the second lists software you don't have, and the third displays all the software that the system knows about whether it's installed or not. In all three cases, you can filter out software by channels and sections, search for specific words in the package name and description, or just show the whole list.

You can mark any package for installation or removal in any of the first four tabs. Actions you have decided to take are listed in the left side of the screen and, in greater detail, in the Pending Actions tab. Only when you click Run Now and confirm all the actions you want to perform will the application remove or install software.

Once you've run a transaction or two, click the History tab to see them listed. This can be very useful if something breaks after a particular software change, and you want to know what you need to undo.

If you're not satisfied with the download performance you get, or with the software available to you, select Edit → Services and add or remove servers. You can even use several services at once, for the maximum variety of software. You'll find a list of additional services at *http://open-carpet.org*.

Using the rug command

Once you understand the general *zmd concepts*, you may find it more convenient to run updates at the command line with *rug*. Each command consists of *rug* followed by an action and any option flags or arguments. All actions also have convenient shorthand notations, which we won't use here, but which you can find in the manpages.

Note that, as with all package management systems, most *rug* actions will require root privileges.

The first action you'll want to use is *rug list-updates*, which displays a list of available updates. If you want to install them, you can then run *rug update*. To search for software, use *rug search* followed by a package name or name fragment. For these and all other *rug* actions, you can get detailed help by running the command *rug action --help*. A complete list of actions is available in the manpage and as the output of the command *rug help*.

More advanced commands for *rug* include package locking, which lets you mark certain packages as not upgradeable. To add a lock, use *rug lock-add packagename*. Locks are listed numerically with the *rug lock-list* command, and deleted using the *rug lock-delete locknumber* command.

Other actions let you check dependencies. For example, *rug what-requires item* tells you what software requires a particular piece of software. You can check dependencies on entire packages, on libraries, commands, or almost anything else. For example:

```
system:/root # rug what-requires libusb

S | Channel      | Package          | Version          | libusb Version
--+--------------+------------------+------------------+----------------
  | suse-92-i586 | ctapi-cyberjack  | 1.0.0-173.1      | (any)
i | suse-92-i586 | pcsc-cyberjack   | 1.1.1-245.1      | (any)
v | suse-92-i586 | pcsc-etoken      | 1.1.1-245.1      | (any)
```

In this example, we see what packages make use of the libusb library. The first column, S, represents the status of the packages in the list. The i next to pcsc-cyberjack denotes that the package is installed. The spaces next to the other packages let us know that they are not installed, and a v indicates that a different version of the package is installed. The second column notes the channel from which the package comes, the third and fourth the package and its version, and the last shows which version of the library is required by the package. In this case, all three packages are content with any version of libusb.

One side effect of being able to check dependencies at a finer level than packages is that you can use the *rug solvedeps* command to install a library without having to worry about versions or packages. For example, if an application you are trying to install demands libfoo greater than 1.5, you can ask it to solve the problem for you with the command *rug solvedeps "libfoo > 1.5"*. You can also tell solvedeps to avoid a package, library, or binary by placing an exclamation point in front of it: *rug solvedeps "!libfoo" "frob > 2.3"*. If it is possible to install *frob* Version 2.3 or greater without installing libfoo, it will do so.

Finally, you can access multiple services through *rug* just like you can with the GUI. Use the *rug service-add* command, followed by the URL for the service. Several services are listed at *http://open-carpet.org*.

Multiple users

Imagine that you are a system administrator and want to update several systems, but that you don't have root access to all of them. How can you do it? During your system install, install *zmd* and configure it to recognize you as a remote user. Then, even when the root password changes, you can still install security updates.

To add a user, use the command *rug user-add username* or, in the GUI, select Edit → Users. You will need to enter a password and select privileges for the user you are creating. Note that these usernames and passwords are totally distinct from system logins.

You can grant the following privileges:

Install
> User can install new software.

Lock
> User can add or delete package locks.

Remove
> User can remove software.

Subscribe
> User can alter channel subscriptions.

Superuser
> User has all access granted to the local root user.

Trusted
> User can install unsigned packages.

Upgrade
> User can upgrade existing software.

View
> User can see what software is installed, and check updates. This is the only privilege that is turned on by default.

Once you have created a user account with the daemon, you can let that user update the system and maintain its software without having to grant them full access to the data on the machine.

To disable remote user connections, use the command *rug set-prefs remote-enabled false*.

To access a remote daemon using the Red Carpet GUI, select File → Connect to Daemon and enter the address of the remote server. To access a remote daemon using *rug*, use the *--host* flag to set the host. Note that the default port for listening is 505.

Operating an update server

Large businesses often want to keep software updates within their firewalls and completely under their control. To do that, they use enterprise-class upgrade servers with sophisticated interfaces and multiple levels of administrator privileges. That's not the kind of update server we're covering here. If you're shipping a few updates to a few systems, or if you're a developer shipping software and want to make it easy to install and update, you don't need a really complicated system. You just want to make sure that the beta testers have the latest version.

Open Carpet is a free server for HTTP, FTP, and Red Carpet access to packages and package metadata. That means that anyone with a web browser can also download the files and install them by hand, just like with a regular file server, but in addition, Red Carpet users can update and resolve dependencies automatically. In some places it's a little rough around the edges, but it works nicely for those willing to fiddle with configuration files a little bit.

To set up your own server, install *open-carpet* and *libredcarpet-python*, available at *http://open-carpet.org*—and of course through the site's own official Open Carpet service. The packages provided contain sample configuration files, normally installed to */usr/share/doc/packages/open-carpet/sample/*. Edit the *server.conf* file first. It's simple enough: enter a name for the server, your email address, and so forth. At the end, it points to a channel directory. Create that directory, put packages in it, and run the *open-carpet* command. If all goes well, you've got a server. To ship updates, just copy them to the channel directories and run the script again.

Upgrading Software Not Provided in Packages

A lot of interesting software is offered outside the package systems, although as it becomes popular, the developers tend to provide Linux packages. In order to install or upgrade applications that don't yet exist as packages, you'll have to obtain the newest release of the software. This is usually available as a *gzip*ped or compressed tar file. Such a package could come in several forms. The most common are *binary distributions*, in which the binaries and related files are archived and ready to unpack on your system, and *source distributions*, in which the source code (or portions of the source code) for the software is provided, and you have to issue commands to compile and install it on your system.

Shared libraries make distributing software in binary form easy; as long as you have a version of the libraries installed that is compatible with the library stubs used to build the program, you're set. However, in many cases, it is easier (and a good idea) to release a program as source. Not only does this make the source code available to you for inspection and further development, but it also allows you to build the application specifically for your system, with your own libraries. Many programs allow you to specify certain options at compile time, such as selectively including various features in the program when built. This kind of customization isn't possible if you get prebuilt binaries.

There's also a security issue at play when installing binaries without source code. Although on Unix systems viruses are nearly unheard of, it's not difficult to write a *Trojan Horse*, a program that appears to do something useful but, in actuality, causes damage to the system.* For example, someone could write an application that includes the "feature" of deleting all files in the home directory of the user executing the program. Because the program would be running with the permissions of the user executing it, the program itself would have the ability to do this kind of damage. (Of course, the Unix security mechanism prevents damage being done to other users' files or to any important system files owned by *root*.)

Although having source code won't necessarily prevent this from happening (do you read the source code for every program you compile on your system?), at least it gives you a way to verify what the program is really doing. Also, if source code is available, it is likely that some people will peruse it, so that using source is a bit safer; however, you can't count on that.

There are techniques for verifying binary packages as well, namely signed packages. The packager can sign a package with his PGP key, and package tools such as *RPM* have means of verifying such a signature. However, you will still have to rely on the packager having packaged correctly and without bad intentions. All the signature tells you is that the package really comes from who it says it comes from, and that it hasn't been tampered with on its way from the packager to your hard disk.

At any rate, dealing with source and binary distributions of software is quite simple. If the package is released as a *tar* file, first use the *tar t* option to determine how the files have been archived. In the case of binary distributions, you may be able to unpack the *tar* file directly on your system—say, from / or */usr*. When doing this, be sure to delete any old versions of the program and its support files (those that aren't overwritten by the new *tar* file). If the old executable comes before the new one on your path, you'll continue to run the old version unless you remove it.

Source distributions are a bit trickier. First, you must unpack the sources into a directory of their own. Most systems use */usr/src* for just this. Because you usually don't have to be *root* to build a software package (although you will usually require

---

* A *virus* in the classic sense is a program that attaches to a "host" and runs when the host is executed. On Unix systems, this usually requires root privileges to do any harm, and if programmers could obtain such privileges, they probably wouldn't bother with a virus.

root permissions to install the program once compiled!), it might be a good idea to make */usr/src* writable by all users, with the command:

```
chmod 1777 /usr/src
```

This allows any user to create subdirectories in */usr/src* and place files there. The first 1 in the mode is the "sticky" bit, which prevents users from deleting each other's subdirectories.

You can now create a subdirectory under */usr/src* and unpack the tar file there, or you can unpack the tar file directly from */usr/src* if the archive contains a subdirectory of its own.

Once the sources are available, the next step is to read any *README* and *INSTALL* files or installation notes included with the sources. Nearly all packages include such documentation. The basic method used to build most programs is as follows:

1. Check the *Makefile*. This file contains instructions for *make*, which controls the compiler to build programs. Many applications require you to edit minor aspects of the *Makefile* for your own system; this should be self-explanatory. The installation notes will tell you if you have to do this. If there is no *Makefile* in the package, you might have to generate it first. See item 3 for how to do this.

2. Possibly edit other files associated with the program. Some applications require you to edit a file named *config.h*; again, this will be explained in the installation instructions.

3. Possibly run a configuration script. Such a script is used to determine what facilities are available on your system, which is necessary to build more complex applications.

   Specifically, when the sources do not contain a *Makefile* in the top-level directory, but instead a file called *Makefile.in* and a file called *configure*, the package has been built with the Autoconf system. In this (more and more common) case, you run the configuration script like this:

   ```
   ./configure
   ```

   The `./` should be used so that the local *configure* is run, and not another *configure* program that might accidentally be in your path. Some packages let you pass options to *configure* that often enable or disable specific features of the package. (You can find out what these options are with *configure --help*.) Once the *configure* script has run, you can proceed with the next step.

4. Run *make*. Generally, this executes the appropriate compilation commands as given in the *Makefile*. In many cases you'll have to give a "target" to *make*, as in *make all* or *make install*. These are two common targets; the former is usually not necessary but can be used to build all targets listed in a *Makefile* (e.g., if the package includes several programs, but only one is compiled by default); the latter is often used to install the executables and support files on the system after compilation. For this reason, *make install* is usually run as *root*.

Even after the installation, there is often one major difference between programs installed from source or from a binary package. Programs installed from source are often installed below *usr/local* by default, which is rarely the case with binary packages.

You might have problems compiling or installing new software on your system, especially if the program in question hasn't been tested under Linux, or depends on other software you don't have installed. In Chapter 21, we talk about the compiler, *make*, and related tools in detail.

Most software packages include manual pages and other files, in addition to the source and executables. The installation script (if there is one) will place these files in the appropriate location. In the case of manual pages, you'll find files with names such as *foobar.1* or *foobar.man*. These files are usually *nroff* source files, which are formatted to produce the human-readable pages displayed by the *man* command. If the manual page source has a numeric extension, such as *.1*, copy it to the directory *usr/man/man1*, where *1* is the number used in the filename extension. (This corresponds to the manual "section" number; for most user programs, it is 1.) If the file has an extension such as *.man*, it usually suffices to copy the file to *usr/man/man1*, renaming the *.man* extension to *.1*.

Upgrading Libraries

Most of the programs on a Linux system are compiled to use shared libraries. These libraries contain useful functions common to many programs. Instead of storing a copy of these routines in each program that calls them, the libraries are contained in files on the system that are read by all programs at runtime. That is, when a program is executed, the code from the program file itself is read, followed by any routines from the shared library files. This saves a great deal of disk space—only one copy of the library routines is stored on disk.

If you're lucky, using the package system means that the right versions of the libraries each program needs are installed along with the programs. The package system is supposed to be aware of dependencies on shared libraries. But because different programs may depend on different versions of libraries, or because you might install a program without using the package system, you occasionally have to understand the conventions for libraries explained in this section.

In some instances, it's necessary to compile a program to have its own copy of the library routines (usually for debugging) instead of using the routines from the shared libraries. We say that programs built in this way are *statically linked*, whereas programs built to use shared libraries are *dynamically linked*.

Therefore, dynamically linked executables depend upon the presence of the shared libraries on disk. Shared libraries are implemented in such a way that the programs compiled to use them generally don't depend on the version of the available libraries. This means that you can upgrade your shared libraries, and all programs that are built to use those libraries will automatically use the new routines. (There is an exception: if major changes are made to a library, the old programs won't work with the new library. You'll know this is the case because the major version number is different; we explain more later. In this case, you keep both the old and new libraries around. All your old executables will continue to use the old libraries, and any new programs that are compiled will use the new libraries.)

When you build a program to use shared libraries, a piece of code is added to the program that causes it to execute *ld.so*, the dynamic linker, when the program is started. *ld.so* is responsible for finding the shared libraries the program needs and loading the routines into memory. Dynamically linked programs are also linked against "stub" routines, which simply take the place of the actual shared library routines in the executable. *ld.so* replaces the stub routine with the code from the libraries when the program is executed.

The *ldd* command can be used to list the shared libraries on which a given executable depends. For example:

```
rutabaga$ ldd /usr/bin/X11/xterm
        linux-gate.so.1 =>  (0xffffe000)
        libXft.so.2 => /usr/X11R6/lib/libXft.so.2 (0x40037000)
        libfontconfig.so.1 => /usr/lib/libfontconfig.so.1 (0x4004b000)
        libfreetype.so.6 => /usr/lib/libfreetype.so.6 (0x40079000)
        libexpat.so.0 => /usr/lib/libexpat.so.0 (0x400e8000)
        libXrender.so.1 => /usr/X11R6/lib/libXrender.so.1 (0x40107000)
        libXaw.so.8 => /usr/X11R6/lib/libXaw.so.8 (0x4010f000)
        libXmu.so.6 => /usr/X11R6/lib/libXmu.so.6 (0x4016b000)
        libXt.so.6 => /usr/X11R6/lib/libXt.so.6 (0x40182000)
        libSM.so.6 => /usr/X11R6/lib/libSM.so.6 (0x401d5000)
        libICE.so.6 => /usr/X11R6/lib/libICE.so.6 (0x401dd000)
        libXpm.so.4 => /usr/X11R6/lib/libXpm.so.4 (0x401f5000)
        libXp.so.6 => /usr/X11R6/lib/libXp.so.6 (0x40205000)
        libXext.so.6 => /usr/X11R6/lib/libXext.so.6 (0x4020d000)
        libX11.so.6 => /usr/X11R6/lib/libX11.so.6 (0x4021c000)
        libncurses.so.5 => /lib/libncurses.so.5 (0x40318000)
        libutempter.so.0 => /usr/lib/libutempter.so.0 (0x4035d000)
        libc.so.6 => /lib/tls/libc.so.6 (0x4035f000)
        libdl.so.2 => /lib/libdl.so.2 (0x40478000)
        /lib/ld-linux.so.2 (0x40000000)
```

Here, we see that the *xterm* program depends on a number of shared libraries, including *libXaw*, *libXt*, *libX11*, and *libc*. (The libraries starting with *libX* as well as *libSM* and *libICE* are all related to the X Window System; *libc* is the standard C library.) We also see the version numbers of the libraries for which the program was compiled (that is, the version of the stub routines used), and the name of the file that contains each shared library. This is the file that *ld.so* will find when the program is executed. The first file in the list, by the way, *linux-gate.so.1*, is not a real shared library, but rather a so-called dynamic shared object provided by the kernel, a technicality that speeds up system calls into the kernel and provides other useful low-level things.

To use a shared library, the version of the stub routines (in the executable) must be compatible with the version of the shared libraries. Basically, a library is compatible if its major version number matches that of the stub routines. The major version number is the part right after the *.so*. In this case, *libX11* (the most basic library used by the X Window System) is used with the major Version 6. The library file *libX11.so.6* (which usually resides in */usr/X11R6/lib*) might very well just be a symbolic link—for example, to *libX11.so.6.2*. This means that the library has the major version number 6 and the minor version number 2. Library versions with the same major version number are supposed to be interchangeable. This way, if a program was compiled with Version 6.0 of the stub routines, shared library Versions 6.1, 6.2, and so forth could be used by the executable. If a new version with the major version number 6 and the minor version number 3 were released (and thus had the filename *libX11.so.6.3*), all you would need to do to use this new version is change the symbolic link *libX11.so.6* to point to the new version. The *xterm* executable would then automatically benefit from any bug fixes or similar that are included in the new version. In "More Fun with Libraries" in Chapter 21, we describe how to use shared libraries with your own programs.

The file */etc/ld.so.conf* contains a list of directories that *ld.so* searches to find shared library files. An example of such a file is:

```
/usr/lib
/usr/local/lib
/usr/X11R6/lib
/opt/kde3/lib
```

ld.so always looks in */lib* and */usr/lib*, regardless of the contents of *ld.so.conf*. Usually, there's no reason to modify this file, and the environment variable LD_LIBRARY_PATH can add additional directories to this search path (e.g., if you have your own private shared libraries that shouldn't be used system-wide). However, if you do add entries to */etc/ld.so.conf* or upgrade or install additional libraries on your system, be sure to use the *ldconfig* command, which will regenerate the shared library cache in */etc/ld.so.cache* from the *ld.so* search path. This cache is used by *ld.so* to find libraries quickly at runtime without actually having to search the directories on its path. For more information, check the manual pages for *ld.so* and *ldconfig*.

Now that you understand how shared libraries are used, let's move on to upgrading them. The two libraries that are most commonly updated are *libc* (the standard C library) and *libm* (the math library). Because naming is a little bit special for these, we will look at another library here, namely *libncurses*, which "emulates" a graphical windowing system on the text console.

For each shared library, there are two separate files:

<library>.a

This is the static version of the library. When a program is statically linked, routines are copied from this file directly into the executable, so the executable contains its own copy of the library routines.*

< library>.so.<version>

This is the shared library image itself. When a program is dynamically linked, the stub routines from this file are copied into the executable, allowing *ld.so* to locate the shared library at runtime. When the program is executed, *ld.so* copies routines from the shared library into memory for use by the program. If a program is dynamically linked, the *<library>.a* file is not used for this library.

For the *libncurses* library, you'll have files such as *libncurses.a* and *libncurses.so.5.4*. The *.a* files are generally kept in */usr/lib*, and *.so* files are kept in */lib*. When you compile a program, either the *.a* or the *.so* file is used for linking, and the compiler looks in */lib* and */usr/lib* (as well as a variety of other places) by default. If you have your own libraries, you can keep these files anywhere, and control where the linker looks with the -L option to the compiler. See "More Fun with Libraries" in Chapter 21 for details.

The shared library image, *<library>.so.version*, is kept in */lib* for most system-wide libraries. Shared library images can be found in any of the directories that *ld.so* searches at runtime; these include */lib*, */usr/lib*, and the files listed in *ld.so.conf*. See the *ld.so* manual page for details.

If you look in */lib*, you'll see a collection of files such as the following:

```
lrwxrwxrwx   1 root     root            17 Jul 11 06:45 /lib/libncurses.so.5 \
    -> libncurses.so.5.4
-rwxr-xr-x   1 root     root        319472 Jul 11 06:45 /lib/libncurses.so.5.4
lrwxrwxrwx   1 root     root            13 Jul 11 06:45 libz.so.1 -> libz.so.1.2.2
-rwxr-xr-x   1 root     root         62606 Jul 11 06:45 libz.so.1.2.2
```

Here, we see the shared library images for two libraries—*libncurses* and *libz*. Note that each image has a symbolic link to it, named *<library>.so.<major>*, where *<major>* is the major version number of the library. The minor number is omitted because *ld.so* searches for a library only by its major version number. When *ld.so* sees a program that has been compiled with the stubs for Version 5.4 of *libncurses*, it looks for a file called *libncurses.so.5* in its search path. Here, */lib/libncurses.so.5* is a symbolic link to */lib/libncurses.so.5.4*, the actual version of the library we have installed.

When you upgrade a library, you must replace the *.a* and *.so.<version>* files corresponding to the library. Replacing the *.a* file is easy: just copy over it with the new

---

* On some distributions, the static versions of the libraries are moved into a separate package and not necessarily installed by default. If this is the case, you won't find the *.a* files unless you install them.

versions. However, you must use some caution when replacing the shared library image, *.so.<version>*; many of the text-based programs on the system depend on shared library images, so you can't simply delete them or rename them. To put this another way, the symbolic link *<library>.so.<major>* must *always* point to a valid library image. To accomplish this, first copy the new image file to */lib*, and then change the symbolic link to point to the new file in one step, using *ln -sf*. This is demonstrated in the following example.

Let's say you're upgrading from Version 5.4 of the *libncurses* library to Version 5.5. You should have the files *libncurses.a* and *libncurses.so.5.5*. First, copy the *.a* file to the appropriate location, overwriting the old version:

> rutabaga# **cp libncurses.a /usr/lib**

Now, copy the new image file to */lib* (or wherever the library image should be):

> rutabaga# **cp libncurses.so.5.5 /lib**

Now, if you use the command *ls -l /lib/libncurses*, you should see something like the following:

```
lrwxrwxrwx    1 root      root               17 Dec 10  1999 /lib/libncurses.so.5 ->
libncurses.so.5.4
-rwxr-xr-x    1 root      root           319472 May 11  2001 /lib/libncurses.so.5.4
-rwxr-xr-x    1 root      root           321042 May 11  2001 /lib/libncurses.so.5.5
```

To update the symbolic link to point to the new library, use the command:

> rutabaga# **ln -sf /lib/libncurses.so.5.5 /lib/libncurses.so.5**

This gives you:

```
lrwxrwxrwx 1 root  root       14 Oct 23 13:25 libncurses.so.5 ->\
    /lib/libncurses.so.5.4
-rwxr-xr-x 1 root  root  623620 Oct 23 13:24 libncurses.so.5.4
-rwxr-xr-x 1 root  root  720310 Nov 16 11:02 libncurses.so.5.5
```

Now you can safely remove the old image file, *libncurses.so.5.4*. You must use *ln -sf* to replace the symbolic link in one step, especially when updating crucial libraries, such as *libc*. If you were to remove the symbolic link first, and then attempt to use *ln -s* to add it again, more than likely *ln* would not be able to execute because the symbolic link is gone, and as far as *ld.so* is concerned, the *libc* library can't be found. Once the link is gone, nearly all the programs on your system will be unable to execute. Be very careful when updating shared library images. For *libncurses*, things are less critical because you will always have command-line programs left to clean up any mess you have made, but if you are used to using *ncurses*-based programs, such as Midnight Commander, this might still be an inconvenience for you.

Whenever you upgrade or add a library to the system, it's not a bad idea to run *ldconfig* to regenerate the library cache used by *ld.so*. In some cases, a new library may not be recognized by *ld.so* until you run *ldconfig*.

One question remains: where can you obtain the new versions of libraries? Several of the basic system libraries (*libc*, *libm*, and so on) can be downloaded from the directory *ftp://ftp.gnu.org/pub/gnu/glibc*. This contains source versions of *libc* and related libraries. Other libraries are maintained and archived separately. At any rate, all libraries you install should include the *.so.version* files and possibly the *.a* files, as well as a set of include files for use with the compiler.

Upgrading the Compiler

One other important part of the system to keep up to date is the C compiler and related utilities. These include *gcc* (the GNU C and C++ compiler itself), the linker, the assembler, the C preprocessor, and various include files and libraries used by the compiler itself. All are included in the Linux *gcc* distribution. Usually, a new version of *gcc* is released along with new versions of the *libc* library and include files, and each requires the other.

You can find the current *gcc* release on the various FTP archives, including *ftp://ftp.gnu.org/pub/gnu/gcc*. The release notes there should tell you what to do. If you don't have Internet access, you can obtain the newest compiler from CD-ROM archives of the FTP sites, as described earlier.

To find out what version of *gcc* you have, use the command:

```
gcc -v
```

This should tell you something like:

```
Reading specs from /usr/lib/gcc-lib/i586-suse-linux/3.3.5/specs
Configured with: ../configure --enable-threads=posix --prefix=/usr --with-local-
prefix=/usr/local --infodir=/usr/share/info --mandir=/usr/share/man --enable-
languages=c,c++,f77,objc,java,ada --disable-checking --libdir=/usr/lib --enable-
libgcj --with-slibdir=/lib --with-system-zlib --enable-shared --enable-__cxa_atexit
i586-suse-linux
Thread model: posix
gcc version 3.3.5 20050117 (prerelease) (SUSE Linux)
```

The last line is the interesting one, telling you the version number of gcc and when it was released. Note that *gcc* itself is just a frontend to the actual compiler and code-generation tools found under

```
/usr/lib/gcc-lib/machine/version
```

gcc (usually in */usr/bin*) can be used with multiple versions of the compiler proper, with the -V option. In "Programming with gcc" in Chapter 21, we describe the use of *gcc* in detail.

We would at this point like to warn you not to try newer compilers without knowing exactly what you are doing. Newer compilers might generate object files that are incompatible with the older ones; this can lead to all kinds of trouble. Version 3.3.x of *gcc* is, at the time of this writing, considered the standard compiler for Linux that everybody expects to find available, even though Versions 3.4.0 and even 4.0.0 are already available. Earlier, when one distributor (Red Hat) started to ship a newer version instead (and even that newer version was not officially released), users ran into lots of trouble. Of course, by the time you read this, another compiler version might be considered the standard. And if you feel adventurous, by all means try newer versions, just be prepared for some serious tweaking.

Archive and Compression Utilities

When installing or upgrading software on Unix systems, the first things you need to be familiar with are the tools used for compressing and archiving files. Dozens of such utilities are available. Some of these (such as *tar* and *compress*) date back to the earliest days of Unix; others (such as *gzip* and the even newer *bzip2*) are relative newcomers. The main goal of these utilities is to archive files (that is, to pack many files together into a single file for easy transportation or backup) and to compress files (to reduce the amount of disk space required to store a particular file or set of files).

In this section, we're going to discuss the most common file formats and utilities you're likely to run into. For instance, a near-universal convention in the Unix world is to transport files or software as a *tar* archive, compressed using *compress*, *gzip*, or *bzip2*. In order to create or unpack these files yourself, you'll need to know the tools of the trade. The tools are most often used when installing new software or creating backups—the subject of the following two sections in this chapter. Packages coming from other worlds, such as the Windows or Java world, are often archived and compressed using the *zip* utility; you can unpack these with the *unzip* command, which should be available in most Linux installations.*

Using gzip and bzip2

gzip is a fast and efficient compression program distributed by the GNU project. The basic function of *gzip* is to take a file, compress it, save the compressed version as *filename.gz*, and remove the original, uncompressed file. The original file is removed only if *gzip* is successful; it is very difficult to accidentally delete a file in this manner. Of course, being GNU software, *gzip* has more options than you want to think about, and many aspects of its behavior can be modified using command-line options.

First, let's say that we have a large file named *garbage.txt*:

```
rutabaga$ ls -l garbage.txt
-rw-r--r--   1 mdw      hack        312996 Nov 17 21:44 garbage.txt
```

---

* Notice that despite the similarity in names, *zip* on the one hand and *gzip* and *bzip2* on the other hand do not have much in common. *zip* is both a packaging and compression tool, whereas *gzip/bzip2* are for compression only—they typically rely on *tar* for the actual packaging. Their formats are incompatible; you need to use the correct program for unpacking a certain package.

To compress this file using *gzip*, we simply use the command:

```
gzip garbage.txt
```

This replaces *garbage.txt* with the compressed file *garbage.txt.gz*. What we end up with is the following:

```
rutabaga$ gzip garbage.txt
rutabaga$ ls -l garbage.txt.gz
-rw-r--r--   1 mdw      hack         103441 Nov 17 21:44 garbage.txt.gz
```

Note that *garbage.txt* is removed when *gzip* completes.

You can give *gzip* a list of filenames; it compresses each file in the list, storing each with a *.gz* extension. (Unlike the *zip* program for Unix and MS-DOS systems, *gzip* will not, by default, compress several files into a single *.gz* archive. That's what *tar* is for; see the next section.)

How efficiently a file is compressed depends on its format and contents. For example, many graphics file formats (such as PNG and JPEG) are already well compressed, and *gzip* will have little or no effect upon such files. Files that compress well usually include plain-text files and binary files, such as executables and libraries. You can get information on a *gzip*ped file using *gzip -l*. For example:

```
rutabaga$ gzip -l garbage.txt.gz
compressed   uncompr. ratio uncompressed_name
   103115    312996  67.0% garbage.txt
```

To get our original file back from the compressed version, we use *gunzip*, as in the following:

```
gunzip garbage.txt.gz
```

After doing this, we get:

```
rutabaga$ gunzip garbage.txt.gz
rutabaga$ ls -l garbage.txt
-rw-r--r--   1 mdw      hack         312996 Nov 17 21:44 garbage.txt
```

which is identical to the original file. Note that when you *gunzip* a file, the compressed version is removed once the uncompression is complete. Instead of using *gunzip*, you can also use *gzip -d* (e.g., if *gunzip* happens not to be installed).

gzip stores the name of the original, uncompressed file in the compressed version. This way, if the compressed filename (including the *.gz* extension) is too long for the filesystem type (say, you're compressing a file on an MS-DOS filesystem with 8.3 filenames), the original filename can be restored using *gunzip* even if the compressed file had a truncated name. To uncompress a file to its original filename, use the *-N* option with *gunzip*. To see the value of this option, consider the following sequence of commands:

```
rutabaga$ gzip garbage.txt
rutabaga$ mv garbage.txt.gz rubbish.txt.gz
```

If we were to *gunzip rubbish.txt.gz* at this point, the uncompressed file would be named *rubbish.txt*, after the new (compressed) filename. However, with the *-N* option, we get the following:

```
rutabaga$ gunzip -N rubbish.txt.gz
rutabaga$ ls -l garbage.txt
-rw-r--r--   1 mdw      hack        312996 Nov 17 21:44 garbage.txt
```

gzip and *gunzip* can also compress or uncompress data from standard input and output. If *gzip* is given no filenames to compress, it attempts to compress data read from standard input. Likewise, if you use the *-c* option with *gunzip*, it writes uncompressed data to standard output. For example, you could pipe the output of a command to *gzip* to compress the output stream and save it to a file in one step:

```
rutabaga$ ls -laR $HOME | gzip > filelist.gz
```

This will produce a recursive directory listing of your home directory and save it in the compressed file *filelist.gz*. You can display the contents of this file with the command:

```
rutabaga$ gunzip -c filelist.gz | more
```

This will uncompress *filelist.gz* and pipe the output to the *more* command. When you use *gunzip -c*, the file on disk remains compressed.

The *zcat* command is identical to *gunzip -c*. You can think of this as a version of *cat* for compressed files. Linux even has a version of the pager *less* for compressed files, called *zless*.

When compressing files, you can use one of the options *-1* through *-9* to specify the speed and quality of the compression used. *-1* (also *--fast*) specifies the fastest method, which compresses the files less compactly, and *-9* (also *--best*) uses the slowest, but best compression method. If you don't specify one of these options, the default is *-6*. None of these options has any bearing on how you use *gunzip*; *gunzip* will be able to uncompress the file no matter what speed option you use.

Compared with the more than three decades long history of Unix, *gzip* is relatively new in the Unix world. The compression programs used on most Unix systems are *compress* and *uncompress*, which were included in the original Berkeley versions of Unix. *compress* and *uncompress* are very much like *gzip* and *gunzip*, respectively; *compress* saves compressed files as *filename.Z* as opposed to *filename.gz*, and uses a slightly less efficient compression algorithm.

However, the free software community has been moving to *gzip* for several reasons. First of all, *gzip* works better. Second, there has been a patent dispute over the compression algorithm used by *compress*—the results of which could prevent third parties from implementing the *compress* algorithm on their own. Because of this, the Free Software Foundation urged a move to *gzip*, which at least the Linux community has embraced. *gzip* has been ported to many architectures, and many others are following suit. Happily, *gunzip* is able to uncompress the *.Z* format files produced by *compress*.

Another compression/decompression program has also emerged to take the lead from *gzip*. *bzip2* is the newest kid on the block and sports even better compression (on the average about 10% to 20% better than *gzip*), at the expense of longer compression times. You cannot use *bunzip2* to uncompress files compressed with *gzip* and vice versa, and because you cannot expect everybody to have *bunzip2* installed on their machine, you might want to confine yourself to *gzip* for the time being if you want to send the compressed file to somebody else. However, it pays to have *bzip2* installed because more and more FTP servers now provide *bzip2*-compressed packages in order to conserve disk space and bandwidth. It is not unlikely that in a few years from now, *gzip* will be as uncommon in the Linux world as *compress* is today. You can recognize *bzip2*-compressed files by their *.bz2* filename extension.

Although the command-line options of *bzip2* are not exactly the same as those of *gzip*, those that have been described in this section are. For more information, see the *bzip2*(1) manual page.

The bottom line is that you should use *gzip/gunzip* or *bzip2/bunzip2* for your compression needs. If you encounter a file with the extension *.Z*, it was probably produced by *compress*, and *gunzip* can uncompress it for you.

Earlier versions of *gzip* used *.z* (lowercase) instead of *.gz* as the compressed-filename extension. Because of the potential confusion with *.Z*, this was changed. At any rate, *gunzip* retains backward compatibility with a number of filename extensions and file types.

Using tar

tar is a general-purpose archiving utility capable of packing many files into a single archive file, while retaining information needed to restore the files fully, such as file permissions and ownership. The name *tar* stands for *tape archive* because the tool was originally used to archive files as backups on tape. However, use of *tar* is not at all restricted to making tape backups, as we'll see.

The format of the *tar* command is:

```
tar functionoptions files...
```

where *function* is a single letter indicating the operation to perform, *options* is a list of (single-letter) options to that function, and *files* is the list of files to pack or unpack in an archive. (Note that *function* is not separated from *options* by any space.)

function can be one of the following:

c   To create a new archive

x   To extract files from an archive

t   To list the contents of an archive

r   To append files to the end of an archive

u   To update files that are newer than those in the archive

d   To compare files in the archive to those in the filesystem

You'll rarely use most of these functions; the more commonly used are c, x, and t.

The most common *options* are

k   To keep any existing files when extracting—that is, to not overwrite any existing files that are contained within the *tar* file.

f *filename*
    To specify that the *tar* file to be read or written is *filename*.

z   To specify that the data to be written to the *tar* file should be compressed or that the data in the *tar* file is compressed with *gzip*.

j   Like *z*, but uses *bzip2* instead of *gzip*; works only with newer versions of *tar*. Some intermediate versions of *tar* used *I* instead; older ones don't support *bzip2* at all.

v   To make *tar* show the files it is archiving or restoring. It is good practice to use this so that you can see what actually happens (unless, of course, you are writing shell scripts).

There are others, which we cover later in this section.

Although the *tar* syntax might appear complex at first, in practice it's quite simple. For example, say we have a directory named *mt*, containing these files:

```
rutabaga$ ls -l mt
total 37
-rw-r--r--  1 root     root           24 Sep 21  2004 Makefile
-rw-r--r--  1 root     root          847 Sep 21  2004 README
-rwxr-xr-x  1 root     root         9220 Nov 16 19:03 mt
-rw-r--r--  1 root     root         2775 Aug  7  2004 mt.1
-rw-r--r--  1 root     root         6421 Aug  7  2004 mt.c
-rw-r--r--  1 root     root         3948 Nov 16 19:02 mt.o
-rw-r--r--  1 root     root        11204 Sep  5  2004 st_info.txt
```

We wish to pack the contents of this directory into a single *tar* archive. To do this, we use the command:

```
tar cf mt.tar mt
```

The first argument to *tar* is the *function* (here, c, for create) followed by any *options*. Here, we use the option f mt.tar to specify that the resulting *tar* archive be named *mt.tar*. The last argument is the name of the file or files to archive; in this case, we give the name of a directory, so *tar* packs all files in that directory into the archive.

Note that the first argument to *tar* must be the function letter and options. Because of this, there's no reason to use a hyphen (-) to precede the options as many Unix commands require. *tar* allows you to use a hyphen, as in:

```
tar -cf mt.tar mt
```

but it's really not necessary. In some versions of *tar*, the first letter must be the *function*, as in c, t, or x. In other versions, the order of letters does not matter.

The function letters as described here follow the so-called "old option style." There is also a newer "short option style" in which you precede the function options with a hyphen, and a "long option style" in which you use long option names with two hyphens. See the Info page for *tar* for more details if you are interested.

Be careful to remember the filename if you use the cf function letters. Otherwise tar will overwrite the first file in your list of files to pack because it will mistake that for the filename!

It is often a good idea to use the v option with *tar*; this lists each file as it is archived. For example:

```
rutabaga$ tar cvf mt.tar mt
mt/
mt/st_info.txt
mt/README
mt/mt.1
mt/Makefile
mt/mt.c
mt/mt.o
mt/mt
```

If you use v multiple times, additional information will be printed:

```
rutabaga$ tar cvvf mt.tar mt
drwxr-xr-x root/root          0 Nov 16 19:03 2004 mt/
-rw-r--r-- root/root      11204 Sep  5 13:10 2004 mt/st_info.txt
-rw-r--r-- root/root        847 Sep 21 16:37 2004 mt/README
-rw-r--r-- root/root       2775 Aug  7 09:50 2004 mt/mt.1
-rw-r--r-- root/root         24 Sep 21 16:03 2004 mt/Makefile
-rw-r--r-- root/root       6421 Aug  7 09:50 2004 mt/mt.c
-rw-r--r-- root/root       3948 Nov 16 19:02 2004 mt/mt.o
-rwxr-xr-x root/root       9220 Nov 16 19:03 2004 mt/mt
```

This is especially useful because it lets you verify that *tar* is doing the right thing.

In some versions of *tar*, f must be the last letter in the list of options. This is because *tar* expects the f option to be followed by a filename—the name of the *tar* file to read from or write to. If you don't specify f *filename* at all, *tar* assumes for historical reasons that it should use the device */dev/rmt0* (that is, the first tape drive). In "Making Backups," in Chapter 27, we talk about using *tar* in conjunction with a tape drive to make backups.

Now, we can give the file *mt.tar* to other people, and they can extract it on their own system. To do this, they would use the following command:

```
tar xvf mt.tar
```

This creates the subdirectory *mt* and places all the original files into it, with the same permissions as found on the original system. The new files will be owned by the user

---

running the *tar xvf* (you) unless you are running as *root*, in which case the original owner is preserved. The x option stands for "extract." The v option is used again here to list each file as it is extracted. This produces:

```
courgette% tar xvf mt.tar
mt/
mt/st_info.txt
mt/README
mt/mt.1
mt/Makefile
mt/mt.c
mt/mt.o
mt/mt
```

We can see that *tar* saves the pathname of each file relative to the location where the *tar* file was originally created. That is, when we created the archive using *tar cf mt.tar mt*, the only input filename we specified was *mt*, the name of the directory containing the files. Therefore, *tar* stores the directory itself and all the files below that directory in the *tar* file. When we extract the *tar* file, the directory *mt* is created and the files placed into it, which is the exact inverse of what was done to create the archive.

By default, *tar* extracts all tar files relative to the current directory where you execute *tar*. For example, if you were to pack up the contents of your */bin* directory with the command:

```
tar cvf bin.tar /bin
```

tar would give the warning:

```
tar: Removing leading / from absolute pathnames in the archive.
```

What this means is that the files are stored in the archive within the subdirectory *bin*. When this *tar* file is extracted, the directory *bin* is created in the working directory of *tar*—not as */bin* on the system where the extraction is being done. This is very important and is meant to prevent terrible mistakes when extracting *tar* files. Otherwise, extracting a tar file packed as, say, */bin* would trash the contents of your */bin* directory when you extracted it.* If you really wanted to extract such a *tar* file into */bin*, you would extract it from the root directory, */*. You can override this behavior using the P option when packing tar files, but it's not recommended you do so.

Another way to create the *tar* file *mt.tar* would have been to *cd* into the *mt* directory itself, and use a command such as:

```
tar cvf mt.tar *
```

This way the *mt* subdirectory would not be stored in the *tar* file; when extracted, the files would be placed directly in your current working directory. One fine point of *tar* etiquette is to always pack *tar* files so that they have a subdirectory at the top level,

---

* Some (older) implementations of Unix (e.g., Sinix and Solaris) do just that.

as we did in the first example with *tar cvf mt.tar mt*. Therefore, when the archive is extracted, the subdirectory is also created and any files placed there. This way you can ensure that the files won't be placed directly in your current working directory; they will be tucked out of the way and prevent confusion. This also saves the person doing the extraction the trouble of having to create a separate directory (should they wish to do so) to unpack the *tar* file. Of course, there are plenty of situations where you wouldn't want to do this. So much for etiquette.

When creating archives, you can, of course, give *tar* a list of files or directories to pack into the archive. In the first example, we have given *tar* the single directory *mt*, but in the previous paragraph we used the wildcard *, which the shell expands into the list of filenames in the current directory.

Before extracting a *tar* file, it's usually a good idea to take a look at its table of contents to determine how it was packed. This way you can determine whether you do need to create a subdirectory yourself where you can unpack the archive. A command such as:

    tar tvf *tarfile*

lists the table of contents for the named *tarfile*. Note that when using the t function, only one v is required to get the long file listing, as in this example:

```
courgette% tar tvf mt.tar
drwxr-xr-x root/root        0 Nov 16 19:03 2004 mt/
-rw-r--r-- root/root    11204 Sep  5 13:10 2004 mt/st_info.txt
-rw-r--r-- root/root      847 Sep 21 16:37 2004 mt/README
-rw-r--r-- root/root     2775 Aug  7 09:50 2004 mt/mt.1
-rw-r--r-- root/root       24 Sep 21 16:03 2004 mt/Makefile
-rw-r--r-- root/root     6421 Aug  7 09:50 2004 mt/mt.c
-rw-r--r-- root/root     3948 Nov 16 19:02 2004 mt/mt.o
-rwxr-xr-x root/root     9220 Nov 16 19:03 2004 mt/mt
```

No extraction is being done here; we're just displaying the archive's table of contents. We can see from the filenames that this file was packed with all files in the subdirectory *mt*, so that when we extract the tar file, the directory *mt* will be created and the files placed there.

You can also extract individual files from a *tar* archive. To do this, use the command:

    tar xvf *tarfile* *files*

where *files* is the list of files to extract. As we've seen, if you don't specify any *files*, *tar* extracts the entire archive.

When specifying individual files to extract, you must give the full pathname as it is stored in the *tar* file. For example, if we wanted to grab just the file *mt.c* from the previous archive *mt.tar*, we'd use the command:

    tar xvf mt.tar mt/mt.c

This would create the subdirectory *mt* and place the file *mt.c* within it.

tar has many more options than those mentioned here. These are the features that you're likely to use most of the time, but GNU *tar*, in particular, has extensions that make it ideal for creating backups and the like. See the *tar* manual page and the following section for more information.

Using tar with gzip and bzip2

tar does not compress the data stored in its archives in any way. If you are creating a tar file from three 200 K files, you'll end up with an archive of about 600 K. It is common practice to compress tar archives with *gzip* (or the older *compress* program). You could create a *gzip*ped *tar* file using the commands:

```
tar cvf tarfile files...
gzip -9 tarfile
```

But that's so cumbersome, and requires you to have enough space to store the uncompressed *tar* file before you *gzip* it.

A much trickier way to accomplish the same task is to use an interesting feature of *tar* that allows you to write an archive to standard output. If you specify - as the *tar* file to read or write, the data will be read from or written to standard input or output. For example, we can create a *gzip*ped *tar* file using the command:

```
tar cvf - files... | gzip -9 > tarfile.tar.gz
```

Here, *tar* creates an archive from the named *files* and writes it to standard output; next, *gzip* reads the data from standard input, compresses it, and writes the result to its own standard output; finally, we redirect the *gzip*ped *tar* file to *tarfile.tar.gz*.

We could extract such a *tar* file using the command:

```
gunzip -c tarfile.tar.gz | tar xvf -
```

gunzip uncompresses the named archive file and writes the result to standard output, which is read by *tar* on standard input and extracted. Isn't Unix fun?

Of course, both commands are rather cumbersome to type. Luckily, the GNU version of *tar* provides the z option, which automatically creates or extracts *gzip*ped archives. (We saved the discussion of this option until now, so you'd truly appreciate its convenience.) For example, we could use the commands:

```
tar cvzf tarfile.tar.gz files...
```

and

```
tar xvzf tarfile.tar.gz
```

to create and extract *gzip*ped tar files. Note that you should name the files created in this way with the *.tar.gz* filename extensions (or the equally often used *.tgz*, which also works on systems with limited filename capabilities) to make their format obvious. The z option works just as well with other *tar* functions, such as t.

Only the GNU version of *tar* supports the z option; if you are using *tar* on another Unix system, you may have to use one of the longer commands to accomplish the same tasks. Nearly all Linux systems use GNU *tar*.

When you want to use *tar* in conjunction with *bzip2*, you need to tell *tar* about your compression program preferences, like this:

```
tar cvf tarfile.tar.bz2 --use-compress-program=bzip2 files...
```

Or, shorter:

```
tar cvf tarfile.tar.bz2 --use-compress-program=bzip2 files...
```

Or, shorter still:

```
tar cvjf tarfile.tar.bz2 files
```

The last version works only with newer versions of GNU *tar* that support the j option.

Keeping this in mind, you could write short shell scripts or aliases to handle cookbook *tar* file creation and extraction for you. Under *bash*, you could include the following functions in your *.bashrc*:

```
tarc ( ) { tar czvf $1.tar.gz $1 }
tarx ( ) { tar xzvf $1 }
tart ( ) { tar tzvf $1 }
```

With these functions, to create a *gzip*ped *tar* file from a single directory, you could use the command:

```
tarc directory
```

The resulting archive file would be named *directory.tar.gz*. (Be sure that there's no trailing slash on the directory name; otherwise, the archive will be created as *.tar.gz* within the given directory.) To list the table of contents of a *gzip*ped tar file, just use

```
tart file.tar.gz
```

Or, to extract such an archive, use:

```
tarx file.tar.gz
```

As a final note, we would like to mention that files created with *gzip* and/or *tar* can be unpacked with the well-known *WinZip* utility on Windows systems. *WinZip* doesn't have support for *bzip2* yet, though. If you, on the other hand, get a file in *.zip* format, you can unpack it on your Linux system using the *unzip* command.

tar Tricks

Because *tar* saves the ownership and permissions of files in the archive and retains the full directory structure, as well as symbolic and hard links, using *tar* is an excellent way to copy or move an entire directory tree from one place to another on the same system (or even between different systems, as we'll see). Using the - syntax described earlier, you can write a tar file to standard output, which is read and extracted on standard input elsewhere.

For example, say that we have a directory containing two subdirectories: *from-stuff* and *to-stuff*. *from-stuff* contains an entire tree of files, symbolic links, and so forth—something that is difficult to mirror precisely using a recursive *cp*. To mirror the entire tree beneath *from-stuff* to *to-stuff*, we could use the commands:

```
cd from-stuff
tar cf - . | (cd ../to-stuff; tar xvf -)
```

Simple and elegant, right? We start in the directory *from-stuff* and create a tar file of the current directory, which is written to standard output. This archive is read by a subshell (the commands contained within parentheses); the subshell does a *cd* to the target directory, *../to-stuff* (relative to *from-stuff*, that is), and then runs *tar xvf*, reading from standard input. No *tar* file is ever written to disk; the data is sent entirely via pipe from one *tar* process to another. The second *tar* process has the v option that prints each file as it's extracted; in this way, we can verify that the command is working as expected.

In fact, you could transfer directory trees from one machine to another (via the network) using this trick—just include an appropriate *rsh* (or *ssh*) command within the subshell on the right side of the pipe. The remote shell would execute *tar* to read the archive on its standard input. (Actually, GNU *tar* has facilities to read or write *tar* files automatically from other machines over the network; see the *tar*(1) manual page for details.)

CHAPTER 13
Networking

So, you've staked out your homestead on the Linux frontier, and installed and configured your system. What's next? Eventually you'll want to communicate with other systems—Linux and otherwise—and the Pony Express isn't going to suffice.

Fortunately, Linux supports a number of methods for data communication and networking. This mostly means TCP/IP these days, but other techniques such as serial communications and even communication via radio links are available. In this chapter, we discuss how to configure your system to communicate with the world.

The *Linux Network Administrator's Guide* (O'Reilly), also available from the Linux Documentation Project, is a wide-ranging guide to configuring TCP/IP and other networking protocols under Linux. For a detailed account of the information presented here, we refer you to that book.

Networking with TCP/IP

Linux supports a full implementation of the Transmission Control Protocol/Internet Protocol (TCP/IP) networking protocols. TCP/IP has become the most successful mechanism for networking computers worldwide. With Linux and an Ethernet card, you can network your machine to a local area network (LAN) or (with the proper network connections) to the Internet—the worldwide TCP/IP network.

Hooking up a small LAN of Unix machines is easy. It simply requires an Ethernet controller in each machine and the appropriate Ethernet cables and other hardware. Or if your business or university provides access to the Internet, you can easily add your Linux machine to this network.

Linux also supports Serial Line Internet Protocol (SLIP) and Point-to-Point Protocol (PPP). SLIP and PPP allow you to have dial-up Internet access using a modem. If your business or university provides SLIP or PPP access, you can dial in to the SLIP or PPP server and put your machine on the Internet over the phone line. Alternatively, if your

Linux machine also has Ethernet access to the Internet, you can configure it as a SLIP or PPP server.

In the following sections, we won't mention SLIP anymore because nowadays most people use PPP.

Besides the *Linux Network Administrator's Guide*, the various HOWTOs at *http://www.tldp.org/HOWTO/HOWTO-INDEX/networking.html* contain lots of information about how to set up particular aspects of networking, including how to deal with unruly hardware like some modems. For example, Linux Ethernet HOWTO at *http://www.tldp.org/HOWTO/Ethernet-HOWTO.html* is a document that describes configuration of various Ethernet card drivers for Linux.

Also of interest is *TCP/IP Network Administration* (O'Reilly). It contains complete information on using and configuring TCP/IP on Unix systems. If you plan to set up a network of Linux machines or do any serious TCP/IP hacking, you should have the background in network administration presented by that book.

If you really want to get serious about setting up and operating networks, you will probably also want to read *DNS and BIND* (O'Reilly). This book tells you all there is to know about nameservers in a refreshingly funny manner.

TCP/IP Concepts

In order to fully appreciate (and utilize) the power of TCP/IP, you should be familiar with its underlying principles. TCP/IP is a suite of *protocols* (the magic buzzword for this chapter) that define how machines should communicate with each other via a network, as well as internally to other layers of the protocol suite. For the theoretical background of the Internet protocols, the best sources of information are the first volume of Douglas Comer's *Internetworking with TCP/IP* (Prentice Hall) and the first volume of W. Richard Stevens' *TCP/IP Illustrated* (Addison Wesley).

TCP/IP was originally developed for use on the Advanced Research Projects Agency network, ARPAnet, which was funded to support military and computer-science research. Therefore, you may hear TCP/IP being referred to as the "DARPA Internet Protocols." Since that first Internet, many other TCP/IP networks have come into use, such as the National Science Foundation's NSFNET, as well as thousands of other local and regional networks around the world. All these networks are interconnected into a single conglomerate known as the Internet.

On a TCP/IP network, each machine is assigned an *IP address*, which is a 32-bit number uniquely identifying the machine. You need to know a little about IP addresses to structure your network and assign addresses to hosts. The IP address is usually represented as a dotted quad: four numbers in decimal notation, separated by dots. As an example, the IP address 0x80114b14 (in hexadecimal format) can be written as 128.17.75.20.

Two special cases should be mentioned here: dynamic IP addresses and masqueraded IP addresses. Both were invented to overcome the current shortage of IP addresses (which will not be of concern any longer once everybody has adopted the new IPv6 standard that prescribes 6 bytes for the IP addresses—enough for every amoeba in the universe to have an IP address).*

Dynamic IP addresses are what most Internet service providers (ISPs) use. When you connect to your ISP's service, whether by dial-up, DSL, or otherwise, you are assigned an IP number out of a pool that the ISP has allocated for this service. The next time you log in, you might get a different IP number. The idea behind this is that only a small number of the customers of an ISP are logged in at the same time, so a smaller number of IP addresses are needed. Still, as long as your computer is connected to the Internet, it has a unique IP address that no other computer is using at that time.

Masquerading (also known as Network Address Translation, NAT) allows several computers to share an IP address. All machines in a masqueraded network use so-called private IP numbers, numbers out of a range that is allocated for internal purposes and that can never serve as real addresses out there on the Internet. Any number of networks can use the same private IP numbers, as they are never visible outside of the LAN. One machine, the "masquerading server," will map these private IP numbers to one public IP number (either dynamic or static) and ensure through an ingenious mapping mechanism that incoming packets are routed to the right machine.

The IP address is divided into two parts: the network address and the host address. The network address consists of the higher-order bits of the address and the host address of the remaining bits. (In general, each *host* is a separate machine on the network.) The size of these two fields depends on the type of network in question. For example, on a Class B network (for which the first byte of the IP address is between 128 and 191), the first two bytes of the address identify the network, and the remaining two bytes identify the host (Figure 13-1). For the example address just given, the network address is 128.17, and the host address is 75.20. To put this another way, the machine with IP address 128.17.75.20 is host number 75.20 on the network 128.17.

In addition, the host portion of the IP address may be subdivided to allow for a *subnetwork address*. Subnetworking allows large networks to be divided into smaller subnets, each of which may be maintained independently. For example, an organization may allocate a single Class B network, which provides 2 bytes of host information, up to 65,534 hosts on the network.† The organization may then wish to dole

---

* Linux supports IPv6, but since most local networks and ISPs do not use it yet, it is not very relevant at this time, unfortunately.

† Why not 65,536 instead? For reasons to be discussed later, a host address of 0 or 255 is invalid.

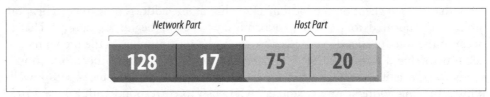

Figure 13-1. IP address

out the responsibility of maintaining portions of the network so that each subnetwork is handled by a different department. Using subnetworking, the organization can specify, for example, that the first byte of the host address (that is, the third byte of the overall IP address) is the subnet address, and the second byte is the host address for that subnetwork (Figure 13-2). In this case, the IP address 128.17.75.20 identifies host number 20 on subnetwork 75 of network 128.17.

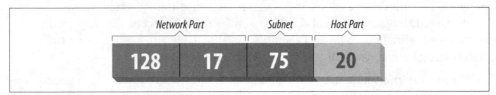

Figure 13-2. IP address with subnet

Processes (on either the same or different machines) that wish to communicate via TCP/IP generally specify the destination machine's IP address as well as a *port address*. The destination IP address is used, of course, to route data from one machine to the destination machine. The port address is a 16-bit number that specifies a particular service or application on the destination machine that should receive the data. Port numbers can be thought of as office numbers at a large office building: the entire building has a single IP address, but each business has a separate office there.

Here's a real-life example of how IP addresses and port numbers are used. The ssh program allows a user on one machine to start a login session on another, while encrypting all the data traffic between the two so that nobody can intercept the communication. On the remote machine, the *ssh* daemon, *sshd*, is listening to a specific port for incoming connections (in this case, the port number is 22).*

The user executing *ssh* specifies the address of the machine to log in to, and the *ssh* program attempts to open a connection to port 22 on the remote machine. If it is successful, *ssh* and *sshd* are able to communicate with each other to provide the remote login for the user in question.

---

* On many systems, *sshd* is not always listening to port 22; the Internet services daemon inetd is listening on its behalf. For now, let's sweep that detail under the carpet.

Note that the *ssh* client on the local machine has a port address of its own. This port address is allocated to the client dynamically when it begins execution. This is because the remote *sshd* doesn't need to know the port number of the incoming *ssh* client beforehand. When the client initiates the connection, part of the information it sends to *sshd* is its port number. *sshd* can be thought of as a business with a well-known mailing address. Any customers who wish to correspond with the *sshd* running on a particular machine need to know not only the IP address of the machine to talk to (the address of the *sshd* office building), but also the port number where *sshd* can be found (the particular office within the building). The address and port number of the *ssh* client are included as part of the "return address" on the envelope containing the letter.

The TCP/IP family contains a number of protocols. Transmission Control Protocol (TCP) is responsible for providing reliable, connection-oriented communications between two processes, which may be running on different machines on the network. User Datagram Protocol (UDP) is similar to TCP except that it provides connectionless, unreliable service. Processes that use UDP must implement their own acknowledgment and synchronization routines if necessary.

TCP and UDP transmit and receive data in units known as *packets*. Each packet contains a chunk of information to send to another machine, as well as a header specifying the destination and source port addresses.

Internet Protocol (IP) sits beneath TCP and UDP in the protocol hierarchy. It is responsible for transmitting and routing TCP or UDP packets via the network. In order to do so, IP wraps each TCP or UDP packet within another packet (known as an IP *datagram*), which includes a header with routing and destination information. The IP datagram header includes the IP address of the source and destination machines.

Note that IP doesn't know anything about port addresses; those are the responsibility of TCP and UDP. Similarly, TCP and UDP don't deal with IP addresses, which (as the name implies) are only IP's concern. As you can see, the mail metaphor with return addresses and envelopes is quite accurate: each packet can be thought of as a letter contained within an envelope. TCP and UDP wrap the letter in an envelope with the source and destination port numbers (office numbers) written on it.

IP acts as the mail room for the office building sending the letter. IP receives the envelope and wraps it in yet another envelope, with the IP address (office building address) of both the destination and the source affixed. The post office (which we haven't discussed quite yet) delivers the letter to the appropriate office building. There, the mail room unwraps the outer envelope and hands it to TCP/UDP, which delivers the letter to the appropriate office based on the port number (written on the inner envelope). Each envelope has a return address that IP and TCP/UDP use to reply to the letter.

To make the specification of machines on the Internet more humane, network hosts are often given a name as well as an IP address. The Domain Name System (DNS) takes care of translating hostnames to IP addresses, and vice versa, as well as handling the distribution of the name-to-IP-address database across the entire Internet. Using hostnames also allows the IP address associated with a machine to change (e.g., if the machine is moved to a different network), without having to worry that others won't be able to "find" the machine once the address changes. The DNS record for the machine is simply updated with the new IP address, and all references to the machine, by name, will continue to work.

DNS is an enormous, worldwide distributed database. Each organization maintains a piece of the database, listing the machines in the organization. If you find yourself in the position of maintaining the list for your organization, you can get help from the *Linux Network Administrator's Guide* or *TCP/IP Network Administration*, both from O'Reilly. If those aren't enough, you can really get the full scoop from the book *DNS and BIND* (O'Reilly).

For the purposes of most administration, all you need to know is that either a daemon called *named* (pronounced "name-dee") has to run on your system, or you need to configure your system to use somebody else's name service—typically your ISP's or one running in your local network. This daemon or name service is your window onto DNS.

Now, we might ask ourselves how a packet gets from one machine (office building) to another. This is the actual job of IP, as well as a number of other protocols that aid IP in its task. Besides managing IP datagrams on each host (as the mail room), IP is also responsible for routing packets between hosts.

Before we can discuss how routing works, we must explain the model upon which TCP/IP networks are built. A network is just a set of machines that are connected through some physical network medium—such as Ethernet or serial lines. In TCP/IP terms, each network has its own methods for handling routing and packet transfer internally.

Networks are connected to each other via *gateways* (also known as *routers*). A gateway is a host that has direct connections to two or more networks; the gateway can then exchange information between the networks and route packets from one network to another. For instance, a gateway might be a workstation with more than one Ethernet interface. Each interface is connected to a different network, and the operating system uses this connectivity to allow the machine to act as a gateway.

In order to make our discussion more concrete, let's introduce an imaginary network, made up of the machines *eggplant*, *papaya*, *apricot*, and *zucchini*. Figure 13-3 depicts the configuration of these machines on the network.

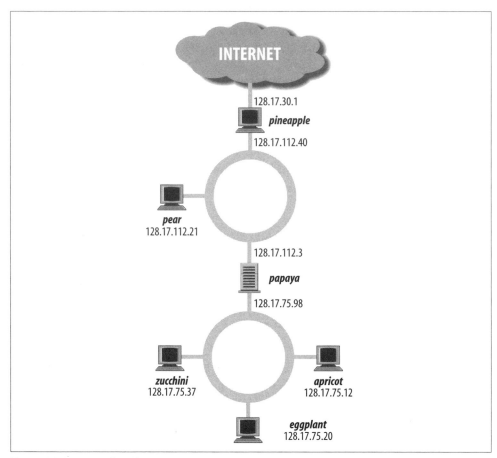

Figure 13-3. Network with two gateways

As you can see, *papaya* has two IP addresses—one on the 128.17.75 subnetwork and another on the 128.17.112 subnetwork. *pear* and *pineapple* are both on network 128.17.112, and *pineapple* is also on 128.17.30.

IP uses the network portion of the IP address to determine how to route packets between machines. To do this, each machine on the network has a *routing table*, which contains a list of networks and the gateway machine for that network. To route a packet to a particular machine, IP looks at the network portion of the destination address. If there is an entry for that network in the routing table, IP routes the packet through the appropriate gateway. Otherwise, IP routes the packet through the "default" gateway given in the routing table.

Routing tables can contain entries for specific machines as well as for networks. In addition, each machine has a routing table entry for itself.

Let's examine the routing table for *eggplant*. Using the command *netstat -rn*, we see the following:

```
eggplant:$ netstat -rn
     Kernel IP routing table
     Destination   Gateway       Genmask         Flags  MSS   Window irtt Iface
     128.17.75.0   128.17.75.20  255.255.255.0   UN     1500  0         0 eth0
     default       128.17.75.98  0.0.0.0         UGN    1500  0         0 eth0
     127.0.0.1     127.0.0.1     255.0.0.0       UH     3584  0         0 lo
     128.17.75.20  127.0.0.1     255.255.255.0   UH     3584  0         0 lo
```

The first column displays the destination networks (and hosts) that the routing table includes. The first entry is for the network 128.17.75 (note that the host address is 0 for network entries), which is the network that *eggplant* lives on. Any packets sent to this network should be routed through 128.17.75.20, which is the IP address of *eggplant*. In general, a machine's route to its own network is through itself.

The Flags column of the routing table gives information on the destination address for this entry; U specifies that the route is "up," N that the destination is a network, and so on. The MSS field shows how many bytes are transferred at a time over the respective connection, Window indicates how many frames may be sent ahead before a confirmation must be made, irtt gives statistics on the use of this route, and Iface lists the network device used for the route. On Linux systems, Ethernet interfaces are named *eth0*, *eth1*, and so on. *lo* is the loopback device, which we'll discuss shortly.

The second entry in the routing table is the default route, which applies to all packets destined for networks or hosts for which there is no entry in the table. In this case, the default route is through *papaya*, which can be considered the door to the outside world. Every machine on the 128.17.75 subnet must go through *papaya* to talk to machines on any other network.

The third entry in the table is for the address 127.0.0.1, which is the *loopback* address. This address is used when a machine wants to make a TCP/IP connection to itself. It uses the *lo* device as its interface, which prevents loopback connections from using the Ethernet (via the *eth0* interface). In this way, network bandwidth is not wasted when a machine wishes to talk to itself.

The last entry in the routing table is for the IP address 128.17.75.20, which is the *eggplant* host's own address. As we can see, it uses 127.0.0.1 as its gateway. This way, any time *eggplant* makes a TCP/IP connection to itself, the loopback address is used as the gateway, and the *lo* network device is used.

Let's say that *eggplant* wants to send a packet to *zucchini*. The IP datagram contains a source address of 128.17.75.20 and a destination address of 128.17.75.37. IP determines that the network portion of the destination address is 128.17.75 and uses the routing table entry for 128.17.75.0 accordingly. The packet is sent directly to the network, which *zucchini* receives and is able to process.

What happens if *eggplant* wants to send packets to a machine not on the local network, such as *pear*? The destination address is 128.17.112.21. IP attempts to find a route for the 128.17.112 network in the routing tables, but none exists, so it selects the default route through *papaya*. *papaya* receives the packet and looks up the destination address in its own routing tables. The routing table for *papaya* might look like this:

```
Destination  Gateway        Genmask       Flags  MSS  Window irtt Iface
  128.17.75.0   128.17.75.98  255.255.255.0  UN    1500  0        0 eth0
  128.17.112.0  128.17.112.3  255.255.255.0  UN    1500  0        0 eth1
  default       128.17.112.40 0.0.0.0        UGN   1500  0        0 eth1
  127.0.0.1     127.0.0.1     255.0.0.0      UH    3584  0        0 lo
  128.17.75.98  127.0.0.1     255.255.255.0  UH    3584  0        0 lo
```

As you can see, *papaya* is connected to the 128.17.75 network through its *eth0* device and to 128.17.112 through *eth1*. The default route is through *pineapple*, which is a gateway to the Wild Blue Yonder (as far as *papaya* is concerned).

Once *papaya* receives a packet destined for *pear*, it sees that the destination address is on the network 128.17.112 and routes that packet to the network using the second entry in the routing table.

Similarly, if *eggplant* wanted to send packets to machines outside the local organization, it would route packets through *papaya* (its gateway). *papaya* would, in turn, route outgoing packets through *pineapple*, and so forth. Packets are handed from one gateway to the next until they reach the intended destination network. This is the basic structure upon which the Internet is based: a seemingly infinite chain of networks, interconnected via gateways.

Hardware Requirements

You can use Linux TCP/IP without any networking hardware; configuring "loopback" mode allows you to talk to yourself. This is necessary for some applications and games that use the loopback network device.

However, if you want to use Linux with an Ethernet TCP/IP network, you'll need an Ethernet adapter card. Many Ethernet adapters are supported by Linux for the ISA, EISA, and PCI buses, as well as USB and PCMCIA adapters. See the Linux Ethernet HOWTO for a complete discussion of Linux Ethernet hardware compatibility. For any reasonably new computer (that was sold in the last, say, two to three years), it is also quite likely that the computer has Ethernet built in, so you do not have install an Ethernet adapter card. You'll recognize this because there is an Ethernet connector socket (type RJ45) somewhere.

Over the last few years, support has been added for non-Ethernet high-speed networking, such as HIPPI. This topic is beyond the scope of this book, but if you are interested, you can get some information from the directory *Documentation/networking* in your kernel sources.

If you have an ADSL connection and use an ADSL router, this looks to Linux just like a normal Ethernet connection. As such, you need neither specific hardware (except an Ethernet card, of course) nor special drivers besides the Ethernet card driver itself. If you want to connect your Linux box directly to your ADSL modem, you still don't need to have any particular hardware or driver, but you do need to run a protocol called PPPoE (PPP over Ethernet); more about this later.

Linux also supports SLIP and PPP, which allow you to use a modem to access the Internet over a phone line. In this case, you'll need a modem compatible with your SLIP or PPP server; for example, many servers require a 56-kbps V.90 modem (most also support K56flex). In this book, we describe the configuration of PPP because it is what most Internet service providers offer.

Finally, there is PLIP, which lets you connect two computers directly via parallel ports, requiring a special cable between the two.

Configuring TCP/IP with Ethernet

In this section, we discuss how to configure an Ethernet TCP/IP connection on a Linux system. Presumably this system will be part of a local network of machines that are already running TCP/IP; in this case, your gateway, nameserver, and so forth are already configured and available.

The following information applies primarily to Ethernet connections. If you're planning to use PPP, read this section to understand the concepts, and follow the PPP-specific instructions in "Dial-Up PPP," later in this chapter.

On the other hand, you may wish to set up an entire LAN of Linux machines (or a mix of Linux machines and other systems). In this case, you'll have to take care of a number of other issues not discussed here. This includes setting up a nameserver for yourself, as well as a gateway machine if your network is to be connected to other networks. If your network is to be connected to the Internet, you'll also have to obtain IP addresses and related information from your access provider.

In short, the method described here should work for many Linux systems configured for an existing LAN—but certainly not all. For further details, we direct you to a book on TCP/IP network administration, such as those mentioned at the beginning of this chapter.

First of all, we assume that your Linux system has the necessary TCP/IP software installed. This includes basic clients such as *ssh* and FTP, system-administration commands such as *ifconfig* and *route* (usually found in */etc* or */sbin*), and networking configuration files (such as */etc/hosts*). The other Linux-related networking documents described earlier explain how to go about installing the Linux networking software if you do not have it already.

A new system administration interface has been developed that unifies the various networking tasks (configurating, routing, etc.) into a single command named ip, provided by the IPROUTE2 package. We won't cover it here, because its value lies mainly in advanced features that most administrators don't use, but once you understand the concepts in this chapter you can figure out how to use those commands if you want to use that package.

We also assume that your kernel has been configured and compiled with TCP/IP support enabled. See "Building a New Kernel" in Chapter 18 for information on compiling your kernel. To enable networking, you must answer yes to the appropriate questions during the *make config* or *make menuconfig* step, rebuild the kernel, and boot from it.

Once this has been done, you must modify a number of configuration files. For the most part this is a simple procedure. Unfortunately, however, there is wide disagreement between Linux distributions as to where the various TCP/IP configuration files and support programs should go. Much of the time, they can be found in *letc* or *letc/sysconfig*, but in other cases they may be found in *lusr/etc*, *lusr/etc/inet*, or other bizarre locations. In the worst case, you'll have to use the find command to locate the files on your system. Also note that not all distributions keep the network configuration files and software in the same location; they may be spread across several directories.

Here we cover how to set up and configure networking on a Linux box manually. This should help you get some insight into what goes on behind the scenes and enable you to help yourself if something goes wrong with automatic setup tools provided by your distribution. It can be a good idea, though, to first try setting up your network with the configuration programs that your distribution provides; many of these are quite advanced these days and detect many of the necessary settings automatically. They are usually available from the menus on your desktop. If you understand the concepts in this chapter, it is not hard to figure out how to use them, but we do not cover them here because they tend to change, and what you mainly need to know is the effects you're aiming to achieve.

This section also assumes use of one Ethernet device on the system. These instructions should be fairly easy to extrapolate if your system has more than one network connection (and hence acts as a gateway).

Here, we also discuss configuration for loopback-only systems (systems with no Ethernet or PPP connection). If you have no network access, you may wish to configure your system for loopback-only TCP/IP so that you can use applications that require it.

Your network configuration

Before you can configure TCP/IP, you need to determine the following information about your network setup. In most cases, your local network administrator or ISP can provide you with this information. If your network is using DHCP, things are going to be a bit different—for example, you do not need to know your IP address, since it will be assigned to you automatically. But it's often easier to test things one step at a time and start with a static IP address. Just make sure with your network administrator or Internet service provider that you are not using one that another computer on the network is already using—that could be very annoying both for you and the other user, because communication will be disturbed, to say the least.

Your IP address

> This is the unique machine address in dotted-decimal format. An example is 128.17.75.98. Your network administrators will provide you with this number.

> If you're configuring loopback mode (i.e., no PPP and no Ethernet card, just TCP/IP connections to your own machine), your IP address is 127.0.0.1.

Your subnetwork mask

> This is a dotted quad, similar to the IP address, which determines which portion of the IP address specifies the subnetwork number and which portion specifies the host on that subnet.

> The subnetwork mask is a pattern of bits, which, when bitwise-ANDed with an IP address on your network, will tell you which subnet that address belongs to. For example, your subnet mask might be 255.255.255.0. If your IP address is 128.17.75.20, the subnetwork portion of your address is 128.17.75.

> We distinguish here between "network address" and "subnetwork address." Remember that for Class B addresses, the first two bytes (here, 128.17) specify the network, while the second two bytes specify the host. With a subnet mask of 255.255.255.0, however, 128.17.75 is considered the entire subnet address (e.g., subnetwork 75 of network 128.17), and 20 the host address.

> Your network administrators choose the subnet mask and therefore can provide you with this information.

> This applies as well to the loopback device. Since the loopback address is always 127.0.0.1, the netmask for this device is always 255.0.0.0.

Your subnetwork address

> This is the subnet portion of your IP address as determined by the subnet mask. For example, if your subnet mask is 255.255.255.0 and your IP address 128.17.75.20, your subnet address is 128.17.75.0.

> Loopback-only systems don't have a subnet address.

Your broadcast address

> This address is used to broadcast packets to every machine on your subnet. In general, this is equal to your subnet address (see previous item) with 255

---

replaced as the host address. For subnet address 128.17.75.0, the broadcast address is 128.17.75.255. Similarly, for subnet address 128.17.0.0, the broadcast address is 128.17.255.255.

Note that some systems use the subnetwork address as the broadcast address. If you have any doubt, check with your network administrators.

Loopback-only systems do not have a broadcast address.

The IP address of your gateway

This is the address of the machine that acts as the default route to the outside world. In fact, you may have more than one gateway address—for example, if your network is connected directly to several other networks. However, only one of these will act as the *default* route. (Recall the example in the previous section, where the 128.17.112.0 network is connected to both 128.17.75.0 through *papaya* and the outside world through *pineapple*.)

Your network administrators will provide you with the IP addresses of any gateways on your network, as well as the networks they connect to. Later, you will use this information with the route command to include entries in the routing table for each gateway.

Loopback-only systems do not have a gateway address. The same is true for isolated networks.

The IP address of your nameserver

This is the address of the machine that handles hostname-to-address translations for your machine. Your network administrators will provide you with this information.

You may wish to run your own nameserver (by configuring and running named). However, unless you absolutely must run your own nameserver (for example, if no other nameserver is available on your local network), we suggest using the nameserver address provided by your network administrators (or your ISP). At any rate, most books on TCP/IP configuration include information on running named.

Naturally, loopback-only systems have no nameserver address.

The network configuration files

Network configuration files are system-wide resource configuration scripts executed at boot time by *init*. They run basic system daemons (such as *sendmail*, *crond*, and so on) and are used to configure network parameters. *rc* files are usually found in the directory */etc/init.d*.

Note that there are *many* ways to carry out the network configuration described here. Every Linux distribution uses a slightly different mechanism to help automate the process. What we describe here is a generic method that allows you to create two network configuration files that will run the appropriate commands to get your machine talking to the network. Most distributions have their own scripts that accomplish more or less the same thing. If in doubt, first attempt to configure networking as suggested by the documentation for your distribution and, as a last resort, use the methods described here. (As an example, the Red Hat distribution uses the script */etc/rc.d/init.d/network*, which obtains network information from files in */etc/sysconfig*. The `control-panel` system administration program provided with Red Hat configures networking automatically without editing any of these files. The SUSE distribution uses */etc/init.d/network*, and lets you configure most networking aspects via the tool *YaST2*. And of course, any new version of either distribution could change this again.)

Here, we're going to describe the network configuration files used to configure TCP/IP in some of the better-known distributions:

Red Hat
> Networking is scattered among files for each `init` level that includes networking. For instance, the */etc/rc.d/rc1.d* directory controls a level 1 (single-user) boot, so it doesn't have any networking commands, but the */etc/rc.d/rc3.d* controlling a level 3 boot has files specifically to start networking.

SUSE
> All the startup files for all system services, including networking, are grouped together in the */etc/init.d* directory. They are quite generic and get their actual values from the system-wide configuration file */etc/sysconfig*. The most important files here are */etc/init.d/network*, which starts and halts network interfaces and configures routing, and */etc/init.d/setserial*, which configures serial ports. If you have ISDN hardware, the file */etc/init.d/isdn* is applicable, too. Note that in general, you do not need to (and should not) edit those files; edit the files */etc/sysconfig* instead (that's what *YaST* does).

Debian
> The network configuration (Ethernet cards, IP addresses, and routing) and the base networking daemons (`portman` and `inetd`) are set up in the file */etc/init.d/networking*.

We'll use two files here for illustrative purposes: */etc/init.d/rc.inet1* and */etc/init.d/rc.inet2*. The former will set up the hardware and the basic networking, and the latter will configure the networking services. A number of distributions follow such a separation, even though the files might have other names.

`init` uses the file */etc/inittab* to determine what processes to run at boot time. To run the files */etc/init.d/rc.inet1* and */etc/init.d/rc.inet2* from `init`, */etc/inittab* might include entries such as:

```
n1:34:wait:/etc/init.d/rc.inet1
n2:34:wait:/etc/init.d/rc.inet2
```

The *inittab* file is described in "init, inittab, and rc Files" in Chapter 17. The first field gives a unique two-character identifier for each entry. The second field lists the run levels in which the scripts are run; on this system, we initialize networking in run levels 3 and 4. The word `wait` in the third field tells `init` to wait until the script has finished execution before continuing. The last field gives the name of the script to run.

While you are first setting up your network configuration, you may wish to run *rc.inet1* and *rc.inet2* by hand (as *root*) in order to debug any problems. Later you can include entries for them in another *rc* file or in */etc/inittab*.

As mentioned earlier, *rc.inet1* configures the basic network interface. This includes your IP and network address and the routing table information for your system. Two programs are used to configure these parameters: *ifconfig* and *route*. Both of these are usually found in */sbin*.

ifconfig is used for configuring the network device interface with certain parameters, such as the IP address, subnetwork mask, broadcast address, and the like. route is used to create and modify entries in the routing table.

For most configurations, an *rc.inet1* file similar to the following should work. You will, of course, have to edit this for your own system. Do not use the sample IP and network addresses listed here; they may correspond to an actual machine on the Internet:

```
#!/bin/sh
# This is /etc/init.d/rc.inet1 - Configure the TCP/IP interfaces

# First, configure the loopback device

HOSTNAME=`hostname`

/sbin/ifconfig lo 127.0.0.1   # uses default netmask 255.0.0.0
/sbin/route add 127.0.0.1     # a route to point to the loopback device

# Next, configure the Ethernet device. If you're only using loopback or
# SLIP, comment out the rest of these lines.

# Edit for your setup.
IPADDR="128.17.75.20"       # REPLACE with your IP address
NETMASK="255.255.255.0"     # REPLACE with your subnet mask
NETWORK="128.17.75.0"       # REPLACE with your network address
BROADCAST="128.17.75.255"   # REPLACE with your broadcast address
GATEWAY="128.17.75.98"      # REPLACE with your default gateway address

# Configure the eth0 device to use information above.
/sbin/ifconfig eth0 ${IPADDR} netmask ${NETMASK} broadcast ${BROADCAST}

# Add a route for our own network.
/sbin/route add ${NETWORK}
```

```
# Add a route to the default gateway.
/sbin/route add default gw ${GATEWAY} metric 1

# End of Ethernet Configuration
```

As you can see, the format of the *ifconfig* command is

```
ifconfig interface device options...
```

For example:

```
ifconfig lo 127.0.0.1
```

assigns the *lo* (loopback) device the IP address 127.0.0.1, and

```
ifconfig eth0 127.17.75.20
```

assigns the *eth0* (first Ethernet) device the address 127.17.75.20.

In addition to specifying the address, Ethernet devices usually require that the sub-network mask be set with the *netmask* option and that the broadcast address be set with *broadcast*.

The format of the *route* command, as used here, is:

```
route add [ -net | -host ] destination [ gw gateway ]
          [ metric metric ] options
```

where *destination* is the destination address for this route (or the keyword default), *gateway* is the IP address of the gateway for this route, and *metric* is the metric number for the route (discussed later).

We use *route* to add entries to the routing table. You should add a route for the loopback device (as seen earlier), for your local network, and for your default gateway. For example, if our default gateway is 128.17.75.98, we would use the command:

```
route add default gw 128.17.75.98
```

route takes several options. Using *-net* or *-host* before *destination* will tell route that the destination is a network or specific host, respectively. (In most cases, routes point to networks, but in some situations you may have an independent machine that requires its own route. You would use *-host* for such a routing table entry.)

The *metric* option specifies a *metric value* for this route. Metric values are used when there is more than one route to a specific location, and the system must make a decision about which to use. Routes with lower metric values are preferred. In this case, we set the metric value for our default route to 1, which forces that route to be preferred over all others.

How could there possibly be more than one route to a particular location? First of all, you may use multiple route commands in *rc.inet1* for a particular destination—if you have more than one gateway to a particular network, for example. However, your routing tables may dynamically acquire additional entries in them if you run routed (discussed later). If you run routed, other systems may broadcast routing information to machines on the network, causing extra routing table entries to be created on your machine. By setting the *metric* value for your default route to 1, you ensure that any new routing table entries will not supersede the preference of your default gateway.

You should read the manual pages for *ifconfig* and *route*, which describe the syntax of these commands in detail. There may be other options to `ifconfig` and `route` that are pertinent to your configuration.

Let's move on. *rc.inet2* is used to run various daemons used by the TCP/IP suite. These are not necessary in order for your system to talk to the network, and are therefore relegated to a separate *rc* file. In most cases you should attempt to configure *rc.inet1*, and ensure that your system is able to send and receive packets from the network, before bothering to configure *rc.inet2*.

Among the daemons executed by *rc.inet2* are *inetd*, *syslogd*, and *routed*. The version of *rc.inet2* on your system may currently start a number of other servers, but we suggest commenting these out while you are debugging your network configuration.

The most important of these servers is `inetd`, which acts as the "operator" for other system daemons. It sits in the background and listens to certain network ports for incoming connections. When a connection is made, `inetd` spawns a copy of the appropriate daemon for that port. For example, when an incoming FTP connection is made, `inetd` forks `in.ftpd`, which handles the FTP connection from there. This is simpler and more efficient than running individual copies of each daemon. This way, network daemons are executed on demand.

`syslogd` is the system logging daemon; it accumulates log messages from various applications and stores them into logfiles based on the configuration information in */etc/syslogd.conf*.

`routed` is a server used to maintain dynamic routing information. When your system attempts to send packets to another network, it may require additional routing table entries in order to do so. `routed` takes care of manipulating the routing table without the need for user intervention.

Here is a sample *rc.inet2* that starts up `syslogd`, `inetd`, and `routed`:

```
#! /bin/sh
# Sample /etc/init.d/rc.inet2

# Start syslogd
if [ -f /usr/sbin/syslogd ]
then
/usr/sbin/syslogd
fi

# Start inetd
if [ -f /usr/sbin/inetd ]
then
/usr/sbin/inetd
```

```
fi

# Start routed
if [ -f /usr/sbin/routed ]
then
/usr/sbin/routed -q
fi
```

Among the various additional servers you may want to start in *rc.inet2* is *named*. *named* is a nameserver: it is responsible for translating (local) IP addresses to names, and vice versa. If you don't have a nameserver elsewhere on the network, or if you want to provide local machine names to other machines in your domain, it may be necessary to run *named*. *named* configuration is somewhat complex and requires planning; we refer interested readers to *DNS and BIND* (O'Reilly).

/etc/hosts

/etc/hosts contains a list of IP addresses and the hostnames they correspond to. In general, */etc/hosts* contains entries for your local machine and perhaps other "important" machines (such as your nameserver or gateway). Your local nameserver provides address-to-name mappings for other machines on the network transparently. It is in fact possible to only get your address-to-name mappings from the */etc/hosts* file, without running a local nameserver at all. If you only have a few machines on your network, that may well be possible. But if you have more, then you would have to change the */etc/hosts* file on each machine for each change, a task that grows quadratic in size with the number of machines and quickly becomes infeasible.

For example, if your machine is *eggplant.veggie.com* with the IP address 128.17.75.20, your */etc/hosts* would look like this:

```
127.0.0.1               localhost
128.17.75.20            eggplant.veggie.com eggplant
```

If you're just using loopback, the only line in the */etc/hosts* file should be for the address 127.0.0.1.

/etc/networks

The */etc/networks* file lists the names and addresses of your own and other networks. It is used by the route command and allows you to specify a network by name instead of by address.

Every network you wish to add a route to using the route command (generally called from *rc.inet1*) should have an entry in */etc/networks* for convenience; otherwise, you will have to specify the network's IP address instead of the name.

As an example:

```
default         0.0.0.0         # default route    - mandatory
loopnet         127.0.0.0       # loopback network - mandatory
veggie-net      128.17.75.0     # Modify for your own network address
```

Now, instead of using the command:

```
route add 128.17.75.20
```

we can use:

```
route add veggie-net
```

/etc/host.conf

The *etc/host.conf* file specifies how your system resolves hostnames. It should contain the following two lines:

```
order hosts,bind
multi on
```

These lines tell the resolver libraries to first check the *etc/hosts* file and then ask the nameserver (if one is present) for any names it must look up. The `multi` entry allows you to have multiple IP addresses for a given machine name in *etc/hosts*.

On systems that use *glibc2* (which applies to most of the newer distributions), *etc/nsswitch.conf* is used instead of *etc/host.conf*. In this case, this file should contain the lines `hosts: files dns` and `networks: files dns`.

/etc/resolv.conf

The *etcresolv.conf* file configures the name resolver, specifying the address of your nameserver (if any) and domains that you want to search by default if a specified hostname is not a fully specified hostname. For example, if this file contains the line:

```
search vpizza.com vpasta.com
```

using the hostname *blurb* will cause the name resolver to try to resolve the names *blurb.vpizza.com* and *blurb.vpasta.com* (in this order). This is convenient because it saves you typing in the full names of often-used domains. On the other hand, the more domains you specify here, the longer the DNS lookup will take.

For example, the machine *eggplant.veggie.com* with a nameserver at address 128.17.75.55 would have the following lines in *etc/resolv.conf*:

```
domain     veggie.com
nameserver 128.17.75.55
```

You can specify more than one nameserver; each must have a `nameserver` line of its own in *resolv.conf*.

Setting your hostname

You should set your system hostname with the `hostname` command. This is usually executed from a file called *etc/init.d/boot.localnet* or similar; simply search your system *rc* files to determine where it is invoked. For example, if your (full) hostname is *eggplant.veggie.com*, edit the appropriate *rc* file to execute the command */bin/host-*

name eggplant.veggie.com. Note that the `hostname` executable may be found in a directory other than */bin* on your system.

Trying out your network

Once you have the various networking configuration files modified for your system, you should be able to reboot (using a TCP/IP-enabled kernel) and attempt to use the network.

When first booting the system, you may wish to disable execution of *rc.inet1* and *rc.inet2* and run them by hand once the system is up. This allows you to catch any error messages, modify the scripts, and retry. Once you have things working, you can enable the scripts from */etc/inittab*.

One good way of testing network connectivity is to simply `ssh` to another host. You should first try to connect to another host on your local network, and if this works, attempt to connect to hosts on other networks. The former will test your connection to the local subnet; the latter, your connection to the rest of the world through your gateway.

You may be able to connect to remote machines via the gateway if connecting to machines on the subnet fails. This is a sign that there is a problem with your subnetwork mask or the routing table entry for the local network.

When attempting to connect to other machines, you should first try to connect using only the IP address of the remote host. If this seems to work, but connecting via the hostname does not, there may be a problem with your nameserver configuration (e.g., */etc/resolv.conf* and */etc/host.conf*) or with your route to the nameserver.

The most common source of network trouble is an ill-configured routing table. You can use the command

```
netstat -rn
```

to display the routing table; in the previous section, we described the format of the routing tables as displayed by this command. The *netstat*(8) manual page provides additional insight as well. Using *netstat* without the *-n* option forces it to display host and network entries by name instead of by address.

To debug your routing tables, you can either edit *rc.inet1* and reboot, or use the `route` command by hand to add or delete entries. The manual page for `route`(8) describes the full syntax of this command. Note that simply editing *rc.inet1* and re-executing it will not clear out old entries in the routing table; you must either reboot or use `route del` to delete the entries.

If absolutely nothing seems to work, there may be a problem with your Ethernet device configuration. First, be sure that your Ethernet card was detected at the appropriate address and/or IRQ at boot time. The kernel boot messages will give you this information; if you are using *syslogd*, kernel boot-time messages are also saved in a file, such as */var/log/messages*.

A good way to determine whether it was really the Ethernet card that created the trouble is to use the command `ifconfig` *interface_name*, as in the following example:

```
ifconfig eth0
```

This will output statistics about the interface. If it has received or sent any packets, it must have been recognized by the kernel, and there cannot be a general hardware problem. If your card is not listed when issuing:

```
ifconfig
```

it wasn't even recognized by the kernel.

If detection of your Ethernet card is faulty, you may have to modify kernel parameters to fix it. The Linux Ethernet HOWTO includes much information on debugging Ethernet card configurations. In many cases, the fix is as simple as specifying the appropriate IRQ and port address at the LILO (or Grub, or whichever boot-loader you are using) boot prompt. For example, booting via LILO with the command:

```
lilo: linux ether=9,0x300,0,1,eth0
```

will select IRQ 9, base address 0x300, and the external transceiver (the fourth value of 1) for the *eth0* device. To use the internal transceiver (if your card supports both types), change the fourth value of the `ether` option to 0.

Also, don't overlook the possibility that your Ethernet card is damaged or incorrectly connected to your machine or the network. A bad Ethernet card or cable can cause no end of trouble, including intermittent network failures, system crashes, and so forth. When you're at the end of your rope, consider replacing the Ethernet card or cable, or both, to determine if this is the source of the problem.[*]

If your Ethernet card is detected but the system is still having problems talking to the network, the device configuration with *ifconfig* may be to blame. Be sure you have specified the appropriate IP address, broadcast address, and subnet mask for your machine. Invoking `ifconfig` with no arguments displays information on your Ethernet device configuration.

Dial-Up PPP

To communicate over TCP/IP using a modem (such as through a dial-up account to an Internet service provider) or through some other serial device (such as a "null modem" serial cable between two machines), Linux provides the Point-to-Point Protocol software suite, commonly known as PPP. PPP is a protocol that takes packets

---

[*] One of the authors once spent three hours trying to determine why the kernel wouldn't recognize an Ethernet card at boot time. As it turned out, the 16-bit card was plugged into an 8-bit slot—*mea culpa*.

sent over a network (such as TCP/IP) and converts them to a format that can be easily sent over a modem or serial wire. Chances are, if you have an Internet account with an ISP, the ISP's server uses PPP to communicate with dial-up accounts. By configuring PPP under Linux, you can directly connect to your ISP account in this way.

SLIP is an earlier protocol that has the same basic features as PPP. However, it lacks certain important qualities, such as the ability to negotiate IP addresses and packet sizes. These days SLIP has more or less been supplanted entirely by PPP.

In this section, we cover configuration of a PPP *client*—that is, a system that will connect to an ISP (or other PPP server) in order to communicate with the Internet. Setting up a Linux machine as a PPP server is also possible but is somewhat more involved; this is covered in the *Linux Network Administrator's Guide* (O'Reilly).

Basic PPP Configuration for Modems

In the U.S. and many parts of the world, people use traditional dial-up modems to send digital data over telephone lines. So we'll cover configuration for modems first. Then we'll show how to configure PPP for the faster and more convenient type of line called Integrated Services Digital Network (ISDN), which is especially popular in Europe and is available but not very well marketed in most of the U.S.

Requirements

Most Linux systems come preinstalled with all the software needed to run PPP. Essentially, you need a kernel compiled with PPP support and the *pppd* daemon and related tools, including the chat program.

Most Linux distributions include PPP support in the preconfigured kernel or as a kernel module that is loaded on demand. However, it may be necessary to compile kernel PPP support yourself; this is a simple matter of enabling the PPP options during the kernel configuration process and rebuilding the kernel. PPP is usually compiled as a separate module, so it is sufficient to recompile only the kernel modules if this is the case. See "Building the Kernel" in Chapter 18 for information on compiling the kernel and modules.

The pppd and chat utilities are user-level applications that control the use of PPP on your system; they are included with nearly every Linux distribution. On Red Hat systems, these utilities are installed in */usr/sbin* and are found in the ppp RPM package.

Also required for PPP usage is a modem that is compatible with both Linux and the type of modems used by your ISP's server. Most 14.4, 28.8, 56 K, and other standard modem types fit into this category; very few modem types are not supported by Linux, and it would be unusual for an ISP to use anything so esoteric as to require you to buy something else.

One type of modem to watch out for is the so-called Winmodem. This was originally a product sold by US Robotics but has now been produced in several varieties by other vendors. Winmodems use the host CPU to convert digital signals into analog signals so that they can be sent over the phone line, unlike regular modems, which have a special chip to perform this function. The problem with Winmodems is that, as of this writing, the programming details for these devices are proprietary, meaning that it is very difficult to write Linux drivers for this class of devices. A lot of work has been done nevertheless on Winmodem drivers, but your mileage using them may vary considerably. Things have become a lot better over the last few years, but we would not advise you to buy a Winmodem if you intend to use it on Linux. If your computer happens to have one built in (as laptops often do), you do have a chance of getting it to work, though (even though some people scoff at the idea of wasting precious CPU cycles to generate modem signals, a job best left to specialized hardware). One perceived advantage of these so-called software modems is that upgrading their functionality is simply a matter of upgrading the operating system driver that controls them, rather than buying new hardware.

Serial device names

Under Windows 95/98/ME and MS-DOS, modems and other serial devices are named COM1 (for the first serial device), COM2 (for the second), and so forth, up to COM4. (Most systems support up to four serial devices, although multiport cards are available that can increase this number.) Under Linux, these same devices are referred to as */dev/ttyS0*, */dev/ttyS1*, on up to */dev/ttyS3*.* On most systems, at installation time a symbolic link called */dev/modem* will be created. This link points to the serial device on which the modem can be found, as shown in the following listing:

```
% ls -l /dev/modem
lrwxrwxrwx  1 root     root       10 May  4 12:41 /dev/modem -> /dev/ttyS0
```

If this link is incorrect for your system (say, because you know that your modem is not on */dev/ttyS0* but on */dev/ttyS2*), you can easily fix it as *root* by entering:

```
# ln -sf /dev/ttyS2 /dev/modem
```

Setting up PPP

Several steps are involved in PPP configuration, and you may want to check first whether your distribution provides some kind of wizard for setting up PPP for you—many do. On the other hand, you won't learn as much as you do when setting things up by hand. The first thing you need to do if you want to roll your own is to write a so-called chat script, which performs the handshaking necessary to set up a PPP connection between your machine and the ISP. During this handshaking phase, various

---

* Older versions of Linux also used special "callout" devices, called */dev/cua0* through */dev/cua3*. These are obsolete as of Linux kernel Version 2.2.

pieces of information might be exchanged, such as your ISP username and password. The second step is to write a script that fires up the pppd daemon; running this script causes the modem to dial the ISP and start up PPP. The final step is to configure your system's /etc/resolv.conf file so that it knows where to find a domain nameserver. We'll go through each step in turn.

Before you start, you need to know the following pieces of information:

- The ISP dial-in account phone number
- Your ISP username and password
- The IP address of the ISP's domain nameserver

Your ISP should have told you this information when you established the account.

In addition, you might need to know the following:

- The IP address of the ISP's server
- The IP address of your system (if not dynamically assigned by the ISP)
- The subnet mask you should use

These last three items can usually be determined automatically during the PPP connection setup; however, occasionally this negotiation does not work properly. It can't hurt to have this information in case you need it.

Writing a chat script

chat is a program that can perform simple handshaking between a PPP client and server during connection setup, such as exchanging usernames and passwords. chat is also responsible for causing your modem to dial the ISP's phone number and other simple tasks.

chat is automatically invoked by *pppd* when started (this is discussed later). All you need to do is write a simple shell script that invokes chat to handle the negotiation. A simple chat script is shown in the following example. Edit the file */etc/ppp/my-chat-script* (as *root*) and place in it the following lines:

```
#!/bin/sh
# my-chat-script: a program for dialing up your ISP
exec chat -v           \
'' ATZ                 \
OK ATDT555-1212        \
CONNECT ''             \
ogin: mdw              \
assword: my-password
```

Specifying ogin and assword without the initial letters allows the prompts to be either Login or login, and Password or password.

Be sure that the file *my-chat-script* is executable; the command *chmod 755 /etc/ppp/my-chat-script* will accomplish this.

Note that each line ending in a backslash should not have any characters *after* the backslash; the backslash forces line-wrapping in the shell script.

The third line of this script runs chat with the options on the following lines. Each line contains two whitespace-delimited fields: an "expect" string and a "send" string. The idea is that the chat script will respond with the send string when it receives the expect string from the modem connection. For example, the last line of the script informs chat to respond with my-password when the prompt assword is given by the ISP's server.

The first line of the handshaking script instructs chat to send ATZ to the modem, which should cause the modem to reset itself. (Specifying an expect string as `` '' means that nothing is expected before ATZ is sent.) The second line waits for the modem to respond with OK, after which the number is dialed using the string ATDT555-1212. (If you use pulse dialing rather than tone dialing, change this to ATDP555-1212. The phone number, of course, should be that of the remote system's modem line.)

When the modem responds with CONNECT, a newline is sent (indicated by `` '' as the send string). After this, chat waits for the prompt ogin: before sending the username, and waits for assword: before sending the password.

The various send strings starting with AT in the previous example are simply Hayes-modem-standard modem control strings. The manual that came with your modem should explain their usage; this is not specific to Linux or any other operating system. As one example, using a comma in a phone number indicates that the modem should pause before sending the following digits; one might use ATDT9,,,555-1212 if a special digit (9 in this case) must be dialed to reach an outside line.

Note that this is a very simple chat script that doesn't deal with timeouts, errors, or any other extraordinary cases that might arise while you're attempting to dial into the ISP. See the *chat* manual pages for information on how to spruce up your script to deal with these cases. Also, note that you need to know in advance what prompts the ISP's server will use (we assumed login and password). There are several ways of finding out this information; possibly, the ISP has told you this information in advance, or supplied a handshaking script for another system such as Windows 95 (which uses a mechanism very similar to chat). Otherwise, you can dial into the ISP server "by hand," using a simple terminal emulator such as *minicom* or *seyon*. The manpages for those commands can help you do this.

Starting up pppd

Now, we're ready to configure the *pppd* daemon to initiate the PPP connection using the chat script we just wrote. Generally, you do this by writing another shell script that invokes *pppd* with a set of options.

The format of the *pppd* command is

```
pppd device-name baudrate options
```

Table 13-1 shows the options supported by *pppd*. You almost certainly won't need all of them.

Table 13-1. Common pppd options

Option	Effect
lock	Locks the serial device to restrict access to *pppd*.
crtscts	Uses hardware flow control.
noipdefault	Doesn't try to determine the local IP address from the hostname. The IP is assigned by the remote system.
user *username*	Specifies the hostname or username for PAP or CHAP identification.
netmask *mask*	Specifies the netmask for the connection.
defaultroute	Adds a default route to the local system's routing table, using the remote IP address as the gateway.
connect *command*	Uses the given *command* to initiate the connection. pppd assumes this script is in /etc/ppp. If not, specify the full path of the script.
local_IP_address:*remote_IP_address*	Specifies the local and/or remote IP addresses. Either or both of these could be 0.0.0.0 to indicate that the address should be assigned by the remote system.
debug	Logs connection information through the *syslog* daemon.

It is common to invoke the *pppd* command from a shell script. Edit the file /etc/ppp/ppp-on and add the following lines:

```
#!/bin/sh
        # the ppp-on script

        exec /usr/sbin/pppd /dev/modem 38400 lock crtscts noipdefault \
        defaultroute 0.0.0.0:0.0.0.0 connect my-chat-script
```

As with the *my-chat-script* file in the earlier example, be sure this is executable and watch out for extra characters after a backslash at the end of a line.

With this script in place, it should be possible to connect to the ISP using the following command:

```
% /etc/ppp/ppp-on
```

You need not be *root* to execute this command. Upon running this script, you should hear your modem dialing, and if all goes well, after a minute PPP should be happily connected. The *ifconfig* command should report an entry for ppp0 if PPP is up and running:

```
# ifconfig
lo        Link encap:Local Loopback
          inet addr:127.0.0.1  Bcast:127.255.255.255  Mask:255.0.0.0
          UP BROADCAST LOOPBACK RUNNING  MTU:3584  Metric:1
```

```
             RX packets:0 errors:0 dropped:0 overruns:0 frame:0
             TX packets:0 errors:0 dropped:0 overruns:0 carrier:0
             collisions:0

   ppp0      Link encap:Point-to-Point Protocol
             inet addr:207.25.97.248  P-t-P:207.25.97.154  Mask:255.255.255.0
             UP POINTOPOINT RUNNING  MTU:1500  Metric:1
             RX packets:1862 errors:0 dropped:0 overruns:0 frame:0
             TX packets:1288 errors:0 dropped:0 overruns:0 carrier:0
             collisions:0
             Memory:73038-73c04
```

Here, we can see that PPP is up, the local IP address is 207.25.97.248, and the remote server IP address is 207.25.97.154.

If you wish to be notified when the PPP connection is established (the *ppp-on* script returns immediately), add the following line to */etc/ppp/ip-up*:

```
/usr/bin/wall "PPP is up!"
```

/etc/ppp/ip-up is executed when PPP establishes an IP connection, so you can use this script to trigger the `wall` command when the connection is complete.

Another simple shell script can be used to kill the PPP session. Edit the file */etc/ppp/ppp-off* as follows:

```
#!/bin/sh
# A simple ppp-off script

kill `cat /var/run/ppp0.pid`
```

Running */etc/ppp/ppp-off* now kills the PPP daemon and shuts down the modem connection.

Configuring DNS

By itself, use of pppd along with chat only establishes a PPP connection and assigns you an IP address; in order to use domain names, you need to configure the system to be aware of the domain nameserver provided by your ISP. You do this by editing */etc/resolv.conf*. The manpage for *resolver* describes this file in detail. However, for most purposes it suffices to simply include lines of two forms: one that specifies the list of domains to search whenever a domain name is used, and another that specifies the address of a DNS server.

A sample */etc/resolv.conf* file might look like this:

```
# Sample /etc/resolv.conf
search cs.nowhere.edu nowhere.edu
nameserver 207.25.97.8
nameserver 204.148.41.1
```

The first line indicates that every time a domain name is used (such as *orange* or *papaya*), it should be searched for in the list of specified domains. In this case, resolver software would first expand a name like *papaya* to *papaya.cs.nowhere.edu* and try to find a system by that name, then expand it to *papaya.nowhere.edu* if necessary and try again.

The lines beginning with nameserver specify the IP address of domain nameservers (which should be provided by your ISP) that your system contacts to resolve domain names. If you specify more than one nameserver line, the given DNS servers will be contacted in order, until one returns a match; in this way, one DNS server is treated as a primary and the others as backups.

Troubleshooting PPP configuration

The PPP configuration described here is meant to be very simple and will certainly not cover all cases; the best sources for additional information are the manpages for pppd and chat as well as the Linux PPP HOWTO and related documents.

Happily, both *chat* and *pppd* log messages on their progress, as well as any errors, using the standard *syslog* daemon facility. By editing */etc/syslog.conf*, you can cause these messages to be captured to a file. To do this, add the following lines:

```
# Save messages from chat
local2.*                                /var/log/chat-log

# Save messages from pppd
daemon.*                                /var/log/pppd-log
```

This will cause messages from chat to be logged to */var/log/chat-log*, and messages from pppd to be logged to */var/log/pppd-log*.

Note that these log messages will contain private information, such as ISP usernames and passwords! It is important that you leave this logging enabled only while you are debugging your PPP configuration; after things are working, remove these two logfiles and remove the lines from */etc/syslog.conf*.

chat will also log certain errors to */etc/ppp/connect-errors*, which is not controlled through the *syslog* daemon. (It should be safe to leave this log in place, however.)

PAP and CHAP

Some ISPs may require you to use a special authentication protocol, such as PAP (Password Authentication Protocol) or CHAP (Challenge Handshake Authentication Protocol). These protocols rely on some form of "shared secret" known to both the client and the server; in most cases, this is just your ISP account password.

If PAP or CHAP is required by your ISP, they are configured by adding information to the files */etc/ppp/pap-secrets* and */etc/ppp/chap-secrets*, respectively. Each file has four fields separated by spaces or tabs. Here is an example of a *pap-secrets* file:

```
# Secrets for authentication using PAP
# client       server            secret          IP or Domain
mdw              *                my-password
```

The first field is your system's name as expected by the remote system—usually your ISP username. The second field specifies the ISP's server name; an asterisk allows this entry to match all ISP servers to which you might connect. The third field specifies the shared secret provided by your ISP; as stated earlier, this is usually your ISP password. The fourth field is primarily used by PPP servers to limit the IP addresses to which users dialing in have access. These addresses can be specified as either IP addresses or domain names. For most PPP client configurations, however, this field is not required.

The *chap-secrets* file has the same four fields, but you need to include an entry other than * for the service provider's system; this is a secret the ISP shares with you when you establish the account.

If PAP or CHAP is being used, it's not necessary for the chat script to include handshaking information after CONNECT is received; *pppd* will take care of the rest. Therefore, you can edit */etc/ppp/my-chat-script* to contain only the following lines:

```
#!/bin/sh
# my-chat-script: a program for dialing up your ISP
exec chat -v        \
'' ATZ              \
OK ATDT555-1212     \
CONNECT ''
```

You will also need to add the user option to the *pppd* command line in */etc/ppp/ppp-on*, as so:

```
#!/bin/sh
# the ppp-on script

exec /usr/sbin/pppd /dev/modem 38400 lock crtscts noipdefault \
user mdw defaultroute 0.0.0.0:0.0.0.0 connect my-chat-script
```

PPP over ISDN

ISDN has offered convenient, high-speed data communications—at a price—for many years; it is particularly popular in Europe, where rates and marketing have been more favorable to its use than in the U.S. ISDN, which integrates data and regular voice transmission over a single line, offers both a faster connection setup and much better throughput than traditional modems.

ISDN lines can transfer 64 kbits per second. And unlike analog lines, they can achieve this speed all the time because their transmission does not depend on the vagaries of analog transmission with interference by various kinds of noise. A newer protocol called ADSL (Asynchronous Digital Subscriber Line) is upping the ante for fast data access over phone lines and is taking over from ISDN in many regions of the world.

In this section, we describe how to configure dial-up access to your Internet provider over an ISDN line. We cover only the most common style of connection, synchronous PPP, not the special mode called *raw IP*. Furthermore, this section discusses just internal ISDN boards, which require a kind of setup that's different from the dial-up access covered in the previous section. To set up external ISDN devices, or the so-called ISDN modems (a term that is an oxymoron because there is no modulation and demodulation), you can use commands similar to those in the previous section because these devices present themselves to the computer and the operating system like a normal modem, albeit one that offers some additional commands, faster connection setup, and higher throughput.

If you want more information beyond what we present here, the source for all ISDN-related information for Linux is *http://www.isdn4linux.de* (despite this domain being registered in Germany, all the information here is in English).

In a way, setting up ISDN connections is much easier than setting up analog connections because many of the problems (bad lines, long connection setup times, and so on) simply cannot occur with digital lines. Once you dial the number, the connection is set up within milliseconds. But this can lead to problems. Because the connections are set up and shut down so fast, a misconfigured system that dials out again and again can cost you a fortune. This is even more problematic because with internal ISDN cards, you hear no clicking and whistling as you do with modems, and there are no lights that inform you that a connection has been made. You can check the status of your ISDN line with some simple programs, though.

Follow these two steps to set up dial-up PPP over ISDN:

1. Configure your ISDN hardware.
2. Configure and start the PPP daemon and change the routing table to use your ISDN line.

We cover those steps in the next sections.

Configuring Your ISDN Hardware

The first step involves making your ISDN board accessible to the kernel. As with any other hardware board, you need a device driver that is configured with the correct parameters for your board.

Linux supports a large number of ISDN hardware boards. We cannot cover every single board here, but the procedure is more or less the same for each one. Reading the documentation for your specific card in the directory *Documentation/isdn* in the Linux kernel sources will help you a lot if your board is not covered here.

We will concentrate here on boards that use the so-called *HiSax* driver. This device driver works with almost all cards that use the Siemens HSCX chipset (and thus with most passive cards available on the market today). That includes, for instance, the

USR Sportster internal TA and the well-known Teles, ELSA, and Fritz boards. Other boards are similarly configured. Even some active cards are supported by Linux, including the well-known AVM B1 and the IBM Active 2000 ISDN card.

The first thing you need to do is configure the kernel so that it includes ISDN support. We advise you to compile everything ISDN-related as modules, especially while you are experimenting with setting it up. You will need the following modules:

- ISDN support.
- Support for synchronous PPP.
- One device driver module for your hardware. If you pick the HiSax driver, you will also have to specify which specific brand of ISDN card you have and which ISDN protocol you want to use. The latter is almost certainly EURO/DSS1 in Europe—unless you live in Germany and have had your ISDN for a long time, in which case it might be 1TR6—and US NI1 in the U.S. If you live elsewhere, or are in doubt, ask your phone company.

Compile and install the modules as described in Chapter 18. Now you are ready to configure your ISDN hardware. Some distributions, such as SUSE, make setting up ISDN lines very easy and comfortable. We cover the hard way here in case your distribution is not so user-friendly, the automatic configuration does not work, or you simply want to know what is going on behind the scenes.

Now you need to load the device driver module using *modprobe*. This will automatically load the other modules as well. All the device driver modules accept a number of module parameters; the hisax module accepts, among others, the following:

id= *boardid*
> Sets an identifier for the ISDN board. You can pick any name you like here, but you cannot have the same identifier for more than one board in your system.

type= *boardtype*
> Specifies the exact board brand and type. For example, a value of 16 for *boardtype* selects the support for the USR Sportster internal TA. See *Documentation/isdn/README.hisax* in the kernel sources for the full list of board types.

protocol= *protocoltype*
> Selects an ISDN subprotocol. Valid values for *protocoltype* are 1 for the old German 1TR6 protocol, 2 for the common EDSS1 (so-called Euro ISDN), and 3 for leased lines.

irq= *irqno*
> Specifies the interrupt line to use. Not all boards need this.

io= *addr*
> Specifies the I/O address to use. Not all boards need this. Some boards need two I/O addresses. In this case, the parameters to use are io0 and io1.

For example, the following command loads the HiSax driver for use with a Teles 16.3 board, Euro ISDN, IO address 0x280, and IRQ line 10 (a very common case):

```
tigger # modprobe hisax type=3 protocol=2 io=0x280 irq=10
```

Please see *Documentation/isdn/README.HiSax* or the equivalent file for your hardware for more information.

This module is not much of a talker; if there is no output from the modprobe command, it is likely that everything went well. You might also want to check your system log at */var/log/messages*. You should see a few lines starting with HiSax: (or the name of the driver you are using); the final line should be

```
HiSax: module installed
```

If the module did not load, you will most likely also find the answer in */var/log/messages*. The most common problem is that the IRQ or I/O address was wrong or that you selected the wrong card type. If all else fails, and you have Windows installed on the same machine, boot up Windows and check what it reports for the IRQ and I/O address lines. Sometimes, it helps to take a look in */proc/ioports* and in */proc/interrupts* to see if the HiSax chipset has the right I/O port and the right interrupt assigned.

You should do one more check before you jump to the next section, and this check involves calling yourself. This can work because, with ISDN, you always have two phone lines at your disposal. Thus, one line will be used for the outgoing "phone call," and the other line will be used for the incoming one.

In order to have the ISDN subsystem report what is going on with your phone lines, you will need to configure it to be more verbose than it is by default. You do this by means of three utility programs that are all part of the *isdn4k-utils* package that you can find at your friendly Linux FTP server around the corner.

The *isdn4k-utils* package contains, among other things, the three utilities *hisaxctrl* for configuring the device driver, *isdnctrl* for configuring the higher levels of the ISDN subsystem, and *isdnlog*, a very useful tool that logs everything happening on your ISDN lines. Although you can use *hisactrl* and *isdnctrl* without any configuration, you will need to provide a small configuration file for *isdnlog*. For now, we will content ourselves with a quick solution, but once your ISDN connection is up and running, you will want to configure *isdnlog* to see where your money is going. So for now, copy one of the sample configuration files contained in the *isdnlog* package to */etc/isdn/isdn.conf*. You will need to edit at least the following lines:

COUNTRYCODE=

Add your phone country code here—for example, 1 for the U.S. and Canada, 44 for the United Kingdom, 46 for Sweden, and so on.

AREAPREFIX=

> If the area codes in your country are prefixed by a fixed digit, put this in here. The prefix is 0 for most European countries, 9 for Finland, and nothing for the U.S., Denmark, and Norway.

AREACODE=

> Put your area code in here. If you have specified an AREAPREFIX in the last step, don't repeat that here. For example, Stockholm, Sweden, has the area code 08. You put 0 into AREAPREFIX and 8 into AREACODE.

Once you have set this up, execute the following commands to make your ISDN system more verbose:

```
tigger # /sbin/hisaxctrl boardid 1 4
tigger # /sbin/isdnctrl verbose 3
tigger # /sbin/lsdnlog /dev/isdnctrl0 &
```

If you are using a driver other than HiSax, you might need to use a different command. For example, for the PCBit driver, the command pcbitctl is available in the *isdn4k-utils* package.

Now you can go ahead and phone yourself. You should try all your MSNs (multiple subscriber numbers, which are your ISDN phone numbers) to see that the board can detect all of them. During or after each call, check */var/log/messages*. You should see lines like the following:

```
Mar 16 18:34:22 tigger kernel: isdn_net: call from 4107123455,1,0 -> 123456
Mar 16 18:34:33 tigger kernel: isdn_net: Service-Indicator not 7, ignored
```

This shows that the kernel has detected a voice call (the service indicator is 0) from the phone number 123455 in the area with the area code (0)4107 to the MSN 123456.

Note how the number called is specified, because you will need this information later. The number is sent with the area code in some phone networks, but without the area code in others. Anyway, congratulations if you have come this far. Your ISDN hardware is now correctly configured.

Setting Up Synchronous PPP

Setting up the PPP daemon again involves several substeps. On Linux, the ISDN board is treated like a network interface that you have to configure with special commands. In addition, you need to specify the username and password that your ISP has assigned you. When everything is configured, you start up the ipppd daemon, which lurks in the background until a connection request is made.

First, let's configure the "network interface." This involves a number of commands that most system administrators simply put into a script that they store in a file, such as */sbin/pppon*. Here is a sample file that you can modify to your needs:

```
/sbin/isdnctrl addif ippp0
/sbin/isdnctrl addphone ippp0 out 0123456789
/sbin/isdnctrl dialmax ippp0 2
/sbin/isdnctrl eaz ippp0 123456
/sbin/isdnctrl huptimeout ippp0 100
/sbin/isdnctrl l2_prot ippp0 hdlc
/sbin/isdnctrl l3_prot ippp0 trans
/sbin/isdnctrl encap ippp0 syncppp
/sbin/ifconfig ippp0 1.1.1.1 pointopoint 123.45.67.89 metric 1
```

Let's go through these commands one by one.

isdnctrl addif ippp0
> Tells the kernel that a new ISDN interface with the name ippp0 will be used. Always use names starting with ippp.

isdnctrl addphone ippp0 out 0123456789
> Tells the ISDN interface which phone number to use. This is the phone number that you use to dial up your provider. If you have used analog dial-up so far, check with your provider, because the phone number for ISDN access could be different.

isdnctrl dialmax ippp0 2
> Specifies how many times the kernel should dial if the connection could not be established, before giving up.

isdnctrl eaz ippp0 123456
> Specifies one of your own MSNs. This is very important—without this, not much will work. In case your provider verifies your access via your phone number, make sure you specify here the MSN that you have registered with your provider.

isdnctrl huptimeout ippp0 100
> Specifies the number of seconds that the line can be idle before the kernel closes the connection (specified by the last number in this command). This is optional, but can save you a lot of money if you do not have a flat phone rate. Thus, if you forget to shut down the connection yourself, the kernel will do that for you.

isdnctrl l2_prot ippp0 hdlc
> Specifies the layer 2 protocol to use. Possible values here are hdlc, x75i, x75ui, and x75bui. Most providers use hdlc. When in doubt, ask your provider.

isdnctrl l3_prot ippp0 trans
> Specifies the layer 3 protocol to use (the l in the option is the letter L). Currently, only trans is available.

isdnctrl encap ippp0 syncppp
> Specifies the encapsulation to use. A number of values are possible here, but if you want to use synchronous PPP (or your provider demands that), you have to specify syncppp here. Another not-so-uncommon value is rawip. But since this

provides only very weak authentication facilities, few providers still use it, even though it gives slightly better throughput because it requires less overhead.

`ifconfig ippp0 1.1.1.1 pointopoint 123.45.67.89 metric 1`

Creates the new network interface. If your IP address is not assigned dynamically (as is the case with most dial-up connections), you need to specify your IP address instead of the 1.1.1.1 here. Also, you need to change the 123.45.67.89 to the IP address of your provider's dial-up server.

If you want, you can also reverse the setup by creating a script that shuts down the interfaces and so on. For example, it would use the `isdnctrl delif` command. But such a script is not strictly necessary, unless you want to disable all dialing at runtime.

Phew! But we are not finished yet. Next, you need to configure the `ipppd` daemon, which you do in the file */etc/ppp/ioptions*. You can also have a configuration file specific to each `ipppd` daemon, but that is necessary only if you want to be able to use different ISDN connections—that is, if you have multiple dial-up accounts.

The following is an *ioptions* file that is generic enough to work with most providers. It does not give maximum throughput but is quite stable. If you want to optimize it, ask your provider about the possible settings and read the manual page for `ipppd(8)`:

```
debug
/dev/ippp0
user yourusername
name yourusername
mru 1500
mtu 1500
ipcp-accept-local
ipcp-accept-remote
noipdefault
-vj -vjccomp -ac -pc -bsdcomp
defaultroute
```

You have to change only two things here: change *yourusername* in the third and fourth lines to the username that your provider has assigned you for connecting to its system. We won't go through all the options here; see the manual page when in doubt.

ISDN access requires the same security as an analog modem. See "PAP and CHAP," earlier in this chapter, for directions on setting up your *pap-secrets* or *chap-secrets* file as required by your service provider.

Now we have got our things together and can start having fun! First run the `ipppd` daemon:

```
tigger # /sbin/ipppd pidfile /var/run/ipppd.ippp0.pid file /etc/ppp/ioptions &
```

The *ipppd* daemon will now wait for connection requests. Since we have not configured it yet to automatically make a connection, we have to manually trigger the connection. You do this with the following command:

```
tigger # isdnctrl dial ipppo
```

You should now check */var/log/messages*. There should be lots of messages that start with *ipppd*. The last of those messages should contain the words local IP address and remote IP address together with the IP addresses. Once you find those messages, you are done. Because we have used the *defaultroute* option previously, the kernel has set up the default route to use the ISDN connection, and you should now be able to access the wide, wide world of the Internet. Start by pinging your provider's IP address. Once you are done and want to shut down the connection, enter

```
tigger # isdnctrl hangup ipppo
```

If you have a flat rate with your ISP, then you can set the *huptimeout* to 0, and you will stay online all the time without ever hanging up. Of course, this is nice to have, but remember that most ISPs reset the connection after 24 hours, and if you have a dynamic IP address, you will possibly be assigned another IP address every 24 hours.

And If It Does Not Work?

If you have no connection even though your hardware was successfully recognized and you have set up everything as described here, */var/log/messages* is again your friend. It is very likely that you will find the cause of the error there, even though it might be buried a bit.

The most common error is specifying the password or the username incorrectly. You know that you have a problem with the authentication if you see a line such as:

```
PAP authentication failed
```

or

```
CHAP authentication failed
```

in the logfile. Check your *chap-secrets* or *pap-secrets* file very carefully. Your provider might also be able to see from its logfiles where exactly the authentication went wrong.

Of course, your provider might not support synchronous PPP as described here, even though most providers do nowadays. If this is the case, ask your provider for exact settings.

If it still does not work, ask your provider. A good ISP has a phone support line and can help you connect your Linux box. If your provider tells you that it "only supports Windows," it's time to switch. Many Linux-friendly providers are out there. Often the support staff is using Linux and can help you even though the provider's official policy is not to support Linux.

If for some reason you are stuck with an uncooperative provider, try finding other customers of this provider who also use Linux. Setting up your connection in non-standard cases means fiddling with the options and parameters of the ISDN subsystem in the kernel and the ipppd daemon, and if somebody else has already found out what to do, you don't have to.

Where to Go from Here?

Once your ISDN connection works and you can access the Internet, you might want to set up some conveniences or other customizations. Here are some suggestions:

- Make *ipppd* dial your remote site automatically. You can do this by setting the default route to the ippp0 device like this:

  ```
  /sbin/route add default netmask 0.0.0.0 ippp0
  ```

  Now, whenever the kernel needs to send an IP packet to an IP address for which it has no specific route configured, it will trigger the *ipppd* daemon to build a connection. Use this only if you have also specified the *huptimeout* option of the ISDN subsystem; otherwise, you could pay a fortune to your telephone company (unless you have a flat rate).

  Since some programs try to build up Internet connections from time to time (Netscape is one of those candidates), setting this up can be dangerous for your wallet. If you use this, make sure to check the state of the connection often (as described later in this section).

- Try tools that monitor your ISDN connection. The *isdn4k-utils* package contains a number of those tools, including the command-line tools imon and imontty and X-based tools.

- Configure *isdnlog* to log exactly what you need, and use *isdnrep* to get detailed reports about the usage of your ISDN line. This works not only for calls to and from computer systems, but also for calls to other ISDN-enabled devices such as phones and fax machines. There is only one caveat: your ISDN board cannot capture outgoing phone numbers for connections being set up by other devices. Most telephone companies provide a service, though, that echoes this phone number back to you and thus lets the ISDN subsystem pick it up. This service is often available for free or for a nominal fee. Ask your telephone company.

- For the truly adventurous: experiment with Multilink-PPP. As you know, with ISDN you have at least two lines. If you need extra-high capacity, why not use both? That's what Multilink-PPP does. To use this, you need to turn on the Support generic MP option during kernel configuration, and read the files *Documentation/isdn/README.syncppp* and *Documentation/isdn/syncppp.FAQ* in the kernel sources for hints on how to do this. Of course, your provider has to support this, too.

ADSL

The 64-Kbps rate that ISDN supports is nice, but if you want to access multimedia files via the Internet or simply are using the Internet a lot, you may want even more bandwidth. Without drawing additional cables to your house or office, ADSL(Asynchronous Digital Subscriber Line), a variant of DSL (Digital Subscriber Line), is a convenient alternative that gives you up to 128 times (depending on your provider and your type of subscription) the bandwidth of standard dial-up access and is run via your ordinary telephone line. A drawback with ADSL is that it only works within a distance of about 5 to 8 kilometers (3 to 5 miles), depending on cable quality around the next switching station, which makes this service unavailable in rural areas. Typical bandwidths are 0.5 to 8 Mbps (megabits per second) downstream (to your computer—download operations, including viewing web pages and retrieving email) and 0.125 to 1 Mbps upstream (from your computer—upload operations, including sending email). Note that there are other technologies with similar-sounding names, such as SDSL. Although these are fundamentally different on the wire level, setting them up on your Linux box should be no different from ADSL.

ADSL is not dial-up access; once you have logged into your account, you are always connected. Some providers cut your connection after a while (often after 24 hours), upon which you have to log in again in order to regain access.[*]

As we have already mentioned, there are no such things as ADSL cards or ADSL drivers. As far as hardware is concerned, an ADSL connection is just a normal Ethernet connection, using the same cables.

How you connect your Linux box to your ADSL line depends a lot on your ISP. With some ISPs, you rent the necessary equipment, such as an ADSL modem and an ADSL router, as part of your subscription. With others, you have to purchase the necessary hardware yourself, either on the free market or from the ISP. Your ISP can give you all the information you need.

There are two ways to use ADSL: either connecting directly to an ADSL modem or with an intervening ADSL router. If you have an ADSL router (either with a built-in ADSL modem, or in addition to one), you plug your Ethernet cable in there and are ready for action. If you want to connect your Linux box directly to your ADSL modem, you still connect the computer and the modem with an Ethernet cable, but you need to run a special protocol, called PPPoE (PPP over Ethernet), on it. This protocol is handled by a special daemon called *pppoed*. How this is set up depends on your distribution and should be documented there. Some distributions also let you set up PPPoE from their respective configuration programs.

---

[*] The reason why the providers do this is that they want to prevent you from running a server, coercing you into upgrading to a more expensive "business" subscription if you wish to do that.

Finally, we should mention that a small number of weirdo ADSL modems are not connected with an Ethernet cable, but rather with a USB cable. This is technically a bad idea, so you should avoid these modems if possible, but if you are stuck with one, you can find more information, including drivers for some devices that run PPPoE on a USB connection (that would be PPP over Ethernet over USB, then!), at *http://eciadsl.flashtux.org* and *http://speedtouch.sourceforge.net*.

Whichever way you use ADSL (with or without an ADSL router), you need to set up the correct IP address. This can either be static (in which case you should find it in the information you have received from your ISP) or dynamic and assigned via DHCP (Dynamic Host Communication Protocol), in which case you can request a dynamic IP address with the following command:

```
dhclient eth0
```

Of course, if the Ethernet card you use has another name, you need to replace the eth0 with the correct name. Instead of *dhclient*, you can also use the utility *pump*. There is also a DHCP daemon called *dhcpcd* that runs in the background and assigns a dynamic IP address whenever necessary.

Finally, many ISPs require that you activate your line from time to time. How you do this depends on your ISP, but often the activation requires nothing more than browsing to a certain web site and entering the credentials there that your ISP has assigned to you. As mentioned before, you may have to repeat this step from time to time.

Cable Modems

When one wants Internet access enough, any wire will do. There are intensive experiments to use even the electricity grid to deliver Internet access. So it's not surprising that companies that built their business plans on delivering laser-crisp pictures of sporting events (the cable TV firms) would realize they could devote one of their channels to a local area network carrying digital data—hence the advent of cable Internet access.

The bandwidth on the cable infrastucture theoretically ranges up to 10 Mb (like an old Ethernet on coaxial cable), but some providers today achieve more throughput. Usually, they span a web of nodes, each of which offers 10 Mb or less. The neighbors who share the node have to share the bandwidth. So if there are two users on the node, each gets 5 Mb. Furthermore, some customers near the center (the central server, which is usually connected via the optical fiber cable to the rest of the Internet) have more bandwidth than those at the periphery. So check your cable network very carefully before you sign up for Internet access. Talk to the technical support first, and if they cannot answer your question, this might be a good indication about how good their support is going to be later.

ISPs that sell clients Internet access through cable modems will usually take responsibility for service all the way to your Ethernet card. They will give you a cable modem with a coaxial cable connected to their cable infrastructure, and an Ethernet (RJ45) connector on your side. To set up your Internet connection, you will need to know the IP address assigned to the cable modem, the network mask, and the gateway; your ISP should provide you with this information together with the cable modem. On your side, you need only start up your (carefully configured) Ethernet card with the data provided to you by your ISP:

```
/sbin/ifconfig eth0 IP_address netmask
```

Next, tell the kernel about the gateway:

```
/sbin/route add default gw gateway metric 1
```

This is the setup for a standalone Linux workstation. If you plan to run a small network behind the Linux machine, you will have to use masquerading, as described earlier in this chapter; you can find help for this in a book that covers Linux firewalling, such as the *Linux Network Administrator's Guide* and the *Linux iptables Pocket Reference* (O'Reilly). Some Linux distributions, such as Slackware, turn off IP forwarding by default, which means that masquerading will not work. If this is the case, add the following line to your startup script:

```
echo 1 >/proc/sys/net/ipv4/ip_forward
```

All cable modems can be configured remotely. If you are unlucky and have an ISP that does not configure the cable modem for you, you have to configure it from scratch; this will require more than average knowledge about how TCP/IP works, and you should probably seek assistance from your ISP (or switch to one that does configure the modem for you).

In some cases, the cable modem is configured such that it is works only with one particular Ethernet card, and you have to give the MAC address of your card to your ISP for configuration purposes. If this is the case, you need to ask your ISP to reconfigure the modem in case you should switch Ethernet cards (or computers).

Network Diagnostics Tools

There are a number of useful tools that can help you diagnose network problems. We discuss three of them here that are generally helpful; a host of others for diagnosing particular problems are available as well.

ping

The first tool we look at is called *ping*. *ping* sends so-called ICMP packets to the server that you specify, the server returns them, and the ping determines the time the round trip took. This is useful to get an idea of the quality of your Internet connection, but we most often use it to see whether we can get a connection somewhere at all. For example, to see whether you have an Internet connection, just ping any computer on the Internet. For example:

```
kalle@tigger:~> ping www.oreilly.com
PING www.oreilly.com (208.201.239.36) 56(84) bytes of data.
64 bytes from www.oreillynet.com (208.201.239.36): icmp_seq=1 ttl=46 time=280 ms
64 bytes from www.oreillynet.com (208.201.239.36): icmp_seq=2 ttl=46 time=250 ms
64 bytes from www.oreillynet.com (208.201.239.36): icmp_seq=3 ttl=46 time=244 ms

--- www.oreilly.com ping statistics ---
3 packets transmitted, 3 received, 0% packet loss, time 2001ms
rtt min/avg/max/mdev = 244.976/258.624/280.430/15.586 ms
```

Notice that we pressed Ctrl-C here after a few seconds—it is not very nice to use the opposite server for this purpose for too long. What can you see from this? Well, first of all, you can see that you are actually able to contact a computer on the Internet. Since you did not type in the numerical IP address, but rather the hostname, you can also see that DNS name resolution worked. The first line of the output shows you the IP address that belonged to *www.oreilly.com*. In the following lines, you can see for each packet sent how long the trip to the server and back took. Of course, the times reported here are going to differ greatly depending on how far that server is away from you network-wise. Also notice the icmp_seq information. Each packet gets a sequence number, and you should receive all of them back. If you don't, if there are gaps in the sequence, then your connection to that host is flakey, or maybe the host is overloaded and drops packets.

It should also be said that *ping* is not completely reliable for diagnosing network problems. Getting no *ping* response may also be due to the server not responding to the ICMP packets—no server is obliged to do so, and some actually don't, in order to reduce their server load and in order to increase security (if you cannot really know that somebody is there, it is difficult to attack that somebody). It is considered good networking practice, though, to answer ping requests.

ping is also interesting to see what does not work. If *ping* does not answer at all, or only answers with network not reachable or a similar output, you know that you have issues with your setup. If you know it, try to ping the IP address of your ISP to see whether the problem is between you and your ISP or further beyond.* If you are using a router that connects your home network with the Internet, ping the IP address of the router; if this already does not work, then it is either the setup of your local computer or the cabling that is faulty. If this works, but you do not get any further to your ISP, then the reason could be that you failed to connect with your ISP, for example, because you have specified the wrong credentials for connecting, or

---

* Computer users are using *ping* as a verb these days.

your ISP is down, or there is a problem with the phone line (your telephone company might be experiencing problems).

Finally, if specifying the hostname does not work, but you know its IP address (maybe from an earlier attempt), and specifying the hostname works:

```
kalle@tigger:~/projects/rl5> ping 208.201.239.36
PING 208.201.239.36 (208.201.239.36) 56(84) bytes of data.
64 bytes from 208.201.239.36: icmp_seq=1 ttl=46 time=249 ms

--- 208.201.239.36 ping statistics ---
2 packets transmitted, 1 received, 50% packet loss, time 1001ms
rtt min/avg/max/mdev = 249.698/249.698/249.698/0.000 ms
```

then you know that you have a problem with DNS name resolution and can continue to look further in that area.

traceroute

The *traceroute* command goes a step further than *ping*. It not only shows you whether you can reach a host on the Internet (or in your own network), but also which route the packets take on their way to get there. That can be useful to diagnose problems that are beyond your reach, such as with central routers on the Internet—not that you could do much about that, but then at least you know that you do not need to debug your own setup.

Here is an example of using *traceroute*. Notice that here we specify the full path to the command. It is usually in a directory that only *root* has in its PATH. *traceroute* can be executed just fine as a normal user, however).

```
kalle@officespace:~> /usr/sbin/traceroute www.oreilly.com
traceroute to www.oreilly.com (208.201.239.36), 30 hops max, 40 byte packets
 1  81.169.166.1  0.204 ms    0.174 ms    0.174 ms
 2  81.169.160.157  0.247 ms    0.196 ms    0.195 ms
 3  81.169.160.37  0.351 ms    0.263 ms    0.320 ms
 4  PC1.bln2-g.mcbone.net (194.97.172.145)  0.256 ms    0.273 ms    0.217 ms
 5  LO.bln2-g2.mcbone.net (62.104.191.140)  0.417 ms    0.315 ms    0.272 ms
 6  loo-0.hnv2-j2.mcbone.net (62.104.191.206)  4.092 ms    4.109 ms    4.048 ms
 7  loo-0.hnv2-j.mcbone.net (62.104.191.205)  4.145 ms    4.184 ms    4.266 ms
 8  LO.dus1-g.mcbone.net (62.104.191.141)  8.206 ms    8.044 ms    8.015 ms
 9  c00.ny2.g6-0.wvfiber.net (198.32.160.137)  92.477 ms    92.522 ms    92.488 ms
10  b0-00.nyc.pos1-35-1.wvfiber.net (63.223.28.9)  166.932 ms    167.323 ms    166.356
    ms
11  b00.chi.pos1-6-1.wvfiber.net (63.223.0.214)  167.921 ms    166.610 ms    166.735 ms
12  63.223.20.53  166.543 ms    166.773 ms    166.429 ms
13  unknown63223030025.wvfiber.net (63.223.30.25)  166.182 ms    165.941 ms    166.042
    ms
14  unknown63223030022.wvfiber.net (63.223.30.22)  165.873 ms    165.918 ms    165.919
    ms
15  unknown63223030134.wvfiber.net (63.223.30.134)  165.909 ms    165.919 ms    165.832
    ms
16  ge7-br02-200p-sfo.unitedlayer.com (209.237.224.17)  165.987 ms    165.881 ms
```

```
      166.022 ms
 17  pos-demarc.sf.sonic.net (209.237.229.26)  168.849 ms   168.753 ms   168.986 ms
 18  0.at-0-0-0.gw4.200p-sf.sonic.net (64.142.0.182)  169.628 ms 0.at-1-0-0.
      gw4.200p-sf.sonic.net (64.142.0.186)  169.632 ms   169.605 ms
 19  0.ge-0-1-0.gw.sr.sonic.net (64.142.0.197)  173.582 ms   173.877 ms   174.144 ms
 20  gig49.dist1-1.sr.sonic.net (209.204.191.30)  176.822 ms   177.680 ms   178.777 ms
 21  www.oreillynet.com (208.201.239.36)  173.932 ms   174.439 ms   173.326 ms
```

Here, the trace was successful, and you can also see how much time the packets took from hop to hop. With some geographical knowledge and some fantasy, you can guess the route along which the packets went. For example, the computer on which this command was executed was located in Berlin, Germany,[*] so it stands to reason that bln2 in lines 4 and 5 is some host in Berlin that belongs to the ISP somehow. Looking at a map of Germany, you might be able to guess that hops 6 and 7 went via Hanover, and hop 8 was in Düsseldorf. That's apparently also where the cable across the big pond starts, because hops 9 and 10 were quite likely in New York City. 11 seems to be Chicago, and 16 to 18 could be San Francisco. That makes sense, given that O'Reilly's headquarters (and therefore the likely location of the machine *www.oreilly.com/www.oreillynet.com*) is in California.

dig

dig is the last diagnostic utility we cover in this section. *dig* is a utility that queries DNS servers and returns the information held about a particular domain. Let's start with an example right away:

```
kalle@tigger:~> dig oreilly.com

; <<>> DiG 9.3.1 <<>> oreilly.com
;; global options:  printcmd
;; Got answer:
;; ->>HEADER<<- opcode: QUERY, status: NOERROR, id: 52820
;; flags: qr rd ra; QUERY: 1, ANSWER: 2, AUTHORITY: 3, ADDITIONAL: 0

;; QUESTION SECTION:
;oreilly.com.                   IN      A

;; ANSWER SECTION:
oreilly.com.            21600   IN      A       208.201.239.36
oreilly.com.            21600   IN      A       208.201.239.37

;; AUTHORITY SECTION:
oreilly.com.            21600   IN      NS      ns2.sonic.net.
oreilly.com.            21600   IN      NS      ns.oreilly.com.
oreilly.com.            21600   IN      NS      ns1.sonic.net.

;; Query time: 252 msec
;; SERVER: 195.67.199.9#53(195.67.199.9)
```

---

[*] While the author was remotely logged in via ssh from Sweden, thanks to the Internet.

```
;; WHEN: Wed Jul  6 13:31:02 2005
;; MSG SIZE  rcvd: 123
```

Now what does this tell you? Have a look at the ANSWER SECTION. It tells you the IP addresses in use by the domain name service serving the domain *oreilly.com*. If you have a problem resolving addresses in this domain, you could try to ping these addresses to see whether the problem is actually with O'Reilly's DNS and not your own. The AUTHORITY SECTION gives you information about the so-called authoritative nameservers for this domain—the ones that are supposed to always give you the correct answer. It is good network administration practice to have at least two, and preferably three, of them, and to have them in different networks, so that the DNS service still works when one of them is down.

The third line from the bottom tells you the nameserver that was used to perform the DNS query; this is taken from your own setup. You can use this information to see whether you have entered the correct information in your DNS setup.

You can also specify a particular nameserver to query. For example, if you wanted to use the nameserver running at 195.67.199.10 instead, you could use:

```
dig @195.67.199.10 oreilly.com
```

Normally, you should get exactly the same result, but if you get a result at all from one of them but not from the other, then it's likely that the one not responding is simply down, or, per your network configuration, not reachable.

CHAPTER 14
Printing

The paperless society has not yet come to pass, and it now seems more likely that we'll just move from conventional paper to electronic paper. Until that time comes, you'll need to communicate with many people by putting your computer documents on bleached dead trees.

Because many distributions set up printing for you, we start this chapter with an introduction to command-line utilities you can use for printing and printer control. Then we'll explain how to configure printing on both local and network printers, focusing on the simple and powerful Common Unix Printing System (CUPS).

Printing

Linux provides various user-level printing options. Traditionally, tools such as the text-mode lpr have been used to print files from the command line. Understanding how to use these and other printing and document formatting commands will enable you to print documents quickly and efficiently. A quick rundown of the *enscript* and *nenscript* utilities will help you create good-looking printouts even from basic text documents. GUI programs present their own user interfaces that you can use to control printing options from such programs. Finally, we describe some of the mechanics behind the printing system. This will help you to manage your printing sessions by giving you an understanding of how it all works, enabling you to use the system to its best effect.

Basic Linux Printing Commands

The *lpr* command prints a document in Linux. You might not always invoke this command directly—you may just press a Print button on some glitzy drag-and-drop graphical interface—but ultimately, printing is handled by lpr and the other print management utilities we describe here.

If you want to print a program listing, you might enter the following:

```
$ lpr myprogram.c
```

Input is also often piped to lpr from another command, as described later. The *lpr* program starts the printing process by storing the data temporarily to a directory called a *print spool*. Other parts of the print management system, which we show you how to set up in "Managing Print Services" later in this chapter remove files from the print queue in the correct order, process the files for printing, and control the flow of data to the printer.

There is at least one print queue for each printer on the system, but each system has one print queue that's marked as the default. (In the old LPD printing systems, this queue was traditionally called lp, but this naming convention is less common with computers that run CUPS.) If you need to specify a queue of a different name, just include a -P option, as in *lpr -Pepson myprogram.c*. If you forget the name of a queue, you can look at queue names in the */etc/printcap* file, access the CUPS web configuration tool (as described in "Managing Print Services"), or type lpstat -a to see the status of all the queues.

 A printer that can be used in different modes of operation, such as for printing faxes as well as letters, may have a separate print queue for each purpose. You can also create multiple queues for a single printer in order to use different resolutions, paper sizes, or other features.

As a user, you do not see whether a printer is connected directly to your computer or somewhere else on the network; all you see and need to know is the name of the printer queue. If you use a printer queue that points to a printer on another machine, the file to print will first be spooled on your machine, then transmitted to the appropriate queue of the machine connected to the printer, and finally be printed. "Managing Print Services" tells you more about setting up printer queues.

Some programs look to the *PRINTER* environment variable to determine what queue to use. Thus, if you want to use a particular printer for most of your printing needs, you can set this environment variable. For instance, if you are using the *bash* shell, you could make epson_360 your personal default queue by putting this command in your *.bashrc* file:

```
$ export PRINTER=epson_360
```

This procedure doesn't work for all programs, though; many ignore the *PRINTER* environment variable. Some complex programs enable you to set a default queue in some other way, such as in a GUI dialog box. Consult your program's documentation for details. In any event, if you use lpr for printing, directly or indirectly, and can change how lpr is called, you can use the -P option to *lpr* to set the destination queue. This option overrides the *PRINTER* environment variable.

Once you know how to print a file, the next problem you might face is finding out what is happening if your file doesn't instantly print as you expect. You can find out the status of files in the print queue by using the *lpq* command. To find out the status of files sent to your default printer, enter:

```
$ lpq
epson_360 is ready and printing
Rank    Owner   Job    File(s)        Total Size
1st     rodsmit 440    (stdin)        2242560 bytes
2nd     rodsmit 441    (stdin)        5199872 bytes
3rd     lark    442    (stdin)        1226752 bytes
```

You see that the printer is running, but large jobs are queued ahead of yours (if you are *lark*). If you just can't wait, you might decide to remove the job from the print queue. You can use the job number of the printing task that lpq reported to remove the printing job:

```
$ lprm 442
```

The spooled print file identified as job 442 is discarded. You can narrow the *lpq* report by asking about a specific print job by task ID (rarely used), by printer, or by user ID. For example, to get a report that identifies spooled files sent to a printer named hp4500, you would enter

```
$ lpq hp4500
ada is ready and printing
Rank    Owner   Job    File(s)        Total Size
active  lovelac 788    (stdin)        16713 bytes
1st     lark    796    (stdin)        70750 bytes
```

If you are the root user, you can kill all pending printing tasks by entering the command:

```
# lprm -
```

If you are not the root user, issuing that command kills only the printing tasks you own. This restriction also holds true if you specify a printer:

```
# lprm ada
```

If you are *root*, the print queue is emptied. If you are a normal user, only the print files you own are removed from the specified print spool. The *lprm* utility reports on the tasks it kills.

The root user can kill all the print tasks issued by any user by specifying:

```
# lprm username
```

If you issue *lprm* with no argument, it deletes the currently active print jobs that you own. This is equivalent to entering:

```
$ lprm yourusername
```

If you want to see whether a queue is down, you can use the *lpc* command:

```
$ /usr/sbin/lpc status epson_360
```

See "Managing Print Services" for details. The *lpc* utility is usually installed in the /*sbin* or /*usr/sbin* directory. Alternatively, the CUPS lpstat command performs a task similar to *lpc* status.

Some Common Command-Line Printing Tasks

Sometimes you want to do more than just send a file that's already been prepared for printing to the printer. For instance, you might want to print a manpage or some other document that's not quite ready for printing. To do so, you can use various Linux utilities, often in pipelines, to do the job. For instance, to get a quick hard-copy printout of the cupsd manual page, enter:

```
$ man cupsd | col -b | lpr
```

The man command finds, formats, and outputs the *cupsd* manual page in an enriched ASCII output that uses backspaces to overstrike and underline characters (in place of italics) for highlighting. The output is piped through *col*, a Unix text filter, whose *-b* option strips the backspace instructions embedded in the manpage, which results in simple text strings while maintaining the layout of the formatted manpage. The output of *col* is piped to *lpr*, which spools the text in a spool directory.

Suppose you want to print the fully enriched manpage with highlighting and all. You might use a command like this:

```
$ gunzip -c /usr/share/man/man8/cupsd.8.gz | groff -man -Tps | lpr
```

The *gunzip -c* command uncompresses the compressed manpage and passes the results to standard output (and hence to the next command in the pipeline). The *groff* command applies the man macros to the file specified, creating PostScript output (specified by *-Tps*). This output is then passed to *lpr*, which spools it, and CUPS applies the default print-processing instructions for the default print queue.

Another useful tool for printing pure-text files is the *pr* command, which formats files in a number of ways. For instance, you can create multicolumn output, documents with headers, numbered lines, and more. Consult the *pr* manpage for details.

Most Linux distributions today use CUPS as the default printing system, but older distributions used the LPRng system or the even older BSD LPD system. (Some distributions ship with two or all three of these systems, but CUPS is usually the default choice.) The BSD LPD and LPRng systems use commands similar to those described here, so even if your distribution uses these older systems, you should be able to use these commands. Some Unix printing systems, such as the SysV printing system, use different commands, such as *lp* for printing. If you've installed such an unusual (for Linux) printing system, you may need to look at its documentation to learn how it works.

CUPS was designed as a drop-in replacement for LPD systems such as BSD LPD and LPRng, as well as for SysV-style printing systems. Thus, CUPS implements the basic printing commands, such as lpr and lp, used by both of these systems.

nenscript and enscript

The *nenscript* utility, now often called *enscript*, is a flexible filter that provides good formatted output for PostScript printers, even from ASCII text files. It isn't a basic Linux utility, but it is included in most Linux distributions and can be retrieved from the usual Linux FTP sites.

Although nenscript and enscript create PostScript output, they can still be used if you have a non-PostScript printer. As described later in this chapter, a properly configured Linux print queue automatically converts PostScript to the formats required by non-PostScript printers.

Suppose you are printing out a C program and want line numbering and a printout on green-striped fanfold paper (not the same format you'd want when printing those graphics you downloaded from the Internet on your nifty PostScript printer). You need to have the program processed, and then insert the line numbers in front of the lines. The solution is to process the file through a filter such as the *enscript* utility. After doing its own processing, enscript passes the file to lpr for spooling and printing to your trusty tractor-feed printer (named here):

```
$ enscript -C -B -L54 -Pdino -M Letter myprogram.c
```

The *enscript* filter numbers each line of the file passed through it when you specify the -C option. (Earlier versions of enscript used -N rather than -C for line numbering.) The -B option suppresses the usual header information from being printed on each page, and the -L54 option specifies formatting at 54 lines per page. The enscript filter just passes the -Pdino option through to lpr, which interprets it and directs the output to dino's print spool for printing. The -M Letter option specifies you want a printout on letter-size paper. (Depending on compile-time options, enscript may default to European A4 paper.)

When called on the command line, enscript automatically passes output to *lpr* unless you specify standard output by supplying the -p option. You don't need to pipe or redirect *enscript* output to *lpr* explicitly.

Suppose you are going to print a lot of program listings today. For convenience, you can set an environment variable for *enscript* to specially process and print your listings each time:

```
$ export ENSCRIPT=" -C -B -L54 -Pdino -M Letter"
```

Now, to print your listing correctly, all you need enter is:

```
$ enscript myprogram.c
```

enscript optionally sends output to a file, which is often useful for preparing Post-Script files on Linux hosts that don't actually have a PostScript printer available. For example, to convert a text file to a PostScript file, formatted for two-column printing on the standard European A4 paper format in 6-point Courier font, you would type:

```
$ enscript -2 -f Courier6 -M A4 -p document.ps document.txt
```

The `-2` option overrides the one-column default, and the `-f Courier6` option over-rides the 7-point Courier default for two-column output. (The one-column default is Courier 10; enscript always uses Courier font when converting plain text into Post-Script, unless told to do otherwise via *-f*.) The `-M A4` option specifies A4 paper size. (To learn what options are available, type *enscript --list-media*.) The `-p` option speci-fies that the output should be stored to *document.ps*, and the filename specified with no option is the input to *enscript*. If no filename had been specified, enscript would have taken standard input as the filename.

As another example, to print the *enscript* manual page as basic text on a PostScript printer, enter:

```
$ man enscript | col -b | enscript
```

The man command retrieves the manual page and formats it for text display. The *col -b* command strips the backspace instructions for highlighting and underlining, leav-ing plain text that is piped to the enscript filter. This turns the plain text into simple PostScript with some "pretty printing" that applies headers, footers, page number-ing, and the like. Finally, the file is passed to *lpr*, which spools the file. CUPS then processes the file in the same way it handles all files, which may involve sending the file directly to a PostScript printer, passing it through Ghostscript, or performing other filtering tasks.

If you specify the *-Z* option with *enscript*, it attempts to detect PostScript files passed to it and passes them through unaltered.

If a PostScript file is passed to enscript and is interpreted as a text file (probably because *enscript* was not called with the *-Z* option), enscript will encapsulate it and pass it through to print. This can result in the PostScript code being printed out literally. Even a small PostScript file can use up a lot of paper in this way.

Note that you could specify the default print queue to use either in PRINTER or as a *-P* argument stored to the ENSCRIPT environment variable. If you set ENSCRIPT to specify a queue to use, that queue will be used every time enscript filters one of your files. We recommend that you set PRINTER rather than *-P* in ENSCRIPT so that you can change the queue specification and have it filtered appropriately.

Printing Using GUI Tools

Most GUI programs use the standard printing tools, such as *lpr*, behind the scenes. These programs display friendly print dialog boxes, such as the one shown in Figure 14-1 (for OpenOffice). Typically, you select your printer from the list near the top (called Name in Figure 14-1). You can also set various program-specific options, such as the number of pages to print and the number of copies. When you've set your options, click a button to begin printing, such as the OK button in Figure 14-1.

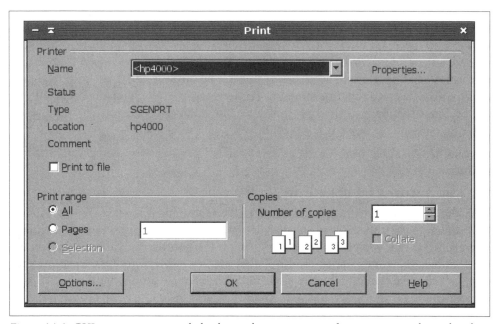

Figure 14-1. GUI programs present dialog boxes that serve as interfaces to more traditional tools

Frequently, there's little you can do to adjust the way a GUI program prints; there are no options that enable you to tell it to use a variant printing command, so you're stuck with whatever options the program provides. Other times, though, the program does present such options. One way to do this that's quite obvious is to present a print dialog box that enables you to enter the print command. For instance, Figure 14-2 shows the *xv* print dialog box. Rather than select a printer from a drop-down list, you enter the print command, including any printer specification, just as you would at a command prompt.

A few programs combine these two approaches, providing both a drop-down list of printers and a way to specify the print command. Some programs also provide configuration options that enable you to set the printing command you want to use. Such options, if present, are usually accessible from the program's preferences or configuration dialog box. Consult your program's documentation if you want to change the way it prints.

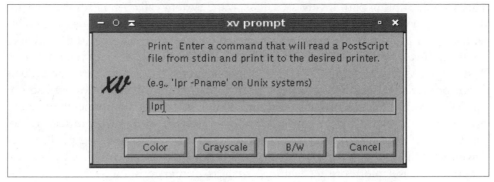

Figure 14-2. Some GUI programs enable you to specify a print command to suit your needs

How the Printing System Processes a File

Generally, after you have handed your document or file that you want printed over to the printing system, you can forget about it until the printed sheet comes out of the printer. But when things go wrong and the sheet does not appear, or if you are simply curious (like us!), you might want to know what goes on behind the scenes between the lpr command and the output tray of your printer. If you want, you can skip this section and come back here later.

Only the root user has the ability to access printers directly, without using the printing system. (That's not a wise thing to do, by the way.) Linux doesn't grant system users the ability to address various physical devices directly because crippling conflicts could result, and also because it's just too much work for them. Instead, utilities call background system processes to schedule your printing. Among other tasks, these processes convert source file data to print to a specific printer using its printer language and protocols, set the print resolution, format the pages, and add (or know not to add) header and footer data and page numbering. Linux configures itself to handle its physical devices when it is booted, including setting up ports and protocols to handle printing.

The print management system is controlled by *cupsd*, the daemon that has necessary privileges to access printers on behalf of the user. (Older Linux systems used BSD LPD or LPRng. These daemons were called *lpd* rather than *cupsd*, but they filled the same basic role.) Once the print management system is installed, cupsd is started every time the Linux system is booted. Files in */etc/cups* provide the control information cupsd needs to manage the files the user wants to print.

Two paths exist for printing on a Linux system that runs CUPS. The first path involves *lpr* or *lp*. These programs are named after the utilities in BSD printing systems (BSD LPD and LPRng) or SysV printing systems, respectively. They accept a file that's to be printed and behave much like their namesakes in the older printing systems, at least as far as the calling application or user is concerned. Behind the scenes, though, these programs are really just gateways into the second printing path.

This second printing path involves CUPS-specific system calls. Applications that use this path can communicate bidirectionally with CUPS. In addition to passing plaintext, PostScript, or other files to the print daemon (as in old-style printing systems), applications can query CUPS about a printer's capabilities. CUPS can then deliver a PostScript Printer Definition (PPD) file to applications. These files describe a PostScript printer's features: its page sizes, printable area, color capabilities, and so on. As described in "Managing Print Services," PPD files are key components of Linux printer driver packages, even for non-PostScript printers. (For such printers, Linux printer driver packages include PPD files that describe the printer's capabilities as driven via Ghostscript.) Because of this bidirectional communication, CUPS-aware programs can set more printer features, such as printer resolution, than can older programs that are not CUPS-aware.

> You can turn some old-style (CUPS-unaware) applications into CUPS-aware applications by changing their printing paths. Specifically, if you call *kprinter* rather than *lpr*, the result is that print jobs will be processed by KDE's printing system, which is CUPS-aware. You can then set CUPS-specific options, such as changing the printer resolution. This option works best for GUI programs because *kprinter* is an X-based application. You could also use this approach for printing from text-mode programs run from within an xterm terminal program.

Whether the program is CUPS-aware or not, once *cupsd* has received a print job, it's stored in the print spool directory (usually */var/spool/cups*), along with a file that describes the print job. CUPS then orders the list of print jobs and sends them to the printer in an organized fashion, preventing conflicts in accessing the printer. Each print queue has associated with it a set of filters, which are programs that process files of particular types. The details of print filter configuration are hidden from view, even from system administrators, unless you dig pretty deeply into the CUPS workings. Typically, applications deliver plain text or PostScript to CUPS. Plain text may be sent on to the printer without processing, but PostScript is usually processed through Ghostscript, which converts the PostScript into a format that the printer can understand.

Managing Print Services

Linux has a fairly complicated printing system, compared with the printing services most PCs use. Configuring the printing system is usually either very easy (because the semiautomated tools get it right) or very hard (because the semiautomated tools fail or because your printer is poorly supported under Linux). The next few pages describe the Linux printing system, beginning with an overview of the software and moving on to hardware configuration and testing, configuring the Common Unix Printing System (CUPS) to enable its web-based configuration tools and network helpers, defining printers in CUPS, fine-tuning printer definitions, managing printer queues, maintaining LPD compatibility, and troubleshooting printers.

Linux Printing Software

Printing in Linux involves the interactions of several different software packages. The most important of these is the Linux printing daemon, which accepts jobs to be printed, keeps them in one or more queues, and sends the jobs to printers in an orderly manner. Additional software includes Ghostscript, which converts between PostScript and a form the printer can understand; Ghostscript printer definitions; and assorted extra tools that can help you create nicely formatted output. Before you can configure Linux printing, you must install all of these components.

Linux printing daemons

A printing daemon's job is to run in the background, accept print jobs from applications, temporarily store those print jobs, and send them to the appropriate printers without interfering with each other. All mainstream Linux distributions ship with at least one printing daemon, and most set them up in at least a minimal way when you install the OS. You may still need to configure your printing daemon so that it knows about your printer, though. This task is described later in this chapter, in "Defining Printers in CUPS."

Traditionally, Linux has used the Berkeley Standard Distribution Line Printer Daemon (BSD LPD) or the updated LPRng package for printing. (For simplicity, both systems are referred to as *LPD* systems from here on.) Basic LPD systems are fairly simple tools; they accept print jobs, store those jobs in queues, and then send them directly to the printer. These systems can be modified to pipe the print jobs through other programs for additional processing, if desired. Unlike printing systems for Windows, Mac OS, and other OSs, LPD printing systems don't provide a two-way communication path. For instance, an application can't query the LPD system about the page width or color capabilities of a printer. Thus, you must tell each application about a printer's special features. LPD systems are, though, network-enabled, which makes it possible for one computer to share its printers with others, or for a computer to print to a network-capable printer.

In 1999, an experimental new printing system was developed: CUPS. This package uses a new network printing protocol and enables applications to query a printer's capabilities and set printer features in ways that aren't possible with LPD systems. By 2004, all major Linux distributions had either switched to CUPS as the default printing system or offered it as an option on equal footing with BSD LPD or LPRng. For this reason, we describe CUPS in this chapter. Although some of the principles and support software are the same for BSD LPD and LPRng as for CUPS, the details are completely different. If you're using an older printing system, you may want to consider upgrading to CUPS.

In most cases, you can install CUPS (if it's not already installed) by using your distribution's package management tools. Look for a package called cups and install it. If your system is already configured to use BSD LPD or LPRng, you should first remove that package. If you prefer, you can download the original CUPS source code from its web page, *http://www.cups.org*.

Ghostscript

The traditional LPD printing system passes a file from an application to a printer. In its most basic form, this means that the application must know how to create a file that the printer can understand. This contrasts with printing under most other OSs, such as Windows, in which the application can use OS calls to help prepare a document for printing. As a practical matter, Unix and Linux applications almost always generate one of two types of output:

Plain text

Programs can send plain text to the printer, under the assumption that the printer is either a dumb line printer (that is, a fast printer with few fancy formatting capabilities) or can at least accept the plain text.

PostScript

Adobe's PostScript language is one of many printer languages. It became popular on laser printers in the 1980s, and most Linux programs that need to print documents with multiple fonts, graphics, or other special formatting almost always do so by generating PostScript output.

Unfortunately, most printers, and particularly the inexpensive consumer and small business printers that are often paired with Linux, don't understand PostScript. The answer is to pipe output through Ghostscript (*http://www.cs.wisc.edu/~ghost/*), which is a PostScript interpreter that can reside on the computer rather than in the printer. Ghostscript converts PostScript into formats that most printers can understand. In effect, the combination of PostScript and Ghostscript becomes the Linux equivalent of the Windows printer driver system.

Although CUPS changes many things about the Linux printing system, it still relies on Ghostscript to convert PostScript into printers' native languages. Thus, you must have Ghostscript installed on your system if you expect to print to a non-PostScript printer. Fortunately, all major Linux distributions ship with Ghostscript. You may want to check to be sure it's installed, though; look for a package called ghostscript.

Ghostscript is actually available in two versions. The most recent version of Ghostscript is AFPL Ghostscript, which is available under a license that permits free use for many purposes, but not free redistribution. After a few months, AFPL Ghostscript is released under the GPL as GNU Ghostscript, and it's this version that comes with most Linux distributions. In most cases, being a few months behind the leading edge of Ghostscript development is unimportant. If you absolutely must have the latest version, though, check the Ghostscript home page.

Ghostscript comes with drivers for many common printers, and it can also output many common graphics file formats. You can even generate Adobe Portable Document Format (PDF) files with Ghostscript. (The ps2pdf shell script helps automate this process.) For more flexibility, you can add Ghostscript drivers for assorted printers.

As a point of interest, you should know that Ghostscript treats all printers as graphics devices. That is, if you print a purely textual document, Ghostscript converts that text into a graphics bitmap and sends the bitmap to the printer. This means that Ghostscript cannot take advantage of fonts that are built into the printer. It also means that Ghostscript sometimes prints more slowly than other software, such as Windows drivers, can print to the same printer. (This effect is usually negligible, but it's sometimes dramatic.) On some very old laser printers, another consequence is that Ghostscript (and hence Linux) requires a printer memory upgrade for the printer to print at full resolution. In practice, though, even Windows treats many printers as graphics-only devices, so Ghostscript's doing so may not make any difference.

Printer definitions

A standard CUPS installation supports a fairly narrow range of printers, typically PostScript models and some Hewlett-Packard and Epson printers. To support more printers, you must install a printer driver package. (In truth, many of these "drivers" are really just printer descriptions coupled to standard Ghostscript drivers, but in practice they're necessary either way.) Several such driver packages exist:

Foomatic
> These drivers, headquartered at *http://www.linuxprinting.org/foomatic.html*, handle many popular printers. They're a good place to start for many printers.

GIMP Print
> The GNU Image Manipulation Program (GIMP) is a popular graphics package that's developed its own set of printer drivers. These have been spun off into a separate printer driver package that can be used with CUPS (or with BSD printing systems). The GIMP Print drivers are often particularly good choices if you want to print graphics. Check *http://gimp-print.sourceforge.net* for more information.

ESP Print Pro
> The original CUPS developers have made a set of printer definitions available on a commercial basis. You can learn more at *http://www.easysw.com/printpro*.

Most distributions ship with Foomatic or GIMP Print, so check for those packages. Sometimes they're called something else, and occasionally they're bundled with still more printer definitions. If you fail to install any printer definitions, you'll see a very limited set of printers when you configure printing.

Sometimes multiple printer definitions are available for a single printer—for instance, separate definitions in the Foomatic and GIMP Print packages, or even multiple definitions in a single package. In such cases, you may want to try all the available definitions to see which one works best with your printer and the types of documents you print. Sometimes the developers give you a hint by specifying in the configuration menus that one definition is recommended over the others.

Additional printing software

CUPS (or an LPD printing system) is a practical necessity for printing from Linux. For most printers, Ghostscript and Ghostscript driver definitions are also practical necessities. Several additional tools are often highly desirable, but may not be necessary in all cases:

enscript *or* nenscript
> These commands were described earlier in this chapter. They help format plain text as PostScript or in other ways, which can be very helpful.

groff
> This program is the open source implementation of the roff typesetting system, which enables creation of prettily formatted documents from text-mode files using troff/nroff markup codes. Although many users today prefer GUI word processors for this task, groff is still required by some tools, and can be used more directly, as well.

TEX and L^ATEX
> The TEX package is a high-end document processing system, and L^ATEX is an extension to this package. These tools are favored by many mathematicians, scientists, computer scientists, and engineers for creating files. Some Linux documentation comes in the form of TEX or L^ATEX files, although such documents are also usually available in other formats.

Lout
> This package is also worthy of consideration as an efficient and compact package to format text documents for PostScript output. It supports Level 2 PostScript and the Adobe Structuring Conventions, takes comparatively little memory, and comes with good enough documentation to learn quickly. Lout doesn't create an intermediate output form; it goes directly from markup input to PostScript output.

netpbm *and* pbmplus
> These programs support a wide variety of graphics file format conversions. (Such formats have to be converted to PostScript before you try to print them.)

Ghostview
> This package provides display tools to view PostScript files in an X Window System environment, and also provides PostScript and PDF support for other packages, such as your web browser.

ImageMagick

> This program lets you display a large number of graphics formats in an X window and convert many file formats to other file formats. (It uses Ghostview and Ghostscript when it needs to display a PostScript image.) Most of the graphics files that you can print can also be displayed using ImageMagick.

Fax packages

> If you want to support fax devices, you can use the *tiffg3* utility with Ghostscript to output Group III fax format files. To control a Class 1 or Class 2 fax modem on your Linux host, you can use the efax package, which is provided in many distributions, or you can install and configure the more capable, but more complex, FlexFax or HylaFax packages.

Some of these tools are covered elsewhere in this book. Most require little configuration, and all are primarily user-level tools. Be aware that this list is not comprehensive; Linux printing tools are extremely plentiful, and range from simple text formatting tools to sophisticated word processors and graphics applications.

Configuring Printer Hardware

The first order of business when configuring a printer is configuring the hardware. You must verify that your printer is compatible with Linux, check its physical interface to the computer, and verify that the interface is working. Failure to check these details can lead to problems when you try to actually configure the printer in Linux, leading to a wild goose chase as you try to debug problems in the wrong subsystems.

Verifying printer compatibility

The main issue with respect to printer compatibility is the language the printer uses. Several languages are common, but many printers use their own unique languages. The more common printer languages include PostScript, HP's Printer Control Language (PCL), and Epson's ESC/P2 language. (ESC/P2 is most common on old dot matrix printers.) Many manufacturers make printers that use each of these languages, but sometimes they bury this detail in their descriptions or refer to it in another way. One common example is a laser printer that uses PCL; the manufacturer may refer to the printer as being "HP-compatible" (usually with a reference to a specific HP printer model).

The best hope for Linux compatibility is to get a printer that supports PostScript. Such printers are typically mid-range to high-end laser printers. Few inkjet or low-end laser printers support PostScript. With a PostScript printer, you needn't be concerned about whether a Ghostscript driver exists for your printer; just configure CUPS to pass the raw PostScript straight through to the printer.

Some printers are advertised as supporting PostScript when in fact they don't. Manufacturers may do this when their printers ship with software that's similar to Ghostscript, but such manufacturer-supplied software usually only runs under Windows. Thus, if you have or are looking for a PostScript-capable printer, try to verify that the Post-Script support is in the printer itself, not in a Windows driver package.

If you don't have a PostScript printer, your best bet for assessing Linux compatibility is to check the Linux Printing web site, and particularly its printer database, located at *http://www.linuxprinting.org/printer_list.cgi*. Locate your printer make and model in the drop-down fields on this site and then click the Show button. You'll then see a description of your printer and its Linux compatibility. The description may also tell you where to find drivers or printer descriptions to use with CUPS, so you can check that you have the appropriate support software.

If your printer is listed on the Linux Printing web site as a "paperweight" (meaning it doesn't work at all under Linux), you may want to try doing a web search on the printer's name and *Linux*. If you're lucky, you'll turn up a new or experimental driver you can try. If not, you may want to look into replacing the printer with one that's more Linux-friendly.

If you have, or are considering buying, a multifunction device (such as one that handles both printing and scanning functions), you should investigate Linux support for all of the device's functions. Sometimes the printer side will work fine but the scanner will be useless, for instance. Typically, support for each function is provided by its own project under Linux, such as Ghostscript for the printer and the Scanner Access Now Easy (SANE) project for scanner support. Occasionally, a project exists to provide all the necessary drivers in one place, such as the HP Office Jet project (*http://hpoj.sourceforge.net*) or Epson's drivers (*http://www.avasys.jp/english/linux_e*). These projects may be independent or sponsored by the device's manufacturer.

Printer interfaces

Printers can be connected to computers in several different ways. Four interface methods are common:

Parallel port
> A very popular interface method. Most x86 computers have a single parallel port that's intended for handling a printer (although some other devices have been designed to use this port, too). The parallel port has the advantage of speed, particularly compared with the RS-232 serial port. Under Linux, the parallel port is usually */dev/lp0*, although it can be */dev/lp1* or higher, particularly if you've added parallel port cards to your computer to support multiple printers.

RS-232 serial port
> Some very old printers use the RS-232 serial port standard. These ports are substantially slower than the parallel port, which is why this interface method hasn't

been a favored one in decades. If you have such a printer, it will probably be accessible as */dev/ttyS0* or */dev/ttyS1*, although higher numbers are possible. Other devices, such as mice and modems, often use RS-232 serial ports, so you may need to study your cabling to determine which one is your printer. You may also need to use the `setserial` program to configure your RS-232 serial port.

USB port

In recent years the Universal Serial Bus (USB) port has eclipsed the parallel port as the favored port for printers. The USB 1.x standard nearly matches the speed of the parallel port, and USB 2.0 exceeds it, so USB provides plenty of speed for printing. Under recent kernels, USB printers are accessed from the */proc/bus/usb* directory tree, and CUPS should be able to automatically detect USB printers; however, the printer must be turned on when the CUPS daemon is started for this to happen. Because CUPS normally starts automatically when the system boots, this means you should ensure that your printer is plugged in and powered on when you boot your system.

Ethernet

Some printers support Ethernet connections, either directly or indirectly. Workgroup printers often have Ethernet ports and show up as if they were computers on the network. Dedicated print server appliances are also available. These devices enable you to connect a USB or parallel printer, effectively turning them into Ethernet printers. These printers support one or more network printing protocols. The best case from a Linux and CUPS perspective is for the printer to understand the Internet Printing Protocol (IPP) that CUPS uses. Failing that, the LPD or Server Message Block/Common Internet File System (SMB/CIFS) protocols will do.

You should be aware of which interface method your printer uses. Some testing and configuration features won't work with some interfaces; for instance, you can't easily bypass the printing system to send a file directly to a USB or Ethernet printer. You must also have appropriate ports on your computer to support your printer, and the necessary cabling. If you lack this hardware, you should buy it. You can purchase add-in cards with any of the necessary port types; or if you have USB ports but no open slots in your computer, you can purchase an adapter so that you can connect a parallel, RS-232 serial, or even an Ethernet printer via a USB port. Be sure Linux drivers exist for the adapter, though!

If your printer supports multiple interface types, USB is generally the best to use, followed by a parallel interface and then RS-232 serial. USB provides more information to the computer about the printer, uses less bulky cables, and (in its 2.0 incarnation) can be faster than the parallel port. A network-enabled printer can be a big advantage if you want it to be accessible to several computers, but if it uses an odd protocol it could be more trouble than it's worth, particularly if you use it on only one system. Of course, you should also consider your available ports and cables; it might be more trouble than it's worth to install a USB card in an older system that you're using as a print server, for instance.

Verifying basic printer connectivity

Before you set up printer services, be sure the printing devices are online. If you also use another operating system, such as Microsoft Windows, you can exercise the hardware to ensure that it is connected properly and working before loading Linux. Successfully printing a document from another operating system immediately eliminates one major source of woe and head scratching. Similarly, if you are going to use printer services on a network, your system should be on the network and all protocols functioning before proceeding.

If you have a parallel or RS-232 serial printer, you can test basic printer functionality by sending a document directly to the printer device file. For instance, you might test a parallel printer by typing this command:

```
# cat /etc/fstab > | /dev/lp0
```

This command copies the */etc/fstab* file to */dev/lp0*, the most common identifier for a parallel printer. If your printer can print a text file, the result should be a printout of your */etc/fstab* file. On some printers, status lights will blink but nothing will emerge. Frequently, pressing a button (marked *Form Feed*, *Continue*, or something similar) on the printer will cause the file to print. This happens because the printer didn't receive a full page of data, and so was waiting until it received more data to continue. This shouldn't happen in normal operation, though—just when testing the printer. Another problem is "stair-stepping," which is a printout that doesn't reset the line starts, like this:

```
/dev/hda1 / ext3 defaults 1 1
                        /dev/hda5 /home ext3 defaults 1 2
```

You might be able to figure out what went wrong here. Text files in Unix use just a newline (also known as a linefeed, ASCII code 10) to terminate each line. MS-DOS uses both a newline and a carriage return. Your printer was therefore set up to use MS-DOS-style line endings with both newline and carriage-return characters at the end of each line. In practice, CUPS normally filters newlines so that printers configured for DOS can understand them. If you still see this problem once you've fully configured printing, though, you can reconfigure your printer to properly return to the start of the line on receipt of a newline character. Often this is simply a matter of setting a dip switch. Check your printer manual. (Be careful about changing your printer characteristics if you use multiple operating systems.)

If you're using a USB printer, you can look for it with the lsusb command:

```
$ lsusb
Bus 005 Device 004: ID 04b8:0807 Seiko Epson Corp.
```

In practice, you're likely to see more output than this; however, this output shows a USB printer—an Epson RX500, to be precise. It's on USB bus 5, device 4. You can learn more about it by viewing the contents of */proc/bus/usb/devices*, but most of the information in that file is likely to look like gibberish to the uninitiated. One feature to look for in this file, though, is Driver=usblp. If a line containing this string is present, it means that Linux has recognized the printer as a printer, which means that CUPS should be able to communicate with it. (Whether you can get output from the printer depends on the status of Ghostscript drivers, though.)

Finally, Ethernet printers can be treated just like other network devices. Specifically, you can use ping to verify that they're connected to the network. More substantial tests of their connectivity depend on the protocols the printer understands. Although low-level diagnostics of these protocols are possible, the simplest approach is usually to try configuring them, as described later in this chapter, in "Defining Printers in CUPS."

Configuring CUPS Security

Before proceeding with configuring CUPS to print, you should review your CUPS security and web-based configuration tool options. Unlike LPD systems, CUPS is best managed through its web-based configuration tool; however, this tool is sometimes disabled or set up in an inconvenient way. (Some distributions provide their own GUI tools for CUPS configuration. When using these distributions, you can either use their GUI tools or use the standard CUPS tools.) Depending on your network configuration, you might want to enable or disable the CUPS *browsing* feature, which enables CUPS servers to communicate their lists of available printers to one another. Browsing greatly simplifies network printer configuration and maintenance, but some distributions disable it by default. On the other hand, in a high-security environment or if your system is connected directly to the Internet, you might want to disable browsing, but some distributions enable it by default. In any event, you should review these settings and be sure they're set appropriately for your environment and needs.

Enabling web-based configuration

The main CUPS configuration file is */etc/cups/cupsd.conf*. This file is modeled after the Apache configuration file, so if you're familiar with Apache, you should feel at home with this file. If you're not familiar with the Apache configuration file, the basics are as follows. The file begins with a series of global directives, which take the form of a directive name followed by the directive's value. For instance, to override the default server name (advertised to other systems), you would enter a directive like this one:

```
ServerName gutenberg.example.com
```

This line sets the server name to *gutenberg.example.com*. CUPS accepts a large number of configuration directives; you should consult its manpage for complete details. Some sets of configuration directives are enclosed in sections delimited by lines that are enclosed in angle brackets:

```
<Location /admin>
AuthType Basic
AuthClass System
Order Deny,Allow
Deny From All
Allow From 127.0.0.1
Allow from 192.168.1.0/24
</Location>
```

This set of lines sets directives that apply only to certain functions of the server—in this case, those handled by the /admin (administrative) subsystem. You can use this feature to selectively modify the CUPS security functions (or other functions). The /admin area is particularly important for controlling access to the CUPS web-based administration tool. The options shown in the preceding example control features you may want to adjust:

AuthType

The *AuthType* directive tells CUPS what type of authentication to require for access to the location. In the case of /admin, this is usually set to Basic, which corresponds to password exchanges in cleartext. If you intend to administer the server from remote systems, you may want to change this to Digest, which adds encryption for the password exchange. (This feature requires that you set a password digest using the *lppasswd* program.) Some subsystems don't normally enable authentication; they use None for the AuthType. This configuration is a common default setting, and enables users to print without providing a password.

AuthClass

This directive tells CUPS what groups of users to accept. Possible values are Anonymous, User, System, and Group. The Anonymous option specifies that no authentication should be performed. User means that any valid username and password will grant access. System means that the user who authenticates must be a member of the CUPS system group. (This option varies from system to system, but it's normally *sys*, *system*, or *root*. You can set it with the SystemGroup option.) The Group option enables you to specify a Linux group name with the AuthGroupName directive, which must appear on another line.

Order

This directive tells CUPS whether to grant or deny access by default. If it's set to Deny,Allow, CUPS denies access unless it's explicitly granted. Setting the value to Allow,Deny grants access unless it's specifically denied.

Deny *and* `Allow`

These directives specify machines or networks from which access should be denied or allowed, respectively. You can specify machines by IP address, by network address, by hostname, by domain name (preceding the name with a dot), by the keywords `All` or `None`, or by the variables `@IF` (followed by a specific interface name in parentheses) or `@LOCAL` (for all local networks).

To enable web-based configuration, you should be sure that your CUPS configuration has an /admin location defined and that it grants access to the 127.0.0.1 address, as shown in the preceding example. That example also gives administrative access to users on the 192.168.1.0/24 network. Generally speaking, you should activate such access only for print servers that you want to administer remotely; opening this option up increases the security risks associated with running CUPS.

If you want to completely disable the CUPS web-based administrative tools (say, because you intend to use your distribution's own CUPS administrative programs instead), you should remove all the `Allow` directives and ensure that the configuration includes a `Deny from All` directive.

Enabling or disabling browsing

While you're digging in the */etc/cups/cupsd.conf* file, you may want to examine the server's browsing options. In the context of CUPS, browsing refers to automatic network printer discovery. This feature, supported by IPP, enables IPP servers to exchange lists of printers with one another. Each server periodically sends out broadcasts to which other IPP servers respond. The result is that you need configure each printer only once, on the computer to which it's connected. That server then propagates the configuration for the printer to other CUPS/IPP servers. Applications on those remote systems will see the new printer appear once they're restarted. This feature can be a great time-saver, particularly on networks on which printers are frequently added or removed.

A couple of caveats are in order concerning browsing, though. First, like many network features, browsing comes with some security baggage. Systems configured to browse could be tricked into displaying bogus printer information, and it's conceivable that a bug in the CUPS browsing code could lead to more serious system compromises. For this reason, some distributions ship with browsing disabled. This fact is the second caveat: if you do want to use browsing, you may need to enable it. If you fail to do so, your system won't automatically detect other printers on your network. Likewise, if you want to tell your system to enable others to print to its printers you must be sure certain options are enabled. You should check several options on your client and server systems:

`BrowseAllow` *and* `BrowseDeny`

These directives tell a CUPS client the addresses from which it should accept or reject browse packets, respectively. They take options with the same form as the

Allow and Deny directives. On a LAN, setting BrowseAllow @LOCAL generally works well to enable a system to automatically detect remote printers. This option tells the system to accept browse packets from all the local interfaces. You can set specific IP addresses or hostnames instead of this option to tighten this security, or specify entire network addresses to loosen or change the security. You can also explicitly exclude computers or networks with BrowseDeny. You can include multiple BrowseAllow and BrowseDeny directives.

Browsing

This directive takes On and Off options. You should be sure that any CUPS server that is to share its printers has this directive set to On, which is the default setting for stock CUPS configurations. (Some distributions change the default to Off, though.)

BrowseAddress

You can tell a CUPS server to which addresses it should send browse packets with this directive, which takes IP addresses, network addresses, and hostnames in the same forms as the Allow and Deny directives. The default is to not send any browse packets, so chances are you'll need to set this line. Using BrowseAddress @LOCAL works well on small networks, but you may need to use multiple lines or configure your system in another way, depending on your network.

These browsing directives are typically set in the global section of the *cupsd.conf* file. They're sometimes set separately or redundantly in the /printers section, though, so check there if you have problems.

 Actually printing to a server requires general access to the /printers section, independent of the browsing access. Thus, CUPS servers typically have one or more Allow directives in their /printers sections. Without these directives (either in this section or set globally), a CUPS server will reject incoming print jobs.

Restarting CUPS

If you make changes to your CUPS configuration, you should restart the CUPS daemon. On most distributions, this is done via the SysV startup script file:

```
# /etc/init.d/cupsd restart
```

This command (or one like it; you may need to change the path to cupsd) shuts down the CUPS daemon and restarts it. The result should be that the system implements any changes you make to the server's configuration.

Defining Printers in CUPS

Now that you've ensured the CUPS administrative tools are available, you can begin using them. To do so, you'll need a web browser. Any modern browser will work:

Mozilla Firefox, Konqueror, Opera, or even the text-mode Lynx, to name just four possibilities. With the help of your web browser, you can add your printer definitions and test your printer configuration.

We describe administering CUPS via its own web-based interface because this approach works with all Linux distributions. Many distributions provide their own tools for CUPS administration, though. For instance, Fedora and Red Hat have the Printer Configuration tool (aka system-config-printer), and SUSE uses its YaST and YaST2 utilities. If you like, you can use such tools. They provide the same basic options as the CUPS printer configuration utility, but the details of their operation differ.

Accessing the printer definition tool

CUPS runs its web-based configuration tool on port 631, so you should be able to access the system by entering *http://localhost:631* in your web browser's address field. If you've configured CUPS to accept administrative input from other systems, you should be able to access the printer configuration tool from another computer by entering the server's hostname, as in *http://gutenberg.example.com:631*.

You cannot use your computer's regular hostname to access the CUPS configuration tools, even from your computer itself, if you restrict administrative access to the localhost interface (127.0.0.1). When you so restrict access, you *must* use the localhost name or 127.0.0.1 IP address.

If CUPS is properly configured and running, the result of accessing a computer's port 631 with a web browser should be a display with a series of links called Do Administration Tasks, Manage Printer Classes, On-Line Help, and so on. If you get an error message from your browser, chances are that something is wrong with your CUPS configuration; review the earlier section "Configuring CUPS Security," and check that the cupsd server is running. If you do see the main CUPS page, you can begin using it to add or reconfigure your printers.

Creating a printer definition

To add a printer to a system, you should select the Manage Printers link on the main CUPS configuration page. The result should resemble Figure 14-3, which shows a CUPS configuration with some remote printers already autodetected.

To create a new printer definition, follow these steps:

1. Ensure that your printer is connected and powered on. In the case of USB printers, if it's not already connected and turned on, you may need to restart CUPS, as described earlier in "Restarting CUPS," after connecting and turning on the printer.

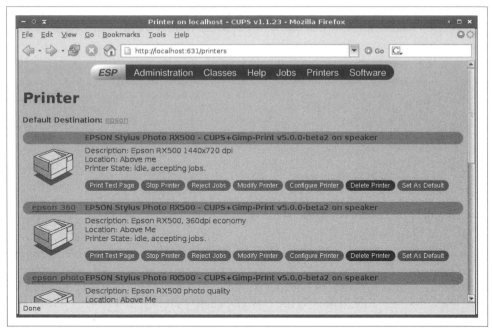

Figure 14-3. The CUPS web-based administrative tool lists all printers, including those detected on other systems

2. Click Add Printer. This link is near the bottom of the page and is not visible in Figure 14-3. Unless you've already done something that requires authentication, the result will probably be a window asking for your username and password. Enter root and the root password. You should now see a new page entitled Add New Printer, in which you enter basic printer identifying information: a name, a location, and a description.

3. Enter the printer's name, location, and description. The printer name is used to identify the printer in applications, and is usually fairly short, such as lexmark or hp4500. One-word names (or multiple words separated by an underscore) work best; multiple words and hyphens tend to confuse CUPS, so don't use them. The location and description fields are purely descriptive, so enter information that will help you distinguish the printer from any others on your network. These fields can and often do contain multiple words. When you're done, click the Continue button.

4. CUPS now displays a Device page, in which you identify the hardware used to connect to the printer. Select the hardware device, which typically appears as follows:

    a. Parallel ports are identified as Parallel Port #1, Parallel Port #2, and so on.

    b. RS-232 serial ports are identified as Serial Port #1, Serial Port #2, and so on.

c. USB printers are identified as USB Printer #1, USB Printer #2, and so on. In addition, the make and model of the printer should appear in parentheses. If it doesn't, you should check that your printer is connected and powered on and then restart CUPS and begin the process again.

d. Network printers are identified by protocol, such as LPD/LPR Host or Printer, Windows Printer via SAMBA, or Internet Printing Protocol. You must know what protocol to use, and depending on the protocol you select, you may need to pick extra options, as described in the sidebar "Printing to Network Printers."

e. Various additional and more obscure options also exist.

Once you've picked your printer device, click Continue.

5. You should now see a Model/Driver page, as shown in Figure 14-4. You should pick the make of your printer from the list and then click Continue. Note that, depending on the printer definition packages you've installed, some makes may appear twice, possibly under different spellings or names, such as HP and Hewlett-Packard. If this is the case for your printer, pick one and if you can't find your specific model, move back and try the other entry. If you don't see your make and it's a common one, such as Epson, Canon, or Lexmark, you should try installing a printer definition package, as described earlier in "Printer definitions." If you don't see your printer make because it's a very obscure one, consult your manual to learn what models your printer emulates and select one of them. Some common printer languages, including PostScript, PCL, and ESC/P2, appear under the Generic brand, so you might try that if your printer is an obscure model that uses such a common printer language.

6. After the first Model/Driver page, CUPS presents a second Model/Driver page in which you select your printer's model, such as the Lexmark Optra Color 45 or the Lexmark Z51. Locate your printer, select it, and click Continue. If you don't see your model, click your browser's Back button and look for another name for your printer manufacturer or select a compatible model and try it. If you still can't find your model, perhaps you need to install more or newer printer definitions; consult the Linux Printing web page for pointers on your model.

7. After clicking Continue on the second Model/Driver page, CUPS should respond with a message to the effect that your printer has been added. If you click Printers at the top of the page, you should see the printer list (Figure 14-3) again, but it should now include the printer you've just defined. You can now exit and fine-tune the printer definition.

If you decide to change any of the features of your printer configuration, you can do so by clicking Modify Printer in the printer's area on the main printer configuration page (Figure 14-3). The result is a run through the original configuration options, except that the defaults have changed to whatever you've entered before. (You will be unable to change the printer's name, but you can change other options.)

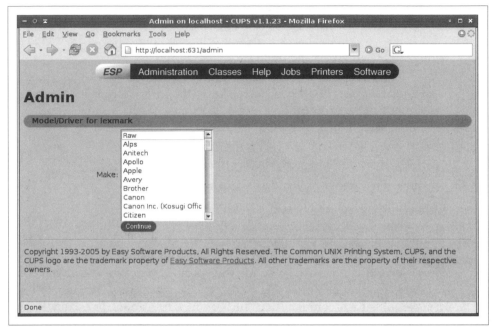

Figure 14-4. CUPS configured with printer definitions

This procedure (or the GUI tools provided by your distribution) is the simplest way to configure a print queue in CUPS. If you happen to know all the values, though, you can use the *lpadmin* command-line utility instead. When used to define a queue, this utility takes the following syntax:

```
lpadmin [-E] [-h server] -p printer option...
```

The *-E* option enables the print queue (a desirable option, typically), while *-h* enables you to modify the configuration of a server other than the local one, and *-p* sets the name of the queue.

The final, trailing options are the tricky part. Typically, the most important of these options are *-i interface*, which sets the interface device, and *-m model*, which points to a PostScript Printer Definition (PPD) file that defines the printer's model and capabilities. You must know the filename of the PPD file for your printer, which may not be obvious unless you've obtained a PPD file specifically for the printer (say, from the printer's manufacturer). As the name implies, a PPD file describes the capabilities of a PostScript printer, so printer manufacturers normally only make these files available for PostScript models. CUPS printer definitions rely on PPD files for all printers, though, and in fact these are the main part of the Foomatic, GIMP Print, and other Linux printer definition packages.

Printing to Network Printers

Network printers require more in the way of identification (described in step 4 of "Creating a printer definition") than local printers do. In all cases, you enter the information in a Device URI screen, which provides a single text-entry field in which you enter a string to identify the remote printer. Precisely what sort of information is required depends on the network protocol in use:

- For LPD printers, you must provide the identifying prefix `lpd://`, the hostname, and the printer queue name. For instance, `lpd://gutenberg/lexmark` allows printing to the `lexmark` printer on `gutenberg`.

- For printers served by Windows systems or Samba using SMB/CIFS, you must provide a hostname and printer queue name, as with LPD printers, but you may also need to provide a username and password. The full URI might resemble

  `smb://printacct:ppass@GUTENBERG/LEXMARK`

  to print to the LEXMARK printer on GUTENBERG using the printacct account and ppass password. Depending on the server's configuration, you may be able to omit the account and possibly the password.

- The best way to manage IPP printers is generally to take advantage of browsing. If that's not possible, though, you can use an `ipp://` prefix, a hostname, and a printer name, much as with LPD printers. Some network-enabled devices that support IPP require variants on this, so consult their documentation.

One type of print queue definition requires special mention: a *raw queue*. You can create a raw queue by selecting a printer make of Raw and model of Raw Queue. Unlike most CUPS printer queues, a raw queue uses no filtering—that is, CUPS won't try to determine the file's type and pass it through programs such as Ghostscript to produce output that's acceptable for your printer. For most Linux purposes, raw queues aren't very useful; however, there are a few cases where you might want to use one. One such instance is if you want to use Linux as a print server for non-Linux systems, such as Windows computers. You might then install Windows drivers on the Windows clients to have them print to the Linux raw queue. Using a raw queue in this instance guarantees that CUPS won't corrupt the Windows print jobs. (Another option for this scenario is to use PostScript drivers on Windows. Each approach has its plusses and minuses.) A second situation where raw queues can be handy is when you use an application that provides its own printer drivers. The GIMP is one such program, and you might get better results using the GIMP's printer drivers than using the standard Ghostscript drivers for your printer.

If in doubt, you should probably create a regular printer queue, which will try to parse the file type and convert it (via Ghostscript or other filtering programs) to your printer's native format. If this doesn't work or if you know you'll need it, though, a raw queue can be the way to go.

Testing your printer definition

Once you've configured your printer queue, you can test it. From the main printer description page (Figure 14-3), click Print Test Page for your queue. CUPS should respond with a message to the effect that a test page has been printed. After a brief delay, the result should be a printer test page being printed. (Precisely how long a delay you'll experience depends on the printer, its configuration, how it's connected to your computer, your computer's CPU speed, and your computer's CPU load.)

The standard CUPS test page includes a color wheel; a circle of fine radial lines (used to assess resolution); information on page size, borders, and nominal resolution; and PostScript interpreter data. Check that the resolution (expressed in dots per inch, or dpi, in the Imageable Area box) is reasonable. If it's not, consult "Fine-Tuning Printer Definitions" for help. Likewise, if a color printer produces merely black-and-white printouts, you will have to adjust your configuration. (This is assuming you know the printer is working correctly; it's entirely possible that the printer's color ink is depleted or clogged!)

If your printer doesn't generate any output at all, consult the section "Printer Troubleshooting," later in this chapter.

Fine-Tuning Printer Definitions

Most modern printers provide options that affect print quality and style. These features include variable resolution, ink- or toner-saving modes, printing modes optimized to particular types of paper, and so on. CUPS provides a way to set defaults for these features for a given queue. From the main print queue list page in the web-based CUPS configuration (Figure 14-3), click Configure Printer in the area for the printer you want to modify. The result is a list of options you can set, as shown in Figure 14-5.

The list of options available for any given printer varies greatly from one printer to another. Some common options you might want to investigate include the following:

Output Mode
> This option sets the color options for the printer: whether it prints in color or black and white, and if in color, how it encodes color information. For most color printers, RGB Color is the best choice.

Print Quality
> This option describes print resolution in imprecise verbal terms (Economy, Standard, High, and so on).

Resolution
> You can set the print resolution in precise numeric terms using this option. Many printers support different horizontal and vertical resolutions. As a general rule of thumb, the higher the resolution, the slower the printing, particularly for inkjet printers.

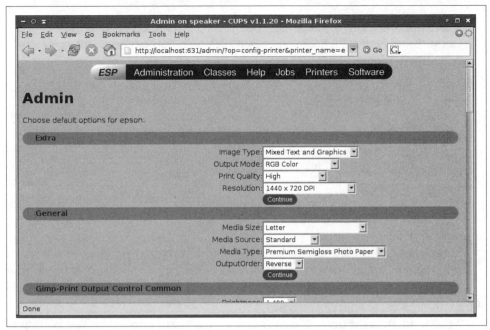

Figure 14-5. CUPS enables you to fine-tune the configuration for each of your print queues

Media Size
> You can tell CUPS what size paper you use with this option. Be sure to check it, because it has a habit of setting itself to the wrong size when you first install a printer.

Media Source
> Many printers support multiple paper feeds, and this option lets you tell CUPS which one to use by default.

Media Type
> This option lets you tell CUPS about the type of paper you're using. This feature can be particularly important for inkjet printers, because different papers absorb ink in different ways. When CUPS knows what type of paper you're using, it can have Ghostscript adjust its output to suit the paper.

Output Order
> Depending on the printer's design, multipage documents may print in such a way that the complete stack is backwards. You can set this option to correct for this problem by having the document print backwards, if you like.

Duplexing and paper handling
> Some drivers enable you to turn on duplexing (printing on both sides of the paper) and other advanced paper-handling options.

Color and brightness options

Many options relate to the brightness, saturation, and color balance of the output of color printers. These options vary from one printer to another. You may need to experiment with these options to find what works best for you.

Dithering options

Ghostscript *dithers* its output—that is, when it's told to print a particular color, it's likely to print a pattern of several different ink colors. The reason is simple: color printers have just a few colors at their disposal, so to match a given color, two or more must be combined in a pattern. Certain dithering algorithms work better for particular applications than others, and personal preference can also play a role. Thus, CUPS lets you tell Ghostscript what dithering algorithm to use. As with color and brightness options, you may need to experiment to determine what works best for you.

Specialty print options

Some printers support borderless (edge-to-edge) printing, printing on CD-R and DVD-R media, and other special options. You can set these options if your Ghostscript driver supports them.

Print direction and interleaving options

Most modern inkjet printers support bidirectional printing—that is, they print in one direction and then in the other to save time. This is handy, but alignment is sometimes improved by printing in one direction alone. Similarly, interleaving options that relate to which ink nozzles fire can improve or degrade print quality while affecting print speed.

Ink options

Some drivers enable you to specify which ink tanks to use, or to tell Ghostscript that you've installed an optional ink set.

Banners

You can have CUPS print a banner page before or after each print job. This page can identify the job and optionally include a brief note, such as `Confidential`.

PostScript level filtering

For some PostScript printers, CUPS can convert the PostScript level to a specified version, such as converting everything to PostScript Level 1. This can be handy if your printer chokes on more recent versions of PostScript.

Because printer capabilities vary so much, we can't describe all the options here. You may need to examine the options and experiment with them. Change an option and see how it affects output. Some options will affect text more than graphics or graphics more than text. Different types of graphics, such as digital photos versus charts and graphs, may also be affected differently by certain options. As a general rule, if you don't understand an option you should probably leave it alone.

In the past, Linux provided applications with limited or no access to printer options such as those described here. In fact, applications built for the old LPD system may not be able to set these options directly; these programs can only use the printer's defaults. To set such options in such applications, you can create multiple print queues for each printer. For instance, suppose you want to be able to print at 360 dpi for quick printouts or at 1440 dpi for slower but higher-quality printouts. You would create two print queues (say, canon_360 and canon_1440). Both queues would connect to a single printer device, but you'd set different default options for the two queues. You'd then choose your desired print resolution by printing to one queue or the other.

Alternatively, if you're running in X and if the application enables you to enter the printing command, you can use kprinter as the printing command. The result is the standard KDE printing dialog box. When you set it to use CUPS (via the listbox near the bottom of the dialog box) and select a print queue, you can click the Properties button in the upper-right corner of the dialog box. The result is the Configuration dialog box shown in Figure 14-6. This dialog box has multiple tabs that correspond to various CUPS configuration options, so you can adjust the resolution (as shown in Figure 14-6) or other printing options.

Another fine-tuning detail is setting the default print queue. In theory, you should be able to do this from the CUPS interface by clicking the Set as Default option; however, in practice this often produces an error message about an unknown operation. To work around this bug, use the *lpadmin* command with its *-d* option, which takes the name of the default queue:

```
# lpadmin -d hp4500
```

This command sets the default queue to hp4500. All subsequent print jobs submitted via *lp* or *lpr* that don't specify a queue will go to the hp4500 queue. This queue will also be the one to appear in print dialog boxes when they first open. In the case of both text-mode and GUI programs, though, you can still print to non-default queues by specifying the one you want to use.

Managing Printer Queues

An important part of printer administration is managing active print queues. Once a system has print queues defined, users start using them, and the result can sometimes be problems. You may need to delete jobs that are too big, temporarily shut down a queue while you reconfigure it, or otherwise manipulate the queue. To handle this task, CUPS provides two basic classes of tools: text-mode and web-based.

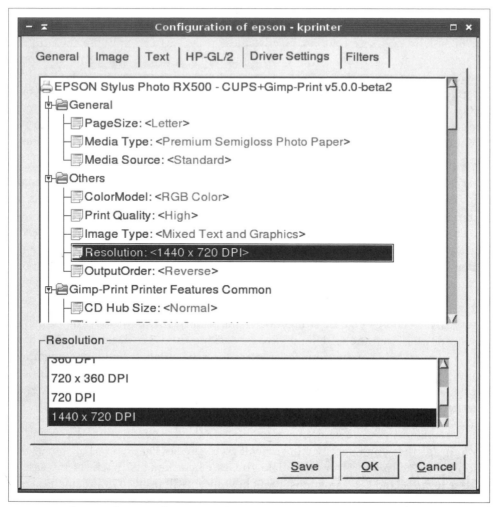

Figure 14-6. kprinter lets you adjust printer features from many CUPS-unaware applications

Using command-line tools

Text-mode CUPS commands enable you to control print queues from a text-mode login, an *xterm* window, or any other text-mode interface. Most of these commands require root privilege to function correctly, but a few can be used by ordinary users:

lpc

This command is named after the main text-mode queue manager in LPD, but the CUPS version is very limited; its only useful option is *status*. Type *lpc* status to see a list of available queues and the status of each (queueing enabled, printing enabled, number of queued jobs, and the availability of a CUPS daemon to manage the queue). You can add a queue name to obtain status on that queue alone.

lpstat

This command lists status information on print jobs, and like *lpc*, it can be used by ordinary users. Type this command by itself to see a list of jobs that are queued for printing on all the system's printers. You can also use various options to modify its output in various ways. For instance, *-p queue* restricts output to the specified queue, *-u users* restricts output to jobs submitted by the specified user or users, and *-d* displays the current default destination.

lpq

Like *lpc*, this command is borrowed from the LPD printing system. It displays information on the status of the current queue, similar in some ways to *lpstat*. It's often used with the *-P queue* option to display information on the specified queue rather than the default one. (Alternatively, -a can be used to display information on all queues.)

lppasswd

This program changes the CUPS digest password—that is, the password used by the system if you set AuthType to Digest in the *cupsd.conf* configuration file.

enable and disable

These commands start or stop a queue, respectively. Both commands take a queue name as an option, and *disable* also takes a few options, the most important of which may be *-c*. This option causes *disable* to cancel all the jobs currently in the queue. The *disable* command also accepts an *-r reason* option, which enters the text string *reason* as an explanation for the printer's unavailability.

 If you receive the error message not a shell builtin when you use the *enable* command, you must provide the complete path to the command, usually */usr/bin/enable*.

accept and reject

These commands cause the specified print queue to begin accepting or rejecting new jobs for printing. This differs from *enable* and *disable* in that *accept* and *reject* affect only the queue's ability to accept new jobs for printing, whereas *enable* and *disable* affect the queue's ability to print jobs in the queue. Like *disable*, *reject* supports a *-r reason* option so that you can register a reason for the queue's unavailability.

lprm

You can remove a job from the queue using this command. It takes an optional queue definition (*-P queue*) and a job identifier (which you can obtain with *lpstat*) as arguments.

lpmove

This command moves a print job from one queue to another. It accepts two arguments: a job identifier and a queue name, as in *lpmove oldqueue-456 newqueue*. This command moves job *oldqueue-456* to the *newqueue* queue.

As an example of these commands in action, suppose you have a problem with the hp4000 queue—perhaps the printer is malfunctioning and needs to be serviced. Thus, you want to disable it and move some of its jobs to another queue (say, the laserwriter queue), and perhaps delete other jobs. You might type commands like these to do all this:

```
# disable hp4000
# lpc status hp4000
hp4000:
        printer is on device '/dev/null' speed -1
        queuing is enabled
        printing is disabled
        no entries
        daemon present
# lpstat
hp4000-433              sholmes          15360   Sun Apr 10 22:20:44 2005
hp4000-434              moriarty          2977   Sun Apr 10 22:21:32
# lpmove hp4000-433 laserwriter
# lprm hp4000-434
# lpstat
laserwriter-433        sholmes          15360   Sun Apr 10 22:20:44 2005
```

In this example, the hp4000 queue is first disabled, and *lpc status hp4000* confirms its disabled status—note the printing is disabled message. The *lpstat* command reveals that two jobs are now stuck in the disabled queue. The first of these, belonging to sholmes, is moved to the laserwriter queue with the *lpmove* command, whereas the second job, belonging to moriarty, is deleted with *lprm*. A subsequent check with *lpstat* shows the moved job under its new name. (This job might not show up if it had been completely accepted by the printer before the command was typed.)

Using the CUPS web-based interface

The CUPS web-based interface provides an alternative means of controlling print queues whose features largely parallel those of the text-based commands. From the main printer list (Figure 14-3), you can stop a queue (equivalent to *disable*) or tell it to reject new jobs (equivalent to *reject*) by clicking the Stop Printer or Reject Jobs links, respectively. Once clicked, these links change to Start Printer and Accept Jobs, respectively, and have the effect of the enable and accept commands.

You can view the contents of print queues by clicking the Jobs link at the top of the page. The result is a process list similar to the one created by *lpstat*. This list includes a Control column with a Hold Job and a Cancel Job link for each job. Click these links to temporarily stop a job from printing or to delete the job entirely, respectively.

Maintaining LPD Compatibility

CUPS is designed as a drop-in replacement for LPD, and in fact it uses many of the same commands for printing as LPD. (These are described in "Printing," earlier in the chapter.) A couple of key LPD compatibility issues are providing an environment that programs designed for LPD will find helpful and accepting print jobs from networked LPD clients.

Maintaining a legacy /etc/printcap file

Many programs that expect to print using LPD examine the */etc/printcap* file to determine what queues are available. Under LPD, this file defines all the available print queues, so it's a critical LPD file. Thus, CUPS tries to maintain a minimal */etc/printcap* file for the benefit of user programs. (CUPS-enabled programs communicate with CUPS in other ways to obtain print queue lists.)

A full LPD */etc/printcap* file contains many types of fields, and any given printer definition is likely to use about half a dozen field types. The simplified needs of CUPS, though, mean that a stripped-down file is sufficient. A typical file looks like this:

```
hp4000|Hewlett-Packard HP LaserJet 4000 Series:rm=nessus:rp=hp4000:
epson|Epson RX500 1440x720 dpi:rm=nessus:rp=epson:
epson_360|Epson RX500, 360dpi economy:rm=nessus:rp=epson_360:
```

These three lines describe three queues: hp4000, epson, and epson_360. Under LPD, print queues may have multiple names, which are separated from one another by vertical bars (|). Typically, a short name begins the entry, and longer names follow. CUPS uses this feature to provide a short name based on the print queue name and a longer name based on the printer description. Subsequent fields in each line are separated by colons (:). In this example, CUPS has generated entries using the rm= and rp= options, which in LPD define the remote server name and remote print queue name for network printers. In this sample, these fields identify the computer on which the file resides and the queue name. CUPS doesn't require this information, nor do most LPD-using programs, but it can help keep a few programs happy to see this minimal information.

Normally, you needn't be concerned with maintaining an */etc/printcap* file, because CUPS does so automatically. If something interferes with this process, though, you might want to create a dummy */etc/printcap* file yourself. At a minimum, the file should hold each queue's correct name and a colon. Adding rm= and rp= fields, as in the preceding example, might help some programs.

Accepting print jobs from LPD systems

As noted earlier, CUPS uses IPP for communicating with other CUPS systems. LPD systems use the older LPD protocol. Thus, if your network contains a mix of CUPS and LPD systems, or a mix of CUPS systems with systems that use some other printing system that nonetheless understands the LPD protocol, you may want to enable LPD support in CUPS. This support will enable a CUPS system to accept print jobs submitted via the LPD protocol. It is not necessary on an all-CUPS network, and is disabled by default on all major Linux distributions.

Enabling LPD support is necessary only to accept print jobs from LPD clients. If you want your CUPS daemon to print to a remote system that runs LPD, you can do so without activating this support. In this case, you need to specify the LPD server as a network print server, as described earlier in "Creating a printer definition."

The CUPS LPD support is provided by a small daemon called, appropriately enough, *cups-lpd*. This server is designed to be run via a super server, such as *inetd* or *xinetd*. On distributions that use xinetd, such as Fedora, Red Hat, and SUSE, look for a *xinetd* configuration file called *cups-lpd* in the */etc/xinetd.d* directory. Look for a line in this file that reads disable = yes and edit it so that it reads disable = no. You can then restart *xinetd* or tell it to reload its configuration, and the *cups-lpd* server should be started. This server will accept print jobs using the LPD protocol just like BSD LPD or LPRng would, but it will redirect the job into the local CUPS queue of the same name.

If your system uses *inetd*, you must add an entry for *cups-lpd* to the */etc/inetd.conf* file:

```
printer stream tcp nowait lp /usr/lib/cups/daemon/cups-lpd cups-lpd
```

Some systems will require changes to this configuration. For instance, you might want to call *cups-lpd* via TCP Wrappers (tcpd) rather than calling *cups-lpd* directly. As with *xinetd*, you must restart *inetd* or tell it to reload its configuration to start *cups-lpd*.

Printer Troubleshooting

With any luck, if you follow the instructions in this chapter, your printer will work with little or no fuss. Unfortunately, CUPS configuration doesn't always work as planned, and printer troubleshooting can be tricky and frustrating. Although we can't provide a sure-fire way to get your printer working, we can provide some suggestions that can help you track down the source of problems and find solutions to them.

- If possible, verify that the printer works in another OS on the same computer. Even a FreeDOS (*http://www.freedos.org*) boot floppy can be handy for such verification, at least for parallel and RS-232 serial printers. If the printer works in another OS, that rules out a lot of pure hardware problems. If not, that suggests (but does not prove) that the problem is hardware-related.

- Try checking all hardware connections, from the power cables to the cables to the computer. Loose or defective cables can cause endless hours of trouble. If your printer has a power switch, check that the printer is turned on. (We know that sounds incredibly basic, but failure to turn on a printer really is a leading cause of problems!) While you're at it, check that you've got paper in the printer's paper trays—all of them, if it has multiple trays.

- Examine the printer's front or top panel for any error signals. Some printers have LCDs that can display short messages such as out of paper or paper jam. Others rely on blinking LEDs. Consult your printer's manual for help interpreting these displays.

- If you have a parallel or RS-232 serial printer, try sending a print job to the printer using its raw device file, as described earlier in "Verifying printer compatibility." If this doesn't work but the printer checks out physically, it could mean you're missing a kernel driver for your device. Loading it with *modprobe* will perhaps do the trick. Another possible cause of such problems is that you're using the wrong device file, so you might want to try others. If the printer's LEDs blink when you try to print, chances are the file is getting through but is in a format that the printer can't understand, so basic hardware functions are probably (but not certainly) working.

- If you have a USB printer, check that the kernel has identified the printer by using the *lsusb* command and by examining the contents of */proc/bus/usb/devices*, as described earlier in "Verifying printer compatibility." If the printer's not showing up, you may be missing kernel drivers or your printer might be an exotic model that's not yet supported by Linux.

- If the printer has a network interface, try using *ping* to verify basic connectivity with the printer. If it doesn't respond, consult the printer's manual to learn how to activate its network interface. You might also need to review your DHCP server's configuration and logfiles to see why the printer's not obtaining an IP address, if it's supposed to do so via DHCP.

- If the printer sports multiple interfaces (such as parallel and USB ports), try using the interface you didn't originally use. If the printer begins working (after appropriate reconfiguration in Linux), it could be that the Linux drivers for the interface you originally tried didn't work, or there could be a hardware defect in the printer, your computer, or a cable. You can either try to track down this problem or continue using the interface that's working.

- If you can get basic printing via a device file working or if you have a USB or network printer that responds in basic ways, you should move on to CUPS configuration.

- From the main CUPS interface (Figure 14-3), check the printer's description. (Alternatively, type *lpc status* at a command prompt.) If the printer is described as stopped or rejecting jobs, you should click the appropriate button or use *enable* or *accept* to get the queue working again.

- If the printer's description includes the phrase waiting for job to complete, it means that something's preventing CUPS from clearing a job from the queue.

This could be a physical connection problem or a software foul-up. Sometimes restarting CUPS will clear this problem.

- If the printer prints, but produces reams of gibberish, it probably means that you've selected the wrong printer when configuring the queue. (Sometimes you'll get gibberish if a job is interrupted and you turn the printer on without clearing the existing jobs from the queue, but this doesn't mean your driver is fouled up.) If the gibberish looks like a PostScript program, you might have selected a PostScript variant of your non-PostScript printer, so selecting the non-PostScript variant might work better. If the gibberish seems utterly random, it's probably a matter of selecting a completely incompatible non-PostScript printer.

- Slow printouts can be a serious problem. You can often improve print speed, particularly for inkjet printers, by reducing the print resolution. This will degrade the print quality, though, and you'll have to decide where a good trade-off point lies. If a USB 2.0 printer is slow, check that you're using a USB 2.0 port and that you've loaded the Linux USB 2.0 (EHCI) drivers. If not, load the appropriate drivers and, if necessary, buy a supplementary USB 2.0 card.

- If printouts don't meet your expectations for quality, review the printer options described in "Fine-Tuning Printer Definitions." You may be able to increase resolution, change dithering options, alter brightness settings, or otherwise change the way Ghostscript and the printer process your printouts to improve the quality. Some of these changes will slow down the printouts, though.

On the whole, printer troubleshooting can be as much of an art as a science. A lot of things can go wrong, and it's hard to predict what's most likely to go wrong. The preceding summary should at least help you narrow the list of potential causes and get you on the right track to fixing the problem, though.

Behind the Scenes: CUPS Files and Directories

Most of the preceding description of CUPS has steered clear of describing specific files and directories. This is because, with the exception of the */etc/cups/cupsd.conf* file, manually editing CUPS configuration files or changing its directories is seldom helpful. CUPS often responds unpredictably to manual changes in its configuration files; you should really use its web-based interface and text-mode commands to configure and control CUPS.

That said, you may need to know about these files and directories. The CUPS configuration files reside in */etc/cups*. The *cupsd.conf* file, as already noted, controls the server on a broad level, and you may need to edit this file. Other important files in this directory include *printers.conf* (which defines local printers) and *lpoptions* (which identifies the default printer). The *ppd* subdirectory holds PPD files for local printers (they're copied from elsewhere, as described shortly).

CUPS stores a great deal of support data in the */usr/share/cups* directory tree. Of particular interest is the */usr/share/cups/model* subdirectory, which holds PPD files (most in subdirectories named after the printers' manufacturers). The Foomatic and GIMP Print packages may install PPD files there. If they don't, and if you can't get these printer definitions recognized, try creating symbolic links in this subdirectory to the actual location of the printer definition package's PPD files. This should enable CUPS to locate the PPD files and install the printers.

In actual operation, CUPS uses the */var/spool/cups* subdirectory to hold print job descriptions and the actual print job files. This directory is owned by *root* and the *lp* group and has 0710 (`rwx--x---`) permissions. CUPS also uses the */var/spool/cups/tmp* directory, which is owned by *root* and the *lp* group and has 1710 (`rwx--x--T`) permissions. (These owners and permissions are typical, but may differ between distributions.) Unlike LPD, CUPS doesn't use separate subdirectories for each printer; print jobs for all printers are dumped into the same directory tree.

CHAPTER 15
File Sharing

In this chapter we give you a quick guide to the two major ways in the Linux world to share resources between systems. First we cover Samba, which uses Microsoft Windows networking protocols to allow users on one system to read and write files on another system, and to send jobs to printers on remote systems. The advantage of using Samba is that Linux and Unix can be integrated almost seamlessly with Microsoft systems, both clients and servers. The Microsoft Windows networking protocols can be used for sharing of files between Linux systems, although the preferred protocol for that really is the NFS protocol.

We present both NFS and NIS, protocols developed by Sun Microsystems and used by Unix systems for decades. NFS, the Network File System, allows systems to share files between Linux and Unix systems in a manner similar to Samba. NIS, the Network Information System, allows user information to be stored in one place and accessed by multiple systems so you don't have to update all the systems when a user or password changes. Although NIS is not a tool for file and printer sharing, we present it in this chapter because it shares some components with its cousin NFS, and because it can make NFS easier to administer because NIS allows each user to have the same account number on all systems.

NFS and NIS are useful at sites where only Linux and variants of Unix are connected. Versions have been created for Microsoft systems, but they are not particularly robust and have never become popular.

Microsoft provides a complimentary NFS client and server implementation for Windows systems that has not been adopted into common use despite it being free of cost. The Microsoft Windows Services for Unix (SFU) package includes an NIS server and over 300 Unix utilities for use under Windows. Even given this free availability Windows sites that wish to secure interoperability between Windows network clients and Linux systems prefer the use of Samba.

In addition to MS Windows networking protocols and NFS, there are several well known file and print sharing protocols. Linux has support for NetWare-style file and print sharing using IPX protocols, Macintosh-based file and print sharing (Apple-Talk protocol), file sharing over protocols such as FISH (File Sharing over SSH), as well as WebDAV-based file services. We do not cover these protocols in this chapter.

Sharing Files with Windows Systems (Samba)

The open source software revolution is not quite over yet, so as a result there still are a huge number of Windows desktop and server systems in common use today. Even though many of us may think that the world will soon be using nothing but a Linux desktop, reality tells us something different: Windows desktops will be around for a long time. So the ability to exchange files across Windows and Linux systems is rather important. The ability to share printers is equally important.

Samba is a very flexible and scalable application suite that allows a Linux user to read and write files located on Windows workstations, and vice versa. You might want to use it just to make files on your Linux system available to a single Windows client (such as when running Windows in a virtual machine environment on a Linux laptop). But you can use Samba to implement a reliable and high-performance file and print server for a network that has thousands of Windows clients. If you use Samba on a site-wide scale, you should probably spend serious time reading the extensive Samba documentation at *http://www.samba.org/samba/docs*, or a book such as *Using Samba* (O'Reilly), which is also part of the Samba distribution.

This section documents the key facets you need to know about file and print interoperability between Windows and Linux systems. First off, we supply an overview of how Windows networking operates, to help avoid some of the anguish and frustration that newcomers often feel during their first attempts to cross the great Windows and Unix divide. Next in line is an overview of the tools available in Linux-land that will help the Linux user to gain access to files and printers that live in Windows-land. The subject of providing Windows users access to files and printers that reside on a Linux system for is covered last—not because it is less important, but because the scope of possibilities it offers is so much greater.

Protocols and Things Windows-Related

Linux users are generally aware that all they need for access to a remote Linux systems is its IP address. In essence, an IP address coupled with the Domain Name System (DNS) is the perfect vehicle for interoperating from any Linux system to a remote Linux system. We can therefore say—with perhaps a little poetic license—that the Linux namespace is the DNS. The namespace of the TCP/IP world places few restrictions on the maximum permissible length of a hostname or a name that may be placed in a DNS database. But human laziness usually limits the maximum number of characters one will tolerate in a hostname.

Life in Windows-land is not quite that easy, and there are good reasons for that too. The Windows networking world has a completely different namespace, one that originates from an attempt to solve a file sharing problem with no immediate plan to use TCP/IP. TCP/IP was an afterthought. Windows did not at first have a TCP/IP protocol stack. Its native networking protocol was NetBEUI, which stands for Network Basic Extended User Interface. For the technically minded, the name is a misnomer because the protocol actually consists of the Server Message Block (SMB) protocol via NetBIOS encapsulated over Logical Link Control (LLC) addressing. The resulting protocol is nonroutable and rather inefficient. The old protocol name, SMB, gave rise to the name Samba for the software project created by developer Andrew Tridgell when he decided to emulate the Windows file-sharing protocol.

Some time around 1996, the Server Message Block protocol was renamed the Common Internet File System (CIFS) protocol. The original CIFS protocol is basically SMB on steroids. The terms are used interchangeably in common use. The SMB/CIFS protocol supports particular features, such as:

- File access
- File and record locking
- File caching, read-ahead, and write-behind
- File change notification
- Ability to negotiate the protocol version
- Extended file and directory attributes
- Distributed replicated virtual filesystems
- Independent name resolution
- Unicode file and directory names

The description of these features is beyond the scope of this book, but suffice it to say that when correctly configured, the protocols work well enough for large-scale business use.

NetBIOS is actually an application programming interface (API) that allows SMB/CIFS operations to be minimally encoded for transmission over a transport protocol of some type. NetBEUI, also known as the NetBIOS Frame (NBF) protocol, happens to use LLC addressing. It originated some time in the 1980s and was apparently first used by IBM as part of its PC-LAN product offering. The use of NetBIOS over TCP/IP was developed later and has been documented in various standards. NetBIOS can be encapsulated over many other protocols, the best known of which is IPX/SPX—the NetWare protocol.

NetBIOS (or, more correctly, SMB) has its own namespace. Unlike the native TCP/IP namespace, all NetBIOS names are precisely 16 characters in length. The - (dash) character may be used in the name, but it is ill-advised to use anything other than alphanumeric characters. Attempts to use a numeric character for the first digit will fail because this will cause systems that implement NetBIOS over TCP/IP to interpret the name as an IP address. The 16th character of a NetBIOS name is a name-type character, which is used by servers and clients to locate specific types of services, such as the network logon service.

The NetBIOS namespace also includes an entity known as a *workgroup*. Machines that have the same workgroup name are said to belong to the same workgroup. IBM LAN Server and Microsoft LAN Manager (as with Windows NT4) used the term *domain* to indicate that some form of magic authentication technology was being used, but at the lowest level a domain is identical with a workgroup name.

 In network environments based on NetBIOS, it is extremely important to configure every machine to use the same networking protocols and to configure all the protocols identically. There can be no deviation from this; every attempt to do otherwise will result in networking failures.

The NetBIOS over TCP/IP protocol (NBT or NetBT) uses two main protocols and ports for basic operation: TCP port 139 (the NetBIOS Session Service port) and UDP port 137 (the NetBIOS Name Server port). UDP port 137 is used for broadcast-based name resolution using a method known as mail-slot broadcasting. This broadcast activity can be significant on a high-traffic network.

The best way to minimize background UDP broadcast activity is to use a NetBIOS Name Server. Microsoft called this kind of server WINS, for Windows Internet Naming Service. WINS is to NetBT as DNS is to TCP/IP. Clients register their NetBIOS names with the WINS server on startup. If all machines are configured to query the WINS server, Windows networking usually proceeds without too many problems. WINS provides a practical and efficient technique to help resolve a NetBIOS name to its IP address.

With the release of Windows 2000, Microsoft introduced a technology called Active Directory (AD) that uses DNS for resolution of machine names to their TCP/IP addresses. In network environments that use only Windows 2000 (or later) clients and servers, Microsoft provides, together with AD, the ability to disable the use of NetBIOS. In its place, the new networking technology uses raw SMB over TCP/IP. This is known as NetBIOS-less TCP/IP. In the absence of UDP-based broadcast name resolution and WINS, both of which are part of the NetBT protocol suite, Net-BIOS-less TCP/IP wholly depends on DNS for name resolution and on Kerberos security coupled with AD services. AD is a more-or-less compliant implementation of the Lightweight Diretory Access Protocol (LDAP) standard, which has an excellent free software implementation called OpenLDAP (mentioned in Chapter 8) and which therefore allows Linux to emulate the most important services offered by AD.

The use of Samba without NetBIOS support effectively means it must be an AD domain member server. Do not disable NetBIOS support unless you configure AD.

Samba Version 2 is capable only of using NetBT. Samba Version 3 is capable of seamless integration into a Windows AD NetBIOS-less network. When configured this way, it will use TCP port 445, using the NetBIOS-less Windows networking protocol. Microsoft Windows networking will also use TCP port 135, for DCE RPC communications. A discussion of these protocols is beyond the scope of this book. The focus in this book is on use of Samba with NetBT.

Samba Version 3 was released in September 2003 after more than two years' development. It implemented more complete support for Windows 200x networking protocols, introduced support for Unicode, added support for multiple password backends (including LDAP), and can join a Windows 200x Active Directory domain using Kerberos security protocols. It remains under active development as the current stable release, with support intentions that will keep it current well into 2007. The Samba team hoped to issue Samba Version 4 beta release towards the end of 2005, after approximately three years' development. Samba Version 4 is a complete rewrite from the ground up. It has extensive support for Active Directory, with the intent of providing Active Directory domain control. It is anticipated that by mid-2006 Samba Version 4 will mature to the point that early adopters will begin to migrate to it.

Where possible, Samba should either be its own WINS server or be used in conjunction with a Microsoft WINS server to facilitate NetBIOS name resolution. Remember that a price will be paid for not using WINS: increased UDP broadcast traffic and nonroutability of networking services.

We start this section with a simple scenario where you want to access files from a Windows server on your Linux system. This assumes that you have established a TCP/IP connection between your Linux and Windows computers, and that there is a directory on the Windows system that is being shared. Detailed instructions on how to configure networking and file sharing on Windows 95/98/Me and Windows NT/2000/XP can be found in *Using Samba* (O'Reilly).

To start with, both your Windows and your Linux systems should be correctly configured for TCP/IP interoperability. This means that:

- Each system has a valid IP address.
- The systems share a correct netmask.
- The systems point to the same gateway (if one of your private networks has routers to multiple network segments).
- Each system has a valid */etc/hosts* and a valid DNS configuration if DNS is in use.

The Windows machine and workgroup names should consist only of alphanumeric characters. If you choose to configure a */etc/hosts* file on the Windows clients, this file must be called *hosts*, without a file extension. On Windows 95/98/Me systems the *hosts* file should be placed in *C:\Windows\System*. On Windows NT/2000/XP systems it is located in *C:\Winnt\System32\drivers\etc\hosts*.

 The example *hosts* file on Windows NT/2000/XP systems has the file extension *sam*. Do not name the working file with this extension because it will not work.

In the rest of this chapter, we use the term *SMB name* to mean the NetBIOS name of the SMB-enabled machine (also known as the machine name). The term *workgroup* means both the workgroup name and the domain name of an SMB-enabled machine. Please note that for all practical network operations, such as browsing domains and workgroups, and browsing machines for shares, the workgroup name and domain name are interchangeable; hence our use of the term *workgroup*.

The Windows machine for our examples is a Windows XP Home machine called EMACHO. The workgroup is called MIDEARTH, with IP address 192.168.1.250. Our Linux system has the hostname loudbell, with IP address 192.168.1.4; our domain is goodoil.biz.

Linux System Preparation and Installing Samba

The services discussed in this chapter require kernel modules and facilities that may not be available on your Linux system as initially installed. Many versions of commercial Linux systems (Novell SUSE Linux and Red Hat Linux) are shipped with the necessary capabilities. If your Linux system is homegrown or one of the roll-your-own distributions, you may need to rebuild the kernel. The steps outlined here should help your preparations. Of course, a recent release of Samba Version 3.0.x will also be required.

First we need to consider the Linux kernel to ensure it is equipped with the tools needed.

The Linux kernel must have support for smbfs and cifsfs. If your Linux system has an older kernel (a version earlier than 2.6.x) the cifsfs facility may not be available. There is a back-port of the cifsfs kernel drivers that you may be able to install. For more information regarding cifsfs visit the CIFS project web site, *http://linux-cifs.samba.org/*. In the event that you need to install this module into your kernel source code tree, be sure to follow the instructions on that site.

The `smbfs` and `cifsfs` Linux kernel modules are not part of Samba. Each is a separate kernel driver project. Both projects depend on helper tools such as `smbmount`, `smbumount`, `mount.smbfs`, and `mount.cifs`, which are part of the Samba distribution tarball, and are required to enable its use.

The Linux kernel source file for Version 2.6.x includes the `cifsfs` module. To find out if your running kernel includes it, install the kernel sources under the directory */usr/src/linux*. Now follow these steps:

1. Configure the kernel source code to match the capabilities of the currently executing kernel:

   ```
   linux:~ # cd /usr/src/linux
   linux:~ # make cloneconfig
   ```

   As the cloning of the kernel configuration finishes, the kernel configuration file will be printed to the console. Do not be concerned, because the contents are also stored in the *.config* file. We examine this file in the next step.

2. To determine the status of `smbfs` support in the kernel, enter:

   ```
   linux:~ # grep CONFIG_SMB_FS .config
   CONFIG_SMB_FS=m
   ```

   The output tells us that `smbfs` support is enabled in the kernel and is available as a kernel loadable module. A value of *y* means it is built into the kernel, which is also acceptable, but a value of *n* means it is not supported.

   In the event that `smbfs` is not supported, use the kernel configuration utility outlined in "Kernel configuration: make config" in Chapter 18 to enable it.

3. Now determine the status of `cifsfs` support in the kernel:

   ```
   linux:~ # grep CONFIG_CIFS .config
   CONFIG_CIFS=m
   ```

   This response means that `cifsfs` support is available in the current kernel. If the value of this option is n, enable it using the kernel configuration utility.

4. If you had to enable support for one of the preceding options, rebuild the kernel and install it.

After rebooting the system, the new kernel will be ready for the steps that follow in this chapter. The next challenge is to ensure that a recent version of Samba is available.

Binary packages of Samba are included in almost any Linux or Unix distribution. There are also some packages available at the Samba home page, *http://samba.org*.

Refer to the manual for your operating system for details on installing packages for your specific operating system. In the increasingly rare event that it is necessary to compile Samba, please refer to the Samba3-HOWTO document, available at *http://*

www.samba.org/samba/docs/Samba3-HOWTO.pdf, for information that may ease the process of building and installing it appropriately.

 If you decide to build and install Samba manually, be sure to remove all Samba packages that have been supplied by the vendor, or that may already have been installed. Failure to do this may cause old binary files to be executed, causing havoc, confusion, and much frustration.

Before building your own Samba binaries, make certain that the *configure* command is given the *--with-smbmount* option. The following commands complete the process of installation of the newly built Samba:

```
linux:~ # make all libsmbclient wins everything
linux:~ # make install
linux:~ # make install-man
```

When the Samba build and installation process has completed, execute the following commands to ensure that the mount.cifs binary file is built and installed:

```
linux:~ # export CFLAGS="-Wall -O -D_GNU_SOURCE -D_LARGEFILE64_SOURCE"
linux:~ # gcc client/mount.cifs.c -o client/mount.cifs
linux:~ # install -m755 -o root -g root client/mount.cifs /sbin/mount.cifs
```

The system is now ready for configuration, so let's get on with some serious exercises in sharing files with the *other world*.

Accessing Remote Windows Files and Printers

Soon we will connect to a file share on a Windows system. We assume that the Windows system has a static IP address, and that we are not using DNS. Name resolution is rather important in networking operations, particularly with Windows clients, so let's configure the */etc/hosts* file so that it has the following entry:

```
192.168.1.250 emacho
```

There should, of course, also be an entry for the IP address of the Linux system we are on.

Now check that the */etc/hosts* entries are working:

```
linux:~ # ping emacho
PING emacho (192.168.1.250) 56(84) bytes of data.
64 bytes from emacho (192.168.1.250): icmp_seq=1 ttl=128 time=2.41 ms
64 bytes from emacho (192.168.1.250): icmp_seq=2 ttl=128 time=2.16 ms
64 bytes from emacho (192.168.1.250): icmp_seq=3 ttl=128 time=2.16 ms
64 bytes from emacho (192.168.1.250): icmp_seq=4 ttl=128 time=2.02 ms
64 bytes from emacho (192.168.1.250): icmp_seq=5 ttl=128 time=2.01 ms
64 bytes from emacho (192.168.1.250): icmp_seq=6 ttl=128 time=3.90 ms

--- emacho ping statistics ---
6 packets transmitted, 6 received, 0% packet loss, time 5004ms
rtt min/avg/max/mdev = 2.015/2.447/3.905/0.667 ms
```

OK, it works. Now we are really ready to begin file sharing.

Using the FTP-like smbclient to access Windows

It makes a lot of sense to first establish that our Linux system can communicate with the Windows system using Samba. The simplest way to do this is to use the Samba client tool, the *smbclient* command, to query the Windows machine so it will tell us what shares are available.

Let's perform an anonymous lookup of the Windows machine:

```
linux:~ # smbclient -L emacho -U%
Domain=[MIDEARTH] OS=[Windows 5.1] Server=[Windows 2000 LAN Manager]

        Sharename       Type        Comment
        ---------       ----        -------
Error returning browse list: NT_STATUS_ACCESS_DENIED
Domain=[MIDEARTH] OS=[Windows 5.1] Server=[Windows 2000 LAN Manager]

        Server          Comment
        ---------       -------

        Workgroup       Master
        ---------       -------
```

This is not very encouraging, is it? The lookup failed, as is evidenced by the reply Error returning browse list: NT_STATUS_ACCESS_DENIED. This is caused by a Windows machine configuration that excludes anonymous lookups. So let's repeat this lookup with a valid user account that has been created on the Windows XP Home machine.

An account we can use on our example system is for the user *lct* with the password 2bblue4u. Here we go:

```
linux:~ # smbclient -L emacho -Ulct%2bblue4u
Domain=[EMACHO] OS=[Windows 5.1] Server=[Windows 2000 LAN Manager]

        Sharename       Type        Comment
        ---------       ----        -------
        IPC$            IPC         Remote IPC
        SharedDocs      Disk
        print$          Disk        Printer Drivers
        Kyocera         Printer     Kyocera Mita FS-C5016N KX
Domain=[EMACHO] OS=[Windows 5.1] Server=[Windows 2000 LAN Manager]

        Server          Comment
        ---------       -------

        Workgroup       Master
        ---------       -------
```

Success! We now know that there is a share called SharedDocs on this machine. In the next step we will connect to that share to satisfy ourselves that we have a working Samba connection.

In this step we connect to the share itself, then obtain a files listing, and then download a file. This is an interesting example of the use of the *smbclient* utility:

```
linux:~ # smbclient //emacho/SharedDocs -Ulct%2bblue4u
Domain=[EMACHO] OS=[Windows 5.1] Server=[Windows 2000 LAN Manager]
smb: \>
```

Success again! This is good. Now for a directory listing:

```
smb:\ dir
  .                            DR       0  Thu May 19 12:04:47 2005
  ..                           DR       0  Thu May 19 12:04:47 2005
  AOL Downloads                D        0  Tue Sep 30 18:55:16 2003
  CanoScanCSUv571a             D        0  Thu May 19 12:06:01 2005
  desktop.ini                  AHS    129  Sun Jul  4 22:12:14 2004
  My Music                     DR       0  Sat Apr 16 22:42:48 2005
  My Pictures                  DR       0  Tue Sep 30 18:36:17 2003
  My Videos                    DR       0  Thu Aug  5 23:37:56 2004

          38146 blocks of size 1048576. 31522 blocks available
smb: \>
```

We can change directory into the *CanoScanCSUv571a* directory:

```
smb: \> cd CanoScanCSUv571a
smb: \CanoScanCSUv571a\>
```

But we want to see what files are in there:

```
smb: \CanoScanCSUv571a\> dir
  .                            D        0  Thu May 19 12:06:01 2005
  ..                           D        0  Thu May 19 12:06:01 2005
  CanoScanCSUv571a.exe         A  3398144  Thu Mar 13 22:40:40 2003
  Deldrv1205.exe               A    77824  Fri Apr 26 14:51:02 2002
  N122U.cat                    A    13644  Tue May 21 02:44:30 2002
  N122u.inf                    A     6151  Tue Apr 16 22:07:00 2002
  N122UNT.cat                  A    15311  Tue May 21 02:44:32 2002
  N122USG                      D        0  Thu May 19 12:10:40 2005
  USBSCAN.SYS                  A     8944  Fri Jun 12 13:01:02 1998

          38146 blocks of size 1048576. 31522 blocks available

smb: \CanoScanCSUv571a\>
```

Good. Everything so far is working. Let's download a file. Fetching and uploading files with *smbclient* works just like an FTP client:

```
smb: \CanoScanCSUv571a\ >get Deldrv1205.exe
getting file \CanoScanCSUv571a\Deldrv1205.exe of size 77824
        as Deldrv1205.exe (275.4 kb/s) (average 275.4 kb/s)
```

It all worked as it should. We are done with this demonstration. Let's quit back to a shell prompt:

```
smb: \CanoScanCSUv571a\> quit
linux:~ #
```

Let's summarize what has been learned so far. We have confirmed the following about our environment:

- There is TCP/IP connectivity between the Linux and Windows systems.
- Anonymous browsing is disabled on the Windows XP Home system.
- Authenticated browsing using a local Windows account and password works.

smbclient was designed to be highly versatile. It is used as part of the `smbprint` utility, where it pipes the print data stream through to a remote SMB/CIFS print queue in a manner analogous to the file transfer example witnessed earlier. For more information regarding the *smbclient* utility, refer to the manpage.

One you have basic SMB/CIFS interoperability, it should not be too difficult to mount the same share using `smbfs`. Let's move on and try that in the next section.

Using Linux-kernel-based smbfs

Before proceeding, let's look at what the `smbfs` filesystem driver does. This tool has some limitations that few people stop to recognize.

The `smbfs` filesystem driver behaves like the *smbclient* utility. It makes an authenticated connection to the target SMB/CIFS server using the credentials of a user, based on the account name and password provided. The filesystem driver then permits the SMB/CIFS connection to be attached to a Linux filesystem mount point. The Linux ownership of the mount point will reflect the user ID and group ID of the Linux user who mounts it, and the permissions will be determined by the UMASK in effect at the time of mounting.

In effect, access to all files and directories will be subject to Linux filesystem permission controls, and on the SMB/CIFS server everything will take place as a single user. Multiple concurrent Linux users who access the file share through the mount point will be making multiple concurrent accesses as a single Windows user, and will do so using a single Windows process.

There is one other, rather significant design limitation when using the `smbfs` filesystem driver. It does not support Unicode, and therefore creates problems when files contain characters other than the English alphabet. It should also be mentioned that this kernel module is somewhat defective and is no longer maintained. So why use it? That is easy to answer. Some Linux systems do not have support for `cifsfs`.

With these caveats stated and in the open, let's mount that SMB/CIFS filesystem:

```
linux:~ # mount -t smbfs //emacho/shareddocs /mnt \
-ousername=lct,password=2bblue4u,uid=jim,gid=users
linux:~ #
```

That was easy! It is time to test whether it works.

```
linux:~ # cd /
linux:~ # ls -ald /mnt
drwxr-xr-x    1 jim  users   4096 May 20 02:50 mnt
```

This demonstrates that the connection is mounted as the local Unix user jim. Let's copy some files to, and from, this system:

```
linux:~ # cd /mnt
linux:~ # ls -al
total 25
drwxr-xr-x   1 lct  users 4096 May 20 02:50 .
drwxr-xr-x  23 root root   560 May 18 15:21 ..
drwxr-xr-x   1 lct  users 4096 Sep 30  2003 AOL Downloads
drwxr-xr-x   1 lct  users 4096 May 19 12:06 CanoScanCSUv571a
dr-xr-xr-x   1 lct  users 4096 Apr 16 22:42 My Music
dr-xr-xr-x   1 lct  users 4096 Sep 30  2003 My Pictures
dr-xr-xr-x   1 lct  users 4096 Aug  5  2004 My Videos
-rwxr-xr-x   1 lct  users  129 Jul  4  2004 desktop.ini

linux:~ # cd CanoScanCSUv571a
linux:~ # ls -al
total 3451
drwxr-xr-x  1 lct users    4096 May 19 12:06 ./
drwxr-xr-x  1 lct users    4096 May 20 02:50 ../
-rwxr-xr-x  1 lct users 3398144 Mar 13  2003 CanoScanCSUv571a.exe*
-rwxr-xr-x  1 lct users   77824 Apr 26  2002 Deldrv1205.exe*
-rwxr-xr-x  1 lct users   13644 May 21  2002 N122U.cat*
-rwxr-xr-x  1 lct users   15311 May 21  2002 N122UNT.cat*
drwxr-xr-x  1 lct users    4096 May 19 12:10 N122USG/
-rwxr-xr-x  1 lct users    6151 Apr 16  2002 N122u.inf*
-rwxr-xr-x  1 lct users    8944 Jun 12  1998 USBSCAN.SYS*

linux:~ # cp USBSCAN.SYS /tmp
linux:~ # cp /var/log/messages .
linux:~ # ls -al messages
-rwxr-xr-x  1 lct users 240117 May 20 02:58 messages
```

This has been a satisfying outcome, because everything works. We were able to copy a file from the SMB/CIFS share. A file was also copied to the share from the Linux filesystem. It is possible to create, change, and delete files on an SMB/CIFS mounted filesystem. Permissions that determine the limits of these operations reflect the operations permitted by the SMB/CIFS server for the effective user at its end. Linux filesystem permissions control user access to the mounted resource.

Now let's dismount the filesystem in preparation for the use of the command-line version of the smbfs toolset:

```
linux:~ # cd /
linux:~ # df /mnt
Filesystem           1K-blocks     Used Available Use% Mounted on
//emacho/shareddocs   39061504  6782976  32278528  18% /mnt
linux:~ # umount /mnt
```

The Samba source tarball includes a set of tools that are meant to be run from the command line. The *smbmount* program is run by the *mount* command when used with the *-t smbfs* option, the way we used it previously. The *smbmount* program calls *smbmnt*, which performs the actual mounting operation. While the shared directory is mounted, the *smbmount* process continues to run, and if you issue a *ps ax* listing, you will see one *smbmount* process for each mounted share.

The *smbmount* program reads the Samba *smb.conf* configuration file, although it doesn't need to gather much information from it. In fact, it is possible to get by without a configuration file, or with one that is empty! The important thing is to make sure the configuration file exists in the correct location, or you will get error messages.

You will learn more about creating and validation of the configuration file later in this chapter. Here is a minimal *smb.conf* file:

```
[global]
workgroup = NAME
```

Simply replace *NAME* with the name of your workgroup, as it is configured on the Windows systems on your network.

The last thing to do is to mount the shared directory. Using smbmount can be quite easy. The command syntax is

```
smbmount UNC_resource_name mount_point options
```

where *mount_point* specifies a directory just as in the mount command. *UNC_resource_name* follows the Windows Universal Naming Convention (UNC) format, except that it replaces the backslashes with slashes. For example, if you want to mount a SMB share from the computer called *maya* that is exported (made available) under the name *mydocs* onto the directory */windocs*, you could use the following command:

```
linux:~ # smbmount //maya/mydocs/ /windocs
```

If a username or password is needed to access the share, *smbmount* will prompt you for them.

Now let's consider a more complex example of an *smbmount* command:

```
linux:~ # smbmount //maya/d /maya-d/ \
-o credentials=/etc/samba/pw,uid=jay,gid=jay,fmask=600,dmask=700
```

In this example, we are using the -o option to specify options for mounting the share. Reading from left to right through the option string, we first specify a credentials file, which contains the username and password needed to access the share. This avoids having to enter them at an interactive prompt each time. The format of the credentials file is very simple:

```
username=USERNAME
password=PASSWORD
```

where you must replace *USERNAME* and *PASSWORD* with the username and password needed for authentication with the Windows workgroup server or domain. The uid and gid options specify the owner and group to apply to the files in the share, just as we did when mounting an MS-DOS partition in the previous section. The difference is that here we are allowed to use either the username and group name or the numeric user ID and group ID. The fmask and dmask options allow permission masks to be logically ANDed with whatever permissions are allowed by the system serving the share. For further explanation of these options and how to use them, see the smbmount(8) manual page.

One problem with *smbmount* is that when the attempt to mount a shared directory fails, it does not really tell you what went wrong. This is where *smbclient* comes in handy—as we saw earlier. See the manual page for *smbclient*(1) for further details.

Once you have succeeded in mounting a shared directory using *smbmount*, you may want to add an entry in your */etc/fstab* file to have the share mounted automatically during system boot. It is a simple matter to reuse the arguments from the *smbmount* command shown earlier to create an */etc/fstab* entry such as the following (all on one line):

```
//maya/d  /maya-d  smbfs
credentials=/etc/samba/pw,uid=jay,gid=jay,fmask=600,dmask=700 0 0
```

Well, that was a lot of information to digest. Let's continue onto the next section, where we will work with the cifsfs kernel driver that is replacing smbfs.

Using Linux-kernel-based cifsfs

The cifsfs filesystem drive is a relatively recent replacement for the smbfs driver. Unlike its predecessor, cifsfs has support for Unicode characters in file and directory names. This new driver is fully maintained by an active development team.

If you have made sure that your kernel has support for the cifsfs module, as described previously in this chapter, try mounting a remote file share with a command like this:

```
linux:~ # mount -t cifs -ouser=lct,password=2bblue4u,uid=lct,gid=users \
//emacho/shareddocs /mnt
linux:~ # ls -ald /mnt
drwxrwxrwx  1 lct users 0 May 19 12:04 /mnt
```

If you compare the mount options with those used with the *smbfs* driver in the previous section, you'll see that the username parameter has changed to just user. The other parameters can be kept identical.

There is one apparent difference in a directory listing:

```
linux:~ # ls -al /mnt/CanoScanCSUv571a/
total 3684
drwxrwxrwx  1 lct users       0 May 20 02:58 .
drwxrwxrwx  1 lct users       0 May 19 12:04 ..
-rwxrwSrwt  1 lct users 3398144 Mar 13  2003 CanoScanCSUv571a.exe
```

```
-rwxrwSrwt  1 lct users   77824 Apr 26  2002 Deldrv1205.exe
-rwxrwSrwt  1 lct users   13644 May 21  2002 N122U.cat
-rwxrwSrwt  1 lct users   15311 May 21  2002 N122UNT.cat
drwxrwxrwx  1 lct users       0 May 19 12:10 N122USG
-rwxrwSrwt  1 lct users    6151 Apr 16  2002 N122u.inf
-rwxrwSrwt  1 lct users    8944 Jun 12  1998 USBSCAN.SYS
-rwxrwSrwt  1 lct users  240117 May 20 02:58 messages
```

Note that the directory node size is now reported as zero. Apart from this minor feature, the use of cifsfs to mount an SMB/CIFS resource cannot really be noticed, except when files that have multibyte (Unicode) characters in them are encountered.

The command used to mount the CIFS/SMB filesystem (*mount -t cifs*) actually causes the execution of the *mount.cifs* binary file. This file is built from the Samba sources, as we saw earlier in this chapter. There are no command-line tools, as there are with the smbfs kernel drivers and the *smbmount* group of tools provided by the Samba package.

Some network administrators insist that a password should never be passed to a Unix command on the command line because it poses a security risk. The good news is that *mount.cifs* permits an alternative to command-line options for obtaining the username and password credentials: it reads the environment variables USER, PASSWD, and PASSWD_FILE. In the variable USER, you can put the username of the person to be used when authenticating to the server. The variable can specify both the username and the password by using the format *username%password*. Alternatively, the variable PASSWD may contain the password. The variable PASSWD_FILE may, instead, contain the pathname of a file from which to read the password. mount.cifs reads a single line of input from the file and uses it as the password.

 If you ever put a cleartext password in a file, be sure to set highly restrictive permissions on that file. It is preferrable that only the processes that must have access to such a file be able to read it.

The username and password can also be stored in a file. The name of this file can be used on the command line as part of the -o option as *credentials=filename*. Many of the options accepted by the *mount -t cifs* command are similar to those frequently used to mount an NFS filesystem. Refer to the *mount.cifs* manpage for specific details.

Using Linux desktop tools with libsmbclient

Office users who make heavy use of the Windows Explorer often feel lost when they first sit down at the Linux desktop. This is not surprising, because the look and feel is a little different. Tools are called by different names, but that does not mean that the capabilities are missing. In fact, thanks to the inclusion of the *libsmbclient* library in all distributions, the Linux desktop file managers (as well as web browsers) have been empowered to browse the Windows network.

Red Hat Linux and Novell SUSE Linux now both include a network browsing facility on the desktop. The environment makes it possible to browse the Windows network and NFS-mounted resources. The level of integration is excellent. Just click on the Windows network browsing icon, and *libsmbclient* will do all the hard work for you. Let's try this with both the KDE desktop and the GNOME desktop.

On Novell SUSE Linux Professional, the default KDE user desktop has an icon labeled *Network Browsing*. A single click opens the application called Konqueror, and very soon displays a separate icon for each networking technology type. The default icons are called FTP, SLP Services, SSH File Browsing, SSH Terminal, VNC Connection, Windows Network, and YOU Server, and there is an icon called Add a Network Folder. When the SMB Share icon is clicked, it reveals an icon for each workgroup and domain on the local network. To use our sample network as an illustration, clicking on the workgroup called `MIDEARTH` displays an icon for each server in that workgroup. An example of this screen is shown in Figure 15-1.

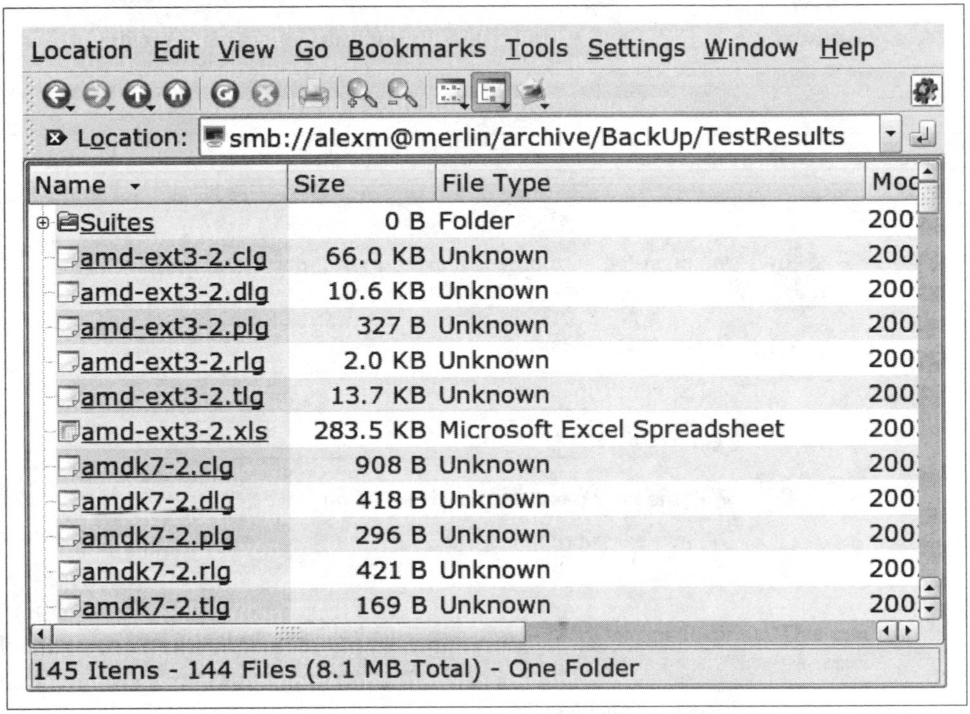

Location Edit View Go Bookmarks Tools Settings Window Help
Location: smb://alexm@merlin/archive/BackUp/TestResults
Name Size File Type Moc
Suites 0 B Folder 200
amd-ext3-2.clg 66.0 KB Unknown 200
amd-ext3-2.dlg 10.6 KB Unknown 200
amd-ext3-2.plg 327 B Unknown 200
amd-ext3-2.rlg 2.0 KB Unknown 200
amd-ext3-2.tlg 13.7 KB Unknown 200
amd-ext3-2.xls 283.5 KB Microsoft Excel Spreadsheet 200
amdk7-2.clg 908 B Unknown 200
amdk7-2.dlg 418 B Unknown 200
amdk7-2.plg 296 B Unknown 200
amdk7-2.rlg 421 B Unknown 200
amdk7-2.tlg 169 B Unknown 200
145 Items - 144 Files (8.1 MB Total) - One Folder

Figure 15-1. KDE Konqueror using the libsmbclient module

The default GNOME desktop has an icon called Network Browsing. A double-click opens the Network Browsing tool to reveal an icon called Windows Network. Click this to reveal an icon for each workgroup and domain that is visible on the network. An example is shown in Figure 15-2. Click on one of the SMB server icons to expose the shared resources that are available. Click on a shared folder to reveal the files within it. If access to any resource requires full user authentication, a login dialog will pop up. An example of the login dialog is shown in Figure 15-3.

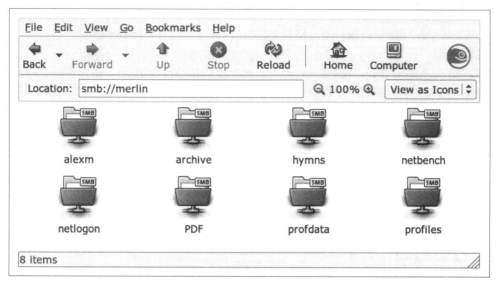

Figure 15-2. GNOME File Manager using the libsmbclient module

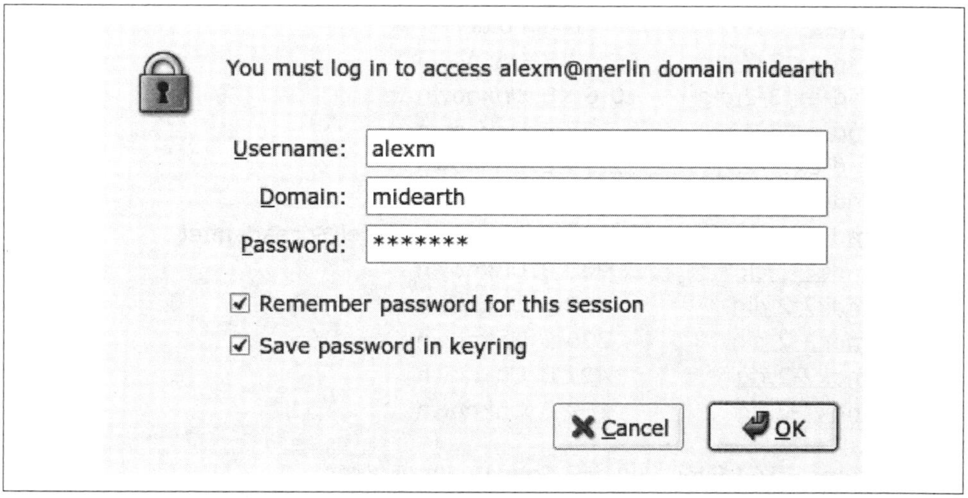

Figure 15-3. GNOME libsmbclient network logon

KDE Konqueror neatly shows the URL in the Location bar. As you browse deeper in the Windows filesystem, the URL is updated to reveal the full effective URL that points to the current network location, for example, *smb://alexm@MERLIN/archive/Music/Haydn/*. The syntax for the URL is given in the libsmbclient manpage as:

```
smb://[[[domain:]user[:password@]]server[/share[/path[/file]]]][?options]
```

When *libsmbclient* is invoked by an application, it searches for a directory called *.smb* in the $HOME directory that is specified in the user's shell environment. It then searches for a file called *smb.conf*, which, if present, will fully override the system */etc/samba/smb.conf* file. If instead libsmbclient finds a file called *~/.smb/smb. conf.append*, it will read the system */etc/samba/smb.conf* file and then append the contents of the *~/.smb/smb.conf.append* file to it.

libsmbclient checks the user's shell environment for the USER parameter and uses its value when the user parameter is omitted from the URL.

The really nice feature of the *libsmbclient* library is that it authenticates access to the remote CIFS/SMB resource on a per-user basis. Each connection (SMB session) is independent, and access to folders and files is permitted just as if the user has logged onto a Windows desktop to perform this access.

Printing to printers on Windows systems

In the earlier years of Samba the sole mechanism for printing from a Unix/Linux system to a printer attached to a Windows machine involved the use of *smbclient* via a sample interface script called *smbprint*. This script is still available in the Samba tarball from the directory *examples/printing*, and remains in use even though it has been superseded by the *smbspool* utility.

When *smbprint* usage was at its prime, the two dominant printing systems in the Unix/Linux world were BSD *lpr/lpd* and AT&T SYSV printing. There was a new tool called LPRng that was trying to edge into the market. The LPRng package was a free open source printing solution that sought to replace the older BSD *lpr/lpd* technology, which was generally considered buggy and in need of replacement. There are still many Unix and Linux systems that use BSD *lpr/lpd* or LPRng. LPRng has a strong following in some areas. Systems that use LPRng tend to still use smbprint as the interface script that makes it possible to send a print job from the Unix/Linux spool to a remote Windows printer.

Commencing around 2000/2001, a new technology started to gain popularity. This package was called CUPS (the Common Unix Print System). The growth of adoption of CUPS has been dramatic. Meanwhile, the development team behind CUPS has gradually expanded its functionality as well as its utility. They created a printing API and have worked with many open source projects to gain a high degree of integration into each software project that requires a printing interface. The CUPS team worked together with the Samba team and contributed a direct interface methodology so that Samba can communicate with CUPS without requiring external interface scripts and utilities. Samba can pipe a print job directly to the CUPS spool management daemon cupsd.

In addition to the improved interface between Samba and CUPS, CUPS is a whole lot smarter than older print systems when sending print jobs to a network-attached

Windows printer. Samba has gained a new printing utility (*smbspool*) that handles all printer interfacing between CUPS and a Windows print server.

Given that CUPS is now the dominant printing technology in Linux, it is best left to the configuration tools provided with either CUPS itself or with the Linux distribution to handle Linux-to-Windows printing. On the other hand, there will always be a situation that is not satisfied by this approach. When it is necessary to send a print job to a Windows printer, it is handy to have knowledge of a suitable tool. The tool of choice in this situation is *smbspool*.

In brief, here are the varieties of command syntax recognized by the *smbspool* utility:

```
smb://server[:port]/printer
```

```
smb://workgroup/server[:port]/printer
```

```
smb://username:password@server[:port]/printer
```

```
smb://username:password@workgroup/server[:port]/printer
```

One of these modes of use will meet all known needs. Each is followed by arguments:

1. This contains the job ID number, and is not presently used by *smbspool*.
2. This contains the print user's name, and is not presently used by *smbspool*.
3. This contains the job title string, and is passed as the remote file name when sending the print job.
4. This contains the number of copies to be printed. If no filename is provided (argument 6), this argument is not used by *smbspool*.
5. This contains the print options in a single string, and is currently not used by *smbspool*.
6. This contains the name of the file to print. If the argument is not specified, the material to print is read from the standard input.

Each parameter should be in the order listed.

Sharing Linux Files and Printers with Windows Users

The previous section outlined the use of tools that make it possible for a Linux desktop user to access files located on Windows workstations and servers using native Windows networking protocols. These tools can also be used in the other direction: to access files that are on a Unix/Linux server.

In this section we explore the use of Samba to provide files that are stored on Linux to Windows clients.

The CIFS/SMB protocol is more complex than some other file-sharing protocols such as NFS. Samba has to be not only protocol-compatible with Microsoft Windows clients, but also compatible with the bugs that are present in each client. In this section, we show you a simple Samba setup, using as many of the default settings as we can.

Setting up Samba involves the following steps:

1. Compiling and installing Samba, if it is not already present on your system.
2. Writing the Samba configuration file *smb.conf* and validating it for correctness.
3. Starting the two Samba daemons *smbd* and *nmbd*.

When correctly configured, a Samba server and the directories shared will appear in the browse lists of the Windows clients on the local network—normally accessed by clicking on the Network Neighborhood or My Network Places icon on the Windows desktop. The users on the Windows client systems will be able to read and write files according to your security settings just as they do on their local systems or a Windows server. The Samba server will appear to them as another Windows system on the network, and act almost identically.

Installing Samba

Correctly compiling Samba can be a challenge, even for an experienced developer, so it makes sense to use prebuilt binary packages where they are available. For most administrators the choice is among the following options:

1. Install from trusted RPM or *.deb* pacakges.
2. Install from contributed RPM or *.deb* packages.
3. Compile and install from the official source tarball.
4. Hire someone else to compile and install from the source tarball.

Most Linux distributions include Samba, allowing you to install it simply by choosing an option when installing Linux. If Samba wasn't installed along with the operating system, it's usually a fairly simple matter to install the package later. Either way, the files in the Samba package will usually be installed as follows:

- Daemons in */usr/sbin*
- Command-line utilities in */usr/bin*
- Configuration files in */etc/samba*
- Logfiles in */var/log/samba*
- Runtime control files in */var/lib/samba*

There are some variations on this. For example, in older releases, you may find logfiles in */var/log*, and the Samba configuration file in */etc*.

If your distribution does not include Samba, you can download the source code, and compile and install it yourself. In this case, all of the files that are part of Samba are installed into subdirectories of *usr/local/samba*.

Either way, you can take a quick look in the directories just mentioned to see whether Samba already exists on your system, and if so, how it was installed.

 If you are not the only system administrator of your Linux system, be careful. Another administrator might have used a source code release to upgrade an earlier version that was installed from a binary package, or vice versa. In this case, you will find files in both locations, and it may take you a while to determine which installation is active.

If you need to install Samba, you can either use one of the packages created for your distribution, or install from source. Installing a binary release may be convenient, but Samba binary packages available from Linux distributors are usually significantly behind the most recent developments. Even if your Linux system already has Samba installed and running, you might want to upgrade to the latest stable source code release.

Obtaining fresh source files. You can obtain the Samba source files from the Samba web site *http://www.samba.org/*. To obtain a development version, you can download Samba from Subversion or using *rsync*.

Samba is developed in an open environment. Developers use Subversion to *check in* (also known as *commit*) new source code. Samba's various Subversion branches can be accessed via anonymous Subversion using SVNweb or using the Subversion client.

To use SVNweb, access the URL *http://svnweb.samba.org*.

Subversion gives you much more control over what you can do with the repository and allows you to check out whole source trees and keep them up-to-date via normal Subversion commands. This is the preferred method of access by Samba developers.

In order to download the Samba sources with Subversion, you need a Subversion client. Your distribution might include one, or you can download the sources from *http://subversion.tigris.org*.

To gain access via anonymous Subversion, use the following steps.

1. Install a recent copy of Subversion. All you really need is a copy of the Subversion client binary.
2. Run the command:
   ```
   linux:~ # svn co svn://svnanon.samba.org/samba/trunk samba.
   ```
   This will create a directory called *samba* containing the latest Samba source code (usually the branch that is going to be the next major release). At the time of writing, this corresponded to the 3.1 development tree.

Other Subversion branches besides the trunk can be obtained by adding *branches/BRANCH_NAME* to the URL you check out. A list of branch names can be found on the Development page of the Samba web site. A common request is to obtain the latest 3.0 release code, which can be done using the following command:

```
linux:~ # svn co svn://svnanon.samba.org/samba/branches/SAMBA_3_0_RELEASE samba_3
```

3. Whenever you want to merge in the latest code changes, use the following command from within the Samba directory:

```
linux:~ # svn update
```

Building Samba from source. To install from source, go to the Samba web site at *http://www.samba.org* and click on one of the links for a download site near you. This will take you to one of the mirror sites for FTP downloads. The most recent stable source release is contained in the file *samba-latest.tar.gz*. This file will give you detailed instructions on how to compile and install Samba. Briefly, you will use the following commands:

```
linux:~ # tar xzvf samba-latest.tar.gz
linux:~ # cd samba-VERSION
linux:~ # su
Password:
linux:~ # ./configure
linux:~ # make
linux:~ # make install
```

Make sure to become superuser before running the *configure* script. Samba is a bit more demanding in this regard than most other open source packages you may have installed. After running the commands just shown, you will be able to find Samba files in the following locations:

- Executables in */usr/local/samba/bin*
- Configuration file in */usr/local/samba/lib*
- Logfiles in */usr/local/samba/log*
- *smbpasswd* file in */usr/local/samba/private*
- Manual pages in */usr/local/samba/man*

You will need to add the */usr/local/samba/bin* directory to your *PATH* environment variable to be able to run the Samba utility commands without providing a full path. Also, you will need to add the following two lines to your */etc/man.config* file to get the man command to find the Samba manpages:

```
MANPATH /usr/local/samba/man
MANPATH_MAP /usr/local/samba/bin /usr/local/samba/man
```

Configuring Samba

The next step is to create a Samba configuration file for your system. Many of the programs in the Samba distribution read the configuration file, and although some of them can get by with a file containing minimal information (even with an empty file), the daemons used for file sharing require that the configuration file be specified in full.

The name and location of the Samba configuration file depend on how Samba was compiled and installed. An easy way to find it is to use the testparm command, shown later in this section. Usually, the file is called *smb.conf*, and we'll use that name for it from now on.

The format of the *smb.conf* file is like that of the *.ini* files used by Windows 3.x: there are entries of the type:

```
key = value
```

When working with Samba, you will almost always see the keys referred to as *parameters* or *options*. They are combined in sections (also called *stanzas*) introduced by labels in square brackets. The stanza name goes by itself on a line, like this:

```
[stanza-name]
```

Each directory or printer you share is called a *share* or *service* in Windows networking terminology. You can specify each service individually using a separate section name, but we'll show you some ways to simplify the configuration file and support many services using just a few sections. One special section called [global] contains parameters that apply as defaults to all services, and parameters that apply to the server in general. Although Samba understands literally hundreds of parameters, it is very likely that you will need to use only a few of them, because most have reasonable defaults. If you are curious which parameters are available, or you are looking for a specific parameter, read the manpage for *smb.conf(5)*. But for now, let's get started with the following *smb.conf* file:

```
[global]
    workgroup = MIDEARTH
        printing = BSD
    wins support = yes

[homes]
        browseable = no
        read only = no

[printers]
        printable = yes
        printing = BSD
        path = /var/spool/samba

[data]
        path = /export/data
        read only = no
        map archive = no
```

Although this is a very simple configuration, you may find it satisfactory for most purposes. We'll now explain each stanza in the file in order of appearance, so you can understand what's going on, and make the changes necessary for it to fit your own system. The parts you most likely need to change are emphasized in boldface in the file listing just shown.

In the [global] section, we set parameters that configure Samba on the particular host system. The workgroup parameter defines the workgroup to which the server belongs. You will need to replace MIDEARTH with the name of your workgroup. If your Windows systems already have a workgroup defined, use that workgroup. If not, create a new workgroup name here and configure your Windows systems to belong to it. Use a workgroup name other than the Windows default of WORKGROUP, to avoid conflicts with misconfigured or unconfigured systems.

For our server's computer name (also called NetBIOS name), we are taking advantage of Samba's default behavior of using the system's hostname. That is, if the system's fully qualified domain name is *dolphin.example.com*, it will be seen from Windows as *dolphin*. Make sure your system's hostname is set appropriately. If you want to explicitly name your Samba server by its hostname, enter a line in the global stanza like this:

```
netbios name = DOLPHIN
```

You can provide a NetBIOS name that differs from the hostname, so it is perfectly acceptable to name the computer like this:

```
netbios name = WHITESHARK
```

 The default hostname used by several Linux distributions is localhost. Please be certain to change that to a valid name, because any machine that has the NetBIOS name of LOCALHOST is completely unusable. This name will always resolve on a Windows network client as the IP address 127.0.0.1, and that is the client itself!

The encrypt passwords parameter tells Samba to expect clients to send passwords in encrypted form, rather than plain text. This parameter should be set on all versions of Samba prior to Version 3.0 because it is necessary in order for Samba to work with Windows 98, Windows NT Service Pack 3, and later versions. Samba version 3.0 and later default to using encrypted passwords, so the parameter is unnecessary, but worth including just to make sure you're doing it right.

 The wins support parameter tells Samba to function as a WINS server, resolving computer names into IP addresses. This is optional, but helps to keep your network running efficiently as described earlier in this chapter in "Protocols and Things Windows-Related." A WINS server is like a DNS server for NetBIOS names, with the key difference that clients register themselves with a WINS server.

The rest of the sections in our sample *smb.conf* are all optional and define the resources Samba offers to the network.

The [homes] stanza defines a meta-service that tells Samba to automatically share home directories. When clients connect to the Samba server, Samba looks up the username of the client in the Linux */etc/passwd* file (or whatever is defined in the name service switch backend), to see if the user has an account on the system. If the account exists and has a home directory, the home directory is offered to the client as a shared directory. The username will be used as the name of the share (which appears as a folder on a Windows client). For example, if a user *diane*, who has an account on the Samba host, connects to the Samba server, she will see that it offers her home directory on the Linux system as a shared folder named diane.

The parameters in the [homes] stanza define how the home directories will be shared. It is necessary to set browseable = no to keep a shared folder named homes from appearing in the browse list.

By default, Samba offers shared folders with read-only permissions. Setting read only = no causes the folder and its contents to be offered in read/write manner to the client. Setting permissions like this in a share definition does not change any permissions on the files in the Linux filesystem, but rather acts to apply additional restrictions. A file that has read-only permissions on the server will not become writable from across the network as a result of read only being set to no. Similarly, if a file has read/write permissions on the Linux system, Samba's default of sharing the file as read-only applies only to access by Samba's network clients.

Samba has the sometimes difficult job of making a Unix filesystem appear like a Windows filesystem to Windows clients. One of the differences between Windows and Unix filesystems is that Windows uses the archive attribute to tell backup software whether a file has been modified since the previous backup. If the backup software is performing an incremental backup, it backs up only files that have their archive bit set. On Unix, this information is usually inferred from the file's modification timestamp, and there is no direct analog to the archive attribute. Samba mimics the archive attribute using the Unix file's execute bit for owner. This allows Windows backup software to function correctly when used on Samba shares, but has the unfortunate side effect of making data files look like executables on your Linux system. We set the map archive parameter to no because we expect that you are more interested in having things work right on your Linux system than being able to perform backups using Windows applications.

The [printers] stanza tells Samba to make printers connected to the Linux system available to network clients. Each section in *smb.conf*, including this one, that defines a shared printer must have the parameter printable = yes. For a printer to be made available, it must have an entry in the Linux system's */etc/printcap* file. This file specifies all the printers on your system and how they are accessed. The printer will be visible to users on network clients with the name it is listed by in the *printcap* file.

With CUPS, the *printcap* file is autogenerated, and should not be modified or edited by the administrator. Some Linux distributions create a symbolic link from */etc/printcap* that points to the autogenerated file, which is named */etc/cups/printcap*. If you want to expose a subset of printers for use by Samba, you can remove the symbolic link and then create your own */etc/printcap* file that exposes only the printers you want Windows users to access. A better way to achieve this (because it does not interfere with the OS printing implementation) is to simply create a file called */etc/samba/smbprintcap*, in which you list the printers that are suitable for Windows client use. This file can then be specified in the *smb.conf* file [global] section parameter `printcap name = /etc/samba/smbprintcap`.

If you have already configured a printer, it may not work properly when shared over the network. Usually, when configuring a printer on Linux, the print queue is associated with a printer driver that translates data it receives from applications into codes that make sense to the specific printer in use. However, Windows clients have their own printer drivers, and expect the printer on the remote system to accept raw data files that are intended to be used directly by the printer, without any kind of intermediate processing. The solution is to add an additional print queue for your printer (or create one, if you don't already have the printer configured) that passes data directly to the printer. In the Unix/Linux world this is sometimes called "raw mode."

The first time the printer is accessed from each Windows client, you will need to install the Windows printer driver on that client. The procedure is the same as when setting up a printer attached directly to the client system. When a document is printed on a Windows client, it is processed by the printer driver, and then sent to Samba. Samba simply adds the file to the printer's print queue, and the Linux system's printing system handles the rest. Historically, most Linux distributions have used BSD-style printing systems, and so we have set `printing = BSD` in the same configuration file to notify Samba that the BSD system is in use. Samba then acts accordingly, issuing the appropriate commands that tell the printing system what to do. More recently, some Linux distributions have used the LPRng printing system or CUPS. If your distribution uses LPRng, set `printing = LPRNG`. If it uses CUPS, set `printing = CUPS`, and also set `printcap name = CUPS`.

We have set the `path` parameter to */var/spool/samba* to tell Samba where to temporarily put the binary files it receives from the network client, before they are added to the print system's queue. You may use another directory if you like. Make sure the directory exists. It must also be world-writable, to allow all clients to access the printer. A security-conscious administrator will object to this because it is a simple matter to hijack someone's print job and turn it into a Trojan horse through which the Linux system may be compromised. The solution to that problem is to set the sticky bit on this directory, thus permitting only the owner to change the file. The sticky bit, together with world read and write permission, can be set on the directory like this:

```
linux:~ # chmod a+rwxt /var/spool/samba
```

The [data] stanza in our example shows how to share a directory. You can follow this example to add as many shared directories as you want, by using a different section name and value for path for each share. In the official Samba documentation you will find that the shared directory is referred to as the *share-point* in the Linux filesystem. The stanza name is used as the name of the share, which will show up on Windows clients as a folder with that name. As in previous sections, we have used read only = no to allow read/write access to the share, and map archive = no to prevent files from having their execute bits set. The path parameter tells Samba what directory on the Linux system is to be shared. You can share any directory, but make sure it exists and has permissions that correspond to its intended use. For our [data] stanza, the directory */export/data* has read, write, and execute permissions set for all of user, group, and other, because it is intended as a general-purpose shared directory for everyone to use.

After you are done creating your *smb.conf* file, run the *testparm* program, which checks your *smb.conf* for errors and inconsistencies. If your *smb.conf* file is correct, testparm should report satisfactory messages, as follows:

```
linux:~ # testparm
Load smb config files from /usr/local/samba/lib/smb.conf
Processing section "[homes]"
Processing section "[printers]"
Processing section "[data]"
Loaded services file OK.
Press enter to see a dump of your service definitions
```

If you have made any major errors in the *smb.conf* file, you will get error messages mixed in with the output shown. You don't need to see the dump of service definitions at this point, so just type Ctrl-C to exit *testparm*.

Smart administrators make a practice of documenting their Samba configuration file. This can be particularly beneficial at a later date when it may be necessary to remember why certain parameters were set. Unfortunately, the practice of documenting the *smb.conf* file is at variance with the way Samba works. The file is reread frequently by *smbd*, so the larger the file becomes because of your documentation, the greater the system impact may be. The solution to this dilemma is to always use a master file in which all parameters are documented as required, then use this command:

```
linux:~ # testparm -s smb.conf.master > smb.conf
```

The resulting *smb.conf* file will be stripped of all comments and contain only those parameters that are not at the default setting. It will be as small as possible while implementing the settings specified. Be warned, though, that the resulting file will be stripped of macros and you may need to edit the file to put them back. For example, include = /etc/samba/%m.conf will be rendered as include=/etc/samba/.conf.

Starting the Samba server

Samba essentially consists of three daemons, of which two are always needed:

nmbd

Handles all name registration and resolution requests. It is the primary vehicle involved in network browsing. It handles all UDP-based protocols. The *nmbd* daemon should be the first command started as part of the Samba startup process.

smbd

Handles all TCP/IP-based connection services for file- and print-based operations. It also manages local authentication. It should be started immediately following the startup of *nmbd*.

winbindd

This daemon should be started when Samba is a member of a Windows NT4 or ADS domain. It is also needed when Samba has trust relationships with another domain. The *winbindd* daemon checks the *smb.conf* file for the presence of the *idmap uid* and *idmap gid* parameters to obtain the values that can be used to map Windows SIDs. The range specified must not conflict with already used on the system. Where no idmap uid or gid ranges are specified *winbindd* will not perform Windows SID mapping and will be capable only of performing user authentication.

You can choose to start *smbd*, *winbindd*, and *nmbd* either as daemons or from *inetd*. Don't try to do both! You wouldn't want two sets of these daemons competing for traffic and stepping on each other.

For intermittently used services where a few users connect sporadically, it might be appropriate to run the services from *inetd* or *xinetd*, which you can do by putting them in *inetd.conf*. However, most administrators just start the services as daemons either from the command line or in */etc/rc.local*. The main advantage of the second method, starting smbd and nmbd as standalone daemons, is that they will respond slightly more quickly to an initial connection request.

See the manpages for details on the command-line options. Take particular care to read the bit about what user you need to have to start Samba. Samba is best run as the *root* user. It will switch to the effective user ID of the user who is accessing Samba resources, but it also needs to be able to run with root privilege for operations that under Linux can be performed only by *root*, such as adding users and groups. Samba Version 3.0.11 and later permit this right and privilege to be assigned to a non-*root* account—however, smbd must run as *root* to be able to do this.

When Samba has been packaged by an operating system vendor, the startup process is typically a custom feature of its integration into the platform as a whole. Please refer to your operating system platform administration manuals for specific information pertaining to correct management of Samba startup.

Starting Samba from inetd.conf. To make sure Samba will run as a service, start by looking at your */etc/services* file. What is defined at port 139/tcp? If nothing is defined, add a line such as this:

```
netbios-ssn    139/tcp
```

Similarly for port 137/udp, you should have an entry such as:

```
netbios-ns        137/udp
```

If you use NIS, NIS+, or LDAP to distribute services maps, they will be consulted instead of the */etc/services* file. However, the steps just shown are worth going through, because systems sometimes fall back on */etc/services*.

Next, edit your */etc/inetd.conf* file and add two lines such as the following:

```
netbios-ssn stream tcp nowait root /usr/local/samba/bin/smbd smbd
netbios-ns dgram udp wait root /usr/local/samba/bin/nmbd nmbd
```

The exact syntax of */etc/inetd.conf* varies between Linux distributions. Look at the other entries in *inetd.conf* for a guide.

> Some distributions already have entries such as netbios_ns (note the underscore) in */etc/services*. You must edit */etc/services* or */etc/inetd.conf* to make them consistent.

Some distributions use *xinetd* instead of *inetd*. Consult the *xinetd* manual for configuration information.

On many systems, you need to use the interfaces option in *smb.conf* to specify the IP addresses and netmasks of your interfaces. Run *ifconfig* as *root* if you do not know this information. *nmbd* tries to determine it at runtime, but fails on some systems.

> On many distributions, a maximum of five arguments are allowed on command lines in *inetd.conf*. One way to avoid hitting this limit is to omit the spaces between options and arguments (e.g., write *-fname* instead of *-f name*). If you absolutely can't stay within the five-option limit, create a one-line script that invokes the command and start the script from *inetd*.

Having enabled Samba operation in *inetd*, you have to restart *inetd*. To do this, just send it a HUP, like this:

```
linux:~ # killall -HUP inetd
```

Starting the Samba daemons with default compilations. If you installed Samba from a source code distribution, you need a script that starts and stops the daemons. You may be able to find and copy such a script from a Samba binary package for your distribution—but check the directory names to make sure they correspond to where you actually built and installed the files. Alternatively, we'll show you how to write and install your own script.

When started from a script, *smbd* and *nmbd* must be started with the -D option, so that they will detach themselves and run as daemons.

After you have tested the script and you are sure it works, create the appropriate symbolic links in your */etc/rcN.d* directories to start Samba in the run level you normally run in, and stop Samba when changing to other run levels.

This information applies to systems on which Samba has been compiled locally using the Samba default arguments to the *configure* command. To start the server as a daemon, you should create a script something like this one, perhaps calling it *startsmb*:

```
#!/bin/sh
/usr/local/samba/bin/smbd -D
/usr/local/samba/bin/winbindd
/usr/local/samba/bin/nmbd -D
```

Make it executable with

```
linux:~ # chmod +x startsmb
```

You can then run startsmb by hand, and add it to a system *rc* script.

If your *smb.conf* file is error-free, it is rare for the daemons to fail to run. Still, you might want to run a ps ax command and check that they are in the list of active processes. If not, take a look at the Samba logfiles, *log.smbd* and *log.nmbd*, for error messages.

To stop Samba, send a kill signal to the *nmbd* and *smbd* processes. On Debian, you can use the killall command, sending them the SIGTERM signal:

```
# killall -TERM smbd nmbd
```

Controlling Samba execution on Debian Linux. The *samba* script can be used to start, stop, or restart Samba.

```
linux:~ # /etc/init.d/samba start
```

Controlling Samba execution on SUSE and Red Hat Linux. SUSE Linux implements individual control over each Samba daemon. A Samba control script that can be conveniently executed from the command line is shown in Example 15-1. This can be located in the directory */sbin* in a file called *samba*. This type of control script should be owned by user *root* and group *root*, and set so that only *root* can execute it.

Example 15-1. A useful Samba control script for SUSE Linux

```
#!/bin/bash
#
# Script to start/stop samba
# Locate this in /sbin as a file called 'samba'

RCD=/etc/rc.d

if [ z$1 == 'z' ]; then
        echo $0 - No arguments given; must be start or stop.
        exit
fi
```

Example 15-1. A useful Samba control script for SUSE Linux (continued)

```
if [ $1 == 'start' ]; then
        ${RCD}/nmb start
        ${RCD}/smb start
        ${RCD}/winbind start

fi
if [ $1 == 'stop' ]; then
        ${RCD}/smb stop
        ${RCD}/winbind stop
        ${RCD}/nmb stop
fi
if [ $1 == 'restart' ]; then
        ${RCD}/smb stop
        ${RCD}/winbind stop
        ${RCD}/nmb stop
        sleep 5
        ${RCD}/nmb start
        ${RCD}/smb start
        ${RCD}/winbind start
fi
exit 0
```

A sample startup script for a Red Hat Linux system is shown in Example 15-2. This file could be located in the directory */etc/rc.d* and can be called *samba* or *smb*. A similar startup script is required to control winbind. If you want to find more information regarding startup scripts, please refer to the packaging section of the Samba source code distribution tarball. The packaging files for each platform include a startup control file.

Example 15-2. A sample Samba control script for Red Hat Linux

```
#!/bin/sh
#
# chkconfig: 345 81 35
# description: Starts and stops the Samba smbd and nmbd daemons \
#              used to provide SMB network services.

# Source function library.
. /etc/rc.d/init.d/functions
# Source networking configuration.
. /etc/sysconfig/network
# Check that networking is up.
[ ${NETWORKING} = "no" ] && exit 0
CONFIG=/etc/samba/smb.conf
# Check that smb.conf exists.
[ -f $CONFIG ] || exit 0

# See how we were called.
case "$1" in
  start)
        echo -n "Starting SMB services: "
```

Example 15-2. A sample Samba control script for Red Hat Linux (continued)

```
            daemon smbd -D; daemon nmbd -D; echo;
            touch /var/lock/subsys/smb
            ;;
  stop)
            echo -n "Shutting down SMB services: "
            smbdpids=`ps guax | grep smbd | grep -v grep | awk '{print $2}'`
            for pid in $smbdpids; do
                    kill -TERM $pid
            done
            killproc nmbd -TERM; rm -f /var/lock/subsys/smb
            echo ""
            ;;
  status)
            status smbd; status nmbd;
            ;;
  restart)
            echo -n "Restarting SMB services: "
            $0 stop; $0 start;
            echo "done."
            ;;
  *)
            echo "Usage: smb {start|stop|restart|status}"
            exit 1
esac
```

Validating that Samba is running. Now that you have Samba installed, configured, and running, try using the smbclient command to list shared resources (the example given here is from an office network on a day when only two people were at work):

```
linux:~ # smbclient -L localhost -U%
added interface ip=172.16.1.3 bcast=172.16.1.255 nmask=255.255.255.0
Domain=[MIDEARTH] OS=[Unix] Server=[Samba 3.0.20]
        Sharename       Type       Comment
        ---------       ----       -------
        archive         Disk       Full Archive Files
        print$          Disk       Printer Drivers
        netlogon        Disk       Network Logon Service
        profiles        Disk       Profile Share
        IPC$            IPC        IPC Service (Main Server)
        ADMIN$          IPC        IPC Service (Main Server)
        kyocera         Printer    FS-C5016N
Domain=[MIDEARTH] OS=[Unix] Server=[Samba 3.0.20]

        Server                     Comment
        ---------                  -------
        AURORA                     Moberg's Magic Machine
        MERLIN                     Main Server
        TINKERBELL                 Mel's Laptop

        Workgroup                  Master
        ---------                  -------
        MIDEARTH                   MERLIN
```

This output demonstrates that a null-session connection could be made to the Samba server. The null session is one that uses no username and no password; it depends only on the availability of the *guest account*, which is usually called *nobody* in the */etc/passwd* file.

If this validation step fails, the cause is usually either that a firewall is blocking the Samba network traffic or that the *guest account* could not be found in the */etc/passwd* file.

Adding users

Network users must be authenticated by Samba before they can access shares. The configuration we are using in this example employs Samba's "user-level" security. This means that users are required to provide a username and password that must match those of a Samba account on the Linux host system. The first step in adding a new Samba user is to make sure that the user has a Linux system account, and, if you have a [homes] share in your *smb.conf*, that the account has an existing home directory.

The tool most frequently used to add user accounts to a Linux system is called use-radd.

```
linux:~ # useradd -m username
```

Samba uses its own password file. It uses the Windows networking passwords and other data it stores in this file to validate the encrypted passwords that are received from clients. For each Samba user, you must run the *smbpasswd* command to add a Samba account for that user:

```
linux:~ # smbpasswd -a username
New SMB password:
Retype new SMB password:
```

Make sure that the username and password you give to *smbpasswd* are both the same as those of the user's Linux account. We suggest you start off by adding your own account, which you can use a bit later to test your installation.

An Office File- and Print-Sharing Solution Using Samba

Now that you are familiar with what Samba is, how to create a basic file server, and how to start and stop it, let's turn our hand to a slightly more complex server configuration. The example we work with here is one that may typically be found in an office of 5 to 50 users. The server can be accessed from old Windows systems using basic workgroup-style Windows networking, but can also serve as a Samba domain controller that provides fully secure authenticated network access services. The complexity is in how it is used, not in the design, and that is the way it should be.

The first priority is to configure simple centralized file sharing and simple printer sharing.

We will consider installation of two types of printers: a network-attached printer and a USB-attached printer. Installation of a network-attached printer is very easy. An HP LaserJet that has a JetDirect network card in it is a typical example of such a printer. This type of printer may be installed using the command-line printer installation tool as follows:

```
linux:~ # lpadmin -p hplj -v socket://192.168.1.25:9100 -E
```

In this example, the HP JetDirect card has been programmed to IP address 192.168.1.25. The CUPS spooler will communicate directly with the printer via TCP port 9100, and the -E option means that the print queue called hplj will be immediately enabled.

This procedure did not install a printer driver, as one was not specified. To install a printer driver, add the *-m model* option. Ensure that you specify the correct model information. In our previous example, we could add *-m LaserJet-laserjet* to the end of the command line.

Installation of a USB-attached Canon BJC-85 printer as a raw printer (i.e., without Linux print filtering) can be achieved by executing:

```
linux:~ # lpadmin -p bj85 -v usb://Canon/BJC-85 -m BJC-85-bjc600 -E
```

Current Linux distributions autodetect the presence of a USB-attached printer or a parallel-port-attached printer, and prompt you to confirm that you want the printer to be automatically configured. In most cases, the printer driver will be autoinstalled without the need to insert a driver disk.

There are two main methods by which a Linux system printer can be made available for use by Windows client users. The first is known as *raw mode*, and the second method is known as *smart mode*.

Raw-mode printing treats the Linux printing system as simply a means of passing a print job directly to the printer without any attempt to intelligently filter the job. This is the most common way that the Berkeley print systems (*lpr/lpd*) and LPRng function in their simplest configurations. CUPS is capable of raw-mode processing also. The Samba cups options = raw parameter permits CUPS to operate as a raw-mode print spooler.

If this parameter is omitted from the *smb.conf* file, and the CUPS print spooler receives a print job containing a character sequence that is not known to the CUPS filters, the print job may be deleted and never reach the printer. Another way to get the job through CUPS (if you fail to specify the cups options = raw parameter) is to edit the */etc/cups/mime.types* and */etc/cups/mime.convs* files to uncomment the line specifying the application/octet-stream MIME type. This permits CUPS to send the print job with the unknown characters directly to the printer.

Raw-mode printing requires the installation of the correct printer driver on every Windows client. The Windows client must fully process all print jobs and render them so they are ready to go directly to the printer.

The smart-mode printing method involves installation of a local print filtering system on the CUPS server. The CUPS server will attempt to interpret the nature of the file that is sent to the printer, and will then filter it with appropriate automatic conversion to suit the printer.

When CUPS printers are used in smart mode, it is possible to use a CUPS PostScript driver (available from the CUPS web site) on all Windows clients, even if the printer is not a PostScript-capable printer. CUPS will convert the print job to the necessary format. It is, however, necessary to install a printer driver that produces an output format known to the CUPS filtering system.

The Samba *smb.conf* file is shown in Example 15-3. This example enables use of raw-mode printing. If the CUPS printer driver is correct, any one of a large number of Windows printer drivers can be used on the Windows clients. For example, it is possible to use a Color LaserJet driver even though the printer may be an Epson Bubble-jet printer.

Example 15-3. Samba smb.conf file for an office network

```
# Global parameters
[global]
        workgroup = GOODOIL
        netbios name = LOUDBELL
        passwd chat = *New*Password* %n\n *Re-enter*new*password* %n\n *Password*changed*
        username map = /etc/samba/smbusers
        syslog = 0
        name resolve order = wins bcast hosts
        printcap name = CUPS
        cups options = raw
        show add printer wizard = No
        add machine script = /usr/sbin/useradd -s /bin/false -d /dev/null '%u'
        logon script = scripts\logon.bat
        logon path =
        logon home = \\%L\%U
        logon drive = H:
        domain logons = Yes
        preferred master = Yes
        wins support = Yes

[homes]
        comment = Home Directories
        valid users = %S
        read only = No
        browseable = No

[printers]
        comment = SMB Print Spool
```

Example 15-3. Samba smb.conf file for an office network (continued)

```
        path = /var/spool/samba
        guest ok = Yes
        printable = Yes
        use client driver = Yes
        default devmode = Yes
        browseable = No

[netlogon]
        comment = Network Logon Service
        path = /var/lib/samba/netlogon
        guest ok = Yes

[officedata]
        comment = Office Files
        path = /data/office
        read only = No
```

Please refer to Chapter 14 for information regarding Linux printer configuration. Samba is capable of communicating directly with CUPS via the *libcups.so* library. To configure Samba to use LPRNG-based printing, simply replace the printcap name = CUPS directive with printcap name = LPRNG. All printers will be automatically exported for use by Samba.

Install the *smb.conf* file in the correct location. Then start Samba following the guidelines shown in "Starting the Samba server," earlier in this chapter.

Create the Linux filesystem directory */data/office* and set the Linux permissions so that the Linux and Windows (Samba) users who need to access it have appropriate access privilege. For example, if all users should be able to read the directory, and the user jamesb needs write capability, execute the following:

```
linux:~ # chown -R jamesb:users /data/office
linux:~ # chmod -R u=rwx,g=rx,o-rwx /data/office
```

After Samba has started, add a user account as shown in "Adding users." When you have created a user account, try out the *smbclient* command described earlier in "Using the FTP-like smbclient to access Windows":

```
linux:~ # smbclient //localhost/officedata -U'username'
password: XXXXXXXXXX
```

Here, *username* is the user account you created, and *XXXXXXXXXX* is the password you entered when adding the Samba account through the *smbpasswd* command.

At the smb:> prompt, you can enter any *smbclient* command. Try the *ls* command, to list the contents of the directory. Then try the *help* command, which will show you all of the commands that are available. The *smbclient* program works very much like *ftp*, so if you are used to *ftp*, you will feel right at home. Now exit *smbclient* (using the *quit* or *exit* command) and try some variations. First, use your server's hostname *loudbell* instead of *localhost* to check that name resolution is functioning properly. Then try accessing your home directory by using your username in place of *officedata*.

And now for the really fun part: go to a Windows system, and log on using your Samba account username and password. (On Windows NT/2000/XP, you will need to add a new user account, using the Samba account's username and password.) Double-click on the Network Neighborhood or My Network Places icon on the desktop. Browse through the network to find your workgroup, and double-click on its icon. You should see an icon for your Samba server in the window that opens. By double-clicking on that icon, you will open a window that shows your home directory, printer, and *officedata* shares. Now you can drag and drop files to and from your home directory and data shares, and, after installing a printer driver for the shared printer, send Windows print jobs to your Linux printer!

We have only touched the surface of what Samba can do, but this should already give you an impression of why Samba—despite not being developed just for Linux—is one of the software packages that have made Linux famous.

Automatic Printer Driver Download

Windows network administrators understand the benefits of easy and reliable printer installations on Windows workstations. Consider, if you will, an example from the daily grind of network administration where printer drivers have not been uploaded to print servers. The network administrator arrives at the desk of a user who requires access to a new printer; he begins to install the printer and discovers that he left the driver disk on his desk. Now he has to walk back to his desk, and in some large businesses that can be a long walk. Alternately, he discovers that the driver does not work and a later driver release is needed. It is so much more convenient to have all printer drivers already installed on the print server!

The trouble with this is that what to some is just part of the holy grail of network administration is to others a great frustration. The following steps will relieve that pain. Follow these steps and you too can enjoy automatic printer driver installation from your print servers. Do follow along carefully, though, because one misstep can cause the process to fail.

First, update your *smb.conf* file as shown in Example 15-4. The changes from the previous example have been highlighted.

Example 15-4. Samba smb.conf file for an office network

```
# Global parameters
[global]
        workgroup = TOPCAT
        netbios name = LOUDBELL
        passwd chat = *New*Password* %n\n *Re-enter*new*password* %n\n *Password*changed*
```

Example 15-4. Samba smb.conf file for an office network (continued)

```
        username map = /etc/samba/smbusers
        syslog = 0
        name resolve order = wins bcast hosts
        printcap name = CUPS
        cups options = raw
        show add printer wizard = Yes
        add machine script = /usr/sbin/useradd -s /bin/false -d /dev/null '%u'
        logon script = scripts\logon.bat
        logon path =
        logon home = \\%L\%U
        logon drive = H:
        domain logons = Yes
        printer admin = jbloggs
        preferred master = Yes
        wins support = Yes

[homes]
        comment = Home Directories
        valid users = %S
        read only = No
        browseable = No

[printers]
        comment = SMB Print Spool
        path = /var/spool/samba
        guest ok = Yes
        use client driver = No
        printable = Yes
        default devmode = Yes
        browseable = No

[print$]
        comment = Printer Drivers
        path = /var/lib/samba/drivers

[netlogon]
        comment = Network Logon Service
        path = /var/lib/samba/netlogon
        guest ok = Yes

[officedata]
        comment = Office Files
        path = /data/office
        read only = No
```

When the *smb.conf* file has been edited as shown, verify that Samba is running.

In our example *smb.conf* file, we have specified that the Windows user *jbloggs* will have the rights to manage printers.

The next step is to create the */var/lib/samba/drivers* directory, as well as the sub-directories beneath it. This is where the Windows printer driver files will be stored. These steps will suffice:

```
linux:~ #  mkdir -p /var/lib/samba/drivers
linux:~ #  cd /var/lib/samba
linux:~ #  mkdir -p drivers/{W32ALPHA,W32MIPS,W32PPC}
linux:~ #  mkdir -p drivers/{W32X86/{2,3},WIN40,COLOR,IA64,x64}
linux:~ #  chown -R jbloggs:root drivers
linux:~ #  chmod -R u+rwx,g+rwx,o+rx-w drivers
```

Install the Linux system printers that you wish to make available for use by MS Windows clients. It does not matter which print spooling and management system you use. LPRng is good, but CUPS has more bells and whistles. In any case, it is a good idea to enable raw-mode printing, even where you do not intend to use it. By enabling raw-mode printing, you may save yourself frustration in the event that some printer driver installed later on a Windows client creates print-job output that can not be handled by a CUPS print filter.

Now you are ready to install the printer drivers onto your Samba server. Keep the printer drivers available within easy reach during the following procedure.

1. Log on to your Windows XP workstation as the Windows user account jbloggs.

2. Launch the My Network Places icon by right-clicking it, and select the Explore option.

3. Browse to the Entire Network, and then to the Microsoft Windows Network. Select the domain or workgroup containing your Samba server. Click on the entry for your Samba server (in our case this is the machine TOPCAT).

4. Click the icon for Printers and Faxes. In the right panel of the Windows Explorer you should now see the printers that have been made available through the Linux printing system.

5. Right-click the icon for the printer that you wish to install drivers for. This will bring up a dialog panel that announces "Device settings cannot be displayed. The driver for the specified printer is not installed, only spooler properties will be displayed. Do you want to install the driver now?" Two choices are displayed: Yes (or Continue, on some systems) and No. Click the No button. Do not click the Yes or the Continue button.

6. Click the Advanced tab of the Windows printer properties panel that is displayed.

7. Click the New Driver button. This will open a printer driver selection panel. Select the printer manufacturer and type, as is appropriate. If you need to install a driver from a CD-ROM or a network share, click the Have Disk button.

8. Follow the prompts in the following dialog boxes. Take careful note as the drivers are being installed; they should be sent to the Samba server (in our case, the

network path is *TOPCAT**print$**W32X86*). At the conclusion of the last drive installation action, the panel can be closed. Congratulate yourself.

As a side effect of the network server printer driver installation process, the printer will also be installed on the workstation that was used to install the network printer drivers. When you visit the next Windows XP workstation, simply click on the printer in the *My Network Places* environment and it should be installed without prompting for driver installation.

Using smbsh for Direct File Manipulation on Remote Systems

The smbsh utility lets you manipulate files on a remote system using standard Unix or Linux commands. To use this command wrapper, execute smbsh from the prompt and enter the username and password that authenticates you to the machine running the Windows NT operating system. Startup looks like this:

```
system$ smbsh
Username: user
Password: XXXXXXX
```

You can now enter commmands on the remote system as if it were local. For example, the command *ls* /*smb* shows a list of workgroups, and the command *ls* /*smb/MYGROUP* shows all the machines in the workgroup MYGROUP. The command *ls* /*smb/MYGROUP/machine-name* shows the share names for that machine. You could also use the *cd* command to change directories, *vi* to edit files, and *rcp* to copy files.

smbsh depends on a facility of dynamic library linking known as *pre-loading*, and uses a pre-loaded library called *smbwrapper.so*. This library intercepts filesystem function calls and routes them through a CIFS/SMB library if the files being operated on lie within the */smb* directory. (If a file lies outside the */smb* directory, the wrapper passes the filesystem function calls on to the standard system library as if the wrapper had not been in place.) Thus, any dynamically linked command you execute from the smbsh shell accesses the */smb* directory using the SMB protocol.

There are two distinct implementations of *smbsh* in the Samba Version 3 tarball. One of them is built from the Samba *source* directory. The other is located in the *examples* directory. The version located in the *source* directory is the original standalone implementation, which no longer works on Linux systems but continues to be in use on such traditional platforms as Sun Solaris, HP-UX, and AIX. It no longer works on Linux because of a decision made by the *glibc* maintainers to change its behavior some time around *glibc* Version 2.1.

The implementation of *smbsh* that is found in the *examples* directory of the Samba tarball does work, although it has a bug. This version uses the *libsmbclient* library. As a result of the bug in this implementation of *smbsh*, it is only possible to list files by performing the *ls* operation from outside the */smb* virtual directory that the utility creates. It is not certain at this time when this bug may be fixed by the Samba Team.

Despite the niggling challenges of the *smbsh* facility, it continues to be used by a number of applications that do not natively support CIFS/SMB and yet need it. This tool may be the only method of supporting CIFS/SMB if the application cannot be updated to use the *libsmbclient* library directly.

NFS and NIS Configuration

When TCP/IP is configured, most Linux distributions support the Network File System (NFS) and the Network Information Service (NIS). NFS allows your system to share files directly with a network of machines. File access across NFS is transparent; you simply access the files as if they were stored on your local disk. In system administration terms, one system mounts another's filesystem on a local directory, just as a local filesystem can be mounted. NFS also allows you to export filesystems, allowing other systems on the network to mount your disks directly.

NIS is a system that allows your host to obtain information automatically on user accounts, groups, filesystem mount points, and other system databases from servers on the network. For example, let's say you have a large collection of machines that should have the same user accounts and groups (information usually found in */etc/passwd* and */etc/group*). Users should be able to log in to any of these machines and access their files directly (say, by mounting their home filesystem from a central location using NFS). Obviously, maintaining user accounts across many machines would be problematic; in order to add a new user, you would need to log in to each machine and create the user account on each. When you use NIS, however, the system automatically consults centrally maintained databases across the network for such information, in addition to local files such as */etc/passwd*. NIS+ is an enhanced NIS service that is coming into use at some sites.

There are two sides to NFS. It is possible to export parts of the filesystem on your server or workstation so that other users can access its files and directories, and it is possible to mount remote resources on your workstation, or server, so they are available locally in like manner to local physical disk resources. NFS resources are exported by an NFS server. Locally mounted NFS resources are available on an NFS client.

You should be aware that NFS provides absolutely no encryption. If you mount your filesystems over the Internet, the transferred files can be interfered and even tampered with at any time (some people joke that NFS is short for "No File Security"). On the other hand, NFS mounts beyond your local network are probably too slow to be useful anyway, unless you are on a really big pipe.

If your Linux system is to interact with other systems on a LAN, it's quite possible that NFS and NIS are in wide use on your LAN. In this section, we show you how to configure your system as an NFS and NIS client—that is, to mount remote filesystems and to participate in an existing NIS domain. It is possible to configure your

---

system as an NFS and NIS server, but many subtle issues are involved in configuring a system as an NFS or NIS server. Instead of providing a dangerously incomplete account of server configuration here, we refer you to O'Reilly's *Managing NFS and NIS* by Hal Stern. If you are already familiar with NFS/NIS configuration on other Unix systems, Linux is really no different; the manual pages and Linux HOWTO documents provide all the specifics.

Configuring Your System as an NFS Client

A few words of warning about NFS. First of all, the client is not very happy when the servers for remote filesystems go down or the network connection fails. When the NFS server is unreachable for any reason, your system prints warning messages to the console (or system logs) periodically. If this is a problem, use the standard *umount* command (introduced in Chapter 10) to unmount any remote filesystems offered by the affected servers.

Another detail to watch out for when mounting NFS filesystems is the user IDs (*uids*) and group IDs (*gids*) of the files on the remote filesystem. In order to access your own files via NFS, the user and group IDs for your own account must match those on the NFS server. One easy way to check this is with an *ls -l* listing: if the *uid* or *gid* does not match any local user, *ls* displays the *uid/gid* of files as numbers; otherwise, the user or group name is printed.

If IDs do not match, you have a few ways to remedy this problem. One is to simply change the *uid* of your user account (and the *gid* of your primary group) to match those on the NFS server (say, by editing your local */etc/passwd* file). This approach requires you to *chown* and *chgrp* all your local files after making the change. Another solution is to create a separate account with matching *uid/gid*. However, the best approach may be to use NIS to manage your user and group databases. With this solution, you do not create your user and group accounts locally; instead, they are provided to you by an NIS server. More on this later.

Another NFS caveat is the restriction of *root* permissions on NFS-mounted filesystems. Unless the NFS server explicitly grants your system *root* access on NFS-mounted filesystems, you will not have total access to files when logged in as *root* on your local system. The reason for this is security: allowing unlimited *root* access to files on a remote-mounted NFS filesystem opens itself up to abuse, especially when the NFS server and the NFS client are maintained or owned by different people.

NFS clients can make use of exported NFS resources in a number of ways:

- Automatic boot-time mounting through the */etc/fstab* file
- Manual mounting from a shell command line
- Automated mount via the *automount* daemon

Discussion of the automount daemon is beyond the scope of this chapter; refer to Chapter 10 for further information. The next sections contain a simplified overview of the two other methods.

Using /etc/fstab NFS client entries

Configuring your system to mount remote filesystems over NFS is a breeze. Assuming that you have TCP/IP configured and that hostname lookup works correctly, you can simply add a line to your */etc/fstab* file such as the following:

```
# device          directory          type  options   dump fsckorder
allison:/usr     /fsys/allison/usr   nfs   defaults  0    0
```

This line is similar to *fstab* for partitions on a local system, but the name of the remote system appears in the first column, and the mount type is nfs. This line will cause the remote */usr* on the machine allison to be mounted at boot time at the directory mount point */fsys/allison/usr*.

As with regular filesystem mounts, be sure to create the mount-point directory (in this case, */fsys/allison/usr*) before letting the system mount the remote directory. The line in the */etc/fstab* example allows your system to mount the directory */usr* from the machine *allison* on the network.

The mount can be specified with various options. Two commonly used options are soft and hard. The soft mounting option means that when a file access request fails, the NFS client will report an error to the process that makes the request. Some application handle that error report gracefully, and some do not. The hard mounting option means that the NFS client will hang when the NFS server ceases to respond to file access requests. You should read the manpage for the mount on your Linux system to explore the finer points of each of the possible options.

Don't forget to check the ro and rw options as well. When exporting a directory, the administrator may choose to make the directory available for *read-only* access, in which case you will not be able to write to the filesystem when mounted on your system. In this case, you should set the options field of the */etc/fstab* line in the previous example to ro instead of defaults.

Make sure the administrator of the remote system has exported the desired directory (see "Adding a directory to the NFS server's exports," later in this chapter) and test your configuration by issuing a mount as *root*:

```
# mount allison:/usr
```

Finding NFS exported resources and diagnosing problems

Sometimes you know that there should be an NFS filesystem resource (a share) on a particular server, but you do not know whether the NFS server is running, or perhaps you do not know the correct name of the shared resource. Here is an example to show how you can find out what is available. In this example there are three NFS servers: *merlin*, *frodo*, and *sunsol*. Let's see what NFS resources are available on each.

The utility that can be used to examine the availabilty of NFS services is called *showmount*. This tool is normally only available to the *root* user. We will examine all three machines as shown here:

```
linux:~ # showmount -e merlin
Export list for merlin:
/srv  *.myworld.org,192.168.1.0/24
/data *.myworld.org,192.168.1.0/24
```

The machine *merlin* has two NFS exports. They may be used only by NFS clients in the *myworld.org* domain, as well as from any IP address in the *192.168.1.0* network. Let's see what surprises the machine sunsol has for you:

```
linux:~ # showmount -e sunsol
Export list for sunsol:
/export (everyone)
```

The */export* directory has been exported to the whole world. It is just as well that this resource is inside a private network and not on a machine that is exposed to the Internet. Just for the record, anyone can mount an export that is world-readable. If it is also capable of being written, that does not make for a particularly secure system!

Finally, let's see what happens when we request NFS export information from a server on which the NFS server service is not running. Let's ask the machine *frodo*, on which the NFS has apparently failed or has been stopped for some reason:

```
linux:~ # showmount -e frodo
mount clntudp_create: RPC: Program not registered
```

You can see that the Remote Procedure Call (RPC) process over which NFS resources are shared is not running. RPC is a protocol for client-server communication. It is possible to check what RPC services are running using the rpcinfo utility. In this case, we will check the difference in services available from the machines merlin and frodo, as shown here:

```
linux:~ # rpcinfo -p merlin
   program vers proto   port
    100000    2   tcp    111  portmapper
    100000    2   udp    111  portmapper
    100003    2   udp   2049  nfs
    100003    3   udp   2049  nfs
    100227    3   udp   2049  nfs_acl
    100003    2   tcp   2049  nfs
    100003    3   tcp   2049  nfs
    100227    3   tcp   2049  nfs_acl
    100024    1   udp   1254  status
    100021    1   udp   1254  nlockmgr
    100021    3   udp   1254  nlockmgr
    100021    4   udp   1254  nlockmgr
    100024    1   tcp   4777  status
```

```
100021    1    tcp    4777    nlockmgr
100021    3    tcp    4777    nlockmgr
100021    4    tcp    4777    nlockmgr
100005    1    udp     645    mountd
100005    1    tcp     648    mountd
100005    2    udp     645    mountd
100005    2    tcp     648    mountd
100005    3    udp     645    mountd
100005    3    tcp     648    mountd
```

The *nlockmgr* RPC service provides file-locking capabilities over NFS-mounted connections, and the *nfs_acl* RPC service provides POSIX Access Control List (ACL) file security controls. Here is the result of asking the same question of the machine frodo:

```
linux:~ # rpcinfo -p frodo
   program vers proto   port
    100000    2    tcp    111    portmapper
    100000    2    udp    111    portmapper
    100024    1    udp  32768    status
    100021    1    udp  32768    nlockmgr
    100021    3    udp  32768    nlockmgr
    100021    4    udp  32768    nlockmgr
    100024    1    tcp  32768    status
    100021    1    tcp  32768    nlockmgr
    100021    3    tcp  32768    nlockmgr
    100021    4    tcp  32768    nlockmgr
```

The *nfs* RPC service is not available. Moments later we executed the command again to obtain this result:

```
linux:~ # rpcinfo -p frodo
rpcinfo: can't contact portmapper: RPC: Remote system error - Connection refused
```

This means that the portmapper service that provides the RPC capabilities has been shut down. This may have been done to permit some maintenance procedures to be performed, or the server may be in the process of being shut down.

By now, you should be getting some clues for finding and diagnosing NFS availability as well as potential causes of NFS problems.

Manual mounting of NFS filesystems

It is possible to determine what NFS filesystems are currently mounted on your Linux system by using the mount utility:

```
linux:~ # mount -t nfs
merlin:/data on /data type nfs (rw,addr=192.168.1.4)
merlin:/srv on /msrv type nfs (rw,addr=192.168.1.4)
sunsol:/export on /mnt type nfs (ro,addr=192.168.1.6)
```

The NFS filesystem resources from the machine *merlin* have been mounted so that they are capable of read/write access. The resource on the machine *sunsol* has been mounted with read-only access capability.

Assuming you want to mount the */export/work* resource from the machine *sunsol* on your Linux workstation at the directory mount point */home/work*, here is the command to use:

```
linux:~ # mkdir /home/work
linux:~ # mount sunsol:/export/work /home/work
```

The `df` command will help to show that it is mounted, as well as the disk space available:

```
linux:~ # df /home/work
Filesystem            1K-blocks      Used Available Use% Mounted on
sunsol:/export/work    17645600   3668352  13800800  21% /home/work
```

When it is necessary to unmount an NFS mounted resource, simply do this:

```
linux:~ # umount /home/work
```

With a little practice, you will soon be an expert at using the NFS client facilities.

Adding a directory to the NFS server's exports

As we said earlier, we will not try to tell you how to configure an NFS server, but we'll briefly explain how to export a directory once the server is running. In our example, the system administrator for the *allison* server must configure it to export the given directory (here, */usr*) to your system. On most Unix systems, this is simply a matter of editing a file, such as */etc/exports*, or running a command that edits the file. It is not necessary for the exported directory to be the root of a filesystem itself; that is, a server can export */usr* even if */usr* does not have its own separate filesystem.

Let's take the role of an administrator on an NFS server now and export the */data/accounts* directory for use by all NFS clients in the *myworld.org* DNS domain. These simple steps will achieve this:

1. Create the */data/accounts* directory:

   ```
   linux:~ # mkdir -p /data/accounts
   linux:~ # chmod 770 /data/accounts
   linux:~ # chown bill:accounting /data/accounts
   ```

   These commands created the exported directory (it did not exist previously), set the permissions so that group members can access the directory, and then set permissions so that the *accounting* group can read and write to the directory. Of course, they can also list any files that may be placed within it.

2. Create the */etc/exports* file with the following contents:

   ```
   /data/accounts   *.myworld.org(rw,no_root_squash,sync)
   ```

   Set the ownership and permissions on this file:

   ```
   linux:~ # chown root:root /etc/exports
   linux:~ # chmod 644 /etc/exports
   ```

Configuring Your System as an NIS Client

NIS is not a tool for file and printer sharing, but we present it in this chapter because it shares some components with its cousin NFS, and because it can make NFS easier to administer because NIS allows each user to have the same account number on all systems.

NIS is a complex system, simply because it is so flexible. It is a general-purpose network database system that allows your machine to transparently access information on user accounts, groups, filesystems, and so forth, from databases stored across the network.

One goal of NIS is to ease network management. Allowing user account information (such as that stored in *etc/passwd*) to be maintained on a single server, for example, makes it easy for many machines to share the same user accounts. In the previous section on NFS, we showed how user and group IDs on the NFS server and client should match in order to effectively access your files remotely. Using NIS allows your *uid* and *gid* to be defined from a remote site, not locally.

If your machine is connected at a site where NIS is used, chances are you can add your machine as an NIS client, thus allowing it to obtain user, group, and other databases directly from the network. To some extent this makes it unnecessary to create local user accounts or groups at all; apart from the locally defined users such as *root*, *bin*, and so forth, all other users will be created from the NIS server. If you couple the use of NIS with mounting user home directories from an NFS server, it's also unnecessary to set aside local storage for users. NIS can greatly lessen the amount of work you need to do as a system administrator.

In an NIS configuration, there may be NIS *servers*, *slaves*, and *clients*. As you can guess, *servers* are the systems where NIS databases originate and are maintained. NIS *slaves* are systems to which the server copies its databases. The slaves can provide the information to other systems, but changes to the databases must be made from the server. Slaves are simply used as a way to ease the load on the NIS server; otherwise, all NIS requests would have to be serviced by a single machine. NIS *clients* are systems that request database information from servers or slaves.

To completely discuss how NIS works and how to maintain an NIS server requires enough material for a whole book (again, see *Managing* NFS *and NIS*). However, when reading about NIS you are likely to come across various terms. NIS was originally named Yellow Pages. This usage has been discontinued because Yellow Pages is trademarked in the United Kingdom (it's the phone book, after all), but its legacy can still be seen in commands containing the letters *yp*.

There are at least two implementations of NIS for Linux: the "traditional" NIS implementation and a separate implementation known as NYS (standing for NIS+, YP, and Switch). The NIS client code for the "traditional" implementation is contained within the standard C library and is already installed on most Linux systems. (This is necessary to allow programs such as login to transparently access NIS databases as well as local system files.) The *glibc2* standard C library that most distributions use these days comes with support for NIS+. The NYS client code is contained within the Network Services Library, *libnsl*. Linux systems using NYS should have compiled programs such as login against this library.

Different Linux distributions use different versions of the NIS or NYS client code, and some use a mixture of the two. To be safe, we'll describe how to configure a system for both traditional NIS and NYS implementations, meaning that no matter which is installed on your system, it should be able to act as a client.

To make matters even more complex, some distributions employ the PAM (Pluggable Authentication Modules) system, mentioned in "PAM and Other Authentication Methods" in Chapter 11. In this case, programs such as login are linked against the PAM library, which in turn loads a PAM library module that implements the authentication system in use on the system, or delegates the task to other libraries.

We assume here that an administrator on your local network has installed and started all the necessary NIS daemon processes (such as *ypbind*) used by traditional NIS to talk to the NIS server. If your Linux system does not appear to have any NIS support, consult documents such as the Linux NIS HOWTO to configure it from scratch. Nearly all current Linux distributions come prepackaged with NIS client (and server) support, and all that's required of you is to edit a few configuration files.

The first step is to set the NIS domain in which your system will be operating. Your network administrator can provide this information to you. Note that the NIS domain name is not necessarily identical to the DNS domain name, which can be set with the hostname command. For example, if the full hostname of your system is *loomer.vpizza.com*, your DNS domain name is *vpizza.com*. However, your NIS domain name could be entirely different—for example, *vpizzas*. The NIS domain name is selected by the NIS server administrators and is not related to the DNS domain name described earlier.

Setting the domain name is usually a matter of running the *domainname* command at boot time, perhaps in one of your system *rc* files (such as */etc/rc.d/rc.inet1*, described earlier). You should first check that *domainname* is not being executed in one of the existing *rc* files. The command takes the format.

```
linux:~ # domainname
domain-name
```

An example is domainname vpizzas. The command is usually found in */sbin/domainname* and may have a slightly different name, such as *domainname-yp*.

A slightly different method sets the domain name under NYS. You should create (or edit) the file */etc/yp.conf*. This file should contain two lines: one specifying the name of your NIS domain, and another specifying the hostname of the NIS server. As an example:

```
linux:~ # domain vpizzas
linux:~ # ypserver allison.vpizza.com
```

sets the NIS domain name to *vpizzas* and specifies that *allison.vpizza.com* should be used as the NIS server. If no ypserver line is included in this file, the system broadcasts a message on the network at boot time to determine the name of the NIS server. Your network administrator can provide you with the hostname of your preferred NIS server.

Once these two steps are complete, your system should be able to transparently access NIS databases. One way to test this is to query the system for a password database entry from the NIS server. The *ypwhich* command queries specific NIS databases. For example:

```
linux:~ # ypwhich username passwd
```

If this returns the line from the NIS *passwd* database for the given user, you have successfully queried the NIS database. (One way to verify that the information returned is correct is to run this same command on another system in your NIS domain whose NIS configuration is known to be working.) The NIS *passwd* database is not identical to the */etc/passwd* file on your system, although it is in the same format. The Linux HOWTO documents contain additional information on troubleshooting your NIS configuration.

## CHAPTER 16

The X Window System

Chapter 3 introduced Linux's graphical desktops, and many subsequent chapters showed you the spiffy and powerful tools you could run on them. Rarely do you have to deal with the underpinnings that make all this possible, but occasionally your screen resolution isn't as good as it could be, or you have trouble getting graphics to start. At these times you notice that error messages are referring to an X server or to various files and libraries with an x in them.

Basically, the X Window System encompasses all the software that lets a CPU understand a video card and get graphics to appear on a monitor. X goes far beyond this, though: it provides an interface of almost unlimited flexibility to let programs display graphics, interact with the user, and exchange data with other graphical programs. KDE and GNOME are both sets of libraries and tools that run on X. In this chapter, we tell you how to install and configure the X Window System in case it was not done by your distribution properly.

A History of X

It's difficult to describe the X Window System in a nutshell. X is a complete windowing graphics interface that runs on almost all computer systems, but was established mostly on Unix and now on Linux. X provides a huge number of options to both the programmer and the user. For instance, at least half a dozen *window managers* are available for X, each one offering a different interface for manipulating windows. Your distribution has chosen a window manager along with a desktop. By customizing the attributes of the window manager, you have complete control over how windows are placed on the screen, the colors and borders used to decorate them, and so forth.

X was originally developed by Project Athena at MIT, by MIT, Digital Equipment Corporation (DEC), and IBM. The version of X current as of the time of writing is Version 11 Revision 6 (X11R6), which was first released in April 1994 and then subsequentially updated in minor versions. Since the release of Version 11, X has virtually taken over as the de facto standard for Unix graphical environments.

Despite its commercial use, the X Window System remains distributable under a liberal license from the Open Group. As such, a complete implementation of X is freely available for Linux systems. X.org, the version most directly based on the X sources, is the version that Linux uses most often. Today, this version supports not only Intel-based systems, but also Alpha AXP, MicroSPARC, PowerPC, and other architectures. Further architectures will follow. Support for innumerable graphics boards and many other operating systems (including Linux) has been added—and X.org implements the latest version, X11R6.8.2.*

We should mention here that commercial X Window System servers are available for Linux that may have advantages over the stock X.org version (such as support for certain video cards). Most people use the X.org version happily, though, so this should certainly be your first stop.

As we mentioned in "Why Use a Graphical Desktop?" in Chapter 3, people who run Linux as a server often don't install X at all. They control the server through remote access only, or using just the text interface.

X Concepts

X is based on a client/server model in which the X *server* is a program that runs on your system and handles all access to the graphics hardware. An X *client* is an applications program that communicates with the server, sending it requests, such as "draw a line" or "pay attention to keyboard input." The X server takes care of servicing these requests by drawing a line on the display or sending user input (via the keyboard, mouse, or whatever) to the client application. Examples of X clients are the now-famous image manipulation program GIMP and the many programs coming out of the aforementioned desktop environments KDE and GNOME—for example, the KDE email program KMail.

It is important to note that X is a network-oriented graphics system. That is, X clients can run either locally (on the same system that the server is running) or remotely (on a system somewhere on a TCP/IP network). The X server listens to both local and remote network sockets for requests from clients. This feature is obviously quite powerful. If you have a connection to a TCP/IP network, you can log in to another system over the network and run an X application there, directing it to display on your local X server.

---

* X.org is a relatively new version. There have been infights in the X Window System community that have led to a split; people have moved from the previously prevailing XFree86 version to the newer X.org version. We will not comment any further on these infights, as they are more a question of personal animosities than of technical benefits.

Further advantages of X are security (if the user so desires), modular separation of functions, and support for many different architectures. All this makes the X Window System technically superior by far to all other window systems.

The X Window System makes a distinction between application behavior and *window management*. Clients running under X are displayed within one or more *windows* on your screen. However, how windows are manipulated (placed on the display, resized, and so forth) and how they are decorated (the appearance of the window frames) are not controlled by the X server. Instead, such things are handled by another X client called a *window manager* that runs concurrently with the other X clients. Your choice of window manager will decide to some extent how X as a whole looks and feels. Most window managers are utterly flexible and configurable; the user can select the look of the window decoration, the focus policy, the meaning of the mouse buttons when the mouse cursor is on the background part of the screen rather than on an application window, and many other things by editing the configuration files of the window manager. More modern systems even let you configure those aspects over a GUI.

To fully understand the concept of window managers, you need to know that the window manager does not affect what the client application does within the window. The window manager is only in charge of painting the window decoration—that is, the frame and the buttons that let you close, move, and resize windows.

There can be only one window manager on any X server. Theoretically, it is even possible to completely do away with window managers, but then you would not be able to move windows around the screen; put a hidden window on top; or minimize, maximize, or resize windows unless the programs themselves provided this functionality.

Let's shortly mention the desktop environments again. A desktop environment such as KDE or GNOME is a collection of applications and tools with a common look and feel as well as many other common properties—for example, the menus of the applications could all be set up according to the same concepts. Desktop environments on X always need a window manager, as described earlier. Some desktop environments provide their own window manager (such as KWin in the KDE desktop environment), whereas others do not have their own window manager. It is up to the user to install a window manager of his or her choice.

Hardware Requirements

As of X.org Version 6.8.2, released in February 2005, the video chipsets listed in this section are supported. The documentation included with your video adapter should specify the chipset used. If you are in the market for a new video card, or are buying a new machine that comes with a video card, have the vendor find out exactly what the video card's make, model, and chipset are. This may require the vendor to call technical support on your behalf; vendors usually will be happy to do this. Many PC hardware vendors will state that the video card is a "standard SVGA card" that "should work" on your system. Explain that your software (mention Linux and X.org!) does not support all video chipsets and that you must have detailed information.

A good source for finding out whether your graphics board is supported and which X server it needs is *http://www.x.org/X11R6.8.2/doc/RELNOTES3.html#9*.

If you are unsure about which chipset you use, you can try to run

```
Xorg -configure
```

This will examine your hardware and create an initial configuration file that you can then tweak according to your needs.

It should be noted that the X.org project instituted an entirely new driver architecture some time ago, which is much more flexible than the old one and will enable more timely support of new graphics hardware.

Video cards using a supported chipset are normally supported on all bus types, including the PCI and AGP.

All these chipsets are supported in 256-color mode, some are supported in mono- and 16-color modes, and some are supported in higher color depths.

This list will undoubtedly expand as time passes. The release notes for the current version of X.org should contain the complete list of supported video chipsets. Please also always see the *README* file for your particular chipset.

Besides those chipsets, there is also support for the framebuffer device starting with the 2.2 kernel series via the fbdev driver. If your chipset is supported by the normal X server drivers, you should use those for better performance, but if it is not, you may still be able to run X by using the framebuffer. On some hardware, even the framebuffer device provides accelerated graphics.

One problem faced by the X.org developers is that some video card manufacturers use nonstandard mechanisms for determining clock frequencies used to drive the card. Some of these manufacturers either don't release specifications describing how to program the card, or require developers to sign a nondisclosure statement to obtain the information. This would obviously restrict the free distribution of the X.org software, something that the X.org development team is not willing to do. So if your board is not supported, this may be the reason why.

It is difficult to specify minimum hardware requirements for running X, as this depends on a lot of external factors, how many graphical programs you are planning to run, what else is going on on your computer, and so on. But any computer sold in the last, say, 5 to 8 years should work just fine, and probably many older ones as well. You should check the documentation for X and verify that your particular card is supported before taking the plunge and purchasing expensive hardware.

Benchmark rating comparisons for various video cards under X.org are posted to the Usenet newsgroups *comp.windows.x.i386unix* and *comp.os.linux.misc* regularly.

As a side note, one author's (Kalle's) tertiary personal Linux system is an AMD K6-2 with 128 MB of RAM and is equipped with a PCI Permedia II chipset card with 8 MB of DRAM. This setup is already a lot faster with respect to display speed than many workstations. X.org on a Linux system with an accelerated SVGA card will give you much greater performance than that found on commercial Unix workstations (which often employ simple framebuffers for graphics and provide accelerated graphics hardware only as a high-priced add-on).

Your machine will need at least 32 MB of physical RAM and 64 MB of virtual RAM (for example, 32 MB physical and 32 MB swap). Remember that the more physical RAM you have, the less frequently the system will swap to and from disk when memory is low. Because swapping is inherently slow (disks are very slow compared with memory), having 32 MB or more of RAM is necessary to run X.org comfortably. A system with 32 MB of physical RAM could run *much* more slowly (up to 10 times more slowly) than one with 64 MB or more.

Installing X.org

X.org does not provide any binary distributions, but you should be able to run those that come with your distribution just fine. On *ftp://ftp.x.org/pub/X11R6.8.2/src*, you can find the full source code, including instructions on how to build binaries yourself, if you really want to. (Of course, the version number of the latest version could have changed by the time you read this.)

Writing an X configuration file (called either *XF86Config-4* or *xorg.conf*, depending on version and distribution) from scratch is a daunting undertaking, and not to be recommended. This section lists three ways of getting at least a start at a configuration file; using the documentation in this chapter, you should be able to change this to match your system in the optimal way.

The first thing you should try (after having tried your distribution's setup tool, of course) is a program called *xorgcfg* that ships with X.org. This is a graphical installation program that works even from the terminal, so that you can use it if you do not have any X set up yet.

If *xorgcfg* should fail you, your next bet would be the command already mentioned, *Xorg -configure*. This fires up the X server in a mode where it attempts to find out as much as possible about your hardware and writes a skeleton configuration file. This skeleton configuration might be sufficient to start up the X server, even though you may want to tune this to your needs.

If even *Xorg -configure* fails you (which, honestly, is quite unlikely), then you can try another text-based configuration tool as a last resort. It is called *xorgconfig*, and should be installed together with X.org. It will guide you through a series of questions about your hardware. If some of the questions are difficult to answer, just go with the default and see what you end up with. In the end, you should again end up with a skeleton configuration file.

Configuring X.org

Setting up X.org is not difficult in most cases. However, if you happen to be using hardware for which drivers are under development, or wish to obtain the best performance or resolution from an accelerated graphics card, configuring X.org can be somewhat time-consuming.

In this section, we describe how to create and edit the *xorg.conf* file, which configures the X.org server. This file is by default located in */etc/X11/*, but is searched for in many other locations, so your distribution might elect to put it elsewhere. In any case, it is best to start out with a skeleton configuration file generated by any of the means described earlier. Then go for a low resolution: a good choice is 640×480, which should be supported on all video cards and monitor types. Once you have X.org working at a lower, standard resolution, you can tweak the configuration to exploit the capabilities of your video hardware. The idea is that you want to make sure X.org works at least minimally on your system and that something isn't wrong with your installation before attempting the sometimes difficult task of setting up X.org for real use. With current hardware, you should easily be able to get up to 1280×1024 pixels (1024×768 on most laptops).

In addition to the information here, you should read the documentation at *http://www.x.org/X11R6.8.2/doc/*, in particular the *README* files for your particular graphics chipset.

The main configuration file you need to create is */etc/X11/xorg.conf*. This file contains information on your mouse, video card parameters, and so on. The file */etc/X11/xorg.conf.install* is provided with the X.org distribution as an example. Copy this file to *xorg.conf* and edit it as a starting point, if any of the other methods did not give you a skeleton configuration file.

The *xorg.conf* manual page explains the format of this file in detail. Read this manual page now if you have not done so already.

We are going to present a sample *xorg.conf* file, piece by piece. This file may not look exactly like the sample file included in the X.org distribution, but the structure is the same. The *xorg.conf* file format may change with each version of X.org; this information is valid only for X.org Version 6.8.2.

Whatever you do, you should not simply copy the configuration file listed here to your own system and attempt to use it. Attempting to use a configuration file that doesn't correspond to your hardware could drive the monitor at a frequency that is too high for it; there have been reports of monitors (especially fixed-frequency monitors) being damaged or destroyed by using an incorrectly configured *xorg.conf* file. The bottom line is this: make absolutely sure your *xorg.conf* file corresponds to your hardware before you attempt to use it.

Now that we have written this warning, we would also like to mention that configuring X.org is much less dangerous than it used to be a few years ago, since the X server has become very good at detecting unsuitable configurations.

Each section of the *Xorg.conf* file is surrounded by the pair of lines Section "*section-name*" and EndSection. The first part of the *Xorg.conf* file is Files, which looks like this:

```
Section "Files"
    FontPath     "/usr/X11R6/lib/X11/fonts/misc:unscaled"
    FontPath     "/usr/X11R6/lib/X11/fonts/local"
    FontPath     "/usr/X11R6/lib/X11/fonts/75dpi:unscaled"
    FontPath     "/usr/X11R6/lib/X11/fonts/100dpi:unscaled"
    FontPath     "/usr/X11R6/lib/X11/fonts/Type1"
    FontPath     "/usr/X11R6/lib/X11/fonts/URW"
    FontPath     "/usr/X11R6/lib/X11/fonts/Speedo"
    FontPath     "/usr/X11R6/lib/X11/fonts/PEX"
    FontPath     "/usr/X11R6/lib/X11/fonts/cyrillic"
    FontPath     "/usr/X11R6/lib/X11/fonts/latin2/misc:unscaled"
    FontPath     "/usr/X11R6/lib/X11/fonts/latin2/75dpi:unscaled"
    FontPath     "/usr/X11R6/lib/X11/fonts/latin2/100dpi:unscaled"
    FontPath     "/usr/X11R6/lib/X11/fonts/latin2/Type1"
    FontPath     "/usr/X11R6/lib/X11/fonts/latin7/75dpi:unscaled"
    FontPath     "/usr/X11R6/lib/X11/fonts/baekmuk:unscaled"
    FontPath     "/usr/X11R6/lib/X11/fonts/japanese:unscaled"
    FontPath     "/usr/X11R6/lib/X11/fonts/kwintv"
    FontPath     "/usr/X11R6/lib/X11/fonts/truetype"
    FontPath     "/usr/X11R6/lib/X11/fonts/uni:unscaled"
    FontPath     "/usr/X11R6/lib/X11/fonts/CID"
    FontPath     "/usr/X11R6/lib/X11/fonts/ucs/misc:unscaled"
    FontPath     "/usr/X11R6/lib/X11/fonts/ucs/75dpi:unscaled"
    FontPath     "/usr/X11R6/lib/X11/fonts/ucs/100dpi:unscaled"
    FontPath     "/usr/X11R6/lib/X11/fonts/hellas/misc:unscaled"
    FontPath     "/usr/X11R6/lib/X11/fonts/hellas/75dpi:unscaled"
    FontPath     "/usr/X11R6/lib/X11/fonts/hellas/100dpi:unscaled"
    FontPath     "/usr/X11R6/lib/X11/fonts/hellas/Type1"
    FontPath     "/usr/X11R6/lib/X11/fonts/misc/sgi:unscaled"
    FontPath     "/usr/X11R6/lib/X11/fonts/xtest"
    FontPath     "/opt/kde3/share/fonts"
    InputDevices "/dev/ttyS0"
    InputDevices "/dev/ttyS1"
    InputDevices "/dev/ttyS2"
```

```
        InputDevices "/dev/ttyS3"
        InputDevices "/dev/ttyS4"
        InputDevices "/dev/ttyS5"
        InputDevices "/dev/ttyS6"
        InputDevices "/dev/ttyS7"
        InputDevices "/dev/ttyS8"
        InputDevices "/dev/psaux"
        InputDevices "/dev/logibm"
        InputDevices "/dev/sunmouse"
        InputDevices "/dev/atibm"
        InputDevices "/dev/amigamouse"
        InputDevices "/dev/atarimouse"
        InputDevices "/dev/inportbm"
        InputDevices "/dev/gpmdata"
        InputDevices "/dev/mouse"
        InputDevices "/dev/usbmouse"
        InputDevices "/dev/adbmouse"
        InputDevices "/dev/input/mice"
        InputDevices "/dev/input/event0"
        InputDevices "/dev/pointer0"
        InputDevices "/dev/pointer1"
        InputDevices "/dev/pointer2"
        InputDevices "/dev/pointer3"
    EndSection
```

There can be many more lines like these. Each `FontPath` line sets the path to a directory containing X11 fonts. In general, you shouldn't have to modify these lines; just be sure there is a `FontPath` entry for each font type you have installed (i.e., for each directory in *usr/X11R6/lib/X11/fonts*). If you add the string `:unscaled` to a `FontPath`, the fonts from this directory will not be scaled. This is often an improvement because fonts that are greatly scaled look ugly. In addition to `FontPath`, you can also set a `RgbPath` for finding the RGB color database (unlikely to be necessary), and a `ModulePath`, to point to a directory with dynamically loaded modules. Those modules are currently used for some special input devices, as well as the PEX and XIE extensions.

The next section is `ServerFlags`, which specifies several global flags for the server. This section is often empty or very small:

```
    Section "ServerFlags"
      Option       "AllowMouseOpenFail"
    EndSection
```

Here, we say that we want the X server to start up even if it cannot find the mouse. For more options, please see the documentation at *http://www.x.org*. Often, options will be autodetected at server startup, so they don't need to be listed here.

The next section is the `Module` section, with which you can dynamically load additional X server modules, such as support for special hardware or graphics libraries such as PEX. It is also used for loading the `freetype` support library and the video and 3D support. Here is a sample `Module` section:

```
Section "Module"
    Load        "v4l"
    Load        "extmod"
    Load        "type1"
    Load        "freetype"
    Load        "dbe"
    Load        "dri"
    Load        "speedo"
    Load        "glx"
EndSection
```

The next sections are InputDevice. You usually have at least two: one for the keyboard and one for the mouse. If you have other input devices, such as a graphics tablet, these will go into additional sections:

```
Section "InputDevice"
    Driver      "kbd"
    Identifier  "Keyboard[0]"
    Option      "Protocol" "Standard"
    Option      "XkbLayout" "us"
    Option      "XkbModel" "pc105"
    Option      "XkbRules" "xfree86"
EndSection


Section "InputDevice"
    Driver      "mouse"
    Identifier  "Mouse[1]"
    Option      "ButtonNumber" "7"
    Option      "Device" "/dev/mouse"
    Option      "Name" "Autodetection"
    Option      "Protocol" "ExplorerPS/2"
    Option      "Vendor" "Sysp"
    Option      "ZAxisMapping" "4 5"
EndSection
```

Again, other options are available as well. The keyboard configurations listed previously are for a U.S. keyboard; for other keyboards, you will need to replace them with lines suitable for your keyboard.

The mouse section tells the X server where the mouse is connected (*/dev/mouse* in this case, which is usually a link to the appropriate port, such as */dev/ttyS0*), what kind of mouse it is (the "Protocol" option) and some other operational details. It is important for the protocol to be right, but the aforementioned configuration programs should usually find out the protocol automatically.

BusMouse should be used for the Logitech busmouse. Note that older Logitech mice that are not bus mice should use Logitech, but newer Logitech mice that are not bus mice use either the Microsoft or the Mouseman protocol. This is a case where the protocol doesn't necessarily have anything to do with the make of the mouse.

If you have a modern serial mouse, you could also try specifying Auto, which will try to autoselect a mouse driver.

It is easy to check whether you have selected the correct mouse driver once you have started up X: when you move your mouse, the mouse pointer on the screen should follow this movement. If it does this, your setup is very likely to be correct. If it doesn't, try another driver, and also check whether the device you specified is correct.

The next section of the *xorg.conf* file is Device, which specifies parameters for your video card. If you have multiple video cards, there will also be multiple Device sections.

```
Section "Device"
   BoardName    "Radeon LW"
   BusID        "1:0:0"
   Driver       "radeon"
   Identifier   "Device[0]"
   Screen       0
   Option       "Rotate" "off"
   VendorName   "ATI"
EndSection
```

The first entry here, BoardName, is simply a descriptive name that reminds you which graphics card you have configured here (important if you have more than one!). Similarly, VendorName is a free-form string that has purely descriptional purposes. Even the Identifier string can be picked freely, but needs to match the Device strings used in later sections of the configuration file. It is customary here to use the names Device[0], Device[1], and so on.

BusID identifies the actual graphics card in terms of the built-in hardware on the PCI bus. PCI:1:0:0, or the shorter 1:0:0, is usually the right choice if you have only one choice. If you are unsure about what to put in here, run the X server as follows:

```
X.org -scanpci
```

and check the output carefully. At least one graphics card should be contained in the output (probably among other hardware not relevant here). For example, a line like:

```
(1:0:0) Matrox unknown card (0x19d8) using a Matrox MGA G400 AGP
```

tells you that you have a Matrox MGA G400 card with an AGP connector installed. The first digits in parentheses are the PCI bus ID, as described earlier.

The Screen section is mandatory on multihead graphics cards, which have more than one monitor output. For single-head graphics cards, always put in 0 here.

Driver is very important, because it determines the actual graphics driver to be loaded by the X server. A good way to find the right driver name is either to use the configuration programs described earlier or to run the X server like this:

```
Xorg -probeonly
```

This will output information the X server has collected about your hardware, including the driver it thinks it should use.

There are lots of other options you can specify in this file, including the chipset, the RAMDAC, and other hardware properties, but the X server is very good at finding these out all by itself, so you usually don't have to do that. If you still want to, check out the driver-specific *README* file, which lists the options and their possible values for that driver.

The next section is `Monitor`, which specifies the characteristics of your monitor. As with other sections in the *xorg.conf* file, there may be more than one `Monitor` section. This is useful if you have multiple monitors connected to a system, or if you use the same *xorg.conf* file under multiple hardware configurations. In general, though, you will need only a single `Monitor` section:

```
Section "Monitor"
    Option      "CalcAlgorithm" "CheckDesktopGeometry"
    DisplaySize 320 240
    HorizSync   28-60
    Identifier  "Monitor[0]"
    ModelName   "THINKPAD 1400X1050 LCD PANEL"
    Option      "DPMS"
    VendorName  "IBM"
    VertRefresh 50-60
    UseModes    "Modes[0]"
EndSection
```

The `Identifier` line is used to give an arbitrary name to the `Monitor` entry. This can be any string; you will use it to refer to the `Monitor` entry later in the *xorg.conf* file.

`HorizSync` specifies the valid horizontal synchronization frequencies for your monitor in kHz. If you have a multisync monitor, this can be a range of values (or several comma-separated ranges), as seen in the `Monitor` section. If you have a fixed-frequency monitor, this will be a list of discrete values, such as the following:

```
HorizSync   31.5, 35.2, 37.9, 35.5, 48.95
```

Your monitor manual should list these values in the technical specifications section. If you do not have this information, you should contact either the manufacturer or the vendor of your monitor to obtain it. There are other sources of information, as well; they are listed later.

You should be careful with these settings. Although the settings `VertRefresh` and `HorizSync` (described next) help to make sure that your monitor will not be destroyed by wrong settings, you won't be very happy with your X setup if you get these values wrong. Unsteady pictures, flickering, or just plain snow can result.

`VertRefresh` specifies the valid vertical refresh rates (or vertical synchronization frequencies) for your monitor in Hz. Like `HorizSync`, this can be a range or a list of discrete values; your monitor manual should list them.

HorizSync and VertRefresh are used only to double-check that the monitor resolutions you specify are in valid ranges. This reduces the chance that you will damage your monitor by attempting to drive it at a frequency for which it wasn't designed.

You can use the ModeLine and Mode directive to specify resolution modes for your monitor. However, unlike earlier versions of X.org, this is not strictly necessary any longer; the Monitor section shown earlier (which comes from a laptop) doesn't have one. Instead, this information is moved into the following section, Modes.

The Modes section, of which there should be one for every monitor you have configured, lists the various video modes that the X server should support. An example:

```
Section "Modes"
  Identifier    "Modes[0]"
  Modeline      "800x600" 36.88 800 832 912 1024 600 601 604 621
  Modeline      "800x600" 40.00 800 840 968 1056 600 601 605 628 +HSync +VSync
  Modeline      "1400x1050" 109.01 1400 1480 1632 1864 1050 1051 1054 1083
  Modeline      "1280x1024" 98.60 1280 1352 1488 1696 1024 1025 1028 1057
  Modeline      "1280x960" 97.68 1280 1352 1488 1696 960 961 964 993
  Modeline      "1152x864" 78.82 1152 1216 1336 1520 864 865 868 894
  Modeline      "1024x768" 61.89 1024 1080 1184 1344 768 769 772 794
  Modeline      "800x600" 36.88 800 832 912 1024 600 601 604 621
  Modeline      "800x600" 40.00 800 840 968 1056 600 601 605 628 +HSync +VSync
  Modeline      "640x480" 23.06 640 656 720 800 480 481 484 497
  Modeline      "1400x1050" 109.01 1400 1480 1632 1864 1050 1051 1054 1083
EndSection
```

The Identifier line refers to a name specified in the Monitor section. The following Modeline lines each specify a video mode. The format of Modeline is:

```
Modeline name dot-clock horiz-values vert-values
```

name is an arbitrary string, which you will use to refer to the resolution mode later in the file. *dot-clock* is the driving clock frequency or *dot clock* associated with the resolution mode. A dot clock is usually specified in MHz and is the rate at which the video card must send pixels to the monitor at this resolution. *horiz-values* and *vert-values* are four numbers each; they specify when the electron gun of the monitor should fire and when the horizontal and vertical sync pulses fire during a sweep across the screen.

How can you determine the Modeline values for your monitor? That's difficult, especially since a lot of the documentation files that used to be shipped with X.org are no longer included, probably because they became outdated and haven't been updated yet. Your best bet is probably to use one of the configuration file generators mentioned in the previous section to get a set of start values and then tweaking these until you reach a satisfactory setting. For example, if while running X the image on the monitor shifts slightly or seems to flicker, tweak the values little by little to try to fix the image. Exactly what you need to adjust is difficult to say because it depends a lot on your actual graphics hardware, but with some experimenting, you usually get good results. Also, be sure to check the knobs and controls on the monitor itself! In many cases it is necessary to change the horizontal or vertical size of the display after starting up X in order for the image to be centered and of the appropriate size. Another option is to use the program *xvidtune* (see the manual page for how to use it), which can help you to get all the numbers for the Modeline, lets you try your changes, and even allows you to undo them if you did something wrong.

Also, X.org has the so-called VESA monitor timings built in, so you might get along without a Modes section altogether. The VESA timings are standard values for the Modeline that work on most display hardware, at the expense of not using the individual hardware to its fullest potential.

Note that the *name* argument to Modeline (in this case "800×600") is an arbitrary string; the convention is to name the mode after the resolution, but *name* can be anything that describes the mode to you.

For each Modeline used, the server checks that the specifications for the mode fall within the range of values specified with HorizSync and VertRefresh. If they do not, the server will complain when you attempt to start up X (more on this later).

You shouldn't insert monitor timing values or Modeline values for monitors other than the model you own. If you attempt to drive the monitor at a frequency for which it was not designed, you can damage or even destroy it.

The next section is Screen, which specifies the monitor/video card combination to use for a particular server:

```
Section "Screen"
  DefaultDepth 24
  SubSection "Display"
    Depth       15
    Modes       "800×600"
  EndSubSection
  SubSection "Display"
    Depth       16
    Modes       "1400×1050"
  EndSubSection
  SubSection "Display"
    Depth       24
    Modes       "1400×1050" "1280×1024" "1280×960" "1152×864" "1024×768"
                "800×600" "640×480"
  EndSubSection
  SubSection "Display"
    Depth       32
    Modes       "800×600"
  EndSubSection
  SubSection "Display"
    Depth       8
    Modes       "800×600"
  EndSubSection
  Device      "Device[0]"
  Identifier  "Screen[0]"
  Monitor     "Monitor[0]"
EndSection
```

This section ties together device, screen, and monitor definitions and lists the color depths to use with the video modes.

Finally, the `ServerLayout` section wraps things up by defining one actual configuration that consists of one or more `Screen` sections and one or more `InputDevice` sections. If you have a so-called multihead system (a system with more than one graphics board and one monitor attached to each, or one of those fancy multihead graphics boards to which you can connect multiple monitors), this section also specifies their relative layout. Here is an example:

```
Section "ServerLayout"
  Identifier   "Layout[all]"
  InputDevice  "Keyboard[0]" "CoreKeyboard"
  InputDevice  "Mouse[1]" "CorePointer"
  InputDevice  "Mouse[3]" "SendCoreEvents"
  Option       "Clone" "off"
  Option       "Xinerama" "off"
  Screen       "Screen[0]"
EndSection
```

Other sections also exist, but these are entirely optional and are not needed to get your X server up and running.

Running X

With your *xorg.conf* file configured, you're ready to fire up the X server and give it a spin. First, be sure that */usr/X11R6/bin* is on your path.

The command to start up X is:

```
startx
```

This is a frontend to `xinit` (in case you're used to using `xinit` on other Unix systems). You can still use `xinit`, which gives you precise control about what exactly is started but requires you to start all necessary programs manually.

This command starts the X server and runs the commands found in the file *.xinitrc* in your home directory. *.xinitrc* is just a shell script containing X clients to run. If this file does not exist, the system default */usr/X11R6/lib/X11/xinit/xinitrc* will be used. You can change the initial display when starting up the X Window System by providing a different *.xinitrc* in your home directory.

Running into Trouble

Often, something will not be quite right when you initially fire up the X server. This is almost always caused by a problem in your *xconf.org* file. Usually, the monitor timing values are off or the video card dot clocks are set incorrectly. If your display seems to roll or the edges are fuzzy, this is a clear indication that the monitor timing values or dot clocks are wrong. Also be sure you are correctly specifying your video card chipset, as well as other options for the Device section of *xconf.org*. These days, there is only one server binary, which loads the module needed for the graphics card in question. The module that loads depends on your Device settings.

If all else fails, try to start X "bare"; that is, use a command such as:

```
Xorg > /tmp/x.out 2>&1
```

You can then kill the X server (using the Ctrl-Alt-Backspace key combination) and examine the contents of */tmp/x.out*. The X server reports any warnings or errors—for example, if your video card doesn't have a dot clock corresponding to a mode supported by your monitor. This output can be very helpful in diagnosing all kinds of problems. Examine it closely if your X server does not start up at all, does not provide the resolutions you wanted, or shows a flaky, snowy, or otherwise insufficient picture. Even if everything works to your satisfaction, you might want to check this file for interesting information that the X server has found out about your hardware. The lines starting with (**) contain data that you provided yourself in the configuration file, whereas lines starting with (--) contain data that the X server has found out itself.

Remember that you can use Ctrl-Alt with the plus or minus keys on the numeric keypad to switch between the video modes listed on the Modes line of the Screen section of *xconf.org*. If the highest-resolution mode doesn't look right, try switching to lower resolutions. This lets you know, at least, that the configurations for those lower resolutions in your X configuration are working correctly.

Also, check the vertical and horizontal size/hold knobs on your monitor. In many cases it is necessary to adjust these when starting up X. For example, if the display seems to be shifted slightly to one side, you can usually correct this using the monitor controls.

The Usenet newsgroup *comp.windows.x.i386unix* is devoted to discussions about X.org. It might be a good idea to watch that newsgroup for postings relating to your video configuration: you might run across someone with the same problems as your own. If this fails, please contact your Linux distributor; their support staff should be able to help you as well.

Hopefully, X is now running for you. You might now want to go back to Chapter 3 and read about the desktop environments that run on top of it. Although it is still possible to run a quite bare-bones X installation with no desktop environment and just a few terminal windows open, this is hardly why you have gone through the trouble of installing X, and the desktop environments are so flexible these days that you can configure them completely to your taste.

X and 3D

Of course, Linux can display not only two-dimensional windows and structures in its graphical environment, but also three-dimensional graphics. There is a de facto standard for programming three-dimensional graphics, OpenGL, which originally came from big-iron Unix workstations, but which Linux supports just fine on inexpensive boards generally available for PCs. In this section, we look at how to set it up.

OpenGL Setup

As with many other subsystems of a free software operating system, Linux gives us a number of choices of OpenGL. Among those are Mesa, TinyGL, and YGL. The most prominent one, and the de facto standard for OpenGL on Linux, is Mesa.

GLX

OpenGL itself is platform neutral, so to "glue" OpenGL to a specific windowing system, an extension is required. For X11 this extension is called GLX. GLX contains X protocol extensions to allow OpenGL to be sent over the X socket to the X server. This is called *indirect rendering*. X.org has another option that is much faster, but works only on the local display. This option is called *direct rendering* and is explained in the following section.

DRI

X.org from Version 4 and up contains a framework for allowing direct access to the graphics hardware in a safe and efficient manner. This framework is called Direct Rendering Infrastructure (DRI), and accelerated OpenGL implementations sit on top of this framework. DRI consists of several components:

- A kernel module for multiplexing the graphics hardware so it can be used by multiple processes. This is called the Direct Rendering Manager (DRM), and the module is hardware specific. The modules are typically located in */lib/modules/2.x.y/kernel/drivers/char/drm*. The kernel will normally autoload the correct module when X is started.

- The 2D X.org driver. For each type of card there is a 2D driver in X.org that initializes the display, performs 2D drawing, and so forth. The drivers are typically located in */usr/X11R6/lib/modules/drivers/*.

- The 3D DRI driver. This component talks to the 3D part of the graphics card and effectively converts OpenGL commands to hardware commands. When using direct rendering, the DRI driver is loaded by *libGL.so* so the application can access the graphics card directly without going through X. The DRI drivers are normally located in */usr/X11R6/lib/modules/dri*.

- *libGL*, which is the OpenGL library that client applications must link to in order to use OpenGL. When using direct rendering, *libGL* loads the DRI driver and uses it directly, and when using indirect rendering (for example, if the X display is remote), it creates GLX commands that are sent to the X server over the regular X socket.

Proprietary drivers

Unfortunately, not all graphics hardware manufacturers want to publish information about how their hardware works. This is especially true for modern 3D accelerated hardware. But fortunately, the X.org XAA driver architecture is binary-compatible even across versions of operating systems (as long as the hardware architecture is the same), so installing a proprieratary binary-only driver is quite easy these days.

NVIDIA and ATI graphics cards are commonly found in PCs today. Newer versions of those cards are not supported by X.org/DRI for 3D hardware accelerated graphics, so we need to use the proprietary drivers published by the manufacturer.

The NVIDIA (*http://www.nvidia.com/*) driver doesn't seem to use DRI, but the overall design is quite similar. The driver comes as a ready-to-run installer-binary file that builds and installs a kernel module (which corresponds to the DRM driver in DRI) and then installs an X.org 2D XAA driver and replaces the *libGL* library on the system with an NVIDIA specific one. Notice that the kernel module comes with source code, but the other two components are binary only. For more details about how to install the NVIDIA driver, please read the information available on the company's web site.

ATI (*http://www.ati.com/*) also provides an accelerated 3D driver for its modern cards for Linux. Unlike NVIDIA's, this one actually uses the DRI framework. Except for that, they work in similar ways: kernel module with source available, binary-only X.org driver, binary-only DRI driver, and a replacement *libGL*.

Configuring X.org for OpenGL

With all the components of OpenGL and the related drivers in place, you can configure your system to use it.

Diagnosis. glxinfo is a valuable tool for setting up X.org for OpenGL. it gives information about the OpenGL capabilities of the current X11 display. Example output from glxinfo is as follows:

```
$ glxinfo|less
name of display: :0.0
display: :0  screen: 0
direct rendering: Yes
server glx vendor string: SGI

server glx version string: 1.2
```

```
server glx extensions:
GLX_ARB_multisample, ...
client glx vendor string: SGI
client glx version string: 1.4
client glx extensions:
GLX_ARB_get_proc_address, ...
GLX extensions:
GLX_ARB_get_proc_address, ...
OpenGL vendor string: Tungsten Graphics, Inc.
OpenGL renderer string: Mesa DRI Radeon 20030328 AGP 1x x86/MMX/SSE2 TCL
OpenGL version string: 1.2 Mesa 6.1
OpenGL extensions:
...
```

This listing shows that we are currently using direct rendering with a Mesa-based DRI driver for an ATI Radeon graphics card. If hardware acceleration was not set up properly or something did not work, it would say *direct rendering: No* instead.

Altering xorg.conf. To get started using DRI, a couple of lines need to be added to the *xorg.conf* file shown earlier in this chapter:

```
Section "Module"
...
# This loads the GLX module
Load       "glx"
# This loads the DRI module
Load       "dri"
EndSection
...
Section "DRI"
Mode 0666
EndSection
```

The *Load* statements take care of loading the modules required for OpenGL into the X server, and the *Mode* statement in the DRI section sets the file permission of the character special file that applications use to communicate with the DRM kernel driver. The special file is */dev/dri/cardN*. Setting the permissions to 0666 allows all users with access to the X display to use hardware-accelerated OpenGL.

Mesa

Mesa is a 3D graphics library with an API very similar to that of OpenGL. The core Mesa library is licensed according to the terms of the X.org copyright (an MIT-style license). Mesa is included with X.org together with the DRI framework, but if you want to use OpenGL on a platform not supported by DRI or want to get started with OpenGL programming, installing your own copy of Mesa can be a good idea—if not for anything else, then for getting the source code for the example programs.

Installing Mesa. If, for some reason, you want to compile Mesa yourself, it is a simple matter of downloading the latest MesaLib (along with MesaDemos) from *http://*

www.mesa3d.org/, unpacking it, and compiling it. The current version of Mesa does not use GNU autoconf; instead it comes with a `Makefile` that contains targets for a large number of operating systems and hardware combinations:

```
$ tar xfj MesaLib-6.2.1.tar.bz2
$ tar xfj MesaDemos-6.2.1.tar.bz2
$ cd Mesa-6.2.1
$ make                  Will write a list of supported build targets
$ make linux-x86        We choose Linux/x86
```

When the build is complete, run some of the demos to check that everything works:

```
$ cd lib
$ export LD_LIBRARY_PATH=$PWD:$LD_LIBRARY_PATH
$ cd ../progs/demos
$ ./gears
```

If the demo application worked, install Mesa like this:

```
$ cd ../../
$ cp -r include/GL /usr/local/mesa/include   Install header files
$ cp -d lib/* /usr/local/mesa/lib            Install libs
```

Hiding the headers and libraries away in */usr/local/mesa* allows you to easily switch between the system-provided OpenGL and Mesa by setting `LD_LIBRARY_PATH` to include or exclude */usr/local/mesa/lib*.

## CHAPTER 17

System Start and Shutdown

Booting the System

There are several ways of booting Linux on your system. The most common methods involve booting from the hard drive or using a boot floppy. In many cases, the installation procedure will have configured one or both of these for you; in any case, it's important to understand how to configure booting for yourself.

Using a Boot Floppy

Traditionally, a Linux boot floppy simply contains a kernel image, which is loaded into memory when you insert the floppy and start the system.[*]

Many Linux distributions create a boot floppy for you in this way when installing the system. Using a boot floppy is an easy way to boot Linux if you don't want to bother booting from the hard drive. (For example, Windows NT/2000/XP's boot manager is somewhat difficult to configure for booting Linux. We talk about this in the next section.) Once the kernel has booted from the floppy, you are free to use the floppy drive for other purposes.

We include some technical information here in order to explain the boot process, but rest assured that in most cases, you can just insert the floppy disk, and booting works. Reading the following paragraphs will help you understand your system, though.

The kernel image is usually compressed, using the same algorithm as the *gzip* or the `bzip2` compression programs (more on this in "Compiling the kernel" in Chapter 18). Compression allows the kernel, which may be several megabytes or more in size, to require only a few hundred kilobytes of disk space. Part of the kernel

---

[*] A Linux boot floppy may instead contain a GRUB boot record, which causes the system to boot a kernel from the hard drive. We discuss this in the next section, when we talk more about GRUB.

code is not compressed: this part contains the routines necessary to uncompress the kernel from the disk image and load it into memory. Therefore, the kernel actually bootstraps itself at boot time by uncompressing into memory.

A number of parameters are stored in the kernel image. Among these parameters is the name of the device to use as the root filesystem once the kernel boots. Another parameter is the text mode to use for the system console. All these parameters may be modified using the rdev command, which we discuss later in this section.

After the kernel has started, it attempts to mount a filesystem on the root device hardcoded in the kernel image itself. This will serve as the root filesystem—that is, the filesystem on /. "Managing Filesystems" in Chapter 10 discusses filesystems in more detail; all that you need to know for now is that the kernel image must contain the name of your root filesystem device. If the kernel can't mount a filesystem on this device, it gives up, issuing a kernel "panic" message. (Essentially, a *kernel panic* is a fatal error signaled by the kernel itself. A panic will occur whenever the kernel is terminally confused and can't continue with execution. For example, if there is a bug in the kernel itself, a panic might occur when it attempts to access memory that doesn't exist. We'll talk about kernel panics more in the section "What to Do in an Emergency" in Chapter 27.)

The root device stored in the kernel image is that of your root filesystem on the hard drive. This means that once the kernel boots, it mounts a hard drive partition as the root filesystem, and all control transfers to the hard drive. Once the kernel is loaded into memory, it stays there—the boot floppy need not be accessed again (until you reboot the system, of course).

Given a reasonably small kernel image, you can create your own boot floppy. On many Linux systems, the kernel itself is stored in the file */boot/vmlinuz*.[*] This is not a universal convention, however; other Linux systems store the kernel in */vmlinuz* or */vmlinux*, and still others in a file such as */Image*. (If you have multiple kernel images, you can use GRUB to select which one to boot. See the next section.) Note that newly installed Linux systems may not have a kernel image on the hard drive if a boot floppy was created for you. In any case, you can build your own kernel. It's often a good idea to do this anyway: you can customize the kernel to include only those drivers for your particular hardware. See "Building the Kernel" in Chapter 18 for details.

---

[*] Why the silly filename? On many Unix systems, the kernel is stored in a file named */vmunix* where *vm* stands for "virtual memory." Naturally, Linux has to be different and names its kernel images *vmlinux*, and places them in the directory */boot* to get them out of the root directory. The name *vmlinuz* was adopted to differentiate compressed kernel images from uncompressed images. Actually, the name and location of the kernel don't matter a bit, as long as you either have a boot floppy containing a kernel, or GRUB knows how to find the kernel image.

All right. Let's say that you have a kernel image in the file *boot/vmlinuz*. To create a boot floppy, the first step is to use *rdev* to set the root device to that of your Linux root filesystem. (If you built the kernel yourself, this should be already set to the correct value, but it can't hurt to check with *rdev*.) We discussed how to create the root device in "Editing /etc/fstab" in Chapter 2.

As *root*, use *rdev -h* to print a usage message. As you will see, there are many supported options, allowing you to specify the root device (our task here), the swap device, ramdisk size, and so on. For the most part, you needn't concern yourself with these options now.

If we use the command *rdev /boot/vmlinuz*, the root device encoded in the kernel found in *boot/vmlinuz* will be printed:

```
courgette:/# rdev /boot/vmlinuz
Root device /dev/hda1
```

If this is incorrect, and the Linux root filesystem is actually on *dev/hda3*, we should use the following command:

```
courgette:/# rdev /boot/vmlinuz /dev/hda3
courgette:/#
```

rdev is the strong, silent type; nothing is printed when you set the root device, so run *rdev /boot/vmlinuz* again to check that it is set correctly.

Now you're ready to create the boot floppy. For best results, use a brand-new, formatted floppy. You can format the floppy under Windows or using `fdformat` under Linux; this will lay down the sector and track information so that the system can autodetect the size of the floppy. (See the section "Managing Filesystems" in Chapter 10 for more on using floppies.)

To create the boot floppy, use *dd* to copy the kernel image to it, as in the following example:

```
courgette:/# dd if=/boot/vmlinuz of=/dev/fd0 bs=8192
```

If you're interested in *dd*, the manual page will be illustrative; in brief, this copies the input file (`if` option) named *boot/vmlinuz* to the output file (`of` option) named *dev/fd0* (the first floppy device), using a block size (`bs`) of 8192 bytes. Of course, the plebian `cp` can be used as well, but we Unix sysadmins love to use cryptic commands to complete relatively simple tasks. That's what separates us from mortal users.

Your boot floppy should now be ready to go. You can shut down the system (see "Shutting Down the System" later in this chapter) and boot with the floppy, and if all goes well, your Linux system should boot as it usually does. It might be a good idea to make an extra boot floppy as a spare. In "What to Do in an Emergency," in Chapter 27, we describe methods by which boot floppies can be used to recover from disaster.

Using GRUB

GRUB is a general-purpose boot manager that can boot whatever operating systems you have installed on your machine, including Linux. There are dozens of ways to configure GRUB. Here, we discuss the two most common methods: installing GRUB on the master boot record of your hard drive and installing GRUB as a secondary bootloader for Linux only.

GRUB is the most common way to boot Linux from the hard drive. (By the expression "boot from the hard drive," we mean that the kernel itself is stored on the hard drive and no boot floppy is required, but remember that even when you use a boot floppy, control is transferred to the hard drive once the kernel is loaded into memory.) If GRUB is installed on your drive's master boot record, or MBR, it is the first code to run when the hard drive is booted. GRUB can then boot other operating systems—such as Linux or Windows—and allow you to select between them at boot time.

 It should be mentioned here that GRUB is not the only boot manager available for booting Linux. There are alternatives, such as the older LILO (Linux Loader) that work just as well. However, because most distributions these days use GRUB, this is what we cover here.

Windows NT and later versions of Windows have boot managers of their own that occupy the MBR. If you are using one of these systems, in order to boot Linux from the hard drive, you may have to install GRUB as the "secondary" bootloader for Linux only. In this case, GRUB is installed on the boot record for just your Linux root partition, and the boot manager software (for Windows NT/2000) takes care of executing GRUB from there when you wish to boot Linux.

As we'll see, however, the Windows NT/2000/XP boot managers are somewhat uncooperative when it comes to booting GRUB. This is a poor design decision, and if you must absolutely use one of these boot managers, it might be easier to boot Linux from floppy instead. Read on. Or, if you really want to go with Linux all the way, you can use GRUB to boot Windows NT/2000/XP and dump the Windows boot managers completely. That is usually a fairly painless way, and the one we recommend. It is also what most distributions install automatically if you try to install Linux on a computer with an existing Windows installation.

Use of GRUB with Windows 95/98/ME/2000/XP is quite simple. You just configure GRUB to boot Windows 95/98/ME/2000/XP (see the next section). However, if you install Windows 95/98/ME/2000/XP after installing GRUB, you need to reinstall GRUB (as the Windows 95/98/ME/2000/XP installation procedure overwrites the MBR of your primary hard drive). Just be sure you have a Linux boot floppy on hand so that you can boot Linux and rerun GRUB.

Before proceeding you should note that a number of Linux distributions are capable of configuring and installing GRUB when you first install the Linux software. It might be a good idea to just let your distribution's installation program do its thing, install GRUB, and then check what it has done; this gives you something working to start with that you can then tweak to your taste.

The /etc/grub.conf file

The first step in configuring GRUB is to set up the GRUB configuration file, which is often stored in */etc/grub.conf*. The */etc/grub.conf* file references other configuration files that we look at later. Often, the */etc/grub.conf* file can be very short.

We are going to look at a sample *grub.conf* file. You can use this file as a base for your own *grub.conf* and edit it for your own system.

It should be said at this point that GRUB is very flexible and can actually drop you into a shell that lets you enter GRUB commands interactively during the boot process. However, most users would find this both tedious and error-prone, which is why we describe another use here, which will provide you with a convenient menu that you can select from (for example, in order to boot different kernels or even different operating systems). With this setup, the *grub.conf* file can be quite concise. Here is an example:

```
root (hd0,0)
install --stage2=/boot/grub/stage2 /grub/stage1 (hd0) /grub/stage2 0x8000
    (hd0,0)/grub/menu.lst
quit
```

The first line specifies the drive to boot from. In this case, it is the first partition on the first hard disk—hd is for hard disk, the first zero is for the first hard disk in the system, and the second zero for the first partition on that particular hard disk (GRUB always starts counting at zero!). It is quite common among Linux users to reserve a small partition (often mounted as */boot*) for the kernel image and booting-related files. Because there have been limits in the past regarding the parts of the disk from which bootloaders could load kernel images, it has become customary to make this partition the very first one. Although these limits are mostly gone with modern hardware, modern BIOSes, and modern bootloaders, this tradition prevails, and it definitely does not hurt to keep it.

A few more examples: (fd0) would mean to boot from the first floppy disk in the system, and (hd3,4) would mean the fifth partition on the fourth hard drive (of one lucky Linux user who apparently can afford lots of hardware). There is also the special name (nd) which is used for booting the kernel image from the network, something that is beyond the scope of this book.

The second line is fairly complex. It would go too far to dissect the complete booting process, but we can at least say that GRUB uses a two-stage booting process, and this command specifies where to get the instructions for the two stages from, at which address to load them into the computer's memory, and what to do then. The "what to do then" part is the most interesting for us; in the example configuration file, it is the (hd0,0)/grub/menu.lst part at the end. Where should this file be located so that GRUB can find it? If you try:

```
pooh:~ # ls /grub/menu.lst
/bin/ls: /grub/menu.lst: No such file or directory
```

you will not find it. But remember that GRUB uses the parentheses to denote a device, in our case a hard disk partition, the first partition on the first hard drive. This could be anywhere, of course, but if you remember that most systems create a small partition that does not contain much except the kernel image and the boot-loader files, and that it is often mounted as *boot*, you can try:

```
pooh:~ # ls /boot/grub/menu.lst
/boot/grub/menu.lst
```

Aha! Of course, if you are installing GRUB from scratch on your system and, unlike us, do not have a preinstalled configuration that you are just fiddling around with, then you will not get a result here either. Rest assured, however, that this is where GRUB will search for the menu file.

What would such a menu file look like? Here is an example of a version that loads two different Linux configurations and MS-Windows, all presented in a convenient menu:

```
default 0
timeout 10

title Linux
    kernel (hd0,5)/boot/vmlinuz root=/dev/hda6 vga=0x314

title Linux Failsafe
    kernel (hd0,5)/boot/vmlinuz root=/dev/hda6 ide=nodma apm=off acpi=off vga=normal
noresume barrier=off nosmp noapic maxcpus=0 3

title Windows
    root (hd0,0)
    chainloader +1
```

The first two lines together mean that when the boot menu is presented by GRUB, the user has 10 seconds (timeout) to make a choice; otherwise, the first entry of the following list will be booted.

After these two initial lines, there are three sections that each start with title. After the title, a string is specified that will be shown in the boot menu at boot time. For the two Linux configurations, there is then a kernel line that shows where the kernel image is loaded from. Everything else is passed directly to the kernel as boot parameters, including what the root device should be, and the terminal mode (vga=0x314). In the so-called failsafe configuration, we specify a lot of kernel parameters that turn off just about any kernel functionality that has the slightest chance of going wrong. Such a system will be slow and not have complete functionality, but if you have misconfigured something, the failsafe kernel may still get along and let you at least boot the system so that you can repair things.

If you type in those commands manually at the GRUB shell, you would have ended with the command boot. The kernel command loads the kernel into memory, but does not actually boot it; the boot command performs the actual booting process. However, if you use the GRUB menu system as we do here, the boot command is implicit and can be left out at the end of each section.

Loading Windows works differently. GRUB is not able to load operating systems other than Linux, the BSD family, and a few others directly. For those other systems, such as Windows, it invokes instead the bootloader that comes with those systems. This is called *chain-loading*, and the GRUB command to do this is not surprisingly called chainloader. The +1 means that GRUB can find the bootloader on the partition specified with the previous *root* command, one sector into the partition.

When you are satisfied with your GRUB setup, you still need to install it. This is best done with the command *grub-install*, which expects to be told the directory in which the stage files and kernel images can be found, and on which device to install the bootloader. This could look like this:

```
pooh:~ # grub-install --root-directory=/boot /dev/hda
```

This installs the bootloader on the first IDE hard drive (/dev/hda), which is typically the one that the computer's BIOS searches for finding the initial booting information.

This was just a short introduction into the world of GRUB. GRUB can do a lot more, such as booting kernel images from the network or over a serial line, providing fancy graphics, and so on. If you plan to do any serious work with GRUB (and since a bootloader is crucial for being able to use the system at all, any changes of configuration files beyond trivial things such as changing the strings of the menu entries, the default entry, or the timeout, can be considered serious in this context), we urge you to read the excellent GRUB documentation that comes as *Info* files, and that you can read nicely in KDE by typing info:grub in Konqueror's location bar.

Specifying boot-time options

When you first installed Linux, more than likely you booted either from a floppy or a CD-ROM, which very likely gave you a GRUB (or other bootloader) boot menu. Selecting an entry and typing e gets you a boot prompt. At this prompt you can enter several boot-time options, such as:

```
hd=cylinders,heads,sectors
```

to specify the hard drive geometry. Each time you boot Linux, it may be necessary to specify these parameters in order for your hardware to be detected correctly. If you are using GRUB to boot Linux from the hard drive, you can specify these parameters in the kernel line in the GRUB configuration file instead of entering them at the boot prompt each time. To the Linux entry, just add a line such as:

```
append = "hd=683,16,38"
```

This causes the system to behave as though hd=683,16,38 were entered at the GRUB boot prompt. If you wish to specify multiple boot options, you can do so with a single append line, as in:

```
append = "hd=683,16,38 hd=64,32,202"
```

In this case, we specify the geometry for the first and second hard drives, respectively. Once you are done with your changes at the boot prompt, press the Esc key to go back to the boot menu, and boot from there.

Note that you need to use such boot options only if the kernel doesn't detect your hardware at boot time, which is unlikely unless you have very old or very uncommon hardware. You should already know if this is necessary, based on your experiences with installing Linux; in general, you should have to specify kernel parameters in the kernel lines in the GRUB menu file only if you had to specify these boot options when first booting the Linux installation media.

There are a number of other boot-time options. Most of them deal with hardware detection, which has already been discussed in Chapter 2. However, the following additional options may also be useful to you:

single
: Boot the system in single-user mode; skip all the system configuration and start a root shell on the console. See "What to Do in an Emergency" in Chapter 27 for hints on using this.

root= *partition*
: Mounts the named *partition* as the Linux root filesystem.

ro
: Mounts the root filesystem as read-only. This is usually done in order to run fsck; see "Checking and Repairing Filesystems" in Chapter 10.

ramdisk= *size*
: Specifies a size, in bytes, for the ramdisk device. Most users need not worry about using the ramdisk; it's useful primarily for installation.

vga= *mode*
: Sets the VGA display mode. Valid modes are normal, extended, ask, or an integer.

mem= *size*
: Tells the kernel how much RAM you have. If you have 64 MB or less, the kernel can get this information from the BIOS, but if you use an older kernel and you have more, you will have to tell the kernel the exact amount, or it will use only the first 64 MB. For example, if you have 128 MB, specify mem=128m. Fortunately, this is no longer necessary with newer kernels.

Any of these options can be entered by hand at the GRUB boot prompt or specified in the kernel line in the GRUB configuration file.

Removing GRUB

If you have GRUB installed on your MBR, the easiest way to remove it on Windows 95/98/ME is to use Windows *FDISK*. The command:

```
FDISK /MBR
```

runs *FDISK* and overwrites the MBR with a valid Windows boot record. On Windows NT/2000/XP, the procedure is a lot more involved.

System Startup and Initialization

In this section, we talk about exactly what happens when the system boots. Understanding this process and the files involved is important for performing various kinds of system configuration.

Kernel Boot Messages

The first step is booting the kernel. As described in the previous section, this can be done from floppy or hard drive. As the kernel loads into memory, it will print messages to the system console, but usually also saves them in the system logfiles as well. As *root*, you can always check the file */var/log/messages* (which contains kernel messages emitted during runtime as well). The command *dmesg* prints out the last lines of the kernel message ring buffer; directly after booting, naturally, you will get the boot messages.

The following few paragraphs go through a couple of the more interesting messages and explain what they mean. These messages are all printed by the kernel itself, as each device driver is initialized. The exact messages printed depend on what drivers are compiled into your kernel and what hardware you have on your system. You are likely to have more, fewer, or different messages; we'll concentrate here on the messages that are quite common.

The line:

```
Linux version 2.6.11.4-21.7-default (geeko@buildhost) (gcc version 3.3.5 2005011
7 (prerelease) (SUSE Linux)) #1 Thu Jun 2 14:23:14 UTC 2005
```

tells you the version number of the kernel, on which machine, when, and with which compiler it was built.

Next, the kernel reports a number of things about the BIOS, the amount of memory found, power management settings, and so one. Here are some of the more interesting lines (of course, depending on your hardware and setup, these may look different for you):

```
...
127MB HIGHMEM available.
896MB LOWMEM available.
...
Kernel command line: root=/dev/hda6 vga=0x314 selinux=0 splash=silent resume=/de
v/hda5
...
Detected 599.481 MHz processor.
...
```

Notice in particular the kernel command line; you can double-check here that you are actually booting the configuration that you think you are booting.

Then, the kernel tells us which console settings it has picked and which console type it has detected:

```
Console: colour dummy device 80x25
```

Note that this involves only the text mode being used by the kernel, not the capabilities of your video card. It also has nothing to do with the X Window System; the kernel is not concerned with that at all.

You'll then see the "BogoMIPS" calculation for your processor:

```
Calibrating delay loop... 1187.84 BogoMIPS (lpj=593920)
```

This is an utterly bogus (hence the name) measurement of processor speed, which is used to obtain optimal performance in delay loops for several device drivers.

The kernel gathers information about the PCI bus and checks for any PCI cards present in the system:

```
PCI: PCI BIOS revision 2.10 entry at 0xfd8d6, last bus=8
PCI: Using configuration type 1
...
PCI: Probing PCI hardware (bus 00)
PCI: Ignoring BAR0-3 of IDE controller 0000:00:1f.1
PCI: Transparent bridge - 0000:00:1e.0
...
```

Linux then sets up networking, the mouse port, and the serial driver. A line such as:

```
ttyS00 at 0x03f8 (irq = 4) is a NS16550A
```

means that the first serial device (*/dev/ttyS00*, or COM1) was detected at address 0x03f8, IRQ 4, using 16550A UART functions. Next comes some more hardware detection, such as the real-time clock and the floppy drive:

```
Real Time Clock Driver v1.12
...
Floppy drive(s): fd0 is 1.44M
FDC 0 is a National Semiconductor PC87306
loop: loaded (max 8 devices)
...
```

The line:

```
Adding 1029632k swap on /dev/hda5.  Priority:42 extents:1
```

tells you how much swap space the kernel has found. Among the further tasks performed during a typical boot are finding and configuring a parallel port (lp1), detecting and configuring the network card, and finally setting up the USB subsystem.

Again, depending on the kernel version and your configuration and hardware, you will see other messages (this was just an excerpt, after all).

init, inittab, and rc Files

Once the device drivers are initialized, the kernel executes the program *init*, which is found in */etc*, */bin*, or */sbin* (it's */sbin/init* on most systems). init is a general-purpose program that spawns new processes and restarts certain programs when they exit. For example, each virtual console has a *getty* process running on it, started by init. Upon login, the *getty* process is replaced with another. After logging out, *init* starts a new *getty* process, allowing you to log in again.

init is also responsible for running a number of programs and scripts when the system boots. Everything *init* does is controlled by the file */etc/inittab*. To understand this file, you need to understand the concept of *runlevels* first.

A runlevel is a number or letter that specifies the current system state, as far as init is concerned. For example, when the system runlevel is changed to 3, all entries in */etc/inittab* containing 3 in the column specifying the runlevels will be executed. Runlevels are a useful way to group entries in */etc/inittab* together. For example, you might want to say that runlevel 1 executes only the bare minimum of configuration scripts, runlevel 2 executes everything in runlevel 1 plus networking configuration, runlevel 3 executes everything in levels 1 and 2 plus dial-in login access, and so on. Today, the Red Hat and SUSE distributions are set up so that runlevel 5 automatically starts the X Window System graphical interface. Debian does so at runlevels 2 through 5—provided you have installed an X display manager such as xdm.

For the most part, you don't need to concern yourself with runlevels. When the system boots, it enters the default runlevel (set in */etc/inittab*, as we will soon show). On most systems, this default is runlevel 3 or 5. After we discuss normal booting, we'll show you how to enter another runlevel that you will sometimes need to use—runlevel 1, or single-user mode. Debian users may want to investigate the *file-rc* package, which lets you configure runlevels in a single file.

Let's take a look at a sample */etc/inittab* file:

```
# Set the default runlevel to three
id:3:initdefault:

# First script to be executed
si::bootwait:/etc/init.d/boot
```

```
# Run /etc/init.d/rc with the runlevel as an argument
l0:0:wait:/etc/init.d/rc 0
l1:1:wait:/etc/init.d/rc 1
l2:2:wait:/etc/init.d/rc 2
l3:3:wait:/etc/init.d/rc 3
l4:4:wait:/etc/init.d/rc 4
l5:5:wait:/etc/init.d/rc 5
l6:6:wait:/etc/init.d/rc 6

# Executed when we press ctrl-alt-delete
ca::ctrlaltdel:/sbin/shutdown -t3 -rf now

# Start agetty for virtual consoles 1 through 6
1:2345:respawn:/sbin/mingetty --noclear tty1
2:2345:respawn:/sbin/mingetty tty2
3:2345:respawn:/sbin/mingetty tty3
4:2345:respawn:/sbin/mingetty tty4
5:2345:respawn:/sbin/mingetty tty5
6:2345:respawn:/sbin/mingetty tty6
```

Fields are separated by colons. The last field is the most recognizable: it is the command that init executes for this entry. The first field is an arbitrary identifier (it doesn't matter what it is as long as it's unique in the file), and the second indicates what runlevels cause the command to be invoked. The third field tells init how to handle this entry; for example, whether to execute the given command once or to respawn the command whenever it exits.

The exact contents of */etc/inittab* depend on your system and the distribution of Linux you have installed.

In our sample file, we see first that the default runlevel is set to 3. The action field for this entry is initdefault, which causes the given runlevel to be set to the default. That's the runlevel normally used whenever the system boots. You can override the default with any level you want by running *init* manually (which you might do when debugging your configuration) and passing in the desired runlevel as an argument. For instance, the following command shuts down all services that belong to the current runlevel, but not to runlevel 5 (warn all your users before doing this!):

```
tigger# init 5
```

GRUB can also boot in single-user mode (usually runlevel 1)—see "Specifying boot-time options," earlier in this chapter.

The next entry tells *init* to execute the script */etc/init.d/boot* when the system boots. (The action field is si [sysinit], which specifies that this entry should be executed when init is first started at system boot.) On other distributions, this file might be elsewhere, but */etc/init.d/boot* is where it belongs according to the Linux Filesystem Hierarchy Standard (FHS). The file is simply a shell script containing commands to handle basic system initialization; for example, swapping is enabled, filesystems are checked and mounted, and the system clock is synchronized with the CMOS clock.

Many of the commands in this file are discussed in "Managing Filesystems" and "Managing Swap Space" in Chapter 10.

Next, we see that the system executes the script */etc/init.d/rc* when it enters any of the runlevels through 6, with the appropriate runlevel as an argument. *rc* is a generic startup script that executes other scripts as appropriate for that runlevel. The action field here is `wait`, which tells *init* to execute the given `command` and to wait for it to complete execution before doing anything else.

rc Files

Linux stores startup commands in files with *rc* in the name, using an old Unix convention. The commands do all the things necessary to have a fully functioning system, such as starting the servers or daemons mentioned in "Processes" in Chapter 10. Thanks to these commands, the system comes up ready with logging facilities, mail, a web server, or whatever you installed and asked it to run. As explained in the previous section, the files are invoked from */etc/inittab*. The commands are standard shell commands, and you can simply read the various *rc* files to see what they do.

In this section, we describe the structure of the *rc* files so that you can understand where everything starts, and so that you can start or stop servers manually in the rare case that they don't do what you want them to do. We use SUSE as our model, but once you get the idea of what to look for, you can find the corresponding files on any Linux distribution. SUSE is pretty good at sticking with the FHS, so other distributions are likely to look fairly similar, or at least will converge to look fairly similar. The Linux FHS is a distribution-neutral initiative to define standard directory names and filenames for important system files. Any Linux distribution that wants to be a good Linux citizen should follow this standard. Debian is another example of a distribution that does so. On Red Hat, the top-level *rc* script is */etc/rc.d/rc*.

In the previous section, you saw how */etc/inittab* invokes the script under a variety of circumstances with different numbers from 0 to 6 as arguments. The numbers correspond to runlevels, and each one causes the *rc* files to invoke a different set of scripts. So our next step is to find the scripts corresponding to each runlevel.

According to the FHS, scripts for each runlevel are stored in the directory */etc/init.d/rcN.d*, where *N* is the runlevel being started. Thus, for runlevel 3, scripts in */etc/rc.d/rc3.d* would be used. Again, slightly different conventions are the rule in other distributions.

Take a look in one of those directories; you will see a number of filenames of the form *Snnxxxx* or *Knnxxxx* where *nn* is a number from 00 to 99, and *xxxx* is the name of some system service. The scripts whose names begin with *K* are executed by */etc/rc.d/rc* first to kill any existing services, and then the scripts whose names begin with *S* are executed to start new services.

The numbers *nn* in the names are used to enforce an ordering on the scripts as they are executed: scripts with lower numbers are executed before those with higher numbers. The name *xxxx* is simply used to help you identify to which system service the script corresponds. This naming convention might seem odd, but it makes it easy to add or remove scripts from these directories and have them automatically executed at the appropriate time by */etc/rc.d/rc*. For customizing startup scripts, you'll find it convenient to use a graphical runlevel editor, such as *KSysV* in KDE (discussed later in this chapter). Some distributions also include a graphical runlevel editor as part of their administration tool.

For example, the script to initialize networking might be called *S10network*, while the script to stop the system logging daemon might be called *K70syslog*. If these files are placed in the appropriate */etc/init.d/rcN.d* directories, */etc/init.d/rc* will run them, in numerical order, at system startup or shutdown time. If the default runlevel of your system is 3, look in */etc/init.d/rc3.d* to see which scripts are executed when the system boots normally.

Because the same services are started or stopped at different runlevels, the SUSE distribution uses symbolic links instead of repeating the same script in multiple places. Thus, each *S* or *K* file is a symbolic link that points to a central directory that stores startup or shutdown scripts for all services, typically */etc/init.d*. On Debian and SUSE, the directory contains a script called *skeleton* that you can adapt to start and stop any new daemons you might write.

Knowing the location of a startup or shutdown script is useful in case you don't want to completely reboot or enter a different runlevel, but need to start or stop a particular service. Look in the *init.d* directory for a script of the appropriate name and execute it, passing the parameter start or stop. For example, on SUSE, if you want the Apache web server to be running but your system is in a runlevel that does not include Apache, just enter the following:

```
tiger# /sbin/init.d/apache start
```

Many distributions are set up such that the script */etc/init.d/boot.local* is executed at the end of the boot process. You can edit this file to accomplish any peculiar or otherwise out-of-place system commands at boot time, or if you're not sure where else they should be executed. For shutting down, there is often the equivalent */etc/init.d/halt.local*.

The next entry, labeled ca, is executed when the key combination Ctrl-Alt-Delete is pressed on the console. This key combination produces an interrupt that usually reboots the system. Under Linux, this interrupt is caught and sent to init, which executes the entry with the action field of ctrlaltdel. The command shown here, /sbin/shutdown -t3 -rf now, will do a "safe" reboot of the system. (See "Shutting Down the System," later in this chapter.) This way we protect the system from sudden reboot when Ctrl-Alt-Delete is pressed.

Finally, the *inittab* file includes entries that execute */sbin/mingetty* for the first six virtual consoles. *mingetty* is one of the several *getty* variants available for Linux. These programs permit logins on terminals; without them the terminal would be effectively dead and would not respond when a user walked up and pressed a key or mouse button. The various *getty* commands open a terminal device (such as a virtual console or a serial line), set various parameters for the terminal driver, and execute */bin/login* to initiate a login session on that terminal. Therefore, to allow logins on a given virtual console, you must be running *getty* or *mingetty* on it. *mingetty* is the version used on a number of Linux systems, but others use *getty* or *agetty*, which have a slightly different syntax. See the manual pages for *getty*, *mingetty*, and *agetty* on your system.

mingetty takes one argument, a device name. The port names for Linux virtual consoles are */dev/tty1*, */dev/tty2*, and so forth. *mingetty* assumes the given device name is relative to */dev*. The baud rate for virtual consoles should generally be 38,400, which is why *mingetty*, unlike, for example, *agetty*, defaults to this value and does not require it to be explicitly specified.

Note that the action field for each *mingetty* entry is respawn. This means that init should restart the command given in the entry when the *mingetty* process dies, which is every time a user logs out.

Single-User Mode

Most of the time, you operate the system in multiuser mode so that users can log in. But there is a special state called *single-user mode* in which Unix is running but there is no login prompt. When you're in single-user mode, you're basically the superuser (*root*). You may have to enter this mode during installation if something goes wrong. Single-user mode is important for certain routine system administration tasks, such as checking corrupted filesystems. (This is not fun; try not to corrupt your filesystem. For instance, always shut down the system through a *shutdown* command before you turn off the power. This is described in the next section.)

Under single-user mode, the system is nearly useless; very little configuration is done, filesystems are unmounted, and so on. This is necessary for recovering from certain kinds of system problems; see "What to Do in an Emergency" in Chapter 27 for details.

Note that Unix is still a multiprocessing system, even in single-user mode. You can run multiple programs at once. Servers can run in the background so that special functions, such as the network, can operate. But if your system supports more than one terminal, only the console can be used. And the X Window System cannot run.

Shutting Down the System

Fortunately, shutting down the Linux system is much simpler than booting and startup. However, it's not just a matter of hitting the reset switch. Linux, like all Unix systems, buffers disk reads and writes in memory. This means disk writes are delayed until absolutely necessary, and multiple reads on the same disk block are served directly from RAM. This greatly increases performance, because disks are extremely slow relative to the CPU.

The problem is that if the system were to be suddenly powered down or rebooted, the buffers in memory would not be written to disk, and data could be lost or corrupted. The kernel flushes dirty buffers (ones that have been changed since they were read from the disk) back to disk every five seconds or so (depending on configuration) to prevent serious damage from occurring should the system crash. However, to be completely safe, the system needs to undergo a "safe" shutdown before rebooting. This will not only ensure that disk buffers are properly synchronized, but also allow all running processes to exit cleanly.

shutdown is the general, all-purpose command used to halt or reboot the system. As *root*, you can issue the command:

```
/sbin/shutdown -r +10
```

to cause the system to reboot in 10 minutes. The -r switch indicates the system should be rebooted after shutdown, and +10 is the amount of time to wait (in minutes) until shutting down. The system will print a warning message to all active terminals, counting down until the shutdown time. You can add your own warning message by including it on the command line, as in the following example:

```
/sbin/shutdown -r +10 "Rebooting to try new kernel"
```

You can also specify an absolute time to shutdown, as in:

```
/sbin/shutdown -r 13:00
```

to reboot at 1:00 p.m. Likewise, you can say:

```
/sbin/shutdown -r now
```

to reboot immediately (after the safe shutdown process).

Using the *-h* switch instead of *-r* will cause the system to simply be halted after shutdown; you can then turn off the system power without fear of losing data. If you specify neither *-h* nor *-r*, the system will go into single-user mode.

As we saw in "init, inittab, and rc Files," you can have init catch the Ctrl-Alt-Delete key sequence and execute a *shutdown* command in response to it. If you're used to rebooting your system in this way it might be a good idea to check that your */etc/inittab* file contains a ctrlaltdel entry. Note that you should never reboot your Linux system by pressing the system power switch or the reboot switch on the front panel of your machine. Unless the system is flat-out hung (a rare occurrence), you should always use *shutdown*. The great thing about a multiprocessing system is that one program may hang, but you can almost always switch to another window or virtual console to recover.

shutdown provides a number of other options. The *-c* switch will cancel a currently running shutdown. (Of course, you can kill the process by hand using *kill*, but *shutdown -c* might be easier.) The *-k* switch will print the warning messages but not actually shut down the system. See the manual page for shutdown(8) if you're interested in the gory details.

A Graphical Runlevel Editor: KSysV

If you think that editing runlevels by copying symbolic links around is too arcane and error-prone, you may want to try a graphical runlevel editor. Your distribution most likely ships one, but if you have installed the KDE Desktop Environment, you probably have KSysV anyway.* You can start this program either from the K menu (as System → Service Configuration → KSysV in KDE's normal distribution) or by invoking ksysv on any command line.

If you are starting KSysV for the first time, it will ask you a few questions about your distribution so that it can determine the right location of your runlevel configuration files. Then it will show its main screen, as seen in Figure 17-1.

To the left, you can see the list of available services, and to the right of it are two lines of boxes; the upper line for entering runlevels, the lower line for leaving them. For each runlevel, one box per line is shown (unless you turn some runlevels off using the checkboxes in the status bar, which can be helpful if you only want to work on a few runlevels).

To add a service to a runlevel, simply use the mouse to drag the service name from the left to the box on the right. Don't forget to do this for both the *Start* and the *Stop* box. To remove an entry from a box, grab it and drag it to the waste bin in the lower-left corner. You can also click any entry in the runlevel boxes to configure it or to manually stop, start, or restart it immediately.

When you are done, use the menu entry File → Save Configuration to save your work. This will only be allowed, however, if you have started KSysV as *root*, as you will otherwise not have write access to the runlevel configuration files. But if you start KSysV from within KDE, it will ask you to supply the *root* password anyway and switch to superuser mode.

---

* The name comes from the fact that the current Linux booting system, as was described in the previous sections, comes from a family of Unix systems called System V. Long ago in Linux history, a different booting system that did not use runlevels was used, but then Linux distributions switched to the so-called SysV system.

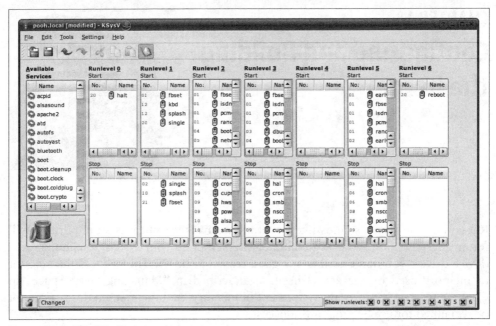

Figure 17-1. The KSysV main window

CHAPTER 18
Configuring and Building the Kernel

Rebuilding the kernel sounds like a pastime for hackers, but it is an important skill for any system administrator. Rebuilding the kernel on your system to eliminate the device drivers you don't need is one good reason to do so. This reduces the amount of memory used by the kernel itself, as described in "Managing Swap Space" in Chapter 10. The kernel is always present in memory, and the memory it uses cannot be reclaimed for use by programs if necessary.

It should be noted here that most distributions today ship with modularized kernels. This means that the kernel they install by default contains only the minimum functionality needed to bring up the system; everything else is then contained in *modules* that add any additionally needed functionality on demand. We will talk about modules in much greater detail later. But even with these stripped-down kernels, distributions have to ship several versions, for example, in order to provide support for both single-processor and multiprocessor machines, as this is something so central that it cannot be moved into a module. The installers that come with distributions are typically smart enough to figure out which kernel you need and install the right one, however.

Why is the ability to select features a win for you? All kernel code and data are "locked down" in memory; that is, they cannot be swapped out to disk. For example, if you use a kernel image with support for hardware you do not have or use, the memory consumed by the support for that hardware cannot be reclaimed for use by user applications. Customizing the kernel allows you to trim it for your needs.

You also need to occasionally upgrade your kernel to a newer version. As with any piece of your system, if you know of important bug fixes or new features in a kernel release, you may want to upgrade to pick them up. Those people who are actively developing kernel code will also need to keep their kernel up-to-date in case changes are made to the code they are working on. Sometimes, it is necessary to upgrade your kernel to use a new version of the compiler or libraries. Some applications (such as the VMware emulator) require a certain kernel version to run.

You can find out what kernel version you are running through the command *uname -a*. This should produce something like the following:

```
rutabaga$ uname -a
Linux pooh 2.6.11.4-21.7-default #1 Thu Jun 2 14:23:14 UTC 2005 i686 i686 i386
GNU/Linux
```

Here, we see a machine running Version 2.6.11.4 of the kernel, which was last compiled on June 2, 2005. We see other information as well, such as the hostname of the machine, the number of times this kernel has been compiled (once), and the fact that the machine is a Pentium Pro or better (as denoted by i686). The manpage for *uname*(1) can tell you more.

Building a New Kernel

The Linux kernel is a many-tentacled beast. Many groups of people work on different pieces of it, and some parts of the code are a patchwork of ideas meeting different design goals. Overall, however, the kernel code is clean and uniform, and those interested in exploring its innards should have little trouble doing so. However, because of the great amount of development going on with the kernel, new releases are made very rapidly—sometimes daily! The chief reason for this is that nearly all device drivers are contained within the kernel code, and every time someone updates a driver, a new release is necessary. Even though almost all device drivers are loadable modules these days, they are still typically shipped together with the kernel as one big package.

Currently, Linus Torvalds maintains the "official" kernel release. Although the GPL allows anyone to modify and rerelease the kernel under the same copyright, Linus's maintenance of an "official" kernel is a helpful convention that keeps version numbers uniform and allows everyone to be on equal footing when talking about kernel revisions. In order for a bug fix or new feature to be included in the kernel, all one must do is send it to Linus (or whoever is in charge for the kernel series in question —Linus himself always maintains the most current kernel), who will usually incorporate the change as long as it doesn't break anything. Linus also makes use of so-called *lieutenants*, very experienced kernel developers, who take care of particular subsystems.

Kernel version numbers follow the convention

```
major.minor.patchlevel
```

major is the major version number, which rarely changes; *minor* is the minor version number, which indicates the current "strain" of the kernel release; and *patchlevel* is the number of the patch to the current kernel version. Some examples of kernel versions are 2.4.4 (patch level 4 of kernel Version 2.4), and 2.6.11.4 (subversion 4 of patch level 11 of kernel Version 2.6).

If you are interested in how the existing kernel versions have evolved, check out *http://www.kernel.org*.

On your system, the kernel sources most probably live in */usr/src/linux* (unless you use the Debian distribution, where you can find the kernel sources in */usr/src/kernel-source-versionsnumber*). If you are going to rebuild your kernel only from the current sources, you don't need to obtain any files or apply any patches (assuming you installed the kernel sources when you installed your system). If you wish to upgrade your kernel to a new version, you need to follow the instructions in the following section.

Obtaining Kernel Sources

The official kernel is released as a *gzipped tar* file, containing the sources along with a series of patch files—one per patch level. The *tar* file contains the source for the unpatched revision; for example, there is a *tar* file containing the sources for kernel Version 2.6.0 with no patches applied. Each subsequent patch level is released as a patch file (produced using *diff*), which can be applied using the *patch* program. In "Patching Files" in Chapter 21, we describe the use of *patch* in detail.

Let's say you're upgrading to kernel Version 2.6, patch level 4. You'll need the sources for 2.6 (the file might be named *v2.6.0.tar.gz*) and the patches for patch levels 1 through 4. These files would be named *patch1*, *patch2*, and so forth. (You need *all* the patch files up to the version to which you're upgrading. Usually, these patch files are rather small, and are *gzip*ped on the archive sites.) All these files can be found in the *kernel* directory of the Linux FTP archive sites; for example, on *ftp://ftp.kernel.org*, the directory containing the 2.6 sources and patches is */pub/linux/kernel/v2.6*. You will find the kernel sources here as *tar* archives, compressed with both *gzip* and *bzip2*.

If you are already at some patch level of the kernel (such as 2.6 patch level 2) and want to upgrade to a newer patch level, you can simply apply the patches from the version you have up to the version to which you'd like to upgrade. If you're upgrading from, say, 2.6 patch level 2 to 2.6 patch level 4, you need the patch files for 2.6.3 and 2.6.4.

Unpacking the sources

First, unpack the source *tar* file from */usr/src* using commands such as:

```
rutabaga# cd /usr/src
rutabaga# mv linux linux.old
rutabaga# tar xzf v2.6.0.tar.gz
```

This saves your old kernel source tree as */usr/src/linux.old* and creates */usr/src/linux* containing the new sources. Note that the tar file containing the sources includes the *linux* subdirectory.

You should keep your current kernel sources in the directory */usr/src/linux* because there are two symbolic links—*/usr/include/linux* and */usr/include/asm*—that point into the current kernel source tree to provide certain header files when compiling programs. (If you are planning on doing any software development, you should always have your kernel sources available so that programs using these include files can be compiled.) If you want to keep several kernel source trees around, be sure that */usr/src/linux* points to the most recent one.

Applying patches

If you are applying any patch files, use the *patch* program. Let's say that you have the files *patch1.gz* through *patch4.gz*, which are *gzip*ped. These patches should be applied from the kernel sources main directory. That doesn't mean the patch files themselves should be located there, but rather that *patch* should be executed from, for example, */usr/src/linux*. For each patch file, use the command:

```
gunzip -c patchfile | patch -p1
```

from */usr/src*. The *-p1* option tells *patch* it shouldn't strip any part of the filenames contained within the patch file except for the first one.

You must apply each patch in numerical order by patch level. This is very important. Note that using a wildcard such as *patch** will not work because the * wildcard uses ASCII order, not numeric order. (Otherwise, if you are applying a larger number of patches, *patch1* might be followed by *patch10* and *patch11*, as opposed to *patch2* and *patch3*.) It is best to run the previous command for each patch file in succession, by hand. This way you can ensure you're doing things in the right order.

You shouldn't encounter problems when patching your source tree in this way unless you try to apply patches out of order or apply a patch more than once. Check the *patch* manual page if you do encounter trouble. If all else fails, remove the new kernel source tree and start over from the original *tar* file.

To double-check that the patches were applied successfully, use the commands:

```
find /usr/src/linux -follow -name "*.rej" -print
find /usr/src/linux -follow -name "*#" -print
```

This lists any files that are "rejected" portions of the patch process. If any such files exist, they contain sections of the patch file that could not be applied for some reason. Look into these, and if there's any doubt, start over from scratch. You cannot expect your kernel to compile or work correctly unless the patch process completes successfully and without rejections.

A handy script for patching the kernel is available and can be found in *scripts/patch-kernel*. But as always, you should know what you are doing before using automated tools—even more so when it comes to the very core of the operating system, the kernel.

Building the Kernel

There are six steps to building the kernel, and they should be quite painless. All these steps are described in more detail in the following pages.

1. Make sure that all the required tools and utilities are installed and at the appropriate versions. See the file *Documentation/Changes* in the kernel source for the list of requirements.

2. Run *make config*, which asks you various questions about which drivers you wish to include. You could also use the more comfortable variants *make menuconfig*, or *make xconfig* (when you are running KDE), or *make gconfig* (when you are running GNOME).

   If you have previously built a kernel and then applied patches to a new version, you can run *make oldconfig* to use your old configuration but be prompted for any new options that may not have been in the old kernel.

3. Some older kernels require you at this point to run *make dep* to gather dependencies for each source file and include them in the various makefiles. This step is not necessary for current kernels (such as the 2.6 series).

4. If you have built a kernel from this source tree before, run *make clean* to clear out old object files and force a complete rebuild.

5. Run *make bzImage* to build the kernel itself.

6. Go have a coffee (or two, depending on the speed of your machine and amount of available memory).

7. Install the new kernel image, either on a boot floppy or via GRUB. You can use *make bzDisk* to put the kernel on a boot floppy.

All these commands are executed from */usr/src/linux*, except for step 5, which you can do anywhere.

A *README* file is included in the kernel sources, which should be located at */usr/src/linux/README* on your system. Read it. It contains up-to-date notes on kernel compilation, which may be more current than the information presented here. Be sure to follow the steps described there, using the descriptions given later in this section as a guide. If you have installed the kernel sources from a package included with your distribution, there may also be a file with distribution-specific notes that tells you how your distribution's packagers have configured the kernel, and whether (and how) the kernel changes have been changed from the pristine sources that you can download from the net.

Kernel configuration: make config

The first step is to run *make config*. This executes a script that asks you a set of yes/no questions about which drivers to include in the kernel. There are defaults for each question, but be careful: the defaults probably don't correspond to what you want. (When several options are available, the default will be shown as a capital letter, as in [Y/n].) Your answers to each question will become the default the next time you build the kernel from this source tree.

Simply answer each question, either by pressing Enter for the default, or pressing y or n (followed by Enter). Some questions don't have a yes/no answer; you may be asked to enter a number or some other value. A number of the configuration questions allow an answer of m in addition to y or n. This option allows the corresponding kernel feature to be compiled as a loadable kernel module, as opposed to building it into the kernel image itself. Loadable modules, covered in the following section, "Loadable Device Drivers," allow portions of the kernel (such as device drivers) to be loaded and unloaded as needed on a running system. If you are unsure about an option, type ? at the prompt; for most options, a message will be shown that tells you more about the option.

The system remembers your configuration options each time you run *make config*, so if you're adding or removing only a few features from your kernel, you need not re-enter all the options.

Some people say that *make config* has so many options now that it is hardly feasible to run it by hand any longer, as you have to concentrate for a long time to press the right keys in response to the right questions. Therefore, people are moving to the alternatives described next.

An alternative to running *make config* is *make xconfig*, which compiles and runs an X-Window-based kernel configuration program. In order for this to work, you must have the X Window System running, have the appropriate X11 and Qt libraries installed, and so forth. Instead of asking a series of questions, the X-based configuration utility allows you to use checkboxes to select which kernel options you want to enable.

Also available is make menuconfig, which uses the text-based *curses* library, providing a similar menu-based kernel configuration if you don't have X installed. *make menuconfig* and *make xconfig* are much more comfortable than *make config*, especially because you can go back to an option and change your mind up to the point where you save your configuration. However, we'll describe the process here in a linear fashion, as *make config* does it.

The following is part of a session with *make config*. When using *make menuconfig* or *make xconfig*, you will encounter the same options, only presented in a more user-friendly fashion (we actually recommend the use of these tools if at all possible, because it is very easy to get confused by the myriad of configuration options):

```
pooh:/usr/src/linux # make config
scripts/kconfig/conf arch/i386/Kconfig
#
# using defaults found in .config
#
```

```
*
* Linux Kernel Configuration
*
*
* Code maturity level options
*
Prompt for development and/or incomplete code/drivers (EXPERIMENTAL) [Y/n/?]
  Select only drivers expected to compile cleanly (CLEAN_COMPILE) [Y/n/?]
*
* General setup
*
Local version - append to kernel release (LOCALVERSION) [-default]
Support for paging of anonymous memory (swap) (SWAP) [Y/n/?]
System V IPC (SYSVIPC) [Y/n/?]
POSIX Message Queues (POSIX_MQUEUE) [Y/n/?]
BSD Process Accounting (BSD_PROCESS_ACCT) [Y/n/?]
  BSD Process Accounting version 3 file format (BSD_PROCESS_ACCT_V3) [Y/n/?]
Sysctl support (SYSCTL) [Y/n/?]
Auditing support (AUDIT) [Y/n/?]
  Enable system-call auditing support (AUDITSYSCALL) [Y/n/?]
Kernel log buffer size (16 => 64KB, 17 => 128KB) (LOG_BUF_SHIFT) [17]
Support for hot-pluggable devices (HOTPLUG) [Y/?] y
Kernel Userspace Events (KOBJECT_UEVENT) [Y/n/?]
Kernel .config support (IKCONFIG) [Y/n/?]
  Enable access to .config through /proc/config.gz (IKCONFIG_PROC) [Y/n/?]
*
* Configure standard kernel features (for small systems)
*
Configure standard kernel features (for small systems) (EMBEDDED) [N/y/?]
  Load all symbols for debugging/kksymoops (KALLSYMS) [Y/?] (NEW) y
    Include all symbols in kallsyms (KALLSYMS_ALL) [N/y/?]
    Do an extra kallsyms pass (KALLSYMS_EXTRA_PASS) [N/y/?]
*
* Loadable module support
*
Enable loadable module support (MODULES) [Y/n/?]
  Module unloading (MODULE_UNLOAD) [Y/n/?]
    Forced module unloading (MODULE_FORCE_UNLOAD) [Y/n/?]
  Module versioning support (EXPERIMENTAL) (MODVERSIONS) [Y/n/?]
  Source checksum for all modules (MODULE_SRCVERSION_ALL) [Y/n/?]
  Automatic kernel module loading (KMOD) [Y/n/?]
*
* Processor type and features
*
Subarchitecture Type
> 1. PC-compatible (X86_PC)
  2. AMD Elan (X86_ELAN)
  3. Voyager (NCR) (X86_VOYAGER)
  4. NUMAQ (IBM/Sequent) (X86_NUMAQ)
  5. SGI 320/540 (Visual Workstation) (X86_VISWS)
choice[1-5]:
Processor family
  1. 386 (M386)
  2. 486 (M486)
```

```
>   3. 586/K5/5x86/6x86/6x86MX (M586)
    4. Pentium-Classic (M586TSC)
    5. Pentium-MMX (M586MMX)
    6. Pentium-Pro (M686)
    7. Pentium-II/Celeron(pre-Coppermine) (MPENTIUMII)
    8. Pentium-III/Celeron(Coppermine)/Pentium-III Xeon (MPENTIUMIII)
    9. Pentium M (MPENTIUMM)
   10. Pentium-4/Celeron(P4-based)/Pentium-4 M/Xeon (MPENTIUM4)
   11. K6/K6-II/K6-III (MK6)
   12. Athlon/Duron/K7 (MK7)
   13. Opteron/Athlon64/Hammer/K8 (MK8)
   14. Crusoe (MCRUSOE)
   15. Efficeon (MEFFICEON)
   16. Winchip-C6 (MWINCHIPC6)
   17. Winchip-2 (MWINCHIP2)
   18. Winchip-2A/Winchip-3 (MWINCHIP3D)
   19. CyrixIII/VIA-C3 (MCYRIXIII)
   20. VIA C3-2 (Nehemiah) (MVIAC3_2)
choice[1-20]:
Generic x86 support (X86_GENERIC) [Y/n/?]
HPET Timer Support (HPET_TIMER) [N/y/?]
Symmetric multi-processing support (SMP) [N/y/?]
Preemptible Kernel (PREEMPT) [N/y/?]
Local APIC support on uniprocessors (X86_UP_APIC) [Y/n/?]
  IO-APIC support on uniprocessors (X86_UP_IOAPIC) [Y/n/?]
  Disable local/IO APIC by default (X86_APIC_OFF) [Y/n/?]
Machine Check Exception (X86_MCE) [Y/n/?]
  Check for non-fatal errors on AMD Athlon/Duron / Intel Pentium 4 (X86_MCE_NONFATAL)
[N/m/y/?]
  check for P4 thermal throttling interrupt. (X86_MCE_P4THERMAL) [Y/n/?]
Toshiba Laptop support (TOSHIBA) [M/n/y/?]

...and so on...
*** End of Linux kernel configuration.
*** Check the top-level Makefile for additional configuration.
*** Next, you may run 'make bzImage', 'make bzdisk', or 'make
install'.
```

If you have gathered the information about your hardware when installing Linux, that information is probably sufficient to answer the configuration questions, most of which should be straightforward. If you don't recognize some feature, it's a specialized feature that you don't need.

It should be noted here that not all Linux device drivers are actually built into the kernel. Instead, some drivers are available only as loadable modules, distributed separately from the kernel sources. (As mentioned earlier, some drivers can be either built into the kernel or compiled as modules. In other cases, you have only one choice or the other.)

If you can't find support for your favorite hardware device in the list presented by *make config*, it's quite possible that the driver is available as a module or a separate kernel patch. Scour the FTP sites and archive CD-ROMs if you can't find what you're looking for. In the next section, "Loadable Device Drivers," kernel modules are covered in detail.

The following questions are found in the kernel configuration for Version 2.6.11.4. If you have applied other patches, additional questions might appear. The same is true for later versions of the kernel. Note that in the following list we don't show all the kernel configuration options; there are simply too many of them, and most are self-explanatory. We have highlighted only those that may require further explanation. Remember that if you're not sure how to answer a particular question, the default answer is often the best choice. When in doubt, it is also a good idea to type ? and check the help message.

Following are the high-level choices and the ramifications of choosing each one.

Prompt for development and/or incomplete code/drivers
> Answer yes for this item if you want to try new features that aren't considered stable enough by the developers. You do not want this option unless you want to help test new features.

System V IPC
> Answering yes to this option includes kernel support for System V interprocess communication (IPC) functions, such as *msgrcv* and *msgsnd*. Some programs ported from System V require this; you should answer yes unless you have a strong aversion to these features.

Sysctl support
> This option instructs the kernel to provide a way to change kernel parameters on the fly, without rebooting. It is a good idea to enable this unless you have very limited memory and cannot tolerate the extra 8 KB that this option adds to the kernel.

Enable loadable module support
> This enables the support for dynamically loading additional modules. You definitely want to enable this.

Module versioning support
> This is a special option that makes it possible to use a module compiled for one kernel version with another kernel version. A number of problems are attached to this; say no here unless you know exactly what you are doing.

Automatic kernel module loading
> If you enable this option, the kernel can automatically load and unload dynamically loadable modules as needed.

Processor family (20 different choices currently) [586/K5/5x86/6x86/6x86MX]
> Here, you have to specify the CPU type that you have. The kernel will then be compiled with optimizations especially geared toward your machine. Note that if you specify a higher processor here than you actually have, the kernel might not work. Choosing an earlier CPU type (such as a Pentium when what you

actually have is a Pentium IV) should work just fine, but your kernel may not run as fast as it could when using more advanced machine-specific features available in newer CPUs.

Symmetric multi-processing support

This enables kernel support for more than one CPU. If your machine has more than one CPU, say yes here; if not, say no.

Power management options (ACPI, APM)

This is an entire subsection for power management, mostly for laptops, but things like suspend-to-disk ("hibernation") could be useful for workstations too. However, power management often leads to problems, including a complete failure to boot. If you experience any problems, try recompiling your kernel without power management, or pass the kernel command-line options noapm and noacpi at boot time to turn off power management.

PCI support

Enable this option if your motherboard includes the PCI bus and you have PCI-bus devices installed in your system. The PCI BIOS is used to detect and enable PCI devices; kernel support for it is necessary for use of any PCI devices in your system.

Parallel port support

Enable this option if you have a parallel port in your system and want to access it from Linux. Linux can use the parallel port not only for printers, but also for PLIP (a networking protocol for parallel lines), Zip drives, scanners, and other things. In most cases, you will need an additional driver to attach a device to the parallel port. If you have a modern printer that reports status back to the computer, you also want to enable the IEEE 1284 transfer modes option.

Normal floppy disk support

Answer yes to this option unless you don't want support for floppy drives (this can save some memory on systems where floppy support isn't required). If you are using one of those attachable floppy drives on IBM Thinkpad laptops, you also need to pass floppy=thinkpad to the kernel at boot time.

Parallel port IDE device support

This option enables support for IDE devices that are attached to the parallel port, such as portable CD-ROM drives.

Packet writing on CD/DVD media

If you have a modern CD or DVD burner, you can enable packet writing (as opposed to track writing) here by selecting this option.

Enhanced IDE/MFM/RLL disk/cdrom/tape/floppy support

Answer yes to this option unless you don't need IDE/MFM/RLL drive support. After answering yes, you will be prompted for types of devices (hard disks, CD-ROM drives, tape drives, and floppy drives) you want to access over the IDE driver. If you have no IDE hardware (only SCSI), it may be safe to disable this option.

SCSI support

If you have a SCSI controller of any kind, answer yes to this option. You will be asked a series of questions about the specific SCSI devices on your system; be sure you know what type of hardware you have installed. All these questions deal with specific SCSI controller chips and boards; if you aren't sure what sort of SCSI controller you have, check the hardware documentation or consult the Linux HOWTO documents.

You will also be asked if you want support for SCSI disks, tapes, CD-ROMs, and other devices; be sure to enable the options appropriate for your hardware.

If you don't have any SCSI hardware, you should answer no to this option; it greatly reduces the size of your kernel.

Old CD-ROM drivers

This is a series of questions dealing with the specific CD-ROM drivers supported by the kernel, such as the Sony CDU31A/33A, Mitsumi, or Sound Blaster Pro CD-ROM. If you have a SCSI or IDECD-ROM controller (and have selected support for it earlier), you need not enable any of these options. Some CD-ROM drives have their own interface boards, and these options enable drivers for them.

Networking support

Answer yes to this option if you want any sort of networking support in your kernel (including TCP/IP, SLIP, PPP, NFS, and so on).

Networking options

If you selected networking support, you will be asked a series of questions about which networking options you want enabled in your kernel. Unless you have special networking needs (in which case you'll know how to answer the questions appropriately), selecting the defaults for these questions should suffice. A number of the questions are esoteric in nature (such as PF_KEY sockets), and you should select the defaults for these in almost all cases.

Network device support

This is a series of questions about the specific networking controllers Linux supports. If you plan to use an Ethernet card (or some other networking controller), be sure to enable the options for your hardware. As with SCSI devices, you should consult your hardware documentation or the Linux HOWTO documents (such as the Ethernet HOWTO) to determine which driver is appropriate for your network controller.

Amateur Radio support

This option enables basic support for networking over public radio frequencies. If you have the equipment to use the feature, enable this option and read the AX25 and the HAM HOWTO.

ISDN subsystem

If you have ISDN hardware in your system, enable this option and select the ISDN hardware driver suitable for your hardware. You will most probably also want to select Support synchronous PPP (see "PPP over ISDN" in Chapter 13). Linux is currently switching from the old so-called ISDN4Linux support to support of the CAPI 2.0 standard. Both should work with most ISDN hardware, but CAPI 2.0 support is going to be used exclusively in the future.

Telephony support

Linux supports some interface cards that let you use a normal telephone set with VoIP (voice-over-IP) Internet telephony. As the documentation says, this has nothing to do with modems, so you have to enable this only if you have such an interface card.

Character devices

Linux supports a number of special "character" devices, such as serial and parallel port controllers, tape drives, and mice with their own proprietary interfaces (not mice that connect to the serial and USB ports, such as the Microsoft serial mouse) or most newer mice.

Sound

This section lets you pick between two different sound systems, the newer ALSA (Advanced Linux Sound Architecture) and the older OSS (Open Sound System). If it supports your sound hardware, go for ALSA.

USB support

Enable this to get support for many USB devices. In particular, if you want to use the popular memory sticks, you need to select USB Mass Storage Support as well. This option also applies to digital cameras that are connected to your computer via the USB port.

Filesystems

This is a series of questions for each filesystem type supported by the kernel. As discussed in the section "Managing Filesystems" in Chapter 10, a number of filesystem types are supported by the system, and you can pick and choose which to include in the kernel. Nearly all systems should include support for the Second Extended and */proc* filesystems. You should include support for the MS-DOS filesystem if you want to access your MS-DOS files directly from Linux, and the ISO 9660 filesystem to access files on a CD-ROM (most of which are encoded in this way).

Kernel hacking

This section contains options that are useful only if you plan on hacking the Linux kernel yourself. If you do not want to do this, answer no.

Preparing the ground: make clean

If you wish to force a complete recompilation of the kernel, you should issue *make clean* at this point. This removes from this source tree all object files produced from a previous build. If you have never built the kernel from this tree, you're probably safe skipping this step (although it can't hurt to perform it). If you are tweaking minor parts of the kernel, you might want to avoid this step so that only those files that have changed will be recompiled. At any rate, running *make clean* simply ensures the entire kernel will be recompiled "from scratch," and if you're in any doubt, use this command to be on the safe side.

Compiling the kernel

Now you're ready to compile the kernel. This is done with the command *make bzImage*. It is best to build your kernel on a lightly loaded system, with most of your memory free for the compilation. If other users are accessing the system, or if you're trying to run any large applications yourself (such as the X Window System, or another compilation), the build may slow to a crawl. The key here is memory. If a system is low on memory and starts swapping, it will be slow no matter how fast the processor is.

The kernel compilation can take anywhere from a few minutes to many hours, depending on your hardware. There is a great deal of code—well over 80 MB—in the entire kernel, so this should come as no surprise. Slower systems with 16 MB (or less) of RAM can expect to take several hours for a complete rebuild; faster machines with more memory can complete it in less than half an hour. Your mileage will most assuredly vary.

If any errors or warnings occur while compiling, you cannot expect the resulting kernel to work correctly; in most cases, the build will halt if an error occurs. Such errors can be the result of incorrectly applying patches, problems with the *make config* step, or actual bugs in the code. In the "stock" kernels, this latter case is rare, but is more common if you're working with development code or new drivers under testing. If you have any doubt, remove the kernel source tree altogether and start over.

When the compilation is complete, you will be left with the file *bzImage* in the directory */usr/src/linux/arch/i386/boot*. (Of course, if you're attempting to build Linux on a platform other than the Intel x86, the kernel image will be found in the corresponding subdirectory under *arch*.) The kernel is so named because it is the executable image of the kernel, and it has been internally compressed using the *bzip2* algorithm. When the kernel boots, it uncompresses itself into memory: don't attempt to use *bzip2* or *bunzip2* on *bzImage* yourself! The kernel requires much less disk space when compressed in this way, allowing kernel images to fit on a floppy. Earlier kernels supported both the *gzip* and the *bzip2* compression algorithms, the former resulting in a file called *zImage*. Because *bzImage* gives better compression results, however, *gzip* should not be used, as the resulting kernels are usually too big to be installed these days.

If you pick too much kernel functionality, you can get a `kernel too big` error at the end of the kernel compilation. This happens rarely because you need only a very limited amount of hardware support for one machine, but it can happen. In this case, there is one way out: compile some kernel functionality as modules (see "Loadable Device Drivers").

You should now run *rdev* on the new kernel image to verify that the root filesystem device, console SVGA mode, and other parameters have been set correctly. This is described in "Using a Boot Floppy" in Chapter 17.

Installing the kernel

With your new kernel in hand, you're ready to configure it for booting. This involves either placing the kernel image on a boot floppy, or configuring GRUB to boot the kernel from the hard drive. These topics are discussed in "Booting the System" in Chapter 17. To use the new kernel, configure it for booting in one of these ways, and reboot the system.

 You should always keep a known good kernel available for booting. Either keep a previous backup kernel selectable from GRUB or test new kernels using a floppy first. This will save you if you make a mistake such as omitting a crucial driver in your new kernel, making your system not bootable.

Loadable Device Drivers

Traditionally, device drivers have been included as part of the kernel. There are several reasons for this. First of all, nearly all device drivers require the special hardware access provided by being part of the kernel code. Such hardware access can't be obtained easily through a user program. Also, device drivers are much easier to implement as part of the kernel; such drivers have complete access to the data structures and other routines in the kernel and can call them freely.

A conglomerate kernel containing all drivers in this manner presents several problems. First of all, it requires the system administrator to rebuild the kernel in order to selectively include device drivers, as we saw in the previous section. Also, this mechanism lends itself to sloppy programming on the part of the driver writers: there's nothing stopping a programmer from writing code that is not completely modular— code which, for example, directly accesses data private to other parts of the kernel. The cooperative nature of the Linux kernel development compounds this problem, and not all parts of the code are as neatly contained as they should be. This can make it more difficult to maintain and debug the code.

In an effort to move away from this paradigm, the Linux kernel supports loadable device drivers—device drivers that are added to or removed from memory at runtime, with a series of commands. Such drivers are still part of the kernel, but they are compiled separately and enabled only when loaded. Loadable device drivers, or *modules*, are generally loaded into memory using commands in one of the boot-time *rc* scripts.

Modules provide a cleaner interface for writing drivers. To some extent, they require the code to be somewhat modular and to follow a certain coding convention. (Note that this doesn't actually prevent a programmer from abusing the convention and writing nonmodular code. Once the module has been loaded, it is just as free to wreak havoc as if it were compiled directly into the kernel.) Using modules makes drivers easier to debug; you can simply unload a module, recompile it, and reload it without having to reboot the system or rebuild the kernel as a whole. Modules can be used for other parts of the kernel, such as filesystem types, in addition to device drivers.

Most device drivers, and a lot of other kernel functionality under Linux, are implemented as modules. One of them is the parallel port driver for PCs (or *parport_pc* driver), for devices that connect to the parallel port (there are also additional drivers for special devices such as printers that report back status to the computer). If you plan to use this driver on your system, it is good to know how to build, load, and unload modules. Although nothing is stopping you from compiling this module statically into your kernel, a parallel port driver is something that you need only rarely (whenever you print to a directly connected printer, maybe a couple of times a day), and its driver shouldn't occupy valuable RAM during the times it is not needed. See the Linux Printing HOWTO for more about parallel port printing.

Installing the Kernel

Now we'll talk about how to load and unload modules from the kernel. The first thing you'll need is the *module-init-tools* package, which contains the commands used to load and unload modules from the kernel. On the FTP archive sites, this is usually found as *module-init-tools-versionnumber.tar.bz2* in the directory where the kernel sources are kept. This package contains the sources to the commands *insmod*, *modprobe*, *rmmod*, and *lsmod*. All reasonably recent Linux distributions include these commands (found in *sbin*) already, so if you already have these commands installed, you probably don't need to get the *modules* package. However, it can't hurt to get the package and rebuild these commands to be sure that you have the most up-to-date version.

To rebuild these commands, unpack *module-init-tools-versionnumber.tar.bz2* (say, in a subdirectory of */usr/src*). Follow the installation instructions contained there; usually all you have to do is execute *make* followed by *make install* (as *root*). The three commands will now be installed in */sbin* and will be ready to use.

Compiling Modules

A module is simply a single object file containing all the code for the driver. For example, the *parport_pc* module might be called *parport_pc.ko*. On most systems, the modules themselves are stored in a directory tree below */lib/modules /kernelversion*, where you can find different directories for the various types of modules. For example, the modules compiled for the 2.6.8 kernel would be below */lib/modules/2.6.8*. You might already have a number of modules on your system; check the appropriate directory. Notice that kernel modules, unlike other compiled object files, have the filename extension *.ko* to show their status as kernel modules. If you are running an older version of Linux, your modules might still have the extension *.o*.

Modules can be either in the kernel sources or external to it. The former is the case for those device drivers, filesystems, and other functionality that are used most often and are maintained as part of the official kernel sources. Using these modules is very easy: during the *make config*, *make menuconfig*, or *make xconfig* step, select to build a certain feature as a module. Repeat this for everything you want to compile as a module. Then, after the *make bzImage* step, execute the following commands:

```
# make modules
# make modules_install
```

This will compile the modules and install them in */lib/modules/kernelversion*.

New modules that are not yet integrated into the official kernel sources, or those that are simply too esoteric to be put into the kernel sources (e.g., a device driver for some custom-built hardware that is not publicly available) can be available as standalone, external modules. Unpack the archive of the module, compile it according to the instructions that are hopefully included, and copy the resulting module file to the appropriate subdirectory of */lib/modules/kernelversion*. Some modules might have an install script or allow you to issue the command *make install* to perform the last step.

Loading a Module

Once you have a compiled module (either from the kernel sources or external), you can load it using the command:

```
insmod module
```

where *module* is the name of the module object file. For example:

```
insmod /lib/modules/2.6.11.4/kernel/drivers/parport/parport_pc.ko
```

installs the *parport_pc* driver if it is found in that file.

Once a module is installed, it may display some information to the console (as well as to the system logs), indicating that it is initialized. For example, the *ftape* driver might display the following:

```
Jul 26 13:08:41 tigger kernel: pnp: Device 00:09 activated.
Jul 26 13:08:41 tigger kernel: parport: PnPBIOS parport detected.
Jul 26 13:08:41 tigger kernel: parport0: PC-style at 0x378, irq 7 [PCSPP,TRISTATE]
```

The exact messages printed depend on the module, of course. Each module should come with ample documentation describing just what it does and how to debug it if there are problems.

It is likely that *insmod* will tell you it could not load the module into the kernel because there were "symbols missing." This means that the module you want to load needs functionality from another part of the kernel that is neither compiled into the kernel nor contained in a module already loaded. In particular, the *parport_pc* module that we have been using as an example depends on the *parport* module that provides the general parallel port functionality. You could now try to find out which module contains those functions, load that module first with *insmod*, and try again. You will eventually succeed with this method, but it can be cumbersome, and this would not be Linux if there weren't a better way.

You first need a module database in the file */lib/modules/kernelversion/modules.dep*. You can create this database by calling:

```
depmod -a
```

This goes through all the modules you have and records whether they need any other modules. With this database in place, you can simply replace the *insmod* command with the *modprobe* command, which checks the module database and loads any other modules that might be needed before loading the requested module. For example, our *modules.dep* file contains—among others—the following line:

```
/lib/modules/2.6.8/kernel/drivers/isdn/i4l/isdn.ko:
/lib/modules/2.6.8/kernel/drivers/net/slhc.ko
```

This means that in order to load the *isdn* module (a device driver for ISDN support), the *slhc* module (containing one of the ISDN protocol implementations) must be loaded. If we now load the *isdn* module with *modprobe* (this example is slightly simplified because the *isdn* module needs additional parameters):

```
modprobe hisax
```

modprobe will detect the dependency and load the *slhc* module. If you have compiled a module for the current kernel, you first need to run *depmod -a*, though, so that *modprobe* can find it.

Some modules need so-called *module parameters*. For example, a device driver might need to be assigned an IRQ. You can pass those parameters in the form *parameter_name=parameter_value* with both the *insmod* and the *modprobe* command. In the following example, several parameters are passed to the *hisax* module, which is a particular (and somewhat outdated) driver for a family of ISDN boards:

```
tigger # modprobe hisax type=3 protocol=2 io=0x280 irq=10
```

The documentation for each module should tell you which parameters the module supports. If you are too lazy to read the documentation, a nifty tool you can use is *modinfo*, which tells you—among other things—which parameters are accepted by the module you specify.

One caveat about modules if you use the Debian distribution: Debian uses a file called */etc/modules* that lists the modules that should be loaded at boot time. If a module that you do not want keeps reappearing, check whether it is listed here.

You can list the drivers that are loaded with the command *lsmod*:

```
rutabaga$ lsmod
Module        Size  Used by
parport       40392 1 parport_pc
```

The memory usage of the module in bytes is displayed as well. The *parport* driver here is using about 40 KB of memory. If any other modules are dependent on this module, they are shown in the third column.

A module can be unloaded from memory using the *rmmod* command, as long as it is not in use. For example:

```
rmmod parport_pc
```

The argument to *rmmod* is the name of the driver as it appears in the *lsmod* listing.

Once you have modules working to your satisfaction, you can include the appropriate *insmod* commands in one of the *rc* scripts executed at boot time. One of your *rc* scripts might already include a place where *insmod* commands can be added, depending on your distribution.

One feature of the current module support is that you must rebuild a module any time you upgrade your kernel to a new version or patch level. (Rebuilding your kernel while keeping the same kernel version doesn't require you to do this.) This is done to ensure that the module is compatible with the kernel version you're using. If you attempt to load a module with a kernel that is newer or older than that for which it was compiled, *insmod* will complain and not allow the module to be loaded. When rebuilding a module, you must be running the kernel under which it will be used. Therefore, when upgrading your kernel, upgrade and reboot the new kernel first, then rebuild your modules and load them. There is an option that allows you to keep your modules when switching kernels, but a number of problems are associated with it, and we recommend against using it.

Loading Modules Automatically

The automatic loading of modules is an especially useful feature implemented by a kernel component called *kmod*. With the help of *kmod*, the kernel can load needed device drivers and other modules automatically and without manual intervention from the system administrator. If the modules are not needed after 60 seconds, they are automatically unloaded as well.

In order to use *kmod*, you need to turn on support for it (Automatic kernel module loading) during kernel configuration in the Loadable module support section.

Modules that need other modules must be correctly listed in */lib/modules /kernelversion/modules.dep*, and there must be aliases for the major and minor number in */etc/modprobe.conf* (and often in subdirectories of */etc/modprobe.d*). See the documentation from the *module-init-tools* package for further information.

If a module has not been loaded manually with *insmod* or *modprobe*, but was loaded automatically by the kernel, the module is listed with the additional string (autoclean) in the *lsmod* output. This tells you that the kernel will remove the module if it has not been used for more than one minute.

We have gone through quite a lot of material now, and you should have all the tools you'll need to build and maintain your own kernels.

## CHAPTER 19

Text Editing

In this chapter, we will look at some editors for editing text. As you have already learned, Linux is rich in configuration files, and even though there are more and more graphical tools for configuring your system, you will not get far without being able to operate at least one text editor. And of course, if you want to author text documents using a real formatting language like those described in the next chapter, or want to write your own software, as described in Chapter 21, you will need text editors even more. There is a good reason why we discuss more than one text editor here. There are the really large and comfortable ones such as XEmacs, but if you just want to change a few characters here or there, firing up such a huge beast may take longer than you are willing to wait, and in this case it is good if you are able to use a smaller editor such as *vi*. Or, you might be connected to your Linux system via a slow, remote link. In this case, you may want to sacrifice some usage convenience for faster redraws in simpler editors.

Editing Files Using vi

This section covers the use of the *vi* (pronounced "vee-eye") text editor. *vi* was the first real screen-based editor for Unix systems. It is also simple, small, and sleek. If you're a system administrator, learning *vi* can be invaluable; in many cases, larger editors, such as (X)Emacs, won't be available in emergency situations (for instance, when booting Linux from a maintenance disk).

vi is based on the same principles as many other Unix applications: that each program provides a small, specific function and is able to interact with other programs. For example, *vi* doesn't include its own spell checker or paragraph filler, but those features are provided by other programs that are easy to fire off from within *vi*. Therefore, *vi* itself is a bit limited, but is able to interact with other applications to provide virtually any functionality you might want.

At first, *vi* may appear to be somewhat complex and unwieldy. However, its single-letter commands are fast and powerful once you've learned them. The next section describes Emacs, a more flexible editor (really an integrated work environment) with an easier learning curve. Do keep in mind that knowing *vi* may be essential to you if you are in a situation where (X)Emacs is not available, so we encourage you to learn the basics, as odd as they may seem. It should also be added that a number of *vi* clones are now available that are much more comfortable to use than the original *vi*, the most popular of which is *vim* (*vi* improved). Chances are that your distribution has things set up so that when starting *vi*, you actually start one of those. We stick to the basics here, though, so that you can use the information presented here no matter which version of *vi* you use. You can find coverage of the newer versions in the book *Learning the vi Editor* by Linda Lamb and Arnold Robbins (O'Reilly).

Starting vi

Let's fire up *vi* and edit a file. The syntax for *vi* is:

    vi *filename*

For example:

    eggplant$ **vi test**

will edit the file *test*. Your screen should look like Figure 19-1.

Figure 19-1. vi when opening a new file

The column of ~ characters indicates that you are at the end of the file.

Inserting Text and Moving Around

While using *vi*, at any one time you are in one of two (or three, depending on how you look at it) modes of operation. These modes are known as *command mode*, *edit mode*, and *ex mode*.

After starting *vi*, you are in command mode. This mode allows you to use a number of (usually single-letter) commands to modify text, as we'll see soon. Text is actually inserted and modified within edit mode. To begin inserting text, press i (which will place you into edit mode) and begin typing. See Figure 19-2.

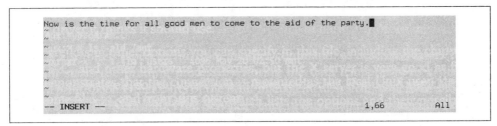

```
Now is the time for all good men to come to the aid of the party.█
~
~
~
~
~
~
~
~
-- INSERT --                                              1,66        All
```

Figure 19-2. Entering text into vi *buffer*

While inserting text, you may type as many lines as you wish (pressing the Enter key after each, of course), and you may correct mistakes using the Backspace key. To end edit mode and return to command mode, press the Esc key.

While in command mode, you can use the arrow keys to move around the file. Alternatively, or when the arrow keys don't work, you may use h, j, k, and l, which move the cursor left, down, up, and right, respectively.

There are several ways to insert text other than using the i command. The a command (for "append") inserts text *after* the current cursor position. For example, use the left arrow key to move the cursor between the words good and men (Figure 19-3).

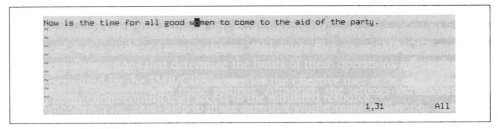

```
Now is the time for all good█men to come to the aid of the party.
~
~
~
~
~
~
~
                                                          1,29        All
```

Figure 19-3. Positioning cursor in vi

Press a, type wo, and then press Esc to return to command mode (Figure 19-4).

```
Now is the time for all good w█men to come to the aid of the party.
~
~
~
~
~
~
                                                          1,31        All
```

Figure 19-4. vi *after insertion*

To open a line below the current one and begin inserting text, use the o command. Press o and type another line or two (Figure 19-5).

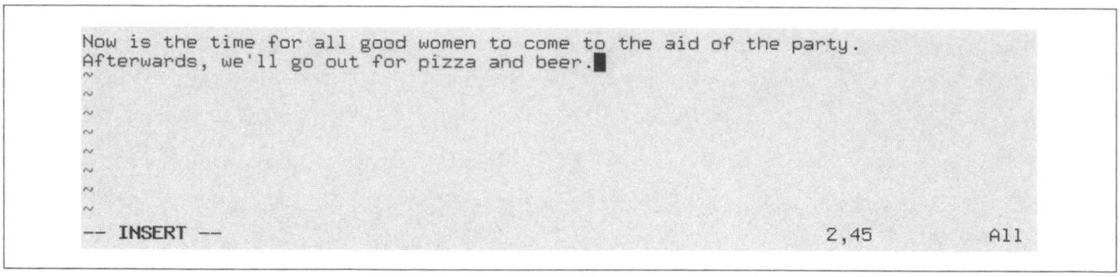

```
Now is the time for all good women to come to the aid of the party.
Afterwards, we'll go out for pizza and beer.█
~
~
~
~
~
~
-- INSERT --                                          2,45        All
```

Figure 19-5. vi *after appending text*

Remember that at any time you're either in command mode (where commands such as i, a, or o are valid) or in edit mode (where you're inserting text, followed by Esc to return to command mode). If you're not sure which mode you're in, press Esc. This takes you out of edit mode, if you are in it, and does nothing except beep if you're already in command mode.

Deleting Text and Undoing Changes

From command mode, the x command deletes the character under the cursor. If you press x five times in our example, you end up with the screen shown in Figure 19-6.

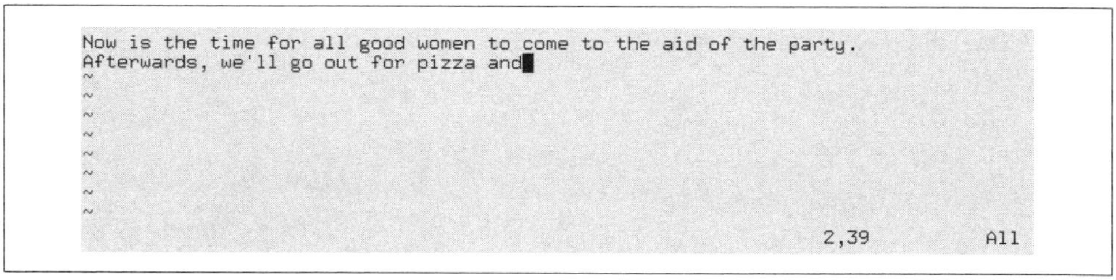

```
Now is the time for all good women to come to the aid of the party.
Afterwards, we'll go out for pizza and█
~
~
~
~
~
~
~
                                                     2,39        All
```

Figure 19-6. vi *after removing text*

Now press a and insert some text, followed by Esc (Figure 19-7).

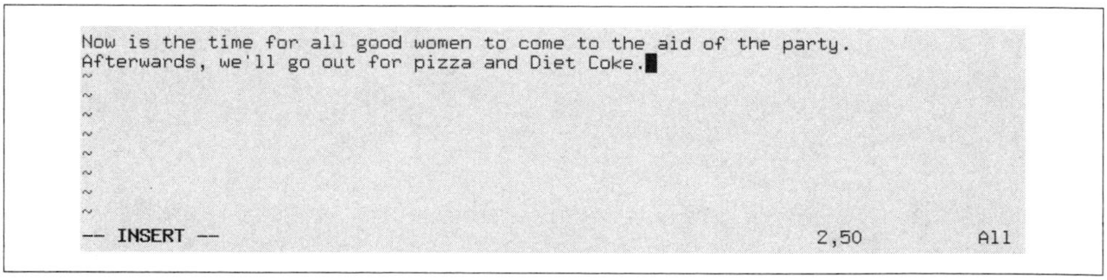

```
Now is the time for all good women to come to the aid of the party.
Afterwards, we'll go out for pizza and Diet Coke.█
~
~
~
~
~
~
-- INSERT --                                          2,50        All
```

Figure 19-7. vi *with new text*

You can delete entire lines using the command dd (that is, press d twice in a row). If your cursor is on the second line in our example, dd will produce the screen shown in Figure 19-8.

Now is the time for all good women to come to the aid of the party.
1,1 All

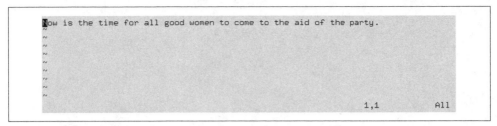

Figure 19-8. vi *after deleting lines*

Text that is deleted may be reinserted using the `p` command (for "put"). Pressing `p` now will return the deleted line to the buffer after the current line. Using `P` (uppercase) instead will insert the text before the current line. By default, `p` and `P` insert text from the "undo buffer"; you can also yank and replace text from other buffers, as we'll see later.

The `u` command undoes the latest change (in this case, pressing `u` after `dd` is equivalent to `p`). If you inserted a large amount of text using the `i` command, pressing `u` immediately after returning to command mode would undo it.

To delete the word beneath the cursor, use the `dw` command. Place the cursor on the word `Diet` and type `dw` (see Figure 19-9).

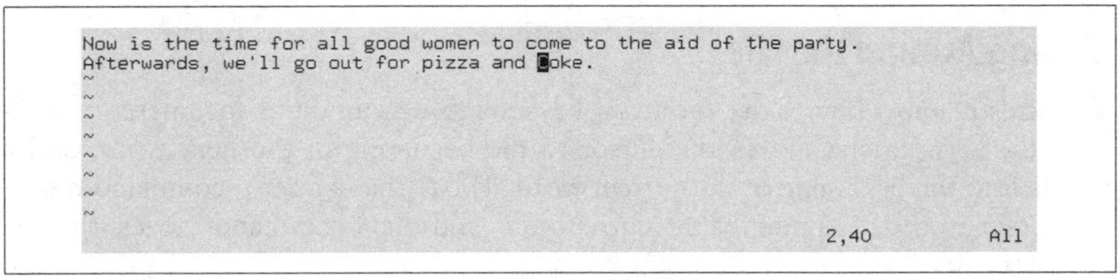

Now is the time for all good women to come to the aid of the party.
Afterwards, we'll go out for pizza and Coke.
2,40 All

Figure 19-9. vi *after deleting a word*

Changing Text

You can replace text using the `R` command, which overwrites the text beginning at the cursor. Place the cursor on the first letter in `pizza`, press `R`, and type (Figure 19-10).

The `r` command replaces the single character under the cursor. `r` does not place you in insert mode per se, so there is no reason to use Esc to return to command mode.

The `~` command changes the case of the letter under the cursor from upper- to lowercase, and vice versa. If you place the cursor on the `o` in `Now` in the previous example, and repeatedly press `~`, you end up with the screen shown in Figure 19-11.

Another useful command for changing words is the `cw` command, which lets you simply type in the new word and—after pressing Esc—removes anything that might

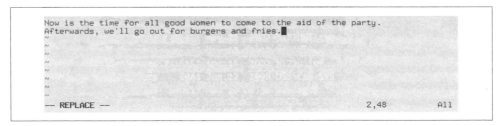

```
    Now is the time for all good women to come to the aid of the party.
    Afterwards, we'll go out for burgers and fries.█
    ~
    ~
    ~
    ~
    ~
    ~
    ~
    ~
    ~
    -- REPLACE --                                                    2,48        All
```

Figure 19-10. vi *after replacing text*

```
    NOW IS THE TIME FOR ALL GOOD WOMEN TO COME TO THE AID OF THE PARTY█
    Afterwards, we'll go out for burgers and fries.
    ~
    ~
    ~
    ~
    ~
    ~
    ~
                                                                     1,67        All
```

Figure 19-11. Changing case in vi

be left over from the original word. If the new text is longer than the one being changed, the space is automatically expanded as needed.

Moving Around the File

You already know how to use the arrow keys to move around the document. In addition, the w command moves the cursor to the beginning of the next word, and b moves it to the beginning of the current word. The 0 (that's a zero) command moves the cursor to the beginning of the current line, and the $ command moves it to the end of the line.

When editing large files, you'll want to move forward or backward through the file one screen at a time. Pressing Ctrl-F moves the cursor one screen forward, and Ctrl-B moves it one screen backward.

To move the cursor to the end of the file, type G. You can also move to an arbitrary line: the command 10G would move the cursor to line 10 in the file. To move to the beginning of the file, use 1G.

Typing / followed by a pattern and the Enter key causes you to jump to the first occurrence of that pattern in the text following the cursor. For example, placing the cursor on the first line of text in our example and typing /burg moves the cursor to the beginning of the word "burgers." Using ? instead of / searches backward through the file.

The pattern following a / or ? command is actually a *regular expression*. Regular expressions are a powerful way to specify patterns for search and replace operations and are used by many Unix utilities. You can find more information about regular expressions in the section "Regular Expressions," later in this chapter. Using regular expressions, you could, for example, search for the next uppercase letter, using the command

```
/[A-Z]
```

Therefore, if the pattern you're searching for is not a static string, regular expressions can be used to specify just what you want.

You can couple navigation commands with other commands, such as deletion. For example, the command d$ will delete everything from the cursor to the end of the line; dG will delete everything from the cursor to the end of the file.

Saving Files and Quitting vi

Most of the commands dealing with files within *vi* are invoked from ex mode. You enter ex mode when you press the : key from command mode. This places the cursor on the last line of the display, allowing you to enter various extended commands.

For example, to write the file being edited, use the command :w. Typing : causes you to enter ex mode, and typing w followed by the Enter key completes the command. The command :wq writes the file and exits *vi*. (The command ZZ—from command mode, without the ":"—is similar to :wq, but checks first whether the file has been changed, and writes it only in this case.)

To quit *vi* without saving changes to the file, use the command :q!. Using :q alone will quit *vi*, but only if modifications to the file have been saved. The ! in :q! means to quit *vi*—and that you really mean it.

Editing Another File

To edit another file, use the :e command. For example, to stop editing *test*, and edit the file *foo* instead, use the command shown at the bottom of Figure 19-12.

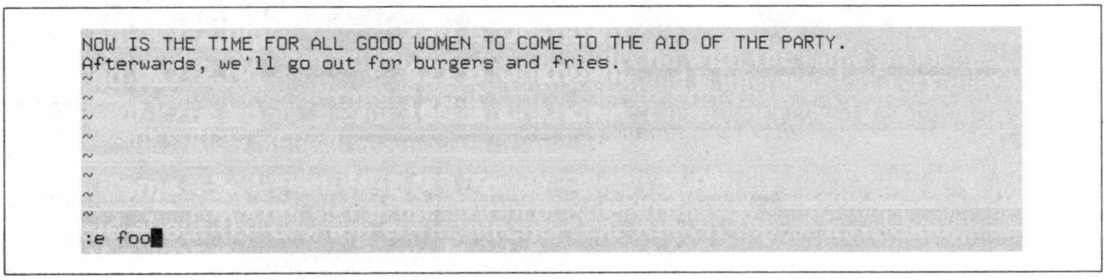

```
NOW IS THE TIME FOR ALL GOOD WOMEN TO COME TO THE AID OF THE PARTY.
Afterwards, we'll go out for burgers and fries.
~
~
~
~
~
~
~
~
~
:e foo
```

Figure 19-12. Editing antoher file with vi

If you use :e without writing the file first, you'll get the following error message:

```
No write since last change (:edit! overrides)
```

At this point, you can use :w to save the original file, and then use :e, or you can use the command :e! foo, which tells *vi* to edit the new file without saving changes to the original. This can be useful if you edit a file and realize that you have screwed up. You can then use the :e! command; if you don't specify a filename, *vi* discards the changes and re-edits the current file.

Including Other Files

If you use the :r command, you can include the contents of another file in the *vi* buffer. For example, the command

```
:r foo.txt
```

inserts the contents of the file *foo.txt* after the current line.

Running Shell Commands

The :! command allows you to enter the name of a shell command, which is executed within *vi*. For example, the command

```
:!ls -F
```

executes the ls command and displays the results on your screen.

The :r! command is similar to :!, but includes the standard output of the command in the buffer. The command:

```
:r!ls -F
```

produces the screen shown in Figure 19-13.

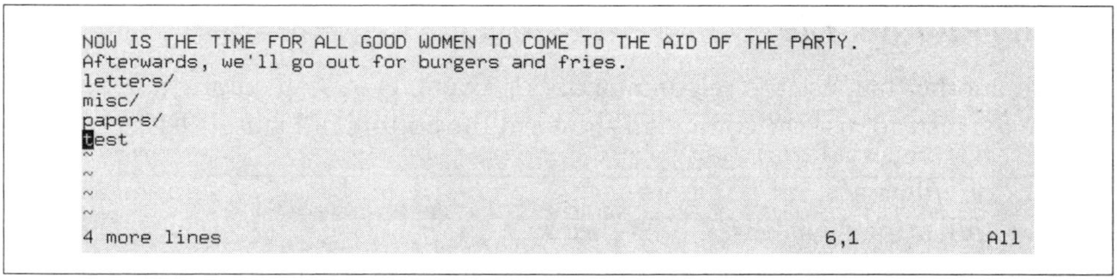

```
NOW IS THE TIME FOR ALL GOOD WOMEN TO COME TO THE AID OF THE PARTY.
Afterwards, we'll go out for burgers and fries.
letters/
misc/
papers/
test
~
~
~
~
4 more lines                                          6,1          All
```

Figure 19-13. Inserting results of a command in vi

If you need to execute a series of shell commands, it's often easier to use the suspend key (usually Ctrl-Z), provided you're using a shell that supports job control, such as zsh or bash.

Global Searching and Replacing

There are many more features of *vi* than are documented here; most of these features are implemented through combinations of the simple features we've seen. Here are one or two other tidbits most *vi* users find useful.

The command

```
:[x,y]s/pattern/replacement/flags
```

searches for *pattern* between lines *x* and *y* in the buffer, and replaces instances of *pattern* with the *replacement* text. *pattern* is a regular expression; *replacement* is literal text but can contain several special characters to refer to elements in the original *pattern*. The following command replaces the first occurrence of weeble with wobble on lines 1 through 10, inclusive:

```
:1,10s/weeble/wobble
```

Instead of giving line-number specification, you can use the % symbol to refer to the entire file. Other special symbols can be used in place of x and y. $ refers to the last line of the file. Leave x or y blank to refer to the current line.

Among the *flags* you can use are g to replace all instances of *pattern* on each line, and c to ask for confirmation for each replacement. In most instances, you will want to use the g flag, unless you want to replace only the first occurrence of *pattern* on each line.

You can also use *marks* to refer to lines. Marks are just single-letter names that are given to cursor locations within the document. Moving the cursor to a location in the file and typing ma will set the mark a at that point. (Marks may be named any of the letters a–z or A–Z.) You can move the cursor directly to the mark a with the command `a (with a backquote). Using a regular single quote (as in 'a) will move the cursor to the beginning of the line that the mark a is on.

Marks allow you to "remember" cursor locations that denote a region of text. For example, if you want to search and replace a block of text, you can move the cursor to the beginning of the text, set a mark, move the cursor to the end of the text, and use the command:

```
:'a,.s/weeble/wobble/
```

where 'a refers to the line containing mark a, and . refers to the current line.

Moving Text and Using Registers

One way to copy and move text is to delete it (using the d or dd commands) and then replace it with the P command, as described earlier. For example, if you want to delete 10 lines, starting with the line that contains your cursor, and paste them somewhere else, just use the command 10dd (to delete 10 lines), move the cursor to the new location for the text, and type p. You can copy text in this way as well: typing 10dd followed by P (at the same cursor location) deletes the text and immediately replaces it. You can then paste the text elsewhere by moving the cursor and using p multiple times.

Similar to dd is the yy command, which "yanks" text without deleting it. You use p to paste the yanked text as with dd. But note that each yank operation will delete the previously yanked text from the clipboard.

The deletion and yank commands can be used on more general regions than lines. Recall that the d command deletes text through a move command; for example, d$ deletes text from the cursor to the end of the line. Similarly, y$ yanks text from the cursor to the end of the line.

Let's say you want to yank (or delete) a region of text. This can be done with marks as well. Move the cursor to the beginning of the text to be yanked and set a mark, such as ma. Move the cursor to the end of the text to be yanked and use the command y`a. This yanks text from the cursor position to the mark a. (Remember that the command `a moves the cursor to the mark a.) Using d instead of y deletes the text from the cursor to the mark.

The most convenient way to cut, copy, and paste portions of text within *vi* is to use registers. A *register* is just a named temporary storage space for text you wish to copy between locations, cut and paste within the document, and so forth.

Registers are given single-letter names; any of the characters a to z or A to Z are valid. The " command (a quotation mark) specifies a register; it is followed by the name of the register, as in "a for register a. The lowercase letters and their uppercase counterparts refer to the same registers: using the lowercase letter overwrites the previous contents of the register, and using the uppercase letter appends to it.

For instance, if we move the cursor to the first line, as in Figure 19-14, and use the command "ayy, the current line is yanked into the register a. We can then move the cursor to the second line, and use the command "ap to paste the text from register a after the current line (see Figure 19-15).

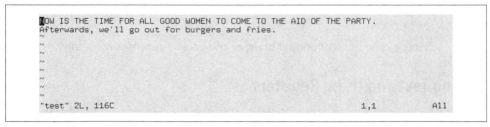

Figure 19-14. vi *buffer before a yank*

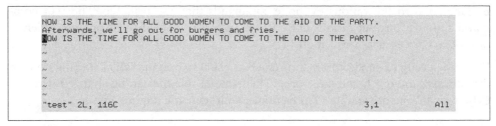

```
       NOW IS THE TIME FOR ALL GOOD WOMEN TO COME TO THE AID OF THE PARTY.
       Afterwards, we'll go out for burgers and fries.
       NOW IS THE TIME FOR ALL GOOD WOMEN TO COME TO THE AID OF THE PARTY.
       ~
       ~
       ~
       ~
       ~
       ~
       "test" 2L, 116C                                              3,1        All
```

Figure 19-15. vi *buffer after a yank*

Similarly, the command "ay`a yanks text from the cursor to mark a into register a. Note that there is no correspondence between mark and register names!

Using registers allows you to copy text between files. Just copy the text to a register, use the :e command to edit a new file, and paste the text from the register.

Extending vi

vi is extensible in many ways. Most of the commands we've introduced can be generalized to arbitrary regions of text. As we've already seen, commands such as d and y operate on the text from the cursor to a move operation, such as $ or G. (dG deletes text from the cursor to the end of the file.) Many other commands operate on text through a move command in the same way. Using marks, you can operate on any region of text.

As we mentioned before, *vi* is just a text editor; it doesn't have facilities for spell checking text, compiling programs, and other such features. However, *vi* executes other programs that you can use to extend the editor. The command:

```
:x,y!command
```

executes the named *command* with the text on lines *x* through *y* as standard input, and replaces the lines with the standard output of the command. As with the s (search and replace) command, other specifications, such as % and $, can be used for the line numbers.

For example, let's say you want to prepend a quote character to all the lines in a region of text. One way to do this is to write a short shell or Perl script (see "Programming Languages and Utilities" in Chapter 1) that reads lines of input and outputs those same lines with the quote character prepended. (Or use a *sed* command— there are many alternatives.) You can then send lines of text through this filter, which replaces them with the quoted text within *vi*. If the script is called *quote*, just use a command such as:

```
:`a,.!quote
```

which quotes the region of text between the cursor location and the mark a.

Be familiar with the various *ex*-mode commands that are available. The `:set` command allows you to set various options; for example, `:set ai` turns on auto indentation of text. (`:set noai` turns it off.)

You can specify *ex*-mode commands (such as `:set`) to execute when starting up *vi* in the file *.exrc* in your home directory. (The name of this file can be changed with the `EXINIT` environment variable.) For example, your *.exrc* file might contain:

```
set ai
```

to turn on auto indentation. You don't need the : before *ex* commands in this file.

A number of good tutorials and references for *vi* are available—both online as well as in print. *Learning the vi Editor* is a good place to look for more information. One popular web site for vi information is The vi Lovers Home Page, *http://thomer.com/vi/vi.html*. The home of *vim* on the Web is *http://www.vim.org*.

The (X)Emacs Editor

Text editors are among the most important applications in the Unix world. They are used so often that many people spend more time within an editor than anywhere else on their Unix system. The same holds true for Linux.

The choice of an editor can be a religious one. Many editors exist, but the Unix community has arranged itself into two major groups: the Emacs camp and the *vi* camp. Because of *vi*'s somewhat nonintuitive user interface, many people (newcomers and seasoned users alike) prefer Emacs over *vi*. However, long-time users of *vi* (and single-finger typists) use it more efficiently than a more complex editor such as Emacs.

If *vi* is one end of the text-editor spectrum, Emacs is the other; they are widely different in their design and philosophy. Emacs is partly the brainchild of Richard Stallman, founder of the Free Software Foundation and author of much of the GNU software.

Emacs is a very large system with more features than any single Unix application to date (some people would even go so far as not to call it an editor but an "integrated environment"). It contains its own LISP language engine that you can use to write extensions for the editor. (Many of the functions within Emacs are written in Emacs LISP.) Emacs includes extensions for everything from compiling and debugging programs to reading and sending electronic mail to X Window System support and more. Emacs also includes its own online tutorial and documentation. The book *Learning GNU Emacs* by Debra Cameron, James Elliott, Marc Loy, Eric S. Raymond, and Bill Rosenblatt (O'Reilly) is a popular guide to the editor.

Most Linux distributions include two variants of Emacs. GNU Emacs is the original version, which is still being developed, but development seems to have slowed down. XEmacs is larger, but much more user-friendly and better integrated with the X Window System (even though you can also use it from the command line, despite its name). If you are not tight on memory and have a reasonably fast computer, we suggest using XEmacs. Another advantage of XEmacs is that many useful packages that you would need to download and install separately with GNU Emacs are already shipped with XEmacs. We will not cover the differences here, though; the discussion in this section applies to both. Whenever we talk about *Emacs* in this section, we mean either version.

Firing It Up

GNU Emacs is simply invoked as follows:

```
$ emacs options
```

Likewise, XEmacs is invoked as follows:

```
$ xemacs options
```

Most of the time, you don't need options. You can specify filenames on the command line, but it's more straightforward to read them in after starting the program.

In Emacs lingo, C-x means Ctrl-X, and M-p is equivalent to Alt-P. As you might guess, C-M-p means Ctrl-Alt-P.

Using these conventions, press C-x followed by C-f to read in a file or create a new one. The keystrokes display a prompt at the bottom of your screen that shows your current working directory. You can create a buffer now to hold what will end up being the content of a new file; let's call the file *wibble.txt*, shown in Figure 19-16.

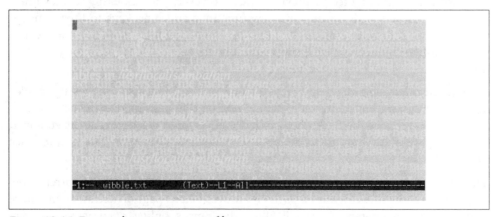

Figure 19-16. Emacs when opening a new file

The mode line at the bottom indicates the name of the file as well as the type of buffer you're in (which here is Fundamental). Emacs supports many kinds of editing modes; Fundamental is the default for plain-text files, but other modes exist for editing C and TEX source, modifying directories, and so on. Each mode has certain key bindings and commands associated with it, as we'll see soon. Emacs typically determines the mode of the buffer based on the filename extension.

To the right of the buffer type is the word All, which means that you are currently looking at the entire file (which is empty). Typically, you will see a percentage, which represents how far into the file you are.

If you're running Emacs under the X Window System, a new window will be created for the editor with a menubar at the top, scrollbars, and other goodies. In "Emacs and the X Window System" later in this chapter we discuss Emacs's special features when used within X.

Simple Editing Commands

Emacs is more straightforward than *vi* when it comes to basic text editing. The arrow keys should move the cursor around the buffer; if they don't (in case Emacs is not configured for your terminal), use the keys C-p (previous line), C-n (next line), C-f (forward character), and C-b (backward character).

If you find using the Alt key uncomfortable, press Esc and then p. Pressing and releasing Esc is equivalent to holding down Alt.

Already we must make the first digression in our discussion of Emacs. Literally every command and key within Emacs is customizable. That is, with a "default" Emacs configuration, C-p maps to the internal function *previous-line*, which moves the cursor (also called "point") to the previous line. However, you can easily rebind different keys to these functions, or write new functions and bind keys to them, and so forth. Unless otherwise stated, the keys we introduce here work for the default Emacs configuration. Later we'll show you how to customize the keys for your own use.

Back to editing: using the arrow keys or one of the equivalents moves the cursor around the current buffer. Just start typing text, and it is inserted at the current cursor location. Pressing the Backspace or Delete key should delete text at the cursor. If it doesn't, we show how to fix it in "Tailoring Emacs" later in this chapter. See Figure 19-17.

The keys C-a and C-e move the cursor to the beginning and end of the current line, respectively. C-v moves forward a page; M-v moves back a page. There are many more basic editing commands, but we'll allow the Emacs online documentation (discussed shortly) to fill those in.

In order to get out of Emacs, use the command C-x C-c. This is the first of the extended commands we've seen; many Emacs commands require several keys. C-x alone is a "prefix" to other keys. In this case, pressing C-x followed by C-c quits Emacs, first asking you if you want to save your changes. If you answer no to this

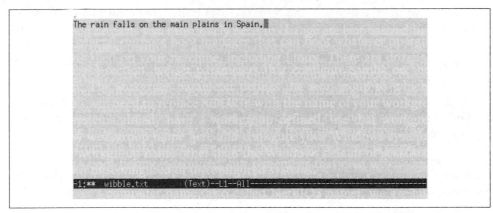

Figure 19-17. Emacs buffer after entering text

question, it will tell you that modified buffers still exist and ask whether you really want to quit without saving changes to those buffers.

You can use C-x C-s to save the current file, and C-x C-f to find another file to edit. For example, typing C-x C-f presents you with a prompt such as:

    Find file: /home/loomer/mdw/

where the current directory is displayed. After this, type the name of the file to find. Pressing the Tab key will do filename completion similar to that used in *bash* and *zsh*. For example, entering:

    Find file: /home/loomer/mdw/**.bash**

and pressing Tab opens another buffer, showing all possible completions, as in Figure 19-18.

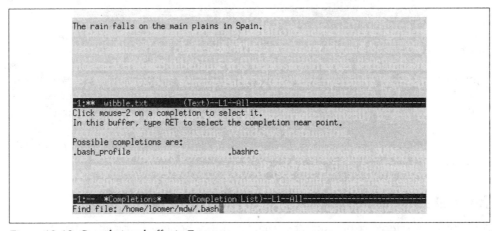

Figure 19-18. Completions buffer in Emacs

After you complete the filename, the *Completions* buffer goes away and the new file is displayed for editing. This is one example of how Emacs uses temporary buffers to present information. If you do not want to use the current directory, instead of deleting everything that's there, you can just append another slash to the displayed path and start over afresh, without having to delete the existing text.

Emacs allows you to use multiple buffers when editing text; each buffer may contain a different file you're editing. When you load a file with C-x C-f, a new buffer is created to edit the file, but the original buffer isn't deleted.

You can switch to another buffer using the C-x b command, which asks you for the name of the buffer (usually the name of the file within the buffer). For example, pressing C-x b presents the following prompt:

```
Switch to buffer: (default wibble.txt)
```

The default buffer is the previous one visited. Press Enter to switch to the default buffer, or type another buffer name. Using C-x C-b will present a buffer list (in a buffer of its own), as shown in Figure 19-19.

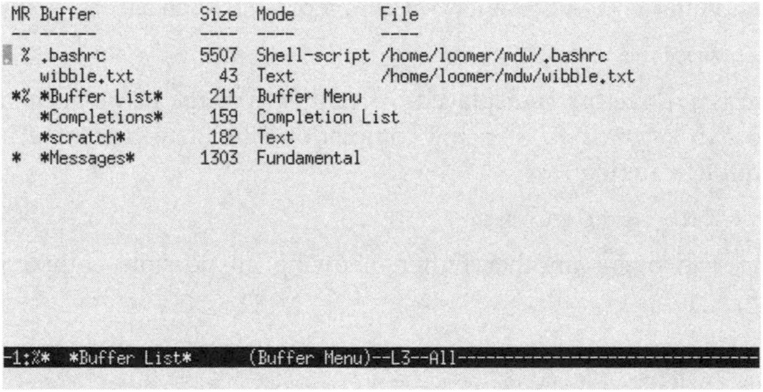

```
MR Buffer          Size  Mode          File
-- ------          ----  ----          ----
 % .bashrc         5507  Shell-script  /home/loomer/mdw/.bashrc
   wibble.txt        43  Text          /home/loomer/mdw/wibble.txt
*% *Buffer List*    211  Buffer Menu
   *Completions*    159  Completion List
   *scratch*        182  Text
 * *Messages*      1303  Fundamental


-1:%*  *Buffer List*     (Buffer Menu)--L3--All------------------------
```

Figure 19-19. Buffer list in Emacs

Popping up the buffer menu splits the Emacs screen into two "windows," which you can switch between using C-x o. More than two concurrent windows are possible as well. In order to view just one window at a time, switch to the appropriate one and press C-x 1. This hides all the other windows, but you can switch to them later using the C-x b command just described. Using C-x k actually deletes a buffer from Emacs's memory.

Tutorial and Online Help

Already Emacs looks a bit complex; that is simply because it's such a flexible system. Before we go any further, it is instructive to introduce Emacs's built-in online help and tutorial. This documentation has also been published in book form as the *GNU Emacs Manual*, by Richard M. Stallman (GNU Press).

Using the C-h command gives you a list of help options on the last line of the display. Pressing C-h again describes what they are. In particular, C-h followed by t drops you into the Emacs tutorial. It should be self-explanatory, and an interactive tutorial about Emacs tells you more about the system than we can hope to cover here.

After going through the Emacs tutorial, you should get accustomed to the Info system, where the rest of the Emacs documentation resides. C-h followed by i enters the Info reader. A mythical Info page might look like this:

```
File: intercal.info,  Node: Top,  Next: Instructions,  Up: (dir)

       This file documents the Intercal interpreter for Linux.

       * Menu:

       * Instructions::      How to read this manual.
       * Overview::          Preliminary information.
       * Examples::          Example Intercal programs and bugs.
       * Concept Index::     Index of concepts.
```

As you see, text is presented along with a menu to other nodes. Pressing m and then entering a node name from the menu will allow you to read that node. You can read nodes sequentially by pressing the spacebar, which jumps to the next node in the document (indicated by the information line at the top of the buffer). Here, the next node is Instructions, which is the first node in the menu.

Each node also has a link to the parent node (Up), which here is (dir), meaning the Info page directory. Pressing u takes you to the parent node. In addition, each node has a link to the previous node, if it exists (in this case, it does not). The p command moves to the previous node. The l command returns you to the node most recently visited.

Within the Info reader, pressing ? gives you a list of commands, and pressing h presents you with a short tutorial on using the system. Since you're running Info within Emacs, you can use Emacs commands as well (such as C-x b to switch to another buffer).

If you think that the Info system is arcane and obsolete, please keep in mind that it was designed to work on all kinds of systems, including those lacking graphics or powerful processing capabilities.

Other online help is available within Emacs. Pressing C-h C-h gives you a list of help options. One of these is C-h k, after which you press a key, and documentation about the function that is bound to that key appears.

Deleting, Copying, and Moving Text

There are various ways to move and duplicate blocks of text within Emacs. These methods involve use of the *mark*, which is simply a "remembered" cursor location you can set using various commands. The block of text between the current cursor location (*point*) and the mark is called the *region*.

You can set the mark using the key C-@ (or C-Space on most systems). Moving the cursor to a location and pressing C-@ sets the mark at that position. You can now move the cursor to another location within the document, and the region is defined as the text between the mark and point.

Many Emacs commands operate on the region. The most important of these commands deal with deleting and yanking text. The command C-w deletes the current region and saves it in the *kill ring*. The kill ring is a list of text blocks that have been deleted. You can then paste (*yank*) the text at another location, using the C-y command. (Note that the semantics of the term *yank* differ between *vi* and Emacs. In *vi*, "yanking" text is equivalent to adding it to the undo register without deleting it, whereas in Emacs, "yank" means to paste text.) Using the kill ring, you can paste not only the most recently deleted block of text, but also blocks of text that were deleted previously.

For example, type the text shown in Figure 19-20 into an Emacs buffer.

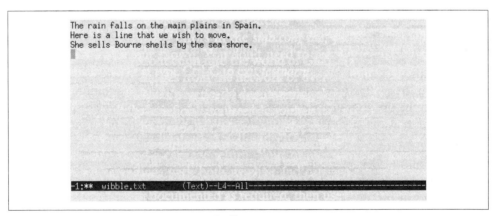

Figure 19-20. Entering text into an Emacs buffer

Now, move the cursor to the beginning of the second line ("*Here is a line...*"), and set the mark with C-@. Move to the end of the line (with C-e), and delete the region using C-w. See Figure 19-21.

To yank the text just deleted, move the cursor to the end of the buffer and press C-y. The line should be pasted at the new location, as shown in Figure 19-22.

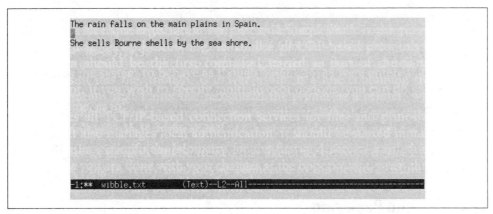

Figure 19-21. Emacs buffer after deletion

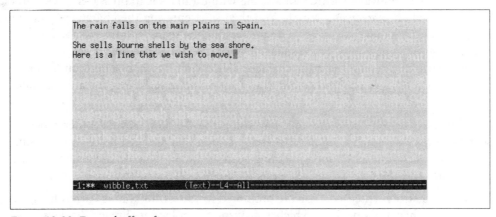

Figure 19-22. Emacs buffer after paste

Pressing C-y repeatedly will insert the text multiple times.

You can copy text in a similar fashion. Using M-w instead of C-w will copy the region into the kill ring without deleting it. (Remember that M- means holding down the Alt key or pressing Esc before the w.)

Text that is deleted using other kill commands, such as C-k, is also added to the kill ring. This means that you don't need to set the mark and use C-w to move a block of text; any command that deletes more than one character will do.

To recover previously deleted blocks of text (which are saved on the kill ring), use the command M-y after yanking with C-y. M-y replaces the yanked text with the previous block from the kill ring. Pressing M-y repeatedly cycles through the contents of the kill ring. This feature is useful if you wish to move or copy multiple blocks of text.

Emacs also provides a more general *register* mechanism, similar to that found in *vi*. Among other things, you can use this feature to save text you want to paste in later. A register has a one-character name; let's use a for this example:

1. At the beginning of the text you want to save, set the mark by pressing the Control key and spacebar together (or if that doesn't work, press C-@).
2. Move point (the cursor) to the end of the region you want to save.
3. Press C-x x followed by the name of the register (a in this case).
4. When you want to paste the text somewhere, press C-x g followed by the name of the register, a.

Searching and Replacing

The most common way to search for a string within Emacs is to press C-s. This starts what is called an *incremental search*. You then start entering the characters you are looking for. Each time you press a character, Emacs searches forward for a string matching everything you've typed so far. If you make a mistake, just press the Delete key and continue typing the right characters. If the string cannot be found, Emacs beeps. If you find an occurrence but you want to keep searching for another one, press C-s again.

You can also search backward this way using the C-r key. Several other types of searches exist, including a regular expression search that you can invoke by pressing M-C-s. This lets you search for something such as jo.*n, which matches names like John, Joan, and Johann. (By default, searches are not case-sensitive.)

To replace a string, enter M-%. You are prompted for the string that is currently in the buffer, and then the one with which you want to replace it. Emacs displays each place in the buffer where the string is and asks you if you want to replace this occurrence. Press the spacebar to replace the string, the Delete key to skip this string, or a period to stop the search.

If you know you want to replace all occurrences of a string that follow your current place in the buffer, without being queried for each one, enter M-x replace-string. (The M-x key allows you to enter the name of an Emacs function and execute it, without use of a key binding. Many Emacs functions are available only via M-x, unless you bind them to keys yourself.) A regular expression can be replaced by entering M-x replace-regexp.

Macros

The name Emacs comes partly from the word *macros*. A macro is a simple but powerful feature that makes Emacs a pleasure to use. If you plan on doing anything frequently and repetitively, just press C-x (, perform the operation once, and then press C-x). The two C-x commands with the opening and closing parentheses remember all the keys you pressed. Then you can execute the commands over and over again by pressing C-x e.

Here's an example you can try on any text file; it capitalizes the first word of each line.

1. Press C-x (to begin the macro.

2. Press C-a to put point at the beginning of the current line. It's important to know where you are each time a macro executes. By pressing C-a, you are making sure the macro will always go to the beginning of the line, which is where you want to be.

3. Press M-c to make the first letter of the first word a capital letter.

4. Press C-a again to return to the beginning of the line, and C-n or the down arrow to go to the beginning of the following line. This ensures that the macro will start execution at the right place next time.

5. Press C-x) to end the macro.

6. Press C-x e repeatedly to capitalize the following lines. Or press C-u several times, followed by C-x e. The repeated uses of C-u are prefix keys, causing the following command to execute many times. If you get to the end of the document while the macro is still executing, no harm is done; Emacs just beeps and stops executing the macro.

Running Commands and Programming Within Emacs

Emacs provides interfaces for many programs, which you can run within an Emacs buffer. For example, Emacs modes exist for reading and sending electronic mail, reading Usenet news, compiling programs, and interacting with the shell. In this section, we introduce some of these features.

To send electronic mail from within Emacs, press C-x m. This opens up a buffer that allows you to compose and send an email message (Figure 19-23).

Simply enter your message within this buffer and use C-c C-s to send it. You can also insert text from other buffers, extend the interface with your own Emacs LISP functions, and so on. Furthermore, an Emacs mode called RMAIL lets you read your electronic mail right within Emacs, but we won't discuss it here because most people prefer standalone mailers. (Usually, these mailers let you choose Emacs as your editor for email messages.)

Similar to the RMAIL mail interface is GNUS, the Emacs-based newsreader, which you can start with the M-x gnus command. After startup (and a bit of chewing on your *.newsrc* file), a list of newsgroups will be presented, along with a count of unread articles for each, as shown in Figure 19-24.

To:
Subject:
--text follows this line--
-1:-- *mail* (Mail)--L1--All-----------------------------------

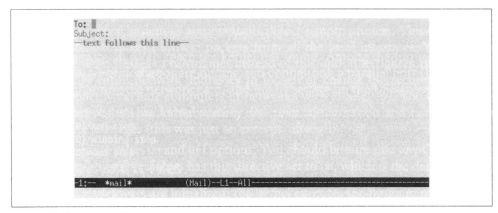

Figure 19-23. Mail in Emacs

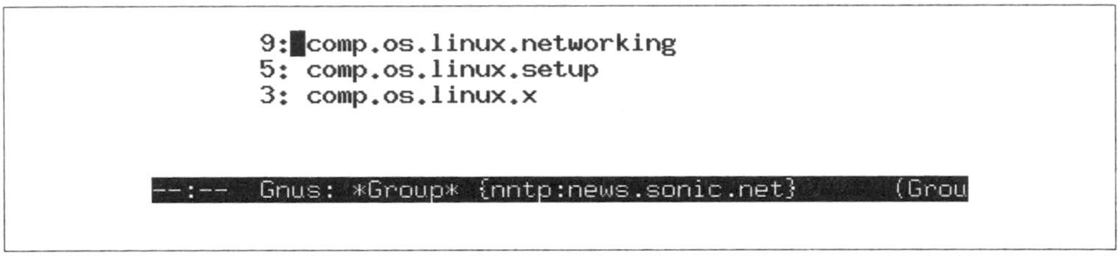

9: comp.os.linux.networking
5: comp.os.linux.setup
3: comp.os.linux.x
--:-- Gnus: *Group* {nntp:news.sonic.net} (Grou

Figure 19-24. Newsgroup reading in Emacs

GNUS is an example of the power of using Emacs interfaces to other tools. You get all the convenience of Emacs's navigation, search, and macro capabilities, along with specific key sequences appropriate for the tool you're using.

Using the arrow keys, you can select a newsgroup to read. Press the spacebar to begin reading articles from that group. Two buffers will be displayed: one containing a list of articles and the other displaying the current article.

Using `n` and `p`, move to the next and previous articles, respectively. Then use `f` and `F` to post a follow-up to the current article (either including or excluding the current article), and `r` and `R` to reply to the article via electronic mail. There are many other GNUS commands; use `C-h m` to get a list of them. If you're used to a newsreader, such as `rn`, GNUS will be somewhat familiar.

Emacs provides a number of modes for editing various types of files. For example, there is C mode for editing C source code, and TeX mode for editing (surprise) TeX source. Each mode boasts features that make editing the appropriate type of file easier.

For example, within C mode, you can use the command `M-x compile`, which, by default, runs `make -k` in the current directory and redirects errors to another buffer. For example, the compilation buffer may contain the following:

```
cd /home/loomer/mdw/pgmseq/
        make -k
        gcc -O -O2 -I. -I../include -c stream_load.c -o stream_load.o
        stream_load.c:217: syntax error before `struct'
        stream_load.c:217: parse error before `struct'
```

You can move the cursor to a line containing an error message and press C-c C-c to make the cursor jump to that line in the corresponding source buffer. Emacs opens a buffer for the appropriate source file if one does not already exist. Now you can edit and compile programs entirely within Emacs.

Emacs also provides a complete interface to the gdb debugger, which is described in "Using Emacs with gdb" in Chapter 21.

Usually, Emacs selects the appropriate mode for the buffer based on the filename extension. For example, editing a file with the extension *.c* in the filename automatically selects C mode for that buffer.

Shell mode is one of the most popular Emacs extensions. Shell mode allows you to interact with the shell in an Emacs buffer, using the command M-x shell. You can edit, cut, and paste command lines with standard Emacs commands. You can also run single shell commands from Emacs using M-!. If you use M-| instead, the contents of the current region are piped to the given shell command as standard input. This is a general interface for running subprograms from within Emacs.

Tailoring Emacs

The Emacs online documentation should be sufficient to get you on track for learning more about the system and growing accustomed to it. However, sometimes it is hard to locate some of the most helpful hints for getting started. Here we present a rundown on certain customization options many Emacs users choose to employ to make life easier.

The Emacs personal customization file is *.emacs*, which should reside in your home directory. This file should contain code, written in Emacs LISP, that runs or defines functions to customize your Emacs environment. (If you've never written LISP before, don't worry; most customizations using it are quite simple.)

One of the most common things users customize are key bindings. For instance, if you use Emacs to edit SGML documents, you can bind the key C-c s to switch to SGML mode. Put this in your *.emacs* file:

```
; C-c followed by s will put buffer into SGML mode."
        (global-set-key "\C-cs" 'sgml-mode)
```

Comments in Emacs LISP start with a semicolon. The command that follows runs the command *global-set-key*. Now you don't have to type in the long sequence M-xsgml-mode to start editing in SGML. Just press the two characters C-c s. This works anywhere in Emacs—no matter what mode your buffer is in—because it is global.

(Of course, Emacs may also recognize an SGML or XML file by its suffix and put it in SGML mode for you automatically.)

A customization that you might want to use is making the text mode the default mode and turning on the autofill minor mode (which makes text automatically wrap if it is too long for one line), like this:

```
; Make text mode the default, with auto-fill
        (setq default-major-mode 'text-mode)
        (add-hook 'text-mode-hook 'turn-on-auto-fill)
```

You don't always want your key mappings to be global. As you use TeX mode, C mode, and other modes defined by Emacs, you'll find useful things you'd like to do only in a single mode. Here, we define a simple LISP function to insert some characters into C code, and then bind the function to a key for our convenience:

```
(defun start-if-block(  )
        (interactive)
        (insert "if (  ) {\n}\n")
        (backward-char 6)
        )
```

We start the function by declaring it `interactive` so that we can invoke it (otherwise, it would be used only internally by other functions). Then we use the `insert` function to put the following characters into our C buffer:

```
if (  ) {
        }
```

Strings in Emacs can contain standard C escape characters. Here, we've used \n for a newline.

Now we have a template for an `if` block. To put on the ribbon and the bow, our function also moves backward six characters so that point is within the parentheses, and we can immediately start typing an expression.

Our whole goal was to make it easy to insert these characters, so now let's bind our function to a key:

```
(define-key c-mode-map "\C-ci" 'start-if-block)
```

The define-key function binds a key to a function. By specifying c-mode-map, we indicate that the key works only in C mode. There is also a tex-mode-map for mode, and a lisp-mode-map that you will want to know about if you play with your *.emacs* file a lot.

If you'd like to write your own Emacs LISP functions, you should read the Info pages for *elisp*, which should be available on your system. Two good books on writing Emacs LISP functions are *An Introduction to Programming in Emacs Lisp*, by Robert J. Chassell (GNU Press).

Now here's an important customization you may need. On many terminals the Backspace key sends the character C-h, which is the Emacs help key. To fix this, you should change the internal table Emacs uses to interpret keys, as follows:

```
(keyboard-translate ?\C-h ?\C-?)
```

Pretty cryptic code. \C-h is recognizable as the Control key pressed with h, which happens to produce the same ASCII code (8) as the Backspace key. \C-? represents the Delete key (ASCII code 127). Don't confuse this question mark with the question marks that precede each backslash. ?\C-h means "the ASCII code corresponding to \C-h." You could just as well specify 8 directly.

So now, both Backspace and C-h will delete. You've lost your help key. Therefore, another good customization would be to bind another key to C-h. Let's use C-\, which isn't often used for anything else. You have to double the backslash when you specify it as a key:

```
(keyboard-translate ?\C-\\ ?\C-h)
```

On the X Window System, there is a way to change the code sent by your Backspace key using the xmodmap command, but we'll have to leave it up to you to do your own research. It is not a completely portable solution (so we can't show you an example guaranteed to work), and it may be too sweeping for your taste (it also changes the meaning of the Backspace key in your xterm shell and everywhere else).

There are other key bindings you may want to use. For example, you may prefer to use the keys C-f and C-b to scroll forward (or backward) one page at a time, as in *vi*. In your *.emacs* file you might include the following lines:

```
(global-set-key "\C-f" 'scroll-up)
        (global-set-key "\C-b" 'scroll-down)
```

Again, we have to issue a caveat: be careful not to redefine keys that have other important uses. (One way to find out is to use C-h k to tell you what a key does in the current mode. You should also consider that the key may have definitions in other modes.) In particular, you'll lose access to a lot of functions if you rebind the *prefix keys* that start commands, such as C-x and C-c.

You can create your own prefix keys, if you really want to extend your current mode with lots of new commands. Use something like:

```
(global-unset-key "\C-d")
        (global-set-key "\C-d\C-f" 'my-function)
```

First, we must unbind the C-d key (which simply deletes the character under the cursor) in order to use it as a prefix for other keys. Now, pressing C-d C-f will execute my-function.

You may also prefer to use another mode besides *Fundamental* or *Text* for editing "vanilla" files. *Indented Text* mode, for example, automatically indents lines of text relative to the previous line so that it starts in the same column (as with the :set ai function in *vi*). To turn on this mode by default, use:

```
; Default mode for editing text
      (setq default-major-mode 'indented-text-mode)
```

You should also rebind the Enter key to indent the next line of text:

```
(define-key indented-text-mode-map "\C-m" 'newline-and-indent)
```

Emacs also provides *minor* modes, which are modes you use along with major modes. For example, *Overwrite* mode is a minor mode that causes newly typed characters to overwrite the text in the buffer, instead of inserting it. To bind the key C-r to toggle *Overwrite* mode, use the following command:

```
; Toggle overwrite mode.
      (global-set-key "\C-r" 'overwrite-mode)
```

Another minor mode is *Autofill*, which automatically wraps lines as you type them. That is, instead of pressing the Enter key at the end of each line of text, you may continue typing and Emacs automatically breaks the line for you. To enable *Autofill* mode, use the commands:

```
(setq text-mode-hook 'turn-on-auto-fill)
      (setq fill-column 72)
```

This turns on *Autofill* mode whenever you enter *Text* mode (through the *text-mode-hook* function). It also sets the point at which to break lines at 72 characters.

Regular Expressions

Even a few regular expression tricks can vastly increase your power to search for text and alter it in bulk. Regular expressions were associated only with Unix tools and languages for a long time; now they are popping up in other environments, such as Microsoft's .NET. Only Unix, however, offers them in a wide variety of places, such as text editors and the grep command, where ordinary users can exploit them.

Let's suppose you're looking through a file that contains mail messages. You're on a bunch of mailing lists with names such as gyro-news and gyro-talk, so you're looking for Subject lines with gyro- in them. You can use your text editor or the grep command to search for:

```
^Subject:.*gyro-
```

This means "look for lines beginning with Subject:, followed by any number of any kind of character, followed by gyro-." The regular expression is made up of a number of parts, some reproducing the plain text you're looking for and others expressing general concepts such as "beginning of line." Figure 19-25 shows what the parts mean and how they fit together.

Just to give a hint of how powerful and sophisticated regular expressions can be, let's refine the one in Figure 19-25 for a narrower search. This time, we know that mailing

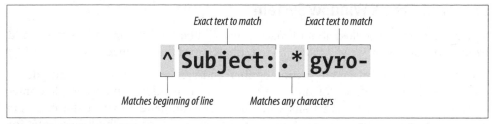

Figure 19-25. Simple regular expression

lists on *gyros* send out mail with Subject lines that begin with the name of the list in brackets, such as Subject: [gyro-news] or Subject: [gyro-talk]. We can search for precisely such lines, as follows:

```
^Subject: *\[gyro-[a-z]*\]
```

Figure 19-26 shows what the parts of this expression mean. We'll just mention a couple of interesting points here.

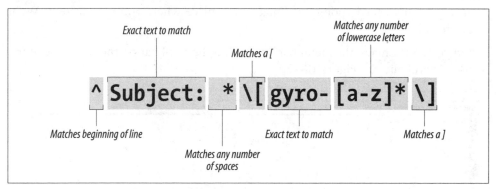

Figure 19-26. Regular expression with more parts

Brackets, like carets and asterisks, are special characters in regular expressions. Brackets are used to mark whole classes of characters you want to search for, such as [a-z] to represent "any lowercase character." We don't want the bracket before gyro to have this special meaning, so we put a backslash in front of it; this is called *escaping* the bracket. (In other words, we let the bracket escape being considered a meta-character in the regular expression.)

The first asterisk in our expression follows a space, so it means "match any number of spaces in succession." The second asterisk follows the [a-z] character class, so it applies to that entire construct. By itself, [a-z] matches one and only one lowercase letter. Together, [a-z]* means "match any number of lowercase letters in succession."

A sophisticated use of regular expressions can take weeks to learn, and readers who want to base applications on regular expressions would do well to read *Mastering Regular Expressions*, by Jeffrey Friedl (O'Reilly).

Emacs and the X Window System

So far, we have only talked about Emacs as it could be run both in an X window and from a console. Now we will take a look at the X support that Emacs has.

The X features in Emacs are getting spiffier and spiffier. They include pull-down menus, different typefaces for different parts of your window, and a complete integration of cut-and-paste functions with the X environment. Most of the concepts here are mainly for the Emacs editor, as the XEmacs editor has built-in menus for many of the things described here. Nevertheless, many of the configurations described in this section work on both versions of Emacs.

Let's start by defining some nice colors for different parts of the Emacs window. Try this command:

```
eggplant$ emacs  -bg ivory  -fg slateblue  -ms orangered  -cr brown
```

You're setting the background color, foreground color, mouse color, and cursor color, respectively. The cursor is the little rectangle that appears in the window, representing what's called "point" in Emacs—the place where you type in text. We'll return to colors soon.

When you start Emacs, the menu bar on top and the scrollbar on the right side of the window stand out. See Figure 19-27.

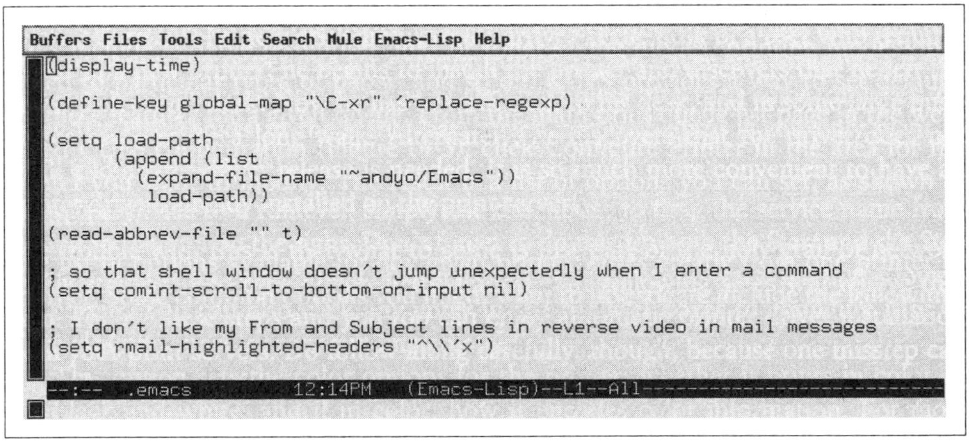

```
 Buffers Files Tools Edit Search Mule Emacs-Lisp Help
(display-time)

(define-key global-map "\C-xr" 'replace-regexp)

(setq load-path
      (append (list
        (expand-file-name "~andyo/Emacs"))
        load-path))

(read-abbrev-file "" t)

; so that shell window doesn't jump unexpectedly when I enter a command
(setq comint-scroll-to-bottom-on-input nil)

; I don't like my From and Subject lines in reverse video in mail messages
(setq rmail-highlighted-headers "^\\'x")

--:--  .emacs        12:14PM   (Emacs-Lisp)--L1--All
```

Figure 19-27. Emacs window

The scrollbar works just like the xterm scrollbar. The menu bar offers a lot of common functions. Some editing modes, such as C and TEX, have their own pull-down menus. The menus are not documented, so you will just have to experiment and try to figure out to which Emacs functions they correspond.

When you want to use a function that doesn't have a simple key sequence—or you've forgotten the sequence—the menus come in handy. For instance, if you rarely use a regular expression search (a quite powerful feature, well worth studying), the easiest way to invoke it is to pull down the Edit menu and choose Regexp Search.

Another useful menu item is Choose Next Paste (Select and Paste on some versions) on the Edit menu. This offers something you can't get any other way: a list of all the pieces of text you've cut recently. In other words, it shows you the kill ring. You can choose the text you want to paste in next, and the next time you press C-y, it's put into your buffer.

If you get tired of the scrollbar and the menu, put the following LISP code in your *.emacs* file to make them go away:

```
(if (getenv "DISPLAY")
        (progn (menu-bar-mode -1)
        (scroll-bar-mode -1))
        )
```

The mouse is the next X feature with interesting possibilities. You can cut and paste text much the same way as in xterm. And you can do this between windows: if you see some output in an xterm window that you'd like to put in a file, you can copy it from the xterm and paste it into your Emacs buffer. Moreover, any text you cut the normal way (such as through C-w) goes into the same selection as text you cut with the mouse. So you can cut a few words from your Emacs buffer and paste them into an xterm window.

The right mouse button works a little unusually. If you select text with the left mouse button, you can click once on the right mouse button to copy it. A second click on the right mouse button removes it. To paste it back, press the middle mouse button.* The text goes just before the character the mouse is currently on. Make a mistake? That's all right—the Undo command reverses it just as for any other Emacs function. (Choose Undo from the Edit menu or just press C-_.)

If you really love mouse work, you can define the buttons to execute any functions you want, just as with keys. Try putting the following command in your *.emacs* file:

```
(define-key global-map [S-mouse-1] 'mail)
```

When you hold down the Shift key and press the left mouse button, a buffer for composing a mail message appears.

We don't recommend you redefine the existing mouse functions, but the Shift, Control, and Alt keys offer plenty of unused possibilities. Combine S-, C-, and M- any way you want in your definitions:

```
(define-key global-map [S-C-mouse-1] 'mail)
```

---

* If you do not have a middle mouse button, chances are that your mouse is configured to emulate a middle mouse button by pressing both the left and the right button simultaneously. Pressing the thumbwheel down could be another option.

Now let's play around a bit with windows. Emacs has had windows of its own for decades, of course, long before the X Window System existed. So an Emacs window is not the same as an X window. What X considers a window, Emacs calls a *frame*.

How would you like to edit in two frames at once? Press C-x 5 2, and another frame appears. The new frame is simply another view onto the same editing session. You can edit different buffers in the two frames, but anything you do in one frame is reflected to the corresponding buffer in the other. When you exit Emacs by pressing C-x C-c, both frames disappear; if you want to close just one frame, press C-x 5 0.

To end our exploration of Emacs on the X Window System, we'll look at a couple of the exciting things you can do with colors. You can change these during an Emacs session, which makes it easy to play around with different possibilities. Press M-x, then type set-background-color and press the Enter key. At the prompt, type ivory or whatever color you've chosen. (Remember, Emacs uses the convention M-x where we use Alt-x in the rest of the book.)

Be careful to make the foreground and background different enough so that you can see the text! In addition to set-background-color, Emacs offers set-foreground-color, set-cursor-color, and set-mouse-color.

Before finishing up this section, we would also like to mention that if Emacs or XEmacs is a bit too much for you, but *vi* is too raw, you will be delighted to know that KDE comes with a variety of text editors that range from quite simple to quite sophisticated. None of these is as big or powerful as (X)Emacs, but they may do the trick.

The two main KDE text editors are called KEdit and Kate; the latter stands for KDE Advanced Text Editor. Kate can be used as a full-blown programmer's editor with syntax coloring, multiple files opened at the same time, and so on. KEdit is similar in feature richness (or poverty) to the Notepad editor on Windows systems. There are also other editors, even (gasp!) a vi version with a KDE interface. You will find all of them in the K menu under the submenu Editors. And finally, if you are using GNOME, you may want to try gedit.

## CHAPTER 20

Text Processing

Now that most of the world uses WYSIWYG word processors, and several good ones are available even for Linux, why use the anachronistic-looking text processors described in this chapter? Actually, text processing (especially in the form of XML) is the wave of the future. People will desire WYSIWYG interfaces, but they will demand a simple, standard, text format underneath to make their documents portable while allowing an unlimited range of automated tools to manipulate the documents.

Because the tools described here are open source and widely available, you can use one of their formats without guilt and reasonably expect your readers to have access to formatters. You can also use an impressive range of tools developed over the years to handle these formats and do sophisticated processing for you, such as to develop a bibliography in TEX. Finally, filters have been developed (although they don't always work perfectly) to convert documents between each of these formats and other popular formats, including the formats used by commercial word processors. So you're not totally locked in, although you will probably have to exert some manual effort to accomplish an accurate conversion.

In Chapter 1, we briefly mentioned various text processing systems available for Linux and how they differ from word processing systems that you may be familiar with. While most word processors allow the user to enter text in a WYSIWYG environment, text processing systems have the user enter source text using a text-formatting language, which can be modified with any text editor. (In fact, Emacs provides special modes for editing various types of text-formatting languages.) Then the source is processed into a printable (or viewable) document using the text processor itself. Finally, you process the output and send it to a file or to a viewer application for display, or you hand it off to a printer daemon to queue for printing to a local or remote device.

TeX and LaTeX

TEX is a professional text processing system for all kinds of documents, articles, and books—especially those that contain a great deal of mathematics. It is a somewhat "low-level" text processing language because it describes to the system how to lay out text on the page, how it should be spaced, and so on. TEX doesn't concern itself directly with higher-level elements of text such as chapters, sections, footnotes, and so forth (those things that you, the writer, care about the most). For this reason, TEX is known as a functional text-formatting language (referring to the actual physical layout of text on a page) rather than a logical one (referring to logical elements, such as chapters and sections). TEX was designed by Donald E. Knuth, one of the world's foremost experts in programming. One of Knuth's motives for developing TEX was to produce a typesetting system powerful enough to handle the mathematics formatting needed for his series of computer science textbooks. Knuth ended up taking an eight-year detour to finish TEX; most would agree the result was well worth the wait.

Of course, TEX is very extensible, and it is possible to write macros for TEX that allow writers to concern themselves primarily with the logical, rather than the physical, format of the document. In fact, a number of such macro packages have been developed—the most popular of which is LATEX, a set of extensions for TEX designed by Leslie Lamport. LATEX commands are concerned mostly with logical structure, but because LATEX is just a set of macros on top of TEX, you can use plain commands as well. LATEX greatly simplifies the use of TEX, hiding most of the low-level functional features from the writer.

In order to write well-structured documents using TEX, you would either have to decide on a prebuilt macro package, such as LATEX, or develop your own (or use a combination of the two). In *The TEX Book* (Addison Wesley), Knuth presents his own set of macros that he used for production of the book. As you might expect, they include commands for beginning new chapters, sections, and the like—somewhat similar to their LATEX counterparts. In the rest of this section, we concentrate on the use of LATEX, which provides support for many types of documents: technical articles, manuals, books, letters, and so on. As with plain TEX, LATEX is extensible as well.

Learning the Ropes

If you've never used a text-formatting system before, there are a number of new concepts of which you should be aware. As we said, text processing systems start with a source document, which you enter with a plain-text editor, such as Emacs. The source is written in a text-formatting language, which includes the text you wish to appear in your document, as well as commands that tell the text processor how to format it.

So, without further ado, let's dive in and see how to write a simple document and format it, from start to finish. As a demonstration, we'll show how to use L^AT_EX to write a short business letter. Sit down at your favorite text editor, and enter the following text into a file (without the line numbers, of course). Call it *letter.tex*:

```
1  \documentclass{letter}
2  \address{755 Chmod Way \\ Apt 0x7F \\
3          Pipeline, N.M. 09915}
4  \signature{Boomer Petway}
5
6  \begin{document}
7  \begin{letter}{O'Reilly and Associates, Inc. \\
8                 1005 Gravenstein Highway North \\
9                 Sebastopol, C.A. 95472}
10
11 \opening{Dear Mr. O'Reilly,}
12
13 I would like to comment on the \LaTeX\ example as presented in
14 Chapter~20 of {\em Running Linux}. Although it was a valiant effort,
15 I find that the example falls somewhat short of what
16 one might expect in a discussion of text-formatting systems.
17 In a future edition of the book, I suggest that you replace
18 the example with one that is more instructive.
19
20 \closing{Thank you,}
21
22 \end{letter}
23 \end{document}
```

This is a complete L^AT_EX document for the business letter that we wish to send. As you can see, it contains the actual text of the letter, with a number of commands (using backslashes and braces) thrown in. Let's walk through it.

Line 1 uses the documentclass command to specify the class of document that we're producing (which is a letter). Commands in L^AT_EX begin with a backslash and are followed by the actual command name, which in this case is documentclass. Following the command name are any arguments, enclosed in braces. L^AT_EX supports several document classes, such as article, report, and book, and you can define your own. Specifying the document class defines global macros for use within the T_EX document, such as the address and signature commands used on lines 2 to 4. As you might guess, the address and signature commands specify your own address and name in the letter. The double backslashes (\\) that appear in the address command generate line breaks in the resulting output of the address.

A word about how L^AT_EX processes input: as with most text-formatting systems, whitespace, line breaks, and other such features in the input source are not passed literally into the output. Therefore, you can break lines more or less wherever you please; when formatting paragraphs, L^AT_EX will fit the lines back together again. Of course, there are exceptions: blank lines in the input begin new paragraphs, and there are commands to force L^AT_EX to treat the source text literally.

On line 6, the command \begin{document} signifies the beginning of the document as a whole. Everything enclosed within the \begin{document} and \end{document} on line 22 is considered part of the text to be formatted; anything before \begin{document} is called the *preamble* and defines formatting parameters before the actual body.

On lines 7 to 9, \begin{letter} begins the actual letter. This is required because you may have many letters within a single source file, and a \begin{letter} command is needed for each. This command takes as an argument the address of the intended recipient; as with the *address* command, double backslashes signify line breaks in the address.

Line 11 uses the *opening* command to open the letter. Following on lines 12 to 18 is the actual body of the letter. As straightforward as it may seem, there are a few tricks hidden in the body as well. On line 13 the \LaTeX\ command generates the logo. You'll notice that a backslash follows as well as precedes the \LaTeX\ command; the trailing backslash is used to force a space after the word "LATEX." This is because TEX ignores spaces after command invocations; the command must be followed by a backslash and a space. Thus, \LaTeX example would print as LATEXexample.

There are two quirks of note on line 14. First of all, a tilde (~) is present between Chapter and 9, which causes a space to appear between the two words, but prevents a line break between them in the output (that is, to prevent Chapter from being on the end of a line, and 9 from being on the beginning of the next). You need only use the tilde to generate a space between two words that should be stuck together on the same line, as in Chapter~9 and Mr.~Jones. (In retrospect, we could have used the tilde in the \begin{letter} and *opening* commands, although it's doubtful TEX would break a line anywhere within the address or the opening.)

The second thing to take note of on line 14 is the use of \em to generate *emphasized text* in the output. TEX supports various other fonts, including **boldface** (\bf) and typewriter (\tt).

Line 20 uses the *closing* command to close off the letter. This also has the effect of appending the signature used on line 4 after the closing in the output. Lines 22 to 23 use the commands \end{letter} and \end{document} to end the letter and document environments begun on lines 6 and 7.

You'll notice that none of the commands in the LATEX source has anything to do with setting up margins, line spacing, or other functional issues of text formatting. That's all taken care of by the LATEX macros on top of the TEX engine. LATEX provides reasonable defaults for these parameters; if you wanted to change any of these formatting options, you could use other LATEX commands (or lower-level TEX commands) to modify them.

We don't expect you to understand all the intricacies of using LATEX from such a limited example, although this should give you an idea of how a living, breathing LATEX document looks. Now, let's format the document in order to print it out.

Formatting and Printing

Believe it or not, the command used to format L^AT_EX source files into something printable is *latex*. After editing and saving the previous example, *letter.tex*, you should be able to use the following command:

```
eggplant$ latex letter
This is pdfeTeX, Version 3.141592-1.21a-2.2 (Web2C 7.5.4)
(letter.tex
LaTeX2e <2003/12/01>
Babel <v3.8d> and hyphenation patterns for american, french, german, ngerman, b
ahasa, basque, bulgarian, catalan, croatian, czech, danish, dutch, esperanto, e
stonian, finnish, greek, icelandic, irish, italian, latin, magyar, norsk, polis
h, portuges, romanian, russian, serbian, slovak, slovene, spanish, swedish, tur
kish, ukrainian, nohyphenation, loaded.
(/usr/share/texmf/tex/latex/base/letter.cls
Document Class: article 2004/02/16 v1.4f Standard LaTeX document class
(/usr/share/texmf/tex/latex/base/size10.clo))
No file letter.aux.
[1] (letter.aux) )
Output written on letter.dvi (1 page, 1128 bytes).
Transcript written on letter.log.
eggplant$
```

latex assumes the extension *.tex* for source files. Here, L^AT_EX has processed the source *letter.tex* and saved the results in the file *letter.dvi*. This is a "device-independent" file that generates printable output on a variety of printers. Various tools exist for converting *.dvi* files to PostScript, HP LaserJet, and other formats, as we'll see shortly.

Instead of immediately printing your letter, you may wish to preview it to be sure that everything looks right. If you're running the X Window System, you can use the *xdvi* command to preview *.dvi* files on your screen. If you are also using the KDE desktop environment, *kdvi* is a more user-friendly version of *xdvi*. What about printing the letter? First, you need to convert the *.dvi* to something your printer can handle. DVI drivers exist for many printer types. Almost all the program names begin with the three characters *dvi*, as in *dvips*, *dvilj*, and so forth. If your system doesn't have one you need, you have to get the appropriate driver from the archives if you have Internet access. See the FAQ for *comp.text.tex* for details.

If you're lucky enough to have a PostScript printer (or have a PostScript filter installed in your system), you can use *dvips* to generate PostScript from the *.dvi* file:

```
eggplant$ dvips -o letter.ps letter.dvi
```

You can then print the PostScript using *lpr*. Or, to do this in one step:

```
eggplant$ dvips letter.dvi | lpr
```

There are printer-specific DVI drivers such as *dvilj* for HP LaserJets as well, but most of these are considered obsolete; use *dvips* and, if necessary, Ghostscript (see below) instead.

It is also possible to ask *dvips* to directly send the PostScript output to a printer, such as to the printer lp in this example:

```
eggplant$ dvips -Plp letter.dvi
```

If you can't find a DVI driver for your printer, you might be able to use Ghostscript to convert PostScript (produced by *dvips*) into something you can print. Although some of Ghostscript's fonts are less than optimal, Ghostscript does allow you to use Adobe fonts (which you can obtain for Windows and use with Ghostscript under Linux). Ghostscript also provides an SVGA preview mode you can use if you're not running X. At any rate, after you manage to format and print the example letter, it should end up looking something like that in Figure 20-1.

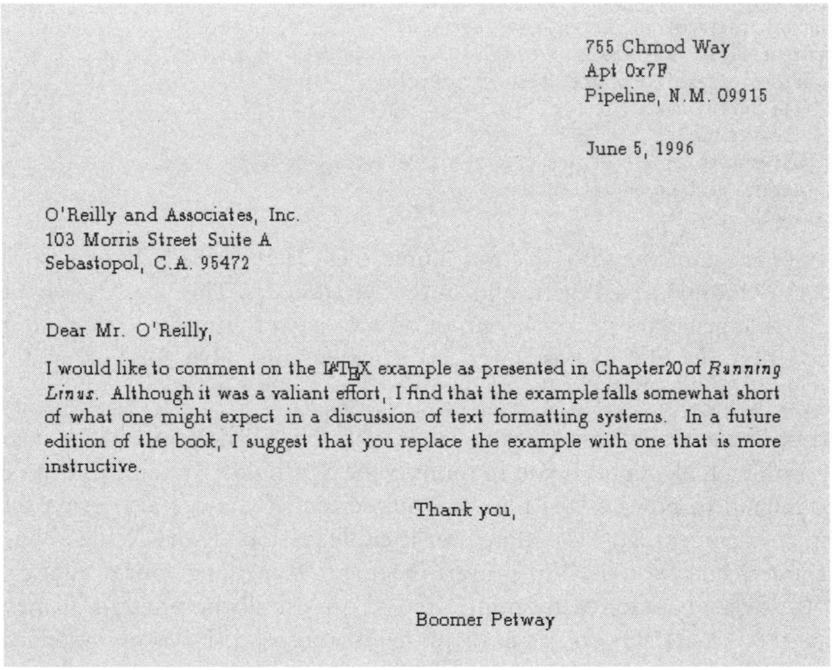

755 Chmod Way
Apt 0x7F
Pipeline, N.M. 09915

June 5, 1996

O'Reilly and Associates, Inc.
103 Morris Street Suite A
Sebastopol, C.A. 95472

Dear Mr. O'Reilly,

I would like to comment on the L^ATEX example as presented in Chapter 20 of *Running Linux*. Although it was a valiant effort, I find that the example falls somewhat short of what one might expect in a discussion of text formatting systems. In a future edition of the book, I suggest that you replace the example with one that is more instructive.

Thank you,

Boomer Petway

Figure 20-1. Sample output from a file

Finally, it should be mentioned that you can also use TEX to create PDF files, either using the *dvipdf* driver or using a special program called *pdftex*.

Further Reading

If L^ATEX seems right for your document-processing needs, and you have been able to get at least this initial example working and printed out, we suggest checking into Leslie Lamport's *L^ATEX User's Guide and Reference Manual* (Addison Wesley), which includes everything you need to know about L^AT_EX for formatting letters, articles, books, and more. If you're interested in hacking or want to know more about the underlying workings of T_EX (which can be invaluable), Donald Knuth's *The T_EX Book* (Addison-Wesley) is the definitive guide to the system.

comp.text.tex is the Usenet newsgroup for questions and information about these systems, although information found there assumes you have access to T_EX and L^AT_EX documentation of some kind, such as the manuals mentioned earlier.

XML and DocBook

XML (and its predecessor SGML) goes one step beyond earlier text markup languages. It imposes a hierarchical structure on the text that shows the relation of each element to the containing elements. This makes it possible to convert the text to a number of output formats, including PostScript and PDF (the Adobe Portable Document Format).

XML itself is just a framework for defining the structure of a document. A so-called Document Type Description (DTD) or schema then defines what kind of markup you are allowed to use in a document.

SGML, the Standard Generalized Markup Language, was the first of these document description languages to be standardized, but it has mostly fallen into oblivion these days. Its two descendants—HTML and XML—are famous, though, and even overly hyped. Essentially, HTML is an implementation of SGML with a fixed set of tags that is useful for formatting web pages. XML, the eXtended Markup Language, is a general solution like SGML, but minus some of its more difficult features. Both SGML and XML allow people to define any set of tags they like; the exact tags and their relationships are specified in the DTD or schema (which are optional in XML).

For each DTD or schema that you want to use, you need to have processing tools that convert the SGML or XML file to the desired output format. Historically, most free systems did this by means of a system called DSSSL (short for Document Style Semantics and Specification Language). XSLT (eXtended Stylesheet Language Template) is now much more popular for converting XML to other formats. As the author of an SGML or XML document, this is nothing you need to be concerned with, but if you are the one to set up the toolchain or want to change the way the output looks, you need to know how the processing is done.

In the field of computer documentation, the most commonly used DTD is DocBook. Among many other things, most of the freely available Linux documentation is written with DocBook, as well as this book. DocBook users include a huge range of companies and well-known organizations, such as Sun Microsystems, Microsoft, IBM, Hewlett-Packard, Boeing, and the U.S. State Department.

To give you an example of how DocBook text can look, here is a fragment of an article for a computer magazine:

```
<!DOCTYPE Article  PUBLIC "-//OASIS//DTD DocBook V4.1.2//EN">
<article>
  <artheader>
    <title>Looping the Froz with Foobar</title>
    <author>
      <firstname>Helmer B.</firstname>
      <surname>Technerd</surname>
      <affiliation>
        <orgname>Linux Hackers, Inc.</orgname>
      </affiliation>
    </author>
  </artheader>
  <abstract>
    <para>This article describes a technique that you can employ to
loop the Froz with the Foobar software package.</para>
  </abstract>
  <sect1>
    <title>Motivation</title>
    <para>Blah, blah, blah, ...
    </para>
  </sect1>
</article>
```

The first line specifies the DTD to be used and the root element; in this case we are creating an article using the DocBook DTD. The rest of the source contains the article itself. If you are familiar with HTML, the markup language used for the World Wide Web (see the O'Reilly book *HTML & XHTML: The Definitive Guide*, by Chuck Musciano and Bill Kennedy), this should look a bit familiar. Tags are used to mark up the text logically.

Describing the whole DocBook DTD is well beyond the scope of this book, but if you are interested, check out *DocBook: The Definitive Guide* by Norman Walsh and Leonard Muellner (O'Reilly).

Once you have your article, documentation, or book written, you will want to transform it, of course, into a format that you can print or view on the screen. In order to do this, you need a complete XML setup, which, unfortunately, is not easy to achieve. In fact, you need so many pieces in place that we cannot describe this here. But there is hope: a number of distributions (including Red Hat, SUSE, and Debian) come with very good XML setups out of the box; just install their respective XML packages. If you have a working SGML or XML system, you should be able to transform the text shown previously to HTML (as one example) with a command like this:

```
tigger$ db2html myarticle.xml
input file was called  -- output will be in myarticle
TMPDIR is db2html.C14157
working on /home/kalle/myarticle.xml
```

```
about to copy cascading stylesheet and admon graphics to temp dir
about to rename temporary directory to "myarticle"
```

The file *myarticle/t1.html* will contain the generated HTML. If you would like to generate PDF instead, use the following command:

```
tigger db2pdf myarticle.xml
tex output file name is /home/kalle/projects/rl5/test.tex
tex file name is /home/kalle/projects/rl5/test.tex
pdf file name is test.pdf
This is pdfeTeX, Version 3.141592-1.21a-2.2 (Web2C 7.5.4)
entering extended mode
(/home/kalle/projects/rl5/test.tex
JadeTeX 2003/04/27: 3.13
(/usr/share/texmf/tex/latex/psnfss/t1ptm.fd)
Elements will be labelled
Jade begin document sequence at 21
(./test.aux) (/usr/share/texmf/tex/latex/cyrillic/t2acmr.fd)
(/usr/share/texmf/tex/latex/base/ts1cmr.fd)
(/usr/share/texmf/tex/latex/hyperref/nameref.sty) (./test.out) (./test.out)
(/usr/share/texmf/tex/latex/psnfss/t1phv.fd) [1.0.49{/var/lib/texmf/fonts/map/p
dftex/updmap/pdftex.map}] [2.0.49] (./test.aux) ){/usr/share/texmf/fonts/enc/dv
ips/psnfss/8r.enc}</usr/share/texmf/fonts/type1/urw/times/utmri8a.pfb></usr/sha
re/texmf/fonts/type1/urw/times/utmr8a.pfb></usr/share/texmf/fonts/type1/urw/hel
vetic/uhvb8a.pfb>
Output written on test.pdf (2 pages, 35689 bytes).
Transcript written on test.log.
```

As you can see, this command uses TEX in the background, or more specifically a special version called Jade that is geared toward documents produced by DSSSL.

This is all nice and good, but if you want to change the way the output looks, you'll find DSSSL is quite cumbersome to use, not least because of the lack of available documentation. We will therefore briefly introduce you here to the more modern mechanism using XSLT and FOP. However, be prepared that this will almost invariably require quite some setup work on your side, including reading ample amounts of online documentation.

In an XSLT setup, the processing chain is as follows: First, the XML document that you have written, plus a so-called stylesheet written in XSL (eXtended Stylesheet Language), are run through an XSLT (eXtended Stylesheet Language Template) processor such as Saxon. XSL is yet another DTD; in other words, the stylesheets are XML documents themselves. They describe how each element in the document to be processed will be converted into other elements or body text. Naturally, the stylesheet needs to fit the DTD you have authored your document in. Also, depending on your output target, you will need to use different stylesheets.

If HTML is your target, you are already done at this point. Because HTML is itself XML-conforming, the stylesheet is able to convert your document into HTML that can be directly displayed in your web browser.

If your target is more remote from the XML input (e.g., PDF) you need to go another step. In this case, you do not generate PDF directly from your document, because PDF is not an XML format but rather a mixed binary/text format. Basic XSLT transformation would be very difficult, if not plain impossible. Instead, you use a stylesheet that generates XSL-FO instead, yet another acronym starting with X (eXtended Stylesheet Language Formatting Objects). The XSL-FO document is another XML document, but one where many of the logical instructions in the original document have been turned into physical instructions.

Next, an FO processor such as Apache FOP is run on the XSL-FO document and generates PDF (or other output, if the FO processor supports that).

Now that you have an idea of the general picture, lets look at what you need to set up. First of all, it may be a good idea to run your XML document through a document validator. This does not do any processing, but just checks whether your document conforms to the specified DTD. The advantage of a document validator is that it does this very fast. Because actual processing can be time-consuming, it is good if you can find out first whether your document is ill-formed and bail out quickly.

One such document validator is *xmllint*. *xmllint* is a part of *libxml2*, a library that was originally developed for the GNOME desktop, but is completely independent of it (and actually also used in the KDE desktop). You can find information about *xmllint* and download it from *http://xmlsoft.org*.

xmllint is used as follows:

```
owl$ xmllint myarticle.xml > myarticle-included.xml
```

The reason that *xmllint* is writing the file to standard output is that it can also be used to process X-Includes. These are a technique to modularize XML files in an author-friendly way, and *xmllint* puts the pieces back together. You can find more information about X-Includes at *http://www.w3.org/TR/xinclude*.

In the next step, the stylesheet needs to be applied. Saxon is a good tool for this. It comes in a Java version and a C++ version. Often, it does not matter much which you install: the C++ one runs faster, but the Java one has a few additional features, such as automatic escaping of special characters in included program listings. You can find information and downloads for Saxon at *http://saxon.sourceforge.net*.

Of course, you also need a stylesheet (often, this is a huge set of files, but it is still usually referenced in the singular). For DocBook, nothing exceeds the DocBook-XSL package, which is maintained by luminaries of the DocBook world. You can find it at *http://docbook.sourceforge.net/projects/xsl*.

Assuming that you are using the Java version of Saxon, you would invoke it more or less as follows for generating XSL-FO:

```
java com.icl.saxon.StyleSheet myarticle-included.xml docbook-xsl/fo/docbook.xsl > \
    myarticle.fo
```

and as follows for generating HTML:

```
java com.icl.saxon.StyleSheet myarticle-included.xml docbook-xsl/html/docbook.xsl > \
    myarticle.html
```

Notice how only the choice of stylesheet determines the output format.

As was already described, for HTML you are done at this point. For PDF output, you still need to run a FOP processor such as Apache FOP, which you can get from *http://xmlgraphics.apache.org/fop*. FOP requires a configuration file; see the documentation for how to create one. Often you can just use the *userconfig.xml* file that ships with FOP. A canonical invocation would look like this, PDF being the standard output format:

```
java org.apache.fop.apps.Fop -c configfile myarticle.fo myarticle.pdf
```

Now you know the general setup and which tools you can use; remember that there are many other similar tools available that might serve your purposes even better. You may ask where your own formatting requirements come in. At this point, all the formatting is determined by the DocBook-XSL stylesheets. And this is also where you can hook into the process. Instead of supplying the *docbook.xsl* file to Saxon, you can also specify your own file. Of course, you do not want to copy the tremendous amount of work that has gone into DocBook-XSL; instead, you should import the DocBook-XSL stylesheet into your stylesheet, and then overwrite some settings. Here is an example for a custom stylesheet:

```
<?xml version='1.0'?>
<xsl:stylesheet xmlns:xsl="http://www.w3.org/1999/XSL/Transform"
                xmlns:fo="http://www.w3.org/1999/XSL/Format"
                version='1.0'
                xmlns="http://www.w3.org/TR/xhtml1/transitional"
                exclude-result-prefixes="#default">

<xsl:import href="docbook-xsl/fo/docbook.xsl"/>
<xsl:param name="paper.type" select="'B5'"/>
<xsl:param name="shade.verbatim" select="1"/>
<xsl:param name="chapter.autolabel" select="1"/>

<xsl:attribute-set name="section.title.level1.properties">
  <xsl:attribute name="color">
    <xsl:value-of select="'#243689'"/>
  </xsl:attribute>
</xsl:attribute-set>

</xsl:stylesheet>
```

What is happening here? After the boilerplate code at the beginning, the `<xsl:import>` element loads the default FOP-generating stylesheet (of course, you would use another stylesheet for HTML generation). Then we set a number of parameters; a lot of settings in DocBook-XSL are parametrized, and a `<xsl:param>` element is all that is needed. In this case, we select a certain output paper format, ask for verbatim blocks to be shaded, and ask for automatic generation of table-of-contents labels for chapters.

Finally, we make a change that cannot be done merely by setting parameters: changing the color of level 1 section titles. Here we overwrite an attribute set with a color attribute of our own. For more complex changes, it is sometimes even necessary to replace element definitions from DocBook-XSL completely. This is not an easy task to do, and you would be well advised to read the DocBook-XSL documentation thoroughly.

XML opens a whole new world of tools and techniques. A good starting point for getting inspired and reading up on this is the web site of the Linux Documentation Project, which, as mentioned before, uses XML/DocBook for all its documentation. You'll find the Linux Documentation Project at *http://www.tlpd.org*.

groff

Parallel to and independent to TEX, another major text processing system emerged in the form of *troff* and *nroff*. These were developed at Bell Labs for the original implementation of Unix (in fact, the development of Unix was spurred, in part, to support such a text processing system). The first version of this text processor was called *roff* (for "runoff"); later came *nroff* and *troff*, which generated output for a particular typesetter in use at the time (*nroff* was written for fixed-pitch printers such as dot matrix printers, *troff* for proportional space devices—initially typesetters). Later versions of *nroff* and *troff* became the standard text processor on Unix systems everywhere. *groff* is GNU's implementation of *nroff* and *troff* that is used on Linux systems. It includes several extended features and drivers for a number of printing devices.

groff is capable of producing documents, articles, and books, much in the same vein as TEX. However, *groff* (as well as the original *nroff*) has one intrinsic feature that is absent from TEX and variants: the ability to produce plain-ASCII output. Although TEX is great for producing documents to be printed, *groff* is able to produce plain ASCII to be viewed online (or printed directly as plain text on even the simplest of printers). If you're going to be producing documentation to be viewed online as well as in printed form, *groff* may be the way to go (although there are other alternatives as well—Texinfo, which is discussed later, is one).

groff also has the benefit of being much smaller than TEX; it requires fewer support files and executables than even a minimal TEX distribution.

One special application of *groff* is to format Unix manual pages. If you're a Unix programmer, you'll eventually need to write and produce manual pages of some kind. In this section, we introduce the use of *groff* through the writing of a short manual page.

As with TEX, *groff* uses a particular text-formatting language to describe how to process the text. This language is slightly more cryptic than TEX but is also less verbose. In addition, *groff* provides several macro packages that are used on top of the basic *groff* formatter; these macro packages are tailored to a particular type of document. For example, the mgs macros are an ideal choice for writing articles and papers, and the man macros are used for manual pages.

Writing a Manual Page

Writing manual pages with *groff* is actually quite simple. In order for your manual page to look like other manual pages, you need to follow several conventions in the source, which are presented in the following example. In this example, we write a manual page for a mythical command *coffee*, which controls your networked coffee machine in various ways.

Enter the following source with your text editor, and save the result as *coffee.man*:

```
 1  .TH COFFEE 1 "23 March 94"
 2  .SH NAME
 3  coffee \- Control remote coffee machine
 4  .SH SYNOPSIS
 5  \fBcoffee\fP [ -h | -b ] [ -t \fItype\fP ] \fIamount\fP
 6  .SH DESCRIPTION
 7  \fIcoffee\fP queues a request to the remote coffee machine at the
 8  device \fB/dev/cf0\fR. The required \fIamount\fP argument specifies
 9  the number of cups, generally between 0 and 15 on ISO standard
10  coffee machines.
11  .SS Options
12  .TP
13  \fB-h\fP
14  Brew hot coffee. Cold is the default.
15  .TP
16  \fB-b\fP
17  Burn coffee. Especially useful when executing \fIcoffee\fP on behalf
18  of your boss.
19  .TP
20  \fB-t \fItype\fR
21  Specify the type of coffee to brew, where \fItype\fP is one of
22  \fBcolombian\fP, \fBregular\fP, or \fBdecaf\fP.
23  .SH FILES
24  .TP
25  \fI/dev/cf0\fR
26  The remote coffee machine device
27  .SH "SEE ALSO"
28  milk(5), sugar(5)
29  .SH BUGS
30  May require human intervention if coffee supply is exhausted.
```

Don't let the amount of obscurity in this source file frighten you. It helps to know that the character sequences \fB, \fI, and \fR are used to change the font to boldface, italics, and roman type, respectively. \fP resets the font to the one previously selected.

Other *groff* requests appear on lines beginning with a dot (.). On line 1, we see that the `.TH` request sets the title of the manual page to `COFFEE` and the manual section to 1. (Manual section 1 is used for user commands, section 2 for system calls, and so forth.) The `.TH` request also sets the date of the last manual page revision.

On line 2, the `.SH` request starts a section entitled `NAME`. Note that almost all Unix manual pages use the section progression `NAME`, `SYNOPSIS`, `DESCRIPTION`, `FILES`, `SEE ALSO`, `NOTES`, `AUTHOR`, and `BUGS`, with extra optional sections as needed. This is just a convention used when writing manual pages and isn't enforced by the software at all.

Line 3 gives the name of the command and a short description, after a dash (\-). You should use this format for the `NAME` section so that your manual page can be added to the *whatis* database used by the *man -k* and *apropos* commands.

On lines 4 to 5, we give the synopsis of the command syntax for *coffee*. Note that italic type (\fI...\fP) is used to denote parameters on the command line in the manual page, and that optional arguments are enclosed in square brackets.

Lines 6 to 10 give a brief description of the command. Italic type generally denotes commands, filenames, and user options. On line 11, a subsection named `Options` is started with the `.SS` request. Following this on lines 11 to 22 is a list of options, presented using a tagged list. Each item in the tagged list is marked with the `.TP` request; the line *after* `.TP` is the tag, after which follows the item text itself. For example, the source on lines 12 to 14:

```
.TP
\fB-h\fP
Brew hot coffee. Cold is the default.
```

will appear as the following in the output:

```
-h      Brew hot coffee. Cold is the default.
```

You should document each command-line option for your program in this way.

Lines 23 to 26 make up the `FILES` section of the manual page, which describes any files the command might use to do its work. A tagged list using the `.TP` request is used for this as well.

On lines 27 and 28, the `SEE ALSO` section is given, which provides cross references to other manual pages of note. Notice that the string `"SEE ALSO"` following the `.SH` request on line 27 is in quotation marks; this is because `.SH` uses the first whitespace-delimited argument as the section title. Therefore, any section titles that are composed of more than one word need to be enclosed in quotation marks to make up a single argument. Finally, on lines 29 and 30, the `BUGS` section is presented.

Formatting and Installing the Manual Page

To format this manual page and view it on your screen, use the following command:

```
eggplant$ groff -Tascii -man coffee.man | more
```

The *-Tascii* option tells *groff* to produce plain-ASCII output; *-man* tells *groff* to use the manual-page macro set. If all goes well, the manual page should be displayed:

```
COFFEE(1)                                                    COFFEE(1)


NAME
       coffee - Control remote coffee machine

SYNOPSIS
       coffee [ -h | -b ] [ -t type ] amount

DESCRIPTION
       coffee  queues  a  request to the remote coffee machine at
       the device /dev/cf0. The required amount  argument  speci-
       fies the number of cups, generally between 0 and 12 on ISO
       standard coffee machines.

   Options
       -h     Brew hot coffee. Cold is the default.

       -b     Burn coffee. Especially useful when executing  cof-
              fee on behalf of your boss.

       -t type
              Specify  the  type of coffee to brew, where type is
              one of colombian, regular, or decaf.

FILES
       /dev/cf0
              The remote coffee machine device

SEE ALSO
       milk(5), sugar(5)

BUGS
       May  require  human  intervention  if  coffee  supply   is
       exhausted.
```

As mentioned before, *groff* is capable of producing other types of output. Using the *-Tps* option in place of *-Tascii* produces PostScript output that you can save to a file, view with Ghostview, or print on a PostScript printer. *-Tdvi* produces device-independent *.dvi* output similar to that produced by TEX.

If you wish to make the manual page available for others to view on your system, you need to install the *groff* source in a directory that is present on the users' MANPATH. The location for standard manual pages is */usr/share/man*, although some systems also use */usr/man* or */usr/local/man*. The source for section 1 manual pages should therefore go in */usr/man/man1*. The command:

eggplant$ **cp coffee.man /usr/man/man1/coffee.1**

installs this manual page in *usr/man* for all to use (note the use of the *.1* filename extension, instead of *.man*). When *man coffee* is subsequently invoked, the manual page will be automatically reformatted, and the viewable text saved in *usr/man/cat1/coffee.1.gz*.

If you can't copy manual page sources directly to *usr/man*, you can create your own manual page directory tree and add it to your MANPATH. See the section "Manual Pages" in Chapter 4.

Texinfo

Texinfo is a text-formatting system used by the GNU Project to produce both online documentation in the form of hypertext Info pages, and printed manuals through TEX from a single-source file. By providing Texinfo source, users can convert the documentation to Info, HTML, DVI, PostScript, PDF, or plain text files.

Texinfo is documented completely through its own Info pages, which are readable within Emacs (using the C-h i command) or a separate Info reader, such as *info*. If the GNU Info pages are installed in your system, complete Texinfo documentation is contained therein. Just as you'll find yourself using *groff* to write a manual page, you'll use Texinfo to write an Info document.

Writing the Texinfo Source

In this section, we present a simple Texinfo source file—chunks at a time—and describe what each chunk does as we go along.

Our Texinfo source file will be called *vacuum.texi* and describe a fictitious *vacuum* command. As usual, you can enter the source using a plain-text editor:

```
\input texinfo @c -*-texinfo-*-
@c %**start of header
@setfilename vacuum.info
@settitle The Empty Info File
@setchapternewpage odd
@c %**end of header
```

This is the header of the Texinfo source. The first line is a TEX command used to input the Texinfo macros when producing printed documentation. Commands in Texinfo begin with the "at" sign, @. The @c command begins a comment; here, the comment -*-texinfo-*- is a tag that tells Emacs this is a Texinfo source file so that Emacs can set the proper major mode. (Major modes were discussed in "Tailoring Emacs" in Chapter 19.)

The comments @c %**start of header and @c %**end of header are used to denote the Texinfo header. This is required if you wish to format just a portion of the Texinfo file. The *@setfilename* command specifies the filename to use for the resulting Info file, *@settitle* sets the title of the document, and *@setchapternewpage odd* tells

Texinfo to start new chapters on an odd-numbered page. These are just cookbook routines that should be used for all Texinfo files.

The next section of the source file sets up the title page, which is used when formatting the document using TeX. These commands should be self-explanatory:

```
@titlepage
@title Vacuum
@subtitle The Empty Info File
@author by Tab U. Larasa
@end titlepage
```

Now we move on to the body of the Texinfo source. The Info file is divided into nodes, where each node is somewhat like a "page" in the document. Each node has links to the next, previous, and parent nodes, and can be linked to other nodes as cross-references. You can think of each node as a chapter or section within the document with a menu to nodes below it. For example, a chapter-level node has a menu that lists the sections within the chapter. Each section node points to the chapter-level node as its parent. Each section also points to the previous and next section, if they exist. This is a little complicated, but will become clear when you see it in action.

Each node is given a short name. The topmost node is called Top. The @node command is used to start a node; it takes as arguments the node name, as well as the names of the next, previous, and parent nodes. As noted earlier, the next and previous nodes should be on the same hierarchical level. The parent node is the node above the current one in the node tree (e.g., the parent of Section 2.1 in a document is Chapter 2). A sample node hierarchy is depicted in Figure 20-2.

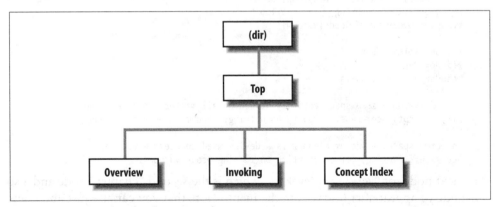

Figure 20-2. Hierarchy of nodes in Texinfo

Here is the source for the Top node:

```
@c     Node, Next, Previous, Up
@node Top ,     ,          , (dir)

@ifinfo
```

```
This Info file is a close approximation to a vacuum. It documents
absolutely nothing.
@end ifinfo

@menu
* Overview::            Overview of Vacuum
* Invoking::            How to use the Vacuum
* Concept Index::       Index of concepts
@end menu
```

The @node command is preceded by a comment to remind us of the order of the arguments to @node. Here, Top has no previous or next node, so they are left blank. The parent node for Top is (dir), which denotes the systemwide Info page directory. Supposedly your Info file will be linked into the system's Info page tree, so you want the Top node to have a link back to the overall directory.

Following the @node command is an abstract for the overall document, enclosed in an *@ifinfo...@end ifinfo* pair. These commands are used because the actual text of the Top node should appear only in the Info file, not the TEX-generated printed document.

The *@menu...@end menu* commands demarcate the node's menu. Each menu entry includes a node name followed by a short description of the node. In this case, the menu points to the nodes Overview, Invoking, and Concept Index, the source for which appears later in the file. These three nodes are the three "chapters" in our document.

We continue with the Overview node, which is the first "chapter":

```
@c      Node,      Next,      Previous, Up
@node Overview, Invoking,          , Top
@chapter Overview of @code{vacuum}

@cindex Nothingness
@cindex Overview
@cindex Vacuum cleaners

A @code{vacuum} is a space entirely devoid of all matter. That means no
air, no empty beer cans, no dust, no nothing. Vacuums are usually found

in outer space. A vacuum cleaner is a device used to clean a vacuum.
See @xref{Invoking} for information on running @code{vacuum}.
```

The next node for Overview is Invoking, which is the second "chapter" node and also the node to appear after Overview in the menu. Note that you can use just about any structure for your Texinfo documents; however, it is often useful to organize them so that nodes resemble chapters, sections, subsections, and so forth. It's up to you.

The *@chapter* command begins a chapter, which has an effect only when formatting the source with TEX. Similarly, the *@section* and *@subsection* commands begin (you guessed it) sections and subsections in the resulting TEX document. The chapter (or section or subsection) name can be more descriptive than the brief name used for the node itself.

You'll notice that the *@code* command is used in the chapter name. This is just one way to specify text to be emphasized in some way. *@code* should be used for the names of commands, as well as source code that appears in a program. This causes the text within the *@code* command to be printed in constant-width type in the TEX output, and enclosed in single quotes (like `'this'`) in the Info file.

Following this are three *@cindex* commands, which produce entries in the concept index at the end of the document. Next is the actual text of the node. Again, *@code* marks the name of the *vacuum* "command."

The *@xref* command produces a cross-reference to another node, which the reader can follow with the *f* command in the Info reader. *@xref* can also make cross-references to other Texinfo documents. See the Texinfo documentation for a complete discussion.

Our next node is Invoking:

```
@node Invoking, Concept Index, Overview, Top
@chapter Running @code{vacuum}

@cindex Running @code{vacuum}
@code{vacuum} is executed as follows:

@example
vacuum @var{options} @dots{  }
@end example
```

Here, *@example* . . . *@end example* sets off an example. Within the example, *@var* denotes a metavariable, a placeholder for a string provided by the user (in this case, the options given to the *vacuum* command). `@dots{  }` produces ellipsis points. The example will appear as:

```
vacuum options ...
```

in the TEX-formatted document, and as:

```
vacuum OPTIONS ...
```

in the Info file. Commands, such as *@code* and *@var*, provide emphasis that can be represented in different ways in the TEX and Info outputs.

Continuing the Invoking node, we have the following:

```
@cindex Options
@cindex Arguments
The following options are supported:

@cindex Getting help
@table @samp
@item -help
Print a summary of options.
```

```
@item -version
Print the version number for @code{vacuum}.

@cindex Empty vacuums
@item -empty
Produce a particularly empty vacuum. This is the default.
@end table
```

Here, we have a table of the options that our fictitious *vacuum* command suppos-edly supports. The command *@table @samp* begins a two-column table (which ends up looking more like a tagged list), where each item is emphasized using the *@samp* command. *@samp* is similar to *@code* and *@var*, except that it's meant to be used for literal input, such as command-line options.

A normal Texinfo document would contain nodes for examples, information on reporting bugs, and much more, but for brevity we're going to wrap up this example with the final node, Concept Index. This is an index of concepts presented in the doc-ument and is produced automatically with the *@printindex* command:

```
@node Concept Index, , Invoking, Top
@unnumbered Concept Index

@printindex cp
```

Here, *@printindex cp* tells the formatter to include the concept index at this point. There are other types of indices as well, such as a function index, command index, and so forth. All are generated with variants on the *@cindex* and *@printindex* commands.

The final three lines of our Texinfo source are as follows:

```
@shortcontents
@contents
@bye
```

This instructs the formatter to produce a "summary" table of contents (*@shortcon-tents*) and a full table of contents (*@contents*), and to end formatting (*@bye*). *@shortcontents* produces a brief table of contents that lists only chapters and appen-dices. In reality, only long manuals would require *@shortcontents* in addition to *@contents*.

Formatting Texinfo

To produce an Info file from the Texinfo source, use the *makeinfo* command. (This command, along with the other programs used to process Texinfo, is included in the Texinfo software distribution, which is sometimes bundled with Emacs.) The command:

```
eggplant$ makeinfo vacuum.texi
```

produces *vacuum.info* from *vacuum.texi*. *makeinfo* uses the output filename specified by the *@setfilename* command in the source; you can change this using the *-o* option.

If the resulting Info file is large, *makeinfo* splits it into a series of files named *vacuum.info-1*, *vacuum.info-2*, and so on, where *vacuum.info* is the top-level file that points to the various split files. As long as all the *vacuum.info* files are in the same directory, the Info reader should be able to find them.

You can also use the Emacs commands M-x makeinfo-region and M-x makeinfo-buffer to generate Info from the Texinfo source.

The Info file can now be viewed from within Emacs, using the C-h i command. Within the Emacs Info mode, you'll need to use the g command and specify the complete path to your Info file, as in the following example:

```
Goto node: (/home/loomer/mdw/info/vacuum.info)Top
```

This is because Emacs usually looks for Info files only within its own Info directory (which may be */usr/local/emacs/info* on your system).

Another alternative is to use the Emacs-independent Info reader, *info*. The command

```
eggplant$ info -f vacuum.info
```

invokes *info*, reading your new Info file.

If you wish to install the new Info page for all users on your system, you must add a link to it in the *dir* file in the Emacs *info* directory. The Texinfo documentation describes how to do this in detail.

To produce a printed document from the source, you need to have TeX installed on your system. The Texinfo software comes with a TeX macro file, *texinfo.tex*, which includes all the macros used by Texinfo for formatting. If installed correctly, *texinfo.tex* should be in the *inputs* directory on your system. If not, you can copy *texinfo.tex* to the directory where your Texinfo files reside.

First, process the Texinfo file using:

```
eggplant$ tex vacuum.texi
```

This produces a slew of files in your directory, some of which pertain to processing and to the index. The *texindex* command (which is included in the Texinfo package) reformats the index into something the display systems can use. The next command to issue is therefore:

```
eggplant$ texindex vacuum.??
```

Using the ?? wildcard runs *texindex* on all files in the directory with two-letter extensions; these are the files produced by Texinfo for generating the index.

Finally, you need to reformat the Texinfo file using TeX, which clears up cross-references and includes the index:

```
eggplant$ tex vacuum.texi
```

This should leave you with *vacuum.dvi*, a device-independent file you can now view with *xdvi* or convert into something printable. See "TeX and LaTeX" earlier in the chapter for a discussion of how to print *.dvi* files.

As usual, there's much more to learn about this system. Texinfo has a complete set of Info pages of its own, which should be available in your Info reader. Or, now that you know the basics, you could format the Texinfo documentation sources yourself using TeX. The *.texi* sources for the Texinfo documentation are found in the Texinfo source distribution.

## PART III

Programming

The tools and practices in this part of the book are not needed by all users, but anyone willing to master them can add a great deal of power to their system. If you've done programming before, this part of the book gets you to a productive state on Linux quickly; if you haven't, it can show you some of the benefits of programming and serve as an introduction to its joys. Chapter 20 shows you two great tools for text editing—*vi* and Emacs—that you should master even if you don't plan to be a programmer. The material in this part of the book can also be a valuable reference as you read other parts.

## CHAPTER 21

Programming Tools

There's much more to Linux than simply using the system. One of the benefits of free software is that you can modify it to suit your needs. This applies equally to the many free applications available for Linux and to the Linux kernel itself.

Linux supports an advanced programming interface, using GNU compilers and tools, such as the *gcc* compiler, the *gdb* debugger, and so on. An enormous number of other programming languages—ranging from such classics as FORTRAN and LISP to modern scripting languages such as Perl, Python, and Ruby—are also supported. Whatever your programming needs, Linux is a great choice for developing Unix applications. Because the complete source code for the libraries and Linux kernel is provided, programmers who need to delve into the system internals are able to do so.*

Many judge a computer system by the tools it offers its programmers. Unix systems have won the contest by many people's standards, having developed a very rich set over the years. Leading the parade is the GNU debugger, *gdb*. In this chapter, we take a close look at this invaluable utility, and at a number of other auxiliary tools C programmers will find useful.

Even if you are not a programmer, you should consider using the Revision Control System (RCS). It provides one of the most reassuring protections a computer user could ask for—backups for everything you do to a file. If you delete a file by accident, or decide that everything you did for the past week was a mistake and should be ripped out, RCS can recover any version you want. If you are working on a larger project that involves either a large number of developers or a large number of directories (or both), Concurrent Versioning System (CVS) might be more suitable for you. It was originally based on RCS, but was rewritten from the ground up and provides many additional features. Currently, another tool, called *Subversion*, is taking

---

* On a variety of Unix systems, the authors have repeatedly found available documentation to be insufficient. With Linux, you can explore the very source code for the kernel, libraries, and system utilities. Having access to source code is more important than most programmers think.

over from CVS and filling in some of the gaps that CVS left in the handling of large projects.* The goal of Subversion is to be "like CVS; just better." Newer installations typically use Subversion these days, but the vast majority still uses CVS. Finally, the Linux kernel itself uses yet another versioning system. It used to use a software called BitKeeper, but when licensing problems arose, Linus Torvalds wrote his own version control system, called *git*, that has been introduced recently.

Linux is an ideal platform for developing software to run under the X Window System. The Linux X distribution, as described in Chapter 16, is a complete implementation with everything you need to develop and support X applications. Programming for X is portable across applications, so the X-specific portions of your application should compile cleanly on other Unix systems.

In this chapter, we explore the Linux programming environment and give you a five-cent tour of the many facilities it provides. Half of the trick to Unix programming is knowing what tools are available and how to use them effectively. Often the most useful features of these tools are not obvious to new users.

Since C programming has been the basis of most large projects (even though it is nowadays being replaced more and more by C++ and Java) and is the language common to most modern programmers—not only on Unix, but on many other systems as well—we start by telling you what tools are available for that. The first few sections of the chapter assume you are already a C programmer.

But several other tools are emerging as important resources, especially for system administration. We examine one in this chapter: Perl. Perl is a scripting language like the Unix shells, taking care of grunt work such as memory allocation so you can concentrate on your task. But Perl offers a degree of sophistication that makes it more powerful than shell scripts and therefore appropriate for many programming tasks.

Several open source projects make it relatively easy to program in Java, and some of the tools and frameworks in the open source community are even more popular than those distributed by Sun Microsystems, the company that invented and licenses Java. Java is a general-purpose language with many potential Internet uses. In a later section, we explore what Java offers and how to get started.

Programming with gcc

The C programming language is by far the most often used in Unix software development. Perhaps this is because the Unix system was originally developed in C; it is the native tongue of Unix. Unix C compilers have traditionally defined the interface standards for other languages and tools, such as linkers, debuggers, and so on.

---

* The name is a very clever pun, if you think about the tool for a while.

Conventions set forth by the original C compilers have remained fairly consistent across the Unix programming board.

gcc is one of the most versatile and advanced compilers around. Unlike other C compilers (such as those shipped with the original AT&T or BSD distributions, or those available from various third-party vendors), *gcc* supports all the modern C standards currently in use—such as the ANSI C standard—as well as many extensions specific to *gcc*. Happily, however, *gcc* provides features to make it compatible with older C compilers and older styles of C programming. There is even a tool called *protoize* that can help you write function prototypes for old-style C programs.

gcc is also a C++ compiler. For those who prefer the more modern object-oriented environment, C++ is supported with all the bells and whistles—including most of the C++ introduced when the C++ standard was released, such as method templates. Complete C++ class libraries are provided as well, such as the Standard Template Library (STL).

For those with a taste for the particularly esoteric, *gcc* also supports Objective-C, an object-oriented C spinoff that never gained much popularity but may see a second spring due to its usage in Mac OS X. And there is *gcj*, which compiles Java code to machine code. But the fun doesn't stop there, as we'll see.

In this section, we cover the use of *gcc* to compile and link programs under Linux. We assume you are familiar with programming in C/C++, but we don't assume you're accustomed to the Unix programming environment. That's what we introduce here.

 The latest *gcc* version at the time of this writing is Version 4.0. However, this is still quite new, sometimes a bit unstable, and, since it is a lot stricter about syntax than previous versions, will not compile some older code. Many developers therefore use either a version of the 3.3 series (with 3.3.5 being the current one at the time of this writing) or Version 3.4. We suggest sticking with either of those unless you know exactly what you are doing.

A word about terminology ahead: Because *gcc* can these days compile so much more than C (for example, C++, Java, and some other programming languages), it is considered to be the abbreviation for GNU Compiler Collection. But if you speak about just the C compiler, *gcc* is taken to mean GNU C Compiler.

Quick Overview

Before imparting all the gritty details of *gcc*, we present a simple example and walk through the steps of compiling a C program on a Unix system.

Let's say you have the following bit of code, an encore of the much overused "Hello, World!" program (not that it bears repeating):

```
#include <stdio.h>
int main(  ) {
  (void)printf("Hello, World!\n");
  return 0; /* Just to be nice */
}
```

Several steps are required to compile this program into a living, breathing executable. You can accomplish most of these steps through a single *gcc* command, but we've left the specifics for later in the chapter.

First, the *gcc* compiler must generate an *object file* from this *source code*. The object file is essentially the machine-code equivalent of the C source. It contains code to set up the main( ) calling stack, a call to the printf( ) function, and code to return the value of 0.

The next step is to *link* the object file to produce an executable. As you might guess, this is done by the *linker*. The job of the linker is to take object files, merge them with code from libraries, and spit out an executable. The object code from the previous source does not make a complete executable. First and foremost, the code for printf( ) must be linked in. Also, various initialization routines, invisible to the mortal programmer, must be appended to the executable.

Where does the code for printf( ) come from? Answer: the libraries. It is impossible to talk for long about *gcc* without mentioning them. A *library* is essentially a collection of many object files, including an index. When searching for the code for printf( ), the linker looks at the index for each library it's been told to link against. It finds the object file containing the printf( ) function and extracts that object file (the entire object file, which may contain much more than just the printf( ) function) and links it to the executable.

In reality, things are more complicated than this. Linux supports two kinds of libraries: *static* and *shared*. What we have described in this example are *static libraries*: libraries where the actual code for called subroutines is appended to the executable. However, the code for subroutines such as printf( ) can be quite lengthy. Because many programs use common subroutines from the libraries, it doesn't make sense for each executable to contain its own copy of the library code. That's where shared libraries come in.*

With *shared libraries*, all the common subroutine code is contained in a single library "image file" on disk. When a program is linked with a shared library, *stub code* is appended to the executable, instead of actual subroutine code. This stub code tells

* It should be noted that some very knowledgeable programmers consider shared libraries harmful, for reasons too involved to be explained here. They say that we shouldn't need to bother in a time when most computers ship with 80-GB hard disks and at least 256 MB of memory preinstalled.

the program loader where to find the library code on disk, in the image file, at runtime. Therefore, when our friendly "Hello, World!" program is executed, the program loader notices that the program has been linked against a shared library. It then finds the shared library image and loads code for library routines, such as printf( ), along with the code for the program itself. The stub code tells the loader where to find the code for printf( ) in the image file.

Even this is an oversimplification of what's really going on. Linux shared libraries use *jump tables* that allow the libraries to be upgraded and their contents to be jumbled around, without requiring the executables using these libraries to be relinked. The stub code in the executable actually looks up another reference in the library itself— in the jump table. In this way, the library contents and the corresponding jump tables can be changed, but the executable stub code can remain the same.

Shared libraries also have another advantage: their ability to be upgraded. When someone fixes a bug in printf( ) (or worse, a security hole), you only need to upgrade the one library. You don't have to relink every single program on your system.

But don't allow yourself to be befuddled by all this abstract information. In time, we'll approach a real-life example and show you how to compile, link, and debug your programs. It's actually very simple; the *gcc* compiler takes care of most of the details for you. However, it helps to understand what's going on behind the scenes.

gcc Features

gcc has more features than we could possibly enumerate here. The *gcc* manual page and Info document give an eyeful of interesting information about this compiler. Later in this section, we give you a comprehensive overview of the most useful *gcc* features to get you started. With this in hand, you should be able to figure out for yourself how to get the many other facilities to work to your advantage.

For starters, *gcc* supports the standard C syntax currently in use, specified for the most part by the ANSI C standard. The most important feature of this standard is function prototyping. That is, when defining a function foo( ), which returns an int and takes two arguments, a (of type char *) and b (of type double), the function may be defined like this:

```
int foo(char *a, double b) {
  /* your code here... */
}
```

This contrasts with the older, nonprototype function definition syntax, which looks like this:

```
int foo(a, b)
char *a;
double b;
```

```
{
    /* your code here... */
}
```

and is also supported by *gcc*. Of course, ANSI C defines many other conventions, but this is the one most obvious to the new programmer. Anyone familiar with C programming style in modern books, such as the second edition of Kernighan and Ritchie's *The C Programming Language* (Prentice Hall), can program using *gcc* with no problem.

The *gcc* compiler boasts quite an impressive optimizer. Whereas most C compilers allow you to use the single switch -O to specify optimization, *gcc* supports multiple levels of optimization. At the highest level, *gcc* pulls tricks out of its sleeve, such as allowing code and static data to be shared. That is, if you have a static string in your program such as Hello, World!, and the ASCII encoding of that string happens to coincide with a sequence of instruction code in your program, *gcc* allows the string data and the corresponding code to share the same storage. How clever is that!

Of course, *gcc* allows you to compile debugging information into object files, which aids a debugger (and hence, the programmer) in tracing through the program. The compiler inserts markers in the object file, allowing the debugger to locate specific lines, variables, and functions in the compiled program. Therefore, when using a debugger such as *gdb* (which we talk about later in the chapter), you can step through the compiled program and view the original source text simultaneously.

Among the other tricks *gcc* offers is the ability to generate assembly code with the flick of a switch (literally). Instead of telling *gcc* to compile your source to machine code, you can ask it to stop at the assembly-language level, which is much easier for humans to comprehend. This happens to be a nice way to learn the intricacies of protected-mode assembly programming under Linux: write some C code, have *gcc* translate it into assembly language for you, and study that.

gcc includes its own assembler (which can be used independently of *gcc* and is called *gas*) (even though the binary often is just called *as* on Linux, since there cannot be confusion with other assemblers as on other Unix operating systems such as Solaris), just in case you're wondering how this assembly-language code might get assembled. In fact, you can include inline assembly code in your C source, in case you need to invoke some particularly nasty magic but don't want to write exclusively in assembly.

Basic gcc Usage

By now, you must be itching to know how to invoke all these wonderful features. It is important, especially to novice Unix and C programmers, to know how to use *gcc* effectively. Using a command-line compiler such as *gcc* is quite different from, say, using an integrated development environment (IDE) such as Visual Studio or C++

Builder under Windows. Even though the language syntax is similar, the methods used to compile and link programs are not at all the same.

 A number of IDEs are available for Linux now. These include the popular open source IDE KDevelop, discussed later in this chapter. For Java, Eclipse (*http://www.eclipse.org*) is the leading choice among programmers who like IDEs.

Let's return to our innocent-looking "Hello, World!" example. How would you go about compiling and linking this program?

The first step, of course, is to enter the source code. You accomplish this with a text editor, such as Emacs or *vi*. The would-be programmer should enter the source code and save it in a file named something like *hello.c*. (As with most C compilers, *gcc* is picky about the filename extension: that is how it distinguishes C source from assembly source from object files, and so on. Use the *.c* extension for standard C source.)

To compile and link the program to the executable *hello*, the programmer would use the command:

```
papaya$ gcc -o hello hello.c
```

and (barring any errors), in one fell swoop, *gcc* compiles the source into an object file, links against the appropriate libraries, and spits out the executable *hello*, ready to run. In fact, the wary programmer might want to test it:

```
papaya$ ./hello
Hello, World!
papaya$
```

As friendly as can be expected.

Obviously, quite a few things took place behind the scenes when executing this single *gcc* command. First of all, *gcc* had to compile your source file, *hello.c*, into an object file, *hello.o*. Next, it had to link *hello.o* against the standard libraries and produce an executable.

By default, *gcc* assumes that you want not only to compile the source files you specify, but also to have them linked together (with each other and with the standard libraries) to produce an executable. First, *gcc* compiles any source files into object files. Next, it automatically invokes the linker to glue all the object files and libraries into an executable. (That's right, the linker is a separate program, called *ld*, not part of *gcc* itself—although it can be said that *gcc* and *ld* are close friends.) *gcc* also knows about the standard libraries used by most programs and tells *ld* to link against them. You can, of course, override these defaults in various ways.

You can pass multiple filenames in one *gcc* command, but on large projects you'll find it more natural to compile a few files at a time and keep the *.o* object files around. If you want only to compile a source file into an object file and forego the linking process, use the -c switch with *gcc*, as in the following example:

    papaya$ **gcc -c hello.c**

This produces the object file *hello.o* and nothing else.

By default, the linker produces an executable named, of all things, *a.out*. This is just a bit of left-over gunk from early implementations of Unix, and nothing to write home about. By using the -o switch with *gcc*, you can force the resulting executable to be named something different, in this case, *hello*.

Using Multiple Source Files

The next step on your path to *gcc* enlightenment is to understand how to compile programs using multiple source files. Let's say you have a program consisting of two source files, *foo.c* and *bar.c*. Naturally, you would use one or more header files (such as *foo.h*) containing function declarations shared between the two programs. In this way, code in *foo.c* knows about functions in *bar.c*, and vice versa.

To compile these two source files and link them together (along with the libraries, of course) to produce the executable *baz*, you'd use the command:

    papaya$ **gcc -o baz foo.c bar.c**

This is roughly equivalent to the following three commands:

    papaya$ **gcc -c foo.c**
    papaya$ **gcc -c bar.c**
    papaya$ **gcc -o baz foo.o bar.o**

gcc acts as a nice frontend to the linker and other "hidden" utilities invoked during compilation.

Of course, compiling a program using multiple source files in one command can be time-consuming. If you had, say, five or more source files in your program, the *gcc* command in the previous example would recompile each source file in turn before linking the executable. This can be a large waste of time, especially if you only made modifications to a single source file since the last compilation. There would be no reason to recompile the other source files, as their up-to-date object files are still intact.

The answer to this problem is to use a project manager such as *make*. We talk about *make* later in the chapter, in "Makefiles."

Optimizing

Telling *gcc* to optimize your code as it compiles is a simple matter; just use the -O switch on the *gcc* command line:

    papaya$ **gcc -O -o fishsticks fishsticks.c**

As we mentioned not long ago, *gcc* supports different levels of optimization. Using -*O2* instead of -*O* will turn on several "expensive" optimizations that may cause compilation to run more slowly but will (hopefully) greatly enhance performance of your code.

You may notice in your dealings with Linux that a number of programs are compiled using the switch -*O6* (the Linux kernel being a good example). The current version of *gcc* does not support optimization up to -*O6*, so this defaults to (presently) the equivalent of -*O2*. However, -*O6* is sometimes used for compatibility with future versions of *gcc* to ensure that the greatest level of optimization is used.

Enabling Debugging Code

The -*g* switch to *gcc* turns on debugging code in your compiled object files. That is, extra information is added to the object file, as well as the resulting executable, allowing the program to be traced with a debugger such as *gdb*. The downside to using debugging code is that it greatly increases the size of the resulting object files. It's usually best to use -*g* only while developing and testing your programs and to leave it out for the "final" compilation.

Happily, debug-enabled code is not incompatible with code optimization. This means that you can safely use the command:

```
papaya$ gcc -O -g -o mumble mumble.c
```

However, certain optimizations enabled by -*O* or -*O2* may cause the program to appear to behave erratically while under a debugger. It is usually best to use either -*O* or -*g*, not both.

More Fun with Libraries

Before we leave the realm of *gcc*, a few words on linking and libraries are in order. For one thing, it's easy for you to create your own libraries. If you have a set of routines you use often, you may wish to group them into a set of source files, compile each source file into an object file, and then create a library from the object files. This saves you from having to compile these routines individually for each program in which you use them.

Let's say you have a set of source files containing oft-used routines, such as:

```
float square(float x) {
  /* Code for square( )... */
}

int factorial(int x, int n) {
  /* Code for factorial( )... */
}
```

and so on (of course, the *gcc* standard libraries provide analogs to these common routines, so don't be misled by our choice of example). Furthermore, let's say that the code for square( ), which both takes and returns a float, is in the file *square.c* and that the code for factorial( ) is in *factorial.c*. Simple enough, right?

To produce a library containing these routines, all you do is compile each source file, as so:

```
papaya$ gcc -c square.c factorial.c
```

which leaves you with *square.o* and *factorial.o*. Next, create a library from the object files. As it turns out, a library is just an archive file created using *ar* (a close counterpart to *tar*). Let's call our library *libstuff.a* and create it this way:

```
papaya$ ar r libstuff.a square.o factorial.o
```

When updating a library such as this, you may need to delete the old *libstuff.a*, if it exists. The last step is to generate an index for the library, which enables the linker to find routines within the library. To do this, use the *ranlib* command, as so:

```
papaya$ ranlib libstuff.a
```

This command adds information to the library itself; no separate index file is created. You could also combine the two steps of running *ar* and *ranlib* by using the *s* command to *ar*:

```
papaya$ ar rs libstuff.a square.o factorial.o
```

Now you have *libstuff.a*, a static library containing your routines. Before you can link programs against it, you'll need to create a header file describing the contents of the library. For example, we could create *libstuff.h* with the contents:

```
/* libstuff.h: routines in libstuff.a */
extern float square(float);
extern int factorial(int, int);
```

Every source file that uses routines from *libstuff.a* should contain an #include "libstuff.h" line, as you would do with standard header files.

Now that we have our library and header file, how do we compile programs to use them? First, we need to put the library and header file someplace where the compiler can find them. Many users place personal libraries in the directory *lib* in their home directory, and personal include files under *include*. Assuming we have done so, we can compile the mythical program *wibble.c* using the following command:

```
papaya$ gcc -I../include -L../lib -o wibble wibble.c -lstuff
```

The *-I* option tells *gcc* to add the directory *../include* to the *include path* it uses to search for include files. *-L* is similar, in that it tells *gcc* to add the directory *../lib* to the *library path*.

The last argument on the command line is *-lstuff*, which tells the linker to link against the library *libstuff.a* (wherever it may be along the library path). The *lib* at the beginning of the filename is assumed for libraries.

Any time you wish to link against libraries other than the standard ones, you should use the *-l* switch on the *gcc* command line. For example, if you wish to use math routines (specified in *math.h*), you should add *-lm* to the end of the *gcc* command, which links against *libm*. Note, however, that the *order* of *-l* options is significant. For example, if our *libstuff* library used routines found in *libm*, you must include *-lm* after *-lstuff* on the command line:

```
papaya$ gcc -Iinclude -Llib -o wibble wibble.c -lstuff -lm
```

This forces the linker to link *libm* after *libstuff*, allowing those unresolved references in *libstuff* to be taken care of.

Where does *gcc* look for libraries? By default, libraries are searched for in a number of locations, the most important of which is */usr/lib*. If you take a glance at the contents of */usr/lib*, you'll notice it contains many library files—some of which have filenames ending in *.a*, others with filenames ending in *.so.version*. The *.a* files are static libraries, as is the case with our *libstuff.a*. The *.so* files are shared libraries, which contain code to be linked at runtime, as well as the stub code required for the runtime linker (*ld.so*) to locate the shared library.

At runtime, the program loader looks for shared library images in several places, including */lib*. If you look at */lib*, you'll see files such as *libc.so.6*. This is the image file containing the code for the *libc* shared library (one of the standard libraries, which most programs are linked against).

By default, the linker attempts to link against shared libraries. However, static libraries are used in several cases—for example, when there are no shared libraries with the specified name anywhere in the library search path. You can also specify that static libraries should be linked by using the *-static* switch with *gcc*.

Creating shared libraries

Now that you know how to create and use static libraries, it's very easy to take the step to shared libraries. Shared libraries have a number of advantages. They reduce memory consumption if used by more than one process, and they reduce the size of the executable. Furthermore, they make developing easier: when you use shared libraries and change some things in a library, you do not need to recompile and relink your application each time. You need to recompile only if you make incompatible changes, such as adding arguments to a call or changing the size of a struct.

Before you start doing all your development work with shared libraries, though, be warned that debugging with them is slightly more difficult than with static libraries because the debugger usually used on Linux, *gdb*, has some problems with shared libraries.

Code that goes into a shared library needs to be *position-independent*. This is just a convention for object code that makes it possible to use the code in shared libraries. You make *gcc* emit position-independent code by passing it one of the command-line switches *-fpic* or *-fPIC*. The former is preferred, unless the modules have grown so large that the relocatable code table is simply too small, in which case the compiler will emit an error message and you have to use *-fPIC*. To repeat our example from the last section:

```
papaya$ gcc -c -fpic square.c factorial.c
```

This being done, it is just a simple step to generate a shared library:[*]

```
papaya$ gcc -shared -o libstuff.so square.o factorial.o
```

Note the compiler switch *-shared*. There is no indexing step as with static libraries.

Using our newly created shared library is even simpler. The shared library doesn't require any change to the compile command:

```
papaya$ gcc -I../include -L../lib -o wibble wibble.c -lstuff -lm
```

You might wonder what the linker does if a shared library *libstuff.so* and a static library *libstuff.a* are available. In this case, the linker always picks the shared library. To make it use the static one, you will have to name it explicitly on the command line:

```
papaya$ gcc -I../include -L../lib -o wibble wibble.c libstuff.a -lm
```

Another very useful tool for working with shared libraries is *ldd*. It tells you which shared libraries an executable program uses. Here's an example:

```
papaya$ ldd wibble
        linux-gate.so.1 =>  (0xffffe000)
        libstuff.so => libstuff.so (0x400af000)
        libm.so.5 => /lib/libm.so.5 (0x400ba000)
        libc.so.5 => /lib/libc.so.5 (0x400c3000)
```

The three fields in each line are the name of the library, the full path to the instance of the library that is used, and where in the virtual address space the library is mapped to. The first line is something arcane, part of the Linux loader implementation that you can happily ignore.

If *ldd* outputs not found for a certain library, you are in trouble and won't be able to run the program in question. You will have to search for a copy of that library. Perhaps it is a library shipped with your distribution that you opted not to install, or it is already on your hard disk but the loader (the part of the system that loads every executable program) cannot find it.

---

[*] In the ancient days of Linux, creating a shared library was a daunting task of which even wizards were afraid. The advent of the ELF object-file format reduced this task to picking the right compiler switch. Things sure have improved!

In the latter situation, try locating the libraries yourself and find out whether they're in a nonstandard directory. By default, the loader looks only in */lib* and */usr/lib*. If you have libraries in another directory, create an environment variable LD_LIBRARY_ PATH and add the directories separated by colons. If you believe that everything is set up correctly, and the library in question still cannot be found, run the command *ldconfig* as root, which refreshes the linker system cache.

Using C++

If you prefer object-oriented programming, *gcc* provides complete support for C++ as well as Objective-C. There are only a few considerations you need to be aware of when doing C++ programming with *gcc*.

First, C++ source filenames should end in the extension *.cpp* (most often used), *.C*, or *.cc*. This distinguishes them from regular C source filenames, which end in *.c*. It is actually possible to tell *gcc* to compile even files ending in *.c* as C++ files, by using the command-line parameter *-x c++*, but that is not recommended, as it is likely to confuse you.

Second, you should use the *g++* shell script in lieu of *gcc* when compiling C++ code. *g++* is simply a shell script that invokes *gcc* with a number of additional arguments, specifying a link against the C++ standard libraries, for example. *g++* takes the same arguments and options as *gcc*.

If you do not use *g++*, you'll need to be sure to link against the C++ libraries in order to use any of the basic C++ classes, such as the cout and cin I/O objects. Also be sure you have actually installed the C++ libraries and include files. Some distributions contain only the standard C libraries. *gcc* will be able to compile your C++ programs fine, but without the C++ libraries, you'll end up with linker errors whenever you attempt to use standard objects.

Makefiles

Sometime during your life with Linux you will probably have to deal with *make*, even if you don't plan to do any programming. It's possible you'll want to patch and rebuild the kernel, and that involves running *make*. If you're lucky, you won't have to muck with the makefiles—but we've tried to direct this book toward unlucky people as well. So in this section, we explain enough of the subtle syntax of *make* so that you're not intimidated by a makefile.

For some of our examples, we draw on the current makefile for the Linux kernel. It exploits a lot of extensions in the powerful GNU version of *make*, so we describe some of those as well as the standard *make* features. Those ready to become thoroughgoing initiates into *make* can read *Managing Projects with GNU Make* (O'Reilly). GNU extensions are also well documented by the GNU *make* manual.

Most users see *make* as a way to build object files and libraries from sources and to build executables from object files. More conceptually, *make* is a general-purpose program that builds *targets* from *dependencies*. The target can be a program executable, a PostScript document, or whatever. The prerequisites can be C code, a T_EX text file, and so on.

Although you can write simple shell scripts to execute *gcc* commands that build an executable program, *make* is special in that it knows which targets need to be rebuilt and which don't. An object file needs to be recompiled only if its corresponding source has changed.

For example, say you have a program that consists of three C source files. If you were to build the executable using the command:

```
papaya$ gcc -o foo foo.c bar.c baz.c
```

each time you changed any of the source files, all three would be recompiled and relinked into the executable. If you changed only one source file, this is a real waste of time (especially if the program in question is much larger than a handful of sources). What you really want to do is recompile only the one source file that changed into an object file and relink all the object files in the program to form the executable. *make* can automate this process for you.

What make Does

The basic goal of *make* is to let you build a file in small steps. If a lot of source files make up the final executable, you can change one and rebuild the executable without having to recompile everything. In order to give you this flexibility, *make* records what files you need to do your build.

Here's a trivial makefile. Call it *makefile* or *Makefile* and keep it in the same directory as the source files:

```
edimh: main.o edit.o
        gcc -o edimh main.o edit.o

main.o: main.c
        gcc -c main.c

edit.o: edit.c
        gcc -c edit.c
```

This file builds a program named *edimh* from two source files named *main.c* and *edit.c*. You aren't restricted to C programming in a makefile; the commands could be anything.

Three entries appear in the file. Each contains a *dependency line* that shows how a file is built. Thus, the first line says that *edimh* (the name before the colon) is built from the two object files *main.o* and *edit.o* (the names after the colon). This line tells *make* that it should execute the following *gcc* line whenever one of those object files changes. The lines containing commands have to begin with tabs (not spaces).

The command:

```
papaya$ make edimh
```

executes the *gcc* line if there isn't currently any file named *edimh*. However, the *gcc* line also executes if *edimh* exists but one of the object files is newer. Here, *edimh* is called a *target*. The files after the colon are called either *dependencies* or *prerequisites*.

The next two entries perform the same service for the object files. *main.o* is built if it doesn't exist or if the associated source file *main.c* is newer. *edit.o* is built from *edit.c*.

How does *make* know if a file is new? It looks at the timestamp, which the filesystem associates with every file. You can see timestamps by issuing the *ls -l* command. Since the timestamp is accurate to one second, it reliably tells *make* whether you've edited a source file since the latest compilation or have compiled an object file since the executable was last built.

Let's try out the makefile and see what it does:

```
papaya$ make edimh
gcc -c main.c
gcc -c edit.c
gcc -o edimh main.o edit.o
```

If we edit *main.c* and reissue the command, it rebuilds only the necessary files, saving us some time:

```
papaya$ make edimh
gcc -c main.c
gcc -o edimh main.o edit.o
```

It doesn't matter what order the three entries are within the makefile. *make* figures out which files depend on which and executes all the commands in the right order. Putting the entry for *edimh* first is convenient because that becomes the file built by default. In other words, typing make is the same as typing make edimh.

Here's a more extensive makefile. See if you can figure out what it does:

```
install: all
        mv edimh /usr/local
        mv readimh /usr/local

all: edimh readimh

readimh: read.o main.o
        gcc -o readimh main.o read.o

edimh: main.o edit.o
        gcc -o edimh main.o edit.o

main.o: main.c
```

```
              gcc -c main.c

   edit.o: edit.c
              gcc -c edit.c

   read.o: read.c
              gcc -c read.c
```

First we see the target install. This is never going to generate a file; it's called a *phony target* because it exists just so that you can execute the commands listed under it. But before install runs, all has to run because install depends on all. (Remember, the order of the entries in the file doesn't matter.)

So *make* turns to the all target. There are no commands under it (this is perfectly legal), but it depends on *edimh* and *readimh*. These are real files; each is an executable program. So *make* keeps tracing back through the list of dependencies until it arrives at the .c files, which don't depend on anything else. Then it painstakingly rebuilds each target.

Here is a sample run (you may need root privilege to install the files in the */usr/local* directory):

```
papaya$ make install
gcc -c main.c
gcc -c edit.c
gcc -o edimh main.o edit.o
gcc -c read.c
gcc -o readimh main.o read.o
mv edimh /usr/local
mv readimh /usr/local
```

This run of *make* does a complete build and install. First it builds the files needed to create *edimh*. Then it builds the additional object file it needs to create *readmh*. With those two executables created, the all target is satisfied. Now *make* can go on to build the install target, which means moving the two executables to their final home.

Many makefiles, including the ones that build Linux, contain a variety of phony targets to do routine activities. For instance, the makefile for the Linux kernel includes commands to remove temporary files:

```
clean:  archclean
        rm -f kernel/ksyms.lst
        rm -f core `find . -name '*.[oas]' -print`
        .
        .
        .
```

It also includes commands to create a list of object files and the header files they depend on (this is a complicated but important task; if a header file changes, you want to make sure the files that refer to it are recompiled):

```
depend dep:
        touch tools/version.h
        for i in init/*.c;do echo -n "init/";$(CPP) -M $$i;done > .tmpdep
        .
        .
        .
```

Some of these shell commands get pretty complicated; we look at makefile commands later in this chapter, in "Multiple Commands."

Some Syntax Rules

The hardest thing about maintaining makefiles, at least if you're new to them, is getting the syntax right. OK, let's be straight about it: *make* syntax is really stupid. If you use spaces where you're supposed to use tabs or vice versa, your makefile blows up. And the error messages are really confusing. So remember the following syntax rules:

- Always put a tab—not spaces—at the beginning of a command. And don't use a tab before any other line.
- You can place a hash sign (#) anywhere on a line to start a comment. Everything after the hash sign is ignored.
- If you put a backslash at the end of a line, it continues on the next line. That works for long commands and other types of makefile lines, too.

Now let's look at some of the powerful features of *make*, which form a kind of programming language of their own.

Macros

When people use a filename or other string more than once in a makefile, they tend to assign it to a macro. That's simply a string that *make* expands to another string. For instance, you could change the beginning of our trivial makefile to read as follows:

```
OBJECTS = main.o edit.o

edimh: $(OBJECTS)
        gcc -o edimh $(OBJECTS)
```

When *make* runs, it simply plugs in main.o edit.o wherever you specify $(OBJECTS). If you have to add another object file to the project, just specify it on the first line of the file. The dependency line and command will then be updated correspondingly.

Don't forget the parentheses when you refer to $(OBJECTS). Macros may resemble shell variables like $HOME and $PATH, but they're not the same.

One macro can be defined in terms of another macro, so you could say something like:

```
ROOT = /usr/local
HEADERS = $(ROOT)/include
SOURCES = $(ROOT)/src
```

In this case, HEADERS evaluates to the directory */usr/local/include* and SOURCES to */usr/local/src*. If you are installing this package on your system and don't want it to be in */usr/local*, just choose another name and change the line that defines ROOT.

By the way, you don't have to use uppercase names for macros, but that's a universal convention.

An extension in GNU *make* allows you to add to the definition of a macro. This uses a := string in place of an equals sign:

```
DRIVERS = drivers/block/block.a

ifdef CONFIG_SCSI
DRIVERS := $(DRIVERS) drivers/scsi/scsi.a
endif
```

The first line is a normal macro definition, setting the DRIVERS macro to the filename *drivers/block/block.a*. The next definition adds the filename *drivers/scsi/scsi.a*. But it takes effect only if the macro CONFIG_SCSI is defined. The full definition in that case becomes:

```
drivers/block/block.a drivers/scsi/scsi.a
```

So how do you define CONFIG_SCSI? You could put it in the makefile, assigning any string you want:

```
CONFIG_SCSI = yes
```

But you'll probably find it easier to define it on the *make* command line. Here's how to do it:

```
papaya$ make CONFIG_SCSI=yes target_name
```

One subtlety of using macros is that you can leave them undefined. If no one defines them, a null string is substituted (that is, you end up with nothing where the macro is supposed to be). But this also gives you the option of defining the macro as an environment variable. For instance, if you don't define CONFIG_SCSI in the makefile, you could put this in your *.bashrc* file, for use with the *bash* shell:

```
export CONFIG_SCSI=yes
```

Or put this in *.cshrc* if you use *csh* or *tcsh*:

```
setenv CONFIG_SCSI yes
```

All your builds will then have CONFIG_SCSI defined.

Suffix Rules and Pattern Rules

For something as routine as building an object file from a source file, you don't want to specify every single dependency in your makefile. And you don't have to. Unix compilers enforce a simple standard (compile a file ending in the suffix *.c* to create a file ending in the suffix *.o*), and *make* provides a feature called suffix rules to cover all such files.

Here's a simple suffix rule to compile a C source file, which you could put in your makefile:

```
.c.o:
        gcc -c $(CFLAGS) $<
```

The `.c.o:` line means "use a *.c* dependency to build a *.o* file." CFLAGS is a macro into which you can plug any compiler options you want: *-g* for debugging, for instance, or *-O* for optimization. The string $< is a cryptic way of saying "the dependency." So the name of your *.c* file is plugged in when *make* executes this command.

Here's a sample run using this suffix rule. The command line passes both the *-g* option and the *-O* option:

```
papaya$ make CFLAGS="-O -g" edit.o
gcc -c -O -g edit.c
```

You actually don't have to specify this suffix rule in your makefile because something very similar is already built into *make*. It even uses CFLAGS, so you can determine the options used for compiling just by setting that variable. The makefile used to build the Linux kernel currently contains the following definition, a whole slew of *gcc* options:

```
CFLAGS = -Wall -Wstrict-prototypes -O2 -fomit-frame-pointer -pipe
```

While we're discussing compiler flags, one set is seen so often that it's worth a special mention. This is the *-D* option, which is used to define symbols in the source code. Since all kinds of commonly used symbols appear in #ifdefs, you may need to pass lots of such options to your makefile, such as *-DDEBUG* or *-DBSD*. If you do this on the *make* command line, be sure to put quotation marks or apostrophes around the whole set. This is because you want the shell to pass the set to your makefile as one argument:

```
papaya$ make CFLAGS="-DDEBUG -DBSD" ...
```

GNU *make* offers something called *pattern rules*, which are even better than suffix rules. A pattern rule uses a percent sign to mean "any string." So C source files would be compiled using a rule such as the following:

```
%.o: %.c
        gcc -c -o $@ $(CFLAGS) $<
```

Here the output file %.*o* comes first, and the dependency %.*c* comes after a colon. In short, a pattern rule is just like a regular dependency line, but it contains percent signs instead of exact filenames.

We see the $< string to refer to the dependency, but we also see $@, which refers to the output file. So the name of the .o file is plugged in there. Both of these are built-in macros; *make* defines them every time it executes an entry.

Another common built-in macro is $*, which refers to the name of the dependency stripped of the suffix. So if the dependency is *edit.c*, the string $*.s would evaluate to *edit.s* (an assembly-language source file).

Here's something useful you can do with a pattern rule that you can't do with a suffix rule: add the string _dbg to the name of the output file so that later you can tell that you compiled it with debugging information:

```
%_dbg.o: %.c
        gcc -c -g -o $@ $(CFLAGS) $<

DEBUG_OBJECTS = main_dbg.o edit_dbg.o

edimh_dbg: $(DEBUG_OBJECTS)
        gcc -o $@ $(DEBUG_OBJECTS)
```

Now you can build all your objects in two different ways: one with debugging information and one without. They'll have different filenames, so you can keep them in one directory:

```
papaya$ make edimh_dbg
gcc -c -g -o main_dbg.o  main.c
gcc -c -g -o edit_dbg.o  edit.c
gcc -o edimh_dbg  main_dbg.o edit_dbg.o
```

Multiple Commands

Any shell commands can be executed in a makefile. But things can get kind of complicated because *make* executes each command in a separate shell. So this would not work:

```
target:
        cd obj
        HOST_DIR=/home/e
        mv *.o $HOST_DIR
```

Neither the *cd* command nor the definition of the variable HOST_DIR has any effect on subsequent commands. You have to string everything together into one command. The shell uses a semicolon as a separator between commands, so you can combine them all on one line:

```
target:
        cd obj ; HOST_DIR=/home/e ; mv *.o $$HOST_DIR
```

One more change: to define and use a shell variable within the command, you have to double the dollar sign. This lets *make* know that you mean it to be a shell variable, not a macro.

You may find the file easier to read if you break the semicolon-separated commands onto multiple lines, using backslashes so that *make* considers them to be on one line:

```
target:
        cd obj ; \
        HOST_DIR=/home/e ; \
        mv *.o $$HOST_DIR
```

Sometimes makefiles contain their own *make* commands; this is called recursive *make*. It looks like this:

```
linuxsubdirs: dummy
        set -e; for i in $(SUBDIRS); do $(MAKE) -C $$i; done
```

The macro $(MAKE) invokes *make*. There are a few reasons for nesting makes. One reason, which applies to this example, is to perform builds in multiple directories (each of these other directories has to contain its own makefile). Another reason is to define macros on the command line, so you can do builds with a variety of macro definitions.

GNU *make* offers another powerful interface to the shell as an extension. You can issue a shell command and assign its output to a macro. A couple of examples can be found in the Linux kernel makefile, but we'll just show a simple example here:

```
HOST_NAME = $(shell uname -n)
```

This assigns the name of your network node—the output of the *uname -n* command—to the macro HOST_NAME.

make offers a couple of conventions you may occasionally want to use. One is to put an at sign before a command, which keeps *make* from echoing the command when it's executed:

```
@if [ -x /bin/dnsdomainname ]; then \
    echo #define LINUX_COMPILE_DOMAIN \"`dnsdomainname`\"; \
else \
    echo #define LINUX_COMPILE_DOMAIN \"`domainname`\"; \
fi >> tools/version.h
```

Another convention is to put a hyphen before a command, which tells *make* to keep going even if the command fails. This may be useful if you want to continue after an *mv* or *cp* command fails:

```
- mv edimh /usr/local
- mv readimh /usr/local
```

Including Other makefiles

Large projects tend to break parts of their makefiles into separate files. This makes it easy for different makefiles in different directories to share things, particularly macro definitions. The line

```
include filename
```

reads in the contents of *filename*. You can see this in the Linux kernel makefile, for instance:

```
include .depend
```

If you look in the file *.depend*, you'll find a bunch of makefile entries: these lines declare that object files depend on particular header files. (By the way, *.depend* might not exist yet; it has to be created by another entry in the makefile.)

Sometimes `include` lines refer to macros instead of filenames, as in the following example:

```
include ${INC_FILE}
```

In this case, `INC_FILE` must be defined either as an environment variable or as a macro. Doing things this way gives you more control over which file is used.

Interpreting make Messages

The error messages from *make* can be quite cryptic, so we'd like to give you some help in interpreting them. The following explanations cover the most common messages.

*** *No targets specified and no makefile found. Stop.*
> This usually means that there is no makefile in the directory you are trying to compile. By default, *make* tries to find the file *GNUmakefile* first; then, if this has failed, *Makefile*, and finally *makefile*. If none of these exists, you will get this error message. If for some reason you want to use a makefile with a different name (or in another directory), you can specify the makefile to use with the *-f* command-line option.

make: *** *No rule to make target 'blah.c', needed by 'blah.o'. Stop.*
> This means that *make* cannot find a dependency it needs (in this case, *blah.c*) in order to build a target (in this case, *blah.o*). As mentioned, *make* first looks for a dependency among the targets in the makefile, and if there is no suitable target, for a file with the name of the dependency. If this does not exist either, you will get this error message. This typically means that your sources are incomplete or that there is a typo in the makefile.

*** *missing separator (did you mean TAB instead of 8 spaces?). Stop.*
> The current versions of *make* are friendly enough to ask you whether you have made a very common mistake: not prepending a command with a tab. If you use

older versions of *make*, *missing separator* is all you get. In this case, check whether you really have a tab in front of all commands, and not before anything else.

Autoconf, Automake, and Other Makefile Tools

Writing makefiles for a larger project usually is a boring and time-consuming task, especially if the programs are expected to be compiled on multiple platforms. From the GNU project come two tools called *Autoconf* and *Automake* that have a steep learning curve but, once mastered, greatly simplify the task of creating portable makefiles. In addition, *libtool* helps a lot to create shared libraries in a portable manner. You can probably find these tools on your distribution CD, or you can download them from *ftp://ftp.gnu.org/gnu*.

From a user's point of view, using *Autoconf* involves running the program *configure*, which should have been shipped in the source package you are trying to build. This program analyzes your system and configures the makefiles of the package to be suitable for your system and setup. A good thing to try before running the *configure* script for real is to issue the command:

```
owl$ ./configure --help
```

This shows all command-line switches that the *configure* program understands. Many packages allow different setups—for example, different modules to be compiled in—and you can select these with *configure* options.

From a programmer's point of view, you don't write makefiles, but rather files called *makefile.in*. These can contain placeholders that will be replaced with actual values when the user runs the *configure* program, generating the makefiles that *make* then runs. In addition, you need to write a file called *configure.in* that describes your project and what to check for on the target system. The *Autoconf* tool then generates the *configure* program from this *configure.in* file. Writing the *configure.in* file is unfortunately way too involved to be described here, but the *Autoconf* package contains documentation to get you started.

Writing the *makefile.in* files is still a cumbersome and lengthy task, but even this can be mostly automated by using the *Automake* package. Using this package, you do not write the *makefile.in* files, but rather the *makefile.am* files, which have a much simpler syntax and are much less verbose. By running the *Automake* tool, you convert these *makefile.am* files to the *makefile.in* files, which you distribute along with your source code and which are later converted into the *makefiles* themselves when the package is configured for the user's system. How to write *makefile.am* files is beyond the scope of this book as well. Again, please check the documentation of the package to get started.

These days, most open source packages use the *libtool/Automake/Autoconf* combo for generating the makefiles, but this does not mean that this rather complicated and involved method is the only one available. Other makefile-generating tools exist as well, such as the *imake* tool used to configure the X Window System.* Another tool that is not as powerful as the *Autoconf* suite (even though it still lets you do most things you would want to do when it comes to makefile generation) but extremely easy to use (it can even generate its own description files for you from scratch) is the *qmake* tool that ships together with the C++ GUI library Qt (downloadable from *http://www.trolltech.com*).

Debugging with gdb

Are you one of those programmers who scoff at the very idea of using a debugger to trace through code? Is it your philosophy that if the code is too complex for even the programmer to understand, the programmer deserves no mercy when it comes to bugs? Do you step through your code, mentally, using a magnifying glass and a toothpick? More often than not, are bugs usually caused by a single-character omission, such as using the = operator when you mean +=?

Then perhaps you should meet *gdb*—the GNU debugger. Whether or not you know it, *gdb* is your friend. It can locate obscure and difficult-to-find bugs that result in core dumps, memory leaks, and erratic behavior (both for the program and the programmer). Sometimes even the most harmless-looking glitches in your code can cause everything to go haywire, and without the aid of a debugger like *gdb*, finding these problems can be nearly impossible—especially for programs longer than a few hundred lines. In this section, we introduce you to the most useful features of *gdb* by way of examples. There's a book on *gdb*: *Debugging with GDB* (Free Software Foundation).

gdb is capable of either debugging programs as they run or examining the cause for a program crash with a core dump. Programs debugged at runtime with *gdb* can either be executed from within *gdb* itself or can be run separately; that is, *gdb* can attach itself to an already running process to examine it. We first discuss how to debug programs running within *gdb* and then move on to attaching to running processes and examining core dumps.

Tracing a Program

Our first example is a program called *trymh* that detects edges in a grayscale image. *trymh* takes as input an image file, does some calculations on the data, and spits out another image file. Unfortunately, it crashes whenever it is invoked, as so:

```
papaya$ trymh < image00.pgm > image00.pbm
Segmentation fault (core dumped)
```

* X.org is planning to switch to *Automake/Autoconf* for the next version as well.

Now, using *gdb*, we could analyze the resulting core file, but for this example, we'll show how to trace the program as it runs.[*]

Before we use *gdb* to trace through the executable *trymh*, we need to ensure that the executable has been compiled with debugging code (see "Enabling Debugging Code," earlier in this chapter). To do so, we should compile *trymh* using the *-g* switch with *gcc*.

Note that enabling optimization (*-O*) with debug code (*-g*) is legal but discouraged. The problem is that *gcc* is too smart for its own good. For example, if you have two identical lines of code in two different places in a function, *gdb* may unexpectedly jump to the second occurrence of the line, instead of the first, as expected. This is because *gcc* combined the two lines into a single line of machine code used in both instances.

Some of the automatic optimizations performed by *gcc* can be confusing when using a debugger. To turn off *all* optimization (even optimizations performed without specifying *-O*), use the *-O0* (that's *dash-oh-zero*) option with *gcc*.

Now we can fire up *gdb* to see what the problem might be:

```
papaya$ gdb trymh
GNU gdb 6.3
Copyright 2004 Free Software Foundation, Inc.
GDB is free software, covered by the GNU General Public License, and you are
welcome to change it and/or distribute copies of it under certain conditions.
Type "show copying" to see the conditions.
There is absolutely no warranty for GDB.  Type "show warranty" for details.
This GDB was configured as "i586-suse-linux".
(gdb)
```

Now *gdb* is waiting for a command. (The command *help* displays information on the available commands.) The first thing we want to do is start running the program so that we can observe its behavior. However, if we immediately use the *run* command, the program simply executes until it exits or crashes.

First, we need to set a *breakpoint* somewhere in the program. A breakpoint is just a location in the program where *gdb* should stop and allow us to control execution of the program. For the sake of simplicity, let's set a breakpoint on the first line of actual code so that the program stops just as it begins to execute. The *list* command displays several lines of code (an amount that is variable) at a time:

```
(gdb) list
12          main( ) {
13
14              FloatImage inimage;
15              FloatImage outimage;
```

---

[*] The sample programs in this section are not programs you're likely to run into anywhere; they were thrown together by the authors for the purpose of demonstration.

```
16          BinaryImage binimage;
17          int i,j;
18
19          inimage = (FloatImage)imLoadF(IMAGE_FLOAT,stdin);
20          outimage = laplacian_float(inimage);
21
(gdb) break 19
Breakpoint 1 at 0x289c: file trymh.c, line 19.
(gdb)
```

A breakpoint is now set at line 19 in the current source file. You can set many break-points in the program; breakpoints may be conditional (that is, triggered only when a certain expression is true), unconditional, delayed, temporarily disabled, and so on. You may set breakpoints on a particular line of code, a particular function, or a set of functions, and in a slew of other ways. You may also set a *watchpoint*, using the *watch* command, which is similar to a breakpoint but is triggered whenever a certain event takes place—not necessarily at a specific line of code within the program. We'll talk more about breakpoints and watchpoints later in the chapter.

Next, we use the *run* command to start running the program. *run* takes as arguments the same arguments you'd give *trymh* on the command line; these can include shell wildcards and input/output redirection, as the command is passed to */bin/sh* for execution:

```
(gdb) run < image00.pgm > image00.pfm
Starting program: /amd/dusk/d/mdw/vis/src/trymh < image00.pgm > image00.pfm

Breakpoint 1, main (  ) at trymh.c:19
19          inimage = (FloatImage)imLoadF(IMAGE_FLOAT,stdin);
(gdb)
```

As expected, the breakpoint is reached immediately at the first line of code. We can now take over.

The most useful program-stepping commands are *next* and *step*. Both commands execute the next line of code in the program, except that *step* descends into any function calls in the program, and *next* steps directly to the next line of code in the same function. *next* quietly executes any function calls that it steps over but does not descend into their code for us to examine.

imLoadF is a function that loads an image from a disk file. We know this function is not at fault (you'll have to trust us on that one), so we wish to step over it using the *next* command:

```
(gdb) next
20          outimage = laplacian_float(inimage);
(gdb)
```

Here, we are interested in tracing the suspicious-looking laplacian_float function, so we use the *step* command:

```
(gdb) step
laplacian_float (fim=0x0) at laplacian.c:21
21          i = 20.0;
(gdb)
```

Let's use the *list* command to get some idea of where we are:

```
(gdb) list
16          FloatImage laplacian_float(FloatImage fim) {
17
18              FloatImage mask;
19              float i;
20
21              i = 20.0;
22              mask=(FloatImage)imNew(IMAGE_FLOAT,3,3);
23              imRef(mask,0,0) = imRef(mask,2,0) = imRef(mask,0,2) = 1.0;
24              imRef(mask,2,2) = 1.0; imRef(mask,1,0) = imRef(mask,0,1) = i/5;
25              imRef(mask,2,1) = imRef(mask,1,2) = i/5; imRef(mask,1,1) = -i;
(gdb) list
26
27              return convolveFloatWithFloat(fim,mask);
28          }
(gdb)
```

As you can see, using *list* multiple times just displays more of the code. Because we don't want to step manually through this code, and we're not interested in the imNew function on line 22, let's continue execution until line 27. For this, we use the *until* command:

```
(gdb) until 27
laplacian_float (fim=0x0) at laplacian.c:27
27              return convolveFloatWithFloat(fim,mask);
(gdb)
```

Before we step into the convolveFloatWithFloat function, let's be sure the two parameters, fim and mask, are valid. The *print* command examines the value of a variable:

```
(gdb) print mask
$1 = (struct {...} *) 0xe838
(gdb) print fim

$2 = (struct {...} *) 0x0
(gdb)
```

mask looks fine, but fim, the input image, is null. Obviously, laplacian_float was passed a null pointer instead of a valid image. If you have been paying close attention, you noticed this as we entered laplacian_float earlier.

Instead of stepping deeper into the program (as it's apparent that something has already gone wrong), let's continue execution until the current function returns. The *finish* command accomplishes this:

```
(gdb) finish
Run till exit from #0  laplacian_float (fim=0x0) at laplacian.c:27
```

```
0x28c0 in main (  ) at trymh.c:20
20        outimage = laplacian_float(inimage);
Value returned is $3 = (struct {...} *) 0x0
(gdb)
```

Now we're back in main. To determine the source of the problem, let's examine the values of some variables:

```
(gdb) list
15        FloatImage outimage;
16        BinaryImage binimage;
17        int i,j;
18
19        inimage = (FloatImage)imLoadF(IMAGE_FLOAT,stdin);
20        outimage = laplacian_float(inimage);
21
22        binimage = marr_hildreth(outimage);
23        if  (binimage == NULL) {
24          fprintf(stderr,"trymh: binimage returned NULL\n");
(gdb) print inimage
$6 = (struct {...} *) 0x0
(gdb)
```

The variable inimage, containing the input image returned from imLoadF, is null. Passing a null pointer into the image manipulation routines certainly would cause a core dump in this case. However, we know imLoadF to be tried and true because it's in a well-tested library, so what's the problem?

As it turns out, our library function imLoadF returns NULL on failure—if the input format is bad, for example. Because we never checked the return value of imLoadF before passing it along to laplacian_float, the program goes haywire when inimage is assigned NULL. To correct the problem, we simply insert code to cause the program to exit with an error message if imLoadF returns a null pointer.

To quit *gdb*, just use the command *quit*. Unless the program has finished execution, *gdb* will complain that the program is still running:

```
(gdb) quit
The program is running.  Quit anyway (and kill it)? (y or n) y
papaya$
```

In the following sections we examine some specific features provided by the debugger, given the general picture just presented.

Examining a Core File

Do you hate it when a program crashes and spites you again by leaving a 20-MB core file in your working directory, wasting much-needed space? Don't be so quick to delete that core file; it can be very helpful. A core file is just a dump of the memory image of a process at the time of the crash. You can use the core file with *gdb* to examine the state of your program (such as the values of variables and data) and determine the cause for failure.

The core file is written to disk by the operating system whenever certain failures occur. The most frequent reason for a crash and the subsequent core dump is a memory violation—that is, trying to read or write memory to which your program does not have access. For example, attempting to write data using a null pointer can cause a *segmentation fault*, which is essentially a fancy way of saying, "you screwed up." Segmentation faults are a common error and occur when you try to access (read from or write to) a memory address that does not belong to your process's address space. This includes the address 0, as often happens with uninitialized pointers. Segmentation faults are often caused by trying to access an array item outside the declared size of the array, and are commonly a result of an off-by-one error. They can also be caused by a failure to allocate memory for a data structure.

Other errors that result in core files are so-called bus errors and floating-point exceptions. Bus errors result from using incorrectly aligned data and are therefore rare on the Intel architecture, which does not pose the strong alignment conditions that other architectures do. Floating-point exceptions point to a severe problem in a floating-point calculation like an overflow, but the most usual case is a division by zero.

However, not all such memory errors will cause immediate crashes. For example, you may overwrite memory in some way, but the program continues to run, not knowing the difference between actual data and instructions or garbage. Subtle memory violations can cause programs to behave erratically. One of the authors once witnessed a bug that caused the program to jump randomly around, but without tracing it with *gdb*, it still appeared to work normally. The only evidence of a bug was that the program returned output that meant, roughly, that two and two did not add up to four. Sure enough, the bug was an attempt to write one too many characters into a block of allocated memory. That single-byte error caused hours of grief.

You can prevent these kinds of memory problems (even the best programmers make these mistakes!) using the Valgrind package, a set of memory-management routines that replaces the commonly used `malloc()` and `free()` functions as well as their C++ counterparts, the operators `new` and `delete`. We talk about Valgrind in "Using Valgrind," later in this chapter.

However, if your program does cause a memory fault, it will crash and dump core. Under Linux, core files are named, appropriately, *core*. The core file appears in the current working directory of the running process, which is usually the working directory of the shell that started the program; on occasion, however, programs may change their own working directory.

Some shells provide facilities for controlling whether core files are written. Under *bash*, for example, the default behavior is not to write core files. To enable core file output, you should use the command:

```
ulimit -c unlimited
```

probably in your *.bashrc* initialization file. You can specify a maximum size for core files other than unlimited, but truncated core files may not be of use when debugging applications.

Also, in order for a core file to be useful, the program must be compiled with debugging code enabled, as described in the previous section. Most binaries on your system will not contain debugging code, so the core file will be of limited value.

Our example for using *gdb* with a core file is yet another mythical program called *cross*. Like *trymh* in the previous section, *cross* takes an image file as input, does some calculations on it, and outputs another image file. However, when running *cross*, we get a segmentation fault:

```
papaya$ cross < image30.pfm > image30.pbm
Segmentation fault (core dumped)
papaya$
```

To invoke *gdb* for use with a core file, you must specify not only the core filename, but also the name of the executable that goes along with that core file. This is because the core file does not contain all the information necessary for debugging:

```
papaya$ gdb cross core
GDB is free software and you are welcome to distribute copies of it
 under certain conditions; type "show copying" to see the conditions.
There is absolutely no warranty for GDB; type "show warranty" for details.
GDB 4.8, Copyright 1993 Free Software Foundation, Inc...
Core was generated by `cross'.
Program terminated with signal 11, Segmentation fault.
#0  0x2494 in crossings (image=0xc7c8) at cross.c:31
31                  if ((image[i][j] >= 0) &&
(gdb)
```

gdb tells us that the core file was created when the program terminated with signal 11. A *signal* is a kind of message that is sent to a running program from the kernel, the user, or the program itself. Signals are generally used to terminate a program (and possibly cause it to dump core). For example, when you type the interrupt character, a signal is sent to the running program, which will probably kill the program.

In this case, signal 11 was sent to the running *cross* process by the kernel when *cross* attempted to read or write to memory to which it did not have access. This signal caused *cross* to die and dump core. *gdb* says that the illegal memory reference occurred on line 31 of the source file *cross.c*:

```
(gdb) list
26                  xmax = imGetWidth(image)-1;
27                  ymax = imGetHeight(image)-1;
28
29                  for (j=1; j<xmax; j++) {
30                    for (i=1; i<ymax; i++) {
31                      if ((image[i][j] >= 0) &&
32                          (image[i-1][j-1] < 0) ||
33                          (image[i-1][j] < 0) ||
```

```
34                              (image[i-1][j+1] < 0) ||
35                              (image[i][j-1] < 0) ||
(gdb)
```

Here, we see several things. First of all, there is a loop across the two index variables i and j, presumably in order to do calculations on the input image. Line 31 is an attempt to reference data from image[i][j], a two-dimensional array. When a program dumps core while attempting to access data from an array, it's usually a sign that one of the indices is out of bounds. Let's check them:

```
(gdb) print i
$1 = 1
(gdb) print j
$2 = 1194
(gdb) print xmax
$3 = 1551
(gdb) print ymax
$4 = 1194
(gdb)
```

Here we see the problem. The program was attempting to reference element image[1][1194]; however, the array extends only to image[1550][1193] (remember that arrays in C are indexed from 0 to *max* − 1). In other words, we attempted to read the 1195th row of an image that has only 1194 rows.

If we look at lines 29 and 30, we see the problem: the values xmax and ymax are reversed. The variable j should range from 1 to ymax (because it is the row index of the array), and i should range from 1 to xmax. Fixing the two for loops on lines 29 and 30 corrects the problem.

Let's say that your program is crashing within a function that is called from many different locations, and you want to determine where the function was invoked from and what situation led up to the crash. The *backtrace* command displays the call stack of the program at the time of failure. If you are like the author of this section and are too lazy to type backtrace all the time, you will be delighted to hear that you can also use the shortcut *bt*.

The *call stack* is the list of functions that led up to the current one. For example, if the program starts in function main, which calls function foo, which calls bamf, the call stack looks like this:

```
(gdb) backtrace
#0  0x1384 in bamf (  ) at goop.c:31
#1  0x4280 in foo (  ) at goop.c:48
#2  0x218 in main (  ) at goop.c:116
(gdb)
```

As each function is called, it pushes certain data onto the stack, such as saved registers, function arguments, local variables, and so forth. Each function has a certain amount of space allocated on the stack for its use. The chunk of memory on the stack for a particular function is called a *stack frame*, and the call stack is the ordered list of stack frames.

In the following example, we are looking at a core file for an X-based animation program. Using *backtrace* gives us the following:

```
(gdb) backtrace
#0  0x602b4982 in _end ( )
#1  0xbffff934 in _end ( )
#2  0x13c6 in stream_drawimage (wgt=0x38330000, sn=4)\
at stream_display.c:94
#3  0x1497 in stream_refresh_all ( ) at stream_display.c:116
#4  0x49c in control_update_all ( ) at control_init.c:73
#5  0x224 in play_timeout (Cannot access memory at address 0x602b7676.
(gdb)
```

This is a list of stack frames for the process. The most recently called function is frame 0, which is the "function" _end in this case. Here, we see that play_timeout called control_update_all, which called stream_refresh_all, and so on. Somehow, the program jumped to _end, where it crashed.

However, _end is not a function; it is simply a label that specifies the end of the process data segment. When a program branches to an address such as _end, which is not a real function, it is a sign that something must have caused the process to go haywire, corrupting the call stack. (This is known in hacker jargon as "jumping to hyperspace.") In fact, the error Cannot access memory at address 0x602b7676 is another indication that something bizarre has occurred.

We can see, however, that the last "real" function called was stream_drawimage, and we might guess that it is the source of the problem. To examine the state of stream_drawimage, we need to select its stack frame (frame number 2), using the *frame* command:

```
(gdb) frame 2
#2  0x13c6 in stream_drawimage (wgt=0x38330000, sn=4)\
at stream_display.c:94
94          XCopyArea(mydisplay,streams[sn].frames[currentframe],\
XtWindow(wgt),
(gdb) list
91
92          printf("CopyArea frame %d, sn %d, wid %d\n",currentframe,sn,wgt);
93
94          XCopyArea(mydisplay,streams[sn].frames[currentframe],\
XtWindow(wgt),
95                  picGC,0,0,streams[sn].width,streams[sn].height,0,0);
(gdb)
```

Well, not knowing anything else about the program at hand, we can't see anything wrong here, unless the variable sn (being used as an index into the array streams) is out of range. From the output of *frame*, we see that stream_drawimage was called with an sn parameter of 4. (Function parameters are displayed in the output of *backtrace*, as well as whenever we change frames.)

Let's move up another frame, to stream_refresh_all, to see how stream_display was called. To do this, we use the *up* command, which selects the stack frame above the current one:

```
(gdb) up
#3  0x1497 in stream_refresh_all (  ) at stream_display.c:116
116          stream_drawimage(streams[i].drawbox,i);
(gdb) list
113      void stream_refresh_all(void) {
114          int i;
115          for (i=0; i<=numstreams; i++) {
116              stream_drawimage(streams[i].drawbox,i);
117
(gdb) print i
$2 = 4
(gdb) print numstreams
$3 = 4
(gdb)
```

Here, we see that the index variable i is looping from 0 to numstreams, and indeed i here is 4, the second parameter to stream_drawimage. However, numstreams is also 4. What's going on?

The for loop on line 115 looks funny; it should read as follows:

```
for (i=0; i<numstreams; i++) {
```

The error is in the use of the <= comparison operator. The streams array is indexed from 0 to numstreams-1, not from 0 to numstreams. This simple off-by-one error caused the program to go berserk.

As you can see, using *gdb* with a core dump allows you to browse through the image of a crashed program to find bugs. Never again will you delete those pesky core files, right?

Debugging a Running Program

gdb can also debug a program that is already running, allowing you to interrupt it, examine it, and then return the process to its regularly scheduled execution. This is very similar to running a program from within *gdb*, and there are only a few new commands to learn.

The *attach* command attaches *gdb* to a running process. In order to use *attach* you must also have access to the executable that corresponds to the process.

For example, if you have started the program *pgmseq* with process ID 254, you can start up *gdb* with

```
papaya$ gdb pgmseq
```

and once inside *gdb*, use the command

```
(gdb) attach 254
Attaching program `/home/loomer/mdw/pgmseq/pgmseq', pid 254
_ _select (nd=4, in=0xbffff96c, out=0xbffff94c, ex=0xbffff92c, tv=0x0)
    at _ _select.c:22
_ _select.c:22: No such file or directory.
(gdb)
```

The No such file or directory error is given because *gdb* can't locate the source file for _ _select. This is often the case with system calls and library functions, and it's nothing to worry about.

You can also start *gdb* with the command

```
papaya$ gdb pgmseq 254
```

Once *gdb* attaches to the running process, it temporarily suspends the program and lets you take over, issuing *gdb* commands. Or you can set a breakpoint or watch-point (with the *break* and *watch* commands) and use *continue* to cause the program to continue execution until the breakpoint is triggered.

The *detach* command detaches *gdb* from the running process. You can then use *attach* again, on another process, if necessary. If you find a bug, you can *detach* the current process, make changes to the source, recompile, and use the *file* command to load the new executable into *gdb*. You can then start the new version of the program and use the *attach* command to debug it. All without leaving *gdb*!

In fact, *gdb* allows you to debug three programs concurrently: one running directly under *gdb*, one tracing with a core file, and one running as an independent process. The *target* command allows you to select which one you wish to debug.

Changing and Examining Data

To examine the values of variables in your program, you can use the *print*, *x*, and *ptype* commands. The *print* command is the most commonly used data inspection command; it takes as an argument an expression in the source language (usually C or C++) and returns its value. For example:

```
(gdb) print mydisplay
$10 = (struct _XDisplay *) 0x9c800
(gdb)
```

This displays the value of the variable mydisplay, as well as an indication of its type. Because this variable is a pointer, you can examine its contents by dereferencing the pointer, as you would in C:

```
(gdb) print *mydisplay
$11 = {ext_data = 0x0, free_funcs = 0x99c20, fd = 5, lock = 0,
  proto_major_version = 11, proto_minor_version = 0,
  vendor = 0x9dff0 "XFree86", resource_base = 41943040,
  ...
```

```
        error_vec = 0x0, cms = {defaultCCCs = 0xa3d80 "",\
    clientCmaps = 0x991a0 "'",
        perVisualIntensityMaps = 0x0}, conn_checker = 0, im_filters = 0x0}
    (gdb)
```

mydisplay is an extensive structure used by X programs; we have abbreviated the output for your reading enjoyment.

print can print the value of just about any expression, including C function calls (which it executes on the fly, within the context of the running program):

```
    (gdb) print getpid( )
    $11 = 138
    (gdb)
```

Of course, not all functions may be called in this manner. Only those functions that have been linked to the running program may be called. If a function has not been linked to the program and you attempt to call it, *gdb* will complain that there is no such symbol in the current context.

More complicated expressions may be used as arguments to *print* as well, including assignments to variables. For example:

```
    (gdb) print mydisplay->vendor = "Linux"
    $19 = 0x9de70 "Linux"
    (gdb)
```

assigns to the vendor member of the mydisplay structure the value "Linux" instead of "XFree86" (a useless modification, but interesting nonetheless). In this way, you can interactively change data in a running program to correct errant behavior or test uncommon situations.

Note that after each *print* command, the value displayed is assigned to one of the *gdb* convenience registers, which are *gdb* internal variables that may be handy for you to use. For example, to recall the value of mydisplay in the previous example, we need to merely print the value of $10:

```
    (gdb) print $10
    $21 = (struct _XDisplay *) 0x9c800
    (gdb)
```

You may also use expressions, such as typecasts, with the *print* command. Almost anything goes.

The *ptype* command gives you detailed (and often long-winded) information about a variable's type or the definition of a *struct* or *typedef*. To get a full definition for the *struct* _XDisplay used by the mydisplay variable, we use:

```
    (gdb) ptype mydisplay
    type = struct _XDisplay {
        struct _XExtData *ext_data;
        struct _XFreeFuncs *free_funcs;
        int fd;
        int lock;
```

```
    int proto_major_version;
    ....
    struct _XIMFilter *im_filters;
} *
(gdb)
```

If you're interested in examining memory on a more fundamental level, beyond the petty confines of defined types, you can use the *x* command. *x* takes a memory address as an argument. If you give it a variable, it uses the *value* of that variable as the address.

x also takes a count and a type specification as an optional argument. The count is the number of objects of the given type to display. For example, x/100x 0x4200 displays 100 bytes of data, represented in hexadecimal format, at the address 0x4200. Use *help x* to get a description of the various output formats.

To examine the value of mydisplay->vendor, we can use:

```
(gdb) x mydisplay->vendor
0x9de70 <_end+35376>:    76 'L'
(gdb) x/6c mydisplay->vendor
0x9de70 <_end+35376>:    76 'L'  105 'i' 110 'n' 117 'u' 120 'x' 0 '\000'
(gdb) x/s mydisplay->vendor
0x9de70 <_end+35376>:      "Linux"
(gdb)
```

The first field of each line gives the absolute address of the data. The second represents the address as some symbol (in this case, _end) plus an offset in bytes. The remaining fields give the actual value of memory at that address, first in decimal, then as an ASCII character. As described earlier, you can force *x* to print the data in other formats.

Getting Information

The *info* command provides information about the status of the program being debugged. There are many subcommands under *info*; use *help info* to see them all. For example, *info program* displays the execution status of the program:

```
(gdb) info program
Using the running image of child process 138.
Program stopped at 0x9e.
It stopped at breakpoint 1.
(gdb)
```

Another useful command is *info locals*, which displays the names and values of all local variables in the current function:

```
(gdb) info locals
inimage = (struct {...} *) 0x2000
outimage = (struct {...} *) 0x8000
(gdb)
```

This is a rather cursory description of the variables. The *print* or *x* commands describe them further.

Similarly, *info variables* displays a list of all known variables in the program, ordered by source file. Note that many of the variables displayed will be from sources outside your actual program—for example, the names of variables used within the library code. The values for these variables are not displayed because the list is culled more or less directly from the executable's symbol table. Only those local variables in the current stack frame and global (static) variables are actually accessible from *gdb*. *info address* gives you information about exactly where a certain variable is stored. For example:

```
(gdb) info address inimage
Symbol "inimage" is a local variable at frame offset -20.
(gdb)
```

By frame offset, *gdb* means that inimage is stored 20 bytes below the top of the stack frame.

You can get information on the current frame using the *info frame* command, as so:

```
(gdb) info frame
Stack level 0, frame at 0xbffffaa8:
 eip = 0x9e in main (main.c:44); saved eip 0x34
 source language c.
 Arglist at 0xbffffaa8, args: argc=1, argv=0xbffffabc
 Locals at 0xbffffaa8, Previous frame's sp is 0x0

 Saved registers:
  ebx at 0xbffffaa0, ebp at 0xbffffaa8, esi at 0xbffffaa4, eip at\
0xbffffaac
 (gdb)
```

This kind of information is useful if you're debugging at the assembly-language level with the *disass*, *nexti*, and *stepi* commands (see "Instruction-level debugging," later in this chapter).

Miscellaneous Features

We have barely scratched the surface of what *gdb* can do. It is an amazing program with a lot of power; we have introduced you only to the most commonly used commands. In this section, we look at other features of *gdb* and then send you on your way.

If you're interested in learning more about *gdb*, we encourage you to read the *gdb* manual page and the Free Software Foundation manual. The manual is also available as an online Info file. (Info files may be read under Emacs or using the *info* reader; see "Tutorial and Online Help" in Chapter 19 for details.)

Breakpoints and watchpoints

As promised, this section demonstrates further use of breakpoints and watchpoints. Breakpoints are set with the *break* command; similarly, watchpoints are set with the *watch* command. The only difference between the two is that breakpoints must break at a particular location in the program—on a certain line of code, for example—whereas watchpoints may be triggered whenever a certain expression is true, regardless of location within the program. Though powerful, watchpoints can be extremely inefficient; any time the state of the program changes, all watchpoints must be reevaluated.

When a breakpoint or watchpoint is triggered, *gdb* suspends the program and returns control to you. Breakpoints and watchpoints allow you to run the program (using the *run* and *continue* commands) and stop only in certain situations, thus saving you the trouble of using many *next* and *step* commands to walk through the program manually.

There are many ways to set a breakpoint in the program. You can specify a line number, as in *break 20*. Or, you can specify a particular function, as in *break stream_ unload*. You can also specify a line number in another source file, as in *break foo.c: 38*. Use *help break* to see the complete syntax.

Breakpoints may be conditional; that is, the breakpoint triggers only when a certain expression is true. For example, using the command:

```
break 184 if (status = = 0)
```

sets a conditional breakpoint at line 184 in the current source file, which triggers only when the variable status is zero. The variable status must be either a global variable or a local variable in the current stack frame. The expression may be any valid expression in the source language that *gdb* understands, identical to the expressions used by the *print* command. You can change the breakpoint condition (if it is conditional) using the *condition* command.

Using the command *info break* gives you a list of all breakpoints and watchpoints and their status. This allows you to delete or disable breakpoints, using the commands *clear*, *delete*, or *disable*. A disabled breakpoint is merely inactive, until you reenable it (with the *enable* command). A breakpoint that has been deleted, on the other hand, is gone from the list of breakpoints for good. You can also specify that a breakpoint be enabled once; meaning that once it is triggered, it will be disabled again.

To set a watchpoint, use the *watch* command, as in the following example:

```
watch (numticks < 1024 && incoming != clear)
```

Watchpoint conditions may be any valid source expression, as with conditional breakpoints.

Instruction-level debugging

gdb is capable of debugging on the processor-instruction level, allowing you to watch the innards of your program with great scrutiny. However, understanding what you see requires not only knowledge of the processor architecture and assembly language, but also some idea of how the operating system sets up process address space. For example, it helps to understand the conventions used for setting up stack frames, calling functions, passing parameters and return values, and so on. Any book on protected-mode 80386/80486 programming can fill you in on these details. But be warned: protected-mode programming on this processor is quite different from real-mode programming (as is used in the MS-DOS world). Be sure that you're reading about native *protected-mode* '386 programming, or else you might subject yourself to terminal confusion.

The primary *gdb* commands used for instruction-level debugging are *nexti*, *stepi*, and *disass*. *nexti* is equivalent to *next*, except that it steps to the next instruction, not the next source line. Similarly, *stepi* is the instruction-level analog of *step*.

The *disass* command displays a disassembly of an address range that you supply. This address range may be specified by literal address or function name. For example, to display a disassembly of the function play_timeout, use the following command:

```
(gdb) disass play_timeout
Dump of assembler code for function play_timeout:
to 0x2ac:
0x21c <play_timeout>:          pushl  %ebp
0x21d <play_timeout+1>:        movl   %esp,%ebp
0x21f <play_timeout+3>:        call   0x494 <control_update_all>
0x224 <play_timeout+8>:        movl   0x952f4,%eax
0x229 <play_timeout+13>:       decl   %eax
0x22a <play_timeout+14>:       cmpl   %eax,0x9530c
0x230 <play_timeout+20>:       jne    0x24c <play_timeout+48>
0x232 <play_timeout+22>:       jmp    0x29c <play_timeout+128>
0x234 <play_timeout+24>:       nop
0x235 <play_timeout+25>:       nop
...

0x2a8 <play_timeout+140>:      addb   %al,(%eax)
0x2aa <play_timeout+142>:      addb   %al,(%eax)
(gdb)
```

This is equivalent to using the command *disass 0x21c* (where 0x21c is the literal address of the beginning of play_timeout).

You can specify an optional second argument to *disass*, which will be used as the address where disassembly should stop. Using *disass 0x21c 0x232* will display only the first seven lines of the assembly listing in the previous example (the instruction starting with 0x232 itself will not be displayed).

If you use *nexti* and *stepi* often, you may wish to use the command:

```
display/i $pc
```

This causes the current instruction to be displayed after every *nexti* or *stepi* command. *display* specifies variables to watch or commands to execute after every stepping command. $pc is a *gdb* internal register that corresponds to the processor's program counter, pointing to the current instruction.

Using Emacs with gdb

(X)Emacs (described in Chapter 19) provides a debugging mode that lets you run *gdb*—or another debugger—within the integrated program-tracing environment provided by Emacs. This so-called Grand Unified Debugger library is very powerful and allows you to debug and edit your programs entirely within Emacs.

To start *gdb* under Emacs, use the Emacs command M-x gdb and give the name of the executable to debug as the argument. A buffer will be created for *gdb*, which is similar to using *gdb* alone. You can then use *core-file* to load a core file or *attach* to attach to a running process, if you wish.

Whenever you step to a new frame (when you first trigger a breakpoint), *gdb* opens a separate window that displays the source corresponding to the current stack frame. You may use this buffer to edit the source text just as you normally would with Emacs, but the current source line is highlighted with an arrow (the characters =>). This allows you to watch the source in one window and execute *gdb* commands in the other.

Within the debugging window, you can use several special key sequences. They are fairly long, though, so it's not clear that you'll find them more convenient than just entering *gdb* commands directly. Some of the more common commands include the following:

C-x C-a C-s
> The equivalent of a *gdb* *step* command, updating the source window appropriately

C-x C-a C-i
> The equivalent of a *stepi* command

C-x C-a C-n
> The equivalent of a *next* command

C-x C-a C-r
> The equivalent of a *continue* command

C-x C-a <
> The equivalent of an *up* command

C-x C-a >
> The equivalent of a *down* command

If you do enter commands in the traditional manner, you can use M-p to move backward to previously issued commands and M-n to move forward. You can also move around in the buffer using Emacs commands for searching, cursor movement, and so on. All in all, using *gdb* within Emacs is more convenient than using it from the shell.

In addition, you may edit the source text in the *gdb* source buffer; the prefix arrow will not be present in the source when it is saved.

Emacs is very easy to customize, and you can write many extensions to this *gdb* interface yourself. You can define Emacs keys for other commonly used *gdb* commands or change the behavior of the source window. (For example, you can highlight all breakpoints in some fashion or provide keys to disable or clear breakpoints.)

Useful Utilities for C Programmers

Along with languages and compilers, there is a plethora of programming tools out there, including libraries, interface builders, debuggers, and other utilities to aid the programming process. In this section, we talk about some of the most interesting bells and whistles of these tools to let you know what's available.

Debuggers

Several interactive debuggers are available for Linux. The de facto standard debugger is *gdb*, which we just covered in detail.

In addition to *gdb*, there are several other debuggers, each with features very similar to *gdb*. DDD (Data Display Debugger) is a version of *gdb* with an X Window System interface similar to that found on the *xdbx* debugger on other Unix systems. There are several panes in the DDD debugger's window. One pane looks like the regular *gdb* text interface, allowing you to input commands manually to interact with the system. Another pane automatically displays the current source file along with a marker displaying the current line. You can use the source pane to set and select breakpoints, browse the source, and so on, while typing commands directly to *gdb*. The DDD window also contains several buttons that provide quick access to frequently used commands, such as *step*, *next*, and so on. Given the buttons, you can use the mouse in conjunction with the keyboard to debug your program within an easy-to-use X interface. Finally, DDD has a very useful mode that lets you explore data structures of an unknown program.

KDevelop, the IDE, comes with its own, very convenient *gdb* frontend; it is also fully integrated into the KDE Desktop. We cover KDevelop at the end of this chapter.

Profiling and Performance Tools

Several utilities exist that allow you to monitor and rate the performance of your program. These tools help you locate bottlenecks in your code—places where performance is lacking. These tools also give you a rundown on the call structure of your program, indicating what functions are called, from where, and how often (in other words, everything you ever wanted to know about your program, but were afraid to ask).

gprof is a profiling utility that gives you a detailed listing of the running statistics for your program, including how often each function was called, from where, the total amount of time that each function required, and so forth.

To use *gprof* with a program, you must compile the program using the *-pg* option with *gcc*. This adds profiling information to the object file and links the executable with standard libraries that have profiling information enabled.

Having compiled the program to profile with *-pg*, simply run it. If it exits normally, the file *gmon.out* will be written to the working directory of the program. This file contains profiling information for that run and can be used with *gprof* to display a table of statistics.

As an example, let's take a program called *getstat*, which gathers statistics about an image file. After compiling *getstat* with *-pg*, we run it:

```
papaya$ getstat image11.pgm > stats.dat
papaya$ ls -l gmon.out
-rw-------   1 mdw       mdw          54448 Feb  5 17:00 gmon.out
papaya$
```

Indeed, the profiling information was written to *gmon.out*.

To examine the profiling data, we run *gprof* and give it the name of the executable and the profiling file *gmon.out*:

```
papaya$ gprof getstat gmon.out
```

If you do not specify the name of the profiling file, *gprof* assumes the name *gmon.out*. It also assumes the executable name *a.out* if you do not specify that, either.

gprof output is rather verbose, so you may want to redirect it to a file or pipe it through a pager. It comes in two parts. The first part is the "flat profile," which gives a one-line entry for each function, listing the percentage of time spent in that function, the time (in seconds) used to execute that function, the number of calls to the function, and other information. For example:

```
Each sample counts as 0.01 seconds.
  %   cumulative   self              self     total
 time   seconds   seconds    calls  ms/call  ms/call  name
45.11     27.49     27.49       41   670.51   903.13  GetComponent
```

16.25	37.40	9.91				mcount
10.72	43.93	6.54	1811863	0.00	0.00	Push
10.33	50.23	6.30	1811863	0.00	0.00	Pop
5.87	53.81	3.58	40	89.50	247.06	stackstats
4.92	56.81	3.00	1811863	0.00	0.00	TrimNeighbors

If any of the fields are blank in the output, *gprof* was unable to determine any further information about that function. This is usually caused by parts of the code that were not compiled with the *-pg* option; for example, if you call routines in nonstandard libraries that haven't been compiled with *-pg*, *gprof* won't be able to gather much information about those routines. In the previous output, the function *mcount* probably hasn't been compiled with profiling enabled.

As we can see, 45.11% of the total running time was spent in the function GetComponent—which amounts to 27.49 seconds. But is this because GetComponent is horribly inefficient* or because GetComponent itself called many other slow functions? The functions Push and Pop were called many times during execution: could they be the culprits?

The second part of the *gprof* report can help us here. It gives a detailed "call graph" describing which functions called other functions and how many times they were called. For example:

```
index % time    self  children    called     name
                                               <spontaneous>
[1]      92.7    0.00    47.30                 start [1]
                 0.01    47.29       1/1           main [2]
                 0.00     0.00       1/2           on_exit [53]
                 0.00     0.00       1/1           exit [172]
```

The first column of the call graph is the index: a unique number given to every function, allowing you to find other functions in the graph. Here, the first function, start, is called implicitly when the program begins. start required 92.7% of the total running time (47.30 seconds), including its children, but required very little time to run itself. This is because start is the parent of all other functions in the program, including main; it makes sense that start plus its children requires that percentage of time.

The call graph normally displays the children as well as the parents of each function in the graph. Here, we can see that start called the functions main, on_exit, and exit (listed below the line for start). However, there are no parents (normally listed above start); instead, we see the ominous word <spontaneous>. This means that *gprof* was unable to determine the parent function of start; more than likely because start was not called from within the program itself but kicked off by the operating system.

---

* Always a possibility where this author's code is concerned!

Skipping down to the entry for GetComponent, the function under suspicion, we see the following:

```
index % time    self  children    called     name
                0.67    0.23       1/41           GetFirstComponent [12]
               26.82    9.30      40/41           GetNextComponent [5]
 [4]     72.6  27.49    9.54       41         GetComponent [4]
                6.54    0.00 1811863/1811863     Push [7]
                3.00    0.00 1811863/1811863     TrimNeighbors [9]
                0.00    0.00       1/1           InitStack [54]
```

The parent functions of GetComponent were GetFirstComponent and GetNextComponent, and its children were Push, TrimNeighbors, and InitStack. As we can see, GetComponent was called 41 times—one time from GetFirstComponent and 40 times from GetNextComponent. The *gprof* output contains notes that describe the report in more detail.

GetComponent itself requires more than 27.49 seconds to run; only 9.54 seconds are spent executing the children of GetComponent (including the many calls to Push and TrimNeighbors). So it looks as though GetComponent and possibly its parent GetNextComponent need some tuning; the oft-called Push function is not the sole cause of the problem.

gprof also keeps track of recursive calls and "cycles" of called functions and indicates the amount of time required for each call. Of course, using *gprof* effectively requires that all code to be profiled is compiled with the *-pg* option. It also requires a knowledge of the program you're attempting to profile; *gprof* can tell you only so much about what's going on. It's up to the programmer to optimize inefficient code.

One last note about *gprof*: running it on a program that calls only a few functions—and runs very quickly—may not give you meaningful results. The units used for timing execution are usually rather coarse—maybe one one-hundredth of a second—and if many functions in your program run more quickly than that, *gprof* will be unable to distinguish between their respective running times (rounding them to the nearest hundredth of a second). In order to get good profiling information, you may need to run your program under unusual circumstances—for example, giving it an unusually large data set to churn on, as in the previous example.

If *gprof* is more than you need, *calls* is a program that displays a tree of all function calls in your C source code. This can be useful to either generate an index of all called functions or produce a high-level hierarchical report of the structure of a program.

Use of *calls* is simple: you tell it the names of the source files to map out, and a function-call tree is displayed. For example:

```
papaya$ calls scan.c
   1    level1 [scan.c]
   2          getid [scan.c]
   3                getc
```

```
    4                      eatwhite [scan.c]
    5                              getc
    6                              ungetc
    7                  strcmp
    8          eatwhite [see line 4]
    9          balance [scan.c]
   10                      eatwhite [see line 4]
```

By default, *calls* lists only one instance of each called function at each level of the tree (so that if printf is called five times in a given function, it is listed only once). The *-a* switch prints all instances. *calls* has several other options as well; using *calls -h* gives you a summary.

Using strace

strace is a tool that displays the system calls being executed by a running program. This can be extremely useful for real-time monitoring of a program's activity, although it does take some knowledge of programming at the system-call level. For example, when the library routine printf is used within a program, *strace* displays information only about the underlying write system call when it is executed. Also, *strace* can be quite verbose: many system calls are executed within a program that the programmer may not be aware of. However, *strace* is a good way to quickly determine the cause of a program crash or other strange failure.

Take the "Hello, World!" program given earlier in the chapter. Running *strace* on the executable *hello* gives us the following:

```
papaya$ strace hello
execve("./hello", ["hello"], [/* 49 vars */]) = 0
mmap(0, 4096, PROT_READ|PROT_WRITE, MAP_PRIVATE|MAP_ANONYMOUS,\
 -1, 0) = 0x40007000
mprotect(0x40000000, 20881, PROT_READ|PROT_WRITE|PROT_EXEC) = 0
mprotect(0x8048000, 4922, PROT_READ|PROT_WRITE|PROT_EXEC) = 0
stat("/etc/ld.so.cache", {st_mode=S_IFREG|0644, st_size=18612,\
 ...}) = 0
open("/etc/ld.so.cache", O_RDONLY)      = 3
mmap(0, 18612, PROT_READ, MAP_SHARED, 3, 0) = 0x40008000
close(3)                                = 0
stat("/etc/ld.so.preload", 0xbffff52c)  = -1 ENOENT (No such\
 file or directory)
open("/usr/local/KDE/lib/libc.so.5", O_RDONLY) = -1 ENOENT (No\
 such file or directory)
open("/usr/local/qt/lib/libc.so.5", O_RDONLY) = -1 ENOENT (No\
 such file or directory)
open("/lib/libc.so.5", O_RDONLY)        = 3
read(3, "\177ELF\1\1\1\0\0\0\0\0\0\0\0\0\3"..., 4096) = 4096
mmap(0, 770048, PROT_NONE, MAP_PRIVATE|MAP_ANONYMOUS, -1, 0) = \
0x4000d000
mmap(0x4000d000, 538959, PROT_READ|PROT_EXEC, MAP_PRIVATE|MAP_\
FIXED, 3, 0) = 0x4000d000
mmap(0x40091000, 21564, PROT_READ|PROT_WRITE, MAP_PRIVATE|MAP_\
```

```
FIXED, 3, 0x83000) = 0x40091000
mmap(0x40097000, 204584, PROT_READ|PROT_WRITE, MAP_PRIVATE|MAP_\
FIXED|MAP_ANONYMOUS, -1, 0) = 0x40097000
close(3)                                    = 0
mprotect(0x4000d000, 538959, PROT_READ|PROT_WRITE|PROT_EXEC) = 0
munmap(0x40008000, 18612)                   = 0
mprotect(0x8048000, 4922, PROT_READ|PROT_EXEC) = 0
mprotect(0x4000d000, 538959, PROT_READ|PROT_EXEC) = 0
mprotect(0x40000000, 20881, PROT_READ|PROT_EXEC) = 0
personality(PER_LINUX)                      = 0
geteuid( )                          = 501
getuid( )                           = 501
getgid( )                           = 100
getegid( )                          = 100
fstat(1, {st_mode=S_IFCHR|0666, st_rdev=makedev(3, 10), ...}) = 0
mmap(0, 4096, PROT_READ|PROT_WRITE, MAP_PRIVATE|MAP_ANONYMOUS,\
 -1, 0) = 0x40008000
ioctl(1, TCGETS, {B9600 opost isig icanon echo ....}) = 0
write(1, "Hello World!\n", 13Hello World!
)           = 13
_exit(0)                            = ?
papaya$
```

This may be much more than you expected to see from a simple program. Let's walk through it, briefly, to explain what's going on.

The first call, execve, starts the program. All the mmap, mprotect, and munmap calls come from the kernel's memory management and are not really interesting here. In the three consecutive open calls, the loader is looking for the C library and finds it on the third try. The library header is then read and the library mapped into memory. After a few more memory-management operations and the calls to geteuid, getuid, getgid, and getegid, which retrieve the rights of the process, there is a call to ioctl. The ioctl is the result of a tcgetattr library call, which the program uses to retrieve the terminal attributes before attempting to write to the terminal. Finally, the write call prints our friendly message to the terminal and exit ends the program.

strace sends its output to standard error, so you can redirect it to a file separate from the actual output of the program (usually sent to standard output). As you can see, *strace* tells you not only the names of the system calls, but also their parameters (expressed as well-known constant names, if possible, instead of just numerics) and return values.

You may also find the *ltrace* package useful. It's a library call tracer that tracks all library calls, not just calls to the kernel. Several distributions already include it; users of other distributions can download the latest version of the source at *ftp://ftp.debian.org/debian/dists/unstable/main/source/utils/*.

Using Valgrind

Valgrind is a replacement for the various memory-allocation routines, such as malloc, realloc, and free, used by C programs, but it also supports C++ programs. It provides smarter memory-allocation procedures and code to detect illegal memory accesses and common faults, such as attempting to free a block of memory more than once. Valgrind displays detailed error messages if your program attempts any kind of hazardous memory access, helping you to catch segmentation faults in your program before they happen. It can also detect memory leaks—for example, places in the code where new memory is malloc'd without being free'd after use.

Valgrind is not just a replacement for malloc and friends. It also inserts code into your program to verify all memory reads and writes. It is very robust and therefore considerably slower than the regular malloc routines. Valgrind is meant to be used during program development and testing; once all potential memory-corrupting bugs have been fixed, you can run your program without it.

For example, take the following program, which allocates some memory and attempts to do various nasty things with it:

```
#include <malloc.h>
int main( ) {
  char *thememory, ch;

  thememory=(char *)malloc(10*sizeof(char));

  ch=thememory[1];     /* Attempt to read uninitialized memory */
  thememory[12]=' ';   /* Attempt to write after the block */
  ch=thememory[-2];    /* Attempt to read before the block */
}
```

To find these errors, we simply compile the program for debugging and run it by prepending the *valgrind* command to the command line:

```
owl$ gcc -g -o nasty nasty.c
owl$ valgrind nasty
= =18037= = valgrind-20020319, a memory error detector for x86 GNU/Linux.
= =18037= = Copyright (C) 2000-2002, and GNU GPL'd, by Julian Seward.
= =18037= = For more details, rerun with: -v
= =18037= =
= =18037= = Invalid write of size 1
= =18037= =    at 0x8048487: main (nasty.c:8)
= =18037= =    by 0x402D67EE: _ _libc_start_main (in /lib/libc.so.6)
= =18037= =    by 0x8048381: _ _libc_start_main@@GLIBC_2.0 (in
/home/kalle/tmp/nasty)
= =18037= =    by <bogus frame pointer> ???
= =18037= =    Address 0x41B2A030 is 2 bytes after a block of size 10 alloc'd
= =18037= =    at 0x40065CFB: malloc (vg_clientmalloc.c:618)
= =18037= =    by 0x8048470: main (nasty.c:5)
= =18037= =    by 0x402D67EE: _ _libc_start_main (in /lib/libc.so.6)
= =18037= =    by 0x8048381: _ _libc_start_main@@GLIBC_2.0 (in
/home/kalle/tmp/nasty)
```

```
= =18037= =
= =18037= = Invalid read of size 1
= =18037= =    at 0x804848D: main (nasty.c:9)
= =18037= =    by 0x402D67EE: __libc_start_main (in /lib/libc.so.6)
= =18037= =    by 0x8048381: __libc_start_main@@GLIBC_2.0 (in
/home/kalle/tmp/nasty)
= =18037= =    by <bogus frame pointer> ???
= =18037= =    Address 0x41B2A022 is 2 bytes before a block of size 10 alloc'd
= =18037= =    at 0x40065CFB: malloc (vg_clientmalloc.c:618)
= =18037= =    by 0x8048470: main (nasty.c:5)
= =18037= =    by 0x402D67EE: __libc_start_main (in /lib/libc.so.6)
= =18037= =    by 0x8048381: __libc_start_main@@GLIBC_2.0 (in
/home/kalle/tmp/nasty)
= =18037= =
= =18037= = ERROR SUMMARY: 2 errors from 2 contexts (suppressed: 0 from 0)
= =18037= = malloc/free: in use at exit: 10 bytes in 1 blocks.
= =18037= = malloc/free: 1 allocs, 0 frees, 10 bytes allocated.
= =18037= = For a detailed leak analysis,  rerun with: --leak-check=yes
= =18037= = For counts of detected errors, rerun with: -v
```

The figure at the start of each line indicates the process ID; if your process spawns other processes, even those will be run under Valgrind's control.

For each memory violation, Valgrind reports an error and gives us information on what happened. The actual Valgrind error messages include information on where the program is executing as well as where the memory block was allocated. You can coax even more information out of Valgrind if you wish, and, along with a debugger such as *gdb*, you can pinpoint problems easily.

You may ask why the reading operation in line 7, where an initialized piece of memory is read, has not led Valgrind to emit an error message. This is because Valgrind won't complain if you pass around initialized memory, but it still keeps track of it. As soon as you use the value (e.g., by passing it to an operating system function or by manipulating it), you receive the expected error message.

Valgrind also provides a garbage collector and detector you can call from within your program. In brief, the garbage detector informs you of any memory leaks: places where a function malloc'd a block of memory but forgot to free it before returning. The garbage collector routine walks through the heap and cleans up the results of these leaks. Here is an example of the output:

```
owl$ valgrind --leak-check=yes --show-reachable=yes nasty
...
= =18081= = ERROR SUMMARY: 2 errors from 2 contexts (suppressed: 0 from 0)
= =18081= = malloc/free: in use at exit: 10 bytes in 1 blocks.
= =18081= = malloc/free: 1 allocs, 0 frees, 10 bytes allocated.
= =18081= = For counts of detected errors, rerun with: -v
= =18081= = searching for pointers to 1 not-freed blocks.
= =18081= = checked 4029376 bytes.
= =18081= =
= =18081= = definitely lost: 0 bytes in 0 blocks.
= =18081= = possibly lost:  0 bytes in 0 blocks.
```

```
=  =18081=  = still reachable: 10 bytes in 1 blocks.
=  =18081=  =
=  =18081=  = 10 bytes in 1 blocks are still reachable in loss record 1 of 1
=  =18081=  =    at 0x40065CFB: malloc (vg_clientmalloc.c:618)
=  =18081=  =    by 0x8048470: main (nasty.c:5)
=  =18081=  =    by 0x402D67EE: __libc_start_main (in /lib/libc.so.6)
=  =18081=  =    by 0x8048381: __libc_start_main@@GLIBC_2.0 (in
/home/kalle/tmp/nasty)
=  =18081=  =
=  =18081=  = LEAK SUMMARY:
=  =18081=  =    possibly lost:   0 bytes in 0 blocks.
=  =18081=  =    definitely lost: 0 bytes in 0 blocks.
=  =18081=  =    still reachable: 10 bytes in 1 blocks.
=  =18081=  =
```

By the way, Valgrind is not just a very useful memory debugger; it also comes with several other so-called skins. One of these is *cachegrind*, a profiler that, together with its graphical frontend *kcachegrind*, has become the profiler of choice for many. *cachegrind* is slowly replacing *gprof* in many projects.

Interface Building Tools

A number of applications and libraries let you easily generate a user interface for your applications under the X Window System. If you do not want to bother with the complexity of the X programming interface, using one of these simple interface-building tools may be the answer for you. There are also tools for producing a text-based interface for programs that don't require X.

The classic X programming model has attempted to be as general as possible, providing only the bare minimum of interface restrictions and assumptions. This generality allows programmers to build their own interface from scratch, as the core X libraries don't make any assumptions about the interface in advance. The X Toolkit Intrinsics (Xt) toolkit provides a rudimentary set of interface widgets (such as simple buttons, scrollbars, and the like), as well as a general interface for writing your own widgets if necessary. Unfortunately this can require a great deal of work for programmers who would rather use a set of premade interface routines. A number of Xt widget sets and programming libraries are available for Linux, all of which make the user interface easier to program.

Qt, a C++ GUI toolkit written by the Norwegian company Trolltech, is an excellent package for GUI development in C++. It sports an ingenious mechanism for connecting user interaction with program code, a very fast drawing engine, and a comprehensive but easy-to-use API. Qt is considered by many as the de facto GUI programming standard because it is the foundation of the KDE desktop (see "The K Desktop Environment" in Chapter 3), which is the most prominent desktop on today's Linux systems.

Qt is a commercial product, but it is also released under the GPL, meaning that you can use it for free if you write software for Unix (and hence Linux) that is licensed under the GPL as well. In addition, (commercial) Windows and Mac OS X versions of Qt are available, which makes it possible to develop for Linux, Windows, and Mac OS X at the same time and create an application for another platform by simply recompiling. Imagine being able to develop on your favorite Linux operating system and still being able to target the larger Windows market! One of the authors, Kalle, uses Qt to write both free software (the KDE just mentioned) and commercial software (often cross-platform products that are developed for Linux, Windows, and Mac OS X). Qt is being very actively developed; for more information, see *Programming with Qt* (O'Reilly).

Another exciting recent addition to Qt is that it can run on embedded systems, without the need for an X server. And which operating system would it support on embedded systems if not Embedded Linux? Many embedded devices with graphical screens already run Embedded Linux and Qt/Embedded—for example, some cellular telephones, car computers, medical devices, and many more. It won't say "Linux" in large letters on the box, but that's what is inside!

Qt also comes with a GUI builder called Qt Designer that greatly facilitates the creation of GUI applications. It is included in the GPL version of Qt as well, so if you download Qt (or simply install it from your distribution CDs), you have the Designer right away. Finally, Python bindings for Qt let you employ its attractive and flexible interface without having to learn a low-level language.

For those who do not like to program in C++, GTK might be a good choice. GTK was originally written for the image manipulation program GIMP. GTK programs usually offer response times that are just as good as those of Qt programs, but the toolkit is not as complete. Documentation is especially lacking. For C-based projects, though, GTK is a good alternative if you do not need to be able to recompile your code on Windows. A Windows port has been developed as well. Good C++ bindings have also been created, so more and more GTK developers are choosing to develop their software in C++ instead of in C.

Many programmers are finding that building a user interface, even with a complete set of widgets and routines in C, requires much overhead and can be quite difficult. This is a question of flexibility versus ease of programming: the easier the interface is to build, the less control the programmer has over it. Many programmers are finding that prebuilt widgets are adequate for their needs, so the loss in flexibility is not a problem.

One of the most popular toolkits in the 1980s and 1990s was the commercial Motif library and widget set, available from several vendors for an inexpensive single-user license fee. Many applications are available that utilize Motif. Binaries statically linked with Motif may be distributed freely and used by people who don't own Motif.

Motif seems to be in use mostly for legacy projects; most programmers have moved on to the newer Qt or GTK toolkits. However, Motif is still being actively developed (albeit rather slowly). It also has some problems. First, programming with Motif can be frustrating. It is difficult, error-prone, and cumbersome because the Motif API was not designed according to modern GUI API design principles. Also, Motif programs tend to run very slowly.

One of the problems with interface generation and X programming is that it is difficult to generalize the most widely used elements of a user interface into a simple programming model. For example, many programs use features such as buttons, dialog boxes, pull-down menus, and so forth, but almost every program uses these widgets in a different context. In simplifying the creation of a graphical interface, generators tend to make assumptions about what you'll want. For example, it is simple enough to specify that a button, when pressed, should execute a certain procedure within your program, but what if you want the button to execute some specialized behavior the programming interface does not allow for? For example, what if you want the button to have a different effect when pressed with mouse button 2 instead of mouse button 1? If the interface-building system does not allow for this degree of generality, it is not of much use to programmers who need a powerful, customized interface.

The Tcl/Tk combo, consisting of the scripting language Tcl and the graphical toolkit Tk, has won some popularity, partly because it is so simple to use and provides a good amount of flexibility. Because Tcl and Tk routines can be called from interpreted "scripts" as well as internally from a C program, it is not difficult to tie the interface features provided by this language and toolkit to functionality in the program. Using Tcl and Tk is, on the whole, less demanding than learning to program Xlib and Xt (along with the myriad of widget sets) directly. It should be noted, though, that the larger a project gets, the more likely it is that you will want to use a language such as C++ that is more suited for large-scale development. For several reasons, larger projects tend to become very unwieldy with Tcl: the use of an interpreted language slows the execution of the program, Tcl/Tk design is hard to scale up to large projects, and important reliability features such as compile- and link-time type checking are missing. The scaling problem is improved by the use of namespaces (a way to keep names in different parts of the program from clashing) and an object-oriented extension called [incr Tcl].

Tcl and Tk allow you to generate an X-based interface complete with windows, buttons, menus, scrollbars, and the like, around your existing program. You may access the interface from a Tcl script (as described in "Other Languages," later in this chapter) or from within a C program.

If you require a nice text-based interface for a program, several options are available. The GNU *getline* library is a set of routines that provide advanced command-line editing, prompting, command history, and other features used by many programs. As an example, both *bash* and *gdb* use the *getline* library to read user input. *getline* provides the Emacs- and *vi*-like command-line editing features found in *bash* and similar programs. (The use of command-line editing within *bash* is described in "Typing Shortcuts" in Chapter 4.)

Another option is to write a set of Emacs interface routines for your program. An example of this is the *gdb* Emacs interface, which sets up multiple windows, special key sequences, and so on, within Emacs. The interface is discussed in "Using Emacs with gdb," earlier in this chapter. (No changes were required to *gdb* code in order to implement this: look at the Emacs library file *gdb.el* for hints on how this was accomplished.) Emacs allows you to start up a subprogram within a text buffer and provides many routines for parsing and processing text within that buffer. For example, within the Emacs *gdb* interface, the *gdb* source listing output is captured by Emacs and turned into a command that displays the current line of code in another window. Routines written in Emacs LISP process the *gdb* output and take certain actions based on it.

The advantage of using Emacs to interact with text-based programs is that Emacs is a powerful and customizable user interface within itself. The user can easily redefine keys and commands to fit her needs; you don't need to provide these customization features yourself. As long as the text interface of the program is straightforward enough to interact with Emacs, customization is not difficult to accomplish. In addition, many users prefer to do virtually everything within Emacs—from reading electronic mail and news to compiling and debugging programs. Giving your program an Emacs frontend allows it to be used more easily by people with this mind-set. It also allows your program to interact with other programs running under Emacs—for example, you can easily cut and paste between different Emacs text buffers. You can even write entire programs using Emacs LISP, if you wish.

Revision Control Tools: RCS

Revision Control System (RCS) has been ported to Linux. This is a set of programs that allow you to maintain a "library" of files that records a history of revisions, allows source-file locking (in case several people are working on the same project), and automatically keeps track of source-file version numbers. RCS is typically used with program source code files, but is general enough to be applicable to any type of file where multiple revisions must be maintained.

Why bother with revision control? Many large projects require some kind of revision control in order to keep track of many tiny complex changes to the system. For example, attempting to maintain a program with a thousand source files and a team of several dozen programmers would be nearly impossible without using something like RCS. With RCS, you can ensure that only one person may modify a given source file at any one time, and all changes are checked in along with a log message detailing the change.

RCS is based on the concept of an *RCS file*, a file that acts as a "library" where source files are "checked in" and "checked out." Let's say that you have a source file *importrtf.c* that you want to maintain with RCS. The RCS filename would be *importrtf.c,v* by default. The RCS file contains a history of revisions to the file, allowing you to extract any previous checked-in version of the file. Each revision is tagged with a log message that you provide.

When you check in a file with RCS, revisions are added to the RCS file, and the original file is deleted by default. To access the original file, you must check it out from the RCS file. When you're editing a file, you generally don't want someone else to be able to edit it at the same time. Therefore, RCS places a lock on the file when you check it out for editing. Only you, the person who checked out this locked file, can modify it (this is accomplished through file permissions). Once you're done making changes to the source, you check it back in, which allows anyone working on the project to check it back out again for further work. Checking out a file as unlocked does not subject it to these restrictions; generally, files are checked out as locked only when they are to be edited but are checked out as unlocked just for reading (for example, to use the source file in a program build).

RCS automatically keeps track of all previous revisions in the RCS file and assigns incremental version numbers to each new revision that you check in. You can also specify a version number of your own when checking in a file with RCS; this allows you to start a new "revision branch" so that multiple projects can stem from different revisions of the same file. This is a good way to share code between projects but ensure that changes made to one branch won't be reflected in others.

Here's an example. Take the source file *importrtf.c*, which contains our friendly program:

```
#include <stdio.h>

int main(void) {
  printf("Hello, world!");
}
```

The first step is to check it into RCS with the *ci* command:

```
papaya$ ci importrtf.c
importrtf.c,v  <--  importrtf.c
enter description, terminated with single '.' or end of file:
NOTE: This is NOT the log message!
>> Hello world source code
>> .
initial revision: 1.1
done
papaya$
```

The RCS file *importrtf.c,v* is created, and *importrtf.c* is removed.

To work on the source file again, use the *co* command to check it out. For example:

```
papaya$ co -l importrtf.c
importrtf.c,v  -->  importrtf.c
revision 1.1 (locked)
done
papaya$
```

will check out *importrtf.c* (from *importrtf.c,v*) and lock it. Locking the file allows you to edit it and to check it back in. If you only need to check the file out in order to read it (for example, to issue a *make*), you can leave the -*l* switch off of the *co* command to check it out unlocked. You can't check in a file unless it is locked first (or if it has never been checked in before, as in the example).

Now you can make some changes to the source and check it back in when done. In many cases, you'll want to keep the file checked out and use *ci* to merely record your most recent revisions in the RCS file and bump the version number. For this, you can use the -*l* switch with *ci*, as so:

```
papaya$ ci -l importrtf.c
importrtf.c,v  <--  importrtf.c
new revision: 1.2; previous revision: 1.1
enter log message, terminated with single '.' or end of file:
>> Changed printf call
>> .
done
papaya$
```

This automatically checks out the file, locked, after checking it in. This is a useful way to keep track of revisions even if you're the only one working on a project.

If you use RCS often, you may not like all those unsightly *importrtf.c,v* RCS files cluttering up your directory. If you create the subdirectory *RCS* within your project directory, *ci* and *co* will place the RCS files there, out of the way of the rest of the source.

In addition, RCS keeps track of all previous revisions of your file. For instance, if you make a change to your program that causes it to break in some way and you want to revert to the previous version to "undo" your changes and retrace your steps, you can specify a particular version number to check out with *co*. For example:

```
papaya$ co -l1.1 importrtf.c
importrtf.c,v  -->  importrtf.c
revision 1.1 (locked)
writable importrtf.c exists; remove it? [ny](n): y
done
papaya$
```

checks out Version 1.1 of the file *importrtf.c*. You can use the program *rlog* to print the revision history of a particular file; this displays your revision log entries (entered with *ci*) along with other information such as the date, the user who checked in the revision, and so forth.

RCS automatically updates embedded "keyword strings" in your source file at check-out time. For example, if you have the string:

```
/* $Header$ */
```

in the source file, *co* will replace it with an informative line about the revision date, version number, and so forth, as in the following example:

```
/* $Header: /work/linux/hitch/programming/tools/RCS/rcs.tex
       1.2 1994/12/04 15:19:31 mdw Exp mdw $ */
```

(We broke this line to fit on the page, but it is supposed to be all on one line.)

Other keywords exist as well, such as $Author$, $Date$, and Log.

Many programmers place a static string within each source file to identify the version of the program after it has been compiled. For example, within each source file in your program, you can place the line:

```
static char rcsid[  ] = "\@(#)$Header$
```

co replaces the keyword $Header$ with a string of the form given here. This static string survives in the executable, and the *what* command displays these strings in a given binary. For example, after compiling *importrtf.c* into the executable *importrtf*, we can use the following command:

```
papaya$ what importrtf
importrtf:
        $Header: /work/linux/hitch/programming/tools/RCS/rcs.tex
                1.2 1994/12/04 15:19:31 mdw Exp mdw $
papaya$
```

what picks out strings beginning with the characters @(#) in a file and displays them. If you have a program that has been compiled from many source files and libraries, and you don't know how up-to-date each component is, you can use *what* to display a version string for each source file used to compile the binary.

RCS has several other programs in its suite, including *rcs*, used for maintaining RCS files. Among other things, *rcs* can give other users permission to check out sources from an RCS file. See the manual pages for *ci*(1), *co*(1), and *rcs*(1) for more information.

Revision Control Tools: CVS

CVS, the Concurrent Versioning System, is more complex than RCS and thus perhaps a little bit oversized for one-person projects. But whenever more than one or two programmers are working on a project or the source code is distributed over several directories, CVS is the better choice. CVS uses the RCS file format for saving changes, but employs a management structure of its own.

By default, CVS works with full directory trees. That is, each CVS command you issue affects the current directory and all the subdirectories it contains, including their subdirectories and so on. You can switch off this recursive traversal with a command-line option, or you can specify a single file for the command to operate on.

CVS has formalized the sandbox concept that is used in many software development shops. In this concept, a so-called *repository* contains the "official" sources that are known to compile and work (at least partly). No developer is ever allowed to directly edit files in this repository. Instead, he checks out a local directory tree, the so-called *sandbox*. Here, he can edit the sources to his heart's delight, make changes, add or remove files, and do all sorts of things that developers usually do (no, not playing Quake or eating marshmallows). When he has made sure that his changes compile and work, he transmits them to the repository again and thus makes them available for the other developers.

When you as a developer have checked out a local directory tree, all the files are writable. You can make any necessary changes to the files in your personal workspace. When you have finished local testing and feel sure enough of your work to share the changes with the rest of the programming team, you write any changed files back into the central repository by issuing a CVS *commit* command. CVS then checks whether another developer has checked in changes since you checked out your directory tree. If this is the case, CVS does not let you check in your changes, but asks you first to take the changes of the other developers over to your local tree. During this update operation, CVS uses a sophisticated algorithm to reconcile ("merge") your changes with those of the other developers. In cases in which this is not automatically possible, CVS informs you that there were conflicts and asks you to resolve them. The file in question is marked up with special characters so that you can see where the conflict has occurred and decide which version should be used. Note that CVS makes sure conflicts can occur only in local developers' trees. There is always a consistent version in the repository.

Setting up a CVS repository

If you are working in a larger project, it is likely that someone else has already set up all the necessary machinery to use CVS. But if you are your project's administrator or you just want to tinker around with CVS on your local machine, you will have to set up a repository yourself.

First, set your environment variable CVSROOT to a directory where you want your CVS repository to be. CVS can keep as many projects as you like in a repository and makes sure they do not interfere with each other. Thus, you have to pick a directory only once to store all projects maintained by CVS, and you won't need to change it when you switch projects. Instead of using the variable CVSROOT, you can always use the command-line switch -*d* with all CVS commands, but since this is cumbersome to type all the time, we will assume that you have set CVSROOT.

Once the directory exists for a repository, you can create the repository with the following command (assuming that CVS is installed on your machine):

```
$tigger cvs init
```

There are several different ways to create a project tree in the CVS repository. If you already have a directory tree but it is not yet managed by RCS, you can simply import it into the repository by calling:

```
$tigger cvs import directory manufacturer tag
```

where *directory* is the name of the top-level directory of the project, *manufacturer* is the name of the author of the code (you can use whatever you like here), and *tag* is a so-called release tag that can be chosen at will. For example:

```
$tigger cvs import dataimport acmeinc initial
... lots of output ....
```

If you want to start a completely new project, you can simply create the directory tree with *mkdir* calls and then import this empty tree as shown in the previous example.

If you want to import a project that is already managed by RCS, things get a little bit more difficult because you cannot use *cvs import*. In this case, you have to create the needed directories directly in the repository and then copy all RCS files (all files that end in *,v*) into those directories. Do not use RCS subdirectories here!

Every repository contains a file named *CVSROOT/modules* that lists the names of the projects in the repository. It is a good idea to edit the *modules* file of the repository to add the new module. You can check out, edit, and check in this file like every other file. Thus, in order to add your module to the list, do the following (we will cover the various commands soon):

```
$tigger cvs checkout CVSROOT/modules
$tigger cd CVSROOT
$tigger emacs modules
... or any other editor of your choice, see below for what to enter ...
$tigger cvs commit modules
$tigger cd ..
$tigger cvs release -d CVSROOT
```

If you are not doing anything fancy, the format of the *modules* file is very easy: each line starts with the name of module, followed by a space or tab and the path within the repository. If you want to do more with the *modules* file, check the CVS documentation at *http://www.loria.fr/~molli/cvs-index.html*. There is also a short but very comprehensive book about CVS, the *CVS Pocket Reference* by Gregor N. Purdy (O'Reilly).

Working with CVS

In this section, we assume that either you or your system administrator has set up a module called dataimport. You can now check out a local tree of this module with the following command:

```
$tigger cvs checkout dataimport
```

If no module is defined for the project you want to work on, you need to know the path within the repository. For example, something like the following could be needed:

```
$tigger cvs checkout clients/acmeinc/dataimport
```

Whichever version of the *checkout* command you use, CVS will create a directory called *dataimport* under your current working directory and check out all files and directories from the repository that belong to this module. All files are writable, and you can start editing them right away.

After you have made some changes, you can write the changed files back into the repository with one command:

```
$tigger cvs commit
```

Of course, you can also check in single files:

```
$tigger cvs commit importrtf.c
```

Whatever you do, CVS will ask you—as RCS does—for a comment to include with your changes. But CVS goes a step beyond RCS in convenience. Instead of the rudimentary prompt from RCS, you get a full-screen editor to work in. You can choose this editor by setting the environment variable CVSEDITOR; if this is not set, CVS looks in EDITOR, and if this is not defined either, CVS invokes *vi*. If you check in a whole project, CVS will use the comment you entered for each directory in which there have been no changes, but will start a new editor for each directory that contains changes so that you can optionally change the comment.

As already mentioned, it is not necessary to set *CVSROOT* correctly for checking in files, because when checking out the tree, CVS has created a directory *CVS* in each work directory. This directory contains all the information that CVS needs for its work, including where to find the repository.

While you have been working on your files, a coworker might have checked in some of the files that you are currently working on. In this case, CVS will not let you check in your files but asks you to first update your local tree. Do this with the following command:

```
$tigger cvs update
M importrtf.c
A exportrtf.c
? importrtf
U importword.c
```

(You can specify a single file here as well.) You should carefully examine the output of this command: CVS outputs the names of all the files it handles, each preceded by a single key letter. This letter tells you what has happened during the update operation. The most important letters are shown in Table 21-1.

Table 21-1. Key letters for files under CVS

Letter	Explanation
P	The file has been updated. The P is shown if the file has been added to the repository in the meantime or if it has been changed, but you have not made any changes to this file yourself.
U	You have changed this file in the meantime, but nobody else has.
M	You have changed this file in the meantime, and somebody else has checked in a newer version. All the changes have been merged successfully.
C	You have changed this file in the meantime, and somebody else has checked in a newer version. During the merge attempt, conflicts have arisen.
?	CVS has no information about this file—that is, this file is not under CVS's control.

The C is the most important of the letters in Table 21-1. It signifies that CVS was not able to merge all changes and needs your help. Load those files into your editor and look for the string <<<<<<<. After this string, the name of the file is shown again, followed by your version, ending with a line containing =======. Then comes the version of the code from the repository, ending with a line containing >>>>>>>. You now have to find out—probably by communicating with your coworker—which version is better or whether it is possible to merge the two versions by hand. Change the file accordingly and remove the CVS markings <<<<<<<, =======, and >>>>>>>. Save the file and once again commit it.

If you decide that you want to stop working on a project for a time, you should check whether you have really committed all changes. To do this, change to the directory above the root directory of your project and issue the command:

```
$tigger cvs release dataimport
```

CVS then checks whether you have written back all changes into the repository and warns you if necessary. A useful option is -d, which deletes the local tree if all changes have been committed.

CVS over the Internet

CVS is also very useful where distributed development teams are concerned because it provides several possibilities to access a repository on another machine.*

Today, both free (like SourceForge) and commercial services are available that run a CVS server for you so that you can start a distributed software development project without having to have a server that is up 24/7.

If you can log into the machine holding the repository with *rsh*, you can use remote CVS to access the repository. To check out a module, do the following:

```
cvs -d :ext:user@domain.com:/path/to/repository checkout dataimport
```

---

* The use of CVS has burgeoned along with the number of free software projects developed over the Internet by people on different continents.

If you cannot or do not want to use *rsh* for security reasons, you can also use the secure shell *ssh*. You can tell CVS that you want to use *ssh* by setting the environment variable CVS_RSH to *ssh*.

Authentication and access to the repository can also be done via a client/server protocol. Remote access requires a CVS server running on the machine with the repository; see the CVS documentation for how to do this. If the server is set up, you can log in to it with:

```
cvs -d :pserver:user@domain.com:path/to/repository login
CVS password:
```

As shown, the CVS server will ask you for your CVS password, which the administrator of the CVS server has assigned to you. This login procedure is necessary only once for every repository. When you check out a module, you need to specify the machine with the server, your username on that machine, and the remote path to the repository; as with local repositories, this information is saved in your local tree. Since the password is saved with minimal encryption in the file *.cvspass* in your home directory, there is a potential security risk here. The CVS documentation tells you more about this.

When you use CVS over the Internet and check out or update largish modules, you might also want to use the -z option, which expects an additional integer parameter for the degree of compression, ranging from 1 to 9, and transmits the data in compressed form.

As was mentioned in the introduction to this chapter, another tool, Subversion, is slowly taking over from CVS, even though CVS is still used by the majority of projects, which is why we cover CVS in detail here. But one of the largest open source projects, KDE, has switched to Subversion, and many others are expected to follow. Many commands are very similar: for example, with Subversion, you register a file with *svn add* instead of *cvs add*. One major advantage of Subversion over CVS is that it handles commits atomically: either you succeed in commiting all files in one go, or you cannot commit any at all (whereas CVS only guarantees that for one directory). Because of that, Subversion does not keep per-file version numbers like CVS, but rather module-global version numbers that make it easier to refer to one set of code. You can find more information about Subversion at *http://subversion.tigris.org*.

Patching Files

Let's say you're trying to maintain a program that is updated periodically, but the program contains many source files, and releasing a complete source distribution with every update is not feasible. The best way to incrementally update source files is with *patch*, a program by Larry Wall, author of Perl.

patch is a program that makes context-dependent changes in a file in order to update that file from one version to the next. This way, when your program changes, you simply release a patch file against the source, which the user applies with *patch* to get the newest version. For example, Linus Torvalds usually releases new Linux kernel versions in the form of patch files as well as complete source distributions.

A nice feature of *patch* is that it applies updates in context; that is, if you have made changes to the source yourself, but still wish to get the changes in the patch file update, *patch* usually can figure out the right location in your changed file to which to apply the change. This way, your versions of the original source files don't need to correspond exactly to those against which the patch file was made.

To make a patch file, the program *diff* is used, which produces "context diffs" between two files. For example, take our overused "Hello World" source code, given here:

```
/* hello.c version 1.0 by Norbert Ebersol */
#include <stdio.h>

int main(  ) {
  printf("Hello, World!");
  exit(0);
}
```

Let's say you were to update this source, as in the following:

```
/* hello.c version 2.0 */
/* (c)1994 Norbert Ebersol */
#include <stdio.h>

int main(  ) {
  printf("Hello, Mother Earth!\n");
  return 0;
}
```

If you want to produce a patch file to update the original *hello.c* to the newest version, use *diff* with the *-c* option:

```
papaya$ diff -c hello.c.old hello.c > hello.patch
```

This produces the patch file *hello.patch* that describes how to convert the original *hello.c* (here, saved in the file *hello.c.old*) to the new version. You can distribute this patch file to anyone who has the original version of "Hello, World," and they can use *patch* to update it.

Using *patch* is quite simple; in most cases, you simply run it with the patch file as input:[*]

```
papaya$ patch < hello.patch
Hmm...  Looks like a new-style context diff to me...
The text leading up to this was:
```

---

[*] The output shown here is from the last version that Larry Wall has released, Version 2.1. If you have a newer version of patch, you will need the *-- verbose* flag to get the same output.

```
--------------------------
|*** hello.c.old       Sun Feb  6 15:30:52 1994
|--- hello.c    Sun Feb  6 15:32:21 1994
--------------------------
Patching file hello.c using Plan A...
Hunk #1 succeeded at 1.
done
papaya$
```

patch warns you if it appears as though the patch has already been applied. If we tried to apply the patch file again, *patch* would ask us if we wanted to assume that *-R* was enabled—which reverses the patch. This is a good way to back out patches you didn't intend to apply. *patch* also saves the original version of each file that it updates in a backup file, usually named *filename~* (the filename with a tilde appended).

In many cases, you'll want to update not only a single source file, but also an entire directory tree of sources. *patch* allows many files to be updated from a single *diff*. Let's say you have two directory trees, *hello.old* and *hello*, which contain the sources for the old and new versions of a program, respectively. To make a patch file for the entire tree, use the *-r* switch with *diff*:

> papaya$ **diff -cr hello.old hello > hello.patch**

Now, let's move to the system where the software needs to be updated. Assuming that the original source is contained in the directory *hello*, you can apply the patch with

> papaya$ **patch -p0 < hello.patch**

The *-p0* switch tells *patch* to preserve the pathnames of files to be updated (so that it knows to look in the *hello* directory for the source). If you have the source to be patched saved in a directory named differently from that given in the patch file, you may need to use the *-p* option without a number. See the patch(1) manual page for details about this.

Indenting Code

If you're terrible at indenting code and find the idea of an editor that automatically indents code for you on the fly a bit annoying, you can use the *indent* program to pretty-print your code after you're done writing it. *indent* is a smart C-code formatter, featuring many options that allow you to specify just what kind of indentation style you wish to use.

Take this terribly formatted source:

```
double fact (double n) { if (n=  =1) return 1;
else return (n*fact(n-1)); }
int main ( ) {
printf("Factorial 5 is %f.\n",fact(5));
printf("Factorial 10 is %f.\n",fact(10)); exit (0); }
```

Running *indent* on this source produces the following relatively beautiful code:

```
#include <math.h>

double
fact (double n)
{
  if (n = = 1)
    return 1;
  else
    return (n * fact (n - 1));
}
void
main ( )
{

  printf ("Factorial 5 is %f.\n", fact (5));
  printf ("Factorial 10 is %f.\n", fact (10));
  exit (0);
}
```

Not only are lines indented well, but also whitespace is added around operators and function parameters to make them more readable. There are many ways to specify how the output of *indent* will look; if you're not fond of this particular indentation style, *indent* can accommodate you.

indent can also produce *troff* code from a source file, suitable for printing or for inclusion in a technical document. This code will have such nice features as italicized comments, boldfaced keywords, and so on. Using a command such as:

```
papaya$ indent -troff importrtf.c | groff -mindent
```

produces *troff* code and formats it with *groff*.

Finally, *indent* can be used as a simple debugging tool. If you have put a } in the wrong place, running your program through *indent* will show you what the computer thinks the block structure is.

Using Perl

Perl may well be the best thing to happen to the Unix programming environment in years; it is worth the price of admission to Linux alone.[*] Perl is a text- and file-manipulation language, originally intended to scan large amounts of text, process it, and produce nicely formatted reports from that data. However, as Perl has matured, it has developed into an all-purpose scripting language capable of doing everything from managing processes to communicating via TCP/IP over a network. Perl is free

---

[*] Truth be told, Perl also exists now on other systems, such as Windows. Many Windows system administrators claim it to be their preferred language. But it is not even remotely as well known and ubiquitous there as it is on Linux.

software originally developed by Larry Wall, the Unix guru who brought us the *rn* newsreader and various popular tools, such as *patch*. Today it is maintained by Larry and a group of volunteers. At the fime of writing, a major effort was underway to create a new, cleaner, more efficient version of Perl, Version 6.

Perl's main strength is that it incorporates the most widely used features of other powerful languages, such as C, *sed*, *awk*, and various shells, into a single interpreted script language. In the past, performing a complicated job required juggling these various languages into complex arrangements, often entailing *sed* scripts piping into *awk* scripts piping into shell scripts and eventually piping into a C program. Perl gets rid of the common Unix philosophy of using many small tools to handle small parts of one large problem. Instead, Perl does it all, and it provides many different ways of doing the same thing. In fact, this chapter was written by an artificial intelligence program developed in Perl. (Just kidding, Larry.)

Perl provides a nice programming interface to many features that were sometimes difficult to use in other languages. For example, a common task of many Unix system administration scripts is to scan a large amount of text, cut fields out of each line of text based on a pattern (usually represented as a *regular expression*), and produce a report based on the data. Let's say we want to process the output of the Unix *last* command, which displays a record of login times for all users on the system, as so:

```
mdw       ttypf   loomer.vpizza.co Sun Jan 16 15:30 - 15:54  (00:23)
larry     ttyp1   muadib.oit.unc.e Sun Jan 16 15:11 - 15:12  (00:00)
johnsonm  ttyp4   mallard.vpizza.c Sun Jan 16 14:34 - 14:37  (00:03)
jem       ttyq2   mallard.vpizza.c Sun Jan 16 13:55 - 13:59  (00:03)
linus     FTP     kruuna.helsinki. Sun Jan 16 13:51 - 13:51  (00:00)
linus     FTP     kruuna.helsinki. Sun Jan 16 13:47 - 13:47  (00:00)
```

If we want to count up the total login time for each user (given in parentheses in the last field), we could write a *sed* script to splice the time values from the input, an *awk* script to sort the data for each user and add up the times, and another *awk* script to produce a report based on the accumulated data. Or, we could write a somewhat complex C program to do the entire task—complex because, as any C programmer knows, text processing functions within C are somewhat limited.

However, you can easily accomplish this task with a simple Perl script. The facilities of I/O, regular expression pattern matching, sorting by associative arrays, and number crunching are all easily accessed from a Perl program with little overhead. Perl programs are generally short and to the point, without a lot of technical mumbo jumbo getting in the way of what you want your program to actually *do*.

Using Perl under Linux is really no different than on other Unix systems. Several good books on Perl already exist, including the O'Reilly books *Programming Perl*, by Larry Wall, Randal L. Schwartz, and Tom Christiansen; *Learning Perl*, by Randal L. Schwartz and Tom Christiansen; *Advanced Perl Programming*, by Sriram Srinivasan; and *Perl Cookbook*, by Tom Christiansen and Nathan Torkington. Nevertheless, we think Perl is such a great tool that it deserves something in the way of an introduction. After all, Perl is free software, as is Linux; they go hand in hand.

A Sample Program

What we really like about Perl is that it lets you immediately jump to the task at hand: you don't have to write extensive code to set up data structures, open files or pipes, allocate space for data, and so on. All these features are taken care of for you in a very friendly way.

The example of login times, just discussed, serves to introduce many of the basic features of Perl. First we'll give the entire script (complete with comments) and then a description of how it works. This script reads the output of the *last* command (see the previous example) and prints an entry for each user on the system, describing the total login time and number of logins for each. (Line numbers are printed to the left of each line for reference):

```
1     #!/usr/bin/perl
2
3     while (<STDIN>) {   # While we have input...
4       # Find lines and save username, login time
5       if (/^(\S*)\s*.*\((.*):(.*)\)$/) {
6         # Increment total hours, minutes, and logins
7         $hours{$1} += $2;
8         $minutes{$1} += $3;
9         $logins{$1}++;
10      }
11    }
12
13    # For each user in the array...
14    foreach $user (sort(keys %hours)) {
15      # Calculate hours from total minutes
16      $hours{$user} += int($minutes{$user} / 60);
17      $minutes{$user} %= 60;
18      # Print the information for this user
19      print "User $user, total login time ";
20      # Perl has printf, too
21      printf "%02d:%02d, ", $hours{$user}, $minutes{$user};
22      print "total logins $logins{$user}.\n";
23    }
```

Line 1 tells the loader that this script should be executed through Perl, not as a shell script. Line 3 is the beginning of the program. It is the head of a simple while loop, which C and shell programmers will be familiar with: the code within the braces from lines 4 to 10 should be executed while a certain expression is true. However, the conditional expression <STDIN> looks funny. Actually, this expression reads a single line from the standard input (represented in Perl through the name STDIN) and makes the line available to the program. This expression returns a true value whenever there is input.

Perl reads input one line at a time (unless you tell it to do otherwise). It also reads by default from standard input unless you tell it to do otherwise. Therefore, this while loop will continuously read lines from standard input until there are no lines left to be read.

The evil-looking mess on line 5 is just an if statement. As with most programming languages, the code within the braces (on lines 7–9) will be executed if the expression that follows the if is true. But what is the expression between the parentheses? Those readers familiar with Unix tools such as *grep* and *sed* will peg this immediately as a *regular expression*: a cryptic but useful way to represent a pattern to be matched in the input text. Regular expressions are usually found between delimiting slashes (/.../).

This particular regular expression matches lines of the form:

```
mdw        ttypf    loomer.vpizza.co Sun Jan 16 15:30 - 15:54  (00:23)
```

This expression also "remembers" the username (*mdw*) and the total login time for this entry (00:23). You needn't worry about the expression itself; building regular expressions is a complex subject. For now, all you need to know is that this if statement finds lines of the form given in the example, and splices out the username and login time for processing. The username is assigned to the variable $1, the hours to the variable $2, and the minutes to $3. (Variables in Perl begin with the $ character, but unlike the shell, the $ must be used when assigning to the variable as well.) This assignment is done by the regular expression match itself (anything enclosed in parentheses in a regular expression is saved for later use to one of the variables $1 through $9).

Lines 6 through 9 actually process these three pieces of information. And they do it in an interesting way: through the use of an *associative array*. Whereas a normal array is indexed with a number as a subscript, an associative array is indexed by an arbitrary string. This lends itself to many powerful applications; it allows you to associate one set of data with another set of data gathered on the fly. In our short program, the keys are the usernames, gathered from the output of *last*. We maintain three associative arrays, all indexed by username: hours, which records the total number of hours the user logged in; minutes, which records the number of minutes; and logins, which records the total number of logins.

As an example, referencing the variable $hours{'mdw'} returns the total number of hours that the user *mdw* was logged in. Similarly, if the username *mdw* is stored in the variable $1, referencing $hours{$1} produces the same effect.

In lines 6 to 9, we increment the values of these arrays according to the data on the present line of input. For example, given the input line:

```
jem        ttyq2    mallard.vpizza.c Sun Jan 16 13:55 - 13:59  (00:03)
```

line 7 increments the value of the hours array, indexed with $1 (the username, *jem*), by the number of hours that *jem* was logged in (stored in the variable $2). The Perl increment operator += is equivalent to the corresponding C operator. Line 8 increments the value of minutes for the appropriate user similarly. Line 9 increments the value of the logins array by one, using the ++ operator.

Associative arrays are one of the most useful features of Perl. They allow you to build up complex databases while parsing text. It would be nearly impossible to use a standard array for this same task. We would first have to count the number of users in the input stream and then allocate an array of the appropriate size, assigning a position in the array to each user (through the use of a hash function or some other indexing scheme). An associative array, however, allows you to index data directly using strings and without regard for the size of the array in question. (Of course, performance issues always arise when attempting to use large arrays, but for most applications this isn't a problem.)

Let's move on. Line 14 uses the Perl foreach statement, which you may be used to if you write shell scripts. (The foreach loop actually breaks down into a for loop, much like that found in C.) Here, in each iteration of the loop, the variable $user is assigned the next value in the list given by the expression sort(keys %hours). %hours simply refers to the entire associative array hours that we have constructed. The function keys returns a list of all the keys used to index the array, which is in this case a list of usernames. Finally, the sort function sorts the list returned by keys. Therefore, we are looping over a sorted list of usernames, assigning each username in turn to the variable $user.

Lines 16 and 17 simply correct for situations where the number of minutes is greater than 60; it determines the total number of hours contained in the minutes entry for this user and increments hours accordingly. The int function returns the integral portion of its argument. (Yes, Perl handles floating-point numbers as well; that's why use of int is necessary.)

Finally, lines 19 to 22 print the total login time and number of logins for each user. The simple print function just prints its arguments, like the *awk* function of the same name. Note that variable evaluation can be done within a print statement, as on lines 19 and 22. However, if you want to do some fancy text formatting, you need to use the printf function (which is just like its C equivalent). In this case, we wish to set the minimum output length of the hours and minutes values for this user to two characters wide, and to left-pad the output with zeroes. To do this, we use the printf command on line 21.

If this script is saved in the file logintime, we can execute it as follows:

```
papaya$ last | logintime
User johnsonm, total login time 01:07, total logins 11.
User kibo, total login time 00:42, total logins 3.
User linus, total login time 98:50, total logins 208.
User mdw, total login time 153:03, total logins 290.
papaya$
```

Of course, this example doesn't serve well as a Perl tutorial, but it should give you some idea of what it can do. We encourage you to read one of the excellent Perl books out there to learn more.

More Features

The previous example introduced the most commonly used Perl features by demonstrating a living, breathing program. There is much more where that came from—in the way of both well-known and not-so-well-known features.

As we mentioned, Perl provides a report-generation mechanism beyond the standard `print` and `printf` functions. Using this feature, the programmer defines a report format that describes how each page of the report will look. For example, we could have included the following format definition in our example:

```
format STDOUT_TOP =
User            Total login time     Total logins
-------------   --------------------  -------------------
.
format STDOUT =
@<<<<<<<<<<<<< @<<<<<<<<            @####
$user,          $thetime,            $logins{$user}
.
```

The `STDOUT_TOP` definition describes the header of the report, which will be printed at the top of each page of output. The `STDOUT` format describes the look of each line of output. Each field is described beginning with the @ character; `@<<<<` specifies a left-justified text field, and `@####` specifies a numeric field. The line below the field definitions gives the names of the variables to use in printing the fields. Here, we have used the variable `$thetime` to store the formatted time string.

To use this report for the output, we replace lines 19 to 22 in the original script with the following:

```
$thetime = sprintf("%02d:%02d", $hours{$user}, $minutes{$user});
write;
```

The first line uses the `sprintf` function to format the time string and save it in the variable `$thetime`; the second line is a `write` command that tells Perl to go off and use the given report format to print a line of output.

Using this report format, we'll get something looking like this:

```
User            Total login time     Total logins
-------------   --------------------  -------------------
johnsonm        01:07                     11
kibo            00:42                      3
linus           98:50                    208
mdw             153:03                   290
```

Using other report formats, we can achieve different (and better-looking) results.

Perl comes with a huge number of modules that you can plug in to your programs for quick access to very powerful features. A popular online archive called CPAN (for Comprehensive Perl Archive Network) contains even more modules: net modules that let you send mail and carry on with other networking tasks, modules for dumping data and debugging, modules for manipulating dates and times, modules for math functions—the list could go on for pages.

If you hear of an interesting module, check first to see whether it's already loaded on your system. You can look at the directories where modules are located (probably under */usr/lib/perl5*) or just try loading in the module and see if it works. Thus, the command

```
$ perl -MCGI -e 1
Can't locate CGI in @INC...
```

gives you the sad news that the *CGI.pm* module is not on your system. *CGI.pm* is popular enough to be included in the standard Perl distribution, and you can install it from there, but for many modules you will have to go to CPAN (and some don't make it into CPAN either). CPAN, which is maintained by Jarkko Hietaniemi and Andreas König, resides on dozens of mirror sites around the world because so many people want to download its modules. The easiest way to get onto CPAN is to visit *http://www.perl.com/CPAN*.

The following program—which we wanted to keep short, and therefore neglected to find a useful task to perform—shows two modules, one that manipulates dates and times in a sophisticated manner and another that sends mail. The disadvantage of using such powerful features is that a huge amount of code is loaded from them, making the runtime size of the program quite large:

```perl
#! /usr/local/bin/perl

# We will illustrate Date and Mail modules
use Date::Manip;
use Mail::Mailer;

# Illustration of Date::Manip module
if ( Date_IsWorkDay( "today", 1) ) {

    # Today is a workday
    $date = ParseDate( "today" );

}
else {

    # Today is not a workday, so choose next workday
    $date=DateCalc( "today" , "+ 1 business day" );

}

# Convert date from compact string to readable string like "April  8"
$printable_date = UnixDate( $date , "%B %e" );
```

```
# Illustration of Mail::Mailer module
my ($to) = "the_person\@you_want_to.mail_to";
my ($from) = "owner_of_script\@system.name";

$mail = Mail::Mailer->new;

$mail->open(
        {
            From => $from,
            To => $to,
            Subject => "Automated reminder",
        }
        );

print $mail <<"MAIL_BODY";
If you are at work on or after
$printable_date,
you will get this mail.
MAIL_BODY

$mail->close;

# The mail has been sent! (Assuming there were no errors.)
```

The reason modules are so easy to use is that Perl added object-oriented features in Version 5. The Date module used in the previous example is not object-oriented, but the Mail module is. The `$mail` variable in the example is a Mailer object, and it makes mailing messages straightforward through methods such as new, open, and close.

To do some major task such as parsing HTML, just read in the proper CGI package and issue a new command to create the proper object—all the functions you need for parsing HTML will then be available.

If you want to give a graphical interface to your Perl script, you can use the Tk module, which originally was developed for use with the Tcl language; the Gtk module, which uses the newer GIMP Toolkit (GTK); or the Qt module, which uses the Qt toolkit that also forms the base of the KDE. The book *Learning Perl/Tk* (O'Reilly) shows you how to do graphics with the Perl/Tk module.

Another abstruse feature of Perl is its ability to (more or less) directly access several Unix system calls, including interprocess communications. For example, Perl provides the functions msgctl, msgget, msgsnd, and msgrcv from System V IPC. Perl also supports the BSD socket implementation, allowing communications via TCP/IP directly from a Perl program. No longer is C the exclusive language of networking daemons and clients. A Perl program loaded with IPC features can be very powerful indeed—especially considering that many client/server implementations call for advanced text processing features such as those provided by Perl. It is generally easier to parse protocol commands transmitted between client and server from a Perl script than to write a complex C program to do the work.

As an example, take the well-known SMTP daemon, which handles the sending and receiving of electronic mail. The SMTP protocol uses internal commands such as *recv from* and *mail to* to enable the client to communicate with the server. Either the client or the server, or both, can be written in Perl and can have full access to Perl's text- and file-manipulation features as well as the vital socket communication functions.

Perl is a fixture of CGI programming—that is, writing small programs that run on a web server and help web pages become more interactive.

Pros and Cons

One of the features of (some might say "problems with") Perl is the ability to abbreviate—and obfuscate—code considerably. In the first script, we used several common shortcuts. For example, input into the Perl script is read into the variable $_. However, most operations act on the variable $_ by default, so it's usually not necessary to reference $_ by name.

Perl also gives you several ways of doing the same thing, which can, of course, be either a blessing or a curse depending on how you look at it. In *Programming Perl*, Larry Wall gives the following example of a short program that simply prints its standard input. All the following statements do the same thing:

```
while ($_ = <STDIN>) { print; }
while (<STDIN>) { print; }
for (;<STDIN>;) { print; }
print while $_ = <STDIN>;
print while <STDIN>;
```

The programmer can use the syntax most appropriate for the situation at hand.

Perl is popular, and not just because it is useful. Because Perl provides much in the way of eccentricity, it gives hackers something to play with, so to speak. Perl programmers are constantly outdoing each other with trickier bits of code. Perl lends itself to interesting kludges, neat hacks, and both very good and very bad programming. Unix programmers see it as a challenging medium to work with. Even if you find Perl too baroque for your taste, there is still something to be said for its artistry. The ability to call oneself a "Perl hacker" is a point of pride within the Unix community.

Java

Java is a network-aware, object-oriented language developed by Sun Microsystems. Java originally engendered a lot of excitement in the computing community because it strived to provide a secure language for running applets downloaded from the World Wide Web. The idea was simple: allow web browsers to download Java applets, which run on the client's machine. Many popular Web browsers—including

Mozilla and Firefox, the GNOME variant Galeon, and the KDE web browser Konqueror (see Chapter 5)—include support for Java. Furthermore, the Java Developer's Kit and other tools have been ported to Linux.

But Java proved suitable for more than applets. It has been used more and more as a general-purpose programming language that offers fewer obstacles for beginners than other languages. Because of its built-in networking libraries, it is often used for programming client/server applications. A number of schools also choose it nowadays for programming courses.

The Promise of Java, or Why You Might Want to Use Java

All this may not sound too exciting to you. There are lots of object-oriented programming languages, after all, and with Mozilla plug-ins you can download executable programs from web servers and execute them on your local machine.

But Java is more than just an object-oriented programming language. One of its most exciting aspects is *platform independence*. That means you can write and compile your Java program and then deploy it on almost every machine, whether it is a lowly '386 running Linux, a powerful Pentium IV running the latest bloatware from Microsoft, or an IBM mainframe. Sun Microsystems calls this "Write Once, Run Anywhere." Unfortunately, real life is not as simple as design goals. There are tiny but frustrating differences that make a program work on one platform and fail on another. With the advent of the GUI library Swing, a large step was made toward remedying this problem.

The neat feature of compiling code once and then being able to run it on another machine is made possible by the Java Virtual Machine (JVM), the piece of software the interprets the byte code generated by the Java compiler: The Java compiler does not generate object code for a particular CPU and operating system like *gcc* does—it generates code for the JVM. This "machine" does not exist anywhere in hardware (yet), but is instead a specification. This specification says which so-called opcodes the machine understands and what the machine does when it encounters them in the object file. The program is distributed in binary form containing so-called *byte codes* that follow the JVM specification.

Now all you need is a program that implements the JVM on your particular computer and operating system. These are available nowadays for just about any platform—no vendor can dare not provide a JVM for its hardware or operating system. Such programs are also called *Java interpreters* because they interpret the opcodes compiled for the JVM and translate them into code for the native machine.

This distinction, which makes Java both a compiled and an interpreted language, makes it possible for you to write and compile your Java program and distribute it to someone else, and no matter what hardware and operating system she has, she will be able to run your program as long as a Java interpreter is available for it.

Alas, Java's platform independence comes at a steep price. Because the object code is not object code of any currently existing hardware, it must pass through an extra layer of processing, meaning that programs written in Java typically run 10 to 20 times slower than comparable programs written in, for example, C. Although this does not matter for some cases, in other cases it is simply unacceptable. So-called *just-in-time compilers* are available that first translate the object code for the JVM into native object code and then run this object code. When the same object code is run a second time, the precompiled native code can be used without any interpretation and thus runs faster. But the speed that can be achieved with this method is still inferior to that of C programs. Newer compilers use a technology called *just-in-time compilation*, but the promise of an execution speed "comparable to C programs" has not been met yet, and it is doubtful whether it ever will.

Java also distinguishes between *applications* and *applets*. Applications are standalone programs that are run from the command line or your local desktop and behave like ordinary programs. Applets, on the other hand, are programs (usually smaller) that run inside your web browser. (To run these programs, the browser needs a Java interpreter inside.) When you browse a web site that contains a Java applet, the web server sends you the object code of the applet, and your browser executes it for you. You can use this for anything from simple animations to complete online banking systems.[*]

When reading about the Java applets, you might have thought, "And what happens if the applet contains mischievous code that spies on my hard disk or even maybe deletes or corrupts files?" Of course, this would be possible if the Java designers had not designed a multistep countermeasure against such attacks: all Java applets run in a so-called sandbox, which allows them access only to certain resources. For example, Java applets can output text on your monitor, but they can't read data from your local filesystem or even write to it unless you explicitly allow them. Although this sandbox paradigm reduces the usefulness of applets, it increases the security of your data. With recent Java releases, you can determine how much security you need and thus have additional flexibility. It should be mentioned that there have been reports of serious security breaches in the use of Java in browsers, although at least all known ones are found and fixed in most current web browsers.

If you decide that Java is something for you, we recommend that you get a copy of *Thinking in Java* (Prentice Hall). It covers most of the things you need to know in the Java world and also teaches you general programming principles. Other Java titles that are well worth looking into include *Learning Java* (O'Reilly) and *Core Java* (Prentice Hall).

---

[*] One of the authors does all his financial business with his bank via a Java applet that his bank provides when browsing a special area of its web server.

Getting Java for Linux

Fortunately, there is a Linux port of the so-called JDK, the Java Developers Kit provided by Sun Microsystems for Solaris and Windows that serves as a reference implementation of Java. In the past, there was usually a gap between the appearance of a new JDK version for Solaris and Windows and the availability of the JDK for Linux. Luckily, this is no longer the case.

The "official" Java implementation JDK contains a compiler, an interpreter, and several related tools. Other kits are also available for Linux, often in the form of open source software. We cover the JDK here, though, because that's the standard. There are other Linux implementations, including a very good one from IBM, as well; you might even have them on your distribution CDs.

One more note: most distributions already contain the JDK for Linux, so it might be easier for you to simply install a prepackaged one. However, the JDK is moving fast, and you might want to install a newer version than the one your distribution contains.

Your one-stop shop for Java software (including environments for Linux) is *http:// java.sun.com*. Here, you will find documentation and news, and of course you can download a copy of the JDK for your machine.

After unpacking and installing the JDK according to the instructions, you have several new programs at your disposal. *javac* is the Java compiler, *java* is the interpreter, and *appletviewer* is a small GUI program that lets you run applets without using a full-blown web browser.

Python

Python has gained a lot of attention lately because it is a powerful mixture of different programming paradigms and styles. For example, it is one of the very few interpreted object-oriented programming languages (Perl being another example, but only relatively late in its existence). Python fans say it is especially easy to learn. Python was written and designed almost entirely by Guido van Rossum, who chose the name because he wrote the interpreter while watching reruns of the British TV show *Monty Python's Flying Circus*. The language is introduced in *Learning Python* and covered in detail in *Programming Python* (both published by O'Reilly).

As nice and useful as Perl is, it has one disadvantage—or at least many people think so—namely, that you can write the same code in many different ways. This has given Perl the reputation that it's easy to write code in Perl, but hard to read it. (The point is that another programmer might do things differently from you, and you might therefore not be used to reading that style.) This means that Perl might not be the right choice for developing code that later must be maintained for years to come.

If you normally develop software in C, C++, or Java, and from time to time you want to do some scripting, you might find that Perl's syntax is too different from what you are normally used to—for example, you need to type a dollar in front of a variable:

```
foreach $user ...
```

Before we look into a bit more detail at what Python is, let us suggest that whether you choose to program in Perl or Python is largely a matter of "religion," just as it is a matter of "religion" whether you use Emacs or *vi*, or whether you use KDE or GNOME. Perl and Python both fill the gap between real languages such as C, C++, and Java, and scripting languages such as the language built into *bash*, *tcsh* or *zsh*.

In contrast to Perl, Python was designed from the beginning to be a real programming language, with many of the constructs inspired from C. This does undoubtedly mean that Python programs are easier to read than Perl ones, even though they might come out slightly longer.

Python is an object-oriented language, but you do not need to program in an object-oriented fashion if you do not want to. This makes it possible for you to start your scripting without worrying about object orientation; as you go along and your script gets longer and more complicated, you can easily convert it to use objects.

Python scripts are interpreted, which means that you do not need to wait for a long compilation process to take place. Python programs are internally byte-compiled on the fly, which ensures that they still run at an acceptable speed. In normal daily use, you don't really notice all this, except for the fact that when you write a *.py* file, Python will create a *.pyc* file.

Python has lists, tuples, strings, and associative arrays (or, in Python lingo, *dictionaries*) built into the syntax of the language, which makes working with these types very easy.

Python comes with an extensive library, similar in power to what we saw previously for Perl. See *http://www.python.org/doc/current/lib/lib.html* for a complete library reference.

Parsing Output from the Last Command Using Python

Most programming languages are best explained using examples, so let's look at a Python version of the *last* log statistics script we previously developed using Perl. Your first impression of the script might very well be that it is way longer than the Perl script. Remember that we are forcing Python to "compete" here in the area where Perl is most powerful. To compensate, we find that this script is more straightforward to read.

Also notice the indentation. Whereas indentation is optional in most other languages and just makes the code more readable, it is required in Python and is one of its characterizing features.

```
1    #!/usr/bin/python
2
3    import sys, re, string
4
5    minutes = {  }
6    count = {  }
7    line = sys.stdin.readline(  )
8    while line:
9      match = re.match( "^(\S*)\s*.*\(([0-9]+):([0-9]+)\)\s*$", line )
10     if match:
11       user = match.group(1)
12       time = string.atoi(match.group(2))*60 + string.atoi(match.group(3))
13       if not count.has_key( user ):
14         minutes[ user ] = 0
15         count[ user ]   = 0
16       minutes[ user ] += time
17       count[user] += 1
18     line = sys.stdin.readline(  )
19
20   for user in count.keys(  ):
21     hour = `minutes[user]/60`
22     min = minutes[user] % 60
23     if min < 10:
24       minute = "0" + `min`
25     else:
26       minute = `min`
27     print "User " + user + ", total login time " + \
28           hour + ":" + minute + \
29           ", total logins " + `count[user]`
```

The script should be self-explanatory, with a few exceptions. On line 3 we import the libraries we want to use. Having imported string, for instance, we may use it as in line 12, where we use the method atoi from the library string.

On lines 5 and 6 we initialize two dictionaries. In contrast to Perl, we need to initialize them before we can assign values to them. Line 7 reads a line from standard input. When no more lines can be read, the readline method returns None, which is the equivalent to a null pointer.

Line 9 matches the line read from stdin against a regular expression, and returns a match object as a result of matching. This object contains a method for accessing the subparts of the match. Line 21 converts the result of the division minutes[user]/60 to a string. This is done using two backquotes.

Developing a Calculator Using Python

In this section we look into developing a slightly more complicated application, which uses classes. The application is a reverse Polish notation calculator, and can be seen in Figure 21-1. For developing the graphical user interface, we use the Qt library, which is a C++ library wrapped for many different languages, such as Perl, Python, and Java.

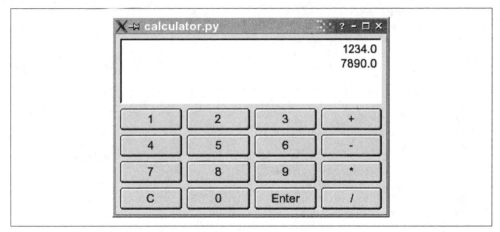

Figure 21-1. A calculator developed in Python

The program consists of two classes: Display, which is the area displaying the numbers, and Calculator, which is a class for the calculator:

```python
1   #!/usr/bin/python
2   import sys, string
3   from qt import *
4
5   class Display(QTextEdit):
6     def __init__( self, parent ):
7       QTextEdit.__init__( self, parent )
8       self.setAlignment( Qt.AlignRight )
9       self.setReadOnly( 1 )
10
11    def pop( self ):
12      lines = self.paragraphs()
13      if lines == 0:
14        return 0
15
16      res = QString.stripWhiteSpace(self.text( lines-1 ))
17      self.removeParagraph(lines-1)
18
19      if ( res.isEmpty() ):
20        return 0
21
22      return res.toFloat()[0]
23
24    def push( self, txt ):
25      self.append( `txt` )
26
27  class Calculator(QDialog):
28    # Constructor
29    def __init__(self, parent):
30      QDialog.__init__(self, parent)
31      vlay = QVBoxLayout( self, 6 )
32      self.insertMode = 0
33
```

```
34        # Create display
35        self.edit = Display( self )
36        vlay.addWidget( self.edit )
37
38        # Create button array
39        index = 0
40        for txt in [ "1", "2", "3", "+", "4", "5", "6", "-", "7", "8", "9", \
41                     "*", "C", "0", "Enter", "/" ]:
42          if (index%4) == 0:
43            hlay = QHBoxLayout( vlay )
44          index = index+1
45
46          but = QPushButton( txt, self )
47          but.setAutoDefault(0)
48          QObject.connect( but, SIGNAL( "clicked()" ), self.buttonClicked )
49          hlay.addWidget( but )
50
51      # Function reacting on button clicks
52      def buttonClicked(self):
53        txt = self.sender().text() # Text on button pressed.
54        if txt == "Enter":
55          self.insertMode = 0
56
57        elif txt in [ "+", "-", "*", "/" ]:
58          val1 = self.edit.pop()
59          val2 = self.edit.pop()
60          self.edit.push( self.evaluate( val2, val1, txt ) )
61          self.insertMode = 0
62
63        elif txt == "C":
64          self.edit.pop()
65          self.insertMode = 0
66
67        else: # A number pressed.
68          if self.insertMode:
69            val = self.edit.pop()
70          else:
71            self.insertMode = 1
72            val = 0
73          val = val*10+ txt.toFloat()[0]
74          self.edit.push(val)
75
76      def evaluate( self, arg1, arg2, op ):
77        if ( op == "+" ):
78          return arg1 + arg2
79        elif ( op == "-" ):
80          return arg1 - arg2
81        elif ( op == "*" ):
82          return arg1 * arg2
83        elif (op == "/" ):
84          return arg1 / arg2
85
86  # Main
87  app=QApplication(sys.argv)
```

```
88  cal = Calculator(None)
89  cal.show( )
90  app.exec_loop( )
```

The code may at first look like a lot of work; on the other hand, with only 90 lines of code we have developed a working application with a graphical user interface. Most of the work is really handled by Qt, and since this is not a book on programming with Qt, we will not delve into these issues too much. Let's have a look at the code snippet by snippet.

Let's start where execution of our application starts—namely, at lines 86 through 90. Of course execution starts on line 1, but the first 85 lines merely defined the classes, which doesn't result in any code being executed.

Line 87 creates an instance of the class QApplication, in contrast to other languages such as Java or C++, you do not use the keyword new to create an instance—you simply name the class. The class QApplication comes from *qt.py*, which we include in a special way on line 3: we say that all symbols from that module should be included into our namespace, so we do not need to write qt.QApplication. Doing it this way is seldom a good idea, but it is OK in our situation, as all classes from Qt already are *namespaced* by an initial letter, namely Q.

The QApplication instance we create on line 87 is the magical object that makes Qt process events and so forth. We start this event processing by calling the method enter_loop( ) on line 90. Details on this are beyond the scope of this book and are not needed for understanding the example.

On line 88 we create an instance of the class Calculator, and on line 89 we call the method show( ), which takes care of mapping the dialog on the screen.

Now let's have a look at the class Display on lines 5 to 25. This class inherits the class QTextEdit, which is a widget for editing multiple lines of text. Inheriting is done on line 5, where we specify the superclass in parentheses. Multiple inheritance is also possible, in which case you would simply write each superclass as a comma-separated list within the parentheses.

Line 6 is the constructor of the class. The constructor is implicitly called whenever an instance of the class is created. The first argument is a reference to the instance itself. This reference is needed whenever a method of the instance is to be called.*

Line 7 is a call to the constructor of the superclass. We need to call the constructor of the superclass to be able to hand on the parent reference to the superclass. The parent reference is, among other things, needed to get the layout working in our GUI.

---

* In languages such as C++ and Java, you do not need to explicitly specify the object when calling methods on it from within member functions. This is needed in Python, however, where we couldn't have replaced line 8 with setAlignment(Qt.AlignRight).

On lines 8 and 9 you see methods called on the object itself. These methods are defined in the superclass, but could of course have been from the class itself.*

On lines 11 to 22 we have a definition of the method pop( ). Again notice how we get a reference to the object itself as the first argument of the function. When calling this method, you do not hand it a reference as the first argument, Python will take care of doing so itself. On line 58 you can see such a call.

The implementation of the pop( ) and push( ) methods involves mostly Qt issues that we do not care about in this context. So let's just shortly outline what they do. The push( ) method appends a number to the end of the text edit, whereas pop( ) does the opposite—namely taking the last line of the text edit, converting it into a number, and returning it.

Now let's turn our focus to the class Calculator, which is our GUI class that you see on screen. To be a Qt dialog, it must inherit QDialog, as we see it do on line 27.

Once again, the code is mostly about Qt, and as such not too interesting in this context. There is one Python construct we still haven't seen, though: instance variables. On lines 32, 55, 61, 65, and 71 we assign to the variable self.insertMode, and on line 68 we read this variable. Due to the self. part of the variable name, it is a variable that is local to the object, which is called an *instance variable*. Had we had several instances of the Calculator class, then each of these objects would have had its own copy of the insertMode variable. In contrast to languages such as C++ and Java, you do not need to declare an instance variable. The first time you assign to it, it will jump into existence, just like local variables do.

You can read all about Python at *http://www.python.org* or in *Learning Python* and *Programming Python*. If you are interested in learning more about Qt, then *Programming with Qt* (O'Reilly) might be interesting to you. There is also at least one book dedicated to developing Qt programs in Python: *Gui Programming With Python: Using the Qt Toolkit* (Opendocs).

Other Languages

Many other popular (and not-so-popular) languages are available for Linux. For the most part, however, these work identically on Linux as on other Unix systems, so there's not much in the way of news there. There are also so many of them that we can't cover them in much detail here. We do want to let you know what's out there, however, and explain some of the differences between the various languages and compilers.

---

* All methods in Python are virtual, as is the case in Java, and unlike how it is in C++.

A recent development in the area of scripting languages, the Ruby language was developed in Japan and has gained an impressive following there. It is an object-oriented scripting language that goes (if possible) even further than Python in its use of objects.

Tcl (Tool Command Language) is a language that was meant as a glue for connecting programs together, but it has become most famous for its included, easy-to-use windowing toolkit, Tk.

LISP is an interpreted language used in many applications, ranging from artificial intelligence to statistics. It is used primarily in computer science because it defines a clean, logical interface for working with algorithms. (It also uses a lot of parentheses, something of which computer scientists are always fond.) It is a functional programming language and is very generalized. Many operations are defined in terms of recursion instead of linear loops. Expressions are hierarchical, and data is represented by lists of items.

Several LISP interpreters are available for Linux. Emacs LISP is a fairly complete implementation in itself. It has many features that allow it to interact directly with Emacs—input and output through Emacs buffers, for example—but it may be used for non-Emacs-related applications as well.

Also available is CLISP, a Common LISP implementation by Bruno Haible of Karlsruhe University and Michael Stoll of Munich University. It includes an interpreter, a compiler, and a subset of CLOS (Common LISP Object System, an object-oriented extension to LISP). CLX, a Common LISP interface to the X Window System, is also available; it runs under CLISP. CLX allows you to write X-based applications in LISP. Austin Kyoto Common LISP, another LISP implementation, is available and compatible with CLX as well.

SWI-Prolog, a complete Prolog implementation by Jan Wielemaker of the University of Amsterdam, is also available. Prolog is a logic-based language, allowing you to make logical assertions, define heuristics for validating those assertions, and make decisions based on them. It is a useful language for AI applications.

Also available are several Scheme interpreters, including MIT Scheme, a complete Scheme interpreter conforming to the R^4 standard. Scheme is a dialect of LISP that offers a cleaner, more general programming model. It is a good LISP dialect for computer science applications and for studying algorithms.

At least two implementations of Ada are available—AdaEd, an Ada interpreter, and GNAT, the GNU Ada Translator. GNAT is actually a full-fledged optimizing Ada compiler. It is to Ada what *gcc* is to C and C++.

In the same vein, two other popular language translators exist for Linux—*p2c*, a Pascal-to-C translator, and *f2c*, a FORTRAN-to-C translator. If you're concerned that these translators won't function as well as bona fide compilers, don't be. Both *p2c* and *f2c* have proven to be robust and useful for heavy Pascal and FORTRAN use.

There is also at least one Object Pascal compiler available for Linux that can compile some programs written with the Delphi product. And finally, there is Kylix, a version of the commercial Delphi environment for Linux.

f2c is Fortran 77–compliant, and a number of tools are available for it as well. *ftnchek* is a FORTRAN checker, similar to *lint*. Both the LAPACK numerical methods library and the *mpfun* multiprecision FORTRAN library have been ported to Linux using *f2c*. *toolpack* is a collection of FORTRAN tools that includes such items as a source-code pretty printer, a precision converter, and a portability checker.

The Mono project is developing a C# compiler plus runtime environment as part of the GNOME desktop, enabling .NET-style programming on Linux.

Among the miscellaneous other languages available for Linux are interpreters for APL, Rexx, Forth, ML, and Eiffel, as well as a Simula-to-C translator. The GNU versions of the compiler tools *lex* and *yacc* (renamed to *flex* and *bison*, respectively), which are used for many software packages, have also been ported to Linux. *lex* and *yacc* are invaluable for creating any kind of parser or translator, most commonly used when writing compilers.

Introduction to OpenGL Programming

Before we finish this chapter with a look at integrated development environments and in particular KDevelop, let's do some fun stuff—three-dimensional graphics programming using the OpenGL libraries!

Of course, it would be far too ambitious to give proper coverage of OpenGL programming in this book, so we just concentrate on a simple example and show how to get started and how OpenGL integrates with two popular toolkits.

GLUT

The GL Utility Toolkit was written by Mark Kilgard of SGI fame. It is not free software, but it comes with full source code and doesn't cost anything. The strength of GLUT is that it is tailored specifically for being very simple to get started with programming OpenGL. Mesa comes with a copy of GLUT included, and a free software reimplementation of GLUT is available from *http://freeglut.sourceforge.net/*. Basically, GLUT helps with initial housekeeping, such as setting up a window and so on, so you quickly can get to the fun part, namely, writing OpenGL code.

To use GLUT, you first need to access its definitions:

```
#include <GL/glut.h>
```

Next, call a couple of initialization functions in `main()`:

```
glutInit(&argc, argv)
```

to initialize GLUT and allow it to parse command-line parameters, and then:

```
glutInitDisplayMode( unsigned int mode )
```

where mode is a bitwise OR of some constants from *glut.h*. We will use GLUT_RGBA|GLUT_SINGLE to get a true-color single-buffered window.

The window size is set using:

```
glutInitWindowSize(500,500)
```

and finally the window is created using:

```
glutCreateWindow("Some title")
```

To be able to redraw the window when the window system requires it, we must register a callback function. We register the function disp( ) using:

```
glutDisplayFunc(disp)
```

The function disp( ) is where all the OpenGL calls happen. In it, we start by setting up the transformation for our object. OpenGL uses a number of transformation matrixes, one of which can be made "current" with the glMatrixMode(GLenum mode) function. The initial matrix is GL_MODELVIEW, which is used to transform objects before they are projected from 3D space to the screen. In our example, an identity matrix is loaded and scaled and rotated a bit.

Next the screen is cleared and a four-pixel-wide white pen is configured. Then the actual geometry calls happen. Drawing in OpenGL takes place between glBegin( ) and glEnd( ), with the parameter given to glBegin( ) controlling how the geometry is interpreted.

We want to draw a simple box, so first we draw four line segments to form the long edges of the box, followed by two rectangles (with GL_LINE_LOOP) for the end caps of the box. When we are done we call glFlush( ) to flush the OpenGL pipeline and make sure the lines are drawn on the screen.

To make the example slightly more interesting, we add a timer callback timeout( ) with the function glutTimerFunc( ) to change the model's rotation and redisplay it every 50 milliseconds.

Here is the complete example:

```
#include <GL/glut.h>

static int glutwin;
static float rot = 0.;

static void disp(void)
{
  float scale=0.5;
  /* transform view */
  glLoadIdentity( );
```

```
    glScalef( scale, scale, scale );
    glRotatef( rot, 1.0, 0.0, 0.0 );
    glRotatef( rot, 0.0, 1.0, 0.0 );
    glRotatef( rot, 0.0, 0.0, 1.0 );

    /* do  a clearscreen */
    glClear(GL_COLOR_BUFFER_BIT);

    /* draw something */
    glLineWidth( 3.0 );
    glColor3f( 1., 1., 1. );

    glBegin( GL_LINES ); /* long edges of box */
    glVertex3f(  1.0,  0.6, -0.4 );    glVertex3f(  1.0,  0.6, 0.4 );
    glVertex3f(  1.0, -0.6, -0.4 );    glVertex3f(  1.0, -0.6, 0.4 );
    glVertex3f( -1.0, -0.6, -0.4 );    glVertex3f( -1.0, -0.6, 0.4 );
    glVertex3f( -1.0,  0.6, -0.4 );    glVertex3f( -1.0,  0.6, 0.4 );
    glEnd( );

    glBegin( GL_LINE_LOOP ); /* end cap */
    glVertex3f(  1.0,  0.6, -0.4 ); glVertex3f(  1.0, -0.6, -0.4 );
    glVertex3f( -1.0, -0.6, -0.4 ); glVertex3f( -1.0,  0.6, -0.4 );
    glEnd( );

    glBegin( GL_LINE_LOOP ); /* other end cap */
    glVertex3f(  1.0,  0.6, 0.4 ); glVertex3f(  1.0, -0.6, 0.4 );
    glVertex3f( -1.0, -0.6, 0.4 ); glVertex3f( -1.0,  0.6, 0.4 );
    glEnd( );

    glFlush( );
}

static void timeout( int value )
{
    rot++; if( rot >= 360. ) rot = 0.;
    glutPostRedisplay( );
    glutTimerFunc( 50, timeout, 0 );
}

int main( int argc, char** argv )
{
    /* initialize glut */
    glutInit(&argc, argv);
    /* set display mode */
    glutInitDisplayMode(GLUT_RGBA | GLUT_SINGLE);
    /* output window size */
    glutInitWindowSize(500,500);
    glutwin = glutCreateWindow("Running Linux 3D Demo");
    glutDisplayFunc(disp);
    /* define the color we use to clearscreen */
    glClearColor(0.,0.,0.,0.);
    /* timer for animation */
    glutTimerFunc( 0, timeout, 0 );
    /* enter the main loop */
```

```
   glutMainLoop( );
   return 0;
}
```

Qt

As an example of how to do OpenGL programming with a more general-purpose
GUI toolkit, we will redo the GLUT example from the previous section in C++ with
the Qt toolkit. Qt is available from *http://www.trolltech.com/* under the GPL license
and is used by large free software projects such as KDE.

We start out by creating a subclass of QGLWidget, which is the central class in Qt's
OpenGL support. QGLWidget works like any other QWidget, with the main difference
being that you do the drawing with OpenGL instead of a QPainter. The callback
function used for drawing with GLUT is now replaced with a reimplementation of
the virtual method paintGL( ), but otherwise it works the same way. GLUT took care
of adjusting the viewport when the window was resized, but with Qt, we need to
handle this manually. This is done by overriding the virtual method resizeGL(int w,
int h). In our example we simply call glViewport( ) with the new size.

Animation is handled by a QTimer that we connect to a method timout( ) to have it
called every 50 milliseconds. The updateGL( ) method serves the same purpose as
glutPostRedisplay( ) in GLUT—to make the application redraw the window.

The actual OpenGL drawing commands have been omitted because they are exactly
the same as in the previous example. Here is the full example:

```
#include <qapplication.h>
#include <qtimer.h>
#include <qgl.h>

class RLDemoGLWidget : public QGLWidget {
  Q_OBJECT
public:
  RLDemoGLWidget(QWidget* parent,const char* name - 0);
public slots:
  void timeout( );
protected:
  virtual void resizeGL(int w, int h);
  virtual void paintGL( );
private:
  float rot;
};

RLDemoGLWidget::RLDemoGLWidget(QWidget* parent, const char* name)
  : QGLWidget(parent,name), rot(0.)
{
  QTimer* t = new QTimer( this );
  t->start( 50 );
  connect( t, SIGNAL( timeout( ) ),
                   this, SLOT( timeout( ) ) );
```

```
    }

    void RLDemoGLWidget::resizeGL(int w, int h)
    {
      /* adjust viewport to new size */
      glViewport(0, 0, (GLint)w, (GLint)h);
    }

    void RLDemoGLWidget::paintGL( )
    {
      /* exact same code as disp( ) in GLUT example */
      ...
    }

    void RLDemoGLWidget::timeout( )
    {
      rot++; if( rot >= 360. ) rot = 0.;
      updateGL( );
    }

    int main( int argc, char** argv )
    {
      /* initialize Qt */
      QApplication app(argc, argv);
      /* create gl widget */
      RLDemoGLWidget w(0);
      app.setMainWidget(&w);
      w.resize(500,500);
      w.show( );
      return app.exec( );
    }
    #include "main.moc"
```

Integrated Development Environments

Whereas software development on Unix (and hence Linux) systems is traditionally command-line-based, developers on other platforms are used to so-called integrated development environments (IDEs) that combine an editor, a compiler, a debugger, and possibly other development tools in the same application. Developers coming from these environments are often dumbfounded when confronted with the Linux command line and asked to type in the *gcc* command.[*]

In order to cater to these migrating developers, but also because Linux developers are increasingly demanding more comfort, IDEs have been developed for Linux as well. There are few of them out there, but only one of them, KDevelop, has seen

---

[*] We can't understand why it can be more difficult to type in a *gcc* command than to select a menu item from a menu, but then again, this might be due to our socialization.

widespread use in the C and C++ communities. Another IDE, Eclipse, is in turn very popular among Java developers.

KDevelop is a part of the KDE project, but can also be run independently of the KDE desktop. It keeps track of all files belonging to your project, generates makefiles for you, lets you parse C++ classes, and includes an integrated debugger and an application wizard that gets you started developing your application. KDevelop was originally developed to facilitate the development of KDE applications, but can also be used to develop all kinds of other software, such as traditional command-line programs and even GNOME applications.

KDevelop is way too big and feature-rich for us to introduce it to you here, but we want to at least whet your appetite with a screenshot (see Figure 21-2) and point you to *http://www.kdevelop.org* for downloads and all information, including complete documentation.

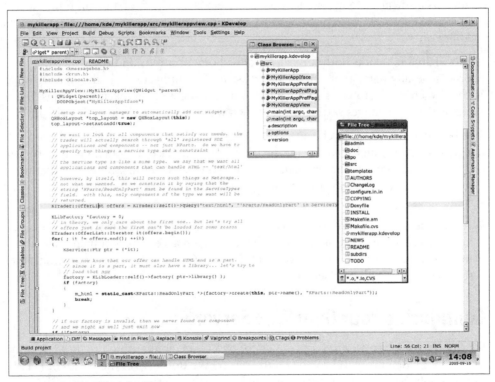

Figure 21-2. The KDevelop IDE

Emacs and XEmacs, by the way, make for very fine IDEs that integrate many additional tools such as *gdb*, as shown earlier in this chapter.

CHAPTER 22

Running a Web Server

Chapter 13 of this book put you on a network. It may have been hard work, but the result was quite an accomplishment: your system is now part of a community. If you are connected to the Internet, the next step is to get access to all the riches this medium offers.

On local area networks both for self-contained organizations and the wider Internet, people generally agree that one of the most useful applications is the World Wide Web. We covered browsers in Chapters 3 and 5. One of the exciting things about Linux is that it facilitates setting up your own web server, the topic of this chapter.

The benefits of having a web server on your system are extensive. Not only can you put up documents and serve up information from databases in a manner that people on any system connected to you can view, but you can also run a range of other tools (for system administration, for instance) that allow remote administration of your system.

With any server, however, you must pay close attention to security, because small errors in configuration can let malicious crackers gain access to documents you don't want, deface web pages, or destroy data. Ponder Chapter 26 before allowing other systems access to your web server.

Configuring Your Own Web Server

Setting up your own web server consists of two tasks: configuring the *httpd* daemon and writing documents to provide on the server. We don't cover the basics of HTML in this book, because knowledge of it is widespread and many people use GUI tools to help them. But we do discuss the basics of dynamic content (web pages created on the fly from databases) in Chapter 25.

httpd is the daemon that services HTTP requests on your machine. Any document accessed with an *HTTP* URL is retrieved using *httpd*. Likewise, *FTP* URLs are accessed using *ftpd*, Gopher URLs using *gopherd*, and so on. There is no single web daemon; each URL type uses a separate daemon to request information from the server.

Many HTTP servers are available. The one discussed here is the Apache server, which is easy to configure and very flexible. There are two major versions of Apache HTTP: the 1.3 family is the older and more widely used, whereas 2.x brings a range of features useful to higher-end sites. The instructions here are valid for either version.

All Linux versions should carry Apache today as their default *httpd* server. However, if you have selected a "minimal" or "desktop" install, it might not have been installed during the installation procedure, and you might have to install it manually afterward. Or you may want to have a newer version than the one that your distribution carries; for example, you might want the latest version in order to be more secure. In that case, you can download both sources and binaries from *http: //httpd.apache.org* and build it yourself. The *httpd.apache.org* web site contains complete documentation for the software.

Apache: The Definitive Guide, by Ben Laurie and Peter Laurie (O'Reilly), covers everything about Apache, including sophisticated configuration issues.

Where the various files of an Apache installation go depends on your distribution or the package you installed, but the following is a common setup. You should locate the various pieces in your system before continuing.

/usr/sbin/httpd
> The binary executable, which is the server itself. On Debian, this is */usr/ sbin/apache* instead.

/etc/httpd
> Contains the configuration files for *httpd*, most notably *httpd.conf*. We discuss how to modify these files later. On Debian systems, this is */etc/apache* instead of */etc/httpd*.

/usr/local/httpd
> Contains the HTML scripts to be served up to the site's clients. This directory and those below it, the *web space*, are accessible to anyone on the Web and therefore pose a severe security risk if used for anything other than public data.

/var/log/httpd
> Holds logfiles stored by the server.

Our task now is to modify the configuration files in the configuration subdirectory. You should notice at least the following four files in this directory: *access.conf-dist*, *httpd.conf-dist*, *mime.types*, and *srm.conf-dist*. (Newer versions of Apache 1.3.x have abandoned the *-dist* suffix in favor of the *.default* suffix, and Apache 2.x places a *-std* fragment before the extension.) Copy the files with names ending in *-dist* and modify them for your own system. For example, *httpd.conf-dist* is copied to *httpd.conf* and edited.

The latest version of Apache pretty much configures itself, but in case things go wrong, we tell you here how to do it manually so that you can fix things yourself.

At *http://httpd.apache.org*, you will find complete documentation on how to configure *httpd*. Here, we present sample configuration files that correspond to an actual running *httpd*.

httpd.conf

The file *httpd.conf* is the main server-configuration file. First, copy *httpd.conf-dist* to *httpd.conf* and edit it. We only cover some of the more important options here; the file *httpd.conf-dist* is vastly commented.

The ServerType directive is used to specify how the server will run—either as a standalone daemon (as seen here) or from *inetd*. For various reasons, it's usually best to run *httpd* in standalone mode. Otherwise, *inetd* must spawn a new instance of *httpd* for each incoming connection.

One tricky item here is the port number specification. You may wish to run *httpd* as a user other than *root* (that is, you may not have *root* access on the machine in question and wish to run *httpd* yourself). In this case, you must use a port numbered 1024 or above. For example, if we specify:

```
Port 2112
```

we may run *httpd* as a regular user. In this case, HTTP URLs to this machine must be specified as in the following example:

> *http://www.ecoveggie.org:2112/…*

If no port number is given in the URL (as is the usual case), port 80 is assumed.

With

```
DocumentRoot /usr/local/httpd/htdocs
```

we specify the DocumentRoot directive, where documents to be provided via HTTP are stored. These documents are written in HTML.

For example, if someone were to access the URL:

> *http://www.ecoveggie.org/fruits.html*

the actual file accessed would be */usr/local/httpd/htdocs/fruits.html*.

The UserDir directive specifies a directory each user may create in his home directory for storing public HTML files. For example, if we were to use the URL:

> *http://www.ecoveggie.org/~mdw/linux-info.html*

the actual file accessed would be *~mdw/public_html/linux-info.html*.

The following lines enable the indexing features of *httpd*:

```
# If a URL is received with a directory but no filename, retrieve this
# file as the index (if it exists).
DirectoryIndex index.html

# Turn on 'fancy' directory indexes
IndexOptions FancyIndexing
```

In this case, if a browser attempts to access a directory URL, the file *index.html* in that directory is returned, if it exists. Otherwise, *httpd* generates a "fancy" index with icons representing various file types. Figure 5-2 shows an example of such an index.

Icons are assigned using the AddIcon directive, as seen here:

```
# Set up various icons for use with fancy indexes, by filename
# E.g., we use DocumentRoot/icons/movie.xbm for files ending
#      in .mpg and .qt
AddIcon /icons/movie.xbm .mpg
AddIcon /icons/back.xbm ..
AddIcon /icons/menu.xbm ^^DIRECTORY^^
AddIcon /icons/blank.xbm ^^BLANKICON^^
DefaultIcon /icons/unknown.xbm
```

The icon filenames (such as *icons/movie.xbm*) are relative to DocumentRoot by default. (There are other ways to specify pathnames to documents and icons—for example, by using aliases. This is discussed later.) There is also an AddIconByType directive, which lets you specify an icon for a document based on the document's MIME type, and an AddIconByEncoding directive, which lets you specify an icon for a document based on the document's encoding (i.e., whether and how it is compressed).

You can also specify an icon to be used when none of the above matches. This is done with the DefaultIcon directive.

The optional ReadmeName and HeaderName directives specify the names of files to be included in the index generated by *httpd*:

```
ReadmeName README
HeaderName HEADER
```

Here, if the file *README.html* exists in the current directory, it will be appended to the index. The file *README* will be appended if *README.html* does not exist. Likewise, *HEADER.html* or *HEADER* will be included at the top of the index generated by *httpd*. You can use these files to describe the contents of a particular directory when an index is requested by the browser:

```
# Local access filename.
AccessFileName .htaccess

# Default MIME type for documents.
DefaultType text/plain
```

The `AccessFileName` directive specifies the name of the *local configuration file* for each directory. (This is described later in this chapter.) The `DefaultType` directive specifies the MIME type for documents not listed in *mime.types*.

The following lines specify directories for useful files:

```
# Set location of icons.
Alias /icons/ /usr/local/html/icons/

# Set location of CGI binaries.
ScriptAlias /cgi-bin/ /usr/local/httpd/cgi-bin/
```

The `Alias` directive specifies an alias for any of the files that would normally not be visible through the web server. Earlier, we used the `AddIcon` directive to set icon names using pathnames such as */icons/movie.xbm*. Here, we specify that the pathname */icons/* should be translated to */usr/local/html/icons/*. Therefore, the various icon files should be stored in the latter directory. You can use `Alias` to set aliases for other pathnames as well.

The `ScriptAlias` directive is similar, but it sets the actual location of CGI scripts on the system. Here, we wish to store scripts in the directory */usr/local/httpd/cgi-bin/*. Any time a URL is used with a leading directory component of */cgi-bin/*, it is translated into the actual directory name. More information on CGI and scripts is included in the book *CGI Programming with Perl*, by Scott Guelich, Shishir Gundavaram, and Gunther Birznieks (O'Reilly).

`<Directory>` entries specify the options and attributes for a particular directory, as in the following:

```
# Set options for the cgi-bin script directory.
<Directory /usr/local/html/cgi-bin>
Options Indexes FollowSymLinks
</Directory>
```

Here, we specify that the CGI script directory should have the access options `Indexes` and `FollowSymLinks`. A number of access options are available. These include the following:

`FollowSymLinks`
> Symbolic links in this directory should be followed to retrieve the documents to which they point. This option is not entirely safe to use on multiuser systems because it allows any user to create a link to some other file or directory (e.g., */etc/passwd*). Use `SymLinksIfOwnerMatch` as a safer (but slightly slower) alternative.

`SymLinksIfOwnerMatch`
> Symbolic links in this directory should be followed only if the target file or directory is owned by the same user ID as the link.

`ExecCGI`
> Allow the execution of CGI scripts from this directory.

Indexes

    Allow indexes to be generated from this directory.

None

    Disable all options for this directory.

All

    Enable all options for this directory.

There are other options as well; see the *httpd* documentation for details.

Next, we configure a very strict default configuration for the complete filesystem.

```
# Default configuration
<Directory />

# Turn all features off
Options None

# Do not allow local files to override configuration.
AllowOverride None

# In fact, do not allow access to any of the files.
Order allow,deny
Deny from all

</Directory>
```

We have started by denying access to the complete filesystem. Now we proceed to explicitly allow access to the files we want Apache to serve. At the very least we need to enable several options and other attributes for */usr/local/httpd/htdocs*, the directory containing our HTML documents. This configuration applies to the base directory and the subdirectories below it.

```
# Configuration for the web server files.
<Directory /usr/local/httpd/htdocs>

# Allow automatic indexes and controlled symbolic links.
Options Indexes SymlinksIfOwnerMatch

# Allow the local access file, .htaccess, to override
# any attributes listed here.
AllowOverride All

# Allow unrestricted access to files in this directory.
Order allow,deny
Allow from all

</Directory>
```

Here, we turn on the `Indexes` and `SymLinksIfOwnerMatch` options for this directory. The `AllowOverride` option allows the local access file (named *.htaccess*) in each directory that contains documents to override any of the attributes given here. The *.htaccess* file has essentially the same format as the global configuration but applies only to the directory in which it is located. This way, we can specify attributes for particular directories by including a *.htaccess* file in those directories instead of listing the attributes in the global file.

The primary use for local access files is to allow individual users to set the access permissions for personal HTML directories (such as *~/public_html*) without having to ask the system administrator to modify the global access file. Security issues are associated with this, however. For example, a user might enable access permissions in her own directory such that any browser can run expensive server-side CGI scripts. If you disable the `AllowOverride` feature, users cannot get around the access attributes specified in the global configuration. This can be done by using:

```
AllowOverride None
```

which effectively disables local *.htaccess* files.

The `<Limit GET>` field is used to specify access rules for browsers attempting to retrieve documents from this server. In this case, we specify `Order allow,deny`, which means that `allow` rules should be evaluated before `deny` rules. We then instate the rule `Allow from all`, which simply means any host may retrieve documents from the server. If you wish to deny access from a particular machine or domain, you could add the line:

```
Deny from ..nuts.com biffnet.biffs-house.us
```

The first entry denies access from all sites in the *nuts.com* domain. The second denies access from the site *biffnet.biffs-house.us*.

srm.conf and access.conf

The *srm.conf* and *access.conf* files should be kept empty. In earlier Apache versions, *srm.conf* stood for Server Resource Map and listed facilities provided by the server, and *access.conf* controlled access to Apache files. All the resources originally placed in those files are now listed in the main *httpd.conf* file.

Starting httpd

Now you're ready to run *httpd*, allowing your machine to service HTTP URLs. As mentioned previously, you can run *httpd* from *inetd* or as a standalone server. Here, we describe how to run *httpd* in standalone mode.

All that's required to start *httpd* is to run the command:

```
httpd -f configuration-file
```

where *configuration-file* is the pathname of *httpd.conf*. For example:

```
/usr/sbin/httpd -f /etc/httpd/httpd.conf
```

starts up *httpd*, with configuration files found in */etc/httpd*.

Watch the *httpd* error logs (the location of which is given in *httpd.conf*) for any errors that might occur when trying to start up the server or when accessing documents. Remember you must run *httpd* as *root* if it is to use a port numbered 1023 or less. Once you have *httpd* working to your satisfaction, you can start it automatically at boot time by including the appropriate *httpd* command line in one of your system *rc* files, such as */etc/init.d/boot.local*.

Apache also provides a utility called *apachectl* that is more convienent for starting, stopping, and reloading the *httpd* process. In particular, calling:

```
apachectl configtest
```

is a good way of checking whether the configuration file is actually correct before starting the server. Finally, we should mention that you can also start, restart, and stop Apache by using */etc/init.d/apache* plus one of the parameters start, restart, or stop.

Of course, in order to request documents via HTTP from your browser, you'll need to write them, something that we cannot cover in this book. Two good sources for HTML information are the O'Reilly books *HTML & XML: The Definitive Guide* and *HTML Pocket Reference* by Jennifer Niederst. To set up a back-end database to your web server, start with Chapter 25.

CHAPTER 23

Transporting and Handling Email Messages

Electronic mail (email) is one of the most desirable features of a computer system. You can send and receive email on your Linux system locally between users on the host and between hosts on a network. You have to set up three classes of software to provide email service. These are the *mail user agent* or mailer, the *mail transport agent* (MTA), and the *transport protocol*.

The mailer provides the user interface for displaying mail, writing new messages, and filing messages. Linux offers you many choices for mailers. They are always being improved, and a particular mailer may provide certain features, such as the ability to serve as a newsreader or as a web browser.

Mailers tend to differ in terms of their MIME support. (MIME stands for Multipurpose Internet Mail Extensions. It is really not multimedia-specific, but more a general standard for describing the contents of email messages.) Some do it better than others. It's difficult to give a recommendation here, though, since all mailers are continually moving toward better MIME support. Also, the problem is often not with the mail software, but rather with the need to register MIME types with the right viewer/handler applications in your environment.

The mailer relies on the MTA to route mail from one user to another, whether locally or across systems. The MTA in turn uses a transport protocol, usually either Unix-to-Unix Copy (UUCP, a very old protocol that was once common and has almost died out in the Western world, but is still common in regions with slow and unreliable dial-up lines) or Simple Mail Transport Protocol (SMTP), to provide the medium for mail transfer.

There are a number of possible scenarios for using email on a Linux system, and depending on those scenarios, you will have to install a different set of software packages. However, no matter which option you choose, you will always need a mailer.

The first scenario applies to dial-up access to the Internet via an Internet service provider (ISP). In this scenario, there is often only one user on the Linux machine, although this is not a requirement. The ISP accepts your mail from the Internet and stores it for you on its hard disks. You can then retrieve the mail whenever you want by using the common Post Office Protocol (POP3) or the newer Internet Message Access Protocol (IMAP). Outgoing mail in this scenario is almost exclusively sent via the SMTP protocol, which is universally used to transport mail over the Internet.

In the easiest case, you use your mailer both to retrieve the mail via POP3 or IMAP and to send it back via SMTP. When you do this, you do not even need to set up an MTA because the mailer handles everything. This is not terribly flexible, but if all you want is to access your mail easily, this might be an option for you. Mailers that support this include KMail from KDE and Mozilla's built-in mail program (both described later).

Browser-based email clients such as *gmail* or GMX are yet another story. They need to operate on a mailbox that is stored on a server; this mailbox could be filled by either POP3 or IMAP, often automatically. These days, it is quite common for browser-based email clients to use IMAP.

If you want more flexibility (which comes at the price of more configuration and maintenance work), you can install an MTA such as Postfix, described in the next section. You will need a program that transports the mail from your provider's POP3 or IMAP server. This program fetches your mail when you ask it to and passes the messages on to the MTA running on your system, which then distributes the mail to the recipients' mail folders. One program that does exactly that is *fetchmail*, which we cover later in this chapter. Outgoing mail is again sent via SMTP, but with an MTA running on your machine, you can choose not to send the outgoing messages directly to your provider's SMTP server, but rather to your own server, which is provided by the MTA. The MTA then forwards the mail to your provider, which in turn sends it to the recipients. With this setup, you can instruct your MTA to send outgoing mail at certain intervals so that you do not always have to make a dial-up connection.

The third scenario is meant for machines that have a permanent connection to the Internet, either because they are in a network that has a gateway with a permanent connection, or because they are using a leased line to your Internet provider. In this case, you might want to receive mail messages as soon as they arrive at your provider and not have them stored there. This also requires setting up an MTA. Incoming mail will be directed to your SMTP server (i.e., your MTA). Your provider will have to set things up accordingly for this to work.

Of course, there are many more scenarios for using mail, and mixtures between the three mentioned are possible as well. If you are going to set up a mail service for a whole network, you will most certainly want to read the *Linux Network Administrator's Guide* (O'Reilly) as well as a book about your MTA.

You have a number of software choices for setting up email on a Linux host. We can't describe all the available email solutions, but we do describe some packages that are often used and quite suitable for their respective tasks. Mail programs for end users, such as KMail and Evolution, have already been described in detail in previous chapters. In this chapter we document what we think are the most popular Linux advanced tools at this time: the Postfix mail transport agent and the *fetchmail* implementation of the POP3 and IMAP protocols. These are relatively simple to configure but provide all the features most users need. In addition, with these tools, you can cover all the scenarios described earlier.

The Postfix MTA

Several MTAs are available for Linux. Historically, the most common MTA on Unix has been *sendmail*, which has been around for a long time. It is generally considered somewhat more difficult to use than the alternatives, but it is thoroughly documented in the book *sendmail*, by Bryan Costales with Eric Allman (O'Reilly).

Postfix is a newer MTA, developed by security guru Wietse Venema as a replacement for *sendmail*. It's designed to be compatible with *sendmail* but to provide a higher level of security and be easier to configure.

Postfix is a highly flexible and secure piece of software that contains multiple layers of protection against would-be attackers. Postfix was also written with performance in mind, and employs techniques to limit slower activities such as creating new processes and accessing the filesystem. It is one of the easier email packages to configure and administer because it uses straightforward configuration files and simple lookup tables for address rewriting. It is remarkable in that it is simple to use as a basic MTA, yet still able to handle much more complicated environments.

Many Linux distributions have Postfix built in, so you may already have it installed on your system. If not, you can find prebuilt packages or compile it yourself from the source code. The Postfix home page (*http://www.postfix.org*) contains links to download both the source code ("Download") and packages for different Linux distributions ("Packages and Ports").

Postfix has two different release tracks: official and experimental. The experimental releases contain all the latest patches and new features, although these might change before they are included in the official release. Don't be put off by the term "experimental"; these releases are very stable and have been tested thoroughly. If you are looking for a feature that is available only in the experimental release, you should feel more than comfortable using it. Read the release notes for both tracks to know what the current differences are.

A Word About DNS

Before setting up Postfix, you should understand that if your system is going to receive mail from others across the Internet, the DNS for your domain has to be configured correctly. DNS is discussed in Chapter 13.

Let's assume for this discussion that you are configuring a host called halo in the domain *example.org* and that you have a user account *michael* on your system. Regardless of how you want to receive mail, your host *halo.example.org* must have a DNS A record that maps its hostname to its IP address.

In this example your email address is going to be either *michael@halo.example.org* or *michael@example.org*. If you want to use the first form, configuring the DNS A record is enough for messages to reach you.

If your system is going to receive all mail for example.org (including *michael@example.org*), the domain should have a DNS MX record pointing to your host halo.example.org. If you are configuring the DNS for your domain yourself, make sure you read the documentation to understand how it works; otherwise, speak to your DNS administrator or ISP about routing mail to your system.

Postfix frequently uses DNS in its normal operation, and it uses the underlying Linux libraries to perform its DNS queries. Make sure your system is configured correctly to perform DNS lookups (see "Configuring DNS" in Chapter 13). Postfix usually has to find an MX record to make its deliveries. Don't assume that if Postfix reports a DNS problem with an address, and you find that the domain resolves correctly, that email delivery should therefore succeed. If Postfix reports a problem, you can be almost certain there is a problem.

Installing Postfix

Although prepackaged distributions are available, you may want to build the package yourself if you want to use any of the add-on libraries or functions that are not included in your distribution. You might also want to get the latest version to obtain a new feature that has not yet been included in your distribution.

Before you install Postfix, be aware that it includes the three commands */usr/bin/newaliases*, */usr/bin/mailq*, and */usr/sbin/sendmail* that are normally used by *sendmail*. Postfix provides replacements that work with the Postfix system rather than with *sendmail*. You should rename your existing *sendmail* commands so that the Postfix installation doesn't overwrite them in case you ever want to use the original *sendmail* binaries again:

```
# mv /usr/bin/newaliases /usr/bin/newaliases.orig
# mv /usr/bin/mailq /usr/bin/mailq.orig
# mv /usr/sbin/sendmail /usr/sbin/sendmail.orig
```

Postfix uses Unix database files to store its alias and lookup table information. You must, therefore, have the *db* libraries installed on your system before building Postfix. These libraries are contained within the *db-devel* RPM package or the Debian *libdb4.3-dev* package. If you are not using a package manager, you can obtain them directly from Sleepycat Software (*http://www.sleepycat.com/*). If you are using RPM, execute the following command to see if the necessary libraries have been installed on your system:

```
# rpm -qa | grep db-devel
db-devel-4.3.27-3
```

You should see a line similar to the second line in the preceding command that displays the *db-devel* package with a version number. If *rpm* returns nothing, you must install the libraries before installing Postfix.

On Debian, you can use *dpkg* to see if the libraries are installed:

```
# dpkg -l libdb4.3-dev
```

If you download a prepackaged Postfix, use your package manager (described in Chapter 12) to install it. If you download the source *postfix-2.2.5.tar.gz*, move that file to a suitable directory (such as your home directory) to unpack it. The numbers in the name of the file represent the version of this release. Your file may have different numbers depending on the current release when you download it.

Follow this basic procedure to build Postfix. Note that you'll have to be the *root* user to create the user and group and to install the package.

1. Rename your *sendmail* binaries as described earlier.
2. Create a user account called *postfix* and a group called *postdrop*. See "Managing User Accounts" in Chapter 11 for information on setting up accounts and groups.
3. Run *gunzip* on the compressed file to produce a file named *postfix-2.2.5.tar*.
4. Execute

   ```
   tar -xvf postfix-2.2.5.tar
   ```

   to unpack the source into a directory called *postfix-2.2.5*.
5. Move to the directory created when you unpacked the file. You'll find a file called *INSTALL* with detailed instructions about building your Postfix system. In most cases, building Postfix should be as simple as typing make in the directory.
6. If your build completes without any errors, type *make install* to install Postfix on your system. You should be able to accept all the defaults when prompted by the installation script.

After installation, you will have Postfix files in the following directories:

/usr/libexec/postfix

This directory contains the various Postfix daemons. Postfix uses a split architecture in which several discrete programs handle separate tasks. The *master* daemon is started first. It deals with starting other programs as they are needed. For the most part, you don't need to worry about any of the programs here. Stopping and starting Postfix is handled with the *postfix* command found in the */usr/sbin* directory.

/etc/postfix

Typically this directory contains dozens of Postfix configuration files, but only *master.cf* and *main.cf* and a few lookup tables are used by Postfix. The rest of the files are examples that document the various parameters used for configuration.

The *master.cf* file controls the various Postfix processes. It includes a line for each component of Postfix. The layout of the file is described by comments in the file itself. Usually, you shouldn't have to make any changes to run a simple Postfix installation.

The *main.cf* file is the global SMTP configuration file. It includes a list of parameters set to one or more values using the format

```
parameter = value
```

Comments are marked with a hash mark (#) at the beginning of the line. You cannot put comments on the same line as parameters. Commented lines can begin with whitespace (spaces or tabs), but they must appear on lines by themselves.

Multiple values for parameters can be separated by either commas or whitespace (including newlines), but if you want to have more than one line for a parameter, start the second and subsequent lines with whitespace. Values can refer to other parameters by preceding the parameter name with a dollar sign ($).

Here's an example of an entry that includes comments, multiple lines, and a parameter reference:

```
# Here are all the systems I accept mail from.
mynetworks = $myhostname
        192.168.75.0/24
        10.110.12.15
```

/usr/sbin

All the Postfix commands are located in */usr/sbin* and have names starting with post. There are commands to create index files, manage the mail queue, and otherwise administer your Postfix system. The *postfix* command, which is used to stop and start Postfix (described later), is found here.

/var/spool/postfix

The Postfix queue manager is an important component of the Postfix system that accepts incoming email messages and arranges with other Postfix components to deliver them. It maintains its files under the */var/spool/postfix* directory.

The queues it maintains are shown next. Postfix provides several tools to manage the queues, such as *postcat*, *postsuper*, and *mailq*, but you might also use the usual Linux commands, such as *find* and *cat*, to inspect your queue.

/var/spool/postfix/incoming

All incoming messages, whether from over the network or sent locally.

/var/spool/postfix/active

Messages that the queue manager is delivering or preparing to deliver.

/var/spool/postfix/deferred

Messages that could not be delivered immediately. Postfix will attempt to deliver them again.

/var/spool/postfix/corrupt

Messages that are completely unreadable or otherwise damaged and not deliverable are stored here for you to look at if necessary to figure out the problem. This queue is rarely used.

/usr/local/man

Postfix installs documentation in the form of manpages on your system. The documentation includes information on command-line utilities, daemons, and configuration files.

As mentioned earlier, Postfix also installs replacements for */usr/bin/newaliases*, */usr/bin/mailq*, and */usr/sbin/sendmail*.

Postfix Configuration

Before you start Postfix for the first time, you have to make sure that the aliases table is formatted correctly and that a few of the critical configuration parameters are set correctly for your system.

Historically, *sendmail* has used the file */etc/aliases* to map one local username to another. Postfix continues the tradition. The */etc/aliases* file is a plain-text file that is used as input to create an indexed database file for faster lookups of aliases on your system. There are at least two important aliases on your system that must be set in your */etc/aliases* file. If you have been running *sendmail* on your system, these aliases are probably already set correctly, but make sure your file has entries for *root* and *postmaster* pointing to a real account that receives mail on your system. Once you have verified the aliases, execute the command *newaliases* to rebuild the index file in the correct format for Postfix.

The */etc/postfix/main.cf* file contains many parameters, but there are just a few important ones that you should verify before starting Postfix; we explain these in this section. If you installed Postfix from a prepackaged distribution, these parameters might already be set correctly. It's also possible that the Postfix defaults work for your system, but edit your */etc/postfix/main.cf* file to make sure.

myhostname

>This is the fully qualified hostname for your system. By default, Postfix uses the name returned by the gethostname function. If this value is not fully qualified, and you have not set this parameter, Postfix will not start. You can check it by executing the command *hostname*. It's probably a good idea to specify your fully qualified hostname here explicitly:
>
>```
>myhostname = halo.example.org
>```

mydomain

>Specifies the domain name for this system. This value is then used as the default in other places. If you do not set it explicitly, Postfix uses the domain portion of myhostname. If you have set myhostname as shown previously and example.org is correct for your system, you do not have to set this parameter.

mydestination

>Specifies a list of domain names for which this system should accept mail. In other words, you should set the value of this parameter to the domain portions of email addresses for which you want to receive mail. By default, Postfix uses the value specified in myhostname. If you are setting up your system to accept mail for your entire domain, specify the domain name itself. You can use the variables $myhostname and $mydomain as the value for this parameter:
>
>```
>mydestination = $myhostname $mydomain
>```

myorigin

>This parameter is used to append a domain name to messages sent locally that do not already include one. For example, if a user on your system sends a message with only the local username in the From: address, Postfix appends this value to the local name. By default, Postfix uses myhostname, but if your system is handling mail for the entire domain, you might want to specify $mydomain instead:
>
>```
>myorigin = $mydomain
>```

Some Linux distributions that already include Postfix configure it to use Procmail by default. Procmail is a separate mail delivery agent (MDA) that can filter and sort mail as it makes deliveries to individual users on your system. We describe Procmail in more detail later in this chapter. If you need the features it provides, you should study the Procmail documentation carefully to understand how it interacts with Postfix. For many systems that don't filter mail for users at the MTA level, Procmail is an unnecessary additional layer of complexity because Postfix can also make local deliveries and provide some of the same functions. Your distribution might be configured to use Procmail in either the mailbox_command or mailbox_transport parameters. If you want Postfix to handle local deliveries directly, you can safely comment out either of these parameters in your */etc/postfix/main.cf* file.

Starting Postfix

Once you have verified the important configuration parameters described earlier and rebuilt your aliases index file, you are ready to start Postfix. As the superuser, execute:

```
postfix start
```

You can stop Postfix by executing:

```
postfix stop
```

Whenever you make changes to either of Postfix's configuration files, you must reload the running Postfix image by executing:

```
postfix reload
```

Once you have Postfix running, all the users on your system should be able to send and receive email messages.

Any of your applications that depend on *sendmail* should still work, and you can use the *sendmail* command as you always did. You can pipe messages to it from within scripts and execute *sendmail -q* to flush the queue. The native Postfix equivalent for flushing the queue is *postfix flush*. Options to *sendmail* that deal with it running as a daemon and setting queue delays do not work because those functions are not handled by the *sendmail* command in Postfix. All the Postfix options are set in its two configuration files. Many parameters deal with the Postfix queue. You can find them in the manpage for *qmgr*(8).

Postfix Logging

After starting or reloading Postfix, you should check the log to see if Postfix reports any problems. (Most Linux distributions use */var/log/maillog*, but you can also check the file */etc/syslog.conf* to be sure.) You can see Postfix's most recent messages by running the command *tail /var/log/maillog*. Since Postfix is a long-running process, it's a good idea to check the log periodically even if you haven't been restarting it. You can execute the following to see if Postfix has reported anything interesting while running:

```
egrep '(reject|warning|error|fatal|panic):' /var/log/maillog
```

In general, Postfix keeps you informed of what is going on with your system by logging lots of good information to *syslogd*. On Linux, *syslogd* uses synchronous writes by default, which means that after every write to the logfile, there is also a sync to force everything in memory to be written to the disk. Therefore, the performance of Postfix (and other processes) can suffer. You can change this default by preceding the name of the logfile with a hyphen in */etc/syslog.conf*. Your entry in *syslog.conf* for mail logging should look like the following:

```
mail.*                  -/var/log/maillog
```

Be sure to have *syslogd* reread its configuration file after you make any changes. You can execute *killall -HUP syslogd* to reinitialize it.

Running Postfix on System Startup

Because of Postfix's compatibility with *sendmail*, if you have your system configured to start *sendmail* at system initialization, more than likely Postfix will start correctly when your system boots. However, system shutdown will probably not work correctly. Most Linux distributions shut down *sendmail* by locating a process called *sendmail* and then killing that process. The Postfix processes, while in many ways compatible with *sendmail*, do not run under the name *sendmail*, so this shutdown fails.

If you would like your system to shut down cleanly, you should create your own *rc* script for Postfix, as described in "rc Files" in Chapter 17. The commands you need to include in your script to start and stop Postfix are the same as those you execute on the command line: *postfix start* and *postfix stop*. Here's an example of a basic script to get you started. You may want to review other *rc* scripts on your system to see if you should add more system checks or follow other conventions and then make your adjustments to this example:

```sh
#!/bin/sh
PATH=""
RETVAL=0

if [ ! -f /usr/sbin/postfix ] ; then
    echo "Unable to locate Postfix"
    exit 1
fi
if [ ! -f /etc/postfix/main.cf ] ; then
    echo "Unable to locate Postfix configuration"
    exit 1
fi

case "$1" in
    start)
        echo -n "Starting Postfix: "
        /usr/sbin/postfix start > /dev/null 2>1
        RETVAL=$?
        echo
        ;;

    stop)
        echo -n "Stopping Postfix: "
        /usr/sbin/postfix stop > /dev/null 2>1
        RETVAL=$?
        echo
        ;;

    restart)
```

```
        echo -n "Restarting Postfix: "
        /usr/bin/postfix reload > /dev/null 2>1
        RETVAL=$?
        echo
        ;;

    *)
        echo "Usage: $0 {start|stop|restart}"
        RETVAL=1

esac
exit $RETVAL
```

Place this script in */etc/rc.d/init.d* or */etc/init.d*, depending on your Linux distribution. Then make the appropriate symbolic links in each of the *rcN.d* directories for each runlevel in which Postfix should start (see "init, inittab, and rc Files" in Chapter 17). For example, if you want to have Postfix start at runlevels 3 and 5 and stop at runlevels 0 and 6, create symbolic links like those that follow for Red Hat. For Debian, the *rcN.d* directories are directly below */etc*.

```
# cd /etc/rc.d/rc3.d
# ln -s .../init.d/postfix S97postfix
# cd /etc/rc.d/rc5.d
# ln -s .../init.d/postfix S97postfix
# cd /etc/rc.d/rc0.d
# ln -s .../init.d/postfix K97postfix
# cd /etc/rc.d/rc6.d
# ln -s .../init.d/postfix K97postfix
```

If you create a Postfix *rc* script, you should configure your system not to start *sendmail* at startup.

Postfix Relay Control

The default installation allows any system on the same subnet as yours to relay mail through your mail server. If you want to override the default, you can set the parameter mynetworks to be a list of hosts or networks that you trust to relay mail through your system. You can specify a list of IP addresses or network/netmask patterns, and any connecting SMTP client that matches will be allowed to relay mail. You can list network or IP addresses that reside anywhere. So, for example, if you want to be able to relay mail through your home Postfix system from your work machine, you can specify the IP address of your machine at work in your home Postfix configuration.

Here's an example that allows mail from the local subnet (192.168.75.0/28) and a single host located elsewhere:

```
mynetworks = 192.168.75.0/28 10.150.134.15
```

If you want to allow relaying for mobile users who do not have static IP addresses, you have to use some kind of SMTP authentication mechanism. Postfix can work with SASL Authentication (which requires that Postfix be compiled with additional

---

libraries, and that users' client software be specially configured) and pop-before-smtp (which requires a POP server running on the same system to first authenticate users).

It is important not to open relay access to anyone except users you trust. In the early days of the Internet, open relays were commonplace. Unfortunately, the current prevalence of spam has precluded that kind of freedom. If your MTA is not protected, you leave yourself and other Internet systems vulnerable to abuse. Spammers constantly scan for open relays, and if you place one on the network, it is only a matter of time before it will be found. Fortunately, the default Postfix installation behaves correctly. However, if you make lots of changes to your Postfix configuration (especially in setting up antispam controls, ironically), you may inadvertently open yourself up to relay abusers. There are some online antispam initiatives that offer to test if your server is configured to correctly deny relaying; try, for example, *http://www.abuse.net/relay.html*.

If you want your own Postfix installation to relay mail through another MTA, specify the IP address of the relay server using the relayhost parameter. Postfix normally figures out where to deliver messages on its own, based on the destination address. However, if your system is behind a firewall, for example, you may want Postfix to hand off all messages to another mail server to make the actual delivery. When you specify a relay server, Postfix normally performs a DNS query to obtain the mail exchanger (MX) address for that system. You can override this DNS lookup by putting the hostname in square brackets:

```
relayhost = [mail.example.org]
```

Additional Configurations

The configuration described here creates a simple Postfix installation to send and receive messages for users on your system. But Postfix is an extremely flexible MTA with many more configuration options, such as hosting multiple virtual domains, maintaining mailing lists, blocking spam, and scanning for viruses. The manpages, HTML files, and sample configuration files that come with Postfix contain a lot of information to guide you in the more advanced configurations.

Procmail

Being a celebrity on the Internet means that you get a lot of attention, just as celebrities do in the real world. The good news is that everyone can become celebrities: simply join a few public mailing lists, get yourself a home page, and you are all set. The bad news is that the attention is from spammers, who send you an enormous amount of suggestions about how you can become richer, extend certain body parts, and take most of their wealth if you want to help them get it out of Iraq.

The virtual bodyguards of your mail are a couple called Procmail and SpamAssassin. Procmail is a general-purpose mail filter, while SpamAssassin is a dedicated mail filter for fighting spam and the like (worms, viruses, etc.). This section discusses Procmail, and the next section is devoted to SpamAssassin.

Procmail Concepts

To understand Procmail, we need to start looking at how it is invoked. The usual sequence is that mail arrives at your account, and your MUA calls Procmail, giving it the mail as argument. The terms *filter* or *rule*, in many mail filtering programs, refer to both a set of conditions to check messages for and an action to perform on the messages that meet those conditions (such as putting them in a particular folder). Procmail refers to this set as a *recipe*, a term we will use throughout this section to describe each set of paired conditions and actions. Procmail goes through each of its recipes until one marks the mail as delivered. If no recipe blocks the mail, it is delivered in your inbox as if Procmail had never been in the picture.

Each recipe consists of two things: a set of conditions and a set of actions. The actions of a recipe are executed if all its conditions are met. In addition, a recipe may mark mail as delivered as described earlier.

The conditions may include the following:

- The letter comes from president@whitehouse.gov.
- The subject contain the text KimDaBa.
- The body of the message contains the text The KDE Image Database.
- All of the above.

The actions may include the following:

- Reply to the sender that you are on holiday.
- Forward the letter to another person.
- Save the letter to a file.
- Change some part of the letter (e.g., add a new header field, add some text to it etc.).

Before you dig too much into the details of this section, you should ask yourself if you really want to use Procmail at all. Many mail clients allow you to sort mail, and if we take KMail as an example, then it is much easier to use than Procmail. The following is a list of reasons why you may still want to use Procmail:

- You are using a number of different mail clients, not always the same. For example, when you are on the road you use a web mail interface, but when you are home you use a normal mail client such as KMail or *mutt*.
- You want to filter your mail the second it arrives, not at a later point when your mail client downloads it—an example of this may be out-of-the-office replies.

- The amount of mail coming to your account is so big that you want filtering to be done before mail is loaded into your client (your client may be slow at filtering mail).

Preparing Procmail for Use

Procmail comes with most modern Linux systems nowadays, but should it not be available for your system, then you should have a look at *http://www.procmail.org*. At this site you will also find a large collection of sample recipes.

When you have ensured that Procmail is on your system, it is time to check if it is invoked by your MUA. The easiest way to do so is to place the following *.procmailrc* file in your home directory, and send yourself an email.

```
SHELL=/bin/sh
MAILDIR=${HOME}/Mail
LOGFILE=${MAILDIR}/procmail.log
LOG="--- Logging ${LOGFILE} for ${LOGNAME}, "
```

If the *~/Mail* directory does not exist, then you need to create it for this script to work. If you store your email elsewhere, replace ${HOME}/Mail with the alternative location. Also please check that */bin/sh* exists (it's quite likely that it does); otherwise, adapt the script.

If Procmail is invoked by default, then the file just shown should give you *~/Mail/procmail.log*, with content similar to the following:

```
--- Logging /home/test/Mail/procmail.log for test, From blackie@blackie.dk  Fri Mar
18 12:25:23 2005
 Subject: Fri Mar 18 12:25:22 CET 2005
  Folder: /var/spool/mail/test
```

If this file didn't come into existence by sending yourself an email, don't panic. All you need to do is to add the following line to the *~/.forward* file:

```
|IFS=' ' && exec /usr/bin/procmail || exit 75 #myid
```

Replace /usr/bin/procmail with the path to your system's Procmail binary, and replace myid with your login name. (This part is necessary to avoid problems with MUAs trying to optimize mail delivery.)

Now send yourself a mail again, and check if it works this time. If you still do not see the file, then it might be a result of a system that is too closed. Check that the *.procmailrc* and *.forward* files are readable by others, and perhaps only writable by yourself. Possibly you also need to add the *x* flag to the attributes of your home directory, which you may do with this command:

```
chmod go+x ~/
```

If things still do not work, then it is time to panic—or at least consult the vendor of your Linux system.

Setting up a sandbox

Are you ready to lose your email while playing with Procmail? If not, then it might be a good idea to create a sandbox for your tests. To do so, create a *Test* directory, and copy your *.procmailrc* file into that directory and name it *proctest.rc*. Now edit this file instead of your *real .procmailrc* file when testing things. In the *Test* directory, create this shell script:

```
#!/bin/sh
#The executable file named "proctest"
#
# You need a test directory.
TESTDIR=~/Test
if [ ! -d ${TESTDIR} ] ; then
  echo "Directory ${TESTDIR} does not exist; First create it"
  exit 0
fi

procmail ${TESTDIR}/proctest.rc < mail.msg
```

You may wish to adjust the LOGFILE line of the *proctest.rc* file so it doesn't write to your existing logfile, but instead simply writes to a logfile in the *Test* subdirectory. You may also want to add the following line to get improved debugging output from Procmail:

```
VERBOSE=yes
LOGABSTRACT=all
```

Finally you are ready to run the tests, which you do by placing a mail message in the file *mail.msg*, and running the script *proctest*. Most email programs allow you to save just one email to a file. Alternatively, send yourself an email, and copy it out of your */var/spool/mail/your-login* file.

Recipe Syntax

With all the preparation done, we may now start looking at recipes. Recipes all follow this style:

```
:0 [flags] [ : [locallockfile] ]
  <0 or more conditions (one per line)>
  <exactly one action line>
```

Conditions start with a leading *. Everything after that character is passed on to the internal *egrep* literally, except for leading and trailing whitespace.

The action line may take several forms:

- If it starts with a !, then the rest of the line is considered an email address to forward to.
- If it starts with a |, then the rest of the line is considered a shell command to be executed.

- If it starts with a {, then everything until the matching } is considered a nested block. Nested blocks consist of a number of recipes.
- Anything else is considered a mailbox name.

The flags are a combination of a number of one-letter flags. The flags are described in Table 23-1 (taken from the procmailrc manpage). There is no need to read the table in detail now; instead, simply look back to it as we show examples in the following sections.

Table 23-1. Procmail flags

Flag	Function
H	Perform an extended regular expression search on the header (default).
B	Perform an extended regular expression search on the body.
D	Check against the regular expression in a case-sensitive manner (default is case-insensitive).
A	Execute the recipe only if there was a match on the most recent recipe without an *A* or *a* flag in the current block nesting level.
a	Same as *A*, but the preceding recipe must have completed successfully.
E	Execute the recipe only if the immediately preceding recipe was not executed. Execution of this recipe also disables any immediately following recipes with the E flag. This allows you to specify else if actions.
e	Execute the recipe only if the immediately preceding recipe was executed but did not complete successfully.
h	Send contents of header to the pipe, file, or mail destination (default).
b	Send contents of body to the pipe, file, or mail destination (default).
c	Create a copy of the mail message so it can be further processed by a later recipe, or delivered.
w	Wait for processing program and check its exit code.
W	Same as *w*, but suppresses any Program failure message.
i	Ignore any write errors (usually due to a closed pipe).
r	Raw mode. Do not ensure that message ends with an empty line.

Conditions are generally regular expressions found in the header or body of the email. Regular expressions are covered in Chapter 19. But some other special conditions can be used. To select them, the condition must start with one of the flags shown in Table 23-2.

Table 23-2. Procmail condition flags

Condition	Function
!	Act only if the specified condition is false.
$	Interpret text with double quotes in the rest of this condition as it would be interpreted in the bash shell
?	Use the exit code.
<	Run recipe on messages with a total length less than the following number.

Table 23-2. Procmail condition flags (continued)

Condition	Function
>	Run recipe on messages with a total length greater than the following number.
variable	Match the following text against the value of this variable, which can be an environment variable or a combination of B for body and H for header
\	Escapes (leaves as a plain character) any of the entries in this table when it should start the line as a plain character without special meaning.

Examples

Procmail recipes are most easily understood through a number of examples, so the rest of this section will show examples of normal Procmail usage. See the manpage procmailex for more examples.

Each of the examples are simple recipes, not complete Procmail scripts, so you still need the initial content shown in "Preparing Procmail for Use."

Finally, when playing with recipes, remember that Procmail processes them in order. Thus, if a recipe marks mail as delivered, it doesn't show up with other recipes.

Making a backup of all incoming mail

When you are playing around with Procmail, there is a risk that you might develop a recipe that throws away messages that should not have been thrown away. It is therefore a very good idea to use the following recipe which is supposed to be the very first recipe in your Procmail setup:

```
:0c:
backup
```

The first line of this recipe has the flag c, which says that even though this recipe matches (which it always will, as the recipe has no conditions), the mail should continue on to other recipes, rather than be stopped here.

After the flag, there is a colon, indicating that the recipe should use a local lock. Thus, before the actions of this recipe can execute, the lock must first be obtained; while the action is executing, the lock will be in place.

The final part of the recipe is the text backup, which indicates that the mail will end in the mailbox named *backup*. If *$MAIL/backup* is a directory, the mail will be put in a unique named file in that directory (this is known as *maildir* storage). Alternatively, if *$MAIL/backup* is a file, the mail will be appended to that file (this is known as *mbox storage*).

Storing mail from a mailing list in a special mailbox

The next recipe might be what you most often do with Procmail—namely, to save mail from a mailing list into a dedicated mailbox. This is done with a recipe looking like this:

```
:0:
* Return-Path:.*kde-devel-bounces
kde-devel
```

Notice that this time we do not use the c flag, because we want mail from this mailing list to stay in the *kde-devel* mailbox, and not get to our inbox.

The line starting with an asterisk is the condition that must be met for this recipe to be triggered. This line is a regular expression that says that the header of the mail must contain the text Return-Path:, then any text (the regular expression .*), and then the text kde-devel-bounces. We got the idea for this regular expression by looking in an email from the mailing list. The trick is always to find a regular expression that will match any mail from the mailing list, but not match any other mail.

Forward messages as SMS

The following recipe forwards a message with a subject starting with the text SMS to a mobile phone in the form of a text message through an imaginary email-to-SMS gateway.

```
:0
* < 1000
* Subject: SMS
! 12345678@smsgateway.com
```

This recipe contains two conditions: the first is that the overall size of the letter be less than 1000 bytes, and the second is that the subject should start with SMS.

The action of this recipe starts with an exclamation mark, which indicates that the message is forwarded to the address following the exclamation mark.

Sending an out-of-office reply

The final example we show is how to send an out-of-office reply. Many systems provide a program named *vacation* that does this in a fairly robust way, but we provide something more customizable here so you can vary the message in any way your scripting skills allow. The basic recipe looks like this:

```
:0c
* !^FROM_DAEMON
* !^X-Loop: your@own.mail.address
{
    SUBJECT=`formail -zx subject:`

    :0
    | (formail -r -I"Precedence: junk" \
```

```
        -A"X-Loop: your@own.mail.address" ; \
        echo "I recived the mail with the subject \"$SUBJECT.\""; \
        echo "I'm out of the office and will answer it as soon as possible") |
    $SENDMAIL -t
  }
```

Starting with the conditions again, this recipe sends an out-of-office reply only if (1) the mail is not from a mailer daemon, and (2) the mail does not contain the header line X-Loop: your@own.mail.address (this should, of course, be replaced with your actual email address). The first condition ensures we do not send out-of-office replies to mailing lists, and the second condition ensures we do not end up in a mail loop with someone else's out-of-office filter.

The action to take when these two conditions are met is a block of recipes. Whatever it says in between the braces is interpreted as if it were a normal Procmail script. If execution makes it to the end of the block (i.e., the mail has not yet been delivered), it will continue execution outside the block. This is, however, not the case in our setup.

The first line of the block is an assignment to the variable SUBJECT. The value comes from standard output from the *formail* command. This is a binary shipped with Procmail; its purpose is to either manipulate the emails or subtract part of them.

The second part of the block is the part that does the core work. It composes an answer and mails it back to the person who originally sent you an email. Let's take it bit by bit.

First we call *formail -r* to create an auto respond header from the incoming mail. That means that it will throw away headers that you do not want in the reply. We also hand the command-line options -I"Precedence: junk" and -A"X-Loop: your@own.mail.address" to *formail*. These two switches basically add new headers to the mail: the first telling the precedence of the mail, and the second adding the line that our condition checks against in order to avoid mail loops.

So far we have echoed the header of the reply mail to standard output. On standard output, we next print the out-of-office reply (i.e., the body part of the email). The whole mail is finally sent to *sendmail*. The -t option tells *sendmail* to look into the mail to figure out who it is meant for.

Filtering Spam

The constant flood of so-called spam (more precisely, unsolicited commercial email) has decreased the usefulness of email as a communication medium considerably. Luckily, there are tools that can help us with that as well. These are called *spam filters*, and what they do is to attempt to categorize each incoming message according to a large number of rules to determine whether it is spam. The filters then mark up the message with either certain additional header lines or a changed subject line. It is then your task (or your mail user agent's task) to sort the messages according to these criteria into separate folders (or, quite dangerously, into the trash can directly). At the end of the day, you decide how aggressively you want to handle spam. You need to make up your mind what is more important to you: to filter out as much spam as possible, or to ensure that no important message (such as a request from a potential customer) will ever get filtered out.

There are two different ways of using a spam filter: either directly on the mail server, or in your email client. Filtering directly on the mail server is advantageous if the mail server serves more than one mail client, because then the same set of filtering rules can be applied and maintained for all users connected to this mail server, and a message coming in to several users on this server only needs to pass the spam filter once, which saves processing time. On the other hand, filtering on the client side allows you to define your own rules and filter spam completely.

The best-known spam filter in the Linux world (even though it is by no means Linux-dependent) is a tool called SpamAssassin. You can find lots of information about SpamAssassin at its home page, *http://spamassassin.spache.org*. SpamAssassin can work both on the server and on the client; we'll leave it to you to read the ample documentation available on the web site for installing SpamAssassin on a Postfix (or other) mail server.

When SpamAssassin is run on a server, the best way to use it is to let it run in client/server mode. That way, the large tables that SpamAssassin needs do not have to be reread for each message. Instead, SpamAssassin runs as a daemon process called *spamd*, which is accessed for each message by a frontend command called *spamc*.

If you want to configure your email client to use SpamAssassin, you need to pipe every incoming email through the command *spamassassin* (you can even use the *spamc/spamd* combo on the client, of course). *spamassassin* will accept the incoming message on standard input, analyze it, and write the changed message to standard output. Most modern mail user agents have facilities for piping all (or just some) incoming messages through an external command, so you should almost always find a way to hook up *spamassassin* somehow.

If SpamAssassin has analyzed your message to be spam, it will add the header line:

    X-Spam-Status: Yes

to your message. It is then up to you to configure the filters in your email client to do to this message whatever you want to be done to spam (sort into a separate folder, move directly to the trash can, etc.). If you want to do more detailed filtering, you can also look at the header line starting with:

    X-Spam-Status:

This marker is followed by a number of stars; the more stars there are, the more likely the message is spam.

Before we look at one email client in more detail, to sum up, you need to do two things in order to set up SpamAssassin on the client:

- Configure your mail client to pipe each incoming message through the *spam-assassin* command.
- According to the header lines added by SpamAssassin, filter the message per your personal requirements.

You can even use the *procmail* command that we covered in the previous section to pass the email messages through *spamassassin*. *http://wiki.apache.org/spamassassin/UsedViaProcmail* has ample information about how to do this.

As an example of how you can set up an email client to support SpamAssassin, we will look at KMail, the KDE email client. KMail allows you to perform the steps just mentioned, of course. But it can also automate the procedure by means of the anti-spam wizard. You can invoke it from Tools → Anti-Spam Wizard. This tool first scans for the available anti-spam tools on your system (searching for a couple more than just SpamAssassin), and then lets you select those that you want KMail to use. It is not a good idea to just select all available tools here, because each additional filtering slows down the processing of incoming email messages.

On the next page of the wizard, you will be given a number of options of what to do with spam. You should check at least "Classify messages using the anti-spam tools" and "Move detected messages to the selected folder." Then select a target folder for messages that are quite sure to be spam, and a target folder for messages where it is a bit less certain. Once you click Finish, KMail sets up all the necessary filter rules for you, and on your next email download, you can watch the spam folders filling. Your inbox should be, if not completely spam-free, then still a lot more free from spam than previously.

SpamAssassin has a lot of functionality that we have not covered at all here. For example, it contains a Bayes filter that operates on statistical data. When a spam message that comes into the system is not marked as spam, you can teach Spam-Assassin to recognize similar messages as spam in the future. Likewise, if a message is erroneously recognized as spam, you can teach SpamAssassin to not consider messages like it as spam in the future (but rather *ham*, as the opposite of spam is often called). Please see the SpamAssassin documentation on how to set this up.

We have now discussed a number of options that you have when setting up your email system. Our advice is to start slowly, setting up one piece at a time and making sure that everything works after each step; trying to perform the whole setup in one go can be quite challenging.

Running an FTP Server

In this chapter, we go through the steps that are necessary to set up your own FTP server. In particular, we concentrate on the *ProFTPD* server, a very stable, open source implementation of an FTP server with many features.

Introduction

ProFTPD is a highly configurable, GPL-licensed FTP server. It strives to be the FTP server equivalent of the Apache web server. It might not be the leanest and meanest FTP server out there, but it is certainly one of the most flexible ones. ProFTPD is used, for example, by SourceForge.

ProFTPD is available from *http://www.proftpd.org*.

Compiling and Installing

If your distribution does not come with ProFTPD, you can either compile and install it from the source tarball or use a package appropriate for your distribution. RPM-based distributions can install the RPM from *http://proftpd.org*. Debian users can enter *apt-get install proftpd*.

RPM Install

Unless there is a specific binary RPM for your distribution, download the source RPM and build it: *rpmbuild --rebuild proftpd-1.2.10-1.src.rpm*. This will produce two installable RPMs: *proftpd-1.2.10-1.i586.rpm*, which contains the actual software, and *proftpd-inetd-1.2.10-1.i586.rpm*, which contains the support files for running ProFTPD from *xinetd*. The *proftpd-inetd* RPM is optional, and we will not cover it in this book. Install the main RPM after the build completes:

```
# rpm -ivh /usr/src/packages/RPMS/i586/proftpd-1.2.10-1.i586.rpm
```

The RPMs seem to be tailored for Red Hat, so if you use SUSE, you need to do a few adjustments. The *rc* script installs to */etc/rc.d/init.d/proftpd*, which isn't the right location on SUSE; also, the script itself will not work. Instead, use the following replacement script and copy it to */etc/rc.d/proftpd*:

```
#!/bin/sh
#
# Startup script for ProFTPD
#
# chkconfig: 345 85 15
# description: ProFTPD is an enhanced FTP server with \
#              a focus toward simplicity, security, and ease of configuration. \
#              It features a very Apache-like configuration syntax, \
#              and a highly customizable server infrastructure, \
#              including support for multiple 'virtual' FTP servers, \
#              anonymous FTP, and permission-based directory visibility.
# processname: proftpd
# config: /etc/proftpd.conf

PROFTPD=/usr/sbin/proftpd
PATH="$PATH:/usr/sbin"

if [ -f /etc/sysconfig/proftpd ]; then
     . /etc/sysconfig/proftpd
fi

. /etc/rc.status
rc_reset

# See how we were called.
case "$1" in
  start)
    echo -n "Starting proftpd: "
    startproc $PROFTPD $OPTIONS
    rc_status -v
    ;;
  stop)
    echo -n "Shutting down proftpd: "
    killproc -TERM $PROFTPD
    rc_status -v
    ;;
  try-restart)
    $0 status
    if test $? = 0; then
      $0 restart
    else
      rc_reset  # Not running is not a failure.
    fi
    # Remember status and be quiet
    rc_status
    ;;
  status)
    checkproc $PROFTPD
```

```
        rc_status -v
        ;;
    restart)
        $0 stop
        $0 start
        rc_status
        ;;
    reload)
        echo -n "Re-reading proftpd config: "
        killproc -HUP $PROFTPD
        rc_status -v
        ;;
    suspend)
        hash ftpshut>/dev/null 2>&1
        if [ $? = 0 ]; then
            if [ $# -gt 1 ]; then
                shift
                echo -n "Suspending with '$*' "
                ftpshut $*
            else
                echo -n "Suspending NOW "
                ftpshut now "Maintanance in progress"
            fi
        else
            echo -n "No way to suspend "
        fi
        echo
        ;;
    resume)
        if [ -f /etc/shutmsg ]; then
            echo -n "Allowing sessions again "
            rm -f /etc/shutmsg
        else
            echo -n "Was not suspended "
        fi
        echo
        ;;
    *)
        echo -n "Usage: $0 {start|stop|restart|try-restart|status|reload|resume"
        hash ftpshut
        if [ $? = 1 ]; then
            echo '}'
        else
            echo '|suspend}'
            echo 'suspend accepts additional arguments which are passed to ftpshut(8)'
        fi
        exit 1
esac
rc_exit
```

Of course, this could be fixed in a later version.

Compiling from Source

Download the tarball, unpack, configure, and build:

```
$ tar xfj proftpd-1.2.10.tar.bz2
$ cd proftpd-1.2.10
$ ./configure --prefix=/usr/local/packages/proftpd
$ make
```

Then, as root, run *make install*. This will install everything to */usr/local/ packages/proftpd/*.

Running ProFTPD

Starting the server
>   When the *rc* script is in place, the server can be started with */etc/rc.d/proftpd start* (*/etc/init.d/proftpd start* on Debian).

Stopping the server
>   To shut the FTP daemon down, run */etc/rc.d/proftpd stop*.

Temporarily suspending the server
>   With */etc/rc.d/proftpd suspend* you can stop ProFTPD from accepting new connections. Users who try to log in will be greeted with a banner telling them that the server is down for maintenance. To resume normal operations, run */etc/rc.d/proftpd resume*.

Debugging
>   While troubleshooting or writing the ProFTPD configuration file, it is often useful to get some extra information about what is going on. *proftpd -vv* will print out some version information, *proftpd --nodaemon* will run the daemon without becoming a background process, and *proftpd -t* will check the syntax of the current configuration file. Output verbosity can be increased by running ProFTPD like this: *proftpd -d9*. The options *-d0* to *-d9* can be combined with the other options.

Configuration

Getting Started

Both the RPM and tarball installations provide a default configuration with a read-only anonymous FTP area and full regular access to users on the system. This is a good starting point if all you want is to offer anonymous FTP access.

The configuration file for ProFTPD is */etc/proftpd.conf* or *$prefix/etc/proftpd.conf* if installed from source. The anonymous FTP users are *chroot( )*ed into the home directory of the FTP user, often something like */srv/ftp/*.

proftpd.conf contains a number of *configuration directives*. A reference of all directives can be found at *http://www.proftpd.org/docs/directives/configuration_full.html*. The configuration file is divided up into a number of *contexts*, each dealing with its own aspect of ProFTPD:

Main server
>   The part of the configuration file that is not inside any other context. This is used for global server settings and is typically found at the beginning of the file.

<Anonymous>
>   This context is used for configuration details for an anonymous FTP server. By default, ProFTPD will allow anonymous access without a password and *chroot( )* to the FTP directory.

<Directory>
>   This context is used to specify configuration details on a per-directory basis. This is typically used to limit or give access.

<Limit>
>   This context is used to control access to FTP commands and groups of FTP commands based on which user is trying to use them.

<Global>
>   This context is used with virtual hosting (i.e., having ProFTPD serving on multiple interfaces with different configurations). Directives in this context are used as if they were in the main server context, with the exception that they can be overridden by any <VirtualHost> context.

<VirtualHost>
>   With <VirtualHost> contexts it is possible to create independent sets of configurations for different network interfaces and ports.

The following sections present two example configurations for ProFTPD: a basic Unix FTP server setup and a more advanced one in which ProFTPD is using its own user database.

Basic Configuration

The example configuration provides us with both an anonymous access area and access to the whole filesystem for regular users:

```
ServerName      "ProFTPD Default Installation"
ServerType      standalone
```

ServerName specifies the banner text that the user sees when accessing the server. ServerType can be either standalone or inetd and specifies whether ProFTPD is listening for incoming connections by itself or is being run from *(x)inetd*.

```
DefaultServer               on
Port                        21
```

`DefaultServer` on means that our server configuration applies to all interfaces of the host, and `Port` specifies the port ProFTPD is listening to (port 21 is the standard FTP port):

```
Umask                          022
MaxInstances                   30
User                           nobody
Group                          nogroup
AllowOverwrite                 on
<Limit SITE_CHMOD>
DenyAll
</Limit>
```

`Umask` is equivalent to the *umask* setting in the shell. `MaxInstances` is the upper limit on concurrent ProFTPD child processes; this limits the number of simultaneous users to 30. `User` and `Group` specify the user and group ProFTPD will run under when not doing privileged operations or running with the privileges of an authenticated user. `AllowOverwrite` on means that users are allowed to overwrite writable files. The `<Limit>` section blocks everybody from using the *site chmod* command.

```
<Anonymous ~ftp>
User                           ftp
Group                          ftp
UserAlias                      anonymous ftp
MaxClients                     10
DisplayLogin                   welcome.msg
DisplayFirstChdir              .message
<Limit WRITE>
DenyAll
</Limit>
</Anonymous>
```

This part of the configuration file sets up a read-only anonymous FTP in the FTP user's home directory (often */srv/ftp*) running as user *ftp*, with a maximum of 10 simultaneous users. `DisplayLogin welcome.msg` will display the contents of the file *welcome.msg* as the login banner, and `DisplayFirstChdir .message` will display the contents of the file *.message* in the current directory when the user first *cd*s into it.

Advanced Configuration

Here we look at a more complex setup in which the users allowed to log in to the FTP server are not taken from the regular Unix user database, but instead from a *passwd* file exclusive to ProFTPD. In addition, we provide limited anonymous access.

The *proftpd.conf* file looks like this:

```
ServerName                     "Acme ftp server"
ServerType                     standalone
DefaultServer                  on
ServerIdent on                 "FTP Server ready."
UseReverseDNS                  off
IdentLookups                   off
```

```
DeferWelcome                    on
Port                            21
MaxInstances                    30
User                            ftp
Group                           nogroup
Umask                           022

<Limit LOGIN>
    Order Deny,Allow
    AllowGroup ftpusers
</Limit>

AuthPAM off
AuthUserFile /etc/proftpd.passwd
AuthGroupFile /etc/proftpd.group
RequireValidShell off
DefaultRoot ~
DirFakeUser on ~
DirFakeGroup on ~

DisplayLogin                    welcome.msg
DisplayFirstChdir               .message

TransferLog        /var/log/xferlog

ScoreboardFile /var/lib/proftpd/scoreFile

<Directory />
  AllowOverwrite                on
</Directory>

<Anonymous /srv/ftp/anonymous>
  User                          ftp
  Group                         ftp
  # We want clients to be able to login with "anonymous" as well as "ftp"
  UserAlias                     anonymous ftp
  # Limit the maximum number of anonymous logins
  MaxClients                    15
  <Limit LOGIN>
    AllowAll
  </Limit>
  # Limit WRITE everywhere in the anonymous chroot
  <Limit WRITE>
    DenyAll
  </Limit>
  TransferRate RETR 40.0:1024
</Anonymous>

<Directory /srv/ftp/joe/upload>
  <Limit WRITE STOR DEL>
        AllowAll
  </Limit>
</Directory>
```

Let us first have a look at how users are handled. FTP is an old protocol that sends passwords unencrypted over the wire, so it is desirable to separate users with "real" accounts from users with FTP-only accounts. To do this, we use two configuration directives,

```
AuthUserFile /etc/proftpd.passwd
AuthGroupFile /etc/proftpd.group
```

to point ProFTPD at alternative *passwd* and *group* files. The format is the same as the regular Linux */etc/passwd* and */etc/group* files. The contents of */etc/proftpd.passwd* for testing purposes are as follows:

```
joe:$1$KdLsLL1G$LNGq21xp9l/4vhF/l/0N1.:20000:20000:Joe User:/srv/ftp/joe:
```

The password is "qwerty" in cleartext and is hashed using the *ftpasswd* utility that can be found in the *contrib* directory in the ProFTPD tarball. */etc/proftpd.group* contains only a single line: ftpusers:x:20000: This is used in conjunction with the

```
<Limit LOGIN>
Order Deny,Allow
AllowGroup ftpusers
</Limit>
```

section in the configuration file to block regular users from logging in and to allow only members of our special group *ftpusers* to log in. Notice that this is not the same as the legacy file */etc/ftpusers*, which can be used for listing system users who are *not* allowed to use FTP. The documentation states that the file specified in AuthUserFile *replaces* the system */etc/passwd* file, but this seems not to be the case currently— hence the special group to only allow users listed in our alternative *passwd* file.

It is possible to have multiple users in */etc/proftpd.passwd* with the same Unix numeric user ID. This is useful if you want to provide FTP access for a huge number of users without running out of user IDs. To make files appear to be owned by the currently authenticated user and group, we put in the:

```
DirFakeUser on ~
DirFakeGroup on ~
```

directives. This is only for cosmetic purposes to give users the nice fuzzy feeling that they in fact own their files. The ScoreboardFile directive specifies the location of the file used for runtime session information. This file is required for utilities such as *ftp-who* and *ftpcount* to work. This completes the main server configuration.

The next part of the config file is a read-only <Anonymous> context for users *anonymous* and *ftp* in */srv/ftp/anonymous*, with a maximum of 15 concurrent users. There is also a download rate limit specified by the TransferRate RETR 40.0:1024 directive. The numbers mean that the download rate is limited to 40 KB per second for all files larger than 1 KB.

The last context of the config file specifies a writable directory */upload* for the user *joe*. By default nothing is writable for any user because of the <Limit WRITE> directive in the main server context, so user *joe* is granted the special privilege to be allowed to upload files to his *upload* directory.

Virtual Hosts

ProFTPD supports virtual hosting via the <VirtualHost> context. The FTP protocol unfortunately does not support host-based virtual hosting, unlike, for example, HTTP, but it is still possible to serve different ports or network interfaces with different configurations. All this will, of course, only work if ProFTPD is run in standalone mode; if run from *inetd*, the ports and interfaces that are listened to are in the hands of *inetd* and not ProFTPD.

Let's look at an example with a few virtual hosts configured:

```
ServerName       "Acme FTP Server"
ServerType       standalone

### Main server config
# Set the user and group that the server normally runs at.
User             nobody
Group            nogroup
MaxInstances     30

# Global creates a "global" configuration that is shared by the
# main server and all virtualhosts.

<Global>
  # Umask 022 is a good standard umask
  # to prevent new dirs and files
  # from being group and world writable.
  Umask          022
</Global>

### Virtual server running on our internal interface
<VirtualHost 127.0.0.1>
   ServerName   "Acme Internal FTP"
   MaxClients       10
   DeferWelcome     on
   <Limit LOGIN>
     DenyAll
   </Limit>
   <Anonymous /srv/ftp/anonymous-internal>
     User           ftp
     Group          ftp
     AnonRequirePassword  off
     # We want clients to be able to login
     # with "anonymous" as well as "ftp"
     UserAlias      anonymous ftp
     <Limit LOGIN>
       AllowAll
     </Limit>
```

```
    # Limit WRITE everywhere in the anonymous chroot
    <Limit WRITE>
      DenyAll
    </Limit>
  </Anonymous>
</VirtualHost>

### Another virtual host on port 4000
<VirtualHost 192.168.1.5>
  ServerName  "Acme Internal FTP upload"
  Port            4000
  MaxClients      10
  MaxLoginAttempts 1
  DeferWelcome    on
  <Limit LOGIN>
    DenyAll
  </Limit>
  <Anonymous /srv/ftp/anonymous-upload>
    User            ftp
    Group           ftp
    AnonRequirePassword  off
    # We want clients to be able to login with
    # "anonymous" as well as "ftp"
    UserAlias       anonymous ftp
    <Limit LOGIN>
      AllowAll
    </Limit>
    # We only allow upload
    <Limit STOR CWD XCWD>
      AllowAll
    </Limit>
    <Limit READ DELE MKD RMD XMKD XRMD>
      DenyAll
    </Limit>
  </Anonymous>
</VirtualHost>
```

The example is a pretty standard main server that allows Unix users access to the filesystem. The interesting parts are the two <VirtualHost> sections. The first one is an anonymous-only server listening to the localhost (127.0.0.1) interface (not particularly useful, I admit), and the second one is an anonymous-only, write-only server listening to port 4000 on the 192.168.1.5 interface.

## PART IV

Network Services

In this part of the book, we introduce you to the things that really make Linux powerful and popular: such tools as a web server, email delivery tools, a database, and some of the other features on the cutting edge of system use. We also show you ways to protect your system and hedge against potential disasters.

## CHAPTER 25

Running Web Applications with MySQL and PHP

Just writing a couple of lines of HTML code is not enough for most web sites; dynamic content is what people want today. To tell the truth, most commercial web sites offer more dynamic content than visitors really want—Flash-driven animations that greet you instead of useful information, for instance, or interactive JavaScript menus that make information harder to retrieve instead of easier—but in this chapter we give you an introduction to offering basic dynamic content that's really useful.

Linux is—you guessed it—an excellent platform for serving dynamic content. A bazillion web sites serving dynamic content are already running on Linux today; this is one of the foremost application areas where Linux excels.

Dynamic content can be achieved by two entirely different ways of programming: server-side programming and client-side programming. JavaScript, Java applets, and the Microsoft-specific ActiveX platform are the most common ways of producing interactive HTML pages with client-side programming.

Because of limitations in these technologies, however, most sites with substantial information to deliver use server-side programs. You can use them in many different flavors with many different software packages, but one combination has become ubiquitous for implementing these techniques. This combination is so common nowadays that it even has received a phony acronym: LAMP, which is short for Linux-Apache-MySQL-PHP. We have already talked about the Apache web server, and this whole book is about Linux, so what we have left to talk about here are the latter two packages—MySQL and PHP—as well as how the four packages go together.

To obtain a working LAMP installation, you will need to have Apache set up as described in "Configuring Your Own Web Server" in Chapter 22, as well as to install MySQL and PHP. We will cover how to get the latter two applications running in this chapter.

Before we get into the technical details, however, we should review why you might want to bother setting up and learning how to use a LAMP system.

LAMP makes it easy to provide a large amount of content and allow users of your web site to navigate through it easily.

Let's say you have a site with lots of JPEGs of photographs you've taken on numerous occasions. Visitors may want to view photographs using a number of different criteria. That is, some visitors want to see photographs of historic buildings, whenever you took them. Others might want to see photographs taken on your latest trip, whenever that was.

To make navigation and retrieval easy, you start by inserting the information about your JPEGs into a MySQL database. (The JPEG files will remain on the filesystem where Apache can get to them quickly.) You organize them any way you want (by subject matter, by trip, and so on) and store all this information in tables within the database. In other words, data is stored in tables, and a number of related tables make up a database.

Now you provide a form on your web site that visitors can fill out to indicate the dimension along which they want to view photographs. The form could be as simple as that shown in Figure 25-1.

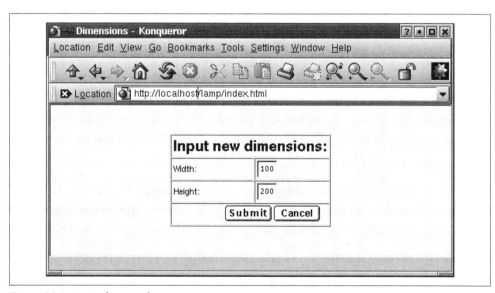

Figure 25-1. A simple input form

Your next page is a dynamic one, along the lines of that which we describe in this chapter. A bit of PHP code retrieves the visitor's request and determines what is displayed in the page. This could look like Figure 25-2.

Where is the MySQL in all this? It's not immediately visible, but it plays a crucial role behind the scenes because it is queried by the PHP code. The combination of inline PHP code and a fast database makes the whole experience fairly pleasant for the visitor.

Figure 25-2. A dynamic web page generated by PHP

MySQL

MySQL is an open source database that is very fast and comparatively easy to administer. If you need the most advanced database features, such as replication or distributed databases, or if you plan to store gigabytes of data, the big-iron databases such as Oracle might be a better choice, but for most intents and purposes, MySQL is an excellent database choice (and it is in fact catching up even when it comes to those very advanced features). It is dual-licensed. If you are using the GPL version, your application must be licensed under the GPL as well; otherwise, you need to buy the commercial version.

MySQL Installation and Initial Configuration

It is very likely that your distribution contains an installable MySQL system, but if you'd rather have the latest and greatest, you can go to *http://www.mysql.com/downloads* and download the package yourself. At the time of this writing, the latest

On the Choice of Databases

We should probably point out that MySQL is not the only choice you have when selecting a database as the backend for dynamic web sites. For example, Postgres, which is installed by default on Red Hat systems, is a very good open source database as well. So, if you want to deploy a "LAPP" system and use Postgres instead, you can very well do that. Most of the information in this chapter will still apply. However, MySQL can be considered the standard database for dynamic web sites on Linux systems. This is due to its ease of use, speed, and versatility. Also, if you are looking for additional documentation on deploying dynamic web sites on Linux (which we strongly recommend you do), you are more likely to find this information (e.g., in the form of dedicated books on this topic) for MySQL than for Postgres.

stable version was 4.1.13. Version 5.0 was stabilizing quickly. If you plan to use MySQL for real-life applications, make sure your Linux kernel is at 2.4 or better.

A problem that can occur with MySQL versions compiled with *gcc* 2.96 is random crashes. This *gcc* version is not an official stable version, but at least one distributor (Red Hat) unfortunately shipped it as the default compiler in one version. So if you experience strange crashes in the database server and are using *gcc* 2.96, try using one of the precompiled binaries or install a more stable (and more recent) compiler version, such as 3.3.5.

If you want to build MySQL on your own, you need to download the source package, unpack it, and install with the following commands:

```
owl$ ./configure --prefix=/usr/local/mysql
owl$ make
owl# make install
```

Note that depending on your system, you might select a different installation path. You will also probably need to be *root* for the third step. You need to remember the installation path because you will need it for the PHP configuration later on.

For the next step, we recommend that you create a user and a group called *mysql* as described in "Creating Accounts" in Chapter 11. Change to this user with *su - mysql* and execute:

```
owl$ scripts/mysql_install_db
```

For security reasons, it might be a good idea to disable logins by the *mysql* user. You can simply do this as *root* by putting a star in the second (password) column in */etc/password* or */etc/shadow*, or both.

After this step, you need to perform just one more command before returning from *root* to your normal user account. The following command starts the MySQL server:

```
owl# /usr/local/mysql/bin/mysqld_safe &
```

You might also want to add either the option -- *log* or the option -- *log-long-format* in order to get a logfile about what is going on in the database server.

To check whether your server was started correctly, you can try (as a normal user again) the following command (you need to change the path, of course, if you have installed MySQL in a different location):

```
owl$ /usr/local/mysql/bin/mysqladmin version
mysqladmin  Ver 8.41 Distrib 4.1.13, for suse-linux on i686
Copyright (C) 2000 MySQL AB & MySQL Finland AB & TCX DataKonsult AB
This software comes with ABSOLUTELY NO WARRANTY. This is free software,
and you are welcome to modify and redistribute it under the GPL license.

Server version          4.1.13
Protocol version    10
Connection              Localhost via UNIX socket
UNIX socket             /var/lib/mysql/mysql.sock
Uptime:                 43 days 11 hours 39 min 17 sec

Threads: 1  Questions: 142  Slow queries: 0  Opens: 160  Flush tables: 1  Open
tables: 13 Queries per second avg: 0.000
```

This should work without entering a password. We would like to point out, though, that it is not a good idea to have a database without a password because that increases the odds that a possible intruder will get at your potentially valuable data in the database. You might perhaps want to leave the database without a password for testing, but you should make sure that you do not forget to set a password after you are done with your tests. Retest to see whether everything works with the password in place. If you have created a password for the *root* database user (or if your distribution has done so for you—check your documentation in case of any problems), you must specify the *-p* option, which makes *mysqladmin* ask you for your password.

We should add here that most distributions include a startup script for the MySQL server that you can use instead of starting the server manually (especially if you have installed MySQL from your installation media). Often, this script is in */etc/init.d/ mysql*.

With the database server started and working, we can start to define database users and create new databases. We would like to point out that a usable tutorial is included with the MySQL sources. You can also find lots of documentation on *http:// www.mysql.com*, so we just cover the very basics here to get you started.

Initial Tasks: Setting Up Users and SQL

There are three ways of communicating with the MySQL engine: you can use a console-based database client, you can write so-called SQL scripts and feed them to the database in order to execute many SQL commands at once, and you can use one of the many bindings to programming languages to access the MySQL database in the programming language of your choice (depending on the access library that you use, this may even mean that you do not have to enter SQL statements at all). SQL stands for Structured Query Language and is the database language used with relational databases; we cover its use later in this chapter. All three ways of executing SQL commands assume that you have the correct username/password combination.

An important thing you need to know about MySQL is that Linux user accounts are different from MySQL user accounts. In other words, MySQL has its own account management. Most people give their MySQL user accounts the same names as their Linux user accounts in order to avoid confusion, though.

By default, there is one MySQL account called *root*, which has no password (talk about "security by default"). This means that you can access the database server with the interactive command-line tool *mysql* as follows:

```
owl$ mysql -u root

Welcome to the MySQL monitor.  Commands end with ; or \g.
Your MySQL connection id is 13 to server version: 4.1.13.

Type 'help;' or '\h' for help. Type '\c' to clear the buffer.

mysql>
```

The *-u* option specifies the database user to use. If this does not work, maybe your MySQL installation has a password set for the *root* user. Try to find this password in the documentation and start the *mysql* program with:

```
owl$ mysql -u root -p
```

which will prompt you for the password.

Assuming that you have been able to log in to the database server, let's try to issue a command:*

```
mysql> show databases;
+-------------+
| Database    |
+-------------+
| mysql       |
| test        |
+-------------+
2 rows in set (0.11 sec)
```

This tells you that two databases are managed by this database server. One is called *mysql* and contains MySQL's internal configuration information, including the usernames, and the other one is called *test* and can be used by you for your experiments.

---

* This is not a real SQL command, but rather a MySQL administration command.

It's also no problem at all to create additional databases; we'll show you how in a minute. As you can see, all SQL commands need to be terminated with a semicolon—probably in order to make the C programmers happy.

Now you should give the *root* account a password (in case it does not have one already). This is done with two SQL commands:

```
mysql> SET PASSWORD FOR root=PASSWORD('new_topsecret_passwd');
mysql> FLUSH PRIVILEGES;
```

Notice again the semicolon at the end of these commands; if you forget to type them before pressing the Enter key, MySQL will just stare at you, waiting for you to enter more.

By the way, SQL commands are case-insensitive; we have written them in uppercase here because that makes it a bit easier to see where the command keywords and the variable parameters are in a SQL script.

Also note the use of the *FLUSH PRIVILEGES* command. This is important because only after this command has been executed will MySQL update its user database.

Now we want to create a new user called *olof*, which has the same access rights as *root*, except that it cannot create new users. Apart from that, *olof* may use and manipulate all MySQL databases on this database server:

```
mysql> GRANT ALL PRIVILEGES ON *.* TO olof@localhost IDENTIFIED BY 'olof_passwd';
mysql> FLUSH PRIVILEGES;
```

The user *olof* can log in to the database only from the local machine. This is a good idea since it leaves one less security issue to think about. We recommend that you only allow access from the local machine unless you have a very good reason not to do it this way. Even in the LAMP combo, local access is enough, because the web server process is running on the local machine, and this is the process that connects to the database, not the user's web browser process.

But if you really require access to the database over the network, you could use these commands instead:

```
mysql> GRANT ALL PRIVILEGES ON *.* TO username@"%"  IDENTIFIED BY 'user_passwd';
mysql> FLUSH PRIVILEGES;
```

If you think that having all access rights except creating new users is a bit too much, let's create another user that may execute the SELECT, INSERT, UPDATE, DELETE, and DROP operations, but only on the database called *test* (and only when connected from the local machine):

```
mysql> GRANT SELECT, INSERT, UPDATE, DELETE, DROP ON test.* TO gonzo@localhost
         IDENTIFIED BY 'gonzo_passwd';
mysql> FLUSH PRIVILEGES;
```

If you haven't worked with SQL databases before, these operations will probably not make much sense to you. Since you are going to need to use them anyway when setting up your LAMP system, we might as well shortly describe them here:

SELECT
> This is the most commonly used SQL command. It queries the database for data with certain properties—for example, you could ask for all customers in a certain town. SELECT never changes anything in the database.

INSERT
> This SQL command inserts new records into a database table. You use this (either interactively or, more likely, as part of a program) to insert a customer record into the customer table in your database, for example.

UPDATE
> This SQL command changes existing records in a database. You could use this to, for example, increase the retail prices of all articles in the database by 15%. (Talk about inflation!)

DELETE
> This SQL command deletes entire records from the database. Be careful with this command, as there is no way of restoring the data short of restoring from a (hopefully available) backup tape.

There are even more SQL commands and corresponding privileges (such as DROP, which lets you delete entire tables or even entire databases), but these are used less often than the "big four" listed here.

Now we want to create a new database, which we can then fill with tables and data later. This is done with the SQL command CREATE DATABASE:

```
mysql> create database test_database;
Query OK; 1 row affected (0.03 sec)
```

The output from MySQL already indicates that everything went fine, but to be really sure, we can ask anew which databases the server manages:

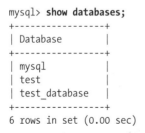
```
mysql> show databases;
+------------------+
| Database         |
+------------------+
| mysql            |
| test             |
| test_database    |
+------------------+
6 rows in set (0.00 sec)
```

Creating and Populating a Database

Now we want to define a table in our new database, but the first thing we need to do is tell the MySQL server that we actually want to use this database:

```
mysql> use test_database
Database changed
```

As you can see, we didn't use a semicolon at the end here, since this is again not a SQL command, but rather a control statement for the MySQL console client. It wouldn't hurt to add a semicolon here, too.

You define a table, which is ultimately where your data will be stored, by means of the SQL command CREATE TABLE. Here is an example:

```
mysql> CREATE TABLE comment_table(
    ->    id INT NOT NULL auto_increment,
    ->    comment TEXT,
    ->    PRIMARY KEY(id));
Query OK, 0 rows affected (0.10 sec)
```

Here we defined a table called comment_table with two columns—that is, there are two data fields in each record. One is called id. This serves as a unique identifier for each record and is therefore marked as the *primary key*, which is just a fancy term in database-speak for "unique identifier." The other column is a variable of type TEXT that can store up to 65,535 characters.

Now we can check which tables we have within our database test_database:

```
mysql> show tables;
+-------------------------+
| Tables_in_test_database |
+-------------------------+
| comment_table           |
+-------------------------+
1 row in set (0.00 sec)
```

Now we know that everything is all right and can start to add data records to our table. This is done with the SQL command INSERT:

```
mysql> INSERT INTO comment_table VALUES ('0','comment');
Query OK, 1 row affected (0.06 sec)
```

Finally, we can check which data our table contains:

```
mysql> SELECT * FROM comment_table;
+----+---------+
| id | comment |
+----+---------+
|  1 | comment |
+----+---------+
1 row in set (0.01 sec)
```

Here we ask for all (*) columns in the table comment_table. But you might have noticed something odd here: we have asked MySQL to insert a 0 in the first column, but instead there is a 1 now. That's because we have defined this column to be of the type INT NOT NULL auto_increment, which means that the column value cannot be NULL and that MySQL will automatically choose the next available value. This is nice because we can insert new records into the table without having to ensure that we pick unique values for the first column:

```
mysql> INSERT INTO comment_table VALUES ('0','comment1');
Query OK, 1 row affected (0.00 sec)

mysql> SELECT * FROM comment_table;
+----+----------+
| id | comment  |
+----+----------+
|  1 | comment  |
|  2 | comment1 |
+----+----------+
2 rows in set (0.00 sec)
```

As you can see, we have specified 0 as the value for the first column again, but MySQL has automatically selected the next available valid value.

At this point, you know already enough about MySQL to experiment yourself or start reading another book about databases and dream about building the next hugely successful e-commerce web site.

But before you enter your dream, take a moment and let us finish our MySQL discussion by letting you in on one more useful feature: SQL scripts.

You do not necessarily need to type in all commands at MySQL's own command-line prompt. You can also execute batch files with SQL commands by piping them to the *mysql* program. For example, if you save the following SQL code as *create_db.sql*:

```
DROP DATABASE IF EXISTS test_database;
CREATE DATABASE test_database;
USE test_database;
CREATE TABLE comment_table( id INT NOT NULL auto_increment,\
 comment TEXT,PRIMARY KEY(id));

INSERT INTO comment_table VALUES ('0','comment');
INSERT INTO comment_table VALUES ('0','comment1');
```

you can execute this script from the ordinary Linux command line with:

```
mysql -u root -p < create_db.sql
```

The line:

```
DROP DATABASE IF EXISTS test_database;
```

is of course pretty dangerous; you should use it only if you don't have important data in your database.

To tell the truth, it is not absolutely necessary (albeit strongly recommended) to create a new database for each project. In theory, you could lump all your data into the *test* database that is preinstalled with MySQL as long as you make sure the table names are all different. In practice, this would be a maintenance nightmare if you had more than a handful of tables.

PHP

To complete our combo of Linux, Apache, PHP, and MySQL, we still need the PHP language interpreter. PHP is a recursive acronym that expands to PHP: Hypertext Preprocessor. It has been in development for several years now; the versions most commonly used are Version 4 and Version 5. We use PHP4 in this chapter, because it was the most often used version at the time of writing. The changes between Versions 4 and 5 are either in underlying implementation or advanced features that will interest you only when you pile up a large number of PHP files.

Some Sample PHP

One of the nice things about PHP is that PHP code can be entered directly into HTML code. The web server will pass everything between <?php and ?> to the PHP module, which will interpret and execute the commands. Here is a very simple example for some PHP code in an HTML page; if you already have set up PHP, you could run this directly from your web server (if not, we'll tell you how to set up PHP shortly):

```
<html>
<body>
<?php
echo "Hi, ";
?>
LAMP enthusiasts.
</body>
</html>
```

As you probably already have expected, your browser will output the following text:

```
Hi, LAMP enthusiasts.
```

This extremely simple example shows how Apache works together with the PHP interpreter: the code between <?php and ?> is passed to the PHP interpreter, which executes the *echo* command, which in turn outputs its parameters to the web browser. In addition to this, the line LAMP enthusiasts is simply added as ordinary HTML text (and since it doesn't have any markup, it doesn't look like HTML).

Of course, PHP can do much more. Like most programming languages, it can use variables and make decisions, as in the following script (we leave out the HTML framework here for brevity):

```
<?php
echo "Dear friends, today's date is: ";
echo date("F d, Y")."\n";
echo "<br>";
echo "We are in the ";

if ( date ("m") <= 6 ) {
        echo "first ";
```

```
        } else {
        echo "second ";
    }
    echo "half of the year ".date("Y");
    ?>
```

You have probably already guessed that this script makes its decision in the `if` statement depending on the current month. Notice that we have used an HTML tag (`<br>`) in the PHP output; this is completely acceptable and a very common technique when using PHP. Your web browser will receive the following data (of course, with other dates, unless your computer clock is wrong or you were trapped in a time warp):

```
Dear friends, today's date is: May 04, 2002
<br>We are in the first half of the year of 2002
```

The web browser will then break the line at the position of the `<br>` tab.

In order to modularize your code, PHP also supports functions, as do most other programming languages. These functions enable you to execute a piece of code in many different places without having to rewrite it over and over again.

PHP comes with very extensive function libraries, and you can download even more from the Net. To include a function library, you can use the `include( )` and the `require( )` statements, which differ only marginally.

If you want to program with PHP, you should familiarize yourself with the documentation of the function libraries that are shipped together with the PHP interpreter, since their use means you do not have to reinvent the wheel when performing common tasks.

Here is the definition of two simple functions—`show_date`, which outputs the current date in a hardcoded date format and appends a line break, and `show_halfyear`, which outputs `first` or `second` depending on the current month:

```
<?php

function show_date( ) {
    echo date("F d, Y") . "\n <br>";
}

function show_halfyear( ) {
    if (date("m") <= 6) {
        echo "first ";
    } else {
        echo "second ";
    }
}

?>
```

Let's call this script *functions.php* and rewrite our initial script using these functions:

```php
<?php

require("functions.php");
echo "Dear friends, the date today is: ";

show_date( );

echo "<br>";
echo "We are in the ";

show_semester( );

echo "semester of " . date("Y");
?>
```

The require( ) statement tells the PHP interpreter to load our function script and make the functions contained therein available to the current script.

Of course, we have only scratched the surface of what PHP can do. If this has whetted your appetite, you might want to look into *Programming PHP*, by Rasmus Lerdorf, the original author of PHP, and Kevin Tatroe (O'Reilly).

Until PHP3, PHP was an interpreted language, the code of which was kept in a buffer. Loops and other often-run pieces of code were parsed over and over again before executing the code. Of course, this led to suboptimal performance.

PHP4 is a complete rewrite and consists of the language core (called "Zend") and the function modules (which are very flexible and extensible). Unlike PHP3, PHP4 can be used in multithreaded environments, which also makes it possible to use PHP as a module in various web servers. PHP5 was yet another rewrite (using the "Zend2" engine) with a new, more intuitive object model, improved performance, and support for exceptions. *http://www.php.net/manual/en/migration5.php* gives you the scoop on the differences between PHP4 and PHP5.

Besides PHP itself, it may be a good idea to download and install *phpMyAdmin*. *phpMyAdmin* is a database administration tool written in PHP that simplifies your daily work when it comes to the administration of MySQL, and handles tasks such as creating and dropping databases and tables. It also can manage privileges, keys and fields, and even more. Besides, it is an excellent example of source code that accesses MySQL databases from PHP code! You can download *phpMyAdmin* from *http://www.phpmyadmin.net*. When you have installed it according to the instructions, you can open the URL *http://localhost/phpMyAdmin* in your browser, and you will see the screen shown in Figure 25-3.

In addition to running PHP4 as a module, you can run it as a CGI program started by the web server, at the expense of some additional overhead. When running PHP as a CGI program, each new page that contains PHP code requires starting a new instance of the PHP interpreter, which in turn requires creating a new process and

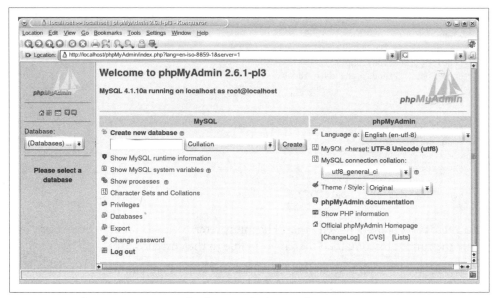

Figure 25-3. Administering MySQL databases with phpMyAdmin

loading the PHP interpreter into this process. When the interpreter is finished creating the page, its process ends, the memory is freed, all file handles are closed, and all database connections are shut down.

As a web server module, the PHP interpreter becomes part of the web server and is always loaded into memory. In addition, it can keep resources such as database connections alive across different pages, which can bring huge performance benefits.

All big-ticket PHP sites use PHP as a module, mostly because of the better performance it affords.

PHP4 as an Apache Module

As we have already said, running the PHP interpreter as a web server module is best for getting good performance. Today, most distributions (including Slackware, Debian, SUSE, and Red Hat) ship both Apache and the PHP4 module for Apache, so it is generally not necessary to build the PHP4 module yourself. It may be a good idea to do so anyway, however.

Because of its vast amount of functionality, the PHP4 module needs quite a number of additional libraries or modules. If you install the module from your installation CDs, the installation program will have automatically installed the necessary modules. However, the modules shipped with distributions are typically loaded with functionality to satisfy all needs and tastes. The result can be a system that's heavier and slower than it needs to be.

Thus, the advantage of building PHP4 by yourself is that you can decide which functionality you want to go into the module. Check the documentation to see which additional libraries you might need to install.

Since we firmly believe that you should know what goes on behind the scenes, even if you use the more comfortable ready-made solutions, we will give you some hints regarding how to work from scratch and how the pieces work together.

To load the PHP4 module into the Apache web server at runtime, you need to have the Apache module *mod_so*. You can check whether this module is presented by issuing:

```
owl$ httpd -l
Compiled-in modules:
        http_core.c
        mod_so.c
```

If this module is not available, please check whether you may have missed installing some of the additional Apache packages in your distribution. If you have built Apache from scratch, follow the documentation to get this module.

It is also possible to compile the PHP4 module directly into Apache, but this requires some very intertwined building of both Apache and PHP4 and does not really give you a big advantage, so we won't cover this here.

Now we need to build PHP and make a dynamic shared object (DSO) out of it. Luckily, this is not as involved as it sounds. Download PHP4 from *http:// www.php.net/download.php*. You will end up with a package called *php-4.4.0.tar.gz* (the actual version number may differ slightly). Unpack the *tar* file and configure PHP with:

```
owl$ ./configure \
                --with-mysql=/usr/lib/mysql\
                --with-ldap=yes\
                --with-gd=yes\
                --with-zlib=yes\
                --with-config-file-path=/etc/\
                --with-apxs=/usr/lib/apache/apxs\
                --enable-versioning\
                --enable-track-vars\
                --enable-thread-safety
```

You can read about numerous additional options in the extensive PHP documentation, but for starters, this will do. Note that you might need to replace some of the paths here with the actual locations on your system. After *configure* is finished, do a *make* and then a *make install* to install PHP (you may need to do the *make install* as *root*).

Next, edit the *httpd.conf* file, Apache's configuration file. If you have installed Apache from your installation CDs, chances are the following lines are already there and you just need to uncomment them. In any case, you should have the following lines in your *httpd.conf*:

```
LoadModule php4_module libexec/libphp4.so
AddModule mod_php4.c

AddHandler application/x-httpd-php .php
```

You may also want to find your existing `DirectoryIndex` line and change it to allow PHP files to be used as default pages:

```
DirectoryIndex index.html index.php
```

Now restart Apache:

```
owl# apachectl restart
```

(The command *apachectl* may be called differently on your distribution; try *rca-pache*.) Once the server is restarted, you should test whether the PHP4 module can be loaded correctly. You can do this by writing a small PHP program, such as the following:

```
<?php
phpinfo( );
?>
```

Save this file as *phpinfo.php* in the *htdocs* directory of your Apache installation (often */usr/local/httpd/htdocs*). Now you should be able to browse this file with your web browser by accessing *http://localhost/phpinfo.php*. If everything is OK, you should see the configuration of the PHP4 module.

The LAMP Server in Action

Now you have all the components for your LAMP server in place; it is time to run a few examples.

If you haven't done so already while following the last section, we suggest that you test your setup now with a very simple PHP file. Save the PHP that you have seen in the last listing in the previous section into a file called *info.php*.

Now place this file in the directory where your Apache web server is looking for its contents files. Often, this is */usr/local/httpd/htdocs*, and it may already contain the files that your distribution has installed for you during installation (at least if you have installed Apache from the installation media). If this doesn't work for you, you should look for the Apache configuration file *httpd.conf*. Often, this file is in the */etc/httpd/* directory, but if this is not the case on your system, you can search for it with

```
locate httpd.conf
```

In this file, look for the line starting with `DocumentRoot`. You should find a directory listed here, and a subdirectory named *htdocs* should be under that directory; put the file *info.php* here. Now you can use any web browser to access the URL *http://local-host/info.php*. This will give you some information about the setup of your PHP module.

PHP comes with a number of built-in functions that manipulate and manage the data stored in MySQL (and other databases).

A relational database consists of a number of tables. If you have sufficient access rights, PHP can query and manipulate data in these tables. We can now write a few PHP scripts to use the database tables. We assume here that you have created the database *test_database* and the table comment_table, as well as the user *olof* as described earlier.

Use your favorite text editor and enter the following code, which creates a small HTML page that lets you add data to this table by means of an HTML form:

```
<html>
<?php
if (isset($_REQUEST["comment"])) {
    $conn = mysql_connect("localhost", "olof", "secret")
     or die("Could not connect to MySQL as olof");

    mysql_select_db("test_database", $conn)
     or die("could not select the test_database");

    if (get_magic_quotes_gpc()) {
        $comment = stripslashes($_REQUEST["comment"]);
    } else {
        $comment = $_REQUEST["comment"];
    }

    $query = "INSERT INTO comment_table VALUES ('0', '"
     . mysql_real_escape_string($comment) . "')";

    mysql_query($query)
     or die(mysql_error(  ));
}
?>

<form action="" method="POST">
    <input type="text" name="comment" size="80"><br>
    <input type="submit">
</form>

</html>
```

When you work with a database, you must take precautions not to allow user input to manipulate your SQL queries. If you don't do this, a malicious user could simply hijack your database. You can make yourself safe by transforming the input data before using it to construct SQL queries. Normally, it is enough to put user input through the mysql_real_escape_string() function. In some situations, you may need to apply the stripslashes() function first. This is because of the special PHP feature called magic_quotes_gpc, which was meant to make all input data safe for the database automatically. Although the idea was noble, the feature does not provide sufficient protection and creates other problems for programmers. We recommend you turn this feature off in your configuration. Otherwise, you first need to detect whether it is enabled, and neutralize its effects if you discover that it is.

You can execute this script by saving it as a file with the extension *.php*, copying it into the document directory of your web server, and accessing the script with your web browser. For example, if you have saved it as *edit.php*, you could access the URL *http://localhost/edit.php* to execute this script. The web server knows that it needs to run everything between <?php and ?> through the PHP module. Thus, the PHP code can be directly embedded into an HTML page.

Now that we can enter comments into our database, we also want to review them. Thus, next up is a script to read from the database:

```
<html>
<?php
$conn = mysql_connect("localhost", "olof", "secret")
  or die("Could not connect to MySQL as olof");

mysql_select_db("test_database", $conn)
  or die("could not select the test_database");

$query = "SELECT * FROM comment_table";
$result = mysql_query($query)
  or die(mysql_error(   ));

$numbers_cols = mysql_num_fields($result);

print "<b>query: $query</b>";
print "<table border=1>\n";
print "<tr>";
print "<td>ID</td>";
print "<td>Comment</td>";
print "</tr>";

while (list($id, $comment) = mysql_fetch_array($result)) {
    print "<tr>";
    print "<td>" . htmlspecialchars($id, ENT_QUOTES) . "</td>";
    print "<td>" . htmlspecialchars($comment, ENT_QUOTES) . "</td>";
    print "</tr>";
}

print "</table>";

?>
</html>
```

As you can see, we are using the HTML tags for laying out tables in order to display the contents of the database, which is a very natural and obvious thing to do. Also note that we did not print the data from the database directly to the HTML page.

This would have allowed a potential adversary to hijack the page by using improper input. Instead, we used the `htmlspecialchars()` function to make the data HTML safe.

It was our intention to keep these examples as simple as possible so as not to overload you with too much information. If you want to dive deeper into the wonderful world of LAMP, we recommend that you read a good book such as *Web Database Applications with PHP & MySQL* (O'Reilly) or *MySQL/PHP Database Applications* (John Wiley & Sons).

## CHAPTER 26

Running a Secure System

In this chapter we discuss basic Linux system security. Security is unfortunately a topic of ever-growing importance, especially with the increasing use of permanently network-connected systems that are vulnerable to remote attacks even while unattended.

Most system security is commonsense good practice. Many of the best techniques are the simplest, yet frequently ignored practices; we cover those first. We then move on to some of the less obvious practices, and we conclude with a short discussion of the complex subject of network security. We also include some firewall recipes to protect simple installations against network attack.

A Perspective on System Security

It's sometimes difficult keeping a balanced perspective on system security. The media tends to sensationalize stories relating to security breaches, especially when they involve well-known companies or institutions. On the other hand, managing security can be a technically challenging and time-consuming task. Many Internet users take the view that their system holds no valuable data, so security isn't much of an issue. Others spend large amounts of effort nailing down their systems to protect against unauthorized use. No matter where you sit in this spectrum, you should be aware that there is always a risk that you will become the target of a security attack. There are a whole host of reasons why someone might be interested in breaching your system security. The value of the data on your system is only one of them; we discuss some others later in the chapter. You must make your own judgment as to how much effort you will expend, though we recommend that you err on the side of caution.

Traditional system security focused on systems that were accessible through either a connected hard-wired terminal or the system console. In this realm the greatest risks typically came from within the organization owning the system, and the best form of defense was physical security, in which system consoles, terminals, and hosts were in locked rooms. Even when computer systems started to become network-connected, access was still very limited. The networks in use were often expensive to gain access to, or were closed networks that did not allow connections to hosts from just anywhere.

The popularity of the Internet has given rise to a new wave of network-based security concerns. An Internet-connected computer is open to potential abuse from tens of millions of hosts around the world. With improved accessibility comes an increase in the number of antisocial individuals intent upon causing nuisance. On the Internet, a number of forms of antisocial behavior are of interest to the system administrator. Those that we address in this chapter are the following:

Denial of service (DoS)
> This kind of attack degrades or disrupts a service on the system.

Intrusion
> This kind of attack accesses the system by guessing passwords or compromising some service. Once an intruder has access to a system, he may then vandalize or steal data or use the target system to launch attacks on some other host.

Snooping
> This kind of attack involves intercepting the data of another user and listening for passwords or other sensitive information. Sometimes this form of attack involves modification of data, too. Snooping usually involves eavesdropping on network connections, but can also be performed by compromising a system to intercept library or system calls that carry sensitive information (e.g., passwords).

Viruses, worms, and Trojan horses
> These attacks each rely on compelling users of your system to execute programs supplied by the attacker. The programs could have been received in an email message, or from a web site, or even from within some other apparently harmless program retrieved from somewhere on the Internet and installed locally.

A DoS attack commonly involves generating an abnormally large number of requests to a service provided by a system. This rush of activity may cause the host system to exhaust its memory, processing power, or network bandwidth. Another way is to provide the service with non-ordinary input in order to exploit a bug in the service and cause a core dump. As a result, further requests to the system are refused, or the system's performance degrades to an unusable point. For this type of attack to work, an attacker must either exploit a poorly designed service or be able to generate a number of requests far exceeding the capacity of the service.

A more insidious form of DoS attack is the distributed denial of service (DDoS). In this form of attack, a large number of computers are used or caused to generate requests against a service. This increases the damage of a DoS attack in two ways: by overwhelming the target with a huge volume of traffic, and by hiding the perpetrator behind thousands of unwitting participants. Using a large number of hosts from which to launch an attack also makes DDoS attacks particularly difficult to control and remedy once they've occurred. Even people who have no concerns about the state of their own data should protect themselves against this form of attack so as to minimize the risk of becoming an unwitting accomplice in a DDoS attack against someone else.

The second form of attack, sometimes known as *cracking*, is the one that most people associate with security.* Companies and institutions often store sensitive data on network-accessible computer systems. A common example of concern to the average Internet user is the storage of credit card details by web sites. Where there is money involved, there is incentive for dishonest individuals to gain access and steal or misuse this kind of sensitive data.

Sometimes the methods that are used to gain unauthorized access or disrupt service are very ingenious, if not unethical. Designing an intrusion mechanism often requires a strong knowledge of the target system to uncover an exploitable flow. Often, once an intrusion mechanism has been discovered, it is packaged in the form of a so-called *rootkit*, a set of programs or scripts that anyone possessing only basic knowledge can use to exploit a security hole. The vast majority of intrusion attacks are launched by "script kiddies" who make use of these prepackaged intrusion kits without any real knowledge of the systems they are attacking. The good news is that it is usually straightforward for a system administrator to protect a system from these well-known attacks; we discuss various ways to secure your system in this chapter.

Initial Steps in Setting Up a Secure System

There are some very simple things you can do to protect a Linux system from the most basic security risks. Of course, depending on your configuration, the ways in which you will be using your system, and so forth, they might be more involved than the simple setup described here. In this section we briefly cover the mechanisms to secure a Linux system from the most common attacks—this is the basic approach one of the authors takes whenever installing a new machine.

Shutting Down Unwanted Network Daemons

The first step in securing a Linux machine is to shut down or disable all network daemons and services that you don't need. Basically, any (external) network port that the system is listening for connections on is a risk, since there might be a security exploit against the daemon serving that port. The fast way to find out what ports are open is to use *netstat -an*, as shown (we've truncated some of the lines, however):

---

* The terms *cracking* and *hacking* are often confused in popular usage. Whereas *cracking* involves immoral or illegal behavior (such as compromising the security of a system), *hacking* is a generic word meaning to program, tinker with, or have an intense interest in something. The popular media often uses the term *hacking* to refer to *cracking*; the Linux community is trying to reassociate *hacking* with positive connotations.

```
# netstat -an
Active Internet connections (servers and established)
Proto Recv-Q Send-Q Local Address          Foreign Address         State
tcp        0      0 0.0.0.0:7120            0.0.0.0:*               LISTEN
tcp        0      0 0.0.0.0:6000            0.0.0.0:*               LISTEN
tcp        0      0 0.0.0.0:22              0.0.0.0:*               LISTEN
```

Here we see that this system is listening for connections on ports 7120, 6000, and 22. Looking at */etc/services*, dropping the *-n* or using the *-p* to *netstat*, can often reveal what daemons are associated with these ports. In this case they are the X font server, the X Window System server, and the *ssh* daemon.

If you see a lot of other open ports—for things such as *telnetd*, *sendmail*, and so forth ask yourself whether you really need these daemons to be running, and to be accessible from other hosts. From time to time, security exploits are announced for various daemons, and unless you are very good at keeping track of these security updates, your system might be vulnerable to attack. Also, *telnetd*, *ftpd*, and *rshd* all involve sending clear-text passwords across the Internet for authentication; a much better solution is to use *sshd*, which encrypts data over connections and uses a stronger authentication mechanism. Even if you never use *telnetd*, it's not a good idea to leave it running on your system, in case someone finds a way to break into it.

Shutting down services is usually a matter of de-installing the corresponding package. If you want to keep the client, but the client and daemon are packaged together (exceedingly rare these days), you need to edit the appropriate configuration files for your distribution and reboot the system (to be sure the daemon is good and dead). On Red Hat systems, for example, many daemons are started by scripts in the */etc/rc.d/init.d* directory; renaming or removing these scripts can prevent the appropriate daemons from starting up. Other daemons are launched by *inetd* or *xinetd* in response to incoming network connections; modifying the configuration of these systems can limit the set of daemons running on your system.

If you absolutely need a service running on your machine (such as the X server), find ways of preventing connections to that service from unwanted hosts. For example, it might be safest to allow *ssh* connections only from certain trusted hosts, such as from machines in your local network. In the case of the X server and X font server, which run on many desktop Linux machines, there is usually no reason to allow connections to those daemons from anything but the local host itself. Filtering connections to these daemons can be performed by TCP wrappers or IP filtering, which are described later in this chapter.

Top 10 Things You Should Never Do

We've made the claim that security is mostly common sense, so what is this common sense? In this section we summarize the most common security mistakes. (There aren't actually 10 items in this list, but there are enough to merit the use of the common "top 10" phrase.) Consistently avoiding them all is harder work than it might first seem.

Never use simple or easily guessed passwords.

Never use a password that's the same as (or closely related to) your user ID, name, date of birth, the name of your company, or the name of your dog. If you're an amateur radio operator, don't use your callsign; if you love cars, don't use the make/model or registration number of your car—you get the idea. Always ensure that your passwords are not simple words that can be found in a dictionary. The best passwords are nonsense strings. One good practice is to use a password based on a simple rule and a phrase that you can remember. For example, you might choose a rule such as using the last letter of each word in the phrase "Mary had a little lamb, its fleece was white as snow"; hence, the password would become ydaebsesesw, certainly not something that will be easily guessed, but a password that will be easily remembered. Another common technique is to use numbers and punctuation characters in the password; indeed, some *passwd* programs insist upon this. A combination of the two techniques is even better. One of our collegues swears by *head -c6 /dev/random | mimencode* as a way to generate hard passwords. Adjust the number of random bytes to use (*-c6*) to taste. Six input characters give eight characters of output, the maximum some Linux distributions accept for passwords.

Don't use the root account unless you have to.

One of the reasons that many common desktop operating systems (such as Windows) are so vulnerable to attack through email viruses and the like is the lack of a comprehensive privilege system, or rather the user's convenience of running applications with administrator privileges. Mind you, some broken applications require to be run with administrator rights. In such systems, any user has permission to access any file, execute any program, or reconfigure the system in any way. Because of this it's easy to coerce a user to execute a program that can do real damage to the system. In contrast, the Linux security model limits a wide range of privileged tasks, such as installing new software or modifying configuration files, to the *root* user. Do not succumb to the temptation to use the *root* account for everything! In doing so you are throwing away one of the more powerful defenses against virus and Trojan horse attacks (not to mention accidental *rm -rf ** commands). Always use a normal user account, and use the *su* or *sudo* commands to temporarily obtain *root* access when you need to undertake privileged tasks. There is an additional benefit in this limited use of the *root* account: logging. The *su* and *sudo* commands write messages to the system logfile when they're invoked, mentioning the ID of the user performing the *su* or *sudo*, as well as the date and time that the command was invoked. This is very helpful for keeping track of when *root* privileges are being used, and by whom.

Don't share your passwords.

Don't tell anybody your passwords, ever. This also means you shouldn't write your passwords on little sticky notes attached to your monitor, or in the diary you keep in the top drawer. If you want to allow people temporary access to your system, create an account for them to use. This allows you some convenience in monitoring what they do, and you can easily clean up afterward. If you really must trust someone with your *root* account, use the *sudo* command, which allows you to give users *root* access to *selected* commands without revealing the root password.

Don't blindly trust binaries that have been given to you.

Although it is very convenient to retrieve and install binary copies of programs on your system, you should always question how much you trust the binary before running it. If you're installing software packages that you've retrieved directly from the official sites of your distribution or from a significant development site, you can be fairly confident the software is safe. If you're getting them from an unofficial mirror site, you need to consider how much you trust the administrators of the site. It is possible that someone is distributing a modified form of the software with back doors that would allow someone to gain access to your machine. Although this is a rather paranoid view, it is nevertheless one that many Linux distribution organizations are embracing. For example, the Debian organization is developing a means of validating a software package to confirm that it hasn't been modified. Other distributions are sure to adopt similar techniques to protect the integrity of their own packaged software.

If you do want to install and execute a program that has been given to you in binary form, there are some things you can do to help minimize risk. Unfortunately, none of these techniques is easy if you're new to the Linux environment. First, always run untrusted programs as a non-*root* user unless the program specifically requires *root* privileges to operate. This will contain any damage the program might do, affecting only files and directories owned by that user. If you want to get some idea of what the program might do before you execute it, you can run the *strings* command over the binaries. This will show you all the hard-coded strings that appear in the code. You should look for any references to important files or directories, such as */etc/passwd* or */bin/login*. If you see a reference to an important file, you should ask yourself whether that is in keeping with the purpose of the program in question. If not, beware. If you're more technically inclined, you might also consider first running the program and watching what it is doing using a program such as *strace* or *ltrace*, which display the system and library calls that the program is making. Look for references to unusual file system or network activity in the traces.

Don't ignore your logfiles

Your system logfiles are your friend, and they can tell you a lot about what is happening on your system. You can find information about when network connections have been made to your system, who has been using the *root* account, and failed login attempts. You should check your logfiles periodically and get to know what is normal and, more usefully, what is abnormal. If you see something unusual, investigate.

Don't let your system get too far out of date.

It's important to keep the software on your system fairly current. That Linux kernel 1.2 system you have running in the corner that's been reliably serving your printers for years might be a great subject at cocktail parties, but it's probably a security incident waiting to happen. Keeping the software on your system up-to-date helps ensure that all bug and security fixes are applied. Most Linux distributions provide a set of packages that are security fixes only, so you don't have to worry about issues such as configuration file and feature changes in order to keep your system secure. You should at least keep track of these updates.

Don't forget about physical security.

Most security breaches are performed by people inside the organization running the target system. The most comprehensive software security configuration in the world means nothing if someone can walk up to your machine and boot a floppy containing exploit code. If your machine uses a BIOS or system PROM that allows the device boot order to be configured, set it so that the floppy and CD-ROM drives boot after the hard drive. If your BIOS provides support for password protection of its configuration, use it. If you can padlock the machine case closed, consider doing so. If you can keep the machine in a physically secure area such as a locked room, that's even better.

TCP Wrapper Configuration

We explained earlier that connecting your system to a network significantly increases the risk of attack. With the commonsense considerations out of the way, it's time to look more closely at basic network security. Here we discuss a simple yet effective method of reducing the risk of unwanted network access, using a tool called TCP wrappers. This mechanism "wraps" an existing service (such as the mail server), screening the network connections that are made to it and refusing connections from unauthorized sites. This is a simple way of adding access control to services that weren't originally designed for it, and is most commonly used in conjunction with the *inetd* or *xinetd* daemons.

TCP wrappers are somewhat equivalent to the security guards, or bouncers, that you might find protecting the entrance to large parties or nightclubs. When you approach a venue, you first encounter the security guard, who may ask you your name and address. The guard then consults a guest list, and if you're approved, the guard moves aside and allows you entry to the party.

When a network connection is made to a service protected by TCP wrappers, the wrapper is the first thing encountered. The wrapper checks the source of the network connection using the source hostname or address and consults a list that describes who is allowed access. If the source matches an entry on the list, the wrapper moves out of the way and allows the network connection access to the actual daemon program.

There are two ways to use TCP wrappers, depending on your Linux distribution and configuration. If you are using the *inetd* daemon for managing services (check to see if the file */etc/inetd.conf* exists), TCP wrappers are implemented using a special daemon called *tcpd*. If you are using the *xinetd* daemon instead (check for the directory */etc/xinetd.d*), *xinetd* is usually configured to use TCP wrappers directly. We describe each case in the following sections.

Using TCP Wrappers with inetd

If your system uses the *inetd* daemon to launch network services, it may be necessary to edit your */etc/inetd.conf* file to use TCP wrappers. Let's use the finger daemon, *in.fingerd*, as an example. The basic idea is that instead of running the actual *in.fingerd* daemon, *inetd* launches the *tcpd* daemon instead. *tcpd* performs the TCP wrapper operation and then runs *in.fingerd* in its place if the connection is accepted.

Configuring TCP wrappers requires a very simple change to */etc/inetd.conf*. For the finger daemon, you might have an entry in this file such as the following:

```
# /etc/in.fingerd finger daemon
finger    stream tcp nowait root  /usr/sbin/in.fingerd  in.fingerd
```

To protect the finger daemon using *tcpd*, simply modify the */etc/inetd.conf* entry, as so:

```
# /etc/in.fingerd finger daemon
finger    stream tcp nowait root  /usr/sbin/tcpd /usr/sbin/in.fingerd
```

Here we've caused the *tcpd* command to be executed instead of the actual *in.fingerd* command. The full pathname of the finger daemon is passed to *tcpd* as an argument, and *tcpd* uses this argument to launch the real daemon after it has confirmed that access should be allowed.

You'll need to make this change for each daemon program you wish to protect. On most Linux systems, you may find that *tcpd* is already configured, so these changes won't be necessary.

Using TCP Wrappers with xinetd

xinetd is a replacement for *inetd* that some distributions (such as Red Hat) are adopting. In most cases, *xinetd* has built-in support for TCP wrappers, so all you'll need to do is modify the TCP wrapper configuration files (*/etc/hosts.allow* and */etc/hosts.deny*) as described in the next section. If you are installing *xinetd* yourself, be sure to compile support for TCP wrappers; this is described in the *xinetd* documentation.

/etc/hosts.allow and /etc/hosts.deny

TCP wrappers use two configuration files, */etc/hosts.allow* and */etc/hosts.deny*. These files are used to specify the access rules for each network daemon protected with TCP wrappers. The files are described in detail in the *hosts_access* manual page, but we cover the mechanics here because common cases are fairly simple.

When a TCP wrapper is invoked, it obtains the IP address of the connecting host and attempts to find its hostname using a reverse DNS lookup. Next, it consults the */etc/hosts.allow* file to see if this host is specifically allowed access to the requested service. If a match is found, access is allowed and the actual network daemon is invoked. If no match is found in the */etc/hosts.allow* file, */etc/hosts.deny* is consulted to see if this host has been specifically denied access. If a match is found here, the connection is closed. If no match is found in either file, access is granted. This simple technique is powerful enough to cover most access requirements.

The syntax of *hosts.allow* and *hosts.deny* is fairly simple. Each file contains a set of rules. Each rule is generally on one line but may be split across multiple lines using a backslash at the end of the line. Each rule has the following general form:

```
daemon_list : client_list : shell_command
```

The daemon list is a comma-separated list of daemons to which the rule applies. The daemons are specified using their command basename—that is, the name of the actual executable daemon program that is executed to fulfill the requested service. The client list is a comma-separated list of hostnames or IP addresses for which the rule will match. We'll demonstrate this later using an example. The shell command is optional, and specifies a command that will be executed when the rule matches. This can be used, for example, to log incoming connections.

daemon_list and *client_list* may contain patterns that allow you to match a number of daemons or hosts without having to explicitly name each one. In addition, you can use a number of predefined tokens to make rules simpler to read and build. The patterns are quite sophisticated, so we don't cover them in detail here; instead, we refer you to the *hosts_access* manual page.

Let's start with a simple *hosts.deny* file that looks like this:

```
# /etc/hosts.deny
ALL: ALL
```

The first line is a comment. The next line is a rule that is interpreted as follows: "Deny access requests to all services from all hosts." If our */etc/hosts.allow* file is empty, this rule will have the effect of denying access to everything from all hosts on the Internet—including the local host! To get around this problem, we can make a simple change to the file:

```
# /etc/hosts.deny
ALL: ALL EXCEPT localhost
```

This is nearly always a safe rule to have in place, as it's a secure default. Remember that the */etc/hosts.allow* rules are consulted *before */etc/hosts.deny*, so by adding rules to *hosts.allow* we can override this default setting in *hosts.deny*. For example, imagine that we want to allow every host on the Internet to access the finger daemon. To do this, we add a rule to */etc/hosts.allow* that looks like the following:

```
# /etc/hosts.allow
in.fingerd: ALL
```

A more common use of TCP wrappers is to restrict the set of hosts that can access a service. Hosts can be specified using an IP address, hostname, or some pattern based on the address or hostname (e.g., to specify a group of hosts). For example, consider making the finger daemon available only to a small set of trusted hosts. In this case, our *hosts.allow* file would be modified as follows:

```
# /etc/hosts.allow
in.fingerd: spaghetti.vpasta.com, .vpizza.com, 192.168.1.
```

In this example we've chosen to allow finger requests from the host named spaghetti.vpasta.com, as well as from any host in the vpizza.com domain, and from any system with an IP address beginning with the pattern 192.168.1.

The host and IP address-matching rules in *hosts.allow* and *hosts.deny* are important to understand, and the presence and location of the period characters are critical. A pattern beginning with a period is assumed to be the name of a domain to which requesting systems must belong. A pattern ending with a period is assumed to specify an IP address pattern. There are other ways of specifying groups of hosts, including NIS netgroups and explicit IP address netmasks. Full details on the configuration syntax of these patterns are available in the hosts_access manual page.

Firewalls: Filtering IP Packets

Although TCP wrappers can be used to restrict the set of hosts that can establish connections to certain services on a machine, in many cases it is desirable to exert finer-grained control over the packets that can enter (or leave) a given system. It's also the case that TCP wrappers only work with services configured using *inetd* or *xinetd*; some services (such as *sshd* on some systems) are standalone and provide their own access control features. Still other services don't implement any access control themselves, so it's necessary to provide another level of protection if we wish to control the connections made to these services.

Today it is commonplace for Internet users to protect themselves against the threat of network-based attacks using a technique called *IP filtering*. IP filtering involves having the kernel inspect each network packet that is transmitted or received and deciding whether to allow it to pass, to throw it away, or to modify it in some way before allowing it through. IP filtering is often called firewalling, because by carefully filtering packets entering or leaving a machine, you are building a firewall between the system and the rest of the Internet. IP filtering won't protect you against virus and Trojan horse attacks or application defects, but it can protect you against many forms of network-based attacks, such as certain types of DoS attacks and IP spoofing (packets that are marked as coming from a system they don't really come from). IP filtering also provides an additional layer of access control that prevents unwanted users from trying to gain access to your system.

To make IP filtering work, we need to know which packets to allow and which to deny. Usually, the decision whether to filter a packet is based on the packet headers, which contain information such as the source and destination IP addresses, the protocol type (TCP, UDP, and so on), and the source and destination port numbers (which identify the particular service for which the packet is destined). Different network services use different protocols and port numbers; for example, most web servers receive requests on TCP port 80. If we wanted to filter out all incoming HTTP traffic from our system, we'd set up an IP filter that rejects all TCP packets destined for port 80.

Sometimes inspecting just the header of a packet is not sufficient to accomplish a particular filtering task, so we need to inspect and interpret the actual data carried within the packet. This technique is sometimes called stateful inspection because a packet is considered in the context of an ongoing network connection rather than in isolation. For example, we might want to allow users inside our network to use FTP servers outside our network. FTP is a complex protocol that uses one TCP connection to send commands to the server, but another to transfer the actual data. Unfortunately, the FTP specification does not mandate a particular port number for data transfers, so the client and server must negotiate port numbers using the command session. Without stateful packet inspection, allowing FTP transfers would require allowing TCP connections to arbitrary ports. Stateful inspection solves this problem by interpreting the port number negotiation between the client and server, and automatically allowing TCP packets on the negotiated port to pass through.

IP filtering is implemented by the Linux kernel, which contains code to inspect each packet that is received and transmitted, applying filtering rules that determine the fate of the packet. The rules are configured using a user-space configuration tool that accepts arguments from the command line and translates them into filter specifications that are stored and used as rules by the kernel.

There have been three generations of kernel-based IP filtering in Linux, and each has had its own configuration mechanism. The first generation was called *ipfw* (for "IP firewall") and provided basic filtering capability but was somewhat inflexible and inefficient for complex configurations. *ipfw* is rarely used now. The second generation of IP filtering, called *IP chains*, improved greatly on *ipfw* and is still in common use. The latest generation of filtering is called *netfilter/iptables*. *netfilter* is the kernel component, and *iptables* is the user-space configuration tool; these terms are often used interchangeably. *netfilter* is not only much more flexible to configure than earlier filters, but is extensible as well. In the following sections we describe *netfilter* and some simple configurations as examples.

netfilter Basics

netfilter is implemented in Linux kernels 2.4.0 and newer. The primary tool for manipulating and displaying the filtering tables is called *iptables* and is included in all current Linux distributions. The *iptables* command allows configuration of a rich and complex set of firewall rules and hence has a large number of command-line options. We address the most common of these here. The *iptables* manpage offers a complete explanation.

Just to whet your appetite, take a look at a sneak preview of where we're heading:

```
iptables -A INPUT -m state --state NEW -m tcp -p tcp --dport 22 -j ACCEPT
```

This command installs an IP filtering rule that accepts new incoming connections to TCP port 22 (the *ssh* service) on our local system. It also uses an extension module called *state* to perform connection tracking. On the following pages we explain how all this works.

An important concept in *netfilter* is the notion of a *chain*, which consists of a list of rules that are applied to packets as they enter, leave, or traverse the system. The kernel defines three chains by default, but the administrator can specify new chains of rules and link them to the predefined chains. The three predefined chains are as follows:

INPUT
> This chain applies to packets that are received by and are destined for the local system.

OUTPUT
> This chain applies to packets that are transmitted by the local system.

FORWARD
> This chain applies whenever a packet will be routed from one network interface to another through this system. It is used whenever the system is acting as a packet router or gateway, and applies to packets that are neither originating from nor destined for this system.

Each rule in a chain provides a set of criteria that specify which packets match the rule, and an action that should be taken on packets that match. Actions that can be taken on a packet include *accepting* the packet (allowing it to be either received or transmitted), *dropping* the packet (simply refusing to receive or transmit it), or passing the packet on to another chain. (The latter is useful when building user-defined chains, which allow complex packet-filtering rules to be built up hierarchically.) A packet traverses each rule in the chain until it is accepted, dropped, or reaches the end of the chain; if it reaches the end, the default action of the chain determines the fate of the packet. The default action of a chain can be configured to either accept or drop all packets.

The Linux *netfilter* supports a number of other interesting things you can do in filtering rules. One of the key advantages of *netfilter* is that it is extensible. It is possible to develop extensions that enhance the way *netfilter* operates. Some examples of more sophisticated packet handling actions are the following:

Packet logging
> You can create rules that do nothing more than log a description of the matching packet so that it can be captured for analysis later. This is very useful for detecting attacks and for testing a filtering configuration.

Stateful inspection
> *netfilter* includes a set of helper modules that can perform stateful connection inspection, such as management of FTP connections, as described earlier.

Network Address Translation
> Network Address Translation (NAT), also called *IP masquerading*, provides a means of rewriting the IP addresses and port numbers of packets as they pass through a chain. NAT is most commonly used to allow systems on a private network to use a connection to the Internet with a single IP address. NAT is a complex subject that we don't discuss at length, but a simple example is provided later in this chapter. You can learn more about NAT in the *NAT HOWTO* or in *TCP/IP Network Administration*, Third Edition (O'Reilly).

Packet and byte accounting
> *netfilter* provides counters that allow you to measure how the network traffic handled each rule. Several IP accounting systems are based on these statistics. These counters are visible when you use *iptables* to list rulesets in verbose mode; we demonstrate this in Example 26-3, later in this chapter.

Using the iptables command

The *iptables* command is used to make changes to the *netfilter* chains and rulesets. You can create new chains, delete chains, list the rules in a chain, flush chains (that is, remove all rules from a chain), and set the default action for a chain. *iptables* also allows you to insert, append, delete, and replace rules in a chain.

The *iptables* command has a large number of command-line arguments and options, but once you've used it a few times, the syntax becomes fairly obvious. In this section we only cover the most common uses of *iptables*, so some arguments and options are left out of the following discussion. Specifically, we don't discuss user-defined chains here. Table 26-1 summarizes the *iptables* arguments that operate on chains, and Table 26-2 summarizes the *iptables* arguments that operate on individual rules.

Table 26-1. iptables operations on chains

Argument	Description
-L *chain*	List the rules in the specified chain or all chains.
-F *chain*	Flush (delete) the rules from the specified chain or all chains.
-Z *chain*	Zero the byte counters in the specified chain or all chains.
-P *chain action*	Set the default action (policy) of the specified chain to *action*.

Table 26-2. iptables operations on rules

Argument	Description
-A *chain rule-specification*	Append a rule to *chain*.
-D *chain rulenum*	Delete the rule with rule number *rulenum* from *chain*.
-R *chain rulenum rule-specification*	Replace rule number *rulenum* in *chain* with *rule-specification*.
-I *chain rulenum rule-specification*	Insert a rule into *chain* at slot number *rulenum* with specification *rule-specification*. If no *rulenum* is specified, 1 is assumed.

Each filtering rule includes parameters that describe which packets match the rule. The most common rule parameters are summarized in Table 26-3. Using an exclamation point (!) before a parameter inverts it. For example, the parameter -dport 80 means "match destination port 80," whereas the parameter -dport ! 80 means "match any destination port except 80."

Table 26-3. iptables rule parameters

Parameter	Matches
-p ! *protocol*	The packet protocol. Valid settings are tcp, udp, icmp, or all.
-s ! *source/mask*	Source address of the packet, specified as a hostname or IP address. *mask* specifies an optional netmask as either a literal netmask or a number of bits. For example, /255.255.255.0 gives the literal netmask, and /24 gives the number of bits in the mask.
-d ! *source/mask*	Destination address of the packet. Uses the same syntax as the source address.
-- sport ! *port*	The source port of the packe, specified as a literal port number or as a service name from /etc/services.
-- dport ! *port*	The destination port of the packet. Uses the same syntax as the source address.
-i ! *interface*	The network interface on which the packet was received.
-o ! *interface*	The network address on which the packet will be sent.

A number of important options are used when building rulesets, summarized in Table 26-4.

Table 26-4. Other important iptables options

Option	Description
-v	Enable verbose output. Most useful when listing rules with -L.
-n	Display IP addresses in numeric form (i.e., avoid DNS lookup).
-m *module*	Load the *iptables* extension named *module*.

In addition to specifying matching parameters, each *netfilter* rule must specify some action to take for each packet matching the rule. Generally, a rule specifies that a packet should be accepted or dropped, as described next. If no action is specified for a rule, the packet and byte counters for that rule will be incremented and the packet will be passed on to the next rule in the chain. This allows a rule to be used for accounting purposes only. To specify an action for a rule, use the following syntax:

    -j *target*

Here, -j stands for "jump," meaning that if a packet matches this rule, processing will jump to the action named by *target*. *target* can be one of the following:

ACCEPT
    Allow this packet to be transmitted or received.

DROP
    Drop the packet.

QUEUE
    Pass the packet to a userspace program for processing.

RETURN
    If used with a user-defined chain, RETURN causes the packet to be returned to the "calling" chain. If used with a built-in chain, it causes the packet to jump to the end of the chain (where it is subject to the default action for that chain).

When using the *-j* option, *target* can also be the name of a user-specified chain, which allows the user to define a "subchain" of rules that will process this packet. As described earlier, the target RETURN is used to cause a packet to return from a user-defined chain back to the "calling" chain.

Developing IP Filtering Rulesets

Often the most difficult part of IP firewall implementation is deciding what you actually want it to do. Do you want to allow outgoing connections freely? Should you allow ICMP packets? What UDP services do you want? What kind of logging do you want to do?

One of the great challenges of building filtering rulesets is that most people aren't accustomed to thinking in terms of addresses, protocols, and port numbers. Instead, we more often think in terms of applications and end users. To build filtering rulesets, we must be able to translate our higher-level requirements into the low-level detail with which the filtering operates.

You can't get around the need to understand a bit about how the services that you are managing with IP filtering actually work. First and foremost, it is important to know whether a service uses TCP or UDP, and which port numbers it uses. The */etc/services* file can often provide a good deal of what you need to know. For example, searching for smtp in this file yields tcp/25, which indicates that the SMTP protocol uses TCP port 25. Likewise, searching for the DNS returns two entries, one for udp/53 and another for tcp/53; this means that the service uses port 53, but uses both the TCP and UDP protocols.

Some protocols, such as FTP, have two related but different entries in */etc/services*. As described earlier, FTP uses one port for the command session (tcp/21) and another for the data transfer sessions (tcp/20). Unfortunately, FTP clients and servers are free to use different ports for the data transfer session. Therefore, FTP has been somewhat of a nuisance for filtering rules. Fortunately, *netfilter* provides some assistance with a feature called *connection tracking*, along with a helper module that specifically understands the FTP service. Because of this, it is necessary only to create a rule for the FTP command session, and *netfilter* will automatically track and allow the data transfer sessions for you. We demonstrate this later in the chapter in Example 26-2.

If */etc/services* doesn't provide enough information, you may need to read the relevant RFC document that specifies the protocol used by the service. Usually you don't need to know much more about a service other than what protocols and ports it uses, which is generally easy to find in the RFC.

IP Filter Management and Script Files

Filtering rules are stored and used by the kernel in much the same way as routing entries: when the system reboots, IP filtering rules must be reconfigured. To ensure that a firewall configuration is reinstated when a reboot occurs, you should place the appropriate *iptables* commands in a script file that is automatically executed at system boot time. Bundled with the *iptables* software package are two programs called *iptables-save* and *iptables-restore* that respectively save the current *netfilter* configuration to a file and restore it from that file. These tools greatly simplify the task of managing firewall configuration.

Each Linux distribution takes a slightly different approach to managing firewall configuration:

Red Hat (versions 7.0 and later)
First configure your IP filtering rules using the appropriate *iptables* commands. Then, execute the following command:

```
/sbin/service iptables save
```

This causes the filtering rules to be saved to */etc/sysconfig/iptables*, which is automatically read at boot time.

Debian
In order to set up *iptables* rules you either need to write a */etc/init.d* script manually or use one of the many packages available that generate firewall rules for you.

SUSE Linux
For a simple, albeit not as flexible, configuration, run *yast2* and select the firewall configuration module Security & Users → Firewall. Otherwise:

- Edit */etc/sysconfig/SUSEfirewall2*. This file is thoroughly documented.
- If necessary, define custom filter rules in */etc/sysconfig/scripts/SUSEfirewall2-custom*. This requires deeper knowledge about how firewalls work on Linux.
- Start the firewall by invoking */sbin/SUSEfirewall2 start*.

Sample netfilter Configurations

In this section we provide some simple but useful IP filtering configurations. The aim here is not to provide you with a set of solutions that you accept uncritically. Instead, we introduce you to what a useful set of IP filtering rules looks like and provide you with a skeleton on which you can base your own configurations.

Simple IP filtering example

Here we demonstrate the basic use of IP filtering, which is similar to our use of TCP wrappers described earlier in the chapter. Here we want to screen out packets from all hosts on the Internet, except for packets destined for the finger daemon from a small set of hosts. Although TCP wrappers can be used to perform the same function, IP filtering can be used to screen many different types of packets (for example, ICMP "ping" packets), and is often necessary to protect services that aren't managed by TCP wrappers.

Unlike TCP wrappers, *iptables* rules cannot use hostnames to identify the origin or destination of a packet; you must use IP addresses when specifying rules. This is a good idea anyway, since reverse hostname lookup is not a completely secure way to identify a packet (it is possible to spoof DNS, making it appear as though an IP address has a different hostname). In Examples 26-1 and 26-2, we use IP addresses instead of hostnames, which can be obtained using a tool such as *host*.

Example 26-1. Simple ipchains example

```
# Load the connection tracking modules if they're not compiled into the
# kernel.
modprobe ip_conntrack
modprobe ip_conntrack_ftp

# Set default policy on the INPUT chain to DROP.
iptables -P INPUT DROP

# ACCEPT packets belonging to an existing connection.
# '-A INPUT' is used to append to the INPUT chain.
# '-m state' uses the stateful inspection module.
iptables -A INPUT -m state --state ESTABLISHED,RELATED -j ACCEPT

# ACCEPT all packets that have come from the loopback interface, that
# is, from the local host. '-i lo' identifies the loopback interface.
iptables -A INPUT -i lo -j ACCEPT

# ACCEPT new incoming connections, and packets belonging to existing
# connections, to port 22 (ssh).
iptables -A INPUT -m state --state NEW -m tcp -p tcp \
        --dport 22 -j ACCEPT

# ACCEPT new incoming FTP connections from 192.168.1/24.
iptables -A INPUT -m state --state NEW -m tcp -p tcp -s 192.168.1/24 \
        --dport 21 -j ACCEPT

# ACCEPT new incoming FTP connections from spaghetti.vpizza.com,
# which has IP address 10.21.2.4.
iptables -A INPUT -m state --state NEW -m tcp -p tcp -s 10.21.2.4 \
        --dport 21 -j ACCEPT

# ACCEPT new incoming FTP connections from *.vpizza.com.
# They have two networks: 172.18.1.0 and 172.25.3.0.
iptables -A INPUT -m state --state NEW -m tcp -p tcp -s 172.18.1/24 \
        --dport 21 -j ACCEPT
iptables -A INPUT -m state --state NEW -m tcp -p tcp -s 172.25.3/24 \
        --dport 21 -j ACCEPT
```

The ruleset specifically accepts all packets that belong to an existing connection. This is needed in the case of FTP, in which the client and server may negotiate an alternate port for the data transfer connection. The connection tracking module (specified with *-m state* in the rules) ensures that the data transfer connection can be accepted.

IP filtering to protect an entire network

The previous example demonstrated IP filtering on a single host. In this section, we deal with the case where a network of machines (such as all the machines in a home or small office) are connected to the Internet through a gateway machine. We can write *netfilter* rules to filter the traffic between the Internet and the internal network. In Example 26-2, we place rules on both the INPUT and FORWARD chains. Recall that INPUT is used to filter incoming packets destined for this host, whereas FORWARD is used for packets being forwarded by the gateway (i.e., packets destined for the internal network or the Internet). Here, we assume that the gateway machine uses the ppp0 interface to communicate with the Internet.

Example 26-2. Using netfilter to protect an IP network

```
# Load the connection tracking modules if they're not compiled into the
# kernel.
modprobe ip_conntrack
modprobe ip_conntrack_ftp

# Set default policy on INPUT and FORWARD chains to DROP.
iptables -P INPUT DROP
iptables -P FORWARD DROP

# ACCEPT all packets from the loopback interface.
iptables -A INPUT -i lo -j ACCEPT

# Create a new user-defined chain. This chain will contain rules
# relevant to both INPUT and FORWARD, so by grouping them together on
# a single chain we avoid stating the rules twice.
iptables -N allowfwdin

# ACCEPT packets belonging to an existing connection.
# Note that this rule (and subsequent rules) are placed
# on the user-defined chain.
iptables -A allowfwdin -m state --state ESTABLISHED,RELATED -j ACCEPT

# ACCEPT new connection requests from machines on the internal network.
# This allows machines on the internal network to establish connections
# to the Internet, but not the other way around. Note the use of
# '-i ! ppp0' to specify packets coming from interfaces other than ppp0.
iptables -A allowfwdin -m state --state NEW -i ! ppp0 -j ACCEPT

# ACCEPT new incoming connections to port 22 (ssh).
iptables -A allowfwdin -m state --state NEW -m tcp -p tcp \
        --dport 22 -j ACCEPT

# ACCEPT new incoming FTP connections from 192.168.1/24.
iptables -A allowfwdin -m state --state NEW -m tcp -p tcp -s 192.168.1/24 \
        --dport 21 -j ACCEPT

# ACCEPT new incoming FTP connections from spaghetti.vpizza.com.
iptables -A allowfwdin -m state --state NEW -m tcp -p tcp -s 10.21.2.4 \
```

Example 26-2. Using netfilter to protect an IP network (continued)

```
        --dport 21 -j ACCEPT

# ACCEPT new incoming FTP connections from *.vpizza.com.
iptables -A allowfwdin -m state --state NEW -m tcp -p tcp -s 172.18.1/24 \
        --dport 21 -j ACCEPT
iptables -A allowfwdin -m state --state NEW -m tcp -p tcp -s 172.25.3/24 \
        fs

# Any packets that have passed through the user-defined chain are now
# subject to the action LOG, which causes them to be logged.
# Use the 'limit' module to prevent logging blocked packets too
# rapidly.
iptables -A allowfwdin -m limit --limit 2/sec -j LOG

# Set default action on the user-defined chain to DROP.
iptables -A allowfwdin -j DROP

# Direct all packets received for INPUT or FORWARD to our user-defined chain.
iptables -A INPUT -j allowfwdin
iptables -A FORWARD -j allowfwdin

# Enable IP routing (required by all IP routers, regardless of the use
# of IP filtering).
echo 1 >/proc/sys/net/ipv4/ip_forward
```

To keep track of any attempts to breach security, we've added a rule that will log any packets that would be dropped. However, if a large number of bad packets were to arrive, this rule might fill up the disk with log entries, or slow down the gateway to a crawl (as it takes much longer to log packets than it does to forward or filter them). So, we use the *limit* module, which controls the rate at which a rule action is taken. In the preceding example, we allowed an average rate of two bad packets per second to be logged. All other packets will pass through the rule and simply be dropped.

To view the rules that have been configured (see Example 26-3), use the *iptables* list option *-L*. Using the verbose mode (*-v*) displays more information than the basic output of the command.

Example 26-3. Listing iptables rulesets forExample 26-2

```
# iptables -L -v
Chain INPUT (policy DROP 0 packets, 0 bytes)
 pkts bytes target     prot opt in     out     source               destination
   16  1328 ACCEPT     all  --  lo     any     anywhere             anywhere
    0     0 allowfwdin all  --  any    any     anywhere             anywhere

Chain FORWARD (policy DROP 0 packets, 0 bytes)
 pkts bytes target     prot opt in     out     source               destination
    0     0 allowfwdin all  --  any    any     anywhere             anywhere

Chain OUTPUT (policy ACCEPT 9756 packets, 819K bytes)
 pkts bytes target     prot opt in     out     source               destination
```

Example 26-3. Listing iptables rulesets forExample 26-2 (continued)

```
Chain allowfwdin (2 references)
 pkts bytes target     prot opt in      out     source               destination
    0     0 ACCEPT     all  --  any     any     anywhere             anywhere   \
    state RELATED,ESTABLISHED
    0     0 ACCEPT     all  --  !ppp0   any     anywhere             anywhere   \
    state NEW
    0     0 ACCEPT     tcp  --  any     any     anywhere             anywhere   \
    state NEW tcp dpt:ssh
    0     0 ACCEPT     tcp  --  any     any     192.168.0.0/24       anywhere   \
    state NEW tcp dpt:ftp
    0     0 ACCEPT     tcp  --  any     any     10.21.2.4            anywhere   \
    state NEW tcp dpt:ftp
    0     0 ACCEPT     tcp  --  any     any     172.18.0.0/24        anywhere   \
    state NEW tcp dpt:ftp
    0     0 ACCEPT     tcp  --  any     any     172.25.0.0/24        anywhere   \
    state NEW tcp dpt:ftp
    0     0 LOG        all  --  any     any     anywhere             anywhere   \
    limit: avg 2/sec burst 5 LOG level warning
    0     0 DROP       all  --  any     any     anywhere             anywhere
```

IP masquerading example

netfilter rules can also be used to implement IP masquerading, a specific type of NAT that rewrites packets from an internal network to make them appear as though they are originating from a single IP address. This is often used in cases where one has a number of machines connected to a LAN, with a single Internet-connected machine with one IP address. This is a common situation in home networks where the ISP has allocated a single IP address; using IP masquerading, however, an entire network of machines can share the address. By having the gateway perform IP masquerading, packets from the internal LAN will appear as though they are originating from the gateway machine, and packets from the Internet will be forwarded to the appropriate host on the internal LAN. You can accomplish all of this with a bit of clever packet rewriting using *netfilter*.

Configuring *netfilter* to support IP masquerading is much simpler than explaining how it works! More complete information about how IP masquerading and NAT are accomplished is provided in the *NAT HOWTO*. We'll show the most basic configuration in Example 26-4.

Example 26-4. Basic IP masquerade configuration

```
# Load the module supporting NAT, if not compiled into the kernel.
modprobe iptables_nat

# Masquerade any routed connections supported by the ppp0 device.
iptables -t nat -A POSTROUTING -p ppp0 -j MASQUERADE

# Enable IP routing.
echo 1 >/proc/sys/net/ipv4/ip_forward
```

In this configuration we assumed that we have a Linux system that will act as a gateway for an internal network. The gateway has a PPP connection to the Internet on interface ppp0, and a LAN connection to the internal network on interface eth0. This configuration allows outgoing connections from the internal network to the Internet, but will block incoming connections from the Internet to machines on the internal network except for the gateway. As it turns out, we don't need to provide explicit commands to achieve this, as it is the default behavior when using NAT in this fashion.

There are some important details to note in this configuration. The NAT functionality is provided in a module of its own, which must be loaded unless it is built into your kernel. The NAT module uses a new chain called POSTROUTING that processes packets after the kernel performs routing operations on them (that is, decides whether the packets are destined for the Internet or for internal LAN machines). The MASQUERADE target does the hard work of address translation and tracking.

Note that this configuration provides no filtering of outgoing connections. All hosts on the private network will be able to establish outgoing connections to any host and any port. The packet filtering HOWTO provides useful information about how to combine IP filtering with address translation.

SELinux

SELinux is a fairly new development in the realm of secure Linux systems. It was developed by the National Security Agency (NSA) in the United States, and presumably fits into its mission of securing U.S. computers and communications. But it's curious that a government agency whose raison d'être includes making it possible to break into people's computers and wiretap their communication would develop a Linux system that is supposed to be more secure against these kinds of attacks. See the book *SELinux* (O'Reilly) for an in-depth guide.

SELinux contains a changed Linux kernel that includes mandatory access controls, as well as a number of utilities for controlling the new kernel features. With SELinux, user programs (and daemons) only get just as much access to resources as they need. A security hole such as a buffer overflow in a web server can therefore not compromise the whole computer anymore. In SELinux, there is no *root* user that has access to everything.

It would be beyond the scope of this book to describe the installation and day-to-day operation of SELinux, but if you are interested in hardened Linux systems, you should have a look at *http://www.nsa.gov/selinux*. Information about how to install an SELinux kernel on a number of distributions can be found on *http://selinux.sf.net*.

## CHAPTER 27

Backup and Recovery

After reading the previous three chapters, you now have all the skills you need to start using your system. But eventually you'll want the information in this chapter too. Some of the activities, such as making backup tapes, are important habits to develop. You may also find it useful to have access to files and programs on Windows. Finally, we'll help you handle events that you hope will never happen, but sometimes do—system panics and corruption.

Making Backups

Making backups of your system is an important way to protect yourself from data corruption or loss in case you have problems with your hardware, or you make a mistake such as deleting important files inadvertently. During your experiences with Linux, you're likely to make quite a few customizations to the system that can't be restored by simply reinstalling from your original installation media. However, if you happen to have your original Linux CD-ROM or DVD-ROM handy, it may not be necessary to back up your entire system. Your original installation media already serve as an excellent backup.

Under Linux, as with any Unix-like system, you can make mistakes while logged in as *root* that would make it impossible to boot the system or log in later. Many newcomers approach such a problem by reinstalling the system entirely from backup, or worse, from scratch. This is seldom, if ever, necessary. In "What to Do in an Emergency," later in this chapter, we talk about what to do in these cases.

If you do experience data loss, it is sometimes possible to recover that data using the filesystem maintenance tools described in "Checking and Repairing Filesystems" in Chapter 10. Unlike some other operating systems, however, it's generally not possible to "undelete" a file that has been removed by *rm* or overwritten by a careless *cp* or *mv* command (for example, copying one file over another destroys the file to which you're copying). In these extreme cases, backups are key to recovering from problems.

Backups are usually made to tape, floppy, CD-R(W), or DVD-R(W). None of these media is 100% reliable, although tape, CD-R(W), and DVD-R(W) are more dependable than floppies in the long term. These days, with the cost of hard disks plummeting and the capacity increasing, backing up to a hard disk is also an option.

Many tools are available to help you make backups. In the simplest case, you can use a combination of *gzip* (or *bzip2*) and *tar* to back up files from your hard drive to removable media. This is the best method to use when you make only occasional backups—no more often than, say, once a month.

If you have numerous users on your system or you make frequent changes to the system configuration, it makes more sense to employ an incremental backup scheme. Under such a scheme, you would make a "full backup" of the system only about once a month. Then, every week, you would back up only those files that changed in the last week. Likewise, each night, you could back up just those files that changed over the previous 24 hours. There are several tools to aid you in this type of backup.

The idea behind an incremental backup is that it is more efficient to make backups in small steps; you use fewer tapes or CDs, and the weekly and nightly backups are shorter and easier to run. With this method, you have a backup that is at most a day old. If you were to, say, accidentally delete your entire system, you would restore it from backup in the following manner:

1. Restore from the most recent monthly backup. For instance, if you wiped the system on July 17, you would restore the July 1 full backup. Your system now reflects the state of files when the July 1 backup was made.

2. Restore from each weekly backup made so far this month. In our case, we could restore from the two weekly backups from July 7 and 14. Restoring each weekly backup updates all the files that changed during that week.

3. Restore from each daily backup during the last week—that is, since the last weekly backup. In this case, we would restore the daily backups from July 15 and 16. The system now looks as it did when the daily backup was taken on July 16; no more than a day's worth of files have been lost.

Depending on the size of your system, the full monthly backup might require 4 GB or more of backup storage—often not more than one DVD-R(W) or tape, but quite a few Zip disks. However, the weekly and daily backups would generally require much less storage space. Depending on how your system is used, you might decide to make the weekly backup on Sunday night and not bother with daily backups for the weekend.

One important characteristic that backups should (usually) have is the ability to select individual files from the backup for restoration. This way, if you accidentally delete a single file or group of files, you can simply restore those files without having to do a full system restoration. Depending on how you make backups, however, this task will be either very easy or painfully difficult.

It's also highly desirable to keep the backup media physically separate from the computer. If you choose to back up to hard disk, consider an external USB, FireWire, or SCSI drive. USB and FireWire are particularly nice because they can be easily plugged into or removed from the system as needed. If you choose to back up to a second, internal hard disk, it would be wise to at least keep the disk unmounted when it's not in use, so that if you were to accidentally delete one or more filesystems, your backup would be spared. An important decision you need to make is evaluating the relative importance of your data's safety and recoverability versus the cost and convenience of the backup media you choose, as well as how you use it.

In this section, we talk about the use of *tar*, *gzip*, and a few related tools for making backups to CD and tape. We even cover the use of tape drives, as well as CD-R in the bargain. These tools allow you to make backups more or less "by hand"; you can automate the process by writing shell scripts and even schedule your backups to run automatically during the night using *cron*. All you have to do is flip tapes. Other software packages provide a nice menu-driven interface for creating backups, restoring specific files from backup, and so forth. Many of these packages are, in fact, nice frontends to *tar* and *gzip*. You can decide for yourself what kind of backup system suits you best.

Simple Backups

The simplest means of making a backup is to use *tar* to archive all the files on the system or only those files in a set of specific directories. Before you do this, however, you need to decide what files to back up. Do you need to back up every file on the system? This is rarely necessary, especially if you have your original installation disks or CD-ROM. If you have made important changes to the system, but everything else is just the way it was found on your installation media, you could get by with only archiving those files you have made changes to. Over time, however, it is difficult to keep track of such changes.

In general, you will be making changes to the system configuration files in */etc*. There are other configuration files as well, and it can't hurt to archive directories such as */usr/lib* and */etc/X11* (which contains the XFree86 configuration files, as we saw in "Installing X.org" in Chapter 16).

You should also back up your kernel sources (if you have upgraded or built your own kernel); these are found in */usr/src/linux*.

During your Linux adventures it's a good idea to keep notes on what features of the system you've made changes to so that you can make intelligent choices when making backups. If you're truly paranoid, go ahead and back up the whole system; that can't hurt, but the cost of backup media might.

Of course, you should also back up the home directories for each user on the system; these are generally found in *home*. If you have your system configured to receive electronic mail (see "The Postfix MTA" in Chapter 23), you might want to back up the incoming mail files for each user. Many people tend to keep old and "important" electronic mail in their incoming mail spool, and it's not difficult to accidentally corrupt one of these files through a mailer error or other mistake. These files are usually found in */var/spool/mail*. Of course, this applies only if you are using the local mail system, not if you access mail directly via POP3 or IMAP.

Backing up to tape

Assuming you know what files or directories to back up, you're ready to roll. You can use the *tar* command directly, as we saw in "Using tar" in Chapter 12, to make a backup. For example, the command:

```
tar cvf /dev/qft0 /usr/src /etc /home
```

archives all the files from */usr/src*, */etc*, and */home* to */dev/qft0*. */dev/qft0* is the first "floppy-tape" device—that is, a tape drive that hangs off of the floppy controller. Many popular tape drives for the PC use this interface. If you have a SCSI tape drive, the device names are */dev/st0*, */dev/st1*, and so on, based on the drive number. Those tape drives with another type of interface have their own device names; you can determine these by looking at the documentation for the device driver in the kernel.

You can then read the archive back from the tape using a command such as:

```
tar xvf /dev/qft0
```

This is exactly as if you were dealing with a *tar* file on disk, as discussed in "Archive and Compression Utilities" in Chapter 12.

When you use the tape drive, the tape is seen as a stream that may be read from or written to in one direction only. Once *tar* is done, the tape device will be closed, and the tape will rewind. You don't create a filesystem on a tape, nor do you mount it or attempt to access the data on it as files. You simply treat the tape device itself as a single "file" from which to create or extract archives.

Be sure your tapes are formatted before you use them. This ensures that the beginning-of-tape marker and bad-blocks information have been written to the tape. For formatting QIC-80 tapes (those used with floppy-tape drivers), you can use a tool called *ftformat* that is either already included with your distribution or can be downloaded from *ftp://sunsite.unc.edu/pub/Linux/kernel/tapes* as part of the *ftape* package.

Creating one *tar* file per tape might be wasteful if the archive requires only a fraction of the capacity of the tape. To place more than one file on a tape, you must first prevent the tape from rewinding after each use, and you must have a way to position the tape to the next file marker, for both *tar* file creation and extraction.

The way to do this is to use the nonrewinding tape devices, which are named */dev/nqft0*, */dev/nqft1*, and so on for floppy-tape drivers, and */dev/nst0*, */dev/nst1*, and so on for SCSI tapes. When this device is used for reading or writing, the tape will not be rewound when the device is closed (that is, once *tar* has completed). You can then use *tar* again to add another archive to the tape. The two *tar* files on the tape won't have anything to do with each other. Of course, if you later overwrite the first *tar* file, you may overwrite the second file or leave an undesirable gap between the first and second files (which may be interpreted as garbage). In general, don't attempt to replace just one file on a tape that has multiple files on it.

Using the nonrewinding tape device, you can add as many files to the tape as space permits. To rewind the tape after use, use the *mt* command. *mt* is a general-purpose command that performs a number of functions with the tape drive. The *mt* command, although very useful and powerful, is also fairly complicated. There's a lot to keep track of to locate a particular record on the tape, and it's easy to get confused. If you're particularly motivated to use your tapes as efficiently as possible, read up on *mt*; the manpage is quite concise. We include a few examples here. The command:

```
mt /dev/nqft0 rewind
```

rewinds the tape in the first floppy-tape device.

Similarly, the command:

```
mt /dev/nqft0 reten
```

retensions the tape by winding it to the end and then rewinding it.

When reading files on a multiple-file tape, you must use the nonrewinding tape device with *tar* and the *mt* command to position the tape to the appropriate file.

For example, to skip to the next file on the tape, use the command:

```
mt /dev/nqft0 fsf 1
```

This skips over one file on the tape. Similarly, to skip over two files, use:

```
mt /dev/nqft0 fsf 2
```

or

```
mt device fsf 1
```

to move to the next file.

Be sure to use the appropriate nonrewinding tape device with *mt*. Note that this command does not move to "file number two" on the tape; it skips over the next two files based on the current tape position. Just use *mt* to rewind the tape if you're not sure where the tape is currently positioned. You can also skip back; see the *mt*(1) manual page for a complete list of options.

Backing up to CD-R

You can back up your files to recordable CD perhaps more easily than to tape. Blank CDs are very inexpensive, widely available, readable on just about any system, and much easier to transport and store than tapes. In this section, we show you the basics of writing backups to CD-R, as well as a couple of tricks. Almost all of the techniques that work for CD-Rs work equally well for the various flavors of recordable DVDs that are available.

By far the most common way to write data to a CD is to create a CD image file on your hard disk, then burn that to CD. This is easy to do, but has one slight disadvantage: you need at least 650 or 700 MB of free disk space to create a full-sized CD image. On modern systems that generally shouldn't be a problem.

CD-ROMs use the ISO 9660 filesystem standard, which can be mounted and read on just about any operating system in common use today. The program *mkisofs* is a full-featured and robust tool for creating such filesystems, which can be used in a number of ways, including burning them to CD-R. The actual burning can be done with *cdrecord*. Both of these programs are usually included with most Linux systems.

Here's how to create an ISO 9660 image and burn it to CD. Let's say you have a directory called */data* that you want to put on CD. Enter:

```
# mkisofs  -T -r -o /tmp/mycd.iso /data
# cdrecord -v -eject -fs=4M speed=8 dev=0,0,0 /tmp/mycd.iso
```

Some of the parameters of *cdrecord* are system-specific. You can run *cdrecord* -*scanbus* to search for the CD burner on your machine. On the machine used for testing the material in this section, the CD burner shows up as device 0,0,0. Even though the author has a 52× burner, he still chooses to record CDs at only 8×, to make sure he doesn't underflow the drive and make a bad disk. Experiment with your hardware and determine what works—you may or may not be able to burn reliably at higher speeds.

A slick, if somewhat less reliable, way to create a CD without writing an image file first is to simply pipe the output of *mkisofs* directly to *cdrecord*:

```
mkisofs -T -r /data  |  cdrecord -v -eject -fs=4M speed=8 dev=0,0,0 -
```

That's not the only possible optimization. If, for some reason, you wanted to treat a CD like a tape, you could skip creating an ISO 9660 filesystem, and just write a tar file directly to a CD. This won't be mountable as a normal CD, and you won't be able to put it in a Windows system, but if you prefer this, it works:

```
tar -czf - /data | cdrecord -v -eject -fs=4M speed=8 dev=0,0,0 -
```

It is important to note that although CD burners are much better than they were a few years ago, it's still quite possible to produce a useless disk if there is anything more than a brief interruption in the flow of data from the source to the burner. These problems are even more apparent when burning from a pipeline as in the last two examples. For this reason, we urge you to check your backups after making them!

In addition to *cdrecord*, *tar*, and *mkisofs*, there are a large number of other programs available on the Web that provide an easy-to-use frontend for creating backups. Some of them are able to span multiple CDs, or manage a rotation of CD-RW disks. If you find that creating CD backups as we've described here doesn't fit your needs, chances are someone has created another program that will work for you.

Backing up to hard disks

As hard disks get bigger and cheaper, one problem is that backup media often don't keep up. Now that 500-GB hard disks are available and affordable by normal people, it may have occurred to you that the only thing you can back a disk that big up to is...another disk that big!

Just about all of the techniques you can use for media in general can apply to hard disks, but there are a few special considerations as well.

If you have a disk mounted at */data*, and you want to back it up to a second hard disk (of equal or greater size) mounted at */backup*, you could do a *tar* and un-*tar* pipeline, like this:

```
cd / ; tar -cvf - /data | (cd /backup ; tar -xf -)
```

If you have room on your backup disk, you can use the remaining space to store incremental backups using the techniques described elsewhere in this chapter. The nice thing about hard disk backups is that you can create any kind of directory structure that makes sense to you. You could have a disk mounted at */backup*, with subdirectories */backup/full* and */backup/incremental*, or any other scheme you choose.

With a combination of *find*, *cron*, *tar*, and *gzip*, you could create a fairly small but powerful script that would mount your backup hard disk, *tar* up the files that have changed since the last time your backup ran, delete the backups older than the last full backup, and unmount the backup disk.

To compress or not to compress?

There are good arguments both for and against compression of *tar* archives when making backups. The overall problem is that neither *tar* nor the compression tools *gzip* and *bzip2* are particularly fault-tolerant, no matter how convenient they are. Although compression using *gzip* or *bzip2* can greatly reduce the amount of backup media required to store an archive, compressing entire *tar* files as they are written to CD-R or tape makes the backup prone to complete loss if one block of the archive is corrupted, say, through a media error (not uncommon in the case of CD-Rs and tapes). Most compression algorithms, *gzip* and *bzip2* included, depend on the coherency of data across many bytes in order to achieve compression. If any data within a compressed archive is corrupt, *gunzip* may not be able to uncompress the file from that point on, making it completely unreadable to *tar*.

This is much worse than if the *tar* file were uncompressed on the tape. Although *tar* doesn't provide much protection against data corruption within an archive, if there is minimal corruption within a *tar* file, you can usually recover most of the archived files with little trouble, or at least those files up until the corruption occurs. Although far from perfect, it's better than losing your entire backup.

A better solution is to use an archiving tool other than *tar* to make backups. Several options are available. *cpio* is an archiving utility that packs files together, similar in fashion to *tar*. However, because of the simpler storage method used by *cpio*, it recovers cleanly from data corruption in an archive. (It still doesn't handle errors well on *gzip*ped files.)

The best solution may be to use a tool such as *afio*. *afio* supports multivolume backups and is similar in some respects to *cpio*. However, *afio* includes compression and is more reliable because each individual file is compressed. This means that if data in an archive is corrupted, the damage can be isolated to individual files, instead of to the entire backup.

These tools should be available with your Linux distribution, as well as from all the Internet-based Linux archives. A number of other backup utilities, with varying degrees of popularity and usability, have been developed or ported for Linux. If you're serious about backups, you should look into them.[*] Among these programs are the freely available *taper*, *tob*, and Amanda, as well as commercial programs such as ARKEIA (free for use with up to two computers), BRU, and Arcserve. Lots of free backup tools can also be found at *http://www.tucows.com/downloads/Linux/IS-IT/FileManagement/BackupRestore*.

Incremental Backups

Incremental backups, as described earlier in this chapter, are a good way to keep your system backups up-to-date. For example, you can make nightly backups of only

---

[*] Of course, this section was written after the author made the first backup of his Linux system in nearly four years of use!

those files that changed in the last 24 hours, weekly backups of all files that changed in the last week, and monthly backups of the entire system.

You can create incremental backups using the tools mentioned previously: *tar*, *gzip*, *cpio*, and so on. The first step in creating an incremental backup is to produce a list of files that have changed since a certain amount of time ago. You can do this easily with the *find* command.* If you use a special backup program, you will most likely not have to do this, but can set some option somewhere that you want to do an incremental backup.

For example, to produce a list of all files that were modified in the last 24 hours, we can use the command:

```
find / -mtime -1 \! -type d -print > /tmp/filelist.daily
```

The first argument to *find* is the directory to start from—here, /, the root directory. The *-mtime -1* option tells *find* to locate all files that changed in the last 24 hours.

The \! *-type d* bit is complicated (and optional), but it cuts some unnecessary stuff from your output. It tells *find* to exclude directories from the resulting file list. The ! is a negation operator (meaning here, "exclude files of type d"), but put a backslash in front of it because otherwise the shell interprets it as a special character.

The *-print* option causes all filenames matching the search to be printed to standard output. We redirect standard output to a file for later use. Likewise, to locate all files that changed in the last week, use:

```
find / -mtime -7 -print > /tmp/filelist.weekly
```

Note that if you use *find* in this way, it traverses all mounted filesystems. If you have a CD-ROM mounted, for example, *find* attempts to locate all files on the CD-ROM as well (which you probably do not wish to backup). The *-xdev* option can be used to limit *find*'s traversal to the local filesystem. Another approach would be to use *find* multiple times with a first argument other than /. See the manual page for *find*(1) for details.

Now you have produced a list of files to back up. Previously, when using *tar*, we specified the files to archive on the command line. However, this list of files may be too long for a single command line (which is usually limited to around 2048 characters), and the list itself is contained within a file.

You can use the *-T* option with *tar* to specify a file containing a list of files for *tar* to back up. In order to use this option, you have to use an alternate syntax to *tar* in

---

* If you're not familiar with *find*, become so soon. *find* is a great way to locate files across many directories that have certain filenames, permissions, or modification times. *find* can even execute a program for each file that it locates. In short, *find* is your friend, and all good system administrators know how to use it well.

which all options are specified explicitly with dashes. For example, to back up the files listed in *tmp/filelist.daily* to the device */dev/qft0*, use the following command:

```
tar -cv -T /tmp/filelist.daily -f /dev/qft0
```

You can now write a short shell script that automatically produces the list of files and backs them up using *tar*. You can use *cron* to execute the script nightly at a certain time; all you have to do is make sure there's a tape in the drive. You can write similar scripts for your weekly and monthly backups. *cron* is covered in Chapter 10.

What to Do in an Emergency

It's not difficult to make a simple mistake as *root* that can cause real problems on your system, such as not being able to log in or losing important files. This is especially true for novice system administrators who are beginning to explore the system. Nearly all new system administrators learn their lessons the hard way: by being forced to recover from a real emergency. In this section, we give you some hints about what to do when the inevitable happens.

You should always be aware of preventive measures that reduce the impact of such emergencies. For example, make backups of all important system files, if not the entire system. If you happen to have a Linux distribution on CD-ROM, the CD-ROM itself acts as a wonderful backup for most files (as long as you have a way to access the CD-ROM in a tight situation—more on this later). Backups are vital to recovering from many problems; don't let the many weeks of hard work configuring your Linux system go to waste.

Also, be sure to keep notes on your system configuration, such as your partition table entries, partition sizes and types, and filesystems. If you were to trash your partition table somehow, fixing the problem might be a simple matter of rerunning *fdisk*, but this helps only as long as you can remember what your partition table used to look like. (True story: one of the authors once created this problem by booting a blank floppy, and had *no* record of the partition table contents. Needless to say, some guesswork was necessary to restore the partition table to its previous state!)

In fact, it's not a bad idea to actually back up the partition tables of each disk in your system. The *sfdisk* program is a very useful tool for viewing, saving, and manipulating partition data. You can capture this data and store it in a file with a command such as

```
sfdisk -d > /partitions.lst
```

This dumps out the partition tables of all the disks in your system and saves them into the file */partitions.lst* (or whatever you want to call it). This output is readable not only by humans, but by *sfdisk* as well. If you need to restore a partition table, you can edit the *partitions.lst* file, remove all the partition info you *don't* want to restore, and rebuild the partition table (for *hda*, for example) like this:

```
sfdisk /dev/hda < partitions.lst
```

Of course, for any of these measures to work, you'll need a way to boot the system and access your files, or recover from backups, in an emergency. This is best accomplished with an "emergency disk," or "root disk." Typically, this is a bootable CD-ROM containing at least enough of a Linux system to be able to recover filesystems and do most kinds of repair work. There are also many full-featured CD-ROMs, such as Knoppix (*http://http://www.knopper.net/knoppix/index-en.html*), that boot into a system with a graphical desktop, Web browser, and everything else you'd want to work comfortably. Either type can be very useful when you need to recover from a disaster.

For systems that can boot only from a floppy, you need a small root filesystem with the basics required to run a Linux system from floppy—just the essential commands and system files, as well as tools to repair problems. Use such a disk by booting a kernel from another floppy (see "Using a Boot Floppy" in Chapter 17) and telling the kernel to use the emergency disk as the root filesystem.

Most distributions of Linux include such a boot/root floppy combination with the original installation floppies. The installation disks usually contain a small Linux system that can be used to install the software as well as perform basic system maintenance. Some systems include both the kernel and root filesystem on one floppy, but this severely limits the number of files that can be stored on the emergency disk. How useful these disks are as a maintenance tool depends on whether they contain the tools (such as *fsck*, *fdisk*, a small editor such as *vi*, and so on) necessary for problem recovery. Some distributions have such an elaborate installation process that the installation floppies don't have room for much else.

At any rate, you can create such a root floppy yourself. Being able to do this from scratch requires an intimate knowledge of what's required to boot and use a Linux system, and exactly what can be trimmed down and cut out. For example, you could dispose of the startup programs *init*, *getty*, and *login*, as long as you know how to rig things so that the kernel starts a shell on the console instead of using a real boot procedure. (One way to do this is to have */etc/init* be a symbolic link to */sbin/bash*, all on the floppy filesystem.)

Although we can't cover all the details here, the first step in creating an emergency floppy is to use *mkfs* to create a filesystem on a floppy (see the section "Creating Filesystems" in Chapter 10). You then mount the floppy and place on it whatever files you'll need, including appropriate entries in */dev* (most of which you can copy from */dev* on your hard drive root filesystem). You'll also need a boot floppy, which merely contains a kernel. The kernel should have its root device set to */dev/fd0*, using *rdev*.

This is covered in "Using a Boot Floppy" in Chapter 17. You'll also have to decide whether you want the root floppy filesystem loaded into a ramdisk (which you can set using *rdev* as well). If you have more than 4 MB of RAM, this is a good idea because it can free up the floppy drive to be used for, say, mounting another floppy containing additional tools. If you have two floppy drives, you can do this without using a ramdisk.

If you feel that setting up an emergency floppy is too hard for you now after reading all this, you might want to try some of the scripts available that do it for you (e.g., *tomsrtbt* at *http://www.toms.net/rb/*). But whatever you do, be sure to try the emergency floppy *before* disaster happens!

At any rate, the best place to start is your installation floppies. If those floppies don't contain all the tools you need, create a filesystem on a separate floppy and place the missing programs on it. If you load the root filesystem from floppy into a ramdisk, or have a second floppy drive, you can mount the other floppy to access your maintenance tools.

What tools do you need? In the following sections, we talk about common emergencies and how to recover from them; this should guide you as to what programs are required for various situations. It is best if the tools you put on the floppy are statically linked in order to avoid problems with shared libraries not being available at emergency time.

Repairing Filesystems

As discussed in "Checking and Repairing Filesystems" in Chapter 10, you can use *fsck* to recover from several kinds of filesystem corruption. Most of these filesystem problems are relatively minor and can be repaired by booting your system in the usual way and running *fsck* from the hard drive. However, it is usually better to check and repair your root filesystem while it is unmounted. In this case, it's easier to run *fsck* from an emergency floppy.

There are no differences between running *fsck* from floppy and from the hard drive; the syntax is exactly the same as described earlier in the chapter. However, remember that *fsck* is usually a frontend to tools such as *fsck.ext3*. On other systems, you'll need to use *e2fsck* (for Second Extended filesystems).

It is possible to corrupt a filesystem so that it cannot be mounted. This is usually the result of damage to the filesystem's *superblock*, which stores information about the filesystem as a whole. If the superblock is corrupted, the system won't be able to access the filesystem at all, and any attempt to mount it will fail (probably with an error to the effect of "can't read superblock").

Because of the importance of the superblock, the filesystem keeps backup copies of it at intervals on the filesystem. Second Extended filesystems (and *ext3*, which is mostly the same) are divided into "block groups," where each group has, by default, 8192 blocks. Therefore, there are backup copies of the superblock at block offsets 8193, 16385 (that's 8192 × 2 + 1), 24577, and so on. If you use the *ext2* or *ext3* filesystem, check that the filesystem has 8192-block groups with the following command:

```
dumpe2fs device | more
```

(Of course, this works only when the master superblock is intact.) This command will print a great deal of information about the filesystem, and you should see something like the following:

```
Blocks per group:        8192
```

If another offset is given, use it for computing offsets to the superblock copies, as mentioned earlier.

If you can't mount a filesystem because of superblock problems, chances are that *fsck* (or *e3fsck*) will fail as well. You can tell *e3fsck* to use one of the superblock copies, instead, to repair the filesystem. The command is:

```
e3fsck -f -b offset device
```

where *offset* is the block offset to a superblock copy; usually, this is 8193. The *-f* switch is used to force a check of the filesystem; when using superblock backups, the filesystem may appear "clean," in which case no check is needed. *-f* overrides this. For example, to repair the filesystem on */dev/hda2* with a bad superblock, we can say:

```
e3fsck -f -b 8193 /dev/hda2
```

Superblock copies save the day. The previous commands can be executed from an emergency floppy system and will hopefully allow you to mount your filesystems again.

Now that journaling filesystems such as *ext3*, *reiserfs* (the Reiser filesystem), and *jfs* come with most Linux distributions by default, it is very unlikely that you will ever have to resort to the superblock-wrangling tricks just described. Because of the "journal," which is a log kept internally by the filesystem of all changes as they are made, modern filesystems are quite resistant to superblock damage. Still, it *can* happen, and it's good to know how to recover from it easily, without having to rebuild your entire filesystem.

Accessing Damaged Files

You might need to access the files on your hard drive filesystems when booting from an emergency floppy or CD-ROM. To do this, simply use the *mount* command as described in "Mounting Filesystems" in Chapter 10, mounting your filesystems under a directory such as */mnt*. (This directory must exist on the root filesystem contained on the rescue disk.) For example,

```
mount -t ext3 /dev/hda2 /mnt
```

will allow us to access the files on the *ext3* filesystem stored on */dev/hda2* in the directory */mnt*. You can then access the files directly and even execute programs from your hard drive filesystems. For example, if you wish to execute *vi* from the hard drive, normally found in */usr/bin/vi*, you would use the command

```
/mnt/usr/bin/vi filename
```

You could even place subdirectories of */mnt* on your path to make this easier.

Be sure to unmount your hard drive filesystems before rebooting the system. If your emergency disks don't have the ability to do a clean shutdown, unmount your filesystems explicitly with *umount*, to be safe.

Two problems that can arise when doing this are forgetting the root password or trashing the contents of */etc/passwd*. In either case, it might be impossible to log in to the system or *su* to *root*. To repair this problem, simply boot from your emergency disks, mount your root filesystem under */mnt*, and edit */mnt/etc/passwd*. (It might be a good idea to keep a backup copy of this file somewhere in case you delete it accidentally.) For example, to clear the root password altogether, change the entry for *root* to

```
root::0:0:The root of all evil:/:/bin/bash
```

Now *root* will have no password; you can reboot the system from the hard drive and use the *passwd* command to reset it.

If you are conscientious about system security, you might have shivered by now. You have read correctly: if somebody has physical access to your system, he or she can change your root password by using a boot floppy. Luckily, there are ways to protect your system against possible assaults. Most effective are, of course, the physical ones: if your computer is locked away, nobody can access it and put a boot floppy into it. There are also locks for the floppy drive only, but notice that you need such protection for the CD-ROM drive as well for floppy-drive locks to be useful. If you don't want to use physical protection, you can also use the BIOS password if your computer supports that: configure the BIOS so that it does not try to boot from CD-ROM or floppy (even if a CD or floppy disk is inserted at boot time) and protect the BIOS settings with a BIOS password. This is not as secure because it is possible to reset the BIOS password with hardware means, but it still protects you against casual would-be intruders. Actually, of course, somebody could steal the whole computer.

Another common problem is corrupt links to shared system libraries. The shared library images in */lib* are generally accessed through symbolic links, such as

/lib/libc.so.5, which point to the actual library, */lib/libc.so.version*. If this link is removed or is pointing to the wrong place, many commands on the system won't run. You can fix this problem by mounting your hard drive filesystems and relinking the library with a command such as:

```
cd /mnt/lib; ln -sf libc.so.5.4.47 libc.so.5
```

to force the *libc.so.5* link to point to *libc.so.5.4.47*. Remember that symbolic links use the pathname given on the *ln* command line. For this reason, the command:

```
ln -sf /mnt/lib/libc.so.5.4.47 /mnt/lib/libc.so.5
```

won't do the right thing: *libc.so.5* will point to */mnt/lib/libc.so.5.4.47*. When you boot from the hard drive, */mnt/lib* can't be accessed, and the library won't be located. The first command works because the symbolic link points to a file in the same directory.

Restoring Files from Backup

If you have deleted important system files, it might be necessary to restore backups while booting from an emergency disk. For this reason, it's important to be sure your emergency disk has the tools you need to restore backups; this includes programs such as *tar* and *gzip*, as well as the drivers necessary to access the backup device. For instance, if your backups are made using the floppy-tape device driver, be sure that the *ftape* module and *insmod* command are available on your emergency disk. See "Loading Modules Automatically" in Chapter 18 for more about this.

All that's required to restore backups to your hard drive filesystems is to mount those filesystems, as described earlier, and unpack the contents of the archives over those filesystems (using the appropriate *tar* and *gzip* commands, for example; see "Making Backups" earlier in this chapter). Remember that every time you restore a backup you will be overwriting other system files; be sure you're doing everything correctly so that you don't make the situation worse. With most archiving programs, you can extract individual files from the archive.

Likewise, if you want to use your original CD-ROM to restore files, be sure the kernel used on your emergency disks has the drivers necessary to access the CD-ROM drive. You can then mount the CD-ROM (remember the *mount* flags *-r -t iso9660*) and copy files from there.

The filesystems on your emergency disks should also contain important system files; if you have deleted one of these from your system, it's easy to copy the lost file from the emergency disk to your hard drive filesystem.

For more information, including some scripts, examples, advice about backups in general, and more, take a look at Charles Curley's Linux Complete Backup and Recovery HOWTO, available at: *http://www.tldp.org/HOWTO/Linux-Complete-Backup-and-Recovery-HOWTO*.

## CHAPTER 28

Heterogeneous Networking and Running Windows Programs

Linux is a remarkably effective operating system, which in many cases can completely replace MS-DOS/Windows. However, there are always those of us who want to continue to use other operating systems as well as Linux. Enterprises considering Linux as an alternative desktop to Microsoft Windows often believe they have some essential Win32 applications or tools that prevent them from changing over. CIOs often eliminate the Linux option because someone advising them failed to mention that Linux can run Win32 applications.

Linux satisfies such yearnings with internal enhancements that allow it to access foreign filesystems and act on their files. It can mount DOS/Windows partitions on the system's hard disk, or access files and printers shared by Windows servers on the network, as we explored in "Sharing Files with Windows Systems (Samba)" in Chapter 15. Linux can also run DOS and Windows applications, using compatibility utilities that allow it to invoke MS-DOS or Windows. It can also access remote systems and run programs on them, using the local keyboard, mouse, and screen for interaction.

We use the term *Windows* somewhat generically in this chapter to refer to any of the operating systems coming from Microsoft, or those compatible with them. Although Windows NT, Windows 2000, and Windows XP are fundamentally different from the old DOS-based systems (up to and including Windows ME), most of the tools in this chapter can accommodate them all.

One of the most common reasons for needing to run Windows is that it often has better support for new hardware products. If you have installed Windows because you need to use a piece of hardware that is supported by Windows but for which there is no Linux driver, do not despair. Although you may have to wait a while for it, most mainstream hardware devices that are supported by Windows will eventually be supported by Linux, too. For example, Linux drivers for USB devices used to be rare and flaky, but now many common USB devices work just fine on Linux. You can get updated information about which USB devices work on Linux at *http://www.linux-usb.org*.

You may also need to run Windows in order to use "standard" applications, such as Photoshop or Microsoft Office. In both of these cases, there are free, open source applications (namely, the GIMP, KOffice, and OpenOffice.org) that can match or even outdo their proprietary, closed-source equivalents. However, it is still sometimes necessary to run Windows to obtain access to software products that have no Linux equivalent, or for which the Linux counterpart is not fully compatible.

There are essentially four ways in which Linux and Windows can cooperate:

- Sharing removable media such as USB keys, CDs, and floppy disks ("sneakernet")
- Sharing a computer by being installed on separate partitions
- Sharing data over a network
- Running concurrently on the same computer using an emulator or virtual machine

When Windows and Linux are running on separate hardware, and the systems are not networked, a floppy disk or CD (either CD-R or CD-RW) can be written on one system and read on the other. Both Windows and Linux have the capability to read and write CDs in industry-standard, ISO 9660 format. The *cdrecord* program, which runs on Linux and other Unix flavors, can create CDs using Microsoft's Joliet extensions to the ISO 9660 standard, making Windows feel right at home with the disk format.

A more cost-effective approach is to install both Windows and Linux on the same computer, each in its own disk partition. At boot time, the user is given the choice of which operating system to run. "Booting the System," in Chapter 17, tells you how to configure a multiboot system. You can then mount your Windows partition directly onto the Linux filesystem and access the Windows files in a manner similar to regular Unix files.

For networked computers, the most outstanding tool for getting Linux and Windows to cooperate is Samba, an open source software suite that lets you access Unix files and printers from Windows. Linux servers running Samba can—depending on the circumstances—serve Windows computers even faster than Windows servers can! In addition, Samba has proven to be very stable and reliable.

The Samba package also includes programs that work with the *smbfs* filesystem supported by Linux, which allows directories shared by Windows to be mounted onto the Linux filesystem. We discuss the *smbfs* filesystem and Samba in enough depth to help you mount shared directories and get a basic, functional server running.

Emulators or virtual computers are forms of software that let you run Windows applications directly under Linux, or even run Windows itself. Wine is an open source project with the goal of directly supporting Windows applications without needing to install Windows. Another approach is used by the commercial VMware application, which is able to concurrently run a number of installations of Windows, Linux, FreeBSD, or some other operating systems. When running Windows under VMware, data is shared with the Linux host using the Samba tools.

Finally, remote desktop applications let users on one system log in to other systems and run applications there, or even control the remote systems.

You should be a little skeptical of some claims of compatibility. You might find, for example, that you need twice the disk storage in order to support two operating systems and their associated files and applications programs, plus file conversion and graphic-format conversion tools, and so on. You may find that hardware tuned for one OS won't be tuned for the other, or that even when you've installed and correctly configured all the necessary software, small compatibility issues remain.

Sharing Partitions

As we've explained in the section "Mounting Filesystems" in Chapter 10, partitions on local hard disks are accessed by mounting them onto a directory in the Linux filesystem. To be able to read and write to a specific filesystem, the Linux kernel needs to have support for it.

Filesystems and Mounting

Linux has filesystem drivers that can read and write files on the traditional FAT filesystem and the newer VFAT filesystem, which was introduced with Windows 95 and supports long filenames. It also can read and (with some caveats) write to the NTFS filesystem of Windows NT/2000/XP.

In "Building a New Kernel" in Chapter 18, you learned how to build your own kernel. In order to be able to access DOS (used by MS-DOS and Windows 3.x) and VFAT (used by Windows 95/98/ME) partitions, you need to enable DOS FAT fs support in the File systems section during kernel configuration. After you say yes to that option, you can choose MSDOS fs support and VFAT (Windows-95) fs support. The first lets you mount FAT partitions, and the second lets you mount FAT32 partitions.

If you want to access files on a Windows NT partition that carries an NTFS filesystem, you need another driver. Activate the option NTFS filesystem support during the kernel configuration. This lets you mount NTFS partitions by specifying the file system type *ntfs*. Note, however, that the current NTFS driver supports just read-only access. There is a version of this driver available that supports writing as well, but at the time of this writing, it was still under development, and not guaranteed to work reliably when writing to the NTFS partition. Read the documentation carefully before installing and using it!

While Linux is running, you can mount a Windows partition like any other type of partition. For example, if the third partition on your first IDE hard disk contains your Windows 98 installation, you can make the files in it accessible with the following command, which must be executed as *root*:

```
# mount -t vfat /dev/hda3 /mnt/windows98
```

The */dev/hda3* argument specifies the disk drive corresponding to the Windows 98 disk, and the */mnt/windows98* argument can be changed to any directory you've created for the purpose of accessing the files. But how do you know that you need (in this case) */dev/hda3*? If you're familiar with the naming conventions for Linux filesystems, you'll know that *hda3* is the third partition on the hard disk that is the master on the primary IDE port. You'll find life easier if you write down the partitions while you are creating them with *fdisk*, but if you neglected to do that, you can run *fdisk* again to view the partition table.

The filesystem drivers support a number of options that can be specified with the *-o* option of the *mount* command. The mount(8) manual page documents the options that can be used, with sections that explain options specific to the *fat* and *ntfs* filesystem types. The section for fat applies to both the *msdos* and *vfat* filesystems, and there are two options listed there that are of special interest.

The *check* option determines whether the kernel should accept filenames that are not permissible on MS-DOS and what it should do with them. This applies only to creating and renaming files. You can specify three values for *check*. relaxed lets you do just about everything with the filename. If it doesn't fit into the 8.3 convention of MS-DOS files, the filename will be truncated accordingly. normal, the default, will also truncate the filenames as needed, and also removes special characters such as * and ? that are not allowed in MS-DOS filenames. Finally, strict forbids both long filenames and the special characters. To make Linux more restrictive with respect to filenames on the partition mounted in our example, the *mount* command could be used as follows:

```
# mount -o check=strict -t msdos /dev/sda5 /mnt/dos
```

This option is used with *msdos* filesystems only; the restrictions on filename length do not apply to *vfat* filesystems.

The *conv* option can be useful, but not as commonly as you might at first think. Windows and Unix systems have different conventions for how a line ending is marked in text files. Windows uses both a carriage return and a linefeed character, whereas Unix only uses a linefeed. Although this does not make the files completely illegible on the other system, it can still be a bother. To tell the kernel to perform the conversion between Windows and Unix text-file styles automatically, pass the *mount* command the option *conv*, which has three possible values: binary, the default, does not perform any conversion; text converts every file; and auto tries to guess whether the file in question is a text file or a binary file. auto does this by looking at the file-name extension. If this extension is included in the list of "known binary extensions," it is not converted; otherwise, it will be converted.

It is not generally advisable to use text, because this will invariably damage any binary files, including graphics files and files written by word processors, spreadsheets, and other programs. Likewise, auto can be dangerous, because the extension-based detection mechanism is not very sophisticated. So we suggest you don't use the *conv* option unless you are sure the partition contains only text files. Stick with *binary* (the default) and convert your files manually on an as-needed basis. See "File Translation Utilities," later in this chapter, for directions on how to do this.

As with other filesystem types, you can mount MS-DOS and NTFS filesystems automatically at system bootup by placing an entry in your */etc/fstab* file. For example, the following line in */etc/fstab* mounts a Windows 98 partition onto */win*:

```
/dev/hda1    /win   vfat   defaults,umask=002,uid=500,gid=500    0  0
```

When accessing any of the *msdos*, *vfat*, or *ntfs* filesystems from Linux, the system must somehow assign Unix permissions and ownerships to the files. By default, ownerships and permissions are determined using the user ID and group ID, and *umasking* of the calling process. This works acceptably well when using the *mount* command from the shell, but when run from the boot scripts, it will assign file ownerships to *root*, which may not be desired. In the previous example, we use the *umask* option to specify the file and directory creation mask the system will use when creating files and directories in the filesystem. The *uid* option specifies the owner (as a numeric user ID, rather than a text name), and the *gid* option specifies the group (as a numeric group ID). All files in the filesystem will appear on the Linux system as having this owner and group. Since dual-boot systems are generally used as workstations by a single user, you will probably want to set the *uid* and *gid* options to the user ID and group ID of that user's account.

File Translation Utilities

One of the most prominent problems when it comes to sharing files between Linux and Windows is that the two systems have different conventions for the line endings in text files. Luckily, there are a few ways to solve this problem:

* If you access files on a mounted partition on the same machine, let the kernel convert the files automatically, as described in "Filesystems and Mounting" earlier in this chapter. Use this with care!

- When creating or modifying files on Linux, common editors such as Emacs and *vi* can handle the conversion automatically for you.

- There are a number of tools that convert files from one line-ending convention to the other. Some of these tools can also handle other conversion tasks as well.

- Use your favorite programming language to write your own conversion utility.

If all you are interested in is converting newline characters, writing programs to perform the conversions is surprisingly simple. To convert from DOS format to Unix format, replace every occurrence of <CR><LF> (\r\f or \r\n) in the file to a newline (\n). To go the other way, convert every newline to a <CR><LF>. For example, we show you two Perl programs that do the job. The first, which we call *d2u*, converts from DOS format to Unix format:

```
#!/usr/bin/perl
while (<STDIN>) { s/\r$//; print }
```

And the following program (which we call *u2d*) converts from Unix format to DOS format:

```
#!/usr/bin/perl
while (<STDIN>) { s/$/\r/; print }
```

Both commands read the input file from the standard input, and write the output file to standard output. You can easily modify our examples to accept the input and output filenames on the command line. If you are too lazy to write the utilities yourself, you can see if your Linux installation contains the programs *dos2unix* and *unix2dos*, which work similarly to our simple *d2u* and *u2d* utilities, and also accept filenames on the command line. Another similar pair of utilities is *fromdos* and *todos*. If you cannot find any of these, then try the *flip* command, which is able to translate in both directions.

If you find these simple utilities underpowered, you may want to try *recode*, a program that can convert just about any text-file standard to any other.

The most simple way to use *recode* is to specify both the old and the new character sets (encodings of text-file conventions) and the file to convert. *recode* will overwrite the old file with the converted one; it will have the same filename. For example, to convert a text file from Windows to Unix, you would enter:

```
recode ibmpc:latin1 textfile
```

textfile is then replaced by the converted version. You can probably guess that to convert the same file back to Windows conventions, you would use:

```
recode latin1:ibmpc textfile
```

In addition to `ibmpc` (as used on Windows) and `latin1` (as used on Unix), there are other possibilities available, such as `latex` for the L^AT_EX style of encoding diacritics and `texte` for encoding French email messages. You can get the full list by issuing:

```
recode -l
```

If you do not like *recode*'s habit of overwriting your old file with the new one, you can make use of the fact that *recode* can also read from standard input and write to standard output. To convert *dostextfile* to *unixtextfile* without deleting *dostextfile*, you could use:

```
recode ibmpc:latin1 < dostextfile > unixtextfile
```

With the tools just described, you can handle text files quite comfortably, but this is only the beginning. For example, pixel graphics on Windows are usually saved as *bmp* files. Fortunately, there are a number of tools available that can convert *bmp* files to graphics file formats, such as *png* or *xpm*, that are more common on Unix. Among these are the GIMP, which is probably included with your distribution.

Things are less easy when it comes to other file formats, such as those saved by office productivity programs. Although the various incarnations of the *.doc* file format used by Microsoft Word have become a de facto lingua franca for word processor files on Windows, it was until recently almost impossible to read those files on Linux. Fortunately, a number of software packages have appeared that can read (and sometimes even write) *.doc* files. Among them are the office productivity suite KOffice, the freely available OpenOffice.org, and the commercial StarOffice 6.0, a close relative to OpenOffice.org. Be aware, though, that these conversions will never be perfect; it is very likely that you will have to manually edit the files afterward. Even on Windows, conversions can never be 100% correct; if you try importing a Microsoft Word file into WordPerfect (or vice versa), you will see what we mean.

In general, the more common a file format is on Windows, the more likely it is that Linux developers will provide a means to read or even write it. Another approach might be to switch to open file formats, such as Rich Text Format (RTF) or Extensible Markup Language (XML), when creating documents on Windows. In the age of the Internet, where information is supposed to float freely, closed, undocumented file formats are an anachronism.

Emulation and Virtual Operating Systems

The next step up from using Windows files within Linux shells and applications is to make Linux act like Windows so it can run Windows applications. In this section we discuss the two most popular ways to do this: Wine (along with CrossOver Office) and VMware.

Wine

Wine can get you out of a number of high-pressure situations, whether it's your friends bugging you to play the latest Half-Life 2 mod, or finding out after you converted your entire corporation to Linux that the CEO can't function without his favorite Access database.

Wine is a free software project that lets you run your favorite Windows programs on Linux. It does this by implementing Microsoft's Win32 application programming interface (only on Intel x86 systems).

The acronym Wine expands to "Wine Is Not an Emulator." Rather than emulating a Windows system, Wine translates between the Windows program and the underlying Linux system. You can think of Wine and its libraries as a piece of middleware that sits between your application and Linux (not unlike those other APIs we mentioned). However, no one will get angry if you call it an emulator because it sort of works like one.

Wine's roots can be traced back to 1993 and the earliest days of Linux. A group of developers thought it might be interesting to get Windows programs to run on Linux. At the time, Microsoft used the Win16 API in Windows 3.1. A newer operating system, Windows NT, was under intense development and was intended to usher in a wide range of new technologies, including the Win32 API. The Wine developers underestimated the amount of work involved with getting Win16 applications to run, and the subsequent Win32 programs that arrived in the next few years added an entirely new complication. Over time it became clearer how to design the architecture to allow Windows programs to run on Linux. Much of the core design was completed by 2000, but the sheer expanse of the Win32 API meant that several more years would be required just to implement its functionality. The latest versions of Wine support advanced APIs such as DirectX, the Microsoft Installer, and COM. A running joke within the Wine community is that it's been six to twelve months from completion for over a decade. However, things have progressed rapidly in the past few years and it's likely that by the time you read this a stable version of Wine exists.

Let's be realistic about what Wine can and can't do for you. A huge number of programs have been written for Windows over the years, and there's a sweet spot where programs tend to work well with Wine.

Anything before Windows 95 tends to run into problems. There are a lot of reasons for this, but the main reason is that the Win16 and DOS parts of Wine don't get used much, so bugs remain.

Similarly, the applications written for the latest and greatest version of Windows sometimes use features not yet implemented in Wine.

Everything in between, which generally means applications written for Windows 98, 2000, and XP, has a decent shot at running. Common applications that people use Wine with include the following:

Microsoft Office
Internet Explorer
Adobe Photoshop
Quicken

You may find some aspects of your application that won't work with Wine, in which case you'll need to evaluate whether they're necessary or whether perhaps a commercially supported version of Wine (described in a later section) can fix it.

Purists may argue that Wine simply degrades Linux and free software. Practically speaking, however, it's undeniable that more software exists for Windows operating systems than for any other. It's also undeniable that a huge amount of Windows software has turned into abandonware over the years as companies have gone out of business. Wine can expand the library of software you have access to and help you solve integration problems. Wine developers would be the first to point out you should always try to use a native Linux solution. If you can't, then maybe Wine can help you.

If you're a software developer, you may be interested in Winelib, which is the Wine version of the Win32 interfaces, exported for applications to link against. Thanks to Winelib, you can take the source code of a Windows program and recompile it on Linux with Wine. There are several advantages to this, such as being able to run a program on versions of Linux other than x86. Creating a Winelib app also means your program will have access to any native Linux library. For example, if you'd like to integrate an application with a native Linux sound system, you could rewrite parts of the application to work with ALSA. Winelib apps still require Wine to facilitate the management of system activities such as Windows threading. Winelib can be found at *http://www.winehq.org/site/winelib*.

Wine can help you solve a wide range of integration problems, though some work may be required on your part to make it function smoothly. Don't give up on Wine if your favorite application doesn't start up the first time you try it. Study the resources we point you to here, to get a feel for what you may need to do. Spend some time with the configuration tools to alter the default settings. If that doesn't work, you may want to download the trial version of CrossOver Office to evaluate whether it will work for you.

Getting and installing Wine

Like most free software, the decision you'll need to make concerning Wine is whether to compile from source code or download a binary version. Both offer advantages, but you should weigh the decision carefully. It's recommended you download a binary version if you can. The source code does utilize standard build tools, so if you're comfortable doing a standard *configure/make* build, you may find it to be a reasonable option. Regardless of which option you choose, you'll want to make sure certain pieces of software have been loaded and configured on your system.

Both the Wine source code and binary packages can be found on the WineHQ web site at *http://www.winehq.org/download*. For some distributions, such as Debian or Ubuntu, you can find additional information for installing packages. All of the individual package selections will redirect you to a download mirror. Wine development moves rapidly, and if your system came preinstalled with it, you should strongly consider upgrading to the latest version on WineHQ.

The Wine project maintains binary packages for the most common Linux distributions, including Red Hat, Mandriva, Fedora, SUSE, Debian, and Slackware. Chances are you can find a package to work with your distribution. Each package has been built specifically for its associated Linux distribution and may even offer some integration you wouldn't ordinarily find from the source distribution. In addition, each binary package has been compiled to work specifically with the set of libraries that come with your distribution. If you're not sure you have all the software installed on your system to compile Wine, download the binary version. Use your Linux distribution's package tool, such as *rpm* or *apt*, to install Wine.

If you choose to download Wine's source code, you'll need a standard build environment. Wine utilizes libraries that are standard on almost every Linux distribution, but you'll need to make sure you have the headers available for things such as X. Building consists of running just a few common commands from within the source code directory:

```
$ ./configure
$ make depend
$ make
```

Be sure to monitor the output from *configure* to make sure everything was found. To actually install the packages, you'll need root access. As *root*, run *make install* from within the source directory. The default installation directories are in */usr/local*, such as */usr/local/bin* and */usr/local/lib/wine*.

If you would like to access the latest development source code of Wine, you can download it from the CVS server. Wine's CVS tree remains relatively stable from day to day, and it's uncommon to run into a build problem. But, as with any software under development, you'll need to carefully evaluate whether it's worth being on the bleeding edge. To access the CVS server, you'll need to let CVS know where the repository is, log in, and then check out the actual source code:

```
$ export CVSROOT=:pserver:cvs@cvs.winehq.org:/home/wine
$ cvs login
$ cvs -z 0 checkout wine
```

For future updates, enter the newly created *wine* directory and simply run *cvs update -PAd*.

A simple example of using Wine

To get started with an application that uses Wine, let's walk through running a simple example. Afterward, we can examine the settings that get automatically configured by Wine. The defaults are sufficient for running simple programs, but you'll want to tweak them later for many applications.

To dive right in, run the Wine task manager application *taskmgr*. If your installation worked, you can enter:

```
$ wine taskmgr
```

Wine's task manager allows you to start, stop, and debug Wine processes.

After running *taskmgr*, you'll notice that a couple of things have been automatically set up in your account. Wine stores its settings in a special directory named *~/.wine* and in subdirectories below that. Within *~/.wine* you'll find that a system registry has been created and stored within three files named *system.reg*, *user.reg*, and *userdef.reg*. In addition, two important directories have been created: *dosdevices* and *drive_c*. The former contains all of the mappings necessary to configure your virtual Windows drives. The latter contains an entire virtual Windows drive with all of the directories you'd expect to find on Windows, such as *c:\windows* and *c:\Program Files*. We discuss each of these in more detail as we go on.

 Never run Wine as *root*. Programs run with Wine have access only to parts of the underlying operating system that the user running it has. Running as *root* can lead to security problems and even corrupt your Linux installation. The default configuration maps a virtual Windows drive to the root of the Linux filesystem, so running a Windows application as *root* would give it the access possible to modify or delete any file on your system.

Configuring Wine

Wine configuration generally involves a couple of graphical tools, but you can also use a regular text editor if you prefer. At the core of Wine's configuration lies the Wine registry. Because Windows applications require a registry to store settings, Wine was forced to implement a completely compatible system. For many years Wine also maintained a separate configuration file (the venerable *config* file.) Having two different configuration mechanisms made no sense, so Wine abandoned its custom mechanism to move its settings directly into the registry. Now you can configure both applications and Wine with one set of tools.

Wine comes with two different tools for configuration: *winecfg* and *regedit*. The first lets you easily control common settings. The second will let you control more obscure settings as well as the settings for your applications. Both tools access the registry files stored in *~/.wine*. Unlike Windows, these registry files are stored in a plain-text format. You can always fire up your favorite text editor and change the keys manually.

Run *winecfg* from the command line to start the program. The first thing you'll notice along the top are a series of tabs to configure applications, libraries, graphics, appearance, drives, and audio. The Applications, Libraries, and Graphics tabs are linked together to allow you to control settings for an individual program. For instance, on the Applications tab you'll notice you can change the Windows version that Wine reports to the program. The default attempts to emulate Windows 2000. You may find that a program responds differently if the Windows version is, say, Windows 98 versus Windows XP. If you happen to know the program explicitly requires Windows 2000, you can use the Add application button to locate your program's executable. Then you can change the Windows Version setting just for that program while leaving the Default Settings as they are. Likewise, all of the settings within the Libraries and Graphics tabs affect the application (or Default Settings) selected within the Applications tab.

The Libraries tab allows you to change the behavior of individual libraries. Wine can optionally use native Windows libraries if you have them available. For instance, if you have a Windows partition on your computer, you can copy the DLLs from *C:\WINDOWS\SYSTEM* to the corresponding directory within your virtual Windows drive.

To utilize one of those libraries, type the name of the library in the text box under "New override for library." For instance, if you copied *FOO.DLL* from Windows, enter foo in the text box and click on the Add button. By default, Wine tries to load the native Windows version followed by the built-in Wine version. You can change that load order to native only, built-in only, or either search combination using the Edit button. Using native Windows libraries can often work around deficiencies within Wine. But keep in mind that you can never replace the core Wine DLLs *kernel32*, *ntdll*, *user32*, or *gdi32*.

Games are the most common reason for changing settings within the Graphics tab. You may find that changing the color depth will enable a game to run better. If you have the XRandR extension available within your X server (and most systems do these days), Wine will attempt to resize your screen if requested by an application. That behavior may not be desirable, though. Therefore, Wine can "Emulate a virtual desktop" of a size of your choosing. The virtual desktop will run an application within an enclosed X window.

The Appearance tab does not affect the running of applications, but just allows you to customize Wine's look. It loads Windows XP themes based on *.msstyles* files.

Windows programs are sandboxed within a contained filesystem environment. The settings within the Drives tab allow you to adjust how much of the underlying Linux filesystem can be seen by an application. This can prevent misbehaving Windows programs from affecting anything else on your system. Wine can modify only files that the Linux user running it can modify. By default, Wine sets up a special virtual Windows drive in *~/.wine/drive_c* and installs Windows applications there. If you look at the drive mappings for your virtual C: drive, you'll see that they point to that location. If you would like to add another drive, click on the Add button and locate the Linux directory you'd like to access. For instance, if you have some removable media, you can add that mount point as a drive.

The final tab that controls audio settings is pretty self-explanatory. If you use the Autodetect button, it attempts to automatically figure out which one of Wine's audio drivers should be used. You can also set this manually using the drop-down box. If you have difficulty getting sound output, be sure to check the mixer settings within your distribution to make sure the volume on your audio device is turned up. Problems with audio are handled in Chapter 9.

In general, *winecfg* operates like Windows' control panels. It simply serves as a graphical interface to the underlying registry settings. And just as on Windows, you can configure these settings directly using the *regedit* tool. Just run *regedit* from the command line to open it. You'll find most of the settings we've discussed stored within the HKEY_CURRENT_USER\Software\Wine branch of the registry. For example, if you drill down through the hierachy using *regedit*, you'll see that the Windows version is stored directly in the key HKEY_CURRENT_USER\Software\Wine with a value of Version containing the data of the version, such as win98. *regedit* can also be useful for examining application settings. Usually these keys follow a naming convention like HKEY_LOCAL_MACHINE\Software*vendor\application*.

The only configuration settings not stored in the registry are drives and ports. The changes made using the Drives tab are stored directly in the filesystem using a series of symbolic links. If you look in the *~/.wine/dosdevices* directory, you'll see that each link points to the location within the filesystem to be accessed by the virtual drive. The default configuration will look something like this:

```
lrwxrwxrwx  1 wineuser wineuser  10 May  6 21:37 c: -> ../drive_c
lrwxrwxrwx  1 wineuser wineuser   1 May  6 21:37 z: -> /
```

Therefore, the virtual Windows drive c: points to *~/.wine/drive_c*. The z: points to the root of your filesystem. Accessing ports is done in a similar manner, and you may find you need to add a symbolic link for *com1* to something like */dev/ttyS0* in order to access the serial port. Of course, Wine will be able to access only the parts of your root filesystem that the user has access to.

Running Wine

To actually run applications, just invoke *wine*. First, locate the actual file you need to run. Most likely this means locating an installation program first. Generally the name will be something like *SETUP.EXE* or *INSTALL.EXE*. To run it, enter:

```
$ wine SETUP.EXE
```

The installation program should then execute and copy all of the files the program requires into your virtual Windows drive. It will also make any necessary registry changes. On Windows, this may mean setting up some special RunOnce registry keys that get executed when Windows reboots. The RunOnce keys will execute just that one time, but they typically perform actions necessary to set up a program for use. To simulate a reboot and execute these keys, run the *wineboot* command. Running that command really can't hurt anything, so you should always plan on running it after installing a program.

Once the program is installed, you need to locate the executable and run it. There's a chance Wine was able to modify your desktop's configuration and create an entry for this new program, so you may see an icon right on your desktop for the new program. You may also see menu entries in GNOME's Panel or KDE's Kicker toolbar. Wine will attempt to set up a special Wine menu containing all of the installed applications.

If that doesn't work, or if you prefer to run your application from the command line, navigate into the directory where you installed the application. Typically this will be something like *~/.wine/drive_c/Program\ Files/application*. Many Windows applications like to be executed from the working directory where the application is installed. From that directory simply enter:

```
$ wine program.EXE
```

At this point, you may find you need to tweak the configuration options using *winecfg* to adjust the Windows version or DLL overrides for the program. If you compiled Wine from source, you'll see FIXME messages printed out informing you of unimplemented Windows functions. Often the FIXME messages can lead you to the library experiencing the problem. Replacing that library with a native one may solve your problem. Installing third-party software may help as well. Internet Explorer and the libraries it comes with can often solve Internet-related issues.

Be sure you have a validly licensed copy of any software or libraries you install.

If you have a text-based application, you can run that with Wine as well. You may want to change the graphics driver to be *winetty.drv* rather than *winex11.drv* so it can run without requiring X Windows. However, some text-based programs misbehave and attempt to use graphical features for backend processing, so you may not be able to run it without X Windows support. To execute a text-based program, run it with the *wineconsole* command:

```
$ wineconsole program.EXE
```

Other programs you can run through *wine* include Wine versions of *Notepad*, *REGEDIT*, and many other common programs provided by Windows. The Wine versions of these programs access Winelib, and all of the graphical elements you see on the screen have been drawn by Wine.

Further help

If you run into problems, check out Wine's web site at *http://www.winehq.org* for more information. It has extensive user documentation. The FAQ might contain the answer to your question. If not, the Wine User Guide contains more in-depth coverage of the topics discussed here as well as other tips and tricks. Finally, several helpful documents have been put together to debunk popular myths, explain in more detail how Wine works, and highlight specific features.

Wine also hosts several resources to help resolve problems. If you look in the Application Database, *http://appdb.winehq.org*, you may find that someone has already solved the same problem you're chasing. If you would like to report a bug, check out Wine's Bugzilla database at *http://bugs.winehq.org*. You may find the mailing lists hosted on WineHQ helpful to solve problems, as well.

Lastly, a wiki has been set up to collect information from the community. If you would like to contribute, or you would like explore more documentation, you can find it at *http://wiki.winehq.org*.

CrossOver Office

If you're struggling with Wine, you may find that a commercial version works better. CodeWeavers' CrossOver Office, available from *http://www.codeweavers.com*, supports a small set of Windows applications. You can download a 30-day trial version for free to get a feel for whether it will work for you.

CodeWeavers actively tests Windows programs with its product, and its supported applications work really well. The current list includes over 30 different popular applications, including Microsoft Word, Excel, PowerPoint, Visio, Access, Quicken, iTunes, FrameMaker, and Lotus Notes. You can also use CrossOver Office to run popular web browser plug-ins, such as QuickTime, Shockwave Director, and Windows Media Player, and have them interoperate with a native Mozilla web browser. CrossOver Office provides a stable and tested version of Wine you can rely on. CodeWeavers also provides consulting services to help you run Windows programs on Linux. If you're looking for a company to provide the warm, fuzzy feeling of commercially supported Wine, CodeWeavers fits the bill.

CrossOver Office can be ordered and downloaded directly from CodeWeavers' web site. You have the option of downloading an RPM installer for Red Hat, SUSE, and other RPM-based distributions, a custom Debian installer, or a Loki-based installer. The Loki-based installer is the preferred method because it can be run entirely in user space.

After downloading the Loki-based installer, be sure to set the execute bit (*chmod +x*) on the installer script. Then you just need to run the following script:

```
$ ./install-crossover-standard-5.0.sh
```

The script will first unpack CrossOver Office and walk you through the installation. At the end it gives you the option to install Windows software. This launches the *cxoffice/bin/cxsetup* configuration tool and gives you a list of supported software you can install. This wizard-like tool will walk you through the process of installing the software and perform any additional steps necessary, such as restarting Wine to simulate a Windows reboot. You can also choose to install unsupported software. CrossOver Office runs many other applications besides the officially supported ones, and you may find your favorite Windows application works better with CrossOver Office than regular old Wine.

Regardless of whether you choose to install supported or unsupported software, you'll be prompted next for the location of the installation file. You can choose from either your vendor CD-ROM or a setup program on your hard drive. Some of the supported software will install automatically, but other software may require the installation program to run. When installation is complete, a simulated reboot of Wine is performed and menu entries are made for your desktop. Your desktop panel—KDE's *Kicker* or GNOME's *Panel*—will contain a new entry called Windows Applications that leads to the programs installed by CrossOver Office.

To configure CrossOver Office, navigate to the CrossOver menu in your desktop's panel and choose Configuration. You'll then be presented with the tab-based *cxsetup* dialog giving you options to Add/Remove programs or Manage Bottles. The first option allows you to manage applications, including the use of the Install button to launch the installation wizard described earlier.

The second option, Manage Bottles, allows you to customize aspects of CrossOver Office. *Bottles* are self-contained directories for sets of installed applications, each holding a complete Wine configuration. After selecting a bottle from the list available, you click on the Configure button to edit things such as menus, set file associations, configure plug-ins, add fonts, open control panel apps, and change bottle settings. Each tab contains a Help button in case you get stuck.

VMware Workstation

VMware (now owned by EMC) distributes proprietary products that permit the running of virtual operating systems on servers and workstations.* The workstation product has achieved a certain popularity by aiding people who want to run different operating systems on their computer desktop; among other things, they can run licensed versions of many different Windows operating systems on Linux. VMware Workstation also sees much use in development and testing. Many claim that it accelerates application deployment.

So what does it actually do?

VMware Workstation 5 allows multiple operating systems and applications to run at the same time on a single physical computer. If you have enough RAM, a decent hard drive, and a modern CPU, VMware performs well.

Figure 28-1 provides a look at VMware Workstation running on Novell Linux Desktop 9 with Windows XP Home Edition installed. This should give you an idea of what you can expect to see if you use this product. Notice on the top of the toolbar that an icon lets you select a full-screen mode. This option makes the screen look just like the guest operating system is running natively.

According to VMware, Workstation Version 5 runs on the following:

32-bit systems
> SUSE LINUX Pro 9.2, SUSE LINUX Enterprise Server 9.0, Mandrake Linux 10, Red Hat Enterprise Linux 4.0, and Windows Server 2003 SP1 beta (experimental support).

64-bit systems
> Red Hat Enterprise Linux 4.0, Red Hat Enterprise Linux 3.0, SUSE LINUX Enterprise Server 9, SUSE LINUX Enterprise Server 9 SP1, SUSE LINUX Enterprise Server 8, Windows Server 2003 SP1 (experimental support), and Windows XP (experimental support).

---

* Xen, which is free software, is another, increasingly popular virtualization tool that allows a large computer server to host multiple versions of Linux and some other operating systems.

Figure 28-1. VMware Workstation 5 on Novell Linux Desktop 9

Users of Fedora Core 3, Gentoo, Red Hat, and Debian have reported that VMware 5 also runs on their systems without difficulty, although the company does not claim to support them. As shown in Figure 28-1, the author found VMware completely functional on NLD 9.

Each guest operating system runs in an isolated virtualized machine. VMware maps a host's computer hardware resources to the virtual machine's resources, so each virtual machine has its own CPU, memory, disks, and I/O devices, so to speak. At least it looks that way to the guest operating system. The virtual machine appears to the guest operating systems as a standard x86 computer.

Once VMware Workstation installs on its host, you can install and run unmodified versions of Windows, Linux, Novell NetWare, and Sun Solaris x86, as well as applications written for those platforms, on one machine. The promise of VMware is for users to derive the benefit of using multiple PCs without the expense, physical setup, and maintenance of various hardware platforms. VMware Workstation makes it easy for Linux users to run Windows applications.

VMware Workstation as a product may turn out to have a limited lifetime. It could be seen as a way to allow Linux users to run their favorite Windows applications while they move toward replacing them with versions that run natively in GNOME, KDE, and other desktop environments. It's worth remembering that the workstation product is just one product among VMware's offerings, and that the future for VMware, the company, probably lies in the server area, where it has given Linux a leg up in the data center.

Still, VMware has an important place in the history and evolution of Linux. Many people still love it and are glad it's around. Hopefully, the company will continue to innovate and make using Windows applications simpler for Linux users while it grows its server business.

Installing VMware Workstation 5

We had some difficulty installing VMware on SUSE Professional 9.2, even though the company listed it as a supported platform. The installation seems simple. One downloads VMware as either a *gunzip*ped tarball or as an RPM. Once the package installs, simply run **vmware-config.pl**. But SUSE 9.2 kept giving this error message:

```
None of the pre-built vmmon modules for VMware Workstation is suitable
for your running kernel. Do you want this program to try to build the
vmmon module for your system (you need to have a C compiler installed
on your system)?
CC [M] /tmp/vmware-config1/vmmon-only/linux/driver.o
/bin/sh: scripts/basic/fixdep: No such file or directory
make[2]: *** [/tmp/vmware-config1/vmmon-only/linux/driver.o] Error 1
make[1]: *** [_module_/tmp/vmware-config1/vmmon-only] Error 2
make[1]: Leaving directory `/usr/src/linux-2.6.11.4-21.7'
make: *** [vmmon.ko] Error 2
make: Leaving directory `/tmp/vmware-config1/vmmon-only'
Unable to build the vmmon module.
```

When we decided to switch and try Novell Linux Desktop, installing it without any updates, VMware installed as well. Afterward, we updated NDL 9 and tested VMware Workstation 5; it continued to work.

We later discovered that SUSE's 9.x kernels have patches that do not come with a stock Linux kernel. Many packages relying on prebuilt modules fail. You can recompile the modules as a workaround. To recompile the modules, use:

```
# cd /usr/src/linux
# make cloneconfig
# make prepare
# vmware-config.pl
```

vmware-config.pl will then find all the necessary files as if a fresh kernel had been compiled.

You also may find some confusion on the VMware site regarding which Linux distributions can operate as "guest" systems and which operate as hosts. Think of this like inviting a guest to your home. You escort them into the living room, where you sit and talk. In VMware terms, when you install VMware, you create a living room for a guest operating system.

In this case, you are running Linux as the host system and install Microsoft Windows as a guest. If you are interested in installing other Linux distributions as guests, make sure you check with the VMware web site for supported guests (as opposed to hosts). Officially supported guest operating systems include the following:

Mandrake Linux 8.2, 9.0, 9.2, 10
Novell Linux Desktop 9
Red Hat Linux 7.0, 7.1, 7.2, 7.3, 8.0, 9.0
Red Hat Enterprise Linux AS/ES/WS 4.0 (32-bit)
Red Hat Enterprise Linux AS/ES/WS 2.1, 3.0
Red Hat Enterprise Linux Advanced Server 2.1
SUSE Linux 7.3, 8.0, 8.1, 8.2, 9.0, 9.1, 9.2
SUSE Linux Enterprise Server 7, 7 patch 2, 8, 9, 9 SP1
Turbolinux 7.0, Enterprise Server 8, Workstation 8
Sun Java Desktop System (JDS) 2

The virtual hardware of VMware 5 runs better than previous versions. With a single Pentium IV or an equivalent AMD processor and 512 MB of RAM, one should be able to run two virtual machines simultaneously. The previous versions would grind to a halt in such a scenario.

VMWare Workstation 5 features

Once you get used to the novelty of seeing another familiar operating system running on your Linux system, you can start to consider the advanced capabilities of VMWare Workstation 5 that turn it into an excellent platform for system testing and group development work.

Operating system snapshots. Version 5 of VMware provides for multiple snapshots so that a user can preserve the state of a guest and revert to an older state after powering down and starting up again. You can configure a virtual machine to take a snapshot and preserve an audit trail. If you need to examine a virus, for example, you can take a snapshot before you introduce the malware. If the virus does damage, you can restore the virtual machine to the state preserved in that snapshot. The same capability can prove valuable when you're testing new code or a patch.

Previous versions of VMware allowed for the taking of snapshots. However, each snapshot would overwrite the previous one. So, for testing purposes, Version 5 provides a significant upgrade.

Virtual networks. Workstation teams allow users to set up a virtual network or lab on a host computer. You can power up multiple virtual machines, as mentioned earlier. You then can configure networking the way you would on any local area network, however, this network would run on a single computer.

Users can work together in what VMware calls a LAN segment. They are invisible to the host computer's network, which creates a virtual safe house for development.

Cloning. VMware Workstation 5 provides interesting deployment capabilities with what the company calls *clones*. In VMware workstation terms, two types of clones exist. One is called a full clone, which we might consider to be similar to a ghosted image used to provision another computer. The second type of clone is called a linked clone. It remains dependent on the original image.

VMware's full clone functions as an independent copy of a virtual machine. Once a user makes the clone, it runs separate from the parent. It then can go off and become a unique instance that you can use to make changes or deploy for whatever purpose you see fit.

VMware's linked clone shares virtual disks with the original or parent, conserving disk space. This permits multiple virtual machines to use the same software installation. Also, linked clones take less time to create than a full clone.

Labs might want to create linked clones to provide identical environments to developers, quality assurance engineers, testers, or maintenance programmers. If you store a linked virtual machine on your local network, other users can make a linked clone quickly. A support team can reproduce a bug in a virtual machine, and an engineer quickly can make a linked clone of that virtual machine to work on the bug.

The files on the parent of a linked clone continue to exist at the time one creates a snapshot, and continue to remain available to the linked clone. Changes to the parent don't affect the linked clone, and changes to the disk of the linked clone don't affect the parent.

Other Programs for Running MS-DOS and Windows Applications on Linux

A number of other attempts have been made by different groups of developers, both open source and commercial, to bring DOS and Windows programs to Linux. The simplest is Dosemu (*http://www.dosemu.org*), which emulates PC hardware well enough for MS-DOS (or compatible systems such as PC-DOS or DR-DOS) to run. It is still necessary to install DOS in the emulator, but since DOS is actually running inside the emulator, good application compatibility is assured. To a limited extent, it is even possible to run Windows 3.1.

Another open source project is Bochs (*http://bochs.sf.net*), which emulates PC hardware well enough for it to run Windows and other operating systems. However, because every 386 instruction is emulated in software, performance is reduced to a small percentage of what it would be if the operating system were running directly on the same hardware.

The *plex86* project (*http://savannah.nongnu.org/projects/plex86*) takes yet another approach, and implements a virtualized environment in which Windows or other operating systems (and their applications) can run. Software running in the virtual machine runs at full speed, except for when it attempts to access the hardware. It is very much like Dosemu, except the implementation is much more robust, and not limited to running just DOS.

At the time this book was written, all of the projects discussed so far in this section were fairly immature, and significantly limited. To put it bluntly, the sayings, "Your mileage may vary" and "You get what you pay for" go a long way here.

You may have better luck with a commercial product, such as VMware (*http://www.vmware.com*) or Win4Lin (*http://www.win4lin.com*). Both of these work by implementing a virtual machine environment (in the same manner as *plex86*), so you will need to install a copy of Windows before you can run Windows applications. The good news is that with VMware, at least, the degree of compatibility is very high. VMware supports versions of DOS/Windows ranging from MS-DOS to .NET, including every version in between. You can even install some of the more popular Linux distributions, to run more than one copy of Linux on the same computer. To varying extents, other operating systems, including FreeBSD, NetWare, and Solaris, can also be run. Although there is some overhead involved, modern multi-gigahertz CPUs are able to yield acceptable performance levels for most common applications, such as office automation software.

Win4Lin is a more recent release than VMware. At the time of this writing, it ran Windows and applications faster than VMware, but was able to support only Windows 95/98/ME, and not Windows NT/2000/XP. As with other projects described in this section, we suggest keeping up-to-date with the product's development, and check once in a while to see if it is mature enough to meet your needs.

Remote Desktop Access to Windows Programs

In this section of the chapter, we switch gears and look at Linux as a thin client for a Microsoft Windows terminal server. Under this scenario, a site's system administrator runs the applications desired by the users on a central Windows system (making sure there are enough licenses to support all the users), and the users access the application transparently through Linux systems. Performance is often better than when users run the same programs locally on Windows PCs!

If you did not know Microsoft offered Terminal Services, the material in this section may come as a pleasant surprise. These services are offered through a feature called Remote Desktop Protocol or Remote Display Protocol (RDP), which can interact with an open source project called *rdesktop*. Thus, *rdesktop* provides the tools Linux needs to run Microsoft Windows software applications natively from NT 4.0, Windows 2000 Server, XP Pro, and Windows Server 2003.

Few people think of a Microsoft Windows server as an application host. When Microsoft released its first viable Network Operating System (NOS), Windows NT Version 3.51 and later 4.0, they did not have such facilities. Windows NOS servers traditionally ran back-office applications such as email, various databases, and web servers. A third-party provider, Citrix, offered Terminal Services through its Win-Frame product, a multiuser technology originally used in NT 3.51 that opened up the NT kernel for multiple sessions per system.

Now Microsoft packages terminal server clients for Windows and Apple desktops. It has allowed Citrix to create terminal extensions and offer solutions to Unix and eventually Linux. But through the directions in this section, Linux can utilize *rdesktop* and Samba to directly access Windows terminal servers without the use of Citrix extensions.

rdesktop and TSCLient

As we stated, *rdesktop* lets a Linux system run Windows applications that reside on a remote Windows system. It also lets Linux participate in the remote Windows administration available with Terminal Services. That allows you the use of both operating systems simultaneously.

Matthew Chapman, a graduate student from the University of New South Wales, Australia, wrote *rdesktop* as an open source client for Windows NT Terminal Server, Windows 2000, Windows XP Professional, and Microsoft Server 2003 Terminal Services. You don't need a license from Microsoft to use *rdesktop* itself (only to use the Microsoft applications). Think of *rdesktop* as you would a Internet browser, or an FTP, Telnet, or SSH client.

A Case Study in Using Linux with RDP

As an example of the benefits of using Linux as a remote desktop, this author set up Microsoft Terminal Services for a workgroup needing access to Exchange Server. We utilized Windows 2003 with Outlook 2000 as the primary application. This allowed our engineers to reply to meeting requests and use the enterprise scheduling system. It also allowed a secretary to manage department personnel's calendars.

Previously, the IT department had purchased laptops for each engineer for the sole purpose of accessing Outlook for meeting management and scheduling. Each laptop cost the department approximately $4,000. Eventually, therefore, the IT department decided to reprovision the laptops to the sales department while setting up a workgroup server for the engineers.

In the new configuration, the workgroup server ran Terminal Services, licensing services, and WINS. Each Linux computer ran Samba and enabled WINS client in its Samba configuration file. The workgroup server utilized local accounts for the department personnel.

Once we could resolve NetBIOS names to IP addresses at the server and workstation level, we added local users to the Remote Desktop Users group. This allowed the Windows server to recognize the Linux hosts and vice versa. The users could then log on and use the multiuser-aware applications.

To use your Linux desktop to run Windows applications, you'll need to configure Windows Terminal Services for applications and remote administration, add the open source *rdesktop* and its popular frontend, TSClient, and configure them for use. Additionally, you can add another component called Virtual Network Computing (VNC) and access Windows, Macintosh OS X, and other Linux desktops remotely using a slightly different approach from Terminal Services.

 You need Microsoft licenses to access and use the company's applications. Microsoft requires a Client Access License (CAL) to access a Microsoft Windows server. You also need a legitimate application product license if you plan to run standard software such as Microsoft Office.

To interoperate with Microsoft's RDP, *rdesktop* uses industry-standard protocols: the Internet Engineering Task Force standards discussed in RFCs 905 and 2126. Those documents implement the Telecommunication Standardization Sector ITU-T.128 application sharing protocol. Matthew released *rdesktop* under the GNU Public License (GPL) as free, open source software.

TSClient is the most popular and easy-to-use graphical interface to *rdesktop*. Most Linux distributions provide *rdesktop* and TSClient in their default configurations.

Occasionally, you might have to specify the RDP components as options when installing Linux or download them from a repository.

Setting up Windows Terminal Services

Unless you have configured a Windows server, you may find it difficult to visualize the kinds of tasks required to enable Linux to use Win32 applications from NT Version 4 or 5. Initially, you will need a Microsoft NOS and the ability to install Terminal Services. You will also need to configure a way for the terminal server to resolve your Linux workstations to a TCP/IP address.

Figure 28-2 provides a look at how a Windows 2000 server sets up Terminal Services. Notice the large screen with the heading Windows 2000 Configure Your Server. On the left side of that window under the heading Application Server, you can see the subheading Terminal Services.

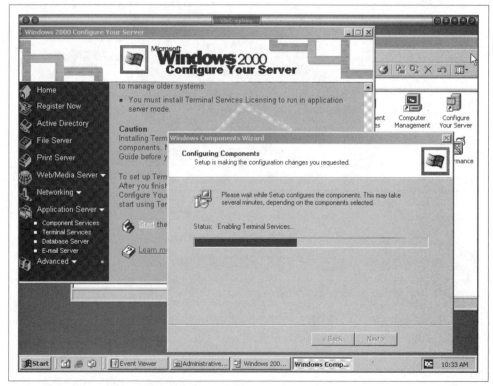

Figure 28-2. Configuring Terminal Services in Windows 2000 and Windows Server 2003

The small window in the foreground of Figure 28-2 shows the progress of installation while the operating system installs the terminal server components in the background. Prior to the release of Windows 2000 Server, you had to order a separate component to run applications from NT. Now, Terminal Services come as an integral part of the NOS.

Figure 28-3 shows the same process for Windows Server 2003. The configuration wizard still displays a dialog screen, but you see a more verbose set of instructions on the wizard screen.

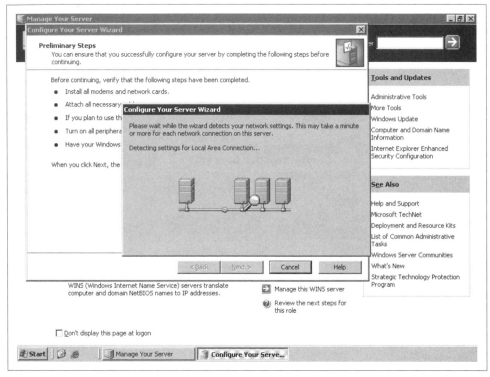

Figure 28-3. The configuration wizard in Windows Server 2003

One of the major differences in the 2003 version of the NOS deals with license management. Microsoft requires activation of Client Access Licenses for its latest server. So, in addition to installing Terminal Services, users must install a license server and activate it over the Internet or by phone.

If you have fewer than 25 users requiring Terminal Services, license services can reside on the same computer. If you have more than 100 users accessing the terminal server, you will want a second computer just to manage the Client Access Licenses.

Figure 28-4 shows how to configure a Windows 2003 server in the role of a terminal server. Select the role and double-click it. You can see, in the highlighted section of this screen, a "Yes" under the column entitled "configured."

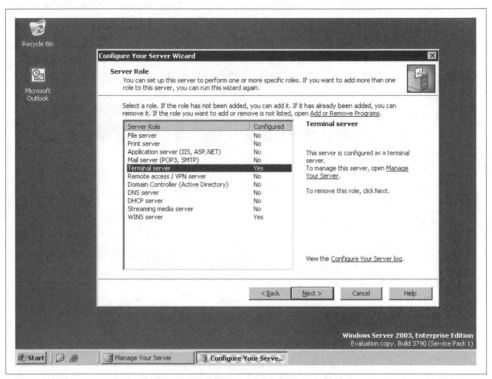

Figure 28-4. Service Options in Windows Server 2003

To summarize what we just covered, remember the following:

1. You must set up Terminal Services on Microsoft servers explicitly by adding it as a Windows component.

2. Terminal Services require Client Access Licenses, and the current Microsoft servers require you to activate the licenses with Microsoft or the server will refuse connection requests.

3. Microsoft applications running in terminal service mode require licenses for each user and require explicit activation.

Connecting to the terminal server

Before you can run a Windows application on your Linux desktop from the terminal server, you need to install and set up *rdesktop*. The best way to run *rdesktop* involves using TSClient. TSClient is simply a graphical interface to *rdesktop*. You can execute the *rdesktop* commands from a console, but the TSClient GUI makes connecting easier for some people. It also allows you to save a configuration file for one or more terminal servers to which you might connect. Figure 28-5 shows TSClient running Microsoft Outlook on a Linux desktop. TSClient provides a Terminal Services configuration dialog box similar to what you see on Windows.

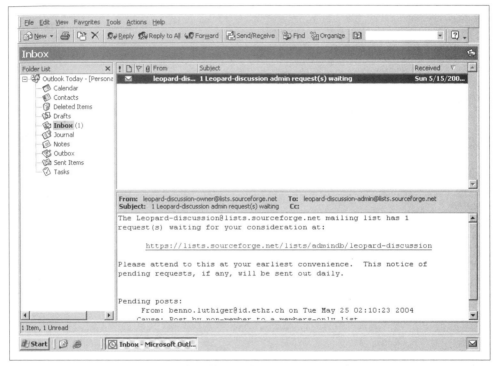

Figure 28-5. Microsoft Outlook displayed by TSClient on a Linux desktop

Making Windows applications multiuser aware

The most common applications used on terminal servers are those in the Microsoft Office suite. Other applications, including custom-written ones, require modifications to run in multiuser mode. The examples here give you an idea of how you might install Microsoft Office.

When installing Office 2000 on a terminal server, you need to install the Office 2000 Resource Kit and specify a *transform* file, which ends with a *.mst* extension. Some people think of such a file as a mini-specification file. The file tells Terminal Services that the installation of the Office 2000 component is for multiuser mode.

At the beginning of the Office installation procedure, you need to specify the path to the transform file in the Office 2000 Resource Kit. For example, the setup command might look like this:

```
E:/Set.exe G:\Program Files\ORKTools\ToolBox\Tools\Terminal Server Tools\TERMSRVR.MST
```

The default Microsoft SDK transform file comes with the Resource Kit. You can also make your own transform file. Some applications, such as Internet Explorer, run from the Windows menu and do not require modifications, unless you wish to change the security settings. But if you use Microsoft Office products including Microsoft Project, Visio, or media tools, most administrators will want to restrict access to those features depending on the needs of the users. Some users don't need templates for doing drafting, so loading the drafting templates is a waste of memory, disk space, and bandwidth. Eliminating features can improve performance.

Office XP on a Terminal Services server gives you the option of using the Office XP Custom Installation Wizard to create a transform file to hold customized settings. You then install Office on the Terminal Services server by using that transform. All Office XP users who log on to the Terminal Services server receive the customized settings you defined in the transform.

On Windows Server 2003, the only version of Office 2003 that supports Terminal Services is Office 2003 Enterprise Edition. It makes installation easier than Office 2000. Setup detects the use of Terminal Services automatically. By default, Microsoft makes some features unavailable. Office 2003 users who log on to the Terminal Services server receive the settings defined by Microsoft and the administrator who installs the Office suite.

Using Windows applications from the Linux desktop

To launch TSClient from Fedora Core 3, simply select Launch → Internet → Terminal Server → Client. Once you have launched TSClient, you need to configure it for use with Windows Terminal Server in order to run applications. Figure 28-6 shows the first set of parameters required to start your client session.

Notice we use the Windows NetBIOS or host alias name of the server in the first line. Other parameters specify the RDP protocol and the Windows domain the system is in, which is known by the system administrator who set up the Windows server. Include your login name and your password on the Windows domain.

If you want to save configuration options for a session so you don't have to retype them next time, you can create a protocol file from the fields you've typed in. Use the Save As button to preserve the information for later use. In this example, we saved a file called *gateway.tsc*. By clicking Open, a user can load that file and it will populate the Terminal Server client with the saved settings.

Figure 28-6. Terminal Server client on a Linux desktop

Notice in Figure 28-6 that five tabs exist toward the top of the screen. Each of these tabs has parameters you can use to configure the look and feel of your session as well as the application that opens when you connect to the server. In Figure 28-7, you can see the options available in the Display tab; among its useful options are altering the size of the display and the color depth. Lowering the color depth can reduce the bandwidth you take up when using Terminal Services. In this display, we used a 16-bit color depth.

The remaining tabs provide additional options. For example, Local Resources allows you to stream sound to your terminal and specify key combinations as well as language options for your keyboard. You can also select a program to start immediately by specifying it in the next tab to the right, entitled Programs. This saves time log-

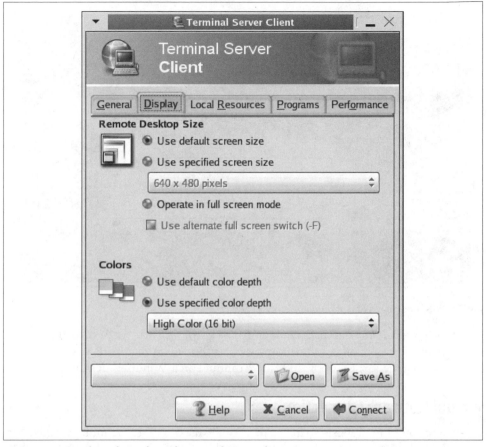

Figure 28-7. Display tab window of Terminal Server client

ging in to the server and selecting icons to launch a program if you use only one application, such as Microsoft Outlook.

The Performance tab allows you to enable bitmap caching, motion events, and a window manager's key bindings and its decorations. You may want to hide the window manager's decorations so that you can immediately tell that you have opened a terminal session.

Once you have pressed the Connect button on the bottom of the Terminal Server client screen, you will see a logon screen for the server. For instance, Figure 28-8 shows the log-on box for a Windows Server 2003 Enterprise Edition.

The remote application screen also appears as a Linux application on the desktop. On the task bar at the bottom of Figure 28-8, you can see that the open application named Gateway Terminal Service Client appears as the second application from the

Figure 28-8. Logging in to a Windows Terminal Server

left. Once you enter your username and password, you can log on to the remote desktop and see an application window such as the one in Figure 28-9, which shows a live calendar view of Outlook 2000 SR-1 running on a Windows desktop.

Virtual Network Connection

In this section our emphasis switches to a widely used remote technology called Virtual Network Connection (VNC). We discuss how VNC works and its value in heterogeneous networks. We also discuss installing it on different hosts and how to use it.

More people use VNC than any other remote desktop tool; several open source VNC projects exist. Servers exist for Linux, Windows, Macintosh, and Unix operating systems. Clients exist for Linux, Windows, Macintosh, Unix, MS-DOS, Palm, and Java. Still, not all Linux users understand how valuable VNC can be.

Perhaps VNC's most powerful feature is to let you control a number of different computers from one keyboard, mouse, and monitor. In a sense, VNC can function as a virtual KVM switch.

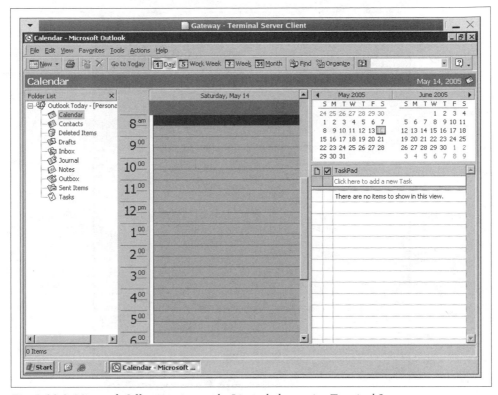

Figure 28-9. Microsoft Office running on the Linux desktop using Terminal Server

 A KVM switch is a hardware device that allows a user to control multiple computers from a single keyboard, video monitor, and mouse. KVM is an acronym for keyboard, video, mouse.

In Figure 28-10, you can see a remote session of VNC running on a Fedora Core 3 GNOME desktop. If you look closely, you can see the GNOME panels at the bottom of the screen. In this figure, we have opened a session of a popular VNC implementation called TightVNC. In the window, you will notice that we have accessed a Microsoft Windows XP desktop and opened the native Remote Desktop client application, which we could use to start a Terminal Services session. VNC displays the entire remote desktop, not just a single application.

VNC requires a client and server to create a session. In the previous example, the server runs on the remote desktop and we used the *vncviewer* command to start the session. It put up the small dialog box shown in Figure 28-11.

Figure 28-10. Opening a remote VNC session in GNOME on Fedora Core 3

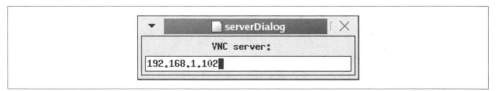

Figure 28-11. Logging on to a remote VNC desktop

Figure 28-11 shows the simplicity of starting a remote session:

- Start *vncviewer* from the command line.
- Enter the TCI/IP address of the remote server in the dialog box and press Enter.
- At the resulting password prompt, enter your password on the remote system.

At that point, you should see a window containing the remote desktop, similar to the one in Figure 28-12.

Figure 28-12 shows some typical activity on a remote Windows XP desktop as viewed from a Fedora Core 3 GNOME desktop. Two events are taking place on the

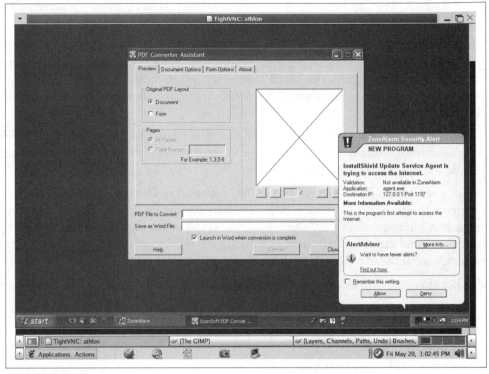

Figure 28-12. Activity on a remote desktop

remote desktop: the Linux user has started a program to convert a PFD file to a Word file, and in response, a security product called ZoneAlarm is informing the user that the application is attempting to access the Internet to check for updates.

VNC allows the user to take control of the remote computer. It is not a remote terminal session, like that provided by Windows Terminal Server, because you do not log in to a server. You do not require a Client Access License. Instead, anything you do on the VNC session will be under the auspices of the user who logged on to the remote desktop.

Let's see how this works.

VNC establishes remote access to a computer over a local area network or over the Internet using TCP/IP. VNC uses Remote Frame Buffer protocol (RFB). The RFB service grabs the screen image and sends it to the client in response to the client's requests. Once the server moves the screen image data, that data becomes compatible with any client ported to supported operating systems. The VNC client takes what the server sends and paints the image of the remote screen in a window on the client desktop. The client transmits mouse and keyboard data back to the server, giving a user control over a remote desktop.

VNC transmits screen data from the server to the client. It compresses the screen data to conform to the bandwidth and CPU power on each end of the connection. Once the client establishes the initial frames and pixels in the viewer window, the server transmits only those areas of the screen that have changed. The frame itself remains the same.

VNC creates stateless sessions. The user can disconnect from a session and then reconnect from a totally different machine to resume work where she left off. Some people use this feature to provide mobility.

Either a server or a client may initiate a VNC connection. Usually, it is the client that connects to the server for remote access operations, but in a tech-support environment it is often useful to have the server connect to a waiting client. The tech support personnel can then lead the user through the resolution of his problem as if in person, even if the two are many miles apart.

Further strengths of VNC include the following:

- It allows a client to connect to any VNC server regardless of the operating system on each side.
- It provides a secure, encrypted connection between client and server.
- It's free, GPL-compliant software.

Current VNC endpoints (clients and servers) are largely based on TCP/IP, enabling them to be used on a very wide range of networks. It is entirely sensible and practical to implement VNC using some other kind of reliable, bidirectional protocol, but such systems are at present almost nonexistent.

Setting up VNC

You can obtain VNC from several sources. Most users prefer either RealVNC or TightVNC, which you can find at *http://www.realvnc.com* and *http://www.tightvnc.com*, respectively. Using either of these web sites, download and install the software on the platforms you want to use. To begin using VNC, you need to run a VNC server and then connect to it from the system running the VNC client through a viewer.

Installing the Windows server, WinVNC, should create a RealVNC group in a Windows Start menu. Then, by running the VNC server as shown in Figure 28-13, you can start the service. With the service running, you can use *vncviewer* to initiate a session from a remote client.

Figure 28-13. Launching WinVNC Server from the RealVNC group in the Start menu

The first time you use a VNC server on a machine, the applications prompt you to set a password. In Windows, a small icon appears in the system tray; by right-clicking on this icon, you can control most aspects of the server. Connecting to the machine from a remote location also requires the password. The initial security uses a challenge/response protocol, which is reasonably secure. From that point on, you will need to find a third-party solution to provide a secure connection between a client and server.

The RFB protocol does not travel over a normal connection in an encrypted mode. For that reason, many people use OpenSSH or some variation on it, and use VNC through an encrypted tunnel. Using VNC with OpenSSH is beyond the scope of this book. However, many articles exist on the Internet that can help you create an encrypted VNC tunnel. When looking, be sure to specify the type of operating systems you will use.

Running a Linux VNC server

With Linux applications, a VNC server appears like an X display. Applications continue running on the remote system whether or not you are connected to it. Start the VNC server on a Linux desktop with the command:

```
$ vncserver
```

You'll probably want to run it in the background because it doesn't exit until you finish your session.

The first time you run the VNC server, the system will prompt you for a system password. This is the password people will use to connect to the machine with an active VNC server. All servers on the same Linux machine will use the same password by default. If you wish to change the password at a later time, you can do so by using the command:

```
$ vncpasswd
```

Once you issue the command, you will be prompted for the current password and the one you wish to use in the future.

With a normal X system, the X display of a workstation uses its hostname and display, in a format such as hostname:0.

On Linux, you can run many VNC servers. They will appear as hostname:1, hostname:2, and so forth, as if each were an additional display. *vncserver* chooses the first available display number and tells you what it is. In some situations, you have pre-existing sessions that you want people to use. You can cause applications to use a pre-existing VNC server rather than the normal X display by setting the DISPLAY environment variable to the VNC server you want, or by starting the application with the *-display* option. For example:

```
$ xterm -display hostname:2 &
```

You can kill a Unix VNC server by using, for example:

```
$ vncserver -kill :2
```

FreeNX: Linux as a Remote Desktop Server

Imagine X server technology with compression so tight that GNOME and KDE sessions run over modems with SSH encryption with impressive response time. FreeNX is an addition to the remote desktop line with stunning performance. Thin clients use small amounts of bandwidth while handling audio and video, printing, and other heavy applications, and permit the use of session suspension instead of termination. As long as you wish to primarily use Linux, FreeNX provides real virtual KVM switches without hardware.

FreeNX differs from both Windows RDP and VNC because it makes Linux the source of the applications people use. So if you want to set up a Linux server and provide OpenOffice.org or Firefox web browsers to remote users with minimal hardware, FreeNX would work for you. Also, if you have clients such as Windows 98 or Mac OS X, you can obtain free clients from *http://nomachine.com* to allow those platforms to connect and run those applications from the Linux server.

Using FreeNX server on Linux creates a secure environment for remote computing. Clients can run on Linux, of course, but FreeNX can also create X client sessions on various operating systems such as Windows and Macintosh without the need to install X. Clients also exist at the time of this writing for PlayStation2, iPAQ, and Zaurus 5XXX.

System administrators like FreeNX because they can control the features and content available to their users. They can also see and operate every Linux server in their data centers with a single keyboard, video console, and mouse. They can do this without a hardwire switch or keyboard, mouse, and video cables. They can also display multiple windows on a single desktop and monitor many servers at once, which they can't do with a KVM switch beccause it is limited to one server at a time.

Gian Filippo Pinzari invented NX by taking the fat and insecure X client/server protocol and utilizing inventive compression to make it very thin. His company, NoMachine.com, released the code under the GPL license in 2003.

Let's see how to set up and use FreeNX. We use an example that utilizes two free Linux distributions, Fedora and Ubuntu. First, we install FreeNX on Ubuntu, after obtaining it from the Ubuntu backports community at *http://backports.ubuntuforums.org*. Follow the directions on the site and add the recommended mirrors to your */etc/apt/sources.list* file. Then run *apt-get install FreeNX* to add FreeNX to your server.

Once installed, add a user, as shown in Figure 28-14.

Following the setup, if you log out and log back in, you will see FreeNX added to the Applications menu under Internet. See Figure 28-15.

Next, obtain and install the RPMs for Fedora from *http://fedoranews.org/contributors/rick_stout/freenx*. Be sure to install both the client and the server. Again, add yourself as a user.

Client configuration involves running a wizard. As the wizard says, "The most important part of the initial connection is the key file. This file, client.id_dsa.key, must be copied from the server to your client machine." Following these directions, I executed the following commands:

```
bash-3.00# scp /var/lib/nxserver/home/.ssh/client.id_dsa.key
username@192.168.1.109:~/
```

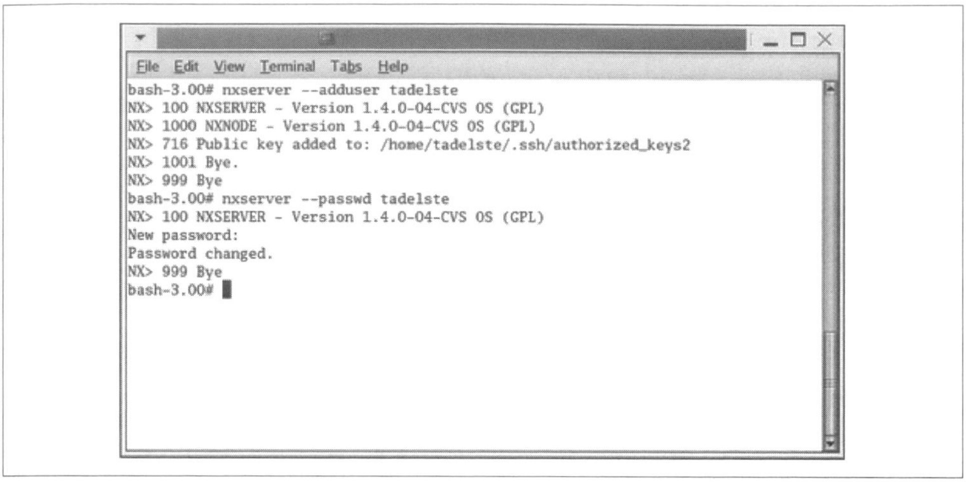

```
File  Edit  View  Terminal  Tabs  Help
bash-3.00# nxserver --adduser tadelste
NX> 100 NXSERVER - Version 1.4.0-04-CVS OS (GPL)
NX> 1000 NXNODE - Version 1.4.0-04-CVS OS (GPL)
NX> 716 Public key added to: /home/tadelste/.ssh/authorized_keys2
NX> 1001 Bye.
NX> 999 Bye
bash-3.00# nxserver --passwd tadelste
NX> 100 NXSERVER - Version 1.4.0-04-CVS OS (GPL)
New password:
Password changed.
NX> 999 Bye
bash-3.00#
```

Figure 28-14. Adding users to the FreeNX server

Figure 28-15. FreeNX on the menu

```
The authenticity of host '192.168.1.109 (192.168.1.109)' can't be
established.
RSA key fingerprint is 40:54:e3:c9:5e:81:39:2d:ac:70:b9:bf:44:a9:ec:a8.
Are you sure you want to continue connecting (yes/no)? yes
Warning: Permanently added '192.168.1.109' (RSA) to the list of known
hosts.
Password: password entered here
client.id_dsa.key                        100%   672      0.7KB/s
00:00
bash-3.00#
```

Once you accomplish these tasks, you should be able to use the FreeNX server to connect as a remote client and see a complete Linux session. If you run into any problems, many support sites exist on the Internet to assist you. You can also find answers on the FreeNX mailing lists or in its archives at *http://developer. berlios.de/projects/freenx.*

FreeNX opens sessions quickly. You will also notice that FreeNX can suspend sessions rather than close them. When you resume a suspended session, the client revalidates but still resumes midsession, at the point where you left off. Although this is not a stateless session in the purest terms, it does save bandwidth; see Figures 28-16 and 28-17.

Figure 28-16. Resuming a session from Fedora to Ubuntu

FreeNX has many advantages for Linux uers. It provides an excellent and free thin client environment. It's fast, and it uses a proven encryption methodology (OpenSSH) that has made it through major FIPS 140 criteria tests in source code form. FreeNX also is available for most commercial Linux distributions. Free distributions of Linux such as the Fedora Project and Ubuntu have extensive community support.

Figure 28-17. Running a FreeNX session on Ubuntu with the server on Fedora Core 3

Finally, FreeNX can use a Linux server as a proxy to VNC and RDP servers. Run either *vcnviewer* or *rdesktop* on the Linux server and use those remote applications to start a Windows session. By using FreeNX, you speed up the VNC sessions, encrypt them, and provide broader access to Windows applications through RDP.

Sources of Linux Information

This appendix lists various online sources of Linux information. Although all these documents are available electronically on the Internet, many are also available in printed form.

Linux distributions often include some of this documentation in the distribution itself and make them available on the runtime system. As mentioned in the text, documentation on a Linux system can be found in a number of places, including Unix manual pages, GNU Info pages, and HTML help documentation (such as that displayed by the KDE Help Center).

Most Linux distributions store documentation on individual programs, such as *README* files and release notes, under the */usr/share/doc* directory. If you have the kernel source installed, the documentation included with the kernel will usually be found in the directory */usr/src/linux/Documentation*.

For information of a more interactive nature, the following sources are commonly used by Linux users:

Usenet newsgroups
    Most newsgroups relevant to Linux are under the *comp.os.linux* hierarchy, but many also are regional, distribution-specific, or dedicated to open source projects.

IRC
    Internet Relay Chat (IRC) is the traditional Unix chat system, and is often used for getting immediate answers to questions from other users.

Mailing lists
    Most Linux and open source projects, from the kernel to KDE, use mailing lists as the primary means for project developers to communicate. Many Linux user groups have mailing lists that can provide a local perspective.

Linux Documentation Project

The primary source of free documentation on Linux is the Linux Documentation Project (LDP). The main LDP web site is *http://www.tldp.org*, but there are many mirror sites around the world, one of which may be closer to you or less busy.

The documentation in the Linux Documentation Project is organized into several types. The *Guides* are long, often book-length, manuals covering in detail such larger topics as networking. The *HOWTOs* are medium-length documents covering specific tasks, such as configuring a sound card. For smaller tasks on specialized topics that don't justify a full HOWTO, there are *mini-HOWTOs*. Finally, there are a number of *FAQs* that answer frequently asked questions on Linux.

The LDP documents are provided in a number of different formats, including HTML, plain text, PDF, and PostScript. Many of the documents have also been translated into different languages by a team of volunteer translators.

FTP Sites

Although your Linux distribution provides precompiled binary packages for many Linux applications, often you need to build them from source code because the software is not available in binary form, you need to look at the source code, or you simply prefer to build it yourself from source. Here are some popular sites for the main sources of software that runs on Linux.

Many of these sites are extremely popular and busy. It is highly recommended that you use a mirror site (another computer system that downloads the software from the primary site on a regular basis) that is closer to you. A mirror site is usually easier to connect to and runs faster.

As well as the FTP sites listed here, many of the web sites listed in this appendix also have corresponding FTP sites for downloads.

FTP site	Description
ftp://ftp.gnu.org	The main download site for the GNU Project
ftp://ftp.ibiblio.org	A large Linux archive site, and one of the first Linux archive sites to be set up (as *sunsite.unc.edu*)
ftp://ftp.x.org	Archive for X Window System software

World Wide Web Sites

This section lists just a few of the thousands of Linux web sites on the Internet, broken down into somewhat arbitrary categories. Due to the dynamic nature of the Web, some of these sites may no longer be active and many new ones will undoubtedly exist by the time you read this.

General Documentation

These sites offer online documentation, articles about Linux, or information geared to specific areas of Linux.

Web site	Description
http://www.andamooka.org	A web site with a number of free online books, some of which are Linux-related, such as *KDE 2.0 Development*
http://www.justlinux.com	A site of news and forums
http://www.linas.org/linux	Linux Enterprise Computing site
http://www.linux-laptop.net	Linux on Laptops site
http://www.linuxfocus.org	*Linux Focus*, a free online magazine
http://www.linuxgazette.com	*Linux Gazette*, a monthly online magazine
http://www.linuxjournal.com	Web site for *Linux Journal* magazine
http://www.linuxmagazine.com	The web site for *Linux Magazine*
http://www.linuxquestions.org	Linux Questions, a very popular and information-rich site
http://www.tldp.org	Main site for the Linux Documentation Project

Open Source Projects

Listed here are web sites for some of the more popular open source and free software projects.

Web site	Description
http://freedesktop.org	Freedesktop.org, a project supported by several vendors to harmonize desktop projects and provide new functionality in common
http://koffice.kde.org	The KDE Office Suite project
http://www.abisource.com	The AbiWord word processor
http://www.alsa-project.org	Alternative Linux Sound Architecture (ALSA) sound driver project
http://www.apache.org	The Apache web server project
http://www.cups.org	The Common UNIX Printing System (CUPS)
http://www.gnome.org	The GNOME Desktop project
http://www.gnu.org	The GNU Project
http://www.isdn4linux.de	ISDN4Linux, supporting ISDN on Linux
http://www.kde.org	The K Desktop Environment (KDE)
http://www.kernel.org	The official Linux kernel site
http://www.linux-usb.org	The Linux USB project
http://www.mozilla.org	The Mozilla web browser project
http://www.mysql.com	The MySQL database
http://www.openoffice.org	The OpenOffice.org office suite project, the open source version of StarOffice
http://www.postfix.org	The Postfix mailer project

Web site	Description
http://www.povray.org	The Persistence Of Vision ray tracer
http://www.winehq.com	The Wine project
http://x.org	Maintainers of the X Window System

Programming Languages and Tools

These sites are related to popular Linux programming languages and to the hosting of Linux software projects.

Web site	Description
http://www.sourceforge.net	A site that hosts many Linux software projects, providing a place for documentation, a source code repository, bug tracking, and software building
http://savannah.gnu.org	GNU Savannah, a site offering features similar to SourceForge, but officially endorsed by the Free Software Foundation because all the hosting software is licensed under the GPL
http://www.blackdown.org	The home page of the Linux Java porting project
http://www.perl.com	Official site of the Perl programming language
http://www.php.net	Web site for the PHP programming language
http://www.python.org	Home page of the Python programming language

News and Information Sites

These sites offer news of interest to Linux users.

Web site	Description
http://www.desktoplinux.com	A site dedicated to Linux on the desktop
http://www.linux.com	A general Linux information and news site (with a very desirable URL)
http://www.linuxtoday.com	Linux Today web site
http://www.lwn.net	Linux Weekly News web site, which has in-depth coverage of the kernel and other developments
http://linuxsecurity.com	News and general information on Linux security issues
http://www.newsforge.com	NewsForge web site
http://www.slashdot.org	The popular news and discussion site that bills itself as "News for Nerds. Stuff that Matters."
http://www.theregister.co.uk	The Register, a UK site for IT industry news with a pro-Linux slant
http://www.varlinux.org	VarLinux news site, for Value Added Resellers (VARs)

Linux Software Directories and Download Sites

Listed here are some sites that maintain large searchable libraries of Linux software with links to download sites.

Web site	Description
http://www.freshmeat.net	A huge directory of Linux and open source software
http://www.icewalkers.com	The large Icewalkers Linux software directory site
http://www.linuxberg.com	The Linuxberg software directory site

Linux Distributions

Here is a long but by no means comprehensive list of some of the different Linux distributions available. These range from those backed by large companies, such as Red Hat, to specialized distributions developed by individuals or small groups. The DistroWatch site (*http://distrowatch.com*) has interesting news and statistics on the many available distributions.

Web site	Description
http://www.debian.org	Debian GNU/Linux, a popular community-developed distribution
http://fedora.redhat.com	Fedora Core, an open source version of Red Hat that undergoes rapid development
http://www.gentoo.org	Gentoo Linux, a fast-moving community project that focuses on source distribution
http://www.knoppix.net	Knoppix, a live CD good for trying out Linux and doing system recovery
http://www.kubuntu.org.uk	Kubuntu Linux, a version of Ubuntu that offers the KDE desktop
http://linspire.com	Linspire, a stable, end-user, desktop commercial product
http://www.lycoris.com	Lycoris
http://www.mandriva.com	Mandriva Linux
http://www.opensuse.org	OpenSUSE, the open source version of SUSE Linux
http://www.redhat.com	Red Hat Linux
http://www.slackware.com	Slackware Linux
http://www.suse.com	SUSE Linux, now distributed by Novell
http://www.turbolinux.com	Turbolinux, a distribution popular in East Asia
http://www.ubuntulinux.org	Ubuntu Linux, an end-user desktop system
http://www.xandros.com	Xandros Desktop Linux
http://www.yellowdoglinux.com	Yellow Dog Linux, a distribution for Macintosh hardware

Commercial Linux Software Companies

Listed here are some companies that offer commercial software and services, other than Linux distributions, for the Linux platform.

Web site	Description
http://www.codeweavers.com	CodeWeavers, developer of CrossOver Office and CrossOver Plugin, products based on the software of the Wine project that offer the ability to run Windows applications on Linux

Web site	Description
http://www.trolltech.com	TrollTech, developer of Qt, a cross-platform graphical toolkit. Qt is used as the basis for the KDE.
http://www.vistasource.com	VistaSource, formerly Applix, is the developer of the Applixware Office Suite.
http://www.vmware.com	VmWare sells virtual machine software that allows running one operating system on top of another, such as Windows on Linux, and vice versa.

Internet RFCs and Other Standards

These are a few of the many sites that host standards used by Linux and the Internet.

Web site	Description
http://www.faqs.org/rfcs	An archive site for Requests For Comments, or RFCs, the technical documents that describe many of the protocols around which the Internet is built. It also includes many other standards documents and FAQs.
http://www.freestandards.org	The Free Standards Group, a nonprofit organization dedicated to accelerating the use and acceptance of open source technologies through the development, application, and promotion of standards.
http://www.linuxbase.org	The Linux Standard Base, a project of the Free Standards Group that develops and promotes a set of standards to increase compatibility among Linux distributions and enable software applications to run on any compliant Linux system.
http://www.w3c.org	The World Wide Web Consortium, an organization that develops specifications, guidelines, software, and tools for the World Wide Web.

Miscellaneous

Finally, here are some sites that defied categorization in any of the other sections.

Web site	Description
http://counter.li.org	The Linux Counter, a unique site that collects data in an attempt to estimate the total number of Linux users worldwide.
http://www.li.org	Linux International, a nonprofit organization that works toward the promotion of Linux and the Linux community.

Index

Symbols

@ (at sign), 701
> (greater-than sign), redirecting output, 116
(hash mark), 697, 781
< (less than sign), redirecting input, 117
/ (slash character), directories, 106
~ (tilde)
    directories, 106
    in vi editors, 628

Numbers

3D, X Window System, 586–589
4Front Technologies, 284

A

AbiWord, 249
absolute mode, 398
accept command (printer), 515
accepting
    packets, 840
    print jobs (LPD systems), 517
access, 561
    Apache web servers, 772
    corrupted files, 862
    databases, 815
    filesystems, 773
    global address books, 259–260
    .htaccess file, 774
    httpd.conf file, 774
    PPP, 440
    printer configuration tool, 505
    Red Carpet, 420
    remote, 529
        FreeNX, 902–906
        VNC, 896–902
        Windows applications, 887–896
    SANE, 498
    SLIP, 440
    TCP wrappers, 834–837
    World Wide Web, 135–142
    (see also connections)
AccessFileName directive, 772
accounting, packets, 840
accounts
    daemons, 384
    GnuCash, 262
        asset, 264
        creating, 266
        deleting, 268
        equity, 265
        expense, 265
        income, 264
        liability, 264
        windows, 265
    root
        prompt, 339
        security, 832
    users
        creating, 49
        MySQL, 813–816
action field (inittab file), 601
Active Directory (see AD)
AD (Active Directory), 525
Ada language, 761
AddIcon directive, 771
AddIconByEncoding directive, 771

We'd like to hear your suggestions for improving our indexes. Send email to *index@oreilly.com*.

D

daemons, 383, 523, 548, 551
    accounts, 384
    automount, 349
    httpd, 768
    inetd, 456, 549
        TCP wrappers, 835
    named, 445
    networks, disabling, 830
    pppd, 461
    printing, 493
    syslogd, 375–378
    xinetd, 836
damaged files, accessing, 862
Data Display Debugger (DDD), 721
[data] section (smb.conf file), 548
data sources (OOoCalc), 229
databases
    access, 815
    applications (commercial), 14
    Kexi, 241
    LAMP servers, 824–827
    MySQL, 811
        configuring, 811–813
        populating, 816–818
        setting up user accounts, 813–816
    packages, 404
    RPM, initializing, 406
    whatis, 670
DCE RPC, 526
dd command, 36
dd option, boot floppy, creating, 592
DDD (Data Display Debugger), 721
Debian, firewalls, 844
debugging, 12, 28, 709
    gcc, 689
    gdb debugger, 16, 686, 689, 704–721
        shared libraries and, 691
    instruction-level, 719
    routing tables, 459
    utilities, 721
    Valgrind package, 709
decryption, 164
default MS Office file formats, 239
default Postfix MTA, editing, 782
default printers, configuring, 485
default templates, 206
DefaultIcon directive, 771
Define Custom Slide Show dialog box, 238
define-key function, 650

defining
    CUPS printers, 504–510
    printers, 495
delete command, 718
Delete key (Emacs), 651
DELETE SQL statement, 816
deleting, 630
    accounts (GnuCash), 268
    directories, 107
    files, 338
    GRUB, 598
    slides, 236
    text, 644
        Emacs, 644
        vi editor, 630
Deny directive (CUPS), 502
dependency line (make files), 694
dependency tracking, 47
deploying VMware Workstation, 881–885
desktop
    environments (GUIs), 17
    Nautilus (GNOME), 91–93
    (see also interfaces)
detach command (gdb), 714
detection, 59
    BIOS, 60
/dev directory, 462
developer tools (KDE), 72
development
    applications, 16
    multimedia, 328–330
    open source model, 25–28
devices
    automounting, 349–351
    busy errors, 331
    conflicts, 330
    creating, 368
    device files, 462
    drivers, loadable, 621–625
    files, 366
        directories, 366
        location, 366
        naming conventions, 367
        security, 337
    loadable drivers, 621–625
    non-PCI/AGP, 57
    SCSI, 59
    Windows support, 865
dial-up
    connection support, 18
    PPP, 460–468

transactions (GnuCash), 268
  scheduling, 271
  split, 270
transition slides, 237
translation
  files, 869–871
  utilities (Windows shares), 869
Transmission Control Protocol (see TCP)
Transmission Control Protocol/Internet
      Protocol (see TCP/IP)
trigger command, 351
troff, 668, 743
troubleshooting, 32, 59, 709
  boot disk, 63
  booting, 63
  CD-ROMs, 60
  cylinders, 60
  Emacs, 642
  email, 373
  filesystems, 861
    mounting, 346
  hardware, 56–61
  installation, 53–66
    booting install media, 54
    overview, 53
  KMail, 154
  LILO, 64
  login, 65
  makefiles, 702
  manual pages, 123–125
  mkfs command, 353
  multimedia applications, 330
  networks, 459, 479–483
  NFS, 564
  online help, 50
  PPP configuration, 467
  printers, 518–520
  root filesystems, 355
  SCSI devices, 59
  security, 831–834
  synchronous PPP, 475
  system emergencies, 859–864
  system functioning, 65
  system log files and, 376
  Windows, 64, 535
  Wine, 879
  X Window Server, 584
trusts, 165
TSClient, 887
  starting, 893

turning off
  Auto-Capitalization feature
      (OOoWriter), 221
  Auto-Replace feature (OOoWriter), 220
  Word Completion feature
      (OOoWriter), 220
tutorials, Emacs, 642
Tux Racer, 190–193
types
  of distributions, 34–36
  of files (OOoWriter), 197
  of filesystems, 10, 45, 341
  of partitions, 39
typing shortcuts, key bindings (Emacs), 649

U

UDF (Universal Disc Format), 282
UDP (User Datagram Protocol), 444
uid field, 386
uid field (passwd file), 385
UMASK, 532, 802
umask command, 399
umount command, 345
UMSDOS filesystem, 342
uname command, 609, 701
uncompress program, 431
uncompressing files, 430
undo command (Emacs), 655
undoing changes, text, 630
Unicode, 532
  filesystem compatibility, 343
Uniform Resource Locators (URLs), 135
uninstalling packages, 405
Universal Disc Format (UDF), 282
Universal Serial Bus (USB), 499, 619
Unix, relation to Linux, 29
Unix standards, 9
Unreal Tournament 2004, 177–182
Unsharp Mask filter (GIMP), 317
up command (gdb), 713
UPDATE SQL statement, 816
updating
  security, 834
  servers, 420
  styles, 211
  Unreal Tournament 2004, 181
upgrading
  compilers, 428
  kernel patches, 611

About the Authors

Matthias Kalle Dalheimer is the president and CEO of Klaralvdalens Datakonsult AB, a Sweden-based consultancy specializing in platform-independent software solutions. He is also a founding member of the KDE project and the current president of the KDE foundation. Kalle has written numerous books for O'Reilly, both in English and in his native German, including *Running Linux* and *Programming with Qt*. In his spare time, he enjoys cross-country skiing and reading history books. Kalle lives with his wife Tanja and his two sons Jan and Tim in the middle of the forest near Hagfors in the Swedish province of Varmland.

Matt Welsh is an assistant professor of computer science in the Division of Engineering and Applied Sciences at Harvard University. His research focuses on wireless sensor networks, including operating systems design, distributed systems, networking, and parallel computing. Matt is a long-time Linux advocate and developer, a role in which he has fielded questions from thousands of Linux users over the years. He was the original coordinator of the Linux Documentation Project and author of the original "Linux Installation and Getting Started" guide. He completed his PhD at Univercity of California, Berkeley.

Colophon

Our look is the result of reader comments, our own experimentation, and feedback from distribution channels. Distinctive covers complement our distinctive approach to technical topics, breathing personality and life into potentially dry subjects.

The image on the cover of *Running Linux,* Fifth Edition is a rearing horse. A horse will often rear to avoid going forward—as a way to avoid either further work or a frightening object. Other factors may include poorly fitted tack or an overly aggressive rider. For some horses, rearing is a learned behavior. Often a very difficult vice to correct, rearing is not a very common problem with most reasonably trained horses, and it is not breed-specific or discipline-specific. Rearing is an unsettling, difficult move to ride, not to mention dangerous. When a horse rears, its rider must lean forward on the horse's neck, to avoid shifting weight and flipping the horse over backward.

Adam Witwer was the production editor for *Running Linux*, Fifth Edition. Argosy Publishing provided production services. Matt Hutchinson and Darren Kelly provided quality control.

Edie Freedman designed the cover of this book, based on a series design by herself and Hanna Dyer. The cover image is a 19th-century engraving from the Dover Pictorial Archive. Karen Montgomery produced the cover layout with Adobe InDesign CS using Adobe's ITC Garamond font.

David Futato designed the interior layout. The chapter opening images are from the Dover Pictorial Archive. This book was converted by Andrew Savikas to FrameMaker 5.5.6 with a format conversion tool created by Erik Ray, Jason McIntosh, Neil Walls, and Mike Sierra that uses Perl and XML technologies. The text font is Linotype Birka; the heading font is Adobe Myriad Condensed; and the code font is LucasFont's TheSans Mono Condensed. The illustrations that appear in the book were produced by Robert Romano, Jessamyn Read, and Lesley Borash using Macromedia FreeHand MX and Adobe Photoshop CS. The tip and warning icons were drawn by Christopher Bing. This colophon was written by Sarah Sherman.

Better than e-books

Buy *Running Linux*, 5th Edition, and access the digital edition FREE on Safari for 45 days.

Go to www.oreilly.com/go/safarienabled
and type in coupon code F5J4-IW3K-XH6P-4ZK1-3AXU

Search
thousands of top tech books

Download
whole chapters

Cut and Paste
code examples

Find
answers fast

Search Safari! The premier electronic reference
library for programmers and IT professionals.

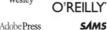

Related Titles from O'Reilly

Linux

Building Embedded Linux Systems

Building Secure Servers
with Linux

The Complete FreeBSD,
4th Edition

Even Grues Get Full

Exploring the JDS Linux
Desktop

Extreme Programming Pocket
Guide

GDB Pocket Reference

Knoppix Hacks

Knoppix Pocket Guide

Learning Red Hat Enterprise
Linux and Fedora,
4th Edition

Linux Cookbook

Linux Desktop Hacks

Linux Desktop Pocket Guide

Linux Device Drivers,
3rd Edition

Linux in a Nutshell,
5th Edition

Linux in a Windows World

Linux iptables Pocket
Reference

Linux Network Administrator's
Guide, *3rd Edition*

Linux Pocket Guide

Linux Security Cookbook

Linux Server Hacks, *Volume 2*

Linux Unwired

Linux Web Server CD
Bookshelf, *Version 2.0*

LPI Linux Certification
in a Nutshell

Managing RAID on Linux

More Linux Server Hacks

OpenOffice.org Writer

Programming with Qt,
2nd Edition

Root of all Evil

Running Linux, *5th Edition*

Samba Pocket Reference,
2nd Edition

Test Driving Linux

Understanding the Linux
Kernel, *3rd Edition*

Understanding Open Source
& Free Software Licensing

User Friendly

Using Samba, *2nd Edition*

Version Control with
Subversion

O'REILLY®

Our books are available at most retail and online bookstores.

To order direct: 1-800-998-9938 • *order@oreilly.com* • *www.oreilly.com*

Online editions of most O'Reilly titles are available by subscription at *safari.oreilly.com*